canadian ninth edition

human
resources
management
in canada

Gary Dessler

Florida International University

Nina D. Cole

Ryerson University

Virginia L. (Gini) Sutherland

Fleming College

PEARSON

Prentice
Hall

Toronto

National Library of Canada Cataloguing in Publication

Dessler, Gary, 1942–
        Human resources management in Canada/Gary Dessler, Nina D. Cole, Virginia
L. (Gini) Sutherland.–Canadian 9th ed.

Canadian 5th ed. published under title: Human resource management in Canada.
Includes index.
ISBN 0-13-121748-8

1. Personnel management. 2. Personnel management–Canada.
I. Cole, Nina D. (Nina Dawn). II. Sutherland, Gini, 1953–. III. Dessler, Gary, 1942–.
Human resource management in Canada. IV. Title.

HF5549.D49 2005   658.3   C2003-906502-2

Vice President, Editorial Director: Michael J. Young
Acquisitions Editor: James Bosma
Director of Marketing, Business and Economics: Bill Todd
Developmental Editor: Madhu Ranadive
Production Editor: Lara Caplan
Copy Editor: Valerie Adams
Proofreader: Ron Jacques

Production Coordinator: Janette Lush
Page Layout: Silver Birch Graphics/Monica Kompter
Permissions Research: Beth McAuley
Photo Research: Amanda McCormick
Art Director: Julia Hall
Cover Design: Martyn Schmoll
Cover Image: Iconica/G&M David de Lossy

Statistics Canada information is used with the permission of the Minister of Industry, as
Minister responsible for Statistics Canada. Information on the availability of the wide
range of data from Statistics Canada can be obtained from Statistics Canada's Regional
Offices, its World Wide Web site at http://www.statcan.ca, and its toll-free access number
1-800-263-1136. The Statistics Canada CANSIM II database can be accessed at
http://cansim2.statcan.ca/.

3 4 5   09 08 07 06 05

Printed and bound in the United States.

Dedication

To my son, Derek

G.D.

To Peggy Martin

N.C.

To my family, David, Jaime, Karen-Lee, Susan, Tom, and Wendy. With thanks for all of your assistance and support. I am indeed blessed.

G.S.

Brief Contents

Table of Contents

Preface

The Canadian ninth edition of *Human Resources Management in Canada* is based on two key premises: 1) that human resources are the most important asset in the majority of Canadian organizations today; and 2) that the effective management of the employment relationship is a responsibility shared by human resources (HR) specialists, all supervisors and managers, and increasingly, employees themselves. A strong foundation in human resources management (HRM) is important for supervisors and managers in every field and employees at every level—not just those working in HR departments or aspiring to do so in the future. This book was designed to provide students specializing in HRM, those in general business or business administration programs, supervisory/managerial staff, and small business owners with a complete, comprehensive review of essential HRM concepts and techniques in a highly readable and understandable form.

As in previous editions, the Canadian ninth edition provides extensive coverage of all essential HRM topics, such as job analysis, HR planning, recruitment, selection, orientation and training, career development, compensation and benefits, performance appraisal, health and safety, and union–management relations. Practical applications are discussed in the Tips for the Front Line and Hints to Ensure Legal Compliance features. Research insights are highlighted, and ethical dilemmas are presented for discussion.

NEW TO THE CANADIAN NINTH EDITION

- **Revised Introductory Chapter** The first two chapters from the eighth edition have been combined into one introductory chapter on strategic HR, and a focus on the strategic importance of all HR topics has been added.
- **Revised Chapter on Managing Quality and Productivity** Chapter 8 has been revised to focus more broadly on strategic organizational renewal, including material on managing change, total quality management, team-based organizations, business process reengineering, and flexible work arrangements.

- **HR Works** We have teamed up with CCH Canadian Limited—one of Canada's largest and most respected business-to-business information service providers—to present you with relevant, timely, and sometimes controversial human resources issues. These items are highlights from CCH's professional newsletters. Students and instructors who wish to receive similar articles on a monthly basis can sign up for the free *CCH HR E-Monthly* electronic newsletter. Just visit the Companion Website for this text and click on the link **www.pearsoned.ca/dessler.**

- **Boxed Features** The articles have been updated and revised in all chapters. To reflect the new material, all five boxed features have been renamed: Strategic HR, Workforce Diversity, Global HRM, HR.Net, and Entrepreneurs and HR.

- **New Running Cases** The running case at the end of each chapter has been updated to a dot-com company called LearnInMotion.com.

- **Web-based Exercises** For additional testing material and class assignments, the web-based exercises have been moved to the *Instructor's Resource Manual with Video Guide*.

KEY FEATURES OF THE CANADIAN NINTH EDITION
Highlighted Themes

- **Workforce Diversity** The Workforce Diversity boxes describe some of the issues and challenges involved in managing the diverse work force found in Canadian organizations. Topics range from attaining work/life balance to ergonomic aids for older workers; the benefits of a multigenerational workforce; gender differences in lying on resumés; reasons for unionizing and workplace violence; potential bias in performance appraisal and job evaluation; designing benefits packages to attract younger workers; and sending female managers abroad.

  WORKFORCE DIVERSITY
  Employment Equity Success at BMO Financial Group

  The BMO Financial Group, one of the largest employers in Canada with almost 34 000 employees, is committed to maintaining an equitable workplace which reflects the diversity of the communities and businesses it serves. One of its strategies to achieve equity involves the advancement of women. Almost 15 years ago, in an attempt to break the glass ceiling, the company developed a statistical demographic profile of men and women at BMO, which found that while three-quarters of permanent employees were women, they represented only 9 percent of executives and 13 percent of senior management. Clearly, there were barriers to women's advancement at BMO, and the company declared its commitment to a diverse workforce in its 1990 corporate strategic plan.

  In order to meet its goals, BMO gathered its senior leaders and executives to create the Chairman's Council on the Equitable Workplace. The group meets quarterly to review and evaluate past initiatives, and to create new plans for an equitable workforce. One of the initiatives to help in the advancement of women within the company was a partnership with an external organization to provide childcare to employees. By 2002, 35 percent of all executives and 30.8 percent of all executive vice-presidents at BMO were women.

  Source: R.M. Patton, "In 12 Years, BMO Women Knock Rose from 9 to 35 Percent," Canadian HR Reporter (December 16, 2002), pp. 13, 16. Reproduced by permission of Canadian HR Reporter, Carswell, One Corporate Plaza, 2075 Kennedy Road, Scarborough, ON M1T 3V4.

- **HR.Net** Throughout the book are examples of how information systems are being used for a wide range of HRM applications, including online mentoring and union organizing, web-based recruitment, and e-learning.

  HR.NET
  Computerized Skills Inventories

  Skill View Enterprise 5.0, a computerized skills inventory program, is available remotely to subscribers via a secure server hosted by its creator, SkillView Technologies. The product's assessment and reporting functions allow employees to record and track their competencies and to perform comparative skill gap analyses against their job position as well as other positions in the organization to aid in personal development and career management. Powerful management reporting capabilities allow managers to easily query department skill gap reports, individual and departmental training needs, and aids in the succession planning process.

  Source: SkillView Technologies Inc. www.skillview.com. Reprinted with permission.

- **Strategic HR** These boxes provide examples that illustrate the ways in which organizations are using effective HRM policies and practices in order to thrive in their product or service market.

  STRATEGIC HR
  Wanted: Strategic VP, HR

  There is a vacant spot waiting to be filled on the executive team at the rapidly growing Research in Motion (RIM). The wireless communications firm is looking to hire its first vice-president of HR and the job description includes a strategic position on the team. "It's an absolutely critical part of our success, for going forward," says Don Morrison, chief operating officer at the Waterloo, Ontario-based RIM. Morrison said the company's 12-member HR department has done exceptional work, but the organization needs the leadership and expertise to bring it to another level. "In all well-run companies this is done. All of these organizations spend a lot of time on [HR policies]. We need a leader who can direct. They contribute to the business strategy," said Morrison.

  Firms like RIM are beginning to realize the possibilities in forging greater relationships with their HR departments. Economic growth and HR expertise have earned them an invitation to the boardroom. RIM, the innovative brains behind the BlackBerry, the handheld e-mail device, has grown exponentially in the last year, from 200 employees to about a thousand. While recruitment remains high on the to-do list, the organization now wants to focus on keeping staff. The new HR role will run the gamut of HR skills, including implementing career development strategies, performance management, succession planning, and compensation. Bringing continuity and a framework to HR practices will be the new hiree's first order of business. Ultimately, said Morrison, the department will help bring structure to the maturing RIM.

  Source: Adapted from L. Cassiani, "Wanted: Strategic VP HR," Canadian HR Reporter (February 26, 2001), p. 9. Reproduced by permission of Canadian HR Reporter, Carswell, One Corporate Plaza, 2075 Kennedy Road, Scarborough, ON M1T 3V4.

- **Entrepreneurs and HR** Suggestions, examples, and practical hints are provided to assist those in smaller businesses with limited time and resources to implement effective HRM policies and procedures.

  ENTREPRENEURS AND HR
  ISO Booklet: ISO 9001 for Small Businesses—What to Do

  ISO 9001 for Small Businesses—What to Do is a booklet that dispels the myth that ISO 9000 is for big companies only. Aimed at managers, it explains the quality system standards in plain language, with the intention of putting improvements in performance, quality, customer satisfaction, and market access within reach of any manufacturing or service organization, regardless of size, through implementation of an ISO 9000 quality system. Quality systems should not be a source of bureaucracy, excessive paperwork, or lack of flexibility. All businesses have a management structure and this should be the basis on which the quality system is built. ISO 9000 is not, therefore, about imposing something totally new.

  The handbook does not set any new ISO 9000 requirements, or add to, or otherwise change the requirements of the standards. It suggests first steps towards a quality system (such as whether to go it alone or use consultants), offers guidance in matters such as training and auditing, and gives a brief outline of the certification process.

  The full text of ISO 9001:2000 is included in boxes, section by section, accompanied by explanations, examples, and implementation guidance in everyday terms. In addition, the handbook includes the eight quality management principles on which the ISO 9000:2000 series is based, plus revised sections on the steps involved in setting up a quality management system—including how to get started—with or without the assistance of a consultant.

  Source: ISO Publishes Advice for the SME on Implementing ISO 9001:2000. International Standards Organization Press Release 827, July 8, 2002. http://www.iso.ch/en/iso9000-14000/tour/smallbus.html. Reprinted with permission of the International Standards Organization. All rights reserved.

- **Global HRM** In recognition of the increasing impact of globalization, topics highlighted in the Global HRM boxes range from international rights and pension plan funding to bringing home foreign workers with "hot" skills, training for international business, executive development in global companies, taking self-managed teams to Mexico, long-term incentives for overseas executives, and the role of unions in protecting human rights internationally.

> **GLOBAL HRM**
> **Recruiting High-Skill Immigrants**
>
> Sometimes companies must recruit highly skilled, specialized workers internationally to help meet particular job requirements, such as in the case of Edmonton-based Fiberex Glass Corporation. There are only 14 firms in the world using the manufacturing procedure they do, and the company wanted to hire a specialist from the Philippines to instruct local staff in the maintenance of fiberglass manufacturing equipment. The Alberta government created the Provincial Nominee Program (PNP) to help employers, such as Fiberex Glass, hire skilled foreign workers and enable them to immigrate to Canada in a matter of months, rather than years.
>
> Employers prepare a business case on behalf of the applicant, stating why they want the candidate and what job skills the person has. The Minister of Economic Development inspects the application and passes it on to the federal government for criminal, security, and health checks. Similar programs are in place in Newfoundland, Prince Edward Island, New Brunswick, Manitoba, Saskatchewan, British Columbia, and the Yukon.
>
> *Source:* A. Tomlinson, "Alberta Matches Employers, Immigrants," *Canadian HR Reporter* (April 22, 2002), p. 12. Reproduced by permission of *Canadian HR Reporter*, Carswell, One Corporate Plaza, 2075 Kennedy Road, Scarborough, ON M1T 3V4.

Additional Features

- *Learning Outcomes* Specific learning goals are defined on each chapter-opening page.

- *Key Terms* Key terms appear in boldface within the text, are defined in the margins, and are listed at the end of the chapter.

- *Current Examples* Numerous real-world examples of HRM policies, procedures, and practices at a wide variety of organizations, ranging from small service providers to huge global corporations, can be found throughout the text.

- *Full-colour Figures, Tables, and Photographs* Throughout each chapter, key concepts and applications are illustrated with strong, full-colour visual materials.

- *Weblinks* Helpful Internet sites are provided throughout the text and are easily identifiable by the Weblinks icon shown here.

- *End-of-Chapter Summaries* At the end of each chapter, the summary reviews key points and links the critical content.

- *End-of-Chapter Review and Discussion Questions* Each chapter contains a set of review and discussion questions.

- *Critical Thinking Questions* New to this edition are end-of-chapter questions designed to provoke critical thinking and stimulate discussion.

- *Running Case* A running case at the end of each chapter illustrates the types of HRM challenges confronted by small business owners and front-line supervisors, and is accompanied by critical thinking questions, which provide an opportunity to discuss and apply the text material.

- *Case Incident* A different case incident can be found at the end of each chapter. These cases present current HRM issues in a real-life setting and are followed by questions designed to encourage discussion and promote the use of problem-solving skills.

- *Experiential Exercises* Each chapter includes a number of individual and group-based experiential exercises, which provide learners with the opportunity to apply the text material and develop some hands-on skills.

Supplements   *Human Resources Management in Canada*, Canadian Ninth Edition, is accompanied by a complete supplements package:

- **Instructor's Resource CD-ROM (0-13-126998-4)** This new supplement for instructors will include the *Instructor's Resource Manual with CBC Video Guide* in PDF and Word format, *Pearson Education Test Generator*, *PowerPoint Lecture Slides*, and access to CBC Videos. These items are now available in one easy-to-access CD-ROM. Below is a description of each item.

  - **Instructor's Manual with CBC Video Guide (0-13-126997-6)** This comprehensive guide contains a detailed lecture outline of each chapter, descriptions of the discussion boxes, answers to review and critical thinking questions, answers to the case questions, hints regarding the experiential and web-based exercises, and helpful video case notes.

  - **Pearson Education Canada Test Generator (0-13-126995-x)** This powerful computerized testing package contains more than 1500 multiple-choice, true/false, and short essay questions. Each question is rated by level of difficulty and includes a text page reference. This state-of-the-art software package in the Windows platform enables instructors to create tailor-made, error-free tests quickly and easily. The Custom Test allows instructors to create an exam, administer it traditionally or online, and evaluate and track students' results—all with the click of the mouse.

  - **PowerPoint Lecture Slides (0-13-126993-3)** This practical set of PowerPoint lecture slides contains over 400 colour images. The presentation outlines key concepts discussed in the text, and includes selected tables and figures from the text.

  -  **Pearson Education Canada/CBC Video Library (0-13-126991-7)** Pearson Education Canada and the CBC have worked together to provide six segments from the CBC series *Venture*. Designed specifically to complement the text, this case collection is an excellent tool for bringing students in contact with the world outside the classroom. These programs have extremely high production quality and have been chosen to relate directly to chapter content.

- **Companion Website (www.pearsoned.ca/dessler)** This Website will be of interest to both instructors and students. Instructors can access the password-protected area of the Website. It includes additional teaching tools, such as downloadable *PowerPoint Lecture Slides* and the *Instructor's Manual with CBC Video Guide*.

For a multitude of practice tests, including true/false, multiple choice, and essay questions, students should take time to explore this site. Also available to students are Weblinks, a glossary, and access to download the CBC Videos featured in the text. New to the Website is a *Student PowerPoint Slides* supplement that can be downloaded from this site. Instructors and students can check out the Companion Website by going to **www.pearsoned.ca/dessler** and selecting the book cover for *Human Resources Management in Canada,* Canadian Ninth Edition, by Dessler, Cole, and Sutherland.

Other Resources

- Gowan, *eHRM: An Internet Guide to Human Resource Management.* Free to adopters, this guide will help you navigate the many tools and resources available on the Internet for human resource managers. (ISBN: 0-13-091283-2)

- Havlovic/Jain, *Human Resource Management: Readings and Exercises.* A virtual textbook, delivered in CD-ROM format. It contains readings and exercises in human resource management. (ISBN: 0-13-027436-4)

- Gowan, *Prentice Hall's Human Resource Management Skills 1.0 CD-ROM*, First Edition. This CD-ROM allows students to explore what every manager needs to know about managing human resources. The CD includes interactive modules with exercises. (ISBN: 0-13-066103-1)

- Cawsey/Deszca/Templer, *Canadian Cases in Human Resources Management*, First Edition. This casebook features 24 Canadian cases in human resource management. (ISBN: 0-13-088455-3)

- Sales/Owen/Lesperance, *Experiential Exercises in Human Resource Management*, First Edition. Designed to accompany texts in the field of management, this resource meets the demand for more real-life, practical, and experiential material in management courses. In each book, the exercises follow an identical and innovative format to guide both instructors and students and to reinforce the goals of the series: increase students' awareness, apply theory, and build skills. (ISBN: 0-13-021805-7)

- *Pearson Custom Publishing* (**www.prenhall.com/custombusiness**). Pearson Custom Publishing can provide you and your students with texts, cases, and articles to enhance your course. Choose material from Darden, Ivey, Harvard Business School Publishing, NACRA, and Thunderbird to create your own custom casebook. Contact your Pearson sales representative for more details.

- *Online Learning Solutions.* Pearson Education Canada supports instructors interested in using online course management systems. We provide text-related content in WebCT and Blackboard. To find out more about creating your online course using Pearson content in one of these platforms, contact your Pearson sales representative.

- *New! Instructor's ASSET.* Pearson Education is proud to introduce Instructor's ASSET, the Academic Support and Service for Educational Technologies. ASSET is the first integrated Canadian service program committed to meeting the customization, training, and support needs for your course. Ask your Pearson sales representative for details!

- *Your Pearson Sales Representative!* Your Pearson rep is always available to ensure you have everything you need to teach a winning course. Armed with experience, training, and product knowledge, your Pearson rep will support your assessment and adoption of any of the products, services, and technologies outlined here to ensure our offerings are tailored to suit your individual needs and the needs of your students. Whether it's getting instructions for TestGen software or specific content files for your new online course, your Pearson Sales Representative is here to help.

ACKNOWLEDGMENTS

The manuscript was reviewed at various stages of its development by a number of peers across Canada, and we wish to thank those who shared their insights and constructive criticism. Among them is:

Gordon Barnard, Durham College

Travor Brown, Memorial University

Susan FitzRandolph, Ryerson University

Rick Jason, Confederation College

Shaista E. Khilji, Carleton University

Barbara Lipton, Seneca College

Fiona McQuarrie, University College of Fraser Valley

Carol Ann Samhaber, Algonquin College

George Vandermey, Conestoga College

At Pearson Education Canada, we are very grateful to James Bosma, Madhu Ranadive, Lara Caplan, Beth McAuley, and Valerie Adams.

A special note of thanks is extended to Kim Campbell, who provided research assistance.

Gary Dessler
Florida International University

Nina D. Cole
Ryerson University

Virginia L. (Gini) Sutherland
Fleming College

Photo Credits

Chapter 13

Chapter 14

Chapter 15

Chapter 16

Chapter 17

Chapter 18

A Great Way to Learn and Instruct Online

The Pearson Education Canada Companion Website is easy to navigate and is organized to correspond to the chapters in this textbook. Whether you are a student in the classroom or a distance learner you will discover helpful resources for in-depth study and research that empower you in your quest for greater knowledge and maximize your potential for success in the course.

[www.pearsoned.ca/dessler]

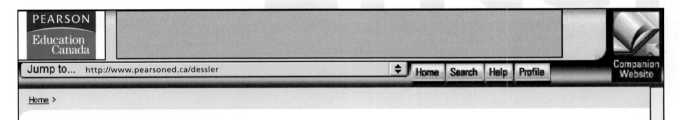

Jump to... http://www.pearsoned.ca/dessler | Home | Search | Help | Profile

Home >

Dessler Companion Website

Human Resources Management in Canada, Canadian Ninth Edition

Student Resources

The modules in this section provide students with tools for learning course material. These modules include:

- Chapter Objectives
- Destinations
- Quizzes
- Internet Exercises
- Net Search
- Glossary

In the quiz modules students can send answers to the grader and receive instant feedback on their progress through the Results Reporter. Coaching comments and references to the textbook may be available to ensure that students take advantage of all available resources to enhance their learning experience.

Instructor Resources

The modules in this section provide instructors with additional teaching tools. Downloadable PowerPoint Presentations, Electronic Transparencies, and an Instructor's Manual are just some of the materials that may be available in this section. Where appropriate, this section will be password protected. To get a password, simply contact your Pearson Education Canada Representative or call Faculty Sales and Services at 1-800-850-5813.

CHAPTER I

The Strategic Role of Human Resources Management

LEARNING OUTCOMES

After studying this chapter, you should be able to:

Define human resources management, *describe* its objectives, and *explain* strategic human resources management.

Explain the five types of activities required of HR managers and line managers with responsibility for HRM.

Discuss the impact of strategic HRM practices on the bottom line.

Describe the internal and external environmental factors affecting human resources management policies and practices, and *explain* their impact.

Describe the three stages in the evolution of management thinking about workers.

Discuss HR challenges in the twenty-first century.

INTRODUCTION TO HUMAN RESOURCES MANAGEMENT

human resources management (HRM) The activities, policies, and practices involved in obtaining, developing, utilizing, evaluating, maintaining, and retaining the appropriate number and skill mix of employees to accomplish the organization's objectives.

strategic human resources management The linking of HRM with strategic goals and objectives in order to improve business performance and develop an organizational culture that fosters innovation and flexibility.

Human resources management (HRM) refers to the management of people in organizations. The goal of HRM is to maximize employees' contributions in order to achieve optimal productivity and effectiveness, while simultaneously attaining individual objectives (such as having a challenging job and obtaining recognition), and societal objectives (such as legal compliance and demonstrating social responsibility).[1]

A growing number of companies are now beginning to view their human resources as a value-adding source of competitive advantage.[2] The realization that employees can be central to achieving competitive advantage has led to the emergence of the field known as **strategic human resources management**, defined as "... the linking of HRM with strategic goals and objectives in order to improve business performance and develop [an] organizational culture that fosters innovation and flexibility ...."[3] The term "strategic HR" recognizes the HR department's partnership role in the strategic planning process, while the term "HR strategies" refers to the specific HR actions that the company uses to achieve its strategic objectives.[4]

All managers must concern themselves with HRM, since they all meet their goals through the efforts of others, which requires the effective management of people. This is particularly true in small and medium-sized firms, where the HR department is small or may not exist at all. Every supervisor and line manager has responsibilities related to a wide range of HRM activities, including analyzing jobs, planning labour needs, selecting employees, orienting and training employees, managing compensation, communicating (which includes counselling and disciplining), and maintaining employee commitment. These responsibilities also include ensuring fair treatment; appraising performance; ensuring employee health and safety; building and maintaining good employee/labour relations; handling complaints and grievances; and ensuring compliance with human rights, occupational health and safety, labour relations, and other legislation affecting the workplace.

According to one expert, "The direct handling of people is, and always has been, an integral part of every ... manager's responsibility, from president down to the lowest-level supervisor."[5] In small organizations, line managers may carry out all of their HRM duties without the assistance of an HR department, and line managers must continually focus on HR matters as they manage their employees day by day. As the organization grows, however, they often need the assistance, specialized knowledge, and advice of a separate human resources staff.[6]

Organization size and complexity are generally major factors in senior management's decision to establish an HR department. As an organization grows, managing human resources effectively and ensuring legal compliance become more of a challenge. Once department managers and first-line supervisors find that HRM activities interfere with their other responsibilities, the benefits of delegating some of their HRM tasks to a separate HR department are generally seen to exceed the costs of establishing such an entity.

Many studies have shown that employees are more committed to their jobs when their participation is valued and encouraged. Here, assembly-line workers in a Tokyo Nissan factory participate in a worker productivity session attended by managers and supervisors.

Human Resource Management Responsibilities

Once an HR department has been created, it is the unit that has overall responsibility for HRM programs and activities. The primary role of the HR department is to ensure that the organization's human resources are utilized effectively and managed in compliance with company policies and procedures, government legislation, and, in unionized settings, collective agreement(s). HR department staff members are involved in five distinct types of activities: serving as consultant and change agent, offering advice, formulating policies and procedures, providing services, and monitoring to ensure compliance.

Serving as Consultants and Strategic Change Agents

In most firms, HR professionals serve as in-house consultants to the managers of other departments in solving HR issues such as executive recruitment, job evaluation, or selecting activities to be outsourced. **Outsourcing**, the practice of contracting with outside vendors to handle specified functions on a permanent basis, has emerged as a worldwide business trend. The rapid emergence of use of the Internet to manage everyday business processes electronically, from supply chain to delivery, is having a dramatic impact on the outsourcing environment —even in the HR field.[7] While using outside experts to provide counselling services has been common for many years, more recently, the outsourcing of specific HR functions and payroll has become popular as a means to enable corporate HR staff to focus on the strategic management of human resources.

For example, the Canadian Imperial Bank of Commerce (CIBC) cut its HR department in half in 2001 when it outsourced all of its non-strategic HR roles to Electronic Data Systems Ltd. (EDS), a business process management firm. Two hundred CIBC HR employees and their work were transferred to EDS. Two years later, the arrangement had proven to be very successful.[8] The Bank of Montreal (BMO) followed suit in early 2003, and 250 BMO employees were transferred to Exult Inc.[9] The United Church of Canada, B.C. Hydro, and Pratt & Whitney Canada are also outsourcing HR activities.[10]

Human resources management converges with strategy implementation through managing change.[11] In addition to serving as consultants, HR specialists are expected to be "change agents" who provide senior managers with "up-to-date information on current trends and new methods of solving problems" to help the organization increase its efficiency and effectiveness.[12] For example, the remaining HR staff at CIBC will be responsible for change management strategies as the bank prepares to "re-brand" itself in the near future.[13]

Offering Advice

Managers at all levels frequently turn to the HR department staff for expert advice and counsel. Members of the HR department are expected to be completely familiar with employment legislation, HR policies and procedures, collective agreements, past practices, and the outcome of recent arbitration hearings and court decisions, so that they can provide sound guidance and suggested solutions.

Formulating Policies and Procedures

HR policies and procedures must be compatible with current economic conditions, collective bargaining trends, and applicable employment legislation. A **policy** is a statement defining the organization's position on a given issue that is established to provide direction in decision making. HR **procedures** specify a prescribed sequence of steps to be followed when implementing HR policies. To maximize effectiveness, HR policies and procedures should be put into writing; they are often compiled in a policy manual or made available online so that they are readily accessible.

---

outsourcing The practice of contracting with outside vendors to handle specified functions on a permanent basis.

CFT Training and Human Resources www.cfthr.com

HR-Dept.Com www.hr-dept.com

---

policy A predetermined guide to thinking, established to provide direction in decision making.

procedure A prescribed sequence of steps to be followed when implementing organizational policies.

HR.NET

@hp

There's a lot of industry buzz about HR portals as the next big thing, but Hewlett-Packard (HP) already has one foot firmly planted in the future. HP's enterprise-wide business-to-employee (b2e) portal, called @hp, offers a standardized look and feel to all corporate information, while offering the ability to perform 150 different automated transactions in eight languages to HP's 88 000 employees in 150 countries, 24 hours a day. The company says it has achieved US$50 million in savings within six months. HP and its business units had 4400 Web sites before the portal was created —now there's just one. In addition, HP was able to eliminate literally thousands of servers. In the next two years, HP plans to standardize its software and go from 12 000 applications to 200.

A by-product of the @hp implementation was to slash the work of the human resources department in half. Many former functions of the HR department were data entry from e-mails and forms that were filled out and sent to HR. The data, such as banking information, address changes, information about dependents, or benefit changes, was moved onto the HR software that was only accessible by HR personnel. The portal now provides a point of entry for direct transactions by employees who input the data into the same HR software. Thus a lot of previous HR tasks were no longer necessary because the portal eliminated the work and about half of the HR jobs. The personnel were deployed elsewhere, and those who remain in HR find their work much more satisfying, because instead of data entry, they are doing the HR-related work that they really like to do.

Other companies are beginning to consider HR portals, but few are willing to go where HP has gone because of the cultural changes that are required. They are not trivial, according to Bill Dupley, Director of Strategy and Business Development for Hewlett-Packard Consulting Canada. This knowledge management tool requires sharing and putting the interests of the company ahead of those of the individual. Thus the portal concept may be ahead of its time at this point.

Source: Based on M. Moralis, "HR's Enterprise-Wide Portal: To Go Where No Intranet Has Gone Before," *Canadian HR Reporter* (May 20, 2002), p. G8. Reproduced by permission of *Canadian HR Reporter*, Carswell, One Corporate Plaza, 2075 Kennedy Road, Scarborough, ON M1T 3V4.

Providing Services The HR department generally provides services in the following areas on an ongoing basis: maintenance of HR records; recruitment and selection; orientation, training and development; performance management; compensation and benefits administration; employee and labour relations; and occupational health and safety. According to a 2002 Towers Perrin survey, more than 90 percent of North American firms are using the Web to provide HR services.[14] Companies such as Canada Post, Oracle Corporation Canada Inc., General Motors, and Rogers Communications Inc. have implemented **electronic human resources (e-HR)**, in order to automate HRM transactions and have employees service themselves as required.[15] Through a Web-based "HR portal" (as illustrated in the HR.Net box), employees have the ability to update personal data, enrol in and make changes to benefits plans, and access online training courses.

electronic HR (e-HR) Self-service HR transactions conducted by employees.

Research ▷
Insight

According to three recent e-HR surveys, e-HR is the number-one cited HR strategy being used by large companies. While the main reason why the over 300 respondents reported implementing self-service HR programs is to improve service to employees, these companies are also reporting that self-service technologies have reduced their HR transaction costs by up to 75 percent. Sixty-seven percent reported improvements in overall organizational efficiency, and 62 percent noted improvement in the HR function in particular.[16]

e-HR not only improves service to employees, it also empowers employees.[17] Of the estimated 17 000 out of 24 000 Alberta government employees who use AGent (Alberta Government Employee Net), a one-stop HR portal, over 88 percent said they agreed, or strongly agreed, with the statement that the AGent is a valuable tool.[18] Improving service and increasing empowerment are not the only reasons why companies have introduced e-HR. With less time spent on administration, experienced HR professionals are finding increased time to focus their expertise on strategic HR.

Monitoring to Ensure Compliance The HR department staff members are generally responsible for monitoring to ensure compliance with established HR policies and procedures and employment legislation. They may analyze data pertaining to absenteeism and turnover or accident rates, for example, to identify problems with policy implementation or failures to comply with specified procedures. They are generally responsible for collecting and analyzing recruitment, selection, and promotion data to monitor compliance with human rights and employment equity legislation. They also assess salary and benefits data to monitor compliance with employment standards and pay equity requirements, and examine accident investigation and grievance reports to monitor compliance with health and safety and labour relations legislation.

STRATEGIC HR: THE IMPACT OF EFFECTIVE HRM PRACTICES ON THE BOTTOM LINE

A 2002 *Globe and Mail* article highlighted how Canada's human resource professionals are in the midst of reinventing themselves—changing what they do for the companies that employ them and how they relate to those on the operations side. Their goal is a seat at the senior management table alongside decision makers like the chief operating, information, and financial officers. The single most important tool they have in their uphill struggle is the intellectual capital held within any corporation, In the past, the profession has focused on winning the hearts of employees; today their aim is to quantify and harness their minds.

The focus is on value added. HRM is in the midst of a fundamental shift from being a cost item on the income statement to being able to justify its existence through return on investment. Historically, the HR department performed administrative functions like payroll, pensions, and benefits administration. That role is changing with the advent of technology and outsourcing. Thus more and more HR professionals are now free to devote their time to developing a new role, one that can help the company reach its strategic objectives.[19]

Research findings indicate that strategic HRM practices have a positive effect on the bottom line, if properly implemented and accompanied by a supportive culture and climate. Research studies have established that 15 percent of the relative profit performance of an organization derives from HR strategy, and a 2002 study by Anderson Consulting found that human capital practices explain just under half of the differences in market value between companies.[20] Strategic HRM can also be very important for small and medium-sized firms, particularly service businesses. One study found that HR systems can affect the probability of new-venture survival by as much as 22 percent.[21]

There is growing research evidence, however, that in addition to high-involvement HR practices, a complementary workplace culture and climate is required. Studies involving more than 1200 Canadian firms and almost 800 local union leaders found that the highest performance levels are associated with high-involvement HR practices combined with a supportive work environment, characterized by participative decision making and open communication.[22]

In addition to these research findings, HR managers now have numbers to take to the boardroom to prove just how much the department can contribute to the bottom line in another form: the Human Capital Index (HCI), developed by Watson Wyatt consultants. Based on a year-long study analyzing the HR practices at more than 400 companies, which were matched with objective financial measures, the HCI outlines 30 key HR practices and indicates, in best-case scenarios, their contributions to shareholder value. These 30 practices were then summarized in five categories: (1) recruiting excellence; (2) clear rewards and accountability; (3) collegial and flexible workplaces; (4) communications integrity; and (5) the imprudent use of resources—the negative impact of poorly implemented HR policies and practices.[23] The impact of each is shown in **Figure 1.1.**

The Watson Wyatt study went beyond previous correlational findings to investigate whether strong HRM drove financial performance or whether successful companies simply had more resources to put into HRM. Results showed that strong human resources management was driving company performance. Looking at 51 large companies in North America and Europe, the study found that those with the best HR practices provided a 64 percent total return to shareholders over a five-year period, more than three times the 21 percent return for companies with weaker HR practices. Bruce Pfau, head of organiza-

---

FIGURE **I.I** HR Return on Investment

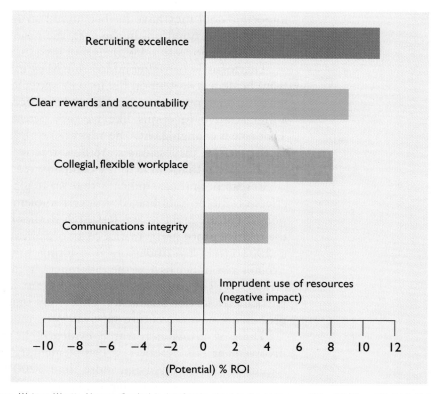

Source: Watson Wyatt, *Human Capital Index Study,* cited in David Brown, "The 30 Ways HR Adds Value to the Bottom Line," *Canadian HR Reporter* (December 13, 1999), p. 1. Reproduced by permission of *Canadian HR Reporter,* Carswell, One Corporate Plaza, 2075 Kennedy Road, Scarborough, ON M1T 3V4.

Strategic HR

Wanted: Strategic VP, HR

There is a vacant spot waiting to be filled on the executive team at the rapidly growing Research in Motion (RIM). The wireless communications firm is looking to hire its first vice-president of HR and the job description includes a strategic position on the team. "It's an absolutely critical part of our success, for going forward," says Don Morrison, chief operating officer at the Waterloo, Ontario-based RIM. Morrison said the company's 12-member HR department has done exceptional work, but the organization needs the leadership and expertise to bring it to another level. "In all well-run companies this is done. All of these organizations spend a lot of time on [HR policies]. We need a leader who can direct. They contribute to the business strategy," said Morrison.

Firms like RIM are beginning to realize the possibilities in forging greater relationships with their HR departments. Economic growth and HR expertise have earned them an invitation to the boardroom. RIM, the innovative brains behind the BlackBerry, the handheld e-mail device, has grown exponentially in the last year, from 200 employees to about a thousand. While recruitment remains high on the to-do list, the organization now wants to focus on keeping staff. The new HR role will run the gamut of HR skills, including implementing career development strategies, performance management, succession planning, and compensation. Bringing continuity and a framework to HR practices will be the new hiree's first order of business. Ultimately, said Morrison, the department will help bring structure to the maturing RIM.

Source: Adapted from L. Cassiani, "Wanted: Strategic VP HR," *Canadian HR Reporter* (February 26, 2001), p. 9. Reproduced by permission of *Canadian HR Reporter*, Carswell, One Corporate Plaza, 2075 Kennedy Road, Scarborough, ON M1T 3V4.

tional effectiveness consulting at Watson Wyatt, and author of the study, says, "Evidence from this new research clearly favours superior human capital management as a leading—rather than lagging—indicator of improved financial outcomes."[24] The bottom line is that effective human capital practices drive business outcomes more than business outcomes lead to good HR practices.[25]

However, a 2001 study of 539 Canadian organizations by the *Canadian HR Reporter* and Watson Wyatt called *HR's Quest for Status: Fantasy or Emerging Reality?* found that while many HR departments in Canadian organizations want to play a more strategic role, they have been slow to adapt practices to capture and showcase their contribution. Results revealed that HR is still often left on the sidelines when it comes to creating business strategy. HR professionals recognize that they should be doing a better job of measuring their contributions, but that time pressure is holding them back. Caught in a vicious circle, HR can't find the time to prove its strategic value, but can't be asked to play a bigger role until it can show that it is strategic. The study concluded that HR professionals must do everything they can to break that cycle.[26]

Watson Wyatt predicts that very soon, human capital will become a business priority and CEOs are going to need somebody with expertise to take a leadership role, or at least guide decisions, about human capital.[27] The Strategic HR box highlights one such company.

Environmental Influences on HRM

Internal and external environmental influences play a major role in HRM. Internal organizational climate, culture, and management practices help to shape HR policies and practices, which, in turn, have an impact on the quality of candidates that a firm can attract, as well as its ability to retain desired workers.

There are also a number of external challenges that are dramatically changing the environment of HRM and requiring it to play an ever more crucial role in organizations.

Internal Environmental Influences

How a firm deals with the following three internal environmental influences has a major impact on its ability to meet its objectives.

First, **organizational culture** consists of the core values, beliefs, and assumptions that are widely shared by members of an organization. Culture is often conveyed through an organization's mission statement, as well as through stories, myths, symbols, and ceremonies. It serves a variety of purposes:

organizational culture The core values, beliefs, and assumptions that are widely shared by members of an organization.

- communicating what the organization "believes in" and "stands for"
- providing employees with a sense of direction and expected behaviour (norms)
- shaping employees' attitudes about themselves, the organization, and their roles
- creating a sense of identity, orderliness, and consistency
- fostering employee loyalty and commitment.

All managers with HR responsibilities play an important role in creating and maintaining the type of organizational culture desired. For example, they may organize recognition ceremonies for high-performing employees, and be involved in decisions regarding symbols such as a logo or the design of new company premises. Having a positive culture earns critical acclaim, and has a positive impact on both retention and recruitment. Lloyd Craig, president and CEO of Surrey Metro Savings Credit Union in British Columbia says, "The most important thing for the head of HR is an appreciation of the culture of the organization. Everything you try to do in HR will fit or not, depending on culture."[28]

Second, **organizational climate** refers to the prevailing atmosphere or "internal weather" that exists in an organization and its impact on employees.[29] It can be friendly or unfriendly, open or secretive, rigid or flexible, innovative or stagnant. The major factors influencing the climate are management's leadership style, HR policies and practices, and amount and style of organizational communication. The type of climate that exists is generally reflected in the level of employee motivation, job satisfaction, performance, and productivity. HR department staff members play a key role in helping managers throughout the firm to establish and maintain a positive organizational climate.

organizational climate The prevailing atmosphere that exists in an organization and its impact on employees.

bureaucratic structure A pyramid-shaped organization, characterized by a hierarchical structure and many levels of management.

empowerment Providing workers with the skills and authority to make decisions that would traditionally be made by managers.

boundaryless organization structure A structure in which relationships (typically joint ventures) are formed with customers, suppliers, and/or competitors, to pool resources for mutual benefit or encourage cooperation in an uncertain environment.

Third, many new management practices are emerging, with many HRM implications. For example, the traditional **bureaucratic structure**, characterized by a pyramid shape and hierarchies with many levels of management, is being replaced by flatter organizational forms. These generally emphasize cross-functional teams and improved communication flow, with corresponding de-emphasis on "sticking to the chain of command" to get decisions made.[30] Since managers have more people reporting to them in flat structures, they cannot supervise their employees as closely. Employee **empowerment** is thus becoming more common. **Boundaryless organization structures** are also emerging. In this type of structure, relationships (typically joint ventures) are formed with customers, suppliers, and/or competitors, to pool resources for mutual benefit or encourage cooperation in an uncertain environment.

External Environmental Influences

To be effective, all managers, including those with responsibility for HR, must monitor the environment on an ongoing basis; assess the impact of any changes; and be proactive in implementing policies and programs to deal with such challenges.

Labour Market Issues

Economic Conditions Economic conditions affect supply and demand for products and services, which, in turn, have a dramatic impact on the **labour force** by affecting the number and types of employees required, as well as an employer's ability to pay wages and provide benefits. The **labour market** is the geographic area from which an organization recruits employees and where individuals seek employment. The labour market is often different for various employee groups within an organization. While clerical and technical employees are generally recruited locally, the labour market for senior managers and highly specialized employees is often national or even international.

When the economy is healthy, companies often hire more workers as demand for products and services increases. Consequently, unemployment rates fall, there is more competition for qualified employees, and training and retention strategies increase in importance.[31] Conversely, during a downturn, some firms reduce pay and benefits in order to retain workers. Other employers are forced to downsize, by offering attractive early retirement and early leave programs or by laying off and terminating employees. Unemployment rates rise, and employers are often overwhelmed with applicants when vacancies are advertised.

As illustrated in **Figure 1.2**, **productivity** refers to the ratio of an organization's outputs (goods and services) to its inputs (people, capital, energy, and materials).[32] For example, a shoe manufacturer could measure worker productivity as the number of shoes produced each year per employee. To improve productivity, managers must find ways to produce more outputs with current input levels or to use fewer resources to produce current output levels. In most organizations today, productivity improvement is essential for long-term success. Canada's relatively low productivity growth rate and high labour costs are of grave concern, since competition with foreign companies has become increasingly important.

Organizations must constantly monitor and track economic trends affecting supply and demand of human resources in order to estimate how difficult it is likely to be to attract and recruit staff. Labour market conditions should also be monitored to determine present and emerging trends (such as the changing composition of the labour force) as well as changing values and expectations, so that policies and programs can be adapted and/or designed in order to recognize and take advantage of these trends.

The Service Sector and the Concept of "Human Capital" As can be seen in **Figure 1.3**, employment trends in Canada have been experiencing dramatic

labour force Individuals who are employed and those actively seeking work.

labour market The geographic area from which an organization recruits employees and where individuals seek employment.

Canada WorkinfoNET
www.workinfonet.ca

productivity The ratio of an organization's outputs (goods and services) to its inputs (people, capital, energy, and materials).

FIGURE **1.2** Productivity Ratio

$$\text{Productivity} = \frac{\text{Outputs (Goods and Services)}}{\text{Inputs (People, Capital, Energy, Materials)}}$$

FIGURE I.3 Employment Trends

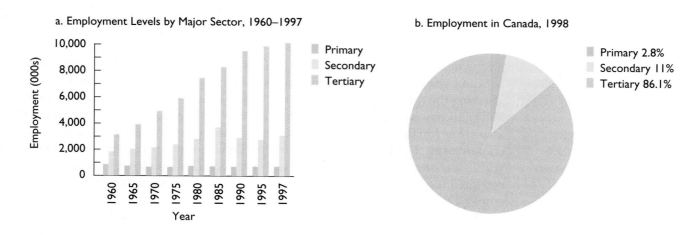

a. Employment Levels by Major Sector, 1960–1997

Primary
Secondary
Tertiary

b. Employment in Canada, 1998

Primary 2.8%
Secondary 11%
Tertiary 86.1%

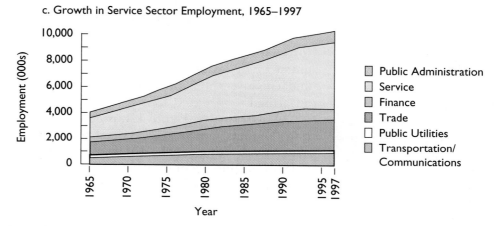

c. Growth in Service Sector Employment, 1965–1997

Public Administration
Service
Finance
Trade
Public Utilities
Transportation/
Communications

Source: Adapted from the Statistics Canada Web site <http://www.statcan.ca/english/Pgdb/labor10a.htm> and <http://www.statcan.ca/english/Pgdb/labor10b.htm>. July 10, 2000, and August 20, 2002.

primary sector Agriculture, fishing and trapping, forestry, and mining.

secondary sector Manufacturing and construction.

tertiary or service sector Public administration, personal and business services, finance, trade, public utilities, and transportation/communications.

knowledge worker An employee who transforms information into a product or service, whose responsibilities include planning, problem solving, and decision making.

change. The **primary sector,** which includes agriculture, fishing and trapping, forestry, and mining, now represents less than 5 percent of jobs. Between 1985 and 2001, employment in the **secondary sector** (manufacturing and construction) dropped by more than 20 percent. The sector of the Canadian economy accounting for the greatest growth in recent decades is the **tertiary or service sector,** which includes public administration, personal and business services, finance, trade, public utilities, and transportation/communications.

Since all jobs in the service sector involve the provision of service, often in person but increasingly through service-providing technologies (such as automated banking machines and cable television), effectively managing and motivating human resources is critical. Although there are some lesser-skilled jobs (in housekeeping and food services, for example), many service-sector jobs demand **knowledge workers,** employees who transform information into a product or service, whose responsibilities include planning, problem solving, and decision making.

human capital The knowledge, education, training, skills, and expertise of a firm's workers.

Management expert Peter Drucker has said that "the foundation of an organization is not money or capital or technology—it's knowledge and education (**human capital**). By 2005, knowledge workers will be the single largest group in the labour force."[33] Many experts believe that the distinguishing characteristic of companies today and tomorrow is this growing emphasis on human capital. Jobs today in all sectors demand a level of expertise far beyond that required of most workers 20 or 30 years ago, which means that human capital is quickly replacing machines as the basis for most firms' success.

For managers, the challenge of fostering intellectual or human capital lies in the fact that knowledge workers must be managed differently than workers of previous generations. New HRM systems and skills are required to select and train such employees, encourage self-discipline, win employee commitment, and spark creativity. 3M is one organization that has learned how to encourage creativity and access the skills and ideas of all of its employees:[34]

> At 3M, there is a corporate policy that 30 percent of its annual revenues must come from products that are less than four years old. Thus, over the years, 3M has mastered the art of motivating employees to come up with new and useful ideas. Scientists and engineers are actively encouraged to form small groups to come up with new ideas and launch new products. If they can't obtain funding from the managers of their own business units, they can seek money from other business groups. If that fails, they can appeal to a panel of scientists from across the firm to obtain a "Genesis Grant," which provides up to $50 000 in funding. For example, 3M executives tried to end the Thinsulate project at least five times. Innovators within 3M persisted, however, and the light, waterproof, synthetic fibre is now used in sporting goods, shoes, and car doors. In short, Thinsulate has become a wildly successful product, but it only saw the light of day because the firm offered ways for creative employees to bring it to the market.

labour union An officially recognized association of employees, practising a similar trade or employed in the same company or industry, who have joined together to present a united front and collective voice in dealing with management.

The Labour Union Movement A **labour union** is an officially recognized association of employees who have joined together to present a united front and collective voice in dealing with management, with the aim of securing and furthering the social and economic interests and well-being of their membership. Once a union has been certified or recognized to represent a specific group of employees, the company is required by law to recognize the union and bargain with it in good faith.

Labour unions affect organizations in several ways. Management has less discretion and flexibility in implementing and administering HR policies, procedures, and practices when dealing with unionized employees. Labour unions also influence the HR policies and practices in non-unionized organizations wishing to remain union-free. Such organizations monitor bargaining activities in their community and industry, and ensure that their employees are provided with terms and conditions of employment equal to or better than those being negotiated by unions.

contingent employees Workers who do not have regular full-time or part-time employment status.

Use of Contingent and Part-Time Employees Many firms are using more **contingent employees**—defined as workers who do not have regular full-time or part-time employment status—to handle vacation and leave coverage, peak-period demands, extra workload, and specialized tasks or assignments. Included are contract workers, seasonal workers, casual and non-regular part-time employees, temporary employees, independent contractors (freelancers), consultants, and leased employees.[35] Contingent workers currently account for about 12 percent of all jobs in Canada, a figure that is expected to reach 25 percent by 2010.[36]

There are more regular part-time employees in Canada than ever before. These are individuals who work fewer hours than full-time core employees, typically during peak periods (such as evenings and weekends in retail stores and restaurants). Approximately 33 percent of all employed women work part-time: two-thirds of them by preference, and the other one-third because they were unable to obtain full-time employment.[37] The fact that part-time workers are often paid less than their full-time counterparts—and may not have benefits coverage at all—has raised some major equity concerns.

Demographic Trends and Increasing Workforce Diversity

Demographics refers to the characteristics of the work force, which include age, sex, marital status, and education level.[38] The fact that Canada's labour force is becoming increasingly diverse is one of the major challenges confronting HR managers today. **Diversity** refers to "... any attribute that humans are likely to use to tell themselves, 'that person is different from me,'" and thus includes such factors as race, gender, age, values, and cultural norms.[39]

Population Growth   The single most important factor governing the size and composition of the labour force is population growth. Since the population growth has slowed to less than 1 percent per year, the average age of the workforce is increasing. Canada admits more immigrants per capita than any other country, which has created a very diverse labour force.

Age   The **baby boomers**, born between 1946 and 1965, are now mostly in their forties and fifties. According to Statistics Canada, between 2001 and 2016, there will be dramatic growth in the 55–69 age groups. In contrast, the youth population, aged 15 to 24, will increase by only 0.3 percent. In fact, the 15 to 19 age group will actually decrease by 7 percent.[40] Since many baby boomers will be retiring over the next 25 years, pension plan and social security benefits issues are starting to present a very serious concern for employers and governments, given the smaller labour force available to support the retirees. At present, there are approximately five active workers to support each retiree—a ratio projected to be reduced to 3.12 over the next 25 years.[41]

The aging of the population has had another impact. Many middle-aged employees are caught in the **Sandwich Generation**, with responsibilities for rearing young dependants as well as assisting elderly relatives who are no longer capable of functioning totally independently. Although some employers, such as the Royal Bank, have been proactive in assisting their "sandwiched" employees, only about 10 percent of Canadian businesses have programs specifically designed to assist workers providing eldercare.[42] A Senate subcommittee has recommended a legislated solution—paid leave for palliative care.[43]

As **Generation X** (individuals born between 1966 and 1980) employees replace aging boomers, flexible work arrangements, continuous skill development, and a balance between work and personal life are becoming increasingly important. They view command- and authority-based cultures with disdain, and believe that security comes from transferability of skills rather than corporate loyalty.[44] The message to employers is that having workers of diverse ages may create a need to bridge the generation gap.

demographics The characteristics of the workforce, which include age, sex, marital status, and education level.

diversity Any attribute that humans are likely to use to tell themselves, "that person is different from me," and thus includes such factors as race, gender, age, values, and cultural norms.

baby boomers Individuals born between 1946 and 1965.

Sandwich Generation Individuals with responsibility for rearing young dependents as well as for assisting elderly relatives who are no longer capable of functioning totally independently.

Generation X Individuals born between 1966 and 1980.

HR Online www.hr2000.com

Education The level of education of the Canadian labour force is increasing at a significant rate. More Canadians are pursuing higher education, through a variety of institutions. Other trends in secondary and post-secondary education include growth in the number of cooperative education programs and of distance education opportunities. Today, the number of Canadians involved in adult education and training activities rivals the number of students enrolled in the entire elementary, secondary, and post-secondary education systems, a trend that many firms encourage through tuition-assistance programs.[45] Given the higher expectations of the better-educated labour force, managers are expected to try to ensure that the talents and capabilities of employees are fully utilized and that opportunities are provided for career growth.

Very few Canadians are illiterate in the sense of not being able to read, but a startlingly high proportion (43 percent) have only marginal literacy skills, defined as the ability to understand and use printed and written documents in daily activities to achieve goals and to develop knowledge and potential.[46] A frightening reality is that inadequate reading and writing skills have replaced lack of experience as the major reason for rejecting entry-level candidates.[47] About one in six working-age Canadians is **functionally illiterate**, unable to read, write, calculate, or solve problems at a level required for independent functioning or the performance of routine technical tasks.[48] Functional illiteracy is exacting a toll, not only on individual social and economic opportunities but also on organizations' accident rates and productivity levels.

Visible and Ethnic Minorities The proportion of visible and ethnic minorities entering the Canadian labour market is growing, largely the result of immigration. More than three-quarters of those who came to Canada during the 1990s were members of a visible minority group.[49] Ethnic diversity is also increasing. Currently, more than 100 different ethnic groups are represented among Canadian residents.[50]

Women The growing presence of women has been one of the dominant trends in Canada's labour force since the 1950s.[51] Factors contributing to the dramatic increase in the female participation rate include smaller family size, increased divorce rate, the need and desire for dual family incomes, increased educational level, and the availability of more-flexible working hours and part-time jobs.

As shown in **Figure 1.4**, between 1946 and the summer of 2000, the employment rate for adult women tripled, while that for men fell by one-fifth.[52] During the 1990s, the unemployment rate for women fell below that of men and stayed there. This trend reflects the fact that women have moved into occupations in which the unemployment rate is low, while men tend to be clustered in jobs in which the risk of unemployment is much higher.[53] There is still strong evidence that women are underutilized in the Canadian workforce, however.

A large number of women in the work force have dependent children. Many organizations are making a determined effort to accommodate working women and shared parenting responsibilities, and offer one or more of the following family-friendly benefits: paid leave banks, childcare information and referral assistance, childcare subsidies, on-site daycare, leave for school functions, emergency childcare support, and flexible work programs (job sharing, a compressed workweek, a shorter workweek, a shorter workday, and/or telecommuting).

functionally illiterate Unable to read, write, calculate, or solve problems at a level required for independent functioning or the performance of routine technical tasks.

AN ETHICAL DILEMMA

The maintenance department supervisor has just come to you, the HR manager, voicing concern about the safety of two of her reporting employees whom she recently discovered are functionally illiterate. What are your responsibilities to these employees, if any?

FIGURE I.4   Employment Rates of Canadian Men and Women (1946–1999)

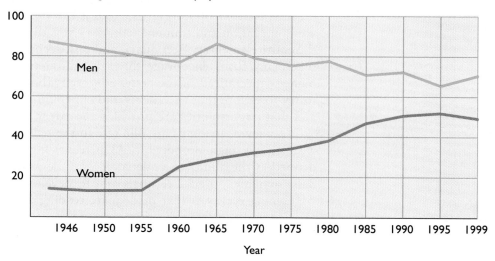

Note: Data from 1976 on have been rebased to the 1996 Census of Population.

Source: Adapted from the Statistics Canada publication *Canadian Social Trends*, Catalogue No. 11-008 (Summer 2000), p. 11.

Aboriginal Peoples Between 1996 and 2006, the number of First Peoples (North American Indians, Inuit, and Métis) in the prime working and family-rearing age group (35 to 54) is expected to increase 41 percent, which will exacerbate their current situation unless drastic measures are taken.[54] First Peoples are still facing considerable difficulty in obtaining jobs and advancing in the workplace.

Persons with Disabilities Despite the fact that human rights legislation in every Canadian jurisdiction prohibits discrimination against individuals with disabilities, Canadians with disabilities continue to confront physical barriers to equality every day. Inaccessibility is still the rule, not the exception. In 1998, 54 percent of persons with disabilities had annual incomes of $15 000 or less.[55] Even though studies show that there are no performance differences in terms of productivity, attendance, and average tenure between employees who classify themselves as having a disability and those who do not, persons with disabilities continue, on average, to experience high rates of unemployment and underemployment, and lower pay.

According to a recent Royal Bank of Canada study, people with disabilities have employment rates about 30 full percentage points below those without a disability, and men with a severe disability who secure full-time employment earn almost 24 percent less than their counterparts without a disability.[56]

Overall, organizations such as the Bank of Montreal have led the way in seeking the benefits of workforce diversity, as described in the Workforce Diversity box.

Technology Manufacturing advances, such as robotics and computer-aided design/computer-aided manufacturing (CAD/CAM), have eliminated many blue-collar jobs, replacing them with fewer but more highly skilled jobs. When

HR Technology www.avantech.ca

WORKFORCE DIVERSITY

At the Bank of Montreal

The Bank of Montreal Group of Companies (BMO) is a prime example of an organization that is opening up the search for talent to all types of people. Creating and maintaining a diverse and equitable workplace is enshrined in the core values of the organization and linked to business initiatives. The organization has won an award for its diversity initiatives from the Conference Board of Canada.

"We ardently look for top talent. That's the reason why we do it. That includes looking at talent pools that traditionally haven't been a focal point in our industry," said Lesya Balych, Vice-President of Workplace Equality at BMO.

There is a two-pronged approach: developing a diverse workforce and developing an equitable workplace. To this end, the firm, headed by very senior executives, developed the Chairman's Council on Equitable Workplace as well as Balych's office of workplace equality.

"Because workplace diversity and equality are a part of our values, it is part of the fabric of our enterprise. It is sewed in to it," says Balych.

The organization has developed employee-led diversity action teams, and offers support to maintain a diverse workplace, like an internal employee assistance program. They recently launched a pilot project to help identify barriers facing persons with disabilities.

The demographics of the organization reflect the success of diversity initiatives at BMO. The number of women holding executive positions has increased to 32.5 percent from 9 percent in 1991; visible minorities account for 18.7 percent of the overall workforce, up from 12.5 percent in 1992; the number of Aboriginal people has also increased from 0.5 percent in 1992 to 1.4 percent; and the number of persons with disabilities is also up from 1.8 percent in 1992 to 3.3 percent. They are also aiming to achieve gender parity at the senior levels by 2007.

Source: L. Cassiani, "Employment Equity Gone Wrong," *Canadian HR Reporter* (June 18, 2002), pp. 1, 14. Reproduced by permission of *Canadian HR Reporter*, Carswell, One Corporate Plaza, 2075 Kennedy Road, Scarborough, ON M1T 3V4.

Robotics is revolutionizing work in many fields. Such technology requires highly trained and committed employees.

AN ETHICAL DILEMMA

How much responsibility does a firm have toward employees whose skills will soon become obsolete due to changing technology?

robots were introduced in the automobile industry, for instance, demand for welders and painters decreased, but a new demand ensued for technicians who could service automated equipment.[57] Similar changes have been occurring in the nature of office work. The overall impact is that labour-intensive blue-collar and clerical jobs have been decreasing, while technical, managerial, and professional jobs are on the increase. Unfortunately, the training of the Canadian labour force has not kept pace with the rate of technological change and innovation, and there is a scarcity of skills in certain fields.

While much of the impact of information technology has been positive, it has also led to some organizational problems. For many employees, it has created anxiety, tension, resentment, and alienation. Unions have consistently expressed concerns about job displacement and health hazards, such as those related to video display terminals. All of these issues must be addressed through effective HRM practices such as information sharing, counselling, ergonomic refitting, job redesign, and training.

Questions concerning data control, accuracy, the right to privacy, and ethics are at the core of a growing controversy brought about by the new information technologies. Sophisticated computerized control systems are used to monitor employee speed, accuracy, and efficiency in some firms. More firms are also monitoring employee e-mail, voice mail, telephone conversations, and computer usage, and some now monitor employee behaviour using video surveillance.[58]

Human Resources Management and Information Technology As discussed earlier, technology is increasingly being used as a delivery mechanism for HR services. Originally, many firms introduced a Human Resources Information System (HRIS) to store detailed information on employees, HR policies and procedures, government laws and regulations, and collective agreements; to track statistics on absenteeism, grievances, and health and safety; to collect data for government statistical reporting and employment equity purposes; to advertise jobs and recruiting candidates; and to communicate with employees.

More recently, some firms have implemented enterprise resource software systems (SAP being the most common) that include a human resources management module. Today, Canadian employers are using HR intranets and e-HR to provide personalized service to employees.[59] As shown in **Figure 1.5**, the majority of Canadian organizations still use HR technology in traditional areas like office and HR administration. A substantial number also use technology for HR transactions, employee research, and document handling. To date, only a few employers have used technology in areas such as payroll and benefit self-service, education, skills inventory, and career planning.[60]

Government Various laws enacted by governments have had and will continue to have a dramatic impact on the employer–employee relationship in Canada. In one recent survey, 70 percent of the HR specialists responding cited changing regulatory requirements as a major factor altering their work environment.[61]

Topics Covered by Legislation Some of the employment-related legislation is aimed at prohibiting discrimination in various aspects and terms and conditions of employment, such as human rights, employment equity, and pay equity. Other laws require employers to meet certain obligations, such as occupational health

Figure I.5 What Is Technology Being Used For?

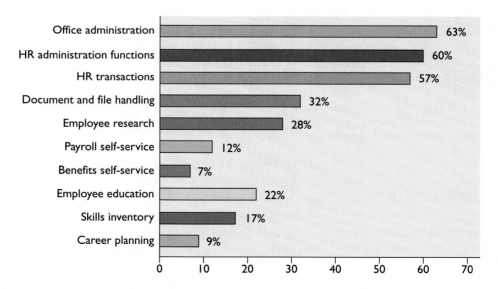

Source: HR's Quest for Status: Fantasy or Emerging Reality? by *Canadian HR Reporter* and Watson Wyatt, August 2001. Reproduced by permission of *Canadian HR Reporter*, Carswell, One Corporate Plaza, 2075 Kennedy Road, Scarborough, ON M1T 3V4.

and safety, employment standards regarding holidays, hours of work, and so on, and labour relations. Still others provide social benefits such as Workers' Compensation, Employment Insurance, and the Canada/Quebec Pension Plans that require financial contributions from employers and employees.

Multiple Jurisdictions One of the factors that make the laws affecting employment in Canada so challenging is the many different jurisdictions involved. Each province and territory (13 in all) has its own human rights, employment standards, labour relations, health and safety, and workers' compensation legislation. While there is some commonality across jurisdictions, there is also considerable variation. Minimum wage, overtime pay requirements, vacation entitlement, and grounds protected under human rights legislation, for example, vary from one province/territory to another. Furthermore, some jurisdictions have pay and employment equity legislation; others do not. This means that companies with employees in more than one jurisdiction have different rules applying to different employees.

To complicate matters even further, employees in certain organizations that operate across Canada are not covered by provincial/territorial legislation, but by federal employment law. These employees represent about 10 percent of the Canadian workforce, including employees of the federal government and Crown corporations, chartered banks, airlines, national railways, and the Canadian armed forces. There are, however, certain laws that apply to all employers and employees across Canada. These federal laws include Employment Insurance and the Canada/Quebec Pension Plan.

Sometimes changes in a federal law will drive changes to provincial/territorial laws. For example, when the Employment Insurance Act was amended in 2000 to provide up to 52 weeks of maternity/parental leave benefits, most provinces/territories provided less than 52 weeks of combined maternity/parental leave. Each jurisdiction then had to consider amendments to its Employment Standards Act to extend combined maternity/parental leave to 52 weeks.

All of the laws mentioned above and their accompanying regulations have important implications for all managers. HR professionals inform managers of changes to the laws, and develop and administer legally compliant policies and practices to avoid losing government contracts, fines or other penalties for noncompliance, and adverse publicity.

Globalization

globalization The tendency of firms to extend their sales or manufacturing to new markets abroad.

Globalization refers to the growing tendency of firms to extend their sales or manufacturing to new markets abroad. Canada currently has approximately 200 international trading partners.[62] As one international business expert put it, "The bottom line is that the growing integration of the world economy into a single, huge marketplace is increasing the intensity of competition in a wide range of manufacturing and service industries."[63]

There are increasing numbers of multinational corporations—firms that conduct a large part of business outside the country in which they are headquartered and that locate a significant percentage of their physical facilities and human resources in other countries. Many organizations are locating new plants in areas where wages and other operating costs are lower. For example, Hewlett Packard's computers are assembled in Mexico, and 3M—the manufacturer of Scotch tape, chemicals, and electrical accessories—has located one of its newest plants in India.[64] Many multinational firms also set up manufacturing plants

Hints to Ensure Legal Compliance

Global HRM

Fairmont Hotels

The old CP Hotels is now Fairmont Hotels and Resorts. Over the last three years, they have purchased Princess Hotels, merged with Fairmont Hotels, and been spun off from their parent company as an independent, publicly traded company. They are now North America's largest luxury hotel chain, with 30 000 employees—a global player in the hotel industry.

"In our industry today, the competitive advantage is service delivery," says Carolyn Clark, Vice President, Human Resources. Clark's strategic HR plan is the foundation for Fairmont's service culture that consistently delivers top service. It is based on four key principles: select the best; lead with the best; train and develop; and recognize and reward. As Fairmont expands globally, this HR strategy is adopted into the new hotels. The secret to success of the Fairmont service culture has been the focus and integration of all four aspects of the HR strategy.

As employers become more global and mergers and acquisitions become more prevalent in business, a critical success factor is the merger of corporate cultures. "If the merger or acquisition is going to fail, quite often it is because the cultures are not aligned," stated Clark. "When we planned the mergers, we put a lot of thought into the human side of it. We asked, 'What are the best practices that each company has to bring?' and from that we moved forward."

From the start of the merger project between Canadian Pacific, Princess, and Fairmont, company-wide communication from the top down was a key component. "We didn't presume that either company had the best practices. We worked together to understand the systems and procedures and cultures of the companies, and together we developed the new culture," said Clark. Clark cautions that the merging of cultures doesn't happen overnight. There needs to be lots of communication.

The international expansion alone has required learning about the cultures and HR practices of different countries. For example, Fairmont is in the midst of opening its first overseas hotel in Dubai, United Arab Emirates. As Fairmont grows and the vision of the company evolves, they plan to stay true to their HR strategy.

Source: Based on R. Langlois, "Fairmont Hotels: Business Strategy with People," *Canadian HR Reporter* (November 5, 2001), pp. 1, 25, 27. Reproduced by permission of *Canadian HR Reporter*, Carswell, One Corporate Plaza, 2075 Kennedy Road, Scarborough, ON M1T 3V4.

abroad to utilize that country's professionals and engineers. From boosting the productivity of a global labour force to formulating selection, training, and compensation policies for expatriate employees, managing globalization and its effects on competitiveness will thus continue to be a major HR challenge in the years to come. The crucial role of HR in the international expansion of Fairmont Hotels and Resorts is described in the Global HR box.

A Brief History of HRM

HRM has changed dramatically over time and has assumed an increasingly important role. The demands on HR department staff members and expectations regarding the types of assistance they should provide have increased correspondingly. HR practices have been shaped by society's prevailing beliefs and attitudes about workers and their rights, which have evolved in three stages.

Scientific Management: Concern for Production

scientific management The process of "scientifically" analyzing manufacturing processes, reducing production costs, and compensating employees based on their performance levels.

Frederick Taylor was the driving force behind **scientific management**, the process of "scientifically" analyzing manufacturing processes, reducing production costs, and compensating employees based on their performance.[65] As a result, management practices in the late 1800s and early 1900s emphasized task simplification and performance-based pay. Such incentives were expected to

Frederick Taylor (1856–1915), the father of scientific management.

human relations movement A management philosophy based on the belief that the attitudes and feelings of workers are important and deserve more attention.

lead to higher wages for workers, increased profits for the organization, and workplace harmony. Taylor's views were not accepted by all management theorists. For example, Mary Parker Follett, a writer ahead of her time, advocated the use of self-management, cross-functional cooperation, empowerment, and managers as leaders, not dictators.[66]

The Human Relations Movement: Concern for People

The primary aim of the **human relations movement**, which emerged in the 1920s and '30s but was not fully embraced until the '40s, was to consider jobs from an employee's perspective. Managers who treated workers as machines were criticized. This management philosophy was based on the results of the Hawthorne Studies, a series of experiments that examined factors influencing worker morale and productivity. The conclusions had a significant and far-reaching impact on management practices.

The researchers discovered that the effect of the social environment was equal to or greater than that of the physical environment. They learned that worker morale was greatly influenced by such factors as working conditions, the supervisor's leadership style, and management's philosophy regarding workers. Treating workers with dignity and respect was found to lead to higher job satisfaction and productivity levels, with economic incentives being of secondary importance. In the many firms embracing the human relations approach, working conditions improved substantially. Managers focused on establishing better channels of communication, allowing employees to exercise more self-direction, and treating employees with consideration. This movement came under severe criticism for overcompensating for the dehumanizing effects of scientific management by failing to recognize the importance of structure and work rules, for oversimplifying the concept of employee motivation, and for failing to recognize individual differences in beliefs, needs, and abilities.

The Human Resources Movement: Concern for People and Productivity

human resources movement A management philosophy focusing on concern for people and productivity.

HRM is currently based on the theoretical assumptions of the **human resources movement**. Arriving at this joint focus on people and productivity involved four evolutionary phases.[67]

Phase One In the early 1900s, HRM—or personnel administration, as it was then called—played a very subservient or nonexistent role. During this era, personnel administrators assumed responsibility for hiring and firing (a duty formerly looked after by first-line supervisors), ran the payroll department, and administered benefits. Their job consisted largely of ensuring that procedures were followed.

Phase Two As the scientific management movement gained momentum, operational efficiency increased but wage increases did not keep up, causing workers to distrust management. The resulting increase in unionization led to personnel departments serving as the primary contact for union representatives. Following the depression of the 1930s, various pieces of legislation were enacted, including a minimum wage act, an unemployment insurance program, and protection of workers' rights to belong to unions. Legal compliance was subsequently added to the responsibilities of personnel managers. During the 1940s and 1950s, personnel managers were also involved in dealing with the impact of the human relations movement. Orientation, performance appraisal, and employee relations responsibilities were added to their portfolio.

Phase Three The third major phase in personnel management was a direct result of government legislation passed during the 1960s, 1970s, and 1980s that affected employees' human rights, wages and benefits, working conditions, and health and safety, and established penalties for failure to meet them. The role of personnel departments expanded dramatically. They continued to provide expertise in areas such as recruitment, screening, and training, but in an expanded capacity. During the latter part of this era, the term "human resources management" emerged. This change represented a shift in emphasis—from maintenance and administration to corporate contribution, proactive management, and initiation of change.[68]

Phase Four The fourth phase of HRM is ongoing. Most managers today believe that workers are motivated primarily by the nature and scope of the job, social influences, the nature of the compensation and incentive systems, organizational culture and climate, management's supervisory style, and individual needs and values. It is widely recognized that employees do not all seek the same rewards and that most sincerely want to make a contribution. To harness this drive and determination, organizations must develop strategies to maximize employee performance and potential, such that the goals and aims of both management and employees are achieved. In today's organizations, employees are often a firm's best competitive advantage. The role of HR departments has thus shifted from protector and screener to planner and change agent.

GROWING PROFESSIONALISM IN HRM

certification Recognition for having met certain professional standards.

Canadian Council of HR
Associations (CCHRA)
www.cchra-ccarh.ca

International Personnel
Management Association
www.ipma-aigp.ca

North American Human Resource
Management Association
(NAHRMA)
**www.shrmglobal.org/nahrma/
index.html**

Today, HR practitioners must be professionals in terms of both performance and qualifications. Every profession has four major characteristics: (1) a common body of knowledge; (2) **certification** of members; (3) self-regulation; and (4) a code of ethics. Every province (except Newfoundland and Prince Edward Island) has an association of HR practitioners that manages these four areas, ensures information exchange and cooperative problem solving, provides HR training and skills updating, and serves as a voice for HR practitioners regarding proposed legislation. The Canadian Council of Human Resources Associations (CCHRA) is the national body through which all provincial and specialist HR associations are affiliated. The International Personnel Management Association (IPMA)—Canada is the national association for public-sector and quasi–public-sector HR professionals.[69]

Other important associations for HR specialists include the Canadian Industrial Relations Association; WorldatWork (formerly the Canadian Compensation Association); health and safety associations such as the Industrial Accident Prevention Association, the Construction Safety Association, and Safe Communities Canada; and groups such as the Ontario Society for Training and Development for training and development professionals.

The Certified Human Resources Professional (CHRP) designation is a nationally recognized certification for Canadian HR professionals. Managed by the CCHRA and administered through provincial HR associations, the CHRP is similar to other professional designations such as the Chartered Accountant (CA) and Professional Engineer (P.Eng.), as it recognizes members' qualifications and experience based on established levels of core competencies.[70] The national certification requirements are shown in **Figure 1.6.**

FIGURE I.6 National CHRP Certification Requirements

A. Initial Certification

To fulfill the academic requirement for the CHRP designation, a candidate must:

1. Become a member of a provincial human resources professionals' association; and

2. Complete all nine required courses listed below (Ontario candidates only); and

3. Pass

(1) the national knowledge examination (assesses knowledge of major human resources functions), and

(2) professional practice assessment (measures human resources "experience"); must be written within 5 years of writing the knowledge exam.

Note: Although not currently necessary, by 2011, all CHRP candidates will require a degree.

Required Courses for the National Knowledge Examination (Ontario candidates only)

Compulsory:

Human Resources Management
Organizational Behaviour
Financial and Managerial Accounting
Compensation
Training & Development
Occupational Health & Safety
Labour Relations
Human Resources Planning
Recruitment & Selection

Optional:

Professional practice workshops on topics like business ethics, HR information management and project management.

B. Recertification

Every three years, all CHRPs will be required to recertify based on a set of professional development criteria, including seminars, conferences, volunteer work, or continuing education.

Source: Based on "Become a Certified Human Resources Professional." *Human Resources Professionals Association of Ontario.* www.hrpao.org. June 6, 2003. Reproduced with permission.

Members of the Canadian Council of Human Resources Associations' professional steering committee celebrate the official launch of national standards for the Certified Human Resources Professional designation in February 2003.

Ethics

The professionalization of HRM has created the need for a uniform code of ethics. Professional associations devise codes of ethics to promote and maintain the highest possible standards of personal and professional conduct among members and assist them in handling ethical dilemmas. Agreement to abide by the code of ethics is one of the requirements of maintaining professional status. The Code of Ethics of HRPAO is shown in **Figure 1.7**. Since what is ethical or unethical is generally open to debate, except in a few very clear-cut cases (such as willful misrepresentation), most codes do not tell employees what they should do. Rather, they provide a guide to help employees discover the best course of action by themselves.[71]

Having a code is not enough, however. According to one noted ethics expert, "The ethical code of conduct is only the first step in the development of an ethical culture."[72] Integrating ethics in the workplace requires specific initiatives aligned with management policies, reporting structures, and

---

FIGURE I.7   Code of Ethics—Human Resources Professionals Association of Ontario (HRPAO)

Human Resources Professionals
Association of Ontario
www.hrpao.org

Ethics Resource Center
www.ethics.org

Human resources professionals shall:

continue professional growth in human resources management, in support and promotion of the goals, objectives and by-laws of the Association;

not knowingly violate or cause to be violated, any legislated act, regulation or by-law that relates to the management of human resources;

commit to the values of respect for human dignity and human rights, and promote human development in the workplace, within the profession and society as a whole;

treat information obtained in the course of business as confidential, and avoid, or disclose, any conflict of interest that might influence personal actions or judgments;

refrain from inappropriately using their position to secure special privileges, gain or benefit for themselves, their employers or the Association;

acknowledge an obligation to the employer community to encourage and foster generally accepted codes of moral behaviour; and,

practise respect and regard for other professional associations.

Source: "HRPAO Code of Ethics." *Human Resources Professionals Association of Ontario.* www.hrpao.org. June 6, 2003. Reproduced with permission.

AN ETHICAL
DILEMMA

Suppose that you, an HR professional, have just discovered that a colleague in the HR department, who is a good friend, has been "leaking" confidential information about employees to other employees. How would you handle this situation?

AN ETHICAL
DILEMMA

Can or should an employee reveal information about a troubled co-worker that was disclosed in confidence, and if so, under what circumstances?

social responsibility The implied, enforced, or felt obligation of managers, acting in their official capacities, to serve or protect the interests of groups other than themselves.

Business for Social Responsibility **www.bsr.org**

Canadian Business for Social Responsibility **cbsr.ca**

reward and promotion systems.[73] Increasingly, HR departments are being given a greater role in communicating the organization's values and standards, providing ethics training, and monitoring to ensure compliance with the code of ethics. Some organizations have such a commitment to ethics that they have a full-time ethics officer. On the other hand, a 2003 U.S. business ethics survey found that more than half of HR professionals had been pressured to act unethically in the previous year.[74]

The most prevalent ethical issues confronting Canadian firms today pertain to security of information, employee and client privacy, environment issues, governance, and conflicts of interest.[75] The major reasons for the failure of ethics programs to achieve the desired results are lack of effective leadership and inadequate training. Positive outcomes associated with properly implemented ethics programs include:

- increased confidence among stakeholders, such as clients, partners, and employees
- greater client/customer and employee loyalty
- decreased vulnerability to crimes committed against the public and legal liability issues, such as those described in the margin
- reduced absenteeism
- increased employee productivity
- reduced losses due to internal theft, and
- increased profits and public trust.[76]

In recent years, the concept of **social responsibility** has frequently been discussed as a complement to ethics. A company that exercises social responsibility attempts to balance its commitments—not only to its investors, but also to its employees and customers, other businesses, and the community or communities in which it operates. The Body Shop, an early and often-cited example of a socially responsible firm, proves that businesses can balance profits and principles. Despite taking a stand on anti-animal testing, human rights protection, and environmental conservation (the three main criteria against which all activities are measured), the firm's annual retail sales amount to more than US$1.4 billion worldwide. Ingredients for the firm's cosmetics products are community traded, which means that the producers get a fair price for their goods and can use the income to improve their own quality of life and that of their communities.

HR AUDITING

HR audit An evaluation of the firm's HR activities and the HR department's effectiveness as a strategic partner.

Just as financial audits are conducted, periodic and systematic evaluations or audits should be conducted to assess how effectively the firm is managing its human resources.[77] Comprehensive **HR audits** encompass three areas:

1. *The HR department's effectiveness as a strategic partner.* HR audits need to begin with a fundamental review of the business strategy of the organization, so that the audit can be carried out with an understanding of the objectives of the business.[78] In order to measure the value of HR, it is necessary to move away from focusing on transactional measures, such as

cost-per-hire, to measures that reflect value creation, such as improvements in customer service following a training course.[79]

2. *Organizational compliance with applicable federal, provincial (or territorial), and municipal laws and regulations.*

3. *The performance of specific HRM programs and functions.* Employee **attitude surveys** are often used to assess how employees feel about a variety of issues and gaining insight into their perceptions of the organization's strengths and weaknesses. Topics surveyed typically include supervision, HR policies and programs, effectiveness of communication strategies, and overall leadership. Survey results should be shared with employees, along with the specific strategies being implemented to address any concerns and/or correct any identified problems.

In addition to surveys, organizations use several other research tools to collect data. Many firms conduct **exit interviews** with departing employees to identify any sources of dissatisfaction contributing to their decision to leave. Some organizations use **focus groups** to obtain in-depth information from a small group of employees. These involve an unstructured group discussion with an unbiased facilitator. A **records analysis** is often included as part of an HR audit. For example, reports pertaining to health and safety, scrap rates, turnover and absenteeism, and grievances are often examined. Internal placement records, selection records, and employee files may also be looked at. A few firms use **field experiments** where experimental and control groups are compared. For example, one group of supervisors might receive hazardous material safety training (the experimental group). Another group of supervisors not receiving the training constitutes the control group. If subsequent safety records reveal a significantly lower rate of hazardous material accidents and injuries for experimental group supervisors, then the training would be considered effective.

To be meaningful, quantifiable audit results should be compared with some accepted external measure of performance, such as industry norms or research findings. Some firms use **benchmarking**, which is a process of comparing organizational performance in a particular area against data from a firm considered to be superior in that area. The value to be derived from conducting HR audits lies in making improvements. When using a benchmarking approach, outstanding performers on a particular dimension can be contacted to determine how the results were achieved. Strategies for performance improvements can thus be identified and targets set to meet survey benchmarks.[80] For example, Royal Victoria Hospital in Barrie, Ontario, noticed that their stress-related absenteeism and disability rates were high compared to other hospitals, so they decided to invest more resources into their employee assistance plan.[81]

HRM CHALLENGES IN THE TWENTY-FIRST CENTURY

Developing and Implementing Corporate Strategy

Perhaps the most striking change in the role of those responsible for HRM is their growing importance in developing and implementing strategy. Traditionally, **strategy**—the company's plan for how it will balance its internal strengths and weaknesses with external opportunities and threats in order to maintain a competitive advantage—was formulated without HR input. Today,

---

attitude survey A survey administered to determine employee thoughts and feelings about organizational issues.

exit interview A conversation with departing employees to learn their opinions of employment with the organization, and reason(s) for leaving.

focus group A group of users of the HR department services, who provide in-depth feedback about the HR activities, programs, and services.

records analysis A review of organizational records to assess compliance with company policies and legislative standards; measure the effectiveness of HR programs in meeting objectives; and identify areas for improvement.

field experiment A research design that enables the comparison of an experimental and control group, to assess the effectiveness of HR programs.

benchmarking A systematic process for comparing some aspect of organizational performance against data from a firm considered to be superior in that particular area.

strategy The company's plan for how it will balance its internal strengths and weaknesses with external opportunities and threats in order to maintain a competitive advantage.

things are very different. Strategies increasingly depend on strengthening organizational responsiveness and building committed work teams, and these put HR in a central role.[82]

Thus, it is increasingly common to involve HR professionals in the earliest stages of developing and implementing the firm's strategic plan, rather than simply letting them react to it. More firms are coming to realize that HR professionals are of greatest benefit when they become strategic partners, responsible for leading organizational change initiatives, developing business strategies in cooperation with operational managers, and building and implementing effective HR strategies. Important skills/competencies for strategic human resources managers are shown in **Figure 1.8.**

Organizations are increasingly viewing the HR department as an equal partner in the strategic planning process. In order to forge the organization's workforce into a competitive advantage, the proponents of this viewpoint believe that the HR department staff members must be equal partners in both formulation and implementation of the firm's organization-wide and competitive strategies.[83]

environmental scanning

Identifying and analyzing external opportunities and threats that may be crucial to the organization's success.

Role in Formulating Strategy HR professionals, often together with line managers, can play a role in what strategic planners call **environmental scanning**, which involves identifying and analyzing external opportunities and threats that may be crucial to the organization's success. These managers can also

---

FIGURE I.8   The Skills to Do the Job

Respondents were asked how important (from completely unimportant to very important) the following competencies are for HR leaders at their organization. The chart represents number of respondents who said the competency was "very important."

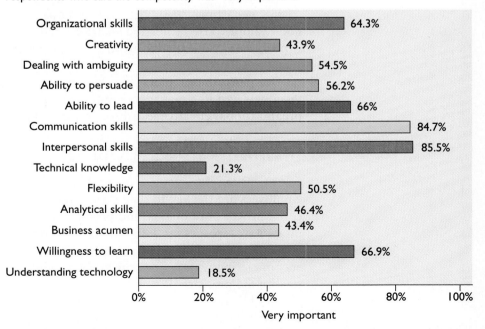

Source: *HR's Quest for Status: Fantasy or Emerging Reality?* by *Canadian HR Reporter* and Watson Wyatt, August 2001. Reproduced by permission of *Canadian HR Reporter*, Carswell, One Corporate Plaza, 2075 Kennedy Road, Scarborough, ON M1T 3V4.

supply *competitive intelligence* that may be useful as the company formulates its strategic plans. Details regarding a successful incentive plan being used by a competitor, employee opinion survey data eliciting information about customer complaints, and information about pending legislative changes are examples.

The HR department also participates in the strategy formulation process by supplying information regarding the company's internal strengths and weaknesses. Once weaknesses have been identified, corrective action can be planned and taken. Some firms even build their strategies around an HR-based competitive advantage. For example, in the process of automating its factories, farm-equipment manufacturer John Deere developed a workforce that was exceptionally talented and expert in factory automation. This, in turn, prompted the firm to establish a new technology division to offer automation services to other companies.[84]

In the Canadian auto industry, a serious labour shortage is looming which could lead to threats to the survival of some auto-parts manufacturers, as big automakers will use suppliers abroad if Canadian firms are unable to meet their needs. But succession planning in the auto-parts industry has been vague and informal, and industry leaders do not seem too understand the critical role of human resources in their future. Without strong emphasis on HR planning, it appears unlikely that strategic objectives will be achieved by some auto-parts manufacturers in the future.[85]

Role in Executing Strategy Leading HR researcher Brian Becker says, "It isn't the content of the strategy that differentiates the winners and losers, it is the ability to execute."[86] Strategy execution has traditionally been the "bread and butter" of HR's strategy role. For example, the competitive strategy may involve differentiating the organization from its competitors by offering superior customer service through a highly committed, competent, and customer-oriented work force.[87]

HR departments support strategy implementation in numerous other ways. For example, HR professionals are heavily involved in the execution of most firms' downsizing and restructuring strategies through establishing training and retraining programs, arranging for outplacement services, instituting pay-for-performance plans, and helping to redesign jobs. In addition, HR professionals and line managers jointly play a critical role in strategies to increase organizational effectiveness through performance management.[88]

Improving Productivity

Organizations known for product and service quality strongly believe that employees are the key to their reputation, and that proper attention to employees improves both quality and productivity. A review of management practices in such companies as GE, FedEx Canada, and 3M Canada indicates that top-level commitment, employee involvement, and a conscious strategy to encourage innovation are critical for productivity improvement.[89] All of these require the presence of enlightened and proactive HR policies and procedures.

The HR department staff members and line managers play a pivotal role in lowering labour costs, the single largest operating expense in many organizations, particularly in the service sector. Doing so might involve introducing strategies developed by HR and/or line managers to reduce turnover, absenteeism, and/or the rate of incidence of occupational illnesses and injuries. It could also mean adopting more effective recruitment, selection, and training programs. At one international tire manufacturing firm, for example, adopting a behaviour-based interview strategy as the basis for selection of entry-level engineers resulted in savings of $500 000 in three years. These savings were due to lower turnover, lower training costs, and improved capabilities of the engineering staff because of a better fit.[90]

For many firms, instituting tough headcount controls is a key strategy in reducing labour costs. The HR department generally plays the central role in planning and implementing corporate downsizings.

Increasing Responsiveness to Change

Making the enterprise more responsive to product/service innovations and technological change is the objective of many management strategies. Flattening the pyramid, empowering employees, and organizing around teams are ways in which HRM can help to improve the design and facilitation of communication among employees so that an organization can respond quickly to its customers' needs and competitors' challenges. People are the ultimate vehicle that enables organizations to become faster and more agile, and leaders realize that boosting speed and agility in talent management will have the greatest leveraging effect inside the organization.[91]

Improving Service

Employee behaviour is particularly important in the service sector, which provides three-quarters of the total employment in Canada.[92] Many service firms, such as banks and retail establishments, have little to differentiate themselves from their competitors except superior service, making them uniquely dependent on their employees' attitudes and motivation—and thus on effective HRM. "Getting customer service right means getting HR right," says Lloyd Craig, president and CEO of Surrey Metro Savings Credit Union. His company has developed an extensive list of HR programs designed to help create and support happy, healthy, engaged employees.[93]

Research Insight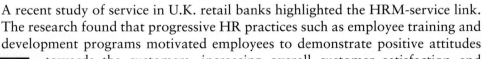

A recent study of service in U.K. retail banks highlighted the HRM-service link. The research found that progressive HR practices such as employee training and development programs motivated employees to demonstrate positive attitudes towards the customers, increasing overall customer satisfaction and retention.[94]

Helping to Build Employee Commitment

Intense global competition and the need for more responsiveness put a premium on employee commitment (sometimes called *engagement*). Building employee commitment requires the joint efforts of HR department staff and managers throughout the firm (see the HR Works box). High-commitment firms also tend to engage in *actualizing practices*, which aim to ensure that employees fully use their skills and gifts at work and become all that they can be. HR practices are crucial here, for instance, in establishing career-oriented performance-appraisal procedures and open job-posting and job-transfer practices.

Employees in fast-food establishments are taught how to provide courteous, efficient customer service.

The Changing Canadian Workplace

... Changing markets, changing competition and changing technology are dramatically affecting the ways in which organizations are structured. Trade has become more global, protection is disappearing, and technology has reduced the importance of large plants with economies of scale. As a result, companies must be flexible in order to respond to opportunities and be competitive. This means that the traditional organizational hierarchies created in the post-war period are now rapidly becoming out of date. Companies now need fewer layers of management, and those managing need to be able to make decisions faster. Training allows companies to respond positively and innovatively to changes in the marketplace and to adapt to new technologies.

At the same time, Canada's environment has also changed. The workforce has become multi-cultural, women have entered the labour force in vast numbers, and legislation has been introduced in many provinces to cover issues of equity, hiring of replacement workers, and other workplace issues.

... There is a growing body of evidence which suggests that good human resource management practice is the key to improving company performance. This can include new ways of organizing companies, less-rigid structures, and good human resource practices, such as HR planning, recruitment policies, thorough job descriptions, entry-level training to upgrade skills, career planning, compensation, and other plans and policies which affect the working lives of individuals in the workplace.

New ways of organizing are emerging based on less-hierarchical forms of work organization, a re-examination of the way in which compensation and rewards are shared in the workplace, a re-examination of how workplace decisions are made, and an increased investment in training....

Source: Excerpted with permission from the *Training and Development Guide*, ¶95,020, published by and copyright CCH Canadian Limited, Toronto, Ontario.

CHAPTER *Review*

Summary

1   Human resources management (HRM) refers to the management of people in organizations. The objective of HRM is to maximize employees' contributions in order to achieve optimal productivity and effectiveness, while simultaneously attaining individual objectives and societal objectives. Strategic HRM involves linking HRM with strategic goals and objectives to improve business performance and develop an organizational culture that fosters innovation and flexibility. In more and more firms, the HR department is becoming a strategic partner, playing a role in strategy formulation and execution.

2   Five activities required of HR managers and other line managers who are responsible for HRM are to formulate policies and procedures; offer HR advice; provide HR services; ensure compliance with HR policies and procedures, and employment legislation; and serve as a consultant and change agent.

3   Research studies have established a link between effective HR practices, employee performance, and the bottom line, if properly implemented and accompanied by a supportive culture and climate. HR has been found to affect profits, new-venture success, and almost half of the differences in market value between companies.

4   Internal environmental factors influencing HRM include organizational culture, which consists of the core values, beliefs, and assumptions that are widely shared by members of the organization; organizational climate, which is the prevailing atmosphere; and management practices such as the shift from traditional bureaucratic structures to flatter organizations where employees are empowered to make more decisions. A number of external factors have an impact on HRM, including economic factors, labour market

issues, demographic trends and increasing workforce diversity, technology, government, and globalization.

5   The three stages in the evolution of management thinking about workers are (1) scientific management, which focused on production; (2) the human relations movement, in which the emphasis was on people; and (3) the human resources movement, in which it was recognized that organizational success is linked to both.

6   HR challenges in the twenty-first century include developing and implementing corporate strategy, improving productivity, increasing responsiveness to change, improving customer service, and building employee commitment.

Key Terms

attitude survey   *(p. 24)*
baby boomers   *(p. 12)*
benchmarking   *(p. 24)*
boundaryless organization structure   *(p. 8)*
bureaucratic structure   *(p. 8)*
certification   *(p. 20)*
contingent employees   *(p. 11)*
demographics   *(p. 12)*
diversity   *(p. 12)*
electronic HR (e-HR)   *(p. 4)*
empowerment   *(p. 8)*
environmental scanning   *(p. 25)*
exit interview   *(p. 24)*
field experiment   *(p. 24)*
focus group   *(p. 24)*
functionally illiterate   *(p. 13)*
Generation X   *(p. 12)*
globalization   *(p. 17)*
HR audit   *(p. 23)*

human capital   *(p. 11)*
human relations movement   *(p. 19)*
human resources management (HRM)   *(p. 2)*
human resources movement   *(p. 19)*
knowledge worker   *(p. 10)*
labour force   *(p. 9)*
labour market   *(p. 9)*
labour union   *(p. 11)*
organizational climate   *(p. 8)*
organizational culture   *(p. 8)*
outsourcing   *(p. 3)*
policy   *(p. 3)*
primary sector   *(p. 10)*
procedure   *(p. 3)*
productivity   *(p. 9)*
records analysis   *(p. 24)*
Sandwich Generation   *(p. 12)*
scientific management   *(p. 18)*
secondary sector   *(p. 10)*
social responsibility   *(p. 23)*
strategic human resources management   *(p. 2)*
strategy   *(p. 24)*
tertiary or service sector   *(p. 10)*

Review and Discussion Questions

1   Differentiate between organizational culture and organizational climate.

2   Describe the multiple jurisdictions related to employment legislation affecting HRM in Canada.

3   Describe scientific management and explain its impact on organizations.

4   Explain why HRM is a profession.

5   Explain why the HR system should be evaluated and describe four auditing techniques used in HRM.

CRITICAL *Thinking Questions*

1   Explain how changing demographics and increasing workforce diversity have had an impact on the organization in which you are working or one in which you have worked.

2   A firm has requested your assistance in ensuring that their multigenerational workforce functions effectively as a team. What strategies and/or programs would you recommend? Why?

3   Identify a company that is known for being both ethical and socially responsible. What types of behaviour and activities typify this organization? How has this behaviour affected the achievement of their corporate strategy?

4 Describe an ethical dilemma that you have confronted, explain how you handled the situation, and critique your performance. Did you handle the situation effectively? If not, what would you do differently if you could do it over again? If so, explain why you feel that you handled the situation appropriately.

APPLICATION *Exercises*

Running Case: LearnInMotion.com

Introduction

The main theme of this book is that HRM—activities like recruiting, selecting, training, and rewarding employees—is not just the job of a central HR group, but rather one in which every manager must engage. Perhaps nowhere is this more apparent than in the typical small service business, where the owner-manager usually has no HR staff to rely on. However, the success of such an enterprise often depends largely on the effectiveness with which workers are recruited, hired, trained, evaluated, and rewarded. To help illustrate and emphasize the front-line manager's HR role, throughout this book we will use a continuing ("running") case, based on an actual small business in Ottawa's high-tech region. Each segment will illustrate how the case's main players—owner-managers Jennifer Lau and Pierre LeBlanc—confront and solve HRM problems each day by applying the concepts and techniques presented in that particular chapter. Here's some background information you'll need to answer questions that arise in subsequent chapters.

LearnInMotion.com: A Profile

Jennifer and Pierre graduated from university as business majors in June 2000, and got the idea for LearnInMotion.com as a result of a project they worked on together their last semester in their entrepreneurship class. The professor had divided the students into two- or three-person teams, and given them the assignment to "create a business plan for a dot-com company." The idea the two came up with was LearnInMotion.com. The basic idea of the Web site was to list a vast array of Web-based, CD-ROM-based, or textbook-based continuing education-type business courses for working people who wanted to take a course from the comfort of their own homes. The idea was that users could come to the Web site to find and then take a course in one of several ways. Some courses could be completed interactively on the Web via the site; others were in a form that was downloadable directly to the user's computer; others (which were either textbook or CD-ROM based) could be ordered and delivered (in several major metropolitan areas) by independent contractor delivery people. Their business mission was "to provide work-related learning when, where, and how you need it."

Based on their research, they knew the market for work-related learning like this was booming. At the same time, professional development activities like these were increasingly Internet-based. Tens of thousands of on- and offline training firms, universities, associations, and other content providers were trying to reach their target customers via the Internet. Jennifer and Pierre understandably thought they were in the right place at the right time. And perhaps they were.

When the two graduated in June 2000, it looked like the Internet boom would go on forever. Jennifer's father had some unused loft space in Kanata, so with about $45 000 of accumulated savings, Jennifer and Pierre incorporated and were in business. They retained the services of an independent programmer and hired two people—a Web designer to create the graphics for the site (which would then be programmed by the programmer), and a content manager whose job was to enter information onto the site as it came in from content providers. By the end of 2000, they also completed upgrading their business plan into a form they could show to prospective venture capitalists. They sent the first version to three Canadian venture capitalists. Then they waited.

And then they waited some more. They never heard back from the first three venture capitalists, so they sent their plan to five more. By now it was October 2001, and a dramatic event occurred: The values of a wide range of Internet and Internet-related sites dropped precipitously on the stock market. But

Pierre and Jennifer pressed on. By day they called customers to get people to place ads on their site, to get content providers to list their available courses, and to get someone—anyone—to deliver textbook- and CD-ROM based courses, as needed, across Canada. By May 2002, they had about 300 content providers offering courses and content through LearnInMotion.com. In the summer, they got their first serious nibble from a venture capital firm. They negotiated with this company through much of the summer, came to terms in the early fall, and closed the deal—getting just over $1 million in venture funding—in November 2002.

After a stunning total of $75 000 in legal fees (they had to pay both their firm's and the venture capital firm's lawyers to navigate the voluminous disclosure documents and agreements), they had just over $900 000 to spend. The funding, according to the business plan, was to go toward accomplishing five main goals: redesigning and expanding the Web site; hiring about seven more employees; moving to a larger office; designing and implementing a personal information manager (PIM)/calendar (users and content providers could use the calendar to interactively keep track of their personal and business schedules); and, last but not least, driving up sales. LearnInMotion was off and running.

Questions

1   Would a company like this with just a few employees and independent contractors have any HR tasks to address? What do you think those might be?

2   What basic HR policies and procedures would you recommend to Jennifer and Pierre?

CASE INCIDENT   *International Electronics Corporation*

International Electronics Corporation (IEC) is an important part of its local economy. It is the largest employer in a rural community just north of Vancouver. It employs almost 10 percent of the local workforce; few alternative job opportunities are available in the area. Scott Tanaka, the human resources director at IEC, was facing a difficult decision:

> Business was going along pretty well despite the economic recession, but I knew that sooner or later we would be affected. At a meeting with the president, Bob Deason, and the rest of the executive team, the possibility of cutting the workforce by 30 percent was discussed. I was to get back to them within a week with a suggested plan. I knew that this plan would not be the final one, because the move was so major, but I knew that Bob Deason and the others were depending on me to provide at least a workable approach.
>
> First, I thought about how the union would react. Certainly, workers would have to be let go in order of seniority. The union would try to protect as many jobs as possible. I also knew that all management actions during this period would be intensely scrutinized. We had to make sure we had our act together.
>
> Then there was the impact on the surrounding community to consider. The local economy had not been in good shape recently. Aside from the effect on individual workers who were laid off, I knew that any IEC cutbacks would further depress the area's economy. I know that a number of government officials and civic leaders would want to know how we were trying to minimize the harm done to the public in the area.
>
> We really had to make the cuts, I believed. I had read news accounts that our biggest competitor, in Calgary, had laid off several hundred workers in a cost-cutting move. To keep our sales from being further depressed, we had to keep our costs as low as those of our competitors. The market for electronic products is very competitive and a cost advantage of even 2 or 3 percent would allow competitors to take many of our customers.
>
> Finally, a major reason for the cutbacks was to protect the interest of our shareholders. A few years ago a shareholder group disrupted our

annual meeting to insist that IEC make certain environmental changes. In general, though, the shareholders seemed to be more concerned with the return on their investment than with social responsibility. At our meeting, the president reminded me that, just like every other manager in the company, I should place the shareholders' interest foremost. I really was quite overwhelmed as I began to work up a personnel plan that would balance all these conflicting interests.

Questions

1   List the elements of the company's environment that will affect Scott's suggested plan. How legitimate are the interests of each of these?

2   Do you agree that Scott should be concerned first and foremost with protecting the interest of shareholders? Why or why not?

Source: Adapted from R.W. Mondy, R.M. Noe, S. R. Premeaux & R.A. Knowles, *Human Resource Management*, 2nd Canadian ed., (Toronto ON: Pearson Education Canada, 2001), pp. 47–48.

EXPERIENTIAL *Exercises*

1   Prepare a summary of the employment legislation affecting all employers and employees who are not under federal jurisdiction in your province or territory. Explain the impact of each of these laws on HRM policies and practices.

2   Working with a small group of classmates, contact several firms in your community to find out whether or not they have a code of ethics. If so, learn as much as possible about the specific initiatives devised to support and communicate the code. If not, find out if the firm is planning to implement such a code. If so, how does the firm intend to proceed? If not, why not?

3   Working alone or with a small group of classmates, interview an HR manager and prepare a short essay regarding his or her role in serving as a consultant and strategic change agent.

CHAPTER 2

The Changing Legal Emphasis: From Compliance to Valuing Diversity

LEARNING OUTCOMES

After studying this chapter, you should be able to:

Explain where the responsibility for employment-related law lies in Canada, the number of jurisdictions involved, and which employees are covered by which jurisdictions.

Differentiate between "equal pay for equal work" and "equal pay for work of equal value."

Discuss at least five common grounds for discrimination prohibited under Canadian human rights legislation and *describe* the requirements pertaining to reasonable accommodation.

Discuss the types of behaviour that could constitute harassment and *describe* employers' responsibilities pertaining thereto.

Describe the six steps involved in implementing an employment equity program.

Discuss the seven characteristics of successful diversity management initiatives.

INTRODUCTION TO THE LEGAL ENVIRONMENT

Government of Canada
www.canada.gc.ca

In Canada, the primary responsibility for employment-related laws resides with the provinces and territories. Today, provincial and territorial statutes (laws) govern approximately 90 percent of Canadian workers. The remaining 10 percent of the workforce, employed in the federal civil service, Crown corporations and agencies, and businesses engaged in transportation, banking, and communications, is governed by federal employment legislation.

Having many separate jurisdictions within one country has some advantages, such as permitting some diversity in legislation to recognize cultural differences. For example, Quebec employment legislation was developed within the culture of francophone Quebec. It also means that there is an opportunity for one jurisdiction to see whether or not a particular legislative change is successful in another jurisdiction before enacting it in its own. The main disadvantage of having many jurisdictions is that it is very time consuming and costly for a company with employees in different provinces to keep track of applicable regulations, and remain current as legislation changes. Ensuring legality across multiple jurisdictions can also be very complex, since it is possible for a policy, practice, or procedure to be legal in one jurisdiction, yet illegal in others.

It is illegal in every jurisdiction in Canada to discriminate on the basis of age.

This chapter will discuss the legal requirements pertaining to employee treatment in the workplace. The focus of such laws has evolved over the years from equality to equal opportunity to equity, primarily due to changing values and social expectations. The ways in which some proactive organizations have moved beyond legal compliance to valuing and capitalizing on workplace diversity will also be discussed.

Discrimination Defined

discrimination As used in the context of human rights in employment, a distinction, exclusion, or preference, based on one of the prohibited grounds, that has the effect of nullifying or impairing the right of a person to full and equal recognition and exercise of his or her human rights and freedoms.

Central to laws mandating equal opportunity and equity is the concept of **discrimination**. When someone is accused of discrimination, it generally means that he or she is perceived to be acting in an unfair or prejudiced manner. The law prohibits unfair discrimination—making choices on the basis of perceived but inaccurate differences, to the detriment of specific individuals and/or groups. Standards pertaining to unfair discrimination have changed over time.

EQUALITY

employment (labour) standards legislation Laws present in every Canadian jurisdiction that establish minimum employee entitlements and set a limit on the maximum number of hours of work permitted per day or week.

All employers and employees in Canada are covered by **employment (labour) standards legislation**. Those under federal jurisdiction are covered by the Canada Labour Code; the ten provinces and three territories each have an employment (or labour) standards act. These laws establish minimum employee entitlements pertaining to such issues as wages; paid holidays and vacations; leave for some mix of maternity, parenting, and adoption; bereavement leave; termination notice; and overtime pay. They also set a limit on the maximum number of hours of work permitted per day or week.

Every jurisdiction in Canada has legislation incorporating the principle of equal pay for equal work. In most jurisdictions, this entitlement is found in the employment (labour) standards legislation; otherwise, it is in the human rights legislation. Equal pay for equal work specifies that an employer cannot pay

National Website for Labour Jurisdiction Information Exchange
www.labour-info-travail.org/E_main.cfm

Jurisdictional Labour Home Pages
www.labour-info-travail.org/E_LabourSites.cfm

male and female employees differently if they are performing the same or substantially similar work. This principle makes it illegal, for example, for a school board to classify male employees as janitors and female employees doing virtually the same work as housekeepers and provide different wage rates based on these classifications. Pay differences based on a valid merit or seniority system, or employee productivity are permitted; it is only sex-based discrimination that is prohibited. Enforcement is complaint-based and violators can be fined.

EQUAL OPPORTUNITY

Equal opportunity legislation makes it illegal to discriminate, even unintentionally, against various groups. Reactive (complaint-driven) in nature, the focus of such legislation is on the types of acts in which employers should *not* engage. Included in this category are:

1. *The Charter of Rights and Freedoms*, federal legislation that is the cornerstone of equal opportunity.
2. *Human rights legislation*, which is present in every jurisdiction.

The Charter of Rights and Freedoms

Charter of Rights and Freedoms Federal law enacted in 1982 that guarantees fundamental freedoms to all Canadians.

The cornerstone of Canada's legislation pertaining to issues of equal opportunity is the Constitution Act, which contains the **Charter of Rights and Freedoms**. The Charter applies directly only to the actions of all levels of government (federal, provincial/territorial, and municipal) and agencies under their jurisdiction. Because it takes precedence over all other laws, however, which means that all legislation must meet Charter standards, it is quite far-reaching in scope.

There are two notable exceptions to this generalization. The Charter allows laws to infringe on Charter rights if they can be demonstrably justified as reasonable limits in a "free and democratic society." Since "demonstrably justified" and "reasonable" are open to interpretation, many issues challenged under the Charter eventually end up before the Supreme Court, its ultimate interpreter. The second exception occurs when a legislative body invokes the "notwithstanding" provision, which allows the legislation to be exempted from challenge under the Charter.

Supreme Court of Canada
www.scc-csc.gc.ca

The Charter provides the following fundamental rights and freedoms to every Canadian:

1. Freedom of conscience and religion.
2. Freedom of thought, belief, opinion, and expression, including freedom of the press and other media of communication.
3. Freedom of peaceful assembly.
4. Freedom of association.

In addition, the Charter provides Canadian multicultural heritage rights, and First People's rights, minority language education rights, the right to live and work anywhere in Canada, the right to due process in criminal proceedings, equality rights, and the right to democracy.[1]

equality rights Section 15 of the Charter of Rights and Freedoms, which guarantees the right to equal protection and equal benefit of the law without discrimination.

Section 15—**equality rights**—guarantees the right to:[2]

equal protection and benefit of the law without discrimination, and, in particular, without discrimination based on race, national or ethnic origin, colour, religion, sex, age, or mental or physical disability.

Some of the major HRM and labour relations issues challenged under the Charter are described briefly below.

The Right to Bargain Collectively, Strike, and Picket

The union movement in Canada was disappointed when the Supreme Court held that the Charter does *not* provide the rights to bargain collectively, strike, or picket. It did not consider these activities to be fundamental freedoms, but rather rights created by law. This means that governments can legislate striking workers back to work and impose binding arbitration, limit unions' ability to negotiate wage and salary increases through wage restraint legislation, mandate compulsory arbitration in place of the right to strike, and that courts can issue injunctions to limit picketing activity.

The Right of Farm Workers to Unionize

In late 2001, the Supreme Court ruled that the exclusion of farm workers from collective bargaining rights under Ontario labour legislation violated their right to association under the Charter.[3]

Mandatory Retirement

The Supreme Court upheld the legality of human rights legislation that protects only individuals of specified ages from discrimination in employment, and therefore allows mandatory retirement at the upper age limit. In British Columbia and Newfoundland, for example, the upper age limit protected under the provincial human rights legislation is 65, and in Saskatchewan it is 64. The court concluded mandatory retirement at that upper age limit, while discriminatory, was "reasonable and justifiable." These rulings do not limit the right of governments to prohibit mandatory retirement should they choose to do so, as the Ontario government did in 2003.

Human Rights Legislation

Every employer in Canada is affected by human rights legislation, which prohibits intentional and unintentional discrimination in its policies pertaining to all aspects and terms and conditions of employment.

Scope

Most employment laws affect only one or two HRM functions. For example, employment (labour) standards legislation primarily impacts the administration of compensation and benefits. Human rights legislation, however, is extremely broad in scope, affecting almost all aspects of HRM. The ways in which employees should be treated on the job every day and the climate in which they work are also addressed by this legislation. An important feature of the human rights legislation is that it supersedes the terms of any employment contract or collective agreement.[4] For these reasons, supervisors and managers must be thoroughly familiar with the human rights legislation, and their legal obligations and responsibilities specified therein.

Overview

Human rights legislation provides equal opportunity for all Canadians in a number of areas, including accommodation, contracts, provision of goods and services, and employment. To review individual provincial and territorial human rights laws would be confusing because of the many but generally minor differences among them, often only in terminology (e.g., some provinces use the term "creed," others "religion"). As indicated in **Figure 2.1**, most provincial/territorial laws are similar to the federal statute in terms of

The Nunavut Handbook
www.nunavut.com

An Ethical Dilemma

Discrimination is not permitted on the basis of family status. Does this mean that employers must accommodate employees' childcare and/or eldercare responsibilities to the point of undue hardship?

Canadian Human Rights Act
Federal legislation prohibiting discrimination on a number of grounds, which applies to federal government agencies and Crown corporations and to businesses and industries under federal jurisdiction.

Canadian Human Rights Commission www.chrc-ccdp.ca

Canadian Human Rights Tribunal www.chrt-tcdp.gc.ca

scope, interpretation, and application. All jurisdictions provide equal opportunity by prohibiting discrimination on the grounds of race, colour, sexual orientation, religion/creed, physical and mental disability, sex (including pregnancy and childbirth), age, and marital status. Some but not all jurisdictions prohibit discrimination on the basis of national or ethnic origin, record of offences/criminal history, and various other grounds. The following discussion will focus on the federal human rights legislation.

The Canadian Human Rights Act

The **Canadian Human Rights Act** covers all businesses under federal jurisdiction. The Canadian Human Rights Commission, the official body responsible for administering the Canadian Human Rights Act, reported that in 2002, 81 percent of all discrimination complaints made were related to employment.[5]

FIGURE **2.1** Prohibited Grounds of Discrimination in Employment by Jurisdiction

Prohibited Grounds of Discrimination	Federal	Alta.	B.C.	Man.	N.B.	Nfld.	N.S.	Ont.	P.E.I.	Que.	Sask.	N.W.T.	Yukon	Nunavut
Race	◆	◆	◆	◆	◆	◆	◆	◆	◆	◆	◆	◆	◆	◆
Colour	◆	◆	◆	◆	◆	◆	◆	◆	◆	◆	◆	◆	◆	◆
Ethnic or national origin	◆		◆	◆	◆	◆	◆	◆	◆	◆	◆	◆	◆	◆
Ancestry or place of origin		◆	◆	◆				◆			◆	◆	◆	◆
Creed or religion	◆	◆	◆	◆	◆	◆	◆	◆	◆	◆	◆	◆	◆	◆
Sex	◆	◆	◆	◆	◆	◆	◆	◆	◆	◆	◆	◆	◆	◆
Marital status	◆	◆	◆	◆	◆	◆	◆	◆	◆	◆	◆	◆	◆	◆
Family status	◆	◆	◆	◆			◆	◆	◆	◆	◆	◆	◆	◆
Age	◆	18+	19–65	◆	◆	19–65	◆	18+	◆	◆	18–64	◆	◆	◆
Mental & physical disability	◆	◆	◆	◆	◆	◆	◆	◆	◆	◆	◆	◆	◆	◆
Pardoned offence	◆		◆						◆	◆		◆	◆	◆
Record of criminal conviction			◆						◆	◆		◆	◆	
Sexual orientation	◆	◆	◆	◆	◆	◆	◆	◆	◆	◆	◆	◆	◆	◆
Dependence on alcohol/drugs	◆	◆	◆	◆	◆	◆	◆	◆	◆	◆	◆			◆

Source: www.chrc-ccdp.ca/publications/prohibit-motifs.asp (July 21, 2003); *Canadian Master Labour Guide: 16th Edition 2002.* Toronto, ON: CCH Canadian Ltd., p. 402; "Recent Changes in Canadian Labour Law—Northwest Territories: Human Rights Act; Bill 1, Assented to October 30, 2002," *Workplace Gazette*, Spring 2003, pp. 95–96; Legislative Assembly of Nunavut, Bill 12 Human Rights Act, www.assembly.nu.ca/english/bills/6th_bill12.pdf, (July 21, 2003); U. Vu, "Ontario to Scrap Mandatory Retirement," *Canadian HR Reporter*, May 19, 2003, p. 1.

Types of Discrimination Prohibited   Both intentional and unintentional discrimination is prohibited.

Intentional Discrimination   Except in specific circumstances that will be described later, intentional discrimination is prohibited. An employer cannot discriminate *directly* by deliberately refusing to hire, train, or promote an individual, for example, on any of the prohibited grounds. It is important to realize that deliberate discrimination is not necessarily overt. In fact, overt (blatant) discrimination is quite rare today. Subtle direct discrimination can be difficult to prove. For example, if a 60-year-old applicant is not selected for a job and is told that there was a better-qualified candidate, it is often difficult for the rejected job-seeker to determine if someone else truly did more closely match the firm's specifications or if the employer discriminated on the basis of age.

An employer is also prohibited from intentional discrimination in the form of *differential or unequal treatment*. No individuals or groups may be treated differently in any aspects or terms and conditions of employment based on any of the prohibited grounds. For example, it is illegal for an employer to request that only female applicants for a factory job demonstrate their lifting skills, or to insist that any candidates with a physical disability undergo a pre-employment medical, unless all applicants are being asked to do so.

It is also illegal for an employer to engage in intentional discrimination *indirectly*, through another party. This means that an employer may not ask someone else to discriminate on his or her behalf. For example, an employer cannot request that an employment agency refer only male candidates for consideration as management trainees, or instruct supervisors that women of childbearing age are to be excluded from consideration for promotions.

Discrimination because of association is another possible type of intentional discrimination listed specifically as a prohibited ground in eight Canadian jurisdictions. It involves the denial of rights because of friendship or other relationship with a protected group member. An example would be the refusal of a firm to promote a highly qualified male into senior management on the basis of the assumption that his wife, who was recently diagnosed with multiple sclerosis, will require too much of his time and attention, and that her needs may restrict his willingness to travel on company business.

unintentional/constructive/ systemic discrimination
Discrimination that is embedded in policies and practices that appear neutral on the surface, and are implemented impartially, but have adverse impact on specific groups of people for reasons that are not job related or required for the safe and efficient operation of the business.

Unintentional Discrimination   **Unintentional discrimination** (also known as **constructive** or **systemic discrimination**) is the most difficult to detect and combat. Typically, it is embedded in policies and practices that, although appearing neutral on the surface and being implemented impartially, have adverse impact on specific groups of people for reasons that are not job related or required for the safe and efficient operation of the business. Examples are shown in **Figure 2.2.**

Examples of Human Rights Legislation Applications   In order to clarify how the human rights legislation is applied, and the types of discrimination prohibited, a few examples follow.

Race and Colour   Discrimination on the basis of race and colour is illegal in every Canadian jurisdiction. For example, a leading research scientist in the field of optics with the National Research Council (NRC) had received excellent recommendations and regular promotions at the NRC. However, when a new director moved into his division, the new director and some other managers

FIGURE 2.2   Examples of Systemic Discrimination

- Minimum height and weight requirements, which screen out dispropor-tionate numbers of women and people from Asia, who tend to be shorter in stature.
- Internal hiring policies or word-of-mouth hiring in workplaces that have not embraced diversity.
- Limited accessibility to company premises, which poses a barrier to per-sons with mobility limitations.
- Culturally biased or non-job-related employment tests, which discrimi-nate against specific groups.
- Job evaluation systems that are not gender-neutral; that is, they under-value traditional female-dominated jobs.
- Promotions based exclusively on seniority or experience in firms that have a history of being white male-dominated.
- Lack of a harassment policy or guidelines, or an organizational climate in which certain groups feel unwelcome and uncomfortable.

Source: Based on material provided by the Ontario Women's Directorate and the Canadian Human Rights Commission.

Urban Alliance on Race Relations
www.tgmag.ca/magic/uarr.html

deliberately and systematically discriminated against the Indian-born scientist because of his race and colour. His research funds and requests for summer assistants and participation in conferences were denied. His research group was disbanded. He was assigned to work under a junior scientist, denied promotion, suffered professional embarrassment, and was eventually fired. At the time the scientist filed a complaint, there were no visible minority managers at the NRC. The tribunal ordered the NRC to stop the discrimination, apologize to the scientist, correct inaccuracies in his employment file, appoint him to a management position, and pay (with interest) his legal costs, lost wages, and payment for humiliation.[6]

Age The use of age as an employment criterion has been receiving increasing attention. Many employers believe that it is justifiable to specify minimum or maximum ages for certain jobs. In actual fact, evidence is rarely available to support the position that age is an accurate indicator of a person's ability to perform a particular type of work.[7]

For example, a 43-year-old employee with Statistics Canada alleged that he was discriminated against on the basis of age when he applied for a position as an economist. The employee did not receive the position, and was not placed on the eligibility list for future economist positions. A statistical profile showed that 97.7 percent of employees holding the position were under the age of 40. It was also found that there was a shortage of recruits for the position of economist during this time period, and therefore there was an incentive for Statistics Canada to place the employee on an eligibility list, and subsequently hire him. The tribunal held that the complainant was discriminated against on the basis of age, and ordered that he be given a position as an economist at the first reasonable opportunity, that he receive an amount of special compensation, and that he be given the difference between the salary actually received in his current position and that which he would have received had he been hired for the economist position.[8]

Pardoned Convicts As indicated in CHRC's *Guide to Screening and Selection in Employment*, included as **Appendix 2.1,** employers cannot ask about arrest records because being arrested is not necessarily an indication of any wrongdoing. Employers in Ontario, Quebec, British Columbia, Nunavut, the Northwest Territories, and the federal jurisdiction cannot ask about conviction records. If information about any criminal record is legitimately needed for employment purposes, the question that can be asked is: "Have you ever been convicted of a criminal offence for which a pardon has not been granted?" In British Columbia, Quebec, Prince Edward Island, and the Yukon, record of criminal conviction is a prohibited ground of discrimination, which means that even this question would be illegal. In all Canadian jurisdictions, it is permissible to ask if an applicant is eligible for bonding, if being bondable is a job requirement. (Bonding involves the firm taking out an insurance policy to cover any losses caused by employee dishonesty.)

Physical and Mental Disability The Canadian Human Rights Act prohibits discrimination in employment policies and practices against an individual on the basis of physical or mental disability, unless accommodation would be impossible (e.g., a person who is blind cannot be employed as a truck driver or bus driver) or accommodating the individual's disability would cause the employer "undue hardship." Organizations must be able to show that any physical standards used for selecting employees for a particular job are truly necessary; otherwise the standards are not permissible since they may constitute systemic discrimination. That is why, for example, the Canadian armed forces no longer have specific height and weight requirements.

In a recent complaint, the employee was a customer service consultant, a job that involved speaking to customers on the phone clearly and continuously, with Rogers Cablesystems. The employee exhibited voice problems, and was diagnosed with vocal cord nodules and laryngitis as a result of voice overuse on the job. Her job performance was rated below average as her voice often cracked or was hoarse. She suffered from temporary voice loss, which eventually led to permanent voice loss. She provided two medical notes to Rogers explaining her voice problems and that she would not be able to return to her present position. She was terminated because of her persistent voice problems that prevented her from doing her job. The tribunal found that the job requirement to talk clearly and consistently for 95 percent of each shift was neutral on its face, but discriminatory in its effect on persons with a voice disability. Rogers was ordered to look for alternative work for the employee.[9]

To ensure that the actual physical demands of the job are identified rather than assumed demands, some employers conduct a physical demands analysis. When such an analysis is distributed to each applicant, as a supplement to the job description, candidates can readily identify any job requirements that might pose a problem for them, so that accommodation strategies can be discussed.

Sexual Orientation Sexual orientation (whether an individual is heterosexual, homosexual, or bisexual) is now a prohibited ground of discrimination in all jurisdictions. The Supreme Court has made it clear that any legislation in which

The Canadian Council on
Rehabilitation and Work
www.workink.com

AN ETHICAL
DILEMMA

Your company president tells you not to hire any gay or lesbian employees to work as part of his office staff because it would make him uncomfortable. What would you do?

the definition of spouse does not include same-sex couples would be declared unconstitutional, if challenged under the Charter. Thus the Canada Pension Plan, Employment Insurance, Old Age Security, the Income Tax Act, the Pension Benefits Standards Act, and other laws have had their definition of "common-law partners" amended to include both same-sex and opposite-sex couples.[10]

Bona Fide Occupational Requirements

Employers are permitted to discriminate if employment preferences are based on a **bona fide occupational requirement (BFOR)**, defined as a justifiable reason for discrimination based on business necessity such as the requirement for the safe and efficient operation of the organization. In some cases, a BFOR exception to human rights protection is fairly obvious. For example, when casting in the theatre, there may be specific roles that justify using age, sex, or national origin as a recruitment and selection criterion. The issue of BFORs gets more complicated in situations in which the occupational requirement is less obvious; the onus of proof is then placed on the employer. There are a number of instances in which BFORs have been established. For example, adherence to the tenets of the Roman Catholic Church has been deemed a BFOR when selecting faculty to teach in a Roman Catholic school.[11] The Royal Canadian Mounted Police has a requirement that guards be of the same sex as prisoners being guarded, which was also ruled to be a BFOR.[12]

A recent precedent-setting case involved Tawney Meiorin, who had been employed by the British Columbia government as part of a three-person Initial Attack Fire-Fighting Crew, when the province introduced a new series of four standardized fitness tests for firefighters. While she successfully completed three of the four tests, she failed the aerobics component in which she was required to run 2.5 kilometres in 11 minutes or less. After four attempts, her fastest time was 49.4 seconds too slow, and she was dismissed. Ms. Meiorin complained that the aerobic standard discriminated against women, as women generally have lower aerobic capacity than their male counterparts. The government argued that this standard was a BFOR for the firefighter position. The Supreme Court determined that this standard was not a BFOR as such a standard was *not* directly related to an individual's performance on the job, and in fact, resulted in systemic discrimination in a prohibited ground.[13]

Requirement for Reasonable Accommodation to the Point of Undue Hardship

The legal principle of **reasonable accommodation** requires the adjustment of employment policies and practices so that no individual is denied benefits, disadvantaged in employment, or prevented from carrying out the essential components of a job on the basis of prohibited grounds of discrimination. This may involve making adjustments to meet needs based on the group to which an individual belongs, such as scheduling adjustments to accommodate religious beliefs, or work station redesign to enable an individual with a physical disability to perform a particular task. Employers are expected to accommodate to the point of **undue hardship,** meaning that the financial cost of the accommodation (even with outside sources of funding) or health and safety risks to the individual concerned or other employees would make accommodation impossible.[14]

Failure to make every reasonable effort to accommodate employees is a violation of the Act.[15] This was established in a case where the complainant joined

---

bona fide occupational requirement (BFOR) A justifiable reason for discrimination based on business necessity (that is, required for the safe and efficient operation of the organization) or a requirement that can be clearly defended as intrinsically required by the tasks an employee is expected to perform.

reasonable accommodation The adjustment of employment policies and practices that an employer may be expected to make so that no individual is denied benefits, disadvantaged in employment, or prevented from carrying out the essential components of a job because of grounds prohibited in human rights legislation.

undue hardship The point to which employers are expected to accommodate under human rights legislative requirements.

Persons with disabilities are now employed in a wide range of fields and occupations. An example is Nancy Thibeault, the telephone operator and receptionist at PAC Corporation.

Tips for the Front Line

The Job Accommodation Network
janweb.icdi.wvu.edu

IBM Canada Web site—
Accommodating Persons with
Disabilities www.austin.ibm.com/
sns/guidelines.htm

Barrier-Free Employees
www.chrc-ccdp.ca/discrimination/
barrier_free-en.asp#barrier

harassment A wide range of behaviour that a reasonable person ought to know is unwelcome, provided that the individual who feels that he or she is being harassed makes it clear that such behaviour is unwelcome and inappropriate and asks that it be discontinued.

Racial Harassment Guide
www.ohrc.on.ca/english/guides/
racial-harassment.shtml

Sexual Harassment Guide
www.ohrc.on.ca/english/guides/
sexual-harassment.shtml

Sexual Orientation Harassment
Guide www.ohrc.on.ca/english/
guides/sexual-orientation.shtml

a religious group, and requested unpaid leave on a specific Monday to observe a church holy day. Because Mondays were particularly busy days at the workplace, his request was refused. The employee observed the holy day, and his employment was terminated. The Supreme Court ruled that the employer had discriminated on the basis of religion in failing to accommodate to the point of undue hardship. The court found that since the employer coped regularly with employees who were absent due to illness on Mondays, there was no reason that it could not accommodate one absence for religious reasons.

In accommodating unionized employees, the employer and union have a joint responsibility. There are two situations in which a union has a duty to accommodate. The first is when the union participated (through collective bargaining) in establishing a work rule that has a discriminatory effect. Refusal by the union to consent to reasonable accommodation measures is considered discrimination. The second situation is one in which the lack of union support would impede the employer's reasonable efforts to accommodate an employee, even where the union was not involved in establishing the work rule with a discriminatory effect.[16]

The duty to accommodate has been evolving and expanding.[17] For example, a union was found to have breached its duty to accommodate by only partially recognizing a disabled member's seniority. A worker at the Toronto Transit Commission claimed that his union, the Amalgamated Transit Union, violated his human rights when it refused to allow him to transfer all of his seniority when he took a new position as part of the employer's accommodation of his disability. A Board of Inquiry found that because the union was able to recognize half of his total seniority in the new department, it could not argue that recognizing all of his seniority would constitute undue hardship. Although in theory the rights of other employees might be affected, there was no evidence that any employee would be seriously prejudiced if the complainant transferred all of his seniority.[18]

Harassment   Some jurisdictions prohibit harassment on all proscribed grounds, while others only expressly ban sexual harassment. **Harassment** includes a wide range of behaviour that a reasonable person "ought to know" is unwelcome. It also encompasses actions and activities that were once tolerated, ignored, and considered horseplay or innocent flirtation, provided that the individual who feels that he or she is being harassed makes it clear that such behaviour is unwelcome and inappropriate and asks that it be discontinued. Harassment generally involves a series of incidents. Examples of the types of behaviour that may constitute harassment are included in **Figure 2.3**.

Employer Responsibility   The Supreme Court has made it clear that protecting employees from harassment is part of an employer's responsibility to provide a safe and healthy working environment. If harassment is occurring, of which they are aware or ought to have been aware, they can be charged as well as the alleged harasser.[19] Employer responsibility includes employee harassment by clients or customers once it has been reported. In a recent racial harassment case, a part-time employee at a personal-care and housekeeping company filed

FIGURE 2.3   Examples of Behaviours That May Constitute Harassment

- unwelcome remarks, slurs, jokes, taunts, or suggestions about a person's body, clothing, race, national or ethnic origin, colour, religion, age, sex, marital status, family status, physical or mental disability, sexual orientation, pardoned conviction, or other personal characteristics
- unwelcome sexual remarks, invitations, or requests (including persistent, unwanted contact after the end of a relationship)
- display of sexually explicit, sexist, racist, or other offensive or derogatory material
- written or verbal abuse or threats
- practical jokes that embarrass or insult someone
- leering (suggestive staring) or other offensive gestures
- unwelcome physical contact, such as patting, touching, pinching, hitting
- patronizing or condescending behaviour
- humiliating an employee in front of co-workers
- abuse of authority that undermines someone's performance or threatens his or her career
- vandalism of personal property
- physical or sexual assault

Source: Anti-Harassment Policies for the Workforce: An Employer's Guide. Canadian Human Rights Commission in co-operation with Human Resources Development Canada and Status of Women. December 2001. www.chrc-ccdp.ca/publications/antih1-lutte.asp?1=e. July 22, 2003. Reprinted with permission.

a complaint of harassment against his employer when a customer of the company cursed the employee and cast racial slurs at him. While the company sent the customer a letter outlining the unacceptable behaviour, the company was still found liable for harassment because if did not have a formal strategy to deal with such issues. In cases of harassment by third parties, the employer is considered to have the greatest control over conditions in the workplace, and is expected to intervene effectively to stop the harassment. The company was not ordered to pay the harassed employee damages, as he did not suffer adversely due to the incident, but it was ordered to provide a written apology to the employee.[20]

Sexual Harassment   The type of harassment that has attracted the most attention in the workplace is **sexual harassment**. Sexual harassment tops the list of complaints heard by provincial human rights commissions. Sixty-four percent of women say they have experienced some form of sexual harassment during their careers, and 48 percent of women executives say they left a job because of an inhospitable organizational culture and harassment.[21]

Sexual harassment can be divided into two categories: sexual coercion and sexual annoyance.[22] **Sexual coercion** involves harassment of a sexual nature that results in some direct consequence to the worker's employment status or some gain in or loss of tangible job benefits. Typically, this involves a supervisor using control over employment, pay, performance appraisal results, or promotion to attempt to coerce an employee to grant sexual favours. If the worker agrees to the request, tangible job benefits follow; if the worker refuses, job benefits are

sexual harassment Harassment on the basis of gender or sexual attractiveness or unattractiveness.

sexual coercion Harassment of a sexual nature that results in some direct consequence to the worker's employment status or some gain in or loss of tangible job benefits.

A poisoned work environment may exist even if no direct threats or promises are made.

sexual annoyance Sexually related conduct that is hostile, intimidating, or offensive to the employee, but has no direct link to tangible job benefits or loss thereof.

denied. For example, Glenn Hill filed a complaint that his employer Dan Barclay, the owner of The Tool Place, has discriminated against him and had caused him to resign because of sexual harassment. The owner would routinely push himself against Hill's body, prod and grab his groin area, make suggestive comments about Hill's sexual orientation, and on one occasion, answered the door nude when Hill came to pick him up for a business trip. Two weeks later, Hill resigned. The tribunal agreed that Hill was sexually harassed, that he perceived that his job depended upon having a sexual relationship with Barclay, and that he tolerated Barclay's conduct for fear of losing work privileges. Barclay was ordered to pay Hill $16 500 in lost wages and $2500 for injury to dignity, feelings, and self-respect.[23]

Sexual annoyance is sexually related conduct that is hostile, intimidating, or offensive to the employee, but has no direct link to tangible job benefits or loss thereof. Rather, a *"poisoned" work environment* is created for the employee, the tolerance of which effectively becomes a term or condition of employment. The following case provides an illustration of this type of harassment, as well as the consequences of management's failure to take corrective action:

> A female employee at Canada Post filed a complaint that her supervisor used an explicit statue to make jokes of a sexual nature as well as compared her to, and made humiliating comments about, a series of posters of female nudes in the station in which she worked. She complained to management about the incidents. Instead of removing the posters, Canada Post transferred her to another station that also had nude photos of women posted. The tribunal ruled that sexual harassment includes any unwelcome conduct of a sexual nature and that the presence of the posters that workers use as the basis of comments and jokes of a sexual nature caused embarrassment, lowered the status of women, and created a poisoned work environment. Although Canada Post did not consent to the harassment, it did nothing to stop it from happening, and was ordered to pay the woman $5700 in damages.[24]

Hints to Ensure Legal Compliance

Harassment Policies   To reduce liability, employers should establish sound corporate harassment policies, communicate such policies to all employees, enforce the policies in a fair and consistent manner, and take an active role in maintaining a working environment that is free of harassment. Most jurisdictions do not require organizations to develop and implement harassment policies. Increasingly, however, organizations are developing policies to deal with harassment, whether or not they are legally required to do so. A few guidelines to effective harassment policies are:[25]

1. The policy should prohibit harassment on all grounds specified in the applicable human rights legislation (as in the example included as **Figure 2.4**).

2. The policy should include a harassment procedure that provides several persons with whom complaints can be filed, guarantees confidentiality to the greatest extent possible, outlines the investigation process and sets time limits for each step, specifies that no record of the complaint will be placed in the HR file of the individual voicing the complaint unless he or she is proven to have filed a false charge with malicious intent, states that no record of a harassment charge will be placed in the file of the accused unless harassment is proven, and provides a range of possible penalties.

3. The policy should require employee training regarding the types of behaviour that may constitute harassment and the specifics of the company policy

FIGURE 2.4   Policy for a Harassment-Free Work Environment

Nova Scotia Construction Safety Association

Sample Harassment Policy

The company, in cooperation with our employees and unions, is committed to a healthy, harassment-free work environment for all employees. The company has developed a company-wide policy intended to prevent harassment of its employees and to deal quickly and effectively with any incident that might occur.

Harassment is any unwelcome physical, visual or verbal conduct. It is against the law. Harassment may include but not be limited to verbal or practical jokes, insults, threats or personal comments. It may take the form of posters, pictures, or graffiti. It may involve touching, striking, pinching, or any unwelcome physical contact. Any behaviour that insults or intimidates is harassment if a reasonable person should have known that the behaviour was unwelcome.

The Human Rights Code protects everyone within provincial jurisdiction from harassment and other forms of discrimination on the basis of race, religion, sex (including pregnancy and sexual orientation), marital status, physical disability, mental disability, political opinion, colour, or ethnic, nation, or social origin, and age.

The company will not tolerate harassment on the basis of any of these protected grounds.

Source: Nova Scotia Construction Safety Association. © 2001. Reprinted with permission of NSCSA. www.nscsa.org/text_only/sample_policiesharassment.html.

and procedure, and should require that each employee sign and return a document indicating that he or she has received harassment training, is now aware of the types of behaviour that may constitute harassment, and is familiar with the company harassment policy and procedure.

4. The policy should state that a thorough, unbiased investigation will be conducted whenever a complaint is filed, and will provide the accused with details regarding the complaint and ample opportunity to respond.

5. The policy should state that when harassment is proven, all relevant factors such as the complainant's wishes and the nature and frequency of the conduct will be considered before deciding upon an appropriate course of action. Options include counselling, a verbal or written apology, a verbal or written warning, a transfer or demotion, a suspension for a period ranging from one day to several months, and termination of employment (court decisions have upheld harassment as just cause for dismissal when circumstances warrant).[26]

6. The policy should state the same range of possible options will be considered when determining an appropriate course of action to deal with an individual found guilty of filing a false accusation with malicious intent.

7. The policy should state that harassment victims will be offered access to counselling and support from the firm's employee assistance program, or from external services.

8. The policy should state that any retaliatory action against an employee who makes a human rights complaint against the company is considered a criminal offence.

FIGURE 2.5   The CHRC Enforcement Process

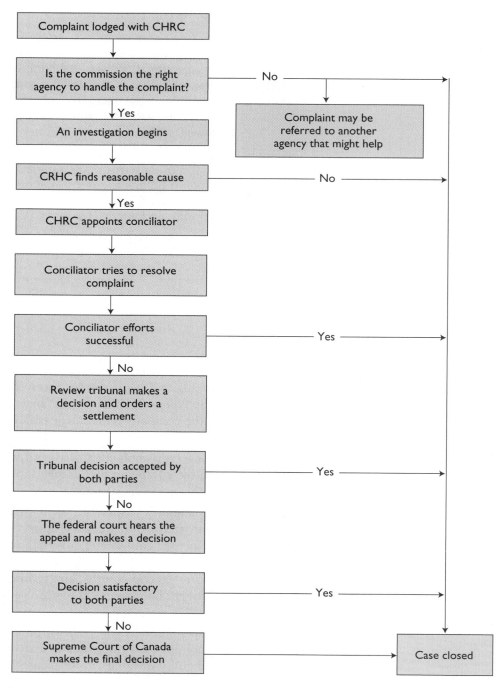

Canadian Human Rights Commission (CHRC) The body responsible for the implementation and enforcement of the Canadian Human Rights Act.

Enforcement Enforcement of the Canadian Human Rights Act is the responsibility of the **Canadian Human Rights Commission (CHRC)**. The steps involved in the enforcement procedure are outlined in **Figure 2.5**. It should be noted that all costs are borne by the CHRC, not by the complainant, which makes the process accessible to all employees, regardless of financial means. The CHRC itself can initiate a complaint if it has reasonable grounds to assume that a party is engaging in a discriminatory practice.

If discrimination is found, a number of remedies can be imposed. The most common is compensation for lost wages, and other remedies include compensation for general damages, complainant expenses, and pain and humiliation. The violator is generally asked to restore the rights, opportunities, and privileges denied the victim, such as employment or promotion. A written letter of apology may be required. If a pattern of discrimination is detected, the employer will be ordered to cease such practices and may be required to attend a training session or hold regular human rights workshops, and may even be ordered to develop and implement an employment equity program.

EQUITY

Catalyst www.catalystwomen.org

occupational segregation The existence of certain occupations that have traditionally been male dominated and others that have been female dominated.

glass ceiling An invisible barrier, caused by attitudinal or organizational bias, which limits the advancement opportunities of qualified designated group members.

Research
Insight ▷

The Charter of Rights legalizes employment equity initiatives, which go beyond human rights laws in that they are proactive programs developed by employers to remedy past discrimination and/or prevent future discrimination. Human rights laws focus on prohibiting various kinds of discrimination; however, over time it became obvious that there were certain groups for whom this complaint-based, reactive approach was insufficient. Investigation revealed that four identifiable groups—women, Aboriginal people, persons with disabilities, and visible minorities—had been subjected to pervasive patterns of differential treatment by employers, as evidenced by lower pay on average, occupational segregation, higher rates of unemployment, underemployment, and concentration in low-status jobs with little potential for career growth.

For example, historically, the majority of women worked in a very small number of jobs, such as nursing, teaching, sales, and secretarial/clerical work. This is known as **occupational segregation**. Advancement of women and other designated group members into senior management positions has been hindered by the existence of a **glass ceiling**, an "invisible" barrier caused by attitudinal or organizational bias, which limits the advancement opportunities of qualified individuals. A recent study by Catalyst (a nonprofit group that works for the advancement of women in business) found that women of colour face an even deeper level of discrimination, now known as the "concrete ceiling."[27]

Several studies have confirmed that the glass ceiling is still intact.[28] A study by the Women's Executive Network found that 55 percent of women executives believed that they have faced more barriers to career advancement than a similarly qualified male would have encountered in their situation. Fifty-nine percent said they had to work harder and 37 percent said they have had fewer opportunities for advancement, compared to their male counterparts. Another recent study involving 500 of Canada's largest companies conducted by Catalyst is highlighted in **Figure 2.6**. In these firms, there is concrete evidence of underutilization of female employees. While women make up almost one-half of the Canadian workforce, they are still underrepresented on executive teams, comprising just under 35 percent of management positions, 14 percent of corporate officers, and less than 10 percent of boards of directors. There seems to be some progress, as the percentage of companies with at least one woman corporate officer jumped from 56 percent in 1999 to 62 percent in 2002 (see **Figure 2.7**), and companies such as BMO Financial Group (as explained in the Workforce Diversity box) are taking proactive initiatives to advance women into leadership roles in the workplace.

FIGURE 2.6   Women Corporate Officers and Top Earners in Canada's 500 Largest Firms

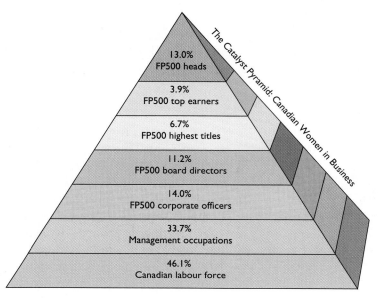

Source: Statistics Canada, Labour Force Survey, 2002.
Catalyst, 2003 Catalyst Census of Women Board Directors of Canada.
Catalyst, 2003 Catalyst Census of Women Corporate Officers and Top Earners of Canada.

FIGURE 2.7   Representation of Women on Corporate Boards in Canada's 500 Largest Firms (Based on Revenue)

	2001	1998
Percentage of Companies with at Least One Female Director	48.6	36.4
Percentage of Companies with Three or More Female Directors	8.6	2.6

Source: Catalyst Census of Women Board of Directors of Canada, 2001. Reproduced with permission of Catalyst. www.catalystwomen.org.

WORKFORCE DIVERSITY

Employment Equity Success at BMO Financial Group

The BMO Financial Group, one of the largest employers in Canada with almost 34 000 employees, is committed to maintaining an equitable workplace which reflects the diversity of the communities and businesses it serves. One of its strategies to achieve equity involves the advancement of women. Almost 15 years ago, in an attempt to break the glass ceiling, the company developed a statistical demographic profile of men and women at BMO, which found that while three-quarters of permanent employees were women, they represented only 9 percent of executives and 13 percent of senior management. Clearly, there were barriers to women's advancement at BMO, and the company declared its commitment to a diverse workforce in its 1990 corporate strategic plan.

In order to meet its goals, BMO gathered its senior leaders and executives to create the Chairman's Council on the Equitable Workplace. The group meets quarterly to review and evaluate past initiatives, and to create new plans for an equitable workforce. One of the initiatives to help in the advancement of women within the company was a partnership with an external organization to provide childcare to employees. By 2002, 35 percent of all executives and 30.8 percent of all executive vice-presidents at BMO were women.

Source: R.M. Patten, "In 12 Years, BMO Women Execs Rise from 9 to 35 Percent," *Canadian HR Reporter* (December 16, 2002), pp. 13, 16. Reproduced by permission of *Canadian HR Reporter*, Carswell, One Corporate Plaza, 2075 Kennedy Road, Scarborough, ON M1T 3V4.

The Plight of the Four Designated Groups

1. Women In most companies, there has tended to be a concentration of women in certain professions, which have been undervalued and underpaid. In 2002, 70 percent of women were working in such traditionally female-dominated occupations as teaching, nursing and other health-related occupations, clerical or administrative positions, and sales and service occupations—down from 74 percent in 1987. Women continue to be underrepresented in engineering, natural sciences, and mathematics, a trend unlikely to change in the near future since women are still underrepresented in university programs in these fields.[29]

Aboriginal Links: Canada & U.S.
www.bloorstreet.com/300block/
aborcan.htm

2. Aboriginals In 2001, there were just over 1.3 million people who reported having some Aboriginal ancestry, representing 4.4 percent of the Canadian population.[30] Almost six out of ten Aboriginal employees in the workforce were largely concentrated in three occupational groups in 2001, namely clerical, skilled crafts, and trade and semi-skilled manual work.[31]

3. People with Disabilities It is estimated that some 3.6 million Canadians—one in eight—have a disability. Among persons with disabilities, the employment rates are 41 percent for men and 32 percent for women. Moreover, working-age Canadians with disabilities earn only 76 percent of the average working-age household's after-tax income.[32]

4. Visible Minorities In 2001, about four million Canadians, or 13 percent of the total population, were visible minority group members, more than double the 6.3 percent figure in 1986. This increase is largely due to immigration. If current immigration rates continue, it is possible that immigration could account for virtually all labour force growth by 2011.[33] According to Statistics

underemployment Being employed in a job that does not fully utilize one's knowledge, skills, and abilities (KSAs).

Canada, 61 percent of immigrants of working age who arrived in the 1990s held trade, college, or university credentials, compared to 51 percent of the total population.[34] Many immigrants obtain employment in jobs that do not take full advantage of their skills and qualifications, thus facing **underemployment**. It has been estimated that underemployment short-changes skilled immigrants by a total of $2.4 billion a year, and discrimination (whether intentional or unintentional) against immigrants is creating a "brain waste" that costs the Canadian economy up to $15 billion each year.[35]

After realizing that simple prohibition of discrimination would not correct these patterns, a number of jurisdictions passed two categories of legislation:

1. *Employment equity*, aimed at identifying and eliminating systemic barriers to employment opportunities that adversely affect these four groups.

2. *Pay equity*, which focuses on mechanisms to redress the imbalance in pay between male-dominated and female-dominated job classes resulting from the undervaluing of work traditionally performed by women.

Employment Equity

Employment equity initiatives are focused on bringing the four traditionally disadvantaged groups identified above into the mainstream of Canada's labour force. The use of the term "employment equity" distinguishes Canada's approach from the "affirmative action" used in the United States. Affirmative action has come to be associated with quotas, a divisive political issue.[36]

Employment Equity Act Federal legislation intended to remove employment barriers and promote equality for the members of four designated groups: women, visible minorities, Aboriginal people, and persons with disabilities.

Federal Contractors Program A provision of the Employment Equity Act that requires firms with 100 or more employees wishing to bid on federal contracts of $200 000 or more to certify their commitment to employment equity in writing and to implement an employment equity program.

employment equity program A detailed plan designed to identify and correct existing discrimination, redress past discrimination, and achieve a balanced representation of designated group members in the organization.

Employment Equity Act The federal **Employment Equity Act** is intended to remove employment barriers and promote equality for the members of the four designated groups. The Act requires that each year, employers (with 100 or more employees) under federal jurisdiction prepare a plan with specific goals to achieve better representation of the designated group members at all levels of the organization, and timetables for goal implementation. Employers must also submit an annual report to HRDC, reporting on the company's progress in meeting its goals, and indicating the representation of designated group members by occupational groups and salary ranges, and information on those hired, promoted, and terminated. Noncompliance can lead to prosecution under the Canadian Human Rights Act. In addition, the CHRC has the authority to conduct random audits.[37]

A large number of employers under provincial/territorial jurisdiction are subject to federal employment equity requirements. Under the **Federal Contractors Program**, a provision of the Employment Equity Act, large firms bidding on federal contracts of $200 000 or more must implement an employment equity program. If a random review reveals that an employer has failed to implement an employment equity program, sanctions are applied, including exclusion of the employer from future government contracts.[38] Unfortunately, a 2001 HRDC report concluded that the program had no substantial positive effects from 1995 to 2000, because of staff cuts and reduced enforcement activity.[39]

Employment Equity Programs Mandatory employment equity programs are virtually nonexistent in provincial and territorial jurisdictions. Some provinces have employment equity policies that encourage employment equity

Alberta Human Rights and
Citizenship Commission
www.albertahumanrights.ab.ca

British Columbia Human Rights
Tribunal www.bchrt.bc.ca/

Manitoba Human Rights
Commission www.gov.mb.ca/hrc

New Brunswick Human Rights
Commission www.gov.nb.ca/hrc-
cdp/e/index.htm

Newfoundland Human Rights
Commission www.gov.nf.ca/hrc

Nova Scotia Human Rights
Commission
www.gov.ns.ca/humanrights

Ontario Human Rights Commission
www.ohrc.on.ca

Prince Edward Island Human
Rights Commission
www.isn.net/peihrc

Québec Commission des droits de
la personne et des droits de la
jeunesse www.cdpdj.qc.ca

Saskatchewan Human Rights
Commission www.gov.sk.ca/shrc

Yukon Human Rights Commission
www.yhrc.yk.ca

stock data Data that provide a
snapshot of the organization at a
particular point in time, in terms
of how many designated group
members are employed, in what
occupations, and at what salaries.
flow data Data tracking designated group members by employment transactions and outcomes.

plans in provincial departments and ministries. Quebec has a contract compliance program where employers in receipt of more than $100 000 in provincial
funding must implement an employment equity plan.[40] Provincial/territorial
human rights commissions often provide assistance to employers wishing to
implement voluntary employment equity programs.

An **employment equity program** is designed to achieve a balanced representation of designated group members in the organization. It is a major management exercise because existing employees must become comfortable working
with others from diverse backgrounds, cultures, religions, and so on, and this
represents a major change in the work environment. A deliberately structured
process is involved, which can be tailored to suit the unique needs of the firm.
The process includes six main steps, each of which will now be described.

Step One: Obtaining Senior-Management Commitment and Support   Senior
management's total commitment to employment equity is essential to a program's success. A *written policy*, endorsed by senior management and strategically posted throughout the organization or distributed to every employee, is an
essential first step. Manitoba Hydro's employment equity policy, shown in
Figure 2.8, illustrates how such a policy statement can convey senior management's approval of and commitment to the program's development and successful implementation. The policy statement should be supplemented by various
communication initiatives. An organization should *appoint a senior official*
(preferably reporting to the CEO) to whom overall responsibility and authority
for program design and implementation is assigned.

Step Two: Data Collection and Analysis   The development of an internal workforce profile is necessary in order to compare internal representation with external workforce availability data, set reasonable goals, and measure progress.
Such profiles must be based on both stock and flow data. **Stock data** provide a
snapshot of the organization at a particular point in time, in terms of how many
designated group members are employed, in what occupations, and at what levels and salaries. **Flow data** track designated group members by employment
transactions and outcomes. This involves determining how many designated
group members apply for jobs with the firm, are interviewed, hired, given
opportunities for training, promoted, and terminated.

FIGURE **2.8**   Manitoba Hydro Employment Equity Policy

Our Commitment to Employment Equity

At Manitoba Hydro, we value the background, experience, perspective and
talents of each individual. We strive to create a workforce that reflects the
diverse populations of the communities in which we serve.

We are committed to the practice of employment equity and we encourage applications from qualified men, women, people of Aboriginal ancestry, persons with disabilities, and members of visible minority groups.

Source: "Our Commitment to Employment Equity." Manitoba Hydro. www.hydro.mb.ca. Reproduced with
permission.

Alliance for Employment Equity
www.web.net/~allforee

To obtain data pertaining to the distribution of designated group members, a self-identification process is often used. Under the federal Employment Equity Act, employers may collect such data, as long as employees voluntarily agree to be identified or identify themselves as designated group members, and the data are only used for employment equity planning and reporting purposes. As explained in the HR.Net box, software is now available to assist employers in complying with federal requirements.

Comparison data must also be collected on the number of designated group members available in the labour markets from which the organization recruits. This data may be obtained from Statistics Canada, HRDC, women's directorates, professional associations, and agencies providing specialized assistance to various designated group members. The comparison of the internal workforce profile with external workforce availability is called a **utilization analysis**. This type of comparison is necessary in order to determine the degree of underutilization and concentration of designated group members in specific occupations or at particular organizational levels.

utilization analysis The comparison of the internal workforce profile with external workforce availability.

Step Three: Employment Systems Review   It is also essential that the organization undertake a comprehensive **employment systems review**. Corporate policies and procedures manuals, collective agreements, and informal practices all have to be examined, to determine their impact on designated group members so that existing intentional or systemic barriers can be eliminated. Typically, employment systems that require review include job classifications and descriptions, recruitment and selection processes, performance appraisal systems, training and development programs, transfer and promotion procedures, compensation policies and practices, and discipline and termination procedures.

employment systems review A thorough examination of corporate policies and procedures, collective agreements, and informal practices, to determine their impact on designated group members so that existing intentional or systemic barriers can be eliminated.

To assist in identifying systemic barriers, the following questions should be asked about each policy, procedure, and practice under review:[41]

- Is it job related?
- Is it valid? (Is it directly related to job performance?)
- Is it applied consistently?

Hints to Ensure Legal Compliance

HR.Net

Employment Equity Reporting

The Employment Equity Computerized Reporting System (EECRS) is Windows-based software that can be used by employers who are implementing an employment equity program, whether legally required or voluntary. It provides a fast and easy way for the user to capture and compile employee data, and then generates the employee equity forms required by each program. EECRS lets the user:

- create reports for different divisions of the company
- create reports for customized regions in Canada
- create reports that are different from the reporting periods under employment equity legislation, such as quarterly or annually

- print forms for areas where a company has less than 100 employees
- print forms by occupational group (based on the National Occupational Classification four-digit groups).

The software is available free of charge, and can be easily downloaded from the HRDC Web site. Technical assistance is also available via the Web site or through the Labour Systems telephone line.

Source: Employment Equity Computerized Reporting System. Human Resources Development Canada, Labour Operations Web site <http://info.load–otea.hrdc-drhc.gc.ca/workplace–equity/software/eecrs.shtml>. July 25, 2003. Reproduced with the permission of the Minister of Public Works and Government Services Canada, 2004.

- Does it have an adverse impact on designated group members?
- Is it a business necessity? (Is it necessary for the safe and efficient operation of the business?)
- Does it conform to human rights legislation?

Step Four: Plan Development Once the workforce profile and systems reviews have been completed, the employment equity plan can be prepared. *Goals and timetables* are the core of an employment equity program, since they help to ensure that changes in representation become a reality. Goals, ranging from short- to long-term in duration, should be flexible and tied to reasonable timetables. *Goals are not quotas.*[42] They are estimates of the results that experts in the firm have established based on knowledge of the workplace and its employees, the availability of individuals with the KSAs required by the firm in the external labour force, and the special measures that are planned. Quantitative goals should be set, specifying the number or percentage of qualified designated group members to be hired, trained, or promoted into each occupational group within a specified period of time. Qualitative goals, referred to as special measures, should also be included.

Occasionally, the courts may impose a specific numerical goal to overcome past discrimination, as happened in the 1980s in the case of Canadian National Railways (CN), and the employer may be accused of **reverse discrimination**.[43] This involves giving preference to designated group members to the extent that nonmembers believe they are being discriminated against. It is possible to avoid the entire issue of reverse discrimination if the approach taken to employment equity is goals rather than quotas. When goals are seen as targets, not quotas, the end result is that a *better-qualified* candidate who is not a protected group member is never denied an employment-related opportunity. However, when there are two *equally qualified candidates*, based on nondiscriminatory job specifications and selection criteria, preference will be given to the designated group member. The term "equally qualified" needs to be explained, since it does not necessarily imply identical educational qualifications or years of work experience, but rather possessing the qualifications required to perform the job. Thus, if a job requires two years of previous related experience, the candidate with four years of related experience is no more qualified than the individual with two.

Three types of special measures are (1) **positive measures** designed to accelerate the entry, development, and promotion of designated group members, such as targeted recruitment; (2) **accommodation measures** to assist designated group members to carry out their essential job duties, such as upgrading facilities for a disabled employee; and (3) **supportive measures** that enable all employees to achieve a better work/life balance, such as flexible work schedules in northern Canada to allow Aboriginal employees to take part in traditional fishing and hunting activities.

Step Five: Implementation Implementation is the process that transforms goals and timetables and special measures into reality. Implementation strategies will be different in every firm, due to each organization's unique culture and climate.

Step Six: Monitoring, Evaluating, and Revising An effective employment equity program requires a control system so that progress and success, or lack thereof,

---

quotas Set goals and timetables for the hiring and promotion of members of each of the designated groups, often externally imposed by government or a regulatory body; a strategy associated with affirmative action in the United States.

reverse discrimination Giving preference to designated group members to the extent that non-members believe they are being discriminated against.

AN ETHICAL DILEMMA

As the hiring manager, how would you inform a white male that he was not selected since preference was given to the equally qualified visible minority candidate in accordance with the firm's employment equity policy?

positive measures Initiatives designed to accelerate the entry, development, and promotion of designated group members, aimed at overcoming the residual effects of past discrimination.

accommodation measures Strategies to assist designated group members.

supportive measures Strategies that enable all employees to achieve better balance between work and other responsibilities.

Managers receiving diversity awards.

can be evaluated. External evaluation occurs through the Employment Equity Merit Awards, as described in the Strategic HR box.

Benefits of Employment Equity A dramatic example of how a more diverse workforce can help a firm to identify differences in customer needs or preferences is provided by DuPont, where a multicultural team increased the company business by $45 million when they changed the way DuPont marketed decorating materials, like its Corian countertops, by recommending a new array of colour that appealed to overseas customers.[44]

Impact of Employment Equity According to the Canadian Human Rights Commission 2002 annual

Strategic HR

Manitoba Hydro Wins Vision Award

Each year, employers who have demonstrated excellence in their employment equity practices under the Employment Equity Act are awarded Employment Equity Merit Awards by HRDC. The prestigious Vision Award was presented to Manitoba Hydro in 2002 in recognition for their efforts to create equity, diversity, and inclusiveness in the workplace. Highlights of their innovative and creative approaches include:

- The corporate targets for Aboriginal employment exceed the labour force demographic to accelerate the level of entry of Aboriginals into the workforce.

- Corporate facilities and workstations were upgraded, renovated, and redesigned to accommodate employees with disabilities.

- Employees who become disabled are encouraged and supported to reintegrate into the workforce through retraining.

- Manitoba Hydro is a founding member of the Manitoba Aboriginal Youth Career Awareness Committee, which is part of a targeted effort to encourage Aboriginal youth to consider a diverse range of careers.

- An Aboriginal pre-placement training program involves a four-week orientation, followed by three electrical trade cycles in northern generating stations; employment follows completion of the training.

- Two "New Generation" scholarships of $30 000 each are provided to Aboriginal students entering the Electrical Engineering field at the University of

Manitoba; winners of the scholarships are guaranteed employment after successfully completing their degrees.

- Eleven employment equity bursaries, with a total value of $120 000 each year, are awarded to students, with the offer of summer employment.

- The company has an employment equity division that was elevated to full department status in 2001.

- Manitoba Hydro's discrimination/harassment policy was revised to clearly state a "zero-tolerance" standard.

- The company employs an Aboriginal employee counsellor who is available to all employees in the company.

- Current exit interview processes are being modified to ensure that they are conducted with all designated group employees voluntarily leaving Manitoba Hydro; results of exit interviews are tracked to reveal any systemic issues that may lead to turnover.

The employment equity program at Manitoba Hydro works. Women represented 23.3 percent of the workforce in 2001, compared to 19.5 percent in 1995; Aboriginal people represented 8.3 percent, up from 5.9 percent; persons with disabilities represented 3.8 percent versus 2.6 percent; and visible minority groups represented 3 percent, compared to 2.2 percent.

Source: Reproduced from J.P. Surrette, "Employment Equity Merit Awards," in Human Resources Development Canada Labour Program, *Workplace Gazette* (Summer 2002), pp. 73–80. Reproduced with the permission of the Minister of Public Works and Government Services Canada, 2004.

report, employment equity can make a difference.[45] The representation of women in the federally regulated private sector improved, rising from 40.1 percent in 1987 to 44.9 percent in 2001. Although this was slightly below their estimated availability of 46.4 percent, it still represents a substantial increase. Women represented in the public sector increased to 52.5 percent in 2002, which is a substantial improvement over 1987, when 42 percent of federal public servants were women. The share of executive positions held by women in the federal public sector increased from 10.7 percent in 1987 to 32 percent in 2002.

Visible minority group members also made some progress in their representation in the federal private sector, more than doubling from 4.9 percent in 1987 to 11.7 percent in 2001. In 1987, visible minorities held 2.7 percent of all positions in the federal public sector. By 2002, their representation had increased to 6.8 percent.

In 1987, only 0.6 percent of federal private sector employees were Aboriginal peoples. While this figure rose to 1.6 percent by 2001, it fell short of the estimated availability of 2.1 percent. Aboriginals fared better in the public sector, where they represented 3.8 percent in 2002, up from 1.8 percent in 1987—higher than their estimated availability.

Of all the designated groups, people with disabilities in the private sector have benefited least from the Act. People with disabilities make up only 2.3 percent of the federal private sector workforce, just a slight increase over the 1.6 percent share reported in 1987 and far below the 6.5 percent labour market availability for this group. The representation of persons with disabilities in the federal public sector increased to 5.3 percent in 2002, up from 2.6 percent in 1987, but still short of their estimated labour market availability.

Pay Equity

The overall wage gap between men and women remains substantial. In 2000, the average woman employed full-time, full-year made 72 percent of what the average man employed full-time, full-year earned.[46] While differences in factors such as level of unionization and the effect of temporary workforce withdrawals account for some of the wage gap, the remaining portion of this wage differential cannot be attributed to differences in the industry of employment, work experience, occupational classification, or major subject studied in postsecondary education.[47] While the wage gap has narrowed since the 1970s, it continues to be persistent.[48] Statistics Canada researchers have concluded that "much of the wage gap still remains a puzzle."[49] Pay equity legislation is aimed at reducing the "unaccounted for" portion of the wage differential.

Pay equity, also known as *equal pay for work of equal value*, requires an employer to provide equal pay to male-dominated job classes and female-dominated job classes of equal "value," as assessed on the basis of skill, effort, responsibility, and working conditions. It may require comparing jobs that are quite different, such as nurses and firefighters.

Six provinces (Ontario, Quebec, Manitoba, Nova Scotia, New Brunswick, and Prince Edward Island) have created separate proactive legislation that specifically requires that pay equity be achieved. Ontario and Quebec require pay equity in both the public and private sectors, whereas the legislation in the remaining provinces applies only to the public sector. In the federal jurisdiction, the Yukon (public sector only), and British Columbia, human rights legislation requires equal pay for work of equal value, determined by comparing skill,

pay equity Providing equal pay to male-dominated job classes and female-dominated job classes of equal value to the employer.

Pay Equity Coalition
www.web.net/~equalpay/

National Committee on Pay Equity
www.pay-equity.org

effort, responsibility, and working conditions (and knowledge in B.C.). In Newfoundland and Saskatchewan, a requirement for equal pay for males and females doing substantially similar work, determined by assessing skill, effort, and responsibility, is incorporated into the human rights legislation (similar wording is included in the Yukon's Employment Standards Act). Although Newfoundland and Saskatchewan do not have specific pay equity legislation, both provinces have formally implemented pay equity in the public sector. There is no requirement for pay equity in Alberta, the Northwest Territories, or Nunavut.[50]

Managing Diversity

diversity management Activities designed to integrate all members of an organization's multicultural workforce and use their diversity to enhance the firm's effectiveness.

Diversity Best Practices
www.diversitybestpractices.com

Workplace Diversity Update
www.diversityupdate.com

Ontario Gateway to Diversity
www.equalopportunity.on.ca

Diversity Central
www.diversitycentral.com

Although many people perceive "management of diversity" to be another term for employment equity, the two are very distinct. Managing diversity goes far beyond legal compliance or even implementing an employment equity plan voluntarily. **Diversity management** is broader and more inclusive in scope, and involves a set of activities designed to integrate all members of an organization's multicultural workforce and use their diversity to enhance the firm's effectiveness.

The ethnocultural profile of Canada has been changing since the 1960s, and will continue to change dramatically over the next 20 years. Canada has seen continued immigration from many lands during the last four decades, and managers are managing an increasingly diverse workforce. While there are ethical and social responsibility issues involved in embracing diversity, there are other more pragmatic reasons for doing so:

1. It makes economic sense. It is estimated that the combined purchasing power of persons with disabilities and visible minorities in Canada is over $420 billion.[51]

2. Employees with different ethnic backgrounds often also possess foreign-language skills, knowledge of different cultures and business practices, and may even have established trade links in other nations, which can lead to competitive advantage.

3. Visible minorities can help to increase an organization's competitiveness and international savvy in the global business arena. Specifically, cultural diversity can help fine-tune product design, marketing, and ultimately customer satisfaction.[52]

Although embracing employee diversity offers opportunities to enhance organizational effectiveness, transforming an organizational culture presents a set of challenges that must be handled properly. Diversity initiatives should be undertaken slowly, since they involve a complex change process. Resistance to change may have to be overcome, along with stereotyped beliefs or prejudices, and employee resentment. Organizations that have been most successful in managing diversity tend to share the following seven characteristics:

1. Top Management Commitment As with any major change initiative, unless there is commitment from the top, it is unlikely that other management staff will become champions of diversity. It is no coincidence that organizations that have established themselves as leaders in diversity management, such as BMO Financial Group, Ernst & Young, and IBM Canada, have had senior-level commitment over an extended period of time.

2. Diversity Training Programs Diversity training programs are designed to provide awareness of diversity issues and to educate employees about specific gender and cultural differences and appropriate ways to handle them. To be successful, diversity training must be ongoing, not a one-day workshop.

3. Inclusive and Representative Communications Organizations wishing to incorporate the value of diversity into their corporate culture must ensure that all of their internal communications and external publications convey this message. Inclusive language (such as gender-neutral terms) and broad representation in terms of age, gender, race, and so on, in company publications are strategies used.

4. Activities to Celebrate Diversity Diversity must also be celebrated in organizational activities. At Dalton Chemical Laboratories Inc., where 70 percent of the employees are new Canadians, they host international luncheons to celebrate the different foods of the world. Everyone in the company brings a dish and employees share the history of their food and culture.[53]

5. Support Groups or Mentoring Programs One goal of diversity programs is to ensure that employees encounter a warm organizational climate, not one that is insensitive to their culture or background. To ensure that no one experiences feelings of alienation, isolation, or tokenism, support groups have been established in some firms to provide a nurturing climate and a means for employees who share the same background to find one another. For example, franchise owner Vince Cardella employs several people with intellectual disabilities at his four Tim Horton's restaurants in southwestern Ontario. The workers learn at a slower pace than others, but Community Living Essex County acts as a support group if any problems arise.[54]

Another option is a mentoring program. At Rogers, a team-based mentoring program is in place across the country. Some mentors and protégés may never actually meet face-to-face. The Women's Executive Network, WXN, is Canada's leading organization dedicated to the advancement and recognition of executive-minded women. WNX partners with Canada's top employers and market leaders, and has created a network of women who are willing to share a vast amount of information and to support other women in business. The e-mentoring program electronically connects a pool of mentors with a pool of young women. E-matches are made by pairing up e-protégés with e-mentors of similar interests, both personal and professional. The WXN Web site is a forum in which e-pairs can communicate with one another. To date, the organization has made over 200 matches.

At Rogers, for example, another ongoing component of the diversity strategy is participation in a Goodwill program, through which call-centre training is provided to youths and people with disabilities who, because of long-term unemployment, are not eligible for employment insurance. After two and a half years of participation, Rogers had fully employed 20 graduates of the Goodwill program, all of whom were still at the firm and performing at an above-average standard at the time a follow-up survey was conducted.[55]

6. Diversity Audits To assess the effectiveness of an organization's diversity initiatives, diversity audits should be conducted. Recommended evaluation criteria include representation of various groups, employee competencies related to diversity KSAs, progress in moving from an initial state of little or no diversity

Women's Executive Network
www.wxnetwork.com/ementoring.htm

WORKFORCE DIVERSITY

Sunny Spot for the Disadvantaged

Pelmorex, owner of the Weather Network, topped the federal government's diversity audit list in 2003. The audit report noted that only one organization in Canada this year earned A's in all four categories— women, Aboriginals, people with disabilities, and visible minorities. No organization earned this honour the year before. Back in 1996, when the federal Employment Equity Act was introduced, Pelmorex enticed managers to sign on to employment equity principles by tying in a year-end bonus to the level of representation of the four designated groups in each team or department. The bonus is still used, but the need for diversity is now ingrained in the way managers think about their staff.

The HR team aggressively networks with groups in the community. They participate in the career sessions at the Six Nations Reserve at Ohsweken, Ontario, and at other Aboriginal events. They sit down with staff at the access office for students with disabilities at universities and colleges to make sure that these students think of Pelmorex when they look for a job.

Ian Campbell, a broadcast IT technician, had a visual impairment and no television experience when he joined the company, but his supervisor worked diligently to bring him up to speed. All the accommodation that he needed was a little patience and a 19-inch monitor. Sometimes accommodation is required in the daily process of getting the work done. For example, one employee has limited mobility, so he needs extra notice of meetings away from his work area. Another employee has a mental condition that means he should not be overloaded with stress, so his desk was situated in a quiet area of the office, out of the way of traffic.

Valerie Morrisette, VP of Human Resources, says, "We just really believe in this. And the more we do this, the more we believe it's just the right thing to do."

Source: U. Vu, "Sunny Spot for the Disadvantaged," *Canadian HR Reporter* (May 19, 2003), p. 2. Reproduced by permission of *Canadian HR Reporter*, Carswell, One Corporate Plaza, 2075 Kennedy Road, Scarborough, ON M1T 3V4.

Human Rights in the Workplace— Pregnancy, Childbirth, and Adoption

The Alberta Human Rights and Citizenship Commission has introduced two new bulletins relating to human rights in the workplace: Rights and responsibilities related to pregnancy, childbirth, and adoption, and Duty to Accommodate.

... It is contrary to the Alberta Human Rights, Citizenship and Multiculturalism Act to discriminate against women with respect to their pregnancy. In fact, if an employee's pregnancy or breastfeeding prevents her from doing part of her job, employers are expected to accommodate that employee up to the

point of undue hardship.... A few examples of what such accommodation could entail [are]:

- changing a pregnant employee's job duties (i.e., limit heavy lifting or other physically demanding duties);

- providing a flexible work schedule to accommodate medical appointments, child care, or breastfeeding;

- ensuring employees can bring their infants in to breastfeed at work, or making other modifications to the workplace as requested; and

- ensuring pregnant employees have full access to benefits such as illness or vacation leave.

Source: Excerpted with permission from the *Workplace Equity Guide Newsletter* (No. 12, June 2002), published by and copyright CCH Canadian Limited, Toronto, Ontario.

commitment and infrastructure to an ideal state in which diversity is integrated into the fabric of the firm, and results measured by the extent to which diversity management strategies are perceived to have succeeded in promoting diversity.[56]

7. Management Responsibility and Accountability Diversity management initiatives will not receive high priority unless supervisors and managers are held accountable and results are part of their formal assessment. The Weather Network is one organization that has followed these guidelines and prospered, as described in the Workforce Diversity box.

CHAPTER *Review*

Summary

1   The responsibility for employment-related law resides with the provinces/territories, except that employees of the federal civil service, Crown corporations and agencies, and businesses engaged in transportation, banking, and communications are federally regulated. There are 14 jurisdictions for employment law—ten provinces, three territories, and the federal jurisdiction. Ninety percent of Canadians are covered by provincial/territorial employment legislation, and 10 percent are covered by federal employment legislation.

2   *Equal pay for equal work* means that an employer cannot pay male and female employees differently if they are performing the same or substantially the same work. *Equal pay for work of equal value* means providing equal pay to male-dominated job classes and female-dominated job classes of equal value, assessed on the basis of skill, effort, responsibility, and working conditions, and may require comparing jobs that are quite different.

3   All jurisdictions prohibit discrimination on the grounds of race, colour, sexual orientation, religion/creed, physical and mental disability, sex (including pregnancy and childbirth), age, and marital status. Employers are required to make reasonable accommodation for employees by adjusting employment policies and practices so

that no one is disadvantaged in employment on any of the prohibited grounds, to the point of undue hardship.

4   Harassment includes a wide range of behaviours that a reasonable person *ought to know* are unwelcome. It includes actions and activities that were once tolerated, ignored, and considered horseplay or innocent flirtation. Employers and managers have a responsibility to provide a safe and healthy working environment. If harassment is occurring, and they are aware or ought to have been aware, they can be charged along with the alleged harasser. To reduce liability, employers should establish harassment policies, communicate these to employees, enforce the policies, and play an active role in maintaining a working environment free of harassment.

5   The six steps involved in implementing an employment equity program are (1) obtaining senior management commitment and support, (2) data collection and analysis, (3) an employment systems review, (4) plan development, (5) plan implementation, and (6) a follow-up process encompassing evaluation, monitoring, and revision.

6   Seven characteristics of successful diversity management programs are (1) include top management commitment, (2) diversity training, (3) inclusive and representative communication, (4) activities to celebrate diversity, (5) support groups or mentoring programs, (6) diversity audits, and (7) management responsibility and accountability.

Key Terms

accommodation measures   *(p. 53)*

bona fide occupational requirement (BFOR)
    (p. 41)

Canadian Human Rights Act   *(p. 37)*

Canadian Human Rights Commission (CHRC)
    (p. 47)

Charter of Rights and Freedoms   *(p. 35)*

discrimination   *(p. 34)*

diversity management   *(p. 56)*

employment (labour) standards legislation   *(p. 34)*

Employment Equity Act   *(p. 50)*

employment equity program   *(p. 50)*

employment systems review   *(p. 52)*

equality rights   *(p. 35)*

Federal Contractors Program   *(p. 50)*

flow data   *(p. 51)*

glass ceiling   *(p. 47)*

harassment   *(p. 42)*

occupational segregation   *(p. 47)*

pay equity   *(p. 55)*

positive measures   *(p. 53)*

quotas   *(p. 53)*

reasonable accommodation   *(p. 41)*

reverse discrimination   *(p. 53)*

sexual annoyance   *(p. 44)*

sexual coercion   *(p. 43)*

sexual harassment   *(p. 43)*

stock data   *(p. 51)*

supportive measures   *(p. 53)*

underemploment   *(p. 50)*

undue hardship   *(p. 41)*

unintentional/constructive/systemic discrimination
    (p. 38)

utilization analysis   *(p. 52)*

Review and Discussion Questions

1 Describe the impact of the Charter of Rights and Freedoms on HRM.

2 Differentiate between the following types of discrimination, and provide one example of each: direct, differential treatment, indirect, because of association, and systemic.

3 Provide five examples of workplace accommodation measures.

4 Define "sexual harassment" and describe five types of behaviour that could constitute such harassment.

5 Define the concepts of occupational segregation, underutilization, underemployment, and the glass ceiling.

6 Explain how diversity management differs from employment equity and explain three reasons (other than ethics and social responsibility) for embracing workforce diversity.

CRITICAL *Thinking Questions*

1 A front-line supervisor has just informed you, the HR manager, that there are certain machine shop jobs for which he feels minimum height and weight requirements are BFORs. You disagree. How would you handle this situation?

2 An employee who has been off for two months with a stress-related ailment has just contacted you, indicating that she would like to return to work next week but won't be able to work full-time for another month or so. How would you handle this?

3 Explain the difference between goals and quotas and discuss the ways in which employers can avoid the issue of reverse discrimination.

APPLICATION *Exercises*

Running Case: LearnInMotion.com

One of the problems that Jennifer and Pierre faced at LearnInMotion.com concerned the inadequacies of the firm's current human resources management practices and procedures. The previous year had been a swirl of activity—creating and testing the business model, launching the site, writing and rewriting the business plan, and finally getting venture funding. And, it would be accurate to say that in all that time, they put absolutely no time into employee manuals, HR policies, or other HR-related matters. Even the 25-page business plan was of no help in this regard. The plan provided considerable detail regarding budgetary projections, competition, market growth, and business strategy. However, it was silent when it came to HR, except for containing short bios of the current employees and projections of the types of positions that would have to be staffed in the first two years.

Almost from the beginning, it was apparent to both Jennifer and Pierre that they were "out of our depth" (as Pierre put it) when it came to the letter and spirit of equal employment opportunity laws. Having both been through business school, they were familiar with the general requirements such as not asking applicants about their ages. However, those general guidelines weren't always easy to translate into practice during the actual applicant interviews. Two incidents particularly concerned them. One of the applicants for a sales position was in his 50s, which made him about twice as old as any other applicant. While Pierre didn't mean to be discriminatory, he found himself asking this candidate questions such as "Do you think you'll be able to get up to speed selling an Internet product?" and "You know, we'll be working very long hours here; are you up to that?"—questions that he did not ask of other, younger candidates. There was also a problem with a candidate for the other, content manager, position. The candidate was a single mother with two children, and Pierre asked her quite pointed questions such as "What are your children's ages and what daycare arrangements do you have?" And, "This job involves quite a bit of overtime and weekend work, are you sure your kids won't get in the way of that?" Jennifer thought questions like these were probably okay, but she wasn't sure.

There was also a disturbing incident in the office. There were already two content management employees, Maya and Dan, whose job it was to actually place the course and other educational content on the Web site. Dan, along with Alex the Web surfer, occasionally used vulgarity, for instance, when referring to the problems the firm was having getting the computer supplier to come to the office and repair a chronic problem with the firm's server. Pierre's attitude was that "boys will be boys." However, Jennifer and Maya cringed several times when "the boys" were having one of these exchanges, and felt strongly that his behaviour had to stop. However, Jennifer was not sure language like this constituted harassment under the law, although she did feel that at a minimum it was uncivil. The two owners decided it was time to institute and implement some HR policies that would ensure their company and its employees adhere to the letter and the spirit of the various employment laws. Now they want you, their management consultant, to help them actually do it. Here's what they want you to do for them.

Questions

1   The company is located in Ontario, it is small, and given the fact that Pierre and Jennifer now have only five employees and are only planning on hiring three or four more, by what legislation is their company actually covered.

2   Were they within their legal rights to ask the age-related and children-related questions? Why or why not?

3   Did Dan and Alex harass Jennifer and Maya? Why or why not? How should this matter be handled?

4   What have Jennifer and Pierre been doing wrong up to now with respect to the various pieces of employment legislation covering the business, and how do you suggest they rectify the situation in the future?

CASE INCIDENT *Harassment*

Maria was hired two months ago to supervise the compensation area of the HR department, which you manage. She seems to have been accepted by her peers and reporting employees but you have noticed that, for the past three weeks, she has been the last to arrive at staff meetings and always sits as far as possible from Bob, another supervisor.

Yesterday afternoon, you had a very upsetting conversation with her. She claimed that for more than a month Bob has been repeatedly asking her to go out with him and that her constant refusals seem to be making the situation worse. Bob has accused her of being unfriendly and suggested that she thinks she is too good for him. She said that he has never touched her but that he discusses how "sexy" she looks with the other men in the department, who seem embarrassed by the whole situation. Maria also said that Bob's advances are escalating the more she refuses him and that his behaviour is interfering with her job performance to such an extent that she is thinking of resigning.

With Maria's consent, you have just spoken to Bob, who denied her allegations vehemently and believably.

Questions

1   How would you proceed in dealing with this situation?

2   What are your responsibilities to Maria and Bob?

3   If Maria is telling the truth, are you or Bob legally liable in any way? If so, under what conditions?

4   How would you resolve this matter?

Source: Based on a case provided in *Equity Works Best*, a publication of the Ontario Women's Directorate.

EXPERIENTIAL *Exercises*

1   Working in teams of six, role-play an investigation of the harassment claim described in the above case. One member of each team is to be assigned the role of Maria, another the role of Bob, and a third the role of the HR manager. The three remaining team members are to assume the roles of other HR department staff. For the purpose of this role-play, assume that Bob has made comments about how "sexy" Maria is and has asked her out, but claims that he didn't realize his behaviour was bothering Maria.

2   Prepare a report outlining legally acceptable questions that may be asked at a selection interview with a young female engineer applying for the job of engineering project manager at an oil field in rural northern Alberta, with an otherwise all-male group.

3   Working with a small group of classmates, contact the HR manager at a company in your community that has an employment equity or diversity management program. Prepare a brief report summarizing its key features.

A Guide to Screening and Selection in Employment

Subject	Avoid Asking	Preferred	Comment
Name	about name change: whether it was changed by court order, marriage, or other reason maiden name		ask after selection if needed to check on previously held jobs or educational credentials
Address	for addresses outside Canada	ask place and duration of current or recent address	
Age	for birth certificates, baptismal records, or about age in general	ask applicants whether they are eligible to work under Canadian laws regarding age restrictions	if precise age required for benefits plans or other legitimate purposes, it can be determined after selection
Sex	males or females to fill in different applications about pregnancy, child-bearing plans, or child-care arrangements	ask applicant if the attendance requirements can be met	during the interview or after selection, the applicant, for purposes of courtesy, may be asked which of Dr., Mr, Mrs, Miss, Ms is preferred
Marital Status	whether the applicant is single, married, divorced, engaged, separated, widowed, or living common law whether an applicant's spouse may be transferred about spouse's employment	if transfer or travel is part of the job, the applicant can be asked if he or she can meet these requirements ask whether there are any circumstances that might prevent completion of a minimum service commitment	information on dependants can be determined after selection if necessary
Family Status	number of children or dependants about child care arrangements	if the applicant would be able to work the required hours and, where applicable, overtime	contacts for emergencies and/or details on dependants can be determined after selection
National or Ethnic Origin	about birthplace, nationality of ancestors, spouse, or other relatives whether born in Canada for proof of citizenship	since those who are entitled to work in Canada must be citizens, permanent residents, or holders of valid work permits, applicants can be asked if they are legally entitled to work in Canada	documentation of eligibility to work (papers, visas, etc.) can be requested after selection
Military Service	about military service in other countries	inquiry about Canadian military service where employment preference is given to veterans by law	
Language	mother tongue where language skills obtained	ask whether applicant understands, reads, writes, or speaks languages required for the job	testing or scoring applicants for language proficiency is not permitted unless job related
Race or Colour	about race or colour, including colour of eyes, skin, or hair		

continued

Subject	Avoid Asking	Preferred	Comment
Photographs	for photo to be attached to applications or sent to interviewer before interview		photos for security passes or company files can be taken after selection
Religion	about religious affiliation, church membership, frequency of church attendance whether applicant will work a specific religious holiday for references from clergy or religious leader	explain the required work shift, asking whether such a schedule poses problems for the applicant	reasonable accommodation of an employee's religious beliefs is the employer's duty
Height and Weight			no inquiry unless there is evidence they are genuine occupational requirements
Disability	for list of all disabilities, limitations, or health problems whether applicant drinks or uses drugs whether applicant has ever received psychiatric care or been hospitalized for emotional problems whether applicant has received workers' compensation	ask whether the applicant has any condition that could affect ability to do the job ask whether the applicant has any condition that should be considered in selection	a disability is only relevant to job ability if it: – threatens the safety or property of others – prevents the applicant from safe and adequate job performance even when reasonable efforts are made to accommodate the disability
Medical Information	whether currently under a physician's care name of family doctor whether receiving counselling or therapy		medical exams should be conducted after selection and only if an employee's condition is related to job duties offers of employment can be made conditional on successful completion of a medical exam
Pardoned Conviction	whether an applicant has ever been convicted if an applicant has ever been arrested whether an applicant has a criminal record	if bonding is a job requirement, ask whether the applicant is eligible	inquiries about criminal record or convictions are discouraged unless related to job duties
Sexual Orientation	about the applicant's sexual orientation		contacts for emergencies and/or details on dependents can be determined after selection
References			the same restrictions that apply to questions asked of applicants apply when asking for employment references

Source: Canadian Human Rights Commission, *A Guide to Screening and Selection in Employment* (Ottawa: CHRC, 2001). www.chrc-ccdp.ca/public/screen.pdf. July 21, 2003. Reprinted with permission of the Minister of Public Works and Government Services Canada.

E-mail Alert

They're gone but not forgotten: corporate e-mails are becoming a primary tool in high-profile court cases, as lawyers dig through hard drives in search of evidence. Now business people are discovering, much to their alarm, that a single incriminating e-mail can expose their companies to big financial risks.

There are many cases where an indiscreet e-mail has led to corporate scandal, and a new industry has been created. Finding e-mails has become a big business, and searching for e-evidence is a huge opportunity. The electronic evidence processing industry uses powerful computers to search for e-mail messages to use against an adversary in court. Juries appear to be more willing to accept what was said in the past as opposed to what is said on the witness stand.

Every day in North America, 500 million e-mail messages are sent, and every company with employees using e-mail is at risk. Why? The candour expressed in e-mails is often astounding. At Merrill Lynch, a stock that was recommended to clients was referred to as a "piece of crap" and a "dog" in employee e-mails. Merrill Lynch settled out of court for $150 million. Even Bill Gates was caught in an e-mail saying he would consider doing a "favour" for a potential client if they adopted a Microsoft system.

The problem is that pressing the delete button doesn't actually delete a message from the hard drive. This only happens when there is enough new data to write over the message. At KPMG Forensics, they find that an e-mail sent once is often copied several times within the computer and also on any PDA that has been synchronized with the computer. In addition, Internet Service Provider data can contain copies of the same message.

Thus, any company that could be the target of litigation, such as consumer products companies, must be particularly careful. Employees should think before they press the send button, and software packages that really do delete e-mail should be considered. However, deletion can be seen as a defensive cover-up activity, even if done accidentally. Thus, there is an increased reluctance to send sensitive information via e-mail, and employees are reverting to using the telephone instead.

Questions

1. Why are people so candid when writing e-mails? What could be done to change this behaviour?

2. How important are e-mail policies, given this situation? Draft some wording for an e-mail policy regarding caution in expressing opinions that could be detrimental to the company's interests.

3. Would you invest in an e-evidence search company? Why or why not?

4. If you were a CEO, would you be in favour of purchasing a software package that would truly delete e-mails?

Video Source: "E-Mail Alert," *CBC Venture 851* (October 27, 2002).

Additional Resource: www.yaletech.com/brochures/eCW%20Brochure-Brokerage.pdf

CHAPTER 3

Designing and Analyzing Jobs

LEARNING OUTCOMES

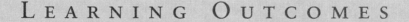

After studying this chapter, you should be able to:

Define job design and *explain* the difference between a job and a position.

Describe the industrial engineering, behavioural, and human engineering considerations involved in job design.

Explain the six steps in job analysis.

Describe four basic narrative methods of collecting job analysis information, and three quantitative methods.

Explain the difference between a job description and a job specification.

Discuss five recent organizational techniques used to foster responsiveness to change and how they have contributed to blurring the concept of a job.

ORGANIZING WORK

organizational structure The formal relationships among jobs in an organization.

organization chart A "snapshot" of the firm at a particular point in time, depicting the organization's structure in chart form.

Example of Online Organization Chart www.IntranetOrgChart.com

Online Organization Charts **www.nakisa.com**

An organization consists of one or more employees, who perform various tasks. The relationships between people and tasks must be structured in such a way that the organization can achieve its goals in an efficient and effective manner.

Organizational structure refers to the formal relationships among jobs in an organization. An **organization chart** is often used to depict the structure. As illustrated in **Figure 3.1**, such a chart indicates the types of departments established, the title of each manager's job, and by means of connecting lines, clarifies the chain of command and shows who is accountable to whom. An organization chart presents a "snapshot" of the firm at a particular point in time, but does not provide details about actual communication patterns, degree of supervision, amount of power and authority, or specific duties and responsibilities. Firms can now use organization chart software to ensure that such charts are kept current and are readily accessible to all employees.

Designing an organization involves choosing a structure that is appropriate, given the company's strategic goals. There are three basic types of organizational structure, as depicted in **Figure 3.2**: bureaucratic, flat, and boundaryless. Bureaucratic designs are becoming less common; flat structures are increasingly the norm; and boundaryless organizations have started to evolve.

FIGURE 3.1   A Sample Organization Chart

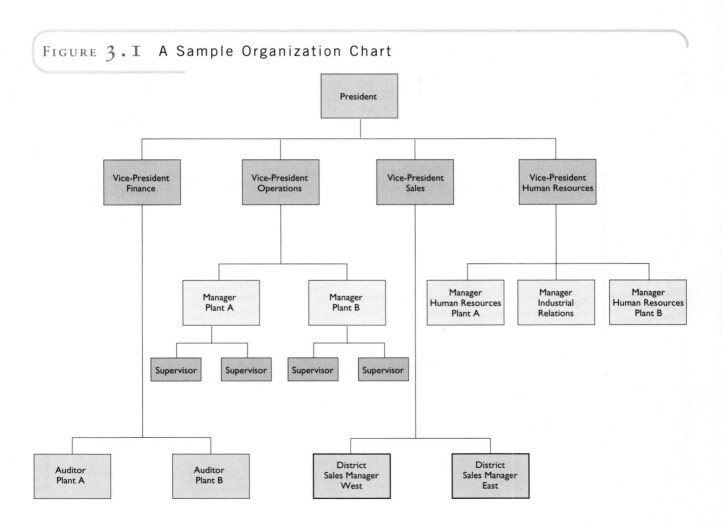

FIGURE 3.2   Bureaucratic, Flat, and Boundaryless Organizational Structures

| Structure | Characteristics |

BUREAUCRATIC

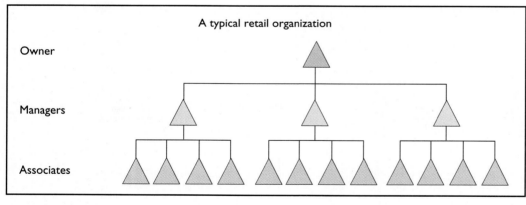

A typical educational institution

President

Vice-presidents

Deans

Chairs

Faculty

- Top-down management approach
- Many levels, and hierarchical communication channels and career paths
- Highly specialized jobs with narrowly defined job descriptions
- Focus on independent performance

FLAT

A typical retail organization

Owner

Managers

Associates

- Decentralized management approach
- Few levels and multi-directional communication
- Broadly defined jobs, with general job descriptions
- Emphasis on teams and on customer service

BOUNDARYLESS

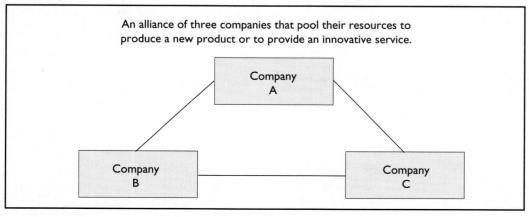

An alliance of three companies that pool their resources to produce a new product or to provide an innovative service.

Company A

Company B

Company C

- Joint ventures with customers, suppliers, and/or competitors
- Emphasis on teams whose members may cross organizational boundaries

JOB DESIGN

job design The process of systematically organizing work into tasks that are required to perform a specific job.

job A group of related activities and duties, held by a single employee or a number of incumbents.

position The collection of tasks and responsibilities performed by one person.

In any organization, work has to be divided into manageable units and ultimately into jobs that can be performed by employees. **Job design** is the process of systematically organizing work into tasks that are required to perform a specific job. An organization's strategy and structure influence the ways in which jobs are designed. In bureaucratic organizations, for example, since there is a hierarchical division of labour, jobs are generally highly specialized. In addition to organizational objectives and structure, however, effective job design also takes into consideration human and technological factors.

A **job** consists of a group of related activities and duties. Ideally, the duties of a job should be clear and distinct from those of other jobs, and involve natural units of work that are similar and related. This helps to minimize conflict and enhance employee performance. A job may be held by a single employee or may have a number of incumbents. The collection of tasks and responsibilities performed by one person is known as a **position**. To clarify, in a department with one supervisor, one clerk, 40 assemblers, and three tow-motor operators, there are 45 positions and four jobs.

Specialization and Industrial Engineering Considerations

The term "job" as it is known today is largely an outgrowth of the efficiency demands of the industrial revolution. As the substitution of machine power for people power became more widespread, experts such as Adam Smith, Charles Babbage, and Frederick Winslow Taylor (the father of scientific management) wrote glowingly about the positive correlation between (1) job specialization, and (2) productivity and efficiency.[1] The popularity of specialized, short-cycle jobs soared—at least among management experts and managers.

work simplification An approach to job design that involves assigning most of the administrative aspects of work (such as planning and organizing) to supervisors and managers, while giving lower-level employees narrowly defined tasks to perform according to methods established and specified by management.

Work simplification evolved from scientific management theory. It is based on the premise that work can be broken down into clearly defined, highly specialized, repetitive tasks to maximize efficiency. This approach to job design involves assigning most of the administrative aspects of work (such as planning and organizing) to supervisors and managers, while giving lower-level employees narrowly defined tasks to perform according to methods established and specified by management.

While work simplification can increase operating efficiency in a stable environment, and may be very appropriate in settings employing individuals with mental disabilities or those lacking in education and training (as in some third-world operations), it is not effective in a changing environment in which customers/clients demand custom-designed products and/or high-quality services, or one in which employees want challenging work. Moreover, among educated employees, simplified jobs often lead to lower satisfaction, higher rates of absenteeism and turnover, and sometimes to a demand for premium pay to compensate for the repetitive nature of the work.

industrial engineering A field of study concerned with analyzing work methods; making work cycles more efficient by modifying, combining, rearranging, or eliminating tasks; and establishing time standards.

Another important contribution of scientific management was the study of work. **Industrial engineering**, which evolved with this movement, is concerned with analyzing work methods and establishing time standards to improve efficiency. Industrial engineers systematically identify, analyze, and time the elements of each job's work cycle and determine which, if any, elements can be modified, combined, rearranged, or eliminated to reduce the time needed to complete the cycle.

To establish time standards, industrial engineers measure and record the time required to complete each element in the work cycle, using a stopwatch or work-sampling techniques, and then combine these times to determine the total. Adjustments are then made to compensate for differences in skill level, breaks, and interruptions due to such factors as machine maintenance or breakdown. The adjusted time becomes the time standard for that particular work cycle, which serves as an objective basis for evaluating and improving employee performance and determining incentive pay.

Since jobs are created primarily to enable an organization to achieve its objectives, industrial engineering cannot be ignored as a disciplined and objective approach to job design. However, too much emphasis on the concerns of industrial engineering—improving efficiency and simplifying work methods—may result in human considerations being neglected or downplayed. What may be improvements in job design and efficiency from an engineering standpoint can sometimes prove to be physiologically or psychologically unsound. For example, an assembly line with its simplified and repetitive tasks embodies the principles of industrial engineering, but may lead to repetitive strain injuries and high turnover and low satisfaction due to the lack of psychological fulfillment. Thus, to be effective, job design must also provide for the satisfaction of human psychological and physiological needs.

Behavioural Considerations

By the mid-1900s, reacting to what they viewed as the "dehumanizing" aspects of pigeonholing workers into highly repetitive and specialized jobs and other problems associated with overspecialization, various management theorists proposed ways of broadening the numbers of activities in which employees engaged. **Job enlargement** involves assigning workers additional tasks at the same level of responsibility to increase the number of tasks they have to perform. Thus, if the work was assembling chairs, the worker who previously only bolted the seat to the legs might take on the additional tasks of assembling the legs and attaching the back, as well. Also known as horizontal loading, job enlargement reduces monotony and fatigue by expanding the job cycle and drawing on a wider range of employee skills. Another technique to relieve monotony and employee boredom is **job rotation**. This involves systematically moving employees from one job to another. Although the jobs themselves don't change, workers experience more task variety, motivation, and productivity. The company gains by having more versatile, multiskilled employees who can cover for one another efficiently.

More recently, psychologist Frederick Herzberg argued that the best way to motivate workers is to build opportunities for challenge and achievement into jobs through **job enrichment**.[2] This is defined as any effort that makes an employee's job more rewarding or satisfying by adding more meaningful tasks and duties. Also known as vertical loading, job enrichment involves increasing autonomy and responsibility by allowing employees to assume a greater role in the decision-making process and become more involved in planning, organizing, directing, and controlling their own work.

job enlargement (horizontal loading) A technique to relieve monotony and boredom that involves assigning workers additional tasks at the same level of responsibility to increase the number of tasks they have to perform.

job rotation Another technique to relieve monotony and employee boredom, which involves systematically moving employees from one job to another.

job enrichment (vertical loading) Any effort that makes an employee's job more rewarding or satisfying by adding more meaningful tasks and duties.

Enriching jobs can be accomplished through such activities as:

- increasing the level of difficulty and responsibility of the job
- assigning workers more authority and control over outcomes
- providing feedback about individual or unit job performance directly to employees
- adding new tasks requiring training, thereby providing an opportunity for growth
- assigning individuals specific tasks or responsibility for performing a whole job rather than only parts of it.

Job design studies explored a new field when behavioural scientists focused on identifying various job dimensions that would simultaneously improve the efficiency of organizations and satisfaction of employees. One of the best-known theories evolving from such research is one advanced by Richard Hackman and Greg Oldham.[3] Their job characteristics model proposes that employee motivation and satisfaction are directly linked to five core characteristics:[4]

1. *Skill variety*. The degree to which the job requires a person to do different tasks and involves the use of a number of different talents, skills, and abilities.
2. *Task identity*. The degree to which the job requires completion of a whole and identifiable piece of work, that is, doing a job from beginning to end, with a visible outcome.
3. *Task significance*. The degree to which the job has a substantial impact on the lives and work of others—both inside and outside the organization.
4. *Autonomy*. The amount of freedom, independence, and discretion the employee has in terms of scheduling work and determining procedures.
5. *Feedback*. The degree to which the job provides the employee with clear and direct information about job outcomes and effectiveness of his or her performance.

These core job characteristics create the conditions that enable workers to experience three critical psychological states that are related to a number of beneficial work outcomes:[5]

1. *Experienced meaningfulness*. The extent to which the employee experiences the work as important, valuable, and worthwhile.
2. *Experienced responsibility*. The degree to which the employee feels personally responsible or accountable for the outcome of the work.
3. *Knowledge of results*. The degree to which the employee understands, on a regular basis, how effectively he or she is performing.

As illustrated in **Figure 3.3**, skill variety, task identity, and task significance are all linked to experienced meaningfulness; autonomy is related to experienced responsibility; and feedback provides knowledge of results.

A job with characteristics that allow an employee to experience all three critical states provides internal rewards that sustain motivation. The benefits to the employer include high-quality performance, higher employee satisfaction, and lower absenteeism and turnover.

FIGURE 3.3   The Job Characteristics Model

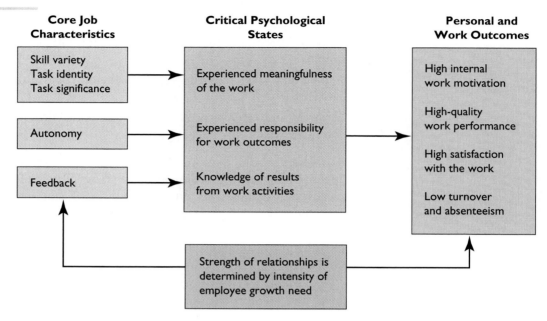

As is no doubt quite apparent, the suggestions of Herzberg, Hackman, and Oldham regarding job design and redesign strategies are quite similar. The benefits of job enrichment also include increased motivation, job satisfaction, and performance.

Job enrichment and the inclusion of the five core dimensions in jobs is not, however, a panacea. Job enrichment programs are more successful in some jobs and settings than in others. Moreover, not all employees want additional responsibility and challenge. Hackman and Oldham stress that the strength of the linkage among job characteristics, psychological states, and work outcomes is determined by the intensity of an individual employee's need for growth.[6] Some people prefer routine jobs and may resist job redesign efforts. In addition, job redesign efforts almost always fail when employees lack the physical or mental skills, abilities, or education needed to perform the job. Furthermore, neither approach will correct job dissatisfaction problems related to inequitable compensation, inadequate benefits, or lack of job security. Unions have sometimes resisted job enrichment, fearing that management will expect workers to take on more responsibility and challenge without additional compensation. Managers, fearing a loss of authority and control or worried about possible elimination of supervisory jobs, have also been sources of resistance.

Team-Based Job Designs   A logical outgrowth of job enrichment and the job characteristics model has been the increasing use of **team-based job designs**, which focus on giving a **team**, rather than an individual, a whole and meaningful piece of work to do. Team members are empowered to decide among themselves how to accomplish the work.[7] Often they are cross-trained, and then rotated to perform different tasks. Team-based designs are best suited to flat and boundaryless organization structures.

team-based job designs Job designs that focus on giving a team, rather than an individual, a whole and meaningful piece of work to do, and empowering team members to decide among themselves how to accomplish the work.
team A small group of people, with complementary skills, who work toward common goals for which they hold joint responsibility and accountability.

At Saturn's auto factory, team members with complementary skills work toward common goals for which they hold joint responsibility and accountability.

AN ETHICAL
DILEMMA

If an organization restructures and adopts a team-based design, how should employees who can't work effectively in teams be dealt with?

General Motors' Saturn Division is an extremely high-profile operation that has mastered the use of team-based job design. Initiated as a completely new venture within GM in an attempt to "reinvent the wheel," the Saturn car assembly process involves self-managed teams with seven to 15 members. Each team operates as a "small business unit" and is responsible for statistical process control tasks, has budgeting responsibilities, and is involved in parts and other supply purchasing decisions. The direction in which teamwork at Saturn has evolved could be representative of the future of team production in the auto industry.[8]

Increasingly, organizations are using "virtual teams"—people working together effectively and efficiently across boundaries of time and space. Livelink software combines a globally recognized methodology for teamwork with state-of-the-art collaboration technology. The software makes team meetings more productive by providing a virtual meeting place, and can be combined with conference calling, real-time broadcasting, shared textpads and whiteboards, group chat, and private instant messaging. Conveniently, all the team's meeting information is captured and stored for future use and reference.[9]

Human Engineering Considerations

human engineering (ergonomics)
An interdisciplinary approach that seeks to integrate and accommodate the physical needs of workers into the design of jobs. It aims to adapt the entire job system—the work, environment, machines, equipment, and processes—to match human characteristics.

Canadian College of Certified Professional Ergonomists
www.ergonomist.ca

Over time, it became apparent that in addition to considering psychological needs, effective job design must also take physiological needs and health and safety issues into account. **Human engineering** (or **ergonomics**) seeks to integrate and accommodate the physical needs of workers into the design of jobs. It aims to adapt the entire job system—the work, environment, machines, equipment, and processes—to match human characteristics. Doing so results in eliminating or minimizing product defects, damage to equipment, and worker injuries or illnesses caused by poor work design.

In addition to designing jobs and equipment with the aim of minimizing negative physiological effects for all workers, human engineering can aid in meeting the unique requirements of individuals with special needs, even as basic as left- and right-handedness, as discussed in the Workforce Diversity box.

WORKFORCE DIVERSITY

Creating a Non-Handed Workplace

While left-handed individuals make up about 10 percent of the general population, there is a tendency to have a right-handed dominance in workplace design. This creates a safety concern for left-handed workers whose safety controls, switches, and blade guards are positioned for right-handed workers. When left-handed workers are forced to use right-handed tools, it affects not only the safety of the worker, but also their productivity level, as they are more easily fatigued and accuracy can be diminished. A second risk that comes from a right-handed dominant workplace is that all workers may develop repetitive strain injuries when they use only their right hands to perform certain tasks.

The solution is to have a non-handed work environment, where the goal is not only to accommodate the left-handed worker, but also to encourage right-handers to use both hands to complete tasks by ensuring that all workers can choose the most comfortable way to perform the task assigned. When the dominant hand is fatigued, the other hand can be used, offering some relief to the worker while maintaining efficiency and productivity levels. In the non-handed workplace, physical demands are more evenly distributed, lowering the risk of the development of repetitive strain injury.

Suggestions for developing a non-handed workplace include:

- Determine how many workers are left-handed and assess their ability to perform tasks right-handed.

- Determine if there are any tasks in the workplace that cannot be modified to accommodate a left-handed worker, (i.e., power tools that have guards that cannot be moved). Minimize or eliminate left-handed workers.

- Make sure all hand tools are designed or purchased to allow for use in both the right and left hands; or, left-handed tools should be made available and clearly identified.

- Ensure that tools are being used safely and correctly.

- Position equipment to allow left-handed workers adequate room to move and reach easily without obstruction.

- Position left-handed workers on the opposite (or most appropriate) side of the production line whenever possible.

- When designing controls and their positioning, consider the frequency, importance of control function, and the dexterity, speed, accuracy, and strength required for control operation. Aim to have controls that both right- and left-handed workers can access.

- Invite left-handed workers to contribute their suggestions for improving the work tools, methods, and environments. Ask workers what methods they use to distribute the work demands from one hand to another.

Source: C. James, "Sinister Dexterity," *OHS Canada*, (December 2000), pp. 38–39.

Research Insight ▷

AN ETHICAL DILEMMA

Since some employees clearly require ergonomic aid while others do not, should ergonomic issues be addressed only in the redesign of special-needs employees' workstations or those of every employee?

It is important to note that the human engineering considerations involved in the design of jobs, workstations, and office space is important to all employees, not just those with special needs. A recent study of 623 full-time employees and 27 HR executives and recruiters revealed that a majority of employees rank design issues second only to compensation as a reason to accept or leave jobs. Besides wanting privacy, employees indicated a desire for access to needed equipment and people, and high-quality workspace lighting and airflow.[10]

Ergonomics has also become a collective bargaining issue. Based on the results of a joint study conducted by researchers at McMaster University and the Canadian Auto Workers Union (CAW), the CAW has determined that its members want to influence the intensity of their work and the design of their jobs, and they want the union to act on their behalf to ensure that these things occur. The CAW is therefore seeking improved job conditions for its members at the bargaining table. The aim is to create workstations that maximize comfort while allowing production standards to be met. For starters, the union wants workers to have a greater say when plants and lines are retooled or when new pieces of equipment are introduced. The union also wants to set "best practice" standards for comparable facilities and ensure that these standards are met.[11]

THE NATURE OF JOB ANALYSIS

job analysis The procedure for determining the tasks, duties, and responsibilities of each job, and the human attributes (in terms of knowledge skills, and abilities) required to perform it.

job description A list of the duties, responsibilities, reporting relationships, and working conditions of a job—one product of a job analysis.

job specification A list of the "human requirements," that is, the requisite knowledge, skills, and abilities (KSAs) needed to perform the job—another product of a job analysis.

Job Analysis **harvey.psyc.vt.edu**

Once jobs have been designed or redesigned, an employer's performance-related expectations need to be defined and communicated. This is best accomplished through job analysis, a process by which information about jobs is systematically gathered and organized. **Job analysis** is the procedure firms use to determine the tasks, duties, and responsibilities of each job, and the human attributes (in terms of knowledge, skills, and abilities) required to perform it. In contrast to job design, which reflects subjective opinions about the ideal requirements of a job, job analysis is concerned with objective and verifiable information about the actual requirements. Once this information has been gathered, it is used for developing **job descriptions** (what the job entails) and **job specifications** (what the human requirements are).[12]

Uses of Job Analysis Information

Job analysis is sometimes called the cornerstone of HRM. As illustrated in **Figure 3.4,** the information gathered, evaluated, and summarized through job analysis is the basis for a number of interrelated HRM activities. Having accurate information about jobs and their human requirements—which has been gathered in a gender-neutral, bias-free manner—is essential for legal compliance in each of these areas, as explained below.

Human Resources Planning   Knowing the actual requirements of jobs is essential in order to plan future staffing needs. As will be explained in the next chapter, when this information is combined with knowledge about the skills and

FIGURE 3.4   Uses of Job Analysis Information

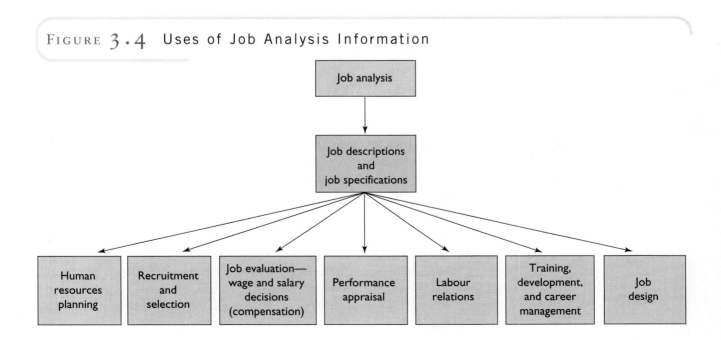

qualifications of current employees, it is possible to determine which jobs can be filled internally and which will require external recruitment. Job analysis information is also extremely helpful in assessing how a firm's employment equity goals can be met most effectively.

Recruitment and Selection

The job description and job specification information should be used to decide what sort of person to recruit and hire. Identifying bona fide occupational requirements, and ensuring that all activities related to recruitment and selection (such as advertising, screening, and testing) are based on such requirements, is necessary for legal compliance in all Canadian jurisdictions, something that was reinforced in a recent Federal Court of Appeal ruling:[13]

> When the Department of Employment and Immigration (now the Ministry of Citizenship and Immigration) advertised for immigration settlement counsellors, five qualifications were listed, one of which was knowledge of relevant legislation, of the branch and of issues concerning immigrant or refugee settlement. During its written and oral testing, however, the department decided to weight these knowledge requirements at only 10 percent, and three of the five candidates subsequently selected failed the knowledge requirement altogether. Two individuals who passed the knowledge requirement but were not hired launched a complaint. The Federal Court of Appeal ruled that the department should have required each candidate to meet each of the qualifications, and that the department should not have eliminated any of the advertised qualifications as this is unfair to people who might otherwise have applied but did not because they did not have all of the advertised qualifications.

> **Hints to Ensure Legal Compliance**

Compensation

Job analysis information is also essential for determining the relative value of and appropriate compensation for each job. Job evaluation should be based on the required skills, physical and mental demands, responsibilities, and working conditions—all assessed through job analysis. The relative value of jobs is one of the key factors used to determine appropriate compensation and justify pay differences if challenged under human rights or pay equity legislation. Information about the actual job duties is also necessary to determine whether a job should be classified as exempt or nonexempt for overtime pay and maximum hours purposes, as specified in employment standards legislation.

Performance Appraisal

To be legally defensible, the criteria used to assess employee performance must be directly related to the duties and responsibilities identified through job analysis. The standards used must also be justifiable. For many jobs involving routine tasks, especially those of a quantifiable nature, performance standards are determined through job analysis. For more complex jobs, performance standards are often jointly established by employees and their supervisors. To be realistic and achievable, such standards should be based on actual job requirements, as identified through job analysis.

Labour Relations

In unionized environments, the job descriptions developed from the job analysis information are generally subject to union approval prior to finalization. Such union-approved job descriptions then become the basis for classifying jobs, and bargaining over wages, performance criteria, and working conditions. Once approved, significant changes to job descriptions may have to be negotiated.

Training, Development, and Career Management By comparing the knowledge, skills, and abilities (KSAs) that employees bring to the job with those that are identified by job analysis, managers can determine the gaps. Training programs can then be designed to bridge these gaps. Having accurate information about jobs also means that employees can prepare for future advancement by identifying gaps between their current KSAs and those specified for the jobs to which they aspire.

Job Design Job analysis is useful for ensuring that all of the duties having to be done have actually been assigned, and identifying areas of overlap. Also, having an accurate description of each job sometimes leads to the identification of unnecessary requirements, areas of conflict or dissatisfaction, and/or health and safety concerns that can be eliminated through job redesign. Such redesign may increase morale and productivity and ensure compliance with human rights and occupational health and safety legislation.

Steps in Job Analysis

The six steps involved in analyzing jobs are as follows:

Step 1   Identify the use to which the information will be put, since this will determine the types of data that should be collected and the techniques used. Some data-collection techniques—such as interviewing the employee and asking what the job entails and what his or her responsibilities are—are good for writing job descriptions and selecting employees for the job. Other job analysis techniques (like the position analysis questionnaire, described later) do not provide qualitative information for job descriptions, but rather numerical ratings for each job; these can be used to compare jobs to one another for compensation purposes.

process chart A diagram showing the flow of inputs to and outputs from the job under study.

Step 2   Review relevant background information such as organization charts, process charts, and job descriptions.[14] As explained earlier, organization charts show how the job in question relates to other jobs and where it fits in the overall organization. A **process chart** provides a more detailed understanding of the workflow than is obtainable from the organization chart alone. In its simplest form, a process chart (like the one in **Figure 3.5**) shows the flow of inputs to and outputs from the job under study. (In Figure 3.5, the inventory control clerk is expected to receive inventory from suppliers, take requests for inventory from the two plant managers, provide requested inventory to these managers, and give information to the plant accountant on the status of in-stock inventories.) Finally, the existing job description, if there is one, can provide a starting point for building the revised one.

Step 3   Select the representative positions and jobs to be analyzed. This is necessary when there are many incumbents in a single job and when a number of similar jobs are to be analyzed, since it would be too time-consuming to analyze every position and job.

Step 4   Next, analyze the jobs by collecting data on job activities, required employee behaviours, working conditions, and human traits and abilities needed to perform the job, using one or more of the job analysis techniques explained later in this chapter.

FIGURE 3.5   Process Chart for Analyzing a Job's Workflow

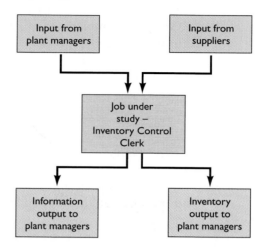

Source: Compensation Management in a Knowledge-based World, 9th edition by Henderson, Richard I., ©
Reprinted by permission of Pearson Education, Inc., Upper Saddle River, NJ.

Step 5 Review the information with job incumbents. The job analysis information should be verified with the worker(s) performing the job and with the immediate supervisor. This will help to confirm that the information is factually correct and complete. By providing an opportunity for review and modification, if necessary, this step can also help gain the employees' acceptance of the job analysis data, as well as the documents derived from this data and subsequent decisions reached.

Step 6 Develop a job description and job specification. A job description and a job specification are the two concrete products of the job analysis. As explained earlier, the job description is a written statement that describes the activities and responsibilities of the job, as well as important features of the job (such as working conditions and safety hazards). The job specification summarizes the personal qualities, traits, skills, and background required. While there may be a separate document describing the human qualifications, job descriptions and specifications are often combined in a single document, generally titled "Job Description."

METHODS OF COLLECTING JOB ANALYSIS INFORMATION

Various qualitative and quantitative techniques are used for collecting information about the duties, responsibilities, and requirements of the job; the most important ones will be discussed in this section. In practice, when the information is being used for multiple purposes, ranging from developing recruitment criteria to compensation decisions, several techniques may be used in combination.

Collecting job analysis data usually involves a joint effort by an HR specialist, the incumbent, and the jobholder's supervisor. The HR specialist (an HR manager, job analyst, or consultant) might observe and analyze the work being done and then develop a job description and specification. The supervisor and incumbent generally also get involved, perhaps by filling out questionnaires. The supervisor and incumbent typically review and verify the job analyst's conclusions regarding the job's duties, responsibilities, and requirements.

Qualitative Job Analysis Techniques

The Interview The interview is probably the most widely used method for determining the duties and responsibilities of a job. Three types of interviews are used to collect job analysis data: individual interviews with each employee; group interviews with employees having the same job; and supervisory interviews with one or more supervisors who are thoroughly knowledgeable about the job being analyzed. The group interview is used when a large number of employees are performing similar or identical work, and it can be a quick and inexpensive way of learning about the job. As a rule, the immediate supervisor attends the group session; if not, the supervisor should be interviewed separately to get that person's perspective on the duties and responsibilities of the job.

Whichever interview method is used, the interviewee should fully understand the reason for the interview, since there's a tendency for such interviews to be misconstrued as "efficiency evaluations." When they are, interviewees may not be willing to accurately describe their jobs or those of their reporting employees.

Typical Questions Some typical interview questions include:

1. What is the major purpose of the job?
2. What are the major duties? What percentage of time is spent on each?
3. What are the major responsibilities?
4. What types of equipment, machinery, and/or tools are used?
5. What are the education, experience, skill, and (where applicable) certification and licensing requirements?
6. What are the basic accountabilities or performance standards that typify the work?
7. What are the job's physical demands? What are its emotional and mental demands?
8. In what physical location(s) is the work performed? What working conditions are involved?
9. What are the health and safety conditions? To what hazard(s) is there exposure, if any?

Most fruitful interviews follow a structured or checklist format. A job analysis questionnaire like the one presented in **Figure 3.6** may be used to interview job incumbents or may be filled out by them. It includes a series of detailed questions regarding such matters as the general purpose of the job; responsibilities and duties; education, experience, and skills required; physical and mental demands; and working conditions. A list like this can also be used by a job analyst who collects information by personally observing the work being done or by administering it as a questionnaire, two methods that will be explained shortly.[15]

FIGURE 3.6 Job Analysis Questionnaire

Job title: _____ Job grade: _____
Department: _____ Location: _____
Prepared by: _____ Date: _____

1. Purpose of job
  • What is the purpose of the job? Why does the job exist?
  _____
  _____
  _____

2. Major responsibilities and essential functions (list in order of importance)
  • What are the responsibilities?   • Why is the activity performed?
  • How are they done?   • What is the measure of success?
  • Percentage of time?   • What direction of others is involved?
  _____
  _____
  _____
  _____

3. Knowledge
  • What techniques and/or practices are necessary? Why?
  _____
  _____

  • List specific education requirement(s).
  _____
  _____

  • List experience requirement(s) and number of years required in each.
  _____
  _____

  • List required licences or certificates.
  _____
  _____

4. Problem solving and decision making
  • List how the jobholder solves problems (i.e., planning, scheduling, creativity techniques, complexity of procedures, degree of independent thinking, and resourcefulness or ingenuity required). List examples of required development of new methods. What are the consequences if problems are not solved?
  _____
  _____
  _____
  _____
  _____

5. Resource responsibility
  • List annual pay of personnel who report to jobholder: _____
  • List annual operating budget (include pay):

- List any other financial resources (i.e., annual project value/cost, shop order value, total sales, total unit payroll, gross sales booked, purchasing/contracts volume, transportation costs, facilities budget, assets, investment income, program development costs, and gross sales billed):

_____

_____

- What is the jobholder's role in planning, organizing, acquiring, or monitoring these resources?

_____

_____

- What is the jobholder's impact in planning, organizing, acquiring, or monitoring these resources?

_____

_____

6. Skills of persuasion
- Describe the communication skills required in the job (e.g., explaining, convincing, and selling).
- Are contacts inside or outside?
- What are the levels of contacts?
- What type of oral or written communications are involved?
- Who is communicated with and why?

_____

_____

_____

_____

_____

_____

7. Working conditions
Read the list of working conditions below and put a check mark if they impact on your job.

Condition	Amount of Exposure		
	Occasional	Regular	Frequent
Dust, dirt, fumes	_____	_____	_____
Heat, cold	_____	_____	_____
Noise	_____	_____	_____
Vibration	_____	_____	_____
Inclement weather	_____	_____	_____
Lighting	_____	_____	_____

Describe any health or safety hazards related to the job.

_____

_____

_____

Source: T.J. Hackett, E.G. Vogeley, S. Weeks, P. Drouillard and D.E. Tyson, "Job Analysis and Job Descriptions," in D.E. Tyson, ed., *Carswell's Compensation Guide* (Toronto: Carswell, March 2002), pp. 21–23. Reprinted by permission of Carswell, a division of Thomson Canada Limited.

Interview Guidelines When conducting a job analysis interview, supervisors and job analysts should keep several things in mind:

1. The job analyst and supervisor should work together to identify the employees who know the job best, as well as those who might be expected to be the most objective in describing their duties and responsibilities.

2. Rapport should be established quickly with the interviewee, by using the individual's name, speaking in easily understood language, briefly reviewing the purpose of the interview (job analysis, not performance appraisal), and explaining how the person came to be chosen.

3. A structured guide or checklist that lists questions and provides spaces for answers should be used. This ensures that crucial questions are identified ahead of time, so that complete and accurate information is gathered, and that all interviewers (if there is more than one) glean the same types of data, thereby helping to ensure comparability of results. However, leeway should also be permitted by including some open-ended questions like, "Was there anything that we didn't cover with our questions?"

4. When duties are not performed in a regular manner—for instance, when the incumbent doesn't perform the same tasks or jobs over and over again many times a day—the incumbent should be asked to list his or her duties *in order of importance* and *frequency of occurrence*. This will ensure that crucial activities that occur infrequently—like a nurse's occasional emergency room duties—aren't overlooked.

5. The data should be reviewed and verified by both the interviewee and his or her immediate supervisor.

Questionnaires Having employees fill out questionnaires to describe their job-related duties and responsibilities is another good method of obtaining job analysis information.

The major decision involved is determining how structured the questionnaire should be and what questions to include. Some questionnaires involve structured checklists. Each employee is presented with an inventory of perhaps hundreds of specific duties or tasks (such as "change and splice wire"), and is asked to indicate whether or not he or she performs each and, if so, how much time is normally spent on it. At the other extreme, the questionnaire can be open-ended and simply ask the employee to describe the major duties of his or her job. In practice, a typical job analysis questionnaire often falls between the two extremes. As illustrated in Figure 3.6, there are often several open-ended questions (such as "state your main job duties"), as well as a number of structured questions (concerning, for instance, job requirements).

Observation Direct observation is especially useful when jobs consist mainly of observable physical activities. Jobs like those of janitor, assembly-line worker, and accounting clerk are examples. On the other hand, observation is usually not appropriate when the job entails a lot of immeasurable mental activity (lawyer, design engineer). Nor is it useful if the employee engages in important activities that might occur only occasionally, such as year-end reports.

Direct observation and interviewing are often used together. One approach is to observe the worker on the job during a complete work cycle. (The cycle is the time that it takes to complete the job; it could be a minute for an assembly-line worker, or an hour, a day, or longer for complex jobs.) All of the observed job activities are noted. Then, after as much information as possible is accumulated, the incumbent is interviewed, asked to clarify points not understood, and asked to explain what additional activities he or she performs that weren't observed. Another approach is to observe and interview simultaneously, while the job-holder performs his or her tasks.

diary/log Daily listings made by employees of every activity in which they engage, along with the time each activity takes.

Participant Diary/Log Another technique involves asking employees to keep a **diary/log** or a list of what they do during the day. Each employee records every activity in which he or she is involved (along with the time) in a log. This can produce a very complete picture of the job, especially when supplemented with subsequent interviews with the employee and his or her supervisor. The employee might, of course, try to exaggerate some activities and underplay others. However, the detailed, chronological nature of the log tends to minimize this problem.

Advantages and Disadvantages of Qualitative Data Collection Methods Interviews, questionnaires, observation, and participant diaries are all qualitative in nature. They are the most popular methods for gathering job analysis data, and provide realistic information about what job incumbents actually do and the qualifications and skills required. Associated with each are certain advantages and disadvantages, as summarized in **Table 3.1**. By combining two or more qualitative techniques, some of the disadvantages can be overcome.

Quantitative Job Analysis Techniques

Although most employers use interviews, questionnaires, observations, and/or diaries/logs for collecting job analysis data, there are many times when these narrative approaches are not appropriate. For example, when the aim is to assign a quantitative value to each job so that jobs can be compared for pay purposes, a more quantitative job analysis approach may be best. The position analysis questionnaire and functional job analysis are two popular quantitative methods.

TABLE 3.1   A Summary of Conventional Data Collection Methods for Job Analysis and the Advantages/Disadvantages of Each

Method	Variations	Brief Description	Advantages	Disadvantages
Observation	Structured	• Watch people go about their work; record frequency of behaviours or nature of performance on forms prepared in advance	• Third-party observer has more credibility than job incumbents, who may have reasons for distorting information	• Observation can influence behaviour of job incumbents
	Unstructured	• Watch people go about their work; describe behaviours/ tasks performed	• Focuses more on reality than on perceptions	• Meaningless for jobs requiring mental effort (in that case, use information processing method)
	Combination	• Part of the form is prepared in advance and is structured; part is unstructured		• Not useful for jobs with a long job cycle

continued

Questionnaire	Structured	• Ask job incumbents/ supervisors about work performed using fixed responses	• Relatively inexpensive • Structured questionnaires lend themselves easily to computer analyses • Good method when employees are widely scattered or when data must be collected from a large number of employees	• Developing and testing a questionnaire can be time-consuming and costly • Depends on communication skills of respondents • Does not allow for probing • Tends to focus on perceptions of the job
	Unstructured	• Ask job incumbents/ supervisors to write essays to describe work performed		
	Combination	• Part of the questionnaire is structured; part is unstructured		
Diary/Log	Structured	• Ask people to record their activities over several days or weeks in a booklet with time increments provided	• Highly detailed information can be collected over the entire job cycle • Quite appropriate for jobs with a long job cycle	• Requires the job incumbent's participation and cooperation • Tends to focus on perceptions of the job
	Unstructured	• Ask people to indicate in a booklet over how long a period they worked on a task or activity		
	Combination	• Part of the diary is structured; part is unstructured		
Individual Interview	Structured	• Read questions and/or fixed response choices to job incumbent and supervisor; must be face to face	• Provides an opportunity to explain the need for and functions of job analysis • Relatively quick and simple way to collect data • More flexible than surveys • Allows for probing to extract information and provides the interviewee with an opportunity to express views and/or vent frustrations that might otherwise go unnoticed • Activities and behaviours may be reported that would be missed during observation	• Depends heavily on rapport between interviewer and respondent • May suffer from validity/ reliability problems • Information may be distorted due to outright falsification or honest misunderstanding
	Unstructured	• Ask questions and/or provide general response choices to job incumbent and supervisor; must be face to face		
	Combination	• Part of the interview is structured; part is unstructured		
Group Interview	Structured	• Same as structured individual interviews except that more than one job incumbent/ supervisor is interviewed	• Groups tend to do better than individuals with open-ended problem solving • Reliability/validity are likely to be higher than with individuals because group members cross check each other	• Cost more because more people are taken away from their jobs to participate • Like individual interviews, tends to focus on perceptions of the job
	Unstructured	• Same as unstructured individual interviews except that more than one job incumbent/supervisor is interviewed		
	Combination	• Same as combination individual interview except more than one job incumbent/supervisor is interviewed		

Source: Adapted from William J. Rothwell and H.C. Kazanas, *Planning and Managing Human Resources: Strategic Planning for Personnel Management*, 2nd ed. (Amherst, MA: Human Resources Development Press, 2003), pp. 66–68. Reprinted by permission of the publisher.

position analysis questionnaire (PAQ) A questionnaire used to collect quantifiable data concerning the duties and responsibilities of various jobs.

PAQ Services Inc. **www.paq.com**

Position Analysis Questionnaire The **position analysis questionnaire (PAQ)** is a very structured job analysis questionnaire, a portion of which is shown in **Figure 3.7**.[16] The PAQ itself is filled in by a job analyst, who should already be acquainted with the particular job to be analyzed. The PAQ contains 194 items, each of which represents a basic element that may or may not play an important role in the job. The job analyst decides whether each item plays a role on the job and, if so, to what extent. If, for example, "written materials" received a rating of four, this would indicate that materials such as books, reports, and office notes play a considerable role in this job.

FIGURE 3.7   Position Analysis Questionnaire (Excerpt)

Extent of Use
0 Does not apply
1 Nominal/very infrequent
2 Occasional
3 Moderate
4 Considerable
5 Very substantial

A1. Visual Sources of Job Information

Using the response scale at the left, rate each of the following items on the basis of the extent to which it is used by the worker as a source of information in performing the job.

1. **Written materials**
   E.g., books, reports, office notes, articles, job instructions, or signs

2. **Quantitative materials**
   Materials that deal with quantities or amounts, e.g., graphs, accounts, specifications, or tables of numbers

3. **Pictorial materials**
   Pictures or picturelike materials used as sources of information, e.g., drawings, blueprints, diagrams, maps, tracings, photographic films, x-ray films, or TV pictures

4. **Patterns or related devices**
   E.g., templates, stencils, or patterns used as sources of information when observed during use (Do not include materials described in item 3.)

5. **Visual displays**
   E.g., dials, gauges, signal lights, radarscopes, speedometers, or clocks

6. **Measuring devices**
   E.g., rules, calipers, tire pressure gauges, scales, thickness gauges, pipettes, thermometers, or protractors used to obtain visual information about physical measurements (Do not include devices described in item 5.)

7. **Mechanical devices**
   E.g., tools, equipment, or machinery that are sources of information when observed during use or operation

8. **Materials in process**
   E.g., parts, materials, or objects which are sources of information when being modified, worked on, or otherwise processed, such as bread dough being mixed, a workpiece being turned in a lathe, fabric being cut, or a shoe being resoled

9. **Materials not in process**
   E.g., parts, materials, or objects not in the process of being changed or modified, which are sources of information when being inspected, handled, packaged, distributed, or selected, such as items or materials in inventory, storage, or distribution channels, or items being inspected

10. **Features of nature**
    E.g., landscapes, fields, geological samples, vegetation, cloud formations, and other natural features that are observed or inspected to provide information

continued

> **11. Constructed features of environment**
> E.g., structures, buildings, dams, highways, bridges, docks, railroads, and other "constructed" or altered aspects of the indoor or outdoor environment which are observed or inspected to provide job information (Do not consider equipment, machines, etc., that individuals use in their work, as covered by item 7.)
>
> **12. Behaviour**
> Observing the actions of people or animals, e.g., in teaching, supervising, or sports officiating, where the behaviour is a source of job information
>
> **13. Events or circumstances**
> Events the worker observed and may participate in, such as flow of traffic, movement of materials, or airport control tower operations
>
> **14. Art or décor**
> Artistic or decorative objects or arrangements used as *sources* of job information, e.g., paintings, sculpture, jewellery, window displays, or interior design

Note: The 194 PAQ elements are grouped into six dimensions. This exhibits 14 of the "information input" questions or elements. Other PAQ pages contain questions regarding mental processes, work output, relationships with others, job context, and other job characteristics.

Source: E.J. McCormick, P.R. Jeanneret, and R.D. Mecham, *Position Analysis Questionnaire.* Copyright 1989 by Purdue Research Foundation, West Lafayette, IN. Reprinted with permission.

The advantage of the PAQ is that it provides a quantitative score or profile of the job in terms of how that job rates on five basic dimensions: (1) having decision-making/communication/social responsibilities, (2) performing skilled activities, (3) being physically active, (4) operating vehicles/equipment, and (5) processing information. Since it allows the assignment of a quantitative score to each job, based on these five dimensions, the PAQ's real strength is in classifying jobs. Results can be used to compare jobs to one another; this information can then be used to determine appropriate pay levels.[17]

Functional Job Analysis   **Functional job analysis (FJA)** rates the job on responsibilities for data, people, and things from simple to complex. This technique also identifies performance standards and training requirements. Thus, FJA allows the analyst to answer the question, "To do this task and meet these standards, what training does the worker require?"[18]

The National Occupational Classification and Job Analysis   The *National Occupational Classification (NOC)*, the product of systematic, field-based research by Human Resources Development Canada (HRDC), is an excellent source of standardized job information.[19] It was updated and revised in 2001, and contains comprehensive descriptions of approximately 30 000 occupations and the requirements for each. To illustrate the types of information included, the *NOC* listing for Specialists in Human Resources is shown in **Figure 3.8.**

The *NOC* and its counselling component, the *Career Handbook*, both focus on occupations rather than jobs. An **occupation** is defined as a collection of jobs that share some or all of a set of main duties. The list of examples of job titles within each of the 530 Unit Groups in the *NOC* provides a frame of reference for the boundaries of that occupational group. The jobs within each group are characterized by similar skills.[20]

functional job analysis (FJA) A quantitative method for classifying jobs based on types and amounts of responsibility for data, people, and things. Performance standards and training requirements are also identified.

National Occupational Classification (NOC) A reference tool for writing job descriptions and job specifications. Compiled by the federal government, it contains comprehensive, standardized descriptions of about 30 000 occupations and the requirements for each.

occupation A collection of jobs that share some or all of a set of main duties.

FIGURE 3.8   *NOC* Job Description for Specialists in Human Resources

Specialists in Human Resources develop, implement, and evaluate human resources and labour relations policies, programs, and procedures and advise managers and employees on personnel matters. Specialists in Human Resources are employed throughout the private and public sectors, or may be self-employed.

Examples of titles classified in this unit group

Business Agent, Labour Union
Employment Equity Officer
Classification Officer
Human Resources Research Officer
Classification Specialist
Job Analyst
Compensation Research Analyst
Labour Relations Officer
Conciliator
Mediator
Consultant, Human Resources
Union Representative
Employee Relations Officer
Wage Analyst

Main duties
Specialists in Human Resources perform some or all of the following duties:

- Develop, implement, and evaluate personnel and labour relations policies, programs, and procedures
- Advise managers and employees on the interpretation of personnel policies, benefit programs, and collective agreements
- Negotiate collective agreements on behalf of employers or workers, and mediate labour disputes and grievances
- Research and prepare occupational classifications, job descriptions, and salary scales
- Administer benefit, employment equity and affirmative action programs, and maintain related record systems
- Coordinate employee performance and appraisal programs
- Research employee benefit and health and safety practices and recommend changes or modifications to existing policies.

Employment requirements

- A university degree or college diploma in a field related to personnel management, such as business administration, industrial relations, commerce, or psychology or Completion of a professional development program in personnel administration is required.
- Some experience in a clerical or administrative position related to personnel administration may be required.

Additional Information
- Progression to management positions is possible with experience.

Classified elsewhere
- *Human Resources Managers* (0112)
- *Personnel and Recruitment Officers* (1223)
- *Personnel Clerks* (1442)
- *Professional Occupations in Business Services to Management* (1122)
- Training officers and instructors (in 4131 *College and Other Vocational Instructors*)

Source: Human Resources Development Canada, *National Occupational Classification*, 2001. Catalogue No. MP 53-25/2001-E. Reproduced with the permission of the Minister of Public Works and Government Services Canada, 2004.

To provide a complete representation of work in the Canadian economy, the *NOC* classifies occupations in Major Groups based on two key dimensions—skill level and skill type. The Major Groups, which are identified by two-digit numbers, are then broken down further into Minor Groups, with a third digit added, and Unit Groups, at which level a fourth digit is added. Within these three levels of classification, a Unit Group provides the actual profile of an occupation.[21] For example:

- Major Group 31—Professional Occupations in Health
- Minor Group 314—Professional Occupations in Therapy and Assessment
- Unit Group 3142—Physiotherapists

These code numbers facilitate the exchange of statistical information about jobs, and are useful for vocational counselling and charting career paths. Since the *NOC* Major Group codes are now being used for employment equity reporting purposes, many companies formerly using *CCDO* and *SOC* codes have switched to *NOC* codes.

One of the benefits of the *NOC* is that it has helped to promote a greater degree of uniformity in job titles and descriptions used by employers across Canada. This has facilitated the exchange of information about salaries and benefits for compensation administration purposes, and about labour supply and demand for human resources planning.

Standardized job descriptions also facilitate the movement of workers from areas experiencing high unemployment to those in which there are more job opportunities.

WRITING JOB DESCRIPTIONS

A job description is a written statement of *what* the jobholder actually does, *how* he or she does it, and *under what conditions* the job is performed. The description in **Figure 3.9**—in this case for a Vice-President, Human Resources, Asia-Pacific Region—provides an example. As can be seen, the description is quite comprehensive and includes such essential elements as identification, summary, and duties and responsibilities, as well as the human qualifications for the job.

No standard format is used in writing job descriptions, but most include the following types of information: job identification, job summary, relationships, duties and responsibilities, authority of incumbent, performance standards, and working conditions. We will describe what is likely to be found under each of these headings shortly. As mentioned previously, job specifications (human qualifications) may also be included, as is the case in Figure 3.9. When writing job descriptions for the first time or updating them to keep them current, the *NOC* and its accompanying *Career Handbook* can be extremely helpful. As explained in the HR.Net box, online assistance is also available.

Job Identification

As in Figure 3.9, the job identification section generally contains several types of information. The *position title* specifies the title of the job, such as vice-president, marketing manager, recruiter, or inventory control clerk. The *department* and

FIGURE 3.9 Sample Job Description

Sample Job Description

Position:	Vice-President, Human Resources, Asia-Pacific
Location:	Hong Kong
Division:	Asia-Pacific
Incumbent:	Y. Tanaka
Department:	Human Resources
Job code:	CAP-HRM-001
Reports to:	President Asia-Pacific (administrative), Vice-President, Human Resources—Corporate (functional)
Written by:	Monica Lim, Joy Analyst
Date:	2 April 2000
Approved by:	J.A. Wong, President, Asia-Pacific (administrative superior) W.J. Smith, Vice-President, Human Resources—Corporate (functional superior)

Job Summary

Under the administrative direction of the President, Asia-Pacific, and the functional guidance of the Vice-President, Human Resources—Corporate, develop, recommend and implement approved HRM strategies, policies and practices that will facilitate the achievement of the company's stated business and HRM objectives.

Duties and Responsibilities

- Develop and recommend HRM strategies, policies, and practices that promote employee commitment, competence, motivation and performance, and that facilitate the achievement of the Asia-Pacific region's business objectives.
- Provide policy guidance to senior management regarding the acquisition, development, reward, maintenance and exist of the division's human resources so as to promote the status of the company as an ethical and preferred employer of choice.
- Identify, analyze, and interpret for Asia-Pacific regional senior management and corporate HR management those influences and changes in the division's internal and external environment and their impact on HRM and divisional business objectives, strategies, policies and practices.

Relationships

Internally, relate with senior line and functional managers within the Asia-Pacific region and corporate headquarters in New York. Externally, successfully relate with senior academic, business, government and trade union personnel. Directly supervise the following positions: Manager, Compensation and Benefits, Asia-Pacific and Manager, Training and Development, Asia-Pacific. Functionally supervise the HR managers in 13 geographic locations within the Asia-Pacific region.

Know-How

University degree is required, along with seven to 10 years broad-based HRM experience in a competitive and international (preferably Asian) business environment. A proven track record in managing change is essential. Fluency in English is essential and fluency in Chinese or Japanese is desirable. Excellent human relations and communication skills are essential. Previous experience in marketing, finance or manufacturing is desirable. The ability to positively represent the company at the most senior levels and to actively contribute as a Director of the Asia-Pacific regional Board is essential.

Problem Solving

Diverse cultures and varying stages of economic development within the Asia-Pacific region create a unique and tough business environment. The incumbent will often face complex HR and business problems demanding solutions that need to be creative and, at the same time, sensitive to local and company requirements.

continued

Authority

This position has the authority to:
- approve expenditures on budgeted capital items up to a total value of $100 000 in any one financial year
- hire and fire subordinate personnel in accord with company policies and procedures
- approve expense accounts for subordinate personnel in accord with company policies and procedures
- authorize all non-capital item expenditures within approved budgetary limit
- exercise line authority over all direct reporting positions

Accountability

Employees: 3000. Sales: $4 billion. Direct budget responsibility: $2.7 million. Assets controlled: $780 000. Locations: Australia, China, Hong Kong, India, Indonesia, Japan, South Korea, Malaysia, New Zealand, the Philippines, Singapore, Taiwan, Thailand.

Special Circumstances

Successful performance requires the incumbent to work long hours, to travel extensively (50–60 percent of the time), to quickly adapt to different cultures and business conditions, to successfully handle high-stress situations and to constantly work under pressure in a complex and very competitive business environment.

Performance Indicators

Performance indicators will include both quantitative and qualitative measures as agreed by the President, Asia-Pacific Division, and Vice-President, Human Resources—Corporate and the incumbent. Indicators may be market based (e.g., share price improvement), business based (e.g., division profitability, budget control, days lost through industrial unrest, positive changes in employee commitment, job satisfaction, and motivation) and individual based (e.g., performance as a leader and manager as assessed by superiors, peers, and subordinates). Performance expectations and performance indicators generally will be defined on an annual basis. A formal performance appraisal will be conducted at least once a year.

Source: R.J. Stone, *Human Resource Management*, 4th edition (Milton, Queensland: John Wiley & Sons, 2002), pp. 131–132. Reprinted with permission of the author.

HR.NET

Writing Job Descriptions Online

Thanks to the Internet, assistance in writing job descriptions may be just a few keystrokes away. A comprehensive, individual, professional job description can be created in minutes—it is fast, easy, and done completely online. At www.jobdescription.com there are more than 3700 built-in job descriptions in the existing job library, and specific competencies can be added to further define and individualize the job description to meet the needs of a specific organization. A step-by-step, easy-to-use wizard is available to aid in the description writing process.

After completing the job description, JobDescription.com helps to create and publish professional job advertisements and generate a job-specific interview form that contains suggested interview questions.

Source: Compiled from the CCHKnowledgePoint Web site at www.jobdescription.com. Used with permission of CCHKnowledgePoint, Petaluma, CA. All Rights Reserved.

location are also indicated, along with the title of the immediate supervisor—in this case under the heading *reports to*. The *date* refers to the date the job description was actually written, and *written by* identifies the person who wrote it. There is also an indication of whom the description was *approved by*. Many job descriptions also include a *job code*, which permits easy referencing. While some firms devise their own coding systems based on wage classification, for example, many use *NOC* codes to facilitate external comparison and employment equity reporting.

Job Summary

The *job summary* should describe the general nature of the job, listing only its major functions or activities. Thus (as in Figure 3.9), the Vice-President, Human Resources, Asia-Pacific "develops, recommends, and implements approved HRM strategies, policies, and practices that will facilitate the achievement of the company's stated business and HRM objectives." For the job of materials manager, the summary might state that she or he "purchases economically, regulates deliveries of, stores, and distributes all material necessary on the production line," while that for a mailroom supervisor might indicate that she or he "receives, sorts, and delivers all incoming mail properly, and he or she handles all outgoing mail including the accurate and timely posting of such mail."[22]

Relationships

The *relationships* section indicates the jobholder's relationships with others inside and outside the organization, as shown in Figure 3.9. Others directly and indirectly supervised are included, along with peers, superiors, and outsiders relevant to the job.

Duties and Responsibilities

This section presents a detailed list of the job's major duties and responsibilities. As in Figure 3.9, each of the job's major duties should be listed separately, and described in a few sentences. In the figure, for instance, the duties of the Vice-President, Human Resources, Asia-Pacific include developing and recommending HRM strategies, policies, and practices; providing policy guidance; identifying, analyzing, and interpreting environmental changes; and contributing to the Asia-Pacific Board of Directors. Typical duties of other jobs might include maintaining balanced and controlled inventories, making accurate postings to accounts payable, maintaining favourable purchase price variances, and repairing production line tools and equipment.

The *NOC* may be a helpful reference tool when itemizing a job's duties and responsibilities. As shown in Figure 3.8, for example, according to the *NOC*, a specialist in human resources might be expected to "develop, implement, and evaluate personnel and labour relations policies, programs, and procedures"; "advise managers and employees on the interpretation of personnel policies, benefit programs, and collective agreements"; and "research and prepare occupational classifications, job descriptions, and salary scales."

Most experts state unequivocally that "one item frequently found that should *never* be included in a job description is a 'cop-out clause' like 'other duties, as assigned,'"[23] since this leaves open the nature of the job and the people needed to staff it, and can be subject to abuse.

While the duties and responsibilities should be described in sufficient detail that training requirements and performance appraisal criteria can be identified, and the qualifications outlined in the job specification can be justified, it is generally possible to make it clear that the incumbent may be asked to perform additional related duties, without resorting to such a "cop-out clause." If not, including a statement such as, "The duties and responsibilities outlined above are representative, but not all-inclusive," may meet the firm's need for flexibility without sacrificing the quality and usefulness of the job description.

Authority

This section of a job description should define the limits of the jobholder's authority, including his or her decision-making authority, direct supervision of other employees, and budgetary limitations. For example, the Vice-President, Human Resources, Asia-Pacific (in Figure 3.9) has the authority to approve all budgeted non-capital expenditures and budgeted capital expenditures up to $100 000; approve expense accounts for subordinates; hire and fire subordinates, and exercise line authority over direct reports.

Performance Standards/Indicators

Some job descriptions also contain a performance standards/indicators section, which indicates the standards the employee is expected to achieve in each of the job description's main duties and responsibilities.

Setting standards is never an easy matter. Most managers soon learn, however, that just telling employees to "do their best" doesn't provide enough guidance to ensure top performance. One straightforward way of setting standards is to finish the statement: "I will be completely satisfied with your work when…" This sentence, if completed for each duty listed in the job description, should result in a usable set of performance standards.[24] Some examples would include the following:

Duty: Accurately Posting Accounts Payable
- All invoices received are posted within the same working day.
- All invoices are routed to the proper department managers for approval no later than the day following receipt.
- No more than three posting errors per month occur on average.
- Posting ledger is balanced by the end of the third working day of each month.

Duty: Meeting Daily Production Schedule
- Work group produces no fewer than 426 units per working day.
- No more than 2 percent of units are rejected at the next workstation, on average.
- Work is completed with no more than 5 percent overtime per week, on average.

Working Conditions and Physical Environment

The job description should also list the general working conditions involved in the job. This section generally includes information about noise level, temperature, lighting, degree of privacy, frequency of interruptions, hours of work, amount of travel, and hazards to which the incumbent may be exposed.

Job Description Guidelines

Some helpful guidelines to assist those writing job descriptions include:[25]

- List duties and responsibilities in logical sequence.
- State separate duties and responsibilities clearly, simply, and concisely.
- Begin each sentence with an action verb.
- Use quantitative terms whenever possible to achieve greater objectivity and clarity.
- Use specific rather than vague terms.
- Use standardized terminology.
- Answer the questions of how, what, and why. This will help produce a complete job description.
- Clearly identify the end results of standards on which performance will be evaluated.

Special guidelines for entrepreneurial and small businesses are provided in the Entrepreneurs and HR box.

Writing Job Descriptions That Comply with Human Rights Legislation
Human rights legislation requires employers to ensure that there is no discrimination on any of the prohibited grounds in any aspect or terms and conditions of employment. To ensure that job descriptions comply with this legislation, a few key points should be kept in mind:

- Job descriptions are not legally required, but are highly advisable.
- Essential job duties should be clearly identified in the job description. Indicating the percentage of time spent on each duty and/or listing duties in order of importance are strategies used to differentiate between essential and nonessential tasks and responsibilities.
- When assessing suitability for employment, training program enrolment, and transfers or promotions, and when appraising performance, the only criteria examined should be KSAs required for the essential duties of the job
- Even when an employee cannot perform one or more of the essential duties due to reasons related to a prohibited ground, such as a physical disability or religion, reasonable accommodation to the point of undue hardship is required.

WRITING JOB SPECIFICATIONS

Writing the job specification involves examining the duties and responsibilities and answering the question, "What human traits and experience are required to do this job?" Both skill and effort factors should be considered, as well as the human implications of the working conditions. Much of this information can be gleaned from the job analysis questionnaire. The job specification clarifies what kind of person to recruit and for which qualities that person should be tested. Often it is presented as part of the job description.[26]

ENTREPRENEURS AND HR

A Practical Approach to Job Analysis and Job Descriptions

Without their own job analysts or (in many cases) their own HR managers, many small-business owners need a more streamlined approach than larger businesses do. Also, there is always the concern that in writing up their job descriptions they will inadvertently overlook duties that should be assigned to employees or assign duties to employees that are usually not associated with such positions. A resource that includes all of the possible positions that they might encounter, with a detailed listing of the duties normally assigned to these positions, exists in the *National Occupational Classification (NOC)* mentioned earlier. The practical approach to job analysis for small-business owners presented next is built around this invaluable reference tool.

Step 1. Develop an organization chart.
Given the organization's strategic plan, the next step should be to develop an organization chart for the firm. A chart should be drawn showing who reports to the owner or CEO and who reports to each of the other managers and supervisors in the firm. Drawing up the organization chart of the present structure comes first. Then, depending upon how far in advance planning is being done, a chart can be produced that shows how the organization should look in the immediate future (say, in two months), as well as two or three other charts showing how the organization is likely to evolve over the next two or three years.

Step 2. Use a job analysis questionnaire.
Next, a job analysis questionnaire can be used to determine what the job entails. A shorter version of one of the more comprehensive job analysis questionnaires, such as that in Figure 3.6 (page 80), may be useful for collecting job analysis data. The information called for should be filled in and the supervisors or the employees themselves should be asked to list their job duties, breaking them into daily duties, periodic duties, and duties performed at irregular intervals. An example of a job summary for a customer service clerk is:

Answers inquiries and gives directions to customers, authorizes cashing of customers' cheques, records and returns lost charge cards, sorts and reviews new credit applications, and works at the customer service desk. An example of one job duty is:

Authorizes cashing of cheques, and authorizes cashing of payroll cheques (up to a specified amount) by customers desiring to make payment by cheque. Requests identification, such as a driver's license, from customers, and examines cheque to verify date, amount, signature, and endorsement. Initials cheque and sends customer to cashier.

Step 3. Obtain a copy of the *National Occupational Classification (NOC)* for reference.
Next, standardized examples of the job descriptions needed should be obtained from the *NOC*. A copy can be found in the reference section of the library in most major centres or purchased through a federal government bookstore or online at http://publications.pwgs.gc.ca.

Step 4. Choose appropriate definitions and copy them for reference.
For each department, the *NOC* job titles and job descriptions that are believed to be appropriate for the enterprise should be chosen and copied for future reference. Particularly when (as is usually the case) only one or two *NOC* definitions apply to the job description being written, the *NOC* definition will provide a firm foundation for the one being created. It will provide a standardized list and constant reminder of the specific duties that should be included. Including the *NOC* codes and definitions will also facilitate conversations with the local human resource centre, should this source be used to help find employees for open positions.

Step 5. Complete the job description.
An appropriate job summary for the job under consideration can then be written. The job analysis information, together with the information gathered from the *NOC*, can be used to create a complete listing of the tasks and duties of each of the jobs. The working conditions section can be completed once all of the tasks and duties have been specified.

Specifications for Trained versus Untrained Employees

Writing job specifications for trained employees might seem relatively straightforward. For example, the specifications for an intermediate-level programming position, accountant, or HR manager tend to focus primarily on length of previous experience required, educational qualifications, and specialized skills or training needed. Once again, however, complying with human rights legislation means keeping a few pointers in mind:

- All listed qualifications must be justifiable, based on the current job duties and responsibilities.

- Unjustifiably high educational and/or lengthy experience requirements can lead to systemic discrimination. For that reason, many employers are no longer indicating that a degree or diploma is mandatory; rather, they specify that the position calls for a university degree in a specific area, a college diploma in that area, or an equivalent combination of education and work experience.

- The qualifications of the current incumbent should not be confused with the minimum requirements, since he or she might be under- or overqualified. To avoid overstating or understating qualifications, it is helpful to ask the question, "What minimum qualifications would be required if this job were being filled in the immediate future?"

- For entry-level jobs, identifying the actual physical and mental demands is critical. Because on-the-job training will be provided, the emphasis tends to be on physical traits, personality, and/or sensory skills, instead of education and/or experience. The goal is to identify those personal traits—the human requirements—that are valid predictors of job success. For example, if the job requires detailed manipulation on a circuit-board assembly line, finger dexterity is extremely important, and is something for which candidates should be tested. A **physical demands analysis**—which identifies the senses used, and type, frequency, and amount of physical effort involved in the job—is often used to supplement the job specification. A sample form is included as **Figure 3.10**. Having such detailed information is particularly beneficial when determining accommodation requirements. The mental and emotional demands of a job are typically missing from job analysis information, and should also be specified so that the mental and emotional competencies of job applicants can be assessed and any need for accommodation can be identified.

physical demands analysis
Identification of the senses used, and type, frequency, and amount of physical effort involved in the job.

- Identifying the human requirements for a job can be accomplished through a judgmental approach or statistical analysis. Basing job specifications on statistical analysis is more legally defensible.

The job specifications for already trained candidates, such as the call centre operators shown here, should clearly indicate which skills, like computer literacy, are job requirements.

FIGURE 3.10   Physical Demands Analysis

Division:	Job Title:
Job Code:	Level:
Date:	Date of Last Revision:

Physical Requirements
Review the chart below. Indicate which of the following are essential to perform the functions of this job, with or without accommodation. Check one box in each section.

Section I					Section 2		Section 3			Section 4	
Incumbent Uses:	NA	Right	Left	Both	Repetitive motion		The job requires the use of the first category up to 2 hours per day	The job requires the use of the first category up to 4 hours per day	The job requires the use of the first category up to 8 hours per day	Frequent breaks: Normal breaks plus those caused by performing jobs outside of the area.	Limited breaks: Two short breaks and one lunch break.
					Y	N					
Hands: (requires manual manipulation)											
Feet: (functions requiring foot pedals and the like)											

Lifting capacity: Indicate, by checking the appropriate box, the amount of lifting necessary for this job, with or without accommodation.

	NA	Occasionally (As Needed)	Often (Up to 4 Hours Per Day)	Frequently (Up to 8 Hours Per Day)
5 kg				
5–10 kg				
10–25 kg				
25–50 kg				
50+ kg				

Mobility: Indicate which category the job functions fall under by placing a check next to those that apply.
☐ Sits constantly (6 hours or more with two breaks and one lunch break)
☐ Sits intermittently (6 hours or more with frequent change, due to breaks and getting up to perform jobs outside of the area)
☐ Stands intermittently (6 hours or more with frequent changes, due to breaks and getting up to perform jobs outside of the area)
☐ Bending constantly (4 hours or more with two breaks and one lunch break)
☐ Bending intermittently (4 hours or more with frequent changes, due to breaks and getting up to perform jobs outside of the area)
☐ Walks constantly (6 hours or more with two breaks and one lunch break)
☐ Walks intermittently (6 hours or more with frequent changes, due to breaks and getting up to perform jobs outside of the area)

Visual acuity: Indicate the minimum acceptable level, with or without accommodation, necessary for the job
☐ Excellent visual acuity
☐ Good visual acuity
☐ Not relevant to the job

Auditory acuity: Indicate the minimum acceptable level, with or without accommodation, necessary for the job.
☐ Excellent auditory acuity
☐ Good auditory acuity
☐ Not relevant to the job

Source: M. Rock and D.R. Berger, eds., *The Compensation Handbook: A State-of-the-Art Guide to Compensation Strategy and Design,* 4th edition, pp. 69–70 © 2000 The McGraw-Hill Companies, Inc.

Job Specifications Based on Judgment

The judgmental approach is based on the educated guesses of job incumbents, supervisors, and HR managers. The usual procedure to obtain the required information is to ask questions on the job analysis questionnaire such as, "What does it take in terms of education, knowledge, training, and the like to do this job?"

When developing job specifications, the *NOC* and *Career Handbook* can provide helpful reference information. Both include the judgments of job analysts and vocational counsellors regarding the education and/or training requirements of all of the occupations included. In addition to the types of information provided in the *NOC* (see Figure 3.8 on page 87), the *Career Handbook* lists desired aptitudes and interests; and the vision, colour discrimination, hearing, body position, limb coordination, and strength demands.[27]

Job Specifications Based on Statistical Analysis

Basing job specifications on statistical analysis is more difficult than using a judgment approach. Basically, the aim is to statistically determine the relationship between (1) some predictor or human trait such as verbal or written communication skills, keyboarding speed, or finger dexterity and (2) some indicator or criterion of job effectiveness (such as performance, as rated by the supervisor). The procedure has five steps: (1) analyze the job and decide how to measure job performance; (2) select personal traits like finger dexterity that are believed to predict successful performance; (3) test job candidates for these traits; (4) measure these candidates' subsequent job performance; and (5) statistically analyze the relationship between the human trait (finger dexterity) and job performance. The objective is to determine whether there is a correlation between them, which means that the former predicts the latter. In this way, the human requirements for performing the job can be statistically ascertained.

Personality-Related Job Requirements The Personality-related Position Requirements Form (PPRF) is a new survey instrument designed to assist managers in identifying potential personality-related traits that may be important in a job. Identifying personality dimensions is difficult using most job analysis techniques, since they tend to be much better suited to unearthing human aptitudes and skills—like manual dexterity. The PPRF uses questionnaire items to assess the relevance of such basic personality dimensions as agreeableness, conscientiousness, and emotional stability to the job under study by asking whether specific items—such as "adapt(s) easily to changes in work procedures"—are "not required," "helpful," or "essential." The relevance of these personality traits can then be assessed through statistical analysis.[28]

As mentioned briefly above, statistical analysis is more legally defensible than the judgmental approach. Human rights legislation forbids using traits that could lead to discrimination on a prohibited ground in any employment decisions, *unless the employer can prove that there is a bona fide occupational requirement.* A statistical validation study provides such proof.

Completing the Job Specification Form

Once the required human characteristics have been determined, whether using statistical analysis or a judgmental approach, a job specification form should be completed. To illustrate the types of information and amount of detail that should be provided in a well-written job specification, a sample has been included as **Figure 3.11**.

FIGURE 3.11 Job Specification

Job Title: Lifeguard   **Location:** Lethbridge Community Pool
Job Code: LG1   **Supervisor:** Head Lifeguard
Department: Recreation   **Division:** Parks and Recreation
Date: May 1, 2004

Job Summary
The incumbent is required to safeguard the health of pool users by patrolling the pool, rescuing swimmers in difficulty, treating injuries, advising pool users of safety rules, and enforcing safety rules.

Skill
Formal Qualifications: Royal Life Saving Society Bronze Medallion or equivalent
    Experience: No prior experience required, but would be an asset.
Communication Skills: Good oral communication skills are required. Proficiency in one or more foreign languages would be an asset. The incumbent must be able to communicate courteously and effectively. Strong interpersonal skills are required. All interaction with the public must be handled with tact and diplomacy.

Effort
Physical Effort: The incumbent is required to stand during the majority of working hours. In the event of an emergency where a swimmer is in distress, the incumbent must initiate rescue procedures immediately, which may involve strenuous physical exertion.
Mental Effort: Continuous mental attention to pool users. Must remain vigilant despite many simultaneous demands on his or her attention.
Emotional Effort: Enforcement of safety rules and water rescue can be stressful. Must maintain a professional demeanour when dealing with serious injuries or death.

Working Conditions
Job is performed in humid indoor environment, temperature-controlled. No privacy. Shift work to cover pool hours from 7 a.m. to 11 p.m., seven days a week. Some overtime and split shifts may be required.

Approval Signatures
Incumbent: _____
Supervisor: _____   Date: _____

Job Analysis in the Twenty-First Century

The concept of a "job" is in the midst of change, as many employees are increasingly expected to adapt what they are doing to reengineered processes, increased empowerment, self-directed work teams, and new technology. Revolutionary forces including accelerating product and technological change, globalized competition, deregulation, political instability, demographic changes, and trends toward a service society and the information age have dramatically increased the need for employees to be flexible and responsive to changes in what they do and how they do it.

The organizational techniques used to foster responsiveness to change have helped to blur the meaning of *job* as a set of well-defined and clearly delineated responsibilities. Here is a sampling of how these techniques have contributed to this blurring.

Flatter Organizations

Human Resource Consultants
www.hrcjobs.com

Instead of pyramid-shaped organizations with seven or more management layers, flat organizations with just three or four levels are becoming more prevalent. Many firms have already cut their management layers from a dozen to six or fewer. As the remaining managers are left with more people reporting to them, they can supervise them less, so every employee's job ends up involving greater breadth and depth of responsibilities.

Work Teams

Centre for the Study of Work Teams
www.workteams.unt.edu

Over the past decade, work has become increasingly organized around teams and processes rather than around specialized functions. Many organizations, such as DuPont, Siemens, GE, and Motorola, have introduced self-managed work teams.[29] In these organizations, employees' jobs change daily; the effort to avoid having employees view their job as a limited and specific set of responsibilities is thus intentional.

In many firms, the widespread use of teams and similar structural mechanisms means that the boundaries that typically separate organizational functions (like sales and production) and hierarchical levels are reduced and made more permeable. In such firms, responsiveness is fostered by encouraging employees to rid themselves of the "it's not my job" attitude that typically creates walls between one employee area and another. Instead, the focus is on defining the job at hand in terms of the overall best interests of the organization, as is the case at WestJet Airlines, which is described in the Strategic HR box.

Because staffing a team must take into account an individual employee's responsibility, with other team members, for the whole team's performance, team staffing requires more than individual job analysis—it requires *teamwork analysis*. In teamwork analysis, performance dimensions and requirements are identified for the team as a whole, rather than individual knowledge, skills, and abilities.[30]

The Boundaryless Organization

Boundaryless organization structures are emerging. In this type of structure, relationships (typically joint ventures) are formed with customers, suppliers,

STRATEGIC HR

WestJet Airlines

While most North American airlines are cutting staff and slashing costs in a desperate fight for survival, Calgary-based WestJet Airlines Ltd. continues to defy the odds and add more jobs. Employees are key to the cost-cutting culture at the no-frill, low-fare airline. When hiring new employees, the company often looks for individuals who are fun-loving, energetic, gregarious, and optimistic, rather than those with previous airline experience. In fact, those with little or no airline experience are preferred as "… they don't bring any preconceived notions of how things are done, because for WestJet we don't do things like traditional airlines do," said company spokesperson Siobhan Vinish.

While the company does set some standards and expectations, training is focused on motivation of employees. The company stresses teamwork, and is managed from the bottom—reducing a costly level of supervisory management. Since there are no job descriptions, employees are given a high degree of latitude to perform their jobs, and are expected to pitch in and perform all tasks necessary to keep the flights on schedule. It is not uncommon to have WestJet pilots unload luggage, and after a plane lands, every employee on the flight, including employees flying on their own time, are expected to join in cleaning the aircraft for its next take-off. Even the CEO helps out during flights and can often be found greeting customers at the ticket counter. This team-based "jobless" culture means an annual savings of $2.5 million and enables a quick turnaround, making WestJet one of the most profitable and successful airlines in North America.

Sources: P. Fitzpatrick, "Wacky WestJet's Winning Ways: Passengers Respond to Stunts that Include Races to Determine Who Leaves the Airplane First," *National Post*, October 16, 2000, pp. C1, C2; J. Bryan, "WestJet Puts Friendly Back in the Skies: The Upstart Western Airline is Praised for Its Low Fares, On-time Flights, Trouble-free Flying, and Helpful, Cheerful Employees," *National Post*, September 6, 1999, p. C6; "WestJet Flies Against Trends by Adding Employees and Aircraft," *Canadian Press Newswire*, September 12, 2002; P. Verburg, "Prepare for Takeoff (Entrepreneur of the Year)," *Canadian Business*, December 25, 2000, pp. 94–96.

and/or competitors, to pool resources for mutual benefit or encourage cooperation in an uncertain environment. As in team-based organizations, barriers are broken down—in this case between the organization and its suppliers, customers, or competitors—and teams are emphasized. The teams may, however, include employees representing each of the companies involved in the joint venture. In such structures, jobs are defined in very general terms, since the emphasis is on the overall best interests of the organizations involved.

Reengineering

Reengineering is defined as "the fundamental rethinking and radical redesign of business processes to achieve dramatic improvements in critical, contemporary measures of performance, such as cost, quality, service, and speed."[31] In their classic book, *Reengineering the Corporation*, Michael Hammer and James Champy argue that the principles that shaped the structure and management of business for hundreds of years—like highly specialized divisions of work—should be retired. Instead, the firm should emphasize combining tasks into integrated, unspecialized processes that are then carried out by committed employees.

Reengineering is achieved in several ways. Specialized jobs are combined into one so that formerly distinct jobs are integrated and compressed into enlarged, enriched ones.[32] A necessary correlate of combining jobs is that workers make more decisions, since each person's responsibilities are generally broader and deeper after reengineering; supervisory checks and controls are reduced; and, indeed, committed employees largely control their own efforts. Finally, workers become collectively responsible for overall results rather than being individually responsible for just their own tasks. As a result, their jobs change dramatically. "They share joint responsibility with their team members for performing the whole process, not just a small piece of it. They not only use a broader range of skills from day to day, they have to be thinking of a far greater picture."[33] Most importantly, "while not every member of the team will be doing exactly the same work... the lines between [the workers' jobs] blur."

E-Business

In the e-business world, speed, agility, and innovation are the drivers of success, and employees who want narrowly defined, rigid, and inflexible jobs are not useful. E-businesses have flexible boundaries between levels of hierarchy, between functional groups, and between suppliers and customers. Employees have complex job roles, with a broad range of responsibilities, and will often work in autonomous teams. This trend is already evident in jobs such as project manager and internal consultant, where roles are broadly defined, encompass a wide array of responsibilities, and are based on empowerment of individuals and teams.[34]

The Future of Job Descriptions

Most firms today continue to utilize job descriptions and to rely on jobs as traditionally defined. However, it is clear that more and more firms are moving toward new organizational configurations, ones built around jobs that are broad and that may change every day. As one writer has said, "In such a situation, people no longer take their cues from a job description or a supervisor's instructions. Signals come from the changing demands of the project. Workers learn to focus their individual efforts and collective resources on the work that needs doing, changing as that changes. Managers lose their 'jobs,' too...."[35]

How To... Accommodate Mental Disabilities: Update Job Descriptions

Employers typically incorporate or append physical demands analyses to job descriptions. If a job requires a certain amount of lifting, bending, twisting or standing, for example, this is identified along with the frequency required. By using physical demands analyses, employers then are able to determine the scope and extent of appropriate physical accommodation. The mental or emotional requirements of a job are rarely mentioned in any job description. Behavioural attributes essential to a job may, however,

be identified. For example, a job may require the ability to juggle competing demands or the ability to make decisions on imperfect information. These attributes certainly can and should be identified. Identification of these attributes in the job description provides a basis upon which to discuss the requirements of the position during a job interview, to inquire as to an applicant's emotional competency and to discuss accommodation, if appropriate.

Source: Excerpted with permission from the *Focus on Canadian Employment & Equality Rights* Newsletter (Vol. 6, No. 2, September 2002), published by and copyright CCH Canadian Limited, Toronto, Ontario.

CHAPTER *Review*

Summary

1   In any organization, work has to be divided into manageable units and ultimately into jobs that can be performed by employees. The process of organizing work into tasks that are required to perform a specific job is known as job design. The term *job* means a group of tasks and duties, and several employees may have the same job. The collection of tasks and responsibilities performed by one person is known as a *position*.

2   Industrial engineering is concerned with analyzing work methods; making work cycles more efficient by modifying, combining, rearranging, or eliminating tasks; and establishing time standards. Behavioural scientists focus on identifying various job dimensions that would simultaneously improve the efficiency of organizations and job satisfaction of employees. Effective job design must also take physiological needs and health and safety issues into account. Human engineering, or ergonomics, seeks to integrate and accommodate the physical needs of workers into the design of jobs.

3   Job analysis involves six steps: (1) determine the use to which the information will be put, (2) collect background information, (3) select the representative positions and jobs to be analyzed, (4) collect data, (5) review the information collected with the incumbents and their supervisors, and (6) develop the job descriptions and job specifications.

4   There are four narrative techniques used to gather job analysis data: interviews, questionnaires, direct observation, and participant logs. Quantitative job analysis techniques include the position analysis questionnaire (PAQ), functional job analysis (FJA), and the *National Occupational Classification (NOC)*.

5   A job description is a written statement of what the jobholder actually does, how he or she does it, and under what conditions the job is performed. The job specification involves examining the duties and responsibilities and answering the question, "What human traits and experience are required to do this job?"

6   Five recent organizational techniques used to foster responsiveness to change have contributed to blurring the concept of a job. These are flatter organizations, work teams, boundaryless organizations, reengineering, and e-business.

Key Terms

diary/log   *(p. 83)*
functional job analysis (FJA)   *(p. 86)*
human engineering (ergonomics)   *(p. 73)*
industrial engineering   *(p. 69)*
job   *(p. 69)*
job analysis   *(p. 75)*
job description   *(p. 75)*
job design   *(p. 69)*
job enlargement   *(p. 70)*
job enrichment   *(p. 70)*
job rotation   *(p. 70)*
job specification   *(p. 75)*
National Occupational Classification (NOC)
   (p. 86)
occupation   *(p. 86)*
organizational structure   *(p. 67)*
organization chart   *(p. 67)*
physical demands analysis   *(p. 95)*
position   *(p. 69)*
position analysis questionnaire (PAQ)   *(p. 85)*
process chart   *(p. 77)*
team   *(p. 72)*
team-based job design   *(p. 72)*
work simplification   *(p. 69)*

Review and Discussion Questions

1   Explain work simplification. In what situations is this approach to job design appropriate?

2   Differentiate between job enlargement, job rotation, and job enrichment, and provide an example of each.

3   What is involved in the human-engineering approach to job design? Why is it becoming increasingly important?

4   Several methods for collecting job analysis data are available—interviews, the position analysis questionnaire, and so on. Compare and contrast these methods, explaining what each is useful for and listing the pros and cons of each.

5   While not legally required, having job descriptions is highly advisable. Why? How can firms

ensure that their job specifications are legally defensible?

CRITICAL *Thinking Questions*

1 Why isn't it always desirable or appropriate to use job enrichment or include the five core dimensions when designing jobs? How would you determine how enriched an individual employee's job should be?

2 Assume that you are the job analyst at a bicycle manufacturing company in British Columbia, and have been assigned responsibility for preparing job descriptions (including specifications) for all of the supervisory and managerial positions. One of the production managers has just indicated that he will not complete the job analysis

questionnaire you have developed. (a) How would you handle this situation? (b) What arguments would you use to attempt to persuade him to change his mind? (c) If your persuasion efforts failed, how would you go about obtaining the job analysis information you need to develop the job description for his position?

3 Since the top job in a firm (such as president, executive director, or CEO) is by nature broader in scope than any of the other jobs, is there less need for a job description for the president? Why or why not?

APPLICATION *Exercises*

Running Case: LearnInMotion.com

Who Do We Have to Hire?

As the excitement surrounding the move into their new offices wound down, the two principal owners of LearnInMotion.com, Pierre and Jennifer, turned to the task of hiring new employees. In their business plan they'd specified several basic goals for the venture capital funds they'd just received, and hiring a team topped the list. They knew their other goals—boosting sales and expanding the Web site, for instance—would be unreachable without the right team.

They were just about to place their ads when Pierre asked a question that brought them to a stop: "What kind of people do we want to hire?" It seemed they hadn't really considered this. They knew the answer in general terms, of course. For example, they knew they needed at least two salespeople, plus a programmer, a Web designer, and several content management people to transform the incoming material into content they could post on their site. But it was obvious that job titles alone really didn't provide enough guidance. For example, if they couldn't specify the exact duties of these positions, how could they decide whether they needed

experienced employees? How could they decide exactly what sorts of experiences and skills they had to look for in their candidates if they didn't know exactly what these candidates would have to do? They wouldn't even know what questions to ask.

And that wasn't all. For example, there were obviously other tasks to do, and these weren't necessarily included in the sorts of things that salespeople, programmers, Web designers, or content management people typically do. Who was going to answer the phones? (Jennifer and Pierre had originally assumed they'd put in one of those fancy automated call directory and voice-mail systems—until they found out it would cost close to $10 000.) As a practical matter, they knew they had to have someone answering the phones and directing callers to the proper extension. Who was going to keep track of the monthly expenses and compile them for the accountants, who'd then produce monthly reports for the venture capitalist? Would the salespeople generate their own leads? Or would LearnInMotion.com have to hire Web surfers to search and find the names of people for the sales staff to call or e-mail? What would happen when the company had to purchase supplies, such as fax paper or computer disks? Would the owners have to do this themselves, or should they have someone in house do it for them? The list, it seemed, went on and on.

It was obvious, in other words, that the owners had to get their managerial act together and draw up the sorts of documents they'd read about as business majors—job descriptions, job specifications, and so forth. The trouble is—it all seemed a lot easier when they read the textbook. Now they want you, their management consultants, to help them actually do it. Here's what they want you to do for them.

Questions

1   Draft a job description for the salesperson and for the Web designer. You may use whatever sources you want, but preferably search the Internet and relevant Web sites, since you want job descriptions and lists of duties that apply specifically to dot-com firms.

2   Next, using sources similar to those in Question 1—and whatever other sources you can think of—draw up a job specification for these two jobs (salesperson and Web designer), including things such as desirable work habits, skills, education, and experience.

3   Next, keeping in mind that this company is on a tight budget, how should it accomplish the other activities it requires, such as answering the phones, compiling sales leads, producing monthly reports, and purchasing supplies?

CASE INCIDENT   *Linking Job Analysis and Pay*

It wasn't until the CEO's secretary, Fay Jacobs, retired that anyone in the Winnipeg Engineering Company's HR department realized how much variation there was in the compensation of the company's secretaries.

To Tina Jessup, compensation specialist, it was quite apparent why there were inconsistent standards for secretarial pay. With the advance of office-automation technology, managers' differing styles of delegation, and secretaries' varying degrees of willingness to take on increasing managerial responsibilities, the job had assumed a variety of profiles. As the jobs now existed, it was quite likely that two individuals with the same title might be performing very different jobs.

Knowing that updated job analysis information was essential, and prepared for resistance from those who might want to protect their status and pay, she decided to use an objective method to gather information about each of the secretaries' jobs. She developed a questionnaire that she planned to distribute to each member of the firm's secretarial staff and his or her manager following a brief explanatory interview. The interviews would, she hoped, give her a chance to dispel fears on the part of any of the secretaries or managers that the purpose of the analysis was to eliminate jobs, reduce salaries, or lower the grade level of positions.

Before finalizing the questionnaire, Tina shared it with a small group of secretaries in her own department. Based on their input, she made some modifications, such as adding questions about the use of office technology and its impact on the job.

The questionnaire now covered nearly every aspect of the secretarial role, from processing mail, to making travel arrangements, to editing and preparing company correspondence, budgets, and reports. The questions also captured information about how much time was spent on each activity and how much supervision each task required. Tina hoped that, in addition to establishing standards on which Winnipeg Engineering could base a more equitable pay structure, the survey would allow the HR staff members to assess training needs, examine the distribution of work, and determine accurate specifications for recruitment and selection and for the development of employment tests to be used in the future.

Just as Tina was about to begin the interviews and distribution of questionnaires, she got a telephone call from Janet Fried, vice-president of sales. Janet had heard about the upcoming analysis and was very upset. She claimed to be worried about how much time Avril, the secretary assisting her, would have to take away from her work in order to meet with Tina and fill out the questionnaire. She also expressed concern that Avril might feel that her job was threatened and start looking for a position elsewhere. Tina agreed to meet with Janet to discuss her reservations, for which Janet thanked her profusely. Just before hanging up, Janet added, "You know, Tina, I sure wouldn't want to see Avril's job rated at a lower grade level than the secretary assisting the vice-president of operations!"

Questions

1   What do you think is the real "problem" from Janet's point of view?

2   How should Tina address each of the concerns that Janet expressed?

3   What can Tina do to prepare herself for any resistance to the job analysis on the part of the secretaries themselves?

4   Given the current advances in office technology, such as sophisticated spreadsheet programs, voice-mail systems, and e-mail, as well as the elimination of many middle-management positions through corporate downsizings, secretaries in many firms are taking on quasi-managerial responsibilities. How can Tina account in her job analyses for the degrees to which individual secretaries at Winnipeg Engineering are doing so?

Experiential Exercises

1   Draw an organization chart to accurately depict the structure of the organization in which you are currently employed or one with which you are thoroughly familiar. Once you have completed this task, form a group with several of your classmates. Taking turns, each member is to show his or her organization chart to the group, briefly describe the structure depicted, explain whether or not the structure seems to be appropriate to him or her, and identify several advantages and disadvantages he or she experienced working within this structure.

2   Working individually or in groups, obtain a copy of the *National Occupational Classification* and/or the *NOC Career Handbook* from your library or nearest HRDC

office. Find the descriptions for any two occupations with which you have some familiarity. Compare the Employment Requirements and/or the Profile Summaries. Based on what you know about these occupations, does the material provided seem accurate? Why or why not? What changes would you recommend, if any?

3   Working individually, prepare a job description (including job specifications) for a position that you know well, using the job analysis questionnaire in this chapter. Once you have done so, exchange job descriptions with someone else in the class. Critique your colleague's job description and provide specific suggestions regarding any additions/deletions/revisions that you would recommend to ensure that the job description accurately reflects the job and is legally defensible.

CHAPTER 4

Human Resources Planning

CHAPTER OUTLINE

- Human Resources Planning

- Forecasting Future Human Resources Needs (Demand)

- Forecasting Future Human Resources Supply

- Planning and Implementing HR Programs to Balance Supply and Demand

- HRP Evaluation

LEARNING OUTCOMES

After studying this chapter, you should be able to:

Explain human resources planning (HRP) and *discuss* its importance.

Describe the relationship between HRP and strategic planning and *explain* the importance of environmental scanning.

Describe five quantitative and two qualitative techniques used to forecast human resources demand.

Briefly *discuss* seven strategies used to forecast internal human resources supply, and four types of market conditions assessed when forecasting external human resources supply.

Describe the ways in which a surplus of human resources can be handled.

Explain how organizations deal with a shortage of human resources.

Describe the HRP evaluation process.

HUMAN RESOURCES PLANNING

human resources planning (HRP)
The process of reviewing human resources requirements to ensure that the organization has the required number of employees, with the necessary skills, to meet its goals.

Human resources planning (HRP) is the process of reviewing human resources requirements to ensure that the organization has the required number of employees with the necessary skills to meet its goals.[1] Also known as employment planning, HRP is a proactive process, which both anticipates and influences an organization's future by systematically forecasting the demand for and supply of employees under changing conditions, and developing plans and activities to satisfy these needs.[2] As illustrated in **Figure 4.1**, key steps in the HRP

FIGURE 4.1   Human Resources Planning Model

Step 1: Forecast Demand for Labour

Considerations
- Organizational strategic plans
- Organizational tactical plans
- Economic conditions
- Market and competitive trends
- Government and legislative issues
- Social concerns
- Technological changes
- Demographic trends

Techniques Utilized
- Trend analysis
- Ratio analysis
- Scatter plot
- Regression analysis
- Computerized forecasting techniques
- Nominal group technique
- Delphi technique
- Managerial judgment
- Staffing tables

Step 2: Analyze Supply

Internal Analysis
- Markov analysis
- Skills inventories

- Management inventories
- Replacement charts and development tracking
- Replacement summaries
- Succession planning

External Analysis
- General economic conditions
- Labour market conditions (national and local)
- Occupational market conditions

Step 3: Implement Human Resources Programs to Balance Supply and Demand

Labour Shortage
- Overtime
- Hire temporary employees
- Subcontract work

- Recruitment
- Transfer
- Promotion

Labour Surplus
- Hiring freeze
- Attrition
- Buy-outs and early retirement programs
- Job sharing
- Part-time work
- Work sharing
- Reduced workweek
- Alternative jobs within the organization
- Layoffs (reverse seniority or juniority)
- Supplemental unemployment benefits (SUBs)
- Termination
- Severance pay
- Outplacement assistance

Canadian Human Resource
Planners **www.chrp.ca**

process include forecasting demand for labour, analyzing labour supply, and planning and implementing HR programs to balance supply and demand. A fundamental HRP decision when demand exceeds supply is whether projected positions will be filled internally or externally. In other words, should the anticipated openings be filled by current employees or is the situation such that some or all vacancies must or should be filled by recruiting outside candidates? Another critical issue is what to do when the labour supply exceeds the anticipated demand. As illustrated in **Figure 4.2**, there are many alternative solutions.

The Importance of HRP

Effective HRP helps an organization to:

- achieve its strategic goals and objectives
- plan and coordinate recruitment, selection, training, career planning, and other staffing and development activities more effectively
- achieve economies in hiring new workers
- make major labour market demands more successfully
- anticipate and avoid shortages and surpluses of human resources
- control and/or reduce labour costs

AN ETHICAL DILEMMA

Is it ethical to hire and/or promote underqualified target group members simply to meet established employment equity goals and timetables?

FIGURE 4.2   Balancing Supply and Demand Considerations

Conditions and Possible Solutions

A. When labour demand exceeds labour supply
- Scheduling overtime hours
- Hiring temporary workers
- Subcontracting
- External recruitment
- Internal promotions and transfers
- ◆ *Performance management, training and retraining, and career development play a critical role.*

B. When labour supply exceeds labour demand
- Hiring freeze: reassigning current workers to job openings
- Attrition: standard employee resignation, retirement, or death
- Incentives to leave the organization: buy-outs or early retirement programs
- Job sharing
- Reducing positions to part-time
- Work sharing and reduced workweek
- Finding employees alternative jobs within the organization
- Employee layoffs
- Termination of employment
- ◆ *Evaluating the effectiveness of layoffs and downsizing is critical, as is managing "survivor sickness."*

C. When labour demand equals labour supply
- Vacancies are filled internally through transfers or promotions, or externally by hiring new employees
- ◆ *Performance management, training, and career development are critical in achieving balance.*

- utilize employees' capabilities more effectively, thereby increasing performance and productivity, and reducing dissatisfaction and turnover
- establish employment equity goals and timetables that are realistic and attainable.

Lack of or inadequate human resources planning within an organization can result in:

- Significant costs—both tangible and intangible. For example, unstaffed vacant positions can lead to costly inefficiencies, particularly when lengthy training is needed for new hires. Requiring employees to work extra hours to perform the duties of such vacant positions can lead to lower productivity, fatigue, stress-related illnesses, and accidents, as well as overtime premium costs. There are also costs associated with overstaffing. For example, if large numbers of employees are being laid off, extended notice periods are required in many jurisdictions, as well as severance pay.
- Situations in which one department is laying off employees, while another is hiring individuals with similar skills, which can have a devastating impact on morale and productivity.
- Inability to develop effective training, development, and career planning programs.
- Turnover—if employees are not qualified when vacancies arise and are therefore denied opportunities for lateral moves or promotions, turnover is the inevitable result, especially among high performers.
- Difficulties in meeting employment equity goals, or inappropriate staffing decisions, such as hiring or promoting underqualified target group members simply to meet established goals and timetables.
- Inability to accomplish short-term operational plans and/or long-range strategic plans.

In their HR planning, employers like Baskin Robbins and others include close monitoring of trends such as the availability of entry-level labour.

The Relationship between HRP and Strategic Planning

Strategic plans are made and carried out by people. Thus, determining whether or not people will be available is a critical element of the strategic planning process. For example, plans to enter new businesses, build new plants, or reduce the level of activities all influence the number and types of positions to be filled. At the same time, decisions regarding how positions will be filled must be integrated with other aspects of the firm's HR plans, for instance, those pertaining to training current and new employees, appraising performance, and terminating, transferring, or promoting staff members. In the words of a noted HRP expert, "Today, virtually all business issues have people implications; all human resource(s) issues have business implications."[3]

While production, financial, and marketing plans have long been recognized as important cornerstones in the strategic planning process, more and more firms are coming to the realization that HR plans are another essential component.[4] It is becoming clear that HRP and strategic planning become effective when there is a reciprocal and interdependent relationship between them.[5]

Failure to integrate HRP and strategic planning can have very serious consequences. In early 1999, the Ontario government announced that it would spend an extra $375 million to hire more than 10 000 nurses in the province—after years of massive cutbacks, and spending more than $400 million on the severance packages of nurses it had laid off the year before. The B.C., Alberta, Saskatchewan, Newfoundland, and Manitoba governments had all taken similar actions in an effort to recruit nurses in response to the national nursing shortage. Despite the fact that the Canadian Nurses Association (CNA) warned governments in 1998 that an aging workforce, greater emphasis on home care, and an inability to attract and retain nurses could leave the system short 113 000 nurses by 2011—a prediction now believed to be too low—a nationwide CNA report showed that low wages, poor working conditions, and a shortage of full-time work were driving 20 percent of new nurses out of the profession and 10 percent south of the border. It was and still is clear that a long-term nationwide HR plan for nurses is needed.[6] In the words of the president of the CNA, "In the past, the approach has been piecemeal. We need a national dialogue and a coordinated approach."[7]

The Importance of Environmental Scanning Environmental scanning is a critical component of HRP and strategic planning processes, since the most successful organizations are prepared for changes before they occur. The external environmental factors most frequently monitored include:

- Economic conditions (general, regional and local).
- Market and competitive trends.
- New or revised laws and the decisions of courts and quasi-judicial bodies.
- Social concerns related to health care, childcare, and educational priorities.
- Technological changes.
- Demographic trends.

Economic conditions affect supply and demand for products and services, which in turn affect the number and types of employees required. In the 1990s, for example, many private-sector firms restructured or downsized. Downsizing used to be relatively rare in the public (government) and quasi-public (such as universities and hospitals) sectors. However, due to cost-cutting strategies, the federal government laid off 45 000 employees in the late 1990s.[8] Staffing cuts have affected employees at all levels and with all types of skills. Evidence that the era of downsizing is not yet over comes from numerous sources.

Probably the most significant environmental factor in HRP in Canada today relates to the dramatic changes in labour-force composition. A few trends of importance include the following:

- Projections indicate that 50 percent of the workforce of 2015 is already in the labour market.[9]
- Currently, the fastest growing groups in the Canadian workforce are women, visible minorities, Aboriginal people, and persons with disabilities.[10]

- By 2015, the number of Canadians between 55 and 69 years of age will increase dramatically; beyond 2015, the Canadian labour force is projected to grow at a rate of less than 0.5 percent per year, while the youth population will grow at a rate of 0.3 percent per year.[11]
- By 2008, one in three Canadians will be age 50 or older.[12]
- Many employers will see one-third to one-half of their management and professional employees reach early retirement thresholds by 2008.[13]

Increasing diversity, the aging workforce, and the shortage of young workers all have major implications for such HR activities as recruitment, selection, training, and compensation. Effective HRP involves monitoring such trends, anticipating their impact, and devising strategies to deal with them.

Elements of Effective HRP

Once the human resources implications of the organization's strategic plans have been analyzed, there are four subsequent processes involved in HRP, which will be discussed next.

1. Forecasting future human resources needs (demand).
2. Forecasting availability of internal and external candidates (supply).
3. Planning and implementing HR programs to balance supply and demand.
4. Monitoring and evaluating the results.

FORECASTING FUTURE HUMAN RESOURCES NEEDS (DEMAND)

A key component of HRP is forecasting the number and type of people needed to meet organizational objectives. Managers should consider several factors when forecasting such requirements.[14] From a practical point of view, the demand for the organization's product or service is paramount.[15] Thus, in a manufacturing firm, sales are projected first. Then, the volume of production required to meet these sales requirements is determined. Finally, the staff needed to maintain this volume of output is estimated. In addition to this "basic requirement" for staff, several other factors should be considered, including:

1. *Projected turnover* as a result of resignations or terminations.
2. *Quality and nature of employees* in relation to what management sees as the changing needs of the organization.
3. *Decisions to upgrade* the quality of products or services *or enter into new markets,* which might change the required employee skill mix.
4. *Planned technological and administrative changes aimed at increasing productivity and reducing employee headcount,* such as the installation of new equipment or introduction of a financial incentive plan.
5. The *financial resources* available to each department. For example, a budget increase may enable managers to pay higher wages and/or hire more people. Conversely, a budget crunch might result in wage freezes and/or layoffs.

In large organizations, needs forecasting is primarily quantitative in nature and is the responsibility of highly trained specialists. *Quantitative techniques* for determining human resources requirements include trend analysis, ratio analysis, scatter plot analysis, regression analysis, and computerized forecasting. *Qualitative approaches* to forecasting range from sophisticated analytical models to informal expert opinions about future needs, such as a manager deciding that the cost of overtime in his or her department is beginning to outweigh that involved in hiring an additional staff member, and making plans to amend his or her staff complement during the next budget year.[16]

Quantitative Approaches

trend analysis Study of a firm's past employment levels over a period of years to predict future needs.

Trend Analysis

Trend analysis involves studying the firm's employment levels over the last five years or so to predict future needs. For example, the number of employees in the firm at the end of each of the last five years—or perhaps the number in each subgroup (such as sales, production, and administration) — might be computed. The purpose is to identify employment trends that might continue into the future.

Trend analysis is valuable as an initial estimate only, since employment levels rarely depend solely on the passage of time. Other factors (like changes in sales volume and productivity) will also affect future staffing needs.

ratio analysis A forecasting technique for determining future staff needs by using ratios between some causal factor (such as sales volume) and number of employees needed.

Ratio Analysis

Another approach, **ratio analysis**, involves making forecasts based on the ratio between (1) some causal factor (such as sales volume) and (2) number of employees required (for instance, number of salespeople). For example, suppose a salesperson traditionally generates $500 000 in sales and that plans call for increasing the firm's sales by $3 million next year. Then, if the sales revenue–salespeople ratio remains the same, six new salespeople would be required (each of whom produces an extra $500 000 in sales).

Ratio analysis can also be used to help forecast other employee requirements. For example, a salesperson–secretary ratio could be computed to determine how many new secretaries will be needed to support the extra sales staff.

Like trend analysis, ratio analysis assumes that productivity remains about the same—for instance, that each salesperson can't be motivated to produce much more than $500 000 in sales. If sales productivity were to increase or decrease, then the ratio of sales to salespeople would change. A forecast based on historical ratios would then no longer be accurate.

scatter plot A graphical method used to help identify the relationship between two variables.

The Scatter Plot

A **scatter plot** is another option. Scatter plots can be used to determine whether two factors—a measure of business activity and staffing levels—are related. If they are, then if the measure of business activity is forecast, HR requirements can also be estimated.

An example to illustrate follows.[17] Legislative changes to the health-care system require that two 500-bed Regina hospitals be amalgamated. Both previously had responsibility for acute, chronic, and long-term care. The government's plan is for one facility to specialize in acute care, while the other assumes responsibility for chronic and long-term care. In general, providing acute care requires staffing with registered nurses (RNs), while chronic and long-term care facilities can be staffed primarily with registered practical nurses (RPNs).

By the end of the calendar year, 200 beds at Hospital *A* must be converted from chronic and long-term care beds to facilities for acute patients. At the same time, Hospital *A*'s 200 chronic and long-term patients must be transferred to Hospital *B*. In a joint meeting, the directors of nursing and HR decide that a good starting point in the planning process would be to calculate the relationship between hospital size (in terms of number of acute beds) and the number of RNs required. After placing telephone calls to their counterparts at eight hospitals in larger centres across Alberta and Saskatchewan, they obtain the following information:

Size of Hospital (Number of Acute Beds)	Number of Registered Nurses
200	240
300	260
400	470
500	500
600	620
700	660
800	820
900	860

In order to determine how many RNs would be needed, they use the data obtained to draw the scatter plot shown in **Figure 4.3**, in which hospital size is shown on the horizontal axis and number of RNs is shown on the vertical axis. If the two factors are related, then the points will tend to fall along a straight line, as they do in this case. Carefully drawing a line that minimizes the distances between the line and each of the plotted points permits an estimate of the number of nurses required for hospitals of various sizes. Thus, since Hospital *A* will now have 500 acute-care beds, the estimated number of RNs needed is 500.

FIGURE 4.3   Determining the Relationship between Hospital Size and Number of Nurses

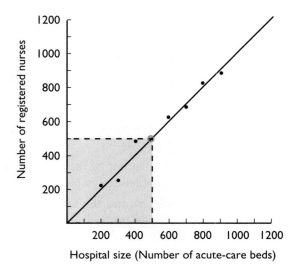

Note: After fitting the line, the number of employees needed, given projected volume, can be extrapolated (projected).

regression analysis A statistical technique involving the use of a mathematical formula to project future demands based on an established relationship between an organization's employment level (dependent variable) and some measurable factor of output (independent variable).

Regression Analysis   **Regression analysis** is a more sophisticated statistical technique to determine the "best-fit" line. It involves the use of a mathematical formula to project future demands based on an established relationship between an organization's employment level (dependent variable) and some measurable factor of output (independent variable) such as revenue, sales, or production level. When there are several dependent and/or independent variables, multiple regression analysis is used.

Computerized Forecasting Techniques   Many employers involved in quantitative forecasting use computers and software packages.[18] Typical data needed include direct labour hours to produce one unit of product (a measure of productivity) and three sales projections—minimum, maximum, and probable—for the product line in question. Based on such data, the program generates a **computerized forecast** of average staff levels required to meet product demands, as well as separate forecasts for direct labour (such as assembly workers), indirect labour (support staff, such as accounting clerks), and senior staff (such as managers).

computerized forecast The determination of future staffing needs by projecting a firm's sales, volume of production, and the human resources requirements to maintain desired volume of output, using computers and software packages.

Radiant Systems Inc.
www.radiantsystems.com

With such systems, employers can quickly translate projected productivity and sales levels into forecasts of human resources needs, and can easily check the impact of various productivity and sales levels on HR requirements.[19] For example, Radiant Systems Inc. has developed comprehensive software to align staffing with the business plan in retail and hospitality businesses. Radiant's forecasting software uses historical and trending models to generate future human resources requirements based on activities within the stores that drive labour needs, such as transactions, customer counts, items, and inventory activities. Human resources requirements forecasts can be adjusted for known events, seasonality, and budgetary constraints to ensure that customer demands are met at all times at acceptable costs.

Qualitative Approaches

In contrast to quantitative approaches, which utilize statistical formulas, qualitative techniques rely solely on expert judgments. Two approaches used to gather such opinions in order to forecast human resources demand (or supply) include the nominal group and Delphi techniques.

nominal group technique A decision-making technique that involves a group of experts meeting face to face. Steps include independent idea generation, clarification and open discussion, and private assessment.

Nominal Group Technique   The **nominal group technique** involves a group of experts (such as first-line supervisors and managers) meeting face to face. While one of its uses is human resources demand forecasting, this technique is used to deal with issues and problems ranging from identifying training needs to determining safety program incentives. The steps involved are as follows:[20]

1. Each member of the group independently writes down his or her ideas on the problem or issue (in this case, the causes of demand).

2. Going around the table, each member then presents one idea. This process continues until all ideas have been presented and recorded, typically on a flipchart or chalkboard. No discussion is permitted during this step.

3. Clarification is then sought, as necessary, followed by group discussion and evaluation.

4. Finally, each member is asked to rank the ideas. This is done independently and in silence.

Advantages of this technique include involvement of key decision makers, a future focus, and the fact that the group discussion involved in Step Three can facilitate the exchange of ideas and greater acceptance of results. Drawbacks include subjectivity and the potential for group pressure to lead to less accurate assessment than could be obtained through other means.

The Delphi Technique   While short-term forecasting is generally handled by managers, the **Delphi technique** is useful for long-range forecasting and other strategic planning issues. It typically involves outside experts as well as company employees, based on the premise that outsiders may be able to assess changes in economic, demographic, governmental, technological, and social conditions and their potential impact more objectively. The Delphi technique involves the following steps:[21]

1. The problem is identified (in this case, the causes of demand) and each group member is requested to submit a potential solution by completing a carefully designed questionnaire. Direct face-to-face contact is not permitted.

2. After each member independently and anonymously completes the initial questionnaire, the results are compiled at a centralized location.

3. Each group member is then given a copy of the results.

4. If there are differences in opinion, each individual uses the feedback from other experts to fine-tune his or her independent assessment.

5. Steps Three and Four are repeated as often as necessary until a consensus is reached.

As with the nominal group technique, advantages include involvement of key decision makers and a future focus. The Delphi technique permits the group to critically evaluate a wider range of views, however. Drawbacks include the fact that judgments may not efficiently use objective data, the time and costs involved, and the potential difficulty in integrating diverse opinions.

Managerial Judgment

While managerial judgment is central to qualitative forecasting, it also plays a key role when using quantitative techniques. It's rare that any historical trend, ratio, or relationship will continue unchanged into the future. Judgment is thus needed to modify the forecast based on anticipated changes.

Summarizing Human Resources Requirements   The end result of the forecasting process is an estimate of short-term and long-range HR requirements. Long-range plans are general statements of potential staffing needs, and may not include specific numbers.

Short-term plans—although still approximations—are more specific, and are often depicted in a **staffing table**. As illustrated in **Figure 4.4**, a staffing table is a pictorial representation of all jobs within the organization, along with the number of current incumbents and future employment requirements (monthly or yearly) for each.

Delphi technique A judgmental forecasting method used to arrive at a group decision, typically involving outside experts as well as organizational employees. Ideas are exchanged without face-to-face interaction and feedback is provided and used to fine-tune independent judgments until a consensus is reached.

staffing table A pictorial representation of all jobs within the organization, along with the number of current incumbents and future employment requirements (monthly or yearly) for each.

FIGURE 4.4   A Sample Staffing Table

Springbrook Utilities Commission Staffing Table														
Job Title (As on Job Description)	**Department**	**Anticipated Openings**												
		Total	Jan.	Feb.	Mar.	Apr.	May	June	July	Aug.	Sept.	Oct.	Nov.	Dec.
General Manager	Administration	1					1							
Director of Finance	Administration	1												1
Human Resources Officer	Administration	2	1					1						
Collection Clerk	Administration	1		1										
Groundskeeper	Maintenance	4						1	1					2
Service and Maintenance Technician	Maintenance	5	1			2					2			
Water Utility Engineer	Operations	3									2			1
Apprentice Lineperson	Operations	10	6						4					
Water Meter Technician	Operations	1												1
Engineering Technician	Operations	3			2							1		
Field Technician	Operations	8						8						
Senior Programmer/ Analyst	Systems	2				1			1					
Programmer/Operator	Systems	4		2						1			1	
Systems Operator	Systems	5					2						3	
Customer Service Representative	Sales	8	4					3				1		

FORECASTING FUTURE HUMAN RESOURCES SUPPLY

Short-term and long-range HR demand forecasts only provide half of the staffing equation by answering the question, "How many employees will we need?" The next major concern is how projected openings will be filled. There are two sources of supply:

1. Internal—present employees who can be transferred or promoted to meet anticipated needs.
2. External—people in the labour market not currently working for the organization. Included are those who are employed elsewhere, as well as those who are unemployed.

Forecasting the Supply of Internal Candidates

Before estimating how many external candidates will need to be recruited and hired, management must determine how many candidates for projected openings will likely come from within the firm. This is the purpose of forecasting the supply of internal candidates.

Markov Analysis

Markov analysis A method of forecasting internal labour supply that involves tracking the pattern of employee movements through various jobs and developing a transitional probability matrix.

Markov Analysis   Estimating internal supply involves much more than simply calculating the number of employees. Some firms use the **Markov analysis** technique to track the pattern of employee movements through various jobs and develop a transitional probability matrix for forecasting internal supply by specific categories, such as position and gender. As illustrated in **Figure 4.5**, such an analysis shows the actual number (and percentage) of employees who remain in each job from one year to the next, as well as proportions promoted, demoted, transferred, and leaving the organization. It is these proportions (probabilities) that are used to forecast human resources supply.

In addition to such quantitative data, the skills and capabilities of current employees must be assessed, and skills inventories prepared. From this information, replacement charts and/or summaries and succession plans can be developed.

Skills Inventories

skills inventories Manual or computerized records summarizing employees' education, experience, interests, skills, etc., which are used to identify internal candidates eligible for transfer and/or promotion.

Skills Inventories   **Skills inventories** contain comprehensive information about the capabilities of current employees. Prepared manually or using a computerized system, data gathered for each employee include name, age, date of employment, current position, present duties and responsibilities, educational background, previous work history, skills, abilities, and interests. Information about current performance and readiness for promotion is generally included, as well. Data pertaining to managerial staff are compiled in

FIGURE 4.5 Hypothetical Markov Analysis for a Manufacturing Operation

2005 → 2006	Plant Manager	Foreperson	Team Leaders	Production Worker	Exit
Plant Manager (n = 5)	80% / 4				20% / 1
Foreperson (n = 35)	8% / 3	82% / 28			10% / 4
Team Leader (n = 110)		11% / 12	70% / 77	7% / 8	12% / 13
Production Worker (n = 861)			6% / 52	72% / 620	22% / 189
Projected Supply	7	40	129	628	

Percentages represent transitions (previous year's actuals).
Actual numbers of employees are shown as whole numbers in each block (projections for 2006 based on current staffing).

management inventories Records summarizing the background, qualifications, interests, and skills of management employees, as well as information about managerial responsibilities and management training, used to identify internal candidates eligible for promotion opportunities.

management inventories. In addition to the information listed above, such inventories also include the number and types of employees supervised, duties of such employees, total budget managed, previous managerial duties and responsibilities, and managerial training received.

To be useful, skills and management inventories must be updated regularly. Failure to do so can lead to present employees being overlooked for job openings. Updating every two years is generally adequate if employees are encouraged to report significant qualifications changes (such as new skills learned and/or courses completed) to the HR department as they occur.

FIGURE 4.6 Skills Inventory Form Appropriate for Manual Storage and Retrieval

HUMAN RESOURCES SKILLS INVENTORY AND DEVELOPMENT RECORD

Date: month, year

Department	Area or sub-department	Branch or section	Location

Company service date (month, day, year)	Birthdate (month, day, year)	Job title

Education — Diploma or degree and major field of study

Grade school 6 7 8 | High school 9 10 11 12

College and/or University 1 2 3 4 5

Courses (company sponsor ed)

Type of course	Subject or course	Year	Type of course	Subject or course	Year

Career and development interests

Are you interested in an alternative type of work? Yes ☐ No ☐

Would you accept transfer to another division? Yes ☐ No ☐

Would you accept lateral moves for further development? Yes ☐ No ☐

If yes, specifically what type?

Comment on any qualifying circumstances

What type of training do you believe you require to:

A) Improve your skills and performance in your present position?

B) Improve your experience and abilities for advancement?

Last name

First name

Middle name

What other assignments do you believe you are qualified to perform now?

Languages	Written		Spoken	
	☐	☐	☐	☐
	☐	☐	☐	☐

Societies and organizations — Memberships in community organizations, etc., within last five years. Indicate name of association and office held, if any.

Skills

Type of skill	Certification, if any	Type of skill	Certification, if any

Other significant work experience. (Omit repetitive experiences)

	Location	From yr.	To yr.	

Comments: Other significant experience, recreational activities, hobbies, interests, or personal data.

Manual Systems Several types of manual systems are used to keep track of employees' qualifications. An example of a skills inventory and development record is shown in **Figure 4.6**. Such a form may be completed by each employee or filled in by a member of the HR department following a face-to-face interview. Once the information has been compiled and recorded, it can be used to determine which current employees are available for and interested in transfer or promotion.

Replacement Charts **Replacement charts** are typically used to keep track of potential internal candidates for the firm's most important positions. As can be seen in **Figure 4.7**, such charts typically indicate the age of potential internal candidates (which cannot be used as a criterion in making selection or promotion decisions, but is necessary to project retirement dates), the current performance level of the employee, and his or her promotion potential. The latter is based on the employee's future career aspirations and a supervisory assessment of readiness for promotion.

replacement charts Visual representations of who will replace whom in the event of a job opening. Likely internal candidates are listed, along with their age, present performance rating, and promotability status.

Canadian Career Partners
www.career-partners.com

FIGURE 4.7 Management Replacement Chart

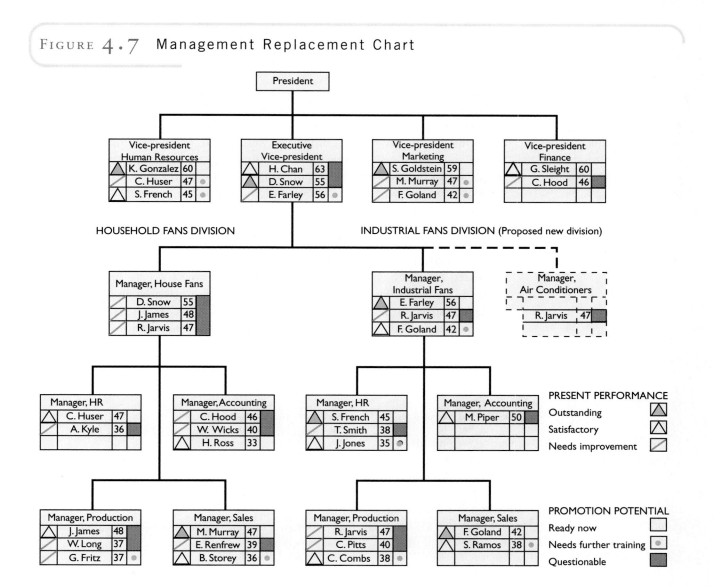

To provide a more objective estimate of future potential, this information may be supplemented by results of psychological tests, interviews with HR specialists, and other selection techniques.

Replacement Summaries

replacement summaries Lists of likely replacements for each position and their relative strengths and wealnesses, as well as information about current position, performance, promotability, age, and experience.

Replacement Summaries   While replacement charts provide an excellent quick reference tool, they contain very little information. For that reason, many firms prefer to use **replacement summaries**. Such summaries list likely replacements for each position and their relative strengths and weaknesses, as well as information about current position, performance, promotability, age, and experience. These additional data can be extremely helpful to decision makers, although caution must be taken to ensure that there is no discrimination on the basis of age, sex, and so on.

SkillView Technologies
www.skillview.com

Computerized Information Systems   HR departments are embracing the latest software to improve their strategic functions, and some of the most popular improvements deal with HR planning and managing the development of existing employees.[22] Skills inventories on hundreds or thousands of employees cannot be adequately maintained manually. Many firms—including Rogers AT&T Wireless—computerize this information to accomplish this task using packaged systems available electronically, as discussed in more detail in the HR.Net box.

succession planning The process of ensuring a suitable supply of successors for current and future senior or key jobs, so that careers of individuals can be effectively planned and managed.

Succession Planning   Forecasting the availability of inside candidates is particularly important in succession planning. In a nutshell, **succession planning** refers to the plans a company makes to fill its most important executive positions. In the days when companies were hierarchical and employees tended to remain with the firm for years, executive succession was often straightforward: staff climbed the ladder one rung at a time, and it wasn't unusual for someone to start on the shop floor and end up in the president's office. While that kind of ascent is still possible, employee turnover and flatter structures mean that the lines of succession are no longer so direct.[23] For example, potential successors for top positions might be routed through the top jobs at several key divisions, as well as overseas, and sent through a university graduate-level, advanced management program. Succession planning for entrepreneurial businesses is particularly important, as discussed in the Entrepreneurs and HR box.

Since succession planning requires balancing the organization's top-management needs with the potential and career aspirations of available candidates, it includes these activities:

HR.NET

Computerized Skills Inventories

Skill View Enterprise 5.0, a computerized skills inventory program, is available remotely to subscribers via a secure server hosted by its creator, SkillView Technologies. The product's assessment and reporting functions allow employees to record and track their competencies and to perform comparative skill gap analyses against their job position as well as other positions in the organization to aid in personal development and career management. Powerful management reporting capabilities allow managers to easily query department skill gap reports, individual and departmental training needs, and aids in the succession planning process.

Source: SkillView Technologies Inc. www.skillview.com. Reprinted with permission.

ENTREPRENEURS AND HR

Who Will Mind the Store?

According to the *National Post*, two-thirds of Canadian small businesses have made no contingency plan if the boss were to die suddenly or be unable to run the company. Entrepreneurs need to plan well in advance for the next stage of their business—the one where they will no longer be in charge. The issue of succession planning for entrepreneurs is assuming a greater importance. With the majority of baby boomers moving into their retirement years in the next decade, small- and medium-sized businesses will be experiencing the same problems as the public sector and large corporations—a large number of employees will be retiring at the same time. There are various succession scenarios available to the business founder, including selling the business outright, employee share ownership plans, partnerships, and family member succession planning. While the very urgency of running a business often prevents owners from dealing with the issue of succession, it is still an essential process. Planning and time are key to a smooth and effective transition of ownership or control, and to be well prepared, entrepreneurs have to start thinking about succession at least five years in advance—and ten years in advance is even better.[1]

The Bank of Montreal's Succession Solution Group is a useful service for the entrepreneur who is looking to retire or sell out. The Group supplies planners who establish what kind of succession team is required and then help the owner determine a fair value for the business.[2]

Notes:

1. P. Quinn, "Who Will Mind the Store?" *National Post*, October 21, 2002, pp. SR1, S7.

2. J. Demers, "Succession Planning in SMEs," *CMA Management*, December 2002/January 2003, p. 12.

Tips for the Front Line

- analysis of the demand for managers and professionals in the company
- audit of existing executives and projection of likely future supply
- planning of individual career paths based on objective estimates of future needs, performance appraisal data, and assessments of potential
- career counselling
- accelerated promotions, with development targeted against future business needs
- performance-related training and development to prepare individuals for future roles
- planned strategic recruitment, aimed at obtaining people with the potential to meet future needs, as well as filling current openings
- the actual activities by which openings are filled.[24]

Several of these activities become much more complex in merger situations, as discussed in the Strategic HR box. It should be noted that replacement charts, replacement summaries, and succession plans are considered to be highly confidential in most organizations.

Forecasting the Supply of External (Outside) Candidates

Some jobs cannot be filled with internal candidates, such as entry-level jobs and jobs for which no current employees are qualified. In these situations, the firm looks for external candidates.

Employer growth is primarily responsible for the number of entry-level openings. While there are some higher-level jobs that require such unique talents

Strategic HR

Forging Top Talent at Alcan

Succession planning poses a challenge for HR in any organization, but when Alcan Inc. merged with Alusuisse Group in 2000, its HR department was faced with the task of assessing the human capital it had acquired. As a leading supplier of primary metals and fabricated products for the automotive and mass transportation markets, and specialty packaging for food, pharmaceutical, and personal care industries, it is a global company with approximately 53 000 employees in 41 countries.

Given the large number of employees involved in the acquisition, and the fact that they were spread out over 38 countries, Alcan's director of executive performance management wanted to ensure that the company had a good knowledge of the quality of the new talent pool and needed to help target "rising stars" for promotion. While the company looked at various traditional HR software products, none were suitable because Alcan operates in so many countries. The solution was the development of tailored Web-based software that could be applied worldwide and which allowed staff anywhere in the world to log on easily. The new software contained two modules—performance management and succession planning.

The employee plays a pivotal role in the performance management process at Alcan because the first step is a self-assessment. Additionally, employees meet with their supervisors at a yearly performance review where they discuss and define goals and objectives for the upcoming year and assess the attainment of goals and objectives set the year before. All the information obtained from its employees is stored in a database. Any questions regarding employees can be accessed through the database, including high-potential and best-performing employees, career interests, development plans, mobility, and language abilities.

Using the database created from the performance module, Alcan uses the succession planning module to mine the data to help in identifying employees who could possibly move up the corporate ladder. Alcan effectively tags junior high-performers to help identify internal candidates to fill strategic positions when they open up. The company is working toward having all staff with university degrees on the system—about 7000 to 8000 employees.

The software has helped Alcan's HR department become more strategic in its planning, as it is better able to focus its efforts on value-added services. In fact, Alcan is so happy with the outcome that it is looking at adding other Web-based modules such as internal job postings, e-recruitment, and e-learning.

Source: T. Humber, "Forging Top Talent," *Canadian HR Reporter* (November 4, 2003), pp. G1, G16. Reproduced by permission of *Canadian HR Reporter*, Carswell, One Corporate Plaza, 2075 Kennedy Road, Scarborough, ON M1T 3V4.

and skills that they are impossible to fill internally, and some jobs are vacated unexpectedly, a key factor in determining the number of positions that must be filled externally is the effectiveness of the organization's training and development and career planning initiatives. If employees are not encouraged to expand their capabilities, they may not be ready to fill vacancies as they arise, and external sources must be tapped.

To project the supply of outside candidates, employers assess general economic conditions, national labour market conditions, local labour market conditions, and occupational market conditions.

General Economic Conditions   The first step is to forecast general economic conditions and the expected unemployment rate. The national unemployment rate provides an estimate of how difficult it is likely to be to recruit new employees in the immediate future. In general terms, the lower the rate of unemployment, the smaller the labour supply and the more difficult it will be to recruit employees. It is important to note, though, that even when unemployment rates are high, some positions will still be difficult to fill, since unemployment rates vary by occupation and geographic location.

Statistics Canada www.statcan.ca

National Labour Market Conditions   Demographic trends have a significant impact on national labour market conditions. Fortunately, there is a wealth of labour market information available from Statistics Canada and other government and private sources.[25] A crucial statistic is that Canada's population is aging. By 2008 one in three Canadians will be 50 years of age or older, and this segment is expected to grow by 50 percent in the next 10 years.[26] To further compound the problem, there will be relatively fewer young workers entering the labour pool, as the portion of the population under the age of 25 has declined.[27] Thus one of the key challenges for employers will be the availability of qualified workers as the "baby boom" generation, about half of Canada's current labour force, enters retirement age in 2020.[28] In 2001, the oldest members of the baby boom generation were 54, beginning the expected large-scale exit of older workers from the labour market.[29]

Research
Insight   ▷

A recent survey indicates a lack of significant preparation for the impending labour shortage. While 54 percent of companies have made some preparations, and 3 percent have undertaken significant planning, 39 percent have made little or no planning efforts to combat the expected labour shortage.[30] Predicting which employees will leave and when are of huge strategic importance, yet few organizations have gathered the employee data to help them answer this question. Of 150 HR executives surveyed, two of three companies do not have an age profile of their workforce.[31]

Highly educated immigrants are the predominant drivers in the growth of the Canadian labour pool.[32] Due to Canada's aging population and declining birth rate, it is expected that by 2011 almost all labour force growth will be made up by immigrant workers. The distribution of immigrants across the country is shown in **Figure 4.8**. Unfortunately, up to 550 000 immigrants have education and experience that is going unrecognized, according to a Conference Board of Canada report entitled *Brain Gain*.[33] As indicated in the Workforce Diversity box, some employers are rethinking their strategies and programs with the overall aim to make the best use of immigrant talent.[34]

FIGURE 4.8   Distribution of Immigrants

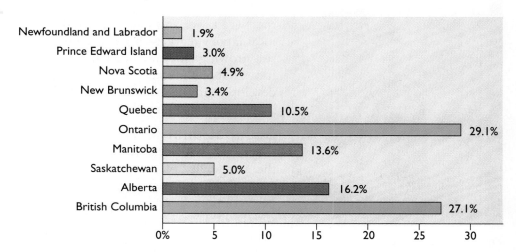

Source: Adapted from the Statistics Canada Web site <http://www12.statcan.ca/english/census01/Products/Analytic/companion/paid/canada.cfm>.

WORKFORCE DIVERSITY

Immigrants Drive IT Growth

In order to help boost productivity levels while the domestic employable population is shrinking, many technology firms are tapping into the knowledge and expertise of the largest growing segment of the Canadian workforce—skilled and highly educated immigrants. Many companies have moved beyond legislative requirements to placing great value on diversity in the workplace simple because it is "good business." Not only do diversity initiatives help quell the impending knowledge and labour shortage, but as Canada becomes more diverse in its interests and structure, a diverse workforce is required in order to service the needs of this marketplace.

Oracle Corporation Canada Inc. has formed partnerships with several external organizations to help cultivate an environment that is inclusive of all employees because "...individual differences present us with opportunities to examine business issues from varying perspectives. Incorporating these different viewpoints gives us greater agility and creativity."[1]

IBM Canada offers ESL classes to employees across the country regardless of their locations, as well as soft-skills training targeted at visible minority groups, which address such topics as communication styles. Diversity is engrained in the IBM culture, and a visible minority council, headed by a diversity director, regularly reviews workplace policies and programs to see if specific needs of visible minority employees are being met.[2]

Lucent Technologies includes workplace diversity as one of the five elements of the culture that is fundamental to their success. It maintains a very broad definition of diversity, and believes that "to sustain momentum in the global communications networking industry and to continue to deliver the results expected of a high-performance company, we must build an operating environment where the talent, contributions, and ideas of all Lucent people can flourish."[3]

Notes:

1. K. Pryma, "Some IT Companies Realize Diversity is Good Business," *Computer World Canada*, August 24, 2001, p. 41.

2. U. Vu, "Labour Force Growth Depends on Immigrants," *Canadian HR Reporter*, March 10, 2003, pp. 1, 3.

3. C. Stephenson, "Corporate Values Drive Global Success at Lucent Technologies," *Canadian Speeches*, November/December 1999, pp. 23–27.

Physiotherapy is a skills-shortage occupation: the demand for physiotherapists exceeds the supply.

Local Labour Market Conditions   Local labour markets are affected by many conditions, including community growth rates and attitudes. Communities that do not support existing businesses may experience declining population as residents move away to find jobs, which then makes it difficult to attract new business, since potential employers fear future local HR supply shortages. The end result is that there are fewer and fewer jobs and more and more people leaving the local labour market—a vicious downward spiral. Conversely, one reason growing cities are attractive to employers is the promise of large future labour markets. Chambers of Commerce and provincial/local development and planning agencies can be excellent sources of local labour market information.

Occupational Market Conditions   In addition to looking at the overall labour market, organizations also generally want to forecast the availability of potential candidates in specific occupations (engineers, drill press operators, accountants, and so on) for which they will be recruiting. In recent years, for example, there has been an undersupply of IT specialists, physiotherapists, nurses, and physicians in many parts of the country. Currently, post-secondary faculty are becoming scarce. At Seneca College in Toronto, half of the faculty is expected to retire between 2003 and 2006.[35] And in Alberta, there are

Human Resources Development
Canada **www.hrdc-drhc.gc.ca**

only 4300 trainees in the pipeline to replace 29 000 engineers, geologists, and geophysicists in the oil industry.[36]

Forecasts for various occupations are available from a number of sources, including Human Resources Development Canada (HRDC). These forecasts are useful for determining whether any projected imbalances will be self-correcting or will require specific intervention on the part of governments and/or private-sector organizations.[37]

PLANNING AND IMPLEMENTING HR PROGRAMS TO BALANCE SUPPLY AND DEMAND

Once the supply and demand of human resources have been estimated, program planning and implementation commence. To successfully fill positions internally, organizations must manage performance and careers. Performance is managed through effective job design and quality of working life initiatives; establishing performance standards and goals, coaching, measuring and evaluating; and implementing a suitable reward structure (compensation and benefits).

To manage careers effectively, policies and systems must be established for recruitment, selection and placement (including transfer, promotion, retirement, and termination), and training and development. Policies and systems are also required for job analysis, individual employee assessment, replacement and succession planning, and career tracking, as well as career planning and development.[38]

Specific strategies must be formulated to balance supply and demand considerations. As was illustrated in Figure 4.2 on page 108, there are three possible scenarios:

- labour supply exceeds demand (surplus)
- labour demand exceeds supply (shortage)
- expected demand matches supply.

Labour Surplus

hiring freeze A common initial response to an employee surplus. Openings are filled by reassigning current employees, and no outsiders are hired.

attrition The normal separation of employees from an organization due to resignation, retirement, or death.

buyout and early retirement programs Strategies used to accelerate attrition, which involve offering attractive buyout packages or the opportunity to retire on full pension, with an attractive benefits package.

A labour surplus exists when the internal supply of employees exceeds the organization's demand. Most employers respond initially by instituting a **hiring freeze**, which means that openings are filled by reassigning current employees, and no outsiders are hired. The surplus is slowly reduced through **attrition**, which is the normal separation of employees due to resignation, retirement, or death. As employees leave voluntarily, the ensuing vacancies are not filled, and the staffing level decreases gradually without any involuntary terminations. In addition to the time it takes, a major drawback of this approach is that the firm has no control over who stays and who leaves.

Some organizations attempt to accelerate attrition by offering incentives to employees to leave, such as **buyout and early retirement programs**. Staffing levels are reduced and internal job openings created by offering attractive buyout packages or the opportunity to retire on full pension, with an attractive benefits package, at a relatively early age (often 50 or 55). To be successful, buyouts must be handled very carefully. Selection criteria should be established to ensure that key people who cannot be easily replaced do not leave the firm. A drawback of buyouts and early retirement packages is that they often require a great deal of money up-front. Care must also be taken to ensure that early retirement is voluntary, since forced early retirement is a contravention of human rights legislation.

Another strategy used to deal with an employee surplus involves reducing the total number of hours worked. **Job sharing** involves dividing the duties of a single position between two or more employees.[39] Reducing full-time positions to *part-time work* is sometimes more effective, especially if there are peak demand periods. Creating a job-share position and/or offering part-time employment can be win–win strategies, since layoffs can be avoided. Although the employees involved work fewer hours and thus have less pay, they are still employed, and may enjoy having more free time at their disposal. The organization benefits by retaining good employees.

For over 25 years, the federal government introduced a **work-sharing** scheme, a layoff-avoidance strategy that involves employees working three or four days a week and receiving EI benefits on their non-workday(s).[40] Similar to work sharing, but without a formal arrangement with government regarding EI benefits, is a **reduced workweek**. Employees simply work fewer hours and receive less pay. The organization retains a skilled workforce, lessens the financial and emotional impact of a full layoff, and yet manages to reduce production costs. The only potential drawback is that it is sometimes difficult to predict in advance, with any degree of accuracy, how many hours of work should be scheduled each week.

Another strategy used to manage an employee surplus is a **layoff**, the temporary withdrawal of employment to workers for economic or business reasons. Layoffs may be short in duration, as when plants close for brief periods to adjust inventory levels or to retool for a new product line, but can last months or even years if caused by a major change in the business cycle. Layoffs are not easy for either managers or workers, but are sometimes necessary if attrition will take too long to reduce the number of employees to the required level.

In unionized settings, layoffs are typically handled on the basis of **reverse seniority**—the employees hired most recently are the first to be laid off and the last to be recalled. When a layoff is expected to be brief, juniority may be used instead. If there is a **juniority clause** in the collective agreement, senior (long-service) workers must be offered the layoff first. Long-service employees may be quite willing to accept a short-term layoff covered by EI benefits to have time off for other pursuits. However, when layoffs are expected to be lengthy or are of unknown duration, long-service employees generally decline to exercise their juniority rights, and employees who are lower in the seniority list are laid off.

A key advantage of seniority and juniority clauses is objectivity. Using length of service as the basis for layoffs is perceived to be fair, and employees themselves can calculate the probability of layoff and recall. The drawback to seniority is that talent and effort are ignored, which can result in less competent employees receiving the same rewards and security as those who are more competent. Also, there is often a disproportionate impact on designated group members, since they are generally more recent hires.

To ease the financial burden of layoffs, some organizations offer **supplemental unemployment benefits (SUBs)**, which increase income levels closer to what an employee would receive if on the job. SUB programs are generally negotiated through collective bargaining. Benefits are payable until the pool of funds set aside has been exhausted.

job sharing A strategy that involves dividing the duties of a single position between two or more employees.

work sharing Employees work three or four days a week and receive employment insurance on their non-work day(s).

reduced workweek Employees work fewer hours and receive less pay.

layoff The temporary withdrawal of employment to workers for economic or business reasons.

reverse seniority The employees hired most recently are the first to be laid off and the last to be recalled.

juniority clause Senior workers (those with the greatest length of service) must be offered layoff first.

supplemental unemployment benefits (SUBs) A top-up to employment insurance to increase income levels closer to what an employee would receive if on the job.

When employees are no longer required, the employment relationship may be severed. **Termination** is a broad term that encompasses permanent separation from the organization for any reason. In situations in which employment is terminated involuntarily, employees with acceptable or better performance ratings are often offered severance pay and outplacement assistance.

Severance pay is a lump sum of money provided to employees who are being terminated. While legally required in certain situations, such as mass layoffs, severance pay is expected when employees are being terminated through no fault of their own. In addition to pay, severance packages often include benefits continuation for a specified period of time. In determining the appropriate package, employers should take salary, years of service, the employee's age, and his or her likelihood of obtaining another job into consideration.[41] Executives may be protected by a *golden parachute clause* in their contract of employment, a guarantee by the employer to pay specified compensation and benefits in the case of termination due to downsizing or restructuring. To soften the blow of termination, *outplacement assistance,* generally offered by an outside agency, can assist affected employees in finding employment elsewhere.

Re-evaluating Restructuring While restructuring initiatives ranging from layoffs to mergers and acquisitions have certainly been prevalent in Canadian firms in recent years, in many instances, the consequences have not been as positive as anticipated.

In a study involving a sample of almost 500 major unionized and non-unionized Canadian organizations ranging in size from under 200 to more than 1000 employees, employers whose firms had undergone workforce reductions reported significant expenditure cuts, a decline in the firm's reputation, difficulty in accomplishing work, a decline in financial performance, pressure on managers to focus on short-term profit or budget goals, a less favourable employee perception of top management, more vocal special interest groups, present employee concern about job security, difficulty in retaining top performers, and increased stress among managers. Permanent workforce reductions were also found to be associated with significantly lower overall employee satisfaction rates; noticeably poorer employer–employee relations (including higher rates of grievances and absenteeism), and more conflict within the organization; and moderately poorer economic performance, including somewhat lower productivity, product/service quality, market share, product/service innovation, and profitability.[42]

As those firms discovered, a high cost associated with downsizing is **survivor sickness**, a range of emotions that can include feelings of betrayal or violation, guilt, and detachment. The remaining employees, anxious about the next round of terminations, often suffer stress symptoms including depression, increased errors, and reduced performance. To avoid survivor sickness in downsizing situations, supervisors should:[43]

- provide abundant, honest communication
- provide assistance to those being laid off
- treat victims and survivors with dignity and respect
- allow remaining employees to grieve and deal with repressed feelings and emotions
- increase their accessibility

- help survivors to recapture their sense of control and self-esteem
- hold special meetings or small-group sessions to provide people with a chance to acknowledge the changes and their reactions to them
- lessen dependency-creating processes by eliminating rewards and recognition based on length of service and encouraging employees to think of themselves as self-employed entrepreneurs.

Labour Shortage

A labour shortage exists when the internal supply of human resources cannot meet the organization's needs. Scheduling overtime hours is often the initial response. Employers may also subcontract work (if not prohibited by the collective agreement) on a temporary or permanent basis. Another short-term solution is to hire temporary employees. Increasingly, these may be older workers. Older workers already make a significant contribution to Canadian society, and will assume an even more important role in the labour market as the population ages. Even now, one in five university-educated individuals older than 65 is still working.[44] As a result, many employers are seeking strategies to increase the workforce participation of older Canadians.

As vacancies are created within the firm, opportunities are generally provided for employee transfers and promotions, which necessitate performance management, training (and retraining), and career development. Of course, internal movement does not eliminate a shortage, which means that recruitment will be required. Hopefully, though, resultant vacancies will be for entry-level jobs, which can be filled more easily externally.

A **transfer** involves lateral movement from one job to another that is relatively equal in pay, responsibility, and/or organizational level. Transfers can lead to more effective utilization of human resources, broaden an employee's skills and perspectives, and help make him or her a better candidate for future promotions. Transfers also offer additional technical and interpersonal challenges and increased variety of work, which may enhance job satisfaction and motivation.

A **promotion** involves the movement of an employee from one job to another that is higher in pay, responsibility, and/or organizational level. Such a move may be based on merit, seniority, or a combination of both. Merit-based promotions are awarded in recognition of a person's outstanding performance in his or her present job, or an assessment of his or her future potential.

In unionized settings, seniority may be the governing factor in promotion and transfer decisions, or the deciding factor in the event of a tie in candidates' skills and abilities. Unions often prefer seniority to be the deciding factor, since length of service is a matter of record and is therefore totally objective. The drawback is that because all workers are not equally capable, the individual who is transferred or promoted may not be the most competent.

Labour Supply Matches Labour Demand

When there is a match between expected supply and demand, organizations replace employees who leave the firm with individuals transferred or promoted

transfer Movement of an employee from one job to another that is relatively equal in pay, responsibility, and/or organizational level.

promotion Movement of an employee from one job to another that is higher in pay, responsibility, and/or organizational level, usually based on merit, seniority, or a combination of both.

from inside or hired from outside. As in shortage situations, performance management, training, and career development play a crucial role.

HRP Evaluation

HR planning should be evaluated on an annual basis to determine its effectiveness in meeting management's expectations. Since HRP links an organization's HRM activities with its strategic goals and objectives, the strength and adequacy of these linkages should be assessed.[45] Whether or not goals were reached, reasons for failure should be determined and areas in need of change should be identified.

Specific criteria often assessed include:

- actual staffing levels versus established staffing requirements
- the ratio of internal placements to external hiring
- actual internal mobility flow (movement of employees within the organization) versus career development plans
- internal mobility flow versus turnover
- employment equity achievements as compared to established goals and timetables.

Labour Market Analysis and Generation X

Labour market analysis is the study of the external supply of labour available to the organization and trends in the market. Examining trends allows the human resources practitioner to consider the factors that may be relevant to turnover. Gaining this kind of understanding is the basis for developing effective retention practices.

... The supply of labour is affected by a number of factors. The foremost factor is the aging of the population. Demographic analysis provides macro-level data that highlight general trends. In Western countries, and particularly in Canada, the Baby Boomer cohorts have been followed by a relatively small group of Generation Xers who, in turn, have been followed by another large cohort. This trend has been well described in the popular bestseller *Boom, Bust and Echo*....

A number of years ago people labelled as Generation X found it difficult to find meaningful full-time employment. They were, in fact, squeezed out of the market by the boomers and the echo. This resulted in a blip in the number of part-time workers. Some analysts interpreted this phenomenon as a growing choice among the employable population. In fact, these part-time workers were merely waiting for an expansion in full-time opportunities.

Supply is irrelevant unless compared to demand. Although the Generation Xers are a smaller cohort, they faced a shortage of available work. This was influenced in some degree by good planning on the part of organizations facing a potential drop in the supply of school-leavers. During the latter part of the 1980s, organizations made long-term structural changes such as flattening the reporting structures that reduced the need for people....

Source: Excerpted with permission from *Secord's A–Z Guide for Human Resources Practitioners*, published by and copyright CCH Canadian Limited, Toronto, Ontario.

Chapter *Review*

Summary

1. Human Resources Planning (HRP) is the process of reviewing HR requirements to ensure that the organization has the required number of employees with the necessary skills to meet its goals. HRP is important because it helps organizations meet their strategic goals and objectives.

2. Strategic plans are made and carried out by people. Thus, determining whether or not people will be available is a critical element of strategic planning processes. HRP and strategic planning become effective when there is a reciprocal and interdependent relationship between them. Environmental scanning is a critical component of the HRP and strategic planning processes. The external environmental factors most frequently monitored include economic conditions; market and competitive trends; government and legislative issues; social concerns related to health care, childcare, and educational priorities; technological changes; and demographic trends.

3. Quantitative techniques for forecasting future HR demand include trend analysis, ratio analysis, scatter plots, regression analysis, and computerized forecasting techniques. Two qualitative techniques used to forecast demand are the nominal group technique and the Delphi technique.

4. Strategies used to forecast internal HR supply are Markov analysis, skills inventories, manual systems, replacement charts, replacement summaries, computerized information systems, computerized skills inventories, and succession planning. Forecasting external HR supply requires an assessment of general economic conditions, national labour market conditions, local labour market conditions, and occupational labour market conditions.

5. Strategies to deal with a labour surplus include the implementation of a hiring freeze and downsizing through attrition; speeding up attrition through attractive buyout and early retirement programs; reducing hours through job sharing, part-time hours, work sharing, or reduced workweeks; laying off workers on the basis of reverse seniority or juniority; and terminating employment.

6. Scheduling overtime is often the initial response to a human resources shortage. Another short-term solution is to hire temporary employees. Employers may also subcontract work (if not prohibited by the collective agreement) on a temporary or permanent basis. As vacancies are created within an organization, opportunities are generally provided for employee transfers and promotions.

7. HR planning should be evaluated on an annual basis to determine its effectiveness in meeting management's expectations. Whether or not goals were reached and reasons for failure should be determined, and areas in need of change identified.

Key Terms

attrition   *(p. 125)*
buyout and early retirement programs   *(p. 125)*
computerized forecast   *(p. 114)*
Delphi technique   *(p. 115)*
hiring freeze   *(p. 125)*
human resources planning (HRP)   *(p. 107)*
job sharing   *(p. 126)*
juniority clause   *(p. 126)*
layoff   *(p. 126)*
management inventories   *(p. 118)*
Markov analysis   *(p. 117)*
nominal group technique   *(p. 114)*
promotion   *(p. 128)*
ratio analysis   *(p. 112)*
reduced workweek   *(p. 126)*
regression analysis   *(p. 114)*
replacement charts   *(p. 119)*
replacement summaries   *(p. 120)*
reverse seniority   *(p. 126)*
scatter plot   *(p. 112)*
severance pay   *(p. 127)*
skills inventories   *(p. 117)*
staffing table   *(p. 115)*
succession planning   *(p. 120)*
supplemental unemployment benefits (SUBs)   *(p. 126)*
survivor sickness   *(p. 127)*
termination   *(p. 127)*
transfer   *(p. 128)*

trend analysis   *(p. 112)*
work sharing   *(p. 126)*

Review and Discussion Questions

1   Describe the costs associated with lack of or inadequate HRP.

2   After analyzing the human resources implications of the organization's strategic plans, what are the four subsequent processes involved in HRP?

3   Differentiate between replacement charts and replacement summaries, and explain why replacement summaries are generally preferred.

4   Discuss various methods of easing the burden of a layoff or termination.

5   Differentiate between the reverse seniority and juniority approaches to layoffs and explain the advantages and disadvantages of each.

6   Differentiate between the seniority and merit-based approaches to promotion and describe the advantages and disadvantages associated with each.

CRITICAL *Thinking Questions*

1   A number of quantitative and qualitative techniques for forecasting human resources demand were discussed in this chapter. Working in groups, identify which strategies would be most appropriate for (a) small versus large companies, (b) industries undergoing rapid change, and (c) businesses/industries in which there are seasonal variations in HR requirements.

2   Suppose that it has just been projected that, due to a number of technological innovations, your firm will need 20 percent fewer clerical employees within the next five years. What actions would you take to try to retain your high-performing clerical staff members?

3   Suppose that you are the HR manager at a firm at which a hiring freeze has just been declared. The plan is to downsize through attrition. What steps would you take to ensure that you reap the advantages of this strategy, while minimizing the disadvantages?

APPLICATION *Exercises*

Running Case: LearnInMotion.com

To Plan or Not to Plan?

One aspect of HRM that Jennifer and Pierre studied at university was HR planning. Their professor emphasized its importance, especially for large organizations. Although LearnInMotion.com was certainly small at this point, with only two employees, they were planning to expand, and it seemed that detailed HRP should be an essential part of their plans. At this point, there is no succession plan—after all, they have just started the business! But they both knew that the market for technology workers, in general, was competitive. Jennifer and Pierre have asked for some assistance with the following questions.

Questions

1   In what ways might HRP benefit LearnInMotion.com?

2   Should they decide to proceed with HRP, what steps should Jennifer and Pierre take?

3   What HRP techniques would be appropriate for them to use?

4   What other issues would have to be addressed to make HRP worthwhile?

CASE INCIDENT *Management Trainees at Nova*

It's that time of year again at Nova! Each year, Carl Adams, recruitment officer at head office of the retail chain, visits colleges and universities across Canada to recruit graduates for sales, marketing, human resources, and purchasing management-trainee positions for its 26 locations.

In order to predict the number of management trainees required, HRP is done each year, based on the budget and forecasted sales. The previous year's plan is also reviewed. There has been virtually no change in the HR plan over the past 10 years.

Natalie Gordon, vice-president of human resources, is feeling rather concerned about what happened last year and is wondering how to ensure that it doesn't happen again. Based on the HR plan, 50 new management trainees were hired. Unfortunately, six months after they started, the company experienced a drastic drop in sales due to a downturn in the economy, combined with increased foreign competition. Half of the recently hired management trainees had to be laid off.

Carl, who started at Nova as a management trainee when he completed the Business Administration–Human Resources Management program at Central Community College, has just returned from an on-campus recruitment campaign, which happened to be at his old alma mater, and reported that his experience was not as pleasant as usual. One of the candidates that he interviewed knew someone who had been hired and laid off last year, and indicated that she was rather worried about considering a position with the firm in light of that fact, despite Nova's excellent reputation for promotion from within and overall stability. (Nova, which currently employs more than 8000 people in its head office and retail stores across the country, has been in business for more than 70 years.)

Carl has just finished telling Natalie how embarrassed he was by this candidate's probing questions about job security and how uncomfortable he felt. He ended up simply reassuring the candidate that such a situation could never happen again. Natalie is now wondering how to make Carl's reassurance a reality.

Questions

1 What are the consequences of poor HRP at Nova?

2 What problems do you see with Nova's present HRP process?

3 What should Natalie do to more accurately forecast the demand for management trainees for the coming year before Carl does any more on-campus recruiting?

EXPERIENTIAL *Exercises*

1 Develop a realistic, hypothetical staffing table for a department or organization with which you are familiar.

2 Contact the HR manager at a firm in your area and find out whether or not the firm uses any of the following: (a) skills/management inventories, (b) replacement charts or summaries, and (c) a succession plan. Prepare a brief summary of the information gathered. Once you have completed these tasks, form a group with several of your classmates. Share your findings with the group members. Were there similarities across firms? Did company size seem to make a difference in terms of strategies used for forecasting the supply of internal candidates? Can you identify any other factors that seem to play a role in the choice of forecasting techniques used?

3 This assignment requires working within teams of five or six. Half of the teams are to assume the role of management at a firm that is about to undergo major downsizing. The other half of the teams are to assume the roles of employees—some of whom will be affected and others of whom will remain. Each management team is paired with an employee team, and must prepare a realistic simulation. Managers should work toward minimizing the negative impact on those who will be affected as well as those who will be remaining. Individuals in employee roles are asked to envision what their thoughts and feelings would be (if they have never actually been in this situation, that is) and to portray them as realistically as possible.

CHAPTER 5

Recruitment

LEARNING OUTCOMES

After studying this chapter, you should be able to:

Define recruitment and *describe* its purposes.

Explain the recruitment process.

Describe the role of job posting, human resources records, and skills inventories in promotion from within.

Identify twelve methods used for external recruitment.

Explain three strategies used to recruit a nonpermanent staff.

Discuss strategies for recruiting a more diverse workforce.

Explain the importance of application forms.

INTRODUCTION

recruitment The process of searching out and attracting qualified job applicants, which begins with the identification of a position that requires staffing, and is completed when résumés and/or completed application forms are received from an adequate number of applicants.

Recruitment is the process of searching out and attracting qualified job applicants. It begins with the identification of a position that requires staffing, and is completed when résumés and/or completed application forms are received from an adequate number of applicants.

The Purposes of Recruitment

According to one expert, recruitment of the right people is a key ingredient of corporate health and well-being.[1] Because the quality of a firm's human resources depends to a great extent upon the quality of its recruits, recruitment is a critical HR function. Its purposes are to:

- ensure that an adequate pool of applicants is generated at minimum possible cost
- eliminate unqualified or poorly qualified candidates, thus improving the success rate of the selection process[2]
- find and attract individuals who not only meet the job requirements, but are also suited to the organization's unique culture and climate
- help the firm to meet its employment equity goals by attracting a diverse applicant pool.

The Role of the HR Department in the Recruitment Process

In firms with an HR department, authority for recruitment is generally delegated to HR staff members. In large organizations, in which recruiting is done on an almost continuous basis, the HR team typically includes specialists, known as **recruiters**, whose job it is to find and attract qualified applicants.

Recruitment tactics are often the first points of personal contact between an organization and a potential employee, and studies suggest that applicants see a connection between the quality of the recruitment efforts and the integrity of the organization. Those companies that can communicate trustworthiness through their recruitment process are more likely to be successful in attracting top candidates.[3]

recruiter A specialist in recruitment, whose job it is to find and attract capable candidates.

Recruiters Café
www.recruiterscafe.com

THE RECRUITMENT PROCESS

As illustrated in **Figure 5.1**, there are a number of steps in the recruitment process:

FIGURE 5.1   An Overview of the Recruitment Process

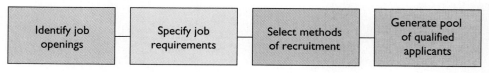

Identify job openings → Specify job requirements → Select methods of recruitment → Generate pool of qualified applicants

1. Job openings are identified through HR planning or manager request. HR plans play a vital role in the identification process, because they indicate present and future openings and specify which should be filled internally and which externally. Openings do arise unexpectedly, however, in which case managers request that a new employee be hired.

2. The job requirements are determined. This involves reviewing the job description and the job specification and updating them, if necessary. Manager comments may also prove helpful in identifying requirements.

3. Appropriate recruiting source(s) and method(s) are chosen. There is no single, best, recruiting technique, and the most appropriate for any given position depends on a number of factors, which will be discussed next.

4. A pool of qualified recruits is generated.

CONSTRAINTS ON THE RECRUITMENT PROCESS

A recruiter must be aware of constraints affecting the recruitment process in order to be successful in his or her job. Constraints arise from organizational policies and plans, job specifications, recruiter preferences, inducements of competitors, and environmental factors.

Organizational Policies

Most firms have a *promote-from-within policy*. While this practice has numerous advantages, having such a policy may mean that a recruiter cannot start recruiting externally for a specified period of time, even if he or she is aware that there are no suitable internal candidates.

Compensation policies regarding the pay structure and benefits package can pose a constraint, since they influence the attractiveness of the job to potential applicants. Recruiters rarely have the authority to exceed established pay ranges, and may be further constrained by an organizational policy specifying that no one can be hired at a rate higher than the midpoint or other set level within the range.

Organizational Plans

The *HR plan* provides valuable guidance to recruiters by indicating how many candidates will be required for various positions and when they will be needed, but may pose some restrictions if such plans specify which positions should be filled internally and which externally.

Whether legally required or voluntarily initiated, if there is an *employment equity plan*, it must be consulted, since it will specify the organization's goals and timetables pertaining to increasing the number of qualified candidates from the designated groups.

Recruitment Budget

The budget established for recruitment also poses some constraints. Some positions can be filled very cheaply; others will require extensive advertising and considerable time and travel. Recruiting for several job openings simultaneously can reduce the cost per recruit. Costs have to be balanced with other considerations, however. For example, relying on three very popular and inexpensive techniques—walk-ins, write-ins, and word-of-mouth hiring—can result in systemic discrimination.

Job Specifications

The job specifications pose some constraints. Highly skilled or specialized workers often have to be hired externally and can often be more difficult to attract than unskilled ones. The length of time required, the scope of the search area (local, regional, national, or international), the amount of compensation required to attract candidates, and the recruitment campaign budget are all linked to the job specifications. Strategic recruitment may be required in order to attract foreign workers with scarce skills, as discussed in the Global HR box.

Recruiter Preferences

With time and success, recruiters acquire preferences that enhance their efficiency. They can also lead to repetition of past mistakes or failure to consider potentially better alternatives. Using the same method repeatedly may make it difficult, if not impossible, to reach employment equity goals, and may result in a pool of employees who share the same strengths and weaknesses.

Inducements of Competitors

Monetary and non-monetary inducements are often used to attract qualified candidates. Inducements offered by competitors impose a constraint, since recruiters must try to meet the prevailing standards or use alternative inducements to overcome limitations. For example, if a competitor is offering excellent pay as an inducement, which the organization cannot match, the recruiter may try to sell the job (interesting projects); the work environment (high level of intellectual stimulation); the firm (reputation as a prestigious blue-chip company); the community (good schools); the location (along the Cabot Trail); or unique benefits (flextime, childcare facilities). The types of inducements offered today range from computers and Internet access at home for a nominal fee to signing bonuses and stock options.[4]

GLOBAL HRM

Recruiting High-Skill Immigrants

Sometimes companies must recruit highly skilled, specialized workers internationally to help meet particular job requirements, such as in the case of Edmonton-based Fiberex Glass Corporation. There are only 14 firms in the world using the manufacturing procedure they do, and the company wanted to hire a specialist from the Philippines to instruct local staff in the maintenance of fiberglass manufacturing equipment. The Alberta government created the Provincial Nominee Program (PNP) to help employers, such as Fiberex Glass, hire skilled foreign workers and enable them to immigrate to Canada in a matter of months, rather than years.

Employers prepare a business case on behalf of the applicant, stating why they want the candidate and what job skills the person has. The Minister of Economic Development inspects the application and passes it on to the federal government for criminal, security, and health checks. Similar programs are in place in Newfoundland, Prince Edward Island, New Brunswick, Manitoba, Saskatchewan, British Columbia, and the Yukon.

Source: A. Tomlinson, "Alberta Matches Employers, Immigrants," *Canadian HR Reporter* (April 22, 2002), p. 12. Reproduced by permission of *Canadian HR Reporter*, Carswell, One Corporate Plaza, 2075 Kennedy Road, Scarborough, ON M1T 3V4.

There is a caution to be noted in the use of inducements, however. The Supreme Court of Canada has made it clear that employers must take extreme care in describing the nature and existence of an employment opportunity to prospective employees. Representations made must be accurate, not misleading, or the firm can be charged with negligent misrepresentation.[5]

Environmental Factors

External environmental factors impose a major constraint on many aspects of employment. Changes in the labour market, unemployment rate, economy and legislation, and the recruiting activities of labour-market competitors all affect a recruiter's efforts. Although environmental scanning is a key step in HRP, the economic environment may change after the HR plan is finalized. Recruiters can use three measures to assess whether the assumptions on which the plan was based are valid at the time of search:

- Leading economic indicators published monthly by Statistics Canada. If these indices signal a sudden downturn or upturn in the economy, recruiting plans may require modification.
- The national want-ads index reported by Statistics Canada. An upward trend in this index indicates a high level of competition for employees who are recruited nationally, such as professionals and managers.
- Actual business activity versus predicted business activity. Since HRP is based on predicted activity levels, variations between what was predicted and what actually happens may necessitate modifications to recruiting plans.

RECRUITING WITHIN THE ORGANIZATION

Although recruiting often brings job boards and employment agencies to mind, current employees are generally the largest source of recruits. Filling open positions with inside candidates has several advantages:

- Employees see that competence is rewarded, thus enhancing commitment, morale, and performance.
- Having already been with the firm for some time, insiders may be more committed to the company's goals and less likely to leave.
- Managers are provided with a longer-term perspective when making business decisions.
- It is generally safer to promote from within, since the firm is likely to have a more accurate assessment of the person's skills and performance level than would otherwise be the case.
- Inside candidates require less orientation than outsiders.

Promotion from within also has a number of drawbacks, however:

- Employees who apply for jobs and don't get them may become discontented. Informing unsuccessful applicants as to why they were rejected and what remedial action they might take to be more successful in the future is thus essential.[6]

- Managers may be required to post all job openings and interview all inside candidates, even when they already know whom they wish to hire, thus wasting considerable time and creating false hope on the part of those employees not genuinely being considered.

- Employees may be less satisfied and accepting of a boss appointed from within their own ranks than they would a newcomer.

- It is sometimes difficult for a newly chosen leader to adjust to no longer being "one of the gang."[7]

- There is a possibility of "inbreeding." When an entire management team has been brought up through the ranks, there may be a tendency to make decisions "by the book" and to maintain the status quo, when a new and innovative direction is needed.

Promotion from within requires using job posting, human resources records, and skills inventories.

job posting The process of notifying current employees about vacant positions.

Job Posting   **Job posting** is a process of notifying current employees about vacant positions. Most companies now use computerized job-posting systems, where information about job vacancies can be found on the company's intranet.[8] This involves a notice outlining the job title, duties (as listed in the job description), qualifications (taken from the job specification), hours of work, pay range, posting date, and closing date, as shown in **Figure 5.2**. Not all firms use intranets. Some post jobs on bulletin boards or in employee publications. As illustrated in **Figure 5.3**, there are advantages and disadvantages to using job postings to facilitate the transfer and promotion of qualified internal candidates.

FIGURE 5.2   Sample Job Posting

Social Work Field Placement Coordinator
Toronto, Ontario, Canada
Posted: June 2, 2003
Position No. 121338_OFT_01
Grade: 11

Department: Social Work
Salary: $40 698.85 - $49 331.93 p.a.
Scale:

Hours of Work: 36.25 hours per week
Start Date: ASAP

Note:
This is a term vacancy with a guarantee to return to home position.

Responsibilities
Assists the Field Education Coordinator in organizing and maintaining high-quality field education placements for social work students. Coordinates students' placements in keeping with the curriculum for their year, their learning needs and career goals. Acts as a liaison with community and institutional-based sites.

Qualifications
- Successful completion of a post-secondary degree in Social Work and at least two years' experience working in the social services fields or in a similar role in a post-secondary educational institution. An equivalent combination of education and experience may be considered.
- Excellent written and verbal communication skills are necessary in order to effectively develop and prepare manuals, procedures, reports and brochures in conjunction with the Coordinator; to counsel and support students in preparation for and during placements; and to consult and assess practicum placement sites to facilitate communication between Ryerson and the site.

- Demonstrated commitment to client service—specifically students, staff, faculty, and external contacts. Excellent interpersonal skills are necessary to explain the placement process and to provide information to students and site contacts.
- An ability to work within a team environment in order to effectively collaborate with the Coordinator and appropriate committees to promote and support instructors at the placement agencies and to coordinate the student application process collaboratively with the Coordinator and others.
- Strong analytical, reasoning, and problem-solving skills to negotiate with students for individual placements that address their learning and career goals; to troubleshoot and assist students with placement needs and issues; and to determine appropriate student/location matches in order to place students and maximize learning potential.
- Experience working with database systems and software applications as well as a good understanding of internet, RISIS and internal e-mail functionalities is required.
- Knowledge of the social work curriculum, practice requirements, and field placement sites is necessary to actively participate in the identification, development, and maintenance of appropriate community-based and institutional-based sites that meet the curricular requirements and individual student needs for practice experience for social work students.
- Good judgment and decision-making skills are required to place students in appropriate practicum sites.
- Demonstrated ability to work independently with minimal supervision.

Note:

Candidates may be asked to demonstrate qualifications through an occupational test. Candidates must have a demonstrated record of dependability/reliability and a commitment to maintain confidentiality.

We thank all candidates for applying; however, only those selected for an interview will be contacted.

Ryerson University has an employment equity program and encourages applications from all qualified individuals, including Aboriginal peoples, persons with disabilities, members of visible minorities, and women.

Qualified candidates can either apply online or attach their résumé and covering letter via e-mail to:

Hiring Committee
Human Resources Department
E-mail: lghent@ryerson.ca

Source: "Careers @ Ryerson: Job Postings." *Ryerson University.* www.ryerson.ca. Reprinted with permission of Ryerson University, Human Resources Department.

FIGURE 5.3   Advantages and Disadvantages of Job Posting

Advantages

- Provides every qualified employee with a chance for a transfer or promotion.
- Reduces the likelihood of special deals and favouritism.
- Demonstrates the organization's commitment to career growth and development.
- Communicates to employees the organization's policies and guidelines regarding promotions and transfers.
- Provides equal opportunity to all qualified employees.

Disadvantages

- Unsuccessful job candidates may become demotivated, demoralized, discontented, and unhappy if feedback is not communicated in a timely and sensitive manner.
- Tensions may rise if it appears that a qualified internal candidate was passed over for an equally qualified or less qualified external candidate.
- The decision about which candidate to select may be more difficult if there are two or more equally qualified candidates.

AN ETHICAL
DILEMMA

Is it ethical to require a manager to post all jobs and interview all internal candidates, even if he or she has already made a decision about the individual who will be selected for the position?

Human Resources Records   Human resources records are often consulted to ensure that qualified individuals are notified, in person, of vacant positions. An examination of employee files, including résumés and application forms, may uncover employees who are working in jobs below their education or skill levels, people who already have the requisite KSAs, or persons with the potential to move into the vacant position if given some additional training.

Skills Inventories   Skills inventories are an even better reference tool. While such inventories may be used instead of job postings, they are more often used as a supplement. Whether computerized or manual, referring to such inventories ensures that qualified internal candidates are identified and considered for transfer or promotion when opportunities arise.

Limitations of Recruiting from Within

It is rarely possible to fill all non-entry-level jobs with current employees. Middle- and upper-level jobs may be vacated unexpectedly, with no internal replacements yet qualified or ready for transfer or promotion; or may require such specialized training and experience that there are no potential internal replacements. Even in firms with a policy of promoting from within, potential external candidates are also considered, because of the potential inbreeding problem described previously. Hiring someone from outside may be preferable in order to acquire the latest knowledge and expertise or gain new ideas and revitalize the department or organization.[9]

RECRUITING OUTSIDE THE ORGANIZATION

Unless there is a workforce reduction, even in firms with a promote-from-within policy, a replacement from outside must eventually be found to fill the job left vacant once all eligible employees have been given the opportunity for transfer and/or promotion. In addition, most entry-level positions must be filled by external candidates. The advantages of external recruitment include:

- generation of a larger pool of qualified candidates, which may have a positive impact on the quality of the selection decision
- availability of a more diverse applicant pool, which can assist in meeting employment equity goals and timetables
- acquisition of skills or knowledge not currently available within the organization and/or new ideas and creative problem-solving techniques
- elimination of rivalry and competition caused by employees jockeying for transfers and promotions, which can hinder interpersonal and interdepartmental cooperation
- potential cost savings resulting from hiring individuals who already have the skills, rather than providing extensive training.

Planning External Recruitment

More than half of Canadian CEOs expect their organizations to be hiring additional employees through 2004 and 2005.[10] When choosing external recruitment method(s), in addition to the constraints mentioned earlier, there are several factors that should be taken into consideration: the type of job, the relationship between the method chosen and quality of hire, the yield ratio, and the amount of lead time.

Type of Job   The type of job to be filled has a major impact on the recruitment method selected. This fact is clearly illustrated by the results of a comprehensive study of the recruiting practices of 718 Canadian firms, representing diverse sectors, industries, and businesses. Sixty-nine percent of the respondents indicated that they normally rely on professional search firms for recruiting executive-level employees. Fifty-four percent indicated that they relied on such firms for recruiting managers/supervisors, 50 percent for recruiting professional/technical employees, and 41 percent for recruiting other salaried employees. In contrast, local newspaper advertising was rated as very useful for recruiting executives by 40 percent of respondents, for recruiting manager/supervisors by 47 percent, for recruiting professional/technical employees by 48 percent, and for recruiting other salaried employees by 54 percent.[11]

Yield Ratios   Yield ratios help to indicate which recruitment methods are the most effective at producing qualified job candidates. A **yield ratio** is the percentage of applicants that proceed to the next stage of the selection process. A recruiting yield pyramid, such as that shown in **Figure 5.4,** can be devised for each method, by calculating the yield ratio for each step in the selection process.

yield ratio The percentage of applicants that proceed to the next stage of the selection process.

The firm in this example typically hires 50 entry-level accountants each year. The firm has calculated that using this method leads to a ratio of offers made to actual new hires of two to one (about half of the candidates to whom offers are made accept). The firm also knows that the ratio of candidates interviewed to offers made is three to two, while the ratio of candidates invited for interviews to candidates actually interviewed is generally four to three. Finally, the firm knows that the ratio between leads generated and candidates selected for interviews is six to one. In other words, of six leads generated through college/university recruiting efforts, one applicant is invited to attend an interview. Given these ratios, the firm knows that, using this particular recruitment method, 1200 leads must be generated in order to hire 50 new accountants.

Amount of Lead Time   The average number of days from when the company initiates a recruitment method to when the successful candidate begins to work is called time-lapse data. Let us assume that the accounting company in the above example found the following: six days elapsed between submission of application forms and résumés to invitation for an interview; five days then

FIGURE 5.4   Recruiting Yield Pyramid

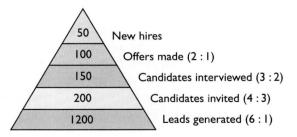

passed from invitation to actual interview; five days from interview to job offer; six days from job offer to acceptance; and 23 days from acceptance of job offer to commencement of work. These data indicate that, using on-campus recruiting, the firm must initiate recruitment efforts at least 45 days prior to the anticipated job opening date.

The Conference Board of Canada reported that in 2002, the average time-to-hire was 15 weeks for executives, nine weeks for management and professional positions, seven weeks for technical positions, and four weeks for clerical support positions.[12] Calculating time-lapse data for each recruitment method means that the amount of lead time available can be taken into account when deciding which strategy or strategies would be most appropriate.

External Recruitment Methods

Recruiting Online www.ilogos.com

Acti-Job Canada www.actijob.com

Canadajobs.com
www.canadajobs.com

Canjobs.com www.canjobs.com

online recruitment Use of the Internet to aid in recruiting.

Online Recruitment
Like so many other facets of business, the Internet has revolutionized human resources recruitment. Currently, 75 percent of the Canadian population has access to the Internet, and one of the most popular online activities is using the Internet as a job search tool.[13] In fact, job seekers have taken to the Internet much faster than employers.[14] A recent survey by Ipsos-Reid found that 50 percent of Canadian adults with an Internet connection have used the Internet to view job postings. The survey also found that 62 percent of these job hunters have researched prospective companies online and have sent a résumé to a company by e-mail.

As the HR profession embraces the Internet as a recruitment tool, new job titles such as Internet Recruiting Specialist and Internet Recruiting Manager are appearing on business cards. Internet recruiting skills are now in demand, and this area is becoming a specialty in its own right.[15] It is projected that the online recruitment industry in North America will grow eight-fold, from US$847 million in 2000 to US$6.6 billion by 2005.[16]

Online recruitment, or use of the Internet to aid in recruiting, significantly increases hiring speed, which in turn reduces the costs of vacant positions.[17] As well, the cost of advertising for a position online can be as little as one-tenth of traditional advertising channels, and is replacing those channels for many firms.[18] For example, Canada's spy agency, the Canadian Security Intelligence Service (CSIS), has now entered the realm of Internet recruiting. An internal report showed that CSIS was less than satisfied with some aspects of past recruitment techniques, and decided to use the Web to increase its reach and attract more visible minorities. Job seekers can now visit their Web site for job openings for intelligence officers and support staff.[19] Online recruitment is an excellent way to reach younger members of the workforce as they are more comfortable using the Internet than traditional media.

Online recruitment is most often conducted through the use of Internet job boards and corporate career Web sites. Each of these will now be discussed.

Internet Job Boards The number of Internet job boards, and the number of job seekers using job boards are both increasing exponentially. Online job boards are fast, easy, and convenient and allow recruiters to search for candidates for positions in two ways. First, for a fee, companies can post a job opening online and customize it using corporate logos and adding details about the company benefits and culture. Job seekers can search through the job postings, often by

Monster Board Canada
www.monster.ca

Workopolis.com
www.workopolis.com

The Canadian Job Board
Comparison
www.careerboards.com

Careerclick.com
www.careerclick.com

CareerMosaic
www.careermosaic.com

HotJobs.com **www.hotjobs.com**

Research
I n s i g h t ▷

job type, region, or other criterion, and apply for the position online through the job board Web site. The popularity of Internet job boards among job seekers is high due to the number of job postings available on one site—Monster.ca has an average of 25 000 job postings available at any given time.

Second, job seekers can also post their own résumés on job boards, and firms can search the database. This allows employers to find talented workers who are not actively searching for a job.[20] Another popular Canadian job board, Workopolis.ca, has a database of over 500 000 Canadian résumés.[21] Hundreds of smaller job boards serve specific fields, from tourism to medicine.[22] Job board meta-crawlers can search more than one job board. For example, actualjobs.com can search 378 job boards and more than 24 000 jobs with one search.[23] Toronto's 411jobs.ca also lets people search multiple job boards with one query, so employers don't have to post their jobs everywhere.

One problem with Internet job boards is their vulnerability to privacy breaches. Fake job postings can lead to identity theft from résumés submitted, and résumés are sometimes copied onto competing job boards or other sites.[24]

Canadians have a success rate four times greater than the global average when it comes to finding employment online. A study by Drake-Beam Morin Canada showed that about 12 percent of Canadians who found a new job in 2002 cited successful Web searches as the reason, compared to 3 percent worldwide, and 6 percent in the US.[25]

Corporate Career Web Sites With the overabundance of applicants now found on most online job boards, employers are now using their own corporate Web sites to recruit. Career pages, also known as recruiting portals, have become a hub of recruiting activity. They provide a single platform for recruitment that promotes the corporate brand, educates the applicant about the company, captures data about the applicant, and provides an important link to job boards where a company's positions may be advertised.[26]

Many firms use Web-enabled applicant tracking system providers, generically known as Application Service Providers (ASPs), to power their career Web sites. The company does not have to worry about maintaining, updating, or administering recruiting software, allowing the HR department to focus on strategic recruitment efforts.[27] Essentially, when applicants hit the career section of a company career page, they are moved over to the ASP Website.[28]

In order to deal with the large numbers of résumés and applications that are submitted through a company's Web site, ASP firms such as Workstream Inc. (formerly e-cruiter.com) provide applicant screening tools to their subscribers, such as a standardized application, or résumé builder, for candidates to fill out online. Standardized applicant information can then be sorted using automated search, screening, and ranking to profile and verify a candidate's qualifications based on the job's specifications. Online applications can incorporate pre-assessment questions to assess the match between the candidate's skills, credentials, and experience and requirements of a particular position. The use of applicant screening tools enables a firm's recruiter to create a short list of candidates for personal interviews.

Combined with résumé databases, corporate Web sites can help the company create a pool of candidates, who have already expressed interest in the organization.[29] The company can also initiate ongoing communication via e-mail to candidates with whom the company feels it would be beneficial to keep in touch.

Corporate career Web sites have a profound impact on a corporation's recruiting strategy in the following areas:

- *Branding.* Organizations are using career Web sites to position their corporate brands to effectively advertise companies and their career opportunities.[30]

- *Response Management.* Career Web sites create a standard application process for candidates from various sources, and help recruiters manage ongoing relationships with candidates.

- *Assessment.* Career Web sites improve recruitment through online screening tools for filtering, scoring, and ranking candidates, thus saving the corporation time and money.

- *Processing.* Career Web sites open the door to streamlining data flow into advanced back-end automated search and tracking tools.[31]

Direct Energy Jobs
www.directyourenergy.com

Direct Energy, a North American energy provider headquartered in Toronto, decided it needed more control over the online hiring process and switched from using job boards to a corporate Web site. The company has filled more that 100 positions with top candidates through the site, and views it as a strategic branding tool in the recruitment process.[32]

Active job seekers are not the only potential future employees that visit corporate Web sites. Customers, investors, and competitors also visit corporate Web sites.[33] Twenty-one percent of those visiting career Web sites are "happily employed" individuals (known as "passive" job seekers) who are likely to arrive at the career site after browsing the company's main pages for other reasons, such as research into products or services.[34] Therefore, it is important that a firm have a prominently positioned link on the homepage leading directly to the careers section to make it easy for passive job seekers to pursue job opportunities within the company.[35]

Best practices for career Web sites include the following:

- Focus on easy navigation and fast download times, not flashy design. Make sure content is fresh and current and present information in easily digestible formats such as graphs and bullet points as opposed to large blocks of text. One in four job seekers reject potential employers based on their Web site.[36]

- Include candid information about the culture, career paths, and business prospects. Some online applicants also want to view virtual tours of the workplace.[37]

- Deliver prompt and appropriate acknowledgements to applicants.[38]

- Include third-party sources of information on your company such as articles, rankings, and awards.[39]

- Design separate sections for different types of job seekers, such as students and part-timers.[40] Leverage the power of the Internet to personalize each job seeker's experience.

- Have a direct link from the home page to the career page.

- Have a job search tool that allows applicants to search open job position by location and job category.
- Have a standardized application or résumé builder to allow for easy applicant screening.
- Utilize "e-mail to a friend" options for visitor referrals.[41]

In an effort to fill 400 job openings, Canadian pharmaceutical company Apotex put up six billboards near the facilities of its competitors around Toronto.

Print Advertising   Print advertising is a very common traditional method of recruiting. For advertising to bring the desired results, two issues must be addressed: the media to be used and the construction of the ad.[42] The selection of the best medium—whether it is the local newspaper, a national newspaper, a technical journal, or even a billboard—depends on the types of positions for which the organization is recruiting. Reaching individuals who are already employed and not actively seeking alternative employment requires a different medium than is appropriate to attract those who are unemployed.

To achieve optimum results from an advertisement, the following four-point guide, called *AIDA*, should be kept in mind as the ad is being constructed:

1. The ad should attract *attention*. The ads that stand out have borders, a company logo or picture, and effective use of empty white space. To attract attention, key positions should be advertised in display ads, rather than classified ads.

2. The ad should develop *interest* in the job. Interest can be created by the nature of the job itself, by pointing out the range of duties and/or the amount of challenge or responsibility involved. Sometimes other aspects of the job, such as its location or working conditions, are useful in attracting interest. To ensure that the individuals attracted are qualified, the job specifications should always be included.

3. The ad should create a *desire* for the job. This may be done by capitalizing on the interesting aspects of the job itself and by pointing out any unique benefits or opportunities associated with it, such as the opportunity for career development or travel. Desire may also be created by stressing the employer's commitment to employment equity. The target audience should be kept in mind as the ad is being created.

4. The ad should instigate *action*. To prompt action, ads often include a closing date and a statement such as "Call today," "Send your résumé today," "Check out our Web site for more information," or "Go to the site of our next job fair."

want ad A recruitment ad describing the job and its specifications, the compensation package, and the hiring employer. The address to which applications and/or résumés should be submitted is also provided.

blind ad A recruitment ad in which the identity and address of the employer are omitted.

When properly constructed, advertisements can be an effective instrument for recruiting, as well as for communicating the organization's corporate image to the general public. A newspaper ad incorporating the AIDA guidelines is shown in **Figure 5.5**.

There are two general types of newspaper advertisements: want ads and blind ads. **Want ads** describe the job and its specifications, the compensation package, and the hiring employer. While the content pertaining to the job, specifications, and compensation is identical in **blind ads**, such ads omit the identity

FIGURE 5.5   Recruitment Advertisement Illustrating AIDA Principles

Grow your career from the ground up.

Are you about to graduate in **Engineering (Systems/Industrial/others), Mathematics/ Operations Research, Logistics or Business** (B.Comm. or MBA combined with a technical degree or diploma)? And are you looking to launch your career with a national leader offering exceptional opportunities from coast to coast? Then Canada Post is where you want to be!

As part of our Development Stream, you will start by providing project support for initiatives that are critical to the success of the business, while acquiring invaluable technical, management and professional competencies, enabling you to assume greater responsibilities in future roles – including management positions. We have a number of opportunities for career-oriented team players with strong analytical skills, who are flexible to travel for extended periods of time, and are interested in growing and developing within our large, diverse organization. Some positions will require the use of both English and French, while others will require either English or French.

While you're learning about the Canada Post family of companies, you'll kick-start your career with assignments in major centres across the country, which may include: **Vancouver, Edmonton, Calgary, Winnipeg, London, Toronto, Ottawa, Montréal, Québec City** and **Halifax.**

Canada Post offers an attractive salary and a comprehensive benefits package, as well as extensive orientation, mentoring, and excellent prospects for career advancement. If you want a career where you'll keep learning, innovating, and contributing to world-class service for all Canadians, don't wait to forward your resumé, preferably by e-mail, **reference #14E2003,** by **April 22, 2003,** to: **Human Resources, Canada Post Corporation, N0030-2701 Riverside Drive, Ottawa, ON K1A 0B1. E-mail: jobs/emplois@canadapost.ca**

We thank all applicants, but advise that only those under consideration will be contacted. Canada Post Corporation is an Employment Equity Employer and welcomes applications from women, Aboriginal peoples, persons with disabilities and members of visible minorities.

CANADA POST   POSTES CANADA

From anywhere...   De partout...
to anyone   jusqu'à vous

www.canadapost.ca

Source: Reproduced with the permission of Canada Post.

and address of the hiring employer. While many job seekers do not like responding to blind ads, since there is always the danger of unknowingly sending a résumé to the firm at which they are currently employed, such ads do result in the opening remaining confidential (which may be necessary if the position is still staffed).

Many factors make advertising a useful recruiting method. Employers can use advertisements to reach and attract potential job applicants from a diverse labour market in as wide or narrow a geographical area as desired. In order to meet employment equity goals and timetables, ads can be placed in publications read by designated group members, such as a minority-language newspaper or the newsletter of a nonprofit agency assisting individuals who have a particular mental or physical disability.

Private Employment Agencies   Private employment agencies are often called upon to provide assistance to employers seeking clerical staff, functional specialists, and technical employees. The "staffing" business has grown into a $4 billion industry that places hundreds of thousands of job seekers each year.[43] Generally, it is the employer who pays the agency fee. It is not uncommon for employers to be charged a fee equal to 15 to 30 percent of the first year's salary of the individual hired through agency referral. This percentage may vary depending on the volume of business provided by the client and type of employee sought.

These agencies take an employer's request for recruits and then solicit job seekers, relying primarily on Internet job boards, advertising, and walk-ins/write-ins. Employment agencies serve two basic functions: expanding the applicant pool and performing preliminary interviewing and screening. Specific situations in which an employment agency might be used for recruiting include the following:

- The organization does not have an HR department or has no one with the requisite time and/or expertise.
- The firm has experienced difficulty in generating a pool of qualified candidates for the position or a similar type of position in the past.
- A particular opening must be filled quickly.
- There is a desire to recruit a greater number of designated group members than the firm has been able to attract on its own.
- The recruitment effort is aimed at reaching individuals who are currently employed and might therefore feel more comfortable answering ads placed by and dealing with an employment agency.

Tips **for the** Front Line

It should be noted, though, that the amount of service provided varies widely, as does the level of professionalism and the calibre of staff. While most agencies carefully screen applicants, some simply provide a stream of applicants and let the client's HR department staff do the screening. Agency staff are usually paid on a commission basis, and their desire to earn a commission may occasionally compromise their professionalism (for example, encouraging job seekers to accept jobs for which they are neither qualified nor suited).

Executive Search Firms   Employers retain executive search firms to fill critical positions in a firm, usually middle- to senior-level professional and managerial employees, with an average compensation level of $168 000.[44] Such firms often specialize in a particular type of talent, such as executives, sales, scientific, or middle-management employees. They typically know and understand the marketplace, have many contacts, and are especially adept at contacting qualified candidates who are employed and not actively looking to change jobs (which is why they have been given the nickname "headhunters").

Fees range from $10 000 to $50 000, and are often payable even if the employer terminates the search for any reason.[45] Generally, one-third of the fee is payable as a retainer at the outset. Compared to the value of the time savings realized by the client firm's executive team, however, such a fee often turns out to be insignificant.

There are some potential pitfalls to using this recruitment method.[46] Executive search firms cannot do an effective job if they are given inaccurate or incomplete information about the job and/or the firm. It is therefore essential for employers to explain in detail the type of candidate required—and why. A few headhunters are more salespeople than professionals, and are more interested in persuading the employer to hire a candidate than in finding one who really meets the job specifications. Some firms have also been known to present an unpromising candidate to a client simply to make their one or two other prospects look that much better. The Association of Canadian Search, Employment and Staffing Services (ACSESS) sponsors the certified personnel consultant (CPC) designation, which signifies that recruiters have met specific educational and testing requirements and confirms an individual's commitment to the best industry practices.[47]

Association of Canadian Search, Employee and Staffing Services (ACSESS) www.acsess.org

Walk-ins and Write-ins

Individuals who go to organizations in person to apply for jobs without referral or invitation are called *walk-ins*. People who submit unsolicited résumés to organizations are known as *write-ins*. Walk-ins and write-ins are an inexpensive recruitment method. Their résumés are generally screened by the HR department and if an applicant is considered suitable, his or her résumé is retained on file for a period of three to six months or passed on to the relevant department manager if there is an immediate or upcoming opening for which he or she is qualified. Some organizations, such as RBC Financial Group, are using computer databases to store the information found on the résumés and application forms of walk-in and write-in candidates. Whether the original document is paper-based or submitted online, it can be scanned and stored on databases for fast, easy access using a few key words.[48]

An Ethical
Dilemma

Is it ethical for HR professionals to engage in "headhunting" activities themselves, rather than relying on executive search firms to do so?

Employee Referrals

Some organizations encourage applications from friends and relatives of current employees by mounting an employee referral campaign. Openings are announced in the company's intranet or newsletter, along with a request for referrals. Cash awards or prizes may be offered for referrals that culminate in a new hire. Because there are no advertising or agency fees involved, paying bonuses such as these still represents a low recruiting cost.

UUNET Canada Inc., a Canadian-based Internet service provider, offers employees referral bonuses of $1500 for successful hires. The bonuses are successful —40 percent of the firm's sales and high-tech positions have been filled using the program.[49] At Edward Jones Investments, one-third of recruits are referred by current representatives.[50]

nepotism A preference for hiring relatives of current employees.

Disadvantages associated with employee referrals include the potential of inbreeding and **nepotism** to cause morale problems, and dissatisfaction of employees whose referral is not hired. Perhaps the biggest drawback, however, is that this method may result in systemic discrimination.

Educational Institutions

Recruiting at educational institutions is extremely effective when candidates require formal training but relatively little full-time work experience. High schools can provide recruits for clerical and blue-collar jobs. For example, the Ontario Trucking Association is recruiting in high schools for truck drivers, due to an impending shortage. Most Canadian universities and community colleges have placement centres that post informa-

Many companies take recruitment campaigns into high schools to sell a career to a younger generation. This type of recruitment helps a variety of industries meet future recruitment demands. Here, students learn how to work on a car.

Career Edge www.careeredge.org

Job Postings (Student Job Magazine) www.jobpostings.ca

Student Connection Program www.scp-ebb.com

tion about job openings provided by employers. Students apply to the placement centre, and a single package containing all applications received is submitted to the employer. The employer then selects those applicants who appear to best fit the job specifications and arranges with the centre to conduct interviews with those individuals on campus.

Most high schools, colleges, and universities have counselling centres that provide job-search assistance to students through activities such as skills assessment testing and workshops on résumé preparation and interview strategies. Sometimes they arrange for on-site job fairs, at which employers set up displays outlining the types of job opportunities available. The Halifax Joint Career Fair, a partnership between three of Nova Scotia's universities and colleges, was created to meet the recruiting demands of the growing film, arts, and culture industries. Every year, the event attracts about 100 companies from across the country, and 1300 to 1500 students.[51]

Cooperative (co-op) education and field placement programs have become increasingly popular in Canada. These programs require students to spend a specified period of time working in organizations as an integral part of their academic program, thereby gaining some hands-on skills in an actual work setting. Co-op programs are now offered in some high schools, as well as in colleges and universities.

Summer *internship programs* hire college and/or university students to complete summer projects between their second-last and final year of study. Their performance is assessed, and those who are judged to be superior are offered permanent positions following graduation. Other firms offer internship opportunities to graduates, thereby enabling them to acquire hands-on skills to supplement their education. As with student internships, outstanding performers are often offered full-time employment at the end of the program. It is now possible for firms to recruit graduate interns online through Career Edge, an organization committed to helping university, college, and high-school graduates gain essential career-related experience through internships. Career Edge uses the Internet as its sole means of bringing companies and youth together. Over 5000 young Canadians have started their careers through the program in over 700 organizations. Within a few months of completing their internship, nearly 85 percent of interns have found permanent employment with competitive salaries and nearly 60 percent of the interns are hired by host organizations on a full-time basis.

Internship, co-op, and field placement programs can produce a win–win result. The employer is provided with an inexpensive opportunity to assess potential employees, while benefiting from the current knowledge and enthusiasm of bright, talented individuals. Because co-op students and interns have been exposed to the organization, they are less likely to leave shortly after permanent hire than recruits with no previous exposure to the firm.[52] Recognizing these benefits has made such programs a major recruitment method in many organizations. Toronto-based Franklin Templeton Investments was awarded the Outstanding Business and Education award for its co-op programs by the Conference Board of Canada in 2001. About 70 percent of the college students who participated in the company's co-op programs return as full-time employees. The company meets its staffing needs and the students obtain sound business experience, creating a win-win situation.[53]

Electronic Labour Exchange (ELE)
www.electroniclabourexchange.
ca

Federal Government Job Bank
www.jobbank.gc.ca

Work Search
www.worksearch.gc.ca

The JobsMARKETS
www.jobsmarket.org

ON-SITE www.epi.ca

CA Source www.casource.com

Human Resources Development Canada (HRDC)

Through various programs, including those for youth, Aboriginals, and persons with disabilities, HRDC helps unemployed individuals to find suitable jobs and employers to locate qualified candidates to meet their needs—at no cost to either party. The Job Bank is the largest Web-based network of job postings available to Canadian employers free of charge, as it provides access to over 46 000 jobs at any given time, with up to 2000 new jobs posted every day. HRDC also operates the Electronic Labour Exchange (ELE), a Web-based recruitment tool that can match employers' skill requirements with individuals' skill sets using the *National Occupational Classification (NOC)*. Job seekers complete a quick and easy skills profile, and registered employers match their job requirements to people with the skills, education, and experience they are looking for. Experience shows that employers find a suitable match about 80 percent of the time.

Professional and Trade Associations

Professional and trade associations can be extremely helpful when recruiters are seeking individuals with specialized skills in fields such as IT, engineering, HR, and accounting, particularly if experience is a job requirement. Many such associations conduct ongoing placement activities on behalf of their members, and most regularly send all of their members newsletters or magazines in which organizations can place job advertisements. Such advertising may attract individuals who hadn't previously thought about changing jobs, as well as those actively seeking employment. For example, the HRPAO has an employment service called the Hire Authority, where for a nominal fee, employers can post an HR-related employment opportunity on the HRPAO Web site, where it can be viewed by HRPAO members. Additionally, employers can pay for access to an online database of member résumés, search, sort, and pre-screen qualified candidates for a vacant position.[54]

Labour Organizations

Some firms, particularly in the construction industry, obtain recruits through union hiring halls. The union maintains a roster of members (typically skilled tradespeople such as carpenters, pipe fitters, welders, plumbers, and electricians), whom it sends out on assignment as requests from employers are received. Once the union members have completed their contracted work at one firm, they notify the union of their availability for another assignment.

Military Personnel   Military reservists are also potential recruits. The Canadian Forces Liaison Council (CFLC) is responsible for promoting the hiring of reservists by civilian employers. The CFLC also encourages civilian employers to give reservists time off for military training. Reserve force training develops skills and attributes sought after in the civilian workforce, such as leadership, planning, coordination, and teamwork.[55] Many organizations—such as Aldeavision Inc. of Quebec and Bristol Aerospace in Winnipeg—have recognized the value of such leave, and have joined the 3200 organizations in Canada that have signed a Statement of Support for the Reserve Forces with the CFLC.[56] More than 550 employers have sent the CFLC copies of HR policies that provide reservists in their employ with time off with no adversarial effects on their employment status.[57] The CFLC's Reserve Employment Assistance Program (REAP) allows employers to place job postings for skilled personnel at more that 300 military units across the country at no charge.[58]

Open Houses and Job Fairs   Another popular recruitment method involves holding an *open house*. Common in retail firms looking to staff a new store from the ground up, open houses have also been the choice of corporations trying to draw out scarce talent in an ultra-tight job market. A similar recruitment method involves holding a *job fair* on-site. At such events, recruiters share information about the organization and job opportunities in an informal, relaxed setting with those attending. Top prospects are invited to visit the firm or to return at a later date for a more in-depth assessment. Recently, job fairs have begun to be held online, as described in the HR.Net box.

The Canadian Force Liaison Council (CFLC)
www.cflc.forces.gc.ca

HR.Net

Virtual Career Fairs

The oil and gas industry in Alberta is facing a severe labour shortage across all areas of the sector, which is only expected to get worse. Over the past few years, employers have been doing everything they could to lure workers from across the country, but have essentially drained the supply. They are now trying to recruit qualified people from oil and gas fields in other countries. Increases in technology and oil exploration efforts have created a greater need for experienced and qualified workers. Many full-time careers and job openings for full-time, year-round employment have been created in an industry that had been plagued with the image of temporary, seasonal employment—as most of the drilling for oil takes place in the winter months when the frozen ground makes it easier to send heavy equipment to remote areas across rugged terrain. But how do you attract international workers to an industry known for low-skilled jobs with little opportunity for growth and development?

The Petroleum Services Association of Canada (PSAC) turned to the Web as a way to attract qualified workers internationally, and created a "virtual" career fair that promoted career opportunities in the industry. By going to the Web site (at www.careersinoilandgas.com), interested individuals can access job listings, training offerings, day-in-the-life tours of several different positions, and other general information about the oil and gas industry in Alberta. PSAC hopes that their efforts will help the companies in the industry with their recruitment efforts for qualified international candidates by dispelling some of the myths about its work environment and career opportunities.

Source: D. Brown, "New HR Strategies Needed to Staff Oil Patch," *Canadian HR Reporter* (January 27, 2003), pp. 1, 6. Reproduced by permission of *Canadian HR Reporter*, Carswell, One Corporate Plaza, 2075 Kennedy Road, Scarborough, ON M1T 3V4.

In today's competitive recruiting environment, creativity, innovation, and use of a combination of recruitment methods can increase the effectiveness of a recruitment campaign, as explained in the Strategic HR box.

Recruiting Nonpermanent Staff

In recent years, many companies have increased their use of contingent workers in order to attain labour flexibility and to acquire employees with special skills on an as-needed basis. In these firms, recruiters are spending more time seeking temporary (term, seasonal, casual) and contract workers and less time recruiting permanent staff.[59] Three sources of nonpermanent staff are temporary help agencies, contract workers, and employee leasing.

Temporary Help Agencies

Temporary help agencies, such as Kelly Services and Office Overload, exist in all major cities in Canada. They specialize in providing temporary workers to cover for employees who are ill, on vacation, or on a leave of absence. Firms also use temporary employees to handle seasonal work, peak workloads, and special projects for which there are no current employees with time and/or expertise. Temporary workers are agency employees, and are reassigned to another employer when their services are no longer required.

Temps provide employers with three major benefits:

1. They cost much less than permanent employees, as they generally receive less compensation than permanent staff. There are also savings related to the hiring and training costs associated with permanent employees. In fact, training has become the central investment in the business strategy of many temporary employment agencies. For example, Accountemps invests in the skills and training of employees after they have worked for a specified

STRATEGIC HR

A Comprehensive Approach to Recruiting

The boom in the video game market means that Electronic Arts (EA), a British Columbia-based video game manufacturer, has to be creative in its attempts to attract top talent. EA employs 38 000 individuals worldwide, and when it needed to fill 130 positions in British Columbia, it turned to its key supporters—its customers. In the back of game manuals, the company has an ad that states, "Get in the game. Want to join the #1 interactive entertainment company?" and directs the potential candidate to the Web site for the company's recruitment page. Trudy Miller, corporate communications manager for EA, says it is a great way for the company to reach the core gamer, "because the one thing that just about everyone in this company has in common is a passion for games."

EA gears the vast amount of its recruiting efforts toward universities and colleges, visiting campuses several times a year. And hosting beer and pizza parties, setting up video games, information sessions, and speeches—anything they can think of that is fun to attract attention—to get to know students and collect résumés. The company also has a separate Web site, called "EA Academy," which lists information about internships and the benefits of working for EA. Open houses, employee referral programs, internships, and co-op programs, as well as involvement with post-secondary institutions, round out what the company calls "a very effective and comprehensive approach to recruiting."

Source: T. Humber, "Playing the Recruitment Game," *Canadian HR Reporter* (May 19, 2003), pp. G3, G6. Reproduced by permission of *Canadian HR Reporter*, Carswell, One Corporate Plaza, 2075 Kennedy Road, Scarborough, ON M1T 3V4.

amount of time. This includes online tutoring in software they may use on the job and tuition reimbursement for skills training.[60]

2. If a temp performs unsatisfactorily, a substitute can be requested immediately. Generally, a suitable replacement is sent to the firm within one business day.

3. Individuals working as temps who are seeking full-time employment are often highly motivated, knowing that many firms choose full-time employees from the ranks of their top-performing temps.

contract workers Employees who develop work relationships directly with the employer for a specific type of work or period of time.

Contract Workers   **Contract workers** are employees who develop work relationships directly with the employer for a specific type of work or period of time.[61] For example, Parc Aviation is a major supplier of contract workers to the airline industry. Airline organizations benefit from the services of contract engineers by having them cover seasonal or unplanned peaks in business, carry out special tasks or projects and reduce the necessity for airlines to downsize permanent staff during cyclical downturns.[62]

Many professionals with specialized skills become contract workers, including project managers, accountants, and lawyers. Some have consciously made a decision to work for themselves; others have been unable to obtain full-time employment in their field of expertise or have found themselves out of a full-time job due to cutbacks. Thus, some wish to remain self-employed; others work a contract in hope of obtaining a full-time position eventually. Some firms hire former employees (such as retirees) on a contract basis.

Contract executives such as CEOs and CFOs now account for 10 percent of Canadian management positions.[63] Executives are often contracted if a company is facing a crisis and needs leadership and expertise, but does not have time for the normal 60- to 90-day search process. Eighty percent of contract executives are filled within 10 days by executive search firms like Caldwell Partners International.[64] CEOs are often put on contract in a start-up or in circumstances where the company feels that in six to twelve months they may need a different type of leader or manager. Contracting executives is an excellent way for a company to access high levels of expertise while maintaining flexibility and keeping costs, such as severance packages, down. Companies that have successfully used interim, contracted executives include Labatt-Interbrew, Thomas Cook, and Sunnybrook & Women's College Health Sciences Centre in Toronto.[65]

employee leasing An arrangement that typically involves a company transferring specific employees to the payroll of an employee leasing firm or Professional Employer Organization (PEO) in an explicit joint-employment relationship.

National Association of Professional Employer Organizations (NAPEO)
www.napeo.org

Employee Leasing   **Employee leasing** arrangements typically involve a company transferring specific employees to the payroll of an employee leasing firm or Professional Employer Organization (PEO) in an explicit joint-employment relationship. These employees then become employees of the PEO, which leases these individuals back to the client company on a permanent basis. The PEO maintains the HR files for the leased employees, handles the administration of their pay and benefits, and performs most of the other functions normally handled by a firm's HR department staff members. In return, the PEO receives a placement fee—typically 2–5 percent of payroll to cover their expenses, plus 9–12 percent of gross wages to pay for benefits and cover their profit.[66]

Not all leasing arrangements are based on the transfer of staff from the client organizations to a PEO. Some leasing companies also hire workers themselves and then lease them out to client organizations. For example, Helmac Products

Corp., with offices in Toronto, Michigan, the U.K. and Hong Kong, has hired a PEO to handle HR, including payroll, for the company's employees.[67]

RECRUITING A MORE DIVERSE WORKFORCE

Recruiting a diverse workforce is not just socially responsible—it's a necessity. As noted previously, the composition of Canada's workforce is changing dramatically. Trends of particular significance include a decrease in the availability of young workers, the increasing necessity for hiring older employees, and an increase in the number of women, visible minorities, Aboriginal people, and persons with disabilities in the workforce.

Attracting Older Workers

Many employers, recognizing the fact that the workforce is aging, are encouraging retirement-age employees to stay with the company or are actively recruiting employees who are at or beyond retirement age. There are significant benefits to hiring and retaining older employees. These include high job satisfaction; a strong sense of loyalty and organizational commitment; a strong work ethic; good people skills; and willingness to work in a variety of roles, including part-time.[68]

In order to make a company attractive to older workers, it is important to deal with stereotypical attitudes toward older workers through education, ensure that HR policies do not discourage recruitment of older workers, develop flexible work options, and redesign jobs to accommodate decreased dexterity and strength.

Attracting Younger Employees

Many firms are recognizing the benefits of a multigenerational workforce, and are not only trying to attract older workers, but are taking steps to address the pending shortage of younger employees. While older employees have comparatively wider experience and wisdom, the young bring energy, enthusiasm, and physical strength to their positions. At any given time, GlaxoSmithKline has 250 life-sciences students in internship or co-op programs in all divisions of the company. This ensures that they have a "robust pipeline of talent." However, there are areas within the company where it is difficult to place candidates with little industry experience. For those, GlaxoSmithKline recently created a handful of positions reserved for high-potential recent graduates with relevant educational background but very little or no experience.[69]

Successful organizations balance these different kinds of experience. McDonald's Restaurants of Canada Ltd. (one of the largest employers of youth in the country and an active recruiter of seniors) feels that it is critical for organizations in the service industry to have employees who mirror their customer base. Their experience is that each member of their multi-age teams brings a particular strength, which leads to synergy, respect, and team-building.[70]

Recruiting Designated Group Members

Most of the recruitment methods discussed previously can be used to attract designated group members, provided that the employer's commitment to equity

Canadian Council for Aboriginal Business www.ccab-canada.com

AboriginalBiz
www.aboriginalbiz.com

Canadian Council for
Rehabilitation and Work—
WORKink www.workink.com

Centre for Advancement in Work
and Living www.cawl.org

Ontario Ministry of Citizenship,
Culture & Recreation—Equal
Opportunity and Disability Access
Branch
www.equalopportunity.on.ca.

and diversity is made clear to all involved in the recruitment process—whether it is employees asked for referrals or private employment agencies. This can also be stressed in all recruitment advertising. Alternative publications targeted at designated group members should be considered for advertising, and linkages can be formed with organizations and agencies specializing in assisting designated group members. Specific examples follow:

- Aboriginal and non-Aboriginal companies and individuals who are members and supporters of the Canadian Council for Aboriginal Business (CCAB) can post jobs of interest to Aboriginal applicants free of charge in the employment section of their business Web site at www.aboriginalbiz. com.[71]

- CCAB has teamed with monster.com to create a national database of résumés of qualified Aboriginal people as well as careers and jobs of interest to Aboriginal people.[72]

- WORKink, a virtual employment centre for people with disabilities, is directed by the Canadian Council on Rehabilitation and Work and is administered in conjunction with provincial/territorial partners. Employers can post job openings free of charge, browse résumés of people with disabilities, or access information on how to adapt the work environment to accommodate disabled persons in their region.[73]

- The Society for Canadian Women in Science and Technology (SCWIST) is a nonprofit, volunteer organization aimed at the improvement of attitudes and stereotypes about, and assistance to, women in scientific, technological, and engineering careers. Employers can access valuable information about resources, such as Web sites, employment agencies, and publications, to attract professional women for employment opportunities in industries where they generally have a low representation.[74]

Two recent publications aimed at ensuring that persons with disabilities are integrated into the workplace are available through the Centre for Management of Community Services. *Opportunity Knocks* is a how-to guide for community agencies to assist them in convincing employers to hire people with disabilities. *It's a Smart Move* targets the corporate sector, and dispels many of the common myths associated with hiring people with disabilities. These include fears that hiring such employees causes Workers' Compensation premiums to rise and that it's impossible to interview candidates with disabilities without violating human rights legislation. Both publications include case studies of organizations committed to adding persons with disabilities to their workforce, such as Canada Trust, McDonald's, Wal-Mart, and the Bank of Montreal. According to the firms interviewed for the employer profiles, there are many advantages to hiring individuals with disabilities, including access to a broader pool of job candidates, enhanced corporate image, a more reliable workforce, lower staff turnover, a workforce better prepared to deal with customers or clients with disabilities, improved staff morale, and better customer service.[75] More information on hiring people with disabilities is provided in the Workforce Diversity box.

WORKFORCE DIVERSITY

Tapping the Talents of People with Disabilities

Employers say they're keen to hire people with disabilities—they just haven't. Obstacles include weak support from line management, union, and employees, lack of resources, and little accountability for results. People with disabilities say that the greatest single barrier is not the disability itself, but the attitudinal barriers and misperceptions about their skills and ability to add value in a workplace setting.

Creating an inclusive culture is an exercise in fundamental change that begins with a directive at the most senior level, is integrated into management practices, and is monitored for progress. Workspace and facility considerations are important: consult with the disabled individual, who is an expert in explaining any needs for accommodation; be flexible and ready to modify jobs; and provide the appropriate technical assistive devices, which range from simple magnification devices to Web browsers with voice synthesizers.

Another problem is the lack of experience going outside "mainstream" sources to find and recruit personnel. The Ontario Ministry of Citizenship's Paths to Equal Opportunity Web site (www.equalopportunity.on.ca) is an excellent place to start, even for organizations not based in Ontario. There are also several national and community-based organizations that provide general information about hiring and accommodating people with disabilities, such as the Canadian

Council on Rehabilitation and Work's WORKink Web site (www.ccrw.org/ccrw/en/wink.htm). Another useful tool is the guidebook *Tapping the Talents of People With Disabilities: A Guidebook for Employers*, which is available through the Conference Board of Canada.

Developing contacts with agencies that serve the needs of people with disabilities can also help. Tricia Pokorny, special needs coordinator at Casino Niagara in Niagara Falls, Ontario found good local contacts through the Niagara Employment Alliance, an umbrella agency that coordinates community and employment services for local chapters of organizations that provide services to people with disabilities. Participation in job fairs for persons with disabilities is another way to let the community know that an organization appreciates diversity. Some leading employers and agencies have partnered to develop intensive, job-specific training programs. An example is the 24-week retail associate training program developed and managed for Wal-Mart Canada by the Canadian Council on Rehabilitation and Work.

After years of exclusion of people with disabilities from the workforce, inclusiveness implies a profound cultural shift. The reward is top-quality recruits—it just so happens that some will be people with disabilities.

Source: R. Wright, "From Exclusion to Inclusion: Tapping the Talents of People with Disabilities," *Canadian HR Reporter* (February 11, 2002), pp. G7–G9. Reproduced by permission of *Canadian HR Reporter*, Carswell, One Corporate Plaza, 2075 Kennedy Road, Scarborough, ON M1T 3V4.

DEVELOPING AND USING APPLICATION FORMS

Most firms require that a standardized company application form be completed, even if a résumé has been submitted.

For most employers, completion of an application form is the last step in the recruitment process. An application form provides an efficient means of collecting verifiable historical data from each candidate in a standardized format; it usually includes information about education, prior work history, and other job-related skills.

A completed application form can provide the recruiter with information on the applicant's education and experience, a brief overview of the applicant's career progress and growth, and information that can be used to predict whether or not the candidate will succeed on the job. Even when detailed résumés have been submitted, most firms also request that a standardized company application form be completed. There are many reasons for this practice:

- Candidate comparison is facilitated because information is collected in a uniform manner.
- The information that the company requires (such as gaps in work history) is specifically requested, rather than just what the candidate wishes to reveal.
- Candidates are typically asked to complete an application form while on the company premises, and thus is a sample of the candidate's own work. (Obtaining assistance with résumés is common, given that many job boards offer online résumé building options.)
- Application forms typically ask the candidate to provide written authorization for reference checking. A photocopy of this section can be provided to individuals being asked for references.
- Candidates are asked to acknowledge that the information provided is true and accurate, which protects the company from applicants who falsify their credentials.
- Many application forms today have an optional section regarding designated group member status. An example is provided in **Figure 5.6**. The data collected are used for employment equity tracking purposes.

FIGURE 5.6   Self-Identification for Employment Equity Purposes

Employee Self-Identification Form

(Confidential when completed)

- This form is designed to collect information on the composition of the Public Service workforce to comply with legislation on employment equity and to facilitate the planning and implementation of employment equity activities. Your response is voluntary and you may identify in more than one designated group.
- The information you provide will be used in compiling statistics on employment equity in the federal Public Service. With your consent (see Box E), it may also be used by the employment equity coordinator of your department for human resource management purposes. This includes referral for training and developmental assignments and, in the case of persons with disabilities, facilitating appropriate accommodation in the workplace.
- Employment equity information will be retained in the Employment Equity Data Bank (EEDB) of the Treasury Board Secretariat and its confidentiality is protected under the *Privacy Act*. You have the right to review and correct information about yourself and can be assured that it will not be used for unauthorized purposes.
- If you need more information or require assistance in completing this form, please contact _____ at _____. This form is also available in Braille, large print and on diskette and audio-cassette.

Step 1:   Complete boxes A to E. In boxes B, C and D, refer to the definitions provided.

Step 2:   Sign and date the form and return it in the attached envelope

Thank you for your cooperation.

TBS/PPB 300-02432
TBS/SCT 330-78 (Rev. 1999–02)

A.

Family Name   Given Name and Initial

continued

Department or Agency/Branch

( )

Telephone # (office)

Personal Record Identifier (PRI)

○ Female   ○ Male

B. A person with a disability (i) has a long-term or recurring physical, mental, sensory, psychiatric, or learning impairment and

a) considers himself/herself to be disadvantaged in employment by reason of that impairment, or

b) believes that an employer or potential employer is likely to consider him/her to be disadvantaged in employment by reason of that impairment, and includes persons whose functional limitations owing to their impairment have been accommodated in their current job or workplace.

ARE YOU A PERSON WITH A DISABILITY?

○ No

○ Yes, check all that apply

11 ○ Coordination or dexterity (difficulty using hands or arms, for example, grasping or handling a stapler or using a keyboard)

12 ○ Mobility (difficulty moving around, for example, from one office to another or up and down stairs)

16 ○ Blind or visual impairment (unable to see or difficulty seeing)

19 ○ Deaf or hard of hearing (unable to hear or difficulty hearing)

13 ○ Speech impairment (unable to speak or difficulty speaking and being understood)

23 ○ Other disability (including learning disabilities, developmental disabilities and all other types of disabilities)

(Please specify) _____

C. An Aboriginal person is a North American Indian or a member of the First Nation, a Métis, or Inuit. North American Indians or members of a First Nation include status, treaty or registered Indians, as well as non-status and non-registered Indians.

ARE YOU AN ABORIGINAL PERSON?

○ No

○ Yes, check the appropriate circle

03 ○ North American Indian/First Nation

02 ○ Métis

01 ○ Inuit

D. A person in a visible minority in Canada is someone (other than an Aboriginal person as defined in C above) who is non-white in colour/race, regardless of place of birth.

ARE YOU IN A VISIBLE MINORITY GROUP?

○ No

○ Yes, check the circle which best describes your visible minority group or origin

41 ○ Black

45 ○ Chinese

51 ○ Filipino

47 ○ Japanese

48 ○ Korean

56 ○ South Asian/East Indian (including Indian from India; Bangladesh; Pakistani; East Indian from Guyana; Trinidad; East Africa; etc.)

58 ○ Southeast Asian (including Burmese; Cambodian; Laotian; Thai; Vietnamese; etc.)

57 ○ Non-White West Asian, North African and Arab (including Egyptian; Libyan; Lebanese; Iranian; etc.)

42 ○ Non-White Latin American (including indigenous persons from Central and South America, etc.)

44 ○ Persons of Mixed Origin (with one parent in one of the visible minority groups listed above)

59 ○ Other Visible Minority Group

(Please specify) _____

E. 99 ○ The information in this form may be used for human resources management.

_____   _____
29 Signature   Date (DD/MM/YY)

Modified: 2003–02-19

Source: Employee Self-Identification Form, www.tbs-sct.gc.ca/ee/survey-sondage/form-formulaire_e.asp, Treasury Board of Canada, Secretariat 2003. Reproduced with the permission of the Minister of Public Works and Government Services, 2004.

Human Rights Legislation and Application Forms

Application forms cannot ask questions that would directly or indirectly classify candidates on the basis of any of the prohibited grounds under human rights legislation. Thus, candidates should not be asked to supply any of the following on an application form:

Hints to Ensure Legal Compliance

- information that could lead to direct, intentional discrimination such as age, gender, sexual orientation, marital status, maiden name, date of birth, place of origin, number of dependants, etc.
- an indication of whether he or she would prefer to be addressed as Mr./Mrs./Miss/Ms.
- his or her social insurance number
- a photograph
- information pertaining to citizenship
- information about height and weight (unless this is a bona fide job requirement)
- an indication of his or her mother tongue or how any language skills possessed were acquired
- the name, address, and dates of educational institutions attended
- information about illnesses, disabilities, or workers' compensation claims
- information on accommodation requirements
- information about military service
- information pertaining to arrests and/or criminal record
- his or her religious affiliation or ability to work on specific religious holidays.

If there are illegal questions on an application form, an unsuccessful candidate may challenge the legality of the entire recruitment and selection processes. In such case, the burden of proof is on the employer. Thus, taking human rights legislative requirements into consideration when designing application forms is imperative. The *Guide to Screening and Selection in Employment* in the Appendix to Chapter 2 provides helpful hints. Specific guidelines regarding questions that can and cannot be asked on application forms are available through the human rights commissions in each jurisdiction. **Figure 5.7**, a sample application form developed by the Ontario Human Rights Commission, illustrates the types of information that can legally be requested.

FIGURE 5.7   Sample Application Form

Sample Application for Employment

Position being applied for _____   Date available for work _____

PERSONAL DATA

Last name _____   Given name(s) _____

Address _____   Apt. No. _____

Home Telephone Number _____

City _____   Province _____   Postal Code _____

Business Telephone Number _____

Are you legally eligible to work in Canada?   Yes ☐   No ☐

Are you 18 years or more and less than 65 years of age?   Yes ☐   No ☐

Are you willing to relocate in Ontario?   Yes ☐   No ☐

Preferred Location _____

To determine your qualification for employment, please provide below and on the reverse, information related to your academic and other achievements including volunteer work, as well as employment history. Additional information may be attached on a separate sheet.

_____

EDUCATION

SECONDARY SCHOOL ☐

BUSINESS OR TRADE SCHOOL ☐

Highest grade or level completed _____   Name of program _____

Length of program _____

Diploma, certificate or license awarded?

Yes ☐   No ☐   Honours ☐   Type: _____

_____

COMMUNITY COLLEGE ☐   UNIVERSITY ☐

Major subject _____   Name of Program _____

Length of Program _____

Degree, diploma or certificate awarded.   Type:

Yes ☐   No ☐   Honours ☐

Other courses, workshops, seminars Licenses, Certificates, Degrees

_____

WORK-RELATED SKILLS

Describe any of your work-related skills, experience, or training that relate to the position being applied.

EMPLOYMENT

Name of present/last employer _____   Job title _____

Period of employment (includes leaves of absence related to maternity/parental leave, Workers' Compensation claims, handicap/disability, or human rights complaints)

From _____   To _____   Salary _____

Reason for leaving (do not include leaves of absence related to maternity/parental leave, Workers' Compensation claims, handicap/disability, or human rights complaints)

Functions/Responsibilities _____

_____

Name of previous employer _____ Job title _____

Period of employment (includes leaves of absence related to maternity/parental leave, Workplace Safety & Insurance claims, disability, or human rights complaints)

From _____ To _____ Salary _____

Reason for leaving (do not include leaves of absence related to maternity/parental leave, Workplace Safety & Insurance claims, disability, or human rights complaints)

Functions/Responsibilities _____

For employment references we may approach:

Your present/last employer?   Yes ☐   No ☐

Your former employer(s)?   Yes ☐   No ☐

List references if different than above on a separate sheet. _____

_____

PERSONAL INTEREST AND ACTIVITIES (civic, athletic, etc.) _____

_____

I hereby declare that the foregoing information is true and complete to my knowledge. I understand that a false statement may disqualify me from employment, or cause my dismissal.

Have you attached an additional sheet?

Yes ☐   No ☐

Signature _____   Date _____

Source: Human Rights at Work (Toronto: Ontario Human Rights Commission, 1999), pp. 108–110. © Queen's Printer for Ontario, 1999. Reproduced with permission.

AN ETHICAL DILEMMA

There is a job that you really want. However, the application form that you have been asked to complete has a number of illegal questions, including date of birth, marital status, number of dependants, and religious affiliation. How would you handle this?

Using Application Forms to Predict Job Performance

Some firms use application forms to predict which candidates will be successful and which will not, in much the same way that employers use tests for screening.

One approach involves designing a **weighted application blank (WAB)**. Statistical studies are conducted to find the relationship between (1) responses on the application form and (2) measures of success on the job. A scoring system is subsequently developed by weighting the different possible responses to those particular items. By scoring an applicant's response to each of those questions and then totalling the scores obtained, a composite score can be calculated for each applicant. Although studies have shown that WABs can be highly valid predictors, and they can be developed fairly easily, such forms are used by relatively few organizations.

Another type of application form that can be used to predict performance is a **biographical information blank (BIB)**, also known as a biodata form.[76] Essentially, it is a more detailed version of an application form, focusing on biographical data found to be predictive of job success. Candidates respond to a series of questions about their background, experiences, and preferences, including willingness to travel and leisure activities, as shown in **Figure 5.8**. Because biographical questions rarely have right or wrong answers, BIBs are difficult to fake. The development of a BIB requires that the items that are valid predictors of job success be identified and that weights be established for

weighted application blank (WAB) A job application form on which applicant responses have been weighted based on their statistical relationship to measures of job success.

biographical information blank (BIB) A detailed job application form requesting biographical data found to be predictive of success on the job, pertaining to background, experiences, and preferences. As with a WAB, responses are scored.

different responses to these items. By totalling the scores for each item, it is possible to obtain a composite score for each applicant.

FIGURE 5.8   Example of a Biographical Information Blank

Example of a Biographical Information Bank

Name _____   Address _____   Number of Dependents_____

How long have you lived at your current address? _____

Do you consider your net worth to be low _____   moderate _____   or high _____?

Have you ever been turned down for a loan?   Yes _____   No _____

How many credit cards do you have? _____

Highest level of education completed: High School _____   Vocational School _____

College _____   University _____   Postgraduate _____

What educational degrees do you have?   B.A. _____   B.Sc. _____   B.Comm. _____

M.B.A. _____   Master's _____   Other _____

What subjects did you major in? _____

What was your grade-point average?   A _____   B _____   C _____   D _____

Did you graduate with honours?   Yes _____   No _____

Did you receive any awards for academic excellence?   Yes _____   No _____

Did you receive any scholarships?   Yes _____   No _____

List any extracurricular activities you participated in during school:

_____

Did you find school stimulating _____   boring _____?

Did you hold a job while attending school?   Yes _____   No _____

How did you pay for your post-high-school training? (Check as many as appropriate)

Parents paid _____   Loans _____   Scholarships _____   Paid own way _____

Have you ever held a job where you earned commissions on sales?   Yes _____   No _____

If "Yes," were your commissions low _____   moderate _____   high _____?

Five years from now, what do you expect your salary to be? _____

Do you enjoy meeting new people?   Yes _____   No _____

How many social phone calls do you receive a week? _____

Do people count on you to "cheer up" others?   Yes _____   No _____

How many parties do you go to in a year? _____

Do you enjoy talking to people?   Yes _____   No _____

Rate your conversational skills:

Excellent _____   Very Good _____   Good _____   Fair _____   Poor _____

How often do you introduce yourself to other people you don't know?

Always _____   Sometimes _____   Never _____

Do you enjoy social gatherings?   Yes _____   No _____

Do you go to social gatherings out of a sense of duty?   Yes _____   No _____

How many times a year do you go out to dinner with friends? _____

Do you enjoy talking to people you don't know?   Yes _____   No _____

What nonwork-related social activities are you engaged in? _____

What are your hobbies?

_____

What sports, recreational, or physical activities do you engage in?

_____

How confident are you in your ability to succeed?

Very Confident _____   Confident _____   Somewhat Confident _____

Common Pitfalls during Recruitment

...Ten common pitfalls [during recruitment] are as follows:

1. There is no real need for the role, which can be met by others, or the role changes rapidly after recruitment. Job analysis and the drawing up of the job specification to accommodate future change will help reduce this risk.

2. Advertising is poorly targeted, or the job undersold, resulting in a poor pool of candidates. A key aim is to ensure that the best possible people apply. A good selection process can be completely negated if selection is among poor candidates.

3. An external candidate is hired to a vacancy not posted internally, giving rise to resentment and a reduction in development opportunities.

4. A job is oversold to a candidate and false promises made to attract a new recruit. These nearly always backfire. Unrealistic expectations result in culture shock and may give rise to claims of wrongful hire.

5. Shortlisting discards good candidates by too rigid a set of criteria of selection (e.g., the inexperienced with high potential may be inappropriately ruled out).

6. Interviews are too short, hurried and conducted poorly. The evidence suggests that with moderate guidance, managers' interviewing skills can be significantly enhanced.

7. Good selection data are wasted by too hasty a final decision-making process and an over-reliance on the hunches of the most senior manager.

8. Psychometric tests are used inappropriately, without due regard to their limitations or issues of adverse impact and unfair discrimination.

9. So-called "experts" (consultants, psychometricians, graphologists ... take over the process so that a line manager feels little ownership of the selection decision. When problems arise, they correctly blame others and try to overturn a decision rather than working with it.

10. A candidate oversells his or her strengths, creating stress and personal discomfort on arrival. Modern recruitment processes encourage individuals to appraise their own skills honestly in relation to a role.

Source: Excerpted with permission from *Secord's A–Z Guide for Human Resources Practitioners*, published by and copyright CCH Canadian Limited, Toronto, Ontario.

CHAPTER *Review*

Summary

1 Recruitment is the process of searching out and attracting qualified job applicants. It begins with the identification of a position that requires staffing, and is completed when résumés and/or completed application forms are received from an adequate number of applicants. The purposes of recruitment are to generate an adequate pool of well-qualified applicants suited to the organization's culture, and to help the organization meet its employment equity goals.

2 There are four steps in the recruitment process. First, job openings are identified through HR planning or manager request. Second, the job description and job specification are then reviewed to determine the job requirements. Third, appropriate recruiting source(s) and method(s) are chosen. Fourth, using these strategies, a pool of qualified candidates is generated.

3 Job posting is the process of notifying existing employees about vacant positions. Human resources records may indicate appropriate applicants for vacant positions. Skills inventories may provide even better information.

4 External recruitment methods include online recruiting, print advertising, private employment agencies, executive search firms, walk-ins/write-ins, employee referrals, educational institutions, HRDC, professional and

trade associations, labour organizations, military personnel, and open houses/job fairs.

5 Three strategies for obtaining nonpermanent staff include using temporary help agencies, hiring contract workers, and leasing employees.

6 Recruiting a diverse workforce is a necessity, given the shrinking labour force. In particular, recruiters are trying to attract older workers, younger workers, women, visible minorities, Aboriginal people, and people with disabilities.

7 Application forms are important because they provide information on the applicant's education and experience, a brief overview of the applicant's career progress, and information that can be used to predict whether an applicant will succeed on the job.

Key Terms

biographical information blank (BIB)   *(p. 161)*
blind ad   *(p. 145)*
contract workers   *(p. 153)*

employee leasing   *(p. 153)*
job posting   *(p. 138)*
nepotism   *(p. 148)*
online recruitment   *(p. 142)*
recruiter   *(p. 134)*
recruitment   *(p. 134)*
want ad   *(p. 145)*
weighted application blank (WAB)   *(p. 161)*
yield ratio   *(p. 141)*

Review and Discussion Questions

1 Discuss the advantages and disadvantages of recruiting within the organization.

2 List the advantages of external recruitment.

3 Explain the difference between an Internet job board and a corporate career Web site.

4 Describe the AIDA guidelines for print advertising.

5 Under what circumstances should a private employment agency be used?

6 Describe three ways to recruit designated group members.

CRITICAL *Thinking Questions*

1 What potential problems could be created by offering referral bonuses to existing employees?

2 Compare and contrast the advantages and disadvantages of traditional and virtual career fairs.

APPLICATION *Exercises*

Running Case: LearnInMotion.com
Getting Better Applicants

If Jennifer and Pierre were asked what the main problem was in running their business, their answer would be quick and short: hiring good people. They were simply astonished at how hard it was to attract and hire good candidates. After much debate, they decided to post openings for seven positions: two salespeople, a Web designer, two content management people, an office manager, and a Web surfer.

Their first approach was to design and place a large display ad in two local newspapers. The dis-

play ad listed all the positions available. Jennifer and Pierre assumed that by placing a large ad with the name of the company prominently displayed and a bold border around the ad, it would draw attention and therefore generate applicants. For two consecutive weekends, the ad cost the fledgling company close to $1000, but it produced only a handful of applicants. After speaking with them by phone, Jennifer and Pierre rejected three outright; two said they weren't interested; and two scheduled interviews but never showed up.

The owners therefore decided to change their approach. They used different recruiting methods for each position. In the paper, they placed ads for the salespeople under "Sales" and for the office manager under "Administrative." They advertised for a Web designer by placing an ad on monster.ca. And for the content managers and Web surfer, they placed neatly typed help wanted ads in the career placement offices of a technical college and a community college about 10 minutes away from their office. They also used this job posting approach to find independent contractors they could use to deliver courses physically to users' homes or offices.

The results were disappointing. Over a typical weekend, literally dozens of want ads for experienced salespeople appear, as well as almost as many for office managers. The ad for salespeople generated about three calls, one of whom Jennifer and Pierre felt might be a viable candidate, although the person wanted a much higher salary than they had planned to pay. One possible candidate emerged for the office manager position.

They decided to change the positioning of the sales ad (since the job involved entirely inside phone sales) in the newspaper from "Salespersons Wanted" to "Phone Sales," which is a separate category. Many of the calls they got (not all of them, but many) were from salespeople who were used to working in what some people called "boiler-room" operations. In other words, they sit at the phone all day making cold calls from lists provided by their employers, selling anything from burglar alarms to investments, all under very high-pressure conditions. They weren't interested in LearnInMotion, nor was LearnInMotion interested in them.

They fared a little better with the Web designer ad, which produced four possible applicants. They got no phone calls from the local college job postings; when they called to ask the placement offices why, they were told that their posted salary of $8 per hour was "way too low." They went back and replaced the job postings with $10 hourly rates.

"I just don't understand it" is the way Jennifer put it. Especially for the sales job, Jennifer and Pierre felt that they were offering perfectly acceptable compensation packages, so the lack of applicants surprised them. "Maybe a lot of people just don't want to work for dot-coms anymore," said Pierre, thinking out loud. "Since the bottom fell out of the dot-com market in March 2000, a lot of good people have gotten burned by working for a series of two or three failed dot-coms, so maybe they've just had enough of the wired world."

Questions

1 Tell Jennifer and Pierre what they're doing wrong.

2 Provide a detailed list of recommendations concerning how they should go about increasing their pool of acceptable job applicants, so they no longer have to hire almost anyone who walks in the door. (Recommendations should include completely worded advertisements and suggestions regarding any other recruiting strategies you would suggest they use.)

CASE INCIDENT   *Expansion at Logans*

Business has been so good at the Logans Department Store outlet in the outskirts of Halifax that management has decided to expand it to include a bakery and deli, a cosmetic department, and a sporting goods department. No other outlets have a bakery and deli, but several have small cosmetics and sporting goods departments. The chain has a reputation for high-quality merchandise and personal attention to customers, standards that new hires will be expected to meet.

Management has estimated that the new departments, scheduled to begin operations in 12 months,

will require 15 new employees. Projected staffing for the bakery and deli includes one baker, one butcher, two customer-service representatives, and one manager. The projected HR requirements for the cosmetics and sporting goods departments are four customer-service representatives and one manager each. These estimates have been based on anticipated customer demand for the new products and services and on the level of service the firm wishes to maintain (i.e., customer-service representative to customer ratio).

Although there is a corporate promote-from-within policy for supervisory and management-level positions, the uniqueness of the new departments makes it unlikely that qualified applicants can be found internally.

Kim Vu has worked as an HR specialist at Logans' corporate offices in downtown Halifax for the past two years. Although she has recruited for a number of positions, she has never previously been asked to conduct a recruitment campaign of this magnitude. She has a challenge ahead of her now, though, since her boss, Vice-President of HR Bea Tjoveld, has asked her to prepare a recruiting plan and budget for staffing the expansion.

Questions

1   Assume that you are Kim. Prepare a recruiting plan and budget to meet the projected staffing needs. Your plan should outline your recommended recruiting sources and methods for each of the positions, accompanied by reasons for each of your recommendations. Your plan should also include cost and lead-time estimates.

2   After you have prepared your plan, assume a scenario in which there is a marked downturn in the economy. How might this affect your recruiting plan?

EXPERIENTIAL Exercises

1   Examine classified and display ads appearing in the help-wanted section of a recent newspaper. Choose three ads and, using the AIDA guidelines presented in this chapter, analyze the effectiveness of each one.

2   Go to your university or college's career centre and gather information on all the services they provide. How many companies come to recruit students through the centre each year? What services does the centre provide to employers seeking to hire graduating students? Employers seeking to hire summer students? Employers seeking to hire students for internships?

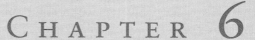

CHAPTER 6

Selection

LEARNING OUTCOMES

After studying this chapter, you should be able to:

Define selection and *discuss* its purpose and importance.

Describe the constraints on the selection process.

Define reliability and validity and *explain* their importance.

Describe at least four types of testing used in selection and *discuss* the conflicting legal concerns related to alcohol and drug testing.

Describe the major types of selection interviews by degree of structure, type of content, and manner of administration.

Explain the importance of reference checking, *describe* strategies to make such checking effective, and *discuss* the legal issues involved.

INTRODUCTION

selection The process of choosing individuals with the relevant qualifications to fill existing or projected job openings.

multiple-hurdle strategy An approach to selection involving a series of successive steps or hurdles. Only candidates clearing the hurdle are permitted to move on to the next step.

Selection is the process of choosing individuals with the relevant qualifications to fill existing or projected job openings. Whether considering current employees for a transfer or promotion, or outside candidates for a first-time position with the firm, information about the applicants must be collected and evaluated. Each step in the selection process, from initial screening to the hiring decision, is performed under legal, organizational, and environmental constraints that protect the interests of both applicant and organization.[1]

Most firms use a sequential selection system involving a series of successive steps—a **multiple-hurdle strategy**. Only candidates clearing a "hurdle" (selection techniques including pre-screening, testing, interviewing, and background/reference checking) are permitted to move on to the next step. Clearing the hurdle requires meeting or exceeding the minimum requirements established for that hurdle. Thus, only candidates who have cleared all of the previous hurdles remain in contention for the position at the time that the hiring decision is being made.

The Selection Process

The types of selection instruments and screening devices used are not standardized across organizations. Even within a firm, the number and sequence of steps often varies with type and level of job, as well as source and method of recruitment. **Figure 6.1** illustrates the steps commonly involved. After describing the constraints on the selection process, and discussing the importance of validity and reliability, we will discuss each of these steps in turn.

FIGURE 6.1   Typical Steps in the Selection Process

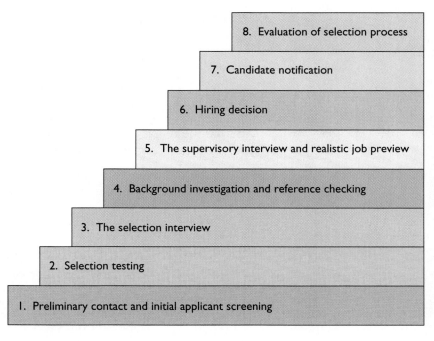

8. Evaluation of selection process

7. Candidate notification

6. Hiring decision

5. The supervisory interview and realistic job preview

4. Background investigation and reference checking

3. The selection interview

2. Selection testing

1. Preliminary contact and initial applicant screening

Purpose and Importance of Selection

The purpose of selection is to find the "best" candidate for the job. Selection is a strategic activity in that the ideal individual will possess the required KSAs, perform well, embrace the corporate mission and values, and fit the organizational culture. Strategic selection is important for three key reasons: (1) its impact on company performance, (2) the costs involved, and (3) its legal implications.

Company Performance

More and more managers have come to the realization that the quality of the company's human resources is often the single most important factor in determining whether the firm is going to survive, be successful in reaching the objectives specified in its strategic plan, and realize a satisfactory return on its investment. In fact, after increasing profits, the top priority of 300 CEOs participating in a recent survey was attracting and retaining key employees.[2]

Cost

In recent years, the cost of recruitment and selection has risen substantially. For example, one expert estimates that the cost of hiring is approximately two to three times an individual's salary.[3] There are also tremendous costs associated with inappropriate selection decisions. If the wrong employee is selected initially, no training program or motivational strategy—no matter how well conceived and designed—is likely to compensate adequately or offset the original hiring error.

When an unsuccessful employee must be terminated while on probation, or quits during this time, the recruitment and selection process must begin all over again, and the successor must be properly oriented and trained. The "hidden" costs are frequently even higher, including the low quality of work performed by the unsuccessful/unhappy employee while on the job, internal disorganization and disruption the employee may have caused, and customer/client ill will or alienation that may have been generated.

More often than not, really unsatisfactory applicants are screened out. However, virtually all organizations have some marginal employees who are really not capable enough to be considered truly satisfactory, and never make a worthwhile contribution to the firm. Once marginal employees are on the payroll, it becomes exceedingly difficult to terminate their employment.

Legal Implications

There are also legal implications associated with ineffective or incompetent selection. *Human rights* legislation in every Canadian jurisdiction prohibits discrimination in all aspects and terms and conditions of employment on such grounds as race, religion or creed, colour, marital status, gender, age, and disability. Firms must ensure that all of their selection procedures are free of both intentional and systemic discrimination. Organizations required by law to implement an employment equity plan must ensure that all of their employment systems, including selection, are bias-free and do not have an adverse impact on members of the four designated groups—women, visible minorities, Aboriginals, and persons with disabilities.

Another legal implication is employer liability for *negligent or wrongful hiring*. Courts are increasingly finding employers liable when employees with unsuitable backgrounds are hired and subsequently engage in criminal activities falling within the scope of their employment. British Columbia has a law that requires schools, hospitals, and employers of childcare workers to conduct criminal record checks for all new employees.[4]

The Role of the HR Department in the Selection Process

While the HR department generally assumes overall responsibility for the selection process, and often handles initial screening, testing, and reference checking, supervisors and managers throughout the firm have an extremely important role to play. The immediate supervisor generally makes the final hiring decision. It is therefore important that all individuals in a supervisory or managerial role understand the purpose and importance of the selection process, as well as the constraints affecting it. They must also be thoroughly trained in the most effective and legally defensible approaches for evaluating applicants.

CONSTRAINTS ON THE SELECTION PROCESS

Those involved in the selection process must be aware of the constraints that come with organizational policies and plans, the job requirements, supply challenges, ethics, and legislative requirements.

Organizational Policies and Plans

Strategic Plan   Through selection, the firm attempts to match its intended strategy with characteristics of persons chosen. As the characteristics of the organization (such as product lines, services provided, market share, and its priorities) change over time, so too must the selection strategies. Many organizations are now focusing on teamwork skills, for example. In firms such as 3M in Brockville, Ontario, the entire team may be involved in the selection process.[5]

Selection Budget   Selection strategies must be cost-effective, and work within budgetary limitations. The selection process is a means through which the organization achieves its objectives. Without limits, employment expenses could be so high that organizational effectiveness would suffer.

Employment Equity Plan   If there is an employment equity plan, it must be taken into consideration when planning the selection process, because selection is one of the main HR activities by which the goals and timetables established by the firm can be reached.

The Job Requirements

It is through job analysis that the duties, responsibilities, and human requirements for each job are identified. By defining bona fide occupational requirements through job analysis and basing selection criteria on these requirements, firms can create a legally defensible hiring system.[6] The skills required, mental and physical demands, responsibilities, and working conditions should provide the basis for the information obtained from the applicant and his or her previous employers and other references, as well as for any employment tests administered. Individuals hired after thorough screening against carefully developed selection criteria (based directly on the job description and job specification) learn their jobs readily, are productive, and generally adjust to their jobs with a minimum of difficulty. As a result, both the individual and organization benefit.

Supply Challenges

Although it is desirable to have a large, qualified pool of recruits from which to select applicants, this is not always possible. In fields in which there is a supply shortage, such as health care and oil and gas, there is often a very small selection ratio.[7] A **selection ratio** is the ratio of the number of applicants hired to the total number of applicants available, as follows:

selection ratio The ratio of the number of applicants hired to the total number of applicants.

$$\frac{\text{Number of Applicants Hired}}{\text{Total Number of Applicants}} = \text{Selection Ratio}$$

A small selection ratio, such as 1:2, means that there are a limited number of applicants from which to select, and may also mean low-quality recruits. If this is the case, it is generally better to start the recruitment process over again, even if it means a hiring delay, rather than taking the risk of hiring an employee who will be a marginal performer at best.

Ethics

It is important that staff involved in hiring decisions have a strong sense of professional ethics. Being offered gifts from a private employment agency wanting the firm's business or being pressured to hire an underqualified designated-group member are examples of ethical dilemmas that those involved in the selection process may encounter. Ethical standards pertaining to privacy and confidentiality are also important.

Legislative Requirements

Organizations must ensure that their selection criteria and screening techniques are legally justifiable, based on the job requirements, and that none leads to discrimination—whether intentional or systemic. Legal compliance concerns also require that employers exercise due diligence in employee screening and reference checking. Suggested guidelines for avoiding negative legal consequences, such as human rights complaints, liability for negligent hiring, and unjust discharge suits, include:[8]

1. Ensuring that all selection criteria and strategies are based on the job description and job specification.

2. Adequately assessing the applicant's ability to meet performance standards or expectations.

3. Carefully scrutinizing all information supplied on application forms and résumés.

4. Obtaining written authorization for reference checking from prospective employees, and checking references very carefully.

5. Saving all records and information obtained about the applicant during each stage of the selection process.

6. Rejecting applicants who make false statements on their application forms or résumés.

Two critical issues related to legal compliance are reliability and validity, which will be discussed next.

An Ethical Dilemma

As the company recruiter, how would you handle a request from the CEO that you hire her son for a summer job, knowing that, given current hiring constraints, the sons and daughters of other employees will not be able to obtain such positions?

Hints to Ensure Legal Compliance

THE IMPORTANCE OF RELIABILITY AND VALIDITY

Reliability

reliability The degree to which interviews, tests, and other selection procedures yield comparable data over a period of time; in other words, the degree of dependability, consistency, or stability of the measures used.

The degree to which interviews, tests, and other selection procedures yield comparable data over a period of time is known as **reliability**. Reliability is thus concerned with the degree of dependability, consistency, or stability of the measures used.[9] For example, a test that results in widely variable scores when it is administered on different occasions to the same individual is unreliable.[10] Reliability also refers to the extent to which two or more methods (such as tests and reference checking) yield the same results or are consistent, as well as the extent to which there is agreement between two or more raters (inter-rater reliability).

When dealing with tests, another measure of reliability that is taken into account is internal consistency. For example, suppose that there were ten items on a vocational interest test, all of which were supposed to measure, in one way or another, the person's interest in working outdoors. To assess internal reliability, the degree to which responses to those ten items vary together would be statistically analyzed. (That is one reason why tests often include questions that appear rather repetitive.) Reliability is also diminished when questions are answered randomly, the test setting is noisy or uncomfortable, and when the applicant is tired or unwell.

Validity

validity The accuracy with which a predictor measures what it is supposed to measure.

Validity refers to the accuracy with which a predictor measures what it is supposed to measure. In the context of selection, validity is an indicator of the extent to which data from a selection technique, such as a test or interview, are related to or predictive of subsequent performance on the job.[11] Selection procedures must, above all, be valid. Without proof of validity, there is no logical or legally permissible reason to continue using the technique to screen job applicants. To ensure that the selection techniques being used are valid, validation studies should be conducted. There are three types of validity that are particularly relevant to selection: criterion-related, content, and construct validity.

criterion-related validity The extent to which a selection tool predicts or significantly correlates with important elements of work behaviour.

Criterion-Related Validity   The extent to which a selection tool predicts or significantly correlates with important elements of work behaviour is known as **criterion-related validity**. Demonstrating criterion-related validity requires proving that those who do well on a test or in an interview, for example, also do well on the job, and that individuals who do poorly on the test or in the interview receive low job-performance ratings.[12]

content validity The extent to which a selection instrument, such as a test, adequately samples the knowledge and skills needed to perform the job.

Content Validity   When a selection instrument, such as a test, adequately samples the knowledge and skills needed to perform the job, **content validity** is assumed to exist. The closer the content of the selection instrument is to actual samples of work or work behaviour, the greater the content validity.[13] For example, asking a candidate for a secretarial position to demonstrate word processing skills, as required on the job, has high content validity.

construct validity The extent to which a selection tool measures a theoretical construct or trait deemed necessary to perform the job successfully.

Construct Validity   The extent to which a selection tool measures a theoretical construct or trait deemed necessary to perform the job successfully is known as **construct validity**. Intelligence, verbal skills, analytical ability, and leadership skills are all examples of constructs. Measuring construct validity

differential validity Confirmation that the selection tool accurately predicts the performance of all possible employee subgroups, including white males, women, visible minorities, persons with disabilities, and Aboriginal people.

requires demonstrating that the psychological trait or attribute is related to satisfactory job performance, as well as showing that the test or other selection tool used accurately measures the psychological trait or attribute.[14]

Separate validation studies should be conducted for different subgroups, such as visible minorities and women, in order to assess **differential validity**. In some cases, a test may be a valid predictor of job success for one group (such as white males), but not for other applicants, thereby leading to systemic discrimination.

STEPS IN THE SELECTION PROCESS

In order to gain as reliable and valid a picture as possible of each applicant's potential for success on the job, organizations typically rely on a number of sources of information. The number of steps in the selection process and their sequence varies with the organization, the recruiting source, and the method. Reference checking with former employers is not generally a step in the selection of an internal candidate for transfer or promotion, for example. Private employment agencies and executive search firms perform screening, and often do testing and reference checking. Thus, when using either of these recruiting methods, the company's selection process may only involve two steps: the supervisory interview (which often includes a realistic job preview) and making the final hiring decision. As illustrated in **Figure 6.2**, after applicants have been pre-screened, the most common selection strategies revealed in a recent study

FIGURE **6.2**   Selection Strategies for Pre-screened Candidates

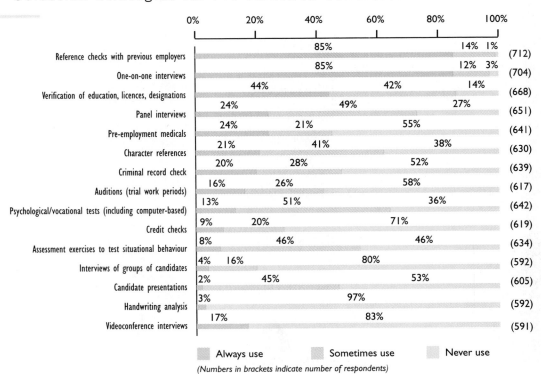

(Numbers in brackets indicate number of respondents)

Source: Murray Axmith & Associates Ltd., *Survey 2000: Canadian Hiring, Retention and Dismissal Practices*, p. 13. Reprinted with permission.

involving 718 Canadian firms include reference checks with previous employers and one-on-one interviews, while the least frequent are handwriting analysis and video interviews.[15]

The type and level of job also make a difference. For example, while 58 percent of those responding to a recent survey of over 200 Canadian organizations indicated that they use letters of reference for at least some jobs, as illustrated in **Figure 6.3**, such letters are requested least frequently for blue-collar jobs and most frequently for white-collar professional positions.[16] Each of the steps commonly involved in the selection process, as identified in Figure 6.1, will now be described.

Step One: Preliminary Contact and Applicant Screening

Many applicants today make first contact through the Web, at a job board or corporate recruiting Web site. Candidates are often required to complete an application form as part of the preliminary contact process online. In some cases, résumés may still be received through the mail or by fax, particularly when responding to print advertisements for jobs.

FIGURE 6.3   Letters of Reference as a Selection Strategy

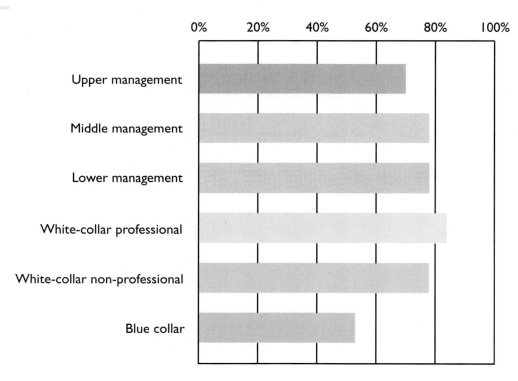

Source: Sean A. Way and James W. Thacker, "Selection Practices: Where Are Canadian Organizations?" *HR Professional* 16, no. 5 (October/November 1999), p. 33. Reprinted with permission of Professor James Thacker.

Initial applicant screening is generally performed by members of the HR department. Application forms and résumés are reviewed. Those candidates not meeting the "must have" selection criteria are eliminated first. Then, the remaining applications are examined and those candidates who most closely match the remaining job specifications are identified and given further consideration.

Some claim that effective applicant screening is what differentiates companies and can create a competitive advantage.[17] The use of technology is becoming increasingly popular to help HR professionals improve the initial screening process. Offerings ranging from applicant-tracking software to Web-based pre-screening tools aim to improve résumé management, simplify applicant tracking, and improve the initial screening process.[18] An increasing number of firms, such as Blockbuster and Home Depot, are using technological applications to help screen large numbers of candidates and generate short-lists of individuals who will move on to the next step in the selection process. Some companies claim that screening technology has helped decrease employee turnover by between 10 and 30 percent by helping to establish a better fit between the candidate and the job.

Kinko's experienced a decrease in their turnover when the company implemented an interactive voice response (IVR) system to automate applicant screening for hourly-rated jobs. Candidates access the system by calling a toll-free telephone number, and by using a touch-tone phone, respond to job-related questions. The questions are set up in a two-tiered series. The first tier asks the applicant questions typically found on employment applications such as experience and availability. If their answers satisfy available job opening specifications, they continue to the second tier of questions that are designed to seek out candidates that match Kinko's culture and business needs. Branch managers can then develop a short-list of candidates that meet their needs for personal interviews. Kinko's has found that the quality of hiring has increased—since instituting IVR, the company has increased its retention and decreased its turnover rates. The IVR system offers a high degree of fairness because all applicants are asked to do the same job-related questions, which eliminates the possibility of any unintended bias on the part of local managers or recruiters.[19]

Step Two: Selection Testing

Selection testing is a common screening device used by organizations to assess specific job-related skills, as well as general intelligence, personality characteristics, mental abilities, interests, and preferences. Testing techniques provide efficient, standardized procedures for screening large numbers of applicants. The use of valid tests can assist in the selection of the most qualified candidate, and increase output substantially.

The use of tests to assist with hiring and/or promotion decisions has been increasing. In a recent study involving over 200 Canadian firms, two-thirds of the respondents indicated that they use at least one type of testing method in their selection process, to supplement interview results.[20] **Table 6.1** indicates the types of testing methods used. In general, testing is more prevalent in larger organizations. This reflects their greater need for efficient, standardized

TABLE 6.1	Selection Testing Methods Used in Canadian Firms (n = 133)						
Paper & Pencil Tests			**Rapid Screening**		**Behavioural**		
Personality	Aptitude	Other	WAB	BIB	Assessment Centre	Work Sampling	Others
25%	36%	23%	3%	6%	12%	29%	7%

Source: Sean A. Way and James W. Thacker, "Selection Practices: Where Are Canadian Organizations?" *HR Professional* 16, no. 5 (October/November 1999), p. 34. Reprinted with permission of Professor James Thacker.

procedures to screen large numbers of applicants, as well as their ability to finance testing programs.

Fundamental Guidelines to Effective Testing

The Canadian Psychological Association has developed and published comprehensive testing standards, covering such areas as test instrumentation, test use and administration, scoring, and reporting.[21] Selection testing involves many different varieties of tests that purport to measure such diverse attributes of candidates as job performance and honesty. It is important, therefore, that firms do a great deal of planning, analysis, and experimentation in order to ensure that the tests they use best satisfy their needs.

Basic guidelines for setting up a testing program include:[22]

Hints to Ensure Legal Compliance

1. Use tests as supplements to other techniques, such as interviews and background checks. Tests are not infallible, and at best, the test score usually accounts for only about 25 percent of the variation in the measure of performance.

2. Validate the tests in the organization. Both legal requirements and good testing practice demand in-house validation. The fact that the same tests have been proven valid in similar organizations is not sufficient.

3. Analyze all current hiring and promotion standards. Questions should be asked, such as: "What proportion of Aboriginal or visible minority applicants are being rejected at each stage of the hiring process?" The burden of proof is always on the organization to show that the predictor (such as intelligence) is related to success or failure on the job.

4. Keep accurate records of why each applicant was rejected, using objective, fact-based statements.

5. Begin a validation program if the firm either does not currently use tests or uses tests that have not been validated. This requires administering a test to applicants, hiring the applicants without referring to the test scores, and at a later date correlating test scores with the employees' performance on the job.

6. Use a certified psychologist. The development, validation, and use of selection standards (including tests) generally require the assistance of a qualified psychologist.

7. Provide appropriate testing conditions. Tests should be administered in a private, quiet, well-lit, and well-ventilated setting, and all applicants must take tests under the same conditions.

Under the Canadian Psychological Association's standards, test takers have the right to expect that:[23]

- results will be treated as highly confidential and used only with their informed consent
- results will be shared only with those having a legitimate need for the information, who are either qualified to interpret the scores or who have been provided with sufficient information to ensure their appropriate interpretation
- tests are equally fair to all test takers in the sense that no one taking a test has any prior information concerning the questions or answers.

Tests of Cognitive Abilities
Included in this category are tests of general reasoning ability (intelligence), tests of emotional intelligence, and tests of specific thinking skills like memory and inductive reasoning.

Intelligence Tests **Intelligence (IQ) tests** are tests of general intellectual abilities. They measure not a single "intelligence" trait, but rather a number of abilities including memory, vocabulary, verbal fluency, and numerical ability. An IQ score is actually a *derived* score, reflecting the extent to which the person is above or below the "average" adult's intelligence score. Intelligence is often measured with individually administered tests, such as the Stanford-Binet Test or the Wechsler Test. Other IQ tests, such as the Wonderlic, can be administered to groups of people.

intelligence (IQ) tests Tests that measure general intellectual abilities, such as verbal comprehension, inductive reasoning, memory, numerical ability, speed of perception, spatial visualization, and word fluency.

emotional intelligence (EI) tests Tests that measure ability to monitor one's own emotions and the emotions of others and use that knowledge to guide thoughts and actions.

Emotional Quotient Inventory
eqi.mhs.com

Emotional Intelligence Tests **Emotional intelligence (EI) tests** measure ability to monitor one's own emotions and the emotions of others and use that knowledge to guide thoughts and actions. Someone with a high emotional quotient (EQ) is self-aware, can control his or her impulses, motivates him- or herself, and demonstrates empathy and social awareness. Many people believe that EQ, which can be modified through conscious effort and practice, is actually a more important determinant of success than having a high IQ. Self-assessment EI tests include the Emotional Quotient Inventory (EQi), the EQ Map, the Mayer Salovey Caruso Emotional Intelligence Test (MSCEIT), and the Emotional Intelligence Questionnaire (EIQ). The Emotional Competence Inventory (ECI) is a 360-degree assessment, where several individuals evaluate one person to get a more complete picture of the individual's emotional competencies.[24]

Specific Cognitive Abilities There are also measures of specific thinking skills, such as inductive and deductive reasoning, verbal comprehension, memory, and numerical ability. Tests in this category are often called **aptitude tests**, since they purport to measure the applicant's aptitudes for the job in question, that is, the applicant's potential to perform the job once given proper training. An example is the test of mechanical comprehension illustrated in **Figure 6.4**. It tests the applicant's understanding of basic mechanical principles. It may therefore reflect a person's aptitude for jobs—like that of machinist or engineer—that require mechanical comprehension. Multidimensional aptitude tests commonly used in applicant selection include the General Aptitude Test Battery (GATB)

aptitude tests Tests that measure an individual's aptitude or potential to perform a job, provided he or she is given proper training.

Microsoft Online Aptitude Testing
www.microsoft.com/skills2000

Aerolaminates, a wind turbine blade manufacturer, used aptitude tests to screen and hire approximately 100 employees following relocation. The company knew that it would have to invest in training new employees, and that candidates' ability to absorb and apply knowledge was key to the start-up effort.

FIGURE 6.4   Two Problems from the Test of Mechanical Comprehension

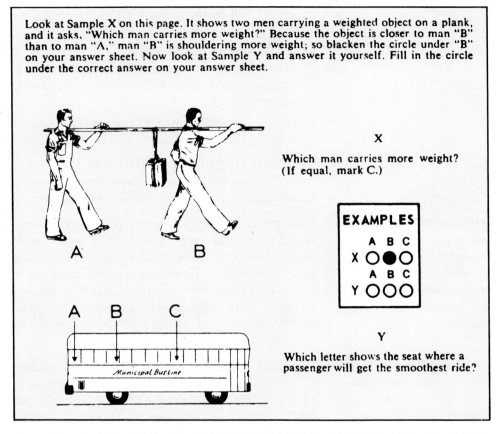

Look at Sample X on this page. It shows two men carrying a weighted object on a plank, and it asks, "Which man carries more weight?" Because the object is closer to man "B" than to man "A," man "B" is shouldering more weight; so blacken the circle under "B" on your answer sheet. Now look at Sample Y and answer it yourself. Fill in the circle under the correct answer on your answer sheet.

X
Which man carries more weight?
(If equal, mark C.)

Y
Which letter shows the seat where a passenger will get the smoothest ride?

To assess the traits on which job success depends, many firms, such as those that rely on computer literacy, administer a skills assessment test before hiring.

The use of the aptitude tests was successful as a screening tool, and the new facility was performing at the same level as the previous facility within six months. The process also helped to raise the company's profile as a credible, professional organization that invests in its employees.[25]

Tests of Motor and Physical Abilities   There are many *motor abilities* that a firm might want to measure. These include finger dexterity, manual dexterity, speed of arm movement, and reaction time. The Crawford Small Parts Dexterity Test, as illustrated in **Figure 6.5**, is an example. It measures the speed and accuracy of simple judgment, as well as the speed of finger, hand, and arm movements. Other tests include the Stromberg Dexterity Test, the Minnesota Rate of Manipulation Test, and the Purdue Peg Board.

Tests of physical abilities may also be required.[26] For example, some firms are now using Functional Abilities Evaluations (FAE) to assist with placement decisions. An FAE, which measures a whole series of physical abilities—ranging

FIGURE 6.5   Crawford Small Parts Dexterity Test

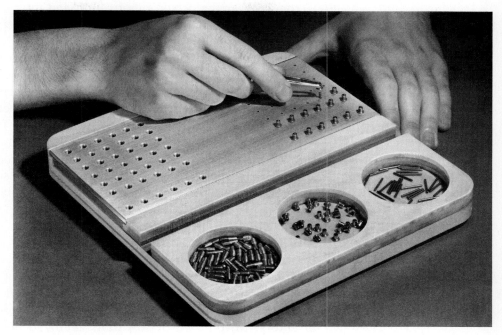

Source: The Psychological Corporation.

Hints to Ensure Legal Compliance

from lifting, to pulling and pushing, sitting, squatting, climbing, and carrying—is particularly useful for positions with a multitude of physical demands, such as firefighter and police officer.[27] Ensuring that physical abilities tests do not violate human rights legislation requires basing such tests on job duties identified through job analysis and a physical demands analysis, ensuring that the tests duplicate the actual physical requirements of the job, developing and imposing such tests honestly and in good faith, ensuring that those administering the tests are properly trained and administer the tests in a consistent manner, and ensuring that testing standards are objectively related to job performance.[28]

If standards have an adverse impact on protected group members, inability to justify them on these grounds can lead to charges of systemic discrimination.[29] In a unanimous decision, the Supreme Court of Canada restored Tawney Meiorin's position as a firefighter with the B.C. Ministry of Forests, ruling that the physical fitness test being used by the province, although developed in good faith, failed to properly take into account the differing physiology of males and females. After three years on the job, Meiorin was permanently laid off when she took 49.4 seconds too long to complete a 2.5-kilometre run (a component of the newly introduced physical testing program), despite the fact that she passed all of the other physical tests. In reaching a decision, the court took into account the fact that 65 to 70 percent of men taking the test were able to pass it on their first attempt, but only 35 percent of the female applicants did so. The Ministry was also unable to prove that inability to run the race in the specified time would pose a serious safety risk to Ms. Meiorin, her fellow employees, or the public at large.

Myers-Briggs Type Indicator
www.psychometrics.com

Measuring Personality and Interests

A person's mental and physical abilities are seldom sufficient to explain his or her job performance. Other factors such as the person's motivation and interpersonal skills are important too. Personality and interest inventories are sometimes used as predictors of such intangibles.

personality tests Instruments used to measure basic aspects of personality, such as introversion, stability, motivation, neurotic tendency, self-confidence, self-sufficiency, and sociability.

Personality tests can measure basic aspects of an applicant's personality, such as introversion, stability, and motivation. The use of such tests for selection assumes that it is possible to find a relationship between a measurable personality trait (such as conscientiousness) and success on the job.[30] Many of these tests are *projective*. In the Thematic Apperception Test, an ambiguous stimulus (like an ink blot or clouded picture) is presented to the test taker, and he or she is asked to interpret or react to it. Since the pictures are ambiguous, the person's interpretation must come from within—he or she supposedly *projects* into the picture his or her own emotional attitudes about life. Thus, a security-oriented person might describe the woman in **Figure 6.6** as "my mother worrying about what I will do if I lose my job."

The Myers-Briggs instrument, which has been in use for over 50 years, is believed to be the most widely used personality inventory in the world. Over 3 million people took the test in 2001 alone as part of such applications as career, organizational, and leadership development, and team building.[31] Another example of a common personality test is the Minnesota Multiphasic Personality Inventory (MMPI), which taps traits like hypochondria and paranoia. FedEx, Wal-Mart, and BASF are all using personality tests to screen candidates for employment at all levels.[32]

An Ethical DILEMMA

As the employment manager, how would you inform an applicant that he or she is being eliminated from a competition based on personality test results?

Research Insight ▷

Recent studies confirm that personality tests can help companies to hire more effective workers. For example, industrial psychologists often talk in terms of the "Big Five" personality dimensions as they apply to employment testing: *extroversion, emotional stability, agreeableness, conscientiousness,* and *openness to experience*.[33] One study focused on the extent to which these dimensions predicted performance (in terms of job and training proficiency, for example) for professionals, police officers, managers, sales workers, and skilled/semi-

FIGURE 6.6   Sample Picture from Thematic Apperception Test

How do you interpret this picture?

skilled workers. Conscientiousness showed a consistent relationship with all performance criteria for every occupation. Extroversion was a valid predictor of performance for managers and sales employees—the two occupations involving the most social interaction. Both openness to experience and extroversion predicted training proficiency for all occupations.[34] Another study involving a sample of 89 university employees concluded that absenteeism was inversely related to extroversion and conscientiousness.[35]

A third study confirms the potential usefulness of personality tests for selection, while underscoring the importance of job analysis. The researchers concluded that the predictive power of a personality test can be quite high.[36] However, they also found that the full potential of personality testing in selection will be realized only when careful job analysis becomes the "standard practice for determining which traits are relevant to predicting performance on a given job..."[37] In summary, personality tests can help employers to predict which candidates will succeed on the job and which will not. However, the job analysis and validation study must be carefully executed.

interest inventories Tests that compare a candidate's interests with those of people in various occupations.

Interest inventories compare a candidate's interests with those of people in various occupations. Thus, a person taking the Strong-Campbell Inventory would receive a report comparing his or her interests to those of people already in occupations such as accountant, engineer, manager, or medical technologist. Interest inventories have many uses. One is career planning, since people generally do better in jobs involving activities in which they have an interest. Another is selection. If the firm can select people whose interests are roughly the same as those of high-performing incumbents in the jobs for which it is hiring, the new employees are more likely to be successful.[38]

achievement tests Tests used to measure knowledge and/or proficiency acquired through education, training, or experience.

Achievement Tests

An **achievement test** is basically a measure of what a person has learned. Most of the tests taken in school are achievement tests. They measure knowledge and/or proficiency in areas such as economics, marketing, or HRM. Achievement tests are also widely used in selection. For example, the Purdue Test for Machinists and Machine Operators tests the job knowledge of experienced machinists with questions like "What is meant by 'tolerance'?" Other tests are available for electricians, welders, carpenters, and so forth. In addition to job knowledge, achievement tests measure the applicant's abilities; a keyboarding test is one example.

Work Sampling for Employee Selection

Work samples focus on measuring job performance directly.[39] A study of various selection methods has found that work sample tests are among the best predictors of job performance.[40] The work sampling technique, which measures how a candidate actually performs some of the job's basic tasks, has a number of advantages:[41]

- Since actual on-the-job tasks are being measured, it is harder for an applicant to fake answers.
- The clear link between the work sample and actual job requirements makes such testing more legally defensible.
- There is virtually no chance of such testing being viewed as an invasion of privacy, since it does not delve into the applicant's personality or psyche.

In developing a work sampling test, experts first list all of the possible tasks that jobholders would be required to perform. Then, by listing the frequency of

A management game or simulation is a typical component in a management assessment centre.

management assessment centre
A strategy used to assess candidates' management potential using a combination of realistic exercises, management games, objective testing, presentations, and interviews.

International Congress on Assessment Center Methods
www.assessmentcenters.org

Assessment Tools
www.behaviourworks.com

performance and relative importance of each task, key tasks are identified. Each applicant then performs the key tasks, and his or her work is monitored by the test administrator, who records the approach taken. Finally, the work sampling test is validated by determining the relationship between the applicants' scores on the work samples and their actual performance on the job. Then, once it is shown that the work sample is a valid predictor of job success, the employer can begin using it for selection.[42]

Management Assessment Centres

In a two- to three-day **management assessment centre**, the management potential of 10 or 12 candidates is assessed by expert appraisers who observe them performing realistic management tasks. The centre may be a plain conference room, but it is often a special room with a one-way mirror to facilitate unobtrusive observations. Examples of the types of activities and exercises involved include:

1. *An in-basket exercise.* Each candidate is faced with an accumulation of reports, memos, messages from incoming phone calls, letters, and other materials collected in the in-basket of the simulated job that he or she is to take over, and is required to take appropriate action. For example, he or she must write letters, return phone calls, and prepare meeting agendas. The trained evaluators then review the results.

2. *A leaderless group discussion.* A leaderless group is given a discussion question and told to arrive at a group decision. The raters evaluate each candidate's interpersonal skills, acceptance by the group, leadership ability, and individual influence.

3. *Management games.* Participants engage in realistic problem solving, usually as members of two or more simulated companies that are competing in the marketplace. Decisions might have to be made about such issues as how to advertise and manufacture and how much inventory to keep in stock.

4. *Individual presentations.* During oral presentations on an assigned topic, each participant's communication skills and persuasiveness are evaluated.

5. *Objective tests.* Candidates may be asked to complete paper-and-pencil or computer-based personality, aptitude, interest, and/or achievement tests.

6. *An interview.* Most centres also require an interview between at least one of the expert assessors and each participant to evaluate interests, background, past performance, and motivation.

situational tests Tests in which candidates are presented with hypothetical situations representative of the job for which they are applying and are evaluated on their responses.

Video-Based Situational Testing

In **situational tests**, candidates are presented with hypothetical situations representative of the job for which they are applying and are evaluated on their responses.[43] Several of the assessment centre exercises described previously are examples. Video-based situational testing is growing in popularity. In a typical test, a number of realistic video scenarios are presented, and each is followed by a multiple-choice question with several possible courses of action, from which candidates are asked to select the "best" response, in their opinion.[44] When combined with a computer application, the level of each candidate's skills can be automatically evaluated, and an

Interactive employment tests administered on the computer are becoming popular as screening devices at many firms.

assessment report can be easily generated, making the simulation easier and less expensive to administer than other screening tools. Job applicants like video-based simulations as they have inherent face validity when compared with other types of pre-employment tests, and provide a realistic job preview by exposing candidates to the types of activities that they will encounter on the job.[45] UPS and Dow Chemical are among the increasing number of companies using simulations during their selection process.[46]

Research
Insight

A recent study of over 4000 retail employees in seven different organizations showed that situational test scores are significantly related to job performance, and are a better predictor of job performance than cognitive tests or employee experience in the retail industry.[47]

Micro-assessments

An entirely performance-based testing strategy that focuses on individual performance is a **micro-assessment**. In a micro-assessment, each applicant completes a series of verbal, paper-based, or computer-based questions and exercises that cover the range of activities required on the job for which he or she is applying. In addition to technical exercises, participants are required to solve a set of work-related problems that demonstrate their ability to perform well within the confines of a certain department or corporate culture. Exercises are simple to develop because they are taken directly from the job. If only the top three performers are subsequently interviewed, such assessments can eliminate 60 to 75 percent of interviews, thereby saving time and money.

micro-assessment A series of verbal, paper-based, or computer-based questions and exercises that a candidate is required to complete, covering the range of activities required on the job for which he or she is applying.

The Polygraph and Honesty Testing

A few firms use the **polygraph** (or "**lie detector**") for honesty testing. This is a device that measures physiological changes like increased perspiration caused by the emotional stress that accompanies lying. Once the person's emotional reaction to giving truthful answers to neutral questions has been ascertained, questions are asked such as, "Have you ever stolen anything without paying for it?" and "Have you ever been convicted of a crime for which a pardon has not been granted?" In theory, the expert can then accurately determine whether or not the applicant is lying. Because of their questionable accuracy, polygraphs are not legally permissible as a selection tool in some Canadian jurisdictions. Thus, even in jurisdictions in which administering polygraphs is legal, employers often choose less offensive and more accurate means to assess applicant honesty.

polygraph (lie detector) A device that measures physiological changes associated with stress, such as increased perspiration, blood pressure, and heart rate.

HR Software www.peoplesoft.com

Paper-and-pencil **honesty tests** are psychological tests designed to predict job applicants' proneness to dishonesty and other forms of counterproductivity.[48] Most measure attitudes regarding things like tolerance of others who steal, acceptance of rationalizations for theft, and admission of theft-related activities. Internal employee theft represents 31 percent of all losses in retail businesses in Canada, and the Retail Council of Canada reports that employee theft costs retailers more than $2 million each day. Therefore, it is imperative that employers try to screen out dishonest individuals who have a propensity for theft. Ironically, most individuals who steal see nothing wrong with it, which makes honesty tests an easy, simple, inexpensive selection test to help weed them out.

honesty tests Psychological tests that measure an individual's attitude toward honest versus dishonest behaviours or lack of candour.

Honesty tests are structured in a way to differentiate between those who have internalized honesty and those who can fake it and give the outward impression of honesty.[49]

Doubt has been expressed regarding the validity of paper-and-pencil honesty-testing instruments. For this and other reasons, honesty testing is not legally permissible in many Canadian jurisdictions. Even if it is, until more widespread evaluations are done, such tests should never be used as the sole selection strategy, but rather as a supplement to other techniques, such as interviewing and reference checking.

graphology The use of handwriting analysis to assess an applicant's basic personality traits.

Graphology   The use of **graphology** (handwriting analysis), based on the premise that handwriting is a rhythmic movement that reflects the writer's personality and is a stable expression of an individual's various traits or tendencies, has some similarity to projective personality tests.[50] In graphology, the handwriting analyst systematically analyzes an applicant's handwriting sample to infer something about the individual's personality, strengths and weaknesses, fit with the organization, or probable job performance.[51] **Figure 6.7** provides examples of how someone's handwriting can be used to assess his or her personality and to determine the jobs best suited for that person. Even though research has shown that graphology is a poor predictor of personality and job performance, its use as a selection tool in increasing in North America.[52] It should definitely not be used as the sole determining factor when hiring.

FIGURE 6.7   Handwriting Exhibit Used by Graphologist

1. Signs of depression after a stroke.

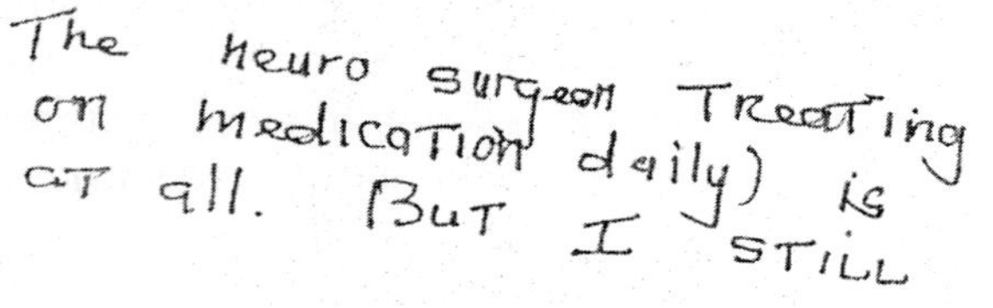

2. Violent handwriting of French Emperor Napoleon Bonaparte.

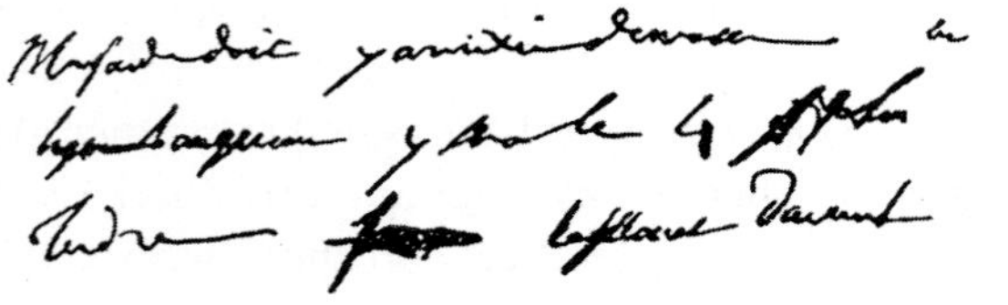

3. Signs of tension in broken and slow handwriting. Excessive muscle tension is preventing the writing hand from moving smoothly.

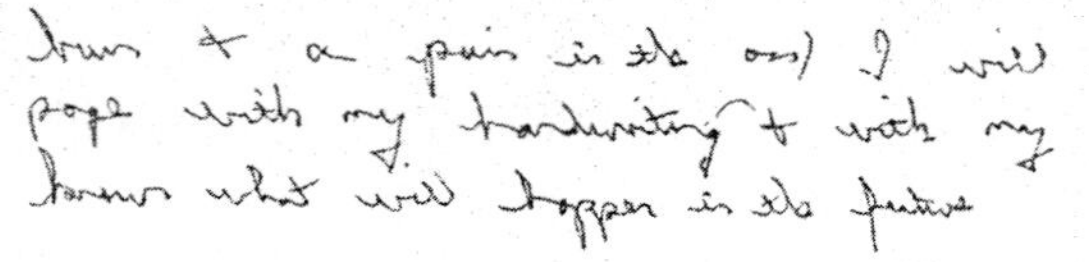

4. This handwriting sample reveals an individual suited to jobs that demand a great deal of responsibility and stable performance such as child care, administration, and accounting.

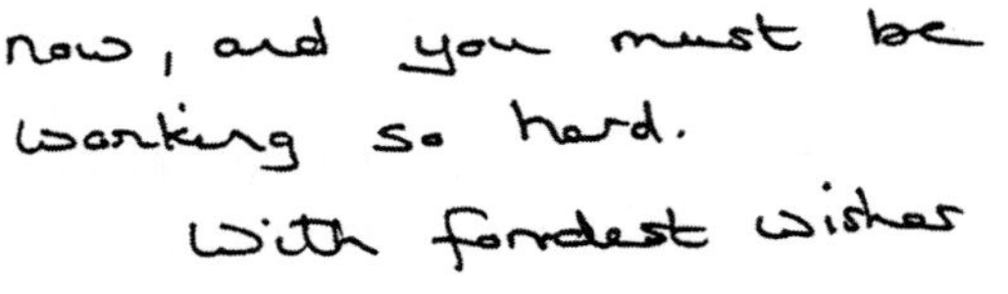

5. Here the handwriting reveals an individual suited to people-oriented fields such as public relations, sales, and journalism.

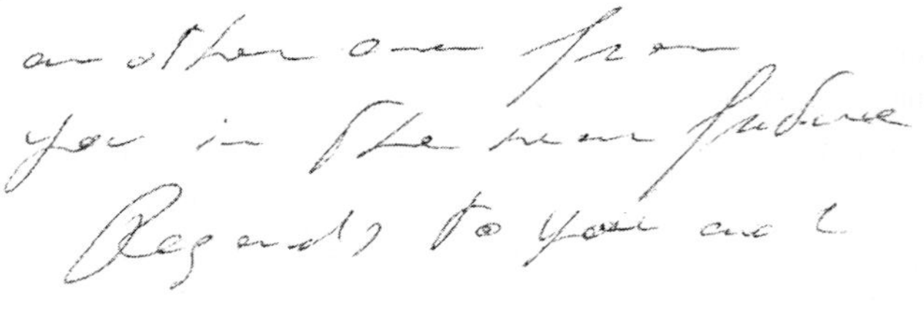

Source: "The Power of the Pen," by Roma Avishai, p. 33. This article was reprinted with permission from the April 1999 issue of *Internal Auditor,* published by The Institute of Internal Auditors, Inc.

Physical Examination   Three main reasons why firms may include a medical examination as a step in the selection process are (1) to determine that the applicant *qualifies for the physical requirements* of the position and, if not, to document any *accommodation requirements;* (2) to establish a *record and baseline* of the applicant's health for the purpose of future insurance or compensation claims; and (3) to *reduce absenteeism and accidents* by enabling the applicant and physician to identify any health- or safety-related issues or concerns that need to be addressed, including communicable diseases of which the applicant may have been unaware. Large firms often employ medical professionals to conduct medical testing. Smaller employers retain the services of consulting physicians to perform such exams, which are paid for by the employer.

When medical testing is a step in the selection process, certain guidelines must be kept in mind:

Hints **to Ensure** **Legal Compliance**

- A medical exam is only permitted after a written offer of employment has been extended (except in the case of bona fide occupational requirements, as in food handlers).

- If used, medical exams must be required of all applicants for the job in question.

- Companies have no right to request information regarding the nature of a candidate's disability, and a person with a disability cannot be rejected for a job if he or she is otherwise qualified and could perform the job duties with reasonable accommodation.

- All medical information should be retained by the examining physician, never placed in employees' HR files.

Substance Abuse Testing   The purpose of pre-employment substance abuse testing is to avoid hiring employees who would pose unnecessary risks to themselves or others and/or perform below expectations. However, in Canada, employers are not permitted to screen candidates for substance abuse.[53] Alcohol and drug addiction is considered to be a handicap under human rights codes, and an employee cannot be discriminated against during the selection process based on a handicap.[54] What complicates the legal situation even further are employers' obligations under health and safety legislation.[55] Certainly, employers can legally discipline employees for being obviously impaired on the job, with sanctions up to and including discharge, but the right to conduct random testing is very limited.

Random *alcohol testing*, such as the use of breathalyzers, can detect current impairment at the time of the test, and therefore is permissible in Canada under certain circumstances. A recent Ontario court case, *Entrop v. Imperial Oil Ltd.*, determined that an employer's right to conduct random alcohol testing for employees in safety-sensitive positions depends on whether the tests are considered to be a bona fide occupational requirement (BFOR). In order to determine if such tests are legally permissible as a BFOR, a company must meet a three-step test as set out by the Supreme Court of Canada:

1. The alcohol test must be adopted for a purpose rationally connected to the performance of the job.

2. The testing provisions must be adopted in an honest and good faith belief that they are necessary to accomplish the company's purpose.

3. The testing provisions must be reasonably necessary to accomplish a company's purpose.

Drug testing remains a grey area for employers. Pre-employment testing is not permitted, even for safety-sensitive positions, as current drug-testing technology does not measure actual impairment at the time of the test—it can only detect past usage. Random testing is generally not permitted, with the possible exception of safety-sensitive positions (such as truck drivers), or upon reinstatement following a workplace incident where impairment affected performance, but only if it is one facet of a larger process of assessment of drug abuse.[56]

Step Three: The Selection Interview

The interview is one of the most common and popular devices used for selecting job applicants. In fact, it was the only selection method being used by 100 percent of the respondents in a recent survey of over 200 Canadian firms.[57] Whether candidates are interviewed prior to or following testing varies greatly. The **selection interview**, which involves a process of two-way communication between the interviewee(s) and the interviewer(s), can be defined as "a procedure designed to predict future job performance on the basis of applicants' oral responses to oral inquiries."[58]

Interviews are considered to be one of the most important aspects of the selection process, and generally have a major impact on both applicants and interviewers. Interviews significantly influence applicants' views about the job and organization, enable employers to fill in any gaps in the information provided on application forms and résumés, and supplement the results of any tests administered. They may also reveal entirely new types of information.

A major reason for the popularity of selection interviews is that they meet a number of objectives of both interviewer and interviewee. Interviewer objectives include assessing applicants' qualifications and observing relevant aspects of applicants' behaviour, such as verbal communication skills, degree of self-confidence, and interpersonal skills; providing candidates with information about the job and expected duties and responsibilities; promoting the organization and highlighting its attractiveness; and determining how well the applicants would fit into the organization.[59] Typical objectives of job applicants include presenting a positive image of themselves; selling their skills and marketing their positive attributes to the interviewer(s); and gathering information about the job and the organization so that they can make an informed decision about the job, career opportunities in the firm, and the work environment.[60]

Types of Interviews   Selection interviews can be classified according to the degree of structure, their content, and the way in which the interview is administered.

The Structure of the Interview   First, interviews can be classified according to the degree to which they are structured. In an **unstructured interview**, questions are asked as they come to mind. Interviewees for the same job thus may or may not be asked the same or similar questions, and the interview's unstructured nature allows the interviewer to ask questions based on the candidate's last statements and to pursue points of interest as they develop. Unstructured inter-

selection interview A procedure designed to predict future job performance on the basis of applicants' oral responses to oral inquiries.

unstructured interview An unstructured, conversational-style interview. The interviewer pursues points of interest as they come up in response to questions.

views lack reliability, and are used for selection purposes by only 17 percent of Canadian firms.[61]

structured interview An interview following a set sequence of questions.

The interview can also be structured. In the classical **structured interview**, the questions and acceptable responses are specified in advance and the responses are rated for appropriateness of content.[62] In practice, however, most structured interviews do not involve specifying and rating responses in advance. Instead, each candidate is asked a series of predetermined, job-related questions, based on the job description and specification. Such interviews are generally high in validity and reliability. On the other hand, a totally structured interview does not provide the flexibility to pursue points of interest as they develop, which may result in an interview that seems quite mechanical to all concerned.

mixed (semi-structured) interview An interview format that combines the structured and unstructured techniques.

Between these two extremes is the **mixed (semi-structured) interview**, which involves a combination of preset, structured questions based on the job description and specification, and a series of preset candidate-specific, job-related questions based on information provided on the application form and/or résumé. The questions asked of all candidates facilitate candidate comparison, while the job-related, candidate-specific questions make the interview more conversational. A realistic approach that yields comparable answers and in-depth insights, the mixed interview format is extremely popular.

Research
Insight   ▷

A recent study of 92 real employment interviews found that the interviewers using high levels of structure in the interview process evaluated applicants less favourably than those who used semi-structured or unstructured interviews, and those applicants who were evaluated using a semi-structured interview were rated slightly higher than those evaluated by unstructured interviews. Additionally, the study found that there are significant differences in the way that female and male interviewers evaluate their applicants. While male interviewers' ratings were unaffected by the interview structure, female interviewers' ratings were substantially higher in unstructured and semi-structured interviews than in highly structured interviews.[63]

situational interview A series of job-related questions that focus on how the candidate would behave in a given situation.

The Content of the Interview Interviews can also be classified according to the content of their questions. A **situational interview** is one in which the questions focus on the individual's ability to project what his or her *future* behaviour would be in a given situation.[64] The underlying premise is that intentions predict behaviour. For example, a candidate for a supervisory position might be asked how he or she would respond to an employee coming to work late three days in a row. The interview can be both *structured* and *situational*, with predetermined questions requiring the candidate to project what his or her behaviour would be. In a structured situational interview, the applicant could be evaluated, say, on whether he or she would try to determine if the employee was experiencing some difficulty in getting to work on time or would simply issue a verbal or written warning to the employee.

behavioural or behaviour descriptive interview (BDI) A series of job-related questions that focus on relevant past job-related behaviours.

The **behavioural interview**, also known as a **behaviour description interview (BDI)**, involves describing various situations and asking interviewees how they behaved *in the past* in such situations.[65] The underlying assumption is that the best predictor of future performance is past performance in similar circumstances.

Finally, *psychological interviews* may be used for selection purposes. Often included in assessment centre evaluations, for example, such psychologist-conducted interviews are used to assess personality traits such as dependability.[66] These interviews generally have a significant unstructured element.

A recent study of 59 candidates for officer training in the Naval branch of the Canadian military and 93 district managers for a national general merchandise chain found that behavioural description interviews (BDI) were a reasonably strong predictor of leadership performance, while situational interviews (SI) were not. BDI is thus generally preferable when interviewing for higher-level positions.[67]

Administering the Interview   Interviews can also be classified based on how they are administered: one-on-one or by a panel of interviewers; sequentially or all at once; and computerized, videotaped, or conducted entirely in person. Most interviews are administered *one-on-one*. Most selection processes are sequential. In a *sequential interview* the applicant is interviewed by several persons in sequence before a selection decision is made. In an *unstructured sequential interview* each interviewer may look at the applicant from his or her own point of view, ask different questions, and form an independent opinion of the candidate. On the other hand, in a *structured sequential* (or serialized) interview, each interviewer rates the candidate on a standard evaluation form, and the ratings are compared before the hiring decision is made.[68]

panel interview An interview in which a group of interviewers questions the applicant.

A **panel interview** involves the candidate being interviewed simultaneously by a group (or panel) of interviewers, including an HR representative, the hiring manager, and potential co-workers, superiors, and/or reporting employees. Panel interviews are becoming increasingly popular. In fact, they are "always" used by 24 percent of the employers responding to a recent survey, and "sometimes used" by 49 percent of respondents.[69] The key advantages associated with this technique are increased likelihood that the information provided will be heard and recorded accurately; varied questions pertaining to each interviewer's area of expertise; minimized time and travel/accommodation expenses as each interviewee only attends one interview; reduced likelihood of human rights/employment equity violations since an HR representative is present; and less likelihood of interviewer error, due to advance planning and preparation.

A more stressful variant of the panel interview is the *mass interview*, which involves a panel simultaneously interviewing several candidates. The panel poses a problem to be solved and then sits back and watches which candidate takes the lead in formulating an answer.

A panel interview is an efficient and cost-effective way of permitting a number of qualified persons to assess a candidate's KSAs.

Increasingly, interviews are computerized. A *computerized selection interview* is one in which a job candidate's oral and/or computerized responses are obtained in response to computerized oral or written questions and/or situations. The basic idea is to present to each applicant a series of questions (often multiple choice) regarding his or her KSAs for the job for which he or she has applied. Once the questions have been answered, they are automatically scored and the candidates are ranked, according to a predetermined weighting scale based on the relative importance of each of the selection criteria.

Research
I n s i g h t

A recent study of 44 video interviews involved Canadian university students who were enrolled in cooperative education programs. Interviewers reported a number of characteristics inherent in the video medium that they believed hindered their assessment of the applicants relative to face-to-face interviews. Forty percent noted difficulties in reading nonverbal behaviours, 28 percent noted audio problems, and 24 percent cited video lag. However, 20 percent indicated that communication skills were easier to assess in the video format than in the face-to-face format, and 12 percent said the same thing about friendliness.

While 76 percent of the interviewers indicated a preference for conducting their interviews in the traditional face-to-face format, the majority of interviewers rated applicants in the video interviews higher than the applicants interviewed face-to-face, and 88 percent reported that they would be willing to use the video technology to conduct employment interviews in the future.[70]

How Useful Are Interviews?   The ironic thing about interviews is that while they are used by virtually all employers, much of the earlier research gave selection interviews low marks in terms of reliability and validity. However, more recent studies affirm that the interview is "generally a much better predictor of performance than previously thought and is comparable with many other selection techniques," as long as the proper administration technique is selected.[71]

Interviewing and the Law   As a selection procedure, interviews must comply with human rights legislation. Doing so requires keeping the following guidelines in mind:

Hints **to Ensure**
Legal Compliance

1. Interviewers cannot ask questions that would violate human rights legislation, either directly or indirectly. Questions cannot be asked about candidates' marital status, childcare arrangements, ethnic background, or workers' compensation history, for example.

2. All interviewees must be treated in the same manner. An interviewer cannot ask only female factory position applicants to demonstrate their lifting abilities, for example, or question female sales applicants about their willingness to travel, but not male candidates.

3. Cutting short an interview based on preconceived notions about the gender or race of the "ideal" candidate should also be avoided, since this is another example of illegal differential treatment.

4. A helpful phrase to keep in mind when designing interview questions is "This job requires..." Interviewers who focus on the job description and job specification can gather all of the information required to assess applicants, without infringing on the candidates' legal rights.

Common Interviewing Mistakes   Several common interviewing errors that can undermine the usefulness of interviews are discussed below.

Poor Planning Many selection interviews are simply not carefully planned, and may be conducted without having prepared written questions in advance. Non-HR supervisors and managers may not know how to plan interviews or understand the importance of doing so.[72] Lack of planning often leads to a relatively unstructured interview, in which whatever comes up gets discussed. Since the end result may be little or no cross-candidate job-related information, the less structured the interview is, the less reliable and valid the evaluation of each candidate will be.[73]

Snap Judgments   One of the most consistent literature findings is that interviewers tend to jump to conclusions—make snap judgments—during the first few minutes of the interview or even before the interview begins, based on the candidates' test scores or résumé data. For example, one study showed that interviewers' access to candidates' test scores led to biased assessments.[74] Another researcher estimated that in 85 percent of the cases, interviewers had made up their minds about candidates before the interview began on the basis of applicants' application forms and personal appearance. Findings like these underscore that it is important for a candidate to start off on the right foot with the interviewer.

Negative Emphasis   Interviewers seem to have a consistent negative bias. They are generally more influenced by unfavourable than favourable information about the candidate. Also, their impressions are much more likely to change from favourable to unfavourable than vice versa. It is thus common for interviewers to turn interviews into a search for negative information, which means that most interviews are probably loaded against the applicant: an applicant who is initially rated highly could easily end up with a low rating, since unfavourable interview information tends to carry more weight, and an interviewee who starts out with a poor rating will find it hard to overcome that first bad impression.[75]

Halo Effect   It is also possible for a positive initial impression to distort an interviewer's rating of a candidate, because subsequent information is judged with a positive bias. This is known as the **halo effect**. An applicant who has a pleasant smile and firm handshake, for example, may be judged positively before the interview even begins. Having gained that positive initial impression, the interviewer may not seek contradictory information when listening to the candidate's answers to the questions posed.

halo effect A positive initial impression that distorts an interviewer's rating of a candidate, because subsequent information is judged with a positive bias.

Poor Knowledge of the Job   Interviewers who do not know precisely what the job entails, and what sort of candidate is best suited for it, usually make their decisions based on incorrect stereotypes about what a good applicant is. Interviewers who have a clear understanding of what the job entails conduct more effective interviews.

Pressure to Hire   Pressure to hire also undermines an interview's usefulness, since interviewers often lower their standards in such situations. In one study, a group of managers was told to assume that they were behind in their recruiting schedule. A second group was told that they were ahead of schedule. Those "behind" evaluated the same recruits much more highly than did those "ahead."[76]

contrast or candidate-order error An error of judgment on the part of the interviewer due to interviewing one or more very good or very bad candidates just before the interview in question.

Contrast (Candidate-Order) Error   **Contrast or candidate-order error** means that the order in which applicants are seen can affect how they are rated. In one study, managers were asked to evaluate a candidate who was "just average" after first evaluating several "unfavourable" candidates. The average candidate was evaluated more favourably than he or she might otherwise have been, since, in contrast to the unfavourable candidates, the average one looked better than he or she actually was.

Influence of Nonverbal Behaviour   Interviewers are also influenced by the applicant's nonverbal behaviour, and the more eye contact, head moving, smiling, and other similar nonverbal behaviours, the higher the ratings. These nonverbal behaviours often account for more than 80 percent of the applicant's rating.[77] This is of particular concern since nonverbal behaviour is tied to ethnicity and cultural background. An applicant's attractiveness and gender also play a role.[78] Research has shown that those rated as being more physically attractive are also rated more suitable for employment, well ahead of those rated average looking and those regarded as physically unattractive. While this bias is considered to be unconscious, it may have serious implications for aging employees.[79]

Telegraphing   Some interviewers are so anxious to fill a job that they help the applicants to respond correctly to their questions by telegraphing the expected answer.[80] An obvious example might be a question like: "This job calls for handling a lot of stress. You can do that, can you not?" The telegraphing is not always so obvious. For example, favourable first impressions of candidates tend to be linked to use of a more positive interview style. This can translate into sending subtle cues regarding the preferred response, such as a smile or nod.[81]

Too Much/Too Little Talking   If the applicant is permitted to dominate the interview, the interviewer may not have a chance to ask his or her prepared questions and often learns very little about the candidate's job-related skills. At the other extreme, some interviewers talk so much that the interviewee is not given enough time to answer questions.[82] One expert suggests using the 30/70 rule: During a selection interview, encourage the candidate to speak 70 percent of the time, and restrict the interviewer speaking to just 30 percent of the time.[83]

Playing Attorney or Psychologist   Since the interviewer often plays the role of gatekeeper in determining whether or not the interviewee gets a job, there is sometimes a tendency to misuse power by playing attorney or psychologist. For example, while it is smart to be alert for inconsistencies in applicants' responses, it is important to guard against turning the interview into a game of "gotcha" in which the interviewer derives pleasure from ferreting out and pouncing on interviewees' inconsistencies. Also inappropriate is playing psychologist, probing for hidden meanings in everything that the applicants say.[84]

Similar-to-Me Bias   Interviewers tend to provide more favourable ratings to candidates who possess similar demographic, personality, and attitudinal characteristics to themselves.[85]

Designing an Effective Interview

Problems like those just described can be avoided by designing and conducting an effective interview. Combining several of the interview formats previously discussed enables interviewers to capitalize on the advantages of each.[86] To allow for probing and to prevent the interview from becoming too mechanical in nature, a semi-structured format is recommended. Given their higher validity in predicting job performance, the focus should be on situational and behavioural questions. Sears Telecatalogue combines several types of interviews and selection tests, as explained in the Strategic HR box.

Designing an effective interview involves composing a series of job-related questions—primarily situational and behavioural—to be asked of all applicants

Strategic HR

Combining Selection Techniques

Sears Telecatalogue has a well-planned and organized system to ensure that hiring is done in the most effective and efficient manner possible. Applicants are first given a mini-application to complete, which includes information about availability. If an applicant's availability meets any job openings, an HR staff member contacts the applicant by telephone to conduct a structured telephone screening interview. The telephone screening interview is considered key to evaluating applicants, as positions with the company involve talking on the telephone. During the interview, applicants are evaluated based on their voice clarity, pace, and grammar.

Upon passing the telephone interview, the applicant is scheduled to come to the facility to complete a more detailed application. Because the jobs with the company involve the use of numbers, candidates complete a math test to measure arithmetic skills as well as a clerical test to identify speed and accuracy in performing routine clerical tasks. The candidate is then asked to complete a multiple-choice-format

computer-assisted interview to assess simple computer skills that are important for the position because the Sears Telecatalogue centre positions require computer use. The PC-based interview was developed specifically for Sears and identifies areas for follow-up to be covered in a personal interview.

The candidate is then scheduled for a personal interview. The supervisor or manager gives the applicant a tour of the workplace and conducts a 30-minute interview consisting of open-ended questions. While waiting for the face-to-face interview, candidates view a video that provides them with a realistic job preview of the position applied for.

Sears Telecatalogue believes that its selection process allows for the most efficient use of time and resources for both applicants and Sears. They believe that the system is effective in promoting the company, because it communicates that they are the kind of employer that treats people with respect through a well-organized, friendly selection process.

Source: Extracted from J.L. MacInnis and B.H. Kleiner, "How to Hire Effectively," *Management Research News* 25, no. 5, 2002, pp. 58–65.

---

for a particular job, as well as a few job-related candidate-specific questions. Doing so involves the following five steps, the first two of which should occur prior to recruitment.[87]

The first step is to decide who will be involved in the selection process and to *develop selection criteria*. Specifying selection criteria involves clarifying and weighting the information in the job description and job specification, and discussion among the interview-team members, especially those most familiar with the job and co-workers.

The second step is to *specify "musts" and "wants"* and weighting the "wants." Once agreed upon, the selection criteria should be divided into two categories: musts and wants.[88] **Must criteria** are those that are absolutely essential for the job, include a measurable standard of acceptability, or are absolute. There tend to be relatively few must criteria for any job; there are often only two: a specific level of education (or equivalent combination of education and work experience) and a minimum amount of prior, related work experience. The must criteria should be listed as mandatory on the job posting and in any recruitment advertising. The **want criteria** include skills and abilities that cannot be screened on paper (such as verbal communication skills), or are not readily measurable (such as leadership ability, teamwork skills, and enthusiasm), as well as qualifications that are desirable but not critical (such as knowledge of the specific word processing software package used at the firm). An example is excellent oral communication skills for a sales position.

must criteria Requirements that are absolutely essential for the job, include a measurable standard of acceptability or are absolute, and can be screened initially on paper.

want criteria Those criteria that have been culled from the must list. They represent qualifications that cannot be screened on paper or are not readily measurable, as well as those that are highly desirable but not critical.

The third step is to determine assessment strategies and to *develop an evaluation form*. Once the must and want criteria have been identified, appropriate strategies for learning about each should be specified. For example, word processing skills are best assessed through hands-on testing (rather than interview questions), and oral communication skills can be judged on the basis of interview performance (not the response to a specific question). For some qualifications, especially those that are critically important, the team may decide to use several assessment strategies. For example, leadership skills might be assessed through behavioural questions, situational questions, a written test, and an assessment centre. Once all want criteria have been agreed upon and weighted, they become the basis for candidate comparison and evaluation, as illustrated in **Figure 6.8**.

The fourth step is to *develop interview questions* to be asked of all candidates. Open-ended questions—primarily situational and behavioural—should then be developed for each of the KSAs to be assessed during the interview. *Job-knowledge questions* and *worker-requirements questions* to gauge the applicants' motivation and willingness to perform under prevailing working conditions should also be included. Examples include questions about shift work, travel, or relocation associated with the job.

The fifth and final step is to *develop candidate-specific questions*. A few open-ended, job-related questions that are candidate-specific should be planned, based on each candidate's résumé and application form.

Conducting an Effective Interview   While the following discussion focuses on a semi-structured panel interview, the steps described should apply to all selection interviews.[89]

Planning the Interview   Prior to the first interview, agreement should be reached on the procedure that will be followed. Sometimes all members of the team ask a question in turn; in other situations, only one member of the team asks questions and the others serve as observers. Immediately before each interview, the panel members should review the applicant's application form and résumé, as well as the interview questions planned in advance. Sitting around a large table in a conference room is much more appropriate and far less stressful than having all panel members seated across from the candidate behind a table or desk, which forms both a physical and psychological barrier. Special planning is required when assessing candidates with disabilities. An example is provided in the Workforce Diversity box.

The rapport established with a job applicant not only puts the person at ease; it also reflects the company's attitude toward its public.

Establishing Rapport   The main reason for an interview is to find out as much as possible about the candidate's fit with the job specifications, something that is difficult to do if the individual is tense and nervous. The candidate should be greeted in a friendly manner and put at ease.

Asking Questions   The questions written in advance should then be asked in order. Interviewers should listen carefully and encourage the candidate to express his or her thoughts and ideas fully, and record the candidate's answers briefly but thoroughly. Taking notes increases the validity of the interview process, since doing so (1) reduces the likelihood of forgetting job-relevant information and subsequently reconstructing forgotten information in accordance with biases and stereotypes; (2) reduces the likelihood of making a snap judgment and helps to prevent

FIGURE 6.8   Worksheet—Comparison of Candidates for a Secretarial Position

Criteria	Wt.	A Smith Info	B Brown Go/No	B Brown Info	B Sc.	B Wt.Sc.	C Yuill Go/No	C Yuill Info	C Sc.	C Wt.Sc.	Go/No
Must											
Education — Office Admin. diploma or equivalent experience (3 years' clerical/secretarial experience)		Office admin. diploma	Go	Office admin. diploma			Go	No diploma, 1 year related experience			No Go
Experience — At least 2 years' secretarial/clerical experience		3 years' experience	Go	2 years' experience			Go				
Wants											
Keyboarding/word processing	10	Word processing test		Word processing test	9	90		Word processing test	10	100	
Good oral communication	9	Interview assessment		Interview assessment	9	81		Interview assessment	9	81	
Good spelling/grammar	9	Test results		Test results	8	72		Test results	9	81	
Organizational ability	9	Interview questions/simulation/ reference checking		Interview questions/simulation/ reference checking	8	72		Interview questions/simulation/ reference checking	9	81	
Initiative	8	Interview questions/simulation/ reference checking		Interview questions/simulation/ reference checking	7	56		Interview questions/simulation/ reference checking	8	64	
High ethical standards	7	Interview questions/simulation/ reference checking		Interview questions/simulation/ reference checking	7	49		Interview questions/simulation/ reference checking	7	49	
Shorthand skills (or speed writing)	4	Interview question and test results		Interview question and test results	4	16		Interview question and test results	0	0	
Designated group member, other than white female	2	Application form		Application form	2	4		Application form	0	0	
						440				456	

TOP CANDIDATE

WORKFORCE DIVERSITY

Looking for a Few Good Workers?

Given the impending labour shortage, hiring persons with disabilities is not only legally required and good public relations—it is a necessity. Employees who are visually impaired are an asset to any organization, as they have excellent attendance records and a greater retention rate in organizations for which they are employed. Many companies that employ visually impaired individuals find that they are very loyal and productive employees. However, when a company encounters a visually impaired candidate, it needs to consider altering its selection processes to help accommodate the applicant. Here are some tips to assist visually impaired applicants:

- Have the application available in electronic form. Visually impaired applicants then can use computers with Braille, speech output, or screen magnification to read and complete the application.

- Provide the application in advance of the interview so the applicant can complete it at home.

- Ask if the applicant wants assistance in an unfamiliar environment. Some people with visual impairments prefer to take someone's arm above the elbow; others prefer to follow verbal directions.

- When entering the interview room, describe the setting to the applicant. For example, you might say, "We are going to sit at a round table. Your chair is on the left."

- If pre-employment tests are routinely administered, discuss accommodations with the applicant to make the test accessible. For example, the test could be given electronically using appropriate assistive technology. Or, another employee could read the questions and record the applicant's answers.

- Focus on an applicant's qualifications, not his or her visual impairment.

- Never pet a guide dog. Although it may be friendly, a guide dog is a working animal.

- Don't be afraid to use expressions like "Do you see what I mean?" Visually impaired people use them too.

Source: Excerpted from K. Tyler, "Looking for a Few Good Workers?" *HR Magazine*, December 2000, pp. 129–134. Reprinted with permission of *HR Magazine* published by the Society for Human Resource Management, Alexandria, VA.

the halo effect, negative emphasis, and candidate-order errors; and (3) helps to ensure that all candidates are assessed on the same criteria.[90]

Closing the Interview Toward the end of the interview, time should be allocated to answer any questions that the candidate may have, and, if appropriate, to advocate the firm and position. All interviews should be ended on a positive note. The interviewee should be thanked and informed about subsequent steps in the selection process.

Reviewing Notes and Evaluating the Candidate Immediately following each interview, the applicant's interview performance should be rated by each panel member independently, based on a review of his or her notes. Since interviews are only one step in the process, and a final decision cannot be reached until all assessments (including reference checking) have been completed, these evaluations should not be shared at this point in time.

Step Four: Background Investigation and Reference Checking

Background investigation and reference checking are extremely important. Such checking serves two key purposes: (1) verifying the accuracy of the information pertaining to job-related educational qualifications and experience provided by candidates on their application forms and résumés, and (2) validating the information obtained during the other steps in the selection process.

In one recent study, for example, 99 percent of employers surveyed reported that they find reference checking to be either useful or very useful. Three-quarters conduct telephone discussions with individuals suggested by executive candidates, and 88 percent conduct such checks for managerial, supervisory, professional, technical, and other salaried candidates. In addition, 97 percent of respondents rated verification of education, licences, or designations as useful or very useful.[91]

Unfortunately, many employers do not check references for lower-level employees, which can have grave consequences. A Toronto-based trucking company could have saved $250 000 had they conducted a background check on a woman they hired to manage their accounts department. Over the course of her two years as a bookkeeper, she siphoned $250 000 from the company's general account. She was ultimately prosecuted for fraud and theft under $5000, and sentenced to three years in jail. If the company had called her previous employer, they would have discovered that the woman they hired had defrauded the other company of $100 000 and was ordered to pay back the money. The former employer said they would have tipped off the company had they been contacted.[92]

Recognizing the critical importance of such checking, but lacking the time or human resources to do a thorough job, some firms use reference-checking services or hire a consultant to perform this task, especially for senior-level positions. For example, third-party specialists were used to conduct reference checking for executive-level candidates by 37 percent of the employers participating in the survey described above.[93] Obtaining such assistance may be a small price to pay to avoid the time and legal costs associated with a wrongful dismissal suit or parting company with an unsuitable employee.

In an ideal world, every applicant's story would be completely accurate, but in real life, this is often not the case. It is estimated that one in four applicants overstates his or her qualifications or achievements, attempts to hide negative information, or is deliberately evasive or untruthful.[94] More than 93 percent of the respondents in a recent survey said that they had found exaggerations on résumés, and 86 percent had found outright misrepresentations.[95] A recent study of Canadian employees found that men are virtually three times more likely to lie on their résumés than women.[96]

Whether requesting reference information in writing or asking for such information over the telephone, questions should be written down in advance. **Figure 6.9** is an example of a form used for written reference checking.

Effectiveness   Handled correctly—by someone other than the interviewer —reference checking can be extremely worthwhile. For example, following an investigation into 7030 Quebec daycare owners, which found that 20 had criminal records, the Quebec government decided to conduct background checks on all of the province's 35 000 daycare workers.[97] If enough time is taken and the proper questions are asked, such checking is an inexpensive and straightforward way of verifying factual information about the applicant. This may include current and previous job titles, salary, dates of employment, and reasons for leaving, as well as information about the applicant's fit with the job and organizational culture. Most employers do not put too much weight on letters of reference provided by former employers.[98] These are often very general, revealing little useful information about ability to perform the job in question, and are typically extremely positive. Furthermore, sometimes such letters have actually been written by the candidate!

FIGURE 6.9   Form Requesting Written Reference Information

We are in the process of considering James Ridley Parrish (SIN Number: 123-45-6789) for a sales position in our firm. In considering him/her, it would be helpful if we could review your appraisal of his/her previous work with you. For your information, we have enclosed a statement signed by him/her authorizing us to contact you for information on his/her previous work experience with you. We would certainly appreciate it if you would provide us with your candid opinions of his/her employment. If you have any questions or comments you would care to make, please feel free to contact us at the number listed in the attached cover letter. At any rate, thank you for your consideration of our requests for the information requested below. As you answer the questions, please keep in mind that they should be answered in terms of your knowledge of his/her previous work with you.

1. When was he/she employed with your firm? From _____ to _____
2. Was he/she under your direct supervision? ☐ Yes ☐ No
3. If not, what was your working relationships with him/her? _____
4. How long have you had an opportunity to observe his/her job performance? _____
5. What was his/her last job title with your firm? _____
6. Did he/she supervise any employees? ☐ Yes ☐ No If so, how many? _____
7 Why did he/she leave your company? _____

Below is a series of questions that deal with how he/she might perform at the job for which we are considering him/her. Read the question and then use the rating scale to indicate how you think he/she would perform based on your previous knowledge of his/her work.

8. For him/her to perform best, how closely should he/she be supervised?
   ☐ Needs no supervision
   ☐ Needs infrequent supervision
   ☐ Needs close, frequent supervision
9. How well does he/she react to working with details?
   ☐ Gets easily frustrated
   ☐ Can handle work that involves some details but works better without them
   ☐ Details in a job pose no problems at all
10. How well do you think he/she can handle complaints from customers?
   ☐ Would generally refuse to help resolve a customer complaint
   ☐ Would help resolve a complaint only if a customer insisted
   ☐ Would feel the customer is right and do everything possible to resolve a complaint
11 In what type of sales job do you think he/she would be best?
   ☐ Handling sales of walk-in customers
   ☐ Traveling to customer locations out-of-town to make sales
12. With respect to his/her work habits, check all of the characteristics below that describe his/her work situation:
   ☐ Works best on a regular schedule
   ☐ Works best under pressure
   ☐ Works best only when in the mood
   ☐ Works best when there is a regular series of steps to follow for solving a problem
13. Do you know of anything that would indicate if he/she would be unfit or dangerous (for example, in working with customers or co-workers or in driving an automobile) in a position with our organization? ☐ Yes ☐ No
   If "yes" please explain. _____
14. If you have any additional comments, please make them on the back of this form.

Your Name: _____
Your Title: _____
Address: _____
            City   State   ZIP
Company: _____
Telephone: _____

Thank you for your time and help. The information you provided will be very useful as we review all application materials.

Note: This form is completed by the reference giver.

Source: From *Human Resource Selection*, fifth edition, by Gatewood/Field. © 2001. Reprinted with permission of South-Western, a division of Thomson Learning: www.thomsonrights.com. Fax 800-730-2215.

Educational qualifications are checked by asking for an original transcript, certificate, diploma, or degree. The use of consumer credit reports by employers as a basis for establishing an applicant's eligibility for employment is fairly restricted in Canada. Such checks must be job related. Positions of trust, such as those that involve the handling of money and financial transactions in banks and other financial institutions, necessitate the use of credit reports, for example. Applicants must agree in writing to a credit report, and have the right to review its contents.

Obtaining Written Permission

Written permission is not only required for credit checking. As a legal protection for all concerned, applicants should be asked to indicate, in writing, their willingness for the firm to check with current and/or former employers and other references. There is generally a section on the application form for this purpose. Many employers will not give out any reference information until they have received a copy of such written authorization.

Making Reference Checks More Effective

Several things can be done to make reference checks more effective. One is to use a structured form to ensure that important questions are not overlooked. Another suggestion is to use the references offered by the applicant as a source for other references who may know of the applicant's performance. Thus, each of the applicant's references might be asked, "Could you please give me the name of another person who might be familiar with the applicant's performance?" In that way, information may be obtained from references who are more objective since they weren't referred directly by the applicant. Making reference checks productive also requires persistence.

Legal Issues Involved in Obtaining and Providing Reference Information

Failure to check references can lead to negligent or wrongful hiring suits that may involve significant damages. In an Ontario case, two nightclub bouncers viciously beat a patron, leaving him with severe and permanent brain damage that rendered him permanently unemployable and incapable of managing his day-to-day affairs. While liability was imposed directly against the bouncers, the court went further and held the employer vicariously liable for failing to properly check the references or criminal backgrounds of the bouncers involved. The application form for one of the bouncers was missing, and the other's application contained false information, which had obviously never been checked. He had also previously been convicted of wounding. Damages of more than $2 million were awarded against the bouncers, the company that operated the bar, and two shareholders, both of whom were officers of the company.

In providing reference information, the concept of qualified privilege is important. Generally speaking, if comments are made in confidence for a public purpose, without malice, and are honestly believed, the defence of "qualified privilege" exists. Thus, if honest, fair, and candid references are given by an individual who is asked to provide confidential information about the performance of a job applicant, then the doctrine of qualified privilege generally protects the reference giver, even if negative information is imparted about the candidate. Nevertheless, with the fear of civil litigation increasing, more Canadian companies are adopting a "no reference" policy regarding previous employees or are only willing to confirm the position held and dates of

An Ethical Dilemma

As the HR manager, how would you balance your ethical responsibilities to those providing reference information and to the job applicant in a situation in which a candidate is being eliminated from a competition based on negative reference information from a number of sources?

employment —especially in the case of discharged employees.[99] In a recent survey, 64 percent of employers responding indicated that they provide only limited reference data with respect to dismissed employees.

Step Five: The Supervisory Interview and Realistic Job Preview

The two or three top candidates typically return for an interview with the immediate supervisor, who usually makes the final selection decision. The supervisory interview is important because the supervisor knows the technical aspects of the job, is most qualified to assess the applicants' job knowledge and skills, and is best equipped to answer any job-specific questions from the candidate. Also, the immediate supervisor generally has to work closely with the selected individual and must feel comfortable with that person. The selected individual must fit with the current members of the hiring department, something that the supervisor is often best able to assess. When a supervisor makes a hiring recommendation, he or she is usually committed to the new employee's success, and will try to provide assistance and guidance. If the new hire is not successful, the supervisor is more likely to accept some of the responsibility.

A **realistic job preview (RJP)** should be provided at the time of the supervisory interview. The purpose of a RJP is to create appropriate expectations about the job by presenting realistic information about the job demands, the organization's expectations, and the work environment.[100] Studies have reported that RJPs lead to improved employee job satisfaction, reduced voluntary turnover, and enhanced communication.[101] While some candidates may choose not to accept employment with the firm after an RJP, those individuals probably would not have remained with the firm long had they accepted the job offer.[102]

realistic job preview (RJP) A strategy used to provide applicants with realistic information—both positive and negative—about the job demands, the organization's expectations, and the work environment.

Step Six: Making the Hiring Decision

To make the hiring decision, information from the multiple selection techniques used must be combined, and the applicant who is the best fit with the selection criteria must be identified. HR department staff members generally play a major role in compiling all of the data. It is the immediate supervisor who is usually responsible for making the final hiring decision, however. Firms generally make a subjective evaluation of all of the information gleaned about each candidate and arrive at an overall judgment. The validity and reliability of these judgments can be improved by using tests that are objectively scored, and devising a candidate-rating sheet based on the weighted want criteria.

Another approach involves combining all of the pieces of information according to a formula, and giving the job to the candidate with the highest score. Research studies have indicated that this approach, called a **statistical strategy**, is generally more reliable and valid than a subjective evaluation.[103] At Toronto Hydro, selection decisions are now made with the assistance of software that enables the selection team to assign numbers to every proposition, comparison, scenario, question, and answer. It is a logical approach that eliminates bias. However, it still requires a human touch, since the hiring-team members have to decide on and weight the selection criteria, determine and weight interview questions, and establish a scale for possible answers. Once these tasks are completed, the software can then track and tabulate all of the numbers as

statistical strategy A more objective technique used to determine to whom the job should be offered, which involves identifying the most valid predictors and weighting them through statistical methods such as multiple regression.

the applicant goes through the process, and eventually the candidate with the best overall score is selected for the position.[104]

Regardless of collection methodology, all information used in making the selection decision should be kept in a file, including interview notes, test results, reference checking information, and so on. In the event of a human rights challenge, negligent hiring charge, or union grievance about the selection decision, such data are critical.

Step Seven: Candidate Notification

AN ETHICAL DILEMMA

As the HR manager, how much feedback should you provide to those individuals not selected for a position?

Once the selection decision has been made, a job offer is extended to the successful candidate. Often, the initial offer is made by telephone, but it should be followed up with a written employment offer that clearly specifies important terms and conditions of employment, such as starting date, starting salary, probation period, and so on. Two copies of the letter should be sent: one for the successful candidate to sign and return to the firm (provided that he or she decides to accept the offer, of course), and the other for the candidate's records.

HR department staff members generally handle offers of employment, both the initial offer by telephone and the follow-up in writing. Candidates should be given a reasonable length of time in which to think the offer over, and not be pressured into making an immediate decision. If there are two candidates who are both excellent, and the second choice would be quite acceptable to all concerned, the runner-up is often not notified until after the first-choice candidate has accepted the position. Should the first-choice candidate decline the offer, the runner-up can then be offered the job. All finalists who are not selected should be notified.

Step Eight: Evaluating the Selection Process

Evaluating the selection process involves considering a number of questions:

- Are the selection procedures used effective in identifying qualified, capable, productive employees?
- Are the techniques used efficient and worth the costs and trouble?
- Are there ways in which the process could be streamlined or improved?

To answer these questions, feedback is required. Retention data and performance appraisal results can help to identify successes. Feedback on failures is typically ample, and includes complaints from supervisors, poor performance ratings, turnover and/or absenteeism, low employee satisfaction, union grievances or unionization attempts, and even legal challenges.

Constructive feedback can also be obtained from employees and supervisors, and through assessment. A questionnaire can be administered to newly hired and newly transferred or promoted employees, asking for their impressions of the steps involved in the selection process. Supervisors can be asked for information about how easily and how well their recent hires seem to be adapting to the job, team, and organizational culture. In addition, an informal assessment of the performance of each newly hired and newly transferred or promoted employee can be made long before a formal appraisal is due.

In the long run, the value of selection procedures must be determined by looking at the quality and productivity of the new hires, as well as the selection costs.

Interview Applicants Appropriately

... If you were hiring a firefighter, you would satisfy yourself that the employee possessed the physical capability to perform the strenuous physical tasks inherent in that position. Passing a series of tests rationally connected to the position might be a prerequisite. In the same way that you would inquire about an applicant's physical ability to perform a physically demanding job, you may wish to assess whether an applicant possesses certain behavioural attributes considered to be essential to the position. Of course, in the same way that you would not ask the applicant whether he or she suffered from a bad back, you would not ask an applicant if he or she suffered from generalized anxiety disorder. You may, however, discuss the demands of the position and you may ask situational questions that would guide you as to how an applicant would handle certain situations. By doing so, you should be in a better position to assess an individual's emotional competency for a job and what, if any, accommodation might be required....

Source: Excerpted with permission from the *Focus on Canadian Employment and Equality Rights* Newsletter (September 2002), published by and copyright CCH Canadian Limited, Toronto, Ontario.

CHAPTER *Review*

Summary

1   Selection is the process of choosing individuals with the relevant qualifications to fill existing or projected job openings. The purpose of selection is to find the "best" candidate. Effective selection is important for three reasons: the quality of the company's human resources is often a competitive advantage in achieving the company's strategic objectives; extremely high costs are associated with ineffective hiring; and there are legal implications related to human rights and employment equity legislation, and liability for negligent or wrongful hiring.

2   There are a number of constraints on the selection process, including the company's strategic plan, selection budget, and employment equity plan; the job requirements; the selection ratio; ethics; and legislative requirements.

3   Reliability (the degree to which selection tools are dependable, consistent, and stable) and validity (which relates to accuracy) are critically important. It is important that all selection procedures be both valid and reliable in order to satisfy legal requirements.

4   The different types of tests used for selection include intelligence tests, emotional intelligence tests, aptitude tests, tests of motor and physical abilities, personality tests, interest inventories, achievement tests, the work-sampling technique, management assessment centres, video-based situational testing, micro-assessments, honesty tests, and graphology. Medical examinations and substance abuse testing must be used with caution due to human rights legislation. Conflicting legal concerns with respect to substance abuse testing arise because on the one hand, employees cannot be discriminated against based on an addiction (as this is considered a disability under human rights law), but on the other hand, employers are responsible for ensuring a safe workplace under occupational health and safety legislation.

5   Selection interviewing can be unstructured, structured, or semi-structured. The content varies between situational interviews (focus on future behaviour), behavioural interviews (focus on past behaviour), and psychological interviews (focus on personality traits). Interviews can be administered on a one-on-one basis, sequentially, using a panel, or by computer.

6   Reference checking is a very important source of information about job candidates. To make

reference checks more effective, written permission should be obtained from each applicant, a structured form should be used, references offered by the applicant should be used as a source for other references, and staff checking references must be persistent. Failure to check references can lead to negligent or wrongful hiring lawsuits. The legal concept of qualified privilege means that if honest, fair, and candid references are given by a reference-giver, he or she is protected from litigation, even if negative information is imparted about the candidate. Nevertheless, the fear of civil litigation is increasing, and more Canadian companies are adopting a policy of "no references" or will only confirm the position held and dates of employment.

Key Terms

achievement tests   *(p. 181)*
aptitude tests   *(p. 177)*
behavioural or behaviour descriptive interview (BDI)   *(p. 187)*
construct validity   *(p. 172)*
content validity   *(p. 172)*
contrast or candidate-order error   *(p. 190)*
criterion-related validity   *(p. 172)*
differential validity   *(p. 173)*
emotional intelligence (EI) tests   *(p. 177)*
graphology   *(p. 184)*
halo effect   *(p. 190)*
honesty tests   *(p. 183)*
intelligence (IQ) tests   *(p. 177)*
interest inventories   *(p. 181)*
management assessment centre   *(p. 182)*
micro-assessment   *(p. 183)*

mixed (semi-structured) interview   *(p. 187)*
multiple-hurdle strategy   *(p. 168)*
must criteria   *(p. 192)*
panel interview   *(p. 188)*
personality tests   *(p. 180)*
polygraph (lie detector)   *(p. 183)*
realistic job preview (RJP)   *(p. 199)*
reliability   *(p. 172)*
selection   *(p. 168)*
selection interview   *(p. 186)*
selection ratio   *(p. 171)*
situational interview   *(p. 187)*
situational tests   *(p. 182)*
statistical strategy   *(p. 199)*
structured interview   *(p. 187)*
unstructured interview   *(p. 186)*
validity   *(p. 172)*
want criteria   *(p. 192)*

Review and Discussion Questions

1   Briefly describe each of the eight steps that may be included in the selection process.

2   Describe any three of the Canadian Psychological Association guidelines for setting up a testing program.

3   Describe any four activities involved in a management assessment centre.

4   Explain the difference between situational and behavioural interviews. Give examples of situational and behavioural interview questions.

5   Briefly discuss any five common interviewing mistakes and explain how such errors can be avoided.

6   Why is the supervisory interview so important in the selection process?

CRITICAL *Thinking Questions*

1   If you were asked to design an effective selection process for retail sales representatives working on a 100 percent commission basis, which of the steps described in this chapter would you include and why? Justify the omission of any steps and explain why the quality of the selection decision will not be compromised by their elimination.

2   Assume that you have just been hired as the employment manager in a firm that has never done any selection testing. Write a memorandum to the CEO describing the types of tests that you would recommend the firm consider using in the future, some of the legal and ethical concerns pertaining to such testing and how

such concerns can be overcome, and the benefits to the firm of using the recommended testing.

3 Describe strategies that you could use to (a) establish rapport with an extremely nervous candidate; (b) get an interviewee who is rambling "back on track"; (c) clarify a statement made by an applicant during an interview; and (d) obtain detailed reference information from an individual who seems reluctant to say much.

APPLICATION *Exercises*

Running Case: LearnInMotion.com

The Better Interview

Like virtually all the other HR-related activities at LearnInMotion.com, the company has no organized approach to interviewing job candidates. Three people, Jennifer, Pierre, and Greg (from the board of directors), interview each candidate, and the three then get together for a discussion. Unfortunately, they usually reach strikingly different conclusions. For example, Greg thought a particular candidate was "stellar" and would not only be able to sell, but eventually assume various administrative responsibilities to take the load off Jennifer and Pierre. Pierre thought this particular candidate was hopeless: "I've been selling for eight years and have hired many salespeople, and there's no way this person's going to be a closer" is the way he put it. Jennifer, noting that a friend of her mother had recommended this particular candidate, was willing to take a wait-and-see attitude: "Let's hire her and see how she does" is the way she put it. Pierre replied that this was no way to hire a salesperson, and, in any case, hiring another administrator was pretty far down their priority list, so "I wish Greg would stick to the problem at hand, namely hiring a 100 percent salesperson."

Jennifer was sure that inadequate formal interviewing practices, procedures, and training accounted for at least some of the problems they were having in hiring and keeping good salespeople. They did hire one salesperson whom they thought was going to be terrific, based on the praise provided by her references and on what they understood her previous sales experience had been; she stayed for a month and a half, sold hardly anything, cost the company almost $10 000 of its precious cash, and then left for another job.

The problem wasn't just with the salespeople. For one thing, they hired a programmer largely based on his assertion that he was expert in various Web-related programming including HTML, XML, and Java script. They followed up with one of his references, who was neutral regarding the candidate's programming abilities. But, being desperate, Jennifer and Pierre hired him anyway—only to have him leave three weeks later, more or less by mutual consent.

"This is a total disaster," said Jennifer, and Pierre could only agree. It was obvious that in some respects their interviews were worse than not interviewing at all: for example, if they didn't have interviews, perhaps they would have used more caution in following up with the candidates' references. In any case, they now want you, their management consultants, to tell them what to do. Here's what they want you to do for them.

Questions

1 Tell Pierre and Jennifer what they're doing wrong.

2 In general, what can LearnInMotion.com do to improve their employee interviewing practices? Should they develop interview forms that list questions for their various jobs? If so, what format should these take?

3 What are five questions they should ask salespeople candidates, and five questions they should ask programmer candidates?

CASE INCIDENT *The Selection Process*

Several weeks ago, Marjorie saw an ad in the local newspaper for a forklift operator to work in the loading dock area at the Three Hills Manufacturing Company. This firm employs you as the HR manager. Marjorie has had seven years of experience in this type of work. Although the thought of having to work on the night shift does not particularly appeal to her, her need for additional money and the fact that the job at Three Hills pays more than she is currently earning prompted her to send in her résumé. She was also impressed by the indication in the ad that employees could qualify for training in more technical areas.

Marjorie was interviewed by Tom, the night shift supervisor, who seemed to have difficulty believing that she had seven years of prior experience. He suggested that she demonstrate her skills by taking a driving test. She complied, even though she was surprised by the request.

Following the test, Tom questioned Marjorie closely about how she would fit into the work environment. He said that she would be the only woman working in that area, and that the group might not appreciate the constraints on their joking and talking that a woman's presence would cause. He also said that she could not expect them to help her out with

tasks "just because she is a woman" and asked how her husband would feel about her being out all night. Marjorie assured Tom that this was a normal work setting for her and one that she had learned to handle long ago.

You have just found out about the situation. Apparently, after learning that she was not being offered a job, Marjorie discovered that six men had been hired, of whom none was asked to take a test and none had as much experience as she. She therefore decided to file a complaint with the Human Rights Commission, a copy of which has just landed on your desk.

Questions

1   Based on the facts given, do you think that Marjorie was treated fairly? Why or why not?

2   "There are a number of problems with the current selection process at Three Hills, including violations of human rights legislation." Explain this statement.

3   As the HR manager, are you legally liable for Tom's behaviour? Why or why not?

4   In resolving this situation, what issues need to be addressed? How would you address them?

Experiential Exercises

1   Design a semi-structured interview questionnaire for a position with which you are extremely familiar, basing the candidate-specific questions on your own résumé. Ensure that behavioural, situational, job-knowledge, and worker-requirements questions are included. Once you have done so, select a partner. Role-play two selection interviews—one based on your questionnaire and the other based on your partner's questionnaire. The individual who wrote the questions is to play the role of interviewee, with

his or her partner serving as the interviewer. Do not forget to build rapport, ask the questions in order, take effective notes, and bring the interview to a close. Once you have completed the two role-plays, critically evaluate each of the interview questionnaires.

2   Create an offer of employment for a successful customer-service representative at a call centre, outlining the terms and conditions of employment. Keep in mind that a copy of the letter should be signed and returned by the new hire and that a signed letter of offer becomes an employment contract.

Résumé Lies

2

Lying on résumés is a very common practice amongst Canadian employees, and many are hired when they do not actually possess the qualifications for the job. If these employees subsequently do not complete their jobs properly, resulting in harm to fellow employees or customers, the employer can be found guilty of negligent hiring and be liable for damages suffered by any negatively affected parties.

HR-department staff typically don't have time to thoroughly check the résumés of job applicants. That's where InfoCheck can help. Partners Clinton Fox and Vincent Tsang assist their 250 corporate clients with reference checking, verifying post-secondary education and professional affiliations, and criminal background checks. They check about 800 résumés per month, from mailroom clerks to CEOs.

About one-third of the résumés they check contain inaccurate information. Applicants embellish, aggrandize, stretch the truth, and lie. Education is the area most often exaggerated. Other commonly misrepresented areas are reasons for leaving a previous job, length of employment, and job responsibilities. One applicant's résumé claimed a university degree and 15 years of experience, whereas in reality, the person had five criminal convictions and had stolen the identity of a dead person.

InfoCheck says that it is better to be truthful, because if an applicant is found to be lying on his or her résumé, they lose credibility and will not get the job.

Questions

1. Would you recommend that employers use the services of a company like InfoCheck to review résumés?

2. Are there any other actions that could be taken in the recruitment process to reduce the likelihood of résumé lies?

3. How much credibility should managers give to letters of reference?

Video Source: "Résumé Lies," *CBC Venture 773* (February 6, 2001).

Additional Resource: **www.infocheck.ca**

CHAPTER 7

Orientation and Training

CHAPTER OUTLINE

- Orienting Employees

- The Training Process

- Training Needs Analysis and Transfer of Training

- Traditional Training Techniques

- E-Learning

- Training for Special Purposes

- Evaluating the Training Effort

LEARNING OUTCOMES

After studying this chapter, you should be able to:

Explain how to develop an orientation program.

Describe the basic training process.

Discuss two techniques used for assessing training needs, and *explain* how to increase transfer of training.

Explain at least five traditional training techniques.

Describe the three types of e-learning.

Explain several common types of training for special purposes.

Describe how to evaluate the training effort.

ORIENTING EMPLOYEES

Once employees have been recruited and selected, the next step is orienting them to their new company and their new job. A strategic approach to recruitment and retention of employees includes a well-integrated orientation program both before and after hiring.[1]

Purpose of Orientation Programs

employee orientation A procedure for providing new employees with basic background information about the firm and the job.

socialization The ongoing process of instilling in all employees the prevailing attitudes, standards, values, and patterns of behaviour that are expected by the organization.

reality shock The state that results from the discrepancy between what the new employee expects from his or her new job, and the realities of it.

Employee orientation provides new employees with basic background information about the employer, and specific information that they need to perform their jobs satisfactorily. Orientation is actually one component of the employer's new-employee socialization process. **Socialization** is the ongoing process of instilling in all employees the prevailing attitudes, standards, values, and patterns of behaviour that are expected by the organization.[2]

The purpose of orientation is to help the employee to perform better by providing necessary information about company rules and practices. It helps to clarify the organization's expectations of an employee regarding his or her job. This can help to reduce the new employee's first-day jitters and the **reality shock** that he or she might otherwise experience (the discrepancy between what the new employee expected from his or her new job, and the realities of it). An important part of any effective orientation program is sitting down and deciding upon work-related goals with the new employee. These goals provide the basis for early feedback, and establish a foundation for ongoing performance management.[3] Orientation is the first step to help the new employee manage the learning curve; it helps new employees to become productive more quickly than they might otherwise. In the long term, a comprehensive orientation can lead to reductions in turnover, increased morale, fewer instances of corrective discipline, and fewer employee grievances. It can also reduce the number of workplace injuries, particularly for young workers.[4]

Some organizations commence orientation activity before the first day of employment. At Ernst & Young, the firm keeps in touch with people who have been hired but have not yet started work by sending them internal newsletters, inviting them to drop by for chats, and hosting dinners for them.[5] Others use orientation as an ongoing "new-hire development process" and extend it in stages throughout the first year of employment, in order to improve retention levels and reduce the overall costs of recruitment.[6]

Content of Orientation Programs

Orientation programs range from brief, informal introductions to lengthy, formal programs. In the latter, the new employee is usually given (over an extended period of time):

- a handbook that covers matters like company history and current mission; working hours and attendance expectations; vacations and holidays; payroll, employee benefits, and pensions; and work regulations and policies
- a tour of the company facilities and introductions to the employee's supervisor and co-workers
- an explanation of job procedures, duties, and responsibilities

- a summary of training to be received (when and why)
- an explanation of performance appraisal criteria, including the estimated time to achieve full productivity.

As illustrated in **Figure 7.1**, other information typically includes HR policies, strategic objectives, company organization and operations, and safety measures and regulations.[7] At Ernst & Young, after a review of best practices, both internally and externally, the orientation program was redesigned to include:[8]

- a presentation providing an overview of the firm
- an administrative checklist of tasks to be conducted prior to a new employee's start date and during the first three months of employment
- a binder explaining the firm's vision, values, strategies, and structures
- computer and voice-mail training
- a form for employee feedback
- an intranet site with information about the firm.

An example of the comprehensive orientation program at General Motors Acceptance Corporation is presented in the HR.Net box.

Note that some courts have found employee handbook contents to represent a contract with the employee. Therefore, disclaimers should be included that make it clear that statements of company policies, benefits, and regulations do not constitute the terms and conditions of an employment contract, either express or implied. Firms should think twice before including statements in the handbook such as, "No employee will be terminated without just cause," or statements that imply or state that employees have tenure; they could be viewed as legal and binding commitments.

Hints to Ensure Legal Compliance

HR.Net

Technology Puts Employees in Orientation Program's Driver Seat

When new employees arrive for their first day on the job at General Motors Acceptance Corporation (GMAC), they take a seat behind the steering wheel of a virtual GM vehicle. Armed with a road map, they proceed to navigate their way through GMAC's orientation program. The virtual dashboard on an employee's computer screen features a steering wheel and a complete selection of functioning buttons and dials. The presentation includes video clips from GM's archives, details on its organization and structure, and information about employee benefits and programs. Before exiting the program, a new employee participates in an interactive quiz and, upon completion, a certificate with his or her name and score is automatically printed.

The GMAC orientation program is delivered via CD-ROM but links to a corporate intranet for information that may be subject to change. This ensures that the orientation program is always up to date. The new orientation program is also used as a reference guide for information throughout an employee's career. When employees transfer to another department, they can review the orientation program to learn about the new area they will be working in.

The bottom line is that GMAC wants employees to be excited about working there. When employees are more knowledgeable about the company, everyone benefits. A self-service orientation will never replace the human touch, but it facilitates the delivery of orientation to a dispersed workforce. It ensures consistency and thoroughness, eliminates any excuses for delaying orientation, and dramatically reduces the burden on HR resources.

Source: Adapted from N. Tollinsky, "Technology Puts Employees in Orientation Program's Driver Seat," *Canadian HR Reporter* (April 9, 2001), pp. 19–20. Reproduced by permission of *Canadian HR Reporter*, Carswell, One Corporate Plaza, 2075 Kennedy Road, Scarborough, ON M1T 3V4.

FIGURE 7.1   Orientation Checklist in a Retail Chain

BIG PICTURE

___ Mission, vision, values, principles
___ History of this business
___ Business ethics
___ Customer service philosophy
___ Target market, customer profile
___ Our key customers
___ What makes our business unique
___ Sales philosophy
___ Merchandising philosophy
___ Housekeeping philosophy
___ Our team
___ Trust and respect
___ Sales and revenue goals
___ Structure and size of business
___ Tour of store(s)

PERSONAL ITEMS

___ Payday, how and when
___ Time sheets, reporting
___ Overtime
___ Bonuses and incentives
___ Benefits and paperwork
___ TD1, CPP, EI, etc.
___ Staff discounts
___ Store hours
___ Work schedules and shifts
___ Parking and restrictions
___ Bus transportation and hours
___ Staff lockers, coat rack
___ Breaks and schedules
___ Where to eat
___ Microwave and fridge
___ Dress code, uniforms, grooming
___ What to do if you are late or sick
___ Vacations
___ Personal telephone calls

SECURITY AND SAFETY

___ Keys and lock-up procedures
___ Key carrier responsibilities
___ Approved entrances and exits a) store, b) mall
___ Fire alarm box, fire extinguishers, fire drills

___ Smoke detector
___ First aid box
___ Police and ambulance
___ Mall security
___ ID badges and photos
___ Smoking areas
___ Reporting accidents, WCB
___ Shoplifting, shrinkage
___ Fitting rooms
___ Internal theft
___ Lifting and carrying boxes/merchandise
___ Use of drugs and alcohol

INTRODUCTION

___ Owner and manager
___ All full-time and part-time staff
___ Mall security
___ Next-door neighbours
___ Head office staff
___ Delivery staff
___ Suppliers
___ Window dressers
___ Customers

SALES AND ADMINISTRATION

___ Point-of-sale (P.O.S.) system
___ Ringing up a sale, refund, return, exchange, lay-away
___ Telephone etiquette
___ Daily sales summary
___ Inventory listings, philosophy, and storage
___ Packing slips, return slips
___ Breakage or damage reports
___ Shipments: short and long
___ Pricing and prices
___ Markdowns and promotional items
___ Re-ordering
___ Transferring stock between stores
___ Guarantees we offer
___ Housekeeping: washrooms, stock room, fitting rooms
___ Seasonal products, hot items
___ Targets and goals on specific

items
___ Target customers
___ Product information sheets, manuals, videos, etc.
___ Features and benefits of products
___ How to approach a customer
___ How to demonstrate a product
___ How to get multiple sales
___ How to handle customer complaints
___ Sales associates' selling responsibilities
___ Test product knowledge, location, and price

MERCHANDISING

___ Philosophy on displaying products
___ Philosophy on window displays
___ Philosophy on signage
___ Seasonal plans
___ Changes: when, how, by whom

COMMUNICATION AND LEARNING

___ Philosophy on communication
___ Philosophy on learning
___ Dealing with constant changes
___ Daily log book
___ Bulletin boards
___ Staff newsletter
___ Customer newsletter
___ Staff meetings
___ Manager availability
___ Ask lots of questions
___ Who to tell? Who needs to know?
___ Telling stories about successes
___ Telling stories about learning opportunities
___ Ask for help
___ Help others
___ Teamwork, buddy system
___ Share new ideas and suggestions
___ The telephone
___ Learning resources

Source: Strategies for Excellence Inc. Used with permission.

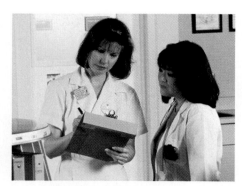

In an orientation, the supervisor explains the exact nature of the job, introduces new colleagues, and familiarizes new employees with the workplace.

Responsibility for Orientation

The first day of the orientation usually starts with the HR specialist, who explains such matters as working hours and vacation. The employee is then introduced to his or her new supervisor, who continues the orientation by explaining the exact nature of the job, introducing the person to his or her new colleagues, and familiarizing the new employee with the workplace. Sometimes, another employee at a peer level will be assigned as a "buddy" or mentor for the newly hired employee for the first few weeks or months of employment. It is a good idea for the HR department to follow up with each new employee about three months after the initial orientation to address any remaining questions.

Special Orientation Situations

Diverse Workforce   In an organization that has not had a diverse workforce in the past, orienting new employees from different backgrounds poses a special challenge. The values of the organization may be new to them if these values were not part of their past experience. New employees should be advised to expect a variety of reactions from current employees to someone from a different background, and be given some tips on how to deal with these reactions. In particular, they need to know which reactions are prohibited under human rights legislation and how to report these, should they occur.

Mergers and Acquisitions   Employees hired into a newly merged company need to receive information about the details of the merger or acquisition as part of the information on company history. They also need to be made aware of any ongoing, as-yet-unresolved difficulties regarding day-to-day operational issues related to their work. A further orientation issue arises with respect to the existing employees at the time of the merger or acquisition: a new company culture will evolve in the merged organization, and everyone will experience a resocialization process. This presents an opportunity for the merged organization to emphasize the new organizational values and beliefs, in order to reinforce corporate culture and further the new organization's business objectives.[9]

Union versus Non-union Employees   New employees in unionized positions need to be provided with a copy of the collective agreement and be told which information relates specifically to their particular job. They also need to be introduced to their union steward, have payroll deduction of union dues explained, and be informed of the names of union executive members. New employees, both unionized and non-unionized, need to be made aware of which jobs are unionized and which ones are not.

Multi-location Organizations   New employees in a multi-location company need to be made aware of where the other locations are and what business functions are performed in each location. The Ontario Ministry of Education is one such organization, and it uses a Web-based online orientation to deliver corporate-level information.[10] All employees have equal access regardless of their location, and the same message is delivered to each one.

Updates can be made instantaneously, and employees can view the information at their own pace.

Problems with Orientation Programs

A number of potential problems can arise with orientation programs. Often, *too much information* is provided in a short time (usually one day) and the new employee is overwhelmed. New employees commonly find themselves inundated with forms to fill out for payroll, benefits, pensions, and so on. Another problem is that *little or no orientation* is provided, which means that new employees must personally seek answers to each question that arises and work without a good understanding of what is expected of them. Finally, the orientation information provided by the HR department can be *too broad* to be meaningful to a new employee, especially on the first day, whereas the orientation information provided by the immediate supervisor may be *too detailed* to realistically expect the new employee to remember it all.

Evaluation of Orientation Programs

Orientation programs should be evaluated to assess whether they are providing timely, useful information to new employees in a cost-effective manner. Three approaches to evaluating orientation programs are:

1. *Employee reaction.* Interview or survey new employees for their opinion of the usefulness of the orientation program.

2. *Socialization effects.* Review new employees at regular intervals to assess progress toward understanding and acceptance of the beliefs, values, and norms of the organization.

3. *Cost/benefit analysis.* Compare: (1) orientation costs such as printing handbooks and time spent orienting new employees by HR staff and immediate supervisors; and (2) benefits of orientation, including reduction in errors, rate of productivity, efficiency levels, and so on.

Executive Integration

An Ethical
Dilemma

Is it ethical to withhold information from an incoming executive about critical problems that he or she will face?

Typically, executives do not participate in formal orientation activities, and there is little planning regarding how they will be integrated into their new position and company. The common assumption is that the new executive is a professional and will know what to do, but full executive integration can take up to 18 months.[11] To make things even more difficult, executives are often brought in as change agents, in which case they can expect to face considerable resistance. Thus a lack of attention to executive integration can result in serious problems with assimilation and work effectiveness. It is common to perceive executive integration as an orientation issue, but integration at senior levels in the organization requires an ongoing process that can continue for months as the new executive learns about the unspoken dynamics of the organization that are not covered in orientation programs, such as how decisions are really made and who holds what type of power.[12]

Research
Insight ▷

Recent research has found three keys to successful executive integration: *roles* must be clarified, a network of trusting *relationships* with key stakeholders must be developed, and the *culture* (norms and values) of the organization must be learned.[13]

Executive integration is of critical importance to a productive relationship between a new executive and his or her organization, and it is important to review previous successes and failures at executive integration on an ongoing basis. Key aspects of the integration process include:

- identifying position specifications (particularly the ability to deal with and overcome jealousy)

- providing realistic information to job candidates and providing support regarding reality shock

- assessing each candidate's previous record at making organizational transitions

- announcing the hiring with enthusiasm

- stressing the importance of listening as well as demonstrating competency, and promoting more time spent talking with the boss

- assisting new executives who are balancing their work to change cultural norms while they themselves are part of the culture itself.[14]

THE TRAINING PROCESS

training The process of teaching new employees the basic skills/competencies that they need to perform their jobs.

Learning Circuits (American Society for Training and Development)
www.learningcircuits.org

Office of Learning Technologies (Human Resources Development Canada) **olt-bta.hrdc-drhc.gc.ca**

Training employees involves a learning process where workers are provided with the information and skills that they need to successfully perform their jobs. Training might thus mean showing a machinist how to operate a new machine, a new salesperson how to sell the firm's product, or a new supervisor how to interview and appraise employees. Whereas training focuses on skills and competencies needed to perform employees' current jobs, *employee and management development* is training of a long-term nature. Its aim is to prepare current employees for future jobs within the organization.

In today's service-based economy, highly knowledgeable workers can be the company's most important assets. Thus it is important to treat training as an investment in human capital, rather than as an expense.[15] It is also important to ensure that business and training goals are aligned, and that training is part of an organization's strategic plan.[16] Some organizations are so serious about employee learning that they are establishing a new executive position called *chief knowledge officer*.[17]

The Ontario Ministry of Economic Development has estimated that, by the year 2010, 60 percent of all new jobs will require skills held by only 22 percent of today's workers.[18] Already, a skills crisis has arisen in the manufacturing sector, where lack of qualified personnel is a major problem. Skills in greatest need for improvement are problem solving, communications, and teamwork.[19] Training is therefore moving to centre stage as a necessity for improving employers' competitiveness. However, a recent Conference Board of Canada study found that Canada lags behind the U.S., Europe, and Asia-Pacific in terms of spending on training and development.[20] Experts warn that this relative under-investment may lead to a gap in essential skills that will be difficult to overcome. For example, project management is a new, highly skilled profession in need of more formal training, as more than 50 percent of project managers receive little or no training, and three-quarters of all projects are finished late and over budget.[21]

The federal government has called for businesses to increase spending on training, and business has asked the government to expand programs for professional immigrants to get Canadian qualifications in their fields.[22] The March 2003 federal budget committed $100 million to the creation of the Canadian Learning Institute to promote best practices in workplace learning.[23] The Quebec government has legislated that all firms with a payroll of more than $250 000 must spend 1 percent of payroll on employee training (or else pay tax in the same amount).[24]

Another benefit of increased training is the fact that training can strengthen employee commitment. It implies faith in the future of the company and of the individual. Few things better illustrate a firm's commitment to its employees than continuing developmental opportunities to improve themselves, and such commitment is usually reciprocated.[25] This is one reason why a high-commitment firm like the Bank of Montreal provides seven days of training per year for all employees.

In summary, to thrive today requires well-trained workers. It also requires responding to customers' needs for quality, variety, customization, convenience, and timeliness. Meeting these new standards requires a workforce that is more than just technically trained: people need to be capable of analyzing and solving job-related problems, working productively in teams, and "switching gears" by shifting from job to job as well.

The Five-Step Training and Development Process

We can conveniently think of a typical training or development program as consisting of five steps, as summarized in **Figure 7.2**. The purpose of the *needs analysis* step is to identify the specific job performance skills needed, to analyze the skills and needs of the prospective trainees, and to develop specific, measurable knowledge and performance objectives. (Managers must make sure that the performance deficiency is amenable to training rather than caused by, say, poor morale due to low salaries.) In the second step, *instructional design*, the actual content of the training program is compiled and produced, including workbooks, exercises, and activities. Next, there may be a third step, *validation*, in which the bugs are worked out of the training program by presenting it to a small representative audience. Fourth, the training program is *implemented*, using techniques like those discussed in this and the following chapter (such as on-the-job training and programmed learning). Fifth, there should be an *evaluation* and follow-up step in which the program's successes or failures are assessed.

Training and Learning

Training is essentially a learning process. To train employees, therefore, it is useful to know something about how people learn. For example, people have three main learning styles: *auditory*, learning through talking and listening; *visual*, learning through pictures and print; and *kinesthetic*, tactile learning through a whole-body experience. Training effectiveness can be enhanced by identifying learning styles and personalizing the training accordingly.[26]

Training and Development
www.ipmaac.org/

FIGURE 7.2   The Five Steps in the Training and Development Process

1. NEEDS ANALYSIS

- Identify specific job performance skills needed to improve performance and productivity.
- Analyze the audience to ensure that the program will be suited to their specific levels of education, experience, and skills, as well as their attitudes and personal motivations.
- Use research to develop specific measurable knowledge and performance objectives.

2. INSTRUCTIONAL DESIGN

- Gather instructional objectives, methods, media, description of and sequence of content, examples, exercises, and activities. Organize them into a curriculum that supports adult learning theory and provides a blueprint for program development.
- Make sure all materials (such as video scripts, leaders' guides, and participants' workbooks) complement each other, are written clearly, and blend into unified training geared directly to the stated learning objectives.
- Carefully and professionally handle all program elements—whether reproduced on paper, film, or tape—to guarantee quality and effectiveness.

3. VALIDATION

- Introduce and validate the training before a representative audience. Base final revisions on pilot results to ensure program effectiveness.

4. IMPLEMENTATION

- When applicable, boost success with a train-the-trainer workshop that focuses on presentation-knowledge and skills in addition to training content.

5. EVALUATION AND FOLLOW-UP

- Assess program success according to:

  REACTION—Document the learners' immediate reactions to the training.

  LEARNING—Use feedback devices or pre- and post-tests to measure what learners have actually learned.

  BEHAVIOUR—Note supervisors' reactions to learners' performance following completion of the training. This is one way to measure the degree to which learners apply new skills and knowledge to their jobs.

  RESULTS—Determine the level of improvement in job performance and assess needed maintenance.

Source: These are adapted from M. D. Carolan, "Today's Training Basics: Some New Golden Rules," *HR Focus* (April 1993), p. 18.

Research
Insight ▷

First, it is easier for trainees to understand and remember material that is meaningful.[27] At the start of training, provide the trainees with an overall picture of the material to be presented. When presenting material, use as many visual aids as possible and a variety of familiar examples. Organize the material so that it is presented in a logical manner and in meaningful units. Try to use terms and concepts that are already familiar to trainees.

Second, make sure that it is easy to transfer new skills and behaviours from the training site to the job site.[28] Maximize the similarity between the training situation and the work situation, and provide adequate training practice. Give trainees the chance to use their new skills immediately upon their return to work. Train managers first and employees second in order to send a message about the importance of the training, and control contingencies by planning rewards for trainees who successfully complete and integrate the new training.[29]

Third, motivate the trainee.[30] Motivation affects training outcomes independently of any increase in cognitive ability. Training motivation is affected by individual characteristics such as conscientiousness and by the training climate.[31] Therefore, it is important to try to provide as much realistic practice as possible. Trainees learn best when correct responses are immediately reinforced, perhaps with a quick "Well done." Finally, trainees learn best at their own pace, so, if possible, let trainees pace themselves.

Fourth, effectively prepare the trainee. Recent research evidence shows that the trainee's pre-training preparation is a crucial step in the training process. It is important to create a perceived need for training in the minds of participants.[32] Also, provide preparatory information that will help to set the trainees' expectations about the events and consequences of actions that are likely to occur in the training environment (and, eventually, on the job). For example, trainees learning to become first-line supervisors might face stressful conditions, high workload, and difficult employees. Studies suggest that the negative impact of such events can be reduced by letting trainees know ahead of time what might occur.[33]

Legal Aspects of Training

Hints to Ensure Legal Compliance

Under human rights and employment equity legislation, several aspects of employee training programs must be assessed with an eye toward the program's impact on designated group members.[34] For example, if relatively few women or visible minorities are selected for the training program, there may be a requirement to show that the admissions procedures are valid—that they predict performance on the job for which the person is being trained. It could turn out that the reading level of the training manuals is too high for many visible minority trainees, which results in their doing poorly in the program, quite aside from their aptitude for the jobs for which they are being trained. The training program might then be found to be unfairly discriminatory.

Negligent training is another potential problem. *Negligent training* occurs when an employer fails to train adequately, and an employee subsequently harms a third party.[35] Also, employees who are dismissed for poor performance or disciplined for safety infractions may claim that the employer was negligent in that the employee's training was inadequate. Precautions here include:[36]

- confirming claims of skill and experience for all applicants
- reducing the risks of harm by extensively training employees who work with dangerous equipment, materials, or processes
- ensuring that the training includes procedures to protect third parties' health and safety (including that of other employees)
- evaluating the training activity to determine its effectiveness in reducing negligence risks.

Training Needs Analysis and Transfer of Training

The first step in training is to determine what training is required, if any. The main task in assessing the training needs of new employees is to determine what the job entails and break it down into subtasks, each of which is then taught to the new employee. Assessing the training needs of current employees can be more complex, since it involves the added task of deciding whether or not training is the solution. For example, performance may be down not because of lack of training but because the standards are not clear or because the person is not motivated.

Task analysis and performance analysis are the two main techniques for identifying training needs. About 19 percent of employers reporting in one survey said that they used **task analysis**—an analysis of the job's requirements—to determine the training required.[37] Task analysis is especially appropriate for determining the training needs of employees who are *new* to their jobs. **Performance analysis** appraises the performance of *current* employees to determine whether training could reduce performance problems (such as excess scrap or low output). Other techniques used to identify training needs include supervisors' reports, HR records, management requests, observations, tests of job knowledge, and questionnaire surveys.[38]

Whichever technique is used—task analysis, performance analysis, or some other—employee input is essential. It is often true that no one knows as much about the job as the people actually doing it, so soliciting employee input is usually wise.[39]

task analysis A detailed study of a job to identify the skills and competencies it requires so that an appropriate training program may be instituted.

performance analysis Verifying that there is a performance deficiency and determining whether that deficiency should be rectified through training or through some other means (such as transferring the employee).

Task Analysis: Assessing the Training Needs of New Employees

Task analysis—identifying the broad competencies and specific skills required to perform job-related tasks—is used for determining the training needs of employees who are new to their jobs. Particularly with entry-level workers, it is common to hire inexperienced people and train them.[40] Thus, the aim is to develop the skills and knowledge required for effective performance—like soldering (in the case of an assembly worker) or interviewing (in the case of a supervisor).

The job description and job specification are helpful here. These list the specific duties and skills required on the job and become the basic reference point in determining the training required to perform the job.

Task Analysis Record Form

Some employers supplement the current job description and specification with a task analysis record form. This consolidates information regarding the job's required tasks and skills in a form that is especially helpful for determining training requirements. As illustrated in **Table 7.1**, a task analysis record form contains six types of information:

1. *Column 1, Task List.* Here, the job's main tasks and subtasks are listed.

2. *Column 2, How Often Performed.* Here, the frequency with which the task and subtasks are performed is indicated.

3. *Column 3, Quantity, Quality Standards.* Here, the standards of performance for each task and subtask are described in measurable terms like "±

TABLE 7.1   Task Analysis Record Form

TASK LIST	WHEN AND HOW OFTEN PERFORMED	QUANTITY AND QUALITY OF PERFORMANCE	CONDITIONS UNDER WHICH PERFORMED	COMPETENCIES AND SPECIFIC KNOWLEDGE REQUIRED	WHERE BEST LEARNED
1. Operate paper cutter	4 times per day		Noisy press room: distractions		
1.1 Start motor					
1.2 Set cutting distance		± tolerance of 0.007 in.		Read gauge	On the job
1.3 Place paper on cutting table		Must be completely even to prevent uneven cut		Lift paper correctly	On the job
1.4 Push paper up to cutter				Must be even	On the job
1.5 Grasp safety release with left hand	100% of time, for safety			Essential for safety	On the job but practice first with no distractions
1.6 Grasp cutter release with right hand				Must keep both hands on releases	On the job but practice first with no distractions
1.7 Simultaneously pull safety release with left hand and cutter release with right hand					
1.8 Wait for cutter to retract	100% of time, for safety			Must keep both hands on releases	On the job but practice first with no distractions
1.9 Retract paper				Wait till cutter retracts	On the job but practice first with no distractions
1.10 Shut off	100% of time, for safety				On the job but practice first with no distractions
2. Operate printing press					
2.1 Start motor					
.					
.					
.					

Note: Task analysis record form showing some of tasks and subtasks performed by a right-handed printing press operator.

tolerance of 0.007 in.," or "Within two days of receiving the order," for instance.

4. *Column 4, Performance Conditions.* This column indicates the conditions under which the tasks and subtasks are to be performed.

International Standards for Core
Competency Training
www.chauncey.com

5. *Column 5, Competencies and Specific Skills Required.* This is the heart of the task analysis form. Here, the competencies and specific skills or knowledge required for each of the tasks and subtasks are listed, specifying exactly what knowledge or skills must be taught. Thus, for the subtask "Set cutting distance," the trainee must be taught how to read the gauge.

6. *Column 6, Where Best Learned.* The decision as to whether the task is learned best on or off the job is based on several considerations. Safety is one: for example, prospective jet pilots must learn something about the plane off the job in a simulator before actually getting behind the controls.

Performance Analysis: Determining the Training Needs of Current Employees

Performance analysis means verifying whether there is a significant performance deficiency, and if so, determining whether that deficiency should be rectified through training or some other means (such as transferring the employee). The first step is to appraise the employee's performance, since to improve it, the firm must first determine the person's current performance compared to what it should be. Examples of specific performance deficiencies follow:

- "Salespeople are expected to make ten new contacts per week, but John averages only six."

- "Other plants our size average no more than two serious accidents per month; we are averaging five."

Distinguishing between *can't do* and *won't do* problems is the heart of performance analysis. First, the firm must determine whether it is a *can't do* problem and, if so, its specific causes. For example, the employees do not know what to do or what the standards are; there are obstacles in the system (such as lack of tools or supplies); job aids are needed; poor selection has resulted in hiring people who do not have the skills to do the job; or training is inadequate. On the other hand, it might be a *won't do* problem. In this case, employees *could* do a good job if they wanted to. If so, the reward system might have to be changed, perhaps by implementing an incentive program.

Transfer of Training

Once training needs have been identified, training objectives can be established. Concrete, measurable training objectives should be set after training needs have been analyzed. Objectives specify what the trainee should be able to accomplish after successfully completing the training program.[41] They thus provide a focus for the efforts of both the trainee and the trainer, and a benchmark for evaluating the success of the training program.

A training program can then be developed and implemented, with the intent to achieve these objectives. It is important to assess the return on investment in human capital made through training by determining whether the training actually achieved the objectives. **Transfer of training** is the application of the skills acquired during the training program into the work environment, and the maintenance of these skills over time.[42] There are a number of actions that can be taken before, during, and after a training program to enhance transfer of training.[43]

transfer of training Application of the skills acquired during the training program into the work environment, and the maintenance of these skills over time.

Before training, potential trainees can be assessed on their level of ability, aptitude, and motivation regarding the skill to be taught, and those with higher levels can be selected for the training program. Trainees can be involved in designing the training, and management should provide active support at this stage.

During the training, it is important to provide frequent feedback, opportunities for practice, and positive reinforcement. After the training program, trainees can use goal setting and relapse prevention techniques to increase the likelihood of applying what they have learned. Management can enhance transfer of training by providing opportunities to apply new skills and by continuing to provide positive reinforcement of the new skills while being tolerant of errors.

TRADITIONAL TRAINING TECHNIQUES

After the employees' training needs have been determined, training objectives can be set, and the training program can be designed and implemented. Although many new computer-based training techniques have been developed over the past decade (these will be discussed later in the chapter), traditional techniques are still widely used. Descriptions of the most popular traditional training techniques follow.

On-the-Job Training

On-the-job training (OJT) involves having a person learn a job by actually performing it. Virtually every employee—from mailroom clerk to company president —gets some on-the-job training when he or she joins a firm. In many companies, OJT is the only type of training available. It usually involves assigning new employees to experienced workers or supervisors who then do the actual training.[44]

There are several types of on-the-job training. The most familiar is the *coaching* or *understudy* method. Here, the employee is trained on the job by an experienced worker or by the trainee's supervisor. At lower levels, trainees may

On-the-job training is structured and concrete. Here, a supervisor teaches an employee to use a drum-forming machine.

acquire skills (e.g., running a machine) by observing the supervisor. This technique is also widely used at top-management levels, where the position of assistant is often used to train and develop the company's future top managers. *Job rotation*, in which an employee (usually a management trainee) moves from job to job at planned intervals, is another OJT technique. *Special assignments* are another on-the-job training technique designed to give lower-level executives firsthand experience in working on actual problems.

OJT has several advantages: it is relatively inexpensive; trainees learn while producing; and there is no need for expensive off-job facilities like classrooms or programmed learning devices. The method also facilitates learning, since trainees learn by actually doing the job and get quick feedback about the quality of their performance.

Several trainer-related factors should be kept in mind when designing OJT programs.[45] The trainers themselves should be carefully trained and given the necessary training materials—in particular, the principles of learning and perhaps the job instruction technique that we address next. (Often, an experienced worker is instead simply told to "go and train John.") A useful step-by-step instruction approach for a trainer giving a new employee on-the-job training follows.

Step 1: Preparation of the Learner

1. Put the learner at ease—relieve the tension.
2. Explain why he or she is being taught.
3. Create interest, encourage questions, and find out what the learner already knows about his or her job or other jobs.
4. Explain the why of the whole job and relate it to some job that the learner already knows.
5. Place the learner as close to the normal working position as possible.
6. Familiarize the learner with the equipment, materials, tools, and trade terms.

Step 2: Presentation of the Operation

1. Explain quantity and quality requirements.
2. Go through the job at the normal work pace.
3. Go through the job at a slow pace several times, explaining each step. Between operations, explain the difficult parts, or those in which errors are likely to be made.
4. Again, go through the job at a slow pace several times; explain the key points.
5. Have the learner explain the steps as you go through the job at a slow pace.

Step 3: Performance Tryout

1. Have the learner go through the job several times, slowly, while explaining each step to you. Correct mistakes and, if necessary, do some of the complicated steps the first few times.
2. Run the job yourself at the normal pace.

3. Have the learner do the job, gradually building up skill and speed.

4. As soon as the learner demonstrates ability to do the job, let the work begin, but do not abandon him or her.

Step 4: Follow-up

1. Designate a person to whom the learner should go for help if he or she needs it.

2. Gradually decrease supervision, checking work from time to time against quality and quantity standards.

3. Correct faulty work patterns that begin to creep into the work, and do it before they become habitual. Show why the learned method is superior.

4. Compliment good work; encourage the worker until he or she is able to meet the quality/quantity standards.

Apprenticeship Training

More employers are going "back to the future" by implementing apprenticeship-training programs, an approach that began in the Middle Ages. Apprenticeship training is a structured process by which individuals become skilled workers through a combination of classroom instruction and on-the-job training. It is widely used to train individuals for many occupations, including those of the electrician and plumber. In Canada, there are close to 170 established trades that have recognized apprenticeship programs, and approximately 1.2 million Canadians register for these programs each year.[46] In 2003, the federal government committed $12 million to promote skilled trades, with a specific goal of doubling the number of Canadians completing apprenticeship programs within ten years.[47] British Columbia has also proposed changes to its apprenticeship training program in order to meet the need for more tradespeople.[48]

Apprenticeship training basically involves having the learner/apprentice study under the tutelage of a master craftsperson.[49] In Germany, for instance, students aged 15 to 18 often divide their time between classroom instruction in vocational schools and part-time work under the master craftsperson. The apprenticeship lasts about three years, and ends with a certification examination.

Informal Learning

About two-thirds of industrial training is not "formal" at all, but rather results from day-to-day unplanned interactions between the new worker and his or her colleagues.[50] Informal learning may be defined as "Any learning that occurs in which the learning process is not determined or designed by the organization."[51]

Although informal learning is not predetermined or predesigned by the organization, some simple things can be done to make sure that such learning takes place. For example, firms can place tools in the cafeteria to take advantage of the work-related brainstorming going on there, or install whiteboards and keep them stocked with markers for quick shift-change notes.

Job Instruction Training

job instruction training (JIT)
Listing of each job's basic tasks, along with key points, in order to provide step-by-step training for employees.

Many jobs consist of a logical sequence of steps and are best taught step by step. This step-by-step process is called **job instruction training (JIT)**. To begin, all necessary steps in the job are listed, each in its proper sequence. Alongside each step, a corresponding "key point" (if any) should be noted. The steps show *what* is to be done, while the key points show *how* it is to be done, and *why*. Here is an example of a job instruction training sheet for teaching a right-handed trainee how to operate a large, motorized paper cutter:

Steps	*Key Points*
1. Start motor	None
2. Set cutting distance	Carefully read scale—to prevent wrong-sized cut
3. Place paper on cutting table	Make sure paper is even—to prevent uneven cut
4. Push paper up to cutter	Make sure paper is tight—to prevent uneven cut
5. Grasp safety release with left hand	Do not release left hand—to prevent hand from being caught in cutter
6. Grasp cutter release with right hand	Do not release right hand—to prevent hand from being caught in cutter
7. Simultaneously pull cutter and safety releases	Keep both hands on corresponding releases —to avoid hands being on cutting table
8. Wait for cutter to retract	Keep both hands on releases—to avoid having hands on cutting table
9. Retract paper	Make sure cutter is retracted; keep both hands away from releases
10. Shut off motor	None

In today's service economy, job instruction training for step-by-step manual work is being superseded by behaviour modelling for service workers. Behaviour modelling is discussed in the next chapter. Other modifications to traditional training techniques may be required when training is undertaken in a family business, as described in the Entrepreneurs and HR box.

Lectures

Classroom training continues to be the primary method of providing corporate training in Canada,[52] and lectures are a widely used method of classroom training delivery. Lecturing has several advantages. It is a quick and simple way of providing knowledge to large groups of trainees, as when the sales force must be taught the special features of a new product. While written material like books and manuals could be used instead, they may involve considerable printing expense, and they do not permit the give and take of questioning that lectures do.

The training room has a significant impact on training effectiveness. It is important to ensure that trainees have a clear map to the room's location, and that the room be as close to pay phones, washrooms, food services, and elevators/ stairs as possible. A display of handouts, reference resources, and items of interest should be set up for trainees to peruse before the session and during breaks. The best training rooms have natural light and temperature controls that work. The room should be the right size for the number of participants, and should be

ENTREPRENEURS AND HR

How to Train Family

Family businesses face some unique challenges that make supplementary training programs necessary.[1] Some of these challenges include issues such as how to make a smooth management transition from one generation to the next, how to smooth conflicts between family members who may hold different positions but equal family status and power, and how to motivate a family member who has access to all rewards regardless of performance.

This means that training programs in family businesses should look at issues beyond simple job duties and performance requirements. Past studies indicate the following as some of the more important areas to focus on in such businesses:

- How to handle family issues which conflict with business issues.

- How to educate the older generation to adapt their past success in the light of emerging realities.

- How to educate the newer generation to work with the older generation and yet be able to infuse newer ideas.

- How to train the management to make a smooth transition from one generation to the next.

- How to help managers to learn from the experiences of other family firms.

- How to manage conflicts among family members over business decisions.

- How to motivate affluent, powerful family members to contribute their share of efforts.

- How to create a smooth relationship between hired, professional employees and family members who are in high positions.

Some of the issues that are unique to family businesses are also worth special attention:

- Managing the transition: How to identify and implement a smooth transition of ownership from one generation to the next.[2]

- Management continuity: How to prepare the next generation professionally and personally to participate in the business. What should they do now and five years from now?

- Establishing the rules of entry: How to establish and communicate a set of consistent rules, standards of performance, and compensation to family members, especially non-nuclear family members.

Over the years, several universities have begun offering family business programs. These programs can assist family businesses by addressing issues that affect their long-term health and survival.

Notes:

1. K. Gersick, J. Davis, M. Hampton, and I. Lansberg, *Generation to Generation*, Boston MA: Harvard Business School Press, 1997; T. Kaplan, G. George, G. Rimler, "University Sponsored Family Business Programs: Program Characteristics, Perceived Quality and Member Satisfaction," *Entrepreneurship Theory and Practice*, Spring 2000, 65–75.

2. A. Pervin, "Remember, Family Before Business," *Globe & Mail*, February 4, 1999, p. B10.

Source: H. Das, *Performance Management* (Toronto: Prentice Hall, 2003), p. 227. Reproduced with permission of Pearson Education Canada.

quiet and clean. Break-out rooms should be arranged in advance so that the instructor knows where small groups will be located.[53]

Audiovisual Techniques

Audiovisual techniques (like films, closed-circuit television, audiotapes, and videotapes) can be very effective and are widely used.[54] Audiovisuals are more expensive than conventional lectures, but offer some advantages. Trainers should consider using them in the following situations:

1. *When there is a need to illustrate how a certain sequence should be followed over time*, such as when teaching wire soldering or telephone repair. The stop-action, instant-replay, or fast- or slow-motion capabilities of audiovisuals can be useful.

2. *When there is a need to expose trainees to events not easily demonstrable in live lectures*, such as a visual tour of a factory or open-heart surgery.

3. *When the training is going to be used organization-wide* and it is too costly to move the trainers from place to place.

There are three options when it comes to video: buying an existing videotape or film; making one; or having a production company produce the video. Dozens of businesses issue catalogues that list audiovisual programs on topics ranging from applicant interviewing to zoo management.

videoconferencing Connecting two or more distant groups using audiovisual equipment.

Videoconferencing, where an instructor is televised live to multiple locations, is now a common method for training employees. It has been defined as "... a means of joining two or more distant groups using a combination of audio and visual equipment."[55] Videoconferencing allows people in one location to communicate live with people in another city or country, or with groups in several other cities. It is particularly important to prepare a training guide ahead of time, as most or all of the learners will not be in the same location as the trainer. It is also important for the trainer to arrive early and test all equipment that will be used.[56]

Programmed Learning

programmed learning A systematic method for teaching job skills that involves presenting questions or facts, allowing the person to respond, and giving the learner immediate feedback on the accuracy of his or her answers.

Whether the programmed instruction device is a textbook or a computer, **programmed learning** consists of three functions:

1. Presenting questions, facts, or problems to the learner.

2. Allowing the person to respond.

3. Providing feedback on the accuracy of his or her answers.

The main advantage of programmed learning is that it reduces training time by about one-third.[57] In terms of the principles of learning listed earlier, programmed instruction can also facilitate learning since it lets trainees learn at their own pace, provides immediate feedback, and (from the learner's point of view) reduces the risk of error. On the other hand, trainees do not learn much more from programmed learning than they would from a traditional textbook. Therefore, the cost of developing the manuals and/or software for programmed instruction has to be weighed against the accelerated but not improved learning that should occur.

vestibule or simulated training Training employees on special off-the-job equipment, as in airplane pilot training, whereby training costs and hazards can be reduced.

Vestibule or Simulated Training

Vestibule training simulates flight conditions at NASA headquarters.

Vestibule or simulated training is a technique by which trainees learn on the actual or simulated equipment that they will use on the job, but are trained off the job. Therefore, it aims to obtain the advantages of on-the-job training without actually putting the trainee on the job. Vestibule training is virtually a necessity when it is too costly or dangerous to train employees on the job. Putting new assembly-line workers right to work could slow production, for instance, and when safety is a concern—as with pilots—vestibule training may be the only practical alternative.

Vestibule training may just place a trainee in a separate room with the equipment that he or she will actually be using on the job; however, it often involves the use of equipment simulators. In pilot training, for instance, the main advantages of flight simulators are safety, learning efficiency, and cost savings (on maintenance costs, pilot cost, fuel cost, and the cost of not having the aircraft in regular service).[58]

E-Learning

e-learning Delivery and administration of learning opportunities and support via computer, networked, and Web-based technology, to enhance employee performance and development.

Click2learn **www.click2learn.com**

Over the past few years, electronic training techniques have been developed that allow training professionals to provide learning in a more flexible, personalized, and cost-effective manner.[59] **E-learning** is the delivery and administration of learning opportunities and support via computer, networked, and Web-based technology, to enhance employee performance and development.[60] The use of e-learning represents a state-of-the-art approach to how knowledge is acquired and human capital is developed. Canadian employers are using e-learning to become more productive and innovative, and to create self-directed, lifelong learners of their employees.[61] By 2004, it is expected that the Canadian corporate market for e-learning will reach about $900 million (about $15 billion in the United States). The increasing popularity of e-learning was spurred on by fears of air travel following the September 11, 2001, terrorist attacks.[62]

According to a Conference Board of Canada survey, three-quarters of all employers in Canada use e-learning technology, and nearly half have used the Internet to deliver training to employees.[63] However, the survey also found that three major obstacles are slowing further investment in e-learning—high costs, lack of time, and content shortage.[64] Consequently, the rate of adoption of e-learning in Canada has been slower than expected.

There are three major types of e-learning—computer-based training, online training, and electronic performance support systems (EPSS).

Computer-Based Training

In computer-based training (CBT), the trainee uses a computer-based system to interactively increase his or her knowledge or skills. Computer-based training almost always involves presenting trainees with integrated computerized simulations and the use of multimedia (including video, audio, text, and graphics) to help the trainee to learn how to do the job.[65]

A new generation of simulations has been developed to simulate role-play situations designed to teach behavioural skills and emotional intelligence. Body language, facial expressions, and subtle nuances are programmed in. These new simulations offer authentic and relevant scenarios involving pressure situations that tap users' emotions and force them to act.[66]

Multimedia training is most often implemented with CD-ROM technology, but is also available through the Internet and other sources.[67] Due to its interactive nature, interactive multimedia has been found to be more effective for training people than text-based instruction.[68]

A higher percentage of Canadian firms use CBT when compared to American firms, primarily because of Canada's geography. CBT is often more cost-effective than traditional training methods requiring instructors and/or trainees to travel long distances to training sites.[69] Alberta Pacific Forest Industries (AL-Pac) has had such good results from using CBT as a staple of its training program that it is about to launch a new component that will enable employees to pick up the skills of another trade. Employees benefit from having training that is accessible 24 hours a day, in order to address shift work and different learning styles. This training program also helps to keep non-union staff members satisfied, as the multi-skilling resulting from CBT enables many employees to rotate jobs.[70]

CBT programs can be very beneficial. Studies indicate that interactive technologies reduce learning time by an average of 50 percent.[71] The new forms of training can also be very cost-effective; while traditional training costs less to develop, new media-based training has a lower cost of delivery over its life span.[72] Other advantages include instructional consistency (computers, unlike human trainers, do not have good days and bad days), mastery of learning (if the trainee does not learn it, he or she generally cannot move on to the next step in the CBT), increased retention, flexibility for the trainee, and increased trainee motivation (resulting from the responsive feedback of the CBT program).

Online Training

Web-based training is the fastest-growing training application in Canada, as shown in **Figure 7.3**.[73] Use of this technology as a tool for workplace learning is here to stay, in part because it is generally estimated that Web-based training costs about 50 percent less than traditional classroom-based training. Also, Web-based learning is ideal for adults, who learn what they want, when they want, and where they want.[74] Online training is often the best solution for

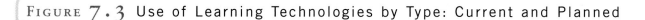

FIGURE 7.3 Use of Learning Technologies by Type: Current and Planned

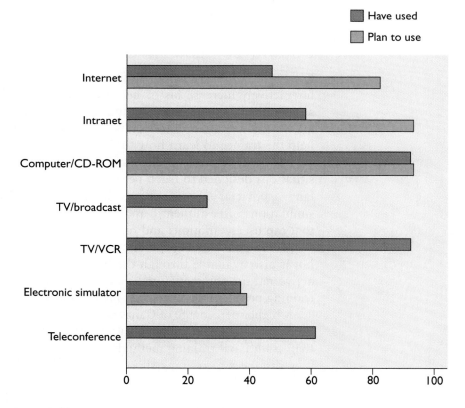

Source: D. Murray, *Keen for the Screen.* © 2000. Reprinted by permission of The Conference Board of Canada, Ottawa.

highly specialized business professionals with little time available for ongoing education.[75] Students (the workers of tomorrow) thrive in online learning environments. They do not find it to be an isolated or lonely experience, and they find that they have more time to reflect on the learning material, which leads to livelier interaction.[76]

However, critics point out that content management, sound educational strategy, learner support and system administration should receive more attention, as they are often the critical determining factors in successful training outcomes.[77] In the last few years, "learner content management systems" have been developed to deliver personalized content in small "chunks" or "nuggets" of learning. These systems complement "learning management systems" that are focused on the logistics of managing learning. Together, they form a powerful combination for an e-learning platform.[78] This development is considered to be part of the "second wave" of e-learning, involving greater standardization and the emergence of norms.[79] Another problem is that the freedom of online learning means that unless learners are highly motivated, they may not complete the training. It is estimated that learners don't complete 50 to 90 percent of Web-based courses.[80] In general, it is important to seek "blended learning" including both personal interaction and online training tools.[81]

Research
Insight

Research studies are beginning to focus on teaching effectiveness in technology-based distance learning programs, to see what teachers can do to be more effective in these kinds of environments. The results of one such study suggest the following:[82]

1. Use cameras and technology layouts that allow instructors to maintain eye contact with both local and remote audiences.

2. Use the variety of media available (CD-ROMs, graphs, videotapes, and so forth).

3. Do not focus on the technology at the expense of the students.

4. Try to emphasize technology that is reliable and of high quality (little delay in audio and video signals is particularly important).

5. Learn how to use the technology effectively and understand the importance of a participative style of teaching.

6. Have adequate technical support staff.

Research comparing the effectiveness of educational television or interactive video to face-to-face instruction has found little or no difference in student achievement.[83] The preliminary evidence, at least, seems to suggest that technology-supported (and particularly video-based) training can be effective.[84] However, this assumes that the technology is effective, and that the instructors are (as previously explained) specially trained to utilize it for maximum impact.

Electronic Performance Support Systems (EPSS)

electronic performance support systems (EPSS) Computer-based job aids, or sets of computerized tools and displays that automate training, documentation, and phone support.

Electronic performance support systems (EPSS) are computer-based job aids, or sets of computerized tools and displays that automate training, documentation, and phone support. EPSS provides support that is faster, cheaper, and more effective than traditional paper-based job aids such as manuals. When a customer calls a Dell Computer service representative about a problem with a new computer, he or she is probably asking questions prompted by an EPSS, which takes the service representative and the customer through an analytical sequence, step by step. Without the EPSS, Dell would have to train its service representatives to memorize an unrealistically large number of solutions. Learners say that EPSS provides significant value in maximizing the impact of training. If a skill is trained at one point in time, but the trainees don't need to use it until several weeks or months later, the learning material is always available through the EPSS.[85]

TRAINING FOR SPECIAL PURPOSES

Training increasingly does more than just prepare employees to perform their jobs effectively. Training for special purposes—increasing literacy and adjusting to diversity, for instance—is required too. The following is a sampling of such special-purpose training programs.

Literacy Training Techniques

Adult Literacy Information Network
www.nald.ca

Tips **for the
Front Line**

Functional illiteracy is a serious problem for many employers. A 2002 survey sponsored by the National Literacy Secretariat and Human Resources Development Canada found that 42 percent of Canadian workers have literacy skills below the level they need to succeed and perform well in most jobs.[86] Yet, as the Canadian economy shifts from goods to services, there is a corresponding need for workers who are more skilled, more literate, and better able to perform at least basic arithmetic skills. Not only does enhanced literacy give employees a better chance for success in their careers, but it also improves bottom-line performance of the employer—through time savings, lower costs, and improved quality of work.[87]

Employers are responding to this issue in two main ways. First, companies are testing prospective employees' basic skills. Second, they are instituting basic skills and literacy programs. One simple approach is to have supervisors focus on basic skills by giving employees writing and speaking exercises. After the exercise has been completed, the supervisor can provide personal feedback.[88] Another approach is to bring in outside professionals like local high-school or community-college teachers to institute, say, a remedial reading or writing program. Having employees attend adult-education or high-school evening classes is another option.

Another approach is to use an interactive video disk (IVD). This technique combines the drama of video with the power of microcomputers.[89] An example is Principles of Alphabet Literacy (PALS). It uses animated video and a computer-stored voice to enable nonreaders to associate sounds with letters and letters with words, and to use the words to create sentences.[90] A second IVD program is called SKILLPAC. This program, subtitled *English for Industry*, was designed mostly for non-native-English speakers. It combines video, audio, and computer technologies to teach language skills in the context of the specific workplace situation in which those skills will be used.[91]

Diversity Training

With increasingly diverse workforces and customers, there is a strong business case for implementing diversity-training programs. Diversity training enhances

Diversity Training Links
www.diversityatwork.com
www.diversityuintl.com
www.diversitytraining.com
www.ideasandtraining.com

cross-cultural sensitivity among supervisors and non-supervisors, with the aim of creating more harmonious working relationships among a firm's employees. It also enhances the abilities of salespeople to provide effective customer service.[92]

Two broad approaches to diversity training are cross-cultural communication training and cultural sensitivity training. *Cross-cultural communication training* focuses on workplace cultural etiquette and interpersonal skills. *Cultural sensitivity training* focuses on sensitizing employees to the views of different cultural groups toward work so that employees from diverse backgrounds can work together more effectively. All employees should be involved in managing diversity, and diversity initiatives should be planned and supported as any other business opportunity would be.[93]

Diversity training is no panacea, and a poorly conceived program can backfire. Potential negative outcomes include reinforcement of group stereotypes and backlash by white males.[94] Diversity experts agree that conflict cannot be avoided when planning and delivering diversity training, or when trying to promote an inclusive workplace.[95]

According to one survey of HR directors, specific training programs aimed at offsetting problems associated with a diverse workforce included (from most used to least used): improving interpersonal skills; understanding/valuing cultural differences; improving technical skills; socializing employees into the corporate culture; reducing stress; indoctrinating into the North American work ethic; mentoring; improving English proficiency; improving basic math skills; and improving bilingual skills for English-speaking employees.[96]

Handidactis, a nonprofit organization in Montreal, provides sensitivity training to help people deal with those who have a disability, including those with impaired vision or hearing, and individuals who have a physical or mental disability. The first step is to ask the person with the disability if he or she needs anything special to do the job. This is often overlooked as people jump in to help someone with a disability, which in effect takes away that person's independence. Furthermore, the person may not need help. The training also involves discovering what it is like to have a disability, through simulated blindness and speech impediments.[97]

Customer-Service Training

More and more retailers are finding it necessary to compete based on the quality of their service, and many are therefore implementing customer-service training programs. The basic aim is to train all employees to (1) have excellent product knowledge, and (2) treat the company's customers in a courteous and hospitable manner. The saying "The customer is always right" is emphasized by countless service companies today. However, putting the customer first requires employee customer-service training.

Until recently, the Canadian retail industry faced a crisis where poorly trained workers were ill equipped to provide quality customer service.[98] Retailers now understand that they need to make a serious investment in their employees.[99] In fact, the Retail Council of Canada is launching a national customer service certification program.[100] At the Liquor Control Board of Ontario, a decision was made to train all 4500 employees through the "That's the Spirit" program, which enhanced customer-service skills and boosted knowledge about distilled spirits. The program stressed empowerment of front-line employees to help customers make better buying decisions. The results have been dramatic—sales of spirits, which had been declining since 1974, have begun to increase.[101]

The next crisis is the competition from online shopping. Surveys have found that one-third of Internet shoppers do so because they don't like dealing with salespeople, and one-quarter say they get better service online than at a store.[102]

Training for Teamwork

An increasing number of firms today use work teams to improve their effectiveness. However, many firms find that teamwork does not just happen, and that employees must be trained to be good team members.

Some firms use outdoor training—such as Outward Bound programs—to build teamwork.[103] Outdoor training usually involves taking a group of employees out into rugged, mountainous terrain, where, by overcoming physical obstacles, they learn team spirit, cooperation, and the need to trust and rely on each other.[104] An example of one activity is the "trust fall." Here, an employee has to slowly lean back and fall backward from a height of, say, three metres into the waiting arms of five or ten team members. The idea is to build trust in one's colleagues.

Not all employees are eager to participate in such activities. Firms such as Outward Bound have prospective participants fill out extensive medical evaluations to make sure that participants can safely engage in risky outdoor activities. Others feel that the outdoor activities are too contrived to be applicable back at work. However, they do illustrate the lengths to which employers will go to build teamwork.

> ### An Ethical Dilemma
>
> Should employees be required to participate in outdoor training, if they do not want to because it is going to take time that they would otherwise be spending on personal and family responsibilities?

Training for First-Time Supervisors

As we progress through the early years of the twenty-first century, baby boomers are heading into retirement, and young employees are rising to positions of authority quickly and in large numbers. They are assuming supervisory roles at a much younger age than their counterparts were only 10 to 15 years ago. Along with the steep learning curve that all first-time supervisors face, the latest group faces generational diversity—supervising boomers, their own Generation Xers, and the "Nexter" generation following them.[105]

New supervisors are often chosen for their technical ability, and their interpersonal and communication skills get overlooked. But it is precisely these skills that will determine success as a supervisor, which requires networking and the ability to get work done through other people. New supervisors also need to learn to define their personal supervisory style, how to give and receive feedback, and how to motivate others.[106]

This transition demands crucial training because first-time supervisors need to learn a new set of skills. Formal training is required, and higher-level managers need to coach, mentor, and provide performance feedback to new young supervisors.[107]

Training for Global Business

Firms competing in the global marketplace often implement special global training programs. The reasons for doing so include avoiding lost business due to cultural insensitivity, improving job satisfaction and retention of overseas staff, and enabling a newly assigned employee to communicate with colleagues abroad.[108]

Research
Insight ▷

Recent research by Healthy Companies International has found that success in the global marketplace is predicted by developing leaders at all levels of business and by placing a high value on multicultural experience and competencies. The research identified four global literacies, or critical competencies, required to succeed in the global economy:

- Personal literacy—understanding and valuing oneself
- Social literacy—engaging and challenging other people
- Business literacy—focusing and mobilizing the business
- Cultural literacy—understanding and leveraging cultural differences.[109]

EVALUATING THE TRAINING EFFORT

After trainees complete their training (or at planned intervals during the training), the program should be evaluated to see how well its objectives have been met and the extent to which transfer of training has occurred. Thus, if assemblers should be able to solder a junction in 30 seconds, or a photocopier technician repair a machine in 30 minutes, then the program's effectiveness should be measured based on whether these objectives are attained. For example, are trainees learning as *much* as they can? Are they learning as *fast* as they can? Is there a *better method* for training them? These are some of the questions that are answered by properly evaluating training efforts.

Overall, there is little doubt that training and development can be effective. Formal studies of training programs substantiate the potential positive impact of such programs. A study conducted in the early 1990s concluded that "firms that establish workplace education programs and reorganize work report noticeable improvements in their workers' abilities and the quality of their products."[110] Another study found that businesses that were operating below their expected labour productivity levels had significant increases in productivity growth after implementing new employee training programs.[111] Profitable companies spend the most on training, and those rated as being among the 100 best companies to work for in Canada spend the most per employee on training.[112]

There are two basic issues to address when evaluating a training program. The first is the design of the evaluation study and, in particular, whether controlled experimentation will be used. The second is the training effect to be measured.

controlled experimentation
Formal methods for testing the effectiveness of a training program, preferably with before-and-after tests and a control group.

Controlled experimentation is the best method to use in evaluating a training program. A controlled experiment uses both a training group and a control group (that receives no training). Data (e.g., on quantity of production or quality of soldered junctions) should be obtained both before and after the training effort in the training group, and before and after a corresponding work period in the control group. In this way, it is possible to determine the extent to which any change in performance in the training group resulted from the training itself, rather than from some organization-wide change like a raise in pay, which would likely have affected employees in both groups equally. In terms of current practices, however, one survey found that something less than half of the companies responding attempted to obtain before-and-after measures from trainees; the number of organizations using control groups was negligible.[113]

Training Effects to Measure

Four basic categories of training outcomes can be measured:[114]

1. *Reaction*. First, evaluate trainees' reactions to the program. Did they like the program? Did they think it worthwhile? One expert suggests at least using an evaluation form like the one shown in **Figure 7.4** to evaluate reaction to the training program.[115]

2. *Learning*. Second, test the trainees to determine whether they learned the principles, skills, and facts that they were supposed to learn.

FIGURE 7.4   A Sample Training Evaluation Form

1. Considering everything, how would you rate this program? (Check one)
   Unsatisfactory ____ Satisfactory ____ Good ____ Outstanding ____
   Please explain briefly the reasons for the rating you have given:

2 Were your expectations (Check one) exceeded ____ matched ____ fallen below ____?

3. Are you going to recommend this training program to other members of your department?
   Yes ____ No ____. If you check "yes," please describe the job titles held by the people to whom you would recommend this program.
   _____

4. Please rate the relative value (1 = very valuable; 2 = worthwhile; 3 = negligible)
   Videocassettes   ____   Role-playing exercises   ____
   Workbooks   ____   Small group discussion   ____
   Small group discussions   ____   Lectures   ____
   Cases   ____   Readings: Articles   ____

5. Please rate the main lecturer's presentation (1 = not effective; 2 = somewhat effective; 3 = effective) in terms of:
   Ability to communicate   ____
   Emphasis on key points   ____
   Handout materials   ____

6. Please rate the following cases, readings, and videocassettes by placing a check mark in the appropriate column:

	Excellent	Good	Fair	Poor
Overcoming Resistance to Change				
Reviewing Performance Goals				
Setting Performance Goals				
Handling Employee Complaints				
Improving Employee Performance				
Slade Co.				
Superior Slate Quarry				
McGregor's Theory X and Y				
Henry Manufacturing				
First Federal Savings				
Claremont Industries				

7. Was the ratio of lectures to cases (Check one): High ____ OK ____ Low ____?

8. Were the videocassettes pertinent to your work? (Check one)
   To most of my work? _____
   To some of my work? _____
   To none of my work? _____

9. To help the training director and the staff provide further improvements in future programs, please give us your frank opinion of each case discussion leader's contribution to your learning. (Place your check marks in the appropriate boxes.)

	Excellent	Above Average	Average	Below Average	Poor
Davis					
Gleason					
Laird					
Martin					
Pontello					
Shall					
Sommers					
Wilson					
Zimmer					

10. How would you evaluate your participation in the program? (Check)
    Overall workload: Too heavy _____   Just right _____   Too light _____
    Case preparation: Too much _____   Just right _____   Too light _____
    Homework assignments: Too heavy _____   Just right _____   Too light _____

11. What suggestions do you have for improving the program?
    _____
    _____

12. Please add any additional comments, criticisms, or suggestions that you think might be helpful for the training group to know before scheduling future programs.
    _____
    _____

Source: Developing and Training Human Resources in Organizations, 3/E by Wexley/Latham. © Reprinted by permission of Pearson Education Inc., Upper Saddle River, NJ.

3. *Behaviour*. Next, ask whether the trainees' behaviour on the job changed because of the training program. For example, are employees in the store's complaint department more courteous toward disgruntled customers than previously? These measures determine the degree of transfer of training.

4. *Results*. Lastly, but probably most importantly, ask: "Did the number of customer complaints about employees drop? Did the reject rate improve? Was turnover reduced? Are production quotas now being met?" and so on. Improved results are, of course, especially important. The training program may succeed in terms of the reactions from trainees, increased learning, and even changes in behaviour, but if the results are not achieved, then in the final analysis, the training had not achieved its goals. If so, the problem may be related to inappropriate use of a training program. For example, training is ineffective when environmental factors are the cause of poor performance.

Some organizations are modifying this traditional approach to the evaluation of training. At TD Bank Financial Group, a fifth measure of training effectiveness is also used. The results data are translated into monetary value and compared to the costs of the training program.[116] In the retail sector, training is being evaluated on "return on expectation" using measures such as time to competence (for employee skills), time to market (for new products), achieved competencies, and achieved expectations.[117]

While the four basic categories are understandable and widely used, there are several things to keep in mind when using them to measure training effects. First, there are usually only modest correlations among the four types of training criteria (i.e., scoring "high" on learning does not necessarily mean that behaviour or results will also score "high," and the converse is true as well). Similarly, studies show that "reaction" measures (e.g., "How well did you like the program?") may provide some insight into how they liked the program, but probably will not provide much insight into what they learned or how they will behave once they are back on the job.

Better, Faster, Cheaper? The e-Learning Market

...According to statistics available to IBM, the e-learning market is projected to reach 90 percent growth by 2002. As impressive as that may sound, many still prefer traditional classroom learning for certain training and development. The general perception, as confirmed by a show of hands within our seminar audience, is that tangible skills are easier to put into e-learning modules while soft (people) skills require traditional classrooms and real interaction among the learners. So, whether e-learning is better than traditional learning will depend upon the skills that need to be taught. Sometimes, the optimal solution combines elements of both learning techniques.

According to the industry, the effectiveness of e-learning can be proved by statistics, such as the one above. But, as always, there is research available to counter these claims, research that says there is no significant difference in the effectiveness of either method. The effectiveness of any learning technique lies in the instructional design, not the technology employed. And when technology is designed correctly, e-learning can offer some advantages over classroom learning....

Determining whether e-learning is cheaper depends on the variables considered. Since most organizations start with cost avoidance when looking at savings, the tangible costs saved are: travel expense; learner non-productive time; and training delivery costs. The intangible costs include: opportunity costs; management attention; improved job performance; currency and relevance of training. However, e-learning does require a significant up-front cost which can sometimes act as a deterrent for many employers unless they look at the whole picture....

Source: Excerpted with the permission from the *Training and Development Guide* Newsletter (No. 23, March 2002), published by and copyright CCH Canadian Limited, Toronto, Ontario.

CHAPTER Review

Summary

1   An orientation program is the joint responsibility of the HR department and the new employee's supervisor. HR should provide the new employee with general information on company history, work regulations, and employee benefits. The immediate supervisor should introduce the new employee to co-workers, conduct a tour of the company premises, and provide specific information on the job, performance criteria, and any training to be provided.

2   The basic training process consists of five steps: needs analysis, instructional design, validation, implementation, and evaluation.

3   Two techniques for assessing training needs are (1) task analysis to determine the training needs of employees who are new to their jobs, and (2)

performance analysis to appraise the performance of current employees to determine whether training could reduce performance problems. Transfer of training to the workplace can be increased by assessing the ability, aptitude, and motivation of potential trainees before training; providing feedback, opportunities for practice, and positive reinforcement during the training; and providing frequent feedback, opportunities for practice, and positive reinforcement after the training.

4 Traditional training techniques include on-the-job-training, apprenticeship training, informal learning, job instruction training, lectures, audiovisual techniques, programmed learning, and vestibule or simulated training.

5 Three types of e-learning are computer-based training, online training, and electronic performance support systems.

6 Today's organizations often provide training for special purposes, including literacy training, diversity training, customer-service training, training for teamwork, training for first-time supervisors, and training for global business.

7 In evaluating the effectiveness of a training program, four categories of outcomes can be measured: reaction, learning, behaviour, and results.

Key Terms

controlled experimentation   *(p. 231)*
electronic performance support systems (EPSS)
    (p. 227)
e-learning   *(p. 225)*
employee orientation   *(p. 207)*
job instruction training (JIT)   *(p. 222)*
performance analysis   *(p. 216)*
programmed learning   *(p. 224)*
reality shock   *(p. 207)*
socialization   *(p. 207)*
task analysis   *(p. 216)*
training   *(p. 212)*
transfer of training   *(p. 218)*
vestibule or simulated training   *(p. 224)*
videoconferencing   *(p. 224)*

Review and Discussion Questions

1 Prepare an orientation program checklist for your current or most recent job.

2 Pick out some task with which you are familiar—such as mowing the lawn or using a chat room—and develop a job instruction training sheet for it.

3 Pierre Belanger is an undergraduate business student majoring in accounting. He has just failed the first accounting course, Accounting 101, and is understandably upset. Explain how you would use performance analysis to identify what, if any, are Pierre's training needs.

4 Think about the jobs that you have had in the past. For which of these jobs could an electronic performance support system be used? Prepare an outline for such a system.

CRITICAL *Thinking Questions*

1 "A well-thought-out orientation program is especially important for employees (like many recent graduates) who have had little or no work experience." Explain why you agree or disagree with this statement.

2 What do you think are some of the main drawbacks of relying on informal on-the-job training for teaching new employees their jobs?

3 This chapter points out that one reason for implementing special global training programs is to avoid business loss due to cultural insensitivity. What sort of cultural insensitivity do you think is referred to, and how might that translate into lost business? What sort of training programs would you recommend to avoid such cultural insensitivity?

4 Most training programs are not formally evaluated past a reaction measure. Why do you think employers do not measure the learning, behaviour, and results effects of training more often?

APPLICATION *Exercises*

Running Case: LearnInMotion.com

The New Training Program

"I just don't understand it," said Pierre. "No one here seems to follow instructions, and no matter how many times I've told them how to do things they seem to do them their own way." At present, LearnInMotion.com has no formal orientation or training policies or procedures. Jennifer believes that is one reason why employees generally ignore the standards that she and Pierre would like employees to adhere to.

Several examples illustrate this. One of the jobs of the Web designer (her name is Maureen) is to take customer copy for banner ads and adapt it for placement on LearnInMotion.com. She has been told several times not to tinker in any way with a customer's logo: Most companies put considerable thought and resources into logo design, and as Pierre has said, "whether or not Maureen thinks the logo is perfect, it's the customer's logo, and she's to leave it as it is." Yet just a week ago, they almost lost a big customer when Maureen, to "clarify" the customer's logo, modified its design before posting it on LearnInMotion.com.

That's just the tip of the iceberg. As far as Jennifer and Pierre are concerned, it is the sales effort that is completely out of control. For one thing, even after several months on the job, it still seems as if the sales people don't know what they're talking about. For example, LearnInMotion has several co-brand arrangements with Web sites like Yahoo!. This means that if they are interested in ordering educational courses or CDs, other sites' users can easily click through to LearnInMotion.com. Jennifer has noticed that during conversations with customers, the two sales people have no idea of which sites co-brand with LearnInMotion, or how to get to the LearnInMotion site from the partner Web site. The salespeople also need to know a lot more about the products themselves. For example, one salesperson was trying to sell someone who produces programs on managing call centres on the idea of listing its products under LearnInMotion's "communications" community. In fact, the "communications" community is for courses on topics like interpersonal com-

munications and how to be a better listener; it has nothing to do with managing the sorts of call centres that, for instance, airlines use for handling customer inquiries. As another example, the Web surfer is supposed to get a specific e-mail address with a specific person's name for the salespeople to use, instead he often just comes back with an "information" e-mail address off a Web site. The list goes on and on.

Jennifer feels the company has had other problems because of the lack of adequate employee training and orientation. For example, a question came up recently when employees found they weren't paid for the Canada Day holiday. They assumed they would be paid, but they were not. Similarly, when a salesperson left after barely a month on the job, there was considerable debate about whether the person should receive severance pay and accumulated vacation pay. Other matters to cover during an orientation, says Jennifer, include company policy regarding lateness and absences; health and hospitalization benefits (there are none, other than workers' compensation); and matters like maintaining a safe and healthy workplace, personal appearance and cleanliness, personal telephone calls and e-mail, substance abuse, and eating on the job.

Jennifer believes that implementing orientation and training programs would help ensure that employees know how to do their jobs. She and Pierre further believe that it is only when employees understand the right way to do their jobs that there is any hope those jobs will in fact be carried out in the way the owners want them to be. Now they want you, their management consultants, to help them. Here's what they want you to do for them.

Questions

1 Specifically, what should be covered in the new employee orientation program, and how should this information be conveyed?

2 In the HR course Jennifer took, the book suggested using a task analysis record form to identify tasks performed by an employee. Should LearnInMoion use a form like this for the salespeople? If so, what, roughly speaking, should the completed, filled-in form look like?

3 Which specific training techniques should be used to train the salespeople, Web designer, and Web surfer, and why?

CASE INCIDENT *TPK Appliances*

When TPK, a manufacturer of small appliances— electric kettles, toasters, and irons—automated its warehouse, the warehouse crew was reduced from 14 to four. Every one of the displaced stock workers was assigned to another department, as TPK had a history of providing stable employment.

Jacob Peters, a stock worker with more than 15 years of service, was transferred to the toaster assembly line to be retrained as a small-parts assembler. When he arrived to begin his new job, the supervisor said, "This may be only temporary, Jacob. I have a full staff right now, so I have nothing for you to do, but come on, I'll find you a locker." As there really was no job for him, Jacob did nothing for the first week except odd jobs such as filling bins. At the beginning of week two, Jacob was informed that a vacancy would be occurring the next day, so he reported for work eager to learn his new job.

The operation was depressingly simple. All Jacob had to do was pick up two pieces of metal, one in each hand, place them into a jig so that they were held together in a cross position, and press a button. The riveting machine then put a rivet through both pieces and an air jet automatically ejected the joined pieces into a bin.

"This job is so simple a monkey could do it," the supervisor told Jacob. "Let me show you how it's done," and he quickly demonstrated the three steps involved. "Now you do it," he said. Of course, Jacob did it right the first time. After watching him rivet two or three, the supervisor left Jacob to his work.

About three hours later, the riveter started to put the rivets in a little crooked, but Jacob kept on working. Finally, a fellow worker stopped by and said, "You're new here, aren't you?" Jacob nodded. "Listen, I'll give you a word of advice. If the supervisor sees you letting the rivets go in crooked like that, he'll give you hell. So hide these in the scrap over there." His new friend then showed Jacob how to adjust his machine.

Jacob's next problem began when the air ejection system started jamming. Four times he managed to clear it, but on the fifth try, he slipped and his elbow hit the rivet button. The machine put a rivet through the fleshy part of the hand, just below the thumb.

It was in the first aid station that the supervisor finally had the opportunity to see Jacob once again.

Questions

1 Comment on the strengths and weaknesses of Jacob's orientation and on-the-job training.

2 Outline how the process should have been conducted.

Source: M. Belcourt, P.C. Wright, and A.M. Saks, *Managing Performance Through Training and Development* (2nd edition). Toronto ON: Nelson Thomson Learning, 2000, pp. 185–186. NOTE: This story is a fictional version of a real-life situation that existed at Canadian General Electric many years ago.

EXPERIENTIAL *Exercises*

1 Obtain a copy of an employee handbook from your employer or from some other organization. Review it and make recommendations for improvement.

2 Working individually or in groups, follow the steps in Figure 7.2, and prepare a training program for a job that you currently hold or have had in the past.

3 In small groups of four to six students, complete the following exercise. JetBlue Airlines has asked you to quickly develop the outline of a training program for its new reservation clerks. Airline reservation clerks obviously need numerous skills to perform their jobs. You may want to start by listing the job's main duties, using the information provided below. In any case, please produce the requested training outline, making sure to be very specific about what you want to teach the new clerks, and what methods and aids you suggest using to train them.

Duties of Airline Reservation Clerks: Customers contact airline reservation clerks to obtain flight schedules, prices, and itineraries. The reservation clerks look up the requested information on the airline's flight schedule systems, which are updated continuously. The reservation clerk must deal courteously and expeditiously with the customer, and be able to quickly find alternative flight arrangements in order to provide the customer with the itinerary that fits his or her needs. Alternative flights and prices must be found quickly, so that the customer is not kept waiting, and so that the reservations operations group maintains its efficiency standards. It is often necessary to look under various routings, since there may be a dozen or more alternative routes between the customer's starting point and destination.

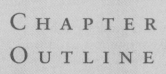

CHAPTER 8

Career Development

LEARNING OUTCOMES

After studying this chapter you should be able to:

Discuss the factors that affect career choices.

Explain how to make a new employee's first assignment more meaningful.

Discuss how to manage promotions and transfers more effectively.

Explain what management development is and why it is important.

Describe on-the-job and off-the-job management-development techniques.

Discuss the five-step executive development process.

CAREER PLANNING AND DEVELOPMENT

boundaryless career A career that spans several organizations and/or industries.

Today, it is widely acknowledged that job security is dead, along with employee loyalty to the employer. Strategically focused employers support their human capital by assisting their employees in managing the career ambiguity associated with this new employment-contract reality, which typically results in multiple-employer careers. Careers that span several organizations, as opposed to the traditional long-term career in a single organization, have become known as **boundaryless careers.**[1]

Instead of a promise of job security, today's emphasis is on employability, and the skills to manage careers both inside and outside of a particular organization. The Conference Board of Canada has developed a list called "Employability Skills 2000+" that are needed to enter, remain, and progress in the world of work. There are three categories of skills:

- *Fundamental skills*—communication, managing information, using numbers, thinking, and solving problems.
- *Personal management skills*—demonstrating positive attitudes and behaviours, being responsible, being adaptable, learning continuously, and working safely.
- *Teamwork skills*—working with others, participating in projects and tasks.[2]

career planning and development The deliberate process through which a person becomes aware of personal career-related attributes, and the lifelong series of activities that contribute to his or her career fulfillment.

Career Planning Exercises
www.careerstorm.com
Career Planning
www.careeraction.org

HRM activities play an important role in **career planning and development.** Career-related programs help HR professionals to maintain employee commitment —an employee's identification with and agreement to pursue the company's or the unit's strategic goals. In the new millennium, when the employee may not be sure that he or she will even have a job there at the end of the year, employee commitment is more adult, more honest, and more realistic. Today, there is widespread recognition that employees can and will reconfigure themselves throughout their careers. This new world of work can actually be liberating, offering much greater room for self-actualization. Employees who are pursuing their need to "be all that they can be" increase their sense of *self-reliance,* and know that the ability to take risks is a key factor in career success. Career expert Barbara Moses suggests that employers help their employees by providing support for individuals who are willing to take responsibility for their own careers, including opportunities for self-assessment and self-determination. She believes that effective career-management programs can prepare employees for the future by fostering self-awareness, helping to improve employee–job "fit," and restoring a sense of self-efficacy and confidence.[3]

Giving employees an opportunity to self-actualize and to develop their potential fosters commitment. Most employees appreciate and respond well to having their potential and skills enhanced, and to knowing that they will be more marketable. Developmental activities, such as providing the educational and training resources required to help employees identify and develop their promotion and career potential, are also important. Career-oriented firms also stress career-oriented appraisals that link the employee's past performance, career preferences, and developmental needs in a formal career plan. Internal job posting systems ensure that the career goals and skills of inside candidates are matched openly, fairly, and effectively with transfer and promotion opportunities.

Career-development activity is becoming widely accepted as a means for organizations to respond to one of their most serious challenges: retaining employees and keeping them motivated and productive in an environment where there are limited opportunities for promotion.[4] Managers face the prospect of high turnover and loss of quality workers unless they take action to value the "knowledge capital" that their employees embody.[5] The key factors in **employee retention** today are opportunities for challenging work, advancement opportunities, and recognition. For example, a 2001 Statistics Canada survey of employees found that new arts and science graduates from high school, trade schools, and community colleges had the highest job search rate (41 percent). Job dissatisfaction due to feeling overqualified, unhappiness with the job not being related to their field of study, and low pay were the main reasons for wanting to change jobs.[6] A 2002 survey by Drake Beam Morin found that high-tech workers stay on the job less than half as much time as other workers, and nearly half of those who leave look for employment in another industry.[7]

Employers should increase the challenge in employees' jobs by including employees in external activities, involving them more closely in the work of senior management, and giving them money to use for developmental purposes of their own choosing.[8] These issues are particularly important for "knowledge workers."[9] In today's downsized, flattened, high-tech, and empowered organizations, employers must also depend on their employees to recognize new opportunities, identify problems, and react quickly with analyses and recommendations. As a result, the need has arisen for encouraging **lifelong learning**— in other words, for providing extensive, continuing training from basic remedial skills to advanced decision-making techniques throughout employees' careers.

Before proceeding, it would be useful to define some of the terms that will be used throughout this chapter.[10] A *career* is a series of work-related positions, paid or unpaid, that help a person to grow in job skills, success, and fulfillment. *Career development* is the lifelong series of activities (such as workshops) that contribute to a person's career exploration, establishment, success, and fulfillment. *Career planning* is the deliberate process through which someone becomes aware of personal skills, interests, knowledge, motivations, and other characteristics; acquires information about opportunities and choices; identifies career-related goals; and establishes action plans to attain specific goals.

Roles in Career Development

The individual, the manager, and the employer all have roles in the individual's career development. Ultimately, however, it is the *individual* who must accept responsibility for his or her own career. This requires an entrepreneurial, goal-oriented approach that requires four key skills: self-motivation, independent learning, effective time and money management, and self-promotion.[11] Networking is the foundation of active career management and is essential for accessing the most valuable career resource—people. Networking is an organized process whereby the individual arranges and conducts a series of face-to-face meetings with his or her colleagues and contacts, plus individuals they

employee retention The extent to which employees are retained by the organization over relatively long periods of time.

lifelong learning Providing extensive continuing training throughout employees' careers.

Career Networking
www.careerkey.com

recommend (not cold calls). Networking does not involve asking for a job, and it is not a one-sided encounter where only the individual benefits, but rather a mutual sharing process. Its objectives are to let people know about background and career goals, and to exchange information, advice, and referrals.[12] A personal networking chart is shown in **Figure 8.1.**

Within the organization, the individual's *manager* plays a role, too. The manager should provide timely and objective performance feedback, offer developmental assignments and support, and participate in career-development discussions. The manager acts as a coach, appraiser, advisor, and referral agent, for instance, listening to and clarifying the individual's career plans, giving feedback, generating career options, and linking the employee to organizational resources and career options.

Finally, the *employer* plays a career-development role. For example, an organization wishing to retain good employees should provide career-oriented training and development opportunities, offer career information and career programs, and give employees a variety of career options. Ultimately, employers need not and should not provide such career-oriented activities purely out of altruism. Most employees will ultimately grade their employers on the extent to which the organization allowed them to excel and to become the people they believed they had the potential to become, and that will help to determine their commitment to their employers and their overall job satisfaction.[13]

FIGURE 8.1   Personal Network Chart

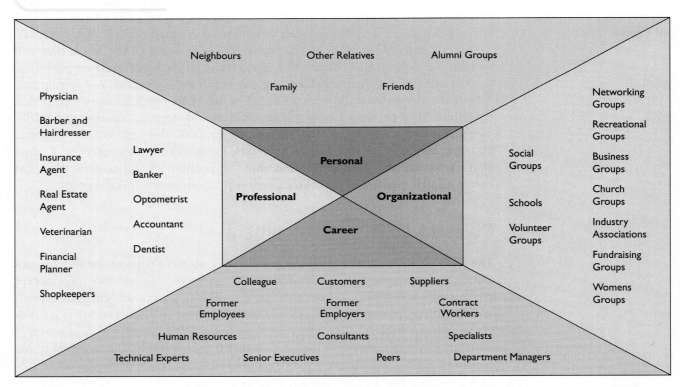

Source: It's Your Move: A Personal and Practical Guide to Career Transition and Job Search for Canadian Managers, Professionals and Executives by M. Watters and L. O'Connor. Published by HarperCollins Publishers Ltd. Copyright © 2001 by Knebel Watters & Associates, Inc. All rights reserved.

Factors That Affect Career Choices

The first step in planning a career is to learn as much as possible about the person's interests, aptitudes, and skills.

Identify Career Stage   Each person's career goes through stages, and the current stage will influence the employee's knowledge of and preference for various occupations. The main stages of this **career cycle** follow.[14]

Growth Stage   The **growth stage** lasts roughly from birth to age 14, and is a period during which the person develops a self-concept by identifying with and interacting with other people, such as family, friends, and teachers. Toward the beginning of this period, role-playing is important, and children experiment with different ways of acting; this helps them to form impressions of how other people react to different behaviours and contributes to their developing a unique self-concept or identity. Toward the end of this stage, the adolescent (who by this time has developed preliminary ideas about what his or her interests and abilities are) begins to think realistically about occupational alternatives.

Exploration Stage   The **exploration stage** is the period (roughly from age 15 to 24) during which a person seriously explores various occupational alternatives. The person attempts to match these alternatives with what he or she has learned about them and about his or her own interests and abilities from school, leisure activities, and work. Tentative broad occupational choices are usually made during the beginning of this period. Toward the end of this period, a seemingly appropriate choice is made and the person tries out for an entry-level job.

Probably the most important task that the person has in this and the preceding stage is to develop a realistic understanding of his or her abilities and talents. Similarly, the person must make sound educational decisions based on reliable sources of information about occupational alternatives.

Establishment Stage   The **establishment stage** spans the period from roughly age 24 to 44 and is the heart of most people's work lives. During this period, it is hoped that a suitable occupation is found and that the person engages in activities that help him or her to earn a permanent place in the chosen field. Often, and particularly in the professions, the person locks into a chosen occupation early. In most cases, however, this is a period during which the person is continually testing his or her capabilities and ambitions against those of the initial occupational choice.

Maintenance Stage   Between the ages of 45 and 65, many people simply slide from the establishment stage into the **maintenance stage**. During this latter period, most efforts are now directed at maintaining the place that the person has typically created in the world of work.

Decline Stage   As retirement age approaches, there may be a deceleration period known as the **decline stage**. Here, many people face the prospect of having to accept reduced levels of power and responsibility, and learn to accept and develop new roles as mentor and confidant for those who are younger. However, it is becoming more common for older workers, despite some decline in physical capabilities, to continue to work until normal retirement age and beyond. Following retirement, the person finds alternative uses for the time and effort formerly expended on his or her occupation.

career cycle The stages through which a person's career evolves.

growth stage The period from birth to age 14, during which the person develops a self-concept by identifying with and interacting with other people, such as family, friends, and teachers.

exploration stage The period from around age 15 to 24, during which a person seriously explores various occupational alternatives, attempting to match these alternatives with his or her interests and abilities.

establishment stage The period, roughly from age 24 to 44, that is the heart of most people's work lives.

maintenance stage The period from about age 45 to 65, during which the person secures his or her place in the world of work.

decline stage The period during which many people are faced with the prospect of having to accept reduced levels of power and responsibility.

occupational orientation The theory, developed by John Holland, that there are six basic personal orientations that determine the sorts of careers to which people are drawn.

Research
Insight ▷

Identify Occupational Orientation

Career-counselling expert John Holland says that a person's personality (including values, motives, and needs) determines his or her **occupational orientation**, which is another important factor in career choices. For example, a person with a strong social orientation might be attracted to careers that entail interpersonal rather than intellectual or physical activities, and to occupations such as social work.

Based on research with his Vocational Preference Test (VPT), Holland found six basic personality types or orientations:[15]

1. *Realistic orientation.* These people are attracted to occupations that involve physical activities requiring skill, strength, and coordination. Examples include forestry, farming, and agriculture.

2. *Investigative orientation.* Investigative people are attracted to careers that involve cognitive activities (thinking, organizing, and understanding) rather than affective activities (feeling, acting, or interpersonal and emotional tasks). Examples include biologists, chemists, and college professors.

3. *Social orientation.* These people are attracted to careers that involve interpersonal rather than intellectual or physical activities. Examples include clinical psychology, foreign service, and social work.

4. *Conventional orientation.* A conventional orientation favours careers that involve structured, rule-regulated activities, as well as careers in which it is expected that the employee subordinate his or her personal needs to those of the organization. Examples include accountants and bankers.

5. *Enterprising orientation.* Verbal activities aimed at influencing others are attractive to enterprising personalities. Examples include managers, lawyers, and public-relations executives.

6. *Artistic orientation.* People here are attracted to careers that involve self-expression, artistic creation, expression of emotions, and individualistic activities. Examples include artists, advertising executives, and musicians.

Most people have more than one orientation (they might be social, realistic, and investigative, for example), and Holland believes that the more similar or compatible these orientations are, the less internal conflict or indecision a person will face in making a career choice.

Identify Skills and Aptitudes

Successful performance depends not just on motivation but also on ability. Someone may have a conventional orientation, but whether he or she has the skills to be an accountant, banker, or credit manager will largely determine the specific occupation ultimately chosen. Therefore, each individual's skills must be identified.

One useful exercise for identifying occupational skills is to write a short essay that describes "The Most Enjoyable Occupational Task That I Have Had." Make sure to go into detail about duties and responsibilities and what it was that made the task enjoyable. Next, on other sheets of paper, do the same thing for two other enjoyable tasks. Now go through the three essays and underline the skills that were mentioned the most often. For example, was it putting together and coordinating the school play as part of a job in the principal's office one year? Was it the hours spent in the library doing research when working one summer as an office clerk?[16]

For career-planning purposes, a person's aptitudes are usually measured with a test battery such as the general aptitude test battery (GATB). This instrument measures various aptitudes, including intelligence and mathematical ability. Considerable work has been done to relate aptitudes, such as those measured by the GATB, to specific occupations.

Identify Career Anchor

career anchor A concern or value that you will not give up if a choice has to be made.

Edgar Schein says that career planning is a continuing process of discovery—one in which a person slowly develops a clearer occupational self-concept in terms of what his or her talents, abilities, motives, needs, attitudes, and values are. Schein also says that as you learn more about yourself, it becomes apparent that you have a dominant **career anchor**, a concern or value that you will not give up if a choice has to be made. Career anchors, as their name implies, are the pivots around which a person's career swings; a person becomes conscious of them as a result of learning about his or her talents and abilities, motives and needs, and attitudes and values. Based on his research, Schein believes that career anchors are difficult to predict ahead of time because they are evolutionary. Some people may not find out what their career anchors are until they have to make a major choice—such as whether to take the promotion to the headquarters staff or strike out on their own by starting a business. It is at this point that all of the person's past work experiences, interests, aptitudes, and orientations converge into a meaningful pattern (or career anchor) that helps to show what is personally the most important in driving the person's career choices. Schein identified five career anchors:[17]

1. *Technical/functional career anchor.* People who have a strong technical/functional career anchor tend to avoid decisions that would drive them toward general management. Instead, they make decisions that will enable them to remain and grow in their chosen technical or functional fields.

2. *Managerial competence as a career anchor.* Other people show a strong motivation to become managers, and their career experience convinces them that they have the skills and values required to rise to general-management positions. A management position of high responsibility is their ultimate goal. Qualifications for these jobs include (1) analytical competence (ability to identify, analyze, and solve problems under conditions of incomplete information and uncertainty); (2) interpersonal competence (ability to influence, supervise, lead, manipulate, and control people at all levels); and (3) emotional competence (the capacity to be stimulated by emotional and interpersonal crises rather than exhausted or debilitated by them, and the capacity to bear high levels of responsibility without becoming paralyzed).

3. *Creativity as a career anchor.* People who become successful entrepreneurs have a need to build or create something that is entirely their own product —a product or process that bears their name, a company of their own, or a personal fortune that reflects their accomplishments. For example, one participant in Schein's research became a successful purchaser, restorer, and renter of townhouses in a large city; another built a successful consulting firm.

4. *Autonomy and independence as career anchors.* Some people seem driven to be on their own, free of the dependence that can arise when a person

works in a large organization where promotions, transfers, and salary decisions make them subordinate to others. Many also have a strong technical/functional orientation. Instead of pursuing this orientation in an organization, however, they decide to become consultants, working either alone or as part of a relatively small firm. Others become professors of business, freelance writers, and proprietors of small retail businesses.

5. *Security as a career anchor.* Some people are mostly concerned with long-run career stability and job security. They seem willing to do what is required to maintain job security, a decent income, and a stable future in the form of a good retirement program and benefits. For those interested in *geographic security*, maintaining a stable, secure career in familiar surroundings is generally more important than pursuing superior career choices, if choosing the latter means injecting instability or insecurity into their lives by forcing them to pull up roots and move to another city. For others, security means *organizational security*. They are much more willing to let their employers decide what their careers should be.

CAREER DEVELOPMENT AND THE RESPONSIBILITIES OF THE MANAGER AND THE EMPLOYER

Along with the employee, the manager and employer both have career-management responsibilities. Some guidelines follow.

Tips for the Front Line

Avoid Reality Shock

Perhaps at no other stage in the person's career is it more important for the employer to be career development-oriented than at the initial entry stage, when the person is recruited, hired, and given a first assignment and boss. This is (or should be) a period of *reality testing* during which his or her initial hopes and goals first confront the realities of organizational life and of the person's talents and needs.

For many first-time workers, this turns out to be a disastrous period, one in which their often-naïve expectations confront unexpected workplace realities such as being relegated to an unimportant low-risk job where he or she "cannot cause any trouble while being tried out," interdepartmental conflict and politicking, or a boss who is neither rewarded for nor trained in the unique mentoring tasks needed to properly supervise new employees.[18]

Provide Challenging Initial Jobs

Most experts agree that one of the most important things is to provide new employees with challenging first jobs. In most organizations, however, providing such jobs seems more the exception than the rule. This imbalance, as one expert has pointed out, is an example of "glaring mismanagement" when one considers the effort and money invested in recruiting, hiring, and training new employees.[19]

Giving an employee responsibility for a major presentation to an important client is one way to front-load entry-level jobs with challenge and to foster employee commitment.

Provide Realistic Job Previews

Providing recruits with realistic previews of what to expect should they be selected to work in the organization—previews that describe both the attractions and possible pitfalls—can be an effective way of minimizing reality shock and improving employees' long-term performance.

Be Demanding

There is often a "Pygmalion effect" in the relationship between a new employee and his or her boss.[20] In other words, the more the supervisor expects and the more confident and supportive he or she is, the better new employees will perform.

Provide Periodic Developmental Job Rotation and Job Pathing

The best way in which new employees can test themselves and crystallize their career anchors is to try out a variety of challenging jobs. By rotating to jobs in various specializations—from financial analysis to production to HR, for example—the employee gets an opportunity to assess his or her aptitudes and preferences. At the same time, the organization gets a manager with a broader, multifunctional view of the organization.[21] One extension of this is called **job pathing,** which means selecting carefully sequenced job assignments.[22]

job pathing Selecting carefully sequenced job assignments to enable employees to test their aptitudes and preferences.

Provide Career-Oriented Performance Appraisals

Supervisors must understand that valid performance appraisal information is, in the long run, more important than protecting the short-term interests of their staff.[23] Therefore, a supervisor needs concrete information regarding the employee's potential career path—information, in other words, about the nature of the future work for which he or she is appraising the employee, or which the employee desires.[24]

Provide Career-Planning Workshops

Employers should also take steps to increase their employees' involvement and expertise in planning and developing their own careers. One option here is to organize periodic career-planning workshops. A **career-planning workshop** has been defined as "a planned learning event in which participants are expected to be actively involved, completing career-planning exercises and inventories and participating in career-skills practice sessions."[25]

career-planning workshop A planned earning event in which participants are expected to be actively involved in career-planning exercises and career-skills practice sessions.

Such workshops usually contain a *self-assessment* activity in which individual employees actively analyze their own career interests, skills, and career anchors. There is then an *environmental assessment* phase in which relevant information about the company and its career options and staffing needs is presented. Finally, a career-planning workshop typically concludes with *goal setting and action planning* in which the individual sets career goals and creates a career plan.

A career-planning workbook may be distributed to employees either as part of a workshop or as an independent career-planning aid. This is "a printed guide that directs its users through a series of assessment exercises, models, discussions, guidelines, and other information to support career planning."[26] The workbook may also contain practical career-related information, such as how to prepare a résumé. Finally, career-planning workbooks usually contain guides for creating a career-development action plan. A career-planning workbook underlines the employee's responsibility to initiate the career-development process, whereas career workshops may reinforce the perception that the employer will do so.[27] Some career-planning activities are now being offered online. At the TD Bank Financial Group, HR managers are utilizing an online career management program called PD@TD, as described in the HR.Net box.

Provide Opportunities for Mentoring

mentoring The use of an experienced individual (the mentor) to teach and train another person (the protégé) with less knowledge in a given area.

Mentoring has traditionally been defined as "the use of an experienced individual (the mentor) to teach and train someone [the protégé] with less knowledge in a given area."[28] Through individualized attention, "the mentor transfers needed information, feedback, and encouragement to the protégé...,"[29] and in that way, the opportunities for the protégé to optimize his or her career success are improved. Effective mentoring builds trust both ways in the mentor–protégé relationship.[30] Mentoring provides benefits to both mentors, who demonstrate enhanced attitudes and job performance, and protégés, who become more self-confident and productive, and experience greater career satisfaction and faster career growth.[31] Group mentoring is another option. A special mentor who offers insight and the wisdom of experience guides four to eight employees, and in addition, each employee's manager plays a key role in developing learning assignments and coaching the employee.[32]

Organizational mentoring may be formal or informal. Informally, of course, middle- and senior-level managers will often voluntarily take up-and-coming

HR.NET

PD@TD

PD@TD is an online, interactive intranet site that combines employee self-assessments with information on TD's businesses, including strategies, job descriptions, workforce statistics, and key success factors, as well as a virtual library of tools and resources that help employees strike a work-life balance. All this is meant to help employees become more career self-reliant—to find their long-term fit within the organization by determining if they are in the right position in the first place. If they are not, they can draft a development plan to help get them there. PD@TD is often referred to a "virtual mentor."

Employees start out by finding out about themselves. They log on and complete three assessments about themselves: interests, skills, and values. From this, the program suggests some positions or types of work the employee would ideally be suited for. Links to the bank's learning and development site provide more information on courses and development programs. Telephone career services are available when needed to assist employees who want to speak to somebody about career development.

To keep employees up to date, the PD@TD site has a "what's new page" and puts advertising banners on other sites on the TD intranet. They try to add a new topic each month, such as résumé building, developing interview skills, networking, integrating work and life, and stress management.

Source: "So You Think Self-service Is a Big Deal," *Canadian HR Reporter* (November 20, 2000), pp. 9, 11. Reproduced by permission of *Canadian HR Reporter*, Carswell, One Corporate Plaza, 2075 Kennedy Road, Scarborough, ON M1T 3V4.

employees under their wings, not only to train them, but to give career advice and to help them steer around political pitfalls. However, many employers also establish formal mentoring programs. Here employers actively encourage mentoring relationships to take place, and may pair protégés with potential mentors. Training may be provided to facilitate the mentoring process and, in particular, to aid both mentor and protégé in understanding their respective responsibilities in the mentoring relationship. A recent study on mentoring across Canada found interesting variations in the gender breakdown between male and female mentors and protégées, based on the type of mentoring program, as shown in **Figure 8.2**.

A recent study by Peer Resources, a nonprofit centre for mentoring in Victoria, B.C., found that mentoring is not being used to its full potential in Canadian workplaces. Almost one-third of Canadian organizations have no mentoring programs. This is surprising, given the emphasis on learning organizations and knowledge workers in today's businesses. Mentoring is one of the best and cheapest ways to transfer knowledge.[33] Mentoring also keeps skilled employees motivated, loyal, and committed to the organization. Ultimately, an effective mentoring program supports corporate strategy by retaining future leaders.[34]

A new development in mentoring is *reverse mentoring* programs where younger employees provide guidance to senior executives on how to use the Web for messaging, buying products and services, finding new business opportunities, and so forth. General Motors, Procter & Gamble, General Electric, and the Wharton Business School are all using reverse mentoring. The relationship that develops often provides benefits to the young mentor when the Web-challenged older manager reciprocates in the form of career advice and guidance.[35]

Become a Learning Organization

Learning is a survival technique for both individuals and organizations. Today, employees at all levels know that they must engage in lifelong learning in order

Mentors—Peer Resources
www.mentors.ca

FIGURE **8.2**   Male/Female Breakdown of Mentors and Mentees

Program Objectives	Mentor male/female ratio	% male	% female	Mentee male/female ratio	% male	% female
Entrepreneur Development	1.1:1	52.2	47.8	0.5:1	35.4	64.5
Retention/Succession Leadership	1.7:1	63.3	36.7	2.1:1	67.3	32.7
Career Entry/ Settlement	1.4:1	58.7	41.3	1.4:1	58.5	41.5
Industry-Specific Mobility	0.1:1	8.7	91.3	0.004:1	3.7	96.3

Source: C. Cuerrier, ed., *Mentoring and the World of Work in Canada: Source Book of Best Practices.* Charlesbourg, QC: Fondation de l'entrepreneurship, 2003. Reprinted with permission of the publisher.

learning organization An organization focused on creating, acquiring, and transferring knowledge, and at modifying its behaviour to reflect new knowledge and insights.

to remain employable and have a satisfying career. A **learning organization** "is an organization skilled at creating, acquiring, and transferring knowledge, and at modifying its behaviour to reflect new knowledge and insights."[36] The HR department is often the driving force behind ensuring that the training and development opportunities necessary to create a learning organization are in place, particularly in the following five activities:

- *Transferring knowledge.* Learning organizations are adept at transferring knowledge. For example, in some firms, rotating assignments are used for transferring knowledge. Other companies organize workers into self-managed teams, the members of which must share their knowledge in order to function successfully.

- *Learning from experience.* Learning organizations also have to review their successes and failures and document the lessons they have learned. Training and development plays an important role in facilitating such learning from past experience. For example, case studies and action learning can be used to study and illustrate what has previously been done correctly or incorrectly.

- *Experimentation.* The learning organization also depends on experimentation, which means systematically searching for and testing new knowledge.[37] It is the role of the HR department to create incentive plans that encourage employees to experiment with new processes or products. For example, the management of 3M company supports the development of new products by encouraging research and development staff to use up to 15 percent of their time on experimentation with new product ideas.[38]

- *Learning from others.* A learning organization is also one that effectively learns from others. Outside training and development activities involving employees from other organizations are important for obtaining such expertise. Employees and managers must also be trained to benchmark, the process through which the best industry practices are uncovered, analyzed, adopted, and implemented.[39]

- *Systematic problem solving.* The learning organization depends on the scientific method, where they gather data and use simple statistical tools to organize data and draw inferences.[40] Training and development is crucial for fostering such systematic problem-solving skills.

Managing Promotions and Transfers

Promotions and transfers are significant career-related decisions that managers make on an ongoing basis. These decisions have important career development implications for the promoted and/or transferred employee and substantial benefits for the organization in terms of creating a pool of potential future managers with broad experience throughout the firm.

Making Promotion Decisions

Employers must decide on the basis on which to promote employees, and the way that these decisions are made will affect the employees' motivation, performance, and commitment.

Decision 1: Is Seniority or Competence the Rule?   From the point of view of motivation, promotion based on competence is best. However, the ability to use competence as the sole criterion depends on several things, most notably whether or not a firm is unionized. Union agreements often contain a clause that emphasizes seniority in promotions, meaning that only *substantial differences in abilities* can be taken into account.[41]

Decision 2: How Is Competence Measured?   If promotion is to be based on competence, how will competence be defined and measured? Defining and measuring *past* performance are relatively straightforward matters, but promotion also requires predicting the person's *potential*; thus, there must be a valid procedure for predicting a candidate's future performance. Many employers simply use good past performance as a guide and assume that the employee will perform well on the new job. Other employers use tests or assessment centres to evaluate promotable employees, and to identify those employees with executive potential.[42]

Decision 3: Is the Process Formal or Informal?   Many employers still depend on an informal system where the availability and requirements of open positions are kept secret. Promotion decisions are then made by key managers from among employees whom they know personally, and also from among those who, for one reason or another, have impressed them.[43] The problem is that when employees are not made aware of the jobs that are available, the criteria for promotion, and how promotion decisions are made, the link between performance and promotion is severed, thereby diminishing the effectiveness of promotion as a reward. For this reason, many employers establish formal, published promotion policies and procedures that describe the criteria by which promotions are awarded. Computerized skill inventories, replacement charts, and replacement summaries can be used to compile detailed information about the qualifications of hundreds or thousands of employees. The net effect of such actions is twofold: (1) An employer ensures that all qualified employees are considered for openings; and (2) promotion becomes more closely linked with performance in the minds of employees.

An Ethical Dilemma

Is it ethical for employers to keep promotion policies and procedures secret in an era of flattened organizations where so many employees who aspire to higher positions will not get them, but might achieve them elsewhere?

Decision 4: Vertical, Horizontal, or Other Career Path?   Finally, employers are increasingly facing the question of how to "promote" employees in an era of flattened organizations that have eliminated many of the higher-management positions to which employees might normally aspire.[44] Some firms have created two parallel career paths: one for managers, and another for "individual contributors" such as engineers, who can move up to nonsupervisory but still more-senior positions, such as "senior engineer," with most of the perks and financial rewards attached to management-track positions at that level.[45] Another option is to provide career-development opportunities by moving the person horizontally, such as a production employee being moved horizontally to HR in order to give him or her an opportunity to develop new skills.

Managing Transfers

Employees may seek transfers into jobs that offer greater possibility for career advancement, opportunities for personal enrichment, or those that are more interesting or more convenient—better hours, location of work, and so on.[46]

Employers may transfer a worker in order to fill a vacant position, or more generally to find a better fit for the employee within the firm. Transfers are thus increasingly a way to give employees opportunities for diversity of job assignment and, therefore, personal and career growth.

Policies of routinely transferring employees from locale to locale, either to give their employees more exposure to a wide range of jobs or to fill open positions with trained employees, have fallen into disfavour, partly because of the cost of relocating employees, and partly because of the assumption that frequent transfers have a bad effect on an employee's family life. Companies are facing a record number of rejections of their relocation offers. About two-thirds of all transfer refusals are due to family or spousal concerns. Providing reassurances that relocation costs will be covered is often no longer enough to persuade employees to upset their lifestyles, their spouses' careers, and their children's activities. To overcome this problem, companies are offering spousal support in the form of career transition programs in order to encourage employees to accept transfers.[47]

MANAGEMENT DEVELOPMENT

management development Any attempt to improve current or future management performance by imparting knowledge, changing attitudes, or increasing skills.

Management development is any attempt to improve managerial performance by imparting knowledge, changing attitudes, or increasing skills. Management development is particularly important today because 60 percent of Canadian organizations are facing a shortage of middle managers.[48] The ultimate aim of management-development programs is to achieve business strategy. For this reason, the management-development process consists of (1) assessing the company's human resources needs to achieve its strategic objectives, (2) creating a talent pool, and then (3) developing the managers themselves.[49]

Some management-development programs are company-wide and involve all or most new (or potential) management recruits. The workers may be rotated through a preprogrammed series of departmental assignments and educational experiences, the aim of which is to identify their management potential and provide the breadth of experience (in, say, production and finance) that will make the new managers more valuable in their first "real" assignment as group product leaders. Superior candidates may then be slotted onto a "fast track," a development program that prepares them more quickly to assume senior-level appointments.

succession planning A process through which senior-level openings are planned for and eventually filled.

On the other hand, the management-development program may be aimed at filling a specific position, such as CEO, perhaps with one of two potential candidates. When it is an executive position to be filled, the process is usually called **succession planning.** Succession planning is particularly challenging in today's downsized organizations, as the pool from which to choose future leaders has grown smaller, and includes employees who are often pursuing professional-development activities to make them marketable for other jobs, not necessarily to move up within their current organizations.[50] However, a formal succession plan that advises high-potential employees they are being considered for senior positions can aid in employee retention by encouraging promising employees to pursue their careers with the firm and offering a reasonable return for loyalty and effort.[51] Thus, a succession plan can be used as an inexpensive form of recognition.[52] Canadian companies like JetForm, Enbridge Inc., and Schering

Canada all believe it is vitally important to tell employees who have been identified as having the potential to fill senior positions.[53] It is important, however, to anticipate the reaction of individuals who are not selected for the "fast track" in order to avoid alienating solid performers who are not chosen.

A succession program typically takes place in stages. First, an *organization projection* is made; here, each department's management needs are anticipated based on strategic factors like planned expansion or contraction. Next, the HR department reviews its *management-skills inventories* to identify the management talent now employed. These inventories contain data on things like education and work experience, career preferences, and performance appraisals. Next *management-replacement charts* are drawn. These summarize potential candidates for each of the management slots, as well as each person's development needs. As shown in **Figure 8.3**, the development needs for a future divisional vice-president might include *job rotation* (to obtain more experience in the firm's finance and production divisions), *executive-development programs* (to provide training in strategic planning), and assignment for two weeks to the employer's *in-house management-development centre*.[54]

Employees should be encouraged to be proactive and accept responsibility for their own career, including seeking out opportunities for leadership training. Employees who feel empowered and motivated to be the initiators of their own management-development process may already be demonstrating leadership potential. Empowering employees in the organization to be part of a mutual succession-planning process increases the potential for its success.[55] However, it may be necessary to pay special attention to providing

FIGURE 8.3 Management Replacement Chart Showing Development Needs of Future Divisional Vice-President

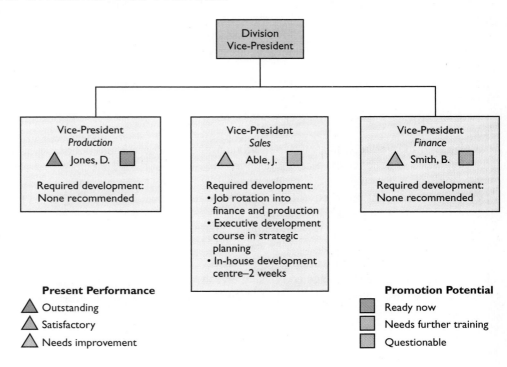

developmental opportunities for female managers, as they have been found to be disadvantaged in this regard, as discussed in the Workforce Diversity box.

A recent study by the Towers Perrin consulting firm surveyed 4500 employees in Canada, and found that only 43 percent of the Canadian managers were rated as performing well in key areas of management behaviour, including inspiring enthusiasm for work and helping employees understand how they impact financial performance (see **Figure 8.4**). This is partly because managers have many other responsibilities in addition to managing their employees, and are typically short of time. However, managing people is difficult, complex work that requires time, resources, organizational support, and role models.[56] A survey by the Center for Creative Leadership found that the most effective leaders are skilled in honest communication, sensitivity to others, and motivating, developing, and retaining staff.[57]

Thus more emphasis on people management is required in management development programs. Management is a discipline with a body of knowledge similar to any science, but is often viewed as an art. Management skills can be taught to and learned by individuals who value the development and success of employees.[58] At the Loyalty Group in Toronto, a three-day program for managers helps them learn how to delegate work, assess whether an employee has the capability and motivation to do the job, and determine which management style will be most effective.[59]

WORKFORCE DIVERSITY

Climbing the Corporate Ladder: Do Male and Female Executives Follow the Same Route?

A recent research study compared matched samples of 69 female executives and 69 male executives to investigate whether the career development experiences and career paths that are related to career success for female executives were different from those for male executives. The results indicated that similar developmental experiences and career history characteristics were related to career success for both genders.

However, the findings suggested that although the developmental experiences and career histories of male and female executives were similar, the women faced greater barriers, relied on different strategies for advancement, and followed different routes up the corporate hierarchy than men. For example, mentoring was more strongly related to success for men than women. Female executives reported greater importance of developing relationships and having a good track record as facilitators of their advancement than did male executives.

The results clearly demonstrated the importance of developmental job assignments. Managing diverse businesses was most strongly related to success and functional diversity was also related to career success. Women reported difficulty getting developmental assignments. Men had more international assignments, and women had more developmental experiences involving non-authority relationships.

In order to advance, women must somehow overcome the reluctance of organizational decision makers to take risks on women—for example, by gaining a powerful sponsor, becoming personally known to organizational decision makers, or meeting a higher standard for promotions than their male counterparts. The authors concluded that organizations that are interested in helping female managers advance should focus on breaking down the barriers that interfere with women's access to developmental experiences.

Source: Karen S. Lyness and Donna E. Thompson, "Climbing the Corporate Ladder: Do Female and Male Executives Follow the Same Route?" *Journal of Applied Psychology* 85, no. 1, 2000, pp. 86–101. Copyright © 2000 by the American Psychological Association. Adapted with permission.

FIGURE 8.4   Ratings of Canadian Management Behaviour

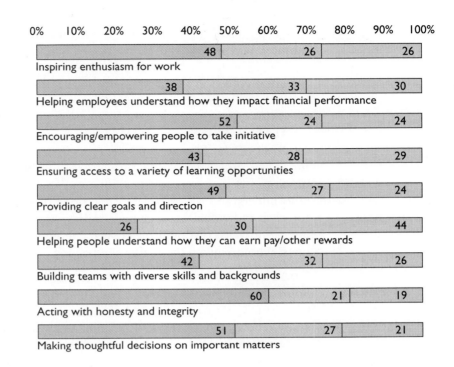

% of employees
rating manager as:

Excellent/good

Fair

Poor/very poor

0%   10%   20%   30%   40%   50%   60%   70%   80%   90%   100%

48 | 26 | 26
Inspiring enthusiasm for work

38 | 33 | 30
Helping employees understand how they impact financial performance

52 | 24 | 24
Encouraging/empowering people to take initiative

43 | 28 | 29
Ensuring access to a variety of learning opportunities

49 | 27 | 24
Providing clear goals and direction

26 | 30 | 44
Helping people understand how they can earn pay/other rewards

42 | 32 | 26
Building teams with diverse skills and backgrounds

60 | 21 | 19
Acting with honesty and integrity

51 | 27 | 21
Making thoughtful decisions on important matters

Source: Working Today: Understanding What Drives Employment Engagement: The Towers Perrin 2003 Talent Report. © Towers Perrin, 2003, Toronto. Used with permission. All rights reserved.

On-the-Job Management-Development Techniques

On-the-job training is one of the most popular development methods. Important techniques here include developmental job rotation, the coaching/understudy approach, and action learning.

developmental job rotation A management-training technique that involves moving a trainee from department to department to broaden his or her experience and identify strong and weak points.

Developmental Job Rotation

Developmental job rotation involves moving management trainees from department to department to broaden their understanding of all parts of the business.[60] The trainee—often a recent college or university graduate—may work for several months in each department; this helps not only to broaden his or her experience, but also helps the trainee discover which jobs he or she prefers.

In addition to providing a well-rounded training experience for each person, job rotation helps to prevent stagnation through the constant introduction of new points of view in each department. It also tests the trainee, and helps to identify the person's strong and weak points.[61] Job rotation does have disadvantages. It encourages generalization, and tends to be more appropriate for developing general line managers than functional staff experts.

There are several ways to improve a rotation program's success.[62] The program should be tailored to the needs and capabilities of the individual trainee, and his or her interests, aptitudes, and career preferences. The length of time that the trainee stays in a job should then be determined by how fast he or she is learning. At Thrifty Foods in British Columbia, no fixed limit is placed on the amount of time a trainee can spend in any of the eight departments they rotate through.[63] Furthermore, the managers to whom these people are assigned should be specially trained themselves to provide feedback and to monitor performance in an interested and competent way. At Thrifty Foods, evaluating potential managers has become such a high priority that four people are involved in the assessments that follow each stage of the rotation—the employee, department manager, store manager, and general manager of retail operations.[64]

At Maple Leaf Foods, a formal management trainee program begins with the selection of the best students from eight Canadian universities, who then go through a three-year process of working on three or four different assignments in various departments of the company. This is the first step in shaping leaders who understand the complete operations of the company. Development plans for each individual management trainee are reviewed monthly, and managers are required to distinguish between the good performers and the exceptional ones, who are given the major challenging assignments they crave.[65]

Coaching/Understudy Approach

In the *coaching/understudy approach*, the trainee works directly with the person that he or she is to replace; the latter is, in turn, responsible for the trainee's coaching. Normally, the understudy relieves the executive of certain responsibilities, thereby giving the trainee a chance to learn the job.[66] This helps to ensure that the employer will have trained managers to assume key positions when such positions are vacated due to retirement, promotion, transfer, or termination.

To be effective, the executive has to be a good coach and mentor. His or her motivation to train the replacement will depend on the quality of the relationship between them. Some executives are also better at delegating responsibility, providing reinforcement, and communicating than are others, and this also affects the results.

action learning A training technique by which management trainees are allowed to work full-time, analyzing and solving problems in other departments.

Action Learning
www.nestadt.com.au/

Action Learning

Action learning releases managers from their regular duties in order that they can work full-time on projects, analyzing and solving problems in departments other than their own.[67] The trainees meet periodically with a project group of four or five people, with whom their findings and progress are discussed and debated.

The idea of developing managers in this way has pros and cons. It gives trainees real experience with actual problems, and to that extent, it can develop skills like problem analysis and planning. Furthermore, working with the others in the group, the trainees can and do find solutions to major problems. The main drawback is that, in releasing trainees to work on outside projects, the employer loses the full-time services of a competent manager.

Off-the-Job Management-Development Techniques

There are many techniques that are used to develop managers off the job, perhaps in a conference room at headquarters or off the premises entirely at a university or special seminar. These techniques are addressed next.

case study method A development method in which a trainee is presented with a written description of an organizational problem to diagnose and solve.

The Case Study Method

The **case study method** presents a trainee with a written description of an organizational problem. The person then analyzes

Trainees participating in a case-study discussion.

the case in private, diagnoses the problem, and presents his or her findings and solutions in a discussion with other trainees.[68] The case method approach is aimed at giving trainees realistic experience in identifying and analyzing complex problems in an environment in which their progress can be subtly guided by a trained discussion leader. Through the class discussion of the case, trainees learn that there are usually many ways to approach and solve complex organizational problems. Trainees also learn that their own needs and values often influence their solutions.

Several things can be done to increase the effectiveness of the case approach. If possible, the cases should be actual scenarios from the trainees' own firms; this will help to ensure that trainees understand the background of the case, as well as to make it easier for trainees to transfer what they learn to their own jobs and situations. Instructors have to guard against dominating the case analysis and make sure that they remain no more than a catalyst or coach. Finally, they must carefully prepare the case discussion and let the participants discuss the case in small groups before class.[69]

management game A computerized development technique in which teams of managers compete with one another by making decisions regarding realistic but simulated companies.

Management Games   In a computerized **management game**, trainees are divided into five- or six-person companies, each of which has to compete with the others in a simulated marketplace. Each company sets a goal (e.g., "maximize sales") and is told that it can make several decisions, such as (1) how much to spend on advertising, (2) how much to produce, (3) how much inventory to maintain, and (4) how many of which product to produce. As in the real world, each company usually cannot see what decisions the other firms have made, although these decisions do affect their own sales. For example, if a competitor decides to increase its advertising expenditures, it may end up increasing its sales at the expense of the other firms.[70] A board game called *Making Sense of Business: A Simulation* designed by Development Dimensions International provides participants with the opportunity to carry out strategic decision-making and learn about the hard decisions and trade-offs that business leaders deal with every day.[71]

Adventure learning participants enhancing their leadership skills, team skills, and risk-taking behaviour.

Management games can be good development tools. People learn best by getting involved in the activity itself, and the games can be useful for gaining such involvement. They help trainees to develop their problem-solving skills and leadership skills, as well as fostering cooperation and teamwork.

Outside Seminars   Many organizations offer special seminars and conferences aimed at providing skill-building training for managers. For example, the Niagara Institute in Niagara-on-the-Lake, Ontario, offers programs aimed at "developing the leaders of the future," and the Institute of Professional Management offers a professional accreditation program leading to the Canadian Management Professional (CMP) designation.[72] Outdoor experiential expeditions, or adventure learning experiences, are sometimes used to enhance leadership skills, team skills, and risk-taking behaviour.[73]

College/University-Related Programs

Colleges and universities provide three types of management-development activities. First, many schools provide *executive-development programs* in leadership, marketing, HRM, operations management, and the like. The Executive Development Centre at Queen's University in Kingston, Ontario, is an example of one of these programs (see **Figure 8.5**). The program uses cases and lectures to provide senior-level managers with the latest management skills, as well as practice in analyzing complex organizational problems. Similar programs are available through many other universities across Canada. Most of these programs take the executives away from their jobs, putting them in university-run learning environments for their entire stay.

Second, many colleges and universities also offer *individualized courses* in areas like business, management, and health-care administration. Managers can take these to fill gaps in their backgrounds. Thus, a prospective division manager with a gap in experience with accounting controls might sign up for a two-course sequence in managerial accounting.

Finally, many schools also offer *degree programs* such as the MBA or Executive MBA.[74] The latter is a Master of Business Administration degree program geared especially to middle managers and above, who generally take their courses on weekends and proceed through the program with the same group of colleagues.

The employer usually plays a role in university-related programs.[75] First, many employers offer *tuition refunds* as an incentive for employees to develop job-related skills. Thus, engineers may be encouraged to enroll in technical courses aimed at keeping them abreast of changes in their field. Supervisors may be encouraged to enroll in programs to develop them for higher-level management jobs. Employers are also increasingly granting technical and professional employees extended *sabbaticals*—periods of time off—for attending a college or university to pursue a higher degree or to upgrade skills.

role-playing A training technique in which trainees act out the parts of people in a realistic management situation.

Role-Playing

The aim of **role-playing** is to create a realistic situation and then have the trainees assume the parts (or roles) of specific persons in that situation.[76] Roles that can be used in an employee discipline role-playing exercise are presented in **Figure 8.6**. When combined with the general instructions for the role-playing exercise, roles like these for all of the participants can trigger a spirited discussion among the role-players, particularly when they all throw themselves into the roles. The idea of the exercise is to solve the problem at hand and thereby develop trainees' skills in areas like leadership and delegation.

The role-players can also give up their inhibitions and experiment with new ways of acting. For example, a supervisor could experiment with both a considerate and an autocratic leadership style, whereas in the real world, the person might not have this harmless avenue for experimentation. Role-playing also trains a person to be aware of and sensitive to the feelings of others.[77]

Role-playing has some drawbacks. An exercise can take an hour or more to complete, only to be deemed a waste of time by participants if the instructor does not prepare a wrap-up explanation of what the participants were to learn. Some trainees also feel that role-playing is childish, while others who may be uncomfortable with acting are reluctant to participate at all. Knowing the audience and preparing a wrap-up are thus advisable.

An Ethical Dilemma

Is it ethical to require employees to participate in role-playing exercises when they are uncomfortable in this situation?

FIGURE 8.5   Programs Offered by Queen's University Executive Development Centre

QUEEN'S EXECUTIVE DEVELOPMENT CENTRE
1.888.EXEC DEV (1.888.393.2338)

Queen's Custom Programs

Queen's Executive Development Centre will help you meet the competitive challenges of today's dynamic business environment. More than 8500 managers from over 1200 Canadian organizations have made Queen's School of Business Canada's leader in executive development. Queen's Custom Programs are designed to meet the particular development needs of a senior executive team and its organization. The program applies the expertise of the *Queen's Executive Development Centre* to the unique objectives of the organization.

Queen's Executive Program

This program focuses on 12 themes: Strategic planning, Leading change, Leadership, Sales management, Strategic alliance, Managing new ventures, Project management, Information technology, Finance, Marketing, Operations, and Human resources. *Three Weeks*

Queen's Marketing Program

Develop marketing strategies that create competitive advantage and improve the positioning of your product or service in the marketplace. *Five Days*

Queen's Public Executive Program

Enhance your policy-making, decision-making, and leadership skills by employing a wide variety of formats to tackle your key management issues. *Two Weeks*

Queen's Sales Management Program

Understand the relationship between sales strategy, sales management systems, and selling behaviour as you benchmark against the best practices of leading organizations. *Five Days*

Queen's Leadership Program

Change the way you think about your leadership responsibilities. Return to work with fresh perspectives on your role as a leader and an action plan for ongoing personal development. *Five Days*

Finance for the Non-Financial Executive

Use modern financial management tools to improve your business decisions. Learn to evaluate capital spending proposals, make lease/buy decisions, and understand the new metrics of EVA, MVA, and free cash flow. *Five Days*

Queen's Information Technology Program

IT affects every aspect of your business, from customer response and product development, to the opening of new channels of distribution and the exploitation of emerging market opportunities. Learn how IT can change the competitive framework of your business. *Five Days*

Queen's Operations Leadership Program

Promote innovation and peak performance within your organization. Lay the groundwork for an operations improvement plan and promote commitment to continuous improvement. *Five Days*

Queen's Human Resources Program

Good human resource policies, procedures, and planning can enhance organizational capabilities and determine your organization's abilities to meet its strategic goals. *Five Days*

Source: Reprinted from *Queen's Executive Education Planning Guide 2003* with permission of Queen's Executive Development Centre.

FIGURE 8.6   Typical Roles in an Employee Discipline Role-playing Exercise

Manager: Dale has failed to adapt to the new requirements for production planning. His/her plans are often incomplete or inadequate. Dale's attitude is defensive and he/she is often nasty to co-workers when they are working on their plans. Dale doesn't seem to understand the importance of the new planning procedure. You have given him/her two verbal warnings in the past. You need to get Dale to understand why production planning is so important in this business. You have just asked Dale to come into your office.

Employee: For 25 years in this job, you have never had any complaints about your work. However, in your performance appraisal last month your manager said that you needed to complete your production planning more quickly. Your manager is also very concerned about the accuracy of your production planning, and has warned you a couple of times to be more careful. He/she has just asked you to come into his/her office, and you think it may be about your production planning work.

behaviour modelling A training technique in which trainees are first shown good management techniques, then asked to play roles in a simulated situation, and finally given feedback regarding their performance.

Tips **for the Front Line**

Behaviour Modelling   **Behaviour modelling** involves (1) showing trainees the right (or "model") way of doing something, (2) letting each person practise the right way to do it, and then (3) providing feedback regarding each trainee's performance.[78] It has been used to train first-line supervisors to better handle common supervisor–employee interactions; this includes giving recognition, disciplining, introducing changes, and improving poor performance. It has also been used to train middle managers to better handle interpersonal situations, such as performance problems and undesirable work habits. Finally, it has been used to train employees and their supervisors to take and give criticism, give and ask for help, and establish mutual trust and respect.

The basic behaviour-modelling procedure can be outlined as follows:

1. *Modelling*. First, trainees watch films or videotapes that show model persons behaving effectively in a problem situation. In other words, trainees are shown the right way to behave in a simulated but realistic situation. The film or video might thus show a supervisor effectively disciplining an employee, if teaching how to discipline is the aim of the training program.

2. *Role-playing*. Next, the trainees are given roles to play in a simulated situation; here they practise and rehearse the effective behaviours demonstrated by the models.

3. *Social reinforcement*. The trainer provides reinforcement in the form of praise and constructive feedback based on how the trainee performs in the role-playing situation.

4. *Transfer of training*. Finally, trainees are encouraged to apply their new skills when they are back on their jobs.

in-house development centre A company-based method for exposing prospective managers to realistic exercises to develop improved management skills.

In-House Development Centres   Some employers have **in-house development centres**, also called "corporate universities." These centres usually combine classroom learning (lectures and seminars, for instance) with other techniques like assessment centres, in-basket exercises, and role-playing, to help develop employees and other managers. The number of corporate universities in North America has grown exponentially over the last several years. Two of the best-known centres in Canada are the Bank of Montreal's Institute for Learning and the CIBC's Leadership Centre.

Organizational Development

organizational development (OD) A method aimed at changing the attitudes, values, and beliefs of employees so that employees can improve the organization.

The Bank of Montreal's Institute for Learning.

Organizational development (OD) is a method that is aimed at changing the attitudes, values, and beliefs of managers and other employees so that they can identify and implement organizational change. OD has several distinguishing characteristics. First, it is usually based on action research, which means collecting data about the organization, and then feeding the data back to the employees to analyze and identify problems. Second, it applies behavioural science knowledge for the purpose of improving the organization's effectiveness. Third, it changes the attitudes, values, and beliefs of employees, so that the employees themselves can identify and implement the changes needed to improve the company's functioning. Fourth, it changes the organization in a particular direction—toward improved problem solving, responsiveness, quality of work, and effectiveness.[79]

The number and variety of OD techniques have increased substantially over the past few years. OD got its start with human-process interventions, which were aimed at understanding one's own and others' behaviour, in order to improve that behaviour for the benefit of the organization. Sensitivity training, team building, confrontation meetings, and survey research are four widely used human-process interventions.

1. Sensitivity Training The basic aim of sensitivity training (also known as T-group training) is to increase the participant's insight into his or her own behaviour and the behaviour of others by encouraging an open expression of feelings in a trainer-guided group.[80] T-group training is obviously quite personal in nature, and is a controversial technique that is used much less frequently now than at the height of its popularity about 20 years ago.

team building Improving the effectiveness of teams through the use of consultants, interviews, and team-building meetings.

2. Team Building The characteristic OD stress on action research is perhaps most evident in **team building**, which refers to the following process of improving team effectiveness. Data concerning the team's performance are collected and then fed back to the members of the group. The participants examine, explain, and analyze the data and develop specific action plans or solutions for solving the team's problems.

3. Confrontation Meetings Confrontation meetings can help to clarify and bring into the open intergroup misconceptions and problems so that they can be resolved. The basic approach here is that the participants themselves provide the input before the meeting; they then confront and thrash out misperceptions in an effort to reduce tensions.

survey feedback A method that involves surveying employees' attitudes and providing feedback so that problems can be solved by the managers and employees.

4. Survey Feedback **Survey feedback** research requires that employees throughout the organization fill out attitude surveys. The data are then used as feedback to the work groups as a basis for problem solving and action planning, In general, such surveys are convenient for unfreezing an organization's management and employees by providing a comparative, graphic illustration of the fact that the organization does have problems that should be solved.[81] The continuing popularity of employee attitude surveys reflects the view that there is validity in employee reports of their experiences. These reports can be very useful as diagnoses of the degree to which a new strategy is being implemented, and the degree to which policies and practices are related to the achievement of strategic goals like customer satisfaction and customer attention.[82]

EXECUTIVE DEVELOPMENT

As we progress through the early years of the twenty-first century, Canada faces a shortage of leadership talent. The demand for leaders is increasing, due to new opportunities being created by economic growth, unplanned early retirements, global "brain drain," a decade of neglected succession planning, lack of organizational commitment to developing talent, problems with traditional job rotation in learning organizations, and mixed success with external recruitment.[83] A recent Conference Board of Canada survey found that only 5 percent of companies believe that they have the leadership capability they need to face the challenges of the new millennium. The report concluded that Canadian companies need a fundamental overhaul of their leadership development practices if they hope to keep up in today's business environment.[84]

Effective executive development is particularly challenging because leaders need the opportunity to acquire knowledge, try it out, and be coached and supported in the process. At the Royal Bank Financial Group, the *Developing People Management Competencies Program* focuses on five areas—change management, achievement motivation, impact and influence, developing others, and teamwork and cooperation. Participants in the program must develop their ability by completing a workplace project.[85]

The Banff Centre for Management in Alberta uses a five-step process that involves competency modelling and learning contracts in order to maximize the effectiveness of its executive development programs:[86]

1. *Evaluation of leadership competencies.* Competency profiles have been researched for the leader's specific position, and can provide a mechanism for peers, colleagues, and supervisors to provide feedback. **Table 8.1** illustrates key competencies for professional development for senior leaders.

2. *The learning contract.* The learning contract ensures individual focus and agreement between the participant, his or her supervisor, and the instructor, on the critical elements for developmental success in the next six to nine months. Even the most capable adult can really only work on improving four or five attributes at once.

3. *The learning process.* The competency profiling and learning contract help focus the learning process, creating links and building strategies. The learning must be hands-on, and provide participants with opportunities to try out new behaviour, receive feedback, and practise again several times.

4. *Re-entry planning.* The learning contract helps the learner plan how he or she will start to apply the learning. Clear implementation plans with timelines and follow-up support will help to ensure that the training actually results in changed behaviour and has an impact on the company.

5. *Measurement of training effectiveness.* The competency profile and learning contract form the basis for measurement of successful changes in behaviour, as well as levels of impact on the sponsoring organization. They can also be used to track continuous improvement by all parties in the learning partnership.

TABLE 8.1 Leading Strategically: Competency Map

Core Competency	Category A Behaviour	Category B Behaviour	Category C Behaviour	Category D Behaviour
1 Fashions clear vision and passion for quality, innovation and business strategy across organization/ division.	Shows a personal sense of quality, passion and innovation for the organization and its products/services.	Engages the team in developing general quality direction/standards for the organization. Key points of contact for decision making around new ideas and processes are clear.	Input from all departments in the organization and customers, is utilized to drive goals and "future state." Customers and stakeholders are regularly tapped to suggest improvements and new processes.	Stakeholder input, competitive benchmarks and organization/ customer knowledge is utilized to create continuously improving standards, values, and goals for the orgaization, department and individuals. High level of passion and commitment to this end is maintained.
2 Is capable of leading strategic planning processes.	Correlates plans and orchestrates activities for short-term results and fire fighting.	Involves key stakeholders in longer-term, strategic discussions on selected issues. Leads own team effectively in business planning process.	Leads a complete strategic planning process (to action plans) with senior management including input from internal stakeholders. Departmental "outcome measures" are defined, business risk assessed, and realignment of organization considered.	Establishes interactive and integrated strategic planning process with all stakeholders based on an accurate scanning of the environment, audience tastes and client needs. Goals and outcomes are clearly defined for the organization within evolving organization.
3 Vision development and enunciation within sector and in keeping with global trends.	Shows a personal sense of the general direction of the organization.	Engages team in developing a common understanding of future direction.	Establishes the process and gathers input from key stakeholders for the purpose of describing a desired future state shared by the management team.	Develops a clear and shared picture of the future state based on an accurate reading of sector, global trends and forces within the environment. Consistently communicates to multistakeholders so it is understood.
4 Is able to recognize "big picture" patterns and relationships and understands how to make balanced decisions suitable for the organization.	Has good problem-solving skills utilizing traditional models. Able to balance competing demands and tends to see/create opportunity from problems.	Engages colleagues in looking at organization and industry trends, issues. Draws connections among them in order to make balanced decisions for his/her team.	Sees clearly how change in one part of the organization affects many others. Works with other departments to develop structures/processes in order to understand and address key issues.	Can conceive and think through systems seeing complex cause and effect relationships. Uses these to keep focus on macro-goals, service outcomes and the larger global context. Sees organization existing within larger industry/community, with attendant responsibilities, impact and challenges.
5 Development of effective differentiation strategies within organization.	Shows an intuitive sense about how their business unit can be/is unique in its products and services.	Engages team to identify strategies that will make the area unique, listens to customer needs, then positions business unit products/services accordingly in the marketplace.	Engages all levels of the business unit to examine their value to customers and finds new ways to build relationships that add value and distinctiveness from competitors.	Partners with customers, stakeholders, and the marketplace, to establish processes that support uniqueness strategies. Creates sustained, value-enhancing, competitive advantage.

Source: Leading Strategically © 2002: Competency Map. Banff, AB: The Banff Centre 2002. www.banffcentre.ca/departments/leadership/competency.map. Reproduced with permission of The Banff Centre.

Entrepreneurs and HR

Executive Development

Small businesses need to develop senior managers because their growth is most often impaired by a lack of management talent. Most smaller enterprises do not have the resources or the time to develop full-blown executive succession programs or to fund many outside programs. Yet, at the same time, the president of a smaller firm has the advantage of working more closely with and knowing more about each of his or her employees than does the CEO of a bigger firm.

For larger companies, there is usually an adequate supply of talent given the ongoing influx of new recruits. For the smaller company, the problem is ensuring that key positions are filled and that the president has the foresight to know when to surrender part of the company's operations. There are thus four main steps in the smaller company's executive development process:

Step 1. Problem Assessment

The executive development process must begin with an assessment of the company's current problems and the owner's plans for the company's future. Obviously, if the owner/entrepreneur is satisfied with the current size of the firm and has no plans to retire in the near future, no additional management talent may be required. On the other hand, if plans call for expansion, or current problems seem to be growing out of control, management development/succession planning might be the key. It often happens, for instance, that as a small company evolves into a larger firm, the management system that adequately served the owner in the past is no longer effective. At this point, the president must assess the problems in his or her firm with an eye toward determining whether and when new management talent is required.

Step 2. Management Audit and Appraisal

One reason management selection and development are so important in small firms is that the "problems" assessed in Step 1 are often just symptoms of inadequate management talent. It is simply not possible for the owner/entrepreneur to run a $5 million company the way he or she did when the company was one-tenth the size. Therefore, the lack of adequate management is a depressingly familiar cause for many of the problems in the small growing firm. The problems found in Step 1 can be used as a starting point in conducting a management audit and appraisal of the people now helping to manage the firm. One simple and effective way to do this is by evaluating them on the traditional management functions of planning, organizing, leading, and controlling.

Step 3. Analysis of Development Needs

The next step is to determine whether any inadequacies uncovered in Step 2 can be remedied via some type of development program. At one extreme, the person may not have the potential to grow beyond what he or she is now, and here development may serve no purpose. At the other extreme, the problems uncovered may just reflect a lack of knowledge. For example, sending a bookkeeper/accountant back to school for a course or two in management accounting could alleviate the problem. Another question to answer here is whether the owner/entrepreneur may be responsible for some of the problems, and whether he or she should attend a management-development program (or move out of the firm altogether).

Step 4. Identify Replacement Needs

The assessment may uncover a need to recruit and select new management talent. Here, the intellectual, personality, interpersonal, and experience criteria to be used should be determined ahead of time. An on-the-job development program that gives the person the breadth of experience that he or she needs to perform the job should also be mapped out.

It is particularly important for entrepreneurs and small business owners to develop future executives in order to grow the company and to ensure that long-term successors are fully prepared to take over, as described in the Entrepreneurs and HR box.

Development and Superior Leadership

Most development processes involve conversations between managers and employees. These conversations are variously referred to as counselling, tutoring, mentoring, or coaching. Whatever the term used, the important point is that these motives for intervention represent a style of management that is very different from previous "top-down" styles of management....

New forms of work organization are designed to accommodate a more flexible workforce with greater participation in production decisions on the part of employees. The current organizational style has been described using different terms such as "empowered," "participative," "decentralized," and "flexible." It vests more power and responsibility with employees....

Because the new forms of work organization are designed to increase flexibility, job skills may be more oriented to producing multi-skilled workers. Training becomes less oriented to narrow product-specific skills and more focused on softer skills such as effective communication, problem-solving, and teamwork.

Not all managers possess the skills necessary to work in this more participative environment, and many see these changes as involving the sacrifice of power they once had themselves. Superior managers, however, recognize that it is the results that matter more than the process, and that both sides stand to benefit from the change.

Source: Excerpted with permission from the *Training and Development Guide*, ¶45, 130, published by and copyright CCH Canadian Limited, Toronto, Ontario.

CHAPTER Review

Summary

1 The first factor affecting career choice is to identify career stage. The main stages in a person's career are growth (roughly birth to age 14), exploration (roughly age 15 to 24), establishment (roughly age 24 to 44, the heart of most people's work lives), maintenance (45 to 65), and decline (pre-retirement). The next step is to identify occupational orientation: realistic, investigative, social, conventional, enterprising, and artistic. Then identify skills and aptitudes. Finally, identify career anchors: technical/functional, managerial, creativity, autonomy, and security.

2 An employee's first assignment can be made more meaningful by adhering to the following guidelines: avoid reality shock, provide challenging initial jobs, provide realistic job previews, be demanding, provide periodic developmental job rotation and job pathing, conduct career-oriented performance appraisals, provide career-planning workshops, provide opportunities for mentoring, and become a learning organization.

3 In making promotion decisions, firms have to (1) decide to promote based on seniority or competence, (2) decide how to measure competence, (3) choose between a formal or informal promotion system, and (4) determine whether career paths will be vertical, horizontal, or other. Transfers offer employees an opportunity for personal and career development, but they have become more difficult to manage because of spousal and family concerns. Thus career-transition programs for spouses are often provided.

4 Management development is any attempt to improve managerial performance and it is aimed at preparing employees for future jobs with the organization. When an executive position needs to be filled, succession planning is often involved. Management development is important because the majority of Canadian companies are facing a shortage of middle managers.

5   Managerial on-the-job training methods include developmental job rotation, coaching, and action learning. Basic off-the-job techniques include case studies, management games, outside seminars, college/university-related programs, role-playing, behaviour modelling, in-house development centres, and organizational development techniques such as sensitivity training, team building, confrontation meetings, and survey feedback.

6   The five-step executive development process involves (1) evaluation of leadership competencies, (2) creating a learning contract, (3) the learning process, (4) re-entry planning, and (5) measurement of training effectiveness based on the competency profile and learning contract.

Key Terms

action learning   *(p. 256)*
behaviour modelling   *(p. 260)*
boundaryless career   *(p. 240)*
career anchor   *(p. 245)*
career cycle   *(p. 243)*
career planning and development   *(p. 240)*
career-planning workshop   *(p. 247)*
case study method   *(p. 256)*
decline stage   *(p. 243)*
developmental job rotation   *(p. 255)*
employee retention   *(p. 241)*
establishment stage   *(p. 243)*
exploration stage   *(p. 243)*
growth stage   *(p. 243)*
in-house development centre   *(p. 260)*
job pathing   *(p. 247)*
learning organization   *(p. 250)*

lifelong learning   *(p. 241)*
maintenance stage   *(p. 243)*
management development   *(p. 252)*
management game   *(p. 257)*
mentoring   *(p. 248)*
occupational orientation   *(p. 244)*
organizational development (OD)   *(p. 261)*
role-playing   *(p. 258)*
succession planning   *(p. 252)*
survey feedback   *(p. 261)*
team building   *(p. 261)*

Review and Discussion Questions

1   Briefly describe each of the five stages in a typical career.

2   What are the six main types of occupational orientation?

3   What is a career anchor? What are the five main types of career anchor?

4   Explain three different ways in which managers can assist in the career development of their employees.

5   What is meant by the term "learning organization"? Explain the five types of activities that learning organizations engage in.

6   Explain the four important decisions to be made in establishing a promotion policy.

7   Explain the three major on-the-job management development techniques.

8   Discuss the four steps in the behaviour modelling procedure.

9   Discuss the five steps in the executive development process used at the Banff Centre for Management.

CRITICAL *Thinking Questions*

1   Do you think developmental job rotation is a good method to use for developing management trainees? Why or why not?

2   Would you tell high-potential employees that they are on the "fast-track"? How might this knowledge affect their behaviour? How might the behaviour of employees who are disappointed at not being included in management development activities be affected?

APPLICATION *Exercises*

Running Case: LearnInMotion.com

What to Do about Succession?

In the second year of operation of LearnInMotion.com, Jennifer was involved in a serious car accident and spent two months in the hospital and another four months in rehabilitation before she was able to return to work. During this six-month period, Pierre had to manage the entire business on his own. It proved to be impossible. Despite some new training, the sales effort continued to falter and sales revenues declined by 25 percent. Staff turnover at LearnInMotion.com increased, as employees found it very frustrating to encounter so much trouble to have even a brief conversation with Pierre. Employees who left were not replaced, as the decline in sales meant that costs had to be reduced. Thus Pierre was spared the difficult job of downsizing—at least for now.

The first day the Jennifer returned to work, Pierre said, "We have to have a succession plan. This business will not survive unless we have other employees who can take over from us temporarily now and permanently in the long term." Jennifer agreed. "Yes, it was difficult for me being unable to work knowing that you were overwhelmed with every problem throughout the entire company. And maybe employees' performance in their current jobs would be enhanced if they knew they had been identified as having management potential, and were provided with specific development opportunities. We'll have to establish a management development program as well."

"I agree," said Pierre, "but we can't afford to spend much money on this." So Pierre and Jennifer had asked for your help in establishing a succession plan and a management development plan. Here's what they've asked you to do.

Questions

1   What is the best way for a small business like LearnInMotion.com to approach succession planning?
2   What on-the-job management development techniques would be most appropriate for LearnInMotion.com?
3   What off-the-job management development techniques, if any, would you recommend for LearnInMotion.com, given their financial constraints?

CASE INCIDENT *Family versus Career—and a Company Caught in the Middle*

Dave and Nora live in the Vancouver area, where Dave works for a major software company. He is very motivated to put in whatever time and effort are needed to complete tasks and projects successfully. Top management recognizes his contributions as important, and his prospects at the company are excellent.

Nora has been married to Dave for five years and knows how devoted he is to his career. Both of them want to start a family and agree that Vancouver isn't where they want to raise their children. Nora, feeling that she can't wait forever to have kids, has been pressuring Dave to find a job in a smaller town.

Understanding Nora's concerns, Dave made a couple of discreet phone calls and was soon asked in for an interview by a company located in a town in Alberta. Dave didn't know what to say when the company made him an offer. The job pays less than his present job and offers fewer opportunities for advancement, but the area is the kind of environment he and Nora want. He knows Nora is thrilled at the prospect of the move, yet he can't help feeling sad. How can he simply walk away from all he has invested in his career at his present company? Maybe there is more to life than his career, but he is already depressed and he hasn't even quit yet.

When Dave told his boss, Terri, about the new job offer, Terri was shocked. Dave is a central figure in the company's plans for the next couple of years, and his expertise is indispensable on a couple of important projects. Terri feels that Dave has blindsided the company. Things will be a mess for a long time if he leaves. But what can the company do to keep him if money isn't the issue?

Questions

1 What preventive measures could Dave's company have taken to avoid the crisis it is faced with? What can the company do now?

2 Should Dave's company involve Nora in any of its attempts to retain Dave? If so, how?

3 Should Dave's company implement any career development programs after this crisis passes? If so, what kind would you recommend? Why?

Source: L.R. Gomez-Mejia, D.B. Balkin, R.L. Cardy, and D. Dimick, *Managing Human Resources*, Canadian 2nd ed. (Scarborough, ON: Prentice-Hall Canada Inc., 2000), p. 283.

EXPERIENTIAL *Exercises*

1 Working individually or in groups, contact a provider of management-development seminars such as the Canadian Institute of Management. Obtain copies of recent listings of seminar offerings. At what levels of managers are the seminar offerings aimed? What seem to be the most popular types of development programs? Why do you think that is the case?

2 Find an older person who is Web-challenged (perhaps a family friend or one of your professors who is having trouble setting up a Web site or getting full use of the e-mail system). Offer to reverse mentor him or her on using the Web for a short time (a few weeks) in return for some career mentoring for yourself. Prepare a short report on the benefits of this experience for both of you.

CHAPTER 9

Managing Strategic Organizational Renewal

LEARNING OUTCOMES

After studying this chapter, you should be able to:

Explain five common types of organizational change, and *discuss* the three steps in the Lewin's change process.

Explain the four steps in establishing and operating a quality circle.

Discuss the ISO 9000 and ISO 14000 quality standards.

Describe several HRM activities that can help to build a team-based organization.

Define business process reengineering and *discuss* the HR department's role in this activity.

Describe four common flexible work arrangements.

ORGANIZATIONAL RENEWAL AND CHANGE

Managing strategic organizational renewal and change involves a broader view of how HRM enables companies to tackle the tough new world of global competition. Organizational change is an ongoing reality, and HRM plays an important role in change efforts, particularly those involving flexible work arrangements, quality management, team-building, and reengineering programs intended to help the organization meet its strategic objectives.

Organizational renewal and change assists in obtaining strategic business objectives by increasing the quality of products and services, and improving the productivity of the workforce. Today, the maturing of technology, the faster pace of work, and globalization are all indicators that the world of work has been transformed. Today's jobs require empowerment rather than restrictive work rules or supervisory practices. Modern businesses depend on employees to provide the responsive and creative solutions that corporate success requires.

These changes are influencing employers' choice of HR methods.[1] In particular, employers are increasingly utilizing techniques like quality improvement programs and flexible work arrangements. Programs like these are aimed at eliciting the best that workers can offer by treating them responsibly and by giving them more discretion over their jobs and the opportunity to use their problem-solving skills at work.

HR plays an important role in the process and techniques of organizational change and renewal. A recent extensive survey of HR practices concluded that "... focusing on strategy, organizational development, and organizational change is a high payoff activity for the HR organization."[2] As more and more HR professionals assume the role of change management in organizations, an understanding of change dynamics has become increasingly important.[3]

What to Change

What is it about a company that can be changed? In practice, several things can be changed, including *strategy, culture, structure, technologies,* and the *attitudes and skills* of the people. But to do so, a thorough knowledge of HR methods is required.

Strategic Change   Organizational renewal often starts with a change in the firm's strategy, mission, and vision—with **strategic change**.

Cultural Change   **Cultural change** means adopting new corporate values—new notions of what employees view as right and wrong, and what they should or shouldn't do. But how can employees be influenced to embrace new values and adopt a new culture? One expert advocates five main ways to change a company's culture, each of which requires HR's support and advice:[4]

1. *Make it clear* to your employees what you pay attention to, measure, and control.

2. *React appropriately* to critical incidents and organizational crises. For example, if you want to emphasize the value that "we have to keep communications lines open," don't react to declining profits by trying to keep that fact a secret.

strategic change A change in a company's strategy, mission, and vision.

cultural change A change in a company's shared values and aims.

Tips **for the**
Front Line

3. *Deliberately role-model*, teach, and coach the values you want to emphasize. For example, Wal-Mart founder Sam Walton embodied the values of hard work, honesty, neighbourliness, and thrift that he wanted Wal-Mart employees to have. So although he was one of the richest men in the world, he drove a pickup truck, a preference he explained by saying, "If I drove a Rolls-Royce, what would I do with my dog?"

4. *Communicate priorities* through the allocation of rewards and status. Leaders communicate priorities and values by how they award pay raises and promotions. For example, top management at General Foods decided several years ago to reorient its strategy from cost minimization to diversification and sales growth. It then had the HR department revise the pay plan to link bonuses to sales volume (rather than just increased earnings, as in the past).

5. *Make your HR procedures and criteria consistent* with the values you hold.

Structural Change

structural change The reorganizing or redesigning of an organization's departmentalization, coordination, span of control, reporting relationships, or decision-making process.

Reorganizing—in other words, redesigning the company's departmental structure, coordination, span of control, reporting relationships, tasks, or decision-making procedures—is a relatively quick and direct way to change an organization. **Structural changes** like these require HRM. For example, downsizings require performance reviews to decide who stays and who goes, and an outplacement effort. Reorganizing requires job analysis, human resources planning, and selection. Flattening the organization may mean consolidating pay levels into fewer, broader bands.

Changes in People, Attitudes, and Skills

All this means that sometimes the employees themselves must change.[5] Here, for example, training and development can provide new or current employees with the skills they need to perform their jobs.

Technological Change

technological change
Modifications to the work methods an organization uses to accomplish its tasks.

Organizational renewal today often entails embracing or modifying technology. For many firms, this means transferring a host of activities to the Internet. For others, it means reengineering work processes, or automating production processes. In any case, managers today realize that **technological change** is futile without employee support. This support requires applying HR methods like building teamwork, drafting new job descriptions, boosting skill and knowledge levels, and installing more flexible work arrangements.

Leading Change: Lewin's Process

Actually implementing and leading an organizational change can be tricky, even for CEOs with lots of clout. The change may require the cooperation of dozens or even hundreds of managers and supervisors; resistance may be considerable; and the change may have to be accomplished while the firm continues to serve its customer base.

Resistance can be a problem. Psychologist Kurt Lewin formulated the classic explanation of how to implement a change in the face of resistance. To Lewin, all behaviour in organizations was a product of two kinds of forces—those striving to maintain the status quo and those pushing for change.

Implementing change thus meant either weakening the status quo forces or building up the forces for change. Lewin's process consisted of these three steps:

1. *Unfreezing*. Unfreezing means reducing the forces that are striving to maintain the status quo, usually by presenting a provocative problem or event to get people to recognize the need for change and to search for new solutions.

2. *Moving*. Moving means developing new behaviours, values, and attitudes, sometimes through structural changes and sometimes through HR-based organizational change.

3. *Refreezing*. Lewin assumed that organizations tend to revert to their former ways of doing things unless you reinforce the changes. How do you do this? By "refreezing" the organization into its new equilibrium. Specifically, Lewin advocated instituting new systems and procedures (such as compensation plans and appraisal processes) to support and maintain the changes.

A 10-Step Change Process

Tips for the Front Line

In practice, accomplishing such a change involves a process like the following:[6]

1. *Establish a sense of urgency*. Once they become aware of the need to change, most leaders start by creating a sense of urgency.

2. *Mobilize commitment through joint diagnosis of problems*. Having established a sense of urgency, leaders then create one or more task forces to diagnose the problems facing the company. Such teams can produce a shared understanding of what they can and must improve, and thereby mobilize the commitment of those who must actually implement the change.

3. *Create a guiding coalition*. Major transformations are sometimes associated with just one or two highly visible leaders. But no one can really implement such changes alone. Most companies create a guiding coalition of influential people, who work together as a team to act as missionaries and implementers.

4. *Develop a shared vision*. Organizational renewal also requires a new leadership vision, or a general statement of the organization's intended direction that evokes feelings of commitment in organization members.

5. *Communicate the vision*. Change expert John Kotter says, "the real power of a vision is unleashed only when most of those involved in an enterprise or activity have a common understanding of its goals and directions."[7] To do this, you have to communicate the vision. The key elements in doing so include:[8]

   - *Keep it simple*. Eliminate all jargon and wasted words. For example: "We are going to become faster than anyone else in our industry at satisfying customer needs."

   - *Use multiple forums*. Try to use every channel possible—big meetings and small, memos and newspapers, formal and informal interaction—to spread the word.

- *Use repetition.* Ideas sink in deeply only after employees have heard them many times.
- *Lead by example.* "Walk your talk"—make sure your behaviours and decisions are consistent with the vision you espouse.

6. *Help employees to make the change.* It's futile to communicate your vision and to have employees want to make it a reality, if they haven't the where-withal to do so. Perhaps a lack of skills stands in the way; or policies, procedures, and the organization chart make it difficult to act; or some bosses may actually discourage employees from acting.

7. *Generate short-term wins.* Changes such as redesigning a firm's control system, or launching a new division, may take time, but the teams working on them need some intermediate reinforcement.[9] For example, one company team set its sights on producing one successful new product about 20 months after the start of the organizational change effort.[10] They selected the product in part because they knew they could meet this goal.

8. *Consolidate gains and produce more change.* Such short-term wins can generate the credibility to move ahead—to change all the systems, structures, and policies that don't fit well with the company's new vision. Leaders continue to produce more change by hiring and promoting new people; by identifying selected employees to champion the continuing change; and by providing additional opportunities for short-term wins by employees.[11]

9. *Anchor the new ways of doing things in the company's culture.* We've seen that organizational changes usually require a corresponding change in culture and values. A "team-based, quality-oriented, adaptable organization" is not going to happen if the values employees share still emphasize selfishness, mediocrity, and bureaucratic behaviour. Leaders thus take steps to role-model and communicate the new values.

10. *Monitor progress and adjust the vision as required.* Finally, monitor how you're doing. One firm appointed an oversight team to monitor the progress and challenges faced by its new self-managing team-based organization.

TOTAL QUALITY MANAGEMENT PROGRAMS

One of the most important contributions that HRM makes toward achieving an organization's strategic objectives is through implementing and maintaining total quality management programs. These programs require the effort and commitment of every employee involved in manufacturing a product or providing a service. **Quality** can be defined as the aggregate of features and characteristics of a product or service that bears on its ability to satisfy customer needs.[12] Improving quality is a necessity for companies all over the world. For highly technical and complex endeavours such as the space program, a focus on quality is critical for achieving goals, as described in the Strategic HR box. Globalization of competition has done more than just force firms to become more efficient; it has raised the quality bar too, by forcing competitors in industries ranging from cars to computers to phone service to meet and exceed the

quality The aggregate of features and characteristics of a product or service that bears on its ability to satisfy customer needs.

STRATEGIC HR

Quality Principles Evident in Space

When you are sitting on 3 billion kg of rocket fuel getting ready to launch into space, the reassurance that quality principles have been an integral part of every procedure and process can be a comforting thought. That was just the position Canadian astronaut and Mission Specialist Chris Hadfield found himself in as he prepared for a 12-day mission to the International Space Station (ISS) on April 19, 2001. After years of intensive simulation training, teamwork, continuous improvement, breakthrough training, and learning, Hadfield made Canadian history on the space shuttle Endeavour. Together with a crew of six astronauts from NASA, European and Russian space agencies, the crew embarked on one of the most technically complex robotics missions in the history of ISS. During the mission, Colonel Hadfield twice stepped into the vacuum of space in two space walks to install the Canadarm 2.

After returning, Colonel Hadfield said, "After four years of training and hundreds of thousands of hours of continually reviewing, improving and visualizing each procedure to the second, we are now involved in a debrief that is as complicated as the training and preparation for the mission." The detailed debriefing examines every facet of the mission with a focus on quality and refinement. "We look at everything, from the way the wash cloths and underwear have been folded to the most complicated of procedures, designs, safety and simulation training," explained Hadfield. "Everything is examined and analyzed as we continually look for areas for improvement. The debrief will be as long and intense as the simulations and training."

The continual improvement of every procedure involves an intense analysis of the crew notes, interviews, and debrief sessions. The developments resulting from such previous mission debriefs in part led to the breakthrough thinking and research that led to the evolution if the Canadarm 2. The technically complex and challenging nature of the mission was successful because of the tremendous dynamics, team effort, and focus on quality by the mission crew, ground crew, and the multitude of agencies that contributed to the effort.

Source: Adapted from Jeannine Pitt-Clark, "Quality Principles Evident in Space," *Excellence Magazine* (Summer 2001), p. 7. Available at the NQI Web site www.nqi.ca/articles/article_details. aspx?ID=54. Used with permission of the National Quality Institute.

quality of the firms with which they compete. Effective HRM plays a central role in improving product and service quality.

A 2002 survey of over 13 000 Canadians conducted by AC Nielsen for Rogers Media and the National Quality Institute regarding service quality found that overall, Canadians feel they get better service in Canada than in the United States. Perceptions of service quality were generally better from Quebec eastward, and service in Toronto, Vancouver, and Calgary received the greatest criticism. Resorts led the list of industries with the best service, and cable TV was rated as having the worst service. Postal services and large retailers improved the most over previous surveys, and airlines and telecommunications companies dropped the most.[13]

total quality management (TQM)
An organizational program aimed at maximizing customer satisfaction through continuous improvements.

Total quality management (TQM) programs are organizational programs aimed at maximizing customer satisfaction through continuous improvement.[14] In North America, this approach often goes by the name *continuous improvement, zero defects,* or *six sigma* (a reference to the statistical unlikelihood of having a defect); in Japan, it is known as *kaizen.*[15] The TQM movement was started in Japan by W. Edwards Deming, and is based on the 14 points shown in **Table 9.1**. The cornerstone of TQM is continuous quality

Chapter 9 Managing Strategic Organizational Renewal   275

TABLE 9.1	Deming's 14 Points of Quality Management

1. Create and publish to all employees a statement of the aims and purposes of the company or other organization. The management must demonstrate constantly their commitment to this statement.

2. Learn the new philosophy, top management, and everybody.

3. Understand the purpose of inspection, for improvement of processes and reduction of cost.

4. End the practice of awarding business based on the price tag alone.

5. Improve constantly and forever the system of production and service.

6. Institute training.

7. Teach and institute leadership.

8. Drive out fear. Create trust. Create a climate for innovation.

9. Optimize toward the aims and purposes of the company the efforts of teams, groups, and staff areas.

10. Eliminate exhortations for the work force.

11a. Eliminate numerical quotas for production. Instead, learn and institute methods for improvement.

11b. Eliminate Management by Objectives. Instead, learn the capabilities of processes, and how to improve them.

12. Remove barriers that rob people of pride of workmanship.

13. Encourage education and self-improvement for everyone.

14. Take action to accomplish the transformation.

Source: W. Edwards Deming, *Out of the Crisis.* © 1986 by The Edwards Deming Institute. Published by MIT Press. Reprinted with permission of the publisher.

improvement, achieved through teams of empowered, customer-focused workers solving problems.

When North American and European companies started to implement TQM in the early 1980s, they assumed that they could simply copy the Japanese model. This assumption proved to be unrealistic. In fact, Japanese companies seem to acknowledge the limitations of TQM, whereas Western companies have been very confident of its benefits.[16] However, Deming's concept of quality management is still seen as a key success factor for Canadian companies in the twenty-first century. In fact, the most successful quality programs are not run in isolation but are part of comprehensive, company-wide quality improvement programs. Successful quality management involves a total corporate focus on meeting and often exceeding customers' expectations and significantly reducing the cost resulting from poor quality by shaping a new management system and corporate culture.[17]

Many believe that the missing component in quality management outside Japan is effective communication.[18] Companies must build interpersonal communication skills in their management teams that support the problem solving required to achieve quality improvements. Further, commitment by employees to quality initiatives will suffer without visible senior- and middle-management support. Weston Foods made a commitment to breaking the information barrier between management and shop floor that, over a five-year period, resulted in significant improvements in five of Weston's seven operating companies.[19]

Quality Circles

quality circle (QC) A group of five to ten specially trained employees who meet on a regular basis to identify and solve problems in their work area.

A **quality circle (QC)** is a group of five to ten specially trained employees who meet for an hour once a week for the purpose of spotting and solving problems in their work area.[20] The circle is usually composed of a work group that produces a specific component or provides a specific service. The HR department usually plays a central role in establishing a QC program. Here are the four steps in establishing and leading a quality circle:

1. *Planning the circle.* The planning phase begins with a top-level executive making the decision to implement the quality circle (QC) technique. A QC *facilitator* is then identified to assist top management in the implementation process. The next task is selecting a cross-functional QC *steering committee,* which has several responsibilities, including the establishment of objectives in terms of *bottom-line improvements* (such as reduced errors and increased attention to problem prevention).

2. *Initial training.* In the second phase, the facilitator and employees interested in being circle leaders meet to be trained in basic QC philosophy, implementation, and operation. This training typically takes several days and includes topics such as the nature and objectives of QCs and QC leadership techniques.

3. *Initiating the circles.* Initiation of a QC begins with department managers conducting QC familiarization meetings with employees. The facilitator and (ideally) an executive participate as speakers. Circle leaders then contact each employee to determine circle membership, which is voluntary, and the circles are constituted.

4. *The circle in operation.* Next, each circle turns to problem solving and analysis. First, circle members identify problems; these are often mundane, such as how to keep the work area cleaner, how to improve the work group's product quality, or how to speed up the packing of the work group's crates.

   Members next select the number-one problem on which they wish to focus, and then collect, collate, and analyze data relating to the problem. Group members analyze and solve the problem. A big benefit of quality circles is the sense of satisfaction that members get from being involved in the actual problem-analysis process—QCs are as much a people-development opportunity as a quality-improving one. Group members then present the recommended solution to management.

Members of a quality circle are responsible for identifying problems in their work area, then analyzing them and proposing solutions.

There are several predictable but avoidable problems with quality circles. One is the feeling on the part of the employees that this is "just another program" that will probably evaporate once the initial excitement wears off. Some employees will complain that the circles are doomed because "management never pays attention to us anyway." Finally, some of the greatest resistance to the circles will come not from the employees but from supervisors, perhaps because they fear that the circles may undermine their traditional authority. Top management's commitment is essential to deal with all of these problems and to let supervisors know that the firm takes this program very seriously.

Case studies of quality circle effectiveness generally confirm that it is spotty at best.[21] In general, instituting QCs without making corresponding changes in management styles and company culture is futile. The bottom-up participation that management wants to encourage must be fostered by a fundamental change in philosophy from top management on down. Managers must make it clear that they will listen to and act on employees' input, create trust and confidence, and show in concrete ways that they mean what they say about wanting employee input.

Quality Awards

Several major awards recognize companies that institute highly effective quality improvement programs. The Deming Prize, named after Dr. W. Edwards Deming and awarded by the Union of Japanese Scientists and Engineers, was the first such award. Miami-based Florida Power & Light Company (FPL), Florida's largest utility, was the first company outside Japan to win the Deming Prize. Awarded annually (and since 1986 outside Japan), the prize recognizes outstanding achievement in quality control management. In 1987, the U.S. Congress established the Malcolm Baldrige National Quality Award to promote quality awareness, recognize quality achievements of U.S. companies, and publicize successful quality strategies.[22]

In Canada, the National Quality Institute (NQI) sponsors the Canada Awards for Excellence, which reward organizations with outstanding achievements in quality. The NQI is an independent, not-for-profit organization dedicated to making Canadian companies more competitive in the global marketplace. The quality awards recognize and reward organizations showing outstanding performance based on a comprehensive quality framework. The seven criteria are:[23]

1. *Leadership*. Strategic direction and involvement in continuous improvement.

2. *Planning for improvement*. Development and implementation of business planning.

3. *Customer focus*. Customer, market, and product knowledge, and management of customer relationships.

4. *People focus*. Human resource planning, participatory environment, continuous learning, and employee satisfaction and well-being.

5. *Process optimization*. Process development, control, and improvement.

6. *Supplier focus*. Partnering with suppliers and management of the partnership.

7. *Organizational performance*. Customer focus, people focus, process management, supplier partnerships, responsibility to society, and owner/shareholder focus.

A team of examiners visits the site of each applicant to verify the information provided. In addition, a random selection of external suppliers and customers of short-listed organizations are contacted.[24]

Features of Two Award-Winning Quality Programs In 2002, two of the winners of the Canada Awards for Excellence were Mullen Trucking in Aldersyde, Alberta, and Dana Corp.'s Spicer Driveshaft Canada facility in Magog, Quebec. David Mullen, vice-president of Mullen Trucking explains, "In 1990, we commenced a very important initiative—one that involved transforming our company into a self-managed organization where all employees could feel empowered to make decisions that supported the stated goals and objectives of the company. There is little doubt that the success of Mullen Trucking is directly related to the commitment and pride that our employees and owner-operators take in their job every day. That is what quality is all about."[25] Dana Canada's facility in Magog, Quebec, was recognized for its overall business system, which is driven by a team atmosphere with initiatives focused on environmental improvements. The facility's employee suggestion program generated 3260 suggestions in 2002—or 20 ideas per employee—with an 88.6 percent implementation rate.[26]

Ontario Centre for Environmental
Technical Advancement
www.oceta.on.ca

HRM and the Quality Improvement Effort

Many HRM actions can help to produce a more effective total quality program. Some HRM guidelines based on the experience of award-winning companies are as follows:

Tips **for the**
Front Line

- *Remember that the first steps need to be taken by top management.* Management must adopt the principles of quality, follow the processes, set examples, and guide others. These programs require reallocation of budgets and other resources.[27]

- *Make sure that all quality efforts are consistent with the firm's goals.*

- *Do not treat the quality improvement program as if it has an end.* It is important to emphasize that a successful quality improvement program is really a systematic way of doing business, one that has no end.

- *Recognize that training is essential.* Quality improvement is successful largely because training continually upgrades the problem analysis and statistics skills of even first-line employees. This training is crucial both to provide the required analytical skills and to emphasize the firm's commitment to the program.

- *Give employees the skills that they need to analyze and solve problems; then get them to analyze and solve the problem, and follow up on their suggestions.* Whether or not the company achieves its quality goals is, although very important, almost secondary. The new culture that emerges is at the heart of the program.

- *Recognize effort and encourage employees.* A main benefit of this type of program is the sense of satisfaction it can foster in employees. This requires encouraging employees to identify and devise countermeasures against problems, and giving them the tools and leeway required to get this job done.

- *Reward individual and team efforts in a concrete manner, not necessarily just with money but with rewards like merchandise or pins.*

International Quality and
Productivity Center **www.iqpc.com**

ISO 9000 and 14000 **www.iso.ch**

Standards Council of Canada
www.scc.ca

Canadian Standards Association
www.csa.ca

Quality Certification Bureau
www.qcbinc.com

ISO 9000 and ISO 14000

Quality standards today are international. Doing business around the world often means that firms must demonstrate their compliance with quality standards set by the International Organization for Standardization (ISO), a worldwide federation formed in 1947. ISO's mission is to promote the development of standardization worldwide, thereby facilitating the exchange of goods and services internationally. Vendors anywhere in the world are able to prove, through their ISO certification, that their quality manuals, procedures, and job instructions all comply with the ISO standards.

A recent survey by the Standards Council of Canada (the Canadian member body of ISO) gathered data from 3000 Canadian companies to assess Canada's experience with ISO 9000, ISO 14000, and QS-9000 (another major international quality standard). Results showed that the standards are widely recognized, accepted, and respected. Companies using the standards found that they provide genuine benefits to the organization, and that their implementation and registration is, despite the costs involved, generally a positive experience. Specific benefits include improved relationships with customers, competitive advantages, and virtually all those registered with ISO intend to maintain their registration.[28]

ISO standards are concerned with quality management in the way work is done, not in the end product or service. The standards were revised in 2000. The ISO 9000 series of standards concerns the features of a product or service that are required by the customer. ISO 9000 has three key standards:

- ISO 9000:2000 Quality Management Systems—Fundamentals and Vocabulary
- ISO 9001:2000 Quality Management Systems—Requirements
- ISO 9004:2000 Quality Management Systems—Guidelines for Performance Improvements

The ISO 9001 standard can be adapted to any type of organization (product or service) and any size of organization. The ISO 9004 standard provides guidelines beyond the basic requirements of ISO 9001 for (1) improving the effectiveness and efficiency of a quality management system, (2) monitoring continual improvement based on measurable criteria, (3) taking a process orientation to quality management, (4) monitoring customer satisfaction, and (5) an emphasis on the role of senior management in developing, implementing, and maintaining a quality management system. It also focuses on stakeholders beyond customers and on the inclusion of financial performance measures linked to quality practices.[29]

The ISO 14000 series of standards is concerned with environmental management, or what the organization does to minimize harmful effects on the environment caused by its activities. ISO 14000 provides a set of tools for determining the environmental aspects of an organization's activities, establishing goals and targets for those aspects, evaluating how well those goals and targets are being achieved, and continuously improving performance. More specifically, it requires a commitment to compliance with applicable environmental legislation, a commitment to continuous improvement, and objective

ENTREPRENEURS AND HR

ISO Booklet: ISO 9001 for Small Businesses—What to Do

ISO 9001 for Small Businesses—What to Do is a booklet that dispels the myth that ISO 9000 is for big companies only. Aimed at managers, it explains the quality system standards in plain language, with the intention of putting improvements in performance, quality, customer satisfaction, and market access within reach of any manufacturing or service organization, regardless of size, through implementation of an ISO 9000 quality system. Quality systems should not be a source of bureaucracy, excessive paperwork, or lack of flexibility. All businesses have a management structure and this should be the basis on which the quality system is built. ISO 9000 is not, therefore, about imposing something totally new.

The handbook does not set any new ISO 9000 requirements, or add to, or otherwise change the requirements of the standards. It suggests first steps towards a quality system (such as whether to go it alone or use consultants), offers guidance in matters such as training and auditing, and gives a brief outline of the certification process.

The full text of ISO 9001:2000 is included in boxes, section by section, accompanied by explanations, examples, and implementation guidance in everyday terms. In addition, the handbook includes the eight quality management principles on which the ISO 9000:2000 series is based, plus revised sections on the steps involved in setting up a quality management system—including how to get started—with or without the assistance of a consultant.

Source: ISO Publishes Advice for the SME on Implementing ISO 9001:2000. International Standards Organization Press Release 827, July 8, 2002. http://www.iso.ch/en/iso9000-14000/tour/smallbus.html. Reprinted with permission of the International Standards Organization. All rights reserved.

evidence that can be audited to demonstrate compliance with the standard. It does not provide specific environmental targets or describe ways to achieve them. ISO 14000 registration can be used to support organizational claims to external stakeholders about its environmental policies, plans, and actions, as well as provide assurances to employees that they are working for an environmentally responsible organization. Specific benefits of an environmental management system include reduced cost of waste management, savings in consumption of energy and materials, lower distribution costs, improved corporate image, and a framework for continuous improvement of environmental performance.[30]

The HR department plays an important role in providing ongoing support to department managers throughout the firm in the preparation for and management of ISO certification, particularly concerning documentation and training.[31] Training for ISO 9000 and ISO 14000 typically covers several topics, including the quality vocabulary associated with the standard, and the requirements of each section of the standard.[32]

The time commitment and costs involved in obtaining ISO certification can be a burden for small businesses. However, some small businesses are joining together with others to share costs. Some industry and professional associations provide assistance in this regard.[33] Further advice for ISO for small businesses is presented in the Entrepreneurs and HR box.

CREATING TEAM-BASED ORGANIZATIONS

Companies today are also increasingly transforming themselves into team-based organizations in an effort to increase quality, productivity, and customer responsiveness. HRM plays a major role in creating such team-based organizations and in ensuring that they function effectively. For many firms, the ideal situation is to organize work around small, close-knit teams whose goals are high and whose aims are the same as the firm's. Many Canadian organizations, including Shell Canada, Brock Telecom, 3M Canada, Norcen Energy Resources Ltd., and even the Government of Ontario, are increasingly organizing the work around small, self-contained teams, which are variously labelled self-managed teams, high-performance teams, autonomous work groups or, simply, superteams.[34]

self-directed teams Highly trained work groups that use consensus decision making and broad authority to self-direct their activities.

Whatever they are called, **self-directed teams** have much in common. Each team generally performs natural sets of interdependent tasks, such as all of the steps needed to assemble a car door. They all use consensus decision making to choose their own team members, solve job-related problems, design their own jobs, and schedule their own break time. In addition, their jobs are always enriched in that they do many of the jobs formerly accomplished by supervisors, such as dealing with vendors and monitoring quality. Self-directed teams are also highly trained to solve problems, design jobs, interview candidates, and understand financial reports. They are, therefore, generally *empowered*: they have the training and ability, as well as the broad authority, to get their jobs done.

Successful team-based organizations have changed from the North American-style, individual-based culture to one oriented around groups. To do so involves changing the corporate mindset to adopt beliefs and values that are very different from those held in the past. Communication and collaboration between managers and employees are considered essential, as are executive-level commitment and employee involvement. Changes in processes, such as reward systems and performance appraisal, signal a commitment to long-term change. It is also important to ensure that team goals are clear, that team members are committed to the goals, and that the team has enough authority, resources, and time to achieve the goal.[35] Surface commitment and lack of cooperation among senior managers are roadblocks to change.

Individuals in most work teams, such as this one at a paper mill, have a high commitment to the group and its work goals, due in part to their shared experiences.

Self-Directed Teams in Action

Let's now consider two examples of self-directed teams. At 3M Canada's manufacturing plant in Brockville, Ontario, teams of six to eight workers handle quality control, logistics, scheduling, and shipping and receiving. Work teams also conduct the entire recruitment process, from initial interviews to various forms of testing. Test results are assessed for problem-solving and interactive skills to see if the applicant can work as part of a team. A dual focus on groups and creativity is crucial, and team members are expected to continually learn new skills and to innovate. Every 3M employee must take courses in risk, handling change, and taking responsibility for his or her job. The Brockville plant is now the model for 3M plants throughout the world.[36]

Honeywell's Scarborough manufacturing operations introduced self-directed work teams over a period of several years, and achieved impressive results—an 80 percent increase in productivity, a 90 percent reduction in scrap and rework, a 95 percent reduction in lost-time accidents, a 70 percent improvement in employee attendance, a reduction of 80 percent in work-in-process inventory, a 97 percent reduction in cycle time, and employee satisfaction ratings in the 70 to 80 percent range.[37]

Several factors contribute to successfully organizing self-directed teams; these include forming a commitment to the principle of teamwork, steeping employees in teamwork terminology and techniques, and fostering employee commitment by enriching the work and empowering the workers.

Three other teamwork success factors deserve emphasis. First, insufficient training is consistently listed as the single biggest barrier to effective self-directed teams. Effective training usually emphasizes problem-solving and communication skills.[38] Second, communication between top management and the teams should be free-flowing so the teams can do their jobs.[39] Making self-directed teams more effective also generally requires that the firm's pay plans be refocused around small-group incentives.[40]

How HRM Helps to Build Productive Teams

Building productive teams requires careful selection, training, and motivation—all HRM-related activities. HRM-related guidelines for building effective teams include:[41]

- *Select members for skill and skill potential.* Select team members for their existing skills and for their potential to learn new ones.
- *Choose people who like teamwork.* Companies like Toyota recruit and select employees who have a history of preferring to work in teams and of being good team members. Loners and unsociable types do not usually make good team members.
- *Train leaders to "coach" and not "boss."* Self–directed work teams are empowered—they have the authority, tools, and information with which to manage themselves. Team leaders must thus learn that their job is not to boss but to support and to coach.

- *Train, train, train.* Team members must have the training required to do their jobs. Training should cover topics such as the philosophy of doing work through teams, how teams make decisions, interpersonal and communication skills for team members, and the technical skills that team members will need to perform their jobs.
- *Cross-train for flexibility.* Members of most teams also need cross-training to learn the jobs of fellow team members either informally or through scheduled rotating assignments. This can help minimize disruptions due to absenteeism and can boost flexibility, since all team members are always ready to fill in when needed.
- *Establish urgent, demanding performance standards.* All team members should believe that the team has urgent and worthwhile purposes, and they need to know what their performance standards are.
- *Challenge the group regularly with fresh facts and information.* New information (such as how the company is doing) helps a team to understand the challenges that it and the company face. Supplying such information there-

by helps the team to shape its common purpose, set clearer goals, and improve its approach.

- *Exploit the power of positive feedback, recognition, and reward.* There are many ways to have team performance recognized and rewarded. For example, a senior executive can speak directly to the team about the urgency of its mission and use special awards to recognize the team's contributions.

BUSINESS PROCESS REENGINEERING

business process reengineering (BPR) The fundamental rethinking and radical redesign of business processes to achieve dramatic improvements in performance.

Another major strategic change initiative in which HR plays a significant role is **business process reengineering (BPR)**, which is defined as "the fundamental rethinking and radical redesign of business processes to achieve dramatic improvements in critical, contemporary measures of performance, such as cost, quality, service, and speed."[42] One of business process reengineering's basic assumptions is that the traditional way of organizing departments and processes around very specialized tasks is inherently duplicative, wasteful, and unresponsive to the firm's customers. These tasks need to be fundamentally changed and reunified into coherent *business processes*. In reengineering a company and its departments and processes, the reengineers, therefore, need to ask themselves: "Why do we do what we do?" and "Why do we do it the way we do?"[43]

Initially, many companies bent on reengineering neglect to simultaneously institute new HR practices; they subsequently fail to win the commitment of their managers and employees to their new reengineered jobs.[44] Senior managers now understand that the HR department plays a crucial role in successfully implementing reengineering. Following are some aspects of the HR department's role:

- *Building commitment to reengineering.* Implementing reengineering successfully means winning employee commitment. HR departments can play a key role in winning such commitment through HR practices like value-based hiring, building a sense of community, and installing effective two-way communication practices.

- *Team building.* Business process reengineering generally results in reorganizing the work force from functional departments to process-oriented teams, such as teams of employees working together to process credit requests. The HR department plays a central role in providing the required training and ensuring that communication between top management and the teams remains open and freely flowing.

- *Changing the nature of the work.* With reengineering, jobs generally change from specialized tasks to multidimensional generalist work. Not only is each worker usually responsible for a broader, more enriched job, but process team members share responsibility for performing the whole process, not just a small piece of it.[45] HR department staff plays a key role in helping managers in hiring high-potential employees and providing them with the training and development that they require.

- *Moving from controlled to empowered jobs.* People working in a reengineered process are of necessity empowered to perform a broader set of tasks with relatively little supervision.[46] This means that companies that reengineer must hire people who have self-discipline and who are "self-starters" with the motivation to do what it takes to please a customer.[47]

- *Moving from training to education.* In companies that reengineer, the emphasis necessarily shifts from training to education. It is no longer enough just to give employees training that shows them "how" to do the job. Instead, the new generalist team members need education: they need to increase their insight and understanding of how to analyze and solve problems and to understand not just the "how" of the job, but the "why" of it.48

- *Shifting focus from activities to results.* Reengineering creates work that is measured in terms of its results—such as serving customers in a timely manner—rather than in terms of completing an activity like taking calls or checking credit. This means that the HR department needs to re-evaluate the compensation system—contribution, performance, and results should be the primary bases for determining compensation.[49]

FLEXIBLE WORK ARRANGEMENTS

Saskatchewan Family Friendly Collective Agreements
www.sfl.sk.ca/policy/
familyfriendlystudy.htm

CAW Child Care Campaign
www.caw.ca

CUPW Child Care Fund Projects
www.cupw-sttp.org

Many organizations find that employees are in a better position to work toward all of these strategic change initiatives if they are provided with work arrangements that enable them to balance work with their non-work responsibilities. Flexible work arrangements, or "family-friendly" policies, are aimed at providing flexibility for employees faced with challenges in work–life balance. Scotiabank is one Canadian employer that offers flexible work arrangements as part of its philosophy regarding their 70 percent female workforce.[50] At IBM Canada, flexible work arrangements help keep employees committed to the workplace.[51] But even more such arrangements are needed. The Health Canada *2001 National Work–Life Conflict Study* surveyed more than 30 000 Canadians, and found that although 70 percent were parents and 60 percent had eldercare responsibilities and were in need of flexible work arrangements, more than 50 percent of Canadians still work a regular nine-to-five workday, as shown in **Figure 9.1**.[52]

The bottom-line impact of this problem is significant—research has demonstrated that an inability to balance work and family life costs Canadian employers an estimated $2.7 billion per year in lost time.[53] Employees experiencing work–family conflict are up to 30 times more likely to experience mental health problems.[54] As a result, unions such as the Canadian Auto Workers, the Canadian Union of Postal Workers, and the United Steelworkers have begun adding work–life balance demands to the collective bargaining process.[55]

Almost half of Canadian workers are experiencing high or moderate levels of stress because of work and family pressures.[56] Employers who ignore this growing trend are left to cope with greater absenteeism and the loss of key workers. Family-friendly policies can result in higher morale, better job satisfaction, and lower turnover.[57] Further, managers play a critical role in workers' ability to manage their work and personal responsibilities. Flexible work arrangements are likely to be ineffective unless they are supported by first-line managers.[58] The results of one Canadian study found that workers who had supervisors who were understanding and accommodating with regard to their

FIGURE 9.1   Regular vs. Flexible Work Arrangements

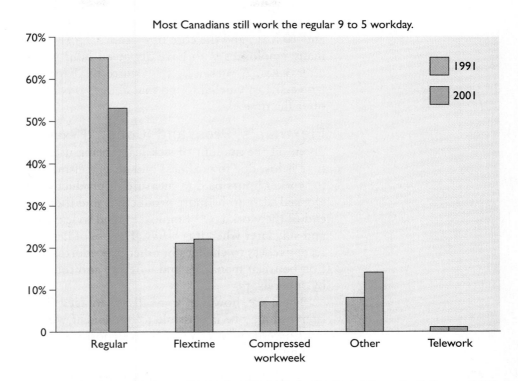

Source: C. Higgins and L. Duxbury, 2001 National Work-Life Conflict Study (Ottawa: Health Canada, 2001). Reproduced with permission of the authors.

home lives missed only half the number of workdays as those with less understanding bosses.[59]

Although flexible work arrangements have traditionally been associated with improving work–family balance, they are increasingly seen as part of a business strategy.[60] This is because they can assist organizations in meeting customer needs when and where they need to be met. For example, one B.C. firm used flexible work arrangements to enhance customer service by offering employees the option to start work at 6:00 A.M. Pacific time in order to deal with customers at 9 A.M. Eastern time.[61]

Overall, flexible work arrangements will continue to expand because they work—for both the employer and the employee.[62] Efforts to assist workers in adapting to ongoing societal and demographic changes can also help organizations to achieve a competitive advantage through increased productivity and lower costs.[63]

Flextime

flextime A plan whereby employees build their workday around a core of midday hours.

Flextime is a plan whereby employees' flexible workdays are built around a core of midday hours, such as 11 A.M. to 2 P.M. Workers determine their own flexible starting and stopping hours. For example, they may opt to work from 7 A.M. to 3 P.M. or from 11 A.M. to 7 P.M. In practice, most employers who use flextime give employees only limited freedom regarding the hours that they work. Typical schedules dictate the earliest starting time, latest starting time, and core periods. Employers often prefer a schedule that is fairly close to the traditional 9 A.M. to 5 P.M. workday. For example, starting times may be between 7 A.M. and 10 A.M., and the core time from 10 A.M. to 3 P.M. The effect of flextime for many employees is to have about an hour or two of leeway before 9 A.M. or after 5 P.M. A survey by the Centre for Families, Work and Well-Being at the University of Guelph found that about 70 percent of small employers in Canada offer flextime.[64]

Flextime's Pros and Cons   Flextime reduces absenteeism and cuts down on the amount of sick leave being used for personal matters. When less time is lost due to tardiness and absenteeism, the ratio of worker-hours worked to worker-hours paid (a measure of productivity) increases. The hours actually worked seem to be more productive, and there is less slowing down toward the end of the workday.[65] Employees tend to leave early when the workload is light and stay later when it is heavy. The use of flextime seems to increase employees' receptiveness to changes in other procedures. It also tends to reduce the distinction between managers and workers and requires more delegation of authority by supervisors.

There are, however, some disadvantages. Flextime is complicated to administer and may be impossible to implement where large groups of workers must work interdependently.[66] Also, the positive effects of flextime have been found to diminish over time.[67]

Conditions for Success   There are several ways in which to make a flextime program more successful. First, supervisory indoctrination is important in order to offset any initial management resistance. Second, flextime is usually more successful with clerical, professional, and managerial jobs, and less so with jobs requiring interdependence among workers. Third, experience indicates that the greater the flexibility of a flextime program, the greater the benefits (although the disadvantages multiply as well). Fourth, careful implementation is important; a flextime project director should be appointed to oversee all aspects of the program, and frequent meetings should take place between supervisors and employees to allay their fears and clear up misunderstandings. A pilot study in one department is advisable.

AN ETHICAL DILEMMA

Is it ethical for an employer to deny employees the right to flexible work arrangements just because managers are concerned about the additional communication required and about losing control over their employees?

Telecommuting

Telecommuting (or teleworking) is the fastest-growing alternative work arrangement.[68] Here, employees work at home, usually with their computers and fax machines, using telephone lines to transmit letters, data, and completed work to the office. Increasingly, wireless technology and even satellite connections are being used, as described in the HR.Net box. Many managers are not comfortable supervising telecommuters, fearing a loss of control. However, according to Jack Nilles, who coined the term "telecommuter," successful telecommuting requires that mutual trust be established between an employee and his or her supervisor. Successful telecommuters are highly motivated and have the self-discipline to work independently.[69]

HR.NET

Satellites Improve Telework Connections

Broadband access is implicit in the telework solution, because of the overwhelming prevalence of broadband connectivity in traditional office settings. However, delivering the same robust level of broadband connectivity to the small office/home office environment as that experienced in the "regular" office is a challenging task. How can teleworkers be provided with fast, secure access and get the uniform level of service and support required? Satellite technology can be one solution.

Satellite connectivity is not dependent on in-the-ground infrastructure, and broadband via satellite is available anywhere. Satellite solutions operate over a standard platform, allowing enterprises to deploy a teleworker program quickly and reliably. In terms of overall network security, satellite offers business users the static Internet protocol addresses that are required to maintain network integrity on virtual private networks, and all data delivered over the network is encrypted for each unique satellite modem.

Satellite can be a great choice for organizations that want to provide teleworkers with a cost-effective, reliable broadband connection. It is available anywhere in North America and can interface with secure virtual private network technology on a common platform.

Source: Adapted from S. Salamoff, "Satellites Improve Telework Connections," *Canadian HR Reporter* (May 20, 2002), p. G6. Reproduced by permission of *Canadian HR Reporter*, Carswell, One Corporate Plaza, 2075 Kennedy Road, Scarborough, ON M1T 3V4.

To overcome resistance and ensure that they learn the planning and communication skills necessary to build such trust, managers who supervise telecommuters need to be properly prepared and trained.[70] Successful teleworking requires approval on the part of management, maintenance of the quantity and quality of work on the part of employees, and respect for existing rules and collective agreements from both management and employees.[71] A legal agreement between the organization and the teleworker is recommended by many experts.[72] Communication is also critical—managers must keep teleworkers informed as to what is going on at the office, and teleworkers must keep in touch with co-workers so that they stay visible and do not become isolated.[73]

Benefits of telecommuting accrue to employers, employees, and the community.[74] For employers, telecommuting can save on office space and related costs, and can increase productivity in some cases.[75] For employees, telecommuting reduces travel time, allows for greater privacy and fewer interruptions, and permits the employee to work whenever he or she is most productive. For communities, telecommuting helps to reduce traffic congestion, air pollution, and daytime residential break-ins, and provides job opportunities for persons with disabilities.

Other Flexible Work Arrangements

job sharing A strategy that involves dividing the duties of a single position between two or more employees.

Employers are taking other steps to accommodate their employees' scheduling needs. **Job sharing** is a strategy that allows two or more employees to share a single full-time job. For example, two people may share a 40-hour-per-week job, with one working mornings and the other working afternoons, or one person working Monday through Wednesday noon, and the other from Wednesday noon through Friday. A *reduced work week* refers to a temporary

compressed workweek An arrangement that most commonly allows employees to work four days of more than eight hours instead of the more usual five eight-hour days.

reduction in work-hours by a group of employees during economic hard times as a way of preventing layoffs; thus 400 employees may all agree to work (and get paid for) only 35 hours per week in order to avoid having the firm lay off 30 workers.

A number of employers have also switched to a **compressed workweek**. The most common arrangement involves employees working four ten-hour days instead of the more usual five eight-hour days. Compressed workweek plans have been fairly successful as they have several advantages. Productivity seems to increase since there are fewer startups and shutdowns. Workers are also more willing to work some evenings and Saturdays as part of these plans. The compressed workweek is generally effective in terms of reducing paid overtime, reducing absenteeism, and improving efficiency. Furthermore, workers also gain; there is a 20-percent reduction in commuter trips and an additional day off per week. Additional savings (e.g., in childcare expenses) may also result.[76] However, there has not been a lot of experience with shortened workweeks, and it is possible that the improvements are short-lived.

There are also disadvantages, and some of them are potentially quite severe. Tardiness, for example, may become a problem. Of more concern is the fact

www.cch.ca

Managing Strategic Organizational Renewal

Human resources practitioners can add great value to any organization through the application of their specialization in introducing breakthrough initiatives that significantly change the attitudes, behaviours and perceptions of employees throughout the organization. Specific initiatives that are identified with the human resources function and underlie change management efforts include:

- *Human resources strategy.* The ... human resources strategy provides a comprehensive and coherent plan for introducing the organization's intended vision, culture and core values.

- *Organizational design.* The practitioner is responsible for consulting with the senior leadership team on the appropriate structures that are consistent with the organization's vision.

- *Cultural change and cultural management.* The practitioner can influence employee behaviours and, therefore, attitudes, through effective use of processes such as the performance management system, training and development strategies and reward and recognition initiatives.

- *Change management.* Many practitioners have inherent facilitation skills to oversee change initiatives and are therefore naturally predisposed to take the lead in change management efforts....

- *Flexibility.* In order to face continuous threats and challenges, many organizations have come to realize that they need to be flexible.... The ultimate flexibility is created in a Learning organization that continuously seeks to improve its processes, products and services through the empowerment of its employees to self-develop persistently.

- *Teams.* The introduction of teams can take many different forms. It may at one level involve teaching peers from different business units how to "act as one." In the extreme, the organization may want to fully empower front-line employees in self-managing work groups....

- *Total quality management.* While not the specific milieu of the human resources practitioner, TQM efforts require the practitioner to become involved in the organizational design aspects to support TQM....

Source: Excerpted with permission from *Secord's A—Z Guide for Human Resources Practitioners*, published by and copyright CCH Canadian Limited, Toronto, Ontario.

that fatigue is a potential drawback of the four-day workweek. (Note that fatigue was a main reason for adopting eight-hour workdays in the first place.)

Still, other employers, especially in Europe, are switching to a plan that they call **flexyear**. Under this plan, employees can choose (at six-month intervals) the number of hours that they want to work each month over the next year. A full-timer, for instance, might be able to work up to 173 hours a month. In a typical flexyear arrangement, an employee who wants to average 110 hours a month might work 150 hours in January (when the children are at school and the company needs extra help to cope with January sales). In February, the employee may work only 70 hours because he or she wants to go skiing.[77]

flexyear A work arrangement under which employees can choose (at six-month intervals) the number of hours that they want to work each month over the next year.

Chapter *Review*

Summary

1   Five common types of organizational change are strategic change; cultural change; structural change; changes in people, attitudes, and skills; and technological change. The three steps in Lewin's change process are (1) unfreezing the status quo; (2) moving toward new behaviours, values, and attitudes; and (3) refreezing the new way of doing business through new systems and procedures.

2   Steps in establishing a quality circle program include planning the circle by establishing a QC facilitator and a QC steering committee; training employees in QC philosophy, implementation, and operation; initiating the circle by soliciting volunteer employees to form QCs; and operating the circle.

3   ISO 9000 and ISO 14000 are worldwide quality standards that facilitate the exchange of goods and services. ISO standards are concerned with quality management in the way work is done, not in the end product or service. ISO 9000:2000 concerns the features of a product or service that are required by the customer. ISO 14000:2000 is concerned with environmental management, or what the organization does to minimize harmful effects on the environment caused by its activities.

4   HRM can help to build a productive team-based organization by selecting team members for skill and skill potential; choosing people who like teamwork; training leaders to "coach," not "boss"; training continuously; cross-training for flexibility; establishing urgent, demanding performance standards; challenging the group regularly with fresh facts and information; and exploiting the power of positive feedback, recognition, and reward.

5   Business process reengineering is the fundamental rethinking and radical redesign of business processes to achieve dramatic improvements in performance. The HR department contributes to reengineering through its effect on building commitment to reengineering, team building, changing the nature of work, empowering jobs, moving from training to education, and shifting focus from activities to results.

6   Flextime is a plan whereby employees' flexible workdays are built around a core of midday hours, such as 10 A.M. to 3 P.M. Telecommuting means working from home using computers and other technology to link to the workplace. Job sharing occurs when two or more employees share one job. A compressed workweek most commonly involves employees working four ten-hour days instead of five eight-hour days.

Key Terms

business process reengineering (BPR)   *(p. 283)*
compressed workweek   *(p. 288)*
cultural change   *(p. 270)*
flextime   *(p. 285)*
flexyear   *(p. 289)*
job sharing   *(p. 287)*
quality   *(p. 273)*

quality circle (QC)   *(p. 276)*
self-directed teams   *(p. 281)*
strategic change   *(p. 270)*
structural change   *(p. 271)*
technological change   *(p. 271)*
total quality management (TQM)   *(p. 274)*

Review and Discussion Questions

1 Explain the ten-step process for organizational change outlined in this chapter.

2 Describe the seven criteria used by the National Quality Institute to determine winners of the Canada Awards for Excellence.

3 Explain the three key standards in ISO 9000:2000.

4 Explain self-directed work teams and the concept of empowerment, and how they change the culture of organizations.

5 What is the fundamental change achieved through business process reengineering?

6 Discuss the reasons why flexible work arrangements are offered by employers.

CRITICAL *Thinking Questions*

1 How can HR management contribute to a firm winning a quality award like the Canada Award for Excellence?

2 Is ISO registration really of value when it does not guarantee the quality of the end product or service?

APPLICATION *Exercises*

Running Case: LearnInMotion.com

Teamwork

Like most companies with fewer than ten employees, LearnInMotion.com doesn't have a formal organization chart. Instead, the company usually has several projects and activities in the works at any one time, each of which is managed by a team. Employees typically serve on at least one team.

The projects and activities are typical of dot-com companies. There is, for instance, the front-page development team, whose task is to see that the overall format of the company's home page (as well as its various subsidiary pages and communities) makes sense in terms of what the company is trying to achieve. In addition to Jennifer and Pierre, the team includes the Web designer, as well as one of the two salespeople (whose job it is to relay information about customer needs). The sales team—charged

with managing the company's sales effort—consists of the two salespeople, as well as Jennifer, Pierre, and Greg (of the Board of Directors).

LearnInMotion.com is creating a Web-based calendar (technically a "personal information manager," or PIM); Pierre is on the calendar committee, as is the representative of the consulting firm that's developing the calendar, as well as the company's programmer/independent contractor. Many dot-coms have a separate "business development" manager, whose role is to conceive and then implement relationships with other Web sites. For example, LearnInMotion.com already has several relationships with job-finding/career Web sites; the assumption is that job hunters may be looking for business courses, and people interested in business courses may be looking for jobs. LearnInMotion.com can't afford its own business development manager, so this is a function that Jennifer fulfills, with help from a business development team that also includes Pierre, Greg, and one of the salespeople.

This all sounds logical, but the problem is, it isn't working. Sales are stagnant, the calendar is two months behind, and the company has been able to finalize only a handful of business development arrangements. Jennifer and Pierre are not sure what to do. There is no way they can afford to go out and hire managers and employees to oversee activities like these. On the other hand, the company is falling behind. Now they want you, their management consultant, to help them figure out what to do. Here's what they want you to do for them.

Questions

1   Tell Jennifer and Pierre what you think the problem is: Is their team approach a good idea?

2   Are there any new approaches, such as total quality management programs, that they should consider applying to their situation?

3   What do you think they should do and why?

CASE INCIDENT *How Much Work Schedule Flexibility Is Too Much Flexibility?*

Jasmine Khan, operations manager at John's Grocery Store, is facing several scheduling problems with her cashiers. Julie Brown is on maternity leave. She is due to come back to work next week, but has been unable to find acceptable daycare for her new daughter because of the baby's special medical needs, and wants to extend her leave. Al Fraser has just requested at least two weeks off to attend to his mother, who is in the early stages of Alzheimer's disease, and needs to have home care and other services organized.

The newest cashier, Bill Bradley, has requested that he only work shifts that finish by 4:30 P.M. so that he can pick up his kids from their daycare centre that closes at 5 P.M. His cousin, who had been taking care of the children between 4:30 P.M. and whenever Bill finished his shift, will be moving to another city shortly and Bill doesn't know anyone else in town that he would trust with his children.

Jasmine' best cashier, Sophia Chan, who has the potential to take over from the current head cashier who will be retiring next year, has recently told Jasmine that she is going back to university next month to finish her degree in business, and will only be able to work part-time for the next eight months. To make matters worse, the head cashier, Shirley Trudeau, has a daughter who is about to become a single mother, and she wants to take three weeks off to help her daughter adjust to the demands of caring for an infant.

John's Grocery Store recently adopted a policy that it would be as flexible as possible to accommodate work–family conflict, which means that Jasmine can't just let cashiers go when they can't work regularly, as she has been able to do in the past. But Jasmine is wondering how can she do that and still operate the store—after all, customers don't care about staffing issues; most just want to buy their groceries and be on their way as quickly as possible.

So far the other five cashiers are available to work regular shifts. Jasmine is considering a variety of flexible work options including regular part-time, temporary part-time, job sharing, compressed workweeks, flextime, and leaves of absence.

Questions

1   What difficulties might Jasmine face if she tries to accommodate all of these requests for flexible work arrangements to cope with work–family issues?

2   Should any of these requests be turned down?

3   How can the remaining requests be accommodated? Make recommendations on how to handle each of them.

EXPERIENTIAL *Exercises*

1 Working in small groups, assume that you are a quality circle and that your task is to identify a problem in your "work area" (classroom) and make recommendations on how to solve it. What aspects of the problem identification, solution, and presentation process seem to contribute to improved personal satisfaction and empowerment, if any? Why?

2 Working individually or in groups, develop a brief example of how you would reengineer a familiar process such as class enrollment at the start of a semester.

CHAPTER 10

Performance Appraisal: The Key to Effective Performance Management

CHAPTER OUTLINE

- Performance Management

- The Performance Appraisal Process

- Defining Performance Expectations

- The Appraisal Itself: Appraisal Methods

- Performance Appraisal: Problems and Solutions

- The Appraisal Interview

- The Role of Appraisals in Managing Performance

LEARNING OUTCOMES

After studying this chapter, you should be able to:

Explain what is meant by the term "performance management" and why it is important to effectively appraise performance.

Describe eight performance appraisal methods and the pros and cons of each.

Discuss the major problems inhibiting effective performance appraisals.

Discuss 360-degree appraisal from multiple sources.

Describe the three types of appraisal interview.

Discuss the use of quality-based appraisals for managing performance.

PERFORMANCE MANAGEMENT

Today's working world requires employee productivity above all else as organizations strive to create a high-performance culture using a minimum number of employees. Thus it has been suggested that better performance management represents a largely untapped opportunity to improve company profitability.[1] In the 1990s, many companies came face-to-face with the reality that their performance management systems were ineffective—they wanted to downsize poor performers, but performance appraisal records indicated that all employees were performing adequately.[2]

performance management The process encompassing all activities related to improving employee performance, productivity, and effectiveness.

Performance management is a process encompassing all activities related to improving employee performance, productivity, and effectiveness. It includes goal setting, merit pay increases, training and development, career management, and disciplinary action. The foundation of performance management is the performance appraisal process. Appraisals provide a concrete basis for analysis of an employee's work performance, and for any action taken to maintain, enhance, or change it. The other aspects of performance management are discussed in other chapters of this text.

THE PERFORMANCE APPRAISAL PROCESS

Performance appraisal is of considerable strategic importance to today's organizations because the most effective way for firms to differentiate themselves in a highly competitive, service-oriented, global marketplace is through the quality of their employees.[3] The performance appraisal process should also link performance criteria to current strategic objectives and implementation plans.[4] Performance appraisal may be defined as any procedure that involves (1) setting work standards; (2) assessing the employee's actual performance relative to these standards; and (3) providing feedback to the employee with the aim of motivating that person to eliminate performance deficiencies or to continue to perform above par.

Unfortunately, most supervisors and employees are dissatisfied with their performance appraisal programs, because they involve so much personal judgment.[5] And it is clear that not all feedback is effective in improving performance. In fact, recent research has shown that about one-third of the time it can actually decrease subsequent performance.[6] The design of any performance appraisal system requires careful thought and consideration of the factors that are likely to make it effective.

Why Should Performance Be Appraised?

There are several reasons to appraise performance.[7] First, appraisals provide *information* with which *promotion and salary decisions* can be made. Second, they provide an opportunity for managers and employees to *review* each employee's work-related behaviour. This in turn enables the manager and employee to reinforce the things that the employee is doing well, and to develop a plan for correction of any deficiencies that the appraisal might have unearthed. Finally, the appraisal should be central to a firm's *career-planning process* because it provides a good opportunity to review each employee's career plans in light of his or her exhibited strengths and weaknesses, and in light of the company's strategic plans.[8]

Performance Appraisal Process
www.uvm.edu/~emplrel/
paprocess.html

The HR Department's Role in Appraisal

The supervisor usually does the actual appraising; therefore, he or she must be familiar with basic appraisal techniques, understand and avoid problems that can cripple an appraisal, and conduct the appraisal fairly.

The HR department serves a policymaking and advisory role. In one survey, for example, about 80 percent of the responding firms said that the HR department provides advice and assistance regarding the appraisal tool to use, but leaves final decisions on appraisal procedures to operating division heads. The rest of the firms in that study said that the HR department staff members prepare detailed forms and procedures and ensure that all departments use them.[9] HR department staff members are responsible, as well, for training supervisors to improve their appraisal skills. Finally, the HR department is also responsible for monitoring the appraisal system's use, and particularly for ensuring that the format and criteria being measured comply with human rights laws and do not become outdated.

Steps in Appraising Performance

A performance appraisal contains three steps: defining performance expectations, appraising performance, and providing feedback. *Defining performance expectations* means making sure that job duties and job standards are clear to all. *Appraising performance* means comparing an employee's actual performance to the standards that have been set; this usually involves some type of rating form. Third, performance appraisal usually requires one or more *feedback sessions* where the employee's performance and progress are discussed and plans are made for any development that is required.

Performance Appraisal Problems

When appraisals fail, they do so for reasons that parallel these three steps—defining performance expectations, appraising performance, and providing feedback.[10] Some appraisals fail because employees are not told ahead of time exactly what is expected of them in terms of good performance. Even if performance standards are defined, they may be irrelevant, subjective, or unrealistic.[11] Others fail because of problems with the forms or procedures used to actually appraise the performance; a lenient supervisor might rate all employees "high," for instance, although many are actually unsatisfactory. Still other problems arise during the interview-feedback session, which include arguing and poor communications. Finally, failure to use evaluations in human resource decision making and career development negates the primary purpose of performance evaluations. Conducting effective appraisals thus begins with defining the job and its performance standards, which will now be discussed.

DEFINING PERFORMANCE EXPECTATIONS

The job description often is not sufficient to clarify what employees are expected to do. All sales associates in the firm might have the same job description, for instance, although each sales manager may have individual ideas about what his or her reporting sales associates are expected to do. For example, the job description may list duties such as "supervise support staff" and "be responsible for all customer liaisons." However, one particular sales associate may be expected to personally sell at least $600 000 worth of products per year by handling the division's two largest accounts, keep the sales assistants happy, and keep customers away from company executives.[12]

To operationalize these expectations, measurable standards should be developed for each. The "personal selling" activity can be measured in terms of how many dollars of sales the associate is to generate personally. "Keeping the sales assistants happy" might be measured in terms of turnover (on the assumption that less than 10 percent of the sales assistants will quit in any given year if morale is high). "Keeping customers away from executives" can be measured with a standard of no more than 10 customer complaints per year being the sales associate's target. In general, employees should always know ahead of time how and on what basis they will be appraised.

THE APPRAISAL ITSELF: APPRAISAL METHODS

The appraisal itself is generally conducted with the aid of a predetermined and formal method like one or more of those described in this section.

Graphic Rating Scale Method

graphic rating scale A scale that lists a number of traits and a range of performance for each. The employee is then rated by identifying the score that best describes his or her level of performance for each trait.

The **graphic rating scale** is the simplest and most popular technique for appraising performance. **Figure 10.1** shows a typical rating scale. It lists traits (such as quality and reliability) and a range of performance values (from unsatisfactory to outstanding) for each one. The supervisor rates each employee by circling or

FIGURE 10.1   One Page of a Two-Page Graphic Rating Scale with Space for Comments

Performance Appraisal

Employee Name _____   Title _____

Department _____   Employee Payroll Number _____

Reason for Review: ☐ Annual   ☐ Promotion   ☐ Unsatisfactory Performance

                     ☐ Merit   ☐ End Probation Period   ☐ Other _____

Date employee began present position ____ / ____ / ____

Date of last appraisal ____ / ____ / ____   Scheduled appraisal date ____ / ____ / ____

Instructions: Carefully evaluate employee's work performance in relation to current job requirements. Check rating box to indicate the employee's performance. Indicate N/A if not applicable. Assign points for each rating within the scale and indicate in the corresponding points box. Points will be totalled and averaged for an overall performance score.

RATING IDENTIFICATION

O–Outstanding–Performance is exceptional in all areas and is recognizable as being far superior to others.

V–Very Good–Results clearly exceed most position requirements. Performance is of high quality and is achieved on a consistent basis.

G–Good–Competent and dependable level of performance. Meets performance standards of the job.

I–Improvement Needed–Performance is deficient in certain areas. Improvement is necessary.

U–Unsatisfactory–Results are generally unacceptable and require immediate improvement. No merit increase should be granted to individuals with this rating.

N–Not Rated–Not applicable or too soon to rate.

GENERAL FACTORS	RATING		SCALE	SUPPORTIVE DETAILS OR COMMENTS
1. Quality–The accuracy, thoroughness and acceptability of work performed.	O V G I U	☐ ☐ ☐ ☐ ☐	100-90 90-80 80-70 70-60 below 60	Points _____ _____ _____ _____
2. Productivity–The quantity and efficiency of work produced in a specified period of time.	O V G I U	☐ ☐ ☐ ☐ ☐	100-90 90-80 80-70 70-60 below 60	Points _____ _____ _____ _____
3. Job Knowledge–The practical/technical skills and information used on the job.	O V G I U	☐ ☐ ☐ ☐ ☐	100-90 90-80 80-70 70-60 below 60	Points _____ _____ _____ _____
4. Reliability–The extent to which an employee can be relied upon regarding task completion and follow up.	O V G I U	☐ ☐ ☐ ☐ ☐	100-90 90-80 80-70 70-60 below 60	Points _____ _____ _____ _____
5. Availability–The extent to which an employee is punctual, observes prescribed work break/meal periods, and the overall attendance record.	O V G I U	☐ ☐ ☐ ☐ ☐	100-90 90-80 80-70 70-60 below 60	Points _____ _____ _____ _____
6. Independence–The extent of work performed with little or no supervision.	O V G I U	☐ ☐ ☐ ☐ ☐	100-90 90-80 80-70 70-60 below 60	Points _____ _____ _____ _____

checking the score that best describes his or her performance for each trait. The assigned values are then totalled.

Instead of appraising generic traits or factors (such as quality and quantity), many firms specify the duties to be appraised. For a payroll coordinator, these might include liaison with accounting and benefits staff, continuous updating of knowledge regarding relevant legislation, maintenance of payroll records, data entry and payroll calculations, and ongoing response to employees' inquiries regarding payroll issues.

Alternation Ranking Method

alternation ranking method

Ranking employees from best to worst on a particular trait.

Ranking employees from best to worst on a trait or traits is another method for evaluating employees. Since it is usually easier to distinguish between the worst and best employees than to rank them, an **alternation ranking method** is most popular. First, list all employees to be rated, and then cross out the names of any not known well enough to rank. Then, on a form such as that in **Figure 10.2**, indicate the employee who is the highest on the characteristic being measured and also the one who is the lowest. Then choose the next highest and the next lowest, alternating between highest and lowest until all of the employees to be rated have been ranked.

FIGURE 10.2   Alternation Ranking Scale

ALTERNATION RANKING SCALE

For the Trait: _____

For the trait you are measuring, list all the employees you want to rank. Put the highest-ranking employee's name on line 1. Put the lowest-ranking employee's name on line 20. Then list the next highest ranking on line 2, the next lowest ranking on line 19, and so on. Continue until all names are on the scale.

Highest-ranking employee

1. _____   11. _____
2. _____   12. _____
3. _____   13. _____
4. _____   14. _____
5. _____   15. _____
6. _____   16. _____
7. _____   17. _____
8. _____   18. _____
9. _____   19. _____
10. _____   20. _____

Lowest-ranking employee

Paired Comparison Method

paired comparison method
Ranking employees by making a chart of all possible pairs of the employees for each trait and indicating which is the better employee of the pair.

The **paired comparison method** helps to make the ranking method more precise. For every trait (quantity of work, quality of work, and so on), every employee is paired with and compared to every other employee.

Suppose that there are five employees to be rated. In the paired comparison method, a chart is prepared, as in **Figure 10.3**, of all possible pairs of employees for each trait. Then, for each trait, indicate (with a + or −) who is the better employee of the pair. Next, the number of times that an employee is rated better is added up. In Figure 10.3, employee Maria ranked highest (has the most + marks) for "quality of work," while Art was ranked highest for "creativity."

Forced Distribution Method

forced distribution method
Predetermined percentages of ratees are placed in various performance categories.

The **forced distribution method** places predetermined percentages of ratees in performance categories. For example, it may be decided to distribute employees as follows:

- 15 percent high performers
- 20 percent high-average performers
- 30 percent average performers
- 20 percent low-average performers
- 15 percent low performers

FIGURE 10.3   Ranking Employees by the Paired Comparison Method

FOR THE TRAIT "QUALITY OF WORK"						FOR THE TRAIT "CREATIVITY"					
	Employee Rated:						Employee Rated:				
As Compared to:	A Art	B Maria	C Chuck	D Diane	E José	As Compared to:	A Art	B Maria	C Chuck	D Diane	E José
A Art		+	+	–	–	A Art		–	–	–	–
B Maria	–		–	–	–	B Maria	+		–	+	+
C Chuck	–	+		+	–	C Chuck	+	+		–	+
D Diane	+	+	–		+	D Diane	+	–	+		–
E José	+	+	+	–		E José	+	–	–	+	
	Maria Ranks Highest Here						Art Ranks Highest Here				

Note: "+" means "better than" and "–" means "worse than." For each chart, add up the number of "+" signs in each column to get the highest-ranked employee.

Similar to bell-curve grading at school, this means that not everyone can get an "A," and that one's performance is always rated relative to that of one's peers. One practical way to do this is to write each employee's name on a separate index card, and then, for each trait being appraised (quality of work, creativity, and so on), place the employee's card in one of the appropriate performance categories. This method has been criticized as demotivating for the considerable proportion of the workforce that is classified as less than average.[13]

Critical Incident Method

critical incident method Keeping a record of uncommonly good or undesirable examples of an employee's work-related behaviour and reviewing it with the employee at predetermined times.

With the **critical incident method**, the supervisor keeps a log of desirable or undesirable examples or incidents of each employee's work-related behaviour. Then, every six months or so, the supervisor and employee meet and discuss the latter's performance using the specific incidents as examples.

This method can always be used to supplement another appraisal technique, and in that role it has several advantages. It provides specific hard facts for explaining the appraisal. It also ensures that a manager thinks about the employee's appraisal throughout the year, because the incidents must be accumulated; therefore, the rating does not just reflect the employee's most recent performance. Keeping a running list of critical incidents should also provide concrete examples of what an employee can do to eliminate any performance deficiencies.

The critical incident method can be adapted to the specific job expectations laid out for the employee at the beginning of the year. Thus, in the example presented in **Table 10.1**, one of the assistant plant manager's continuing duties is to supervise procurement and to minimize inventory costs. The critical incident shows that the assistant plant manager let inventory storage costs rise 15 percent; this provides a specific example of what performance must be improved in the future.

TABLE 10.1	Examples of Critical Incidents for an Assistant Plant Manager	
CONTINUING DUTIES	**TARGETS**	**CRITICAL INCIDENTS**
Schedule production for plant	Full utilization of employees and machinery in plant; orders delivered on time	Instituted new production scheduling system; decreased late orders by 10 percent last month; increased machine utilization in plant by 20 percent last month
Supervise procurement of raw materials and inventory control	Minimize inventory costs while keeping adequate supplies on hand	Let inventory storage costs rise 15 percent last month; overordered parts "A" and "B" by 20 percent; underordered part "C" by 30 percent
Supervise machinery maintenance	No shutdowns due to faulty machinery	Instituted new preventative maintenance system for plant; prevented a machine breakdown by discovering faulty part

The critical incident method is often used to supplement a ranking technique. It is useful for identifying specific examples of good and poor performance and planning how deficiencies can be corrected. It is not as useful by itself for comparing employees, nor, therefore, for making salary decisions.

Narrative Forms

Some employers use narrative forms to evaluate employees. For example, the form in **Figure 10.4** presents a suggested format for identifying a performance issue and presenting a *performance improvement plan*. The performance problem is described in specific detail, and its organizational impact is specified. The improvement plan identifies measurable improvement goals, provides directions regarding training and any other suggested activities to address the performance issue, and encourages the employee to add ideas about steps to be taken to improve performance. Finally, the outcomes and consequences, both positive and negative, are explicitly stated. A summary performance appraisal discussion then focuses on problem solving.[14]

Behaviourally Anchored Rating Scales

behaviourally anchored rating scale (BARS) An appraisal method that aims to combine the benefits of narratives, critical incidents, and quantified ratings by anchoring a quantified scale with specific narrative examples of good and poor performance.

A **behaviourally anchored rating scale (BARS)** combines the benefits of narratives, critical incidents, and quantified ratings by anchoring a quantified scale with specific behavioural examples of good or poor performance, as in **Figure 10.5.** Its proponents claim that it provides better, more equitable appraisals than do the other tools that have been discussed.[15]

Developing a BARS typically requires five steps:[16]

1. *Generate critical incidents.* Persons who know the job being appraised (jobholders and/or supervisors) are asked to describe specific illustrations (critical incidents) of effective and ineffective performance.

FIGURE 10.4   Performance Improvement Plan

PERFORMANCE IMPROVEMENT PLAN

Employee Name: Brent Goldman   **Department:** Purchasing
Date Presented: August 8, 2004   **Supervisor:** Paul Reisman

Incident Description and Supporting Details: Include the following information: Time, Place, Date of Occurrence, and Persons Present as well as Organizational Impact.

Brent,

On August 1, you conducted a telephone conversation with Morris Kirschenbaum, a wholesaler, regarding the price of switchplates for an upcoming sale. Specifically, you told Mr. Kirschenbaum that the best bid that you currently had was $.20 each for a lot. Another wholesaler, Fred Schiller, whom we've worked with for the past two and a half years, learned of your disclosure to Mr. Kirschenbaum. Mr. Schiller later refused to honor our original bid and consequently severed our working relationship because you disclosed confidential information to a third party.

This disclosure of confidential pricing information violates policy 3.01, "Confidential Information," which states: "All sales price bids is to be strictly confidential. Release of prior sales or present bids is strictly prohibited."

Performance Improvement Plan

1. Measurable/Tangible Improvement Goals. Brent, I expect you to abide by all established policies and procedures. I also expect that you will never again display such a serious lack of judgment or discretion by sharing bid prices in advance of a sale.

2. Training or Special Direction to Be Provided: Policy 3.01 is attached. Please read this policy immediately and see me with any questions that you may have.

3. Interim Performance Evaluation Necessary? No

4. Our Employee Assistance Program (EAP) Provider, Prime Behavioral Health Group, can be confidentially reached to assist you at (800) 555-5555. This is strictly voluntary. A booklet regarding the EAP's services is available from Human Resources.

5. In addition, I recognize that you may have certain ideas to improve your performance. Therefore, I encourage you to provide your own Personal Improvement Plan Input and Suggestions:

_____
_____
_____

(Attach additional sheets if needed.)

Outcomes and Consequences

Positive: If you meet your performance goals, no further disciplinary action will be taken regarding this issue. In addition, you will help our company remain profitable by ensuring that our bids are competitive and that our relationships with our vendors remain solid.

Negative: If you ever again divulge confidential company information regarding pricing, bids, or any other protected areas of information, disciplinary action up to and including dismissal may result. A copy of this document will be placed in your personnel file.

Scheduled Review Date: None

Employee Comments and/or Rebuttal
_____
_____
_____

(Attach additional sheets if needed.)

                                                          X_____
                                                          Employee Signature

---

FIGURE 10.5   Behaviourally Anchored Rating Scale

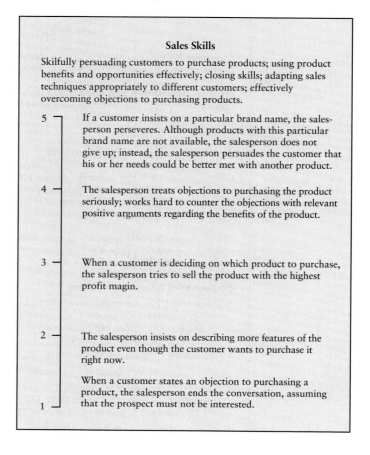

Sales Skills

Skilfully persuading customers to purchase products; using product benefits and opportunities effectively; closing skills; adapting sales techniques appropriately to different customers; effectively overcoming objections to purchasing products.

5 — If a customer insists on a particular brand name, the salesperson perseveres. Although products with this particular brand name are not available, the salesperson does not give up; instead, the salesperson persuades the customer that his or her needs could be better met with another product.

4 — The salesperson treats objections to purchasing the product seriously; works hard to counter the objections with relevant positive arguments regarding the benefits of the product.

3 — When a customer is deciding on which product to purchase, the salesperson tries to sell the product with the highest profit magin.

2 — The salesperson insists on describing more features of the product even though the customer wants to purchase it right now.

1 — When a customer states an objection to purchasing a product, the salesperson ends the conversation, assuming that the prospect must not be interested.

2. *Develop performance dimensions*. These people then cluster the incidents into a smaller set of performance dimensions (say, five or ten). Each cluster (dimension) is then defined.

3. *Reallocate incidents*. Another group of people who also know the job then reallocate the original critical incidents. They are given the clusters' definitions and the critical incidents, and are asked to reassign each incident to the cluster that they think it best fits. Typically, a critical incident is retained if some percentage (usually 50 percent to 80 percent) of this second group assigns it to the same cluster as did the group in Step 2.

4. *Scale the incidents*. This second group is generally asked to rate the behaviour described in the incident as to how effectively or ineffectively it represents performance on the appropriate dimension (seven- or nine-point scales are typical).

5. *Develop final instrument*. A subset of the incidents (usually six or seven per cluster) is used as behavioural anchors for each dimension.

Advantages   Developing a BARS can be more time consuming than developing other appraisal tools, such as graphic rating scales. But BARS may also have important advantages:[17]

1. *A more accurate measure.* People who know the job and its requirements better than anyone else develop BARS. The result should therefore be a good measure of performance on that job.

2. *Clearer standards.* The critical incidents along the scale help to clarify what is meant by extremely good performance, average performance, and so forth.

3. *Feedback.* The critical incidents may be more useful in providing feedback to appraisees than simply informing them of their performance rating and not providing specific behavioural examples.

4. *Independent dimensions.* Systematically clustering the critical incidents into five or six performance dimensions (such as "knowledge and judgment") should help to make the dimensions more independent of one another. For example, a rater should be less likely to rate an employee high on all dimensions simply because he or she was rated high in "conscientiousness."

5. *Consistency.* BARS evaluations also seem to be relatively consistent and reliable in that different raters' appraisals of the same person tend to be similar.[18]

The Management by Objectives (MBO) Method

management by objectives (MBO)
Involves setting specific measurable goals with each employee and then periodically reviewing the progress made.

Stripped to its essentials, **management by objectives (MBO)** requires the manager to set specific measurable goals with each employee and then periodically discuss his or her progress toward these goals. A manager can implement a modest MBO program by jointly setting goals with employees and periodically providing feedback. However, the term *MBO* almost always refers to a comprehensive, *organization-wide, goal setting and appraisal program* that consists of six main steps:

1. *Set the organization's goals.* Establish an organization-wide plan for next year and set goals.

2. *Set departmental goals.* Here department heads and their superiors jointly set goals for their departments.

3. *Discuss departmental goals.* Department heads discuss the department's goals with all employees in the department (often at a department-wide meeting) and ask them to develop their own individual goals; in other words, how can each employee contribute to the department's attainment of its goals?

4. *Define expected results* (set individual goals). Here, department heads and employees set short-term performance targets.

5. *Performance reviews: Measure the results.* Department heads compare the actual performance of each employee with expected results.

6. *Provide feedback.* Department heads hold periodic performance review meetings with employees to discuss and evaluate progress in achieving expected results.

Problems to Avoid   There are three problems in using MBO. *Setting unclear, unmeasurable objectives* is the main one. An objective such as "will do a better job of training" is useless. On the other hand, "will have four employees promoted during the year" is a measurable objective.

Second, MBO is *time-consuming*. Taking the time to set objectives, to measure progress, and to provide feedback can take several hours per employee per year, over and above the time already spent doing each person's appraisal.

Third, setting objectives with an employee sometimes turns into a *tug of war*, with the manager pushing for higher goals and the employee pushing for lower ones. It is thus important to know the job and the person's ability. To motivate performance, the objectives must be fair and attainable. The more a manager knows about the job and the employee's ability, the more confident he or she can be about the standards set.

Mixing the Methods

Most firms combine several appraisal techniques; an example of a form used to appraise the performance of managers in a large airline is shown in **Figure 10.6**. Note that it is basically a graphic rating scale with descriptive phrases included to define the traits being measured, but there is also a section for comments below each trait. This lets the rater jot down several critical incidents. The quantifiable ranking method permits comparisons of employees, and is therefore useful for making salary, transfer, and promotion decisions. The critical incidents provide specific examples of good and poor performance.[19]

Some firms utilize computerized approaches. Several relatively inexpensive performance appraisal software programs are on the market. Ottawa-based Halogen Software's eAppraisal is one such Web-based performance appraisal system. It reduces the administrative burden of conducting employee reviews, and allows line managers to create appraisals from any Web-connected workstation. The system is flexible and customizable to suit each organization's needs. It assists human resources professionals in managing the process by approving appraisal forms, monitoring their status, and sending automatic e-mail notifications to managers. Employees benefit from having 24/7 Web access to present and past performance plans, objectives, and appraisals.[20]

Computerized Performance Appraisal
www.successfactors.com

Technology has updated the appraisal process. New software programs enable employees to check their own performance against prescribed criteria.

FIGURE IO.6 One Page from a Typical Management Appraisal Form

MAJOR PERFORMANCE STRENGTHS/WEAKNESSES

Read the definitions of each management factor below and choose the ranking that most accurately describes the employee. If, after reading the definition, it is determined that the skill area was not demonstrated because of the nature of the employee's position, indicate as Non-Applicable (N/A). The evaluation on each of the management factors below should relate directly to the employee's actual performance on the job.

PLANNING SKILL – Degree to which incumbent:	Ranking Code	(CHECK ONE)	
– Assessed and established priorities of result areas.	5	Far exceeds requirements	
– Designed realistic short- and long-range plans.	4	Usually exceeds requirements	
– Formulated feasible timetables.	3	Fully meets requirements	
– Anticipated possible problems and obstacles toward reaching required results.	2	Usually meets requirements	
	1	Fails to meet requirements	

Comments:

_____

_____

_____

ORGANIZING SKILL – Degree to which incumbent:	Ranking Code	(CHECK ONE)	
– Grouped activities for optimal use of human and material resources in order to achieve goals.	5	Far exceeds requirements	
– Clearly defined responsibilities and authority limits of employees.	4	Usually exceeds requirements	
	3	Fully meets requirements	
– Minimized confusion and inefficiencies in work operations.	2	Usually meets requirements	
	1	Fails to meet requirements	

Comments:

_____

_____

_____

CONTROLLING SKILL – Degree to which incumbent:	Ranking Code	(CHECK ONE)	
– Established appropriate procedures to be kept informed of employee's work progress.	5	Far exceeds requirements	
	4	Usually exceeds requirements	
– Identified deviations in work goal progress.	3	Fully meets requirements	
– Adjusted to deviations in work to ensure that established goals were met.	2	Usually meets requirements	
	1	Fails to meet requirements	

Comments:

_____

_____

_____

Note: This is one page from a multipage form used to appraise managers.

PERFORMANCE APPRAISAL: PROBLEMS AND SOLUTIONS

Few of the things a manager does are fraught with more peril than appraising employees' performance. Employees in general tend to be overly optimistic about what their ratings will be, and also know that their raises, career progress, and peace of mind may well hinge on how they are rated. Thus, an honest appraisal inevitably involves an emotional component, which is particularly difficult when managers are not trained in appraisal interview skills. The result is often dishonest appraisals or avoidance of appraisals.[21]

Even more problematic, however, are the numerous structural problems that can cast serious doubt on just how fair the whole process is. Fortunately, research shows that action by management to implement a more acceptable performance appraisal system can increase employee trust in management.[22] A 2002 Conference Board of Canada survey found that while many Canadian businesses remain unhappy with their performance management programs, there have been significant improvements in quite a few organizations.[23] Some of the main appraisal problems and how to solve them, as well as several other pertinent appraisal issues, will now be reviewed.

Performance Measurement Resources
www.zigonperf.com/performance.htm

Validity and Reliability

Appraisal systems must be based on performance criteria that are valid for the position being rated, and reliable in that their application must produce consistent ratings for the same performance. Employee concerns about appraisal fairness are influenced by these characteristics of the performance appraisal system.

Validity   Criteria used in performance appraisal must be accurate, or valid, in order to produce useful results. Criteria must be (1) relevant to the job being appraised; (2) broad enough to cover all aspects of the job requirements; and (3) specific. For example, including a broad criterion such as "leadership" may not be relevant to non-management jobs, and may be so vague that it can be interpreted in many different ways.

Reliability   Effective appraisal criteria are precise enough to result in consistent measures of performance when applied across many employees by many different raters. This is difficult to achieve without quantifiable and measurable criteria.

Dealing with Rating Scale Problems

Seven main problems can undermine appraisal tools such as graphic rating scales: unclear standards, the halo effect, central tendency, leniency or strictness, appraisal bias, the recency effect, and the similar-to-me bias.

unclear performance standards
An appraisal scale that is too open to interpretation of traits and standards.

Unclear Standards   The problem of **unclear performance standards** is illustrated in **Table 10.2**. Although the graphic rating scale seems objective, it would probably result in unfair appraisals because the traits and degrees of merit are open to interpretation. For example, different supervisors would probably differently define "good" performance, "fair" performance, and so on. The same is true of traits such as "quality of work" or "creativity." There are several ways in which to rectify this problem. The best way is to develop and include descriptive phrases that define each trait, as in Figure 10.1 There, the

TABLE 10.2 A Graphic Rating Scale with Unclear Standards			
	EXCELLENT	**GOOD**	**FAIR**	**POOR**
Quality of work				
Quantity of work				
Creativity				
Integrity				

Note: For example, what exactly is meant by "good," "quantity of work," and so forth?

form specified what was meant by "outstanding," "very good," and "good" quality of work. This specificity results in appraisals that are more consistent and more easily explained.

halo effect In performance appraisal, the problem that occurs when a supervisor's rating of an employee on one trait biases the rating of that person on other traits.

Halo Effect   The **halo effect** means that the rating of an employee on one trait (such as "gets along with others") biases the way that the person is rated on other traits (such as "quantity of work"). This problem often occurs with employees who are especially friendly (or unfriendly) toward the supervisor. For example, an unfriendly employee will often be rated unsatisfactory for all traits rather than just for the trait "gets along well with others." Being aware of this problem is a major step toward avoiding it. Supervisory training can also alleviate the problem.[24]

central tendency A tendency to rate all employees in the middle of the scale.

Central Tendency   Many supervisors have a **central tendency** when filling in rating scales. For example, if the rating scale ranges from one to seven, they tend to avoid the highs (six and seven) and lows (one and two) and rate most of their employees between three and five. If a graphic rating scale is used, this central tendency could mean that all employees are simply rated "average." Such a restriction can distort the evaluations, making them less useful for promotion, salary, or counselling purposes. Ranking employees instead of using a graphic rating scale can avoid this central tendency problem, because all employees must be ranked and thus cannot all be rated average.

Leniency or Strictness   Some supervisors tend to rate all of their employees consistently high (or low), just as some instructors are notoriously high graders and others are not. Fear of interpersonal conflict is often the reason for leniency.[25] On the other hand, evaluators tend to give more weight to negative attributes than to positive ones.[26] This **strictness/leniency** problem is especially serious with graphic rating scales, since supervisors are not necessarily required to avoid giving all of their employees high (or low) ratings. On the other hand, when ranking employees, a manager is forced to distinguish between high and low performers. Thus, strictness/leniency is not a problem with the ranking or forced distribution approaches.

strictness/leniency The problem that occurs when a supervisor has a tendency to rate all employees either high or low.

appraisal bias The tendency to allow individual differences such as age, race, and sex to affect the appraisal ratings that these employees receive.

Appraisal Bias   Individual differences among ratees in terms of a wide variety of characteristics such as age, race, and sex can affect their ratings, often quite apart from each ratee's actual performance.[27] In fact, recent research shows that less than half of performance evaluation ratings are actually related to employee performance, and that most of the rating is based on idiosyncratic factors.[28] This is known as **appraisal bias**. Not only does this bias

Canadian Human Rights
Commission www.chrc-ccdp.ca

result in inaccurate feedback, but it is also illegal under human rights legislation. Although age-related bias is typically thought of as affecting older workers, one study found a negative relationship between age and performance evaluation for entry-level jobs in public accounting firms.[29] A related issue is described in the Workforce Diversity box.

Interestingly, the friendliness and likeability of an employee have been found to have little effect on that person's performance ratings.[30] However, an employee's previous performance can affect the evaluation of his or her current performance.[31] The actual error can take several forms. Sometimes the rater may systematically overestimate improvement by a poor worker or decline by a good worker, for instance. In some situations—especially when the change in behaviour is more gradual—the rater may simply be insensitive to improvement or decline. In any case, it is important to rate performance objectively. Factors such as previous performance, age, or race, should not be allowed to influence results.

recency effect The rating error that occurs when ratings are based on the employee's most recent performance rather than performance throughout the appraisal period.

similar-to-me bias The tendency to give higher performance ratings to employees who are perceived to be similar to the rater in some way.

Recency Effect
The **recency effect** occurs when ratings are based on the employee's most recent performance, whether good or bad. To the extent that this recent performance does not exemplify the employee's average performance over the appraisal period, the appraisal is biased.

Similar-to-Me Bias
If a supervisor tends to give higher ratings to employees with whom he or she has something in common, the **similar-to-me bias** is occurring. This bias can be discriminatory if it is based on similarity in race, gender, or other prohibited grounds.

How to Avoid Appraisal Problems

There are at least three ways in which to minimize the impact of appraisal problems such as bias and central tendency. First, raters must be familiar with the problems just discussed. Understanding the problem can help to prevent it.

WORKFORCE DIVERSITY

Gender and Performance Appraisal

Numerous studies have found that supervisors rate women lower than men for similar levels of performance, suggesting that for female employees, good performance alone may not lead to fair ratings. Two recent studies have provided further results regarding gender issues in performance appraisal.

One study investigated whether the gender composition of the supervisor–subordinate dyad affected ratings. Based on data from supervisor–subordinate dyads in four organizations, researchers found that both male and female supervisors exhibited a positive bias toward subordinates of the same sex and rated members of the same gender higher.[1]

Another study conducted among officers in the Israeli Defense Forces found that women's performance was rated lower than that of men when the women were token members of their units. However, the performance of women was rated higher than that of men when they constituted a higher proportion of officers in the unit.[2] Thus the number of women in a work group may have some bearing on performance evaluation results.

Both studies concluded that further investigation of gender differences in performance appraisal are needed to extend knowledge regarding this complex situation.

1. A. Varma and L.K. Stroh, "The Impact of Same-Sex LMX Dyads on Performance Evaluations," *Human Resource Management*, 40 (Winter 2001), pp. 309–20.

2. A. Pazy and I. Oron, "Sex Proportion and Performance Evaluation Among High-Ranking Military Officers," *Journal of Organizational Behavior*, 22 (2001), pp. 689–702.

Second, choose the right appraisal tool. Each tool, such as the graphic rating scale or critical incident method, has its own advantages and disadvantages. For example, the ranking method avoids central tendency but can cause ill feelings when employees' performances are in fact all "high" (see **Table 10.3**).

Third, training supervisors to eliminate rating errors such as halo, leniency, and central tendency can help them to avoid these problems.[32] In a typical training program, raters are shown a videotape of jobs being performed and are asked to rate the worker. Ratings made by each participant are then placed on a flip chart and the various errors (such as leniency and halo) are explained. For example, if a trainee rated all criteria (such as quality, quantity, and so on) about the same, the trainer might explain that a halo error had occurred. Typically, the trainer gives the correct rating and then illustrates the rating errors made by the participants.[33] According to one study, computer-assisted appraisal training improved managers' ability to conduct performance appraisal discussions with their employees.[34]

Rater training is no panacea for reducing rating errors or improving appraisal accuracy. In practice, several factors—including the extent to which pay is tied to performance ratings, union pressure, employee turnover, time constraints, and the need to justify ratings—may be more important than training. This means that improving appraisal accuracy calls not only for training but also for reducing outside factors, such as union pressure and time constraints.[35] It has also been found that employee reaction to current performance reviews is affected by prior appraisal feedback, which is beyond the control of the current manager.[36]

TABLE 10.3 Important Advantages and Disadvantages of Appraisal Tools

	ADVANTAGES	DISADVANTAGES
Graphic rating scale	Simple to use; provides a quantitative rating for each employee.	Standards may be unclear; halo effect, central tendency, leniency, and bias can also be problems.
Alternation ranking	Simple to use (but not as simple as graphic rating scale). Avoids central tendency and other problems of rating scales.	Can cause disagreements among employees and may be unfair if all employees are, in fact, excellent.
Forced distribution method	End up with a predetermined number of people in each group.	Appraisal results depend on th adequacy of the original choice of cutoff points.
Critical incident method	Helps specify what is "right" and "wrong" about the employee's performance; forces supervisor to evaluate employees on an ongoing basis.	Difficult to rate or rank employees relative to one another.
Behaviourally anchored rating scale	Provides behavioural "anchors." BARS is very accurate.	Difficult to develop.
Management by objectives	Tied to jointly agreed-upon performance objectives.	Time consuming.

Legal and Ethical Issues in Performance Appraisal

Ethics should be the bedrock of a performance appraisal. Accurate, well-documented performance records and performance appraisal feedback are necessary to avoid legal penalties and to defend against charges of bias based on grounds prohibited under human rights legislation, such as age, sex, and so on. As one commentator puts it:

> The overall objective of high-ethics performance reviews should be to provide an honest assessment of performance and to mutually develop a plan to improve the individual's effectiveness. That requires that we tell people where they stand and that we be straight with them.[37]

Ashland Canada Ltd., an automotive products marketing company in British Columbia, was fined $20 000 for dismissing a sales employee based on an "unacceptable" performance rating even though the employee had exceeded his sales goals. The British Columbia Supreme Court found that the performance rating was unwarranted and undeserved, and criticized Ashland's human resources department for a "reprehensible and substantial departure" from good faith dealings with the employee.[38] In another case, a worker in a government mental health facility was terminated for unsatisfactory performance after ten years of work with no performance evaluations and no disciplinary record. An adjudicator determined that the employer had failed to establish that her job performance was unsatisfactory, that she had not been given a chance to improve, and that the employer did not have just cause for termination. The employer was required to pay compensation in lieu of reinstatement.[39]

Guidelines for developing an effective appraisal process include the following:[40]

1. Conduct a job analysis to ascertain characteristics (such as "timely project completion") required for successful job performance. Use this information to create job-performance standards.

2. Incorporate these characteristics into a rating instrument. (The professional literature recommends rating instruments that are tied to specific job behaviours, that is, BARS.)

Hints to Ensure Legal Compliance

The best performance appraisal systems are those in which the supervisor or manager makes an ongoing effort to coach and monitor employees, instead of leaving evaluation to the last minute.

3. Make sure that definitive performance standards are provided to all raters and ratees.

4. Use clearly defined individual dimensions of job performance (like "quantity" or "quality") rather than undefined, global measures of job performance (like "overall performance").

5. When using a graphic rating scale, avoid abstract trait names (for example, "loyalty," "honesty") unless they can be defined in terms of observable behaviours.

6. Employ subjective supervisory ratings (essays, for instance) as only one component of the overall appraisal process.

7. Train supervisors to use the rating instrument properly. Give instructions on how to apply performance appraisal standards ("outstanding," and so on) when making judgments. Ensure that subjective standards are not subject to bias.[41]

8. Allow appraisers regular contact with the employee being evaluated.

9. Whenever possible, have more than one appraiser conduct the appraisal, and conduct all such appraisals independently. This process can help to cancel out individual errors and biases.

10. Utilize formal appeal mechanisms and a review of ratings by upper-level managers.

11. Document evaluations and reasons for any termination decision.

12. Where appropriate, provide corrective guidance to assist poor performers in improving their performance.

Who Should Do the Appraising?

Who should actually rate an employee's performance? Several options exist.

Appraisal by the Immediate Supervisor Supervisors' ratings are still the heart of most appraisal systems. Getting a supervisor's appraisal is relatively easy and also makes a great deal of sense. The supervisor should be—and usually is—in the best position to observe and evaluate the performance of employees reporting to him or her and is responsible for their performance.

Using Peer Appraisals The appraisal of an employee by his or her peers can be effective in predicting future management success. There is a high correlation between peer and supervisor ratings.[42] Peers have more opportunity to observe ratees, and to observe them at more revealing times than supervisors.[43] From a study of military officers, for example, we know that peer ratings were quite accurate in predicting which officers would be promoted and which would not.[44] In another study that involved more than 200 industrial managers, peer ratings were similarly useful in predicting who would be promoted.[45] One potential problem is *logrolling*; here, all the peers simply get together to rate each other highly.

With more firms using self-managing teams, peer or team appraisals are becoming more popular. One study found that peer ratings had an immediate positive impact on perceptions of open communication, motivation, group cohesion, and satisfaction, and these were not dependent on the ratio of positive to negative feedback.[46] Thus, peer appraisals would appear to have great

This food service supervisor is conducting a feedback session about an employee's performance during today's major banquet, to keep communications open and build employee commitment.

potential for work teams. At Ciba in Mississauga, Ontario, peer reviews were implemented as part of its transition to self-directed work teams. There was some uneasiness at first, but over time, a trusting relationship developed between co-workers.[47]

Rating Committees   Many employers use rating committees to evaluate employees. These committees are usually composed of the employee's immediate supervisor and three or four other supervisors. Using multiple raters can be advantageous. While there may be a discrepancy in the ratings made by individual supervisors, the composite ratings tend to be more reliable, fair, and valid.[48] Several raters can help cancel out problems like bias and the halo effect on the part of individual raters. Furthermore, when there are variations in raters' ratings, they usually stem from the fact that raters often observe different facets of an employee's performance; the appraisal ought to reflect these differences.[49] Even when a committee is not used, it is common to have the appraisal reviewed by the manager immediately above the one who makes the appraisal.

Self-Ratings   Employees' self-ratings of performance are also sometimes used (generally in conjunction with supervisors' ratings). Employees value the opportunity to participate in performance appraisal more for the opportunity to be heard than for the opportunity to influence the end result.[50] Nevertheless, the basic problem with self-ratings is that employees usually rate themselves higher than they are rated by supervisors or peers.[51] In one study, for example, it was found that when asked to rate their own job performance, 40 percent of the employees in jobs of all types placed themselves in the top 10 percent ("one of the best"), while virtually all remaining employees rated themselves either in the top 25 percent ("well above average"), or at least in the top 50 percent ("above average"). Usually no more than 1 percent or 2 percent will place themselves in a below-average category, and then almost invariably in the top below-average category. However, self-ratings have been found to correlate more highly with performance measures if employees know that this comparison will be made, and if they are instructed to compare themselves with others.[52]

Supervisors requesting self-appraisals should know that their appraisals and the self-appraisals may accentuate appraiser–appraisee differences, and rigidify positions.[53] Furthermore, even if self-appraisals are not formally requested, each employee will enter the performance review meeting with his or her own self-appraisal in mind, and this will usually be higher than the supervisor's rating.

Appraisal by Employees   Traditionally, supervisors feared that being appraised by their employees would undermine their management authority.[54] However, with today's flatter organizations and empowered workers, much managerial authority is a thing of the past, and employees are in a good position to observe managerial performance.[55] Thus, more firms today are letting employees anonymously evaluate their supervisors' performance, a process many call *upward feedback*.[56] When conducted throughout the firm, the process helps top managers to diagnose management styles, identify potential "people" problems, and take corrective action with individual managers as required. Such employee ratings are especially valuable when used for developmental rather than evaluative purposes.[57] Managers who receive feedback from employees who identify themselves view the upward appraisal process more positively than do managers who receive anonymous feedback; however, employees (not surprisingly) are more comfortable giving anonymous responses and those who have to identify themselves tend to provide inflated ratings.[58] Research comparing employee and peer ratings of managers found them to be comparable.[59]

How effective is upward feedback from reporting employees in terms of improving the supervisor's behaviour? Considerably effective, to judge from the research evidence. One study examined data for 92 managers who were rated by one or more reporting employees in each of four administrations of an upward feedback survey over 2.5 years.[60] Managers were based in North America, Europe, Asia/Pacific, the Caribbean, and Central/South America. The reporting employees were asked to rate themselves and their managers in surveys that consisted of 33 behavioural statements. The feedback to the managers also contained results from previous administrations of the survey so that they could track their performance over time.[61]

According to the researchers, "managers whose initial level of performance (defined as the average rating from reporting employees) was low improved between administrations one and two, and sustained this improvement two years later."[62] Interestingly, the results also suggest that it is not necessarily the specific feedback that caused the performance improvement, since low-performing managers seemed to improve over time even if they did not receive any feedback. Instead, learning what the critical supervisory behaviours were (as a result of themselves filling out the appraisal surveys), plus knowing that they might be appraised may have been enough to result in the improved supervisory behaviours. In a sense, therefore, it is the existence of the formal upward feedback program rather than the actual feedback itself that may signal and motivate supervisors to get their behaviours in line with what they should be.

360-Degree Appraisal

Many Canadian firms, including B.C. Gas Utility Ltd., Aetna Life Insurance, Scotiabank, Goodyear Canada, and Hallmark Cards, are now using what is called **360-degree appraisal**, or "*multisource feedback*."[63] Here, as shown in **Figure 10.7**, performance information is collected "all around" an employee, from his or her supervisors, employees reporting to the appraisee, peers, and internal or external customers.[64] This feedback was originally used only for training and development purposes, but has rapidly spread to use in the management of performance and pay.[65] The 360-degree approach supports the activities of performance feedback, coaching, leadership development, succession planning, and rewards and recognition.[66]

360-degree appraisal A performance appraisal technique that uses multiple raters including peers, employees reporting to the appraisee, supervisors, and customers.

There are a number of reasons for the rapid growth of 360-degree appraisal despite the significant investment of time required for it to function successfully. Today's flatter organizations mean a more open communication climate conducive to such an approach, and it fits closely with the goals of organizations committed to continuous learning. A multiple-rater system is also more meaningful in today's reality of complex jobs, with matrix and team reporting relationships. Further, the widespread lack of confidence in traditional performance appraisals conducted only by a supervisor, and the fear associated with such

FIGURE 10.7   360-Degree Performance Appraisals

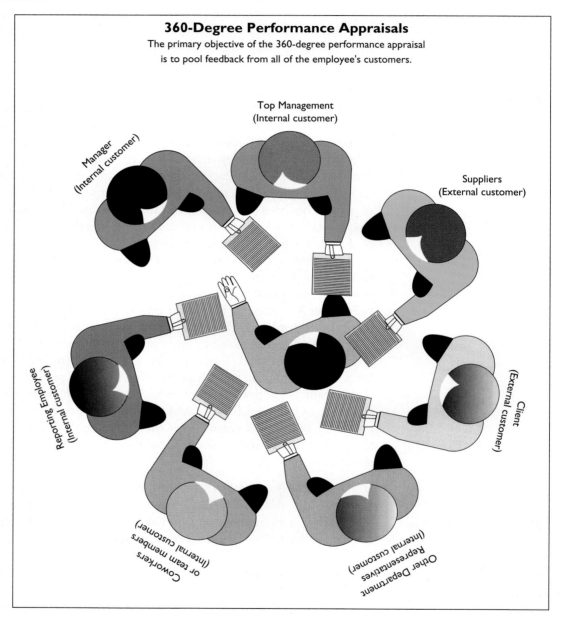

360-Degree Performance Appraisals
The primary objective of the 360-degree performance appraisal
is to pool feedback from all of the employee's customers.

Source: J.F. Milliman, R.A. Zawacki, C. Norman, L. Powell, and J. Kerksey, "Companies Evaluate Employee from All Perspectives," *Personnel Journal*, 73, no. 11 (November 1994), p. 100. Illustration by Tim Barker, copyright November 1994. Used with permission. All rights reserved.

appraisals on the part of both parties, have reduced the credibility of that approach.[67] A 360-degree appraisal can be perceived as a jury of peers, rather than the supervisor as a single judge, which enhances perceptions of fairness.[68]

Most 360-degree appraisal systems contain several common features. They are usually applied in a confidential and anonymous manner. Appropriate parties—peers, supervisors, employees reporting to the appraisee, and customers, for instance—complete survey questionnaires about an individual. The questionnaires must be custom-designed and linked to the organization's strategic direction, and its vision and values.[69] All of this information is then compiled into individualized reports. When the information is being used for self-development purposes only, the report is presented to the person being rated, who then meets with his or her own supervisor (and possibly with reporting employees) and information pertinent for the purpose of developing a self-improvement plan is shared.[70] When the information is being used for management of performance or pay, the information is also provided to the ratee's supervisor, and a supportive and facilitative process to follow up is required to ensure that the behavioural change required for performance improvement is made.[71]

Research Insight ▷

There is a limited amount of research data on the effectiveness of 360-degree feedback. Some organizations have abandoned it for appraisal purposes because of negative attitudes from employees and inflated ratings.[72] Some studies have found that the different raters often disagree on performance ratings.[73] A recent study by researchers at Concordia University in Montreal found that 360-degree feedback is popular among Canadian employers, despite problems such as the amount of time and effort involved, lack of trust in the system by employees, and lack of fit with strategic goals and other HR practices. The results showed that organizations that successfully implemented 360-degree feedback were the most clear on what their objectives in doing so were to begin with. Organizations that rely exclusively on external consultants to establish 360-degree appraisal have less success than those that are more sensitive to contextual factors such as the readiness of employees and the culture of the organization.[74]

Some experts suggest using 360-degree feedback for developmental purposes only.[75] In general, it is advisable to use 360-degree feedback for developmental/career-planning purposes initially, and then determine whether the organization is ready to use it for evaluative appraisal purposes. A pilot test in one department is often recommended. Once a decision to use 360-degree appraisal has been made, organizations should consider the following advice:[76]

An Ethical
Dilemma

Is it fair to factor in employee self-ratings in 360-degree performance appraisal, when we know that these appraisals tend to be inflated?

Tips **for the**
Front Line

- Have the performance criteria developed by a representative group that is familiar with each job.
- Be clear about who will have access to reports.
- Provide training for supervisors, raters, and ratees.
- Assure all raters that their comments will be kept anonymous.
- Plan to evaluate the 360-degree feedback system for fine-tuning.

Internet-based 360-degree feedback systems are now available, as described in the HR.Net box. One sample page of output from a feedback report is shown in **Figure 10.8.**

FIGURE I0.8   Summary of Internet-Based 360-Degree Feedback

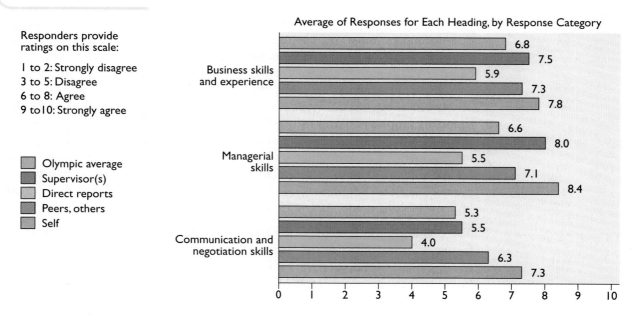

Responders provide ratings on this scale:

1 to 2: Strongly disagree
3 to 5: Disagree
6 to 8: Agree
9 to 10: Strongly agree

- Olympic average
- Supervisor(s)
- Direct reports
- Peers, others
- Self

Average of Responses for Each Heading, by Response Category

Business skills and experience: 6.8, 7.5, 5.9, 7.3, 7.8

Managerial skills: 6.6, 8.0, 5.5, 7.1, 8.4

Communication and negotiation skills: 5.3, 5.5, 4.0, 6.3, 7.3

Source: "Panoramic Feedback." Panometrics Inc. www.panoramicfeedback.com. April 2003. Reprinted with permission of Panometrics Inc.

HR.NET

Internet Addresses 360-Degree Feedback Concerns

Early 360-degree performance appraisal systems were paper-intensive and time consuming. But today's computer-based 360-degree feedback models require few technical skills on the part of the user, and the project organizer can set up a survey quickly from a personal computer. Respondents can reply via the Internet from work or home—a big advantage for people who don't have very much privacy at the office.

Immediately after the last reply has been entered, the organizer can print out a detailed, full-colour report. Until that point, it is a near-paperless process. There can be as little as a week between the initial preparation of the survey and the compilation of the final reports.

Users say they appreciate the simplicity of the set-up and the ease of customizing questionnaires on the Internet. Respondents find the surveys simple—they just click on some buttons, type in their comments, and the data is stored securely off-premises. Subjects react positively to the clear, attractive presentation of the reports.

Each provider has a different structure to their product. Here is what to look for in a computer-based 360-degree feedback program:

1. *Technical requirements.* Internet/intranet access is essential, but are paper questionnaires available for employees who are not online?

2. *Support.* Is the manual comprehensive? Is technical support free? Is a workbook provided for subjects?

3. *Customization.* Can you design your own survey?

4. *Simplicity.* Is set-up straightforward? Are sample competency lists provided?

5. *Speed.* Can you set up surveys at once, generating reports within a week or two?

6. *Cost.* Initial registration can range from $1500 to $2500. Does your supplier's fee include a free report? Will there be an annual renewal charge or training costs? Each assessment can cost from $20 to $300. Are there any other charges per respondent? Are quantity discounts available?

Source: Adapted from T. Bentley, "Internet Addresses 360-degree Feedback Concerns," *Canadian HR Reporter* (May 8, 2000), pp. G3, G15. Reproduced by permission of *Canadian HR Reporter*, Carswell, One Corporate Plaza, 2075 Kennedy Road, Scarborough, ON M1T 3V4 .

THE APPRAISAL INTERVIEW

appraisal interview An interview in which the supervisor and employee review the appraisal and make plans to remedy deficiencies and reinforce strengths.

An appraisal typically culminates in an **appraisal interview**. This is an interview in which the supervisor and employee review the appraisal and make plans to remedy deficiencies and reinforce strengths. This discussion is often avoided by supervisors and managers who have not been trained to provide constructive feedback and to deal with defensive employees. According to the International Society for Performance Improvement, 80 percent of problems with job performance are a result of insufficient feedback, where employees are unaware of performance standards and of the consequences of not meeting those standards.[77] One survey found that over 50 percent of respondents found their performance feedback to be insignificant.[78]

Types of Interviews

There are three basic types of appraisal interviews, each with its own objectives:[79]

Appraisal Interview Type	Appraisal Interview Objective
(1) Satisfactory performance—Promotable employee	(1) Make development plans
(2) Satisfactory performance—Unpromotable employee	(2) Maintain performance
(3) Unsatisfactory performance—Correctable	(3) Plan correction

If the employee is unsatisfactory and the situation uncorrectable, there is usually no need for any appraisal interview because the person's performance is not correctable anyway. The person's poor performance is either tolerated for now, or he or she is dismissed.

Satisfactory—Promotable   Here, the person's performance is satisfactory and there is a promotion ahead. This is the easiest of the three appraisal interviews. The objective is to discuss the person's career plans and to develop a specific action plan for the educational and professional development that the person needs in order to move to the next job.

Satisfactory—Not Promotable   This interview is for employees whose performance is satisfactory but for whom promotion is not possible. Perhaps there is no more room in the company. Some employees are also happy where they are and do not want a promotion.[80] The objective here is not to improve or develop the person, but to maintain satisfactory performance.

This is not easy. The best option is usually to find incentives that are important to the person and enough to maintain satisfactory performance. These might include extra time off, a small bonus, additional authority to handle a slightly enlarged job, and reinforcement, perhaps in the form of an occasional "Well done!"

Unsatisfactory—Correctable   When the person's performance is unsatisfactory but correctable, the interview objective is to lay out an action plan (as explained later) for correcting the unsatisfactory performance.

How to Prepare for the Appraisal Interview

Tips for the Front Line

There are three things to do in preparation for the interview.[81] First, assemble the data. Study the person's job description, compare the employee's performance to the standards, and review the files of the employee's previous appraisals. Next, prepare the employee. Give the employee at least a week's notice to review his or her work, read over the job description, analyze problems, and gather questions and comments. Finally, choose the time and place. Find a mutually agreeable time for the interview and allow a period long enough for the entire interview. Interviews with non-supervisory staff (like clerical workers and maintenance people) should take no more than an hour. Appraising management employees often takes two or three hours. Be sure that the interview is done in a private place where there will be no interruptions by phone calls or visitors.

How to Conduct the Interview

There are four things to keep in mind when conducting an appraisal interview:[82]

1. *Be direct and specific.* Talk in terms of objective work data. Use examples, such as absences, tardiness, quality records, inspection reports, scrap or waste, orders processed, productivity records, material used or consumed, timeliness of tasks or projects, control or reduction of costs, numbers of errors, costs compared to budgets, customers' comments, product returns, order processing time, inventory level and accuracy, accident reports, and so on.

2. *Do not get personal.* Do not say, "You are too slow in producing those reports." Instead, try to compare the person's performance to a standard ("These reports should normally be done within 10 days"). Similarly, do not compare the person's performance to that of other people ("He is quicker than you are").

3. *Encourage the person to talk.* Stop and listen to what the person is saying; ask open-ended questions, such as "What do you think we can do to improve the situation?" Use a phrase such as "Go on," or "Tell me more." Restate the person's last point as a question, such as, "You do not think that you can get the job done?"

4. *Develop an action plan.* Do not get personal, but do make sure that the person leaves knowing specifically what he or she is doing right and doing wrong. Give specific examples, make sure that the person understands, and get agreement before he or she leaves on how things will be improved, and by when. Develop an action plan showing steps and expected results, as in **Figure 10.9.**

Tips for the Front Line

How to Handle a Defensive Employee   Defences are a very important and familiar aspect of our lives. When a person is accused of poor performance, the first reaction will sometimes be denial. By denying the fault, the person avoids having to question his or her own competence. Others react to criticism with anger and aggression. This helps them to let off steam and postpones confronting the immediate problem until they are able to cope with it. Still others react to criticism by retreating into a shell.

Figure 10.9   Example of an Action Plan

ACTION PLAN

Date: May 18, 2004

For: John, Assistant Plant Manager
Problem: Parts inventory too high
Objective: Reduce plant parts inventory by 10% in June

Action Steps	When	Expected Results
Determine average monthly parts inventory	6/2	Establish a base from which to measure progress
Review ordering quantities and parts usage	6/15	Identify overstock items
Ship excess parts to regional warehouse and scrap obsolete parts	6/20	Clear stock space
Set new ordering quantities for all parts	6/25	Avoid future overstocking
Check records to measure where we are now	7/1	See how close we are to objective

Understanding and dealing with defensiveness is an important appraisal skill. In his book, *Effective Psychology for Managers*, psychologist Mortimer Feinberg suggests the following:

1. *Recognize that defensive behaviour is normal.*

2. *Never attack a person's defences.* Do not try to "explain someone to themselves" by saying things like, "You know the real reason you are using that excuse is that you cannot bear to be blamed for anything." Instead try to concentrate on the act itself ("sales are down") rather than on the person ("you are not selling enough").

3. *Postpone action.* Sometimes it is best to do nothing at all. People frequently react to sudden threats by instinctively hiding behind their "masks." Given sufficient time, however, a more rational reaction takes over.

4. *Recognize human limitations.* Do not expect to be able to solve every problem that comes up, especially the human ones. More important, remember that a supervisor should not try to be a psychologist. Offering employees understanding is one thing; trying to deal with deep psychological problems is another matter entirely.

Argumentative behaviour on the part of the manager during a performance appraisal meeting undermines the usefulness of the evaluation process.

How to Constructively Criticize an Employee's Performance
When criticism is required, it should be done in a manner that lets the person maintain his or her dignity and sense of

worth. Specifically, criticism should be provided constructively in private. Provide examples of critical incidents and specific suggestions of what could be done and why. Avoid a once-a-year "critical broadside" by giving feedback on a daily basis, so that at the formal review there are no surprises. Never say the person is "always" wrong (since no one is ever "always" wrong or right). Finally, criticism should be objective and free of any personal biases.

How to Ensure That the Appraisal Interview Leads to Improved Performance

It is important to clear up job-related problems by setting improvement goals and a schedule for achieving them. In one study, researchers found that whether or not employees expressed satisfaction with their appraisal interview depended mostly on three factors: not feeling threatened during the interview; having an opportunity to present their ideas and feelings and to influence the course of the interview; and having a helpful and constructive supervisor conduct the interview.[83]

However, it is not enough for employees to be satisfied with their appraisal interviews. The main objective is to get them to improve their subsequent performance. Here, researchers have found that clearing up job-related problems with the appraisee and setting measurable performance targets and a schedule for achieving them are the actions that consistently lead to improved performance.

How to Handle a Formal Written Warning

There will be times when an employee's performance is so poor that a formal written warning is required. Such written warnings serve two purposes: (1) they may serve to shake the employee out of his or her bad habits; and (2) they can help the manager to defend his or her rating of the employee, both to his or her boss and (if needed) to a court or Human Rights Commission.

Hints to Ensure Legal Compliance

Written warnings should identify the standards under which the employee is judged, make it clear that the employee was aware of the standard, specify any violation of the standard, indicate that the employee has had an opportunity to correct his or her behaviour, and specify what the employee must now do to correct his or her behaviour.

THE ROLE OF APPRAISALS IN MANAGING PERFORMANCE

Appraisals serve several purposes, including providing information upon which promotion and salary decisions are made. Increasingly, though, HR specialists are emphasizing appraisal's related role as a central player in performance management. It is therefore useful to close this chapter by looking more closely at appraisal's role as a component in a company's performance management system, specifically how appraisals can be used to better manage employee performance.

Should Appraisals Be Abolished?

Many experts feel that traditional appraisals do not help in managing performance and may actually backfire. They argue that most performance appraisal systems neither motivate employees nor guide their development.[84] Furthermore, "…they cause conflict between supervisors and employees and lead to dysfunctional behaviours."[85] The traits measured are often personal in nature and "...Who likes the idea of being evaluated on his or her: honesty, integrity, teamwork, compassion, cooperation [objectivity]...?"[86]

Similarly, proponents of quality management programs (including the late W. Edwards Deming) generally argue in favour of eliminating performance appraisals.[87] They believe that the organization is a system of interrelated parts and that an employee's performance is more a function of factors like training, communication, tools, and supervision than of his or her own motivation.[88] They also suggest that performance appraisals can have unanticipated consequences. Thus, employees might make themselves look better in terms of customer service by continually badgering customers to send in letters of support. Deming particularly argued against forced distribution appraisal systems because of their potential for undermining teamwork.[89]

Criticisms like these appear to be supported by surveys of how managers view appraisal systems. A 2002 Conference Board survey (see **Figure 10.10**) of the effectiveness of performance management systems found that only 5 percent of systems were considered "very effective." Twenty-one percent were rated as "requiring improvement," and 43 percent were "acceptable, but not effective."[90] There is little doubt that most appraisals are viewed with skepticism.

Yet, while these criticisms have merit, it is not practical to eliminate performance appraisals. Managers still need some way to review employees' work-related behaviour. In addition, although Deming reportedly hated performance reviews, "... he really did not offer any concrete solution to the problem or an alternative, other than just [to] pay everybody at the same salary."[91] The solution is to create instead performance appraisal systems that make it possible to manage performance in today's team-oriented and quality-oriented

> **AN ETHICAL**
> **DILEMMA**
>
> Is it ethical to use the forced distribution method, where we classify some employees as having low performance, when we know we do not continue to employ workers whose performance really is poor?

FIGURE **IO.IO** Effectiveness of Performance Management Systems

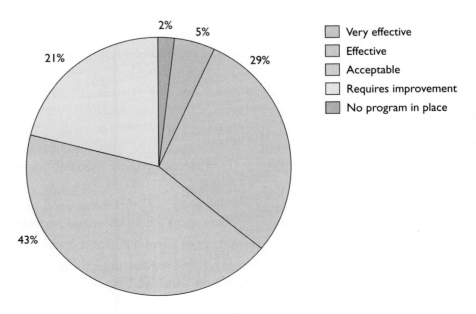

Source: Compensation Planning Outlook 2003. Reprinted by permission of The Conference Board of Canada, Ottawa.

environments. Creating more effective appraisals, as described in this chapter, is one way to do this. Others suggest also taking a quality-based approach, which is explained next.

Quality-Based Appraisals for Managing Performance

Quality management programs are organization-wide programs that integrate all functions and processes of the business such that all aspects—including design, planning, production, distribution, and field service—are aimed at maximizing customer satisfaction through continuous improvements.[92] Deming said that such programs are built on a number of principles, including ceasing dependence on inspection to achieve quality, aiming for continuous improvement, instituting extensive training on the job, driving out fear so that everyone may work effectively for the company, breaking down barriers between departments, eliminating work standards (quotas) on the factory floor, removing barriers that rob employees of their right to pride of workmanship (in particular, abolishing the annual merit rating and all forms of management by objectives), and instituting a vigorous program of education and self-improvement.[93]

Quality management principles like these can be applied to designing quality-based performance management systems. The aim of performance management in TQM-oriented companies is to establish systems that encourage employees to become committed partners in the tasks of boosting quality and performance. Employees here are not just "told what to do." Instead, they are relied upon to make suggestions, improve performance, and generally act like owners of the business. According to proponents, performance appraisals in TQM environments therefore do not force managers to give questionable feedback; instead, they facilitate open, job-related discussions between the supervisor and the employee.[94] The characteristics of such a system would include:

1. An appraisal scale that contains relatively few performance categories and avoids a forced distribution.[95]

2. Objective ways to measure results, avoiding subjective criteria such as teamwork and integrity.[96]

3. A determination about whether any performance deficiency is a result of (1) employee motivation, (2) inadequate training, or (3) factors (like poor supervision) that are outside the employee's control.

4. 360-degree feedback from a number of different sources, not just supervisors but internal and possibly external "customers" of the employee as well.[97]

5. Adequate "samples" of work behaviour: "regular observations of their staff members' work behaviours and performance."[98]

6. An atmosphere of partnership and constructive advice.[99]

7. A thorough analysis of key external and internal customers' needs and expectations on which to base performance appraisal standards. (For example, if accurately completing the sales slip is important for the accounting department, then the retail sales clerk should be appraised in part on this dimension).

Performance Evaluation

Based on the Customer Contact Strategy Forum, an association of senior executives involved in call centre management, "Maximizing the ROI in Human Resources," held May 18, 2002.

Separate systems should be devised for individual performance and for the efficiency and effectiveness of the team/program as a whole. In evaluating performance, the manager should avoid concentrating solely on the *quantity results* or *efficiency statistics*, which are often easier to compile and understand, therefore missing the picture of the *quality results* or *effectiveness statistics*.... [To counteract this problem, employers suggest that] employees are only entitled to receive their bonuses accumulated from quantity results after achieving a prescribed mark on the qual-

ity results. This can ensure optimal service quality in the figure- and deadline-driven environment.... [Managers are] warned to avoid misrepresenting or obscuring figures and results in the reports to senior management. Report everything as is, so that senior management knows the progress and experiments that are happening. This also makes it easier to request capital resources from senior management when need arises. Evaluation tools should be designed "to account for both success and failure," [participants at the session advised].... Results should trigger proper reward, discipline or development of the programs or individuals concerned....

Source: Excerpted with permission from the *Training and Development Guide Newsletter*, written by Anna Wong (No. 21, December 2001), published by and copyright CCH Canadian Limited, Toronto, Ontario.

CHAPTER *Review*

Summary

1 Performance management is a process encompassing all activities related to improving employee performance, productivity, and effectiveness. It includes goal setting, merit pay increases, training and development, career management, and disciplinary action. The foundation of performance management is the performance appraisal process. It is important to appraise performance effectively because appraisals provide the opportunity for managers and employees to review each employee's work performance, which provides information for making promotion and salary decisions, and an opportunity to review each employee's career plans. Before the appraisal, the expected performance should be clarified so that each employee knows what he or she should be striving for. Employees need feedback regarding how they are doing, and appraisal provides an opportunity to give them that feedback on a formal basis.

2 Graphic rating scales are simple to use and facilitate comparison of employees, but the perform-

ance standards are often unclear, and bias can be a problem. Alternation ranking is a simple method and avoids central tendency, but can be unfair if most employees are doing well. Paired comparison ensures that all employees are compared to each other, but can also be unfair if most employees are performing similarly. Narrative forms provide concrete information to the employee, but are time consuming and can be subjective. The forced distribution method ensures differentiation of performance ratings, but can be demotivating for employees classified as less than average. The critical incident method is very specific about the employee's strengths and weaknesses and forces the supervisor to evaluate employees on an ongoing basis, but makes it difficult to compare employees. BARS is very accurate, but is difficult and time consuming to develop. MBO ties performance ratings to jointly agreed-upon performance objectives, but is time consuming to administer.

3 Appraisal problems to beware of include unclear standards, the halo effect, central tendency, leniency or strictness, appraisal bias, the recency effect, and the similar-to-me bias.

4   The use of 360-degree feedback has grown rapidly. Performance information is collected from the individual being appraised, his or her supervisor, other employees reporting to the person being appraised, and customers. This approach supports the activities of performance appraisal, coaching, leadership development, succession planning, and employee rewards and recognition.

5   There are three types of appraisal interviews. When performance is unsatisfactory but correctable, the objective is to set out an action plan for correcting performance. For employees whose performance is satisfactory but for whom promotion is not possible, the objective is to maintain satisfactory performance. Finally, the satisfactory-and-promotable interview has the main objective of discussing the person's career plans and developing a specific action plan for the educational and professional development that the person needs in order to move on to the next job.

6   Appraisals should also ideally serve a performance management role by providing a concrete basis for an analysis of an employee's work-related performance. A quality-based approach is one way to achieve this goal. Characteristics of a quality-based approach include making the appraisal scale as broadly descriptive as possible so that it contains relatively few performance categories and avoids a forced distribution; measuring results objectively; specifically identifying if the performance deficiency is a result of motivation, training, or factors outside the employee's control; using 360-degree feedback; including adequate samples of work behaviour; addressing problems in an atmosphere of partnership and constructive advice; and basing performance standards on an analysis of key external and internal customers' needs and expectations.

Key Terms

alternation ranking method   *(p. 297)*
appraisal bias   *(p. 307)*
appraisal interview   *(p. 317)*
behaviourally anchored rating scale (BARS)   *(p. 300)*
central tendency   *(p. 307)*
critical incident method   *(p. 299)*
forced distribution method   *(p. 298)*
graphic rating scale   *(p. 296)*
halo effect   *(p. 307)*
management by objectives (MBO)   *(p. 303)*
paired comparison method   *(p. 298)*
performance management   *(p. 294)*
recency effect   *(p. 308)*
similar-to-me bias   *(p. 308)*
strictness/leniency   *(p. 307)*
360-degree appraisal   *(p. 313)*
unclear performance standards   *(p. 306)*

Review and Discussion Questions

1   Explain what is meant by the term "performance management."

2   Describe the three steps in appraising performance.

3   Explain how to ensure that the performance appraisal process is carried out ethically, and without violating human rights laws.

4   Discuss the pros and cons of using different potential raters to appraise a person's performance.

5   What are the four key factors in conducting an appraisal interview.

6   Explain how to handle a defensive employee in a performance appraisal interview.

CRITICAL *Thinking Questions*

1   Given the numerous problems with performance appraisal, and the negative consequences that often ensue, should performance appraisal be abolished?

2   How can the problem of inconsistency between managers who are rating workers be solved, or at least diminished? Make two or more suggestions.

APPLICATION *Exercises*

The Performance Appraisal

Jennifer and Pierre disagree over the importance of having performance appraisals. Pierre says it's quite clear whether any particular LearnInMotion.com employee is doing his or her job. It's obvious, for instance, if the salespeople are selling, if the Web designer is designing, if the Web surfer is surfing, and if the content management people are managing to get the customers' content up on the Web site in a timely fashion. Pierre's position, like that of many small-business managers, is that "we have 1000 higher-priority things to attend to" such as boosting sales and creating the calendar. And in any case, he says, the employees already get plenty of day-to-day feedback from him or Jennifer regarding what they're doing right and what they're doing wrong.

This informal feedback notwithstanding, Jennifer believes that a more formal appraisal approach is required. For one thing, they're approaching the end of the 90-day "introductory" period for many of these employees, and the owners need to make decisions about whether they should go or stay. And from a practical point of view, Jennifer just believes that sitting down and providing formal, written feedback is more likely to reinforce what employees are doing right, and to get them to modify what they may be doing wrong. "Maybe this is one reason we're not getting enough sales," she says. They've been debating this for about an hour. Now, they want you, their management consultants, to advise them on what to do. Here's what they want you to do for them.

Questions

1 Is Jennifer right about the need to evaluate the workers formally? Why or why not? If you think she's right, how do you explain away Pierre's arguments?

2 Develop a performance appraisal method for the salespeople, Web designer, or Web surfer. Please make sure to include any form you want the owners to use.

CASE INCIDENT *Objectives?*

It was performance appraisal time again and Hans Funderburk knew that he would receive a low evaluation this time. Janet Stevens, Hans's boss, opened the appraisal interview with this comment, "The sales department had a good increase this quarter. Also, departmental expenses are down a good bit. But we have nowhere near accomplished the ambitious goals you and I set last quarter."

"I know," said Hans. "I thought we were going to make it though. We would have, too, if we had received that big Sears order and if I could have gotten us on the Internet a little earlier in the quarter."

"I agree with you, Hans," said Janet. "Do you think we were just too ambitious or do you think there was some way we could have made the Sears sale and sped up the Web page design?"

"Yes," replied Hans, "we could have gotten the Sears order this quarter. I just made a couple of concessions to Sears and their purchasing manager tells me he can issue the order next week. The delay with the Internet was my responsibility; I thought I knew what I was doing, but it was a little more complicated than I expected."

The discussion continued for about 30 minutes longer. Hans discovered that Janet was going to mark him very high in all areas despite his failure to accomplish the goals they had set.

Prior to the meeting, Janet had planned to suggest that the unattained goals for last period be set as the new goals for the coming quarter. After she and Hans had discussed matters, however, they both decided to establish new, somewhat higher goals. As he was about to leave the meeting, Hans said, "Janet, I feel good about these objectives, but I don't believe we have more than a 50 percent chance of accomplishing them."

"I believe you can do it," replied Janet. "If you knew for sure, though, the goals wouldn't be high enough."

"I see what you mean," said Hans, as he left the office.

Questions

1 What was wrong or right with Janet's appraisal of Hans's performance?

2 Should the new objectives be higher or lower than they are? Explain

Source: R.W. Mondy, R.M. Noe, S.R. Premeaux, and R.A. Knowles, *Human Resource Management*, 2nd Canadian edition (Toronto, ON: Pearson Education, 2001), p. 254.

EXPERIENTIAL *Exercises*

1 Working individually or in groups, develop a graphic rating scale for a retail sales associate and a fast food restaurant manager.

2 Working individually or in groups, develop, over the period of a week, a set of critical incidents covering the classroom performance of one of your instructors.

Under 21 (Young Entrepreneurs)

Starting a small business isn't easy at any stage of a person's career. But how many of us would have the courage to attempt it right out of the gate, at the start of our careers? Well, two members of the next generation of entrepreneurs are taking it all in stride.

Evan Clifford is hip, urban, and 21 years old. He quit high school and started his own clothing design business. His first client was his former school, where he designed new physical education uniforms—ones that students actually wanted to wear. The school was so pleased that they ordered more uniforms. Then other schools placed orders. Evan has a retail store on trendy Queen Street West in Toronto, and has established a solid customer base. He exhibits a natural astuteness in financial management, as he tries to collect enough money at the time an order is placed to cover his costs.

Alexandra Hickey had a secure government job but didn't feel fulfilled. She made the decision to give it up, then took a chef's course and started her own business as a personal chef. She and Evan are examples of the recent boom of young entrepreneurs aged 15 to 24. There has been a 25 percent increase in young people starting their own companies. Many feel that the risks inherent in starting a business are no greater than the risks of a job in the corporate world.

This new breed of entrepreneur is not just about making money, however. They are giving back to the community; call it capitalism with a conscience. Alexandra cycles to her clients' homes in order to contribute to a cleaner environment. Evan Clifford works with a hip-hop artist to design a clothing line for disadvantaged youth, and distributes long distance phone cards to street youth at Christmastime so they can call someone close to them. Evan and Alexandra see contributions to the community as a part of business life and believe that small changes can make big differences.

Questions

1. Why do these young people feel it is just as risky in the corporate world as it is for entrepreneurs?

2. Is Evan Clifford just lucky, or does he have a natural flair for business?

3. Why does this group of individuals seem to have a conscience, when so many corporations today are accused of unethical and immoral behaviour?

Video Source: "Under 21 (Young Entrepreneurs)," *CBC Venture 856* (December 1, 2002).

Additional Resources: **www.youngentrepreneur.com; www.yea.ca**

CHAPTER **11**

Establishing Strategic Pay Plans

LEARNING OUTCOMES

After studying this chapter, you should be able to:

Discuss four basic factors determining pay rates.

Explain in detail each of the five basic steps in establishing pay rates.

Discuss skill/competency-based pay.

Describe the five basic elements of compensation for managers.

Define pay equity and *explain* its importance today.

BASIC ASPECTS OF TOTAL REWARDS

total rewards All forms of pay or compensation provided to employees and arising from their employment.

Canadian Payroll Association
www.payroll.ca

Total rewards refers to all forms of pay or other compensation provided to employees and arising from their employment.[1] For a typical employer, payroll is the largest budget item, making up approximately 50 percent of operating costs. Reward systems are now widely viewed as a strategic tool with which to improve performance and contribute to the achievement of an organization's strategic goals. Thus, total rewards is an important issue for both employees and employers.[2] In this millennium, organizations are adopting new thinking, new practices, and more strategic direction in total rewards, as they experience reductions in organizational hierarchy and the evolution of more flexible jobs. Three strategic approaches are emerging:[3]

- Paying the person for his or her skills and competencies, rather than on the basis of his or her job description.

- Rewarding excellence through pay for performance.

- Individualizing pay systems by providing flexibility and choice to an increasingly diverse workforce.

Two traditional components comprise total rewards. There are direct financial payments in the form of wages, salaries, incentives, commissions, and bonuses, and indirect payments in the form of financial benefits like employer-paid insurance and vacations. Increasing attention is now being given to a third component—the work experience.

In turn, there are essentially two bases for direct financial payments to employees: increments of time, and performance. Most employees are still paid primarily based on the time that they put in on the job. For example, blue-collar workers are usually paid hourly or daily wages. Some employees—executive, administrative, and professional—are salaried. They are compensated on the basis of a longer period of time (like a week, month, or year), rather than an hour or a day.

The second option is to pay for performance. Piecework is an example: it ties compensation directly to the amount of production (or number of "pieces") that the worker produces, and is popular as an incentive pay plan. For instance, a worker's hourly wage is divided by the standard number of units that he or she is expected to produce in one hour. Then, for each unit produced over and above this standard, the worker is paid an incentive. Salespeople's commissions are another example of compensation tied to output (in this case, sales).

In this chapter, we will explain how to formulate plans for paying employees a fixed wage or salary; succeeding chapters will cover financial incentives and bonuses, and employee benefits and services.

Psychologists know that people have many needs, of which only some can be satisfied directly with money. In some countries, cash is by far the most sought-after reward, as outlined in the Global HR box.

Other needs—for challenging work, affiliation, flexible hours, or career development, for instance—also motivate behaviour but can only be satisfied indirectly (if at all) by money.[4] As organizations face increasing pressure to win

GLOBAL HRM

Hong Kong and China: The Cash Mentality

In China and Hong Kong, cash is still the main motivator. In Hong Kong, many people have arrived there as refugees and do not have deep roots in the community. When combined with uncertainty and insecurity in the region, people tend to have a short-term perspective and a low level of trust, commitment, and confidence in the company they work for and the government. Money is important for daily living and also allows them to have autonomy and freedom. This refugee mentality fosters a cash mentality. Cash remains king in Hong Kong among all other compensation components.

In China, the "iron rice bowl" of lifetime employment regardless of performance is fading away. The massive influx of foreign investment, along with Western management philosophies and practices, has created major changes in compensation systems. Fixed wages are being replaced by market economy reward systems such as performance-based pay, paid vacations, and other benefits.

A survey of over 500 management and non-management employees in Hong Kong and senior and middle-level managers from 121 companies in China found that base salary was the most effective form of compensation for attracting and motivating employees. Clearly, cash increases feelings of security in the current era of uncertainty. Also, in the Chinese culture, adults are expected to be self-reliant, financially independent, and socially successful. Finally, people in metropolitan cities such as Hong Kong, and in developing countries, such as China, can be very materialistic, capitalistic, individualistic, and egoistic. Cash supports all these goals.

In the long term, Western research suggests that extrinsic rewards such as cash may undermine intrinsic motivation and create negative consequences on performance. Researchers will be tracking the long-term effects of the cash mentality on job turnover, life satisfaction, job satisfaction, and intrinsic motivation in China and Hong Kong.

Source: Adapted from R.K. Chiu, T. Li-Ping and V. Wai-Mei Luk, "Hong Kong and China: The Cash Mentality Revisited," *Compensation and Benefits Review*, May/June 2001, pp. 66–72. © 2001. Used with permission of Sage Publications, Inc.

Towers Perrin
www.towersperrin.com

the war for talent, it is important to keep the relative importance of pay in perspective. Two Canadian reports issued in 2001 indicated (1) that there is a persistent gap between what companies are offering employees and what the employees want, and (2) that employees care more about having good relationships and other intrinsic rewards from work than about pay and benefits. Specifically, employees want a better working environment, more fairness and respect, more support and recognition, and more honesty and commitment on the part of employers.[5]

A 2002 Canadian study by Towers Perrin consultants investigated the reasons behind employee retention and employee engagement (getting employees to invest their energy and deliver the kind of performance that produces results) based on four components of total rewards (pay, benefits, work environment, and learning and development). As shown in **Figure 11.1** and **Figure 11.2**, work environment and opportunities for learning and development are more important than pay and benefits in both cases. Career advancement opportunity was the key to retention, while senior management interest in employee well being is most important for engagement. Most of the factors driving retention and engagement were the same, but had different levels of importance in each case.[6]

FIGURE 11.1 Six Key Drivers of Employee Retention*

Pay	Benefits
③ Competitive base pay	⑤ Overall satisfaction with benefits needed in day-to-day life ⑥ Work/life balance

Learning and Development	Work Environment
① Career advancement opportunities ④ Challenging work	② Retaining employees with skills needed

*In Canada, there are only six factors with a statistically meaningful effect on retention.

Source: Working Today: Understanding What Drives Employment Engagement: The Towers Perrin 2003 Talent Report. © Towers Perrin, 2003, Toronto. Used with permission. All rights reserved.

FIGURE 11.2 Ten Key Drivers of Employee Engagement

Pay	Benefits

Learning and Development	Work Environment
② Challenging work ⑤ Career advancement opportunities ⑩ Manager helps me understand contribution to corporate financial success	① Senior management interest in employee well-being ③ Overall work environment ④ Input into decision making ⑥ Resources to get the job done ⑦ Senior management ensuring long-term success ⑧ Company reputation ⑨ Teamwork

Source: Working Today: Understanding What Drives Employment Engagement: The Towers Perrin 2003 Talent Report. © Towers Perrin, 2003, Toronto. Used with permission. All rights reserved.

Basic Considerations in Determining Pay Rates

Four basic considerations influence the formulation of any pay plan: legal requirements, union issues, compensation policy, and equity.

Legal Considerations in Compensation

There are a number of laws affecting compensation in Canada. These laws vary between the provinces and territories, and there are similar laws at the federal level that cover employees in interprovincial operations (including highway, rail, and air transportation, pipelines, telecommunications, banking, federal crown corporations, and others). The territory of Nunavut, created on April 1, 1999, was formerly part of the Northwest Territories, and the federal legislation that created Nunavut declared that the Northwest Territories' legislation would apply to Nunavut until it passed its own legislation. Federal government employees are covered under yet another law (the Public Service Staff Relations Act). Thus, HR managers must pay careful attention to which legislation affects their employees. Further, these laws are constantly changing, and require continual monitoring to ensure compliance. Legislation affecting compensation administration is discussed below.

Employment/Labour Standards Acts (Canada Labour Code)
These laws set minimum standards regarding pay, including minimum wage, maximum hours of work, overtime pay, paid vacation, paid statutory holidays, termination pay, record keeping of pay information, and more. There are variations in some of the minimum standards for students, trainees, domestics, nannies, seasonal agricultural workers, and others. Executive, administrative, and professional employees are generally exempt from the overtime pay requirements.

Pay Equity Acts
Pay equity legislation has been enacted in all Canadian jurisdictions other than the Northwest Territories and Nunavut. These laws apply to public-sector employees only, except in Ontario, Quebec, British Columbia, and the federal jurisdiction where the laws cover employees in both the public and private sectors. Pay equity laws were enacted to redress the historical undervaluation of "women's work" by providing equal pay for work of equal (or comparable) value performed by men and women. Employers are required to identify male- and female-dominated jobs, and then use a gender-neutral job evaluation system based on specific compensable factors (such as skill, effort, responsibility, and working conditions) in order to evaluate the jobs. Pay for female-dominated jobs that are equivalent in value to male-dominated jobs must be increased to the pay level of the comparable male-dominated job.

Human Rights Acts
All jurisdictions have enacted human rights laws to protect Canadians from discrimination on a number of grounds in employment and other areas. These grounds differ somewhat between jurisdictions, but most prohibit discrimination on the basis of age, sex, colour, race/ancestry/place of origin, religion/creed, marital/family status, and physical or mental disability.

Canada/Quebec Pension Plan
All employees and their employers must contribute to the Canada/Quebec Pension Plan throughout the employee's

working lifetime. Pension benefits based on the employee's average earnings are paid during retirement. Details of these and other benefits are provided in Chapter 13.

Other Legislation Affecting Compensation   Each of the provinces and territories, as well as the federal government, has its own *workers' compensation laws*. The objective of these laws is to provide a prompt, sure, and reasonable income to victims of work-related accidents and illnesses. The *Employment Insurance Act* is aimed at protecting Canadian workers from total economic destitution in the event of employment termination that is beyond their control. Employers and employees both contribute to the benefits provided by this act. This act also provides up to 45 weeks of compensation for workers unemployed through no fault of their own (depending on the unemployment rate in the claimant's region, and other factors). Maternity and parental leave benefits are also provided under the Employment Insurance Act.

Association of Workers'
Compensation Boards of Canada
www.awcbc.org

Union Influences on Compensation Decisions

Unions and labour relations laws also influence how pay plans are designed. Historically, wage rates have been the main issue in collective bargaining. However, other issues—including time off with pay, income security (for those in industries with periodic layoffs), cost-of-living adjustment, and pensions—are also important.[7]

The Canada Labour Relations Board and similar bodies in each of the provinces and territories oversee employer practices and ensure that employees are treated in accordance with their legal rights. Their decisions underscore the need to involve union officials in developing the compensation package.

Work stoppages may reflect employee dissatisfaction with pay plans and other forms of compensation such as benefits.

Union Attitudes toward Compensation Decisions
Several classic studies shed light on union attitudes toward compensation plans and on commonly held union fears.[8] Many union leaders fear that any system (like a time and motion study) used to evaluate the worth of a job can become a tool for management malpractice. They tend to believe that no one can judge the relative value of jobs better than the workers themselves. In addition, they believe that management's usual method of using several compensable factors (like "degree of responsibility") to evaluate and rank the worth of jobs can be a manipulative device for restricting or lowering the pay of workers. One implication seems to be that the best way in which to gain the cooperation of union members in evaluating the worth of jobs is to get their active involvement in this process and in assigning fair rates of pay to these jobs. On the other hand, management has to ensure that its prerogatives—such as the right to use the appropriate job evaluation technique to assess the relative worth of jobs—are not surrendered.

Compensation Policies

An employer's compensation policies provide important compensation guidelines regarding the wages and benefits that it pays. One consideration is whether the organization wants to be a leader or a follower regarding pay. Other important policies include the basis for salary increases, promotion and demotion policies, overtime pay policy, and policies regarding probationary pay and leaves for military service, jury duty, and holidays. Compensation policies are usually written by the HR or compensation manager in conjunction with senior management.[9]

Economists have proposed what they call segmented labour markets theories to emphasize that there are high- and low-wage employers.[10] Some employers choose to be leaders regarding pay, and some followers, and as a result one U.S. study noted that "a worker who moves from a low- to a high-wage employer within a U.S. city can usually increase his or her pay by over 50 percent with no change in job description." Compensation policies have also been found to have measurable effects on workplace attitudes and behaviours.[11] Not surprisingly, workers receiving high wages are "...less likely to quit, are more satisfied with their pay, and report that they work harder than they have to."[12]

Equity and Its Impact on Pay Rates

A crucial factor in determining pay rates is the need for equity, specifically *external equity* and *internal equity*. Externally, pay must compare favourably with rates in other organizations, or an employer will find it hard to attract and retain qualified employees. Pay rates must also be equitable internally: each employee should view his or her pay as equitable given other pay rates in the organization. Some firms administer surveys to learn employees' perceptions and feelings about their compensation system. Questions typically addressed include these:

- "How satisfied are you with your pay?"
- "What criteria were used for your recent pay increase?"
- "What factors do you believe are used when your pay is determined?"[13]

Research by Hay Group compensation consultants has indicated that employee perceptions of fairness are one of the three key conditions for effective reward programs.[14]

ESTABLISHING PAY RATES

In practice, the process of establishing pay rates, while ensuring external and internal equity, requires five steps:

1. Determine the worth of each job within the organization through job evaluation (to ensure internal equity).

2. Group similar jobs into pay grades.

3. Conduct a salary survey of what other employers are paying for comparable jobs (to help ensure external equity).

4. Price each pay grade by using wage curves.

5. Fine-tune pay rates.

Each of these steps will now be explained in turn.

Step 1. Determine the Worth of Each Job: Job Evaluation

job evaluation A systematic comparison to determine the relative worth of jobs within a firm.

Purpose of Job Evaluation   **Job evaluation** is aimed at determining a job's relative worth. It is a formal and systematic comparison of jobs within a firm to determine the worth of one job relative to another, and eventually results in a job hierarchy. The basic procedure is to compare the content of jobs in relation to one another, for example, in terms of their effort, responsibility, skills, and working conditions. Once the compensation specialist knows (based on salary survey data and compensation policies) how to price key **benchmark jobs**, and can use job evaluation to determine the worth of all the other jobs in the firm relative to these key jobs, he or she is well on the way to being able to pay all jobs in the organization equitably.

benchmark job A job commonly found in other organizations and/or critical to the firm's operations that is used to anchor the employer's pay scale and acts as a reference point around which other jobs are arranged in order of relative worth.

Compensable Factors   There are two basic approaches for comparing jobs. The first is an intuitive approach. It might be decided that one job is "more important" or "of greater value or worth" than another without digging any deeper into why in terms of specific job-related factors.

As an alternative, jobs can be compared by focusing on certain basic factors that they have in common. In compensation management, these basic factors are called **compensable factors**. They are the factors that determine the definition of job content, establish how the jobs compare to each other, and set the compensation paid for each job.

compensable factor A fundamental, compensable element of a job, such as skill, effort, responsibility, and working conditions.

Some employers develop their own compensable factors. However, most use factors that have been popularized by packaged job evaluation systems or by legislation. For example, most of the pay equity acts in Canada focus on four compensable factors: *skill, effort, responsibility,* and *working conditions*. As another example, the job evaluation method popularized by the Hay consulting firm focuses on four compensable factors: *know-how, problem solving, accountability,* and *working conditions*. Often, different job evaluation systems are used for different departments, employee groups, or business units.

Identifying compensable factors plays a pivotal role in job evaluation. All jobs in each employee group, department, or business unit are evaluated *using the same compensable factors*. An employer thus evaluates the same elemental components for each job within the work group, and is then better able to compare jobs—for example, in terms of the degree of skill, effort, responsibility, and working conditions present in each.[15]

Planning and Preparation for Job Evaluation   Job evaluation is largely a judgmental process, and one that demands close cooperation between supervisors, compensation specialists, and the employees and their union representatives. The main steps involved include identifying the need for the program, getting cooperation, and then choosing an evaluation committee; the latter then carries out the actual job evaluation.[16]

Identifying the need for job evaluation should not be difficult. Employee dissatisfaction with the inequities of paying employees different rates for similar jobs may be reflected in high turnover, work stoppages, or arguments.[17] Managers may express uneasiness about an existing informal way of assigning pay rates to jobs, accurately sensing that a more systematic means of assigning pay rates would be more equitable and make it easier to justify compensation practices.

Next, since employees may fear that a systematic evaluation of their jobs may actually reduce their wage rates, *getting employee cooperation* for the evaluation is a second important step. Employees can be told that as a result of the impending job evaluation program, wage rate decisions will no longer be made just by management whim, job evaluation will provide a mechanism for considering the complaints that they have been expressing, and no present employee's rate will be adversely affected as a result of the job evaluation.[18]

The next step is *choosing a job evaluation committee*. There are two reasons for doing so. First, the committee should bring to bear the points of view of several people who are familiar with the jobs in question, each of whom may have a different perspective regarding the nature of the jobs. Second, assuming that the committee is composed at least partly of employees, the committee approach can help to ensure greater acceptance by employees of the job evaluation results.

The group usually consists of about five members, most of whom are employees. The presence of managers can be viewed with suspicion by employees, but an HR specialist can usually be justified on the grounds that he or she has a more impartial image than other managers and can provide expert assistance in the job evaluation. The HR specialist may serve in a nonvoting capacity. Union representation is also desirable and may be required by pay equity legislation. In some cases, the union's position is that it is accepting job evaluation only as an initial decision technique and is reserving the right to appeal the final pay decisions through grievance or bargaining channels.

The evaluation committee performs three main functions. First, the members usually identify 10 or 15 key benchmark jobs. These will be the first jobs to be evaluated and will serve as the anchors or benchmarks against which the relative importance or value of all other jobs can be compared. Next, the committee may select compensable factors (although the human resources department will usually choose these as part of the process of determining the specific job evaluation technique to be used). Finally, the committee turns to its most important function—actually evaluating the worth of each job. For this, the committee will probably use one of the following job evaluation methods: the ranking method, the job classification method, the point method, or the factor comparison method.

Ranking Method of Job Evaluation

The simplest job evaluation method ranks each job relative to all other jobs, usually based on some overall factor like "job difficulty." There are several steps in the job **ranking method**:

1. *Obtain job information.* Job analysis is the first step. Job descriptions for each job are prepared, and these are usually the basis on which the rankings are made.

2. *Group the jobs to be rated.* It is often not practical to make a single ranking of all jobs in an organization. The more usual procedure is to rank jobs by department or in "clusters" (such as factory or clerical workers). This eliminates the need for having to compare directly, say, factory jobs and clerical jobs.

3. *Select compensable factors.* In the ranking method, it is common to use just one factor (such as job difficulty) and to rank jobs on the basis of the whole job. Regardless of the number of factors chosen, it is advisable to explain the definition of the factor(s) to the evaluators carefully so that they evaluate the jobs consistently.

Tips for the Front Line

ranking method The simplest method of job evaluation, which involves ranking each job relative to all other jobs, usually based on overall difficulty.

4. *Rank jobs.* Next the jobs are ranked. The simplest way is to give each rater a set of index cards, each of which contains a brief description of a job. These cards are then ranked from lowest to highest. Some managers use an "alternation ranking method" for making the procedure more accurate. Here, the committee members arrange the cards by first choosing the highest and the lowest, then the next highest and next lowest, and so forth until all of the cards have been ranked. A job ranking is illustrated in **Table 11.1**. Jobs in this small health facility are ranked from cleaner up to director of operations. The corresponding pay scales are shown on the right.

5. *Combine ratings.* It is usual for several raters to rank the jobs independently. Then the rating committee (or employer) can simply average the rankings.

Pros and Cons This is the simplest job evaluation method, as well as the easiest to explain, and it usually takes less time to accomplish than other methods. Some of its drawbacks derive more from how it is used than from the method itself. For example, there is a tendency to rely too heavily on "guesstimates." Similarly, ranking provides no yardstick for measuring the value of one job relative to another. For example, the highest-ranked job may in fact be five times "more valuable" than the second highest-ranked job, but with the ranking system one only knows that one job ranks higher than the other. Ranking is often used by small organizations that are unable to afford the time or expense of developing a more elaborate system.

Another potential drawback relates to legal compliance requirements. The "whole job" approach to ranking, just described, cannot be used by employers covered by pay equity legislation. Instead, separate rankings must be completed for each of four compensable factors (skill, effort, responsibility, and working conditions), and judgment used to combine the results. Furthermore, pay equity legislation requires that jobs be ranked across clusters or departments, not separately.

Classification (or Grading) Evaluation Method The **classification (or grading) method** is a simple, widely used method in which jobs are categorized into groups. The groups are called **classes** if they contain similar jobs, or **grades** if they contain jobs that are similar in difficulty but otherwise different.

classification (or grading) method
A method for categorizing jobs into groups.

classes Groups of jobs based on a set of rules for each class, such as amount of independent judgment, skill, physical effort, and so forth. Classes usually contain similar jobs—such as all secretaries.

grades Groups of jobs based on a set of rules for each grade, where jobs are similar in difficulty but otherwise different. Grades often contain dissimilar jobs, such as secretaries, mechanics, and fire-fighters.

Hints to Ensure Legal Compliance

TABLE 11.1 Job Ranking by Olympia Health Care

Ranking Order	Annual Pay Scale
1. Director of Operations	$60 000
2. Head nurse	54 000
3. Accountant	50 000
4. Nurse	40 000
5. Cook	26 000
6. Nurse's aide	24 000
7. Cleaner	20 000

After ranking, it becomes possible to slot additional jobs between those already ranked and to assign an appropriate wage rate.

The federal government's UT (University Teaching) job group is an example of a job class because it contains similar jobs, involving teaching, research, and consulting. On the other hand, the AV (Audit, Commerce, and Purchasing) job group is an example of a job grade because it contains dissimilar jobs, involving auditing, economic development consulting, and purchasing.

There are several ways in which to categorize jobs. One is to draw up class descriptions (similar to job descriptions), and place jobs into classes based on their correspondence to these descriptions. Another is to draw up a set of classifying rules for each class (for instance, the amount of independent judgment, skill, physical effort, and so on, that the class of jobs requires). Then the jobs are categorized according to these rules.

grade/group description Written description of the level of compensable factors required by jobs in each grade. Used to combine similar jobs into grades or classes.

The usual procedure is to choose compensable factors and then develop class or grade descriptions that describe each class in terms of amount or level of compensable factor(s) in jobs. The federal government's classification system, for example, employs different compensable factors for various job groups. Based on these compensable factors, a **grade/group description** (like that in **Figure 11.3**) is written. Then, the evaluation committee reviews all job descriptions and slots each job into its appropriate class or grade.

FIGURE **11.3**   Example of Group Definition in the Federal Government

GROUP DEFINITION—AUDIT, COMMERCE AND PURCHASING (AV)

The Audit, Commerce and Purchasing Group comprises positions that are primarily involved in the application of a comprehensive knowledge of generally accepted accounting principles and auditing standards to the planning, delivery and management of external audit programs; the planning, delivery and management of economic development policies, programs, services and other activities; and the planning, development, delivery and management of policies, programs, systems or other activities dealing with purchasing and supply in the Public Service.

Inclusions

Notwithstanding the generality of the foregoing, for greater certainty, it includes positions that have, as their primary purpose, responsibility for one or more of the following activities:

1. audit—the application of a comprehensive knowledge of generally accepted accounting principles and auditing standards to the auditing of the accounts and financial records of individuals, businesses, non-profit organizations, or provincial or municipal governments to determine their accuracy and reasonableness, to establish or verify costs, or to confirm the compliance of transactions with the provisions of statutes, regulations, agreements or contracts;

2. commerce—the planning, development, delivery and management of economic development policies, programs, services and other activities designed to promote the establishment, growth and improvement of industry, commerce and export trade; and the regulation of trade and commerce including:

   (a) the promotion of the more efficient use of resources in particular geographic areas through the conduct of studies and investigations and the implementation of programs and projects for this purpose;

   (b) the promotion of the development and use of modern industrial technologies;

(c) the promotion of economic development directed towards groups, regions, industries or the Canadian economy as a whole;

(d) the promotion of the export of Canadian goods and services, including the tourist industry;

(e) the expansion of Canada's share of global trade by providing advice to Canadian companies, trade associations or other agencies of government, by safeguarding and promoting Canadian trading relationships, or by bringing the export aspects to bear in Canada's aid and financing programs;

(f) the study and assessment of developments in international trade and trading arrangements, and their implications for the Canadian economy;

(g) the administration and enforcement of competition legislation and legislation relating to restraints of trade; and

(h) the examination of records and reports of registered insurance, trust and loan companies, money lenders and small loan companies, fraternal benefit societies and co-operative credit associations to ensure their solvency and compliance with legislation and regulations controlling their operations;

3. purchasing—the planning, development, delivery and management of purchasing and supply notices, programs, services and other activities to meet the needs of Public Service departments and agencies including one or more subsidiary activities, such as in the areas of asset management and disposal, contracting, procurement of goods and services, inventory management, cataloguing, warehousing or traffic management;

4. the provision of advice in the above fields; and

5. the leadership of any of the above activities.

Exclusions

Positions excluded from the Audit, Commerce and Purchasing Group are those whose primary purpose is included in the definition of any other group or those in which one or more of the following activities is of primary importance:

1. the evaluation of actuarial liabilities and the determination of premiums and contributions in respect of insurance, annuity and pension plans;

2. the planning and conduct of internal financial audits;

3. the planning, development, delivery or management of the internal comprehensive audit of the operations of Public Service departments and agencies;

4. the application of a comprehensive knowledge of economics, sociology or statistics to the conduct of economic, socio-economic and sociological research, studies, forecasts and surveys;

5. the planning, development, delivery and promotion of Canada's diplomatic, commercial, human rights, cultural, promotional and international development policies and interests in other countries and in international organizations through the career rotational foreign service;

6. the design of trade exhibits or displays or activities dealing with the explanation, promotion and publication of federal government programs, policies and services;

7. the writing of specifications and technical descriptions that require the continuing application of technical knowledge; and

8. the receipt, storage, handling and issue of items held in stores.

Source: Audit, Commerce and Purchasing Occupational Group Definition, http://www.tbs-sct.gc.ca/
Classification/OrgGroupStruct/OGDe.asp, Treasury Board Secretariat, 2003. Reproduced with the permission of the Minister of Public Works and Government Service, 2004.

Pros and Cons The job classification method has several advantages. The main one is that most employers usually end up classifying jobs anyway, regardless of the job evaluation method that they use. They do this to avoid having to work with and price an unmanageable number of jobs; with the job classification method, all jobs are already grouped into several classes. The disadvantages are that it is difficult to write the class or grade descriptions, and considerable judgment is required in applying them. Yet many employers (including the Canadian government) use this method with success.

Point Method of Job Evaluation

point method The job evaluation method in which a number of compensable factors are identified and then the degree to which each of these factors is present in the job is determined and an overall point value is calculated.

The **point method** (also known as the point factor method) is widely used. It requires identifying several compensable factors, each with several degrees. A different number of points is then assigned for each degree of each factor. Next the extent/degree to which each of these factors is present in the job is evaluated. Once the degree to which each factor is present in the job is determined, all that remains is to add up the corresponding number of points for each factor and arrive at an overall point value for the job.[19] Here are the steps:

1. *Determine clusters of jobs to be evaluated.* Because jobs vary widely by department, the same point-rating plan is not usually used for all jobs in the organization. Therefore, the first step is usually to cluster jobs, for example, into shop jobs, non-union jobs, and so forth. Then, the committee will generally develop a point plan for one group or cluster at a time.

2. *Collect job information.* Perform a job analysis and write job descriptions and job specifications.

3. *Select and define compensable factors.* Select compensable factors, like mental requirements, physical requirements, or skill. Each compensable factor must be carefully defined. This is done in order to ensure that the evaluation committee members will apply the factors with consistency. Examples of definitions are presented in **Figure 11.4.** The definitions are often drawn up or obtained by a human resources specialist.

FIGURE 11.4 Example of One Factor in a Point Factor System

Responsibility for the Safety of Others:

this subfactor measures the degree of care required to prevent injury or harm to others

Level Description of Characteristics and Measures

1   Little degree of care required to prevent injury or harm to others
   e.g., closing of file drawers.

2   Some degree of care required to prevent injury or harm to others
   e.g., posting of "wet floor" signs; stacking supplies.

3   Considerable degree of care required to prevent injury or harm to others
   e.g., use of heavy equipment; yard duty.

4   High degree of care required to prevent injury or harm to others
   e.g., use of hazardous materials; administering medication; driving school bus.

Source: Adapted from the *CUPE Gender-Neutral Job Evaluation Plan.* Jointly developed by the Medicine Hat School District #76 and CUPE Local 829. Revised February 2000, p. 21. Used with permission.

4. *Define factor degrees.* Next, definitions of several degrees for each factor are prepared so that raters may judge the amount or degree of a factor existing in a job. Thus, the factor "complexity" might have six degrees, ranging from "job is repetitive" through "requires initiative." (Definitions for each degree are shown in Figure 11.4.) The number of degrees usually does not exceed five or six, and the actual number depends mostly on judgment. Thus, if all employees work either in a quiet, air-conditioned office or in a noisy, hot factory, then two degrees would probably suffice for the factor "working conditions." It is not necessary to have the same number of degrees for each factor, and degrees should be limited to the number necessary to distinguish among jobs.

5. *Determine factor weights.* The next step is to decide how much weight (or how many total points) to assign to each factor. This is important because, for each cluster of jobs, some factors are bound to be more important than others. Thus, for executives, the "mental requirements" factor would carry far more weight than would "physical requirements." The opposite might be true of factory jobs.

   The relative values or weights to be assigned to each of the factors can now be determined. Assigning factor weights is generally done by the evaluation committee. The committee members carefully study factor and degree definitions and then determine the relative value of the factors for the cluster of jobs under consideration. For example,

Skill	30 percent
Effort	30 percent
Responsibility	30 percent
Working Conditions	<u>10 percent</u>
	100 percent

6. *Assign point values to factors and degrees.* Now, points are assigned to each factor, as in **Table 11.2**. For example, suppose that it is decided to use a total number of 500 points in the point plan. Then, since the factor "skill" had a weight of 30 percent, it would be assigned a total of 30 percent × 500 = 150 points.

   Thus, it was decided to assign 150 points to the skill factor. This automatically means that the highest degree for the skill factor would also carry 150 points. Then, points are assigned to the other degrees for this factor, in equal amounts from the lowest to the highest degree. This step is repeated for each factor (as in Table 11.2).

TABLE 11.2 Evaluation Points Assigned to Factors and Degrees

Factor	First-Degree Points	Second-Degree Points	Third-Degree Points	Fourth-Degree Points	Fifth-Degree Points
Skill	30	60	90	120	150
Effort	30	60	90	120	150
Responsibility	30	60	90	120	150
Working Conditions	10	20	30	40	50

7. *Write the job evaluation manual.* Developing a point plan like this usually culminates in a job evaluation manual. This simply consolidates the factor and degree definitions and point values into one convenient manual.

8. *Rate the jobs.* Once the manual is complete, the actual evaluations can begin. Raters (usually the committee) use the manual to evaluate jobs. Each job, based on its job description and job specification, is evaluated factor by factor to determine the number of points that should be assigned to it. First, committee members determine the degree (first degree, second degree, and so on) to which each factor is present in the job. Then, they note the corresponding points (see Table 11.2) that were previously assigned to each of these degrees (in Step 6 above). Finally, they add up the points for all factors, arriving at a total point value for the job. Raters generally start with rating key jobs and obtain consensus on these, and then they rate the rest of the jobs in the cluster.

Pros and Cons   Point systems have their advantages, as their wide use suggests. They involve a quantitative technique that is easily explained to and used by employees. On the other hand, it can be difficult and time consuming to develop a point plan and to effectively train the job evaluation user group. This is one reason that many organizations opt for a plan developed and marketed by a consulting firm. In fact, the availability of a number of ready-made plans probably accounts in part for the wide use of point plans in job evaluation.

factor comparison method A method of ranking jobs according to a variety of skill and difficulty factors, adding these rankings to arrive at an overall numerical rating for each given job, and then incorporating wage rates.

Factor Comparison Job Evaluation Method

The **factor comparison method** is the most complex job evaluation method. It is actually a refinement of the ranking method. Each benchmark job is ranked several times—once for each compensable factor chosen. For example, jobs might be ranked first in terms of the factor "skill." Then they are ranked according to their "mental requirements." Next they are ranked according to their "responsibility," and so forth. Then the wage rate for each job is distributed by factor, and a job-comparison scale is constructed, as shown in **Table 11.3**. The scale is then used by slotting all the other jobs to be evaluated, factor by factor, into the job-comparison scale.

Pros and Cons   This method has two main advantages: first, it is an accurate, systematic method. Second, jobs are compared to other jobs to determine a relative value. Thus, it enables the determination of how much more of each compensable factor is required in one job versus all the others. This type of calibration is not possible with the ranking or classification methods. Complexity is probably the most serious disadvantage of the factor comparison method.

Research
Insight

A study assessing the reliability of four job evaluation methods—ranking, classification, factor comparison, and point—found that ratings from the point method and the job classification method were most consistent, taking overall job evaluation ratings and individual job ratings into account.[20]

The job evaluation step often takes the longest amount of time. Once it has been completed, the next step is to group similar jobs into pay grades.

Step 2. Group Similar Jobs Into Pay Grades

If the committee used the ranking, point, or factor comparison methods, it could assign pay rates to each individual job. For a larger employer, however, such a

TABLE 11.3 Factor Comparison Scale

$	Mental Requirements	Physical Requirements	Skill Requirements	Responsibility	Working Conditions
.25	. . . . .	. . . . .	. . . . .	. . . . .	Data Entry Clerk
.30	. . . . .	. . . . .	. . . . .	. . . . .	Security Guard
.40					
.50	. . . . .	. . . . .	. . . . .	. . . . .	Crane Operator
.60					
.70					
.75					
.80					
.90	. . . . .	. . . . .	. . . . .	. . . . .	Nurse
1.00	. . . . .	Crane Operator	. . . . .	. . . . .	Welder
1.10	. . . . .	. . . . .	Security Guard		
1.20					
1.30					
1.40					
1.50	Data Entry Clerk	. . . . .	. . . . .	Data Entry Clerk	
1.60					
1.70	Security Guard	Security Guard			
1.80					
1.90					
2.00	Crane Operater	Data Entry Clerk	Data Entry Clerk	Crane Operator	
2.25	. . . . .	. . . . .	Crane Operator		
2.40	. . . . .	. . . . .	. . . . .	Security Guard	
2.50					
2.80					
3.00	Welder	Nurse	Welder	Welder	
3.20					
3.40					
3.50	. . . . .	Welder			
3.80					
4.00	Nurse	. . . . .	Nurse	Nurse	
4.20					
4.40					
4.60					
4.80					

pay plan would be difficult to administer, since there might be different pay rates for hundreds or even thousands of jobs. Even in smaller organizations, there is a tendency to try to simplify wage and salary structures as much as possible. Therefore, the committee will probably want to group similar jobs (in terms of their ranking or number of points, for instance) into grades for pay purposes. Then, instead of having to deal with hundreds of pay rates, it might only have to focus on, say, 10 or 12.

pay grade A pay grade comprises jobs of approximately equal value.

A **pay grade** comprises jobs of approximately equal value or importance as determined by job evaluation. If the point method was used, the pay grade consists of jobs falling within a range of points. If the ranking plan was used, the grade consists of all jobs that fall within two or three ranks. If the classification system was used, then the jobs are already categorized into classes or grades. If the factor comparison method was used, the grade consists of a specified range of pay rates. Ten to 16 grades per logical grouping such as factory jobs, non-union jobs, and so on, are common in large organizations. The next step is to obtain information on market pay rates by conducting a wage/salary survey.

Step 3. Conduct a Wage/Salary Survey

Compensation or **wage/salary surveys** play a central role in the pricing of jobs. Virtually every employer therefore conducts such surveys for pricing one or more jobs.[21]

An employer may use wage/salary surveys in three ways. First, survey data are used to price benchmark jobs that serve as reference points, which are used to anchor the employer's pay scale and around which its other jobs are then slotted based on their relative worth to the firm. Second, an increasing number of positions are being priced directly in the marketplace (rather than relative to the firm's benchmark jobs), based on a formal or informal survey of what similar firms are paying for comparable jobs.[22] As a result of the current shift away from long-term employment, compensation is increasingly shaped by the market wage and less by how it fits into the hierarchy of jobs in one organization. Finally, surveys also collect data on benefits like insurance, sick leave, and vacation time, and so provide a basis on which to make decisions regarding employee benefits.

There are many ways to conduct a salary survey, including:

- informal communication with other employers
- reviewing newspaper and Internet job ads
- surveying employment agencies
- buying commercial or professional surveys
- reviewing online compensation surveys
- conducting formal questionnaire-type surveys with other employers.

Data from the Hay consulting group indicate that large organizations participate in an average of 11 compensation surveys, and use information from seven of them to administer their own compensation practices.[23]

Upward bias can be a problem regardless of the type of compensation survey.[24] At least one compensation expert argues that the way in which most surveys are constructed, interpreted, and used leads almost invariably to a situation in which firms set higher wages than they otherwise might. For example, "Companies like to compare themselves against well-regarded, high-paying, and high-performing companies," so that baseline salaries tend to be biased upward.[25] Similarly, "Companies that sponsor surveys often do so with an implicit (albeit unstated) objective: to show the company [is now] paying either competitively or somewhat below the market, so as to justify positive corrective action."[26] For these and similar reasons, it is probably wise to review survey results with a skeptical eye and to acknowledge that upward bias may exist and should perhaps be adjusted for.

Whatever the source of the survey, the data must be carefully assessed for accuracy before they are used to make compensation decisions. Problems can arise when the organization's job descriptions only partially match the descriptions contained in the survey, the survey data were collected several months prior to the time of use, the participants in the survey do not represent the appropriate labour market for the jobs being matched, and so on.[27]

Formal and Informal Surveys by the Employer   Most employers rely heavily on formal or informal surveys of what other employers are paying.[28] Informal telephone surveys are good for collecting data on a relatively small number of easily identified and quickly recognized jobs, such as when a bank's HR director wants to determine the salary at which a newly opened customer service representative's job should be advertised. Informal discussions among human resources specialists at regular professional association meetings are other occasions for informal salary surveys. Some employers use formal questionnaire surveys to collect compensation information from other employers, including things like number of employees, overtime policies, starting salaries, and paid vacations.

Commercial, Professional, and Government Salary Surveys   Many employers also rely on surveys published by various commercial firms, professional associations, or government agencies. For example, Statistics Canada provides monthly data on earnings by geographic area, by industry, and by occupation. **Table 11.4** provides an example of earnings data by industry and occupation.

TABLE 11.4 Weekly Wages by Industry and Occupation 2001–2002

		Weekly wage	
		2001	2002
		$	
Total Industry		**634.30**	**650.10**
	Agriculture	421.85	432.34
	Forestry, fishing mining oil, and gas	927.27	985.73
	Utilities	960.97	1 003.87
	Construction	753.74	769.66
	Manufacturing	717.66	731.94
	Trade	471.55	477.65
	Transportation and warehousing	708.15	725.18
	Finance, insurance, real estate and leasing	703.88	731.36
	Professional, scientific and technical services	834.76	856.55
	Management, administrative and other support	470.00	481.59
	Educational services	733.29	762.04
	Health care and social assistance	593.40	618.62
	Information, culture and recreation	639.98	617.97
	Accommodation and food services	303.52	305.22
	Other services	525.59	533.30
	Public administration	787.48	816.39
Occupation	Management	1 072.05	1 117.25
	Business, finance and administrative	591.53	613.15
	Natural and applied sciences	962.40	979.79
	Health	661.34	688.95
	Social science, education, government service and religion	807.08	834.49
	Art, culture, recreation and sport	568.22	579.47
	Sales and service	391.98	395.63
	Trades, transport and equipment operators	710.00	721.72
	Occupations unique to primary industry	617.71	620.44
	Processing, manufacturing and utilities	613.64	621.02

Source: Adapted from the Statistics Canada publication "Perspectives on Labour and Income," Catalogue No. 75-001, Spring 2003, p. 94.

The Toronto Board of Trade conducts five compensation surveys annually, covering executive; middle-management; professional, supervisory, and sales; information technology; and administrative and support positions. In all, the surveys include information from small, medium, and large employers in the Greater Toronto Area, for over 250 positions. A separate survey of employee benefits and employment practices is also conducted.

Private consulting and/or executive recruiting companies like Watson Wyatt, Mercer Human Resources Consulting, and Hewitt Associates annually publish data covering the compensation of senior and middle managers and members of boards of directors. Professional organizations like the Certified General Accountants Association and Professional Engineers Ontario conduct surveys of compensation practices among members of their associations, as shown in **Figure 11.5**.

FIGURE 11.5   Compensation Survey

If you are a **full-time wage earner** as of April 1, 2003, please complete the entire questionnaire. **If not**, please answer only the first six questions in order to complete the questionnaire. **Self-employed members** should only complete as far as Question #10.

1. Demographics
(Optional)
Sex   ☐¹ M   ☐² F
Age _____ Years (on April 1, 2003)

2. Year of Bachelor Degree
or degree accepted as requirement for registration (i.e.

_____
(year)

☐   *(Check this box & leave year blank if you entered the profession by exam route)*

3. Engineering Field/Discipline
(Check 1 box only)
☐¹ Aeronautical & aerospace
☐² Biomedical, biological
☐³ Chemical
☐⁴ Civil
☐⁵ Computer, systems
☐⁶ Electrical, electronics
☐⁷ Environmental
☐⁸ Geological, geotechnical
☐⁹ Mechanical, industrial
☐¹⁰ Metallurgical, materials, mining
☐¹¹ Nuclear
☐¹² Systems Design
☐¹³ Other (please specify _____

4. Highest Degree Obtained
(Check 1 box only)
☐¹ BASc, BEng or equivalent
☐² MASc, MEng
☐³ PhD (Engineering)
☐⁴ MBA
☐⁵ Other (please specify) _____

5. Occupational Status
☐¹ Employed full-time [(min. 30hrs/wk), (permanent salary)]
☐² Employed full-time [(min. 30hrs/wk), (contract, temporary)]
☐³ Self-employed full-time (owner, principal)
☐⁴ Part-time employee (contract or permanent)
☐⁵ Unemployed
☐⁶ Retired
☐⁷ Student
☐⁸ Other (please specify) _____

6. Region
(Current work location)
☐¹ I work in Canada
If in Canada, please provide the first three digits of your Postal Code:
☐² ☐³ ☐⁴
☐⁵ I work outside Canada (Postal Code not required)

7. Income
(From principal source of employment)
Basic annual salary as of April 1, 2003 $ _____
Other cash income received in the last 12 months as follows:
Cash bonus $ _____
Profit sharing $ _____
Commission $ _____
Overtime (On-call & shift premiums) $ _____
Consulting fees $ _____
Other (please specify) $ _____
(exclude deferred profit sharing, car allowances, fringe benefits)
Total Income $ _____

8. Work Category
☐¹ Largely or entirely engineering
☐² Not purely engineering but associated with, or job requirement that you be an engineer
☐³ In no way associated with engineering

9. Principal Function
(Check 1 box only)
☐¹ General management
☐² Engineering management

☐³ Administration (finance, personnel, public relations)
☐⁴ Computer services/systems
☐⁵ Research & development
☐⁶ Planning
☐⁷ Marketing/sales
☐⁸ Production engineering
☐⁹ Project engineering
☐¹⁰ Instrumentation/control
☐¹¹ Maintenance engineering
☐¹² Design
☐¹³ Quality assurance
☐¹⁴ Teaching (university)
☐¹⁵ Teaching (other)
☐¹⁶ Environmental/pollution
☐¹⁷ Health & Safety
☐¹⁸ Regulatory/standards
☐¹⁹ Consulting
☐²⁰ Other engineering (please specify) _____
☐²¹ Other non-engineering (please specify) _____

10. Industry Sector

(Check 1 box only)

Manufacturing
☐¹ Chemical & pharmaceutical
☐² Heavy electrical
☐³ Electronics, electrical products
☐⁴ Machinery (except electrical)
☐⁵ Metals
☐⁶ Petroleum products
☐⁷ Pulp & paper, wood products
☐⁸ Aerospace & aircraft products
☐⁹ Food, beverages, tobacco
☐¹⁰ Transportation equipment (except aircraft)
☐¹¹ Plastics & rubber
☐¹² Other manufacturing (please specify) _____

Non-Manufacturing
☐¹³ Construction
☐¹⁴ Consulting engineer
☐¹⁵ Consulting, other
☐¹⁶ Mining
☐¹⁷ Electrical utilities
☐¹⁸ Utilities, other
☐¹⁹ Communications services
☐²⁰ Transportation services
☐²¹ Petroleum
☐²² Data processing
☐²³ Computer systems development
☐²⁴ Other (services, trade, business, research, professional associations, etc.) _____

Educational & Government (excludes crown corporations)
☐²⁵ Federal government
☐²⁶ Provincial government
☐²⁷ Municipal government
☐²⁸ Educational institutions

Instruction: *Self-employed members—do not complete questions 11 to 15.*

11. Responsibility Level

(Use the classification guide presented on the last page if you are unsure of your level)

☐¹ A   ☐⁵ E
☐² B   ☐⁶ F
☐³ C   ☐⁷ F+

☐⁴ D

12. Size of Employer Organization

(In Canada)
☐¹ 2–25 employees
☐² 26–100 employees
☐³ 101–500 employees
☐⁴ more than 500 employees

13. Length of Time with Current Employer

_____ Years _____ Months employed with current organization

14. Benefits and Working Conditions

(Provided by employer)

Benefit	Yes	No
Pension	☐¹	☐²
Group life	☐¹	☐²
Hospitalization	☐¹	☐²
Drug Plan	☐¹	☐²
Dental Plan	☐¹	☐²
Vision care	☐¹	☐²
Long-term disability	☐¹	☐²

Overtime
Are you eligible for paid overtime?
        Yes ☐¹   No ☐²
If Yes, at what rate?
☐¹ Straight pay
☐² Greater than straight pay
☐³ Credit toward time off
☐⁴ Combination of above

Working Week
Base work week (max. 40 hrs.) _____ (# of hours)
Actual work week _____ (# of hours)

Vacation
_____ (# of weeks)

Collective Agreement
Are your salary and working conditions part of a collective agreement?
        Yes ☐¹   No ☐²

15. Hiring and Professional Development

Does your employer plan to hire engineers this year?
        Yes ☐¹   No ☐²   Don't Know ☐³
Does your employer reimburse you for professional development costs (e.g., seminars, courses, etc.)?
        Yes ☐¹   No ☐²
If Yes, limit of reimbursement _____ ($/yr.)

Thank your for your participation!

Please go to www2.researchdimensions.com/engineersurvey to complete this survey on-line or return it by mail postmarked no later than **April 21, 2003** to:

Research Dimensions
30 Soudan Ave., 6th floor
Toronto, ON M4S 1V6

You may also fax your completed survey to 1-800-582-7559. Please direct any questions to Research Dimensions at 1-800-663-2973. Engineers who complete the survey in our secure on-line site will be entered into a draw to win a **HP Digital Camera!** Please check www.ospe.onca. for details.

Source: Excerpt from the 2003 Membership Salary Survey Questionnaire. Used with permission of the Ontario Society of Professional Engineers.

Monster.ca Salary Centre
salary.monster.ca

wage curve A graphic description
of the relationship between the
value of the job and the average
wage paid for this job.

An Ethical
Dilemma
What should employers
do when there is a short-
age of a certain type of
skills and they cannot
attract any workers
unless they pay a market
rate above the maximum
of their salary range for
that job? How should
other jobs in the same
salary range be paid?

For some jobs, salaries are determined directly based on formal or informal salary surveys. In most cases, though, surveys are used to price benchmark jobs, around which other jobs are then slotted based on their relative worth, as determined through job evaluation. Now all of the information necessary to move to the next step—constructing wage curves—has been obtained.

Step 4. Price Each Pay Grade—Wage Curves

The next step is to assign pay rates to each of the pay grades. (Of course, if jobs were not grouped into pay grades, individual pay rates would have to be assigned to each job.) Assigning pay rates to each pay grade (or to each job) is usually accomplished with a **wage curve**.

The wage curve graphically depicts the pay rates currently being paid for jobs in each pay grade, relative to the points or rankings assigned to each job or grade by the job evaluation committee. An example of a wage curve is presented in **Figure 11.6.** Note that pay rates are shown on the vertical axis, while the pay grades (in terms of points) are shown along the horizontal axis. The purpose of the wage curve is to show the relationship between (1) the value of the job as determined by one of the job evaluation methods and (2) the current average pay rates for each job or grade.

The pay rates on the graph are traditionally those now paid by the organization. If there is reason to believe that the present pay rates are substantially out of step with the prevailing market pay rates for these jobs, then benchmark jobs within each pay grade are chosen and priced via a compensation survey. These new market-based pay rates are then used to plot a new wage curve.

There are several steps in pricing jobs with a wage curve using grades. First, *find the average pay for each pay grade,* since each of the pay grades consists of several jobs. Next, *plot the pay rates* for each pay grade, as was done in Figure

Figure 11.6   Plotting a Wage Curve

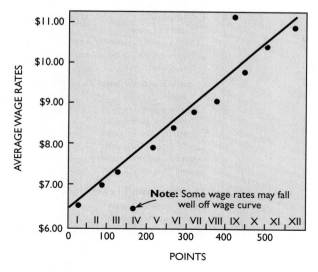

Note: The average pay rate for jobs in each grade (Grade I, Grade II, Grade III, etc.) are plotted, and the wage curve is fitted to the resulting points.

11.6. Then fit a line (called a *wage line*) through the points just plotted. This can be done either freehand or by using a statistical method known as regression analysis. Finally, *price jobs*. Wages along the wage line are the target wages or salary rates for the jobs in each pay grade. If the current rates being paid for any of the jobs or grades fall well above or well below the wage line, that rate may be "out of line"; raises or a pay freeze for that job may be in order. The next step, then, is to fine-tune the pay rates.

Step 5. Fine-Tune Pay Rates

Fine-tuning involves correcting out-of-line rates and (usually) developing rate ranges.

Developing Rate Ranges

rate ranges A series of steps or levels within a pay grade, usually based upon years of service.

Most employers do not just pay one rate for all jobs in a particular pay grade. Instead, they develop **rate ranges** for each grade so that there might, for instance, be ten levels or "steps" and ten corresponding pay rates within each pay grade. This approach is illustrated in **Table 11.5**, which shows the pay rates and levels for some of the federal government pay grades. As of the time of this pay schedule, for instance, employees in positions that were classified in grade AU-3 could be paid annual salaries between $58 415 and $69 575, depending on the level at which they were hired into the grade, the amount of time they were in the grade, and their merit increases (if any). Another way to depict the rate ranges for each grade is with a wage structure, as in **Figure 11.7**. The wage structure graphically depicts the range of pay rates (in this case, per hour) to be paid for each grade.

There are several benefits to using rate ranges for each pay grade. First, the employer can take a more flexible stance with respect to the labour market. For example, it makes it easier to attract experienced, higher-paid employees into a pay grade where the starting salary for the lowest step may be too low to attract such experienced people. Rate ranges also allow employers to provide for performance differences between employees within the same grade or between those with differing seniority. As in Figure 11.7, most employers structure their rate ranges to overlap a bit so that an employee with greater experience or seniority may earn more than an entry-level person in the next higher pay grade.

TABLE 11.5 Federal Government Pay Schedules AU-3 to AU-5*

| | RATE LEVELS WITHIN GRADE | | | | | |
GRADE	1	2	3	4	5	6
AU-3	58 415	60 813	63 089	65 253	67 413	69 575
AU-4	66 623	68 603	71 086	73 527	75 974	78 420
AU-5	73 833	76 312	78 797	81 283	83 766	86 249

*Salary scales apply for the duration of the collective agreement (December 19, 2001 to June 21, 2003).

Source: Treasury Board of Canada Secretariat, *Agreement Between the Treasury Board and the Professional Institute of the Public Service of Canada—Audit, Commerce and Purchasing*, Appendix A: Auditing (AU) Annual Rates of Pay, www.tbs-sct.gc.ca/pubs_pol/hrpubs/coll_agre/av2_e.asp#_Toc535911661. Reproduced with the permission of the Minister of Public Works and Government Services Canada, 2003.

FIGURE 11.7   Wage Structure

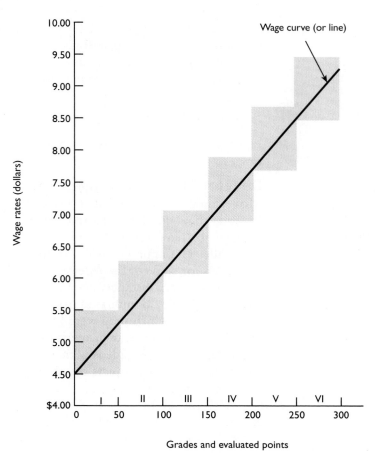

The rate range is usually built around the wage line or curve. Some employers allow the rate range for each grade to become wider for the higher pay ranges, reflecting the greater demands and performance variability inherent in these more complex jobs.

Broadbanding

broadbanding Reducing the number of salary grades and ranges into just a few wide levels or "bands," each of which then contains a relatively wide range of jobs and salary levels.

The trend today is for employers to reduce their salary grades and ranges from ten or more down to three to five, a process that is called **broadbanding**. Broadbanding means collapsing salary grades and ranges into just a few wide levels or "bands," each of which then contains a relatively wide range of jobs and salary levels.

Broadbanding a pay system involves several steps. First, the number of bands is decided upon and each is assigned a salary range. The bands usually have wide salary ranges and also overlap substantially. As a result, there is much more flexibility to move employees from job to job within bands and less need to "promote" them to new grades just to get them higher salaries.

The bands are then typically subdivided into either specific jobs or skill levels (see **Figure 11.8**). For example, a band may consist of a number of jobs each assigned a market value. More often, bands are subdivided into several skill levels. Ontario Hydro used three skill levels for its executive group: developmental, mature, and expert.[29] With this approach, workers are not paid above market value just for doing a job well or for having seniority. Instead, they must increase their competencies such as skills, knowledge, and abilities.[30]

Broadbanding's basic advantage is that it injects greater flexibility into employee compensation.[31] Broadbanding is especially sensible where firms flatten their hierarchies and organize around self-managing teams. The new, broad salary bands can include both supervisors and those reporting to them, and can also facilitate moving employees slightly up or down along the pay scale without accompanying promotional raises or demotional pay cuts.

Broadbanding also facilitates the sorts of less specialized, boundaryless jobs and organizations being embraced by many firms like General Electric Canada Inc. Less specialization and more participation in cross-departmental processes generally mean enlarged duties or capabilities and more possibilities for alternative career tracks; broader, more inclusive salary bands facilitate this. One expert argues that traditional quantitative evaluation plans actually reward unadaptability.[32] The argument here is that being slotted into a job that is highly routine as defined by a compensable factor such as "know-how" is unlikely to encourage job incumbents to think independently or be flexible. Instead, the tendency may be for workers to concentrate on the specific, routine jobs to which they are assigned and for which they are rewarded.

General Electric Canada Inc. and Ontario Hydro are two organizations that have broadbanded their pay scales. GE Canada was able to restructure non-union salaried employees into just six broad compensation bands: two for the executive level and four for non-union salaried employees. Ontario Hydro initially applied

FIGURE 11.8   Broadbanding

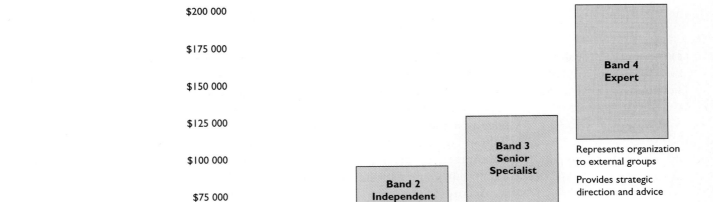

Source: H. Risher, "Planning a 'Next Generation' Salary System," *Compensation and Benefits Review,* November/December 2002, p. 16. © 2002. Reprinted with permission of Sage Publications, Inc.

broadbanding at the executive level, and is now working toward applying broadbanding at other levels.[33]

Correcting Out-of-Line Rates

The actual wage rate for a job may fall well off the wage line or well outside the rate range for its grade, as shown in Figure 11.7. This means that the average pay for that job is currently too high or too low, relative to other jobs in the firm. If a point falls well below the line, a pay raise for the job may be required. If the plot falls well above the wage line, pay cuts or a pay freeze may be required.

Underpaid employees should have their wages raised to the minimum of the rate range for their pay grade, assuming that the organization wants to retain the employees and has the funds. This can be done either immediately or in one or two steps.

Pay rates of overpaid employees are often called **red circle**, flagged, or over-rates, and there are several ways to cope with this problem. One is to freeze the rate paid to employees in this grade until general salary increases bring the other jobs into line with it. A second alternative is to transfer or promote some or all of the employees involved to jobs for which they can legitimately be paid their current pay rates. The third alternative is to freeze the rate for six months, during which time attempts are made to transfer or promote the overpaid employees. If this is not possible, then the rate at which these employees are paid is cut to the maximum in the pay range for their grade.

red circle pay rate A rate of pay that is above the pay range maximum.

Current Trends in Compensation

Skill/competency-based pay and customized job evaluation are two important current trends in compensation. They will give us a glimpse into the future of compensation management.

Skill/Competency-Based Pay

competencies Individual skills, knowledge, and behaviours that are critical to successful individual or corporate performance.

Competencies are individual skills, knowledge, and behaviours that are critical to successful individual or corporate performance. Competencies are one means of characterizing the human capital of an organization.[34] With skill/competency-based pay, employees are paid for the range, depth, and types of skills and knowledge that they are capable of using, rather than for the job that they currently hold.[35] For many of today's leading organizations, key competencies reflect the importance of managing change, including technical knowledge, flexibility/adaptability, creativity/resourcefulness, and the ability to lead/manage.[36]

According to one expert, there are several key differences between skill-based pay (SBP) and job evaluation-driven, job-based pay (JBP).[37]

Competence Testing

With JBP, employees receive the pay attached to their jobs regardless of whether or not they develop the competence needed to perform the job effectively. With SBP, base pay is tied not to the job, but to the employee's skills and competencies.

Effect of Job Change

With JBP, pay usually changes automatically when the employee switches jobs. With SBP, that is not necessarily so. Before getting a pay raise, an employee must first demonstrate proficiency at the skills/competencies required by the new job.

Seniority and Other Factors

Pay in JBP systems is often tied to "time in grade," or seniority. In other words, the longer the employee is in the job, the more he or she gets paid, regardless of performance. SBP systems are based on skills, not seniority.

Construction workers today are often compensated for their work through the method of skill-based pay.

Advancement Opportunities

There tend to be more opportunities for advancement with SBP plans than with JBP plans, because of the company-wide focus on skill building. A corollary to this is that SBP enhances organizational flexibility by making it easier for workers to move from job to job because their skills/competencies (and thus their pay) may be applicable to more jobs and thus more portable.

In a manufacturing plant setting, workers are sometimes paid based on their attained skill levels. For example, in a three-level plan:

1. Level One would indicate limited ability, such as knowledge of basic facts and ability to perform simple tasks without direction.
2. Level Two would mean that the employee has attained partial proficiency and could, for instance, apply technical principles on the job.
3. Level Three would mean that the employee is fully competent in the area and could, for example, analyze and solve production problems.

Typically, employees are continually rotated between different production areas. This system encourages the learning of new skills, and can foster flexibility by encouraging workers to learn multiple skills and willingly switch tasks.

Experience has shown that skill-based pay is more efficient in the first years of its existence.[38] The greatest challenge is measurement of skills, abilities, and competencies. As time goes on, employees often become dissatisfied if skill measurements are not valid, or if the people responsible for assessing competencies are considered incompetent or biased. Another major employee concern is that pay be linked sufficiently to performance as well as skills/competencies. Some compensation consultants suggest that firms should not pay for competencies at the exclusion of rewards for high-performance results. For example, competencies could be linked to the determination of base salary, combined with bonuses that are based on performance.[39]

Research
I n s i g h t   ▷

One longitudinal study found that skill-based pay plans, which provide training and are better understood and communicated, will lead to an increased general perception of fairness, which, in turn, will lead to more positive evaluations of the plan a year later.[40]

Customized Job Evaluation Plans

Despite the trend away from job-based pay, quantitative job evaluation systems (primarily the point plan) are still widely used in Canada, partly due to the requirements of pay equity legislation. There are several other reasons for this trend. Proponents argue that individual differences in skill attainment can be taken into consideration even when point-type plans are used, since most firms use salary ranges for groups of similar jobs. Each individual's pay can vary to reflect differences in the skills attained by several people who may be working on the very same job.[41]

Furthermore, neither skill/competency-based pay nor market-based pay entirely eliminates the need for evaluating the worth of one job relative to others. However, traditional job evaluation systems give little or no weight to teamwork, customer relations, or interpersonal communication, which have all become key behaviours for success in today's marketplace. Skill has traditionally been defined as years of education and experience, but has not included the IT knowledge required for many of today's jobs. Responsibility has traditionally been defined in terms of the number of employees supervised, but not for coaching and developing team members. Therefore, if an organization wants to reward technical knowledge and encourage teamwork, its job evaluation system needs to be updated to reflect the current organizational priorities, and be flexible and easy to adapt to the ever-increasing rate of change in organizations. As leading Canadian compensation consultant Nadine Winter says:[42]

> This means that traditional one-size-fits-all job evaluation systems are being rejected in favour of systems customized to reflect an organization's values, priorities and changing job roles.

In the final analysis, their relative ease of use and security are probably the major reasons for the continued widespread use of quantitative plans. Quantitative plans have also recently been facilitated by computerized packages, as explained in the HR.Net box.

A Glimpse into the Future

The future is now for leading-edge firms that are using emerging practices in compensation management, including an increasing emphasis on flexibility and empowerment. There is an increasing emphasis on paying employees for their

HR.Net

Computerized Job Evaluation

Link HR Systems Inc., compensation specialists, has been applying information technology to more than 350 job evaluation processes over 15 years, and has found that radical reductions in effort and cost can be achieved. Internet technology can change job evaluation from a bureaucratic committee-centred process to a simpler exercise where information is collected rapidly and inexpensively directly from employees and their managers over the Internet.[1]

HR-Dept.com is a virtual HR department that offers a variety of tools for HR management. One of these is the "Job Evaluation Assistant," which is intended to accomplish job evaluation while eliminating job evaluation committee meetings. The software provides a customizable job information questionnaire online, allows for prompted employee completion, and includes an embedded workflow for approval of the questionnaire. The job evaluation process is built in by allowing committee members to access the job questionnaires and the job evaluation plan and to enter their assessment of the job requirements. A roll-up feature allows the compensation specialist to call up all of the results, deal with the exceptions, and manage the feedback reporting process all with a few clicks of the mouse. This software can reduce job evaluation time significantly without reducing the effectiveness of the process.[2]

Information technology also offers the possibility to improve the accuracy and integrity of the job evaluation process. A computerized job evaluation system can collect fact-based information as the basis for job evaluation, use analytic tools to assure consistency across organizational units, and provide a complete audit trail of the decision process.[3]

1. T. Hull and R. Heneman, *Submission to the Canadian Federal Pay Equity Task Force* (June 2002), p. 3.

2. www.hr-dept.com/products/performance/index.cfm (April 30, 2003).

3. Hull and Heneman, *Submission to the Canadian Federal Pay Equity Task Force*, p. 3.

FIGURE I I.9 Reward and Organizational Systems Alignment Model

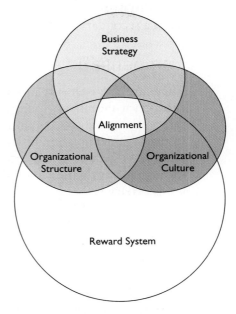

Source: R.L. Heneman and K.E. Dixon, "Reward and Organizational Systems Alignment: An Expert System," *Compensation and Benefits Review*, November/December 2001, p. 22. © 2001. Reprinted with permission of Sage Publications, Inc.

competencies rather than just for the job's responsibilities and activities. Measurement systems and rewards are increasingly emphasizing paying for results.

This is all part of what is known as *strategic pay*. As two strategic pay consultants put it:[43]

> Today, compensation systems must support the mission and culture of the organization, and communicate to employees what is important, why they are important, and what their role is in ensuring the ongoing viability of the organization.

Figure 11.9 provides a strategic model for reward and organizational systems alignment. Organizations using strategically designed pay systems have been found to outperform those that do not, based on financial measures such as earnings per share, return on assets, profit per employee, and cash flow.[44]

PAY FOR MANAGERIAL AND PROFESSIONAL JOBS

Developing a compensation plan to pay executive, managerial, and professional employees is similar in many respects to developing a plan for other employees.[45] The basic aims of the plan are the same in that the goal is to attract good employees and maintain their commitment. Furthermore, the basic methods of job evaluation—classifying jobs, ranking them, or assigning points to them, for instance—are about as applicable to managerial and professional jobs as to production and clerical jobs.

Yet for managerial and professional jobs, job evaluation provides only a partial answer to the question of how to pay these employees. Managers and professionals are almost always paid based on their performance as well as on the basis of static job demands like working conditions. Developing compensation plans for managers and professionals, therefore, tends to be relatively complex, and job evaluation, while still important for determining base salary, usually plays a secondary role to non-salary issues like bonuses, incentives, and benefits.

Compensating Managers

There are five elements in a manager's compensation package: salary, benefits, short-term incentives, long-term incentives, and perquisites.[46] The amount of salary that managers are paid usually depends on the value of the person's work to the organization and how well the person is discharging his or her responsibilities. As with other jobs, the value of the person's work is usually determined through job evaluation and salary surveys and the resulting fine-tuning of salary levels. Salary is the cornerstone of executive compensation, because it is the element on which the others are layered, with benefits, incentives, and perquisites normally awarded in some proportion to the manager's base pay.

Executive compensation tends to emphasize performance incentives more than do other employees' pay plans, since organizational results are likely to reflect the contributions of executives more directly than those of other employees. A recent Canadian research study by Johnson Smith International on the relationship between executive pay and corporate performance found that organizations that make some part of compensation dependent on individual performance perform better than others, and also increase the pool of money available for employee compensation.[47]

The heavy incentive component of executives' compensation can be illustrated using some of Canada's best-paid executives.[48] In 2001, Frank Stronach, CEO of Magna International, received a base salary of $310 000, an annual bonus of $2 323 000, and long-term incentives of $55 546 000, for a total of $58 178 000. Frank Dunn, CEO of Nortel Networks, received a base salary of $1 277 000, no annual bonus (given Nortel's disastrous results), and long-term incentives of $16 889 000. Gerald Schwartz, CEO of Onex Corp., received a base salary of $975 000, an annual bonus of $16 271 000, and no long-term incentives. There is considerable disagreement regarding what should determine executive pay and, therefore, whether top executives are worth what they are paid.

A major review of the results of many previous studies of CEO pay determined that firm size accounts for 40 percent in the variance of total CEO pay, while firm performance accounts for less than 5 percent of the variance.[49]

In 2001, total compensation for CEOs of the 100 largest companies on the Toronto Stock Exchange climbed 54 percent, despite an average corporate earnings decline of 13 percent.[50] For example, pay for the CEO of BCE Inc. increased 452 percent, while the return to shareholders dropped 14 percent.[51] Some observers call this "insane," while others believe it is necessary to attract and retain top talent.[52] The job of an executive is increasingly difficult in the post-Enron world. The stakes are high and job tenure often short. Expectations are higher, the questions from shareholders are more direct, and the challenge of navigating an organization through difficult economic times has never been so great. Board members who hire CEOs must find the right balance between the need to hire the right person, to offer an attractive employment situation, and to protect shareholder interests.[53]

AN ETHICAL DILEMMA

Is it right that CEOs earn enormous amounts of money when most employees are getting small increases each year (sometimes even less than inflation)?

Research Insight ▷

Shareholder activism regarding executive pay has attempted to tighten up the restrictions on what firms pay their top executives.[54] For example, the Ontario Securities Commission has rules regarding disclosure of executive compensation (salary, bonus, stock options, and other compensation) for companies listed on the Toronto Stock Exchange.[55] The chief executive officer's pay must always be disclosed, as well as that of the next four highest-paid employees. A related development for public-sector employees is the Ontario government's requirement that public disclosure be made of salaries for provincial government employees earning $100 000 or more.[56] This requirement also applies to employees in the broader public sector, including hospitals, universities, school boards, crown agencies, and municipalities. However, some believe that this disclosure has actually contributed to the growth in senior executive pay, rather than reduced it, because many CEOs now compare their pay against their peers and will not accept pay below the average. Over time, this results in higher and higher average earnings.[57]

The general trend today is to reduce the relative importance of base salary and boost the importance of short- and long-term executive incentives.[58] The main issue here is identifying the appropriate performance measures for each type of incentive and then determining how to link these to pay. Typical short-term measures of shareholder value include revenue growth and operating profit margin. Long-term shareholder value measures include rate of return above some predetermined base.

Compensating Professional Employees

Compensating nonsupervisory professional employees like engineers and scientists presents unique problems. Analytical jobs require creativity and problem solving, compensable factors not easily compared or measured. Furthermore, the professional's economic impact on the firm is often related only indirectly to the person's actual efforts; for example, the success of an engineer's invention depends on many factors, like how well it is produced and marketed.

In theory, the job evaluation methods explained previously can be used for evaluating professional jobs.[59] The compensable factors here tend to focus on problem solving, creativity, job scope, and technical knowledge and expertise. The job classification method is commonly used—a series of grade descriptions are written, and each position is slotted into the grade having the most appropriate definition.

In practice, traditional methods of job evaluation are rarely used for professional jobs since it is so difficult to identify compensable factors and degrees of factors that meaningfully capture the value of professional work.[60] "Knowledge and the skill of applying it," as one expert notes, "are extremely difficult to quantify and measure."[61]

As a result, most employers use a *market-pricing approach* in evaluating professional jobs. They price professional jobs in the marketplace to the best of their ability to establish the values for benchmark jobs. These benchmark jobs and the employer's other professional jobs are then slotted into a salary structure. Specifically, each professional discipline (like mechanical engineering or electrical engineering) usually ends up having four to six grade levels, each of which requires a fairly broad salary range. This approach helps ensure that the employer remains competitive when bidding for professionals whose attainments vary widely and whose potential employers are found literally worldwide.[62]

IMPORTANT CURRENT ISSUES IN COMPENSATION MANAGEMENT

Four important issues in compensation management will now be discussed: pay equity, pay secrecy, salary compression, and cost-of-living differentials.

The Issue of Pay Equity

Historically, the average pay for Canadian women has been considerably lower than that for men. In 1967, women's average wages were 46.1 percent of men's average wages. This "wage gap" of 53.9 percent means that for every dollar earned by a man, a woman earned 46.1 cents. The gap has slowly narrowed to a low of 35.2 percent in 1995. **Table 11.6** shows the most recent wage gap statistics. Some of this gap is due to the fact that women do more part-time work than men, but even when full-year, full-time workers are compared, the gap is 28.3 percent. The wage gap is narrower for single women than for those who are married, and for younger women compared to those who are older.[63]

Moreover, the gap persists even when women have the same qualifications and do the same type of work as men. For example, the 2002 membership salary survey of the Professional Engineers of Ontario shows that female engineers earn an average of $10 000 less per year than males (a 13 percent wage gap). Female engineers occupy the majority of nonsupervisory engineering jobs, while males occupy the majority of higher-paying supervisory and management engineering jobs.[64]

pay equity Providing equal pay to male-dominated job classes and female-dominated job classes of equal value to the employer.

Although such factors as differences in hours worked, experience levels, education levels, and level of unionization contribute to the wage gap, systemic discrimination is also present.[65] The purpose of pay equity legislation is to redress systemic gender discrimination in compensation for work performed by employees in female-dominated job classes. **Pay equity** requires that equal wages be

TABLE 11.6 Male/Female Average Earnings Ratio*

Year	Full-Year Full-Time Workers			All Earners		
	Women $	Men $	Earnings Ratio (percent)	Women $	Men $	Earnings Ratio (percent)
1991	30 866	44 447	69.4	20 757	33 871	61.3
1992	32 200	44 838	71.8	21 459	33 665	63.7
1993	31 750	44 040	72.1	21 235	33 120	64.1
1994	31 550	45 289	69.7	21 432	34 555	62.0
1995	32 288	44 221	73.0	21 895	33 783	64.8
1996	31 799	43 679	72.8	21 678	33 633	64.5
1997	31 704	45 786	69.2	21 857	34 544	63.3
1998	33 839	46 902	72.1	22 832	35 649	64.0
1999	32 676	47 091	69.4	23 101	36 076	64.0
2000	33 774	47 085	71.7	23 796	37 210	64.0

*Earnings stated in constant year 2000 dollars.

Source: Adapted from the Statistics Canada Web site <http://www.statcan.ca/english/Pgdb/labor01b.htm>, and from the Statistics Canada CANSIM database <http://cansim2.statcan.ca>, Table 202-0102.

paid for jobs of equal value or "worth" to the employer, as determined by gender-neutral (that is, free of any bias based on gender) job evaluation techniques. The federal government recently agreed (after 14 years of court action) to pay $3.6 billion in pay equity adjustments to 230 000 current and former civil servants in female-dominated jobs.[66] Twenty-two thousand Bell Canada operators and clerical staff have been involved in a pay equity court battle since the early 1990s. The case is now before the Supreme Court of Canada. Bell could be ordered to pay about $150 million if the employees win the case.[67]

Six provinces (Ontario, Quebec, Manitoba, Nova Scotia, New Brunswick, and Prince Edward Island) have created separate proactive legislation that

specifically requires that pay equity be achieved. Ontario and Quebec require pay equity in both the public and private sectors, whereas the legislation in the remaining provinces applies only to the public sector. In the federal jurisdiction, the Yukon (public sector only), and British Columbia, human rights legislation requires equal pay for work of equal value, determined by comparing skill, effort, responsibility, and working conditions (and knowledge in B.C.). In Newfoundland and Saskatchewan, a requirement for equal pay for males and females doing substantially similar work, determined by assessing skill, effort, and responsibility, is incorporated into the human rights legislation (similar wording is included in the Yukon's Employment

Saskatchewan workers demonstrate for pay equity.

Standards Act). Although Newfoundland and Saskatchewan do not have specific pay equity legislation, both provinces have formally implemented pay equity in the public sector. There is presently no requirement for pay equity in Alberta, the Northwest Territories, or Nunavut.[68]

The effect of pay equity on the wage gap is still being assessed, and so far results have showed that pay equity legislation has narrowed the wage gap, it has not eliminated it, and there is still no explanation other than systemic discrimination for much of the gap that persists.[69] The pay equity legislation for federally regulated employees is under review.[70]

The Pay Equity Commission (Ontario) www.gov.on.ca/lab/pec

Pay Equity and Job Evaluation

One of the challenges of implementing pay equity is ensuring that there is no gender bias in the job evaluation plan itself. In particular, some traditional job evaluation point plans "tend to result in higher point totals for jobs traditionally held by males than for those traditionally held by females."[71] As an example, the factor "supervisory responsibility" might heavily weight chain-of-command factors such as number of employees supervised and downplay the importance of functional authority or gaining the voluntary cooperation of other employees. The solution here is to rewrite the factor rules in job evaluation plans so as to give more weight to the sorts of activities that female-dominated positions frequently emphasize.[72]

In an attempt to better conform to the principles of pay equity, the federal government spent five years attempting to update and streamline their job evaluation system to a Universal Classification System to replace the 70-plus classifications currently in use. They concluded that the universal approach is unworkable, as it creates a single pay line, which results in a system that is too rigid.[73]

Implications In the long term, the best way to remove the portion of the wage gap resulting from systemic discrimination is to eliminate male- and female-dominated jobs by ensuring that women have equal access to, and are equally represented in, all jobs.

To avoid pay equity problems, questions to ask include:

1. Are job duties and responsibilities clearly documented either by a job analysis questionnaire or a job description? Are they reviewed and updated annually?

2. Is the pay system clearly documented in a salary administration manual? If not, the credibility and defensibility of pay practices are ripe for challenge.

3. When was the pay system last reviewed? If more than three years have passed, serious inequities could exist. Maintenance of pay equity is a requirement of pay equity legislation.

4. Are the pay equity laws being monitored and adhered to in each province/territory in which the organization has employees? There are differences in the legislation between jurisdictions.

> **Hints to Ensure Legal Compliance**

The Issue of Pay Secrecy

There are two points of view with respect to whether employees should know what other employees in the organization are being paid. The basic argument for "open pay" is that it improves employee motivation. If employees believe that greater effort results in greater rewards, then, generally speaking, greater effort will be forthcoming. On the other hand, if employees do not see a direct relationship between effort and rewards, then greater effort will not result. Proponents of open pay contend that workers who do not know each other's pay cannot easily assess how effort and rewards are related, or whether they are equitably paid and, as a result of this, motivation tends to suffer.

The opposing argument is that, in practice, there are usually real inequities in the pay scale, perhaps because of the need to hire someone "in a hurry," or because of the superior negotiating ability of a particular applicant. In addition, even if the employee in a similar job who is being paid more actually deserves the higher salary because of his or her effort, skill, or experience, it is possible that lower-paid colleagues may convince themselves that they are underpaid relative to the higher-paid individual.

The Issues of Inflation and Salary Compression

Inflation and how to cope with it has been another important issue in compensation management.[74] Salary compression refers to the situation that occurs over time when starting salaries increase rapidly at levels often greater than inflation (so as to attract new employees); meanwhile, existing employees receive salary increases equal to, or sometimes less than, inflation. Its symptoms include (1) higher starting salaries, which compress current employees' salaries; and (2) unionized hourly pay increases that overtake supervisory and non-union hourly rates.[75]

Dealing with salary compression is a tricky problem.[76] On the one hand, long-term employees should not be treated unfairly. On the other hand, mediocre performance or lack of assertiveness, rather than salary compression, may in many cases explain the low salaries.

In any case, there are several solutions.[77] As distasteful as it may be, a program of providing raises based on seniority can be instituted in the form of across-the-board salary increases either in lieu of or in addition to performance-based merit increases. Second, a much more aggressive merit pay program can be installed. Third, supervisors can be authorized to recommend "equity" adjustments for selected incumbents who are both highly valued by the organization and also viewed as unfairly victimized by pay compression. Fourth, the compensation mix is sometimes changed to decrease the emphasis on taxable income like wages and salary and to substitute nontaxable benefits like flexible work hours, dental plans, daycare centres, and group legal and auto insurance plans.[78]

Finally, the cost-of-living adjustment (or COLA) clause is sometimes pushed by unions as another way to cope with inflation.[79] The COLA clause is designed to maintain the purchasing power of the wage rate and operates as follows. Specified increases in the Consumer Price Index trigger increases in the wage rate, with the magnitude of the increase depending on the negotiated COLA formula. Non-union employees often receive a similar adjustment.

The Issue of Cost-of-Living Differentials

Cost-of-living differences between localities have escalated from occasional inconveniences to serious compensation problems. For example, an employee living in Toronto with an annual salary of $36 000 would only need to make $31 830 for the same standard of living in Calgary.[80] Employers often handle cost-of-living differentials by increasing the employee's base salary rate in an amount equal to the amount by which living costs in the new locale exceed those in the old, in addition to any other promotion-based raise the employee may get.

Reward Management— Compensation Policies

...Until recently, there was little strategic direction in reward management and changes came about as reactions to immediate pressures in competitive labour markets. Since the mid-1980s, reward management has moved from a back office administration role to a major management role for change. Organizations have become aware of the importance of "culture" to the success of the enterprise and the compensation system can play a major part in shaping the culture. In particular, there has been a great emphasis on creating a pay-for-performance environment. Senior managers now recognize that compensation policy is an important ingredient of business strategy.

Reward management processes work best if they are part of a coherent set of people management activities, which are carried out within the context of the process of strategic management and Human Resources Management. Human Resources Management is a strategic, management-driven approach to the management of the organization's most important assets—the people working there....

Source: Excerpted with permission from *Secord's A–Z Guide for Human Resources Practitioners*, published by and copyright CCH Canadian Limited, Toronto, Ontario.

CHAPTER *Review*

Summary

1 Four basic factors determining pay rates are legal considerations, union influences, compensation policies, and equity.

2 Establishing pay rates involves five steps: evaluating jobs, developing pay grades, conducting a salary survey, using wage curves, and fine-tuning pay rates. Job evaluation is aimed at determining the relative worth of jobs within a firm. It compares jobs to one another based on their content, which is usually defined in terms of compensable factors like skill, effort, responsibility, and working conditions. Most managers group similar jobs into wage or pay grades for pay purposes. These comprise jobs of approximately equal value or importance as determined by job evaluation. Salary surveys collect data from other employers in the marketplace who are competing for employees in similar kinds of positions. The wage curve (or line) shows the average target wage for each pay grade (or job). It illustrates what the average wage for each grade should be, and whether any present wages or salaries are out of line.

3 Skill/competency-based pay plans provide employee compensation based on the skills and knowledge that they are capable of using, rather than the job that they currently hold.

4 The five basic elements of compensation for managers are salary, benefits, short-term incentives, long-term incentives, and perquisites.

5 Pay equity is intended to redress systemic gender discrimination as measured by the wage gap, which indicates that full-time working women make about 70 cents for every dollar made by full-time working men. Pay equity requires equal pay for female-dominated jobs of equal value to male-dominated jobs (where value is determined through job evaluation).

Key Terms

benchmark job   *(p. 335)*
broadbanding   *(p. 350)*
classes   *(p. 337)*
classification (or grading) method   *(p. 337)*
compensable factor   *(p. 335)*
competencies   *(p. 352)*
factor comparison method   *(p. 342)*
grade/group description   *(p. 338)*
grades   *(p. 337)*
job evaluation   *(p. 335)*
pay equity   *(p. 358)*
pay grade   *(p. 343)*
point method   *(p. 340)*
ranking method   *(p. 336)*
rate ranges   *(p. 349)*
red circle pay rate   *(p. 352)*
total rewards   *(p. 329)*
wage curve   *(p. 348)*
wage/salary survey   *(p. 344)*

Review and Discussion Questions

1 Describe what is meant by the term "benchmark job."

2 What are the pros and cons of the following methods of job evaluation: ranking, classification, factor comparison, point method?

3 What are the pros and cons of broadbanding? Would you recommend that your current employer (or some other firm you are familiar with) use it? Why or why not?

4 Explain the model for strategic alignment of reward and organizational systems.

5 Explain what is meant by the market-pricing approach in evaluating professional jobs.

6 Discuss the issues of inflation, salary compression, and cost-of-living adjustments.

CRITICAL *Thinking Questions*

1   It was recently reported in the news that the average pay for most university presidents was around $200 000 per year, but that a few earned closer to $500 000 per year. What would account for such a disparity in the pay of university CEOs?

2   Based on your experience and knowledge, which of the two points of view on pay secrecy do you subscribe to? Explain why.

APPLICATION *Exercises*

Running Case: LearnInMotion.com

The New Pay Plan

LearnInMotion.com does not have a formal wage structure, nor does it have rate ranges or use compensable factors. Jennifer and Pierre base wage rates almost exclusively on those prevailing in the surrounding community, and temper these by trying to maintain some semblance of equity between what workers with different responsibilities are paid. As Jennifer says, "Deciding what to pay dot-com employees is an adventure: Wages for jobs like Web designer and online salesperson are always climbing dramatically, and there's not an awful lot of loyalty involved when someone else offers you 30 percent or 40 percent more than you're currently making." Jennifer and Pierre are therefore continuously scanning various sources to see what others are paying for positions like theirs. They peruse the want ads almost every day, and conduct informal surveys among their friends in other dot-coms. Once or twice a week, they also check compensation Web sites like Monster.ca.

While the company has taken a somewhat unstructured, informal approach to establishing its compensation plan, the firm's actual salary schedule is guided by several basic pay policies. For one thing, the difficulty they had recruiting and hiring employees caused them to pay salaries 10 to 20 percent above what the market would seem to indicate. Jennifer and Pierre write this off to the need to get and keep good employees. As Jennifer says, "If you've got 10 Web designers working for you, you can afford to go a few extra weeks without hiring another one, but when you need one designer and you have none, you've got to do whatever you can to get that one designer hired." Their somewhat informal approach has also led to some potential inequities. For example, the two salespeople—one a man, the other a woman—are earning different salaries, and the man is making about 30 percent more. If everything was going fine—for instance, if sales were up, and the calendar was functional—perhaps they wouldn't be worried. However, the fact is that the two owners are wondering if a more structured pay plan would be a good idea. Now they want you, their management consultants, to help them decide what to do. Here's what they want you to do for them.

Questions

1   Is the company at the point where it should be setting up a formal salary structure complete with job evaluations? Why or why not?

2   Is the company's policy of paying more than the prevailing wage rates a sound one? What do you base that on?

3   Is the salesperson's male–female differential wise? If not, why not?

4   What would you suggest they do now?

CASE INCIDENT *Salary Inequities at Acme Manufacturing*

Joe Blackenship was trying to figure out what to do about a problem salary situation that he had in his plant. Blackenship recently took over as president of Acme Manufacturing. The founder, Bill George, had been president for 35 years. The company is family-owned and located in a small eastern Manitoba town. It has approximately 250 employees and is the largest employer in the community. Blackenship is a member of the family that owned Acme, but he had never worked for the company prior to becoming president. He has an MBA and a law degree, plus 15 years of management experience with a large manufacturing organization, where he was senior vice-president of human resources when he made his move to Acme.

A short time after joining Acme, Blackenship started to notice that there was considerable inequity in the pay structure for salaried employees. A discussion with the HR director led him to believe that salaried employees' pay was very much a matter of individual bargaining with the past president. Hourly-paid factory workers were not part of the problem, because they were unionized and their wages were set by collective bargaining. An examination of the salaried payroll showed that there were 25 employees, whose pay ranged from that of the president to that of the receptionist. A closer examination showed that 14 of the salaried employees were female. Three of these were front-line factory supervisors, and one was the HR director. The rest were nonmanagement employees.

This examination also showed that the HR director appeared to be underpaid, and that the three female supervisors were paid somewhat less than any of the male supervisors. However, there were no similar supervisory jobs in which there were both male and female incumbents. When asked, the HR director said that she thought the female supervisors may have been paid at a lower rate mainly because they were women, and perhaps George did not think that women needed as much money because they had working husbands. However, she added the thought that they might be paid less because they supervised lesser-skilled employees than did male supervisors. Blackenship was not sure that this was true.

The company from which Blackenship had moved had a good job evaluation system. Although he was thoroughly familiar and capable with this compensation tool, Blackenship did not have time to make a job evaluation study at Acme. Therefore, he decided to hire a compensation consultant from a nearby university to help him. Together, they decided that all 25 salaried jobs should be in the same job evaluation cluster, that a modified ranking system of job evaluation should be used, and that the job descriptions recently completed by the HR director were current, accurate, and usable in the study.

The job evaluation showed that there was no evidence of serious inequities or discrimination in the nonmanagement jobs, but that the HR director and the three female supervisors were being underpaid relative to comparable male salaried employees.

Blackenship was not sure what to do. He knew that if the underpaid supervisors took their case to the local pay equity commission, the company could be found guilty of sex discrimination and then have to pay considerable back wages. He was afraid that if he gave these women an immediate salary increase large enough to bring them up to where they should be, the male supervisors would be upset and the female supervisors might comprehend the total situation and want back pay. The HR director told Blackenship that the female supervisors had never complained about pay differences, and they probably did not know the law to any extent.

The HR director agreed to take a sizeable salary increase with no back pay, so this part of the problem was solved. Blackenship believed that he had four choices relative to the female supervisors:

- to do nothing
- to increase the female supervisors' salaries gradually
- to increase their salaries immediately
- to call the three supervisors into his office, discuss the situation with them, and jointly decide what to do.

Questions

1   What would you do if you were Blackenship?

2   How do you think the company got into a situation like this in the first place?

3   Why would you suggest that Blackenship pursue your suggested alternative?

Source: Based on a case prepared by Professor James C. Hodgetts of the Fogelman College of Business and Economics at the University of Memphis. All names are disguised. Used with permission.

EXPERIENTIAL *Exercises*

1   Working individually or in groups, conduct salary surveys for the positions of entry-level accountant and entry-level chemical engineer. What sources did you use, and what conclusions did you reach? If you were the HR manager for a local engineering firm, what would you recommend that each job be paid?

2   Obtain information on the pay grades and rate ranges for each grade at your college or university. Do they appear to be broad bands? If not, propose specific broad bands that could be implemented.

CHAPTER 12

Pay-for-Performance and Financial Incentives

LEARNING OUTCOMES

After studying this chapter, you should be able to:

Discuss how piecework, standard hour, and team or group incentive plans are used.

Explain how to use short-term and long-term incentives for managers and executives.

List the main advantages and disadvantages of salary plans and commission plans for salespeople.

Explain why money is somewhat less important as an incentive for professional employees than it is for other employees.

Describe three types of organization-wide incentive plans.

Explain under what conditions it is best to use an incentive plan.

Explain the emerging emphasis on employee recognition.

CHAPTER OUTLINE

- Money and Motivation: Background and Trends

- Incentives for Operations Employees

- Incentives for Managers and Executives

- Incentives for Salespeople

- Incentives for Other Managers/Professionals

- Organization-wide Incentive Plans

- Developing Effective Incentive Plans

- Employee Recognition Programs

MONEY AND MOTIVATION: BACKGROUND AND TRENDS

Frederick Taylor University
www.ftu.edu

variable pay Any plan that ties pay to productivity or profitability.

The use of financial incentives—financial rewards paid to workers whose production exceeds some predetermined standard—is not new, but was popularized by Frederick Taylor in the late 1800s. As a supervisory employee of the Midvale Steel Company, Taylor had become concerned with the tendency of employees to work at the slowest pace possible and produce at the minimum acceptable level. What especially intrigued him was the fact that some of these same workers still had the energy to run home and work on their cabins, even after a hard 12-hour day. Taylor knew that if he could find some way to harness this energy during the workday, huge productivity gains would be achieved.

Today's efforts to achieve the organization's strategy through motivated employees include financial incentives, pay-for-performance, and variable compensation plans. These types of compensation are now commonly called **variable pay**, meaning any plan that links pay with productivity, profitability, or some other measure of organizational performance. Employers have put increasing emphasis on variable pay plans in order to maximize their return on "human capital," the only unlimited and self-renewing organizational resource.[1] Linking pay to performance has become a global trend, and the Global HRM box provides details of the variable pay system in Singapore.[2]

GLOBAL HRM

Variable Pay in Singapore

Singapore is a resource-scarce country and yet is often regarded as one of the most celebrated cases of economic development. Without doubt, it is the country's pool of human resources and the qualities of its workforce that have always been regarded by the government as the key factors in scaling the economic ladder. Income policy in Singapore shapes the country's competitiveness, and in order to understand the structure of the pay system and workers' wage expectations in Singapore, it is important to appreciate the role played by the National Wages Council (NWC), a tripartite body made up of representatives from unions, employers, and government. Although the wage and other recommendations given out by the NWC are not binding on individual employers and unions, they do provide a basis for constructive negotiation and reference. The aim of the NWC deliberations is to come up with a win–win situation so that the country's competitiveness and the welfare of its citizens will not be jeopardized. Because the underpinnings of these guidelines have been thoroughly discussed and agreed on, it is less likely that the outcome will be strongly in favour of one particular group of stakeholders.

Competitiveness at both the national and enterprise levels remains the foremost concern in the country's compensation structure. Over the years since the 1985–1986 recession, the pay system has been improved to enhance the responsiveness of its adjustment mechanisms. This was done through building up the variable component of the flexible wage system to 80 percent basic wage and 20 percent annual variable component. Almost 85 percent of the unionized companies in Singapore adopted the flexible wage system, as did about 70 percent of the non-unionized ones.

The 1997–1998 economic downturn gave the NWC a good opportunity to assess the variable component of the total pay package. It was found that the existing flexible wage structure was not flexible enough for companies to weather a sudden business downturn. The addition of a new component was strongly recommended by the NWC, resulting in a compensation structure of 70 percent basic wages, 20 percent annual variable component, and a 10 percent monthly variable component. These ongoing efforts to develop a flexible wage structure are intended to reduce the need for reductions in government unemployment/retirement programs and excessive corporate retrenchments in any future economic downturn.

Source: Adapted from D. Wan and C.H. Ong, "Compensation Systems in Singapore," *Compensation and Benefits Review*, July/August 2002, pp. 23–32. © 2002. Used with permission of Sage Publications, Inc.

Variable pay facilitates management of total compensation costs by keeping base pay inflation controlled.[3] The fundamental premise of variable pay plans is that top performers must get top pay in order to secure their commitment to the organization.[4] Thus, accurate performance appraisal or measurable outcomes is a precondition of effective pay-for-performance plans. Another important prerequisite for effective variable pay plans is "line of sight," or the extent to which an employee can relate his or her daily work to the achievement of overall corporate goals. Employees need to understand corporate strategy and how their work as individual employees is important to the achievement of strategic objectives.[5]

The entire thrust of such programs is to treat workers like partners, and get them to think of the business and its goals as their own. It is thus reasonable to pay them more like partners, too, by linking their pay more directly to performance. For example, Canadian steel-maker Dofasco announced in early 2000 that it was providing each of its 7000 employees with a cash bonus of $7900 as a result of the company's best year in a decade.[6]

Organizations are increasingly using more than one type of variable pay program, according to a 2002 study by Hewitt Associates.[7] **Figure 12.1** shows the increase in the use of variable pay plans by Canadian organizations from 2001 to 2002. This figure shows that pay plans based solely on internal and external equity are giving way to skill-based plans, and being supplemented by the sorts of spot awards, team incentives, and gainsharing plans discussed in this chapter.

FIGURE **12.1** Variable Pay Programs 2001–2002

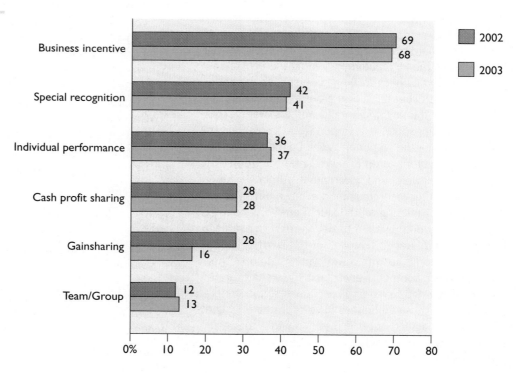

Types of Incentive Plans

There are several types of incentive plans.[8] *Individual incentive programs* give income over and above base salary to individual employees who meet a specific individual performance standard.[9] **Spot bonuses** are awarded, generally to individual employees, for accomplishments that are not readily measured by a standard, such as "to recognize the long hours that this employee put in last month," or "to recognize exemplary customer service this week."[10] For example, Cisco Systems provides up to a $2000 spot bonus for exceptional performance.[11] *Group incentive programs* are like individual incentive plans, but they give pay over and above base salary to all team members when the group or team collectively meets a specified standard for performance, productivity, or other work-related behaviour.[12] *Profit-sharing plans* are generally organization-wide incentive programs that provide employees with a share of the organization's profits in a specified period.[13] *Gainsharing programs* are organization-wide pay plans designed to reward employees for improvements in organizational productivity. They generally include employee suggestion systems, and focus on reducing labour costs through employee suggestions and participation.[14]

For simplicity, we will discuss these plans as follows: incentives for operations employees; incentives for managers and executives; incentives for salespeople; incentives primarily for white-collar and professional employees (merit pay); and organization-wide incentives.

INCENTIVES FOR OPERATIONS EMPLOYEES

Piecework Plans

Several incentive plans are particularly well suited for use with operations employees, such as those doing production work. **Piecework** is the oldest incentive plan and still the most commonly used. Earnings are tied directly to what the worker produces; the person is paid a *piece rate* for each unit that he or she produces. Thus, if Tom Smith gets $0.40 per piece for stamping out door jambs, then he would make $40 for stamping out 100 a day and $80 for stamping out 200.

Developing a workable piece-rate plan requires both job evaluation and (usually) industrial engineering. Job evaluation enables firms to assign an hourly wage rate to the job in question. The crucial issue in piece-rate planning is the production standard, however, and this standard is usually developed by industrial engineers. Production standards are stated in terms of a standard number of minutes per unit or a standard number of units per hour. In Tom Smith's case, the job evaluation indicated that his door-jamb stamping job was worth $8 per hour. The industrial engineer determined that 20 jambs per hour was the standard production rate. Therefore, the piece rate (for each door jamb) was $8.00 ÷ 20 = $0.40 per door jamb.

With a **straight piecework plan**, Tom Smith would be paid on the basis of the number of door jambs that he produced; there would be no guaranteed minimum wage. However, after passage of employment/labour standards legislation, it became necessary for most employers to guarantee their workers a minimum wage. With a **guaranteed piecework plan**, Tom Smith would be paid the

spot bonus A spontaneous incentive awarded to individuals for accomplishments not readily measured by a standard.

piecework A system of pay based on the number of items processed by each individual worker in a unit of time, such as items per hour or items per day.

straight piecework plan A set payment for each piece produced or processed in a factory or shop.

guaranteed piecework plan The minimum hourly wage plus an incentive for each piece produced above a set number of pieces per hour.

minimum wage whether or not he stamped out the number of door jambs required to make minimum wage, for example, 11 pieces if minimum wage is $4.40 per hour. As an incentive he would, however, also be paid at the piece rate of $0.40 for each unit that he produced over the number required to make minimum wage.

Piecework generally implies straight piecework, a strict proportionality between results and rewards regardless of the level of output. Thus, in Smith's case, he continues to get $0.40 apiece for stamping out door jambs, even if he stamps out many more than planned (say, 500 per day). On the other hand, certain types of piecework incentive plans call for a sharing of productivity gains between worker and employer such that the worker does not receive full credit for all production above normal.[15]

Advantages and Disadvantages

Piecework incentive plans have several advantages. They are simple to calculate and easily understood by employees. Piece-rate plans appear equitable in principle, and their incentive value can be powerful since rewards are directly tied to performance.

Piecework also has some disadvantages. A main one is its somewhat unsavoury reputation among many employees, based on some employers' habits of arbitrarily raising production standards whenever they found their workers earning "excessive" wages. In addition, piece rates are stated in monetary terms (like $0.40 per piece). Thus, when a new job evaluation results in a new hourly wage rate, the piece rate must also be revised; this can be a big clerical chore. Another disadvantage is more subtle: since the piece rate is quoted on a per-piece basis, in workers' minds production standards become tied inseparably to the amount of money earned. When an attempt is made to revise production standards, it meets considerable worker resistance, even if the revision is fully justified.[16]

In fact, the industrial-engineered specificity of piecework plans represents the seeds of piecework's biggest disadvantage these days. Piecework plans tend to be tailor-made for relatively specialized jobs in which employees do basically the same narrow tasks over and over again many times a day. This, in turn, fosters a certain rigidity: employees become preoccupied with producing the number of units needed, and are less willing to concern themselves with meeting quality standards or switching from job to job (since doing so could reduce the person's productivity).[17] Employees tend to be trained to perform only a limited number of tasks. Similarly, attempts to introduce new technology or innovative processes may be more likely to fail, insofar as they require major adjustments to engineered standards and negotiations with employees. Equipment tends not to be as well maintained, since employees are focusing on maximizing each machine's output.

Problems such as these have led some firms to drop their piecework plans (as well as their standard hour plans, discussed next), and to substitute team-based incentive plans or programs such as gainsharing, which will also be discussed later in this chapter.

Standard Hour Plan

standard hour plan A plan by which a worker is paid a basic hourly rate plus an extra percentage of his or her base rate for production exceeding the standard per hour or per day. It is similar to piecework payment, but is based on a percentage premium.

The **standard hour plan** is like the piece-rate plan, with one major difference. With a piece-rate plan, the worker is paid a particular rate for each piece that he or she produces. With the standard hour plan, the worker is rewarded by a *premium that equals the percentage by which his or her performance exceeds the standard.* The plan assumes the worker to have a guaranteed base rate.

As an example, suppose that the base rate for Smith's job is $8 per hour. (The base rate may, but need not, equal the hourly rate determined by the job evaluation.) Assume also that the production standard for Smith's job is 20 units per hour, or three minutes per unit. Suppose that in one day (eight hours) Smith produces 200 door jambs. According to the production standard, this should have taken Smith 10 hours (200 divided by 20 per hour); instead it took him eight hours. He produced at a rate that was 25 percent (40 divided by 160) higher than the standard rate. The standard rate would be eight hours times 20 (units per hour) = 160: Smith actually produced 40 more, or 200. He will, therefore, be paid at a rate 25 percent above his base rate for the day. His base rate was $8 per hour times eight hours, which equals $64, so he will be paid 1.25 times 64 or $80.00 for the day.

The standard hour plan has most of the advantages of the piecework plan and is fairly simple to compute and easy to understand. The incentive is expressed in units of time instead of in monetary terms (as it is with the piece-rate system). Therefore, there is a lesser tendency on the part of workers to link their production standard with their pay. Furthermore, the clerical job of recomputing piece rates whenever hourly wage rates are re-evaluated is avoided.[18]

Team or Group Incentive Plans

team or group incentive plan A plan in which a production standard is set for a specific work group, and its members are paid incentives if the group exceeds the production standard.

There are several ways in which to implement **team or group incentive plans.**[19] One is to set work standards for each member of the group and maintain a count of the output of each member. Members are then paid based on one of three formulas: (1) all members receive the pay earned by the highest producer; (2) all members receive the pay earned by the lowest producer; or (3) all members receive payment equal to the average pay earned by the group.

The second approach is to set a production standard based on the final output of the group as a whole; all members then receive the same pay, based on the piece rate that exists for the group's job. The group incentive can be based on either the piece rate or standard hour plan, but the latter is somewhat more prevalent.

A third option is to choose a measurable definition of group performance or productivity that the group can control. For instance, broad criteria such as total labour-hours per final product could be used: piecework's engineered standards are thus not necessarily required here.[20]

There are several reasons to use team incentive plans. Sometimes, several jobs are interrelated, as they are on project teams. Here, one worker's performance reflects not only his or her own effort but that of co-workers as well; thus, team incentives make sense. Team plans also reinforce group planning and problem solving and help to ensure that collaboration takes place.[21] In Japan, employees are rewarded as a group in order to reduce jealousy, make group members indebted to one another (as they would be to the group), and encourage a sense of cooperation.[22] There tends to be less bickering among group members over who has "tight" production standards and who has loose ones. Group incentive plans also facilitate on-the-job training, since each member of the group has an interest in getting new members trained as quickly as possible.[23]

A group incentive plan's chief disadvantage is that each worker's rewards are no longer based solely on his or her own effort. To the extent that the person does not see his or her effort leading to the desired reward, a group plan may be less effective at motivating employees than an individual plan.

Research
I n s i g h t   ▷

Group incentive plans have been found to be more effective when there are high levels of communication to employees about the specifics of the plan, strong worker involvement in the plan's design and implementation, and when group members perceive the plan as fair.[24]

INCENTIVES FOR MANAGERS AND EXECUTIVES

The Conference Board of Canada
www.conferenceboard.ca

Most employers award their managers and executives a bonus or incentive because of the role that managers play in determining divisional and corporate profitability.[25] A Conference Board of Canada survey of 327 organizations found that long-term incentive plans (like stock options), which are intended to motivate and reward management for the corporation's long-term growth and prosperity, were used by 47 percent of the Canadian firms surveyed.[26]

Short-Term Incentives: The Annual Bonus

annual bonus Plans that are designed to motivate short-term performance of managers and are tied to company profitability.

More than 85 percent of firms in Canada with variable pay plans provide an **annual bonus**.[27] Unlike salaries, which rarely decline with reduced performance, short-term incentive bonuses can easily result in an increase or decrease of 25 percent or more in total pay relative to the previous year. There are three basic issues to be considered when awarding short-term incentives: eligibility, fund-size determination, and individual awards.

Eligibility
Eligibility is usually decided in one of three ways. The first criterion is *key position*. Here, a job-by-job review is conducted to identify the key jobs (typically only line jobs) that have a measurable impact on profitability. The second approach to determining eligibility is to set a *salary-level* cutoff point; all employees earning over that threshold amount are automatically eligible for consideration for short-term incentives. Finally, eligibility can be determined by *salary grade*. This is a refinement of the salary cutoff approach and assumes that all employees at a certain grade or above should be eligible for the short-term incentive program.[28] The simplest approach is just to use salary level as a cutoff.[29]

The size of the bonus is usually greater for top-level executives. Thus, an executive earning $150 000 in salary may be able to earn another 80 percent of his or her salary as a bonus, while a manager in the same firm earning $80 000 can earn only another 30 percent. Similarly, a supervisor might be able to earn up to 15 percent of his or her base salary in bonuses. Average bonuses range from a low of 10 percent to a high of 80 percent or more: a typical company might establish a plan whereby executives could earn 45 percent of base salary, managers 25 percent, and supervisors 12 percent.

Frank Stronach, CEO of Magna Corp., receives very high bonuses in addition to his regular compensation.

How Much to Pay Out (Fund Size)
Next, a decision must be made regarding fund size—the total amount of bonus money that will be available—and there are several formulas to do this. Some companies use a *nondeductible formula*. Here a straight percentage (usually of the company's net income) is used to create the short-term incentive fund. Others use a *deductible formula* on

the assumption that the short-term incentive fund should begin to accumulate only after the firm has met a specified level of earnings.

In practice, what proportion of profits is usually paid out as bonuses? There are no hard-and-fast rules, and some firms do not even have a formula for developing the bonus fund.[30] One alternative is to reserve a minimum amount of the profits, say 10 percent, for safeguarding shareholders' investments, and then to establish a fund for bonuses equal to 20 percent of the corporate operating profit before taxes in excess of this base amount. Thus, if the operating profits were $100 000, then the management bonus fund might be 20 percent of $90 000, or $18 000.[31] Other illustrative formulas used for determining the executive bonus fund are as follows:

- 10 percent of net income after deducting 5 percent of average capital invested in the business

- 12.5 percent of the amount by which net income exceeds 6 percent of shareholders' equity

- 12 percent of net earnings after deducting 6 percent of net capital.[32]

Determining Individual Awards

The third issue is determining the *individual awards* to be paid. In some cases, the amount is determined on a discretionary basis (usually by the employee's boss), but typically a target bonus is set for each eligible position and adjustments are then made for greater or less than targeted performance. A maximum amount, perhaps double the target bonus, may be set. Performance ratings are obtained for each manager and preliminary bonus estimates are computed. Estimates for the total amount of money to be spent on short-term incentives are thereby made and compared with the bonus fund available. If necessary, the individual estimates are then adjusted.

A related question is whether managers will receive bonuses based on individual performance, team performance, corporate performance, or some combination of these. Keep in mind that there is a difference between a profit-sharing plan and a true, individual incentive bonus. In a profit-sharing plan, each person gets a bonus based on the company's results, regardless of the person's actual effort. With a true individual incentive, it is the manager's individual effort and performance that are rewarded with a bonus.

Here, again, there are no hard-and-fast rules. Top-level executive bonuses are generally tied to overall corporate results (or divisional results if the executive is, say, the vice-president of a major division). The assumption is that corporate results reflect the person's individual performance. However, as one moves further down the chain of command, corporate profits become a less accurate gauge of a manager's contribution. For supervisory staff or the heads of functional departments, the person's individual performance, rather than corporate results, is a more logical determinant of his or her bonus.

Many experts argue that, in most organizations, managerial and executive-level bonuses should be tied to both organizational and individual performance, and there are several ways to do this.[33] Perhaps the simplest is the *split-award method*, which breaks the bonus into two parts. Here, the manager actually gets two separate bonuses, one based on his or her individual effort and one based on the organization's overall performance. Thus, a manager might be eligible for an individual performance bonus of up to $10 000 but receive an

Tips for the Front Line

AN ETHICAL DILEMMA

Is it ethical to provide potentially large bonuses to managers and executives on a purely discretionary basis?

individual performance bonus of only $8000 at the end of the year, based on his or her individual performance evaluation. In addition, though, the person might also receive a second bonus of $8000 based on the company's profits for the year. Thus, even if there were no company profits, the high-performing manager would still get an individual performance bonus.

One drawback to this approach is that it pays too much to the marginal performer, who, even if his or her own performance is mediocre, at least gets that second, company-based bonus. One way to get around this problem is to use the *multiplier method*. For example, a manager whose individual performance was "poor" might not even receive a company-performance-based bonus, on the assumption that the bonus should be a *product* of individual *and* corporate performance. When either is very poor, the product is zero.

Whichever approach is used, outstanding performers should get substantially larger awards than do other managers. They are people that the company cannot afford to lose, and their performance should always be adequately rewarded by the organization's incentive system. Conversely, marginal or below-average performers should never receive awards that are normal or average, and poor performers should be awarded nothing. The money saved on those people should be given to above-average performers.[34]

Long-Term Incentives

Long-term incentives are intended to motivate and reward top management for the firm's long-term growth and prosperity, and to inject a long-term perspective into executive decisions. If only short-term criteria are used, a manager could, for instance, increase profitability by reducing plant maintenance; this tactic might, of course, reduce profits over two or three years. This issue has received considerable attention in the past few years as shareholders have become increasingly critical of management focus on short-term returns at the expense of long-term increase in stock price.[35] Long-term incentives are intended also to encourage executives to stay with the company by giving them the opportunity to accumulate capital (like company stock) based on the firm's long-term success. Long-term incentives or **capital accumulation programs** are most often reserved for senior executives, but have more recently begun to be extended to employees at lower organizational levels.[36]

There are six popular long-term incentive plans (for capital accumulation) in Canada: stock options, book value plans, stock appreciation rights, performance achievement plans, restricted stock plans, and phantom stock plans.[37] The popularity of these plans changes over time due to economic conditions and trends, internal company financial pressures, changing attitudes toward long-term incentives, and changes in tax law, as well as other factors.

Stock Options   The **stock option** is by far the most popular long-term incentive in Canada. Over 80 percent of organizations using long-term incentives provide stock options.[38] A stock option is the right to purchase a specific number of shares of company stock at a specific price during a period of time. Sometimes a vesting (waiting) period is required to ensure that the employee has contributed to any increase in stock price. The executive thus hopes to profit by exercising his or her option to buy the shares in the future but at today's price. The assumption is that the price of the stock will go up, rather than going down

capital accumulation programs Long-term incentives most often reserved for senior executives. Six popular plans include stock options, book value plans, stock appreciation rights, performance achievement plans, restricted stock plans, and phantom stock plans.

stock option The right to purchase a stated number of shares of a company stock at today's price at some time in the future.

or staying the same. As shown in **Figure 12.2,** if shares provided at an option price of $20 per share are exercised (bought) later for $20 when the market price is $60 per share, and sold when the market price is $80 per share, a cash gain of $60 per share results if the shares are then sold on the stock market. Often, part of the gain is needed to meet income tax liabilities that are triggered when the options are exercised. Stock options are attractive from a taxation perspective in Canada, as only 75 percent of the gain on exercising the options is taxable. Thus, stock option plans are often seen as a cash windfall with no downside risk but unlimited upside potential.[39]

Unfortunately, stock price depends to a significant extent on considerations outside the executive's control, such as general economic conditions and investor sentiment. An executive performing valiantly in a declining market or troubled industry may receive nothing, since stock options are worthless if share prices don't rise.[40] This is a particularly important concern in today's volatile stock market.[41] However, stock price is affected relative to the overall stock market by the firm's profitability and growth, and to the extent that the executive can affect these factors, the stock option can be an incentive.

One of the interesting trends in stock options as long-term incentives is that, increasingly, they are not just for high-level managers and executives—or even just managers and executives—anymore. Pepsico, Starbucks, the Gap, TELUS, Corel, and many other companies have broad-based stock option plans that include employees below the executive level.[42] The trend toward broad-based plans is aimed at providing support for the competitive strategies being pursued by many firms today. Such companies have been asking more from employees than ever before, but employees often feel that they are corporate "partners" in name only, working harder but receiving little in return. In response,

> Companies are increasingly interested in drawing employees into the new deal by implementing broad-based stock option plans. By giving stock options to non-executives,

FIGURE **12.2** Stock Options

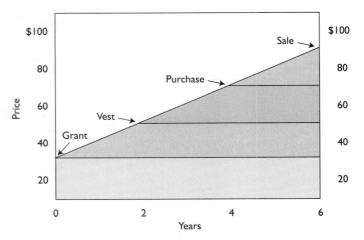

Source: B.R. Ellig, "Executive Pay: A Primer," *Compensation and Benefits Review,* January/February 2003, p. 48. © 2003. Reprinted with permission of Sage Publications, Inc.

companies make good the promise of letting employees share in the company's success.[43]

Figure 12.3 illustrates the expansion in the use of stock options during 2001 and 2002. Internet technologies can then help companies to manage such broad-based plans by providing employees with an easy way to check option status, place market orders, and receive updated information.[44]

In the post-Enron world, stock options have come under attack as the motive for short-term managerial focus and questionable accounting practices. Proposals have been made to require that stock options be shown as an expense on company financial statements because the excessive issuing of options dilutes share values for shareholders and creates a distorted impression of the true value of a company. The Canada Pension Plan Investment Board stated in its *2003 Proxy Voting Principles and Guidelines,*

> Stock options are problematic in many areas, including their effectiveness in aligning management interests with those of shareholders, (and) their tendency to focus management on short-term issues.[45]

Some organizations, such as TD Bank, Bank of Montreal, and Microsoft are doing so voluntarily. Others are considering individual performance in eligibility for stock options. In addition, other forms of capital accumulation plans are becoming more prominent as some companies look for alternatives to stock options. However, the use of stock options continues, as companies continue to face the importance of attracting and retaining human capital in the face of fluctuating economic conditions.[46]

FIGURE I2.3 Stock Option Growth 2001–2002

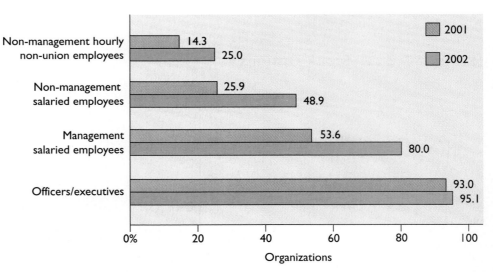

Source: Reprinted from 29th Annual Total Salary Increase Budget Survey, © 2002 with permission from WorldatWork, 14040 N. Northsight Blvd., Scottsdale, AZ 85260; phone: 877-951-9191; fax: 480-483-8352; www.worldatwork.org, © 2002, WorldatWork. Unauthorized reproduction or distribution is strictly prohibited.

Book Value Plan

A book value plan is one alternative to stock options. Here, managers are permitted to purchase stock at current book value, a value anchored in the value of the company's assets. Executives can earn dividends on the stock they own and, as the company grows, the book value of their shares may grow too. When these employees leave the company, they can sell the shares back to the company at the new higher book value.[47] The book value approach avoids the uncertainties of the stock market, emphasizing instead a company's growth. Book value plans are used by privately held companies, as publicly traded companies cannot issue book value stock.

Other Plans

There are several other popular long-term incentive plans. *Stock appreciation rights* (SARs) are usually combined with stock options; they permit the recipient either to exercise the regular stock option (by buying the stock) or to take any appreciation in the stock price in cash, stock, or some combination of these. A *performance achievement plan* awards shares of stock for the achievement of predetermined financial targets, such as profit or growth in earnings per share. A variation on this plan is to provide stock options that are only exercisable after a performance target has been achieved. With *restricted stock plans*, shares are usually awarded without cost to the executive but with certain restrictions that are imposed by the employer. For example, there may be a risk of forfeiture if an executive leaves the company before the specified time limit elapses. Finally, under *phantom stock plans*, executives receive not shares but "units" that are similar to shares of company stock. Then, at some future time, they receive an amount (usually in cash) equal to the appreciation of the "phantom" stock that they own.[48] Some phantom stock plans even provide the full original unit value plus the amount of appreciation.

Whichever long-term plan is used, a main concern today is that traditional executive incentives often do not build in any real risk for the executive. Often, for instance, options can be exercised with little or no cash outlay by the executive, who then turns around and quickly sells his or her stock. There is, therefore, a growing emphasis on long-term executive incentives that build more executive risk into the formula.[49]

Performance Plans

The need to tie executives' pay more clearly to the firm's performance while building in more risk has led many firms to institute *performance plans*. Performance plans "are plans whose payment or value is contingent on financial performance measured against objectives set at the start of a multi-year period."[50] The executive may be granted "performance units" similar to an annual bonus but with a measurement period of longer than a year. For example, an executive might be granted $100 000 in units valued at $50 per unit, in proportion to his or her success in meeting assigned financial goals. In Canada, these plans are usually limited to three years due to income tax rules.

Long-Term Incentives: Cash versus Stock Options

A study by consultants McKinsey and Company, Inc., suggests that giving managers stock options may be the simplest and wisest way to provide long-term incentives for top executives. In the McKinsey study, about one-half of the companies surveyed had stock options only, and about one-half had performance-based cash plans. The results indicated that in most cases the return to shareholders of companies with long-term cash performance incentives did not differ significantly from that of companies that had only stock-based incentive plans (like stock options). Their most serious problem in awarding cash bonuses lay in identifying the proper performance measures.

On the other hand, consultants Watson Wyatt suggest that it is not clear that stock options are the best compensation tools for rewarding senior executives because they do not reward strategies that (1) maximize current dividend payouts, or (2) preserve existing share values in the short term, because executives do not have their own money at risk.[51]

Relating Strategy to Executive Compensation   Executive compensation is more likely to be effective if it is appropriately linked to corporate strategy.[52] Few HR practices have as much connection to strategy as does how the company crafts its long-term incentives. Whether expanding sales through joint ventures abroad, consolidating operations and downsizing the workforce, or some other tactic, few strategies can be accomplished in just one or two years. As a result, the long-term signals that are sent to executives regarding the results and activities that will (or will not) be rewarded can have an impact on whether or not the firm's strategy is implemented effectively. For example, a strategy to boost sales by expanding abroad might suggest linking incentives to increased sales abroad. A cost-reduction strategy might instead emphasize linking incentives to improved profit margins.

Compensation experts therefore suggest defining the strategic context for the executive compensation plan before creating the compensation package itself, as follows:[53]

1. Define the internal and external issues that face the company and its business objectives—boosting sales abroad, downsizing, and so on.

2. Based on the strategic aims, shape each component of the executive compensation package and then group the components into a balanced whole. Include a stock option plan to give the executive compensation package the special character it needs to meet the unique needs of the executives and the company.

3. Check the executive compensation plan for compliance with all legal and regulatory requirements and for tax effectiveness.

4. Install a process for reviewing and evaluating the executive compensation plan whenever a major business change occurs.

INCENTIVES FOR SALESPEOPLE

Sales compensation plans have typically relied heavily on incentives (sales commissions), although this varies by industry. In the real estate industry, for instance, salespeople are paid entirely via commissions, while in the pharmaceutical industry, salespeople tend to be paid a salary. However, the most prevalent approach is to use a combination of salary and commissions to compensate salespeople.[54]

The widespread use of incentives for salespeople is due to three factors: tradition, the unsupervised nature of most sales work, and the assumption that incentives are needed to motivate salespeople. The pros and cons of salary, commission, and combination plans follow.

Sales Compensation
www.davekahle.com/getem.htm

Salary Plan

In a salary plan, salespeople are paid a fixed salary, although there may be occasional incentives in the form of bonuses, sales contest prizes, and the like.[55] There are several reasons to use straight salary. It works well when the main sales objective is prospecting (finding new clients) or when the salesperson is mostly involved in account servicing, such as developing and executing product training programs for a distributor's sales force or participating in national and local trade shows.[56] Jobs like these are often found in industries that sell technical products. This is one reason why the aerospace and transportation equipment industries have a relatively heavy emphasis on salary plans for their salespeople.

There are advantages to paying salespeople on a straight salary basis. Salespeople know in advance what their income will be, and the employer also has fixed, predictable sales force expenses. Straight salary makes it simple to switch territories or quotas or to reassign salespeople, and it can develop a high degree of loyalty among the sales staff. Commissions tend to shift the salesperson's emphasis to making the sale rather than to prospecting and cultivating long-term customers. A long-term perspective is encouraged by straight salary compensation.

The main disadvantage is that salary plans do not depend on results.[57] In fact, salaries are often tied to seniority rather than to performance, which can be demotivating to potentially high-performing salespeople who see seniority—not performance—being rewarded.

Commission Plan

Commission plans pay salespeople in direct proportion to their sales: they pay for results, and only for results. The commission plan has several advantages. Salespeople have the greatest possible incentive, and there is a tendency to attract high-performing salespeople who see that effort will clearly lead to rewards. Sales costs are proportional to sales rather than fixed, and the company's selling investment is reduced. The commission basis is also easy to understand and compute.

The commission plan, too, has drawbacks, however. Salespeople focus on making a sale and on high-volume items; cultivating dedicated customers and working to push hard-to-sell items may be neglected. Wide variances in income between salespeople may occur; this can lead to a feeling that the plan is inequitable. More serious is the fact that salespeople are encouraged to neglect non-selling duties like servicing small accounts. In addition, pay is often excessive in boom times and very low in recessions.

Recent research evidence presents further insights into the impact of sales commissions. One study addressed whether paying salespeople on commission "without a financial net" might induce more salespeople to leave. The participants in this study were 225 field sales representatives from a telecommunications company. Results showed that paying salespersons a commission accounting for 100 percent of pay was the situation with by far the highest turnover of salespersons. Turnover was much lower in the situation in which salespersons were paid a combination of a base salary plus commissions.[58] These findings suggest that while 100-percent commissions can drive higher

AN ETHICAL DILEMMA
Is it fair to compensate sales employees on a 100-percent commission basis with no financial security?

Research Insight ▷

sales by focusing the attention of strong-willed salespeople on maximizing sales, it can also undermine the desire of salespeople to stay without a financial safety net.

The effects on the salesperson of a commission pay plan could also depend on that person's personality. A second study investigated 154 sales representatives who were responsible for contacting and renewing existing members and for identifying and adding new members.[59] A number of the sales reps in this study were more extroverted than were the others—they were more sociable, outgoing, talkative, aggressive, energetic, and enthusiastic.[60] It might be expected that extroverted salespeople would usually generate higher sales than less extroverted ones, but in this study, extroversion was positively associated with higher performance (in terms of percentage of existing members renewing their memberships, and the count of new members paying membership fees) *only when the salespeople were explicitly rewarded for accomplishing these tasks.* Thus, being extroverted did not always lead to higher sales; extroverts only sold more than those less extroverted when their rewards were contingent on their performance.

Combination Plan

There has been a definite movement away from the extremes of straight commission or fixed salary to combination plans for salespeople.[61] Combination plans provide some of the advantages of both straight salary and straight commission plans, and also some of their disadvantages. Salespeople have a floor to their earnings. Furthermore, the company can direct its salespeople's activities by detailing what services the salary component is being paid for, while the commission component provides a built-in incentive for superior performance.

However, the salary component is not tied to performance, and the employer is therefore trading away some incentive value. Combination plans also tend to become complicated, and misunderstandings can result. This might not be a problem with a simple "salary plus commission" plan, but most plans are not so simple. For example, there is a "commission plus drawing account" plan, whereby a salesperson is paid basically on commissions but can draw on future earnings to get through low sales periods. Similarly, in the "commission plus bonus" plan, salespeople are again paid primarily on the basis of commissions. However, they are also given a small bonus for directed activities like selling slow-moving items.

An example can help to illustrate the complexities of the typical combination plan. In one company, for instance, the following three-step formula is applied:

- Step 1: Sales volume up to $18 000 a month. Base salary plus 7 percent of gross profits plus 0.5 percent of gross sales.
- Step 2: Sales volume from $18 000 to $25 000 a month. Base salary plus 9 percent of gross profits plus 0.5 percent of gross sales.
- Step 3: Sales volume over $25 000 a month. Base salary plus 10 percent of gross profits plus 0.5 percent of gross sales.

In all cases, base salary is paid every two weeks, while the earned percentage of gross profits and gross sales is paid monthly.[62] It should be remembered that setting sales goals or targets is complex, and requires careful planning and analysis. Answers to questions such as why $18 000 and $25 000 were chosen as break points must be available.[63]

The sales force also may get various special awards. Trips, home stereos, TVs, VCRs, and video cameras are commonly used as sales prizes. Access to the latest technology (such as notebook computers with customer and product databases, portable printers, digital cell phones, and so on) can also have a strong behavioural impact on field sales staff.[64]

Sales Compensation in the E-Commerce Era

Traditional product-based sales compensation focuses on the amount of product sold. In the Internet age, an integrated team of individuals works together to position the company with prospects, make sales, and service accounts. All sales team members work to deepen customer relationships. This new approach is due to the fact that for customers who know what they want, rapid low-cost purchases can be made over the Internet. Face-to-face sales are now reserved for high-volume customers and higher-margin services.

In the future, sales teams will be the norm, and there will be three separate sales roles—marketing managers, sales closers, and relationship managers (only for high-cost, high-value-added products). Sales incentive plans will have to encourage the sales force to focus on the customer, integrate with e-commerce, and support rapid change. Cross-selling incentives (making multiple sales of different product lines to the same customer) will be more important, as will incentives for relationship management and customer satisfaction. Experts recommend setting sales salaries at 50 percent to 75 percent of total expected compensation, plus incentives. A portion of the incentive should be tied to team-based sales results, in order to encourage sharing, handoffs, and peer pressure.[65]

INCENTIVES FOR OTHER MANAGERS/PROFESSIONALS

merit pay (merit raise) Any salary increase awarded to an employee based on his or her individual performance.

Merit pay or a **merit raise** is any salary increase that is awarded to an employee based on his or her individual performance. It is different from a bonus in that it usually represents a continuing increment, whereas the bonus represents a one-time payment. Although the term *merit pay* can apply to the incentive raises given to any employees—office or factory, management or non-management—the term is more often used with respect to white-collar employees and particularly professional, office, and clerical employees.

Merit pay has both advocates and detractors and is the subject of much debate.[66] Advocates argue that only pay or other rewards tied directly to performance can motivate improved performance. They contend that the effect of awarding pay raises across the board (without regard to individual performance) may actually detract from performance by showing employees that they will be rewarded the same regardless of how they perform.

On the other hand, merit pay detractors present good reasons why merit pay can backfire. One is that the usefulness of the merit pay plan depends on the validity of the performance appraisal system, since if performance appraisals are viewed as unfair, so too will the merit pay that is based on them.[67] Second, supervisors often tend to minimize differences in employee performance when computing merit raises. They give most employees about the same raise, either

Tips for the Front Line

because of a reluctance to alienate some employees, or a desire to give everyone a raise that will at least help them to stay even with the cost of living. A third problem is that almost every employee thinks that he or she is an above-average performer; being paid a below-average merit increase can thus be demoralizing.[68] However, while problems like these can undermine a merit pay plan, there seems to be little doubt that merit pay can and does improve performance. It is critical, however, that performance appraisals be carried out effectively.[69]

Traditional merit pay plans have two basic characteristics: (1) merit increases are usually granted to employees at a designated time of the year in the form of a higher base salary (or *raise*); and (2) the merit raise is usually based exclusively on individual performance, although the overall level of company profits may affect the total sum available for merit raises.[70] In some cases, merit raises are awarded in a single lump sum once a year, without changing base salary. Occasionally, awards are tied to both individual and organizational performance.

Incentives for Professional Employees

Professional employees are those whose work involves the application of learned knowledge to the solution of the employer's problems. They include lawyers, doctors, economists, and engineers. Professionals almost always reach their positions through prolonged periods of formal study.[71]

Pay decisions regarding professional employees involve unique problems. One is that, for most professionals, money has historically been somewhat less important as an incentive than it has been for other employees. This is true partly because professionals tend to be paid well anyway, and partly because they are already driven—by the desire to produce high-calibre work and receive recognition from colleagues.

However, that is not to say that professionals do not want financial incentives. For example, studies in industries like pharmaceuticals and aerospace consistently show that firms with the most productive research and development groups have incentive pay plans for their professionals, usually in the form of bonuses. However, professionals' bonuses tend to represent a relatively small portion of their total pay. The time cycle of the professionals' incentive plans also tends to be longer than a year, reflecting the long time spent in designing, developing, and marketing a new product.

There are also many non-salary items that professionals must have to do their best work. Not strictly incentives, these range from better equipment and facilities and a supportive management style to support for professional journal publications.

ORGANIZATION-WIDE INCENTIVE PLANS

Many employers have incentive plans in which virtually all employees can participate. These include profit-sharing, employee stock ownership, and Scanlon plans.

Profit-Sharing Plans

profit-sharing plan A plan whereby most or all employees share in the company's profits.

In a **profit-sharing plan**, most or all employees receive a share of the company's profits. Approximately 20 percent of Canadian organizations offer profit-sharing plans.[72] These plans are easy to administer and have a broad appeal to employees and other company stakeholders. The weakness of profit-sharing plans regards "line of sight." It is unlikely that most employees perceive that they personally have the ability to influence overall company profit. It has been found that these plans produce a one-time productivity improvement, but no change thereafter. Another weakness of these plans is that they typically provide an annual payout, which is not as effective as more frequent payouts.[73]

There are several types of profit-sharing plans. In *cash plans*, the most popular, a percentage of profits (usually 15 percent to 20 percent) is distributed as profit shares at regular intervals. One example is Atlas-Graham Industries Limited in Winnipeg. A profit-sharing pool is calculated by deducting 2 percent of sales from pre-tax profit, and then taking 30 percent of the result. The pool is distributed equally among all employees. Other plans provide cash and deferred benefits. Fisheries Products International Limited in St. John's, Newfoundland, contributes 10 percent of pre-tax income to a profit-sharing pool that is divided up, just before Christmas, based on each employee's earnings. The first 75 percent of each employee's share is paid in cash, and the remaining 25 percent is allocated to pension plan improvements.[74]

There are also *deferred profit-sharing plans*. Here, a predetermined portion of profits is placed in each employee's account under the supervision of a trustee. There is a tax advantage to such plans, since income taxes are deferred, often until the employee retires and is taxed at a lower rate.

Employee Share Purchase/Stock Ownership Plan

employee share purchase/stock ownership plan (ESOPs) A trust is established to hold shares of company stock purchased for or issued to employees. The trust distributes the stock to employees on retirement, separation from service, or as otherwise prescribed by the plan.

National Centre for Employee Ownership **www.nceo.org**

Hints to Ensure Legal Compliance

Employee share purchase/stock ownership plans (ESOPs) are in place at approximately 50 percent of Canadian organizations with publicly traded stock.[75] A trust is established to purchase shares of the firm's stock for employees using cash from employee (and sometimes employer) contributions. Employers may also issue treasury shares to the trust instead of paying cash for a purchase on the open market. The trust holds the stock in individual employee accounts and distributes it to employees, often upon retirement or other separation from service. Some plans distribute the stock to employees once a year.

The corporation receives a tax deduction equal to the fair market value of the shares that are purchased by the trustee using employer contributions, but not for any treasury shares issued. The value of the shares purchased with employer contributions, and of any treasury shares issued, is a taxable benefit to the employees in the year of purchase of the shares. This tax treatment can create two problems. First, if the plan requires employees to complete a certain period of service before taking ownership of the shares, and the employee leaves before being eligible for ownership, the employee has paid tax on the value of shares that she or he never owns. Therefore, most plans have immediate vesting.[76] Second, if the value of the shares drops, employees may have paid tax on a greater amount than they receive when they eventually sell the shares.

ESOPs can encourage employees to develop a sense of ownership in and commitment to the firm, particularly when combined with good communication, employee involvement in decision making, and employee understanding of the business and the economic

General Printers' president, David Fors (far left), credits an employee share ownership plan with the company's turnaround.

environment.[77] For example, General Printers, in Oshawa, Ontario, achieved a dramatic turnaround following the introduction of an ESOP. The firm had been a chronic money-loser, but became profitable the year that the plan was introduced, and has remained so in the years since that time. The value of the company has grown 80 percent since the ESOP was introduced, profits are up, spoiled orders are down 50 percent, and far less supervision of employees is required.[78]

Scanlon Plan

Scanlon plan An incentive plan developed in 1937 by Joseph Scanlon and designed to encourage cooperation, involvement, and sharing of benefits.

Few would argue with the fact that the most powerful way of ensuring commitment is to synchronize the organization's goals with those of its employees. Many techniques have been proposed for obtaining this idyllic state, but few have been implemented as widely or successfully as the **Scanlon plan**, an incentive plan developed in 1937 by Joseph Scanlon, a United Steelworkers Union official.[79]

The Scanlon plan is remarkably progressive, considering that it was developed over 60 years ago. As currently implemented, Scanlon plans have the following basic features.[80] The first is the *philosophy of cooperation* on which it is based. This philosophy assumes that managers and workers have to rid themselves of the "us" and "them" attitudes that normally inhibit employees from developing a sense of ownership in the company. A pervasive philosophy of cooperation must exist in the firm for the plan to succeed.[81]

A second feature of the plan is what its practitioners refer to as *identity*. This means that to focus employee involvement, the company's mission or purpose must be clearly articulated and employees must fundamentally understand how the business operates in terms of customers, prices, and costs, for instance.

Competence is a third basic feature. The plan assumes that hourly employees can competently perform their jobs as well as identify and implement improvements, and that supervisors have leadership skills for the participative management that is crucial to a Scanlon plan.

The fourth feature of the plan is the *involvement system*.[82] Productivity-improving suggestions are presented by employees to the appropriate departmental-level committees, the members of which transmit the valuable ones to the executive-level committee. The latter group then decides whether to implement the suggestion.

The fifth element of the plan is the *sharing of benefits formula*. Basically, the Scanlon plan assumes that employees should share directly in any extra profits resulting from their cost-cutting suggestions. If a suggestion is implemented and successful, all employees usually share in 75 percent of the savings. For example, assume that the normal monthly ratio of payroll costs to sales is 50 percent. (Thus, if sales are $600 000, payroll costs should be $300 000.) Assume that suggestions are implemented and result in payroll costs of $250 000 in a month when sales were $550 000 and payroll costs would otherwise have been $275 000 (50 percent of sales). The saving attributable to these suggestions is $25 000 ($275 000 – $250 000). Workers would typically share in 75 percent of this ($18 750), while $6250 would go to the firm. In practice, a portion, usually one-quarter of the $18 750, is set aside for the months in which labour costs exceed the standard.

The Scanlon plan has been quite successful at reducing costs and fostering a sense of sharing and cooperation among employees. Yet Scanlon plans do fail, and there are several conditions required for their success. They are usually more effective when there is a relatively small number of participants, generally fewer than 1000. They are more successful when there are stable product lines and costs, since it is important that the labour costs/sales ratio remain fairly constant. Good supervision and healthy labour relations also seem essential. In addition, it is crucial that there be strong commitment to the plan on the part of management, particularly during the confusing phase-in period.[83]

Gainsharing Plans

The Scanlon plan is actually an early version of what today is known as a **gainsharing plan,** an incentive plan that engages many or all employees in a common effort to achieve a company's productivity objectives; any resulting incremental cost-saving gains are shared among employees and the company.[84] In addition to the Scanlon plan, other popular types of gainsharing plans include the Rucker and Improshare plans.

The basic difference among these plans is in the formula used to determine employee bonuses.[85] The Scanlon formula divides payroll expenses by total sales. The Rucker formula uses sales value minus materials and supplies, all divided into payroll expenses. The Improshare plan creates production standards for each department. The Scanlon and Rucker plans include participative management systems using committees. Improshare does not include a participative management component but instead considers participation an outcome of the bonus plan. According to one recent survey, just under 10 percent of Canadian organizations use gainsharing plans.[86]

The financial aspects of a gainsharing program can be quite straightforward.[87] Assume that a supplier wants to boost quality. Doing so would translate into fewer customer returns, less scrap and rework, and therefore higher profits. Historically, $1 million in output results in $20 000 (2 percent) scrap, returns, and rework. The company tells its employees that if next month's production results in only 1 percent scrap, returns, and rework, the 1 percent saved would be a gain, to be split 50/50 with the workforce, less a small amount for reserve for months in which scrap exceeds 2 percent. Awards are often posted monthly but allocated quarterly.[88]

Making the Plan Work   Several factors contribute to a gainsharing plan's successful implementation. While the focus may be on just one goal (like quality), many firms use a "family of measures." For example, one firm chose seven variables (productivity, cost performance, product damage, customer complaints, shipping errors, safety, and attendance) and set specific goals for each (such as zero lost-time accidents, for safety). Then specific monthly bonuses were attached to each goal achieved.[89] Quality, customer service, productivity, and cost represent another familiar family of measures.[90]

Successful gainsharing programs have several other key ingredients, according to a study by compensation consultants Sibson and Company.[91] Regardless of industry or size of operation, five key factors enabled the successful design, implementation, and ongoing operation of gainsharing plans:

- a cooperative relationship between management and labour
- joint development of the plan

gainsharing plan An incentive plan that engages employees in a common effort to achieve productivity objectives and share the gains.

Tips **for the**
Front Line

- effective communication
- clear guidelines regarding changing the plan
- setting achievable goals.

Gainsharing works well in stable organizations with predictable goals and measures of performance, but is less flexible and useful in dynamic industries that require rapid business adjustment. In general, most of their cost savings are generated in the early years.[92]

At-Risk Variable Pay Plans

In recent years, some firms have implemented new at-risk variable pay plans. These are plans that put some portion of the employee's base pay at risk, subject to the firm meeting its financial goals. At DuPont Canada, for instance, the employee's at-risk pay is 4 percent. This means that each employee will be paid 96 percent of his or her nominal salary. The employee can then earn up to 10 percent of that nominal salary based on company performance, payable in cash or company stock. The at-risk approach is aimed, in part, at paying employees like partners. It is actually similar to much more extensive programs in Japan in which the at-risk portion might be 50 percent to 60 percent of a person's yearly pay. To the extent that at-risk pay is part of a more comprehensive program aimed at turning employees into committed partners—a program stressing trust and respect, extensive communications, and participation and opportunities for advancement, for instance—at-risk programs should be successful.

DuPont Canada **ca.dupont.com**

DEVELOPING EFFECTIVE INCENTIVE PLANS

There are two major practical considerations in developing an effective incentive plan—when to use it and how to implement it.

When to Use Incentives

While there are no hard-and-fast rules, there are some conditions under which straight salary or pay based on time on the job—*not* on an incentive—makes somewhat more sense such as when:

- units of output are difficult to distinguish and measure
- employees are unable to control quantity of output
- delays in the work are frequent and beyond employees' control
- quality is a primary consideration.

Therefore, in general, it makes more sense to use an incentive plan when:

- units of output can be measured
- there is a clear relationship between employee effort and quantity of output
- the job is standardized, the work flow is regular, and delays are few or consistent

- quality is less important than quantity, or, if quality is important, it is easily measured and controlled.[93]

How to Implement Incentive Plans

Unfortunately, many companies find that variable pay plans do not produce desired business results. This is usually due to poor design and implementation of the plans.[94] There are several specific common-sense considerations in establishing any incentive plan. Of primary importance is "line of sight." The employee or group must be able to see their own impact on the goals or objectives for which incentives are being provided.[95] The Strategic HR box describes how one Canadian company, Maritime Life, has successfully implemented a variety of incentive plans.

Research
Insight ▷

Recent research indicates that there are seven principles that support effective implementation of incentive plans that lead to superior business results:[96]

1. Pay for performance—and make sure that performance is tied to the successful achievement of critical business goals.

2. Link incentives to other activities that engage employees in the business, such as career development and challenging opportunities.

STRATEGIC HR

Maritime Life Assures Employee Rewards

Employees at Maritime Life Assurance in Halifax are given extra incentive to treat their customers right. The company reinforces top-notch service by offering a yearly bonus for all staff based on customer satisfaction. In fact, that's one of the reasons Maritime Life was listed as one of Canada's top 50 companies to work for two years in a row.

"Maritime Life has been measuring customer satisfaction for a long time. The intention is to ensure that customer service and satisfaction is high and it has been within the company's value system for years," said Steve Christie, Director of Compensation and Benefits at Maritime Life.

Maritime usually sets target satisfaction rates of about 90 percent, and if that is achieved, staff will receive a bonus. Employees receive their payouts at the end of the year and the bonus ranges from $500 to $1000 per worker. However, the overall payout is the same for everyone, from senior manager to front-line worker, regardless of their position in the organization.

But employees don't have to wait until the end of the year to get rewarded. They could receive a Lighthouse Award at any time throughout the year,

which recognizes individual contributions. And it doesn't have to be handed out by top management. Peers can award other peers, managers can recognize staff both in their departments and other departments, and vice-presidents can do the same. Staff can also provide them to managers. The awards come complete with a certificate and voucher that can be used at the company's store, which sells Maritime Life paraphernalia. There is a maximum voucher of $75.

Cash bonuses and vouchers aren't the only things on Maritime's recognition roster. Top management and HR make sure employees know there is room for advancement. Employees even have access to their own Career Investment Account to facilitate career growth. About 2–4 percent of every employee's salary is allocated to this account. They can use the account for learning in terms of attending conferences, seminars, or workshops. As part of the performance review process when employees sit down with their managers, they're expected to look at what their development opportunities are and where they want to go in the company.

Source: Adapted from A. Tomlinson, "Maritime Life Assurance Employee Rewards," *Canadian HR Reporter* (March 11, 2002), p. 7. Reproduced by permission of *Canadian HR Reporter*, Carswell, One Corporate Plaza, 2075 Kennedy Road, Scarborough, ON M1T 3V4.

3. Link incentives to measurable competencies that are valued by the organization.

4. Match incentives to the culture of the organization—its vision, mission, and operation principles.

5. Keep group incentives clear and simple—employee understanding is the most important factor differentiating effective from ineffective group incentive plans.

6. Overcommunicate—employees become engaged when they hear the message that they are neither faceless nor expendable.

7. Remember that the greatest incentive is the work itself. For example, highly skilled engineers at MacDonald Detweiler and Associates Ltd. in Richmond, B.C., feel valued and appreciated when they are chosen by their peers to work on project teams to work on the Canada space arm or a project to save the rainforest, and they don't require large financial incentives to work hard.[97]

Why Incentive Plans Do Not Work

1. *Performance pay cannot replace good management.* Performance pay is supposed to motivate workers, but lack of motivation is not always the culprit. Ambiguous instructions, lack of clear goals, inadequate employee selection and training, unavailability of tools, and a hostile workforce (or management) are just a few of the factors that impede performance.

2. *Firms get what they pay for.* Psychologists know that people often put their effort where they know they will be rewarded. However, this can backfire. An incentive plan that rewards a group based on how many pieces are produced could lead to rushed production and lower quality. Awarding a plant-wide incentive for reducing accidents may simply reduce the number of reported accidents.

3. *"Pay is not a motivator."*[98] Psychologist Frederick Herzberg makes the point that money only buys temporary compliance, and that as soon as the incentive is removed the "motivation" disappears too. Instead, Herzberg says, employers should provide adequate financial rewards and then build other motivators, like opportunities for achievement and psychological success, into their jobs.

4. *Rewards rupture relationships.* Incentive plans have the potential for reducing teamwork by encouraging individuals (or individual groups) to blindly pursue financial rewards for themselves.

5. *Rewards may undermine responsiveness.* Since the employees' primary focus is on achieving some specific goal, like cutting costs, any changes or extraneous distractions mean that achieving that goal will be harder. Incentive plans can, therefore, mediate against change and responsiveness.

Potential pitfalls like these do not mean that financial incentive plans cannot be useful or should not be used. They do suggest, however, that goals need to be reasonable and achievable, but not so easily attained that employees view incentives as entitlements.[99] In general, any incentive plan is more apt to succeed if implemented with management support, employee acceptance, and a

Nelson Motivation Inc.
www.nelson-motivation.com

supportive culture characterized by teamwork, trust, and involvement at all levels.[100] This probably helps to explain why some of the longest-lasting incentive plans, like the Scanlon and Rucker plans, depend heavily on two-way communication and employee involvement in addition to incentive pay.

Research
I n s i g h t ▷

Recent research by two professors at the University of Alberta reviewed 145 major studies on rewards, motivation, and performance. Their investigation was designed to resolve a longstanding debate about whether extrinsic rewards can backfire by reducing intrinsic motivation, or whether extrinsic rewards boost performance and enhance intrinsic motivation. The authors concluded that *careful* management of rewards does enhance performance. Common problem areas to be avoided include not tying rewards to performance, not delivering on all rewards initially promised, and delivering rewards in an authoritarian style or manner. Guidelines for effective management of rewards include setting performance goals, linking rewards and career advancement, providing rewards for what employees really don't like doing, and letting workers design and implement rewards themselves.[101]

EMPLOYEE RECOGNITION PROGRAMS

Stephanie Kwolek, a DuPont scientist, received the company's highest award, the Lavoisier Medal for Technical Achievement.

Although appreciated at the time of receipt, monetary rewards are quickly spent and offer no lasting symbol of recognition.[102] There is a growing awareness that, in tough competitive times, when organizations need all of the skill and talents of all of their people, demonstrating appreciation of employees' achievements is more important than ever.[103] Why? Because lack of recognition and praise is the number-one reason that employees leave an organization.[104] The traditional role of recognition plans has been to reward employees for long service. Today, employees value being appreciated by an employer even more than the reward itself.[105]

Adrian Gostick of the recognition firm O.C. Tanner described another reason for increased management focus on recognition:

The September 11 tragedy put things in perspective for many North American businesses. Since then we have been reminded that companies are comprised of living, feeling, human beings who more than ever must be led, motivated and inspired. The job of manager has never been more important. It has also never been harder.... If we do it right, if we care enough to recognize and reward our people, we will emerge from this tragedy stronger than we entered.[106]

Recognition Plus **www. recognition-plus.com/index.html**

National Association for Employee Recognition **www.recognition.org**

O.C. Tanner Recognition Co. **www.octanner.com**

Employees consistently say that they receive little recognition.[107] One study found that only 50 percent of managers give recognition for high performance, and that up to 40 percent of workers feel that they never get recognized for outstanding performance.[108] Nurses are one group of employees that has long suffered from lack of respect. They feel ignored and undervalued as subservient assistants to doctors. The shortage of nurses in Canada has forced employers to consider treating nurses with the respect and recognition they deserve as invaluable contributors of knowledge and skills to the health-care system.[109]

Some believe that this lack of recognition occurs because expressing generous appreciation means talking about feelings in public, which may make managers feel vulnerable.[110] However, when lack of recognition and praise is resulting in the loss of valued employees, managers need to confront such apprehension and

Corporate Gifts
www.corporategift.com

start recognizing their employees for their achievements.[111] Why? Because employees favour recognition from supervisors and managers by a margin of two-to-one over recognition from other sources.[112]

Recognition is also cost-effective. It takes 5–15 percent of pay to have an impact on behaviour when a cash reward is provided, but only 3–5 percent when a non-cash form of reward is used (such as recognition and modest gifts).[113] More and more companies are using the Web to establish online recognition programs to reduce administration costs, as described in the HR.Net box.

Making time to recognize the individual in front of his or her colleagues is critical to the success of the program. Personal attention and public celebration create recognition that is personal in nature, and that addresses the deep needs that we all have for belonging and contributing to something worthwhile.[114] Effective recognition is sincere, immediate, meaningful, consistent, and visible.[115] If it is memorable, it will continue to evoke emotion and make the employee feel that his or her individual effort made a difference.[116] Company DNA, an incentives provider, offers an online points system where recognition points can be spent on merchandise with merchant partners such as Eddie Bauer, La Senza, Canadian Tire, and Future Shop.[117]

Recognition programs are more effective than cash in achieving improved employee attitudes, increased workloads and hours of work, and productivity (speed of work/intensity of work). They can build confidence, create a positive and supportive environment, build a sense of pride in accomplishments, inspire

HR.NET

Click on Rewards: Recognition Goes Online

North Americans have flocked to the Internet in staggering numbers. Growing in parallel to the Internet is the development of company-specific intranet sites used to inform employees and gather information from them in a wide variety of areas. The latest addition to the growing list of online, self-managed employee programs is employee recognition programs. However, building a successful online recognition program is not as easy as merely transferring a current paper-based catalogue program to an intranet or Internet site, nor is it restricted to technically savvy companies with huge IT budgets and personnel. As with any successful recognition program, companies that choose to go this route need to assess a number of determining factors, including employee Web access, award choices, award presentations, Web site development costs, and program administration.

Building an online recognition program and dedicated program Web site can be an expensive proposition. But given the flexibility and increased efficiency that online programs provide, these costs are well worth the investment. The investment associated with a printed brochure is eliminated and these budgeted dollars can be used to develop an electronic brochure. The online brochure is a virtual document with the flexibility to change levels, awards, policies, and program details without expensive reprinting costs.

An online recognition service provider allows program coordinators to set up their own private-label service-award program in minutes. Each Web site is fully customizable and features the client's logo, colours, photos, and messages. The Web site and awards can be modified at any time. A PDF version of the awards program can be printed off for employees who do not have e-mail access. Administration is also managed through the online program. The use of online-delivered HR programs will continue to grow. They are more convenient, offer greater efficiency, operate 24/7, and have the potential to lower HR's operating costs.

Source: Adapted from J. Mills, "Click on Rewards: Recognition Goes Online," *Canadian HR Reporter*, March 11, 2002, pp. 7, 12. Reproduced by permission of *Canadian HR Reporter*, Carswell, One Corporate Plaza, 2075 Kennedy Road, Scarborough, ON M1T 3V4.

people to increase their efforts, and help people feel valued.[118] Recognition can act as a strategic change effort if recognition criteria are aligned with business strategy, employee input is solicited regarding program design and implementation, and a recognition culture is created.[119]

Recognition is also important for high performers, who focus on what needs to be done to exceed expectations. These employees are driven by internal motivation, and look to reward programs to add fuel to their achievements. Recognition satisfies "wants" rather than "needs" (where cash bonuses often go), they eliminate guilt about owning luxury items, they provide bragging rights, and maintain a lasting impression in the employees' memory.[120]

Finally, recognition programs are key corporate communication tools that can achieve several goals—saying thank you, encouraging good workers, and encouraging good behaviour.[121] IBM, Labatt Breweries Ontario, Shell Canada, 3M Canada, Maple Leaf Sports and Entertainment Ltd., PricewaterhouseCoopers, and Warner Lambert are just some of the Canadian companies that are reaping the benefits of employee recognition programs.

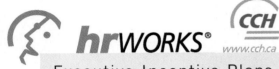

Executive Incentive Plans

The purpose of [executive] incentive compensation is to stimulate the best efforts of the executives. Incentive compensation plans will typically provide relatively high rewards for exceptional achievements, lower rewards for average achievements and no rewards for poor achievements.

Incentive compensation plans may provide rewards in the form of cash, additional deferred compensation, stock ownership or a combination of all three forms....

In designing incentive compensation plans, it is vital that the key purpose of the plan be documented.

For example, why does the plan exist? How does the plan relate to the business strategy of the company? What company division/department goals does the plan support? How are the following objectives weighted in the plan: attraction; retention; motivation; team building; building a proprietary interest in the company; motivation towards individual performance goals?

The plan's purpose must be consistent with a long term strategy of the organization while the actual design of the plan may incorporate more short term goals.

Source: Excerpted with permission from *Benefits and Pensions*, published by and copyright CCH Canadian Limited, Toronto, Ontario.

CHAPTER *Review*

Summary

1 Piecework is the oldest type of incentive plan. Here, a worker is paid a piece rate for each unit that he or she produces. The standard hour plan rewards workers by a premium that equals the percentage by which their performance is above standard. Group incentive plans are useful where the workers' jobs are highly interrelated.

2 Most management employees receive a short-term incentive, usually in the form of an annual bonus linked to company or divisional profits. Long-term incentives are intended to motivate and reward top management for the firm's long-term growth and prosperity, and to inject a long-term perspective into executive decisions.

3 Salary plans for salespeople are effective when the main sales objective is finding new clients, or servicing accounts. The main disadvantage of salary plans is that pay is not tied to performance. Commission plans attract high-performing salespeople who see that performance will clearly lead to rewards. The problem with straight commission plans is that there is a tendency to focus on "big-ticket" or "quick-sell" items and to disregard long-term customer relationships.

4 Money is somewhat less important as an incentive for professional employees than it is for other employees because professionals are already driven by the desire to produce high-calibre work and because the time cycle of professionals' incentive plans tends to be longer than one year, reflecting time for research, design, and development of new products and services. Professionals seek recognition and support in the form of the latest equipment and support for journal publications.

5 Profit-sharing plans, employee share purchase/stock ownership plans, and gainsharing plans, such as the Scanlon plan, are examples of organization-wide incentive plans. Profit-sharing plans provide a share of company profits to all employees in the organization. The problem with such plans is that sometimes the link between a person's efforts and rewards is unclear. Stock purchase plans provide a vehicle for employees to purchase company stock with their own and sometimes employer contributions. Gainsharing plans engage employees in a common effort to achieve a company's productivity objectives, and incremental cost-savings are shared among employees and the company. All of these plans are intended to increase employee commitment to the organization and motivate workers.

6 Incentive plans are particularly appropriate when units of output are easily measured, employees can control output, the effort–reward relationship is clear, work delays are under employees' control, and quality is not paramount.

7 Employee recognition plans are growing in popularity as a cost-effective method of retaining employees by praising their achievements. Recognition has the most impact when it is sincerely and meaningfully provided by the supervisor in a public presentation format.

Key Terms

annual bonus   *(p. 372)*
capital accumulation programs   *(p. 374)*
employee share purchase/stock ownership plan   *(p. 383)*
gainsharing plan   *(p. 385)*
guaranteed piecework plan   *(p. 369)*
merit pay (merit raise)   *(p. 381)*
piecework   *(p. 369)*
profit-sharing plan   *(p. 382)*
Scanlon plan   *(p. 384)*
spot bonus   *(p. 369)*
standard hour plan   *(p. 370)*
stock option   *(p. 374)*
straight piecework plan   *(p. 369)*
team or group incentive plan   *(p. 371)*
variable pay   *(p. 367)*

Review and Discussion Questions

1 What are two prerequisites for effective pay-for-performance plans?

2 Describe the three basic issues to be considered when awarding short-term management bonuses.

3 Explain how stock options work. What are some of the reasons that stock options have been criticized in recent years?

4 When and why should a salesperson be paid a salary? A commission? Salary and commission combined?

5 What is a Scanlon plan? What are the five basic features of these plans?

6 Explain five reasons why incentive plans fail.

7 Why are recognition plans useful for motivating high performers?

CRITICAL *Thinking Questions*

1 A university recently instituted a "Teacher Incentive Program" (TIP) for its faculty. Basically, faculty committees within each of the university's colleges were told to award $5000 raises (not bonuses) to about 40 percent of their faculty members based on how good a job they did in teaching undergraduates, and how many of these students they taught per year. What are the potential advantages and pitfalls of such an incentive program? How well do you think it was accepted by the faculty? Do you think that it had the desired effect?

2 Do you think that it is a good idea to award employees with merit raises? Why or why not? If not, what approach would you take to incentive compensation?

3 In this chapter, we listed a number of reasons that experts give for not instituting a pay-for-performance plan in a vacuum (such as "rewards rupture relationships"). Do you think that these points (or any others) are valid? Why or why not?

APPLICATION *Exercises*

Running Case: LearnInMotion.com

The Incentive Plan

Of all its HR programs, those relating to pay for performance and incentives are LearnInMotion.com's most fully developed. For one thing, the venture capital firm that funded it was very explicit about reserving at least 10 percent of the company's stock for employee incentives. The agreement with the venture capital firm also included very explicit terms and conditions regarding LearnInMotion.com's stock option plan. The venture fund agreement included among its 500 or so pages the specific written agreement that LearnInMotion.com would have to send to each of its employees, laying out the details of the company's stock option plan.

While there was some flexibility, the stock option plan details came down to this:

- Employees would get stock options (the right to buy shares of LearnInMotion.com stock) at a price equal to 15 percent less than the venture capital fund paid for those shares when it funded LearnInMotion.com.

- The shares will have a vesting schedule of 36 months, with one-third of the shares vesting once the employee has completed 12 full months of employment with the company, and one-third

vesting upon successful completion of each of the following two full 12 months of employment.

- If an employee leaves the company for any reason prior to his or her first full 12 months with the firm, the person is eligible for no stock options.

- If the person has stock options and leaves the firm for any reason, he or she must exercise the options within 90 days of the date of leaving the firm, or lose the right to exercise them.

The actual number of options an employee gets depends on the person's bargaining power and on how much Jennifer and Pierre think the person brings to the company. The options granted generally ranged from options to buy 10 000 shares for some employees up to 50 000 shares for others, but this has not raised any questions to date. When a new employee signs on, he or she receives a letter of offer. This provides minimal details regarding the option plan; after the person has completed the 90-day introductory period, he or she receives the five-page document describing the stock option plan, which Jennifer or Pierre, as well as the employee, signs.

Beyond that, the only incentive plan is the one for the two salespeople. In addition to their respective salaries, both salespeople receive about 20 percent of any sales they bring in, whether those sales are from advertising banners or course listing fees. It's not clear to Jennifer and Pierre whether this incentive is effective. Each salesperson gets a base salary regardless of what he or she sells (one gets about $50 000, the other about $35 000). However, sales have simply not come up to the levels anticipated. Jennifer and Pierre are not sure why. It could be that Internet advertising has dried up. It could be that their own business model is no good, and there's not enough demand for their company's services. They may be charging too much or too little. It could be that the salespeople can't do the job due to inadequate skills or inadequate training. Or, of course, it could be the incentive plan. ("Or it could be all of the above," as Pierre somewhat dejectedly said late one Friday evening.) They want to try to figure out what the problem is. They want you, their management consultants, to help them figure out what to do. Here's what they want you to do for them.

Questions

1 Up to this point they've awarded only a tiny fraction of the total stock options available for distribution. Should they give anyone or everyone additional options? Why or why not?

2 Should they put other employees on a pay-for-performance plan that somehow links their monthly or yearly pay to how well the company is doing sales-wise? Why or why not? If so, how should the company do it?

3 Is there another incentive plan you think would work better for the salespeople? What is it?

4 On the whole, what do you think the sales problem is?

CASE INCIDENT *Loafers at Interlake Utility Company*

Interlake Utility Company provides electrical power to a district with 50 000 households. Pamela Johnson is the manager in charge of all repair and installation crews. Each crew consists of approximately seven employees who work closely together to respond to calls concerning power outages, fires caused by electrical malfunctions, and installation of new equipment or electrical lines. Fourteen months ago, Johnson decided to implement a team-based incentive system in which an annual bonus would be provided to each crew that met certain performance criteria. Performance measures included such indicators as average length of time needed to restore power, results of a customer satisfaction survey, and number of hours required to complete routine installation assignments successfully. At the end of the first year, five crews received an average cash bonus of $12 000 each, with the amount divided equally among all crew members.

Soon after Johnson announced the recipients of the cash bonus, she began to receive a large number of complaints. Some teams not chosen for the award voiced their unhappiness through their crew leader. The two most common complaints were that the teams working on the most difficult assignments were penalized (because it was harder to score higher on the evaluation) and that crews unwilling to help out other crews were being rewarded.

Ironically, members of the crews that received the awards also expressed dissatisfaction. A surprisingly large number of confidential employee letters from the winning teams reported that the system was unfair because the bonus money was split evenly among all crew members. Several letters named loafers who received "more than their share" because they were frequently late for work, took long lunches and frequent smoking breaks, and lacked initiative. Johnson is at a loss about what to do next.

Questions

1 What major issues and problems concerning the design and implementation of pay-for-performance systems does this case illustrate? Explain.

2 Are team-based incentives appropriate for the type of work done by Johnson's crews?

3 Might it be desirable to use a combination of team-based and individual incentives at Interlake Utility Company? How might such a plan be structured?

Source: L. R. Gomez-Mejia, D.B. Balkin, R. L. Cardy, and D.E. Dimick, "Loafers at Interlake Utility Company." In *Managing Human Resources*, Canadian second edition (Scarborough, ON: Prentice Hall, 2000), pp. 342–43.

EXPERIENTIAL Exercises

1 Working individually or in groups, develop an incentive plan for each of the following positions: Web designer, hotel manager, and used-car salesperson. What factors had to be taken into consideration?

2 Explain why employee recognition plans are growing in popularity. How would you go about recognizing your favourite professor?

3 Express Automotive, an automobile mega-dealership with over 600 employees that represents 22 brands, has just received a very discouraging set of survey results. It seems their customer satisfaction scores have fallen for the ninth straight quarter. Customer complaints included the following:

- It was hard to get prompt feedback from mechanics by phone.
- Salespeople often did not return phone calls.
- The finance people seemed "pushy."
- New cars were often not properly cleaned or had minor items that needed immediate repair or adjustment.
- Cars often had to be returned to have repair work redone.

The following table describes Express Automotive's current compensation system.

The class is to be divided into five groups. Each group is assigned to one of the five teams in column one. Each group should analyze the compensation package for its team. Each group should be able to identify the ways in which the current compensation plan (1) helps company performance and/or (2) impedes company performance. Once the groups have completed their analysis, the following questions are to be discussed as a class:

(a) In what ways might your group's compensation plan contribute to the customer service problems?

(b) Are rewards provided by your department that impede the work of other departments?

(c) What recommendations would you make to improve the compensation system in a way that would likely improve customer satisfaction?

Team	Responsibility	Current Compensation Method
Sales Force	Persuade buyers to purchase a car.	Very small salary (minimum wage) with commissions. Commission rate increases with every 20 cars sold per month.
Finance Office	Help close the sale; persuade customer to use company finance plan.	Salary, plus bonus for each $10 000 financed with the company.
Detailing	Inspect cars delivered from factory, clean and make minor adjustments.	Piecework paid on the number of cars detailed per day.
Mechanics	Provide factory warranty service, maintenance and repair.	Small hourly wage, plus bonus based on (1) number of cars completed per day and (2) finishing each car faster than the standard estimated time to repair.
Receptionists/ phone service personnel	Primary liaison between customer and sales force, finance, and mechanics.	Minimum wage.

CHAPTER 13

Employee Benefits and Services

LEARNING OUTCOMES

After studying this chapter, you should be able to:

List and describe the five main categories of employee benefits.

Describe four government-sponsored benefits.

Explain why the cost of health insurance benefits is increasing and how employers can reduce these costs.

Describe recent trends in retirement benefits.

Discuss three types of personal employee services and six types of job-related services offered by many organizations.

Explain how to set up a flexible benefits program.

THE CHANGING ROLE OF EMPLOYEE BENEFITS

employee benefits Indirect financial payments given to employees. They may include supplementary health and life insurance, vacation, pension, education plans, and discounts on company products, for instance.

Employee benefits and services can be defined as all of the indirect financial payments that an employee receives during his or her employment with an employer.[1] Benefits are generally available to all of a firm's employees, and include such things as time off with pay, supplementary health and life insurance, and employee assistance plans. Employee services, traditionally a minor aspect of compensation, are becoming more sought after by today's employees in the post-job-security era. Research indicates that benefits do matter to employees, and that if they are aligned with business strategy, they can help to attract and retain the right people to achieve business objectives.[2] Flight Centre Ltd., one of the *Report on Business* "Best Companies to Work for in Canada" uses benefits to motivate staff, as described in the Strategic HR box.

Employee benefits are an important part of most employees' compensation; particularly given today's reality of modest salary increases.[3] For the aging workforce, health-care benefits are becoming increasingly important.[4] Employee benefits are in the midst of an evolution, based on the aging population, the looming labour shortage in Canada, and advances in health care. Each of these factors is expected to increase the cost of benefits, which are already at an all-time high.[5]

Administering benefits today represents an increasingly specialized task because workers are more financially sophisticated and demanding, and because benefit plans must comply with a wide variety of laws. Providing and administering benefits is also an increasingly expensive task. Benefits as a percentage of

STRATEGIC HR

Top Shops Deliver More than Flashy Perks

The number one ranked company to work for in Canada is Flight Centre Ltd., an international travel agency with a division in Toronto. With its beginnings in Australia, it has become the leading travel agency down under and ranks seventh in the world. They have a very humble work philosophy. They work by a "no privileges unless everyone has them" motto, which means no receptionists (not even for the head honchos), no individual offices, and no cleaners.

"We even take the garbage out ourselves," says Grahame Hubbard, managing director for Eastern Canada.

Everything is shared including an emergency fund created by Hubbard. After being diagnosed with a brain tumour that was operated on and was benign, he discovered there's a lot an insurance package can't cover. Now every store in Eastern Canada saves $100 per month to go towards a company fund that helps employees in times of need. One employee suffers from a disorder called alopecia and all her hair fell out last year, and the emergency fund money was used to buy a wig for her. It's important for Hubbard

to know his employees and share things with them that go beyond how many sales are made, so they don't feel like they're just a number.

"I want them to feel that I appreciate them for who they are. That I give them enough respect to know about them and what makes them tick and I offer the same in return," said Hubbard.

Considering his staff is 75 percent female, he's also planning to build a free on-site daycare centre that will stay open late in the evening. Right now it's an absolute nightmare to find a daycare centre that's open until 10 o'clock at night, says Hubbard. And Flight Centre employees stay out later than that at their monthly "buzz night" socials where they cheer on other employees, talk about their lives, and have a drink or two.

"Our employees have a lot in common and it's not just Flight Centre talk. It brings togetherness to the team."

Source: A. Tomlinson, "Top Shops Deliver More than Flashy Perks," *Canadian HR Reporter* (January 28, 2002), pp. 1, 3. Reproduced by permission of *Canadian HR Reporter*, Carswell, One Corporate Plaza, 2075 Kennedy Road, Scarborough, ON M1T 3V4.

payroll (for public and private sectors combined) are about 37 percent today (compared to about 15 percent in 1953). That translates to around $17 500 in total annual benefits per employee.[6] Most employees do not realize the market value and high cost to the employer of their benefits, so prudent employers list the benefits' true costs on each employee's pay stub.

Most Canadian companies provide some form of employee benefits. Almost all employers provide group life insurance, and most provide health and dental care insurance and retirement benefits. In the remainder of this chapter, we will describe the following types of benefits and services: (1) government-sponsored benefits, (2) pay for time not worked, (3) insurance benefits, (4) retirement benefits, and (5) employee services.

GOVERNMENT-SPONSORED BENEFITS

Canada has one of the world's finest collections of social programs to protect its citizens when they cannot earn income. Employers and employees provide funding for these plans, along with general tax revenues. In 2000, the average cost to employers for government-sponsored benefits was 11 percent of payroll.[7]

Employment Insurance (EI)

employment insurance A federal program that provides income benefits if a person is unable to work through no fault of his or her own.

Employment insurance is a federal program that provides weekly benefits if a person is unable to work through no fault of his or her own. It does not apply to workers who are self-employed. EI provides benefits for employees who are laid off, terminated without just cause, or who quit their job for a justifiable reason such as harassment. EI benefits are not payable when an employee is terminated for just cause—for example, for theft of company property—or when an employee quits for no good reason. Workers may also be eligible for special EI benefits in cases of illness, injury, or quarantine where the employer has no sickness or disability benefits (or once such benefits have been exhausted), and for maternity/parental leaves.

In order to receive benefits, an employee must first have worked a minimum number of hours during a minimum number of weeks called a qualifying period (the number of hours and weeks varies between regions of the country). Then there is a waiting period from the last day of work until benefits begin. The waiting period varies, but is often two weeks. If the employee was provided with severance pay or holiday pay at the time of losing the job, these payments must run out before the waiting period begins.

The EI benefit is generally 55 percent of average earnings during the last 14 to 26 weeks of the qualifying period, depending on the regional unemployment rate. The benefit is payable for up to 45 weeks, depending on the regional unemployment rate and other factors. In order to receive EI benefits, individuals must demonstrate that they are actively seeking work. Claimants are encouraged to work part-time, as they can earn up to 25 percent of their EI benefit amount before these earnings will be deducted from the benefit. Illness benefits are payable for up to 15 weeks, and maternity/parental leave benefits are payable for up to 50 weeks.

The EI program is funded by contributions from eligible employees and their employers. Employee contributions are collected by payroll deduction, and employers pay 1.4 times the employee contribution. Employer contributions can be reduced if the employer provides a wage loss replacement plan for employee sick leave.

A supplemental unemployment benefit (SUB) plan is an agreement between an employer and the employees (often the result of collective bargaining) for a plan that enables employees who are eligible for EI benefits to receive additional benefits from an SUB fund created by the employer. The purpose of an SUB plan is to supplement EI benefits so that employees can better maintain their standard of living during periods of unemployment resulting from a variety of circumstances (including layoffs, maternity/parental leave, and illness) by receiving a combined benefit closer to their actual working wage. One Canadian study found that 80 percent of employers who provide SUBs do so for maternity leaves.[8] SUBs are often found in heavy-manufacturing operations, such as the auto and steel industries, where layoffs are common. The amount of the SUB benefit is usually determined based on length of service and wage rate. Eighty percent of Canadian SUBs provide benefits of 90 percent of the working wage or greater.[9] Work-sharing programs are a related arrangement where employees work a reduced workweek and receive EI benefits for the remainder of the week. The EI Commission must approve SUB plans and work-sharing programs.

Canada/Quebec Pension Plan (C/QPP)

The **Canada/Quebec Pension Plans (C/QPP)** were introduced in 1966 to provide working Canadians with a basic level of financial security upon retirement or disability. Over 35 years later, these benefits do indeed provide a significant part of most Canadians' retirement income. Almost all employed Canadians between the ages of 18 and 65 are covered, including self-employed individuals. Casual and migrant workers are excluded, as are people who are not earning any employment income, such as homemakers. The benefits are portable, meaning that pension rights are not affected by changes in job or residence within Canada. Both contributions and benefits are based only on earnings up to the "Year's Maximum Pensionable Earnings" (intended to approximate the average industrial wage) as defined in the legislation. Benefits are adjusted based on inflation each year in line with the consumer price index.

Three types of benefits are provided: retirement pensions, disability pensions, and survivor benefits. The *retirement pension* is calculated as 25 percent of the average earnings (adjusted for inflation up to the average inflation level during the last five years prior to retirement) over the years during which contributions were made. Plan members can choose to begin receiving benefits at any time between the ages of 60 and 70. Benefits are reduced upon early retirement before age 65 and are increased in the case of late retirement after age 65. *Disability benefits* are only paid for severe disabilities that are expected to be permanent or to last for an extended period of time. The disability benefit is 75 percent of the pension benefit earned at the date of disability, plus a flat-rate amount per child. *Survivor benefits* are paid upon the death of a plan member. A lump sum payment is made to survivors, and a monthly pension is also payable to the surviving spouse.

Contributions made by employees (4.95 percent of pensionable earnings) are matched by employers. The amount of contributions was gradually increased

Canada/Quebec Pension Plan (C/QPP) Programs that provide three types of benefits: retirement income; survivor or death benefits payable to the employee's dependants regardless of age at time of death; and disability benefits payable to disabled employees and their dependants. Benefits are payable only to those individuals who make contributions to the plans and/or their family members.

Canada Pension Plan
www.cpp-rpc.gc.ca

from 1987 to 2003 due to concerns about the ability of these plans to pay benefits to members of the baby-boom generation when they retire.[10]

Workers' Compensation

workers' compensation Workers' compensation provides income and medical benefits to victims of work-related accidents or illnesses and/or their dependants, regardless of fault.

Workers' compensation laws are aimed at providing sure, prompt income and medical benefits to victims of work-related accidents or illnesses and/or their dependants, regardless of fault. Every province and territory, and the federal jurisdiction, has its own workers' compensation law. These laws impose compulsory collective liability for workplace accidents and work-related illnesses. This means that employees and employers cannot sue each other regarding the costs of workplace accidents or illnesses. Workers' compensation is, in effect, a "no fault" insurance plan designed to help injured or ill workers get well and return to work. For an injury or illness to be covered by workers' compensation, one must only prove that it arose while the employee was on the job. It does not matter that the employee may have been at fault; if he or she was on the job when the injury or illness occurred, he or she is entitled to workers' compensation. For example, suppose all employees are instructed to wear safety goggles when working at their machines, and one does not and is injured. Workers' compensation benefits will still be provided. The fact that the worker was at fault in no way waives his or her claim to benefits.

Employers collectively pay the full cost of the workers' compensation system, which can be an onerous financial burden for small businesses. The amount of the premiums (called assessments) varies by industry and by actual employer costs. Employer premiums are tax-deductible. Workers' Compensation Boards (Workplace Safety and Insurance Board in Ontario) exist in each jurisdiction to determine and collect assessments from employers, determine rights to compensation, and pay workers the amount of benefit to which they are entitled under the legislation in their jurisdiction. Employers and employees have some representation on these boards, but usually both parties believe they should have more control.

Although safety gear is always recommended, failure to wear it does not invalidate an employee's claim for benefits under workers' compensation laws.

Workers' compensation benefits include payment of expenses for medical treatment and rehabilitation, income benefits during the period of time in which the worker is unable to work (temporarily or permanently) due to his or her disability (partial or total). Survivor benefits are payable if a work-related death occurs. All benefits are nontaxable.

Controlling Workers' Compensation Costs

In most provinces, workers' compensation costs skyrocketed during the 1980s and 1990s. Unfunded liabilities for future pensions across the country reached over $15 billion. As a result, a number of provinces amended their workers' compensation legislation to reduce benefit levels, limit benefit entitlements for stress-related illnesses and chronic pain, reduce inflation indexing of benefits, and put more emphasis on rehabilitation and return to work. Several provinces followed the lead of Alberta in using sound business principles and practices to streamline the large administrative bureaucracies that had developed and to eliminate unfunded liabilities, while still providing the benefits required by law and generating surplus funds to return to employers.

All parties agree that a renewed focus on accident prevention is the best way to manage workers' compensation costs over the long term. Minimizing the number of workers' compensation claims is an important goal for all employers. While the Workers' Compensation Board pays the claims, the premiums for most employers depend on the number and amount of claims that are paid. Minimizing such claims is thus important.

In practice, there are two main approaches to reducing workers' compensation claims. First, firms try to reduce accident- or illness-causing conditions in facilities by instituting effective safety and health programs and complying with government safety standards. Second, since workers' compensation costs increase the longer an employee is unable to return to work, employers have become involved in instituting rehabilitation programs for injured or ill employees. These include physical therapy programs and career counselling to guide such employees into new, less strenuous or stressful jobs to reintegrate recipients back into the workforce. Workers are required to cooperate with return-to-work initiatives such as modified work.[11]

Provincial Health-Care Plans

provincial health-care plans
Provincial health-care plans pay for basic medically required hospital and medical services with no direct fee to patients.

All provinces and territories sponsor **provincial health-care plans** that provide basic medical and hospital services with no direct fee to patients. The provinces of British Columbia and Alberta finance their health-care plans by requiring monthly premiums to be paid by each resident. These premiums may be subsidized by employers. Ontario, Quebec, Manitoba, and Newfoundland levy a payroll tax to partially fund the cost of their health-care plans. Saskatchewan, Prince Edward Island, New Brunswick, Nova Scotia, the Northwest Territories, Nunavut, and the Yukon Territory use general tax revenues to pay for their plans.

The services paid for by these plans include medically required procedures provided by physicians, nurses, and other health-care professionals, standard ward hospital accommodation, drugs and medication administered in hospital, laboratory and diagnostic procedures, and hospital facilities such as operating rooms. Some of the services that are not covered by the provincial plans are prescription drugs, dental care, eyeglasses, private-duty nursing, cosmetic surgery, and semi-private or private hospital accommodation.

PAY FOR TIME NOT WORKED

pay for time not worked Benefits for time not worked such as vacation and holiday pay, and sick pay.

Pay for time not worked is typically one of an employer's most expensive benefits because of the large amount of time off that many employees receive. Common time-off-with-pay periods include holidays, vacations, sick leave, notice periods on termination of employment, and some leaves of absence. While some of these (such as holidays and vacations) can also be viewed as legally required benefits, the fact is that pay for time not worked is a substantial part of almost every employer's payroll expense. In this section some of the major time-off-with-pay elements will be discussed, specifically vacation and holiday pay, short-term disability/sick leave, leaves of absence, and pay on termination of employment.

Vacations and Holidays

Labour/employment standards legislation sets out a minimum amount of paid vacation that must be provided to employees, usually two weeks per year, but the requirements vary by jurisdiction. The actual number of paid employee vacation days also varies considerably from employer to employer. Even within the same organization, the number of vacation days usually depends on how long the employee has worked at the firm. Thus, a typical vacation policy might call for:

- two weeks for the first five years of service
- three weeks for six to ten years of service
- four weeks for 11 to 15 years of service
- five weeks for 16 to 25 years of service
- six weeks after 25 years of service.

The average number of annual vacation days is generally greater in European countries. For example, employees in Sweden and Austria can expect 30 vacation days; in France 25 days; and in the United Kingdom, Spain, Norway, Finland, and Belgium 20 to 25 days. There is some pressure from younger Canadian employees to increase vacation time, to assist with work–life balance.[12]

Several practical questions must be addressed in formulating an employer's vacation policies. For example, some vacation plans give the employee his or her regular base rate of pay while on vacation, while others provide for vacation pay based on average earnings (which may include overtime). The statutory minimum accrued vacation time must be paid if an employee leaves before taking it. Consideration must also be given to whether to penalize an employee who takes his or her annual vacation and then resigns before fully earning the vacation time that he or she has already taken.

The number of paid holidays similarly varies considerably from one jurisdiction to another, from a minimum of five to a maximum of nine. The most common paid holidays include New Year's Day, Good Friday, Canada Day, Labour Day, Thanksgiving Day, and Christmas Day. Other common holidays include Victoria Day, Remembrance Day, and Boxing Day. Additional holidays may be observed in each province, such as Saint Jean-Baptiste Day in Quebec and the Alberta Family Day.

A number of holiday pay policy issues must also be addressed. For example, provisions must be made for holidays that fall on a Saturday or Sunday: employees are often given the following Monday off when the holiday falls on a Sunday, and Friday off when it falls on a Saturday. Most labour/employment standards legislation also provides for some pay premium—such as time and a half—when employees must work on a holiday.

Short-Term Disability/Sick Leave

EmployEase www.employease.com

short-term disability/sick leave
Plans that provide pay to an employee when he or she is unable to work because of a non-work-related illness or injury.

Short-term disability plans (also known as salary continuation plans) provide a continuation of all or part of an employee's earnings when the employee is absent from work due to non-work-related illness or injury. Usually a medical certificate is required if the absence extends beyond two or three days. These plans typically provide full pay for some period of time (often two or three weeks) and then gradually reduce the percentage of earnings paid as the period of absence lengthens. The benefits cease when the employee returns to work or when the employee qualifies for long-term disability. These plans are sometimes provided through an insurance company.

Sick leave plans operate quite differently from short-term disability plans. Most sick leave policies grant full pay for a specified number of permissible sick days—usually up to about 12 per year (often accumulated at the rate of one day per month of service). Newfoundland, the Yukon, Quebec, and the federal jurisdiction require sick leave (unpaid), as a minimum standard. Sick leave pay creates difficulty for many employers. The problem is that while many employees use their sick days only when they are legitimately sick, others simply utilize their sick leave as extensions to their vacations, whether they are sick or not. Also, seriously ill or injured employees get no pay once their sick days are used up.

Employers have tried several tactics to eliminate or reduce the problem. Some now buy back unused sick leave at the end of the year by paying their employees a daily equivalent pay for each sick leave day not used. The drawback is that the policy can encourage legitimately sick employees to come to work despite their illness.[13] Others have experimented with holding monthly lotteries in which only employees with perfect monthly attendance are able to participate; those who participate are eligible to win a cash prize. Still others aggressively investigate all absences, for instance, by calling the absent employees at their homes when they are off sick.

Leaves of Absence

All of the provinces and territories, and the federal jurisdiction, require unpaid leaves of absence to be provided to employees in certain circumstances. Some employers provide full or partial pay for all or part of these leaves. Maternity/pregnancy leave is provided in every jurisdiction, and each has one or more of paternity, parental, and adoption leave available as well. The amount of maternity leave is 17 or 18 weeks in each jurisdiction (usually after one year of service), but parental and adoption leaves range from eight to 52 weeks. Employees who take these leaves of absence are guaranteed their old job or a similar job when they return to work.

Bereavement leave upon the death of a family member is provided for employees in some, but not all, jurisdictions. The amount of time off varies by jurisdiction, and depends on the closeness of the relationship between the employee and the deceased. Bereavement leave is usually unpaid, but in some cases it can be partially or fully paid.

Sabbatical leaves are becoming more common as a trend to retain employees and avoid employee burnout, particularly for employees struggling with work–life balance. Sun Media Corporation has led the way in Canada. Sabbatical leaves are usually unpaid, but some employers provide partial or full pay.[14]

Having a clear procedure for any leave of absence is essential. An application form such as the one in **Figure 13.1** should be the centrepiece of any such procedure. In general, no employee should be given a leave until it is clear what the leave is for. If the leave is for medical or family reasons, medical certification should be obtained from the attending physician or medical practitioner. A form like this also places on record the employee's expected return date and the fact that, without an authorized extension, his or her employment may be terminated.

FIGURE 13.1   Sample Application for Leave of Absence

APPLICATION FOR LEAVE OF ABSENCE WITHOUT PAY

NAME:			
	Surname	*First Name*	*Initial*

I.D #

WORK LOCATION:
- ☐ King Edward Campus   ☐ City Centre Campus
- ☐ Other: _____
  Please specify

DEPARTMENT:

EMPLOYEE GROUP:
- ☐ Support Staff (CUPE)   ☐ VCCFA Instructors
- ☐ Administrators   ☐ VCCFA Health Nurses

PERIOD OF LEAVE REQUESTED (Includes Weekends):

FROM (First Calendar Day of Leave):	**TO (Last Calendar Day of Leave):**
Day Month Year	Day Month Year

If period of Leave requested is 15 (fifteen) * calendar days or less, you must complete this section:

Number of Duty Days on Leave: _____

Total Number of hours on Leave: _____

Working under Compressed Work Week Schedule: ☐ Yes   ☐ No

If Leave is One Duty Day or Less, Indicate Hours of Leave: _____

For Faculty Members:

This unpaid Leave of Absence will not count as "duty days" for the purpose of regularization of appointment nor for the purpose of time-status increase.

REASON FOR REQUEST:

☐ **PERSONAL**   ☐ **ILLNESS** (Exhaustion of Sick Leave Credits) _____
                                                              First Date of Absence

☐ **MATERNITY** (Please attach Doctor's note indicating Expected Date of Confinement)

☐ **OTHER** _____
             Please Specify

EMPLOYEES SIGNATURE:		**DATE:**	
APPROVAL-DEPARTMENT HEAD:		**DATE:**	
APPROVAL-HUMAN RESOURCES:		**DATE:**	
THIS SECTION FOR PAYROLL USE:			

The information on this form is collected under the authority of the Collective Agreement between the College and its bargaining units. The information provided will be used to process your leave. If you have any questions about the collection and use of this information, please contact the Department of Human Resources.

Completed "Original" Form to be Forwarded to the Department of Human Resources for Processing

Source: Human Resources Department, Vancouver Community College. © 2003. Reproduced with permission.

While most leaves are unpaid, it is incorrect to assume that the leave is cost-less to the employer. For example, one study concluded that the costs associated with recruiting new temporary-replacement workers, training replacement workers, and compensating for the lower level of productivity of these workers could represent a substantial expense over and above what employers would normally pay their full-time employees.[15]

Pay on Termination of Employment

Employment/labour standards legislation requires that employees whose employment is being terminated by the employer be provided with termination pay when they leave. In most cases, this is pay for time not worked. The amount to be paid varies between jurisdictions and with the circumstances, as follows.

Pay in Lieu of Notice
An employee must be provided with advance written notice if the employer is going to terminate his or her employment (unless the employee is working on a short-term contract, or is being fired for just cause). The amount of advance notice that is required increases with the length of employment of the employee (often one week per year of employment to a specified maximum), and varies between jurisdictions. Many employers do not provide advance written notice. Instead, they ask the employee to cease working immediately and provide the employee with a lump sum equal to their pay for the notice period. This amount is called "pay in lieu of notice."

Severance Pay
Employees in Ontario and the federal jurisdiction may be eligible for severance pay in addition to pay in lieu of notice in certain termination situations. In Ontario, employees with five or more years of service may be eligible for severance pay if (1) the employer's annual Ontario payroll is $2.5 million or more, or (2) the employer is closing down the business and 50 or more employees will be losing their jobs within a six-month period. The amount of the severance pay is one week's pay for each year of employment (maximum 26 weeks). In the federal jurisdiction, employees who have been employed for 12 months or more receive the greater of (1) two days' wages per year of employment and (2) five days' wages.

Pay for Mass Layoffs
The provinces of British Columbia, Manitoba, Ontario, New Brunswick, and Newfoundland require that additional pay be provided when a layoff of 50 or more employees occurs. In Nova Scotia and Saskatchewan, additional pay is required if 10 or more employees are being laid off. The amount of additional pay ranges from six weeks to 18 weeks, depending on the province and the number of employees being laid off.

INSURANCE BENEFITS

Life Insurance

group life insurance Insurance provided at lower rates for all employees, including new employees, regardless of health or physical condition.

Virtually all employers provide **group life insurance** plans for their employees. As a group, employees can obtain lower rates than if they bought such insurance as individuals. In addition, group plans usually contain a provision for coverage of all employees—including new ones—regardless of health or physical condition.

In most cases, the employer pays 100 percent of the base premium, which usually provides life insurance equal to about two years' salary. Additional life insurance coverage is sometimes made available to employees, on an optional, employee-paid basis. *Accidental death and dismemberment* coverage provides a fixed lump-sum benefit in addition to life insurance benefits when death is accidental. It also provides a range of benefits in case of accidental loss of limbs or sight, and is often paid for by the employer. In general, there are three key policy areas to be addressed: the amount of benefit to be paid (benefits are usually tied to the annual earnings of the employee); supplemental benefits (continued life insurance coverage after retirement, and so on); and financing (the amount of the cost that the employee contributes).[16]

Critical illness insurance provides a lump-sum benefit to an employee who is diagnosed with and/or survives a life-threatening illness. This benefit bridges the gap between life insurance and disability insurance by providing immediate funds to relieve some the financial burden associated with the illness (such as paying for out-of-country treatment or experimental treatment) or enabling employees to enjoy their remaining time by pursuing activities that would normally be beyond their financial means.[17]

Supplementary Health-Care/Medical Insurance

Most employers provide their employees with supplementary health-care/medical insurance (over and above that provided by provincial health-care plans). Along with life insurance and long-term disability, these benefits form the cornerstone of almost all benefit programs.[18] Supplementary health-care insurance is aimed at providing protection against medical costs arising from accidents or illness as a result of off-the-job causes. **Figure 13.2** illustrates the results of a Canadian survey on health care showing that employees consider drug plans to be the most important benefit, closely followed by disability plans.

FIGURE 13.2 "Very Important" Benefits According to Employees

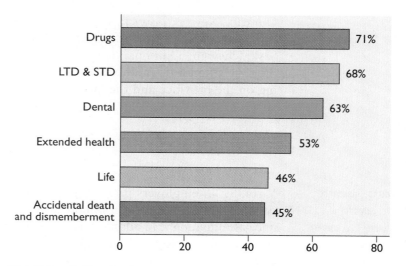

Source: "Not All Benefit Plans Are Equal," *Benefits Briefly*, Winter 2001. Reprinted with permission of RBWS Inc.

Most supplementary health insurance plans provide insurance at group rates, which are usually lower than individual rates and are generally available to all employees—including new ones—regardless of health or physical condition. Supplementary health-care plans provide major medical coverage to meet medical expenses not covered by government health-care plans (including prescription drugs, private or semi-private hospital rooms, private duty nursing, physiotherapy, medical supplies, ambulance services, and so on) that result from normal health problems or from long-term or serious illnesses. In most employer-sponsored drug plans, employees must pay a specified amount of **deductible** expense (typically $25 or $50) per year before plan benefits begin. Many employers also sponsor health-related insurance plans that cover expenses like vision care, hearing aids, and dental services, often with deductibles. In a majority of cases, the participants in such plans have their premiums paid for entirely by their employers.[19]

deductible The annual amount of health/dental expenses that an employee must pay before insurance benefits will be paid.

Reducing Health Benefit Costs

Dramatic increases in health-care costs are the biggest issue facing benefits managers in Canada today. **Figure 13.3** shows how increases in medical and dental plan costs have escalated since 1990. The main reasons for these increases are increased use of expensive new drugs, rising drug utilization by an aging population, and reductions in coverage under provincial health-care plans.[20] Despite government health-care plans, Canadian employers pay about 30 percent of all health-care expenses in Canada, most of this for prescription drugs.[21] The latest research from the Canadian Life and Health Insurance Association shows that annual employer health benefit payments total $12.5 billion.[22] In late 2002, two reports commissioned by the federal government both recommended that the government pay for "catastrophic" drug costs beyond a certain limit each year for each Canadian. If implemented, employer costs would be significantly reduced.[23]

FIGURE $\mathrm{I}3.3$ Health Plan Costs versus Inflation

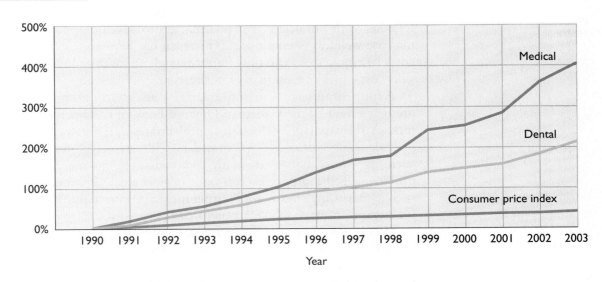

Source: Jason Billard, "Communicating Can Ease the Pain of Rising Benefits Costs," *Canadian HR Reporter* (June 17, 2002), pp. G3, G11. Reproduced by permission of *Canadian HR Reporter*, Carswell, One Corporate Plaza, 2075 Kennedy Road, Scarborough, ON, M1T 3V4.

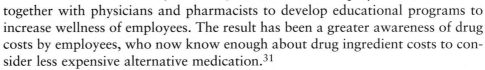

Tips for the Front Line

coinsurance The percentage of expenses (in excess of the deductible) that are paid for by the insurance plan.

Many Canadian managers now find controlling and reducing health-care costs topping their to-do lists. The simplest approach to reducing health-benefit costs is to *increase the amount of health-care costs paid by employees.* This can be accomplished by increasing employee premiums, increasing deductibles, reducing company **coinsurance** levels, instituting or lowering annual maximums on some services, or even eliminating coverage for spouses, private hospital rooms, and other benefits.[24] An Angus Reid poll of 1500 Canadians found that three-quarters of the respondents were willing to pay higher premiums to cover the high cost of prescription drugs.[25] In the U.S., smokers pay more for benefits than their non-smoking co-workers, but this has not yet happened in Canada. A positive approach, such as providing rewards for employees in smoking cessation programs, may be more in line with the Canadian tradition of freedom of choice.[26]

Another cost-reduction strategy is to publish a *restricted list of the drugs* that will be paid for under the plan, to encourage the use of generic rather than more expensive brand-name drugs. New drugs may not be covered if equally effective, cheaper alternatives are available. This approach should be combined with employee education to effectively manage the demand for drugs.[27]

A third approach is *health promotion.* In-house newsletters can caution workers to take medication properly and advertise programs on weight management, smoking cessation, exercise classes, on-site massage therapy, nutrition counselling, and other wellness programs.[28] After ten years of providing an on-site exercise program for employees, Canada Life Insurance Company found that absenteeism dropped 24 percent for employees who exercised two to three times per week.[29] It is estimated that the Canadian economy loses $2 billion every year because of employee absenteeism due to illness and stress—conditions that can be reversed through physical exercise.[30] Employee assistance programs can help to combat alcohol and drug addiction, and provide stress-management counselling. Some companies are developing innovative approaches to creating a healthy workforce. In Timmins, Ontario, several local employers have banded together with physicians and pharmacists to develop educational programs to increase wellness of employees. The result has been a greater awareness of drug costs by employees, who now know enough about drug ingredient costs to consider less expensive alternative medication.[31]

An on-site employee fitness centre.

A fourth approach is to implement *risk assessment* programs. Such programs are being used by the Canadian Imperial Bank of Commerce and other companies. A third party conducts a confidential survey of the health history and lifestyle choices of employees in order to identify common health risk factors, such as those associated with heart disease or mental health, so that problem-specific programs can be implemented.[32] Pharmaceutical companies such as Bayer Inc. and Astra Pharma Inc. have moved into the business of helping organizations to manage benefit costs this way.[33]

Finally, *health services spending accounts* are offered by over 90 percent of Canadian employers, either alone or in combination with a standard health-care plan.[34] The employer establishes an annual account for each employee containing a certain amount of money (determined by the employer). This provides cost control for the employer. Then the employee can spend the money on health-care costs as he or she wishes. This provides flexibility for the employee. These accounts are governed by the Income Tax Act, which allows expenses not normally covered under employer-sponsored health-care plans (such as laser eye surgery) and defines dependents more broadly than most employer plans.[35]

Retiree Health Benefits

Another concern is the cost of health benefits provided to retirees. These benefits typically include life insurance, drugs, and private/semi-private hospital coverage. Some continue coverage to a surviving spouse.[36] Retiree benefit costs are already exceeding the costs for active employees in some organizations, partly due to encouragement of early retirement during the recession/restructuring of the 1990s.[37] Many early retirees between the ages of 50 and 65 are not yet eligible for government health benefits that start at age 65.[38] Since January 1998, Canadian employers have been required to disclose liabilities for retiree benefits in their financial statements.[39] These liabilities are not required to be pre-funded, and thus are at risk in the case of business failure.[40]

As members of the baby-boom generation retire with increasing life expectancies, these costs will increase rapidly. For example, **Figure 13.4** shows the projected increases in hospital stays in Canada over the next 25 years. Almost 90 percent of the projected increase is attributable to seniors.[41] Employers can cut costs by increasing retiree contributions, increasing deductibles, tightening eligibility requirements, and reducing maximum payouts.[42] Reducing existing retiree coverage might appear to be another way to reduce costs, but Navistar International, a London, Ontario-based truck manufacturer, was sued by its employees for reducing post-retirement benefits—and the employees won.[43] Thus, it is advisable for firms to support wellness and disease prevention programs for active employees so that their retirement health-care costs will be minimized.[44]

Canadian Health Network
www.canadian-health-network.ca

Health Promotion Network
www.healthpromotionnetwork.org

AN ETHICAL
DILEMMA
Should it be the employer's responsibility to cover health-care costs for early retirees until they become eligible for government health-care benefits at age 65?

FIGURE 13.4   Projected Hospital Stays in Canada

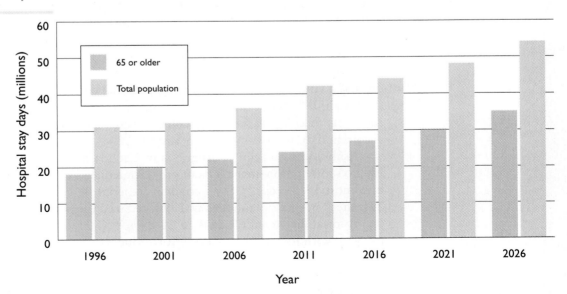

Source: M. Warren, "Retiree Benefits Coming of Age," *Benefits Canada* (May 2000), pp. 73–77. © Rogers Media Inc. Used with permission.

National Institute of Disability
Management and Research
www.nidmar.ca

Canadian Council on
Rehabilitation and Work
www.ccrw.org/ccrw

disability management A proactive, employer-centred process that
coordinates the activities of the
employer, the insurance company,
and health-care providers in an
effort to minimize the impact of
injury, disability, or disease in a
worker's capacity to successfully
perform his or her job.

Long-Term Disability

Long-term disability insurance is aimed at providing income protection or compensation for loss of income due to long-term illness or injury that is not
work-related. The disability payments usually begin when normal short-term
disability/sick leave is used up and may continue to provide income to age 65 or
beyond.[45] The disability benefits usually range from 50 percent to 75 percent of
the employee's base pay.

The number of long-term disability claims in Canada is rising sharply.[46] An
average disability claim can cost up to $78 000 per injury, including production
delays, product and material damage due to inexperienced replacement staff,
clerical and administrative time, and loss of expertise, on top of the actual benefit payments.[47] Therefore, disability management programs with a goal of
returning workers safely back to work are becoming a priority in many organizations.

Disability management is a proactive, employer-centred process that coordinates the activities of the employer, the insurance company, and health-care
providers in an effort to minimize the impact of injury, disability, or disease on
a worker's capacity to successfully perform his or her job.[48] Maintaining contact with a worker who is ill or injured is imperative in disability management
so that the worker can be involved in the return-to-work process from the
beginning. Ongoing contact also allows the employer to monitor the employee's
emotional well-being, which is always affected by illness and/or injury.[49]
Effective disability management programs include prevention, early assessment
and intervention regarding employee health problems, monitoring and management of employee absences, and early and safe return-to-work policies.[50]

The three most common approaches to returning a worker with a disability
to work are reduced work hours, reduced work duties, and workstation modification.[51] Evaluating the physical capabilities of the worker is an important
step in designing work modifications to safely reintegrate injured workers.[52] A
study by the Institute for Work and Health found that employees with back
injuries who were offered modified work spent only 60 days on workers' compensation, compared to 103 days for employees who were not offered modified
work.[53]

In many cases, the cost of accommodating an employee's disability can be
quite modest. For example, employees with disabilities who are unable to type
can use a voice recognition system for personal computers, which now costs less
than $1000.[54] One study found that the majority of workplace accommodation
costs less than $500, with 31 percent occurring at no cost. Only 5 percent of
accommodations cost more than $5000.

Disability management programs in Canada have had dramatic results. BC
Hydro's joint union–management program reduced long-term disability days off
by almost 14 percent.[55] The Canadian Imperial Bank of Commerce's "Working
Together" program, launched in 1998, reduced the average number of days lost
due to disability from 60 days to 23 days.[56] Canada Post saved $54.6 million
per year with its return-to-work efforts, due to a drop in employee absenteeism
from 20 days to 10 days per employee per year.[57] The City of Medicine Hat,
Alberta, reduced the number of employees on long-term disability by 31 percent
in one year.[58]

Mental Health Benefits   Almost half of non-occupational disabilities are attributable to psychological conditions.[59] Costs associated with mental health problems relate to short- and long-term disability, and increased drug usage.[60] Psychiatric disabilities are the fastest growing of all occupational disabilities, with depression being the most common (even though it is underreported by employees who don't want to admit it to their employer).[61] Depression has been described as a "clear and present danger" to business, as it manifests itself in alcoholism, absenteeism, injury, physical illness, and lost productivity.[62] Estimates suggest that the employee with depression who goes untreated costs the company twice what treatment costs per year.[63] Overall, depression, anxiety, and stress account for up to 25 percent of disability claims. At the Canadian Imperial Bank of Commerce, antidepressants are one of the most common drug claims. At the Royal Bank of Canada, 31 percent of short-term absenteeism is related to mental illness and addiction.[64] A Harvard University study projects that, by 2020, depression will become the biggest source of lost workdays in developed countries.[65]

For Canadian employers, the cost of mental health benefits is about $30 billion annually.[66] Many companies are trying to help reduce costs with prevention and early intervention programs including psychiatric counselling and peer-support groups.[67]

World Federation for Mental Health
www.wfmh.org/wmhday

RETIREMENT BENEFITS

pension plans Plans that provide income when employees reach a predetermined retirement age.

Employer-sponsored **pension plans** are intended to supplement an employee's government-sponsored retirement benefits, which on average make up 50 percent of the average Canadian's retirement income.[68] Unlike government-provided retirement benefits, employer-sponsored pension plans are pre-funded. Money is set aside in a pension fund to accumulate with investment income until it is needed to pay benefits at retirement. Pension fund assets have grown rapidly over the last 35 years. Much of this money is invested in Canadian stocks and bonds, due to laws restricting the investment of these assets in foreign securities.

defined benefit pension plan A plan that contains a formula for determining retirement benefits.
defined contribution pension plan A plan in which the employer's contribution to the employees' retirement fund is specified.

Pension plans fall into two categories—defined benefit pension plans and defined contribution pension plans.[69] A **defined benefit pension plan** contains a formula for determining retirement benefits so that the actual benefits to be received are defined ahead of time. For example, the plan might include a formula such as 2 percent of final year's earnings for each year of service, which would provide a pension of 70 percent of final year's earnings to an employee with 35 years of service. A **defined contribution pension plan** specifies what contribution the employer will make to a retirement fund set up for the employee. The defined contribution plan does not define the eventual benefit amount, only the periodic contribution to the plan. In a defined benefit plan, the employee knows ahead of time what his or her retirement benefits will be upon retirement. With a defined contribution plan, the employee cannot be sure of his or her retirement benefits until retirement, when his or her share of the money in the pension fund is used to buy an annuity. Thus, benefits depend on both the amounts contributed to the fund and the retirement fund's investment earnings. The prevalence of these two types of plans is shown in **Figure 13.5.**

Canadian Association for Retired Persons www.fifty-plus.net

Benefits and Pensions Monitor www.bpmmagazine.com

Association of Canadian Pension Management www.acpm.com

Retirement Council of Canada www.rcoc.net

FIGURE I3.5 Registered Pension Plans

Type of Plan	Number of Plans	Percentage of Plans Registered	Number of Canadians Covered	Percentage of Total Plan Membership
Defined benefit	7 010	45.7	4 569 808	84.1
Defined contribution	8 055	52.5	768 781	14.2
Combination DB/DC	209	1.4	58 012	1.1
Other	81	0.4	35 077	0.6

Source: Adapted from Statistics Canada publication *Pension Plans in Canada: Statistical Highlights and Key Tables,* Catalogue No. 74-401-SPB, Table 7, October 2000.

There are two other types of defined contribution arrangements. Under a group registered retirement savings plan (Group RRSP), employees can have a portion of their compensation (which would otherwise be paid in cash) put into an RRSP by the employer. The employee is not taxed on those set-aside dollars until after he or she retires (or removes the money from the plan). One attraction of RRSPs is that employees may have a range of investment options for the RRSP funds, including mutual funds and bond funds.[70] Employers must be sure to monitor Group RRSP investments to avoid potential employee lawsuits if investment losses are severe.[71]

Most employers do not match all or a portion of what the employee contributes to the Group RRSP because employer contributions are considered taxable income to employees. Instead, the employer often establishes a **deferred profit-sharing plan** (DPSP), and contributes a portion of company profits into the DPSP fund, where an account is set up for each employee. No employee contributions to a DPSP are allowed under Canadian tax law. Group RRSP/DPSP combinations are popular in Canada because no tax is paid until money is received from the plans at the time of the employee's death or termination of employment (at retirement or otherwise).

The entire area of pension planning is complicated, partly because of the laws governing pensions. For example, companies want to ensure that their pension contributions are tax deductible and must, therefore, adhere to the Income Tax Act. Each province and the federal jurisdiction also has a law governing employer-sponsored pension plans.[72] Sometimes the complicated and overlapping federal and provincial legislation can make employers question whether or not to sponsor a pension plan.[73] Legislation regarding pension plans varies around the world, as described in the Global HRM box.

While an employer usually must develop a pension plan to meet the organization's unique needs, there are several legal and policy issues to consider.[74]

deferred profit-sharing plan A plan in which a certain amount of company profits is credited to each employee's account, payable at retirement, termination, or death.

Hints to Ensure Legal Compliance

- *Membership requirements.* For example, at what minimum number of years of service do employees become eligible to join the plan?

GLOBAL HRM

Cultural Issues in Retirement Plans

Cultural differences can have an impact on international pension planning. The Asia Pacific region will expect a different level of pension planning because of a heightened level of respect for the elderly. Whereas North American government social security benefits are provided on a defined benefit basis, many countries in the Asia Pacific region provide a Provident Fund, which is a defined contribution approach. The legislative environment in Asia Pacific is also a bit more relaxed than in other regions in the world, with the exception of Japan, where the market is heavily regulated. Taiwan only recently passed a labour standards law.

In Europe, there is a greater sense of entitlement than in Asia or parts of Latin America. All of Europe has a sophisticated tax and financial system, with the exception of parts of Eastern Europe. While the U.K. is changing from defined benefit to defined contribution, Germany is, by nature, a defined benefit culture. The continent as a whole is headed toward defined contribution plans. There are many ways to deliver defined contribution plans, and European countries such as Spain, Italy, and the U.K. have recently passed legislation affecting the design of such plans.

In Latin America, the working population is much younger than that of the rest of the world. The emphasis is less on retirement benefits and more on medical and life insurance benefits. In the 1990s, Chile revamped legislation on its social security policies that is known today as the Chilean model. It is a defined contribution model based on sound ideas; however, it was passed without any strict investment regulations, and Chile found its system in serious financial difficulty. New legislation now restricts the amount of commission that can be received on contributions from employees and guaranteed returns that must be met.[1]

In Africa, different issues arise. For example, in Nigeria, a mandatory retirement age of 65 has been legislated for academic faculty. The monthly pension payable is 50 percent of the employee's basic pay, and a gratuity of 75 percent of monthly basic pay multiplied by the number of years of service is also payable. Despite this requirement, many Nigerian pensioners have suffered severe economic deprivation when they exit from the labour market. The nonpayment of gratuity at the time of retirement and frequent delays in the payment of monthly pensions to retired civil servants have influenced employees' attitudes toward retirement. There is now a general trend for prospective pensioners to falsify their birth records or make a new age declaration to circumvent the mandatory retirement age policy in the civil service.[2]

1. R. Polak, "Finding a Path to Global Benefits," *Workspan* (February 2003), pp. 32–35.

2. Y.B. Yehudah, "Nigerian Academic Faculty: Issues in Compensation and Retirement Benefits," *Compensation and Benefits Review* (November/December 2002), pp. 55–58.

- *Benefit formula* (defined benefits plans only). This usually ties the pension to the employee's final earnings, or an average of his or her last three to five years' earnings.

- *Retirement age*. The normal retirement age in Canada is 65. However, some employer plans may permit early or late retirement, and plans covering employees in provinces that have outlawed mandatory retirement cannot require these employees to retire at age 65. In companies such as General Motors, for example, only a small proportion of production and office workers retire as late as 65.[75] Partly due to union pressure and partly because early retirement helps to open up jobs for younger employees, many employers have encouraged early retirement. For example, some plans call for "30 and out." This permits an employee to retire after 30 years of continuous service, regardless of the person's age.[76]

- *Funding*. The question of how the plan is to be funded is another key issue. One aspect is whether the plan will be contributory or noncontributory. In the former, contributions to the pension fund are made by both employees and the employer. In a noncontributory fund, only the employer contributes.

vesting Provision that employer money placed in a pension fund cannot be forfeited for any reason.

- *Vesting*. Employee **vesting** rights is another critical issue in pension planning. Vesting refers to the money that the employer has placed in the pension fund that cannot be forfeited for any reason. The employees' contributions can never be forfeited. An employee is vested when he or she has met the requirements set out in the plan, whereby, upon termination of employment, he or she will receive future benefits based on the contributions made to the plan by the *employer* on behalf of the employee. In most provinces, pension legislation requires that employer contributions be vested once the employee has completed two years of service. Plans may vest more quickly than required by law. If the employee terminates employment before being vested, he or she is only entitled to a refund of his or her own contributions, plus interest (unless the employer has decided to be more generous). Once an employee is vested, all contributions are "locked in," and cannot be withdrawn by the employee on termination of employment; that is, employees must wait until retirement to receive a pension from the plan. Most plans permit the employee to transfer the amount into a locked-in RRSP (see the discussion on portability below), but the money cannot be accessed until retirement.

portability A provision that employees who change jobs can transfer the lump-sum value of the pension they have earned to a locked-in RRSP or their new employer's pension plan.

- *Portability*. Canadian employers today are being required by pension legislation to make their pensions more "portable" for employees upon termination of employment. This means that employees in defined contribution plans can take the money in their company pension account to a new employer's plan or roll it over into a locked-in RRSP. For defined benefit plans, the lump-sum value of the benefit earned can be transferred. **Portability** represents a shift in pension planning away from the original intent behind pension plans, which was to keep workers from changing jobs.

Recent Trends

Rapid Growth of Defined Contribution Plans

It is expected that defined benefit plans will continue to be used in large organizations where long tenure is the norm. Defined contribution plans have until recently been considered ideal for the growing number of today's businesses with a relatively young workforce of highly skilled professional and technical people who expect to work with several employers over the course of their careers.[77] The cost and complexity of sponsoring a defined benefit plan in an increasingly fragmented legislative environment is another reason that employers are increasingly switching to defined contribution plans. Defined contribution plan sponsors benefit from predictable costs and employees find the plan easier to understand.[78]

However, poor returns in the stock market over the last few years have highlighted the importance of employees making sound investment decisions and the employer responsibility for educating their employees about investment choices.[79] A recent survey found that two-thirds of Canadian employers offering defined contribution plans permit employees to make their own investment decisions, but only one-quarter of these companies offer any financial counselling to assist employees in making these decisions.[80] This is problematic because the Canadian Association of Financial Planners estimates that over 50 percent of Canadians do not know how much money they need for a comfortable retirement. Expected changes in pension legislation will make employers responsible for providing advice and education to employees.[81]

Employees in defined contribution plans make decisions about the investment of the pension fund assets, which means that member communication is one of the most critical challenges facing defined contribution plan sponsors.[82] Employers must pay careful attention to their obligation to educate and inform plan members about pension investments. There have been cases where plan members who were unhappy with the information provided by the employer and surprised by small benefits have sued their employers and won.[83] On the other hand, the University of Western Ontario plan converted to defined contribution in 1970, and faculty members are retiring with incomes greater than their working salaries.[84] Multicultural workplaces present special communication challenges, as outlined in the Workforce Diversity box.

Still other employers are offering "hybrid plans," which combine defined benefit and defined contribution features. For example, an employer-paid defined benefit plan can be offered with an employee-paid defined contribution component (which could have partially matching employer contributions).[85]

Same-Sex Benefits   Over the last several years, numerous court challenges based on human rights laws prohibiting discrimination on the basis of

WORKFORCE DIVERSITY

Communications in a Multicultural Workplace

Pension plans can be hard enough to understand when one's mother tongue is English or French—for employees fluent in neither official language, multilingual services can help. Plan sponsors have a statutory and fiduciary responsibility to provide information to plan members. Now that risk management in many plans rests with the individual employee, the plan sponsor has a responsibility to educate employees in a manner that is appropriate to the audience. In a multicultural workplace the customary meetings, brochures, and Internet sites may not go far enough to ensure that employees get information in useable form.

Sun Life Financial recently introduced live multilingual interpretation for members of its group retirement or savings plans. The call centre is able to set up a three-way connection between the caller, an interpreter, and the customer service rep. The caller asks questions in the language of his or her choice. The interpreter relays the question and translates the information provided by the subject area specialist.

"It takes a few minutes longer to complete the call," says Susan Hunt, director of marketing for group retirement services at Sun Life, "but we know the information is reaching clients in a language they understand."

"We started this service because plan sponsors wanted to be certain that all their employees were in a position to make informed decisions about managing their defined contribution plans. They did not want anyone missing out as the result of a language barrier."

Hunt says, "The interpretation service is one more tool enabling members to manage their pension plans more effectively. The interpreters give callers information that is specific to their company plan, as well as broader information on how a group plan works and the role of the plan member."

"More than 150 languages are available at the call centre from 8:00 A.M. to 8:00 P.M. EST using a third-party provider, On Line Interpreters."

Mandarin and Vietnamese are the primary languages requested, along with Russian and Finnish.

Source: S. Singh, "Communications in a Multi-cultural Workplace," *Canadian HR Reporter* (June 17, 2002), p. G2. Reproduced by permission of *Canadian HR Reporter*, Carswell, One Corporate Plaza, 2075 Kennedy Road, Scarborough, ON M1T 3V4.

sexual orientation have led most of the jurisdictions in Canada to change their pension laws to permit same-sex couples to be entitled to spousal and survivor benefits in the same way as common-law couples and married couples.[86] In most cases, the new definition of spouse applies to other benefits as well.

early retirement window A type of early retirement incentive by which employees are encouraged to retire early, the incentive being liberal pension benefits plus perhaps a cash payment.

Phased Retirement   During the downsizing of the 1990s, **early retirement windows** were used to avoid dismissals by offering special retirement packages to specific employees (often age 50+). The "window" represents the fact that the company opens up (for a limited time only) the chance for an employee to retire earlier than usual. The financial incentive was usually a combination of improved or liberalized pension benefits.[87]

However, the looming labour shortage when baby boomers start retiring is now resulting in employers seeking to retain older employees.[88] At the same time, many Canadians often hope to retire at age 55 or 60, but find that they are not in a financial position to do so, and that they need to continue working to age 60, 65, or even later.[89] The vast majority of workers between the ages of 55 and 64 plan to get another job after they retire. Overall, the number of older workers is increasing.[90]

phased retirement An arrangement whereby employees gradually ease into retirement using reduced workdays and/or shortened workweeks.

The idea of **phased retirement**, whereby employees gradually ease into retirement using reduced workdays and/or shortened workweeks, has been in place in Europe for some time, and this approach is gradually appearing in North America.[91] The Canadian Auto Workers have negotiated phased retirement plans with DaimlerChrysler, Ford, and General Motors, as well as with Air Canada.[92] The Quebec government recently amended its pension legislation so that employees choosing phased-in retirement can receive an annual payout from their pension plan during their phased-in retirement period.[93]

Supplemental Employee Retirement Plans (SERPs)   It is estimated that in 2005, one in four salaried employees in Canada will have their pension benefits capped (due to income tax legislation) at less than what the maximum allowable benefit formula (under pension legislation) could provide. Over half of Canadian employers promise employees affected by this situation that they will pay them the difference at retirement. Two-thirds do not pre-fund these extra benefits, and almost 10 percent provide no formal documentation.[94]

EMPLOYEE SERVICES

While an employer's time off and insurance and retirement benefits account for the largest portion of its benefits costs, many employers also provide a range of services including personal services (such as counselling), job-related services (such as childcare facilities), and executive perquisites (such as company cars and planes for executives).

Personal Services

First, many companies provide personal services that most employees need at one time or another. These include credit unions, counselling, employee assistance plans, and social and recreational opportunities.

Credit Unions   Credit unions are usually separate businesses established with the assistance of the employer. Employees usually become members of a credit union by purchasing a share of the credit union's stock for $5 or $10. Members can then deposit savings that accrue interest at a rate determined by the credit union's board of directors. Perhaps more importantly to most employees, loan eligibility and the rate of interest paid on the loan are usually more favourable than those found in banks and finance companies.

Counselling Services   Employers are also providing a wider range of counselling services to employees. These include *financial counselling* (e.g., in terms of how to overcome existing indebtedness problems); *family counselling* (for marital problems and so on); *career counselling* (in terms of analyzing one's aptitudes and deciding on a career); *job placement counselling* (for helping terminated or disenchanted employees find new jobs); and *pre-retirement counselling* (aimed at preparing retiring employees for what many find is the trauma of retiring). Many employers also make available to employees a full range of *legal counselling* through legal insurance plans.[95]

employee assistance plan (EAP) A company-sponsored program to help employees cope with personal problems that are interfering with or have the potential to interfere with their job performance, as well as issues affecting their well-being and/or that of their families.

Employee Assistance Plans (EAPs)   An **employee assistance plan (EAP)** is a formal employer program that provides employees with confidential counselling and/or treatment programs for problems such as mental health issues, marital/family problems, work/life balance issues, stress, legal problems, substance abuse, and other addictions such as gambling.[96] **Figure 13.6** provides statistics on EAP utilization by industry sector and by type of problem. They are particularly important for helping employees who suffer workplace trauma—ranging from harassment to physical assault.[97] The number of EAPs in Canada is growing because they are a proactive way for organizations to reduce absenteeism and disability costs. A very general estimate is that 10 percent of employees use EAP services. With supervisory training in how to identify employees that may need an EAP referral, usage can be expanded to more employees who need help.[98]

There are four basic models in use today.[99] In the *in-house model*, the entire assistance staff is employed by the company. In the *out-of-house model*, the company contracts a vendor to provide employee assistance staff and services in its own offices, the company's offices, or a combination of both. In the *consortium model*, several companies pool their resources to develop a collaborative EAP program. Finally, in the *affiliate model*, a vendor already under contract to the employer subcontracts to a local professional rather than using its own salaried staff. This is usually to service employees in a client company location in which the EAP vendors do not have an office. Whatever the model, an EAP provider should be accessible to employees in all company locations, timely in providing service, and confidential, and should offer highly educated counsellors and provide communication material to publicize the plan to employees. They should also provide utilization reports on the number of employees using the service, and the types of services being provided, without compromising confidentiality.[100]

Other Personal Services   Finally, some employers also provide various social and recreational opportunities for their employees, including company-sponsored athletic events, dances, annual summer picnics, craft activities, and parties.[101] In practice, the benefits offered are limited only by creativity in thinking up new benefits. For example, pharmaceutical giant Pfizer Inc. provides employees with free drugs made by the company, including Viagra![102]

FIGURE 13.6 EAP Utilization

Warren Shepell
www.warrenshepell.com

TOP 10 SECTORS WITH HIGHEST USE OF EAP SERVICES
(presented in alphabetical order)

- Communications/Media
- Computer Hardware/Software
- Consulting
- Manufacturing—Consumer Goods
- Entertainment
- Government—Municipal
- Government—Provincial
- Insurance
- Religious/Social Service Agencies
- Utilities

TOP 10 REASONS FOR ACCESSING EAPS
(ranked by frequency)

The top ten primary issues for which individuals seek EAP services. Note that these issues, and the order in which they appear, are fairly consistent across industries.

Problem
- Marital/Relationships
- Stress—Personal
- Child-Related Issues
- Depression Symptoms
- Stress—Workplace
- Separation (divorce)
- Anxiety Symptoms
- Work-Related Conflict
- Grief
- Parenting

OTHER REASONS FOR USING EAPS
(no particular order, may vary significantly by industry)

In addition to the top ten presented above, other primary presenting issues for which people seek EAP assistance include:

Problem
- Extended Family Relations
- Career
- Anger
- Alcohol Abuse/Addiction
- Post Trauma
- Life Transition
- Blended Family
- Other's Addiction
- Drug Abuse/Addiction

Source: The WarrenShepell Research Group, a division of WarrenShepell. Data collected for the year 2002 from 1,806 organizations with a WarrenShepell EAP. For more information, contact WarrenShepell at 1-800-461-9722, or visit www.warrenshepell.com.

Job-Related Services

Job-related services aimed directly at helping employees perform their jobs, such as educational subsidies and daycare centres, constitute a second group of services.

Subsidizing daycare facilities for children of employees has many benefits for the employer, including lower employee absenteeism.

Subsidized Childcare Today large numbers of Canadian women with children under six years old are in the workforce. Subsidized daycare is one increasingly popular benefit stemming directly from that trend.[103] Many employers simply investigate the daycare facilities in their communities and recommend certain ones to interested employees, but more employers are setting up company-sponsored daycare facilities themselves, both to attract young parents to the payroll and to reduce absenteeism. In this case, the centre is a separate, privately run venture, paid for by the firm. IKEA, Husky Injection Moldings, IBM, and the Kanata Research Park have all chosen this option.[104] Where successful, the hours of operation are structured around parents' schedules, the daycare facility is close to the workplace (often in the same building), and the employer provides 50 percent to 75 percent of the operating costs. An emerging benefit is daycare for mildly ill children who are not accepted at regular daycare. Mildly ill childcare centres are more expensive than regular daycares as they offer medical supervision, usually by a registered nurse, and infection control measures.[105]

To date, the evidence regarding the actual effects of employer-sponsored childcare on employee absenteeism, turnover, productivity, recruitment, and job satisfaction is positive, particularly with respect to reducing obstacles to coming to work and improving workers' attitudes.[106]

Eldercare With the average age of the Canadian population rising, eldercare is increasingly a concern for many employers and individuals. Eldercare is designed to assist employees who must help elderly parents or relatives who are not fully able to care for themselves, up to and including palliative care of the dying.[107] It is a complex, unpredictable, and exhausting process that creates stress for the caregiver, their family, and co-workers.[108] Eldercare is expected to become a more common workplace issue than childcare as we progress through the twenty-first century.[109] On average, 32 percent of Canadians have eldercare responsibilities.[110]

From the employer's point of view, eldercare benefits are important for much the same reason as are childcare benefits: the responsibility for caring for an aging relative can and will affect the employee's performance at work.[111] A number of employers are, therefore, instituting eldercare benefits, including flexible hours, support groups, counselling, free pagers, and adult daycare programs. Referral services to help employees connect with the wide variety of services for the elderly are particularly helpful for employees with eldercare responsibilities.[112]

Subsidized Employee Transportation Some employers also provide subsidized employee transportation.[113] An employer can negotiate with a transit system to provide free year-round transportation to its employees. Other employers just facilitate employee car-pooling, perhaps by acting as the central clearinghouse to identify employees from the same geographic areas who work the same hours.

Food Services Food services are provided in some form by many employers; they let employees purchase meals, snacks, or coffee, usually at relatively low prices. Even employers that do not provide full dining facilities generally make available food services such as coffee wagons or vending machines for the convenience of employees.

Educational Subsidies

Educational subsidies such as tuition refunds have long been a popular benefit for employees seeking to continue or complete their education. Payments range from all tuition and expenses to some percentage of expenses to a flat fee per year of, say, $500 to $600. Most companies pay for courses directly related to an employee's present job. Many also reimburse tuition for courses that are not job-related (such as a secretary taking an accounting class) that pertain to the company business and those that are part of a degree or diploma program.[114] In-house educational programs include remedial work in basic literacy and training for improved supervisory skills.

Ford Motor Company and Delta Airlines recently announced that they will provide all of their employees (350 000 at Ford, 72 000 at Delta) with computers and Internet access at home, for a small fee. The purpose is to enable employees to be on the leading edge of technology and to connect more closely to customers.[115]

Family-Friendly Benefits

One of the top drivers of workforce commitment in Canada is management's recognition of personal and family life.[116] Ninety percent of responding employees in one survey said work/life benefits were "important" or "very important" to them.[117] Recognition of the pressures of balancing work and family life have led many employers to bolster what they call their "family-friendly" benefits.

While there is no single list of what does or does not constitute a "family-friendly" benefit, they are generally those like childcare, eldercare, providing light-duty work for pregnant women whose jobs required heavy lifting or long periods of standing, and flexible work hours that enable employees to better balance the demands of their family and work lives.[118] One recent Canadian survey found that 80 percent of firms polled provided leaves for family illness, and almost 75 percent provided leaves for other personal and family duties such as eldercare.[119] Ford Motor Company now considers it a disability when a woman has to miss work to find shelter from domestic violence.[120]

The family-friendly benefits at several companies are illustrative. Eddie Bauer, Inc., reportedly "believes its associates shouldn't confuse having a career with having a life."[121] Since 1994, Eddie Bauer has therefore introduced more than 20 new family-friendly benefits ranging from on-site mammography to emergency childcare services. Also included in the firm's existing family-friendly benefits are a casual dress code, subsidies for liberal paid parental leave, alternative transportation options, a compressed workweek, and telecommuting.[122]

Research Insight ▷ Having family-friendly benefits assumes that work–family conflicts spill over to the employee's job and somehow undermine the person's job satisfaction and performance. A recent study suggests that this is the case.[123] Two researchers reviewed two computer databases, to find all studies focusing on work and family conflict, job satisfaction, and life satisfaction. They found that "the relationship between job satisfaction and various [work–family] conflict measures is strong and negative across all samples; people with high levels of [work–family] conflict tend to be less satisfied with their jobs."[124] Similarly, there was a strong negative correlation between work–family conflict and measures of "life satisfaction," in other words, the extent to which the employees were satisfied with their lives in general. Managers should therefore understand that offering employees family-friendly benefits and letting them use them can apparently have very positive effects on the employees, one of which is making them more satisfied with their work and their jobs.

Executive Perquisites

Perquisites (perks, for short) are usually given to only a few top executives. Perks can range from the substantial to the almost insignificant. A bank chairperson may have a chauffeur-driven limousine and use of a bank-owned property in the Caribbean. Executives of large companies often use a corporate jet for business travel. At the other extreme, perks may entail little more than the right to use a company car.[125]

A multitude of popular perks falls between these extremes. These include: management loans (which typically enable senior officers to use their stock options); salary guarantees (also known as *golden parachutes*) to protect executives if their firms are the targets of acquisitions or mergers; financial counselling (to handle top executives' investment programs); and relocation benefits, often including subsidized mortgages, purchase of the executive's current house, and payment for the actual move.[126] A potpourri of other executive perks include cell phones, outplacement assistance, company cars, chauffeured limousines, security systems, company planes and yachts, executive dining rooms, legal services, tax assistance, liberal expense accounts, club memberships, season tickets, credit cards, and subsidized children's education. Perks related to wellness and quality of life (such as physical fitness programs) are highly valued in today's stressful environment.[127] An increasingly popular new perk is concierge service, intended to carry out errands for busy executives.[128] Employers have many ways of making their hard-working executives' lives as pleasant as possible!

Indeed, this tendency continues in the face of growing populist sentiment and despite a decade of corporate downsizings, restructurings, and more restrictive tax laws.[129] Some of the most visible status perks—such as executive apartments, company planes, and full-time chauffeurs—are more rare. However, many companies still provide executives with personal or leased automobiles, supplemental life insurance, and reserved parking spots.

An Ethical Dilemma

Is it fair that senior executives get financial perks such as subsidized mortgages in addition to their higher amounts of cash compensation, when other lower-paid employees may be struggling to meet mortgage payments?

FLEXIBLE BENEFITS PROGRAMS

Research conducted over 25 years ago found that an employee's age, marital status, and sex influenced his or her choice of benefits.[130] For example, preference for pensions increased significantly with employee age, and preference for the family dental plan increased sharply as the number of dependants increased. Thus, benefits which one worker finds attractive may be unattractive to another. In the last few years in Canada, there has been a phenomenal increase in **flexible benefits programs** that permit employees to develop individualized benefits packages for themselves by choosing the benefits options they prefer.[131] According to a 2002 survey by benefit consultants Hewitt Associates, more than half of Canadian benefits plans have some form of flexibility, or plan to implement flexible benefits during the next two years. Only 7 percent of respondents said they were not interested in flexible plans.[132]

flexible benefits program
Individualized benefit plans to accommodate employee needs and preferences.

Employers derive several advantages from offering flexible benefit plans, the two most important being cost containment and the ability to meet the needs of an increasingly diverse workforce. A 2002 Hewitt Associates employer survey found that 71 percent of respondents offering flexible plans had realized the cost savings they had planned for, and 94 percent said that their flexible plan met or exceeded their expectations for providing choice and empowerment to employees. The biggest employer concern is the cost of administration of flexible plans, which are much more complicated than traditional plans. However, as experience with these plans has progressed, the designs have become less complex, and Internet technology permits employees to perform much of the administration themselves.[133]

Flexible benefits plans empower the employee to put together his or her own benefit package, subject to two constraints. First, the employer must carefully limit total cost for each total benefits package. Second, each benefit plan must include certain non-optional items. These include, for example, Canada/Quebec Pension Plan, workers' compensation, and employment insurance. Subject to these two constraints, employees can pick and choose from the available options. Thus, a young parent might opt for the company's life and dental insurance plans, while an older employee opts for an improved pension plan. The list of possible options that the employer might offer can include many of the benefits discussed in this chapter: vacations, insurance benefits, pension plans, educational services, and so on.

As an example, a flexible plan was instituted at Unilever Canada in 1996. Unilever employees who were covered by the plan automatically got core benefits including provincial health care, life insurance of 50 percent of their base pay, business travel accident insurance of three times their base pay, short-term disability that pays 100 percent or 70 percent of base pay (depending on length of service), and long-term disability benefits of 70 percent of base pay that begin after a 26-week absence. In addition, the company also provides flexible benefit credits that the employee can use to pay for extra benefits including medical coverage, dental care, life insurance, and accident insurance. Any leftover credits can be taken in cash or deposited in a health-care spending account to pay extra health and dental expenses. Employees may supplement their flexible benefit credits with payroll deduction. Those employees who wish to may opt out of the plan and take their credits as cash (which will constitute taxable income).

Advantages and disadvantages of flexible benefit programs are summarized in **Figure 13.7.** The flexibility is, of course, the main advantage. Although most employees favour flexible benefits, some do not like to spend time choosing among available options, and some choose inappropriate benefits. Communication regarding the choices available in a flexible plan is considered the biggest challenge for employers.[134] However, over three-quarters of employers surveyed in 2002 are expecting to provide communication material on their intranet site or by using the Internet within the next three years, as compared to about 50 percent in 2002.[135] Various firms have developed user-friendly interactive software for personal computers that helps employees to make choices under a flexible benefits program.[136] The recent rapid increase in the number of flexible plans in Canada indicates that the pros outweigh the cons.

A few firms are moving beyond flexible benefits to "total flexible compensation" where employees at all levels design an individual compensation pack-

Benefits Design Inc.
www.benefitsdesign.com

International Federation of
Employee Benefit Plans
www.ifebp.org

FIGURE 13.7   Advantages and Disadvantages of Flexible Benefit Programs

ADVANTAGES

1. Employees choose packages that best satisfy their unique needs.

2. Flexible benefits help firms meet the *changing* needs of a *changing* workforce.

3. Increased involvement of employees and families improves understanding of benefits.

4. Flexible plans make introduction of new benefits less costly. The new option is added merely as one among a wide variety of elements from which to choose.

5. Cost containment—the organization sets the dollar maximum. Employee chooses within that constraint.

DISADVANTAGES

1. Employees make bad choices and find themselves not covered for predictable emergencies.

2. Administrative burdens and expenses increase.

3. Adverse selection—employees pick only benefits they will use. The subsequent high benefit utilization increases its cost.

Source: G.T. Milkovich and J.M Newman, *Compensation*, p. 433. © 2002. The McGraw-Hill Companies, Inc.

age (cash, benefits, vacation, incentives, and so on). Total flexible compensation provides employees with control over their compensation, and employers maximize the effectiveness of their compensation dollars.[137]

BENEFITS ADMINISTRATION

Canadian Pension and Benefits Institute **www.cpbi-icra.ca**

Whether it is a flexible benefits plan or a more traditional one, benefits administration is a challenge. Even in a relatively small company with 40 to 50 employees, the administrative problems of keeping track of the benefits status of each employee can be a time-consuming task as employees are hired and separated, and as they utilize or want to change their benefits. Many companies make use of some sort of benefits spreadsheet software to facilitate tracking benefits and updating information. For example, the program tracks vacation eligibility and will trigger an e-mail to a supervisor when one of the employees in his or her department is overdue for some time off. Another approach is outsourcing benefits administration, including record keeping, administration, and participant communication, to a third-party expert. The major advantages are greater efficiency and consistency, and enhanced service.[138]

Keeping Employees Informed

Benefits communication, particularly regarding pension plans and flexible benefits, is increasingly important as a large number of people are approaching retirement.[139] Correct information must be provided in a timely, clear manner. Pension legislation across Canada specifies what information must be disclosed to plan members and their spouses. Court challenges concerning information on benefits plans are on the rise, as people's awareness of their right to information grows.[140]

Increasingly, organizations are utilizing new technology such as intranets to ensure that up-to-date information is provided in a consistent manner.[141] Some companies are now using real-time e-statements, as described in the HR.Net box. At Hewlett Packard (Canada) Ltd., an electronic pension booklet is available on the company's intranet, and a pension-modelling tool can be accessed through the Web. The modelling software allows employees to fill in their personal information to calculate various "what if" scenarios.[142]

HR.Net

Communicating Total Rewards Real-Time

Traditional employee benefits statements are snapshots of information that show data from some arbitrary point in the past. It has been difficult to get current, accurate, real-time account balances and benefits data from employers. But the vision of real-time data is becoming a reality.

Employer-provided e-statements are integrated, Web-based statements that provide information on a range of employer-sponsored benefits. Real-time e-statements pull together a current view of an employee's total compensation package and, in doing so, clearly communicate the value of the employer's benefit programs and the firm's commitment to the well-being of its workforce.

Key employee advantages include personalization, privacy and security, and one-stop shopping with no need for multiple passwords and separate sites. Benefits for employers include leveraging of prior technology investments, enhanced communication through personalized content and messages to employees, and attraction and retention of employees through the ability to provide real-time benefits information.

Quebecor World is one employer that has recognized the potential of e-statements, so much so that they placed kiosks on the floor of 80 plants to provide their mostly hourly workers with online access. Simultaneously, they approved an overhaul of the existing benefits self-serve system. The crisp, user-friendly design reflected the familiar HR icons, plus plenty of white space and intuitive navigation.

Employee feedback was positive. Within the first few weeks, 20 percent of the workforce accessed their e-statements and spent time reviewing other Web-based software such as the health risk assessment and online summary plan descriptions.

"With the e-statements, we have been able to provide our employees with personalized, useful information by tapping into our established benefits programs via the Web," said Shari Davidson, global vice president of benefits for Quebecor World. "The e-statements reflect our existing benefits material and go a long way toward extending HR's brand."

E-statements help HR to live up to its strategic role, giving employers an opportunity for repeated, targeted messaging. They also provide employees with a tool to help them better understand and appreciate their compensation and benefits program.

Source: Excerpt from S. Constantin and C. Bell, "Linking a Global Workforce," *workspan*, March 2002, pp. 22–28. Reprinted with permission of WorldatWork, Scottsdale, AZ. http://www.worldatwork.org.

Canadian Workers Stressed Out

According to a recent study, Canadian employees are stressed out, depressed and less loyal to their employers than they were 10 years ago.... Most people have family commitments outside of work. A large number of workers are experiencing greater challenges in balancing their job with their life commitments. According to the study, this conflict results in

- Increased workload and hours of work—In 1991, the average employee spent 42 hours a week at work, which has increased to 45 hours in 2001.

- More stress—High stress at work is twice as common today as it was ten years ago.

- Poor physical and mental health—Employees visit the doctor more often, and suffer from depression more often today than they did ten years ago.

- Increased absenteeism—Employees who are experiencing high work–life conflict have absenteeism rates three times those of employees with low work–life conflict.

- Lower job satisfaction—62% of employees were highly satisfied with their jobs in 1991, but only 45% are highly satisfied with their job in 2001.

- Lower commitment to employers—The number of employees who are highly committed to their organization has decreased from 66% in 1991 to only 50% in 2001.

All of these factors have a negative impact on the employer's business and productivity. For example, the authors of the study estimate that absenteeism resulting from work–life conflict costs Canadian employers almost $3 billion each year.

...The study makes a number of recommendations to decrease the number of work–life conflicts experienced by employees. They recommend that employers offer flexible work hours and work locations; increase employees' sense of control over their work; increase the number of supportive managers; and focus on the creation of family-friendly work environments.

Further, the paper recommends that governments introduce legislation to protect an employee's right to refuse overtime, take time off in lieu of overtime pay, and entitle employees to take five personal leave days each year. It also suggests that the federal government work with the provinces to establish national childcare and eldercare programs.

Source: Excerpted with permission from the *Canadian Benefits and Pensions Newsletter* (No. 493, December 2001), published by and copyright CCH Canadian Limited, Toronto, Ontario.

CHAPTER Review

Summary

1 Five categories of employee benefit plans are government-sponsored benefits, pay for time not worked, insurance benefits, retirement benefits, and employee services.

2 Government-sponsored benefits include employment insurance, Canada/Quebec Pension Plan, workers' compensation, and provincial health-care plans.

3 Health insurance costs are rising because of expensive new drugs, rising drug utilization by an aging population, and reductions in coverage under provincial health-care plans. These costs can be reduced by increasing the amount of health-care costs paid by employees, publishing a restricted list of the drugs that will be paid for under the plan, implementing health and wellness promotion plans, using risk assessment programs, and offering health services spending accounts.

4 Recent trends in retirement benefits include the rapid growth of defined contribution plans, same-sex benefits, the shift away from early retirement incentives to phased retirement, and increasing use of supplemental employee retirement plans (SERPs).

5   Three types of personal employee services offered by many organizations include credit unions, counselling services, and employee assistance plans. Six types of job-related services offered by many employers include subsidized childcare, eldercare, subsidized employee transportation, food services, educational subsidies, and family-friendly benefits.

6   The flexible benefits approach allows the employee to put together his or her own benefit plan, subject to total cost limits and the inclusion of certain compulsory items. The employer first determines the total cost for the benefits package. Then a decision is made as to which benefits will be compulsory, including but not limited to Canada/Quebec Pension Plan, workers' compensation, and employment insurance. Then other benefits are selected for inclusion in the plan, such as life insurance, health and dental coverage, short- and long-term disability insurance, and retirement plans. Sometimes vacations and employee services are included as well. Then employees select the optional benefits they prefer with the money they have available to them under the total plan.

Key Terms

Canada/Quebec Pension Plan   *(p. 399)*
coinsurance   *(p. 408)*

deductible   *(p. 407)*
deferred profit-sharing plan   *(p. 412)*
defined benefit pension plan   *(p. 411)*
defined contribution pension plan   *(p. 411)*
disability management   *(p. 410)*
early retirement window   *(p. 416)*
employee assistance plan (EAP)   *(p. 417)*
employee benefits   *(p. 397)*
employment insurance   *(p. 398)*
flexible benefits program   *(p. 421)*
group life insurance   *(p. 405)*
pay for time not worked   *(p. 401)*
pension plans   *(p. 411)*
phased retirement   *(p. 416)*
portability   *(p. 414)*
provincial health-care plans   *(p. 401)*
short-term disability/sick leave   *(p. 402)*
vesting   *(p. 414)*
workers' compensation   *(p. 400)*

Review and Discussion Questions

1   Explain two main approaches to reducing workers' compensation claims.

2   Explain the difference between sick leave plans and short-term disability plans.

3   Why are long-term disability claims increasing so rapidly in Canada?

4   Outline the kinds of services provided by EAPs.

CRITICAL *Thinking Questions*

1   You are applying for a job as a manager and are at the point of negotiating a salary and benefits. What questions would you ask your prospective employer concerning benefits? Describe the benefits package that you would try to negotiate for yourself.

2   What are pension "vesting" and "portability"? Why do you think these are (or are not) important to a recent university or college graduate?

3   You are the HR consultant to a small business with about 40 employees. At the present time, the business offers only the legal minimum number of days for vacation and paid holidays, and legally mandated benefits. Develop a list of other benefits that you believe should be offered, along with your reasons for suggesting them.

APPLICATION *Exercises*

Running Case: LearnInMotion.com

The New Benefits Plan

LearnInMotion.com provides only legislatively required benefits for all of its employees. These include participation in employment insurance, Canada/Quebec Pension Plan, and workers' compensation. No employee services are provided.

Jennifer can see several things wrong with the company's policies regarding benefits and services. First, she wants to determine whether similar companies' experiences with providing health and life insurance benefits suggest it makes hiring easier and/or reduces employee turnover. Jennifer is also concerned that the company has no policy regarding vacations or for sick leave. Informally, at least, it is understood that employees get a one-week vacation after one year's work. However, the policy regarding pay for days such as New Year's and Thanksgiving has been inconsistent: Sometimes employees on the job only two or three weeks are paid fully for one of these holidays; sometimes employees who have been with the firm for six months or more get paid for only half a day. No one really knows what the company's chosen "paid" holidays are. Jennifer knows these policies must be more consistent.

She also wonders about the wisdom of establishing some type of retirement plan for the firm. While everyone working for the firm is still in their 20s, she believes a defined contribution plan in which employees contribute a portion of their pre-tax salary, to be matched up to some limit by a contribution by LearnInMotion.com, would contribute to the sense of commitment she and Pierre would like to create among their employees. However, Pierre isn't so sure. His position is that if they don't get sales up pretty soon, they're going to burn through their cash. Now they want you, their management consultants, to help them decide what to do. Here's what they want you to do for them.

Questions

1   Draw up a policy statement regarding vacations, sick leave, and paid days off for LearnInMotion.com, based on sources such as those discussed in this and the previous two chapters.

2   What are the advantages and disadvantages to LearnInMotion.com of providing its employees with health insurance and disability programs?

3   In terms of competitors and any other information that you think is relevant, do you or do you not think it's a good idea for LearnInMotion.com to establish a defined contribution retirement plan for its employees? If they were to establish such a plan, briefly summarize the plan as you see it.

CASE INCIDENT *Barrie Shipping Ltd.*

Heath Proctor, Benefits Manager at Barrie Shipping Ltd., was faced with the task of redesigning the company's health-care plans. Costs had risen to an unacceptable level, largely due to prescription drug and dental plan costs. Two-thirds of employees were over age 45, and drug utilization had increased along with the average age of the workforce. The remaining employees, like their older counterparts, tended to be smokers, drinkers, and bar brawlers, who were unconcerned about their health—a common situation among workers in Great Lakes shipping companies.

The current prescription drug plan had an annual deductible of $20, and coinsurance of 100 percent. The dental plan had an annual deductible of $25, and coinsurance of 90 percent. Insurance company premiums were fully paid by Barrie Shipping. Retirees were also covered under these plans, but they paid 25 percent of the premiums.

Heath had proposed the idea of a flexible benefits plan in the past, but management had not seen any need to change from the standard benefit package they had offered for many years. Furthermore, none of their competitors had flexible plans, and the three large companies in the industry traditionally offered similar human resources programs.

Heath knew that the company had to cut drug costs immediately. He had read something about proactive measures that could be taken and wondered if any of these should be considered by Barrie Shipping in the longer term.

Heath's boss, Leo Santini, the vice-president of Human Resources, asked him to investigate different options for reducing health benefit costs and to pre-

pare a short presentation describing each option and making some recommendations about which options might be most effective for Barrie Shipping.

Questions

1   What methods of health-care cost control should Heath include in his presentation? What are the advantages and disadvantages of each?

2   Should Barrie Shipping continue to provide health-care coverage to retirees? Why or why not?

3   What recommendations should Heath Proctor make to Leo?

EXPERIENTIAL *Exercises*

1   Working individually or in groups, compile a list of the perks available to the following individuals: the head of your local public utilities commission, the president of your college or university, and the president of a large company in your area. Do they all have certain perks in common? What do you think accounts for any differences?

2   Working individually or in groups, contact your provincial Workers' Compensation Board (or Workplace Safety and Insurance Board in Ontario) and compile a list of their suggestions for reducing workers' compensation costs. What seem to be their main recommendations?

Rewards

Companies have traditionally offered employees special rewards and incentives at Christmastime, or in appreciation for special effort. Back in the 1980s, expensive trips, big-screen TVs, and fur coats were not uncommon rewards, and trade shows featuring incentive manufacturers and their products were crowded. However, by the mid-1990s, times had changed, with rewards being scaled back to items such as plastic watches; the only trips were a few days in a Florida condo, not including airfare. The trade shows attracted very few people. And now, in the new millennium, many employees report getting no special incentives or rewards at all.

But there is a glimmer of hope. Brenda McDonald, an incentive manufacturer, says her business is up 10 percent. She says her customers want to make employees feel better and give them a sense of belonging so that they will remain with the company. She sells pens, rings, chocolates, and watches to employers who give the gifts as tokens of appreciation to employees, many of whom have worked hard despite severe cutbacks. Her personal incentive is the opportunity to work in a peaceful Southern Ontario town.

For their part, employees say they value being acknowledged by management in some way. Some want a thank-you note, an employee-of-the-month plaque, or a pat on the back for a job well done. Others prefer time off work, or perhaps a plant or clock radio for their desk. And, of course, there are always those who just want cash.

Questions

1. These "rewards" are really forms of employee recognition. What kinds of recognition items would you prefer? Why?

2. The employees shown in the video seem to be happy with the idea of recognition items of relatively modest value. Why don't they want more expensive items?

Video Source: "Rewards," *CBC Venture 804* (December 2, 2001).

Additional Resources: www.helicanada.com/incentives.html; www.incentivestointrigue.com

CHAPTER 14

Occupational Health and Safety

LEARNING OUTCOMES

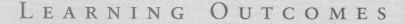

After studying this chapter, you should be able to:

Discuss the responsibilities and rights of employees and employers under occupational health and safety legislation.

Explain WHMIS.

Explain in detail three basic causes of accidents.

Describe how accidents at work can be prevented.

Explain why employee wellness programs are becoming increasingly popular.

Discuss six major employee health issues at work and *explain* how they should be handled.

STRATEGIC IMPORTANCE OF OCCUPATIONAL HEALTH AND SAFETY

Ceremonies are held across Canada every April 28 to mark the National Day of Mourning for workers killed or injured on the job. In Moncton, New Brunswick, Pauline Farrell lays roses in memory of her husband Bill Kelly, who was killed over 30 years ago.

Health and safety initiatives are part of a strategic approach to human resources management. Service provided to clients and customers is a function of how employees are treated, and employee health, safety, and wellness management are important determinants of employee perceptions regarding fair treatment by the organization. Further, investment in disability management and proactive wellness programs create measurable bottom-line returns.[1]

Another reason that safety and accident prevention concern managers is that the work-related accident figures are staggering. According to the Association of Workers' Compensation Boards of Canada, in 2001 there were 920 deaths and 373 216 injuries resulting from accidents at work.[2] These figures do not include minor injuries that do not involve time lost from work beyond the day of the accident. Furthermore, these figures do not tell the full story. They do not reflect the human suffering incurred by injured or ill workers and their families, or the economic costs incurred by employers. On April 28 each year, a day of mourning is observed for Canadian workers killed or injured on the job.[3]

Workplace health concerns are also widespread. One study found that two-thirds of employed Canadian adults believed that they were being exposed to some sort of occupational health hazard, the most common being exposure to airborne dust and fibres, and working with a computer screen or terminal. Thirty-two percent believed that these exposures had a negative effect on their health.[4]

BASIC FACTS ABOUT OCCUPATIONAL HEALTH AND SAFETY LEGISLATION

occupational health and safety legislation Laws intended to protect the health and safety of workers by minimizing work-related accidents and illnesses.

All provinces, territories, and the federal jurisdiction have **occupational health and safety legislation** based on the principle of joint responsibility shared by workers and employers to maintain a hazard-free work environment and to enhance the health and safety of workers.[5]

Purpose

These laws fall into three categories: general health and safety rules; rules for specific industries (e.g., mining); and rules related to specific hazards (e.g., asbestos). In some jurisdictions, these are combined into one overall law with regulations for specific industries and hazards, while in others they remain separate. The regulations are very complex and cover almost every conceivable hazard in great detail, as can be seen in **Figure 14.1**. Provisions of occupational health and safety legislation differ significantly across Canada, but most have certain basic features in common.

FIGURE 14.1   Ontario Occupational Health and Safety Act—Construction Regulations

> **O.REG.213/91**
>
> **68. A sign used to direct traffic,**
> (a) shall be diamond shaped, 450 millimetres wide and 450 millimetres long, with the diamond mounted at one corner on a pole 1.2 metres long; (b) shall be made of material that has at least the rigidity of six millimetres thick plywood; (c) shall be reflective fluorescent and coloured, (i) red-orange on one side with the corner areas coloured black, so that the red-orange area forms a regular eight-sided figure, with the word "STOP" written in legible white letters 150 millimetres high in a central position on the sign, and (ii) chartreuse on one side, with the word "SLOW" written in legible black letters 150 millimetres high in a central position on the sign; and (d) shall be maintained in a clean condition.

Responsibilities and Rights of Employers and Employees

In all jurisdictions, employers are responsible for taking every reasonable precaution to ensure the health and safety of their workers. This is called the "due diligence" requirement. Specific duties of the employer include filing government accident reports, maintaining records, ensuring that safety rules are enforced, and posting safety notices and legislative information.

Employees are responsible for taking reasonable care to protect their own health and safety and, in most cases, that of their co-workers. Specific requirements include wearing protective clothing and equipment, and reporting any contravention of the law or regulations. Employees have three basic rights under the joint responsibility model: (1) the right to know about workplace safety hazards; (2) the right to participate in the occupational health and safety process; and (3) the right to refuse unsafe work if they have "reasonable cause" to believe that the work is dangerous. "Reasonable cause" usually means that a complaint about a workplace hazard has not been satisfactorily resolved, or a safety problem places employees in immediate danger. If performance of a task would adversely affect health and safety, a worker cannot be disciplined for refusing to do the job.

Joint Health and Safety Committees

The function of joint health and safety committees is to provide a non-adversarial atmosphere where management and labour can work together to ensure a safe and healthy workplace. Most jurisdictions require a joint health and safety committee to be established in each workplace with a minimum number of workers (usually 10 or 20). In the other jurisdictions, the government has the power to require a committee to be formed. Committees are usually required to consist of between two and twelve members, at least half of whom must represent workers. In small workplaces, one health and safety representative may be required.

This woman's loose hair creates an unsafe condition for use of the band saw.

Canadian Centre for OH&S
www.ccohs.ca

The committee is generally responsible for making regular inspections of the workplace in order to identify potential health and safety hazards, evaluating the hazards, and implementing solutions.[6] Hazard control can be achieved by addressing safety issues before an accident or injury happens, identifying ways in which a hazardous situation can be prevented from harming workers, and establishing procedures to ensure that a potential hazard will not recur.[7] Health and safety committees are also responsible for investigating employee complaints, accident investigation, development and promotion of measures to protect health and safety, and dissemination of information about health and safety laws and regulations. In Ontario, at least one management and one labour representative must be certified in occupational health and safety through a provincial training program. Committees are often more effective if the company's health and safety manager acts as an independent expert rather than a management representative.[8]

Enforcement of Occupational Health and Safety Laws

In all Canadian jurisdictions, occupational health and safety law provides for government inspectors to periodically carry out safety inspections of workplaces. Health and safety inspectors have wide powers to conduct inspections, and employers are required to assist them.[9] Safety inspectors may enter a workplace at any time without a warrant or prior notification, and may engage in any examination and inquiry that they believe necessary to ascertain whether the workplace is in compliance with the law. Safety inspectors may order a variety of actions on the part of employers and employees, including orders to stop work, stop using tools, install first aid equipment, and stop emission of contaminants.

Penalties consist of fines and/or jail terms. Governments across Canada are increasingly turning to prosecutions as a means of enforcing health and safety standards. Fines have increased dramatically, with penalties now being as high as $900 000.[10] General Motors of Canada was fined $325 000 after pleading guilty to a health and safety violation that led to a worker's death. The fine was the highest in GM's 92 years in business in Canada.[11]

Canadian corporate executives and directors may be held directly responsible for workplace injuries. In 2002, a corporate officer in Ontario was sentenced to 45 days in prison for health and safety violations that led to the serious injury of a young worker—the first time a corporate officer rather than a supervisor has been convicted.[12] An amendment to the Criminal Code has been proposed, introducing a criminal offence called "corporate killing," which would impose criminal liability on corporate decision makers who blatantly and systematically fail to ensure that their company maintains an appropriate level of safety in the workplace. A House of Commons committee recommended this action following a public inquiry into the Westray mine explosion in Nova Scotia that killed 26 workers in 1992.[13]

Control of Toxic Substances

Most occupational health and safety laws require basic precautions with respect to toxic substances, including chemicals, biohazards (such as HIV/AIDS and SARS), and physical agents (such as radiation, heat, and noise). An accurate inventory of these substances must be maintained, maximum exposure limits for airborne concentrations of these agents adhered to, the substances tested, and their use carefully controlled.

Workplace Hazardous Materials Information System (WHMIS) A Canada-wide legally mandated system designed to protect workers by providing information about hazardous materials in the work-place.

The **Workplace Hazardous Materials Information System (WHMIS)** is a Canada-wide legally mandated system designed to protect workers by providing crucial information about hazardous materials or substances in the workplace. WHMIS was the outcome of a cooperative effort between the federal, provincial, and territorial governments, together with industry and organized labour. The WHMIS legislation has three components:[14]

1. Labelling of hazardous material containers to alert workers that there is a potentially hazardous product inside (see **Figure 14.2** for examples of hazard symbols).

FIGURE I4.2   WHMIS Symbols

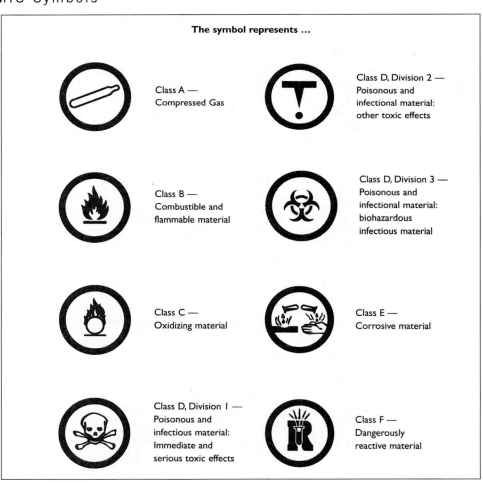

The symbol represents ...

Class A — Compressed Gas

Class B — Combustible and flammable material

Class C — Oxidizing material

Class D, Division I — Poisonous and infectious material: Immediate and serious toxic effects

Class D, Division 2 — Poisonous and infectional material: other toxic effects

Class D, Division 3 — Poisonous and infectional material: biohazardous infectious material

Class E — Corrosive material

Class F — Dangerously reactive material

Source: From *Management of Occupational Health and Safety*, Second Edition, by Montgomery/Kelloway. © 2001. Reprinted with permission of Nelson, a division of Thomson Learning: www.thomsonrights.com. Fax 800-730-2215.

2. Material safety data sheets (MSDS) to outline a product's potentially hazardous ingredients and the procedures for safe handling of the product (see **Figure 14.3** for a sample MSDS).

3. Employee training to ensure that employees can identify WHMIS hazard symbols, read WHMIS supplier and workplace labels, and read and apply the information on an MSDS.

FIGURE I4.3   Material Safety Data Sheet (MSDS)

MATERIAL SAFETY DATA SHEET	Name of Product:				
SECTION I—HAZARDOUS INGREDIENTS					
Chemical Activity	Concentration	CAS Number	PIN Number	LDso Species and Route	LCso Species and Route

SECTION II—PREPARATION INFORMATION		
Prepared by (Group, Department, Etc.)	Phone Number	Date of Preparation

SECTION III—PRODUCT INFORMATION

Product Identifier	
Manufacturer's Name	Supplier's Name
Street Address	Street Address

City	Province	City	Province
Postal Code	Emergency Tel. No.	Postal Code	Emergency Tel. No.

Product Use

SECTION IV—PHYSICAL DATA

Physical State	Odour and Appearance		Odour Threshold
Specific Gravity (water = 1)	Co-efficient of Water/Oil Distribution		Vapour Pressure
Boiling Point (°C)	Freezing Point (°C)	pH	Vapour Density (Air = 1)
Evaporation Rate (BuAc = 1)		Percent Volatile (by volume)	

continued

MATERIAL SAFETY DATA SHEET	Name of Product:		
SECTION V—FIRE OR EXPLOSION HAZARD			
Conditions of Flammability			
Means of Extinction			
Explosion Data Sensitivity to Mechanical Impact	Sensitivity to Static Discharge		
Flashpoint (°C) and Method	Upper Flammable Limit %	Lower Flammable Limit %	
Autoignition Temperature (°C)	Hazardous Combustion Products		
SECTION VI—REACTIVITY DATA			
Stability			
Incompatible Materials			
Conditions of Reactivity			
Hazardous Decomposition Products			
SECTION VII—TOXICOLOGICAL PROPERTIES			
Route of Entry ☐ Skin Contact ☐ Skin Absorption ☐ Eye Contact ☐ Inhalation ☐ Ingestion			
Effects of Acute Exposure to Product			
Effects of Chronic Exposure to Product			
Exposure Limits	Irritancy of Product		Synergistic Products
Evidence of Carcinogenicity, Reproductive Toxicity, Teratogenicity or Mutagenicity?			Sensitization to Product

Occupational Health and Safety and Other Legislation

Health and safety, human rights, labour relations, and employment standards laws are in force in every jurisdiction in Canada in an interlaced web of legislation. Situations arise in which it is difficult to know which law is applicable, or which one takes precedence over another.[15] For example, are the human rights of one employee to wear a ceremonial knife related to a religion more important than the safety of other employees; how much discipline is acceptable to labour arbitrators for health and safety violations; should fights in the workplace be considered a safety hazard; is sexual harassment a safety hazard; and how long does an employer have to tolerate poor performance from an alcoholic employee whose attempts at treatment fail? In Saskatchewan, human rights and occupational health and safety legislation overlap because sexual harassment is considered to be a workplace hazard.[16]

MATERIAL SAFETY DATA SHEET	Name of Product:

SECTION VIII—PREVENTIVE MEASURES

Personal Protective Equipment

Gloves (specify)	Respiratory (specify)
Eye (specify)	Footwear (specify)

Other Equipment (specify)

Engineering Controls (e.g. ventilation, enclosed process, specify)

Leak and Spill Procedure

Waste Disposal

Handling Procedures and Equipment

Storage Requirements

Special Shipping Information

SECTION IX—FIRST AID MEASURES

Inhalation

Ingestion

Eye Contact

Skin Contact

Additional Information	Sources Used

Source: From *Management of Occupational Health and Safety*, Second Edition, by Montgomery/Kelloway. © 2001. Reprinted with permission of Nelson, a division of Thomson Learning: www.thomsonrights.com. Fax 800-730-2215.

THE SUPERVISOR'S ROLE IN SAFETY

Most jurisdictions impose a personal duty on supervisors to ensure that workers comply with occupational health and safety regulations, and place a specific obligation on supervisors to advise and instruct workers about safety.[17] In June 2000, an Ontario court sentenced a business owner (who pleaded guilty as a supervisor) to 20 days in jail after a 17-year-old worker was killed on the job.[18] Safety-minded managers must aim to instill in their workers the desire to work safely. Minimizing hazards (by ensuring that spills are wiped up, machine guards are adequate, and so forth) is important, but no matter how safe the workplace is, there will be accidents unless workers want to and do act safely. Of course, supervisors try to watch each employee closely, but most managers know that this will not work. In the final analysis, the best (and perhaps only) alternative is to get workers to want to work safely. Then, when needed, safety rules should be enforced.[19]

Top-Management Commitment

Most safety experts agree that safety commitment begins with top management. Historically, DuPont's accident rate worldwide has been much lower than that of the chemical industry as a whole. (In its U.S. plants, DuPont had an annual rate of 0.12 accidents per 100 workers, which was one twenty-third of the average rate for all manufacturers in that year.) If DuPont's record had been average, it would have spent more than $26 million in additional compensation and other costs, or 3.6 percent of its profits. To recover the difference, DuPont would have had to boost sales by about $500 million, given the company's 5.5 percent net return on sales at that time.[20] This good safety record is probably partly due to an organizational commitment to safety, which is evident in the following description:

> One of the best examples I know of in setting the highest possible priority for safety takes place at a DuPont plant in Germany. Each morning at the DuPont Polyester and Nylon Plant the director and his assistants meet at 8:45 to review the past 24 hours. The first matter they discuss is not production, but safety. Only after they have examined reports of accidents and near misses and satisfied themselves that corrective action has been taken do they move on to look at output, quality, and cost matters.[21]

In summary, without full commitment at all levels of management, any attempts to reduce unsafe acts by workers will meet with little success. The first-line supervisor is a critical link in the chain of management. If the supervisor does not take safety seriously, it is likely that those under him or her will not either.

WHAT CAUSES ACCIDENTS?

There are three basic causes of workplace accidents: (1) chance occurrences, (2) unsafe conditions, and (3) unsafe acts on the part of employees. A 1995 accident in a Toronto subway tunnel, in which three passengers were killed, provides a vivid example of all of these factors. Signal problems that had been reported by eight other drivers throughout the day had not been addressed as crews were sent to the wrong tunnel, the rookie driver ran three red signal lights, a trip alarm failed, a call for help rang 15 times and then got a voice-mail direction to call another number, emergency crews were sent to look for an "odour," the radio system did not work in the tunnels, and the drivers had no evacuation training.[22]

Chance Occurrences

Chance occurrences (such as walking past a plate-glass window just as someone hits a ball through it) contribute to accidents but are more or less beyond management's control: We will therefore focus on *unsafe conditions* and *unsafe acts*.

Unsafe Conditions

unsafe conditions The mechanical and physical conditions that cause accidents.

Safety Council
www.safety-council.org

Unsafe conditions are one main cause of accidents. They include such factors as:

- improperly guarded equipment
- defective equipment
- hazardous procedures in, on, or around machines or equipment
- unsafe storage (congestion, overloading)
- improper illumination (glare, insufficient light)
- improper ventilation (insufficient air change, impure air source).[23]

The basic remedy here is to eliminate or minimize the unsafe conditions. Government standards address the mechanical and physical conditions that cause accidents. Furthermore, a checklist of unsafe conditions can be used to conduct a job hazard analysis. Common indicators of job hazards include increased numbers of accidents, employee complaints, poor product quality, employee modifications to workstations, and higher levels of absenteeism and turnover.[24]

In addition to unsafe conditions, three other work-related factors contribute to accidents: the *job itself*, the *work schedule*, and the *psychological climate* of the workplace.

Certain *jobs* are inherently more dangerous than others. According to one study, for example, the job of crane operator results in about three times more accident-related hospital visits than does the job of supervisor. Similarly, some departments' work is inherently safer than others'. An accounting department usually has fewer accidents than a shipping department.

Work schedules and fatigue also affect accident rates. Accident rates usually do not increase too noticeably during the first five or six hours of the workday. Beyond that, however, the accident rate increases quickly as the number of hours worked increases. This is due partly to fatigue. It has also been found that accidents occur more often during night shifts.

Many experts believe that the *psychological climate* of the workplace affects the accident rate. For example, accidents occur more frequently in plants with a high seasonal layoff rate and those where there is hostility among employees, many garnished wages, and blighted living conditions. Temporary stress factors such as high workplace temperature, poor illumination, and a congested workplace are also related to accident rates. It appears that workers who work under stress, or who consider their jobs to be threatened or insecure, have more accidents than those who do not.[25]

Unsafe Acts

unsafe acts Behaviour tendencies and undesirable attitudes that cause accidents.

Most safety experts and managers know that it is impossible to eliminate accidents just by improving unsafe conditions. People cause accidents, and no one has found a sure-fire way to eliminate **unsafe acts** by employees such as:

- throwing materials
- operating or working at unsafe speeds (either too fast or too slow)
- making safety devices inoperative by removing, adjusting, disconnecting them

- using unsafe equipment or using equipment unsafely
- using unsafe procedures in loading, placing, mixing, combining
- taking unsafe positions under suspended loads
- lifting improperly
- distracting, teasing, abusing, startling, quarrelling, and instigating horse-play.

Unsafe acts such as these can undermine even the best attempts to minimize unsafe conditions.[26] A model summarizing how personal characteristics are linked to accidents is presented in **Figure 14.4**. Personal characteristics (personality, motivation, and so on) can serve as the basis for certain "behaviour tendencies," such as the tendency to take risks, and undesirable attitudes. These behaviour tendencies in turn result in unsafe acts, such as inattention and failure to follow procedures. It follows that such unsafe acts increase the probability of someone having an accident.[27]

Research
Insight

Years of research have failed to unearth any set of traits that accident repeaters seemed to have in common. Today, most experts doubt that accident proneness is universal—that there are some people who will have many accidents no matter what situation they are put in. Instead, the consensus is that the person who is accident prone on one job may not be on a different job—that accident proneness is situational. For example, *personality traits* (such as emotional stability) may distinguish accident-prone workers on jobs involving risk; and *lack of motor skills* may distinguish accident-prone workers on jobs involving coor-

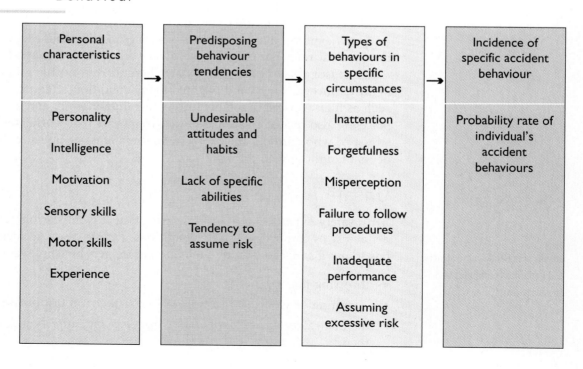

FIGURE 14.4   How Personal Factors May Influence Employee Accident Behaviour

dination. In fact, many human traits *have* been found to be related to accident repetition *in specific situations*, as the following discussion illustrates.[28]

Vision
Vision is related to accident frequency for many jobs. For example, passenger car drivers, intercity bus drivers, and machine operators who have high visual skills have fewer injuries than those who do not.[29]

Managing Young Workers
www.youngworker.ca

Canadian LifeQuilt
www.youngworkerquilt.ca

Age
Accidents are generally most frequent among people between the ages of 17 and 28, declining thereafter to reach a low in the late 50s and 60s.[30] While different patterns might be found with different jobs, this age factor repeats year after year. Across Canada, young workers between the ages of 15 and 24 (often students in low-paying summer jobs) represent about 17 percent of all workplace accidents.[31] For example, Felice D'Ascario, age 19, of Etobicoke, Ontario, was struck in the head by part of a skid (a wooden platform used to move crates) and killed on September 23, 1998—his third day on the job. He was especially happy that morning as he was to purchase his first car after work that day.[32] Many injuries and fatalities occur in the first few days of employment, which raises questions about the supervision and training of young workers. Suggestions regarding training of young workers are provided in the Workforce Diversity box.

Perceptual versus Motor Skills
One researcher concludes that "where [a worker's] perceptual skill is equal to, or higher than, his or her motor skill, the employee is a relatively safe worker. But where the perception level is lower than the motor level, the employee is accident prone and his or her accident proneness becomes greater as this difference increases."[33] This theory seems to be a twist on the "look before you leap" theme—a worker who reacts more quickly than he or she can perceive is more likely to have accidents.

WORKFORCE DIVERSITY

Training Young Workers in Safety Basics

Young workers think differently from most experienced employees:

- Young workers tend to take risks and are unrealistic about their own mortality.

- Young people may be reluctant to ask questions for fear of appearing unknowledgeable.

- Due to a lack of understanding, young workers may decide to make changes to the job in unexpected and possibly risky ways.

To reduce the likelihood of accidents and injuries to young people in the workplace, the Canadian Centre for Occupational Health and Safety suggests:

1. *Assign suitable work.* Avoid assigning jobs that require long training times, a high degree of skill, a lot of responsibility, critical or risky tasks, or working alone.

2. *Provide training.* Tell young workers not to perform any task until they have been properly trained.

3. *Ensure hazardous equipment training is provided and protective equipment is used.* Make sure that any young worker who must use hazardous equipment is given detailed training on safety features. If young workers must wear protective equipment, make sure they know when they need to wear it, where to find it, how to use it, and how to care for it.

Source: "Training Young Workers in Safety Basics," *Canadian HR Reporter* (May 5, 2003), p. 8. Reproduced by permission of *Canadian HR Reporter*, Carswell, One Corporate Plaza, 2075 Kennedy Road, Scarborough, ON M1T 3V4.

In summary, these findings provide a partial list of the human traits that have been found to be related to higher accident rates, and suggest that, for specific jobs, it seems to be possible to identify accident-prone individuals and to screen them out.

Research
I n s i g h t ▷

There is usually no single cause—whether acts or conditions—of workplace injuries; instead, accident causes tend to be multifaceted. This is illustrated by a recent study of employed adolescents.[34] Participants were 319 adolescents recruited by the researcher through advertisements at three colleges and 37 high schools. To be eligible, the student had to be between 16 and 19 years old, currently working for pay in a formal organization at least five hours per week, and a full-time student. The students were asked to complete detailed questionnaires, which measured both possible predictors of workplace injuries (such as gender) and the number and nature of any job injuries actually suffered.

It was clear that several factors or predictors were related to the number of workplace injuries that these adolescents suffered. For example, gender was important: adolescent boys reported more work injuries than did adolescent girls (perhaps because they also reported greater exposure to physical hazards on the job). Personality was important: for example, "negative affectivity"—the extent to which individuals experience negative moods and emotional reactivity, as measured by items such as "Often, I get irritated at little annoyances"—was positively related to work injuries. Other predictors related to work injuries included job tenure (the longer on the job, the more injuries, perhaps because more experienced workers got the jobs involving higher skill levels and greater exposure to risks), exposure to physical hazards, excessive workloads, job boredom, poor physical health, and on-the-job substance abuse.

The results of a study focusing on adolescents do not necessarily apply to working adults. However, one apparent implication of this study is that employers need comprehensive safety programs since accidents seem to have multiple causes. With that in mind, we now turn to a discussion of how to prevent accidents.

HOW TO PREVENT ACCIDENTS

In practice, accident prevention involves reducing unsafe conditions and reducing unsafe acts.

Reducing Unsafe Conditions

Reducing unsafe conditions is an employer's first line of defence. Safety engineers should design jobs to remove or reduce physical hazards. In addition, supervisors and managers play a role in reducing unsafe conditions. A brief checklist can be used to identify and remove potential hazards. However, only 4 percent of accidents stem from unsafe working conditions, and therefore we will concentrate mainly on accident prevention methods that focus on changing behaviours.[35]

Reducing Unsafe Acts

Selection and Placement Reducing unsafe acts is the second basic approach, and one way to do this is to screen out accident-prone persons before

they are hired. The basic technique is to identify the human trait (such as visual skill) that might be related to accidents on the specific job, and then determine whether scores on this trait are related to accidents on the job.[36] For example:

- *Measures of muscular coordination.* We know that coordination is a predictor of safety for certain jobs.
- *Tests of visual skills.* Good vision plays a part in preventing accidents in many occupations, including driving and operating machines.
- *Employee reliability tests.* Several studies suggest that a test such as the Employee Reliability Inventory (ERI) can help employers to reduce unsafe acts at work. The ERI measures reliability dimensions such as emotional maturity, conscientiousness, safe job performance, and courteous job performance.[37]
- *Behaviour-based interviewing.* Behavioural interviews and observations made in a test situation can also help to determine the likelihood that the candidate will be a safe worker.[38]

Research
Insight ▷

A study conducted in a major industrial plant in Ontario compared injury costs for a group of employees that were subjected to post-offer screening to assess their physical capability to perform job duties, and another group that did not receive post-offer screening. Injury costs over five years for the screened group were $6500 and for the non-screened group were $2 073 000—a highly significant difference.[39]

Hints to Ensure Legal Compliance

Canadian human rights legislation has particular relevance for safety-related screening decisions. Many employers would like to inquire about applicants' workers' compensation history prior to hiring, in part to avoid habitual workers'-compensation claimants and accident-prone individuals. However, inquiring about an applicant's workers' compensation injuries and claims can lead to allegations of discrimination based on disability. Similarly, applicants cannot be asked whether they have a disability nor can they be asked to take tests that tend to screen out those with disabilities.

Employers can ask each applicant whether he or she has the ability to perform the essential duties of the job and ask, "Do you know of any reason why you would not be able to perform the various functions of the job in question?"[40] Candidates can also be asked to demonstrate job-related skills, provided that every applicant is required to do so. Any selection test that duplicates the physical requirements of the job at realistic levels and type of work expected does not violate human rights law, as long as it is developed and imposed honestly and in good faith to test whether or not the applicant can meet production requirements.[41]

Training and Education   Safety training is a third technique for reducing accidents. Safety associations, such as the Industrial Accident Prevention Association (IAPA), are available to partner in training efforts. All employees should be required to participate in occupational health and safety training programs, and opportunities for employee input into the content and design of such programs is advisable.[42] The training should include instructions on safe work practices and procedures, warnings of potential hazards, the development of worker awareness about health and safety issues, and emphasis on commitment to responsible and appropriate workplace behaviour. It should include a practical evaluation process to ensure that workers are applying the acquired

Industrial Accident Prevention
Association www.iapa.on.ca

knowledge and following recommended safety procedures. Such training is especially appropriate for new employees. This training can be delivered through a variety of media, including classroom training, printed material, computer, videos, intranets, and the Internet.[43] The HR.Net box describes two successfully developed Web-based health and safety training programs.

Safety posters can also help reduce unsafe acts. However, posters are no substitute for a comprehensive safety program; instead, they should be combined with other techniques like screening and training to reduce unsafe conditions and acts.[44] Posters with pictures may be particularly valuable for immigrant workers. One study found that 68 percent of Canadian immigrant workers who did not speak English said they were not aware of workplace safety practices, and 72 percent said they had never received formal safety training.[45]

AN ETHICAL DILEMMA

Is it ethical to provide safety training in English to immigrant workers who speak little English, in order to save money?

Positive Reinforcement   Safety programs based on positive reinforcement are a fourth strategy for improving safety at work.[46] Employees often receive little or no positive reinforcement for performing safely. One approach is to establish and communicate a reasonable goal (in terms of observed incidents performed safely) so that workers know what is expected of them in terms of good performance. Employees are then encouraged to consider increasing their performance to the new safety goal, for their own protection and to decrease costs for the company. Next, various observers (such as safety coordi-

HR.NET

Online Health and Safety Training

Two health and safety organizations have recently begun to use the Web for delivering health and safety training. First, the Industrial Accident Prevention Association (IAPA) decided to develop health and safety training software in 2000. To combat traditional learners' desire for an "in-person classroom" program, the IAPA wanted to create a virtual classroom that would mirror the "in-person classroom" by including the same ingredients.

Three existing courses were redeveloped to accommodate the Web medium. Web course template software was selected to develop and pilot the courses. Digital media such as pictures, short video/audio clips, and animations were included, as well as exercises and testing in the form of a self-assessment quiz. A virtual instructor functioning as a facilitator and other online supports were added to the mix to ensure that participants were guided through the Web course process and to increase completion rates.

Registration occurred online via the IAPA home page. Between October 2000 and August 2001, Web participation increased steadily, and the Web courses were completed by 500 learners.

Second, the Canadian Centre for Occupational Health and Safety (CCOHS) has worked with youth across the country to build Job One (http://job-one.ccohs.ca), a site designed to attract youth and teach them about health and safety. The site is aimed at the 16 to 25 age group. It features information on hours of work and wages, real stories of young workers who have had accidents, as well as games and quizzes. It also has information on occupational health and safety laws in different jurisdictions and what to do if injured in the workplace. The true-life stories, in particular, have proven to be a popular part of the site.

"Youth talk amongst each other about what types of Web sites they visit," said Kerilyn Molinski, the Manitoba representative on the youth committee that helped brainstorm the site. "They say, 'Hey Tommy. I visited this really cool Web site last night and you should check it out.' If there is stuff out there they like, they'll pass that information on to their friends, so we're relying a lot on work-of-mouth to get the message out."

Source: Adapted from E. Lederman, "Building a Virtual Classroom," *Canadian HR Reporter* (October 22, 2001), pp. G10–G11; and T. Humber, "Telling Stories, Learning Lessons Online," *Canadian HR Reporter* (May 5, 2003), p. 7.

nators and senior managers) should walk through the plant regularly, collecting safety data. The results can then be posted on a graph charting the percentage of incidents performed safely by the group as a whole, thus providing the workers with feedback on their safety performance. Workers can thereby compare their current safety performance with their assigned goal. In addition, supervisors should praise workers when they perform selected activities safely.[47]

Top-Management Commitment
One of the most consistent findings in the literature is that successful health and safety programs require a strong management commitment.[48] This commitment, a fifth approach to accident reduction, manifests itself in senior managers: being personally involved in safety activities on a routine basis; giving safety matters high priority in company meetings and production scheduling; giving the company safety officer high rank and status; and including safety training in new workers' training. HR managers have an important role to play in communicating the importance of health and safety to senior management, by demonstrating how it affects the bottom line.[49]

Managers who want to emphasize safety are advised to:[50]

- praise employees when they choose safe behaviours
- listen when employees voice suggestions, concerns, or complaints
- be a good example (e.g., by following every safety rule and procedure)
- continually improve and simplify plant safety (e.g., by removing hazards where possible)
- visit plant areas regularly
- maintain open safety communications (e.g., by telling employees as much as possible about safety activities such as testing alarms and changing safety equipment or procedures).

Linking managers' bonuses to safety improvements can reinforce a firm's commitment to safety and encourage managers to emphasize safety. One company reduced its workers' compensation costs with an HR policy that requires managers to halve accidents or forfeit 30 percent of their bonuses.[51]

Monitoring Work Overload and Stress
In one recent study, "role overload" (formally defined as the degree to which the employee's performance was seen as being affected by inadequate time, training, and resources) was significantly associated with unsafe behaviours.[52] Similarly, other researchers have suggested that as work overload increases, workers are more likely to adopt more risky work methods. Thus, a sixth approach to reducing unsafe acts is having employers and supervisors monitor employees (particularly those in relatively hazardous jobs) for signs of stress and overload.

Controlling Workers' Compensation Costs
Workers' compensation costs are often the most expensive benefit provided by an employer. For example, the average workplace injury in Ontario costs over $59 000 in workers' compensation benefits. Indirect costs are estimated to be about four times the direct costs.[53] Employers' workers' compensation premiums are proportional to the firm's workers' compensation experience rate. Thus, the more workers' compensation claims a firm has, the more the firm will pay in premiums.

There are several steps in reducing workers' compensation claims:

Before the Accident The appropriate time to begin "controlling" workers' compensation claims is before the accident happens, not after. This involves taking all of the steps previously summarized. For example, firms should remove unsafe conditions, screen out employees who might be accident prone for the job in question (without violating human rights legislation), and establish a safety policy and loss control goals.

After the Accident The occupational injury or illness can obviously be a traumatic event for the employee, and the employer's way of handling it can influence the injured worker's reaction to it. The employee is going to have specific needs and specific questions, such as where to go for medical help and whether he or she will be paid for any time off. Employers should provide first aid and make sure that the worker gets quick medical attention; make it clear that they are interested in the injured worker and his or her fears and questions; document the accident; file any required accident reports; and encourage a speedy return to work.[54]

Facilitate the Employee's Return to Work According to one discussion of managing workers' compensation costs:

> Perhaps the most important and effective thing an employer can do to reduce costs is to develop an aggressive return-to-work program, including making light-duty work available. Surely the best solution to the current workers' compensation crisis, for both the employer and the employee, is for the worker to become a productive member of the company again instead of a helpless victim living on benefits.[55]

Specific actions to encourage early return to work can be internal and/or external to the organization. Internally, an employer can set up rehabilitation committees to identify modified work, including relevant stakeholders such as the employee and his or her colleagues, HR professionals, union representatives, and managers.

Functional abilities evaluations (FAEs) are an important step in facilitating return to work. The FAE is conducted by a health-care professional, in order to:

- improve the chances that the injured worker will be safe on the job
- help the worker's performance by identifying problem areas of work that can be addressed by physical therapy or accommodated through job modification
- determine the level of disability so that the worker can either go back to his or her original job or be accommodated.[56]

Externally, the employer can work with the employee's family to ensure that they are supportive, mobilize the resources of the EAP to help the employee, ensure that physical and occupational therapists are available, and make the family physician aware of workplace accommodation possibilities.[57] A study by consultants Sobeco, Ernst & Young found that 90 percent of companies have formal return-to-work programs, but only 62 percent of those are applying the program to all employees with disabilities.[58]

The City of Toronto uses software that can develop alternative career paths for employees who are physically or psychologically unable to perform a particular job by matching their restricted abilities with jobs whose physical and

Tips for the Front Line

psychological demands they are able to meet. The City's savings from returning employees to productivity have been estimated at $800 000 to $1.2 million.[59]

EMPLOYEE WELLNESS PROGRAMS

employee wellness program A program that takes a proactive approach to employee health and well-being.

Strength-Tek Fitness and Wellness Consultants **www.strengthtek.com**

Healthy Workplace Week **www.healthyworkplaceweek.ca**

There are three elements in a healthy workplace—the physical environment, the social environment, and health practices. **Employee wellness programs** take a proactive approach to all of these areas of employee well-being (as opposed to EAPs, which provide reactive management of employee health problems).[60] Wellness should be viewed as a management strategy to achieve measurable outcomes related to increased levels of employee health, such as reduced health and safety costs, decreased absenteeism, lower workers' compensation costs, fewer long-term disability claims, reduced time off for short-term disability/sickness, increased morale, decreased health-care costs, and fewer employees in high-risk health categories (such as smokers).[61]

One expert predicts that over the next 25 years, prevention and wellness will be the next great leap forward in health care, as employees become more broadly recognized as the most important assets of organizations. A focus on wellness will also be driven by the shrinking workforce, an increase in postponed retirement, increased awareness of mental health, and medical and technological advances.[62]

Wellness initiatives often include stress management, nutrition and weight management, smoking cessation programs, tai chi, heart health (such as screening cholesterol and blood pressure levels), physical fitness programs, and workstation wellness through ergonomics.[63] Wellness and prevention efforts need to be understood and undertaken as a process—a long-term commitment to a holistic focus on the total person. B.C. Telus has a 50-year-old wellness program where managers are held accountable—if absenteeism increases in their department, their bonus decreases![64] Telus believes that a focus on wellness and enhancing corporate competitiveness are one and the same. Its long-term experience has netted a savings of three dollars for every dollar spent on wellness.

Although wellness programs tend to be associated with large companies, smaller employers can also benefit from wellness programs, as outlined in the Entrepreneurs and HR box.

A ten-year study of the wellness program at Canada Life Assurance Company found substantial benefits to be gained from wellness programs, including decreased absenteeism and turnover and decreased costs for health and drug benefits, with an average of three dollars saved for every dollar invested.[65] NCR Canada saved $600 000 in direct and indirect costs during the first year of its wellness program, and absenteeism was cut by more than half after 12 months and was still one-third lower after 36 months.[66] The National Quality Institute (NQI) gave its 2002 Healthy Workplace Award to MDS Nordion for a wellness program that cut absenteeism from 5.5 to 4 days annually, and cut turnover to half the industry average.[67] NQI's five key design principles for

DaimlerChrysler Canada is partnering with labour and local health units to promote wellness. The automaker's new workplace wellness program in Windsor, Ontario, includes a health risk assessment tool and various health promotion initiatives such as health fairs.

ENTREPRENEURS AND HR

Novo Nordisk Canada Inc.

Novo Nordisk is an international pharmaceutical company, with its Canadian office located in Mississauga, Ontario. About 50 employees work there, with 50 more sales personnel spread across Canada. In the spring of 2000, a committee was formed to explore the development of a wellness program, which was launched that summer. It is run by employees, who wrote a mission statement for the program. They choose, organize, and lead activities after receiving appropriate training from a wellness professional who visits the site once a week.

The program is intended to foster an environment where a healthy and safe lifestyle is encouraged through awareness, education, and participation. Three goals support the company's mission:

- to provide a supportive work environment that fosters optimal health, safety, and well-being

- to provide resources and programs to help employees adopt positive health behaviours, and

- to educate employees about the importance of physical activity and provide opportunities for employees to increase their level of physical activity.

Employees participate enthusiastically in healthy lifestyle initiatives that include lunch-and-learn workshops, roving wellness clinics, walking days, incentive challenges, on-site massage therapy, stretch breaks, and health fairs. A conference room is also used for "low sweat" or "showerless" workouts.

Novo Nordisk is an example of a relatively small employer that has successfully adopted a strategy to enhance workplace wellness using creativity and flexibility. According to Marie Percival, the company's director of human resources and proud sponsor of its wellness program, "Wellness initiatives are completely aligned with our values and business strategy."

Source: V. Marsden, "Workplace Wellness: Small Companies Can't Afford to be Left Behind," *Canadian HR Reporter* (April 22, 2002), p. 28. Reproduced by permission of *Canadian HR Reporter*, Carswell, One Corporate Plaza, 2075 Kennedy Road, Scarborough, ON M1T 3V4.

FIGURE 14.5   Corporate Wellness Initiatives

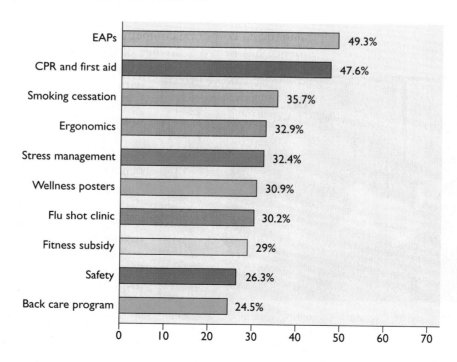

Source: Corporate Wellness Initiatives, Health Canada, © 2002. Reproduced with the permission of the Minister of Public Works and Government Services Canada, 2004.

successful wellness programs are personal control, social support, interactivity, wide appeal, and convenience.[68]

One recent survey found that 17 percent of Canadian companies have implemented wellness programs, compared to 37 percent in the United States (where 67 of the Fortune 100 companies have invested in wellness).[69] Almost 64 percent of Canadian organizations offer some form of wellness initiatives such as smoking cessation programs, as shown in **Figure 14.5**.[70] Another survey found that the number of Canadian companies implementing some form of wellness program has grown, but that most are not measuring their effectiveness.[71] Both MDS Nordion and Husky Injection Moulding Systems have innovative wellness programs, as described in the Strategic HR box.

STRATEGIC HR

Creating a Culture of Wellness

MDS Nordion and Husky Injection Moulding Systems Ltd. are two organizations with innovative healthy workplace programs that are using them as strategic HR initiatives for now and in the future. MDS Nordion engineers spend their lunch playing volleyball. They used to play bridge, but then they asked about a volleyball net. It's just one example of how the company's holistic approach to a healthy workplace is paying off and changing behaviour. MDS Nordion makes sure it talks to staff about what their needs and wants are before they implement things like a fitness centre. Employees were asked if they would support a fitness centre by signing up in advance of the company formally committing to it. They hoped to get 25 percent of their 800 employees at corporate headquarters to sign up. They met that target, and now 38 percent of employees have memberships.

The company has 21 hectares of land complete with a hockey rink, soccer field, and baseball diamond—all of which hum with activity. In 1991, only one female staff member participated in a 10-kilometre run sponsored by the company. In 2002, there were 137—another indication of changing norms and behaviour. The company offers a health and well-being reimbursement program where employees can get weight management, golf memberships, and ski programs subsidized by 50 percent to a maximum of $150 per year.

The company feels ready to handle the changing demographics of the workforce in the coming years. It recently launched an intranet site on work–life balance and augmented its flextime, compressed workweek, and telework programs.

At Husky Injection Moulding's Bolton, Ontario, headquarters, the cafeteria provides a perfect example of what its healthy workplace program is all about. A vegetarian meal costs about $1.50 less than other meals because it is subsidized by the company. There are three main components of Husky's healthy workplace program for its 1300 workers—a wellness centre, a fitness centre, and the nutrition program.

The wellness centre is an on-site medical facility that treats occupational and non-occupational healthcare concerns. The facility, open Monday to Friday from 8 A.M. to 5:30 P.M., is busy. In 2001, it had 7900 patient visits and took in another 7600 in 2002. The services are all paid for by provincial health care or the company. The fitness centre is open 24 hours and employs a full-time fitness coordinator. Workers get an extra vacation day every year if they commit to physical fitness and have an annual medical check-up. The nutrition program means that all the food served in the cafeteria is low in fat and the only meats available are fish and poultry. Pop is available, but nothing with aspartame, and there are no donuts in sight.

The company received a rebate of nearly $500 000 from the Ontario Workplace Safety and Insurance Board in 2003, which they believe is due to the effects of the wellness program in improving employee health. As far as dealing with the aging workforce, the company plans to stay in close touch with the workforce, and listen and develop programs as the need arises. For example, the wellness centre is treating a lot of back complaints, so a back-care program is being developed so staff can do something for themselves to prevent or help manage back pain.

Source: T. Humber, "Creating a Culture of Wellness," *Canadian HR Reporter* (April 7, 2003), pp. 21, 26. Reproduced by permission of *Canadian HR Reporter*, Carswell, One Corporate Plaza, 2075 Kennedy Road, Scarborough, ON M1T 3V4.

OCCUPATIONAL HEALTH ISSUES AND CHALLENGES

A number of health-related issues and challenges can undermine employee performance at work.[72] These include alcoholism and substance abuse, stress and burnout, repetitive strain injuries, smoking, workplace toxins, and workplace violence.

Alcoholism and Substance Abuse

Alcoholism is a serious and widespread disease with staggering costs. The effects of alcoholism on the employee and his or her work are severe. Both the quality and quantity of the work decline sharply, and a form of "on-the-job absenteeism" (also known as "presenteeism") occurs as efficiency declines. The problem is particularly severe in the manufacturing sector, where employees have substance abuse rates at nearly twice the national norm.[73]

The use of drugs, especially in the workplace, is a growing concern for Canadian companies and has led to increased numbers of alcohol and drug abuse counselling programs.

In Ontario alone, the annual cost of workers' compensation payouts related to alcohol and drug abuse is up to $240 million.[74] The Canadian Centre on Substance Abuse estimates the annual lost productivity due to substance abuse at close to $11.8 billion nationwide.[75] Employers can expect between 3 and 7 percent of their workforce to be alcoholics, 10 to 30 percent of workers to drink to excess, and 2 to 7 percent to have a problem with illicit drug use, according to the Ontario Centre for Addiction and Mental Health.[76] Overall, about thirty percent of Canadian companies report having problems with drugs and alcohol in the workplace.[77]

Recognizing the alcoholic on the job can pose a problem. The early symptoms can be similar to those of other problems, and thus hard to classify. Alcohol-related problems range from tardiness in the earliest stages of alcohol abuse to prolonged unpredictable absences in its later stages.[78] Supervisors should be the company's first line of defence in combating substance abuse in the workplace, but should not try to be company detectives or medical diagnosticians. Guidelines that supervisors should follow include these:

- If an employee appears to be under the influence of drugs or alcohol, ask how the employee feels and look for signs of impairment, such as slurred speech. An employee judged to be unfit for duty may be sent home but not fired on the spot.

- Make a written record of observed behaviour and follow up each incident. In addition to issuing a written reprimand, managers should inform workers of the number of warnings that the company will tolerate before requiring termination. Regardless of any suspicion of substance abuse, concerns should be focused on work performance, expected changes, and available options for help.[79]

- Troubled employees should be referred to the company's employee assistance program.

Traditional Techniques
The four traditional techniques for dealing with alcoholism and substance abuse are discipline, discharge, in-house counselling, and referral to an outside agency. Discharge is used to deal with alcoholism and drug problems only after repeated attempts at rehabilitation have failed.[80]

Tips for the Front Line

Hints to Ensure Legal Compliance

In-house counselling, often one component of an employee assistance program, can be used to assist alcoholics and drug users. In most cases the counselling is offered by the HR department or the employer's medical staff. Immediate supervisors with special training also provide counselling in many instances. Many companies use outside agencies such as Alcoholics Anonymous, psychiatrists, and clinics to assist employees with alcoholism and drug problems. In Timmins, Ontario, a broad-based community coalition assembled by the local Chamber of Commerce created the very successful "Withdrawal Management Service." The service uses a mix of professional staff and trained volunteers to intervene early with people having drug or alcohol problems—while they remain at home.[81] The cost per client is $437, compared to $1308 per client in a residential detox centre.

Workplace Substance Abuse and the Law   Because of the seriousness of the problem, most employers are taking additional steps to deal with alcohol and substance abuse on the job. This is difficult in Canada, because employers must balance conflicting legal obligations. On the one hand, Canadian human rights and privacy laws must be respected. Alcoholism and drug addiction are generally considered to be disabilities under human rights legislation. On the other hand, under occupational health and safety legislation, employers are responsible for maintaining due diligence. Thus, it makes sense to utilize drug testing to assess whether employees in "safety-sensitive" positions are drug- and alcohol-free at work. "Safety sensitive" refers to the actual functions being carried out by the employee rather than to his or her overall job. Thus, an aircraft mechanic would not be considered to be doing safety-sensitive work during an all-day training session on retirement planning.[82]

For example, the Ontario Human Rights Commission decided that Imperial Oil's pre-employment and random drug testing discriminated against a recovering alcoholic employee because the company had not established that drug testing was relevant in assessing whether the employee could perform the job safely.[83] This conundrum is all the more important for employers because of a British Columbia Supreme Court decision that an employer who supplies alcohol to employees has the obligation to monitor employees' consumption of alcohol and prevent an employee from driving if he or she is likely to be impaired.[84]

Drug tests are most commonly used to determine whether an employee is in violation of a company policy on alcohol and drug use. These tests should be conducted only in certain circumstances, including where there are reasonable grounds based on direct observation to believe that the employee is unfit for duty, as part of an accident investigation, as a condition of employment after a rule violation, to monitor an employee after drug treatment, or as a final condition for a job offer in a safety-sensitive position.[85]

So far, it appears that employers can have a policy forbidding drugs and alcohol in the workplace, they can require random drug testing for employees in safety-sensitive jobs, and they can conduct mandatory drug testing after an accident or near-accident if the employer has reasonable or probable grounds to suspect that such abuse contributed to the accident.[86] Beyond that, the situation is less clear.

Substance Abuse Policies   In general, a clear, well-communicated substance abuse policy that is reasonably and consistently enforced is the employer's best approach. The Centre for Addiction and Mental Health recommends that the policy components should include:[87]

- The prohibition of alcohol and drug use (or coming to work drugged or drunk) during work hours and company special events; with clearly defined business circumstances, if any, in which alcohol consumption is considered appropriate.

- Clearly defined roles and responsibilities of workers and management in meeting company expectations regarding alcohol and drug use, and seeking help if problems arise.

- Disciplinary measures for infractions (these must meet human rights legal requirements that addictions be considered a disability).

- Communication procedures to ensure that all employees know and understand the policy.

- Preventive education to ensure that employees are knowledgeable about alcohol and drug abuse.

- Training to ensure that front-line supervisors and union stewards can identify employees with suspected substance abuse problems, complete thorough documentation of job performance problems, and refer the employees to a company-sponsored or external treatment program.

- Provision for confidential assistance and treatment programs for employees with drug and alcohol problems.

Finally, organizations should remember that health promotion and drug education programs can help to prevent employee drug and alcohol problems from developing in the first place. Overall, employers need to balance measures to control or deter substance abuse, such as drug testing, with preventive measures such as education and EAPs.

Job Stress

Workplace stress is a pervasive problem that is getting worse.[88] In a nationwide poll, over half of all Canadian workers said that they experience "a great deal of stress at work."[89] Forty-one percent of those surveyed were of the opinion that their employer was not doing "nearly enough" to help them manage stress in the workplace. Another nationwide survey found that 45 percent of Canadians said that working conditions were the biggest source of stress in their lives.[90] Organizations begin to suffer when too many employees feel that the relentless pace of work life is neither sustainable nor healthy.[91] Why is this happening? Downsizing has resulted in employees being asked to do more with less, creating work overload, increased time pressures, and tighter deadlines.[92] Also, technology and the sheer volume of e-mail and voice mail is imposing terrific amounts of pressure and distraction on employees, taking a toll on their emotional equilibrium. The result is a corporate climate characterized by fatigue, depression, and anxiety.[93] Employment insurance claims for illness benefits showed a dramatic increase in 1999, and the financial impact of stress on the Canadian workplace has been estimated at more than $20 billion per year.[94]

There are two main sources of job stress: environmental factors and personal factors.[95] First, a variety of external, *environmental factors* can lead to job stress. The top ten sources of workplace stress are shown in **Table 14.1.** Two factors are particularly stress-inducing. The first is a high-demand job, such as one with constant deadlines coupled with low employee control. The second is high levels of mental and physical effort combined with low reward in terms of compensation or acknowledgement.[96]

However, no two people react to the same job in an identical way, since *personal factors* also influence stress. For example, Type A personalities—people who are workaholics and who feel driven to always be on time and meet deadlines—normally place themselves under greater stress than do others. Similarly, one's patience, tolerance for ambiguity, self-esteem, health and exercise, and work and sleep patterns can also affect how one reacts to stress. Add to job stress the stress caused by non-job problems like divorce, postpartum depression, seasonal affective disorder, and work/family time conflict, and many workers are problems waiting to happen.

Job stress has serious consequences for both the employee and the organization. Mental illness costs Canadian organizations up to $30 billion per year.[97] The human consequences of job stress include anxiety, depression, anger, and various physical consequences, such as cardiovascular disease, headaches, and accidents. One study found that even isolated episodes of workplace stress can as much as double the risk of a heart attack.[98] A national health survey by Statistics Canada found that employees working long hours are more likely to indulge in a harmful combination of more cigarettes, more alcohol, and more unhealthy food.[99] Stress also has serious consequences for the organization, including reductions in the quantity and quality of job performance, increased absenteeism and turnover, increased grievances, and escalating short- and long-term disability claims.[100]

Yet stress is not necessarily dysfunctional. Too little stress creates boredom and apathy. Performance is optimal at a level of stress that energizes but does not wear someone out.[101] Others find that stress may result in a search that leads to a better job or to a career that makes more sense, given the person's aptitudes. A modest level of stress may even lead to more creativity if a competitive situation results in new ideas being generated.

TABLE 14.1   Top Ten Sources of Workplace Stress

1. Feeling of not contributing and having a lack of control.
2. Lack of two-way communication up and down the chain of command.
3. Being unappreciated.
4. Inconsistent performance management. Raises but no reviews. Positive feedback and then laid off with no understanding of why.
5. Career/job ambiguity. Things happen without employees knowing why.
6. Unclear company direction and policies.
7. Mistrust. Vicious office politics disrupts positive behaviour.
8. Doubt. Employees are uncertain about what is happening and where things are headed in their position, department or organization.
9. Random interruptions.
10. Treadmill syndrome. Too much to do at once, requires 24-hour workday.

Source: Adapted from *Top 10 Sources of Workplace Stress* (Toronto: Global Business and Economic Roundtable on Addiction and Mental Health, 2003). Available online: http://www.mentalhealthroundtable.ca/aug_round_pdfs/Top%20Ten%20Sources%20of%20Stress.pdf. Reprinted with the permission of Global Business and Economic Roundtable on Addiction and Mental Health.

AN ETHICAL
DILEMMA

Is it ethical to ignore the issue of job stress entirely, or should organizations at least analyze sickness and disability claims to assess whether there are one or more workplace issues contributing to employee job stress?

Reducing Job Stress   There are things that a person can do to alleviate stress, ranging from common-sense remedies such as getting more sleep, eating better, and taking vacation time, to more exotic remedies such as biofeedback and meditation. Finding a more suitable job, getting counselling through an EAP or elsewhere, and planning and organizing each day's activities are other sensible responses.[102]

The organization and its HR specialists and supervisors can also play a role in identifying and reducing job stress. One expert, Dr. John Yardley of the Brock University Wellness Institute, predicts that due diligence for health and safety could soon include an obligation for employers to ensure that employees are not faced with excessive amounts of stress.[103] Offering an EAP is a major step toward alleviating the pressure on managers to try to help employees cope with stress.[104] About 40 percent of EAP usage is related to stress at work.[105] For the supervisor, important activities include monitoring each employee's performance to identify symptoms of stress, and then informing the person of the organizational remedies that may be available, such as EAPs, job transfers, or other counselling. Also important are fair treatment and permitting the employee to have more control over his or her job.[106] The HR specialist's role includes using attitude surveys to identify organizational sources of stress, refining selection and placement procedures to ensure effective person–job match, and providing career planning aimed at ensuring that the employee moves toward a job that makes sense in terms of his or her aptitudes.

The Business and Economic Roundtable on Mental Health has recommended that HR executives take a more aggressive role in helping to combat workplace depression.[107] After years of selling executive decisions about downsizing and restructuring to employees, HR executives now need to become advocates for employee health within the senior management team. Today's highly valued employees who are driving corporate productivity, innovation, and performance tend to be young knowledge workers, precisely the type of worker most prone to depression and stress. Unfortunately, there is still a stigma associated with mental illness, which drives a lot of it underground and unreported to employers or even health-care providers.[108] The roundtable group is calling for stimulation of EAP usage and for the creation of special EAPs specifically targeting depression, which affects about 10 percent of the labour force.[109] **Figure 14.6** illustrates 12 steps recommended by the roundtable group to eradicate depression and work-generated stress.

Managers should also be aware of probable gender differences in job stress. Studies suggest that women competing in a male-dominated environment are subject to chronic stress, which is partly attributable to distinct stressors for women, such as harassment and particularly sexual harassment.[110] This suggests the importance of reducing gender-related potential stressors such as sexual harassment and "glass-ceiling" impediments to advancement.

Research
Insight   ▷

Giving employees more control over their job can also mediate the effects of job stress. This is illustrated by the results of a study in which the psychological strain caused by job stress was reduced by the amount of control that employees had over their job.[111] The less stressful jobs did have high demands in terms of quantitative work load, the amount of attention that the employees had to pay to their work, and work pressure. However, they also ranked high in task clarity, job control, supervisory support, and employee skill utilization.[112] The researchers conclude that "to achieve a balanced system, that is, to reduce psy-

FIGURE 14.6   Twelve Steps to End Depression

1. **CEO Briefing**—The CEO and executives should be briefed and educated about depression.
2. **Financial Targets**—Targets should be set to reduce depression within the organization.
3. **EAP and Group Health Plan Reforms**—These should be redesigned to support managers dealing with the privacy issues inherent in dealing with employees with depression.
4. **Create a Healthy Work Climate**—Organizational and employee health should go to the top of the business agenda. Employees should be surveyed to identify the main causes of their stress.
5. **Reduce E-Mail Enslavement**—E-mail should be recognized as a potential source of stress and employees should be trained in the most efficient use of e-mail and voice mail.
6. **Return-to-Work Strategies**—Programs should be implemented to help employees re-enter the workforce following a depression-based absence.
7. **Depression-Related Disabilities**—HR executives, health professionals, and managers should be educated about heart disease, stroke, and immune system problems.
8. **Inventory of Emotional Work Hazards**—An inventory of emotional work hazards (including office politics) should be taken and a plan put in place to decrease the risks associated with them (including confronting and eliminating office politics).
9. **Work/Life Strategies**—Programs such as flextime, home-care services, workplace daycare, and eldercare should be instituted.
10. **The Rule-out Rule**—Employers should implement a process to differentiate between employee performance problems stemming from depression as opposed to other problems.
11. **Company-wide Health Index**—An overall health benchmark for the company should be established.
12. **Goals**—Employers should aim to reduce disability rates by 15 to 25 percent a year by targeting mental health issues; to dramatically increase EAP usage; and to reduce or eliminate the top 10 sources of workplace stress.

Source: J. Hampton, "HR Executives Key to Combatting Workplace Depression," *Canadian HR Reporter* (August 14, 2000), pp. 1, 3. The Twelve Steps are Drawn from the Business and Economic Roundtable on Mental Health. © Carswell, Thomson Professional Publishing. Reproduced by permission of *Canadian HR Reporter*, Carswell, One Corporate Plaza, 2075 Kennedy Road, Scarborough, ON M1T 3V4.

chological strain, [job] demands and [ambiguity regarding the future of the job] need to be lowered, while skill utilization, task clarity, job control, and supervisor support need to be increased."[113]

burnout The total depletion of physical and mental resources caused by excessive striving to reach an unrealistic work-related goal.

Burnout   Many people fall victim to **burnout**—the total depletion of physical and mental resources—due to excessive striving to reach an unrealistic work-related goal. Burnout begins with cynical and pessimistic thoughts, and leads to apathy, exhaustion, withdrawal into isolation, and eventually depression.[114] Burnout is often the result of too much job stress, especially when that stress is combined with a preoccupation with attaining unattainable work-related goals. Burnout victims often do not lead well-balanced lives; virtually all of their energies are focused on achieving their work-related goals to the exclusion of other activities, leading to physical and sometimes mental collapse. This need not be limited to upwardly mobile executives: for instance, social-work counsellors caught up in their clients' problems are often burnout victims.

What can a candidate for burnout do? Here are some suggestions:

**Tips for the
Front Line**

- *Break patterns.* First, survey how you spend your time. Are you doing a variety of things, or the same thing over and over? The more well-rounded your life is, the better protected you are against burnout. If you have stopped trying new activities, start them again—for instance, travel or new hobbies.
- *Get away from it all periodically.* Schedule occasional periods of introspection during which you can get away from your usual routine, perhaps alone, to seek a perspective on where you are and where you are going.
- *Reassess goals in terms of their intrinsic worth.* Are the goals that you have set for yourself attainable? Are they really worth the sacrifices that you will have to make?
- *Think about work.* Could you do as good a job without being so intense or while also pursuing outside interests?
- *Reduce stress.* Organize your time more effectively, build a better relationship with your boss, negotiate realistic deadlines, find time during the day for detachment and relaxation, reduce unnecessary noise around your office, and limit interruptions.

Workers' Compensation and Stress-Related Disability Claims   Workers' compensation laws in several provinces prohibit compensation for chronic mental stress, or impose severe limitations on what is covered. The rationale is that stress has multiple causes, including family situations and personal disposition. Research suggests, however, that a significant portion of chronic stress is often work-related. In particular, high-demand/low-control jobs (such as an administrative assistant with several demanding bosses) are known to be "psychotoxic."[115] Consequently, employees who are denied workers' compensation benefits for chronic stress that they believe to be work-related are suing their employers. The courts are recognizing these claims and holding employers responsible for actions of supervisors who create "poisoned work environments" through harassment and psychological abuse.[116] Courts are finding that a fundamental implied term of any employment relationship is that the employer will treat the employee fairly and with respect and dignity, and that the due diligence requirement includes protection of employees from psychological damage as well as physical.[117] Ontario is considering providing workers' compensation benefits for chronic mental stress caused by ongoing harassment in the workplace.[118]

Repetitive Strain Injuries

Repetitive strain injuries (RSIs) are the greatest single contributor to workers' compensation claims, and cost the Canadian economy nearly $800 million each year.[119] The physical demands of new technologies have brought a new set of RSIs, most notably *carpal tunnel syndrome* (a tingling or numbness in the fingers caused by the narrowing of a tunnel of bones and ligaments in the wrist).

RSI Clinic www.rsiclinic.com

Human Systems Inc.
www.humansys.com

Human Factors and Ergonomics
Society www.hfes.org

ergonomics The art of fitting the
workstation and work tools to the
individual.

RSIs have three causes: repetitive movements, awkward postures, and forceful exertion. The risk of developing RSIs increases with exposure to vibration and cold, and pre-existing conditions such as arthritis can exacerbate RSIs.[120] Warning signs of RSI include tightness or stiffness in the hands, elbow, wrists, shoulder, and neck; numbness and tingling in the fingertips; hands falling asleep; and frequent dropping of tools. The most common symptoms are neck and shoulder strain.[121] A four-year research study by the Institute for Work and Health found that giving employees more control over their work and over the choice of office equipment can reduce the number of RSIs.[122]

Ergonomics   Fortunately, RSIs are extremely preventable. Poorly designed workstations and bad posture are among the primary conditions leading to RSIs. **Ergonomics** is the art of fitting the workstation and work tools to the individual, which is necessary because there is no such thing as an average body. **Figure 14.7** shows the difference between a conventional tool and an ergonomically designed one. The most important preventive measure is to have employees take short breaks every half-hour or hour to do simple stretches at their

FIGURE 14.7   Ergonomic Hammer Configuration

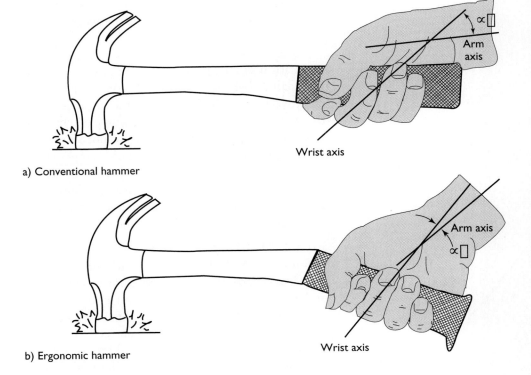

*Source: From Management of Occupational Health and Safety, Second Edition, by Montgomery/Kelloway.
© 2001. Reprinted with permission of Nelson, a division of Thomson Learning: www.thomsonrights.com.
Fax 800-730-2215.*

workstations.[123] Software is now available that counts keystrokes over time and flashes a message to the employee to take a break and do the exercise shown on the screen.[124]

For example, the Ergowatch software developed at the University of Waterloo, and originally designed to assess and reduce the risk of back injuries in industrial settings, is being transformed into a broader tool that will also be able to evaluate the risk of repetitive stress injuries in workers' hands and arms. The software can assess the load or impact of a task—the combination of weight that is lifted and cumulative time spent in a position or posture, linking that with a worker's physical characteristics (size, age, sex) to predict potential pain and injury. Ergowatch can also be used to prioritize ergonomics projects by comparing data from different ergonomics improvement projects. It can also conduct a physical demand analysis based on a checklist required by workers' compensation boards to determine what an injured employee can safely do when returning to work.[125]

Ergonomically designed workstations have been found to increase productivity and efficiency, as well as reduce injuries. One study found that ergonomic improvements reduced errors by 93 percent, and increased efficiency by 33 percent, while musculoskeletal problems decreased by 50 percent.[126] Ergonomics will become more and more important as the workforce ages, and physical demands of work will need to be adapted to accommodate some of the many physical changes typically associated with aging, including changes in muscular strength, hand function, cardiovascular capacity, vision, and hearing.[127] In fact a recent survey found that the workers most likely to suffer from ergonomically related problems are females over the age of 50 with a professional occupation who spend between 75 and 100 hours a week at their desk.[128]

In the mid-1990s, Canadian Tire Acceptance Corporation Ltd., in Welland, Ontario, was facing increasing employee complaints of pain and stiffness, but no related lost-time injuries. A root cause analysis found that 60 percent of employees had RSI symptoms, and 50 percent had sought medical attention for them. The company launched a comprehensive RSI prevention program using internal and external community resources. The program included modification of workstations, wellness initiatives, stress management, education on risk factors, and proactive occupational therapy for RSI sufferers. Three years later, the company had no RSI-related disability claims. The success of the program was attributed to process champions, stakeholder participation, and management commitment to employees' well-being.[129]

Video Display Terminals   The fact that many workers today must spend hours each day working with video display terminals (VDTs) is creating new health problems at work. Short-term eye problems like burning, itching, and tearing, as well as eye strain and eye soreness are common complaints among video display operators. Backaches and neckaches are also widespread among display users. These often occur because employees try to compensate for display problems like glare and immovable keyboards by manoeuvring into awkward body positions. Researchers also found that employees who used VDTs and had heavy workloads were prone to psychological distress like anxiety, irritability, and fatigue. There may also be a tendency for computer users to suffer from RSI, such as carpal tunnel syndrome, caused by repetitive use of the hands and arms at uncomfortable angles.[130]

General recommendations regarding the use of VDTs include giving employees rest breaks every hour, designing maximum flexibility into the workstation so that it can be adapted to the individual operator, reducing glare with devices such as shades over windows and terminal screens, and giving VDT workers a complete pre-placement vision exam to ensure that vision is properly corrected for reduced visual strain.

Workplace Toxins

The leading cause of work-related deaths around the world is cancer, as shown in **Figure 14.8.** Hundreds of Canadian workers die from occupational cancer each year. There is an erroneous perception that cancer-causing agents in the workplace are disappearing. Employers often face significant costs in order to eliminate carcinogens in the workplace, and unions are often so preoccupied with wage and benefit increases that they don't bring the issue to the bargaining table. In addition to known carcinogens, such as asbestos and benzene, new chemicals and substances are constantly being introduced into the workplace

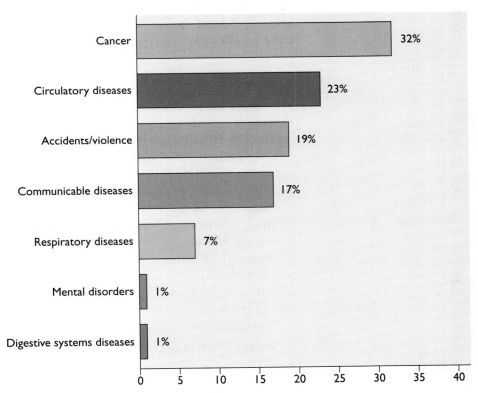

FIGURE 14.8   Deaths Attributed to Work Worldwide

According to the International Labour Organization, there was an estimated two million work-related deaths around the globe in the year 2000. Out of eight work-related diseases, cancer was cited as the number one cause of death.

Source: Introductory Report: Decent Work–Safe Work, Table 1 (http://www.ilo.org/public/english/protection/safework/wdcongrs/ilo_rep.pdf). Copyright © 2002 International Labour Oganization.

without adequate testing.[131] In 2002, Manitoba's workers' compensation law was amended to provide benefits to firefighters who develop any of five specific job-related cancers. This new law could set a precedent for other occupations and other jurisdictions.[132]

Workplace Smoking

Smoking is a serious problem for employees and employers. Employers face higher costs deriving from higher supplementary health-care and disability insurance, as smoking is associated with numerous health problems. Smoking employees have reduced productivity and a significantly greater risk of occupational accidents than do non-smokers. In general, "smoking employees are less healthy than non-smokers, are absent more, make more and more expensive claims for health and disability benefits, and endanger co-workers who breathe smoky air."[133] A 1999 Labour Canada study determined that it costs an additional $2460 per year to employ a smoker.[134]

Smokers who are also exposed to other carcinogens in the workplace, such as asbestos, have dramatically higher rates of lung cancer. The effects of on-the-job exposure to radon on lung cancer rates were found to last up to 14 years, and the cancer rates were greatly increased for smokers.[135]

Governments across Canada have taken the lead in banning smoking in an increasing number of workplaces. British Columbia has declared second-hand tobacco smoke to be an occupational hazard. In 2003, Employment insurance benefits were awarded to a Nova Scotia casino worker who quit her job because of second-hand smoke. Overall, the movement to eliminate smoking in all indoor public places is gathering strength.[136]

Violence at Work

Workplace violence is defined by the International Labour Organization as incidents in which an employee is abused, threatened, or assaulted in circumstances relating to work, and includes harassment, bullying, intimidation, physical threats, assaults, and robberies.[137] Violence against employees at work has become increasingly common in Canada. In fact, Canadians are more likely to be assaulted in their workplaces than Americans are. A 2003 Quebec study found that one-third of workers in that province had witnessed violence on the job, including physical, psychological, verbal, and sexual aggression.[138] Victims are often women in health-care professions.[139] A study of 45 000 nurses reported that 68 percent had suffered physical violence, ranging from slaps to jaw-breaking punches. One author noted that when police officers are attacked, charges of assault or resisting arrest are laid, whereas for nurses, being attacked is seen as part of the job.[140]

Workplace violence arises in three situations:

1. An employee is angry with management or a co-worker.

2. A customer/client is angry with the provider/denier of a product or service.

3. A violent outsider attacks by chance.[141]

Workplace violence is about fear, about people losing control, and about implicit contracts between employer and employee being broken. Triggers for workplace violence include poor management relations, ambiguous work standards, inconsistent rule enforcement, ignoring cultural concerns, failure to address threats of violence, and insufficient worksite security.[142] Often, not enough is being done to address situations where employees are threatened, harassed, or intimidated.[143] Such behaviour constitutes psychological violence.[144] Thus, two-way communication programs, EAPs, and fair treatment programs can all contribute to reducing the possibility of violence in the workplace. Many EAPs also offer trauma counselling when violence occurs.[145] One psychologist suggests that violence is a reaction to unbearable stress, and warns that internal threats cannot be effectively handled through standard disciplinary and HR procedures.[146] Years of constant change—including mergers, restructuring, downsizing, and new technology—have contributed to extremely high levels of stress in Canadian workplaces today.[147]

Employers want to avoid such violence on humanitarian grounds, but there are legal reasons to do so as well. Employers may be found liable for the violent acts of their employees.[148] For example, an employer may be sued directly by the victim of an employee's violent act on the basis that the employer negligently hired or negligently retained someone whom the employer should reasonably have known could cause the violent act. Even if the employee was not negligently hired or retained, employers may still in general be liable for employees' violent acts when the employees' actions were performed within the scope of employment. In two recent B.C. court cases relating to sexual abuse of children in government-funded youthcare facilities, the government was found to be vicariously liable.[149] Further, violence is costly in terms of burnout and turnover, reduced morale, higher absenteeism, lower performance and productivity, and time spent dealing with disruption in the workplace.[150]

Workplace Violence and the Law

Legal safeguards against workplace violence in Canada are vague and fragmented. British Columbia and Saskatchewan have included workplace violence as an occupational hazard under occupational health and safety legislation. The federal labour code requires employers to take steps to protect employees from violence. Human rights laws across the country prohibit various forms of harassment. Overall, employers are being held to an increasingly high standard regarding the protection of employees from workplace violence—particularly when employers are aware of violent incidents and fail to respond.[151] Courts across Canada have provided damages to employees who have been victims of psychological violence in the form of bullying. Employers have been held vicariously liable in these situations, and are expected by the courts to ensure that employees are treated respectfully by their co-workers.[152]

Prevention and Control of Workplace Violence

There are several concrete steps that employers can take to reduce the incidence of workplace violence. These include instituting a workplace violence policy, enhancing security arrangements, improving employee screening, and training for violence reduction.

Institute a Workplace Violence Policy Firms should develop, support, and communicate a workplace violence policy that clearly communicates management's commitment to preventing violent incidents.[153]

Heighten Security Measures Heightened security measures are an employer's first line of defence against workplace violence, whether that violence derives

Hints to Ensure Legal Compliance

Workplace Violence Research Institute
www.noworkviolence.com

Canadian Initiative on Workplace Violence
www.workplaceviolence.ca

from co-workers, customers, or outsiders. Sensible precautions for reducing the risk of workplace violence[154] include improving external lighting; using drop safes to minimize cash on hand and posting signs noting that only a limited amount of cash is on hand; installing silent alarms and surveillance cameras; increasing the number of staff members on duty; and closing establishments during high-risk hours late at night and early in the morning.[155] Most of all, managers should be vigilant and heed all warning signs such as troubled relationships, prejudice, or intimidation.[156]

In workplaces where members of the public are served in person, some important precautions for employee safety include providing staff training in conflict resolution and defusing anger; ensuring that offices have large windows that allow others to see in; having security staff to refuse admittance to anyone who appears intoxicated, visibly angry, or threatening; and instituting a recognizable "help" signal to alert other staff members that assistance is required.[157]

Improve Employee Screening Screening out potentially explosive internal and external applicants is the employer's next line of defence. At a minimum, this means instituting a sound pre-employment investigation. A detailed employment application should be completed, and each applicant's employment history, education background, and references should be solicited.[158] A personal interview, job-related testing, and a review and verification of all information provided should also be included in the selection process. Sample interview questions to ask might include, for instance, "What frustrates you?" and "Who was your worst supervisor and why?"[159]

Certain background circumstances should raise a red flag indicating the need for a more in-depth background investigation to help screen out potentially violent employees. The investigation report provides a record that everything that could have been done was done to screen out the violent employee. Red flags include:[160]

- an unexplained gap in employment
- incomplete or false information on the résumé or application
- a negative, unfavourable, or false reference
- prior insubordinate or violent behaviour on the job
- a history involving harassing or violent behaviour
- a prior termination for cause with a suspicious explanation (or none)
- strong indications of instability in the individual's work or personal life suggested, for example, by frequent job changes or geographic moves
- lost licences or accreditations.[161]

As sensible as it is to try to screen out potentially violent employees, doing so incurs the risk of liability and lawsuits. Human rights legislation limits the use of criminal records in hiring decisions. Eliminating workplace violence while safely navigating the legal shoals is, therefore, a tricky business.

Provide Workplace Violence Training Enhanced security and screening can be supplemented with workplace violence training. Video training programs

"Sick Building Syndrome"

Mould as an occupational health hazard is a fairly recent phenomenon. In the 1990s, several highly publicized cases of "sick building syndrome" ("SBS")—of which mould is one possible cause—brought the issue to the forefront of the health and safety field. Perhaps the most notorious case in Canada involved the Newmarket courthouse north of Toronto.

Employees at the provincial courthouse in Newmarket began experiencing health problems shortly after building renovations commenced in February 2000. The most common health complaint was the development of occupational asthma. A health survey ordered by the Ontario Ministry of Labour ("MOL") found that 40 per cent of the employees had acquired symptoms of asthma. Many sick employees—including 13 out of 25 judges and justices of the peace who worked in the building—exercised their right to refuse dangerous work under subsection 43(3) of the Occupational Health and Safety Act. In June 2000, the Attorney General of Ontario ordered the Newmarket courthouse closed. It remained closed for a full year while all "toxic mould" was removed from the building and it reopened in June 2001....

...Employers in all Canadian jurisdictions are required to take all reasonable steps to protect the health and safety of workers. Individual employees with a work-related illness that has been diagnosed by a physician must be accommodated. There are currently no established exposure limits to moulds in workplace buildings, but in Ontario the MOL has shown itself willing to issue orders to correct problems with mould. The Newmarket courthouse is not the only example of a building that was closed and its employees relocated. In the fall of 2001, a courthouse in Etobicoke was closed after the MOL had issued 10 orders to address mould and other indoor air quality concerns in the building.

Employers also need to be aware of the potential for litigation. In the Newmarket case, a $32 million class action suit was filed (and later dismissed). South of the border, litigation on this issue is virtually exploding....

Source: Excerpted with permission from the *Employment Health and Safety Guide Newsletter*, written by Lisa Duncan (No. 265, October 2002), published by and copyright CCH Canadian Limited, Toronto, Ontario.

explain what workplace violence is, identify its causes and signs, and offer tips on how to prevent it and what to do when it occurs.[162] Supervisors can also be trained to identify the types of multiple clues that typically precede violent incidents. One of the most common precursors to violence is a change in the behaviour of an employee.[163] Other common signs include:[164]

- *Verbal threats.* Individuals often talk about what they may do. An employee might say, "Bad things are going to happen to so-and-so," or "That propane tank in the back could blow up easily."

- *Physical actions.* Troubled employees may try to intimidate others, gain access to places in which they do not belong, or flash a concealed weapon in the workplace to test reactions.

- *Frustration.* Most cases do not involve a panicked individual; a more likely scenario would involve an employee who has a frustrated sense of entitlement to a promotion, for example.

- *Obsession.* An employee may hold a grudge against a co-worker or supervisor, and some cases stem from romantic interest.[165]

Dealing with Angry Employees What should a supervisor do when confronted by an angry, potentially explosive employee? Here are some suggestions:[166]

1. Make eye contact.
2. Stop any other work and give full attention to the employee.
3. Speak in a calm voice and create a relaxed environment.
4. Be open and honest.
5. Let the person have his or her say.
6. Ask for specific examples of what the person is upset about.
7. Be careful to define the problem.
8. Ask open-ended questions and explore all sides of the issue.

CHAPTER *Review*

Summary

1 Employers and employees are held jointly responsible for maintaining the health and safety of workers, including participation on joint health and safety committees. Employers are responsible for "due diligence"—taking every reasonable precaution to ensure the health and safety of their workers. Employees are responsible for protecting their own health and safety and that of their co-workers. Employees have the right to know about workplace safety hazards, the right to participate in the occupational health and safety process, and the right to refuse unsafe work.

2 The Workplace Hazardous Materials Information System (WHMIS) law is a Canada-wide legally mandated system designed to protect workers by providing crucial information about hazardous materials and substances in the workplace. WHMIS requires labelling of hazardous material containers, material safety data sheets, and employee training.

3 There are three basic causes of accidents: chance occurrences, unsafe conditions, and unsafe acts on the part of employees. In addition, three other work-related factors (the job itself, the work schedule, and the psychological climate) also contribute to accidents.

4 One approach to preventing accidents is to reduce unsafe conditions by identifying and removing potential hazards. Another approach to improving safety is to reduce unsafe acts—for example, through selection and placement, education and training, positive reinforcement, top-management commitment, and monitoring work overload and stress.

5 Employee wellness programs aim to improve employees' health and reduce costs for sickness and disability claims, workers' compensation, and absenteeism. Wellness initiatives include physical fitness programs, smoking cessation programs, relaxation classes, and heart health monitoring.

6 *Alcoholism and other substance abuse* are important and growing health problems among employees. Techniques to deal with these challenges include disciplining, discharge, in-house counselling, and referrals to an outside agency. *Stress, depression, and burnout* are other potential health problems at work. Job stress can be reduced by ensuring that employees take breaks each day, counselling, and giving employees more control over their jobs. *Repetitive strain injuries* occur as a result of repetitive movements, awkward postures, and forceful exertion. Ergonomics is very effective at reducing RSIs. *Workplace toxins* can be carcinogenic, and some governments are providing workers' compensation benefits to workers with job-related cancer. *Employees who smoke* have reduced productivity and greater health costs. Governments across Canada have increasingly banned workplace smoking. *Violence* against employees is a serious problem at work. Steps that can reduce workplace violence include improved security arrangements, better employee screening, and workplace violence training.

Key Terms

burnout   *(p. 455)*

employee wellness program   *(p. 447)*

ergonomics   *(p. 457)*

occupational health and safety legislation   *(p. 431)*

unsafe acts   *(p. 439)*

unsafe conditions   *(p. 439)*

Workplace Hazardous Materials Information System (WHMIS)   *(p. 434)*

Review and Discussion Questions

1   Discuss the purpose of occupational health and safety legislation and how it is enforced.

2   Explain the supervisor's role in safety.

3   Explain what causes unsafe acts.

4   Describe how to reduce workers' compensation costs, both before and after an accident.

5   Explain the four traditional techniques for dealing with alcoholism and substance abuse.

6   Analyze the legal and safety issues concerning workplace toxins.

7   Explain how to reduce violence at work.

CRITICAL *Thinking Questions*

1   What is your opinion on the question: "Is there such a thing as an accident-prone person?"

2   What guidelines would you suggest for determining the point at which to terminate an employee who shows signs of being prone to violence?

APPLICATION *Exercises*

Running Case: LearnInMotion.com

The New Health and Safety Program

At first glance, a dot-com is one of the last places you would expect to find potential health and safety hazards—or so Jennifer and Pierre thought. There is no danger of moving machinery, no high-pressure lines, no cutting or heavy lifting, and certainly no forklift trucks. However, there are health and safety problems.

In terms of unsafe conditions, for instance, the one thing dot-com companies have lots of is cables and wires. There are cables connecting the computers to each other and to the servers, and in many cases separate cables running from some computers to separate printers. There are ten telephones in the office, all on five-metre phone lines that always seem to be snaking around chairs and tables. There is, in fact, an astonishing amount of cable considering that this is an office with fewer than ten employees. When the installation specialists wired the office (for

electricity, high-speed DSL, phone lines, burglar alarms, and computers), they estimated that they used over five kilometres of cable of one sort or another. Most of the cables are hidden in the walls, or ceilings, but many of them snake their way from desk to desk, and under and over doorways.

Several employees have tried to reduce the nuisance of having to trip over wires whenever they get up by putting their plastic chair pads over the wires closest to them, However, that still leaves many wires unprotected. In other cases, they brought in their own packing tape, and tried to tape down the wires in those spaces where they are particularly troublesome, such as across doorways.

The cables and wires are one of the more obvious potential accident-causing conditions. The firm's programmer, before he left the firm, had tried to repair the main server while the unit was still electrically alive. To this day, they are not exactly sure where he stuck the screwdriver, but the result was that he was "blown across the room" as Pierre puts it. He was all right, but it was still a scare. And while they have not received any claims yet, every employee spends hours at his or her computer, so carpal tunnel syndrome is a risk, as are eyestrain and strained backs. One recent incident particularly scared them. The firm uses independent contractors to deliver the firm's book- and CD-ROM-based course in Toronto and two other cities. A delivery person was riding his bike at the corner of King and Bay Streets in Toronto, where he was struck by a car. Luckily he was not hurt, but the bike's front wheel was wrecked, and the close call got Pierre and Jennifer thinking about their lack of a safety program.

It's not just the physical conditions that concern the company's two owners. They also have some concerns about potential health problems such as job stress and burnout. While the business may be (relatively) safe with respect to physical conditions, it is also relatively stressful in terms of the demands it makes in hours and deadlines. It is not at all uncommon for employees to get to work by 7:30 or 8 o'clock in the morning and to work through until 11 or 12 o'clock at night, at least five, and sometimes six or seven days per week. Just getting the company's new calendar fine-tuned and operational required 70-hour workweeks for three weeks from five of LearnInMotion.com's employees. The bottom line is that both Jennifer and Pierre feel quite strongly that

they need to do something about implementing a health and safety plan. Now they want you, their management consultants, to help them to actually do it. Here's what they want you to do for them.

Questions

1 Based upon your knowledge of health and safety matters, and your actual observations of operations that are similar to LearnInMotion.com, make a list of the potential hazardous conditions employees and others face at this company. Make specific recommendations to reduce the potential severity of the top five hazards.

2 Would it be advisable for the company to set up a procedure for screening out stress-prone or accident-prone individuals? Why or why not? If so, how should they be screened?

3 If a decision is made to screen applicants, what are the legal implications? Can they do this legally? How?

4 What specific topics should be included in their health and safety training program?

CASE INCIDENT   *Introducing Ergonomics: What Went Wrong?*

HR manager Roger Scanlon was flipping through a business magazine as he rode the train home one night when he read that the post office had recently saved more than $10 million with a new ergonomics program in its automated mail sorting system. Roger was impressed, and the next morning he began putting together a plan for research and training in ergonomics at his own firm, Harbour Office Supply. He told his boss that he was sure Harbour could realize financial savings and a reduction in absenteeism and turnover if the workplace could be made more ergonomically streamlined.

Roger knew that Harbour relied heavily on its many data entry clerks, particularly since several of the firm's major corporate customers had adopted stockless purchasing operations and now placed their office supply orders directly with Harbour's clerks. Over the last few years, as business increased, absenteeism rose as well, and various work-related

health complaints seemed to be on the rise. Despite brighter lighting and posters reminding employees to take frequent short breaks, the clerks often reported headaches, backaches, eyestrain, and even some cases of carpal tunnel syndrome.

Roger began by surveying the data entry supervisors to learn their observations of worker behaviour. Were people wringing their wrists, stretching their necks and backs, or bringing pillows and backrests from home in their attempt to make their workstations more comfortable? He asked the supervisors to question employees about the kinds of problems that they were experiencing, and to give him a tally of reported problems. Next, he researched the injury and illness records, looking for reasons for absenteeism and sick leave, and even for transfer requests and employee turnover.

It seemed to Roger that Harbour's records and the supervisors' reports indicated that there were several ways in which to improve the firm's ergonomic profile and achieve the promised improvements in cost and performance. He decided to implement a two-step program that would consist of training and some office renovation. With management's approval, he developed a two-hour training program for the entire staff that focused on showing employees how to correct their posture at their workstations, how to adjust the lighting around their computer screens, how to schedule regular breaks in their work, and how to use stretching and mild exercise to prevent stiffness and strain. Supervisors were given an extra training session on spotting potential health problems in their reporting employees that could be caused by excessively repetitive work, poor posture, and inadequate light and ventilation.

The second part of the program was to include training in ergonomic principles for the purchasing staff, and the purchase and installation of new ergonomic workstations, adjustable chairs, and accessories like slanted keyboards and screen filters. Roger had even arranged for the clerks' work areas

to be redesigned to put more clerks near the windows. Before this part of the plan could be put into action, however, Roger discovered that instead of the decrease in complaints that he expected, the first few weeks after the training session had actually brought an increase in the rates of illness and injury reported by the clerks. Roger's boss told him that the CEO was now questioning whether to spend the money on the renovation and new equipment. She asked him to attend a meeting in which the three of them would discuss what had gone wrong.

Questions

1 What went wrong in this case?

2 What elements of Roger's plan could be improved?

3 What do you think accounts for the increase in reported illness and injury?

4 Given your answer to Question 3, do you think that Harbour should go ahead with the renovation?

EXPERIENTIAL *Exercises*

1 In a group of four to six students, spend about 30 to 45 minutes in and around one of the buildings on your campus identifying health and safety hazards. Research whether or not these unsafe conditions violate the applicable health and safety legislation.

2 Contact a workplace violence consultant. Ask him or her for information on what advice is provided to clients on preventing workplace violence, and ask for a sample workplace violence policy. Prepare a brief presentation to the class on your findings.

CHAPTER 15

Fair Treatment:
The Foundation of Effective Employee Relations

LEARNING OUTCOMES

After studying this chapter, you should be able to:

Explain three techniques for building effective two-way communication in organizations.

Discuss the three foundations of a fair and just disciplinary process.

Define wrongful dismissal and *explain* how to handle a wrongful dismissal lawsuit.

Explain the six steps in the termination interview.

List important HR considerations in adjusting to downsizings and mergers.

CHAPTER OUTLINE

- The Importance of Fair Treatment

- Building Two-Way Communication

- Fair Treatment Programs

- Fairness in Discipline

- Managing Dismissals

- Managing Separations: Layoffs and Retirements

- Retirement

THE IMPORTANCE OF FAIR TREATMENT

It makes sense for employers to focus on fair treatment of employees for several reasons. From a practical point of view, an increasingly litigious workforce makes it almost a necessity that employers institute disciplinary and discharge procedures that will survive the scrutiny of arbitrators and the courts. Quite aside from legal constraints, however, employers must show employees that their policies and procedures are fair in order to foster improved commitment and reduce grievances and morale problems. Over 25 years of organizational research clearly indicates that employees are sensitive to the treatment they receive, particularly the perceived fairness of processes used to make decisions that affect them, and to the perceived fairness of the interpersonal treatment they receive at work.[1]

While it is impossible to guarantee that every employee will perceive that he or she is being treated fairly, there are steps that employers can take to move in that direction. As will be explained in this chapter, these steps include building two-way communication, implementing fair treatment and employee discipline appeals procedures, protecting employees' privacy, and doing a better job of managing dismissals and other types of separations (such as layoffs and retirements).

BUILDING TWO-WAY COMMUNICATION

Consider the following example of how poor communication can work against corporate objectives. Wal-Mart Canada prides itself on its open communication policy with employees, yet the Windsor, Ontario, store became the world's first unionized Wal-Mart when the Ontario Labour Relations Board certified a union, despite a large majority of employees voting against it. The Board believed that employees feared losing their jobs if they voted for the union, because employees who asked managers whether the store would remain open if the union were voted in were told that the company had no comment. This communication was considered by the Board to be a management threat, constituting an unfair labour practice, and thus, as will be explained in Chapter 16, the union was automatically certified.[2]

In general, courts in Canada have found that the employee–employer relationship is a special relationship that gives rise to a duty of care, including communication regarding employment issues. The legal basis used in many employee communication court challenges is "negligent misrepresentation." An employer can be found liable of negligent misrepresentation if it is demonstrated that:[3]

> **Hints to Ensure Legal Compliance**

- The employer owed the employee a duty of care based on a "special relationship."
- The information provided to employees is "untrue, inaccurate, or misleading" or was misrepresented.
- The employer was negligent in providing the information.
- The information was relied on by the employee in a reasonable manner.
- The employee suffered damages as a result of relying on the information provided by the employer.
- The employer did not take reasonable care to ensure the accuracy of the information communicated to employees.

Treating employees fairly begins with good listening and effective two-way communication. What follows are four examples of such programs: *Speak Up! programs* for voicing concerns and making inquiries, periodic *survey-type programs* for expressing opinions, various *top-down programs* for keeping employees informed, and *fair treatment programs* for filing grievances and complaints.

"Speak Up!"-Type Programs

Speak Up! programs
Communication programs that allow employees to register questions, concerns, and suggestions about work-related matters.

Grievance matters are the tip of the iceberg when it comes to the concerns of employees. These concerns run the gamut from malfunctioning vending machines to unlit parking lots to a manager's spending too much of the department's money on travel. IBM Canada's **Speak Up! program** aims to give employees a confidential channel for speaking their minds about such issues.[4] Anonymity makes the program unique. Employees may ask questions or make comments and get a reply without revealing their identity to anyone except the Speak Up! administrator.

The investigator is usually the highest-level manager familiar with the Speak Up! concern. Answers are provided within ten working days unless more extensive investigation is required. The Speak Up! administrator first checks all responses for accuracy and completeness. He or she then personally addresses and mails the answer to the employee's home.

The program lets employees jump the normal chain of command to communicate directly with someone who is responsible for the activity in question. Employees are encouraged to write Speak Up! requests at any time, but are told that they might first consider talking to their own manager, reviewing the employee handbook, or calling the department involved to get a direct answer. Similarly, the IBM Canada suggestion program is generally used to propose ideas that could save the company time or money.

Dofasco Inc.'s suggestion program has been a success story for decades. Employees can receive cash awards of up to $50 000, depending on the savings realized by implementing the suggestion. Another organization with a successful suggestion plan is the Royal Bank of Canada. One suggestion made in the mid-1990s, for streamlining computer backup procedures and reducing the required amount of data storage equipment, saved the bank almost $8 million over three years. Employees receive monetary rewards for suggestions that are implemented, but most of all, they say they want to improve operations and productivity for the bank and its customers.[5]

Programs like these have several benefits. They let management continuously monitor employees' feelings and concerns, they make it clear that employees have several channels through which to communicate concerns and get responses, and the net effect is that there is less likelihood that small problems will grow into big ones.

Employee Opinion Surveys

opinion surveys Communication devices that use questionnaires to ask for employees' opinions about the company, management, and work life.

Many firms also administer periodic anonymous **opinion surveys**. For maximum benefit, surveys should be conducted regularly and the results must be provided to participants.[6] **Figure 15.1** provides a list of survey "dos" and "don'ts."

IBM Canada's organizational effectiveness survey regularly asks employees their opinions about the company, management, and work-life. The survey's

FIGURE **15.1**   Survey Dos and Don'ts

Do	Don't
Create an effective team (two to 10 members) with representatives from corporate HR, corporate communication and business/front-line employees.	Announce really good news (everyone is getting a bonus) or really bad news (staff cutbacks) when handing out surveys.
Identify communication strategy and training needs.	Promise to listen and then don't.
Determine final project objectives: scope, timelines, deliverables, success measures, outcomes.	Say you will act on the findings and then don't.
Define key audiences (internal and external).	Promise anonymity or confidentiality and then break that promise.
Identify core survey content, as well as customized, business-specific content.	Make the survey too long, complicated and technical.
Finalize the method of survey administration.	Forget to add the due date and where to return the completed survey.
Distribute the survey according to predetermined information needs: Do you survey the entire population or a sample?	Think you know how to analyze the data because you have mastered multiplication tables.
Have a communication plan—pre-survey, mid-survey and post-survey. Consider key messages and distribution channels.	Search the data until you find that nasty little tidbit you knew was there if you only looked hard enough.
Once the survey closes, determine the level of analysis required (simple descriptive statistics, predictive modelling, correlations).	Release write-in comments without figuring out what to do about any included names of employees, managers and leaders, foul language, slanderous remarks, serious workplace health and safety issues or harassing or discriminatory comments.

Source: Douglas, "Bad Surveys Beat Great Technology," *Canadian HR Reporter* (March 10, 2003), p. G3. Reproduced by permission of *Canadian HR Reporter*, Carswell, One Corporate Plaza, 2075 Kennedy Road, Scarborough, ON M1T 3V4.

purpose is to assess the morale of employees. The standard practice is to have department heads conduct feedback sessions with their department members after the survey results are compiled in order to share the results and work on solutions.

The Survey Feedback Action (SFA) program at FedEx Canada is typical. SFA includes an anonymous survey that allows employees to express feelings about the company and their managers, and to some extent feelings about service, pay, and benefits. Each manager then has an opportunity to use the results to help design a blueprint for improving work group commitment.

SFA has three phases. First, the survey itself is a standard, anonymous questionnaire given each year to every employee. The second phase is a feedback session between the manager and his or her work group. The feedback meeting leads to a third, "action plan" phase. The plan itself is a list of actions that the work group will take to address employees' concerns and boost results.

A new employee satisfaction survey, called the Employee Feedback System (EFS), has been developed by the National Quality Institute and the Brock University Wellness Institute.[7] The EFS examines 15 areas ranging from job satisfaction and co-worker cohesion to quality focus and employee commitment. The plan is to promote the EFS as a national standard for employee feedback surveys.

Top-Down Communication Programs

top-down communication programs Communication activities including in-house television centres, electronic bulletin boards, and newsletters that provide continuing opportunities for the firm to update employees on important matters.

It is hard for employees to feel committed when their boss will not tell them what is going on. Some firms, therefore, give employees extensive data on the performance of and prospects for their operations. Employers have used a number of **top-down communication programs** over the years. Traditionally, newsletters and verbal presentations were the methods used to disseminate information from the company to employees. More recently, organizations have utilized videos and high-tech communication using computers—e-mail, electronic bulletin boards, and intranets.[8]

There are a number of advantages to technology-based communication. Immediacy means that information can get to employees before it gets to the press, which is particularly important with major reorganizations and adverse news such as downsizing. A second advantage is that the message can be tailored to individual employees when it relates to personal information such as benefits. Individualized messages tell the employee that he or she matters.

Toyota's management works hard to share what it knows with every team member. There are three-times-per-shift, five-minute team information meetings at job sites, where employees get the latest news about the plant. There are monthly "roundtable" discussions between top management and selected non-supervisory staff, as well as a bi-monthly news bulletin reporting current events in Toyota worldwide, and a bi-weekly local newsletter. The firm's president is often in the plant—fielding questions, providing performance information, and ensuring that all in the company are aware of Toyota's goals and where the company is heading.

FAIR TREATMENT PROGRAMS

There is always potential for employee grievances and discontent stemming from perceived unfairness. Discipline cases and seniority issues in promotions, transfers, and layoffs probably top the list. Others include grievances growing out of job evaluations and work assignments, overtime, vacations, incentive plans, and holidays.

fair treatment programs Employer programs that are aimed at ensuring that all employees are treated fairly, generally by providing formalized, well-documented, and highly publicized vehicles through which employees can appeal any eligible issues.

Fair Treatment Programs at Work

Whatever the source, many firms today (and virtually all unionized ones) give employees **fair treatment programs** through which to air grievances. A grievance procedure helps to ensure that every employee's grievance is heard and treated fairly, and unionized firms do not hold a monopoly on such fair treatment.

Programs such as FedEx Canada's Guaranteed Fair Treatment Procedure (GFTP) go beyond most grievance procedures: (1) special, easily available forms make filing the grievance easy; (2) employees are encouraged to use the system; and (3) the highest levels of top management are routinely involved in reviewing complaints. The net effect is twofold: complaints do not get a chance to accumulate; and all managers think twice before doing anything unfair, since their actions will likely be brought to their bosses' attention.

Eligible Concerns   GFTP is available to all permanent FedEx Canada employees. It covers concerns regarding matters such as job promotion and discipline affecting the individual complainant. The firm's handbook points out that any recipient of discipline has access to the GFTP.

Steps   The FedEx guaranteed fair treatment procedure contains three steps.

In Step One, *management review*, the complainant contacts an employee representative from the HR department, who helps him or her to submit a written complaint to a member of management (manager or senior manager of the employee's department) within seven calendar days of the occurrence of the eligible issue. The decision to uphold, modify, or overturn management's action is communicated within ten calendar days of receipt of the complaint.

In Step Two, *officer complaint*, the complainant submits a written complaint to the managing director of his or her functional area within seven calendar days of the Step-One decision. The decision to uphold, overturn, or modify management's action, or initiate a review of the facts of the case is communicated to the complainant with copies to the department's HR representative and the complainant's manager within ten calendar days of receipt of the complaint.

Finally, in Step Three, *executive appeals review*, the complainant submits a written complaint within seven calendar days of the Step-Two decision to the employee relations department, which investigates and prepares a GFTP case file for the international appeals board executive review. The appeals board—the president of FedEx Canada, the vice-president of human resources (Canada), and the employee's departmental vice-president—then makes a decision within 14 calendar days of receipt of the complaint either to uphold, overturn, or initiate a review of the facts of the case, or to take other appropriate action. Barring a request for a further review, the appeals board's decision is final.

IBM Canada's **open-door program** gives every employee the right to appeal his or her supervisor's actions. Programs like IBM's do not have as much structure and formality as FedEx's guaranteed fair treatment program; however, they do help to ensure that healthy communication occurs regarding disciplinary matters and that employees' voices are heard.

open-door program A fair treatment program that gives every employee the right to appeal the actions of his or her supervisor by taking the concern to successively higher levels of management.

Electronic Trespassing and Employee Privacy

The advent of the Internet and e-mail has led to concerns about misuse of company time and property for personal and possibly illegal uses.[9] Individuals are concerned with privacy—their control over information about themselves, and their freedom from unjustifiable interference in their personal life. On the other hand, employers must maintain the ability to effectively manage their employees, and prevent liability to the company, as companies can be held legally liable

Angry about the installation of video cameras in their workplace, employees of Smurfit-Stone protest outside the Bathurst, New Brunswick, paper mill.

Privacy Commission of Canada
www.privcom.gc.ca

Information and Privacy
Commission of Ontario
www.ipc.on.ca

**Hints to Ensure
Legal Compliance**

for the actions of their employees.[10] For example, police in Toronto have clearly stated that an employer may be held liable of it knows an employee has offensive material on a workplace computer, but does nothing.[11]

Today's employers are grappling with the problem of how to deal fairly with the issue of electronic trespassing and employee privacy. Around the world, about 27 million employees have their e-mail and Internet use tracked.[12] Modern technological advances have put employees' privacy rights on a potential collision course with their employers' access and monitoring of information.[13] Research indicates that task performance declines when employees are being monitored unless they have control over the monitoring.[14] Nevertheless, employers want to monitor the use of computer-related activities in the workplace in order to eliminate time wastage (on Web surfing, playing computer games, and so on), and abuse of company resources.[15]

The issue boils down to the manner in which workers' privacy interests are balanced with the employer's "right to know." Potential justifications for access and/or monitoring include productivity measurement, harassment/defamation cases, activity involving obscenity and pornography, security issues, workplace investigations, and protection of confidentiality. For example, in 2002, the Catholic Children's Aid Society in Toronto fired six employees, suspended 26 others without pay, and sent letters of warning to six others for e-mailing hardcore pornography and offensive jokes.[16] Electronic monitoring is becoming easier and less expensive as new software is developed that can track Web sites visited by workers and the time spent on each.

George Radwanski, Canada's former privacy commissioner, stated that "...employees have a fundamental, inherent right to privacy in the workplace," and that he was opposed to broad monitoring of e-mails or computer use.[17] Privacy of employee information has recently been addressed in a new law stating that any information about an employee beyond name, title, business address, and telephone number is regarded as personal and private. This includes health-related information provided to insurers. Originally applicable to federally regulated employees, the law was extended to cover all employees across the country on January 1, 2004.[18]

In general, courts in Canada have permitted electronic surveillance as long as there is proper balancing of opposing interests. Because Internet and e-mail usage occur over telephone lines, previous case law determining that cell phone conversations are not "private" because the transmission is being done through a device that can be intercepted by someone other than the intended recipient has been deemed to apply. Thus, at the present time, employers are given substantial leeway in monitoring their employees' use of the Internet and e-mail. Employers are in an even stronger position if there is a written policy in place. A typical policy includes the following elements:[19]

- A caution alerting employees that e-mail/Internet systems are for business use and that the employer retains the rights to all material sent over and stored in the system.

- A warning that the computer system should not be used to communicate anything improper or illegal.

- A warning that deletion of a message or file may not fully eliminate it from the system.

- A clear statement that violation of the policy may result in disciplinary action.

- A requirement that employees sign a consent form indicating their understanding of the company's policy.

The Strategic HR box provides details on how Carswell Publishing Company developed an effective Internet usage policy for its employees.

STRATEGIC HR

Carswell's Internet and E-mail Policy

When Carswell Publishing Company gave almost all of its nearly 600 employees access to the Internet at work, they set out to develop a clear Internet and e-mail usage policy. The first step in setting up the policy was meeting with the company's lawyer. In this case, the lawyer had a sample policy that had been implemented at a sister company. Carswell's HR department took the sample to the director of information systems to make sure it was relevant to the systems and procedures in place. Then the sample was taken to the executive team to ensure they were on board with what was being proposed. They made some minor revisions, sent it back to the lawyer to go over the fine points, and the policy was set. All in all, it took about five weeks from the day the decision was made to implement the policy until the completed draft was ready to present to the employees.

Carswell uses software that blocks employees from accessing prohibited Web sites. This approach is more proactive than what the company was originally doing, which consisted of generating reports of sites accessed and having someone go through them looking for anything offensive. The Internet policy was easy to create, but the issue of monitoring e-mail was more difficult. There was a lot of conversation around privacy, and the company didn't want to go too far in monitoring employees.

"We were trying to balance privacy with making sure we had a policy that said there are certain things that are not acceptable and make sure you understand that," said Barb Conway, Vice-President of Human Resources. "There were some interesting perspectives on people's rights to privacy versus the organization's right to do these types of things."

Eventually, Carswell decided to block inappropriate external e-mail from coming in by using filtering software but chose not to monitor e-mail being sent by employees around and outside the company. Instead, they came up with a written policy that sets out clearly what employees can, and can't, use e-mail for.

"The key to us was that we communicated what the policy was, what the procedures were going to be, and I have not had a lot of personal concern expressed," said Conway. "We want to be really clear that the systems are for business purposes and we have to make sure that we're protecting our reputation."

The policy is also communicated to new employees who are required to sign a business conduct policy that includes e-mail and Internet use. Conway said it's also important to remember that the policy needs to keep changing as time and technology change the way business is done.

Source: T. Humber, "Developing an Internet Use Policy is Painless —and Crucial," *Canadian HR Reporter* (November 4, 2002), p. G4. Reproduced by permission of *Canadian HR Reporter*, Carswell, One Corporate Plaza, 2075 Kennedy Road, Scarborough, ON M1T 3V4.

FAIRNESS IN DISCIPLINE

discipline A procedure intended to correct an employee's behaviour because a rule or procedure has been violated.

The purpose of **discipline** is to encourage employees to adhere to rules and regulations. Courts have repeatedly articulated the rights of employees to fair treatment not only during the term of employment, but also during the disciplinary and termination process.[20] A fair and just disciplinary process is based on three foundations: *rules and regulations*, a *system of progressive penalties*, and an *appeals process*.

A set of clear *rules and regulations* is the first foundation. These rules address things like theft, destruction of company property, drinking on the job, and insubordination. Examples of rules include:

- Poor performance is not acceptable. Each employee is expected to perform his or her work properly and efficiently and to meet established standards of quality.

- Liquor and drugs do not mix with work. The use of either during working hours and reporting for work under the influence of either are both strictly prohibited.

- Safety rules must be followed at all times.

The purpose of these rules is to inform employees ahead of time as to what is and is not acceptable behaviour. Employees must be told, preferably in writing, what is not permitted. This is usually done during the employee's orientation. The rules and regulations are generally listed in the employee orientation handbook.

A *system of progressive penalties* is a second foundation of effective discipline. Penalties may range from verbal warnings to written warnings to suspension from the job to discharge. The severity of the penalty is usually a function of the type of offence and the number of times the offence has occurred. For example, most companies issue warnings for the first instance of unexcused lateness. However, for a fourth offence, discharge is the more usual disciplinary action.

Finally, there should be an *appeals process* as part of the disciplinary process; this helps to ensure that discipline is meted out fairly and equitably. Programs like FedEx's GFTP and IBM's open-door program help to assure their employees a real appeals process. Several important discipline guidelines are summarized in **Figure 15.2**.

AN ETHICAL DILEMMA

Is it ethical to apply disciplinary action in cases of ongoing absenteeism and tardiness due to family responsibilities? What other approach could be used?

Research Insight ▷

Research has shown that there are six general components of fairness relating to a disciplinary discussion between a manager and an employee. Managers should do the following:[21]

1. Take a counselling approach to the problem.
2. Exhibit a positive nonverbal demeanour, not angry or anxious.
3. Provide the employee with some control over the disciplinary process and outcome.
4. Provide a clear explanation of the problem behaviour.
5. Ensure that the discussion occurs in private.
6. Ensure that the discipline is not arbitrary; that is, it is consistent with other similar situations.

FIGURE 15.2   Discipline Guidelines

Make sure that the evidence supports the charge of employee wrongdoing. In one study, "the employer's evidence did not support the charge of employee wrongdoing" was the reason arbitrators gave most often for reinstating discharged employees or for reducing disciplinary suspensions.

Ensure that the employees' due process rights are protected. Arbitrators normally reverse discharges and suspensions that are imposed in a manner that violates basic notions of fairness of employee due process procedures. For example, follow established progressive discipline procedures, and do not deny the employee an opportunity to tell his of her side of the story.

Adequately warn the employee of the disciplinary consequences of his or her alleged misconduct.

Ensure that the rule that allegedly was violated is "reasonably related" to the efficient and safe operation of the particular work environment (since employees are usually allowed by arbitrators to question the reason behind any rule or order).

Management must fairly and adequately investigate the matter before administering discipline.

Ensure that the investigation produces substantial evidence of misconduct.

Apply rules, orders, or penalties even-handedly and without discrimination.

Ensure that the penalty is reasonably related to the misconduct and to the employee's past work history.

Maintain the employees' right to counsel. All union employees have the right to bring a union representative when they are called in for an interview that they reasonably believe might result in disciplinary action.

Do not rob the employee of his or her dignity. Discipline employees in private (unless they request counsel).

Remember that the burden of proof is on the employer. In our society, a person is always considered innocent until proven guilty.

Get the facts. Do not base disciplinary decisions on hearsay evidence or on general impressions.

Do not act while angry. Very few people can be objective and sensible when they are angry.

Discipline without Punishment

Traditional discipline has two major potential flaws. First, although fairness guidelines like those previously mentioned can help, no one ever feels good about being punished. There may, therefore, be residual bad feelings among all involved. A second shortcoming is that forcing the rules on employees may gain their short-term compliance but not their active cooperation when supervisors are not on hand to enforce the rules.

Discipline without punishment (or nonpunitive discipline) is aimed at avoiding these disciplinary problems. This is accomplished by gaining the employees' acceptance of the rules and by reducing the punitive nature of the discipline itself. Here is an example. Assume that there has been a breach of discipline (such as disregarding safety rules) or unsatisfactory work performance (such as carelessness in handling materials). In such a case, the following steps would constitute a typical nonpunitive approach to discipline:[22]

- *Step 1.* First, issue an oral reminder. The goal here is to get the employee to agree to solve the problem by reminding the employee of (1) the reason for the rule, and (2) the fact that he or she has a responsibility to meet performance standards. Keep a written record of the incident in a separate working file in the supervisor's desk rather than in the employee's HR file.

- *Step 2.* Should another incident arise within six weeks, issue the employee a formal written reminder, a copy of which is placed in the HR file. In addition, privately hold a second discussion with the employee to express confidence in the person's ability to act responsibly at work. Should another such incident occur in the next six weeks, you may decide to hold a follow-up meeting to investigate the possibility that the person is ill-suited to or bored with the job. Usually, though, the next step after the written reminder would be a paid one-day leave.

- *Step 3.* The next step is a paid one-day "decision-making leave." If another incident occurs in the next six weeks or so after the written warning, tell the employee to take a one-day leave with pay, to stay home and consider whether or not the job is right for him or her and whether or not the person wants to abide by the company's rules. The fact that the person is paid for the day is a final expression of the company's hope that the employee can and will act responsibly with respect to following the rules. When the employee returns to work, he or she should be asked to provide a decision regarding whether or not the rules will be followed. Assuming that there is a positive response, the supervisor should work out a brief action plan to help the person change his or her behaviour.

- *Step 4.* If no further incidents occur in the next year or so, the one-day paid suspension is purged from the person's file. If the behaviour is repeated, dismissal is required.

The process must, of course, be changed in exceptional circumstances. Criminal behaviour or in-plant fighting might be grounds for immediate dismissal, for instance. In addition, if several incidents occurred at very close intervals, Step 2—the written warning—might be skipped.

Nonpunitive discipline can be effective. Employees seem to welcome the less punitive aspects and do not seem to abuse the system by misbehaving to get a day off with pay. Grievances, sick leave usage, and disciplinary incidents all seem to drop in firms that use these procedures. However, there will still be times when dismissals will be required.

MANAGING DISMISSALS

dismissal Involuntary termination of an employee's employment.

Just Cause **www.labourlaw.com**

Dismissal is the most drastic disciplinary step that can be taken toward an employee, and one that must be handled with deliberate care. Specifically, the dismissal should be fair in that *sufficient cause* exists for it. Furthermore, the dismissal should occur only after *all reasonable steps* to rehabilitate or salvage the employee have failed. However, there are undoubtedly times when dismissal is required, and in these instances it should be carried out forthrightly.[23]

Grounds for Dismissal

There are four bases for dismissal: unsatisfactory performance, misconduct, lack of qualifications for the job, and changed requirements of (or elimination of) the job. *Unsatisfactory performance* may be defined as a persistent failure to perform assigned duties or to meet prescribed standards on the job.[24] Specific reasons here include excessive absenteeism, tardiness, a persistent failure to meet normal job requirements, or an adverse attitude toward the company, supervisor, or fellow employees. *Misconduct* can be defined as deliberate and willful violation of the employer's rules and may include stealing, rowdyism, and insubordination. The Retail Council of Canada reports that employee theft costs Canadian businesses about $2 million per day.[25] For example, Air Canada estimates that it loses up to 9 percent of its cabin stock each year due to employee theft, or about $9 per day per employee.[26]

Lack of qualifications for the job is defined as an employee's incapability of doing the assigned work although the person is diligent. Since the employee in this case may be trying to do the job, it is especially important that every effort be made to salvage him or her. *Changed requirements of the job* may be defined as an employee's incapability of doing the assigned work after the nature of the job has been changed. Similarly, an employee may have to be dismissed when his or her job is eliminated. Here again, the employee may be industrious, so every effort should be made to retrain or transfer this person, if possible.

Insubordination, a form of misconduct, is sometimes the grounds for dismissal, although it may be relatively difficult to prove. Stealing, chronic tardiness, and poor-quality work are fairly concrete grounds for dismissal, while insubordination is sometimes harder to translate into words. To that end, it may be useful to remember that some acts are or should be considered insubordinate whenever and wherever they occur. These include:[27]

insubordination Willful disregard or disobedience of the boss's authority or legitimate orders; criticizing the boss in public.

1. Direct disregard of the boss's authority. At sea, this is called mutiny.
2. Flat-out disobedience of, or refusal to obey, the boss's orders—particularly in front of others.
3. Deliberate defiance of clearly stated company policies, rules, regulations, and procedures.
4. Public criticism of the boss. Contradicting or arguing with him or her is also negative and inappropriate.
5. Blatant disregard of the boss's reasonable instructions.
6. Contemptuous display of disrespect; making insolent comments, for example; and, more important, portraying these feelings in the attitude shown while on the job.
7. Disregard for the chain of command, shown by going around the immediate supervisor or manager with a complaint, suggestion, or political manoeuvre. Although the employee may be right, that may not be enough to save him or her from the charges of insubordination.
8. Participation in (or leadership of) an effort to undermine and remove the boss from power. If the effort does not work (and it seldom does), those involved will be "dead in the water."

As in most human endeavours, there may be extenuating circumstances for the apparent insubordination. Cases like these should therefore be reviewed by the supervisor's boss. For example, an Ontario millwright was fired when he pushed a company manager down the steps of a construction trailer, narrowly missing construction debris and a passing front-end loader. The manager had been reprimanding the millwright for taking a day off to go hunting, which had forced the company to hire a private electrical contractor. The millwright grieved his termination, and the arbitrator ruled that a four-month suspension would be more appropriate, as the assault was not premeditated, but the result of momentary anger in reaction to provocation by the supervisor.[28]

The Employment Contract, Reasonable Notice, and Wrongful Dismissal

In Canada, the employer–employee relationship is governed by an employment contract—a formal agreement (in writing or based on mutual understanding) made between the two parties. If the contract is for a specific length of time, the contract ends at the expiration date, and the employee cannot be prematurely dismissed without just cause.

Employees are often hired under an implied contract where the understanding is that employment is for an indefinite period of time and may be terminated by either party only when *reasonable notice* is given.[29] Employers cannot hire and fire employees at will, as is the case in the United States. Canadian employers can only terminate an employee's employment without reasonable notice when just cause exists. If just cause is not present, then a termination without notice is considered **wrongful dismissal**.

wrongful dismissal An employee dismissal that does not comply with the law or does not comply with a written or implied contractual arrangement.

Just cause is usually considered to include disobedience, incompetence, dishonesty, insubordination, fighting, and persistent absence or lateness.[30] However, just cause cannot be assessed in isolation, and may vary depending on the possible consequences of the misconduct, the status of the employee, and the circumstances of the case. The burden of proof rests with the employer. In Canada, courts often do not accept the assertion of just cause by the employer, and unions almost never do—one union alleged that a death threat made by an employee to his supervisor was "mild insubordination."[31] One Canadian researcher found that, since 1980, the courts agreed with employers in only 25 percent of cases alleging incompetence, 40 percent for misconduct, 54 percent for insubordination, and 66 percent for conflict of interest/competing with the employer.[32]

In any termination where just cause is not involved, the employer must provide reasonable notice to the employee (often three to four weeks per year of service). The employee sometimes continues to work during the period of notice given, but usually ceases work at the time that the notice of termination is given. In the latter case, the employee receives a lump sum of money equal to his or her pay for the period of notice.

Often, the amount considered reasonable is beyond the minimum notice requirements of employment/labour standards legislation. The employee can accept the notice given or can sue for wrongful dismissal if the notice is considered unacceptable. The court will review the circumstances of the dismissal, and make a final decision on the amount of notice to be provided. The courts generally award a period of notice based on their assessment of how long it will take the employee to find alternative employment, taking into account the employee's age, salary, length of service, the level of the job, and other factors. Rarely have notice periods exceeded 24 months.[33]

A major change in the law of wrongful dismissal occurred in 1997 when the Supreme Court of Canada ruled that "bad faith conduct" on the part of the employer in dismissing an employee is a new factor to be considered in determining the period of reasonable notice.[34] At a minimum, employers are required to be candid, reasonable, honest, and forthright with their employees in the course of dismissal, and should refrain from engaging in conduct that is unfair or in bad faith, such as being untruthful, misleading, or unduly insensitive. Since the Supreme Court decision, many employees suing for wrongful dismissal have also claimed notice on the basis of "bad faith" conduct on the part of their employer, and there have been no limits on what kinds of conduct have been considered "bad faith." The resulting additional periods of notice (known as "Wallace damages") have been unpredictable, often about three to six months, no matter the context.[35] This has resulted in a few cases where the notice period has exceeded 24 months. It is clear that employers must treat employees with honesty and respect at all times, especially at the time of dismissal.[36]

In extreme cases, employers may also be ordered to pay punitive damages for harsh and vindictive treatment of an employee, and/or damages for aggravated or mental distress if the employee suffered undue distress from not being given adequate notice of termination.[37] The employee has the responsibility to make every effort to find alternative employment as soon as possible, although not at a position inferior to the one from which he or she was terminated.

Avoiding Wrongful Dismissal Suits

With the increased likelihood that terminated employees can and will sue for wrongful dismissal, it behooves employers to protect themselves against wrongful dismissal suits. The time to do that is before mistakes have been made and suits have been filed.

Ten steps to take in order to avoid wrongful dismissal suits are:[38]

Hints to Ensure Legal Compliance

1. Avoid inducements to lure employees away from other secure employment.

2. Avoid promising permanent employment.

3. Use employment contracts with a termination clause and wording to ensure that the ability to dismiss without cause during the probationary period is clear.

4. Document all disciplinary action.

5. Do not allege cause for dismissal unless it can be proven.

6. Time the termination so that it does not conflict with birthdays, holidays, or other disappointments in an employee's life.

7. Use termination letters in all cases, clearly stating the settlement offer.

8. Schedule the termination meeting in a private location at a time of day that will allow the employee to clear out belongings with a minimal amount of contact with other employees.

9. Conduct the termination meeting with two members of management.

10. Provide honest references.

constructive dismissal The employer makes unilateral changes in the employment contract that are unacceptable to the employee, even though the employee has not been formally terminated.

Restructuring Tips
www.hr.cch.com

If a wrongful dismissal suit is taken against the company, it should:[39]

- Review the claim carefully before retaining a lawyer.
- Choose a lawyer who practices in the area of employment law.
- Ask for a legal opinion on the merits of the case.
- Work with the lawyer and provide all relevant facts and documentation.
- Never allege cause if none exists.
- Investigate for other improper conduct.
- Avoid defamatory statements.
- Discuss any possible letter of reference with the lawyer.
- Offer to settle in order to save time and money.
- Consider mediation as an option.

Constructive Dismissal

Constructive dismissal can be considered to occur when the employer makes unilateral changes in the employment contract that are unacceptable to the employee, even though the employee has not been formally terminated.[40] The most common changes in employment status that are considered to constitute constructive dismissal are demotion, reduction in pay and benefits, forced resignation, forced early retirement, forced transfer, and changes in job duties and responsibilities. An employee who believes that he or she has been constructively dismissed can sue the employer for wrongful dismissal. If the judge agrees that constructive dismissal occurred, he or she will determine a period of notice to be provided to the employee. An executive at the Toronto-Dominion Bank who was deemed to have been constructively dismissed when many of his duties were transferred to someone else received $2 million as a result of wrongful dismissal litigation.[41]

Dismissal Procedures

In the event of a dismissal, a number of steps should be followed:

- Hold warning discussions before taking any final action. An employee must be made aware that he or she is not performing satisfactorily.
- Get written confirmation of the final warning.
- Prepare a checklist of all property that should be accounted for, including computer disks and manuals.
- Change security codes and locks previously used by discharged individuals.
- Always prepare for the possibility that the discharged individual may act irrationally or even violently, either immediately or in weeks to come.
- Decide beforehand how other employees will be informed about this person's dismissal. An informal departmental meeting of those directly involved with this person is usually sufficient.

Consider having a lawyer create an employee release form. Such releases are obtained from employees who have asserted claims against the company or who are the subject of employment actions such as discharges and layoffs. They release the employer from claims by giving the employee something of value—"consideration" in legal terms.[42] Any such release should include (1) a general release of the employee's claims; (2) a covenant not to sue the employer; and (3) an indemnification and payback provision relating to breaches of the release and covenant-not-to-sue provisions.[43]

Research Insight ▷ A recent study of 996 recently fired or laid-off workers found that wrongful dismissal claims were strongly correlated with the way workers felt they had been treated at the time of termination. They also found a "vendetta effect" where the instances of wrongful dismissal claims became stronger as negative treatment became extreme, as shown in **Figure 15.3**. The researchers concluded that many wrongful dismissal lawsuits could be avoided if effective human resource practices, specifically treating employees fairly, were employed. Providing clear, honest explanations of termination decisions and handling the termination in a way that treats people with dignity and respect can be especially effective.[44]

The Termination Interview Dismissing an employee is one of the most difficult tasks that a manager will face at work.[45] The dismissed employee, even

FIGURE **15.3** Fair Treatment and Wrongful Dismissal Claims: The Vendetta Effect

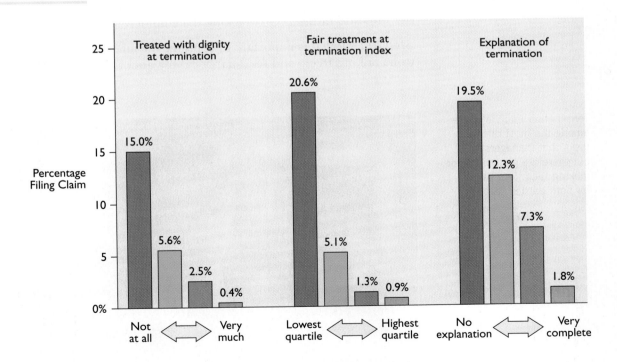

Source: E.A. Lind, J. Greenberg, K.S. Scott and T.D. Welchans, "The Winding Road from Employee to Complainant: Situational and Psychological Determinants of Wrongful-Termination Claims," *Administrative Science Quarterly*, September 2000, p. 557–590. Reproduced by permission of *Administrative Science Quarterly*.

termination interview The interview in which an employee is informed of the fact that he or she has been dismissed.

if warned many times in the past, will often still react with total disbelief or even violence. Guidelines for the **termination interview** itself are as follows.

Step 1: Plan the Interview Carefully According to experts at Hay Associates, this means:

- Schedule the meeting on a day early in the week.
- Never inform an employee over the phone.
- Allow ten to fifteen minutes as sufficient time for the interview.
- Avoid Fridays, pre-holidays, and vacation times when possible.
- Use a neutral site, never your office.
- Have employee agreements, human resources file, and release announcement (internal and external) prepared in advance.
- Be available at a time after the interview in case questions or problems arise.
- Have phone numbers ready for medical or security emergencies.

Step 2: Get to the Point As soon as the employee arrives, give the person a moment to get comfortable and then inform him or her of the decision.

Step 3: Describe the Situation Briefly, in three or four sentences, explain why the person is being let go. For instance, "Production in your area is down 4 percent, and we are continuing to have quality problems. We have talked about these problems several times in the past three months and the solutions are not being followed through. We have to make a change."[46] Remember to describe the situation rather than attacking the employee personally.

Step 4: Listen It is important to continue the interview until the person appears to be talking freely and reasonably calmly about the reasons for his or her ter-

Termination interviews are among the most difficult tasks that managers face, but there are guidelines for making them less painful for both parties.

mination and the severance package that he or she is to receive. Behavioural indications can be used to help gauge the person's reaction and to decide how best to proceed. Five major reactions often occur.

First, some employees will be *hostile and angry*, expressing hurt and disappointment. In such case, remain objective while providing information on any outplacement or career counselling to be provided, being careful to avoid being defensive or confronting the person's anger.

Second, some employees may react in a *defensive, bargaining* manner, based on their feelings of fear and disbelief. In this case, it is important to acknowledge that this is a difficult time for the employee, and then provide information regarding outplacement counselling without getting involved in any bargaining discussions.

Third, the employee may proceed in a *formal, controlled* manner, indicative of a suppressed, vengeful reaction, and the potential for legal action. In this case, allow the employee to ask any questions pertaining to his or her case (avoiding side issues) in a formal tone while leading into information about the outplacement counselling to be provided.

Fourth, some employees will maintain a *stoic* façade, masking their shock, disbelief, and numbness. In this case, communicate to the employee that his or her shock is recognized, and that the details can be handled later if the employee prefers, and then answer any questions arising at that point, as well as providing information on outplacement counselling.

A fifth reaction is an *emotional* one involving tears and sadness, indicating grief and worry on the part of the employee. Allow the person to cry and provide tissues. When the person regains his or her composure, explain the outplacement counselling process.

Step 5: Review All Elements of the Severance Package Describe severance payments, benefits, and the way in which references will be handled. However, under no conditions should any promises or benefits beyond those already in the severance package be implied. The termination should be complete when the person leaves.

Step 6: Identify the Next Step The terminated employee may be disoriented, so explain where he or she should go upon leaving the interview. Remind the person whom to contact at the company regarding questions about the severance package or references.

outplacement counselling A systematic process by which a terminated person is trained and counselled in the techniques of self-appraisal and securing a new position.

Outplacement Counselling

Outplacement counselling provides career counselling and job search skills training for terminated employees. The counselling itself is done either by the employer's in-house specialist or by outside consultants. The outplacement counselling is considered part of the terminated employee's severance package.[47]

Outplacement counselling is usually conducted by outplacement firms, such as Drake Beam Moran Inc. and Right Associates Inc. Middle- and upper-level managers who are let go will typically have office space and secretarial services that they can use at local offices of such firms, in addition to the counselling services. Some outplacement providers are experimenting with Internet-delivered services, as described in the HR.Net box.

HR.Net

Keeping Up with Outplacement

Traditional outplacement provided recently released employees with the work-like environment they were accustomed to and couldn't get while in a job search from home. Today, the services offered by sites such as Workopolis.com and Monster.ca have reduced the need for assistance with résumé writing and company research, and personally empowered the job seeker. Also, many employees have a comfortable setting and the necessary technology at home.

Therefore, some outplacement companies have offered Internet-delivered job search programs on a self-administered basis. However, these programs are missing the "human factor." When someone loses a job, that person hurts and is in a great deal of emotional pain. A computer is about as sensitive as a vacuum cleaner or refrigerator. This problem has led some outplacement specialists to use a new hybrid approach, combining the efficiencies of technology with face-to-face personal coaching.

A professional outplacement counsellor can be in attendance at the termination to help the individual cope and will then meet again with the terminated

employee to help design the outplacement program. Meetings can be held in coffee shops that provide a neutral setting close to the employee's home where they feel comfortable and can converse in a more candid and informal manner.

The employee has access to around-the-clock Web-based and telephone support, and is encouraged to at least start working on a résumé within 48 hours. It is during the first 48 hours that the panic and anger set in, and when the terminated employee is most likely to hire a lawyer and challenge the company's decision. By producing at least a starter résumé, the individual is challenged to move forward.

When a terminated individual regains employment quickly, litigation challenges drop significantly and the "survivor" employees, who probably still remain in contact with the terminated employee, are much happier, more stable, and productive.

Source: Adapted from B. Delaney, "Keeping Up with Outplacement," *Canadian HR Reporter* (June 17, 2002), pp. 15, 19. Reproduced by permission of *Canadian HR Reporter*, Carswell, One Corporate Plaza, 2075 Kennedy Road, Scarborough, ON M1T 3V4.

MANAGING SEPARATIONS: LAYOFFS AND RETIREMENTS

group termination laws Laws that require an employer to notify employees in the event that an employer decides to terminate a group of employees.

Hints to Ensure Legal Compliance

Nondisciplinary separations are a fact of life in organizations, and can be initiated by either employer or employee. For the employer, reduced sales or profits may require layoffs or downsizings, while employees may terminate their own employment in order to retire or to seek better jobs.

Group termination laws require employers who are terminating a large group of employees to give them more notice than that required upon termination of an individual employee. The laws are intended to assist employees in situations of plant closings and large downsizings. Most jurisdictions in Canada require employers who are terminating a group of employees (some specify 10 or more, others 25 or more) within a short period of time to give advance notice to employees, and sometimes to their union. The amount of notice varies by jurisdiction, and with the number of employees being terminated, but generally ranges from 6 weeks to 18 weeks.

The laws do not prevent the employer from closing down, nor do they require saving jobs. They simply give employees time to seek other work or retraining by giving them advance notice of the termination. The law is not clear about how the notice to employees must be worded. However, a letter to the individual employees to be terminated might include a paragraph toward the end of the letter as follows:

Please consider this letter to be your official notice, as required by law, that your current position with the company will end 60 days from today because of a (layoff or closing) that is now projected to take place on (date). After that day, your employment with the company will be terminated, and you will no longer be carried on our payroll records or be covered by any company benefit programs. Any questions concerning this notice will be answered in the HR office.[48]

Managing Layoffs

layoff The temporary withdrawal of employment to workers for economic or business reasons.

A **layoff,** in which workers are sent home for a time, is a situation in which three conditions are present: (1) there is no work available for the employees; (2) management expects the no-work situation to be temporary and probably short-term; and (3) management intends to recall the employees when work is again available.[49] A layoff is therefore not a termination, which is a permanent severing of the employment relationship. However, some employers do use the term *layoff* as a euphemism for discharge or termination.

bumping/layoff procedures
Detailed procedures that determine who will be laid off if no work is available; generally allowing employees to use their seniority to remain on the job.

Bumping/Layoff Procedures

Employers who encounter frequent business slowdowns and layoffs often have detailed **bumping/layoff procedures** that allow employees to use their seniority to remain on the job. In unionized organizations, these procedures are negotiated with workers.

Most such procedures have the following features in common:[50]

1. For the most part, seniority is the ultimate determinant of who will work.
2. Seniority can give way to merit or ability, but usually only when none of the senior employees is qualified for a particular job.
3. Seniority is usually based on the date the employee joined the organization, not the date he or she took a particular job.
4. Because seniority is usually company-wide, an employee in one job is usually allowed to bump or displace an employee in another job provided that the more senior employee is able to do the job in question without further training.

> **Tips for the Front Line**

Alternatives to Layoffs

Many employers today recognize the enormous investments that they have in recruiting, screening, and training their employees. As a result, they are more hesitant to lay off employees at the first signs of business decline. Instead, they are using new approaches to either blunt the effects of the layoff or eliminate the layoffs entirely.

For example, the Honeywell division in Amherstburg, Ontario, decided to make every effort to resist layoffs during the last quarter of 2001. They wanted to maintain staffing levels because they were predicting their market to pick up in early 2003 and they knew they would need those people then. Like many other organizations, not long before, Honeywell was struggling to find good employees, particularly at the managerial and supervisory level. In the past when people at that level would leave, it would take up to six months to find replacements. The company had also gained a much better sense of exactly who its essential people were,

As more firms relocate their manufacturing plants to foreign countries in order to minimize costs, workers protest the signing of any free trade agreements, which they think encourage such actions.

and retention strategies had been put into place to make sure they wouldn't be lured away. When Honeywell finds somebody who they think has a lot of potential but there doesn't appear to be anywhere on the organization chart for that person to go, share options will be offered and a development plan structured to encourage him or her to stay.[51]

There are several alternatives to layoff. With the *voluntary reduction in pay plan*, all employees agree to reductions in pay in order to keep everyone working. Other employers arrange to have all or most of their employees accumulate their vacation time and to concentrate their vacations during slow periods. Other employees agree to take *voluntary time off*, which again has the effect of reducing the employer's payroll and avoiding the need for a layoff. Another way to avoid layoffs is the use of *contingent employees*. Temporary supplemental employees can be hired with the understanding that their work is of a temporary nature where they may be laid off at any time. Then, when layoffs come, the first group to be laid off is the cadre of contingent workers.[52] The use of contingent workers in Canada is growing, and is expected to continue to increase.[53] Finally, the *Work Sharing Program* available through Human Resources Development Canada allows employers to reduce the workweek by one to three days and for the time not worked, employees can claim employment insurance. In 2003, this program was used to avoid layoffs at Toronto-area hotels hit hard by the SARS crisis.[54]

Adjusting to Downsizing and Mergers

downsizing Refers to the process of reducing, usually dramatically, the number of people employed by the firm.

Downsizing refers to the process of reducing, usually dramatically, the number of people employed by the firm. Although it is not clear why, most firms do not find that their operating earnings improve after major staff cuts are made. There are probably many ways to explain this anomaly, but declining employee morale as a result of downsizing is one plausible reason. Therefore, firms that are downsizing must also give attention to the remaining employees. Certainly those "downsized-out" should be treated fairly, but it is around the employees retained that the business will be built.

When dealing with the survivors immediately after the downsizing, one of two situations must be faced right away. First, if no further reductions are anticipated at that time, workers can be reassured accordingly. Second, if it is expected that more reductions will probably take place, be honest with those who remain, explaining that while future downsizings will probably occur, they will be informed of these reductions as soon as possible.

Specific Steps to Take
A major downsizing program instituted at Duracell Canada illustrates the steps involved in a well-conceived program. The criteria used for planning decisions were employee dignity and respect—which are among the company's core values. The program began with *announcement activities*. The first was a full staff meeting at the facility, where senior management announced the downsizing. This meeting was immediately followed by small-group meetings between the employees who were losing their jobs, their manager, and an outplacement counsellor. Information about the support services and assistance being provided to those leaving was also made available to survivors.

Next there was an *immediate follow-up* phase during the two weeks after the announcement. Workshops were provided by outplacement counsellors to help employees begin the job search process, and one-on-one counselling was also available to those who wanted it. A career centre with internal and external job postings was set up inside the company's premises. During this period, all employees continued working, and productivity increased.

A mechanism for providing *long-term support* was also built into the program. Key managers were encouraged to meet with the remaining staff frequently and informally in order to provide them with ongoing support in an open-door atmosphere.

A critical responsibility of human resources managers in any downsizing is to ensure that the bad news is delivered in a humane manner.[55] Department managers need to be trained in how to deliver unwelcome news effectively (by participating in role-plays for practice), and how to listen to and observe other managers. These managers also need to identify and recognize their own personal values that will anchor them during the difficult communication process. The responsibility for delivering tough news humanely, treating people with dignity and respect, and advising people of all support services available to them must be emphasized. It helps if managers work with a partner who acts as a coach when preparing for a termination interview, and debriefs them on the experience when it is over. Finally, every effort should be made to deliver downsizing news in a one-on-one manner, and to anticipate the emotional reactions from everyone involved, including the manager.

Handling a Merger/Acquisition

About two-thirds of all corporate mergers fail to reach their forecasted goals of increased efficiency and cost-effectiveness.[56] The merging organizations often underestimate the difficulty involved in merging two distinct work cultures (and in many cases, ethnic cultures). A human resources department with credibility and strong two-way communication programs enabling it to assess morale in merger situations can find great opportunity to take on the responsibility for facilitating the change process.

Dismissals and downsizings in the case of mergers or acquisitions are usually one-sided. One company essentially acquires the other, and it is often the employees of the latter who find themselves out looking for new jobs. In such a situation, the employees in the acquired firm will be hypersensitive to mistreatment of their colleagues. It thus behooves managers to ensure that those who are let go are treated with courtesy. Seeing former colleagues fired is bad enough for morale; seeing them fired under conditions that look like bullying rubs salt in the wound and poisons the relationship for years to come. As a rule, therefore, managers should:[57]

- Avoid the appearance of power and domination.
- Avoid win/lose behaviour.
- Remain businesslike and professional in all dealings.
- Maintain as positive a feeling about the acquired company as possible.
- Remember that the degree to which the organization treats the acquired group with care and dignity will affect the confidence, productivity, and commitment of those remaining.

RETIREMENT

The Retirement Centre
www.iretire.org

Financial Knowledge Inc.
www.financialknowledgeinc.com

T.E. Financial Consultants
www.tefinancial.com

With Canada's rapidly aging population, retirement issues are becoming increasingly important and complex.[58] Retirement for most employees is bittersweet. For some, it is the culmination of their careers, a time when they can relax and enjoy the fruits of their labour without worrying about the problems of work. For others, it is the retirement itself that is the trauma, as the once-busy employee tries to cope with suddenly being "nonproductive." For many retirees, in fact, maintaining a sense of identity and self-worth without a full-time job is the single most important task they will face. It is one that employers are increasingly trying to help their retirees cope with as a logical last step in the career management process.

The Conference Board of Canada's 2002 report *Leaving Work: Managing One of Life's Pivotal Transitions* identified six key life lessons as vital to a successful transition to retirement:[59]

- View retirement as a journey, not a destination.
- Get a life while you are still working; develop other interests.
- Be prepared to leave; it happens sooner or later. Adjust your work pace as retirement nears.
- Cut yourself some slack after leaving; take time to adjust.
- Renew and rediscover relationships on your journey.
- Make the most out of this phase of your life.

Pre-retirement Counselling

pre-retirement counselling
Counselling provided to employees some months (or even years) before retirement, which covers matters such as benefits advice, second careers, and so on.

Most employers provide some type of formal **pre-retirement counselling** aimed at easing the passage of their employees into retirement.[60] Court decisions have confirmed that employers do have some legal responsibility to help employees prepare for retirement.[61] Retirement education and planning firms provide services to assist upcoming retirees with issues such as lifestyle goals, (including part-time or volunteer work and/or moving to another country), financial planning, relationship issues, and health issues. Both individual and group transition counselling are offered in seminars and workshops featuring workbooks, questionnaires, discussions, group exercises, and software products. In the end, employees who are taking control of their retirement plans often have reduced absenteeism and health-care costs.[62]

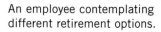

An employee contemplating different retirement options.

Stay on Track during Trying Transitional Times

If your company is going through a layoff, reorganization, or merger, employee morale may dip and productivity may slide. How can you keep morale and productivity up during such trying transitional times? According to Janelle Brittain of the Dynamic Performance Institute, LLC, employers need to know how their individual employees react to stress, be able to motivate employees effectively, and take steps to keep teams focused on productivity.... Everybody wants to know what's going on during an organizational change, advises Brittain. When there isn't enough information, it will be made up and misinfor-

mation will spread quickly. If information is withheld, morale can be destroyed quickly. Brittain therefore advises employers to share information as soon as it is obtained, unless it will cause damage to the company's stock position or hinder the progress of the merger or acquisition. It must also reduce employee fear of the unknown and help employees remain productive. How should you present it? Information must be presented to everyone and everyone must hear the same message, urges Brittain. One way to ensure this happens is to use technology, simulcasts, or the computer. All spoken words must also be in writing.

Source: Excerpted with permission from the *Ideas and Trends* #542-1 and #542-2, September 4, 2002, published by CCH Incorporated, United States.

CHAPTER *Review*

Summary

1 Three techniques for building effective two-way communication in organizations are Speak Up! programs, employee opinion surveys, and top-down communication programs.

2 A fair and just disciplinary process is based on three prerequisites: rules and regulations, a system of progressive penalties, and an appeals process.

3 Employees who are dismissed without just cause must be provided with reasonable notice. This means paying them for several weeks or months in addition to the legally required notice period on termination. If the employee does not believe that the period of notice is reasonable, he or she may file a wrongful dismissal lawsuit. In order to avoid wrongful dismissal suits, firms should avoid constructively dismissing employees by placing them in lower-paying jobs in hopes of a resignation, avoid promising permanent employment, document all disciplinary action, use employment contracts with a termination clause, and use termination letters clearly stating the settlement offer.

4 The six steps in the termination interview are plan the interview carefully, get to the point, describe the situation, listen until the person has expressed his or her feelings, discuss the severance package, and identify the next step.

5 HR considerations in adjusting to downsizings and mergers include avoiding the appearance of power and domination, avoiding win/lose behaviour, remaining businesslike and professional in all dealings, maintaining as positive a feeling about the acquired company as possible, and remembering that the degree to which the organization treats the acquired group with care and dignity will affect the confidence, productivity, and commitment of those remaining.

Key Terms

bumping/layoff procedures *(p. 487)*
constructive dismissal *(p. 482)*
discipline *(p. 476)*
dismissal *(p. 478)*
downsizing *(p. 488)*
fair treatment programs *(p. 472)*
group termination laws *(p. 486)*
insubordination *(p. 479)*
layoff *(p. 487)*
open-door program *(p. 473)*

Review and Discussion Questions

1 Explain the role of communication and fair treatment programs in establishing a foundation for effective employee relations.

2 Describe specific techniques that you would use to foster top-down communication in an organization.

3 Explain how fairness in employee discipline can be ensured, particularly the prerequisites to discipline, discipline guidelines, and the "discipline without punishment" approach.

4 Describe the four main reasons for dismissal.

5 What are the techniques that can be used as alternatives to layoffs?

6 Discuss some of the issues that should be covered in a pre-retirement counselling program.

CRITICAL *Thinking Questions*

1 Describe the similarities and differences between a program such as FedEx Canada's guaranteed fair treatment program and a typical union grievance procedure.

2 Describe the similarities and differences between the "discipline without punishment" approach and a typical progressive discipline procedure.

APPLICATION *Exercises*

Running Case: LearnInMotion.com

Fair Treatment in Disciplinary Action

Because the employees used high-cost computer equipment to do their jobs, Jennifer and Pierre have always felt strongly about not allowing employees to eat or drink at their desks. Jennifer was therefore surprised to walk into the office one day to find two employees eating lunch at their desks. There was a large pizza in its box, and the two of them were sipping soft drinks and eating slices of pizza and submarine sandwiches from paper plates. Not only did it look messy, but there were also grease and soft drink spills on their desks and the office smelled of onions and pepperoni. In addition to looking unprofessional, the mess on the desks increased the possibility that the computers could be damaged. One of the employees continued to use his computer with greasy fingers between bites.

While this was a serious matter, neither Jennifer nor Pierre believes that what the employees were doing is grounds for immediate dismissal, partly because there was no written policy on eating at the workstations. They just assumed that people would use their common sense. The problem is that they do not know what to do. It seems to them that the matter calls for more than just a warning, but less than dismissal. As their management consultants, here's what they want you to do for them.

Questions

1 Advise them whether there should be formal policies and rules regarding employee behaviour. What should these include?

2 Should a disciplinary system be established at LearnInMotion.com? Why or why not?

3 If such a system is introduced, what should it cover, and how should the company deal with employees who break the rules?

CASE INCIDENT *Job Insecurity at IBM*

For over 50 years, IBM was known for its policy of job security. Throughout all those years, it had never laid off any employees, even as the company was going through wrenching changes. For example, in the late 1970s and 1980s, IBM had to close down its punch card manufacturing plants and division, but the thousands of employees who worked in those plants were simply given an opportunity to move to comparable jobs in other IBM divisions.

Unfortunately, IBM's full-employment policy eventually evaporated, and fast. As IBM's computer industry market share dropped throughout the 1980s, both its sales revenue and profits began to erode. By 1991, it had become apparent that a drastic restructuring was needed. The firm therefore accelerated its downsizing efforts, instituting various early retirement and incentive plans aimed at getting employees to leave voluntarily. Numerous imaginative schemes were introduced, including spinning off certain operations to groups of employees who then quit IBM while becoming independent consultants, doing tasks very similar to those they used to do while employees of IBM. By 1992, however, at least 40 000 more employees still had to be trimmed, and by 1993 it had become apparent that IBM's cherished long-term employment policy had to be discarded. For the first time, IBM began laying off employees, and eventually tens of thousands more employees were let go, beginning with about 300 employees of the firm's Armonk, New York, headquarters.

Questions

1   What accounts for the fact that a company like IBM can have high commitment but still lose market share, sales, and profitability? In other words, why did employee commitment not translate into corporate success as well as it might have at IBM?

2   What sorts of steps should IBM have taken in order to continue to avoid layoffs? If it appears that any such steps were not feasible, explain why.

3   Given IBM's experience with its long-term employment policy, what are the implications for other companies that are thinking of instituting similar employment policies of their own?

EXPERIENTIAL *Exercises*

1   Working individually or in groups, obtain copies of the student handbook for a college or university and determine to what extent there is a formal process through which students can air grievances. Would you expect the process to be effective? Why or why not? Based on contacts with students who have used the grievance process, has it been effective?

2   Working individually or in groups, determine the nature of the academic discipline process in a college or university. Does it appear to be an effective one? Based on this chapter, should any modification be made to the student discipline process?

3   A computer department employee made an entry error that ruined an entire run of computer reports. Efforts to rectify the situation produced a second batch of improperly run reports. As a result of the series of errors, the employer incurred extra costs of $2400, plus a weekend of overtime work by other computer department staffers. Management suspended the employee for three days for negligence, and also revoked a promotion for which the employee had previously been approved.

Protesting the discipline, the employee stressed that she had attempted to correct her error in the early stages of the run by notifying the manager of computer operations of her mistake. Maintaining that the resulting string of errors could have been avoided if the manager had followed up on her report and stopped the initial run, the employee argued that she had been treated unfairly in being severely punished because the manager had not been disciplined at all even though he had compounded the problem. Moreover, citing her "impeccable" work record and management's acknowledgment that she had always been a "model employee," the employee insisted that the denial of her previously approved promotion was "unconscionable."

(a) in groups, determine what your decision would be if you were the arbitrator. Why?

(Your instructor will inform you of the actual arbitrator's decision when you discuss this exercise in class.)

(b) Do you think that the employer handled the disciplinary situation correctly? Why? What would you have done differently?

CHAPTER 16

The Dynamics of Labour Relations

CHAPTER
OUTLINE

- Introduction to Labour–Management Relations

- Management's Labour Relations Strategy

- Canada's Labour Laws

- The Labour Movement in Canada Today

- The Labour Relations Process

- The Impact of Unionization on HRM

LEARNING OUTCOMES

After studying this chapter, you should be able to:

Describe the labour relations strategies managers can adopt.

Discuss the key elements of Canada's labour laws.

Outline the five steps in the labour relations process.

Explain why workers might desire unionization.

Describe the five steps in a union organizing campaign.

Discuss the three ways in which a union can obtain recognition as a bargaining unit.

Introduction to Labour–Management Relations

labour union (union) An officially recognized association of employees, practising a similar trade or employed in the same company or industry, who have joined together to present a united front and collective voice in dealing with management.

labour–management relations The ongoing economic and social interactions between labour unions and management in organizations.

collective agreement (union contract) A signed, written agreement between an employer (or employer's organization) and the union representing a group of the organization's employees, containing provisions outlining the terms and conditions of their employment.

collective bargaining The negotiations that take place between a labour union, collectively representing the employees of a firm or industry, and the employer or employer's association, to arrive at a mutually acceptable collective agreement.

bargaining unit The group of employees in a firm, plant, or industry that has been recognized by an employer or certified by a Labour Relations Board (LRB) as appropriate for collective bargaining purposes.

Human Resources Development Canada—Labour Program
labour-travail.hrdc-drhc.gc.ca

Canadian Labour and Business Centre **www.clbc.ca**

A **labour union (or union)** is an officially recognized body representing a group of individuals who have joined together to present a collective voice in dealing with management. The term **labour–management relations** refers to the ongoing economic and social interactions between labour unions and management in organizations. The presence of a labour union alters the relationship between employees and the firm. Managerial discretion and flexibility in dealing with employees and in implementing and administering HR policies and procedures are reduced. For example, union seniority provisions in the **collective agreement** (**union contract**), negotiated through **collective bargaining**, govern the selection of employees for transfers, promotions, and training programs, and specify the order in which employees can be laid off and recalled. Many other terms and conditions of employment for **bargaining unit** members are determined and standardized through collective bargaining, rather than being left to management's discretion.

In the context of labour–management relations, the term *management* refers to all individuals with HRM responsibilities—those who supervise employees. Employees typically seek union representation because they are dissatisfied with certain aspects of the job, feel that they lack influence with management and have relatively little power in their relations with supervisors, and see unionization as a way of pursuing their interests and solving their problems.[1] If supervisors communicate effectively with employees, deal with their concerns, and treat them fairly, employees are far less likely to be interested in forming or joining a union. A work environment that is not conducive to unionization is one that is participative and acknowledges the individual, and where managers understand their obligations to workers.[2]

Once a union has been recognized, the industrial relations (IR) specialist in the HR department assumes primary responsibility for negotiations and contract administration. However, first-line supervisors play a critical role in shaping the labour–management relationship, because of their day-to-day involvement in administering the collective agreement.

Purposes of Unionization

The purposes of unionization are to:

- influence HR policies and practices affecting bargaining unit members, such as pay and benefits, discipline, transfers, promotions, grievances, and layoffs
- achieve greater control over the jobs being performed, greater job security and improved working conditions
- increase job satisfaction and meet employees' affiliation needs.

Management's Labour Relations Strategy

An organization's *labour relations (LR) strategy*, one component of its HR strategy, is its overall plan for dealing with unions, which sets the tone for its

Ontario Ministry of Labour, Labour
Management Services
www.gov.on.ca/lab/lms/lmse.htm

Canada LabourWatch Association
www.labourwatch.com

union–management relationship. The decision to accept or avoid unions is the basis of an organization's LR strategy.[3]

Union Acceptance Strategy

Managers in firms choosing a union acceptance strategy view the union as the legitimate representative of the firm's employees. They accept collective bargaining as an appropriate mechanism for establishing workplace rules and the terms and conditions of employment for the bargaining unit members. In such a setting, the management negotiation team strives for a mutually acceptable collective agreement, and all supervisors are (ideally) thoroughly familiar with the terms of the collective agreement and committed to abiding by them. As described in the Strategic HR box, such a relationship can lead to innovative initiatives and win–win outcomes.

Union Avoidance Strategy

Managers select a union avoidance strategy when they believe that it is preferable to operate in a non-unionized environment. There are two approaches that firms can adopt in order to avoid unionization—one is proactive and the other employs hardball tactics.[4]

STRATEGIC HR

DaimlerChrysler and the Canadian Auto Workers—A Unique Initiative

DaimlerChrysler Canada's unique initiative with the Canadian Auto Workers (CAW) is an excellent example of union and management working together. The company had to cut up to 2700 employees from its Canadian workforce due to a reduced volume requirement. At the Brampton, Ontario, plant, the company was not able to offset the number of layoffs with early retirement options, as they had done in other locations, because of its relatively young workforce in Brampton. The company did not want their laid-off employees to go away resenting the company, so they came up with two remedies, jointly developed by the union and the company.

First, they authorized payment for a training program to prepare employees for layoffs. Second, the company and the union opened up an "action centre"—funded by the federal and provincial governments—which helped laid-off workers find and develop new careers. About 80 percent of the workers that were laid off registered with the centre and actively participated.

DaimlerChrysler also ran an ad in *The Globe and Mail*, in late November 2001, encouraging other employers to hire their laid-off workers. This was done on the advice of the "action centre" board members who felt the centre should be promoted, as well as their unemployed workers who were searching for jobs.

This open relationship with the union did not come easily, but was the result of 15 years of negotiations and discussion. Today, DaimlerChrysler considers the CAW to be its partner, which translates into a culture of engaging participation in the company's objectives. Phil Bezaire, vice-president of human resources for DaimlerChrysler Canada says, "Things work well if you listen. Sometimes you don't like what you hear but it's through dialogue that you can come up with a workable compromise and that's really the way our manufacturing management works." Buzz Hargrove, president of the CAW says, "You're in it for the long term and there's absolutely nothing to be gained by either side taking a short-term advantage. So, any successful company has to have the long term in mind when dealing with the union and its members."

Source: Adapted from A. Tomlinson, "Layoffs or Fewer Hours? Neither Thank You," *Canadian HR Reporter* (January 14, 2002), pp. 1, 6. Reproduced by permission of *Canadian HR Reporter*, Carswell, One Corporate Plaza, 2075 Kennedy Road, Scarborough, ON M1T 3V4.

union substitution (proactive HRM) approach A union avoidance strategy that involves removing the incentives for unionization by ensuring that employees' needs are met.

Hints **to Ensure**
Legal Compliance

Union Substitution   The **union substitution (proactive HRM) approach** involves becoming so responsive to employees' needs that there is no incentive for them to unionize. Managers ensure that the treatment employees receive, as well as their pay, benefits, and working conditions, are equal to or better than that in comparable unionized firms. For example, Dofasco, a large steel-manufacturing firm in Hamilton, Ontario, which has used unionized Stelco as a frame of reference over the years, has remained non-union by developing a reputation for fair treatment and concern for employee well-being. Management has taken numerous steps to ensure that the firm lives up to its motto, "Our product is steel. Our strength is people."

Union Suppression   Firms adopt a union suppression approach when there is a desire to avoid a union at all costs. This is a rather high-risk strategy that was prevalent in the early years of the union movement, but is rarely adopted today. One legal tactic to try to prevent a union from gaining a foothold is to make it difficult for a newly certified union to negotiate its first collective agreement, since failure to reach an agreement within a one-year period following certification can lead to automatic decertification in some jurisdictions. This strategy will not be successful in jurisdictions in which a breakdown in first contract negotiations can lead to a collective agreement imposed through arbitration. Union suppression tactics can sometimes backfire. In some jurisdictions, a union may receive automatic certification if management is found guilty of unfair labour practices.

CANADA'S LABOUR LAWS

Canadian labour laws have two general purposes:
1. To provide a common set of rules for fair negotiations.
2. To ensure the protection of the public interest, by preventing the impact of labour disputes from inconveniencing the public.

Jurisdiction

As with other employment-related legislation, primary jurisdiction for labour laws resides with the provinces and territories. Today, provincial and territorial statutes govern approximately 90 percent of labour–management relations. The remaining 10 percent, mainly federal departments, crown corporations and agencies, and businesses engaged in transportation, banking, and communications, are governed by federal labour relations legislation.

One advantage of this system is that there is an opportunity for one jurisdiction to see whether or not a particular legislative change is successful in another jurisdiction before enacting it in its own. The main disadvantage is that ensuring legality across multiple jurisdictions can be very complex, since it is possible for a policy, practice, or procedure to be legal in one jurisdiction, yet illegal in others.

The key federal statute affecting labour–management relations in Canada today is the Canada Labour Code, which applies to all employ-

When public-sector employees strike, they may be ordered back to work, through special legislation, to avoid causing undue public hardship.

ees under federal jurisdiction, except federal civil servants and individuals working in federal agencies, who are covered by the Public Service Staff Relations Act (PSSRA).

The content of the provincial and territorial laws is fairly similar to that of the federal law. Although these laws vary across the country, there are a number of common characteristics in the LR legislation across Canada, which can be summarized as follows:

- Procedures for the certification of a union.
- The requirement that a collective agreement be in force for a minimum of one year.
- Procedures that must be followed by one or both parties before a strike or lockout is legal.
- The prohibition of strikes or lockouts during the life of a collective agreement.
- The requirement that disputes over matters arising from interpretation of the collective agreement be settled by final and binding arbitration.
- Prohibition of certain specified "unfair practices" on the part of labour and management.
- Establishment of a labour relations board or the equivalent.

Labour Relations Boards

Labour Relations Board (LRB) The legally recognized body responsible for interpreting, administering, and enforcing the LR legislation.

Public Service Staff Relations Board (PSSRB)
www.pssrb-crtfp.gc.ca

Ontario Labour Relations Board
www.gov.on.ca/lab/olrb/eng/homeeng.htm

There is a **Labour Relations Board (LRB)** in every Canadian jurisdiction—called the Canada Labour Relations Board in the federal jurisdiction, the Public Service Staff Relations Board (PSSRB) for civil servants, and the Labour Court (with 20 Commissioners) in Quebec. The LRBs are tripartite—composed of representatives of union and management, and a neutral chair or a vice-chair, typically a government representative. They are empowered to interpret, administer, and enforce the Act and to investigate alleged violations. LRBs are more flexible than traditional courts, and their decisions are final and binding.

The LRBs have the power to:

- decide whether a proposed bargaining unit is appropriate for collective bargaining purposes and accept or modify the unit described in the union's application
- decide whether an individual is eligible for union membership and whether or not an employee is a trade union member
- determine whether a collective agreement is in force and whether the parties are bound by it
- investigate allegations of unfair labour practices
- supervise certification elections.

For example, the British Columbia LRB rebuked Wal-Mart in 2003 for interfering with a union certification effort, and ordered that union leaders be given 30 minutes with employees without management present to discuss the benefits of unionization.[5]

Employer and Employee Rights

The labour relations legislation attempts to balance employees' statutory rights to engage in union activities with employers' proprietary and commercial rights. In order to protect employers from interfering with employee rights, managers are prohibited from interfering with and discriminating against employees who are exercising their rights under the LR legislation. Other examples of prohibited unfair labour practices by employers include:[6]

Hints to Ensure Legal Compliance

- Interfering with the employees' right to select the union of their choice for collective bargaining purposes or discriminating against employees for union activity.
- Unilaterally changing the terms of collective agreements or changing or threatening to change the wages and working conditions during certification proceedings or collective bargaining, if the purpose is to undermine the union.
- Refusing to bargain in good faith—that is, failing to make a serious attempt to reach a collective agreement.
- Suspending, discharging, or imposing any penalty on an employee for refusing to perform the duties of another employee who is participating in a legal strike.

Canadian labour laws also place limitations on the conduct of labour unions. Unfair labour practices by unions include:

- Attempting to persuade an employee to become or continue to be a union member, at the workplace, during working hours, unless employer consent has been obtained.
- Refusing to bargain in good faith.
- Intimidating or coercing employees to become or remain members of the union.
- Failing to provide fair representation for all employees in the bargaining unit.
- Calling or authorizing an unlawful strike, or threatening to do so, or disciplining members who refuse to participate in an unlawful strike.

THE LABOUR MOVEMENT IN CANADA TODAY

business unionism The activities of labour unions focusing on economic and welfare issues, including pay and benefits, job security, and working conditions.

The primary goal of the labour unions active in Canada is to obtain economic benefits and improved treatment for their members. It may involve lobbying for legislative changes pertaining to these issues. This union philosophy, with its emphasis on economic and welfare goals, has become known as **business unionism**. This term acknowledges the fact that unions can only survive if they deliver necessary services to members in a businesslike manner.[7]

Unions strive to ensure *job security* for their members in layoff or termination situations, as well as protection against unjust treatment such as arbitrary termination. They also provide job security by lobbying for legislative changes, such as increased notice requirements in large-scale layoff situations; helping to establish the rules governing the work environment; and resisting actions that might result in loss of members' work, such as increased use of part-time workers. Unions protect the job security of members with the longest service by negotiating seniority provisions requiring that major HR decisions, such as transfers, promotions, layoffs, and recalls, be based on seniority.

The goal of attaining *improved economic conditions* for their members is pursued by negotiating higher wages and benefits improvements. Unions have successfully negotiated *better working conditions* for their members, and have been instrumental in convincing politicians of the need for comprehensive health and safety legislation. The results of such efforts include shorter workweeks, safer working conditions, longer breaks, and voluntary rather than compulsory overtime. Recently, unions have been adding work–life balance demands to the bargaining table.[8]

Most unions today also become involved in broader political and social issues affecting their members. Activities aimed at influencing government economic and social policies are known as **social (reform) unionism**. Social unionism involves lobbying and speaking out on proposed legislative reforms, such as the introduction of employment equity legislation or amendments to LR acts.

Achieving the objectives of social and business unionism may present unions with multiple, and sometimes conflicting, demands. For example, negotiating a significant pay increase may result in some members being laid off. Supporting more aggressive health and safety legislation may result in improved working conditions, but significant employer costs, such that less money is available for improvements in pay or benefits.[9] Determining the appropriate course of action when confronted with such conflicting demands is a source of much debate among bargaining unit members.

Types of Unions

The labour unions in Canada can be divided according to (a) type of worker eligible for membership, (b) geographical scope, and (c) labour congress affiliation.

Types of Worker Eligible for Membership
All of the early trade unions in Canada were **craft unions**—associations of persons performing a certain type of skill or trade (e.g., carpenters or bricklayers). Examples include the United Brotherhood of Carpenters and Joiners of America, the British Columbia Teachers' Federation, and the Ontario Nurses' Association. An **industrial union** is a labour organization comprising all of the workers eligible for union membership in a particular company or industry, irrespective of the type of work performed.

There is a long history of membership competition between craft and industrial unions. Over time, industrial unions started representing all workers eligible for union membership in a particular company or industry, including skilled tradespersons. The Canadian Union of Postal Workers is an example of an industrial union, as is the Communications, Energy and Paperworkers Union of Canada. While the distinction between craft and industrial unions still exists, technological changes and increasing competition for members have blurred it. Although there are still some craft unions with members possessing a particular skill or "craft," many craft unions now represent all of the workers in a plant.

Geographic Scope
Labour unions that charter branches in both Canada and the United States are known as *international unions*. Such unions have their

---

social (reform) unionism
Activities of unions directed at furthering the interests of their members by influencing the social and economic policies of governments at all levels, such as speaking out on proposed legislative reforms.

craft union Traditionally, a labour organization representing workers practising the same craft or trade, such as carpentry or plumbing.

industrial union Traditionally, a labour organization representing unskilled and semiskilled workers in a particular organization or industry, irrespective of the type of work performed. Over time, the term came to refer to a labour organization representing all workers eligible for union membership in a particular company or industry, including skilled tradespersons.

Construction Labour Relations
www.clra.org

head office in the United States, the country in which the majority of their members work and reside. Due to their larger membership base, international unions are generally the strongest financially. In recent years, Canadian branches have been breaking away from the parent unions and forming their own Canadian unions, a trend known as **succession**. The most dramatic breakaway occurred in 1985, when the Canadian Auto Workers Union (CAW) separated from its American parent, the United Auto Workers (UAW).

Labour unions that charter branches in Canada only and have their head office in this country are known as *national unions*. As with international unions, national unions provide a wide range of services to their branches (known as "locals"), including assistance with organizing activities, negotiations, grievance handling, arbitration, and strikes. Some national unions, such as the CAW, actually bargain an industry-wide contract on behalf of their locals. Other examples of national unions include the Canadian Union of Public Employees (CUPE) and the Public Service Alliance of Canada. As illustrated in **Table 16.1**, about 66 percent of union members in Canada belong to national unions, and 29 percent to international unions. This is a complete reversal of the situation of about 30 years ago, when only 30 percent of union members belonged to national unions.

There are two types of labour unions in Canada that are purely local in geographical scope. The first is the *independent local union*, which is not affiliated

succession The act of a Canadian branch of an international union breaking away from the parent union and forming its own Canadian union.

International Labour News
www.labourstart.org

TABLE 16.1   Union Membership by Type of Union and Affiliation, 2002

Type and Affiliation	Number of Unions	Number of Locals	Membership Number	Membership Percent
International Unions	**46**	**3 233**	**1 196 990**	**28.7**
AFL–CIO/CLC	39	3 155	1 171 400	28.1
AFL–CIO only	4	65	24 540	0.6
Unaffiliated unions	3	13	1 050	0.0†
National Unions	**220**	**13 368**	**2 772 105**	**66.4**
CLC	64	7 441	1 865 565	44.7
CSN	10	2 481	272 600	6.5
CEQ	15	381	104 720	2.5
CCU	7	27	9 670	0.2
CSD	2	93	11 120	0.3
Unaffiliated unions	122	2 945	507 430	12.2
Directly Chartered Unions	**316**	**50 430**		**1.2**
CSD	309	50 000		1.2
CLC	7	430		0.0†
Independent Local Organizations	**304**	**154 475**		**3.7**
Total	886	16 601	4 174 000	100.0

Note: Due to rounding, sums may not always equal totals. † Less than 0.1 percent.

Source: Human Resources Development Canada, Workplace Information Directorate, as reproduced in *Workplace Gazette* (Fall 2002), p. 44. Reproduced with the permission of the Minister of Public Works and Government Services Canada, 2004.

with any other labour organization. The second type is a *directly chartered local union* that has been organized by and received its charter directly from the Canadian Labour Congress. Such locals are not part of a national or international union. As shown in Table 16.1, membership in independent local unions and directly chartered local unions is very small.

Labour Congress Affiliation   A third way of distinguishing between labour unions is according to affiliation with one or another central labour organization. These central organizations include:

1. *Canadian Labour Congress (CLC).* As illustrated in **Table 16.2,** the CLC is the major central labour organization in Canada, and has the largest number of affiliated union members. Most international and national unions belong, and all directly chartered local unions, local/district labour councils, and provincial/territorial federations of labour are affiliated with the CLC. The CLC, the structure of which is illustrated in **Figure 16.1,** is financed through dues based on membership numbers.

   The purpose of the CLC is primarily political: to act as the spokesperson for organized labour throughout Canada, particularly in Ottawa. The CLC also ensures that the provincial/territorial federations of labour and local/district labour councils exert political influence at the provincial and local levels, respectively, and represents the Canadian labour movement internationally. Another role of the CLC is to monitor the behaviour of its member organizations. In its "watchdog" role, the CLC imposed sanctions on the CAW in 2000, when the CAW was found guilty of raiding (stealing dues-paying members) from another CLC member, U.S.-based SEIU, in its bid to represent 30 000 Ontario Jockey Club workers—an act in violation of the CLC's constitution.[10]

TABLE 16.2   Union Membership by Congress Affiliation, 2002

Congress Affiliation	Membership Number	Percent
CLC	**3 037 395**	**72.8**
AFL–CIO/CLC	1 171 400	28.1
CLC only	1 865 995	44.7
CSN	**272 600**	**6.5**
AFL–CIO only	**24 540**	**0.6**
CSQ	**104 720**	**2.5**
CSD	**62 120**	**1.5**
CCU	**9 670**	**0.2**
Unaffiliated International Unions	**1 050**	**0.0†**
Unaffiliated National Unions	**507 430**	**12.2**
Independent Local Organizations	**154 475**	**3.7**
Total	**4 174 000**	**100.0**

Note: Due to rounding, sums may not always equal totals. † Less than 0.1 percent.

Source: Human Resources Development Canada, Workplace Information Directorate, as reproduced in *Workplace Gazette* (Fall 2002), p. 41. Reproduced with the permission of the Minister of Public Works and Government Services Canada, 2004.

FIGURE 16.1   Structure of the Canadian Labour Congress

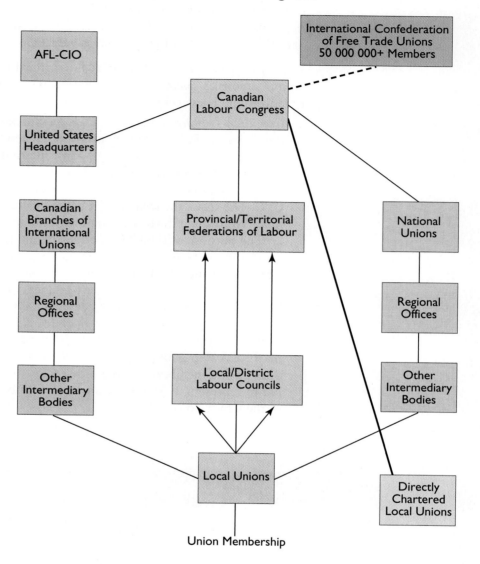

2. *Confédération des syndicats nationaux (CSN)*—in English, Confederation of National Trade Unions (CNTU). This organization is the Quebec counterpart of the CLC.

3. *American Federation of Labor—Congress of Industrial Organizations (AFL-CIO).* The American counterpart of the CLC is the AFL–CIO. Although the two organizations operate independently, since most international unions in the CLC are also members of the AFL–CIO, a certain degree of common interest exists.

Structure and Functions

Other than those unions that are strictly local in geographic scope, most unions have central offices in each province/territory in which they have members.

They may also have regional offices in major metropolitan centres, with various departments, as well as a number of geographically dispersed smaller branches, called *locals*. The central and/or regional office staff assist locals with organizing activities, applications for certification, negotiations, grievances, and strike activities, as the need arises.

local The basic unit of the labour union movement in Canada, formed in a particular plant or locality.

grass-roots unionism A term referring to the fact that the Canadian labour movement tends to be driven from the bottom up, meaning that union locals tend to have a high degree of autonomy.

The basic unit of the labour union movement in Canada is the **local,** formed in a particular plant or locality. For HR managers and front-line supervisors, the union locals are generally the most important part of the union structure, due to Canada's system of **grass-roots unionism** with a high degree of local autonomy or decentralization. Each local has its own constitution, draws up its own bylaws, and has responsibility for obtaining new members, handling grievances, collective bargaining, and organizing recreational activities. An executive committee—headed by a president and vice-president, and sometimes a business agent—usually exercises power. As illustrated in **Figure 16.2**, there are generally a number of committees, each of which is assigned responsibility for specific activities.

FIGURE **16.2**   Structure of a Typical Union Local

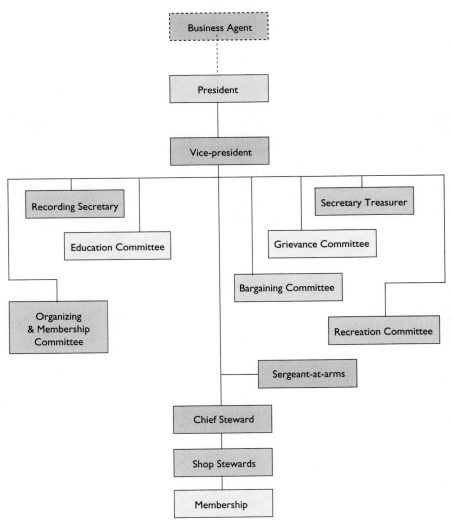

union steward A union member elected by workers in a particular department or area of a firm to act as their union representative.

Key players within the local are the elected officials known as **union stewards,** who are responsible for representing the interests and protecting the rights of bargaining unit employees in their department or area. Functions performed by such stewards include resolving complaints and grievances; informing members about union policies and meetings; and recruiting new members. The senior steward for a particular area or division is known as the *chief steward.* In smaller locals, all executive positions are filled on a voluntary part-time basis by union members working at their regular jobs, who are elected by members of the local for a specified term of office. In larger locals, there is often a full-time **business agent,** whose salary is paid by the local or the national/international office.

business agent A full-time, elected or appointed, paid official of a union local, whose duties involve handling grievances and helping to enforce the terms of the collective agreement.

Membership Trends

As shown in **Table 16.3,** the number of persons belonging to labour unions fluctuated between 1989 and 2002, reaching an all-time high in 2002, when union membership stood at 4 174 000, representing 25.7 percent of the civilian labour force and 31.1 percent of non-agricultural paid workers. However, the membership in unions as a percentage of the civilian labour force has been decreasing since 1994. This decline has not been dramatic as in the United States. In 2002, organized labour as a share of the workforce in the U.S. was less than 15 percent of all non-agricultural paid workers, down from a peak of about 34 percent in 1955.[11] Although Canada's unionization rate is more than twice that of

TABLE 16.3   Union Membership in Canada, 1989–2002

Year	Union Membership (thousands)	Civilian Labour Force (thousands)	Total Non-Agricultural Paid Workers (thousands)	Union Membership as a Percentage of Civilian Labour Force	Union Membership as a Percentage of Non-Agricultural Paid Workers
1989	3 944	13 779	11 340	28.6	34.8
1990	4 031	14 047	11 598	28.7	34.8
1991	4 068	14 241	11 679	28.6	34.8
1992	4 089	14 330	11 414	28.5	35.8
1993	4 071	14 362	11 303	28.3	36.0
1994	4 078	14 505	11 310	28.1	36.1
1995	4 003	14 627	11 526	27.4	34.7
1996	4 033	14 750	11 764	27.3	34.3
1997	4 074	14 900	11 802	27.3	34.5
1998	3 938	15 153	12 031	26.0	32.7
1999	4 010	15 418	12 295	26.0	32.6
2000	4 058	15 721	12 707	25.8	31.9
2001	4 111	15 999	13 146	25.7	31.3
2002	4 174	16 242	13 414	25.7	31.1

Note: Labour Force and non-agricultural paid employment data shown for each year are annual averages of the preceding year; data for union membership are as of January of the years shown.

Source: Adapted from the Statistics Canada Labour Force Survey, Labour Statistics Division.

the U.S., it is small in comparison to many European nations such as Iceland (83.3 percent), Sweden (81.9 percent), and Denmark (81.8 percent).[12]

Various factors are responsible for membership decline, including a dramatic increase in service-sector and white-collar jobs, combined with a decrease in employment opportunities in the industries that have traditionally been highly unionized, such as manufacturing. More effective HR practices in non-unionized firms are another contributing factor, as is the major restructuring in firms over the past 10 years, which has resulted in the loss of thousands of jobs.[13] In order to offset these losses, some unions have started organizing activities in areas outside their traditional field. For instance, the United Steelworkers recently organized clerical workers at the University of Toronto, and the International Association of Machinists and Aerospace Workers now represents individuals working in organizations ranging from pulp and paper mills to office furniture manufacturing plants, school boards and transit commissions.[14] Unions are also searching for new ways to meet the needs of members and potential members, a topic discussed in more detail in the HR.Net box.

Not all industries and sectors have the same degree of unionization. Sectors that are highly unionized include education, utilities, public administration, and health care. The agriculture, professional, scientific and technical, and accommodation and food sectors have the lowest rates of unionization.[15] As shown in **Figure 16.3**, there are also differences in the degree of unionization in various parts of Canada. Another important development that has had significant implications for unions is the change in membership demographics. While the unionization of women has historically tended to be less than that of men, this trend has reversed over the last decade. Unions have worked hard to increase female membership, as outlined in the Workforce Diversity box.

In 2002, for the first time, the unionization rate for women (30.2 percent) was virtually the same as for men (30.3 percent).[16] While this increase was mainly due to rapid growth in the highly unionized public and quasi-public sectors in the 1990s, this trend also reflects the movement of women into traditionally male-dominated jobs, and the increasing unionization of part-time and service-sector workers.[17] Accompanying this growth in female membership has

HR.NET

Computers Help Union Leaders to Meet Changing Member Needs

Unions are now using computer technology to meet the changing needs of members and potential members. The Canadian Union of Public Employees (CUPE) uses its Web site (www.cupe.ca) to allow members to download forms, find information regarding collective agreements and bargaining, and change the personal information that the union has about them. CUPE has also eliminated much of the paper-based communication with its members by providing chat rooms, message boards, and e-mail lists for its membership.

The Web site is not only used for communication between the union and its membership. Online Actions is a feature where members can send e-mail to employers, Members of Parliament, or provincial government representatives. With no special software or technical knowledge required, the features are easy to use, and initiators can see how many people have sent letters and easily follow-up information to those who request it. The CUPE national site also hosts Web sites for its division, locals, councils, and committees.

Source: Adapted from "Online Actions." Canadian Union of Public Employees (CUPE). www.cupe.ca. Reprinted with the permission of CUPE.

FIGURE 16.3   Percentage of the Workforce in a Union, by Province

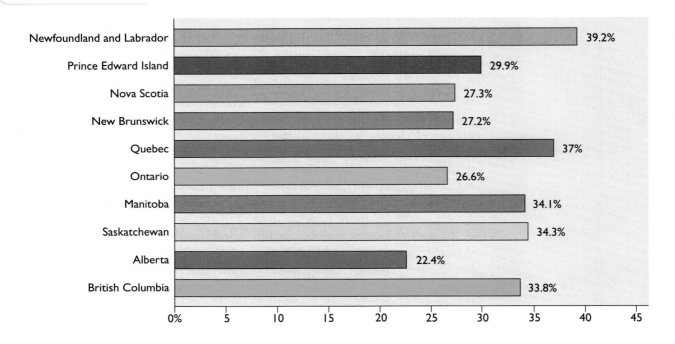

Source: Workplace Gazette (Fall 2002), p. 40. Reproduced with the permission of the Minister of Public Works and Government Services Canada, 2004.

WORKFORCE DIVERSITY

Unions Seek More Women Members

In the spring of 2002, the Canadian Labour Congress embarked on a campaign to double the number of unionized women in Canada in just three years. While working men and women have nearly equal unionization rates (34 and 32 percent respectively), women are much more likely to work temporary, part-time, and low-wage jobs, and therefore a larger number of women would gain from union membership. The median wage is about $17 000 for women and more than $28 600 for men. "This campaign isn't about unions needing more women. It is about more women needing unions," said Nancy Riche, secretary-treasurer of the Canadian Labour Congress.

Source: "Labour Seeks More Women Members," *Canadian HR Reporter* (April 22, 2002), p. 2. Reproduced by permission of *Canadian HR Reporter*, Carswell, One Corporate Plaza, 2075 Kennedy Road, Scarborough, ON M1T 3V4.

been a shift in bargaining priorities. Unions have begun to put more emphasis on pay and employment equity, and issues pertaining to the balancing of work and family responsibilities, such as family-related leaves and childcare.

The two largest unions in Canada in 2002 represented public-sector employees: CUPE and the National Union of Public and General Employees (NUPGE). The largest union representing federal sector employees, and seventh largest union in Canada, was the Public Service Alliance of Canada (PSAC). **Table 16.4** lists the 15 largest unions in Canada, as of 2002.

TABLE 16.4	The 15 Largest Unions in Canada, 2002	
Ranking (Size)	Union Organization	Membership (thousands)
1	Canadian Union of Public Employees—CUPE	521.6
2	National Union of Public and General Employees—NUPGE	325.0
	National Automobile, Aerospace, Transportation and General Workers Union of Canada—CAW-Canada	238.0
4	United Food and Commercial Workers International Union—UFCW	220.0
5	United Steelworkers of America—USWA	180.0
6	Communications, Energy and Paperworkers Union of Canada—CEP	150.0
7	Public Service Alliance of Canada—PSAC	150.0
8	International Brotherhood of Teamsters—IBT	102.0
9	Fédération de la santé et des services sociaux—FSSS	101.3
10	Service Employees International Union, Canada—SEIUC	90.0
11	Laborers' International Union of North America—LIUNA	72.5
12	Fédération des syndicats de l'enseignement—FSE	67.6
13	Elementary Teachers' Federation of Ontario—ETFO	63.5
14	International Brotherhood of Electrical Workers—IBEW	54.8
15	United Brotherhood of Carpenters and Joiners of America—UBC	53.0

Source: Workplace Gazette (Fall 2002), p. 40. Reproduced with the permission of the Minister of Public Works and Government Services Canada, 2004.

Current Challenges to the Canadian Labour Movement

As with employers, global competition and technological advances pose challenges for the union movement. Unions also have to deal with challenges pertaining to the privatization and the unionization of white-collar employees, managers, and professionals; and innovative work practices that have the potential to decrease employee interest in unionization.

Global Competition and Technological Change   Increased global competition and massive importation of consumer electronics, cars, clothing, textiles, and shoes has led to job losses for Canadian union members.[18] Furthermore, foreign subsidiaries of Canadian-owned corporations, have been accused by union leaders of deliberately trying to decrease union membership by exporting Canadian jobs to plants offshore.[19] Canadian unions were highly opposed to NAFTA, claiming that Canadian jobs would be lost to low-wage Mexican workers, as well as to the anti-union environment that exists in many U.S. states. Some unions have taken more direct action. The United Electrical Workers, for example, subsidized organizers at Mexican plants of U.S.-owned General Electric company.[20]

Technological advances pose another challenge to unions.[21] Such advances have decreased the effectiveness of strikes in some sectors, because highly automated organizations can remain fully operational with minimal staffing levels during work stoppages. Even more significant is the fact that improvements in computer technology have lowered the demand for blue-collar workers, and resulted in a decline in union membership in the auto, steel, and other manufacturing industries. E-commerce work (such as processing credit card claims) is highly portable, and can be shifted, almost literally, at the touch of a button from one centre to another—even overseas. To deal with such threats, some unions have negotiated collective agreement protection for workers whose skills are threatened by technological obsolescence.

Privatization and the Unionization of White-Collar Employees

In the past, many white-collar employees tended to identify more with owners or managers than with their blue-collar colleagues, often enjoying certain privileges and status symbols available to salaried employees only. Because the improvements in pay, benefits, and working conditions that were negotiated by the union representing their blue-collar co-workers were often extended to them as a matter of course, there was little perceived need to unionize. In recent years, however, the growth in the size of many organizations has tended to distance them from management, which has made unionization more attractive. Increasing difficulties in attempting to resolve grievances, combined with a lack of job security related to downsizing in all sectors, as well as the privatization of services ranging from hydro to home care, has also led to increased interest in unionization among white-collar workers.[22]

This McDonald's, in Squamish, B.C., was the first to unionize of the chain's more than 15 000 North American outlets.

At the same time that white-collar employees began to experience increased interest in unionization, union leaders came to realize that organizing such employees was a key to their ongoing viability and survival, and started to increase their efforts to organize white-collar employees. Service-oriented organizations, such as insurance agencies, banks, retail stores, fast-food chains, and government agencies have been targeted for organizing campaigns. Even small businesses are being organized. To attract white-collar employees, unions are now focusing more on work–family issues. Unions are also capitalizing on the health and safety risks associated with white-collar jobs, such as the effects of working at video display terminals and the potential for repetitive strain injury.

Another group that has been targeted for unionization includes managers and professionals, whose job security has been seriously threatened by privatization and extensive downsizing in both public- and private-sector organizations. According to Statistics Canada, more than 9 percent of employees in management positions are union members, and more than 12 percent of non-unionized managers are covered by a collective agreement.[23] More and more statistics are showing that employees in professional jobs, such as management and finance, are seeking union representation due to concerns over compensation, increases in workload, and communication problems with employers. This was evident when more than three-quarters of the 8000 managers at Bell Canada expressed interest in joining a union, and subsequently approached the Communication, Energy and Paperworkers' Union of Canada (CEP) to seek certification in late 2000.[24]

Innovative Workplace Practices

In workplaces in which employees participate in decision making, have a high degree of autonomy and little supervision, and are paid based on their performance or the knowledge/skills they have attained, there may be less perceived need for a union.[25] Some individuals argue that such innovative workplace practices as semi-autonomous work teams, skill-based pay, profit sharing, and employee stock ownership plans undermine union power by co-opting employees and aligning employee interests with those of management.[26] On the other hand, in workplaces in which the unions have supported such changes, the end result may be better communication and more cooperation, a win–win situation.[27]

THE LABOUR RELATIONS PROCESS

As illustrated in **Figure 16.4**, the labour relations (LR) process consists of five steps, the first three of which will be described next. The last two are the focus of Chapter 17.

Step One: Employees Seek Collective Representation

A tremendous amount of time and money have been spent trying to analyze why workers unionize, and many theories have been proposed. It has become apparent that there is no simple answer, partly because each individual may become interested in unionizing for very unique reasons.

FIGURE 16.4   An Overview of the Labour Relations Process.

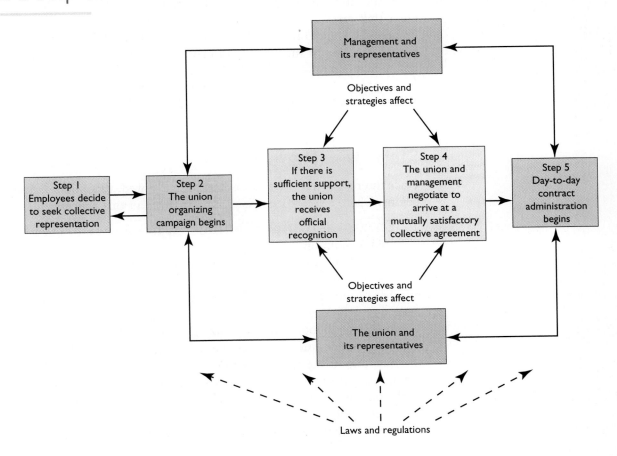

Research

Insight   ▷

Based on numerous research studies, however, there are a number of factors that can clearly be linked to the desire to unionize:[28]

- job dissatisfaction, especially with pay, benefits, and working conditions
- lack of job security
- unfair or biased administration of policies and practices
- perceived inequities in pay
- lack of opportunity for advancement
- lack of a desired amount of influence or participation in work-related decisions
- the belief that unions can be effective in improving pay and working conditions.

Both union members and nonmembers have their highest expectations of union performance regarding the "bread and butter" issues of collective bargaining.[29] Given the fact that unionized employees in Canada earn 8 percent more than non-unionized workers, these expectations seem quite justifiable.[30] While the difference in average earnings is not entirely a reflection of unionization, being unionized does have an impact. Being a union member also has an impact on female workers' ability to achieve pay equity. On average, full-time female unionized workers earned 90 percent of the hourly wages of their male counterparts, and those working part-time earned 9 percent *more than* their male counterparts.[31]

It should be pointed out, however, that research studies have made it quite clear that dissatisfaction alone will not lead to unionization. More important seems to be the employees' belief that it is only through unity that they can get a fair share of the "pie" and protect themselves from the arbitrary whims of management. *In other words, it is only when workers are dissatisfied and believe that they are without the ability to change the factors causing dissatisfaction, except through collective action, that they become interested in unionizing.*[32]

Step Two: The Union Organizing Campaign

Once interest in joining a union has been aroused, the union organizing process begins. There are five steps typically involved in this process:

1. Employee/Union Contact   A formal organizing campaign may be initiated by a union organizer or by employees acting on their own behalf. Most organizing campaigns are begun by employees who get in touch with an existing union.[33] However, large unions such as the CAW and the Teamsters, have a number of *union organizers* on staff, who are responsible for identifying organizing opportunities and launching organizing campaigns. For example, the CEP began a Nova Scotia-wide organizing blitz in 2002, following success in both New Brunswick and Newfoundland during the previous two years, including the first organizing of Canadian offshore oil rig workers at the Hibernia platform.[34] No matter how large or sophisticated a union's organizing department is, the outcome of an organizing campaign depends primarily on the employees. Even the most experienced organizers find it difficult to organize a truly well-managed, successful organization.

Promoting the benefits of unionization.

Regardless of how the contact is initiated, the first step begins when employees and union officials make contact and explore the possibility of unionization. During these discussions, employees investigate the advantages of union representation, and the union officials start to gather information about the employees' sources of dissatisfaction, to see if a case can be built in support of the union.

Since organizing campaigns can be expensive, union leaders carefully evaluate their chances of success and the possible benefits to be gained from their efforts. Important in this evaluation is the employer's vulnerability to unionization.[35] Union leaders also consider the effect that allowing the firm to remain non-union might have on their strength in the community. A non-union employer, for example, can hinder a union's efforts to standardize employment conditions within an industry or geographic area, as well as weaken the union's bargaining power with employers that it has successfully organized.

Research
Insight ▷

A recent survey of 205 Canadian unions reported a total of 242 staff working full-time on organizing and recruitment efforts, and 42 percent indicated that they have specific organizing or recruitment targets. Less than one-half (44.8 percent) reported the presence of a person who has overall responsibility for organizing and recruiting new members. While the public service sector remains the highest priority in current attempts to organize new members (45.8 percent), 30.8 percent indicated that the private sector was a very high priority for organization and recruitment efforts.[36]

2. Initial Organizational Meeting

Once convinced that the expense of an organizing campaign is justified, the union organizer generally schedules an initial meeting with the individuals who first expressed an interest in unionization and co-workers who subsequently expressed their support. The aim is to identify employees who would be willing to help the organizer direct the campaign.

3. Formation of an In-house Organizing Committee

A key step in the success of an organizing campaign is the formation of an in-house organizing committee, a group of employees, dedicated to the goal of unionization, who are willing to assist the union organizer. The role of such volunteers is to devote the time and effort necessary to contact employees, present the case for unionization, and sign members up.

4. The Organizing Campaign

Once the committee is formed, the union organizing campaign begins. First, the members gather together information about the firm—its products, customers, finances, employees, and so on—and information about other firms in the community that employ the same types of workers. Once these data have been collected, analyzed, and discussed, the committee can start to plan the most effective type of appeal to convince employees of the benefits of unionization. The next step in the campaign generally involves obtaining an accurate, up-to-date list of all employees that is used to record the responses received to membership solicitations and keep track of the level of support among the eligible employees. Then the committee members begin contacting employees; usually those who are believed to favour unionization are approached first.

Some unions are now harnessing the power of the Web and making this initial contact online. For example, the Hotel, Restaurant and Culinary Employees and Bartenders Union, Local 40 in British Columbia has an organizing Web site that informs those who log on that employees have legal rights, and that joining a union will enhance their rights. It urges that any decision about whether or not to join a union be based on facts. The site is designed to answer some common questions that are asked during an organizing campaign, and urges people to browse through the site for more information. And of course, each person who logs on is urged to join their union! The site includes a link to an organizing brochure, entitled "Be Wise ... Organize," that contains a ten-item questionnaire for those who log on to rate their employer as good, average, or "you need a union." It explains the benefits of joining a union, explains what happens in an organizing campaign, and stresses that all inquiries made to the union are kept strictly confidential.[37]

authorization card A card signed by an employee that indicates his or her willingness to have the union act as his or her representative for purposes of collective bargaining.

Whether in person, by mail, or online, the aim of this contact is to encourage as many employees as possible to sign an **authorization card** that indicates their willingness to be represented by the union in question in collective bargaining with their employer. Once a signed authorization card has been obtained, the union canvasser turns it over to the union office or organizer. The number of signed cards is typically kept a closely guarded secret until a substantial number of eligible employees have been signed up.

5. The Outcome   There are a number of possible outcomes to a unionization campaign, including rejection by the majority of eligible employees. In order for a union to become the bargaining unit for a group of employees, it must be certified by an LRB or receive official recognition from the employer.

Signs of Organizing Activity   A firm is susceptible to unionization if there has been a sudden increase in unionization activity in the community or industry; major changes are being planned that will impact the size of the workforce, such as a merger or acquisition; or there have been recent legislative changes that make it easier to unionize. As mentioned earlier, however, even in these circumstances, a union rarely succeeds in organizing a well-managed firm in which employees are treated fairly. On the other hand, if the organization's wages and benefits have fallen behind industry or community averages, employees feel that their complaints have been and/or will be ignored, and there is evidence of low job satisfaction (such as high rates of absenteeism and turnover), unionization is a definite possibility.

Supervisors or small-business owners who suspect that a unionization attempt may be underway should watch for a number of the following signs:[38]

Tips for the Front Line

- disappearance of employee lists or directories
- more inquiries than usual about benefits, wages, promotions, and other HR policies and procedures
- questions about their opinions of unions
- an increase in the number or nature of employee complaints or grievances
- a change in the number, composition, and size of informal groups at lunch and coffee breaks

- the sudden popularity of certain employees (especially if they are the informal leaders)
- the sudden cessation of employee conversation when a member of management approaches or an obvious change in employees' behaviour toward members of management, expressed either formally or informally
- the appearance of strangers in the parking lot
- the distribution of cards or flyers or pro-union buttons.

When such signs are present, it does not mean that an organizing campaign is definitely underway. Managers and small business owners should keep their eyes and ears open to determine if their suspicions are justified, but must be extremely careful not to engage in any unfair practices. Because of their positions of authority, even a friendly inquiry about unionization activities may be perceived as intimidation by employees. For this reason, asking employees any direct questions on the subject is not recommended.

Employer Response to an Organizing Campaign

Once it is evident that an organizing campaign is underway, if the employer prefers that the group seeking unionization retain its non-union status, a careful campaign is usually mounted to counteract the union drive. Normally, HR department staff members head up the campaign, although they may be assisted by a consultant or labour lawyer.

Absolutely critical to the success of a company's counter-campaign is supervisory training. Supervisors need to be informed about what they can and cannot do or say during the organizing campaign, to ensure that they do not violate LR legislation, and avoid actions that might inadvertently provide fuel for the union's campaign. When a supervisor commits an unfair labour practice, it can result in a lawsuit or even in automatic certification of the union. Even when management actions are legal, union leaders may claim credit for any new policies or practices that are favourable to employees.

When planning a counter-campaign, data collection is essential. As much information about the union as possible should be obtained, pertaining to dues, strike record, salaries of officers, and any other relevant facts that might cause employees to question the benefits of unionization. Armed with this detailed information, communication strategies can be planned, with the aim of reminding employees about the company's good points, pointing out disadvantages of unionization, and refuting any misleading union claims. The employer's case for remaining non-union should be presented in a factual, honest, and straightforward manner.

Answering questions is an important part of an effective counter-campaign. A good strategy is to set up an "information line," so that supervisors and employees can get quick answers to questions. Other communication strategies include preparing speeches outlining the benefits of remaining non-union, writing factual articles for the company newsletter, or preparing a letter to send to the home of each employee.

Under the law, employers are granted the right to do the following:

- Express their views and opinions regarding unions.
- State their position regarding the desirability of remaining non-union.

Labour Management Services (Ontario)
www.gov.on.ca/lab/lms/lmse.htm

Hints to Ensure Legal Compliance

Hints to Ensure Legal Compliance

- Prohibit distribution of union literature on their own property on company time.
- Increase wages, make promotions, and take other HR actions, as long as they would do so in the normal course of business. In most jurisdictions, however, once an application for certification is received by the LRB, wages, benefits, and working conditions are frozen until the application is dealt with.
- Assemble employees during working hours to state the company's position, as long as employees are advised of the purpose of the meeting in advance, attendance is optional, and threats and promises are avoided (employers have no obligation to give the union the same opportunity).

Employers must ensure that they do *not*:

- hold "captive audience" speeches (where employee attendance is mandatory)
- question employees about union activities
- increase wages and benefits in a manner that could be perceived as a bribe for remaining non-union
- use coercion, intimidation, threats, promises, or undue influence
- refuse to answer legitimate employee questions about the impact of unionization.

> ### An Ethical Dilemma
>
> Knowing that head office plans to close the facility should a unionization bid be successful, how should you, as a manager, respond to inquiries from employees about the impact of a union?

The distinction between expressing one's views and exerting undue influence is not always clear, and many of the cases that come before the LRBs pertaining to organizing campaigns revolve around this issue. Where there is evidence of strong anti-union propaganda, for example, what might ordinarily appear to be innocent language or actions could be viewed by the Board as less than benign.[39] The highly publicized Wal-Mart case provides an excellent example of the fine line that an employer must walk:[40]

> The case arose out of a 1996 certification drive by the United Steelworkers of America at a Wal-Mart store in Windsor, Ontario. After obtaining 91 authorization cards from the 205 staff at the store, the union filed for certification. Based on the level of membership support indicated, the Board ordered that a certification vote be held. At the vote, the union was rejected by a margin of 151 to 43. The union subsequently alleged that the employer's conduct prior to the vote constituted unfair practices that unlawfully influenced the outcome of the election and was sufficiently serious to justify disregarding the results of the vote and granting automatic certification to the union.

After hearing the evidence, the LRB concluded that the union should succeed and certified the Steelworkers as the bargaining agent. Factors influencing the Board's decision included the fact that the company allowed an anti-union employee to make a speech at a company meeting, which, in the Board's opinion, contained the employee's belief that Wal-Mart would not stand for a union and that a union would harm job security. They also concluded that five managers who circulated throughout the store for a number of days exerted a subtle form of intimidation, since it appeared to be an effort to identify union supporters. Also, the LRB found that despite the company's open communication policy, management refused to answer the question as to whether the Wal-Mart store would close if it was unionized, which was perceived by the Board to be a subtle, but intentional, threat to employee job security.

Step Three: Union Recognition

There are three basic ways in which a union can obtain recognition as a bargaining unit for a group of workers: (1) voluntary recognition, (2) the regular certification process, and (3) a pre-hearing vote. Bargaining rights can also be terminated in various ways.

Voluntary Recognition
An employer in every Canadian jurisdiction, except Quebec, can voluntarily recognize a union as the bargaining agent for a group of its employees, if it considers the bargaining unit to be appropriate and believes that the majority of employees, without having been subjected to undue pressure, have indicated their desire to be represented by that union. The voluntary recognition process is an alternative to certification and does not require the involvement of a third party. Although fairly rare, it may occur if an employer has adopted a union acceptance strategy, and believes that representation by that union is what the employees desire.

certification The procedure whereby a labour union obtains a certificate from the relevant LRB declaring that the union is the exclusive bargaining agent for a defined group of employees in a bargaining unit that the Board considers appropriate for collective bargaining purposes.

Regular Certification
While all jurisdictions differ slightly in their union **certification** procedure, the norm is for unions to present evidence of at least a minimum level of membership support for a bargaining unit that they have defined, in the form of signed authorization cards, to the appropriate LRB, along with an application for certification. The minimum level of support required to apply for certification varies by jurisdiction, from 25 percent of the bargaining unit in Saskatchewan to 65 percent in Manitoba.[41] The LRB then determines whether the bargaining unit defined by the union is appropriate for collective bargaining purposes.

In most jurisdictions, LRBs can grant *automatic certification*, which means certification without a vote, if the applicant union can demonstrate that it has a high enough level of support for the proposed bargaining unit (generally 50 or 55 percent). Automatic certification may also be granted in some jurisdictions if the employer has engaged in unfair practices. If the level of support is not sufficient for automatic certification, but is above a specified minimum level (between 25 and 45 percent, depending on jurisdiction), the LRB will order and supervise a **representation vote**.[42] Eligible employees have the opportunity to cast a secret ballot, indicating whether or not they wish the union to be certified. In some jurisdictions, to gain certification, the voting results must indicate that *more than 50 percent of the potential bargaining unit members* are in support of the union. In other jurisdictions, the standard is the support of *more than 50 percent of those voting*.[43] If the union loses, another election cannot be held among the same employees for at least one year. Only about 20 percent of certifications are the result of a vote—roughly four out of five certifications are the result of authorization cards alone.[44]

representation vote A vote conducted by the LRB in which employees in the bargaining unit indicate, by secret ballot, whether or not they wish to be represented, or continue to be represented, by a labour union.

pre-hearing vote An alternative mechanism for certification, used in situations in which there is evidence of irregularities early in the organizing campaign, such as unfair management practices.

Pre-hearing Votes
In most jurisdictions, a **pre-hearing vote** may be conducted where there is evidence of irregularities early in an organizing campaign, such as an employer's use of unfair labour practices. In such a case, the LRB may order a vote prior to holding a hearing to determine the composition of the bargaining unit. The intent is to determine the level of support for the union as quickly as possible, before the employer's intimidation tactics can taint the outcome. The ballot box is then sealed until the Board determines whether the bargaining unit is appropriate and, if so, which employees are eligible for membership. If the bargaining unit is deemed appropriate by the LRB, only the

votes of potential bargaining unit members are counted, and if the majority of the ballots cast support the union, it is certified.

Termination of Bargaining Rights   Just as it is possible for a labour union to become the legally certified or recognized bargaining agent for a group of employees, it is also possible for a union to lose such rights. In the case of a union that received voluntary employer recognition, its bargaining rights may be terminated upon application by any employee in the bargaining unit or by the labour union, during the first year of the collective agreement (or within one year of signing the recognition agreement if no collective agreement has been signed). If termination of such rights is the desire of the majority of bargaining unit members, the union loses its recognition status.

All LR acts provide procedures for workers to apply for the **decertification** of their unions. Generally, members may apply for decertification if the union has failed to negotiate a collective agreement within one year of certification, or if they are dissatisfied with the performance of the union. Applications must be submitted to the appropriate LRB, along with evidence (in the form of a voluntarily signed document) that a significant percentage of the employees in the bargaining unit no longer wish to be represented by the union. In such case, the LRB is required to satisfy itself that the majority of the employees are in favour of the termination of the union's bargaining rights by holding a secret-ballot vote. If more than 50 percent of the ballots cast (or bargaining unit members, depending on jurisdiction) are in opposition to the union, the union will be decertified.

If it is determined that the union obtained its certification through fraudulent acts, the union will be decertified immediately. Once the LRB has declared that the union no longer represents the bargaining unit employees, any collective agreement negotiated between the parties is void. A labour union also has the right to notify the LRB that it no longer wishes to continue to represent the employees in a particular bargaining unit. This is known as "termination on abandonment." Although generally rare, decertifications are becoming more common, in part because of changes to B.C. legislation permitting more freedom for employers to communicate during certification and decertification drives, and new Ontario legislation requiring employers to post and circulate annually to unionized employees a document explaining how to decertify an union.[45]

decertification The process whereby a union is legally deprived of its official recognition as the exclusive bargaining agent for a group of employees.

Ontario Decertification Brochure
www.gov.on.ca/lab/english/about/leg/decert_br.html

THE IMPACT OF UNIONIZATION ON HRM

Following certification or voluntary recognition, both the employer and the union are legally required to bargain in good faith to arrive at terms and conditions of employment for the bargaining unit members. Unionization results in a number of changes relating to HRM.

Organizational Structure

Once an organization is unionized, the HR department is typically expanded by the addition of an LR specialist or section. In a large firm with a number of bargaining units, human resources and labour relations may form two divisions within a broader department, often called industrial relations or labour relations. In such situations, the LR staff members specialize in negotiations and contract administration issues, while those working in the HR section continue to oversee all of the other HR functions.

Management Decision Making

Union leaders are typically involved in decisions pertaining to any issues that will affect bargaining unit members, such as subcontracting of work, productivity standards, and job content. While management continues to claim exclusive rights over certain matters, union leaders may challenge these rights. In a unionized setting, management has less freedom to make unilateral changes. All HR policies must be consistent with the terms of the collective agreement. To gain union cooperation in the administration of policies and procedures, union representatives are often involved in the formulation of any policies that affect bargaining unit members—such as those pertaining to disciplinary rules and regulations—or are at least consulted as such policies are being drafted.

Centralization of Record Keeping and Standardization of Decision Making

Unionization generally results in greater centralization of employee record keeping and standardization of decision making to ensure equity, consistency, and uniformity. More centralized coordination is typically required in the enforcement of HR policies and procedures, which creates an expanded role for members of the LR department, as does the increased need for documentation to support decisions.

Supervisory Authority and Responsibility

The major impact of unionization is at the first-line level, since it is the supervisors who are responsible for administering the terms of the collective agreement on a day-to-day basis. Greater standardization of decision making and centralization of record keeping may lead supervisors to feel that they have lost some of their authority, which can cause resentment, especially since they inevitably find that unionization results in an increase in their responsibilities. Supervisors are often required to produce more written records than ever before, since documentation is critical at grievance and arbitration hearings. They must ensure that all of their decisions and actions are in accordance with the terms of the collective agreement. Even decisions that abide by the agreement may be challenged by the union.

An Ethical Dilemma

As the HR manager, how would you handle a situation in which a supervisor has knowingly violated the collective agreement when scheduling overtime?

Conclusion

In every organization, whether union or non-union, ultimate responsibility for the firm's performance and the effective utilization of its human resources rests with management. While unionization does have an impact on the way in which managers perform their HR responsibilities, when union leaders are treated as partners, they can provide a great deal of assistance with HR functions. When there is a cooperative and harmonious working relationship between management and union leaders, the result can be a win–win situation.

Case Law: Duty to Bargain in Good Faith

The union was engaged in strike action against the employer. During the strike the two parties continued to negotiate. An impasse occurred when a union representative informed the employer that an offer must contain a specific item or it would not be accepted. The employer was not prepared to accede to that demand and refused to continue to bargain. The union filed a complaint alleging failure to bargain in good faith. The complaint was dismissed. The obligation to bargain is not a hollow one. Its purpose is to conclude a collective agreement. In the absence of any reasonable indication that discussions are likely to bear fruit, there is no obligation to meet or to commence a dialogue. However, [once] the impasse no longer existed the Board recommended that the parties recommence collective bargaining. International Association of Machinists and Aerospace Workers, Lodge 2309 v. Nordair Ltd., (1985) LRB (Can.) 85 CLLC ¶16,023.

Source: Excerpted with permission from the *Canadian Labour Law Reporter*, ¶1975, published by and copyright CCH Canadian Limited, Toronto, Ontario.

CHAPTER *Review*

Summary

1 An organization's labour relations (LR) strategy is its overall plan for dealing with unions, which sets the tone for its union–management relationship. Possible strategies include union acceptance and union avoidance. There are two avoidance strategies: union substitution and union suppression.

2 Canada's labour laws provide a common set of rules for fair negotiations and ensure the protection of public interest by preventing the impact of labour disputes from inconveniencing the public. Tripartite Labour Relations Boards across the country administer labour relations laws. These laws try to balance employees' rights to engage in union activity with employers' management rights.

3 There are five steps in the LR process: (1) employees decide to seek collective representation, (2) the union organizing campaign, (3) official recognition of the union, (4) negotiation of a collective agreement, and (5) day-to-day contract administration.

4 Workers desire unionization because of dissatisfaction with pay, benefits, and working conditions; lack of job security; unfair or biased administration of policies and practices; perceived inequities in pay; lack of opportunity for advancement; desire for more participation in work-related decisions; and a belief that unions can improve pay and working conditions.

5 The union organizing process involves five steps, which typically include (1) employee/union contact, (2) an initial organizational meeting, (3) the formation of an in-house organizing committee, (4) an organizing campaign, and (5) the outcome —certification, recognition, or rejection.

6 There are three basic ways in which a union can obtain recognition as a bargaining unit for a group of workers: (1) voluntary recognition, (2) the regular certification process, and (3) a pre-hearing vote.

Key Terms

authorization card   *(p. 514)*
bargaining unit   *(p. 496)*
business agent   *(p. 506)*
business unionism   *(p. 500)*
certification   *(p. 517)*
collective agreement (union contract)   *(p. 496)*
collective bargaining   *(p. 496)*
craft union   *(p. 501)*

decertification   *(p. 518)*
grass-roots unionism   *(p. 505)*
industrial union   *(p. 501)*
labour–management relations   *(p. 496)*
Labour Relations Board (LRB)   *(p. 499)*
labour union (union)   *(p. 496)*
local   *(p. 505)*
pre-hearing vote   *(p. 517)*
representation vote   *(p. 517)*
social (reform) unionism   *(p. 501)*
succession   *(p. 502)*
union steward   *(p. 506)*
union substitution (proactive HRM)
    approach   *(p. 498)*

Review and Discussion Questions

1   Summarize the common characteristics in the LR legislation across Canadian jurisdictions.

2   Cite three examples of unfair labour practices on the part of management and three on the part of unions.

3   Explain the role of union locals and describe their structure.

4   Explain three of the challenges facing the union movement in Canada today.

5   Describe five signs to which managers should be alert in order to detect an organizing campaign.

6   Discuss the impact of unionization on HRM.

CRITICAL *Thinking Questions*

1   "If supervisors communicate effectively with employees, deal with their concerns, and treat them fairly, employees are far less likely to be interested in forming or joining a union." Do you agree or disagree with this statement? Why?

2   Differentiate between business and social unionism and provide three examples of conflicts that might arise between these two philosophies.

3   Two possible approaches to labour relations are union acceptance and union avoidance (union substitution or union suppression). Determine which of these strategies seems to have been adopted in a firm in which you have been employed or with which you are familiar. Provide evidence to back up your answer.

APPLICATION *Exercises*

Running Case: LearnInMotion.com

Potential Unionization

The employees at dot-coms like LearnInMotion.com are young, well paid, and technologically sophisticated, and they're doing interesting, creative work with flexible hours. They are, in other words, exactly the sort of employees you might assume would have no interest in joining a union. Jennifer, however, was surprised to find that unions are actively attempting to organize several dot-coms. For example, one article she happened to come across said that union activity at Canadian Internet companies is on the increase and claims that unions receive enquiries from young dot-com workers regarding union membership. "That's all we'd need is to have some dis-

gruntled current or former employee call a union in on us," said Pierre.

The fact that LearnInMotion.com is in Ottawa (which has a relatively high proportion of union workers due to the heavily unionized federal civil service) and that several employees have left under less-than-pleasant circumstances suggest to Jennifer that perhaps she should be vigilant, and take steps now to prevent a problem later. The question is, what should she and Pierre do? Now they want you, their management consultants, to help them decide what to do. Here's what they want you to do for them.

Questions

1   Use the Internet to determine if any union organized or tried to organize a dot-com in the Ottawa area in the past two years.

2 What could Jennifer and Pierre do now to increase the chances of their employees deciding to remain non-unionized?

3 Explain how to tell the first, early stages of an organizing campaign are underway. Explain how to find out for sure.

CASE INCIDENT *Western College*

Sean O'Sullivan is the HR manager at Western College, a medium-sized institution located in Bradley, Manitoba, which is approximately 240 km north of Winnipeg. Bradley has a population of 120 000, and many of the residents are employees of the federal or provincial governments or Via Rail Canada. Western College, like many other Canadian educational institutions, is under severe pressure to restrict and meet budgets in the wake of recent provincial government announcements of reduced spending on education. There have been some staff reductions already and it is likely that there will be more, affecting virtually all areas of the college.

Sean is mulling over how he should handle a situation that Ruth Ann Zimmer, a supervisor in the maintenance and housekeeping department, has just brought to his attention. According to Ruth Ann, she is quite certain that an organizing campaign has begun among the employees reporting to her, who maintain and clean the on-campus residences. She indicated that she actually witnessed a CUPE representative meeting with a number of the employees, and urging them to sign union authorization cards. She also observed several of those who report to her "cornering" other employees to talk to them about joining the union and urge them to sign cards. Some of this activity occurred during working hours, as the employees were carrying out their normal duties. She indicated that a number of employees have come to her, asking her opinion about unions, in general, and CUPE, in particular. They informed her that several other supervisors in the department had told their reporting employees not to sign any union authorization cards and not to talk about the union while they were on campus. Of particular concern to Sean is Ruth Ann's statement that one of her fellow supervisors told his reporting employees in a meeting that anyone who was caught talking about the union or signing an authorization card would be disciplined and perhaps terminated.

According to Ruth Ann, the employees are very dissatisfied with their wages and many of the conditions that they have endured because of students, supervisors, and other staff members. She said that several employees told her that they had signed union cards because they believed that the only way to get the college administrators to pay any attention to their concerns was to have a union represent them. Ruth Ann mentioned that she made a list of employees whom she felt had already signed authorization cards or were seriously considering doing so, and said that she would be prepared to share this list with Sean if he wanted to deal with those individuals personally. Since her pager went off, she had to leave Sean's office rather abruptly. Just before departing, she stated that she and the other supervisors wanted to know what they should do in order to "stomp out" the threat of unionization in their department.

Questions

1 Assuming that Ruth Ann is correct, why do you think some of the maintenance and housekeeping staff members might be interested in forming a union at this point in time? (That is, what factors may have led to their contact with CUPE?)

2 How can Sean determine if Ruth Ann's information is correct?

3 What unfair labour practices have been committed by members of the union and/or management? Are there any legal ramifications?

4 How should Sean respond to Ruth Ann's offer to give him a list of those who have signed cards or are likely to do so?

5 What should Sean do to deal with all of the other issues that Ruth Ann has raised, including her desire and that of some of the other supervisors to "stomp out" the threat of unionization in their department?

EXPERIENTIAL *Exercises*

1 Assume that you are the vice-president of HR at relatively new non-union firm that has been experiencing rapid growth. In view of the management team's desire to remain non-union, you have been asked to prepare a report to the other senior management team members, making spe- cific recommendations regarding strategies that the firm should adopt to help to ensure that the employees will have no desire to unionize.

2 Working with two or three classmates, devise a management counter-campaign to a unionization attempt, ensuring that all recommended courses of action are legal.

CHAPTER 17

Collective Bargaining and Contract Administration

LEARNING OUTCOMES

After studying this chapter, you should be able to:

Explain the requirements of good-faith bargaining.

Describe typical steps involved in preparation for negotiations.

Differentiate between distributive and integrative bargaining, and *describe* three types of integrative bargaining.

Describe conciliation, mediation, strikes, lockouts, and interest arbitration as possible responses to a bargaining impasse.

Briefly *describe* five typical collective agreement provisions.

Explain the typical steps in a grievance procedure.

Describe strategies that can be used to build effective labour–management relations.

INTRODUCTION TO COLLECTIVE BARGAINING

Collective bargaining is the process by which a formal collective agreement is established between labour and management. The negotiation of a collective agreement involves discussions, concessions, and mutual tradeoffs between the union negotiating team and management representatives. Collective bargaining may also involve the use of third-party assistance, and economic pressure by either union (a strike) or management (a lockout) or third-party intervention.

The purposes of collective bargaining include:

- negotiating, in "good faith," a collective agreement that describes the scope of management and union rights and responsibilities
- arriving at an agreement that is acceptable to both management and union members
- developing a framework for labour relations (LR) in the organization, including a mechanism to resolve conflicts or disputes pertaining to the contract provisions
- specifying the manner in which management and bargaining unit members will treat each other and conduct themselves during the term of the collective agreement.

Collective Bargaining
www.gov.on.ca/LAB/english/lr/
pubs_type.html

The Collective Agreement

For a collective agreement to be valid, it must be made between an employer's organization and a trade union or council of trade unions, contain provisions regarding the terms and conditions of employment of bargaining unit members, and be in writing. The collective agreement is the cornerstone of the Canadian LR system. In addition to serving the functions listed above, its provisions are used as the basis for determining the legality or illegality of the activities of the employer, trade union, and bargaining unit members. Negotiating such a contract is complex and, at times, time consuming and difficult. To try to ensure that the process is as smooth as possible, both parties are legally required to bargain in good faith.

Good-Faith Bargaining

good-faith bargaining The legal requirement that the parties negotiating a collective agreement bargain honestly, fairly, and sincerely.

Good-faith bargaining requires that union and management representatives communicate and negotiate, that proposals be matched with counterproposals, and that both parties make every reasonable effort to arrive at an agreement.[1] The line between hard bargaining and bargaining in bad faith is not always clear. However, as interpreted by LRBs and the courts, activities that violate the requirement to bargain in good faith include:[2]

> **Hints to Ensure Legal Compliance**

surface bargaining Going through the motions of collective bargaining with no intention of arriving at a mutually acceptable agreement.

- *Surface bargaining.* **Surface bargaining** involves going through the motions of bargaining, without any real intention of reaching a mutually acceptable agreement.
- *Failing to make concessions or withdrawing previously granted concessions.* Although neither party is required to make concessions, the definition of good faith suggests that a willingness to compromise is an

essential ingredient. Withdrawing previously granted concessions is considered to be bad-faith bargaining.

- *Failing to make reasonable proposals and demands.* Failure to advance proposals is considered a sign of bad-faith bargaining, as is the failure to advance realistic proposals.

- *Dilatory tactics.* The parties must meet and confer at reasonable times and intervals. Refusing to meet does not constitute good-faith bargaining, nor does the use of frequent delaying tactics, such as postponement of scheduled sessions. Any of these may be considered **dilatory tactics**.

dilatory tactics Actions tending to or intended to cause delay.

- *Imposing unreasonable conditions.* Attempts to impose conditions that are onerous or unreasonable may constitute bad-faith bargaining. Insisting that striking employees return to work before resuming negotiations would be an example of an unreasonable condition on the part of an employer.

- *Making unilateral changes in conditions.* Making changes in the bargaining unit members' conditions of employment during negotiations without consulting the union constitutes bad-faith bargaining, and is considered as an indication that the employer is not bargaining with the intent of reaching an agreement.

- *Bypassing the representatives.* The duty to bargain in good faith is violated when either party refuses to negotiate with the selected representatives of the other. Management is prohibited from overriding the bargaining process by making an offer directly to the employees. This practice, called *Boulwarism*, was named after Lemuel Boulware, vice-president of General Electric, who used this strategy in the 1950s. For example, in November 2001, just before a strike vote by the faculty union, representatives of Dalhousie University in Halifax sent an offer directly to the union members. Because the university bypassed the faculty negotiators, thus showing disrespect for the collective bargaining process, the union members voted 71 percent in favour of a strike.[3]

- *Committing unfair labour practices during negotiations.* Such actions may reflect upon the good faith of the guilty party.

- *Failing to provide information.* Information must be supplied to the other negotiating team, upon request, that will enable the members to understand and intelligently discuss the issues raised. Neither party can deliberately distort information or mislead the other party.

THE COLLECTIVE BARGAINING PROCESS

Steps typically involved in the collective bargaining process include (1) preparation for bargaining, (2) face-to-face negotiations, and (3) obtaining approval for the proposed contract. When talks do not go as smoothly as might be desired, there are two possible additional steps. First, when talks break down, third-party assistance is required by law in every jurisdiction except Saskatchewan.[4] Even when impartial third parties are brought in to assist the union and management negotiating teams, there is always the possibility of arriving at a bargaining impasse, resulting in the second additional step, a strike/lockout or interest arbitration. Each of these steps will be described next.

Preparation for Negotiations

Good preparation leads to a greater likelihood that desired goals will be achieved. Preparation for negotiations involves planning the bargaining strategy and process and assembling data to support bargaining proposals. Assuming that the collective agreement is not the first to be negotiated by the parties, preparations for the next round of negotiations should commence soon after the signing of the current collective agreement, while the experience is still fresh in the minds of the members of both negotiating teams.

Management Strategies   The organization's LR specialists are generally the key players in management's preparations. In addition to reviewing the strengths and weaknesses of any previous negotiating sessions, management's preparations involve the following activities:[5]

- *Reviewing the organization's strategic plan.* Preparation for bargaining typically begins with a review of the organization's strategic plan. The firm's overall objectives, intermediate and long-term plans, upcoming changes in their product or service mix, and major technological innovations must all be taken into consideration as an initial bargaining strategy is being prepared.

- *Gathering data on economic trends.* Data are then gathered on general economic conditions, cost-of-living trends, and wage rates for the general geographic area. Data obtained from government sources (such as HRDC's Workplace Information Directorate and Statistics Canada) can help to support the employer's position during negotiations, as can information from newspapers and reports published by the Conference Board of Canada.

- *Conducting wage and benefit surveys and analyzing ability to pay.* Surveys are almost always conducted to compile data about the compensation policies, wage rates, and benefits and services offered by union and non-union competitors. Since unions generally try to negotiate wages and benefits in line with those offered by labour market competitors, having these data enables managers to anticipate likely union demands and plan their monetary proposals. The employer's ability to pay has to be taken into consideration, so accurate data about the firm's current financial situation must be obtained.

- *Analyzing other collective agreements.* This includes a section-by-section comparison with other benchmark collective agreements, since they often provide a framework that one side or the other may seek to follow in negotiations. **Pattern bargaining** occurs when unions negotiate provisions covering wages and other benefits that are similar to those already negotiated for another bargaining unit within the region or industry. Such bargaining enables unions to provide their members with wages and benefits similar to those negotiated elsewhere, and helps to ensure that employers' labour costs are comparable with those of their competitors. The collective agreements negotiated by the Canadian Auto Workers (CAW) and the Big-Three automakers (Ford, GM, and DaimlerChrysler), set important precedents for many areas in the Canadian economy, often setting the benchmark for wages and benefits not only in the automotive industry, but for all unionized and non-unionized hourly workers across Canada.[6]

pattern bargaining A bargaining tactic whereby a union uses a settlement negotiated with one employer as a "pattern" (or model) and seeks to secure a similar settlement from other employers in the region or industry.

- *Obtaining multi-employer coordination.* Coordination can range from the exchange of general information among loosely connected employers to the formation of a multi-employer bargaining association (where legally permissible).

- *Obtaining supervisory input.* Input from first-line supervisors is integrated into the planning process because they can identify current provisions that have proven to be difficult to implement, and to suggest possible amendments, deletions, or additions.

- *Reviewing the union's organizing-campaign promises or the existing contract.* Promises made during the union organizing campaign or unmet demands from previous negotiations are reviewed to anticipate likely union demands. An existing collective agreement is reviewed carefully to identify any unclear contract language.

- *Conducting an audit and analysis of grievances.* Such an audit provides information about the types of grievances filed, and the interpretation of contract provisions through grievance settlements and arbitration awards. It often points out weaknesses in contract language or provisions.

- *Canvassing relevant arbitration awards and LRB rulings.* Examination of such decisions may point out the need for contract language amendments.

- *Costing.* Management must have accurate data about the costs of any current contract provisions, as well as the costs of anticipated union demands. Often, accounting or finance staff assume major responsibility for costing.

- *Contingency planning.* The likelihood of a strike or lockout is often assessed, and contingency plans drawn up for dealing with a bargaining impasse if it is deemed to be a possibility.

Preparing an Initial Bargaining Plan and Strategy Once the above steps have been completed, an initial bargaining plan and strategy are formulated. Generally, these are submitted to the senior management team for approval. The composition and size of the bargaining team are generally based on industry practices and previous bargaining history. Normally, union and management teams each comprise four to six representatives. The chief negotiator for management is generally the vice-president or manager of LR. Team members typically include HR or LR staff, especially those with expertise in such areas as compensation and benefits administration, training, and occupational health and safety; first-line supervisors; a legal expert; and a representative of the accounting or finance department.

Guidelines are then prepared and submitted for senior management approval in order to provide a framework for the negotiating team and ensure that the chief negotiator has the authority to reach a settlement. A procedure is generally established to modify the guidelines, as circumstances dictate, once the negotiations are underway. The chief negotiator must know exactly how far the organization is willing to go in meeting union demands and whether or not a strike or lockout would even be considered.

The plans and strategy are then refined, with input from the team members. The data on which such proposals are based are typically rechecked for accuracy, and the finalized proposals are submitted to senior management for approval. A procedure is typically established to provide the senior management team with periodic updates during negotiations, and to ensure that the chief negotiator has ready access to the CEO once talks are underway.

Union Strategies   The union's preparation for negotiations involves a number of parallel steps:

- *Obtaining information on union policy objectives.* Some of the local's demands may be shaped by the overall policy objectives of the international or national union with which the local is associated, if any.

- *Gathering data on general economic trends.* The union negotiating team requires data on economic conditions, unemployment rates, cost-of-living trends, and wage rates for the general geographic area, just as the management negotiating team does.

- *Obtaining data on collective bargaining trends and settlements.* The national, international, or regional office staff and business agent (if applicable) are excellent sources of information about collective bargaining trends and settlements.

- *Obtaining data about the organization's finances.* In public companies, information about the financial health of the organization is often obtained from company financial reports. Privately held companies are not required to disclose financial information to the union. Unions recognize that despite trends elsewhere, there is a limit on each employer's ability to pay. Demanding a settlement beyond that point may result in a lengthy strike, resulting in little or no gain or even in plant closure.

- *Analyzing other collective agreements.* This includes a section-by-section comparison with other benchmark collective agreements, which typically provide suggestions regarding language revisions or new provisions that could be negotiated.

- *Obtaining input from stewards and others.* Since stewards and chief stewards play a key role in day-to-day contract administration, they are best equipped to identify current provisions that have resulted in complaints or grievances, and to suggest possible amendments, deletions, or additions. Based on experiences with other locals, central or regional office staff members often suggest demands that should be placed on the table to solve existing problems or to avoid anticipated future problems.

- *Obtaining input from the membership.* Unions generally hold a meeting that is open to all bargaining unit members, at which individual members have the opportunity to suggest items for inclusion in the union's demands. The Internet is being used increasingly for this purpose and for many other aspects of union business.

- *Gathering data about the bargaining unit members.* Data about the demographic composition of the bargaining unit members are extremely helpful in assessing bargaining priorities. For instance, if the majority of members are over 50, provisions regarding job security and pensions may be bargaining priorities. For example, the United Steelworkers at Stelco in Hamilton, Ontario, ratified an agreement in 2002 where virtually all of the increases went to pensions and none to wages.[7] If there is a large number of women in the bargaining unit, provisions pertaining to family-friendly benefits or flexible working hours may be high on the priority list.

- *Reviewing organizing-campaign promises or the existing contract.* Promises made during the organizing campaign must be addressed during the negotiation of a first collective agreement. Where there is an existing collective agreement, it is generally subjected to a comprehensive review, to identify any unclear contract language that has led or could potentially lead to divergent interpretations.

- *Conducting an audit and analysis of grievances.* Such an audit provides information about grievances that have been filed, as well as information about the interpretation of contract provisions through grievance settlements and arbitration awards.

- *Costing.* Typically, financial experts from the central or regional office are responsible for costing monetary demands. It is not uncommon for management to indicate, toward the end of negotiations, the overall percentage or amount that the organization is willing to commit to monetary issues. In such a case, the union negotiating team must be aware of the cost of every monetary item in order to decide on the best allocation of available funds.

- *Contingency planning.* The likelihood of a strike or lockout is generally assessed, and contingency plans are drawn up for dealing with a bargaining impasse if it is deemed to be a possibility.

- *Establishing a bargaining team.* In some situations, the union negotiating committee consists of union officials, such as the president of the local, vice-president, secretary/treasurer, recording secretary, and chief stewards. In others, the bargaining unit members select individuals to serve on their negotiating team by means of a special election. If there is a business agent, he or she is generally on the negotiating team. He or she, or a representative of the regional or central office, often serves as the chief negotiator for the union.

- *Finalizing bargaining strategy and proposals.* The union's proposals are then finalized in writing, and the data on which the proposals are based are rechecked for accuracy. The finalized proposals are then generally approved by the membership at a union meeting.

Face-to-Face Negotiations

Under LR legislation, representatives of either union or management can give written notice to the other party of their desire to bargain to negotiate a first collective agreement or renew an existing one. Where there is an existing collective agreement, the time period is generally specified therein. For example:[8]

This Agreement shall be in effect from _____ and shall continue in full force and effect until _____. The agreement shall be considered to be automatically continued in all of its provisions, unless, no earlier than ninety (90) days and no later than sixty (60) days before its termination date, either party gives written notice of its intent to bargain for renewal or modification of the agreement or of any of its provisions.

Early in the negotiating process, demands are exchanged— often before the first bargaining session. Generally included in

Negotiating a collective agreement.

each side's proposals are some that the negotiating team believes must be achieved, some that they would like to achieve, and some that are put on the table primarily for trading purposes. Very often, after the proposals have been exchanged, each party is asked to explain to the other the intent of its proposals, to ensure that they are properly understood, and may also be asked for justification of its demands.

At this stage, the company and union negotiating teams generally make a private assessment of the other team's demands. Usually, each team finds some items with which they can agree quite readily and others on which compromise seems likely. Tentative conclusions are also made regarding which items, if any, are potential strike or lockout issues.

Location, Frequency, and Duration of Meetings

Negotiations are generally held at a neutral, off-site location, such as a hotel meeting room, so that there is no psychological advantage for either team, and so that interruptions and work distractions can be kept to a minimum. Each side generally has another room in which intra-team meetings, known as **caucus sessions**, are held.

Generally, meetings are held as often as either or both parties consider desirable, as long as the sessions are helping the parties to move closer to a settlement. Meetings generally last as long as progress is being made. A caucus session or an adjournment can be suggested by either party, when deemed appropriate. Marathon bargaining sessions, such as those lasting all night, are not typical until conciliation has been exhausted and the clock is ticking rapidly toward the strike/lockout deadline.

Initial Bargaining Session

The initial meeting of the bargaining teams is extremely important in establishing the climate that will prevail during the negotiating sessions that follow. A cordial attitude, with occasional humour, can help to relax tension and ensure that negotiations proceed smoothly. Generally, the first meeting is devoted to an exchange of demands (if this has not taken place previously) and the establishment of rules and procedures that will be used during negotiations.

Subsequent Bargaining Sessions

In traditional approaches to bargaining, each party argues for its demands and resists those of the other at each negotiating session. At the same time, both are looking for compromise alternatives that will enable an agreement to be reached. Regardless of its degree of importance, every proposal submitted must be resolved in order to reach a settlement. A proposal may be withdrawn temporarily or permanently, accepted by the other side in its entirety, or accepted in a modified form. Ideally, both sides should come away from negotiations feeling that they have attained many of their basic bargaining goals (even if in slightly modified form), and confident that the tentative agreement reached will be acceptable to senior management and/or the board, and the members of the bargaining unit not involved on the negotiating team.

In order for each issue on the table to be resolved satisfactorily, the point at which agreement is reached must be within limits that the union and employer are willing to accept, often referred to as the **bargaining zone**. As illustrated in **Figure 17.1**, if the solution desired by one party exceeds the limits of the other party, then it is outside of the bargaining zone. Unless that party modifies its

caucus session A session in which only the members of one's own bargaining team are present.

An Ethical Dilemma

Is it ethical for a union negotiator to state in the opening bargaining session that the union is prepared to strike unless the firm grants a wage increase of 5 percent in year one and 4 percent in year two, knowing that the membership will be satisfied with 3 percent and 2 percent, respectively?

bargaining zone The area defined by the bargaining limits (resistance points) of each side, in which compromise is possible, as is the attainment of a settlement satisfactory to both parties.

FIGURE 17.1   The Bargaining Zone and Characteristics of Distributive
Bargaining

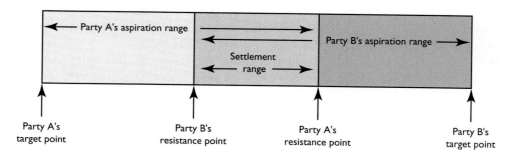

Source: P. Robbins and N. Langton, *Organizational Behaviour*, 3rd edition (Don Mills, ON: Pearson Education Canada, 2003), p. 307. Reprinted with permission by Pearson Education Canada Inc.

demands sufficiently to bring them within the bargaining zone, or the other party extends its limits to accommodate such demands, a bargaining deadlock is the inevitable result.[9]

Monetary versus Non-monetary Issues   Very often, the parties separate the bargaining demands into two categories: monetary and non-monetary. *Monetary issues* include all items with direct cost implications, such as wages, overtime pay rates, shift premiums, changes in hours of work, vacation entitlement, and holidays. *Non-monetary issues* include such items as contract language, procedural matters, and administrative issues, which do not involve direct cents-per-hour cost implications. However, non-monetary items may have an indirect impact on an employer's costs. For example, negotiated seniority provisions pertaining to layoffs can lead to situations in which a less-qualified and less-productive employee replaces an outstanding performer, thereby increasing labour costs.

Bargaining Strategies   Typically, non-monetary issues are discussed first, based on the assumption that such items will be easier to resolve, and a pattern of give and take can be established. When a deadlock subsequently occurs, the sense of past progress may increase the resolve of both sides to find a compromise by offering counterproposals that take the other party's objections into account. Sometimes, progress is made simply by dropping the contentious issue temporarily and moving on to other items. Further progress on other issues may lead to compromises regarding the earlier impasse.

It is important to retain some flexibility around issues, as compromises are at the heart of the negotiation process. Effective negotiators respect the importance of saving face for all those involved. They also consider the impact of present negotiations on those in future years. The support of a conciliator should be enlisted if an impasse is reached and no further progress seems possible.

Negotiating is a complex process consisting of four types of activity: distributive bargaining, integrative bargaining, attitudinal structuring, and intra-organizational bargaining.

distributive bargaining A win–lose negotiating strategy, such that one party gains at the expense of the other.

integrative bargaining A negotiating strategy in which the possibility of win–win, lose–win, win–lose, and lose–lose outcomes is recognized, and there is acknowledgement that achieving a win–win outcome will depend on mutual trust and problem solving.

productivity bargaining The attempt to improve organizational productivity and competitiveness, resulting in greater job security for bargaining unit members.

concessionary bargaining A strategy that is used when employers are experiencing severe economic problems. In return for freezes or roll-backs in wages and benefits, bargaining unit members receive greater job security, and often participate in productivity improvements through a gainsharing plan.

Distributive bargaining is an approach often typified as "win–lose" bargaining, because the gains of one party are normally achieved at the expense of the other.[10] It is appropriately involved when the issues being discussed pertain to the distribution of things that are available in fixed amounts, such as wage increases and benefits improvements. However, it may also be used when there is a history of distrust and adversarial relations, even when dealing with issues on which a more constructive approach is possible.

As indicated in Figure 17.1, distributive bargaining is characterized by three distinct components: the initial point, the target point, and the resistance point. The initial point for the union is usually higher than what the union expects to receive from management. The union target point is next, and represents the negotiating team's assessment of what is realistically achievable from management. The union's bargaining zone limit is its resistance point, which represents its minimally acceptable level.

These points are essentially reversed for management. The management team's initial point is its lowest level, which is used at the beginning of negotiations. Next is its target point, the desired agreement level. Management's resistance point forms the other boundary of the bargaining zone.

Integrative bargaining is an approach that assumes that a win–win solution can be found, but also acknowledges that one or both sides can be losers if the bargaining is not handled effectively.[11] Integrative bargaining strategies require that both management and union negotiators adopt a genuine interest in the joint exploration of creative solutions to common problems.

Issues pertaining to work rules, job descriptions, and contract language can often be handled effectively using an integrative approach, in situations in which management negotiators are not intent on retaining management rights and both sides are committed to seeking a win–win solution. Wage rates and vacation entitlements are more likely to be fixed-sum issues that are handled by a distributive approach.

Productivity and concessionary bargaining are subcategories of integrative bargaining. One of the primary purposes of **productivity bargaining** is to improve the effectiveness of the organization by eliminating work rules and inefficient work methods that inhibit productivity. Getting union agreement is not always easy, since there is often a fear that this might eventually lead to the loss of union jobs and a weakening of the union's power base. A union's willingness to negotiate new, improved work rules and practices is generally due to the belief that the job security of bargaining unit members will increase with improvements in the employer's ability to compete in its product or service market. An example is provided by the Industrial Wood and Allied Workers of Canada (IWA). Through its Negotiated Partnership Policy, the IWA assumes responsibility for productivity, product development, and marketing, in exchange for an increase in worker job security.[12]

Concessionary bargaining is a special type of bargaining strategy that is utilized when organizations are experiencing financial problems. In such circumstances, employers may seek agreement from the union to freeze economic rewards such as wages and benefits, or seek benefits and/or wage reductions, known as "roll-backs." While this may initially appear to be a losing situation for the union and a win for management, it is actually a win–win situation if it leads to company survival and prevents layoffs. In exchange for such concessions, management usually guarantees the job security of the bargaining unit members. For example, members of the United Steelworkers of America Local 7085 agreed to a new three-year contract in 2003 that would allow Noranda Inc., Canada's largest mining company, to freeze wages and reduce the workforce by 20 percent due to low prices of lead. Instead of cutting jobs through layoffs due to declining production in the plant, the company will cut 70 jobs through early retirement incentives.[13]

The objective of integrative bargaining is to establish a creative negotiating relationship that benefits labour and management. Becoming increasing popular these days is a relatively new integrative approach, known as mutual gains or interest-based bargaining.

Mutual gains (interest-based) bargaining is aimed at seeking win–win solutions to LR issues. As part of the process, all key union and management negotiators are trained in the fundamentals of effective problem solving and conflict resolution. Such training is often extended to as many other employees as possible, with the aim of ensuring that the principles of mutual gains (interest-based) bargaining are incorporated into the organization's value system, so that promoting cooperation becomes a year-round corporate objective.[14]

Ninety-three percent of respondents to a recent survey of 25 employer and 20 union negotiators, representing 32 collective agreements, showed that their primary motivation for using interest-based bargaining was a desire to make the negotiation process more satisfying so that it would lead to concrete and lasting results. A majority of both management and union negotiators reported that their experiences were positive—marked by open communications and respectful attitudes among participants—and resulted in a win–win outcome. While 58 percent of employers rated hours of work and overtime easy to negotiate through interest-based bargaining and 59 percent of union representatives noted personnel changes as easiest, not all issues lent to ease of negotiation through interest-based bargaining, and almost three-quarters of the negotiators stated that they had changed approaches in the course of the negotiation process depending on the issue at stake—reverting to either the traditional distributive bargaining approach or a mixed distributive/interest-based approach. While none of the negotiators had used an interest-based approach to bargaining before, a large majority from both the employee and union representatives expressed an interest in applying the interest-based approach not only to formal collective bargaining, but also to day-to-day labour relations problems and in developing ways to maintain cooperation beyond the negotiation period.[15]

In interest-based bargaining, the order in which items are discussed is typically based on mutual agreement, and generally begins with problems involving common interests. Each problem is explored in detail. Joint fact-finding may be involved. Brainstorming is used to generate alternative solutions, which are subsequently discussed. To be agreed upon, solutions must take the interests of each party into account, and may have to meet certain pre-agreed-upon standards. Proponents of this approach to bargaining at other organizations point out that a joint sense of accountability is fostered between union and management representatives and that ongoing joint initiatives are the result of the negotiating process. In addition, the tools that are used at the bargaining table can be applied to the resolution of all workplace issues.[16] While more widely used in the private sector, interest-based bargaining is becoming more and more prevalent in the public sector—such as between the Canadian Union of Postal Workers and Canada Post, and the Ontario Nurses Association and the Ontario

---

mutual gains (interest-based) bargaining A win–win approach, based on training in the fundamentals of effective problem solving and conflict resolution, in which trainees are taught to take the interests of all stakeholders into account, so that the solutions developed are better and more permanent.

Research
Insight ▷

Hospital Association—where union–management relationships had been historically adversarial.[17] While mutual gains (interest-based) bargaining has been becoming increasingly popular, experts warn that implementation is difficult as it requires a grassroots culture change.

As should by now be apparent, **attitudinal structuring**, which is the shaping of such attitudes as trust or distrust, and cooperation or hostility, has a major impact on bargaining outcomes. Management and union negotiating team members must keep in mind the fact that they have to work together after the bargaining sessions are over and must live with the agreement negotiated. Thus, management's bargaining strategy and philosophy are critically important, as are the attitudes of the union negotiating team.

Attitudinal structuring behaviours such as showing willingness to trust and reinforcing the other party's willingness to trust can assist in building the trusting relationship on which many successful negotiations are based.[18]

attitudinal structuring The shaping of such attitudes between the parties as trust or distrust, and cooperation or hostility, which have a major impact on bargaining outcomes.

Research
I n s i g h t

A 2002 study by the Canadian Labour and Business Centre polled 6000 labour leaders and managers across Canada to assess the current state of labour–management relations. Results showed that management are more positive than unions in their perceptions of the current state of labour–management relations, as shown in **Figure 17.2**. In the public sector, 62 percent of labour leaders and 28 percent of managers said that relations were poor. In the private sector, 48 percent of labour leaders and 27 percent of managers also felt that relations were poor. In Quebec, labour–management relations appear amicable compared to the rest of Canada. Eighty-two percent of managers and 73 percent of labour leaders in that province said that their relationships were acceptable or better. However, in British Columbia, labour relations are deteriorating, particularly in the public sector where 76 percent of labour leaders and 47 percent of managers

FIGURE 17.2   Perceptions of the Current State of Labour–Management Relations

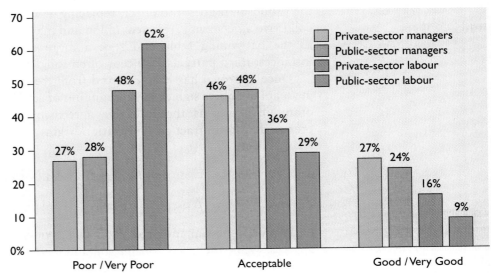

Source: Canadian Labour and Business Centre, *Viewpoints 2002: Labour-Management Relations in Canada.* © 2002. Reprinted by permission of the Canadian Labour and Business Centre, Ottawa, ON.

felt that things had worsened since 2000. The province had the highest number of managers and labour leaders who were unhappy.[19]

Intra-organizational bargaining also plays a major role in contract negotiations. This is the manoeuvring required to achieve a consensus within (rather than between) the union and management organizations. Within the union organization, the preferences and priorities of skilled workers, semiskilled workers, and unskilled workers often differ; as do those of young, middle-aged, and older employees; and those of male and female members. There are also differences sometimes between the priorities of the local and those of the national or international office staff. On the employer's side, there are also often conflicting points of view that have to be resolved.

Thus, the negotiating process is far more complex than it may appear to a casual observer. There are different types of bargaining strategies involved, and each side arrives at the bargaining table with political and organizational interests at stake.

The Contract Approval Process

As mentioned previously, collective agreements must be written documents. Verbal understandings between management and labour are not collective agreements and will not be enforced as such. However, the parties do not normally execute a formal written document until some time after the bargaining process has been completed. Instead, the terms and conditions agreed to by the parties are usually reduced to a **memorandum of settlement,** and submitted to the constituent groups for final approval.

Generally, final approval for the employer rests with the senior management team. In most cases, the union bargaining team submits the memorandum of settlement to the bargaining unit members for **ratification**. In some jurisdictions, such as Ontario, ratification is required by law, and all members of the bargaining unit, whether or not they are trade union members, must be given ample opportunity to cast a secret-ballot vote indicating approval or rejection of the proposed contract. If the majority of bargaining unit members vote in favour of the proposal, it goes into effect, replacing any prior agreement. If the proposed collective agreement is rejected, union and management negotiators must return to the bargaining table and seek a more acceptable compromise. In such instances, third-party assistance is often sought.

Once approval has been received from the constituent groups, the bargaining team members sign the memorandum of settlement. Once signed, this memorandum serves as the collective agreement until the formal document is prepared, and contract administration begins.

THIRD-PARTY ASSISTANCE AND BARGAINING IMPASSES

Third-Party Assistance: Conciliation and Mediation

Legislation in all Canadian jurisdictions provides for conciliation and mediation services. While the terms *conciliation* and *mediation* are often used interchangeably, in most jurisdictions they have quite distinct and different meanings.

Conciliation is usually defined as the intervention of a neutral third party whose primary purpose is to bring the parties together and keep them talking to

---

memorandum of settlement Summary of the terms and conditions agreed to by the parties that is submitted to the constituent groups for final approval.

ratification Formal approval by the bargaining unit members of the agreement negotiated between union and management bargaining team members by means of a secret-ballot vote.

conciliation The use of a neutral third party to help an organization and the union representing a group of its employees to come to a mutually satisfactory collective agreement.

Conciliation and Mediation
www.gov.on.ca/lab/english/lr/faq/
lr_faq2.html

enable them to reach a mutually satisfactory collective agreement. The only means available to a conciliator to bring the parties to agreement is persuasion; he or she is not permitted to have any direct input into the negotiation process, or to impose a settlement. Conciliation is typically requested after the parties have been negotiating for some length of time and are starting to reach a dead-lock, or after talks have broken down. The aim of conciliation is to try to help the parties avoid the hardship of a strike or lockout.

In all jurisdictions except Saskatchewan, strikes and lockouts are prohibited until third-party assistance has been undertaken. (Conciliation is required in all but two jurisdictions.) In most jurisdictions in which third-party assistance is mandatory, strikes/lockouts are prohibited until conciliation efforts have failed and a specified time period has elapsed.[20] Some jurisdictions provide for a two-stage conciliation process involving the appointment of a three-person con-ciliation board if the conciliation officer fails to obtain a settlement. In practice, conciliation boards are not appointed, and the conciliation process involves a conciliation officer alone. In such jurisdictions, the parties are in a legal strike or lockout position following a specified number of days (ranging from seven days to two weeks) after the minister of labour releases a "no-board report" (the report indicating that a conciliation board will not be appointed).[21]

mediation The use of a neutral third party to help an organization and the union representing its employees to reach a mutually sat-isfactory collective agreement. Unlike conciliation, mediation is usually voluntary.

Mediation is the intervention of a neutral third party whose primary purpose is to help the parties to fashion a mutually satisfactory agreement. Whereas con-ciliation is required by statute prior to a strike or lockout in most jurisdictions, mediation is usually a voluntary process. Typically, mediators become involved during the countdown period prior to a strike or lockout or during the strike or lockout itself. The mediator's role is an active one. It often involves meeting with each side separately and then bringing them together in an attempt to assist them in bridging the existing gaps. He or she is allowed to have direct input into the negotiation process, but cannot impose a settlement.

Bargaining Impasses: Strikes, Lockouts, and Interest Arbitration

When the union and management negotiating teams are unable to reach an agreement, and once the conciliation process has been undertaken (where required), the union may exercise its right to strike or request interest arbitra-tion, and the employer may exercise its right to lock out the bargaining unit members. Alternatively, bargaining unit members may continue to work with-out a collective agreement once the old one has expired, until talks resume and an agreement is reached.

strike The temporary refusal by bargaining unit members to con-tinue working for the employer.
strike vote Legally required in some jurisdictions, it is a vote seeking authorization from bar-gaining unit members to strike if necessary. A favourable vote does not mean that a strike is inevitable.

Strikes
A **strike** can be defined as a temporary refusal by bargaining unit members to continue working for the employer. When talks are reaching an impasse, unions will often hold a **strike vote**. Legally required in some jurisdic-tions, such a vote seeks authorization from bargaining unit members to strike if necessary. A favourable vote does not mean that a strike is inevitable. In fact, a highly favourable strike vote is often used as a bargaining ploy to gain conces-sions that will make a strike unnecessary. The results of a strike vote also help the union negotiating team members to determine their relative bargaining strength. Unless strike action is supported by a substantial majority of bargain-ing unit members, union leaders are rarely prepared to risk a strike, and must

Striking member of the Public Service Alliance of Canada.

therefore be more willing to compromise, if necessary, to avoid a work stoppage.

It should be noted that more than 95 percent of labour negotiations are settled without a work stoppage.[22] As illustrated in **Figure 17.3**, major work stoppages accounted for only 0.09 percent of overall working time lost in 2000, much less than the 3.2 percent lost due to illness/disability and personal/family demands.[23]

Since a strike can have serious economic consequences for bargaining unit members, the union negotiating team must carefully analyze the prospects for its success. The members' willingness to endure the personal hardships resulting from a strike must be estimated, based in part on the results of the strike vote, particularly if the strike may be lengthy.[24] Striking union members receive no wages and often have no benefits coverage until they return to work, although they may draw some money from the union's strike fund. A long strike tends to lead to a decline in member support and sometimes exhausts the strike fund, thereby putting extreme pressure on the union negotiating team to make concessions in order to get the bargaining unit members back to work.

Work stoppages are costly for employers as well. When employees at Inco Ltd. in Sudbury, Ontario, stopped working following the expiry of their collective agreement in June 2003, the company's total production of nickel declined

FIGURE **17.3**   Major Work Stoppages—1992 to 2002: Time Not Worked as a Percentage of Total Working Time

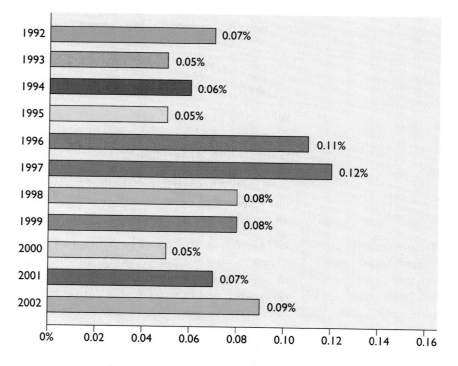

Source: Reproduced from the Human Resources Development Canada Web site, http://labour.hrdc-drhc.gc.ca/millieudetravail_workplace/chrono/index.cfm/doc/english. July 15, 2003. Reproduced with the permission of the Minister of Public Works and Government Services Canada, 2004.

by 50 percent—enough to supply 9 percent of the world demand for nickel. It is estimated that the cost of the strike for the company was US$20 million per month.[25]

Another factor that must be taken into consideration is the employer's ability to continue operating in the event of a strike, through the use of supervisors and other nonstriking employees and **replacement workers** where legally permitted. (Quebec has "anti-scab" legislation, forbidding the use of replacement workers during a strike, and B.C. has legislation that places some restrictions on the use of such workers.)[26] The greater the organization's ability to continue operations, the less the union's chances of gaining its demands through strike action.

When a union goes on strike, bargaining unit members often **picket** the employer. To ensure as many picketers as possible, the union may make strike pay contingent on picket duty. Picketers stand at business entrances, carrying signs advertising the issues in dispute, and attempt to discourage people from entering or leaving the premises. Unions cannot picket on any privately owned property without permission, nor can they legally block entrances and exits. Even when there is a relatively small number of picketers, they may succeed in closing the entire operation if they can convince enough people to refuse to cross the picket line. (There are many people who refuse to cross picket lines, as a matter of principle.) Subjecting people who attempt to cross a picket line to verbal insults or physical restraint is illegal. If employees on the picket line become disruptive, the employer can apply to the LRB or court to have a restriction placed on the number of picketers.

Secondary picketing, legal as of 2002 in Canada, is used to delay or disrupt the regular course of business in companies that are affiliated with or are clients of the employer in an attempt to put pressure on the company to settle the dispute. While secondary picketing can delay or disrupt a business, workers must refrain from intimidation, property damage, or criminal behaviour.[27]

Another economic weapon available to unions is a **boycott**, which is a refusal to patronize the employer. A boycott occurs when a union asks its members, other union members, the employer's customers/clients, and supporters in the general public, not to patronize the business involved in the labour dispute. Such action can harm the employer if the union is successful in gaining a large number of supporters. As with a strike, a boycott can have long-term consequences if former customers/clients develop a bias against the employer's products or services or make a change in buying habits or service provider that is not easily reversed.

The duration and ultimate success of a strike depends on the relative strength of the parties. The side that experiences the most economic hardship during a strike is more likely to compromise in order to reach a settlement. Failure to achieve a desired settlement on the part of the union negotiating team may result in the union executive members being voted out of office, or even in union decertification.

Once a strike is settled, striking workers return to their jobs. During a labour dispute many people are put under remarkable pressure, and relationships essential to effective post-settlement work dynamics can be tarnished—especially in firms that rely heavily on teamwork. Post-settlement work environments are often riddled with tension, derogatory remarks, and hostility. Relationships are a critical factor in how quickly and effectively business gets back to normal, and

replacement workers Individuals hired to perform the work of striking employees, often referred to as "scabs."

picket Stationing groups of striking employees, usually carrying signs, at the entrances and exits of the struck operation to publicize the issues in dispute and discourage people from entering or leaving the premises.

secondary picketing Picketing used to delay or disrupt the regular course of business in companies that are affiliated with or are clients of the employer in an attempt to put pressure on the company to settle the dispute.

boycott An organized refusal of bargaining unit members and supporters to buy the products or utilize the services of the organization whose employees are on strike, in an effort to exert economic pressure on the employer.

Tips **for the** Front Line

HR managers returning to the workplace after a settlement must work to repair damaged relationships that infect working environments and hinder productivity. By doing some pre-strike planning, HR managers can more effectively address issues that arise later. Some ways to improve a post-settlement work environment include:

- Hold a welcome back meeting within the first few hours of the first day back.
- Meet with picket captains in the first couple of days after the strike settlement to repair relationships and to clearly indicate that roles assumed during the strike are no longer applicable to the workplace. (Picket captains, usually union leaders, are individuals who control picket lines during a strike, and after a strike settlement, they often bring their leadership style back to the workplace and present an authority problem.)
- Hold return-to-work workshops, post-settlement trauma briefings, or other support services. Review EAP options and ensure that management and employees are aware of the programs available.
- Establish ground rules about the importance of business resumptions and zero tolerance for inappropriate behaviour such as harassment.
- Ensure that management has clearly defined expectations about the return to work and the possible actions to take in case a negative situation occurs.[28]

lockout Temporary refusal of a company to continue providing work for bargaining unit employees involved in a labour dispute, which may result in closure of the establishment for a period of time.

Lockout   Although not a widely used strategy in Canada, a **lockout** is legally permissible. This involves the employer prohibiting the bargaining unit employees from entering the company premises, as a means of putting pressure on the union negotiating team to agree to the terms and conditions being offered by management. Sometimes the employer chooses to close operations entirely, which means that nonstriking employees are also affected. Most employers try to avoid this option, since doing so means that the well-being of innocent parties is threatened, and a lockout may damage the firm's public image. However, in May 2003, for the second time in five years, the Toronto Catholic School Board locked out approximately 3700 teachers at 170 schools, leaving over 69 000 Ontario elementary school children out of class. Although the teachers had not been on strike, they had been on a week-long work-to-rule campaign at the time of the lockout, after having worked for almost 10 months without a contract. The school board refused to send the contract dispute to voluntary arbitration, saying it would be too expensive. The teachers filed a suit asking for damages of approximately $1.3 million a day since the lockout began. Thirteen days later, the Ontario government legislated an end to the lockout.[29]

As illustrated in **Table 17.1**, the number of work stoppages and person-days not worked due to work stoppages fluctuated considerably between 1992 and 2002.

Unlawful Strikes and Lockouts   An unlawful strike is one that contravenes the relevant LR legislation, and lays the union and its members open to charges and possible fines and/or periods of imprisonment if found guilty. For example, it is illegal for a union to call a strike involving employees who do not have the right to strike because of the essential nature of their services, such as nurses or police officers. In all jurisdictions, it is illegal to call a strike during the term of an existing collective agreement.

AN ETHICAL DILEMMA

Is it ethical for a firm to close the establishment during a labour dispute if that results in nonstriking employees being laid off?

TABLE 17.1 Work Stoppages—A Chronological Perspective—1992 to 2002			
Year	Total Number	Workers Involved	Person-Days Not Worked
1992	404	149 940	2 110 180
1993	381	101 784	1 516 640
1994	374	80 856	1 606 580
1995	328	149 159	1 583 061
1996	330	281 816	3 351 820
1997	284	257 664	3 610 206
1998	381	244 367	2 443 836
1999	413	158 288	2 498 581
2000	379	143 456	1 656 790
2001	381	220 499	2 198 870
2002	293	168 640	3 025 657

Source: Reproduced from the Human Resources Development Canada Web site, http://labour.hrdc-drhc.gc.ca/millieudetravail_workplace/chrono/index.cfm/doc/english. July 15, 2003. Reproduced with the permission of the Minister of Public Works and Government Services Canada, 2004.

wildcat strike A spontaneous walkout, not officially sanctioned by the union leadership, which may be legal or illegal, depending on its timing.

Arbitration
www.gov.on.ca/lab/english/lr/faq/lr_faq4.html

arbitration The use of an outside third party to investigate a dispute between an employer and union and impose a settlement.

interest dispute A dispute between an organization and the union representing its employees over the terms of a collective agreement.

interest arbitration The imposition of the final terms of a collective agreement.

A **wildcat strike** is a spontaneous walkout, not officially sanctioned by the union leaders, which is illegal if it occurs during the term of a collective agreement. For example, 500 unionized employees at TrentonWorks, a rail-car plant in New Glasgow, Nova Scotia, walked off the job in September 2002 to protest the installation of video cameras in the plant's main production area without the union's knowledge. The company claimed that the cameras were installed due to recent vandalism, while employees felt that the cameras would be used to spy on honest workers. The wildcat strike ended the next day when the company agreed to remove the cameras for ten days while management and the union worked out a solution to the issue.[30]

An unlawful lockout contravenes the applicable LR statute, laying the employer open to charges and penalties similar to those involved in illegal strike situations. Locking out employees during the term of a collective agreement is illegal in every jurisdiction, prior to the exhaustion of conciliation procedures in most, and within a prescribed number of hours of a strike vote in a few.

Interest Arbitration

Arbitration involves the use of an outside third party to investigate a dispute between an employer and union, and impose a settlement. A sole arbitrator or three-person arbitration board may be involved. Arbitration decisions are final and binding and cannot be changed or revised.

Arbitration may be used to settle an **interest dispute** regarding the terms of a collective agreement. Known as **interest arbitration,** this process results in the imposition of the terms of the collective agreement. The right to interest arbitration is legally mandated for workers who are not permitted to strike, such as hospital and nursing home employees, police officers and firefighters in most jurisdictions, and public servants in some.[31] Federal civil servants can choose between the right to strike and interest arbitration in each set of negotiations. Interest arbitration is also involved when special legislation is passed, ordering striking or locked-out parties back to work, due to public hardship. Because the right to strike or lock out is, in effect, removed by such legislation, any terms of the collective agreement that are still in dispute are investigated by an arbitrator, and a settlement is imposed based on his or her judgment of a fair course of action.

The Collective Agreement: Typical Provisions

The eventual outcome of collective bargaining, whether negotiated by the parties, or imposed by an arbitrator, is a formal, written, collective agreement. The length and scope of this document vary depending on organization size, type of relationship between the parties, and duration of the bargaining relationship.

Typical contract provisions include:

- union recognition clause
- union security/checkoff clause
- no-strike-or-lockout provision
- management rights clause
- grievance procedure
- arbitration clause
- disciplinary procedures
- compensation rates and benefits
- hours of work and overtime pay provisions
- health and safety provisions
- employee security/seniority provisions
- contract expiration date.

Of the twelve items listed above, five deserve closer scrutiny.

Union Recognition Clause

A *union recognition clause* clarifies the scope of the bargaining unit by specifying the employee classifications included therein or listing those excluded. This clause recognizes the union as the exclusive bargaining agent for the employees in the bargaining unit. For example:[32]

> The company recognizes the union as the exclusive bargaining agent for all its employees, save and except employees charged with management and supervisory responsibilities, clerical and secretarial staff, professional and technical employees, and security staff.

Union Security/Checkoff Clause

union security clause The contract provisions protecting the interests of the labour union, dealing with the issue of membership requirements and, often, the payment of union dues.

closed shop A security clause specifying that only union members in good standing may be hired by the employer to perform bargaining unit work.

All Canadian jurisdictions permit the inclusion of a **union security clause** in the collective agreement to protect the interests of the labour union. This clause deals with the issue of membership requirements and, often, the payment of union dues. There are various forms of union security clauses, the most common of which will be described next:[33]

- *Closed shop.* A **closed shop** is the most restrictive form of union security. Only union members in good standing may be hired by the employer to

union shop A type of security arrangement in which union membership and dues payment are mandatory conditions of employment.

modified union shop A type of security arrangement in which the individuals who were bargaining unit members at the time of certification or when the collective agreement was signed are not obliged to join the union, although they must pay dues, but all subsequently hired employees must do both.

maintenance-of-membership arrangement A security arrangement that requires individuals voluntarily joining the union to remain members during the life of the collective agreement.

Rand formula (dues shop/agency shop) A popular security arrangement that does not require union membership, but does require all bargaining unit members to pay union dues.

AN ETHICAL DILEMMA

Given the fact that some workers have religious or other objections to unions, is a dues shop arrangement ethical?

open shop The weakest type of security arrangement, in which union membership is voluntary, and nonmembers are not required to pay dues.

checkoff Contract provisions requiring the employer to deduct union dues from the paycheques of bargaining unit members and forward the money to the union.

perform bargaining unit work. This type of security clause is common in the construction industry.

- *Union shop*. In a **union shop**, membership and dues payment are mandatory conditions of employment. Although individuals do not have to be union members at the time that they are hired, they are required to join the union on the day on which they commence work or on completion of probation.

- *Modified union shop*. In a **modified union shop**, the individuals who were bargaining unit members at the time of certification or when the collective agreement was signed are not obliged to join the union, although they must pay dues, but all subsequently hired employees must do both.

- *Maintenance-of-membership arrangement*. Under a **maintenance-of-membership arrangement**, individuals voluntarily joining the union must remain members during the term of the contract. Membership withdrawal is typically permitted during a designated period around the time of contract expiration. Dues payment is generally mandatory for all bargaining unit members.

- *The Rand formula*. A setting in which the **Rand formula** is applied may also be known as a **dues shop** (in Canada) or an **agency shop** (in the U.S.). This is a popular union security arrangement that does not require union membership, but does require that all members of the bargaining unit pay union dues. It is a compromise arrangement, suggested by former Chief Justice of the Supreme Court of Canada Ivan C. Rand, that recognizes the fact that the union must represent all employees in the bargaining unit and should therefore be entitled to their financial support, but also provides the choice to join or not join the union.

- *Open shop*. An **open shop** is a type of security arrangement whereby union membership is voluntary and nonmembers are not required to pay dues.

The process by which union dues are collected by the employer via payroll deduction and remitted to the union is known as **checkoff**. Today, nearly 90 percent of collective agreements in Canada have a checkoff provision whereby employers deduct dues from unionized employees' paycheques and remit the dues with a list of dues-paying (and dues-equivalent-paying under the Rand formula) employees.[34] Employers in every Canadian jurisdiction must deduct union dues when authorized to do so by the employee.[35] Where there are *voluntary checkoff* arrangements, the employer only deducts union dues from the paycheques of employees who authorize such deductions in writing. Such arrangements cannot exist in a union or closed shop. Some jurisdictions now require employers to deduct union dues from the paycheques of all bargaining unit members and remit them to the union.[36] This is known as *compulsory checkoff*. In these jurisdictions, the minimum union security provision in collective agreements generally involves the Rand formula.

No-Strike-or-Lockout Provision

There must be a clause in every contract in Canada forbidding strikes or lockouts while the collective agreement is in effect. The intent is to guarantee some degree of stability in the employment relationship during the life of the collective agreement, which must be at least one year. Saskatchewan and Quebec are the only jurisdictions that impose a maximum duration of three years.[37] In general, the duration of collective agreements in Canada is increasing. In 1991, the average duration was 18.2 months, but by 2000 the average duration had risen to 35.0 months.[38]

Management Rights Clause

The *management rights clause* clarifies the areas in which management may exercise its exclusive rights without agreement from the union, and the issues that are not subject to collective bargaining. It typically refers to the rights of management to operate the organization, subject to the terms of the collective agreement. Any rights not limited by the clause are reserved to management. For example:[39]

> The management of the plant and the direction of its working force is the sole responsibility of the company. These functions are broad in nature and include the right to schedule work and shift beginning and ending times, the right to schedule overtime, and the right to contract out work. The company also has the right to discipline and discharge employees for cause providing the terms of this agreement are met, and the right to determine the makeup of its workforce and to transfer, lay off or demote employees. In the fulfillment of these functions, the company agrees not to violate the terms of this agreement nor to discriminate against any member of the union.

Arbitration Clause

All Canadian jurisdictions require that collective agreements contain a clause providing for the final and binding settlement, by arbitration, of all disputes arising during the term of a collective agreement. Such disputes may relate to the application, interpretation, or administration of that agreement, as well as alleged contraventions by either party.

Impact of Societal Changes on Contract Provisions

As with HR policies and procedures, collective agreement language and provisions change over time. Many contracts now include clauses that reflect increasing environmental awareness and activism.[40] Legislative issues and demographic changes can also affect contract language and provisions, as explained in the Workforce Diversity box.

CONTRACT ADMINISTRATION

After a collective agreement has been negotiated and signed, the contract administration process begins. Both union and management are required to abide by the contract provisions. It is also in day-to-day contract administration that the bulk of labour–management relations occurs. Regardless of the amount of time, effort, care, and attention put into the wording of the contract, it is almost inevitable that differences of opinion will arise regarding the application and interpretation of the agreement.

With the exception of the management rights clause, most contract provisions limit the types of actions that managers can take. Because such provisions

WORKFORCE DIVERSITY

Accommodation in Collective Agreements

The collective agreement between the Saskatchewan Association of Health Organizers and CUPE includes an agreement to introduce a representative Aboriginal workforce and to facilitate literacy training and educational counselling. The parties also agreed to implement educational opportunities for all employees to deal with misconceptions and dispel myths about Aboriginal people. The employer and the union will make every reasonable effort to accommodate an employee who wishes to attend or participate in a spiritual or cultural observation required by faith or culture.[1]

Bell Canada and the Canadian Telecommunications Employees Association have negotiated a workforce diversity and employment equity program. Three hours of training will be given to employee groups who could be challenged by issues of diversity and respect of other workers. Also, the importance of reasonable accommodation and the respective responsibilities of managers and other employees will be highlighted by various training and communication initiatives. Local initiatives such as diversity days or multicultural days will be organized to improve awareness.[2]

"Reserved Jobs" positions for permanently disabled employees have been negotiated between INCO Ltd. in Thompson, Manitoba, and the United Steelworkers of America. Certain positions will be identified and forwarded to the joint rehabilitation committee. Employees working in those classifications identified as reserved will not be removed; however, when the job becomes vacant, permanently disabled employees will have the opportunity to move into the job. These employees will be placed in accordance with seniority and their regular job will be protected as a temporary vacancy.[3]

1. T. Plante, "Innovative Workplace Practices," *Workplace Gazette* (Spring 2002), p. 37.

2. B. Aldridge, "Innovative Workplace Practices," *Workplace Gazette* (Winter 2002), p. 36.

3. B. Aldridge, "Innovative Workplace Practices," *Workplace Gazette* (Winter 2002), p. 36.

not only place restrictions on management but are often subject to different interpretations, seniority and discipline issues are a major source of disagreement between union and management.

Seniority

seniority Length of service in the bargaining unit.

Unions typically prefer to have employee-related decisions determined by **seniority**, which refers to length of service in the bargaining unit. In many collective agreements, seniority is the governing factor in layoffs and recalls (the most senior employees are the last to be laid off and the first to be recalled), and a determining factor in transfers and promotions. In some collective agreements, seniority is also the determining factor in decisions pertaining to work assignments, shift preferences, allocation of days off, and vacation time.

The principle of seniority is sometimes accepted as an equitable and objective decision-making criterion, ensuring that there is no favouritism. However, in other cases, there is disagreement about the amount of weight that should be placed on seniority as compared to ability. Managers often prefer to place greater weight on ability or merit, while unions want more emphasis placed on seniority. Since employers are generally unwilling to accept seniority as the sole criterion for transfers and promotions or for layoffs due to lack of work, *sufficient ability* and *relative ability* clauses are very common.

Discipline

Almost all collective agreements give the employer the right to make reasonable rules and regulations governing employees' behaviour and to take disciplinary action if the rules are broken. In every collective agreement, bargaining unit members are given the right to file a grievance if they feel that any disciplinary action taken was too harsh or without just cause.

Most collective agreements restrict an employer's right to discipline employees by requiring proof of just or reasonable cause for the disciplinary action imposed. Since just or reasonable cause is open to different interpretations, disciplinary action is a major source of grievances. Managers must therefore be extremely careful not only that disciplinary issues are handled in accordance with the terms of the collective agreement, but also that they are backed by evidence. The need for proof requires careful documentation (and thus, often, more paperwork for first-line supervisors). Even when disciplinary action is handled carefully, the union steward representing the employee involved may argue that there were extenuating circumstances that should be taken into consideration. Supervisors have to strike a delicate balance between fairness and consistency.

When discipline cases end up at arbitration, two independent decisions are made. The first is whether the employee actually engaged in some form of misconduct. Then, if that question is answered in the affirmative, an assessment must be made of whether such misconduct warrants the particular discipline imposed, as well as whether such disciplinary action violated the collective agreement.

Grievance Resolution and Rights Arbitration

A **grievance** is a written allegation of a contract violation generally involving a disagreement about its application or interpretation. Disagreements may also arise because of misunderstandings, unclear contract language, and changing circumstances. When such alleged violations or disagreements arise, they are settled through the grievance procedure. A multi-step grievance procedure, the last step of which is final and binding arbitration, is found in virtually all collective agreements. Such procedures have been very effective in resolving day-to-day problems arising during the life of the collective agreement.

The primary purpose of the grievance procedure is to ensure the application of the contract with a degree of justice for both parties. Secondary purposes include providing the opportunity for the interpretation of contract language, such as the meaning of "sufficient ability"; serving as a communications device through which managers can become aware of employee concerns and areas of dissatisfaction; and bringing to the attention of both union and management those areas of the contract requiring clarification or modification in subsequent negotiations.

Steps in the Grievance Procedure
The grievance procedure involves systematic deliberation of a complaint at progressively higher levels of authority in the company and union. Grievances are usually filed by individual bargaining unit members. If the issue in contention is one that may affect a number of union members, either at the time or in the future, the union may file a *policy grievance*. Management also has the right to use the grievance procedure

---

AN ETHICAL DILEMMA

Is it ethical to insist that all similar grievances be resolved in a consistent manner, regardless of specific circumstances, to avoid setting a precedent?

grievance A written allegation of a contract violation, filed by an individual bargaining unit member, the union, or management.

to process a complaint about the union, although such use is rare. All contracts contain a grievance procedure, and most provide for arbitration as a final step. While the number of steps and people involved at each vary, **Figure 17.4** illustrates a typical grievance procedure.

FIGURE 17.4   A Typical Grievance Procedure

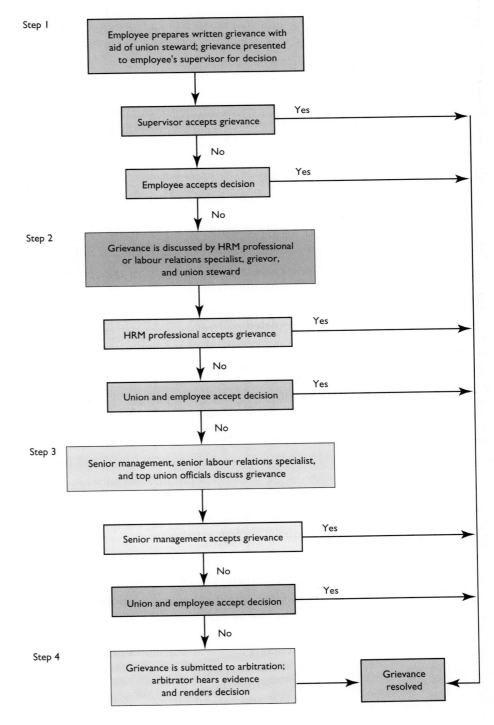

As illustrated in Figure 17.4, the typical first step of the grievance procedure in a collective agreement occurs when an aggrieved employee or a union steward on his or her behalf files a written complaint with the employee's immediate supervisor. If the problem is not resolved to the satisfaction of the employee at the first step, he or she may then take the problem to the next higher managerial level designated in the contract, and so on through all of the steps available. There are generally three internal steps prior to arbitration. Time limits are typically provided for resolution at each step. Failure to respond within the specified time limit may result in the grievance being automatically processed at the next step, or being deemed to have been withdrawn or resolved. Ninety percent or more of all grievances are settled, abandoned, or withdrawn prior to arbitration.

Handling Complaints/Grievances

When handling complaints or formal grievances, supervisors must walk a fine line, since they need to treat employees fairly, while maintaining management's rights. To accomplish this goal, some helpful guidelines to keep in mind follow:[41]

> ### Tips for the Front Line

Do:
- investigate each and every case as though it might eventually result in an arbitration hearing; visit and inspect the work area involved, and interview any witnesses
- treat the union steward and the complainant as equals
- examine the HR records of the complainant regarding any past complaints and/or disciplinary action
- require the union to identify the specific contractual provisions allegedly violated
- comply with the time limits specified in the collective agreement.

Do not:
- allow grievances over issues that are not covered by the collective agreement; these should be handled as informal complaints
- hold back the remedy if the company is wrong
- admit to the binding effect of a past practice
- settle grievances on the basis of what seems "fair"; the collective agreement should be the standard
- make arrangements with individual employees that are inconsistent with the collective agreement.

Common Difficulties with Grievance Procedures

Some employee "grievances" stem from perceived injustices or injured feelings rather than from actual contract violations. The union then has to decide whether to process the complaint as a formal grievance or to attempt to pacify the employee. Management must also decide how to handle such complaints. One approach is for the steward and/or supervisor to attempt to assess the emotional and social aspects of the complaint and deal with the problem at that level. Simply permitting the employee to vent his or her feelings may provide a partial solution, and careful listening may help to identify the real underlying issue.

Another difficulty with the grievance procedure is the possibility of its becoming a vehicle for the respective parties to test their relative strengths. For example, in settings in which union–management relations are poor, the union may file grievances at every opportunity in order to wring concessions from management, or a union official may decide to press a particular case to test his or her strength or to "get back" at management. Similarly, management may fight every grievance in an attempt to restrict the union's rights and power.

A third difficulty may arise due to political pressures. A union steward, for example, may be subjected to considerable pressure from an aggrieved worker to push a grievance to further steps within the organization even if its legitimacy is somewhat questionable. Similarly, the LR manager may be pressured by other members of management to settle or not to settle a particular grievance, depending on the current LR climate within the firm.

Rights Arbitration   Grievance arbitration is a process through which disputes arising out of the application and interpretation of a collective agreement are resolved. It is a quasi-judicial system created for each collective bargaining relationship. Differences concerning the interpretation or administration of the collective agreement are known as **rights disputes**. Thus, if the parties are unable to resolve a grievance issue themselves, it must be referred to an arbitrator or three-person arbitration board for a final and binding decision. The process involved in resolving such issues is known as **rights arbitration**.

Many collective agreements provide for a three-person arbitration board, rather than a sole arbitrator. In such cases, each party appoints a delegate to represent it on the board (the union and management nominees), and these two nominees are responsible for choosing a neutral chair (generally a lawyer or professor skilled in arbitration). If they cannot reach agreement on a suitable chairperson, within specified timelines, the chair is generally appointed by the applicable minister of labour. The advantage of using a board relates to the fact that a representative of each of the parties is directly involved in the decision-making process. The disadvantage is that boards generally take more time to reach a decision and are more costly. When a three-person board is used, each party pays its nominee's expenses, and the expenses of the chair and costs involved in meeting room rental are shared.

Role of the Arbitrator/Arbitration Board The collective agreement is recognized as the fundamental source of the subject matter that is within an arbitrator's jurisdiction.[42] In the grievance-arbitration process, the arbitrator's role is generally considered quasi-judicial, that is, similar to that of a judge. He or she is expected to listen to evidence, weigh it impartially and objectively, and make a decision based on the contract language. There are some significant differences between the arbitrator's role and that of a judge, however.

Firstly, arbitration hearings tend to be much more informal than courtroom proceedings. The parties may or may not have legal counsel present at the hearings, and the proceedings are not bound by the rules of evidence as in the court of law. However, it is expected that the proceedings will be conducted with dignity and fairness. They generally include the cross-examination of the parties or witnesses and the submission of documents as evidence.

Secondly, the arbitrator is not bound by precedents to the extent that a judge is usually held.[43] Although an arbitrator may study decisions of other arbitrators in order to further his or her understanding of the issues, and even though

rights dispute A disagreement between an organization and the union representing its employees regarding the interpretation or application of one or more clauses in the current collective agreement.

rights arbitration The process involved in the settlement of a rights dispute.

both parties may cite previous arbitration decisions in support of their positions, an arbitrator is not bound by such decisions.

Thirdly, both the law and court decisions have given the arbitration function considerable power and freedom. The substance or content of arbitration decisions cannot be appealed to the courts except under certain stringent circumstances. Decisions of arbitrators can become orders of the court and are thereby legally enforceable.[44]

The Arbitration Award A written arbitration award is issued at the conclusion of most rights arbitration cases, indicating that the grievance has been upheld (which means that the griever's arguments are deemed to be correct) or overturned (which means that the actions that launched the grievance have been deemed to be correct). In disciplinary cases, it is also possible for an arbitration award to substitute a penalty that is more or less severe than the one proposed by union or management. Generally, such an award includes the decision and the rationale behind it, which can provide guidance to both union and management regarding the interpretation of the collective agreement and the ways in which future disputes arising from its administration should be handled. When there is a three-person arbitration board, an award is commonly issued with one dissenting opinion, that of the nominee of the unsuccessful party. However, it is possible to have an award with two dissenting opinions if both union and management nominees are dissatisfied with the decision made by the neutral chair.

Problems with Rights Arbitration In most organizations, whenever possible, HR managers try to resolve grievances with the union without seeking third-party assistance. In addition to the deterioration in labour–management relations that tends to result when the majority of grievance cases end up at arbitration, and the often-lengthy delay between the alleged violation and arbitration hearing date(s), there are two other potential problems with rights arbitration: the costs involved, and the fact that there is the potential for an arbitration decision to alter management's rights drastically. The substitution of a lesser penalty in a disciplinary case, for example, means that similar future cases must be afforded the same penalty. Otherwise, a grievance is the inevitable result.

BUILDING EFFECTIVE LABOUR–MANAGEMENT RELATIONS

In many organizations, union and management leaders recognize that an effective working relationship is in their mutual interests.[45] A 2002 Conference Board of Canada study found that there is a high degree of maturity in Canadian labour relations, and that both parties have acknowledged that their individual interests are inextricably linked.[46] When managers wish to build a more harmonious and effective relationship, a number of strategies can help.

Instituting an Open-Door Policy

When the key managers involved in labour–management relations welcome employees into their offices to discuss any problems or concerns, and employees feel comfortable in doing so, many issues can be resolved informally. For example, if the president of the local knows that he or she can approach the LR manager "off the record" and that anything discussed in such sessions will be kept strictly confidential, fewer grievances and a more trusting and harmonious relationship often result.

Extending the Courtesy of Prior Consultation

While every management decision does not require union approval, if any actions that might affect union members are discussed with the union executive first, the likelihood of grievances is greatly reduced.

Demonstrating Genuine Concern for Employee Well-Being

When managers are genuinely concerned about employee well-being, and demonstrate that concern, mutual trust and respect are often established. This involves fair treatment and communication going well above and beyond the requirements of the collective agreement.

Forming Joint Committees

Forming labour–management committees to investigate and resolve complex issues can lead to innovative and creative solutions, as well as to a better relationship. In 2000, 67 percent of all Canadian collective agreements contained at least one joint union–management committee.[47] An excellent example of such cooperation is described in the Strategic HR box.

Holding Joint Training Programs

When a contract is first signed, it can be beneficial to hold a joint training program to ensure that supervisors and union stewards are familiar with the terms and conditions specified therein and that they understand the intent of the negotiating teams. Such training can reduce misunderstandings and the likelihood of

STRATEGIC HR

Union–Management Collaboration in the Canadian Steel Industry

In the 1980s, the United Steelworkers of America and steel industry representatives converged to form the Canadian Steel Trade Employment Congress (CSTEC) to deal with a massive industry downturn that resulted in the loss of one-third of its workforce. Faced with massive layoffs and workers with few outside skills, CSTEC developed the Worker Adjustment Program, a shared initiative between government, labour, and management, involving peer counselling, career development, and career training.

Now, 20 years later, the situation is that in the next five to ten years, one-third of the steel industry's workforce will have to be replaced. What started as an outplacement program now encompasses a wide range of entry-level and pre-employment training. Employers can't keep up with the pace of change if their employees are not trained to do the work, and they can't meet business goals if they can't hire people with the right skills.

Thus, unions and management in the steel industry are learning to leverage their resources to fulfill both their needs. The CSTEC has been able to get results, and it is these results that will determine the quality of cooperation and future collaboration efforts.

Source: L. Cassiani, "Strength in Numbers: Union, Management Join Forces on Training — Competitive Business Climate Requires Cooperation for Survival," *Canadian HR Reporter* (March 26, 2001), pp. 3, 11. Reproduced by permission of *Canadian HR Reporter*, Carswell, One Corporate Plaza, 2075 Kennedy Road, Scarborough, ON M1T 3V4.

disagreement regarding interpretation of contract language. Joint training programs can also be extremely helpful in building the cooperation necessary to deal more effectively with other employment-related issues of concern to both parties, such as employee health and safety.

Meeting Regularly

Whether required by the collective agreement or voluntarily instituted, regularly scheduled union–management meetings can result in more effective communication and the resolution of problems/concerns before they become formal grievance issues.

Using Third-Party Assistance

To build a better relationship, it is often beneficial to bring in a consultant or a government agency representative to help identify common goals and objectives and ways in which trust and communication can be strengthened.

The Grievance Process—Sign of a Healthy Environment?

The grievance process can potentially be designed as an effective relationship builder. In a healthy environment, grievances would be welcomed as opportunities to initiate a dialogue over areas of mutual concern. In conjunction with other processes, including collective bargaining, consultations and harmony meetings, the grievance process can be used to promote a positive employee relations environment. In this environment, the absence of grievances would be viewed as a signal that something was wrong. Giving employees an opportunity to readily access a forum where their voices are heard is the sign of a healthy and growing organization.

Source: Excerpted with permission from *Industrial Relations and Personnel Developments* (September 2003), published by and copyright CCH Canadian Limited, Toronto, Ontario.

CHAPTER *Review*

Summary

1   Good-faith bargaining requires that union and management representatives communicate and negotiate, that proposals be matched with counterproposals, and that both parties make every reasonable effort to arrive at an agreement. Surface bargaining and dilatory tactics are two practices that violate good-faith bargaining.

2   Preparations for negotiations include reviewing strategic objectives, gathering data on economic trends, conducting wage and benefit surveys (company) and collecting data on collective bargaining settlements (union), analyzing other collective agreements, obtaining input from supervisors (company) and stewards (union), conducting an audit and analysis of grievances, costing, contingency planning, establishing a bargaining team, and finalizing bargaining strategies and proposals.

3   *Distributive bargaining* is a "win–lose" approach where gains of one party are achieved at the expense of the other. *Integrative bargaining* is an approach that assumes a win–win solution can be found. Three specific types of integrative bargaining are (1) *productivity bargaining* aimed at improving the productivity and effectiveness of the organization, (2) *concessionary bargaining*

used when the employer is experiencing financial difficulty and is seeking "roll-backs," and (3) *mutual gains (interest-based) bargaining* aimed at seeking win–win solutions to all LR issues.

4   Conciliation involves the use of a neutral third party to assist the parties involved in bargaining to come to a mutually satisfactory agreement. Mediation also involves the use of a neutral third party, but mediators play a more active role than conciliators. When a bargaining impasse has been reached and the conciliation process has been undertaken, the union may exercise its right to strike, the employer may exercise its right to lock out the bargaining unit members, or the parties may request interest arbitration. Interest arbitration addresses disputes arising over the terms of a collective agreement, and results in the imposition of the terms of the collective agreement.

5   Five typical collective agreement provisions include a union recognition clause, a union security/checkoff clause, a no-strike-or-lockout provision, a management rights clause, and an arbitration clause.

6   Typical steps in a grievance procedure involve presenting a written grievance to (1) the worker's immediate supervisor, (2) an HR/LR specialist, (3) senior management, and (4) an arbitrator for final and binding rights arbitration.

7   In many organizations, union and management leaders recognize that an effective working relationship is in their mutual best interest. A number of strategies can help, such as instituting an open-door policy, prior consultation, demonstrating genuine concern for employee well-being, forming joint study committees, holding joint training programs, meeting regularly, and using third-party assistance when doing so would be beneficial.

Key Terms

attitudinal structuring   *(p. 535)*
arbitration   *(p. 541)*
bargaining zone   *(p. 531)*
boycott   *(p. 539)*
caucus session   *(p. 531)*
checkoff   *(p. 543)*
closed shop   *(p. 542)*

concessionary bargaining   *(p. 533)*
conciliation   *(p. 536)*
dilatory tactics   *(p. 526)*
distributive bargaining   *(p. 533)*
good-faith bargaining   *(p. 525)*
grievance   *(p. 546)*
integrative bargaining   *(p. 533)*
interest arbitration   *(p. 541)*
interest dispute   *(p. 541)*
lockout   *(p. 540)*
maintenance-of-membership arrangement   *(p. 543)*
mediation   *(p. 537)*
memorandum of settlement   *(p. 536)*
modified union shop   *(p. 543)*
mutual gains (interest-based) bargaining   *(p. 534)*
open shop   *(p. 543)*
pattern bargaining   *(p. 527)*
picket   *(p. 539)*
productivity bargaining   *(p. 533)*
Rand formula (dues shop/agency shop)   *(p. 543)*
ratification   *(p. 536)*
replacement workers   *(p. 539)*
rights arbitration   *(p. 549)*
rights dispute   *(p. 549)*
secondary picketing   *(p. 539)*
seniority   *(p. 545)*
strike   *(p. 537)*
strike vote   *(p. 537)*
surface bargaining   *(p. 525)*
union security clause   *(p. 542)*
union shop   *(p. 543)*
wildcat strike   *(p. 541)*

Review and Discussion Questions

1   Describe the purposes of collective bargaining and cite five examples of violations of the principle of bargaining in good faith.

2   Describe the typical steps and issues involved in the face-to-face negotiating process.

3   Explain the bargaining zone and draw a diagram to illustrate this concept.

4   Explain the concepts of strikes, picketing, secondary picketing, boycotts, and lockouts.

5   Explain the six common forms of union security clause.

6   Explain how arbitration differs from conciliation and mediation, and differentiate between interest arbitration and rights arbitration.

CRITICAL *Thinking Questions*

1   As the LR specialist, what steps would you take in order to prepare the firm and management team if you believed that a strike was a possible outcome of the upcoming negotiations?

2   "Seniority and discipline issues are a major source of disagreement between union and management during the contract administration

process." Discuss this statement and explain why these two issues often lead to grievances.

3   Think of an organization with which you are familiar, in which there is a harmonious labour–management relationship. Compare and contrast the steps taken to build such a relationship with the guidelines provided in this chapter.

APPLICATION *Exercises*

Running Case: LearnInMotion.com
The Grievance

When coming in to work one day, Pierre was surprised to be taken aside by Jason, one of their original employees, who met him as he was parking his car. "Jennifer told me I was suspended for two days without pay because I came in late last Thursday," said Jason. "I'm really upset, but around here Jennifer's word seems to be law, and it sometimes seems like the only way anyone can file a grievance is by meeting you like this in the parking lot."

Pierre was very disturbed by this revelation and promised the employee that he would discuss the situation with Jennifer. He began mulling over possible alternatives.

Questions

1   Do you think that it is important for LearnInMotion.com to have a formal grievance procedure? Why or why not?

2   Based on what you know about LearnInMotion.com, outline the steps that you think should be involved in the firm's grievance process, should they decide to implement one.

3   What else could Jennifer and Pierre do, other than implementing a grievance process, to ensure that complaints and grievances get expressed and handled?

CASE INCIDENT *Strategy*

"They want what?" the mayor exclaimed.

"Like I said," the town clerk replied, "17 percent over two years."

"There is no way that the taxpayers will accept a settlement anywhere near that," reiterated the mayor. "I don't care if the garbage doesn't get collected for a century. We can't go more than 8 percent over the next two years."

The town clerk looked worried. "How much loss of service do you think the public will accept? Suppose they do go on strike? I'm the one who always gets the complaints. Then there's the health problem with rats running all over the place!

Remember over in Neibringtown, when that little kid was bitten? There was a hell of an outcry."

The mayor agreed: "Garbage collectors always have strong bargaining power, but, if I don't fight this, I'll be voted out in the next election. I say we offer 6 percent over 18 months. Then we can go either way—6 percent over 12 months or 8 percent over two years."

"I wonder if we have any other options?" worried the town clerk.

"Well, we could threaten not to hire any more union personnel and to job out the collection service to private contractors if the union wasn't cooperative," mused the mayor.

"That's a good idea!" The town clerk sounded enthusiastic. "Also, we can mount a newspaper advertising campaign to get the public behind us. If we play on the fear of massive tax increases, the garbage collectors won't have much public sympathy."

"What about asking the union to guarantee garbage collection for old people during a strike? If they refuse, they'll look bad in the public eye; if they accept, we are rid of a major problem. Most people can bring their trash to a central collection point. Not all old people can," chuckled the mayor, "We can't lose on that issue!"

"Okay then," said the town clerk. "It looks like we have the beginning of a bargaining strategy here. Actually, I feel better now. I think we're in a rather strong position."

Questions

1 Discuss the plight of public sector unions faced with the reality of a limited tax base and public pressure to lower taxes.

2 Is the town clerk right? Is the town in a good bargaining position? Explain your answer.

3 What strengths does the union have in its position?

4 If you were a labour relations consultant, would you agree with the present strategy? What alternatives, if any, would you propose?

Source: R.W. Mondy, R.M. Noe, S.R. Premeaux, and R.A. Knowles, *Human Resource Management,* 2nd Canadian ed. (Toronto, ON: Pearson Education Canada, 2001, p. 386).

EXPERIENTIAL *Exercises*

1 Working with several of your classmates, use role-playing to differentiate between distributive, integrative, and intra-organizational bargaining. Then use role-playing to differentiate between mutual gains (interest-based) bargaining and the more traditional position-based approach.

2 Obtain a copy of two collective agreements. Compare and contrast the following provisions: union recognition, management rights, union security/checkoff, grievance procedure, arbitration clause, and contract expiry date.

5

Alabama Auto Jobs

What an incredible week in the car business! Chrysler workers went to the brink in a contract dispute, narrowly avoiding a massive strike. Then came the news that Navistar is shutting its plant in Chatham, Ontario. Two thousand workers will be out of jobs. Pressure is building for the government to smooth out what appears to be some very big bumps on the road this industry is travelling.

A massive strike of DaimlerChrysler workers was averted at the last minute when union and management agreed that production could be cancelled at the Windsor plant (resulting in 1200 lost jobs), but that DaimlerChrysler would build a new plant in a few years if the Canadian government provides support and incentives. A similar agreement had previously been reached with Ford Canada.

Anil Verma, professor of industrial relations at the University of Toronto, says that this is a perfect example of strategic bargaining—labour-management bargaining with political implications; in other words, a squeeze play by the Canadian Auto Workers, where the Canadian government can be blamed if jobs are lost because incentives are not provided to automakers to locate here. This is all part of a global trend by governments to entice automakers to choose their location for new plants.

It started when the state of Alabama, which had no auto jobs, enticed Mercedes to locate there with $250 million in incentives, including free employee training, free construction of a highway overpass into the plant, expansion financing, and tax breaks. Alabama, with its low-wage, no-union landscape, has been transformed into "Detroit South," with Mercedes, Honda, Hyundai, and auto parts companies located there, turning out 600 000 autos per year. People are moving into the state to take auto jobs, creating a booming construction business.

Canada offers a built-in incentive in the form of its government health-care system, which reduces company health-care costs relative to the United States. Nevertheless, DaimlerChrysler recently decided to locate in Georgia instead of Windsor, due to the incentives offered to them in Georgia. The mayor of Windsor is now pressuring Ottawa to match these kinds of incentives. Thus, it appears that Canadian economic growth could be limited without further government incentives, particularly support for employee training. According to Professor Verma, there is really no choice in the foreseeable future.

Questions

1. Is it ethical for unions and management to exert pressure on the Canadian government through the use of strategic bargaining?

2. Why would the Canadian Auto Workers agree to close a plant now when they cannot be sure that the government will provide incentives in the future?

3. How likely is it that the Canadian government will begin providing incentives to automakers to build plants in Canada?

Video Source: "Alabama Auto Jobs," *CBC Venture 850* (October 20, 2002).

Additional Resources: www.caw.ca; www.newswire.ca/en/releases/archive/July2003/30/c6400.html

CHAPTER 18

Managing Human Resources in an International Business

LEARNING OUTCOMES

After studying this chapter, you should be able to:

Explain how intercountry differences have an impact on HRM.

Explain how to improve international assignments through employee selection.

Answer the question, "What sort of special training do overseas candidates need?"

Discuss the major considerations in formulating a compensation plan for overseas employees.

Describe the main considerations in repatriating employees from abroad.

The Internationalization of Business

It is clear that international business is important to companies here and abroad. Huge global companies like Noranda, Labatt, and Molson have long had extensive overseas operations. With the ongoing European market unification, the opening of Eastern Europe, and the rapid development of demand in the Pacific Rim and other areas of the world, however, the vast majority of companies are finding that their success depends on their ability to market and manage overseas. Of course, to foreign companies like Toyota, Canada is "overseas," and thousands of foreign firms already have thriving operations in Canada.

As a result of this internationalization, companies must increasingly be managed globally, but globalization confronts managers with several challenges. For instance, market, product, and production plans must be coordinated on a worldwide basis, and organization structures capable of balancing centralized home-office control with adequate local autonomy must be created. Some of the most pressing challenges concern globalization's impact on an employer's HR management system, and specifically the techniques used to recruit, select, train, compensate, and maintain the quality of work-life of employees who are based abroad.[1] As shown in **Figure 18.1**, HR is one of the top three most important business functions for executing global strategy.

FIGURE 18.1   Value Added by HR in Executing Global Strategy

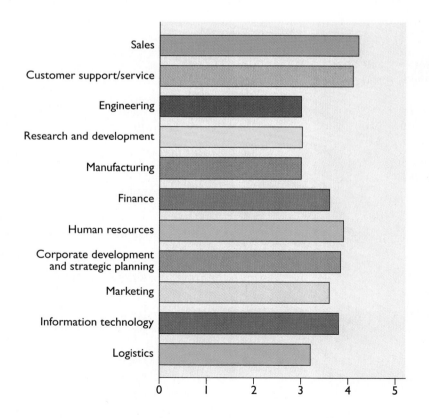

Source: *The Accenture High-Performance Workforce Study 2002/2003.* © 2003 Accenture. Reprinted by permission of Accenture, Toronto. All rights reserved.

HR and the International Business Challenge

As companies have gone global, the number of their employees abroad has increased. In terms of employees overseas, for instance, a recent survey of 351 companies found that virtually every firm had at least one employee on international assignment; about 67 percent of the firms had between one and 40 employees abroad, while the remaining firms have 41 or more employees on international assignment. About 20 percent of the assignments were short term (up to one year), while 50 percent were for up to three years, and about 30 percent were for more than three years.[2] There is a trend toward short-term global assignments instead of permanent relocations, due to the prevalence of dual-career families and a host of other issues.[3]

With more employees abroad, HR departments have had to tackle new global challenges. For example, senior international HR managers in eight large companies were recently asked questions such as, "What are the key global pressures affecting HRM practices in your firm currently and for the projected future?"[4] The three broad global HR challenges that emerged were as follows:

International HRM Association
www.ihrim.org

Mobility Services International
www.msimobility.com

Monster Board Moving
www.monstermoving.com/
International

- *Deployment.* Easily getting the right skills to where they are needed in the organization regardless of geographical location.

- *Knowledge and innovation dissemination.* Spreading state-of-the art knowledge and practices throughout the organization regardless of where they originate.

- *Identifying and developing talent on a global basis.* Identifying who has the ability to function effectively in a global organization and developing these abilities.[5]

Dealing with such challenges means that most employers have had to scramble to develop HR policies and procedures just for handling global assignments. This process itself can be very complex: for example, consider some of the factors needed to address a decision about whom to deploy to an overseas assignment and how to pay that person. From a practical point of view, one has to address issues such as the following:[6]

1. *Candidate identification, assessment, and selection.* In addition to the required technical and business skills, key traits to consider for global assignments include cultural sensitivity, interpersonal skills, and flexibility.

2. *Cost projections.* The average cost of sending an employee and family on an overseas assignment is reportedly between three and five times the employee's pre-departure salary; as a result, quantifying total costs for a global assignment and deciding whether to use an expatriate or a local employee are essential in the budgeting process.

3. *Assignment letters.* The assignee's specific job requirements and associated pay will have to be documented and formally communicated in an assignment letter.

4. *Compensation, benefits, and tax programs.* There are many ways in which to compensate employees who are transferred abroad, given the vast differences in living expenses around the world. Some common approaches to international pay include home-based pay plus a supplement and destination-based pay.

5. *Relocation assistance.* The assignee will probably have to be assisted with such matters as maintenance of the person's home and automobiles, shipment and storage of household goods, and so forth. Flexible relocation benefit packages are becoming more common.[7]

6. *Family support.* Cultural orientation, educational assistance, and emergency provisions are just some of the matters to be addressed before the family is shipped abroad.[8]

The last two issues relate to the heightened focus on work–life balance that is so necessary in today's climate of relocation refusals due to concerns about a mother-in-law's home care, the children's education, a spouse's career, and the difficulty of adjusting to new surroundings while juggling family responsibilities at the same time as focusing on the job. Four major work–life balance relocation challenges are career assistance for the spouse, eldercare assistance, education and school selection assistance, and cross-cultural adjustment.[9]

That is just the tip of the iceberg. Cross-cultural, technical, and language training programs will probably be required. The complex and differentiated tapestry of labour laws and rules from country to country and provisions for reassimilating the expatriate when he or she returns home are some of the other issues that must be addressed. In the future, it is expected that some of these issues will be dealt with virtually, as the relocation industry transforms itself into an e-commerce platform accessible to relocated employees, as explained in the HR.Net box.

Research
Insight ▷

The need to take local customs and laws into consideration is illustrated by a recent study of the facility of NCR Corporation in Dundee, Scotland. The researcher collected information on several HRM activities at Dundee, including the strategic role of HRM, recruitment, employee training and development, compensation, industrial relations, and flexible working patterns.[10] The findings suggested that any attempt to simply transfer home-office HR best practices to a host country facility without accommodating cultural and other differences would be futile. For example, although in many respects Dundee HR "follows the parent company's overall policies ... to a fair extent senior managers in Dundee do things as they choose to do."[11] "Almost all, some 95 percent of the education and training policies and specific programs implemented in Dundee are defined [there]."[12] On the other hand, compensation and benefits tend to "follow the parent company's policies, and the system is fairly centralized with this respect" although there are instances where "these policies are translated into practices and procedures in a manner that is specific to NCR Dundee."[13]

New Destinations

Sending employees abroad and managing HR globally is complicated by the nature of the countries into which many firms are expanding. Employers today are not just transferring employees into the relatively lush surroundings of industrialized countries. Today's expatriates are heading to China (increasingly the most likely destination for a foreign assignment), India, Brazil, Russia, Mexico, Singapore, and Hong Kong.

Notice the range of HR-related challenges that an employer can expect when assigning employees in some of these countries. In China, for instance, special insurance should cover emergency evacuations for serious health problems; tele-

HR.Net

Global Relocation of the Future

In this techno-charged global arena with its incredible rate of change, HR professionals struggle to allow their imaginations to keep pace with technological advancements. Technology is framing and setting the pace for the future, and has indeed already done so in the field of global relocation.

Statistics tell the story. According to the *2000 Global Relocation Trends Survey*, conducted by GMAC Global Relocation Services, the U.S.-based National Foreign Trade Council and the Institute for International Human Resources, 23 percent of companies use a dedicated Web site to communicate with expatriates. Of those respondents whose companies did not have an expatriate Web site, 41 percent indicated plans to build one. Respondents report that these intranets are highly effective for relocation program administration.

Expatriates themselves said that technology is very important to them. Ninety-two percent said that the Internet is critical to their lives, and 96 percent said they use it daily for personal or business communications, according to a 2001 survey, *Maximizing Your Expatriate Investment*, sponsored by WorldatWork, the National Foreign Trade Council, and Cigna International Expatriate Benefits.

The big innovation to watch for will be "relocation stores" on the Internet. It is inevitable that the relocation industry will transform itself into an e-commerce platform, whereby relocation companies will create locations on the Internet for corporations and consumers to access. While they will not replace the HR relocation function entirely, they will certainly ease the burden and create greater self-sufficiency on the part of transferees.

Some of these Web sites already exist:

- Homestore.com helps today's transferees with information on housing prices and selling their homes and information on communities and mortgages.

- HRToolbox.com helps manage expatriates by providing administrators with a system that helps calculate compensation.

- Expataccess.com provides information and connections between individual expatriates, managers responsible for expatriation, and companies providing products and services to these groups.

- Expatspouse.com helps HR by providing support to expatriate families throughout the expatriation cycle so they can successfully navigate the transitions associated with global relocation.

Relocation stores will provide access to all relocation services people require, in whatever languages they are most comfortable, thereby reducing the need for HR involvement with the expatriate employee. Given the increase in international activity, coupled with the shorter tenure of assignments, self-directed Internet services will become more necessary.

Source: M. Schell, "Global Relocation of the Future," *Canadian HR Reporter* (September 24, 2001), pp. 7, 12. Reproduced by permission of *Canadian HR Reporter*, Carswell, One Corporate Plaza, 2075 Kennedy Road, Scarborough, ON M1T 3V4.

phone communication can be a "severe handicap" in Russia; medical facilities in Russia may not meet international standards; and the compensation plan for employees in Mexico may have to deal with an inflation rate that approaches 52 percent per year.[14]

HOW INTERCOUNTRY DIFFERENCES AFFECT HRM

To a large extent, companies operating only within Canada's borders have the luxury of dealing with a relatively limited set of economic, cultural, and legal variables. Notwithstanding the range from liberal to conservative, for instance, Canada is basically a capitalist competitive society. In addition, while a multitude of cultural and ethnic backgrounds are represented in the Canadian workforce, various shared values (such as an appreciation for democracy) help to blur the otherwise sharp cultural differences.

While vacationers like these in Luxembourg are legally entitled to five weeks' holiday, standards vary widely even within Europe.

A company that is operating multiple units abroad is generally not blessed with such relative homogeneity. For example, minimum legally mandated holidays may range from none in the United States to five weeks per year in Luxembourg. In addition, while there are no formal requirements for employee participation in Italy, employee representatives on boards of directors are required in companies with more than 30 employees in Denmark.

Another troubling issue is the need for tight security and terrorism awareness training for employees sent to countries such as Colombia, where kidnapping of foreign executives is commonplace.[15] Some employers are experiencing post-9/11 resistance to foreign assignments, particularly into regions of high political or economic volatility.[16] And two-thirds of the world's nations are corrupt places to conduct business.[17] The point is that the management of the HR functions in multinational companies is complicated enormously by the need to adapt HR policies and procedures to the differences among countries in which each subsidiary is based. The following are some intercountry differences that demand such adaptation.[18]

Cultural Factors

Wide-ranging cultural differences from country to country demand corresponding differences in HR practices among a company's foreign subsidiaries. We might generalize, for instance, that the cultural norms of the Far East and the importance there of the patriarchal system will mould the typical Japanese worker's view of his or her relationship to an employer as well as influence how that person works. Japanese workers have often come to expect lifetime employment in return for their loyalty. As well, incentive plans in Japan tend to focus on the work group, while in the West the more usual prescription is still to focus on individual worker incentives.[19] Similarly, in a recent study of about 330 managers from Hong Kong, China, and the United States, American managers tended to be most concerned with getting the job done, while Chinese managers were most concerned with maintaining a harmonious environment; managers in Hong Kong fell between these two extremes.[20]

A well-known study by Professor Geert Hofstede underscores other international cultural differences. Hofstede says that societies differ first in *power distance*; in other words, they differ in the extent to which the less powerful members of institutions accept and expect that power will be distributed unequally.[21] He concluded that the institutionalization of such an inequality is higher in some countries (such as Mexico) than in others (such as Sweden).

His findings identified several other cultural differences. *Individualism versus collectivism* refers to the degree to which ties between individuals are normally loose rather than close. In more individualistic countries, "all members are expected to look after themselves and their immediate families."[22] Individualistic countries include Canada and the United States. Collectivist countries include Indonesia and Pakistan.

Masculinity versus femininity refers, said Hofstede, to the extent to which society values assertiveness ("masculinity") versus caring (what he called "femininity"). Japan and Austria ranked high in masculinity; Denmark and Chile ranked low.

Such intercountry cultural differences have several HR implications. First, they suggest the need for adapting HR practices such as testing and pay plans to local cultural norms. They also suggest that HR staff members in a foreign subsidiary are best drawn from host-country citizens. A high degree of sensitivity and empathy for the cultural and attitudinal demands of co-workers is always important when selecting employees to staff overseas operations. However, such sensitivity is especially important when the job is HRM and the work involves "human" jobs like interviewing, testing, orienting, training, counselling, and (if need be) terminating. As one expert puts it, "An HR staff member who shares the employee's cultural background is more likely to be sensitive to the employee's needs and expectations in the workplace—and is thus more likely to manage the company successfully."[23]

Economic Factors

Differences in economic systems among countries also translate into intercountry differences in HR practices. In free enterprise systems, for instance, the need for efficiency tends to favour HR policies that value productivity, efficient workers, and staff cutting where market forces dictate. Moving along the scale toward more socialist systems, HR practices tend to shift toward preventing unemployment, even at the expense of sacrificing efficiency.

Labour Cost Factors

Differences in labour costs may also produce differences in HR practices. High labour costs can require a focus on efficiency, for instance, and on HR practices (like pay-for-performance) aimed at improving employee performance. Along with differences in wages and salaries, wide gaps exist in hours worked. Thus, workers in Portugal average about 1980 hours of work annually, while workers in Germany average 1648 hours. Employees in Europe generally receive four to six weeks of vacation as compared with two or three weeks in Canada. Several European countries, including the United Kingdom and Germany, require substantial severance pay to departing employees, usually equal to at least two years' service in the United Kingdom and one year in Germany.[24]

Industrial Relations Factors

Industrial relations, and specifically the relationship between the worker, the union, and the employer, vary dramatically from country to country and have an enormous impact on HRM practices. In Germany, for instance, *codetermination* is the rule. Here, employees have the legal right to a voice in setting company policies. In this and several other countries, workers elect their own representatives to the supervisory board of the employer, and there is also a vice-president for labour at the top management level.[25] On the other hand, in many other countries, the state interferes little in the relations between employers and unions. In Canada, for instance, HR policies on most matters such as wages and benefits are set not by the government but by the employer, or by the employer in negotiations with its labour unions. In Germany, conversely, the various laws on codetermination largely determine the nature of HR policies in many German firms.

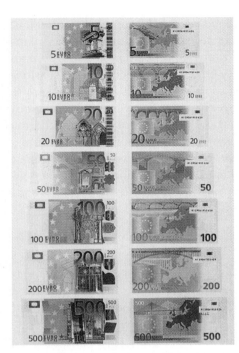

Among the many changes taking place in the international business arena is the introduction of the euro, the new single currency used by the European Union since 1999.

The European Union (EU)

In 1992, 12 separate countries in Europe were unified into a common market for goods, services, capital, and even labour.[26] Since that time, the EU has expanded to 15 members, and will soon increase to 25.[27] Generally speaking, tariffs for goods moving across borders from one EU country to another no longer exist, and employees (with some exceptions) find it easier to move relatively freely between jobs in various EU countries. Also, the EU hopes that its unique blend of social and economic policy will provide a competitive advantage.[28]

However, differences remain. Many countries have a minimum wage while others do not, and maximum hours permitted in the workday and workweek vary. Other differences are apparent in matters like minimum annual holidays, minimum notice to be given by employer, termination formalities, and employee participation.

The impact of the EU will be to gradually reduce these sorts of differences. Social legislation and examinations by the union's European Parliament and its administrative European Commission are slowly narrowing some gaps. However, even if all of the differences are eventually eliminated, HR practices will still vary from country to country; cultural diversity will require that, no doubt. Even into the near future, in other words, and even just within Europe, managing human resources multinationally will present tricky problems for HR managers.

Summary

In summary, intercountry variations in culture, economic systems, labour costs, and legal and industrial relations systems complicate the task of selecting, training, and managing employees abroad. These variations result in corresponding differences in management styles and practices from country to country, and such differences "...may strain relations between headquarters and subsidiary personnel or make a manager less effective when working abroad than at home."[29] International assignments thus run a relatively high risk of failing unless special steps are taken in selecting, training, and compensating international assignees.

IMPROVING INTERNATIONAL ASSIGNMENTS THROUGH SELECTION

Canadian companies have reported low failure rates for employees on foreign assignments relative to other countries, particularly the United States.[30] Failure is defined as the premature return of employees to their home country or the inability of expatriates to achieve their business goals. Although the exact number of failures is understandably difficult to quantify, one survey of American, European, and Japanese multinationals concluded that three-quarters of U.S. multinational companies experience expatriate assignment failure rates of 10 percent or more.[31] European and Japanese multinationals reported lower failure rates, with only about one-sixth of Japanese multinationals and 3 percent of European multinationals reporting more than a 10 percent expatriate recall rate.

The reasons reported for expatriate failure differ between the U.S., European, and Japanese multinationals. A 2002 survey by Runzheimer International consultants showed that for North American multinationals, the top two reasons were family ties and spousal employment, as shown in **Figure 18.2**.[32] Managers of European firms emphasized only the inability of the manager's spouse to adjust as an explanation for the expatriate's failed assignment. Japanese firms emphasized (in descending order) inability to cope with larger overseas responsibility, difficulties with the new assignment, personal or emotional problems, lack of technical competence, and finally, inability of the spouse to adjust.[33]

These findings underscore a truism regarding selection for international assignments, namely, that it is usually not inadequate technical competence but family and personal problems that undermine the international assignee.[34] As one expert puts it:

> The selection process is fundamentally flawed. Expatriate assignments rarely fail because the person cannot accommodate to the technical demands of the job. The expatriate selections are made by line managers based on technical competence. They fail because of family and personal issues and lack of cultural skills that haven't been part of the process.[35]

FIGURE 18.2   Reasons for Relocation Refusals/Failures

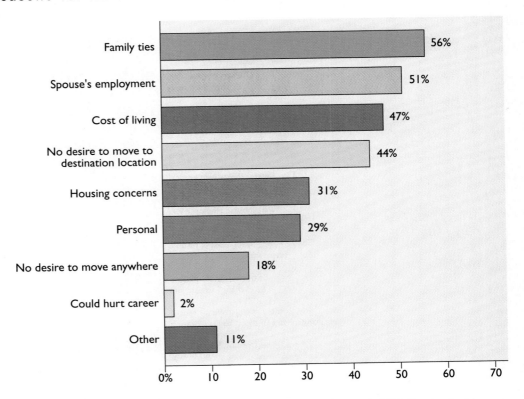

Source: Survey and Analysis of Employee Relocation Policies and Costs. © 2002. Reprinted with permission of Runzheimer International. www.runzheimer.com.

The Canadian experience is unique.[36] Factors identified by Canadian firms as important to expatriate success include flexibility, language ability, and family adjustment. However, these factors were not identified by Canadian companies as having been part of the selection and training process for expatriates. There are three potential explanations for this result. First, Canadians may be more culturally adaptable than their foreign counterparts because they are already familiar with bilingualism and multiculturalism. Second, Canadian expatriates are so few in number that they can be dealt with on an individual basis. Thus their firms may be doing more to prepare and support them than they report, because their systems are not formalized. Third, Canadian expatriate assignments have tended to be in culturally similar situations, which makes successful adaptation more likely.

Some organizations have moved away from full-scale relocation of an employee and his or her family to alternatives such as frequent extended business trips with corresponding time spent back at home, short-term assignments of between three months and a year with frequent home leave (once every 12 weeks on average), and the dual household arrangement where the employee's family remains at home and the employee sets up a small household for him- or herself in the foreign country. Overall, relocation policies are becoming more flexible.[37] **Figure 18.3** provides the results of a survey of 520 multinationals

FIGURE 18.3   Expatriate Spousal Re-employment Assistance

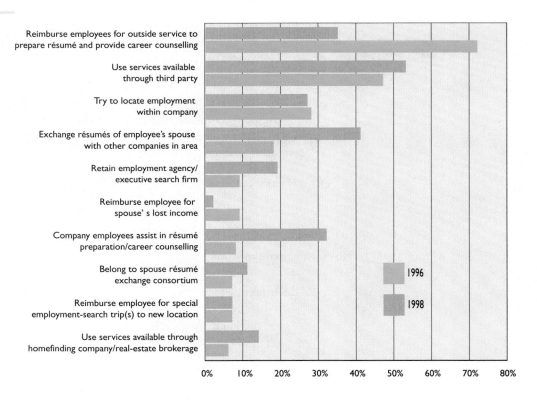

Source: *Runzheimer Reports on Relocation.* © 2000. Reprinted with permission of Runzheimer International. www.runzheimer.com.

(including 50 Canadian companies) regarding relocation services provided for short-term international assignments. The majority of all services are provided on a case-by-case basis, indicating flexibility.[38] Often, firms neglect to prepare employees for short-term assignments in the same way as they do for the long-term variety, which leads to problems such as lack of cross-cultural awareness, extreme loneliness, and feeling undervalued upon returning to the home office.[39]

International Staffing

International Labour Organization
www.ilo.org

Sources of Managers   There are several ways in which to classify international managers. *Locals* are citizens of the countries where they are working. *Expatriates* are non-citizens of the countries in which they are working.[40] *Home-country nationals* are the citizens of the country in which the multinational company's headquarters is based.[41] *Third-country nationals* are citizens of a country other than the parent or the host country—for example, a British executive working in a Tokyo subsidiary of a Canadian multinational bank.[42]

Expatriates represent a minority of managers. Thus, "most managerial positions are filled by locals rather than expatriates in both headquarters or foreign subsidiary operations."[43] There are several reasons to rely on local, host-country management talent for filling the foreign subsidiary's management ranks. Many people simply prefer not to work in a foreign country, and in general the cost of using expatriates is far greater than the cost of using local management talent.[44] The multinational corporation may be viewed locally as a "better citizen" if it uses local management talent, and indeed some governments actually press for the "nativization" of local management.[45] There may also be a fear that expatriates, knowing that they are posted to the foreign subsidiary for only a few years, may overemphasize short-term projects rather than focus on perhaps more necessary long-term tasks.[46]

There are also several reasons for using expatriates—either home-country or third-country nationals—for staffing subsidiaries. The major reason is reportedly technical competence: in other words, employers cannot find local candidates with the required technical qualifications.[47] Multinationals also increasingly view a successful stint abroad as a required step in developing top managers. For instance, the head of General Electric's Asia-Pacific region was transferred back to a top executive position of vice-chair at GE in 1995. Control is another important reason. Multinationals sometimes assign home-country nationals from their headquarters staff abroad on the assumption that these managers are more steeped in the firm's policies and culture and more likely to unquestioningly implement headquarters' instructions.

Canadian Employee Relocation
Council **www.cerc.ca**

Transition Dynamics
www.transition-dynamics.com

The Expatriate Group
www.expat.ca

International Staffing Policy   Multinational firms' top executives are often classified as either ethnocentric, polycentric, or geocentric.[48] In an *ethnocentric* corporation, the prevailing attitude is that home-country managers are superior to those in the host country.[49] In the *polycentric* corporation, there is a belief that only host-country managers can understand the culture and behaviour of the host-country market; and therefore, foreign subsidiaries should have local managers.[50] The *geocentric* approach, which is becoming more common, assumes that management candidates must be searched for globally, on the assumption that the best manager for any specific position anywhere on the globe may be found in any of the countries in which the firm operates.

These three multinational attitudes translate into three international staffing policies. An ethnocentric staffing policy is one in which all key management positions are filled by parent-country nationals.[51] At Royal Dutch Shell, for instance, virtually all financial controllers around the world are Dutch nationals. Reasons given for ethnocentric staffing policies include lack of qualified host-country senior management talent, a desire to maintain a unified corporate culture and tighter control, and the desire to transfer the parent firm's core competencies (e.g., a specialized manufacturing skill) to a foreign subsidiary more expeditiously.[52]

A polycentric-oriented firm would staff foreign subsidiaries with host-country nationals and its home-office headquarters with parent-country nationals. This may reduce the local cultural misunderstandings that expatriate managers may exhibit. It will also almost undoubtedly be less expensive. One expert estimates that an expatriate executive can cost a firm up to three times as much as a domestic executive because of transfer expenses and other expenses such as schooling for children, annual home leave, and the need to pay income taxes in two countries.[53]

A geocentric staffing policy "seeks the best people for key jobs throughout the organization, regardless of nationality."[54] This may allow the global firm to use its human resources more efficiently by transferring the best person to the open job, wherever he or she may be. It can also help to build a stronger and more consistent culture and set of values among the entire global management team. Team members here are continually interacting and networking with each other as they move from assignment to assignment around the globe and participate in global development activities.

Selecting International Managers
There are common traits which managers to be assigned domestically and overseas will obviously share. Wherever a person is to be posted, he or she will need the technical knowledge and skills to do the job and the intelligence and people skills to be a successful manager.[55] In addition, foreign assignments make demands on expatriate assignees that are different from what the manager would face if simply assigned to a management post in his or her home country. There is the need to cope with a workforce and management colleagues whose cultural inclinations may be drastically different from one's own, and the considerable stress that being alone in a foreign land can bring to bear on the single manager.

If the employee's spouse and children share the assignment, there are also the complexities and pressures that the family will have to confront, from learning a new language to shopping in strange surroundings, to finding new friends and attending new schools. Perceived organizational support and fairness regarding family issues can reduce intentions to return home early.[56]

Research
I n s i g h t   ▷

Selecting managers for expatriate assignments, therefore, means screening them for traits that predict success in adapting to what may be dramatically new environments. A recent study of 338 international assignees from many countries and organizations identified five factors perceived by international assignees to contribute to success in a foreign assignment. They were job knowledge and motivation, relational skills, flexibility/adaptability, extracultural openness, and family situation.[57] Specific items—including managerial ability, organizational ability, administrative skills, and creativity—were statistically combined into a single "job knowledge and motivation" factor. Respect, courtesy and tact, display of respect, and kindness were some of the items comprising the "relational skills" factor. "Flexibility/adaptability" included such items as resourcefulness, ability to deal with stress, flexibility, and emotional stability. "Extracultural openness" included a variety of outside interests, interest in foreign countries, and openness. Finally, several items (including adaptability of spouse and family, spouse's positive opinion, willingness of spouse to live abroad, and stable marriage) comprise the "family situation" factor.[58]

The five factors were not equally important in the foreign assignee's success, according to the responding managers. As the researchers conclude, "Family situation was generally found to be the most important factor, a finding consistent with other research on international assignments and transfers."[59] Therefore, while all five factors were perceived to be important to the foreign assignee's success, the company that ignores the candidate's family situation does so at its own peril.

Research
Insight ▷

A recent study by researchers of the University of Southern California provides an additional perspective. In this case, 838 managers from six international firms and 21 countries were evaluated.[60] The researchers specifically studied the extent to which personal characteristics (such as "sensitive to cultural differences") could be used to distinguish between managers who had high potential as international executives and those whose potential was not as high. Results showed that personal characteristics successfully distinguished the managers identified by their companies as "high potential." Consistent with results such as those mentioned previously, the characteristics—such as flexibility, integrity, the courage to take a stand, seeking and using feedback, business knowledge, bringing out the best in people, taking risks, and openness to criticism—reflect a blend of technical expertise, openness, and flexibility in dealing with people and getting things done.

Adaptability Screening Adaptability screening is generally recommended as an integral part of the expatriate selection process. Generally conducted by a professional psychologist or psychiatrist, adaptability screening aims to assess the family's probable success in handling the foreign transfer and to alert the couple to personal issues (such as the impact on children) that the foreign move may involve.[61]

Past experience is often the best predictor of future success. Companies like Colgate-Palmolive, therefore, look for overseas candidates whose work and non-work experience, education, and language skills already demonstrate a commitment to and facility in living and working with different cultures.[62] Even several summers spent successfully travelling overseas or participating in foreign student programs would seem to provide some concrete basis for believing that the potential transferee can accomplish the required adaptation when he or she arrives overseas.

Realistic job previews at this point are also crucial. Again, both the potential assignee and his or her family require all of the information that can be provided on the problems to expect in the new job (such as mandatory private schooling for the children) as well as any information obtainable about the cultural benefits, problems, and idiosyncrasies of the country in question. A preassignment visit to the new location by the employee and his or her family can provide an opportunity to make an informed decision about a potential relocation assignment.[63] International HR managers speak about avoiding culture shock in much the same way as we discussed using realistic job previews to avoid reality shock among new employees. In any case, the rule here is to spell it out ahead of time, as firms like Ciba-Geigy do for their international transferees.[64]

There are also paper-and-pencil tests that can be used to more effectively select employees for overseas assignments. The Overseas Assignment Inventory is one such assessment tool. Based on 12 years of research with more than 7000 candidates, the test's publisher contends that it is useful in identifying characteristics and attitudes that such candidates should have.[65]

TRAINING AND MAINTAINING INTERNATIONAL EMPLOYEES

Painstaking screening is just the first step in ensuring that the foreign assignee is successful. The employee may then require special training and, additionally, international HR policies must be formulated for compensating the firm's overseas managers and maintaining healthy labour relations.

Orienting and Training Employees for International Assignments

When it comes to providing the orientation and training required for success overseas, the practices of most North American firms reflect more form than substance. One consultant says that, despite many companies' claims, there is generally little or no systematic selection and training for assignments overseas. One relevant survey concluded that a sample of company presidents and chairpersons agreed that international business was growing in importance and required employees to be firmly grounded in the economics and practices of foreign countries. However, few of their companies actually provided such overseas-oriented training to their employees.[66] This is unfortunate, because a positive relationship exists between realistic expectations and cross-cultural adjustment.[67]

Orientation and training for international assignments can help employees (and their families) to avoid "culture shock" and better adjust to their new surroundings.

What sort of special training do overseas candidates need? One firm specializing in such programs prescribes a four-step approach.[68] Level One training focuses on the impact of cultural differences, and on raising trainees' awareness of such differences and their impact on business outcomes. Even transfers to the United States from Canada can involve culture shock.[69] Level Two training focuses on attitudes, and aims at getting participants to understand how attitudes (both negative and positive) are formed and how they influence behaviour. (For example, unfavourable stereotypes may subconsciously influence how a new manager responds to and treats his or her new foreign employees.) Finally, Level Three training provides factual knowledge about the target country, while Level Four provides skill building in areas like language and adjustment and adaptation skills. The depth of training is of the utmost importance. If firms are going to provide cross-cultural training, it needs to be in-depth and done with care.[70] For example, language training must include nonverbal communication awareness, as it varies so widely across the world.[71]

Many organizations offer spousal assistance in the form of reimbursement for continuing education, job search assistance, résumé preparation, or recertification.[72] **Figure 18.4** provides the results of a survey by Runzheimer consultants of 43 relocation professionals on the types of spousal re-employment assistance offered in formal relocation programs.

Beyond these special training practices, there is also the need for more traditional training and development of overseas employees. At IBM, for instance, such development includes using a series of rotating assignments that permits overseas IBM managers to grow professionally. At the same time, IBM and other major firms have established management development centres around the world where executives can go to hone their skills. Beyond that, classroom programs (such as those at the London Business School, or at INSEAD in France) provide overseas executives with the opportunities that they need to hone their functional skills.

In addition to honing functional skills, international management development often aims to foster improved control of global operations by building a unified corporate culture. The assumption here is that the firm should bring together managers from its far-flung subsidiaries and steep them for a week or two in the firm's cherished values and current strategy and policies. The managers should then be more likely to adhere consistently to these values, policies, and aims once they return to their assignments abroad.

International Compensation

The whole area of international compensation management presents some tricky problems. Compensation programs throughout a global firm must be integrated for overall effectiveness, yet differentiated to effectively motivate and

Engage Relocation
www.engagerelocation.ca

Relocation Resources International
www.myrriworld.com

Relocation Links
www.workindex.com

FIGURE 18.4   Relocation Services

Type of Service	Never Provided	Always Provided	Provided on a Case by Case basis
Orientation and Settling in Assistance	28%	17%	55%
Security Briefings	29%	20%	51%
Cross Cultural Training	34%	12%	54%
Language Training	28%	13%	59%

Source: Reprinted from Canadian News, third quarter 2002 with permission from WorldatWork, 14040 N. Northsight Blvd., Scottsdale, AZ 85260; phone: 877-951-9191; fax: 480-483-8352; www.worldatwork.org, © 2002, WorldatWork. Unauthorized reproduction or distribution is strictly prohibited.

meet the specific needs of the various categories and locations of employees.[73] On the one hand, there is a certain logic in maintaining company-wide pay scales and policies so that, for instance, divisional marketing directors throughout the world are all paid within the same narrow range. This reduces the risk of perceived inequities and dramatically simplifies the job of keeping track of disparate country-by-country wage rates. However, most multinational companies have recognized the need to make executive pay decisions on a global level, and executive pay plans are gradually becoming more uniform.[74] Dow Chemical has shifted all of its HRM processes from a local focus to a global one, as described in the Strategic HR box.

Yet, the practice of not adapting pay scales to local markets can present an HR manager with more problems than it solves. The fact is that living in Tokyo is three times more expensive than living in Calgary, while the cost of living in Bangalore, India, is 30 percent lower than that in Toronto.[75] If these cost-of-

STRATEGIC HR

Linking a Global Workforce

As a leading science and chemical company with customers in more than 170 countries, the Dow Chemical Company is truly a global organization. The company's shift to a global, business-based structure has created a unique series of total rewards challenges and opportunities for Dow's human resources department, as it seeks to integrate the needs of its 50 000 worldwide employees with the goals of Dow's various businesses.

Prior to the 1990s, Dow maintained a geographic focus and carried out processes on a country-by-country basis. In the past decade, however, the world has gotten smaller and many boundaries have disappeared. The advantages of being geographically structured are no longer valid. As a result, it became clear that the successful management of people could no longer be done on a geographic basis. Managers with employees reporting to them from multiple countries wanted their people processes to be as simple and as straightforward as possible.

Dow's HR department aspires to be highly strategic in nature to help the businesses bring out the best in their workforce. This is reflected in Dow's HR mission statement "Enabling Business Success Through People." Dow HR works closely with Dow leaders so they can understand the impact of their actions and how employees are affected by the business decisions they make.

The primary framework for supporting these efforts is called People Success, Dow's global, integrated, competency-based HR system. It is delivered through Dow's intranet and is accessible to each of Dow's 50 000 worldwide employees 24/7. This global delivery method offers a streamlined, consistent delivery of programs, including compensation structures, learning resources, and Dow's Job Announcement System. With the new system, an employee in Belgium receives the same information as an employee in Mexico.

Dow's Global Pay Planning Process uses an electronic tool that enables annual global pay planning. Leaders use this system around the world to determine their employees' compensation. This allows managers to evaluate employees in the same way, regardless of their location, and the process is applicable across business units, functions, and international boundaries, while at the same time being appropriately calibrated to the local market in each country. Leaders make decisions on base pay, bonuses, and long-term incentives online, where a second-level leader reviews them. Employee compensation is based on a similar set of criteria, regardless of location.

Whenever possible, HR leverages the capabilities of the organization on a global basis, based on the principle of "Think Globally, Act Locally." By developing the framework for global standard processes that are then implemented locally, HR manages to serve localized needs without duplicating efforts or wasting resources.

Source: Excerpt from S. Constantin and C. Bell, "Linking a Global Workforce," *workspan*, March 2002, pp. 22–28. Reprinted with permission of WorldatWork, Scottsdale, AZ. http://www.worldatwork.org.

living differences are not considered, it may be almost impossible to get managers to take "high-cost" assignments.

However, the answer is usually not just to pay, say, marketing directors more in one country than in another. For one thing, the firm could thereby elicit resistance when telling a marketing director in Tokyo who is earning $3000 per week to move to a division in Spain, where his or her pay for the same job (cost of living notwithstanding) will drop by half. One way to handle the problem is to pay a similar base salary company-wide and then add on various allowances according to individual market conditions.[76]

Determining equitable wage rates in many countries is no simple matter. There is a wealth of "packaged" compensation survey data already available in North America, but such data are not so easy to come by overseas. As a result, "one of the greatest difficulties in managing total compensation on a multinational level is establishing a consistent compensation measure between countries that builds credibility both at home and abroad."[77] Compensation professionals must face the challenge of designing programs that motivate local employees in each country as well as internationally mobile employees of all nationalities.[78]

Some multinational companies deal with this problem for local managers by conducting their own annual compensation surveys. Others use a global career progression framework that includes the flexibility to accommodate local practices and still maintain organization-wide consistency.[79]

The Balance Sheet Approach

The most common approach to formulating expatriate pay is to equalize purchasing power across countries, a technique known as *the balance sheet approach*.[80] The basic idea is that each expatriate should enjoy the same standard of living that he or she would have had at home. With the balance sheet approach, four main home-country groups of expenses—income taxes, housing, goods and services, and reserve—are the focus of attention. The employer estimates what each of these four expenses is for the expatriate's home country, and also what each is expected to be in the expatriate's host country. Any differences—such as additional income taxes or housing expenses—are then paid by the employer.

In practice, this usually boils down to building the expatriate's total compensation around five or six separate components. For example, *base salary* will normally be in the same range as the manager's home-country salary. In addition, however, there might be an *overseas or foreign service premium*. This is paid as a percentage of the executive's base salary, in part to compensate the manager for the cultural and physical adjustments that he or she will have to make.[81] There may also be several *allowances*, including a housing allowance and an education allowance for the expatriate's children. Income taxes represent another area of concern. In many cases, a Canadian manager posted abroad may have to pay not only Canadian taxes, but income taxes to the country to which he or she is posted as well.

Incentives

One international compensation trend is the use of equity participation and stock options for expatriates.[82] Since the performance of the company's stock on a Canadian stock market may have little relevance to, say, a manager in a German subsidiary, the incentive value of such a reward is highly suspect. This is particularly true because, regardless of size, a foreign subsidiary's influence on its parent company's stock price is more likely to result from exchange rate movements than from management action.[83]

The answer here, more multinationals are finding, is to formulate new long-term incentives specifically for overseas executives. Multinationals are thus devising performance-based long-term incentive plans that are tied more closely to performance at the subsidiary level. These can help to build a sense of ownership among key local managers while providing the financial incentives needed to attract and keep the people required for overseas operations.

International EAPs
EAPs are going global, helping expatriates to take care of their mental health, which is often affected by the stressful relocation process.[84] The approach is to proactively contact employees before departure to explain the program's services, then about three months after arrival families are contacted again. By this time, they have usually run into some challenges from culture shock and will welcome some assistance. The expatriates and their families have then established a connection with the EAP to use for ongoing support. Online stress counselling and career services are beginning to be made available.[85]

Problems such as homesickness, boredom, withdrawal, depression, compulsive eating and drinking, irritability, marital stress, family tension and conflict are all common reactions to culture shock. Employees on short-term assignment without their families can experience extreme loneliness. Treatment for psychiatric illnesses varies widely around the world, as do the conditions in government-run mental health institutions, and consultation with an EAP professional having extensive cross-cultural training may be critical in ensuring that appropriate medical treatment is obtained.[86]

Expat Forum www.expatforum.com

Performance Appraisal of International Managers

Several issues complicate the task of appraising an expatriate's performance.[87] For one thing, the question of who actually appraises the expatriate is crucial. Obviously, local management must have some input into the appraisal, but the appraisal may then be distorted by cultural differences. Thus, an expatriate manager in India may be evaluated somewhat negatively by his host-country bosses, who find his use of participative decision making inappropriate in their culture. On the other hand, home-office managers may be so geographically distanced from the expatriate that they cannot provide valid appraisals because they are not fully aware of the situation that the manager actually faces. This can be problematic: the expatriate may be measured by objective criteria such as profits and market share, but local events such as political instability may undermine the manager's performance while remaining "invisible" to home-office staff.

Two experts make five suggestions for improving the expatriate appraisal process:[88]

1. Stipulate the assignment's difficulty level. For example, being an expatriate manager in China is generally considered to be more difficult than working in England, and the appraisal should take such difficulty-level differences into account.

2. Weight the evaluation more toward the on-site manager's appraisal than toward the home-site manager's distant perceptions of the employee's performance.

3. If, however (as is usually the case), the home-site manager does the actual written appraisal, he or she should use a former expatriate from the same overseas location to provide background advice during the appraisal process. This can help to ensure that unique local issues are considered during the appraisal process.

4. Modify the normal performance criteria used for that particular position to fit the overseas position and characteristics of that particular locale. For example, "maintaining positive labour relations" might be more important in Chile, where labour instability is more common, than it would be in Canada.

5. Attempt to give the expatriate manager credit for relevant insights into the functioning of the operation and specifically the interdependencies of the domestic and foreign operations. In other words, do not just appraise the expatriate manager in terms of quantifiable criteria like profits or market share. His or her recommendations regarding how home-office/foreign-subsidiary communication might be enhanced, and other useful insights, should also affect the appraisal.

International Labour Relations

Firms opening subsidiaries abroad will find substantial differences in labour relations practices among the world's countries and regions. The following synopsis illustrates some of these differences by focusing on Europe. However, keep in mind that similarly significant differences would exist in South and Central America and Asia. Some important differences between labour relations practices in Europe and North America include the following:[89]

1. *Centralization.* In general, collective bargaining in Western Europe is likely to be industry-wide or regionally oriented, whereas North American collective bargaining generally occurs at the enterprise or plant level.

2. *Union structure.* Because collective bargaining is relatively centralized in most European countries, local unions in Europe tend to have much less autonomy and decision-making power than in North America, and they basically concentrate on administrative and service functions.

3. *Employer organization.* Due to the prevalence of industry-wide bargaining, the employer's collective bargaining role tends to be performed primarily by employer associations in Europe; individual employers in North America generally (but not always) represent their own interests when bargaining collectively with unions.

4. *Union recognition.* Union recognition for collective bargaining in Western Europe is much less formal than in North America. For example, in Europe there is no legal mechanism requiring an employer to recognize a particular union; even if a union claims to represent 80 percent of an employer's workers, another union can try to organize and bargain for the other 20 percent.

5. *Union security.* Union security in the form of formal closed-shop agreements is largely absent in continental Western Europe.

6. *Labour–management contracts.* As in North America, most European labour–management agreements are legally binding documents, except in Great Britain where such collective agreements are viewed as "gentlemen's agreements" existing outside the law.

7. *Content and scope of bargaining.* North American labour–management agreements tend to focus on wages, hours, and working conditions. European agreements, on the other hand, tend to be brief and simple and to specify minimum wages and employment conditions, with employers being free to institute more generous terms. The relative brevity of the European agreements is a function of two things: industry-wide bargaining makes it difficult to write detailed contracts applicable to individual enterprises, and in Europe the government is much more heavily involved in setting terms of employment such as vacations and working conditions.

8. *Grievance handling.* In Western Europe, grievances occur much less frequently than in North America; when raised, they are usually handled by a legislated machinery outside the union's formal control.

9. *Strikes.* Generally speaking, strikes occur less frequently in Europe. This is probably due to industry-wide bargaining, which generally elicits less management resistance than in North America, where demands "… cut deeper into the individual enterprise's revenues."[90]

10. *Government's role.* In Europe, governments generally do not regulate the bargaining process but are much more interested in directly setting the actual terms of employment than is the case in North America.

11. *Worker participation.* Worker participation has a long and relatively extensive history in Western Europe, where it tends to go far beyond such matters as pay and working conditions. The aim is to create a system by which workers can participate in a meaningful way in the direct management of the enterprise. Determining wages, hours, and working conditions is not enough; employees should participate in formulating all management decisions. In many countries in Western Europe, works councils are required. A *works council* is a committee in which plant workers consult with management about certain issues or share in the governance of the workplace.[91] Codetermination is a second form of worker participation in Europe. *Codetermination* means that there is mandatory worker representation on an enterprise's board of directors. It is especially prevalent in Germany.

Safety and Fair Treatment Abroad

Making provisions to ensure employee safety and fair treatment does not stop at a country's borders. While Canada has often taken the lead with respect to matters such as occupational safety, other countries are also quickly adopting such laws, and, in any event, it is hard to make a legitimate case for being less safety conscious or fair with workers abroad than with those at home.

Having employees abroad does raise some unique safety and fair treatment issues, however. As one security executive at an oil company put it, "It's crucial for a company to understand the local environment, local conditions and what

Interlink Consulting Services
www.interlinkconsulting.com

International SOS
www.internationalsos.com

threat exists."[92] For example, "kidnapping has become a way of life" in some countries in Central and South America, and in many places—"Brazil, Nigeria, the Philippines, Russia and New Guinea, to name a few—street crime is epidemic, although tourists and business people are rarely kidnapped or assassinated," as illustrated in the Global HRM box.[93]

Kidnap and ransom insurance is a rapidly growing benefit, given that between 10 000 and 15 000 kidnappings of foreigners for ransom occur each year, with about 80 percent in Latin America. The insurance policy usually covers:

- ransom money and coverage on the money while in transit
- professional negotiators
- consultant to handle media, law, and family communications
- bodily injury of abductee
- security company fees
- extortion against company property, product contamination, and computer systems
- travel expenses for negotiator, family and employee
- lost salary of abductee
- psychological counselling for employee and family.[94]

Keeping business travellers out of crime's way is a specialty all its own but suggestions include the following:[95]

- Provide expatriates with general training about travelling and living abroad, and specific information about the place that they are going to, so they are better oriented when they get there.
- Have travellers arrive at airports as close to departure time as possible and wait in areas away from the main flow of traffic where they are not as easily observed.
- Equip the expatriates' car and home with adequate security systems.
- Tell employees to vary their departure and arrival times and take different routes to and from work.
- Keep employees current on crime and other problems by regularly checking travel advisory service and consular information sheets; these provide up-

GLOBAL HRM

Really Hard Bargaining

The CEO of a Zimbabwe security company was taken hostage for six days by a group of his workers, only being released after agreeing to pay them the more than (Cdn) $6 million they claimed they were owed as part of a severance package. The security guards claimed the CEO was planning to leave the country without paying the laid-off employees their severance, according to a report in the *Daily News* of Zimbabwe. The company's leaders said paying the money will force them to shut down.

Source: "Really Hard Bargaining," *Canadian HR Reporter* (October 21, 2002), p. 14.

to-date information on possible threats in almost every country of the world.

- Advise employees to remain confident at all times: body language can attract perpetrators, and those who look like victims often become victimized.[96]

Wages paid to foreign nonmanagement workers abroad are a well-publicized aspect of employee fair treatment today. For example, high-profile companies, including Nike Inc., have recently received bad publicity for the working conditions, long hours, and low pay rates for their factory workers in countries such as Indonesia.[97] Many companies, including Nike, have therefore taken steps to increase wages for foreign workers.

Repatriation: Problems and Solutions

Repatriation is often a bittersweet experience for the returning expatriate. *Repatriation*, the process of moving back to the parent company and country from the foreign assignment, means returning one's family to familiar surroundings and old friends.[98] The returning employee all too often discovers, however, that in many respects his or her employer has ignored the manager's career and personal needs. Up to 40 percent of expatriates leave the company within one year of their return home.[99]

Several repatriation problems are very common. One is the expatriate's fear that he or she has been "out of sight, out of mind" during an extended foreign stay and has thus lost touch with the parent firm's culture, top executives, and those responsible for the firm's management selection processes. Indeed, such fears can be well founded: Many repatriates are temporarily placed in mediocre or makeshift jobs.[100] Ironically, the company often undervalues the cross-cultural skills acquired abroad, and the international posting becomes a career-limiting, rather than career-enhancing, move.[101] Many are shocked to find that the executive trappings of the overseas job (private schools for the children and a company car and driver, for instance) are lost upon return, and that the executive is again just a small fish in a big pond. Perhaps more exasperating is the discovery that some of the expatriate's former colleagues have been more rapidly promoted while he or she was overseas. Even the expatriate's family may undergo a sort of reverse culture shock, as spouse and children face the often-daunting task of picking up old friendships and habits or starting schools anew upon their return. Expatriates who experience problems fitting back into the organization often leave, and the firm loses a valuable resource.[102]

Progressive multinationals anticipate and avoid these problems by taking a number of sensible steps. These can be summarized as follows:[103]

1. *Write repatriation agreements.* Many firms use repatriation agreements, which guarantee in writing that the international assignee will not be kept abroad longer than some period (such as five years), and that on return he or she will be given a mutually acceptable job.

2. *Assign a sponsor.* The employee should be assigned a sponsor/mentor (such as a senior manager at the parent firm's home office). This person's role is to look after the expatriate while he or she is away. This includes keeping

the person apprised of significant company events and changes back home, monitoring his or her career interests, and nominating the person to be considered for key openings when the expatriate is ready to come home.

3. *Provide career counselling.* Provide formal career counselling sessions to ensure that the repatriate's job assignments upon return will meet his or her needs.[104]

4. *Keep communication open.* Keep the expatriate "plugged in" to home-office business affairs through management meetings around the world, frequent home leave combined with stays at headquarters to work on specific problems, and regularly scheduled meetings at headquarters.[105]

5. *Offer financial support.* Many firms pay real estate and legal fees and help the expatriate to rent or in some other way to maintain his or her residence, so that the repatriate and his or her family can actually return "home."

6. *Develop reorientation programs.* Finally, provide the repatriate and his or her family with a reorientation program to facilitate the adjustment back into the home culture.

7. *Build in return trips.* One study concluded that, particularly when they come from a more homogeneous culture (in this case Finland) and are sent to a more "novel" culture, expatriates can benefit from more frequent trips to the home country "to ensure that expatriates stay in touch with home-country norms and changes during their international assignment."[106]

"In North America the Squeaky Wheel Gets the Grease. In Korea the Nail That Stands Out Gets Pounded In."

...Eastern cultures have societies and systems that are very different from those in the [W]est... In Japan [for example], the word for "individualism" has negative connotations. Groups tend to value cooperation more [in the East] than in the [W]est.... [G]roup rather than individual achievement and an approach [that] tends to be more holistic in thinking—looking for the collective good rather than the individual good—[is valued]. Individuals tend often to do better on projects that have a social conte[x]t, where [their] own output can be perceived as part of the bigger picture. This is very different from the [W]est, where being "best" or "top of the class" has been the traditional underlying theme that affects both education and training. It is this attitude that has caused many organizations such problems and stress in attempting to develop new forms of organization based upon teams and teamwork. This has traditionally been alien to the Western workforce despite the lip service paid to it....

Source: Excerpted with permission from the *Training and Development Guide,* ¶67,075, published by and copyright CCH Canadian Limited, Toronto, Ontario.

CHAPTER *Review*

Summary

1 Intercountry differences have an impact on HRM. *Cultural factors* (such as Hofstede's power distance, individualism versus collectivism, and masculinity versus femininity) suggest differences in values, attitudes, and therefore behaviours and reactions of people from country to country. *Economic factors* and *labour cost factors* help to determine whether the human resources emphasis should be on efficiency, commitment building, or some other approach. *Industrial relations factors*—and specifically the relationship between the worker, the union, and the employer—manifest themselves in concepts such as Germany's codetermination; these in turn influence the nature of a company's specific HR policies from country to country. Even within the relatively unified *European Union*, substantial variations in matters like minimum wage laws and length of workday exist between member countries.

2 Selecting managers for expatriate assignments means screening them for traits that predict success in adapting to dramatically new environments. Such expatriate traits include adaptability and flexibility, job knowledge and motivation, relational skills, extracultural openness, and family situation. Adaptability screening that focuses on the family's probable success in handling the foreign transfer can be an especially important step in the expatriate selection process.

3 Prior to the assignment, training for expatriate managers typically focuses on cultural differences, on how attitudes influence behaviour, on factual knowledge about the target country, and on language and cultural adjustment/adaptation skills.

4 The most common approach to formulating expatriate pay is to equalize purchasing power across countries, a technique known as the balance sheet approach. With this approach, the employer estimates expenses for income taxes, housing, goods and services, and reserve, and pays supplements to the expatriate in such a way as to maintain the same standard of living that he or she would have had at home.

5 Repatriation problems are very common but can be minimized. They include the often-well-founded fear that the expatriate is "out of sight, out of mind," and difficulties in re-assimilating the expatriate's family back into home-country culture. Suggestions for avoiding these problems include using repatriation agreements, assigning a sponsor/mentor, offering career counselling, keeping the expatriate plugged in to home-office business, building in return trips, providing financial support to maintain the expatriate's home-country residence, and offering reorientation programs to the expatriate and his or her family.

Review and Discussion Questions

1 What are some of the specific uniquely international activities that an international HR manager typically engages in?

2 Explain three broad global HR challenges.

3 What special training do overseas candidates need? In what ways is such training similar to and different from traditional diversity training?

4 How does appraising an expatriate's performance differ from appraising that of a home-office manager? How can some of the unique problems of appraising the expatriate's performance be avoided?

5 What accounts for the fact that worker participation has a long and relatively extensive history in Europe? How has this relatively extensive participation affected the labour relations process?

6 Describe five actions that can be taken by expatriate managers in other countries to increase their personal safety.

CRITICAL *Thinking Questions*

1 You are president of a small business. In what ways do you expect that being involved in international business activity will affect HRM in your business?

2 A firm is about to send its first employees overseas to staff a new subsidiary. The president asks why such assignments fail, and what can be done to avoid such failures. Write a memo in response to these questions.

APPLICATION *Exercises*

Running Case: LearnInMotion.com

Going Abroad

According to its business plan, and in practice, LearnInMotion.com "acquires content globally but delivers it locally." In other words, all the content and courses and other material that it lists on its site come from content providers all over the world. However, the "hard copy" (book and CD-ROM) courses are delivered, with the help of independent contracting delivery firms, locally, in Ontario and Quebec.

Now the company is considering an expansion. While the most logical strategic expansion would probably entail adding cities in Canada, one of its major content providers—a big training company in England—believes there is a significant market for LearnInMotion.com services in England, and particularly in London, Oxford, and Manchester (all of which are bustling business centres, and all of which have well-known universities). The training company has offered to finance and co-own a branch of LearnInMotion.com, in London. They want it housed in the training firm's new offices in Mayfair, near Shepherds Market. This is an easily accessible (if somewhat expensive) area, within easy walking distance of Hyde Park and not far from the London Underground Piccadilly line, which runs directly through the city to Heathrow airport.

Everyone concerned wants to make sure the new operation can "hit the ground running." This means either Jennifer or Pierre will have to move to London almost at once, and take one salesperson and one of the content management people along. Once there, this small team could hire additional employees locally, and then, once the new operation is running

successfully, return to Ottawa, probably within three or four months.

Jennifer and Pierre have decided to go ahead and open the London office, but this is not a decision they've taken lightly, since there are many drawbacks to doing so. The original, Ottawa-based site is not generating anywhere near the sales revenue it was supposed to at this point, and being short three key employees is not going to help. Neither the board of directors nor the representatives of the venture capital fund were enthusiastic about the idea of expanding abroad, either. However, they went along with it; and the deciding factor was probably the cash infusion that the London-based training firm was willing to make. It basically provided enough cash to run not just the London operation but the Ottawa one for an additional six months.

Having made the decision to set up operations abroad, Jennifer and Pierre now need to turn to the multitude of matters involved in the expansion—for instance, obtaining the necessary licences to open the business in England, and arranging for phone lines (all carried out with the assistance of the London-based training firm). However, it's also obvious to Jennifer and Pierre that there are considerable human resource management implications involved in moving LearnInMotion.com employees abroad, and in staffing the operation once they're there. Now, they want you, their management consultants, to help them actually do it. Here's what they want you to do for them.

Questions

1 What are the main HR-related implications and challenges as a result of opening the operation in London?

2 How should the person who will be the permanent manager for the new operation be chosen?

Should he or she be hired locally, or should one of the people from the existing operation be used? Why?

3 Based upon any sources available to you, including the Internet, research the comparative cost of living of London and Ottawa, including housing and transportation, as well as comparative salaries.

4 Write a short position paper on the subject: "a list of the HR-related things we need to do in sending our three people abroad."

EXPERIENTIAL *Exercises*

1 Choose three traits that are useful for selecting international assignees, and create a straightforward test (not one that uses pencil and paper) to screen candidates for these traits.

2 Describe the most common approach to formulating expatriate pay. Use a library source to determine the relative cost of living in five countries as of this year, and explain the implications of such differences for drafting a pay plan for managers being sent to each country.

Border Security

Border anxiety—it's certainly not business as usual for companies trying to cross into the United States. They've discovered that they can't count on the same easy access to the American market that they had prior to September 2001. The ground rules to timely border crossing have been shifting, and not always fairly.

Many Canadians are now afraid to try to cross the border because they are being challenged, and companies are having to review their staff to find out who is "good to go" to the U.S. In a B.C. communication tower plant, managers meet their lawyer and find that sending their Russian engineer to the U.S. may be asking for problems, so they must find someone else to travel to the U.S. and install the towers.

John Ashcroft, Attorney-General of the United States, speaks about a new adversary of his country, one that enters in the form of business people and students. Anyone who was born in or has recently visited certain countries is considered "ethnically at risk." For example, someone born in Iran will be fingerprinted and have their entry delayed. Therefore, this employee will not be able to do business easily, and clients will become unhappy when meetings are cancelled or delayed. If the employer is lucky, they can send someone else.

This situation creates problems for Canada, which has a diverse population and workforce. Ashcroft's colleague, the more moderate Secretary of State Colin Powell, says that the U.S. wants to respect Canadian citizens but must protect the American interest. However, the reality is that people have been stripsearched or told to go away and get more documentation, and some border guards overexert their authority by pushing people around. The rules can change in an instant with a directive from Washington.

A Canadian with a minor criminal record from a youthful indiscretion may be denied entry or asked for new documents—to say nothing of the issue of his or her boss discovering the criminal record. Even someone who was turned back at the border years ago for possession of marijuana, who was not arrested, charged, or convicted, may be denied entry. Tens of thousands of people could be affected by these sorts of regulations.

Questions

1. Do you agree with the U.S. government and its changes in border security? Why or why not?

2. Do you think it is fair that Canadian citizens are being turned back at the U.S. border when crossing on business? Why or why not?

3. What alternative actions could the U.S. take to protect itself from terrorism but not unduly inconvenience innocent Canadian business people?

4. What can Canadians with minor criminal records or previous border-crossing problems do about their current problems crossing into the U.S. on business?

Video Source: "Border Security," *CBC Venture 854* (November 17, 2002).

Additional Resources: http://gocanada.about.com/cs/bordercrossing/a/crossing.htm; www.mto.gov.on.ca/english/trucks/checklist.htm

Notes

Chapter 1

1. J. D. Ross, "A Definition of Human Resources Management," *Personnel Journal* (October 1982), pp. 781–783.

2. R. Amit and M. Belcourt, "Human Resources Management Processes: A Value-Creating Source of Competitive Advantage," *European Management Journal* (April 1999), pp. 174–181. See also G.R. Ferris, W.A. Hochwarter, M.R. Buckley, G. Harrell-Cook &D.D. Frink, "Human Resource Management: Some New Directions," *Journal of Management*, 25 (1999), pp. 385–415.

3. For a discussion see, for example, J. Galbraith, "Positioning Human Resources as a Value-adding Function: The Case of Rockwell International," *Human Resource Management* (Winter 1992), pp. 287–300; and A. Lado and M. Wilson, "Human Resource Systems and Sustained Competitive Advantage: A Competency-based Perspective," *Academy of Management Review*, 19(4), 1994, pp. 699–727. Quote from C. Truss and L. Gratton, "Strategic Human Resource Management: A Conceptual Approach," *The International Journal of Human Resource Management* (September 1994), p. 663.

4. Truss and Gratton, "Strategic Human Resource Management," p. 663.

5. See R. Saltonstall, "Who's Who in Personnel Administration," *Harvard Business Review* 33 (July–August 1955), pp. 75–83, reprinted in P. Pigors, C. Meyers, and F.P. Malm, *Management of Human Resources* (New York: McGraw-Hill, 1969), pp. 61–73.

6. Saltonstall, "Who's Who?" p. 63.

7. Based on the definition provided in the handout distributed by the Bell Canada Trainer at Workshop One in the seminar series titled "Be There: A Series of e-Business Workshops Presented by Bell Canada and the Peterborough Chamber of Commerce," Thursday, May 18, 2000, p. 2; J. Simke, "Emerging Trends in Outsourcing," *CMA Management*, February 2000, pp. 26–27.

8. D. Brown, "CIBC HR Department Halved as Non-Strategic Roles Outsourced," *Canadian HR Reporter* (June 4, 2001), pp. 1, 6. See also D. Brown, "Lessons from HR Outsourcing Pioneers," *Canadian HR Reporter*, January 16, 2003, pp. 1, 12.

9. P. Brieger, "HR Joins Outsourcing Trend," *Financial Post* (May 7, 2003), p. 6.

10. L. McKibbin-Brown, "Who Is Outsourcing What?," *HR Professional* (June–July 2002), p. 33; P.J. Labrie and J. Berard, "Outsourcing Training at Pratt & Whitney Canada," *HR Professional* (June–July 2002), p. 43; and P. Brieger, "HR Joins Outsourcing Trend," *Financial Post* (May 7, 2003), p. 6.

11. D. Brown, "The Future Is High for Strategic HR," *Canadian HR Reporter* (June 17, 2002), p. 7.

12. F.K. Foulkes and H. Morgan, "Organizing and Staffing the Personnel Function," *Harvard Business Review* 56 (May–June 1977), p. 149.

13. D. Brown, "Measuring the Value of HR," *Canadian HR Reporter* (September 24, 2001), pp. 1, 5.

14. *e-Track*. Towers Perrin (September, 2002). Quoted in G. Downey, "Use of Self-Service HR Skyrockets: Survey Reveals Training, Benefits Most Commonly Accessed Via the Web," *Computing Canada* (February 1, 2002), pp. 1, 6.

15. M. Morales, "e-HR: A Work in Progress: Despite Bumps in the Road, Organizations Embracing e-HR and Self-Service Will Win the Race," *Canadian HR Reporter* (May 20, 2002), p. G4; C. Collet, "Business-to-Employee: Automating the HR Function," *CMA Management* (October 1, 2001), pp. 20–23; B. Leonard, "GM Drives HR to the Next Level," *HR Magazine*, March 2002, pp. 46–50; J. Brown, "Rogers Orders Self-Service Portal," *Computing Canada*, June 7, 2002, p. 23.

16. R. Zampetti and L. Adamson, "Web-Based Employee Self-Service." In A.J. Walker, ed., *Web-based Human Resources: The Technologies and Trends are Transforming HR*. New York: McGraw-Hill, 2001, pp. 19–20; and "Three New Surveys Track the Growth of e-HR," *HR Focus* (April 2002), pp. 4–6.

17. "Three New Surveys Track the Growth of e-HR."

18. L. Lahey, "Virtual HR Helps Alberta Government Employees Take Matters Into Their Own Hands," *Technology in Government* (July 1, 2002), p. 17.

19. T. Belford, "HR Focusing on How It Can Add Value," *The Globe & Mail* (March 25, 2002), p. B11.

20. D. Brown, "HR Gets Credit for Market Value," *Canadian HR Reporter* (May 20, 2002), pp. 1, 12.

21. M. Belcourt, "Making A Difference... And Measuring It With the 5 C's," *Human Resources Professional* (December 1996/January 1997), pp. 20–24.

22. T. H. Wagar, "Do HRM Practices and Policies Matter? The Survey Says ..." *The HRM Research Quarterly* (Spring 1999), pp. 1–4.

23. Watson Wyatt, *Human Capital Index Study*, cited in D. Brown, "The 30 Ways HR Adds Value to the Bottom Line," *Canadian HR Reporter* (December 13, 1999), pp. 1, 20, 31. See also "Human Resources Key to Financial Performance," *The Globe & Mail* (September 25, 2002), p. C6.

24. "Good HR Equals Good Performance," *Workplace Today* (January 2002), p. 7.

25. D. Brown, "Profit Driven by Good HR, Study Finds," *Canadian HR Reporter* (November 19, 2001), p. 3.

26. D. Brown, "The Measure of a Function," *Canadian HR Reporter* (November 19, 2001), pp. 1, 7.

27. D. Brown, "The Measure of a Function."

28. "CEOs Talk," *Canadian HR Reporter* (March 11, 2002), pp. 17–19.

29. R. Stringer, *Leadership and Organizational Climate* (Upper Saddle River NJ: Prentice-Hall, 2002).

30. S. Nador, "Designing Your Own Best Practices to Attract and Retain Talent," *HR Professional* (August/September 1999), pp. 42–43.

31. "Highly Skilled Workers Still Hard to Find," *Canadian HR Reporter* (February 3, 1999), p. 6.

32. W.B. Werther, Jr., W.A. Ruch, and L. McClure, *Productivity Through People* (St. Paul: West Publishing, 1986), pp. 3–5.

33. P. Drucker, "Knowledge Work," *Executive Excellence* (April 2000), p. 11.

34. J. Zeidenberg, "HR and the Innovative Company," *Human Resources Professional* (June, 1996), pp. 12–15.

35. This is the Conference Board of Canada's definition used in its 1997 report titled *Contingent Work in Canada*, cited in J. Garland and E. Cousineau, "Recognizing Contingent Workers a Full-time Job," *Canadian HR Reporter* (September 6, 1999), p. 33.

36. J. Kettle, "Casual Work Gets Serious," *The Globe & Mail* (November 20, 1997), p. B4.

37. "Women in the Labour Force" (Ottawa: Statistics Canada, 1994), Cat. No. 75-507E, p. 5.

38. S. Ostry and M.A. Zaidi, *Labour Economics in Canada*, 2nd ed. (Toronto: MacMillan of Canada, 1972).

39. G. Ferris, D. Frink, and M. C. Galang, "Diversity in the Workplace: The Human Resources Management Challenge," *Human Resource Planning* 16(1), p. 42.

40. Based on CANSIM, Statistics Canada's online statistical database, "Population Projections for 2001," www.statcan.ca/english/Pgdb/People/Population/demo23a.htm, and "Population Projections for 2016,"

www.statcan.ca/english/Pgdb/People/Population/demo23b.htm, Matrix 6900, extracted July 6, 2000.

41. Cited in S. Pellegrini, "Keep Benefits Costs Low By Assessing Retiree Health," *Canadian HR Reporter* (June 14, 1999), pp. 9–10.

42. M. Miller, "The New Entrant to the Work/Life Balancing Act: Eldercare," *HR Professional* (August/September 1999), pp. 40–41; D. Brown, "Senate Proposes Leave Benefits for Palliative Care," *Canadian HR Reporter* (July 17, 2000), p. 6.

43. Brown, "Senate Proposes Leave Benefits," pp. 1, 6.

44. Based on material cited in "News and Views: Flex Appeal," compiled by M. Griffin, *HR Professional* (February/March 1999), p. 10; and research reported by P.I Nyhof in "Managing Generation X: The Millennial Challenge," *Canadian HR Reporter* (May 22, 2000), pp. 7–8.

45. Statistics Canada, *The Canada Year Book 1999,* (Ottawa: Minister of Industry, 1998), Catalogue No. 11-402-XPE, p. 158.

46. Statistics Canada, *The Canada Year Book 1999,* p. 160; International Adult Literacy Survey (IALS) definition, cited in W. Clark, "Adult Literacy in Canada, the United States, and Germany," *Canadian Social Trends* (Winter 1996), Statistics Canada Catalogue No. 11-008-XPE, p. 28.

47. *Workforce 2000* (Toronto: Hudson Institute Canada and Towers Perrin, 1993).

48. Clark, "Adult Literacy in Canada," pp. 28–33; Statistics Canada, *The Canada Year Book 1999,* p. 160.

49. 1996 Census data cited in "The Diversity of Visible Minorities," *Worklife Report,* (March 1, 1999), pp. 2–3.

50. Statistics Canada, *The Canada Year Book 1999,* p. 74.

51. Statistics Canada, *The Canada Year Book 1999,* p. 228.

52. S. Crompton and M. Vickers, "One Hundred Years of the Labour Force," *Canadian Social Trends* (Summer 2000), Statistics Canada Catalogue No. 11-008, p. 8.

53. Based on B. Little, "Women Profit From Labour Trends," *The Globe & Mail* (April 2, 2000), and CANSIM, Statistics Canada's online statistical database, "Labour Force, Employed and Unemployed, Numbers and Rates," www.statcan.ca/english/Pgdb/People/Labour/labor07a.htm, Matrices 3472-3482, extracted July 6, 2000.

54. Canadian Human Rights Commission, *Annual Report of 1998,* p. 33.

55. Canadian Human Rights Commission, *Annual Report of 1998,* p. 24.

56. From a Royal Bank of Canada study, cited in A-M. Tobin, "Increase Hiring of Disabled, Bank Urges," *Toronto Star* (April 4, 2000).

57. E. McGregor, "Emerging Careers," *Occupational Outlook Quarterly,* 34 (Fall 1990), p. 22.

58. B. Orr, "Privacy in the Workplace a Growing Challenge for Employers," *Canadian HR Reporter* (January 25, 1999), pp. 8–10.

59. "HR Intranet Popularity Grows," *Canadian HR Reporter* (March 24, 2003), p. 3; "e-HR Victim of Unrealistic Expectations," *Canadian HR Reporter* (March 11, 2002), pp. 1, 6; and D. Brown, "When Managers Balk at Doing HR's Work," *Canadian HR Reporter* (January 13, 2003), pp. 1, 6, 8.

60. "HR's Quest for Status: Fantasy or Emerging Reality?" *Canadian HR Reporter* and Watson Wyatt (August 2001).

61. G. Betcherman, K. McMullen, N. Leckie, and C. Caron, *The Canadian Workplace in Transition* (Kingston, ON: IRC Press, Queen's University, 1994).

62. A. Purvis, "Super Exporter," *Time* (April 28, 1997), pp. 34–38.

63. C. W. Hill, *International Business* (Burr Ridge, IL: Irwin, 1994), p. 6.

64. B. O'Reilly, "Your New Global Workforce," *Fortune* (December 14, 1992), pp. 52–66.

65. F.W. Taylor, "The Principles of Scientific Management," J.M. Sharfritz and J.S. Ott (editors), *Classics of Organization Theory,* 2nd ed. (Chicago: The Dorsey Press, 1987), pp. 66–81.

66. D.G. Nickels, J.M. McHugh, S.M. McHugh, and P.D Berman, *Understanding Canadian Business* 2nd ed. (Toronto: Irwin, 1997), p. 220.

67. This discussion is based on E.E. Lawler III, "Human Resources Management," *Personnel* (January 1988) pp. 24–25.

68. R.J. Cattaneo and A.J. Templer, "Determining the Effectiveness of Human Resources Management," T.H. Stone (editor), *ASAC: Personnel and Human Resources Division Proceedings* (Halifax: St. Mary's University, June 1988), p. 73.

69. L. Young, "National Public-Service Association Explores International Outreach Initiatives," *Canadian HR Reporter* (June 5, 2000), p. 2.

70. D. Brown, "Canada Gets National HR Designation," *Canadian HR Reporter* (July 15, 2002), pp. 1, 13.

71. D. McDougall, "Employees Want an Ethical Work Environment," *Canadian HR Reporter* (April 10, 2000), p. 4.

72. L. Brooks, Professor of Business Ethics and Executive Director of the Clarkson Centre for Business Ethics at the University of Toronto, cited in L. Young, "Companies Not Doing Right by Their Ethics Codes," *Canadian HR Reporter* (April 10, 2000), p. 17.

73. *KPMG's Ethics Survey 2000—Managing for Ethical Practice,* cited in Young, "Companies Not Doing Right," p. 17.

74. D. Brown, "HR Feeling Pressure to Act Unethically," *Canadian HR Reporter* (May 19, 2003), pp. 1, 9.

75. *KPMG's Ethics Survey 2000—Managing for Ethical Practice,* cited in Young, "Companies Not Doing Right," p. 17.

76. Based on *Walker Information Canada Inc. Study,* cited in J. Martin, "Studies Suggest a Link Between Employees' Perception of a Firm's Ethics—and Loyalty," *Recruitment & Staffing, Supplement to Canadian HR Reporter* (September 20, 1999), p. G.7; and McDougall, "Employees Want an Ethical Work Environment," p. 4.

77. The section on HR auditing is based on two sources, except as noted: G.E. Biles and R.S. Schuler, *Audit Handbook of Human Resources Management Practices* (Alexandria, VA: American Society for Personnel Administration, 1986); and J.J. Phillips "13 Ways to Show You Are Worth It: A Guide to HR Evaluation," *Human Resources Professional* 4, no. 2 (February 1992), pp. 59–63.

78. S. Hodkinson, "Aligning HR with Business," *Canadian HR Reporter* (November 18, 2002), p. 4.

79. B. Becker, "Measuring the Value of HR," *Canadian HR Reporter* (September 24, 2001), pp.1, 5; and D. Brown, "The Measure of a Function," *Canadian HR Reporter* (November 19, 2001), p. 17.

80. Colin Dawes, "Measuring HR's Pulse," *Human Resources Professional* 13, no. 5 (July/August 1996), pp. 13–15.

81. D. Brown, "Benchmarking Should Be More Than Cliché," *Canadian HR Reporter* (November 4, 2002), pp. 3, 6.

82. D. Brown, "HR's Role in Business Strategy: Still a Lot of Work to Be Done," *Canadian HR Reporter* (November 5, 2001), pp. 1, 20.

83. For discussions see, for example, R. Schuler, P. Dowling, and H. DeCieri, "An Integrative Framework of Strategic International Human Resource Management," *Journal of Management,* 19(2), 1993, pp. 419–59; V. Scarpello, "New Paradigm Approaches in Strategic Human Resource Management," *Group and Organization Management* 19(2), June 1994, pp. 160–64; and S. Peck, "Exploring the Link Between Organizational Strategy and the Employment Relationships: The Role of Human Resources Policies," *Journal of Management Studies* 31(5), September 1994, pp. 715–36.

84. W. Henn, "What the Strategist Asks from Human Resources," *Human Resource Planning* 8(4), 1985, p. 195; quoted in Greer, *Strategy and Human Resources,* p. 105.

85. D. Brown, "Auto-Parts Makers Need to Value HR: Study," *Canadian HR Reporter* (May 19, 2003), pp. 1, 10.

86. B.E. Becker, M.A. Huselid and D. Ulrich, *The HR Scorecard: Linking People, Strategy and Performance,* (Boston, MA: Harvard Business School Press, 2001); see also D. Brown, "Measuring the Value of HR," *Canadian HR Reporter* (September 24, 2001), pp. 1, 5.

87. R. Schuler and S. Jackson, "Linking Competitive Strategies with Human Resource Management Practices," *Academy of Management Executive* 1(3), 1987, pp. 207–19.

88. D. Brown, "HR Must Ensure Individual Goals are Met," *Canadian HR Reporter* (February 25, 2002), p. 12.

89. K. Mark, "No More Pink Slips," *Human Resources Professional* (November 1996), pp. 21–3; L. Young, "Recognition a Learning Experience," *Canadian HR Reporter* (January 31, 2000), p. 10.

90. D. S. Cohen, "Behaviour-based Interviewing," *Human Resources Professional* (April/May 1997), p. 29.

91. R. Gandossy, "The Need for Speed," *The Journal of Business Strategy* (January/February 2003), pp. 29–30.

92. "The Service Economy at a Glance: Overview of Canada's Service Economy," *Industry Canada* (March 2001), p. 11.

93. "CEOs Talk," *Canadian HR Reporter* (March 11), 2002, p. 19.

94. I. Papasolomou-Doukakis, "The Role of Employee Development in Customer Relations: The Case of UK Retail Banks," *Corporate Communications*, 7(1), 2002, pp. 62–76.

Chapter 2

1. *Canadian Charter of Rights and Freedoms*, as part of the Constitution Act of 1982.

2. *Canadian Charter of Rights and Freedoms*, Section 15(1).

3. D. Brown, "Supreme Court Gives Labour Historic Win," *Canadian HR Reporter* (January 28, 2002), p. 3.

4. *Annual Report of the Canadian Human Rights Commission* (Ottawa: Government of Canada, 1991), p. 65.

5. *Annual Report of the Canadian Human Rights Commission* (Ottawa: Minister of Public Works and Government Services, 2002), p. 18.

6. *Race, Colour, National or Ethnic Origin: Anti-Discrimination Handbook* (Ottawa: Canadian Human Rights Commission, 2001), pp. 8–9.

7. *Annual Report of the Canadian Human Rights Commission*, (Ottawa: Government of Canada, 1985), p. 25.

8. *Attorney General of Canada v. Singh*, Canadian Labour Law Reporter (2000), pp. 145 217–145 227.

9. *Conte v. Rogers Cablesystems Ltd.*, Canadian Labour Law Reporter (1999), pp. 145 058–145 069.

10. "Key Provisions of Ottawa's Same-Sex Legislation," *Canadian HR Reporter* (March 27, 2000), p. 11.

11. A.P. Aggarwal, *Sex Discrimination: Employment Law and Practices* (Toronto: Butterworths Canada, 1994).

12. H.J. Jain, "Human Rights: Issues in Employment," *Human Resources Management in Canada* (Toronto: Prentice-Hall Canada, 1995), p. 50 036.

13. *Bona Fide Occupational Requirements and Bona Fide Justifications Under the Canadian Human Rights Act: The Implications of Meiorin and Grismer* (Ottawa: Canadian Human Rights Commission, January 2003); see also A. Wahl, "Where There's Fire, There's Smoke," *Canadian Business* (October 8, 1999), pp. 16, 20.

14. Ontario Human Rights Commission, *Human Rights at Work* (Toronto: Government of Ontario, 1999), pp. 63–64.

15. *Annual Report of the Canadian Human Rights Commission* (Ottawa: Government of Canada, 1991), p. 63.

16. B.G. Humphrey, "Employer/Union Joint Responsibilities," *Human Resources Professional* (October 1996), pp. 23–26, 31.

17. R. LeClair, "The Evolution of Accommodation," *Canadian HR Reporter* (January 24, 2003), p. 7.

18. "Union's Duty," *Canadian HR Reporter* (February 24, 2003), p. 7.

19. Based on Canadian Human Rights Commission, *Harassment Casebook*, p. 3.

20. Clarendone Foundation v. Ontario Public Service Employees' Union, Local 593 (Mitchell Grievance, 2000). Cited in *Focus on Canadian Employment & Equality Rights* (June 2000), p. 240.

21. B. Orser, *Sexual Harassment Is Still a Management Issue* (Ottawa, ON: Conference Board of Canada). Cited in L. Cassiani, "Sexual Harassment Persists Despite Workplace Fallout," *Canadian HR Reporter* (April 9, 2001), pp. 1, 5.

22. A.P. Aggarwal, *Sexual Harassment in the Workplace*, 2nd ed. (Toronto: Butterworths Canada, 1992), pp. 10–11.

23. *Hill v. Dan Barclay Enterprises Ltd.* (1999). Cited in "Case Notes," *Focus on Canadian Employment & Equity Rights* (December 1999), p. 188.

24. *Pond v. Canada Post*. Cited in *Anti-Harassment Policies for the Workplace: An Employer's Guide* (Ottawa: Canadian Human Rights Commission with Human Resources Development Canada and Status of Women, December 2001). www.chrc-ccdp.ca/publications/antih1-luttel.asp1=e (July 22, 2003).

25. M. MacKillop, "Dismissal If Necessary; Not Necessarily Dismissal," *Human Resources Professional* 13, no. 2 (April 1996), pp. 24–25.

26. *Himmelman v. King's-Edgehill School* (1985), 7 CCEL 16 (N.S.S.C.).

27. A. Tomlinson, "Concrete Ceiling Harder to Break Than Glass for Women of Colour," *Canadian HR Reporter* (December 17, 2001), pp. 7, 13.

28. This section based on *Moving Forward 2002: Barriers and Opportunities for Executive Women in Canada* (Toronto, ON: Women's Executive Network); *2002 Catalyst Census of Women Corporate Officers and Top Earners of Canada* (Toronto, ON: Catalyst), cited in D. Brown, "Progress Slow, Incremental for Women in Business," *Canadian HR Reporter* (April 7, 2003), p. 11.

29. *Women in Canada: Work Chapter Updates*. Statistics Canada Catalogue No. 89F0133XIE, 2003. Statistics Canada—Housing, Family and Social Statistics Division.

30. *2001 Census: Analysis Series—Aboriginal Peoples of Canada: A Demographic Profile*. Statistics Canada Catalogue No. 960030XIE2001007, 2003, p. 5.

31. *2002 Annual Report—Employment Equity Act*. Human Resources Development Canada, p. 4.

32. *Advancing the Inclusion of Persons with Disabilities* (Ottawa: Government of Canada, 2002), p. 2.

33. *Canada's Ethnocultural Portrait: The Changing Mosaic*. 2001 Census: Analysis Series, Statistics Canada (January 21, 2003), p. 18; *Changing Profile of Canada's Labour Force*. Statistics Canada. www12.statcan.ca/english/census01/products/analytic/companion/paid/shaping.cfm (July 24, 2003).

34. *Changing Profile of Canada's Labour Force*.

35. P. Gorrie, "Discrimination Costly: Study," *Toronto Star* (March 20, 2002), p. A23.

36. R.S. Abella, *Equality in Employment: A Royal Commission Report* (Ottawa: Supply and Services Canada, 1984).

37. *Employment Equity Act and Reporting Requirements* (Ottawa: Employment and Immigration Canada, 1986); and material found on the CHRC Web site: www.chrc-ccdp.ca/publications/hrchrc-dpccdp.asp?/ (August 20, 2000). See also L. Thanasse, "Count on Employment Equity Audits," *WorldatWork Canadian News* (Third Quarter 2003), pp. 9–11.

38. *Employment Equity Act and Reporting Requirements*.

39. "Equity Hiring Program a Failure, Study Says," *Toronto Star* (July 13, 2001), p. A3.

40. A.B. Bakan and A. Kobyashi, *Employment Equity Policy in Canada: An Interprovincial Comparison* (Ottawa: Status of Women Canada, March 2000), pp. 9–10.

41. *Employment Equity: A Guide for Employers* (Ottawa: Employment and Immigration Canada, May 1991), Cat. No. LM-143.

42. M.B. Currie, "Destined for Equity," *Human Resources Professional* (July/August 1993), pp. 7–8.

43. *Annual Report of the Canadian Human Rights Commission* (Ottawa: Government of Canada, 1985).

44. J. Gandz, "A Business Case for Diversity," *Paths to Equal Opportunity* (Ontario Ministry of Citizenship, 2001). www.equalopportunity.on.ca/userfiles/item/5859/BusCase.pdf (July 23, 2003).

45. This section is based on *2002 Canadian Human Rights Commission Annual Report*.

46. "Average Earnings by Sex and Work Pattern," Statistics Canada www.stat-can.ca/english/Pgbd/Labor01b.htm (April 30, 2003), from CANSIM II Table 202-0102.

47. M. Drolet, "The Male–Female Wage Gap," *Perspectives*, Spring 2002, pp. 29–37. Statistics Canada Catalogue No. 75-001-XPE.

48. "The Male–Female Wage Gap."

49. Statistics Canada, *The Persistent Gap: New Evidence on the Canadian Gender Wage Gap*, cited in David Brown, "StatsCan Unable to Explain Gender Wage Gap," *Canadian HR Reporter* 12, no. 2 (January 31, 2000), p. 3.

50. *Canadian Master Labour Guide 2002*, 16th Edition (Toronto, ON: CCH Canadian Ltd., 2002), pp. 549–590.

51. B. Siu, "Beyond Quotas: The Business Case for Employment Equity," *Canadian HR Reporter*, June 4, 2001, p. 20.

52. J. Schilder, "The Rainbow Connection," *Human Resources Professional*, April 1994, pp. 13–5.

53. "CEOs Talk," *Canadian HR Reporter* (May 19, 2003), pp. 15–17.

54. www.acl.on.ca/Daily_News/2002/July_02/july25.htm (July 24, 2003).

55. Based on L. Young, "Mentoring Program is One Diversity Step in a Series at Rogers," *Canadian HR Reporter* (March 27, 2000), p. 8.

56. B. Siu, "Making Sense of Diversity Assessment Approaches," *Canadian HR Reporter* (November 1, 1999), p. 10.

Chapter 3

1. C. Babbage, *On the Economy of Machinery and Manufacturers* (London: Charles Knight, 1832), pp. 169–76; reprinted in Joseph Litterer, *Organizations* (New York: John Wiley and Sons, 1969), pp. 73–75.

2. F. Herzberg, "One More Time, How Do You Motivate Employees?" *Harvard Business Review* 46 (Jan–Feb 1968), pp. 53–62.

3. J.R. Hackman and G. Oldham, "Motivation Through the Design of Work: Test of a Theory," *Organizational Behavior and Human Performance* 16 (August 1976), pp. 250–79.

4. Hackman and Oldham, "Motivation," pp. 257–58.

5. D.A. Nadler, J.R. Hackman, and E.E. Lawler, *Managing Organizational Behavior* (Boston: Little, Brown, 1979).

6. J.R. Hackman and G. Oldham, "Motivation Through the Design of Work: Test of a Theory," pp. 255–56.

7. G. M. Parker, *Cross-Functional Teams: Working with Allies, Enemies and Other Strangers*. San Francisco, CA: Jossey-Bass, 2003, p. 68.

8. B. Gebor, "Saturn's Grand Experiment," *Training* (June 1992), pp. 27–35.

9. "Collaboration for Virtual Teams," *HR Professional* (December 2002/January 2003), p. 44.

10. Based on L. Young, "Latest HR Strategy Tied to Office Space Design," *Canadian HR Reporter* 12, no. 14 (August 9, 1999), pp. 1–11.

11. Reported in R. Stang, "Democracy Fails in Workplace?" *Workplace News* 5 (May 1999), p. 3.

12. For a good discussion of job analysis, see J. Clifford, "Job Analysis: Why Do It, and How Should It be Done?" *Public Personnel Management* 23, no. 2 (Summer 1994), pp. 321–40.

13. Based on J. Miller, "Top Court Speaks on Hiring, Re-Classification," *Canadian HR Reporter* 13 (June 19, 2000), pp. 5, 9.

14. R. I. Henderson, *Compensation Management in a Knowledge-based World* (Upper Saddle River, NJ: Prentice-Hall, 2003), pp. 135–138. See also P.W. Wright and K. Wesley, "How to Choose the Kind of Job Analysis You Really Need," *Personnel* 62 (May 1985), pp. 51–55; C.J. Cranny and M.E. Doherty, "Importance Ratings in Job Analysis: Note on the Misinterpretation of Factor Analyses," *Journal of Applied Psychology* (May 1988), pp. 320–322.

15. Henderson, *Compensation Management*, pp. 139–140.

16. Note that the PAQ (and other quantitative techniques) can also be used for job evaluation.

17. E. Corrnelius III, F. Schmidt, and T. Carron, "Job Classification Approaches and the Implementation of Validity Generalization Results," *Personnel Psychology* 37 (Summer 1984), pp. 247–260; E. Cornelius III, A. DeNisi,

and A. Blencoe, "Expert and Naïve Raters Using the PAQ: Does It Matter?" *Personnel Psychology* 37 (Autumn 1984), pp. 453–464; L. Friedman and R. Harvey, "Can Raters with Reduced Job Description Information Provide Accurate Position Analysis Questionnaire (PAQ) Ratings?" *Personnel Psychology* 34 (Winter 1986), pp. 779–789; R. J. Harvey et al., "Dimensionality of the Job Element Inventory, A Simplified Worker-oriented Job Analysis Questionnaire," *Journal of Applied Psychology* (November 1988), pp. 639–646; S. Butler & R. Harvey, "A Comparison of Holistic Versus Decomposed Rating of Position Analysis Questionnaire Work Dimensions," *Personnel Psychology* (Winter 1988), pp. 761–772.

18. This discussion is based on H. Olson et al., "The Use of Functional Job Analysis in Establishing Performance Standards for Heavy Equipment Operators," *Personnel Psychology* 34 (Summer 1981), pp. 351–64.

19. Human Resources Development Canada, *National Occupation Classification Career Handbook* (Ottawa: Minister of Supply and Services Canada, 2001), Catalogue No. MP53-25/2001E.

20. Human Resources Development Canada, *National Occupation Classification Career Handbook*.

21. Human Resources Development Canada, *National Occupation Classification Career Handbook*.

22. J. Evered, "How to Write a Good Job Description," *Supervisory Management* (April 1981), pp. 14–19; R. J. Plachy, "Writing Job Descriptions That Get Results," *Personnel* (October 1987), pp. 56–58. See also M. Mariani, "Replace with a Database," *Occupational Outlook Quarterly* 43 (Spring 1999), pp. 2–9.

23. Evered, "How to Write," p. 16.

24. Evered, "How to Write," p. 18

25. R.J. Stone, *Human Resources Management* (Milton, Queensland: John Wiley & Sons Australia, 2002), p. 132.

26. Based on E.J. McCormick and Joseph Tiffin, *Industrial Psychology* (Englewood Cliffs, NJ: Prentice-Hall, 1974), pp. 56–61.

27. Human Resources Development Canada, *National Occupation Classification Career Handbook*.

28. P.H. Raymark, M. J. Schmidt, and R. M. Guion, "Identifying Potentially Useful Personality Constructs for Employee Selection," *Personnel Psychology* 50 (1997) pp. 723–26.

29. D. Davidson. "Transformation to a High-Performance Team," *Canadian Business Review* 21 (1994), pp. 18–19; and C. Kapel, "Master Copy," *Human Resources Professional* 11 (August 1994), pp. 17–18.

30. R.J. Klimoski and L.B. Zukin in E.D. Sundstrom & Associates, *Supporting Work Team Effectiveness: Best Management Practices for Fostering High Performance* (San Francisco, CA: Jossey-Bass, 1999).

31. M. Hammer and J. Champy, *Reengineering the Corporation* (New York: Harper Business, 1993), p. 32.

32. Hammer and Champy, *Reengineering*, p. 51.

33. Hammer and Champy, *Reengineering*, p. 68.

34. B. Gomolski, "New E-commerce Food Chain Breaks the Bond Between Employee and Employer," *Network World Canada* (November 2000), p. 28.

35. Bridges, "The End of the Job," p. 68.

Chapter 4

1. N.C. Agarwal, "Human Resources Planning," *Human Resources Management in Canada* (Toronto: Prentice-Hall Canada Inc., 1983), p. 20 011.

2. J.W. Walker, *Human Resource Planning* (New York: McGraw-Hill, 1980), p. 10.

3. J.W. Walker, "Integrating the Human Resource Function with the Business," *Human Resource Planning* 14(2), 1996, pp. 59–77.

4. J.W. Walker, "Human Resource Planning, 1990s Style," *Human Resource Planning* 13(4), 1990, pp. 229–40.

5. D. Ulrich, "Strategic and Human Resource Planning: Linking Customers and Employees," *Human Resource Planning* 15(2), 1992, pp. 47–62.

6. L. Young, "Government's Unique Incentive Plan Falls Short of Retention Mark, Nurses Contend," *Canadian HR Reporter* (March 13, 2000), p. 8.

7. Cited in Young, "Government's Unique Incentive Plan," p. 8.

8. D. Sheremata, "Art, Tell Them What They've Won," Alberta Report, *Newsmagazine* (July 31, 1995), pp. 6–7.

9. K.L. Johnson, D.S. Lero, and J.A. Rooney, *Work-Life Compendium 2001: 150 Canadian Statistics on Work, Family and Well-Being.* Centre for Families, Work and Well-Being, University of Guelph (Ottawa, ON: Human Resources Development Canada, 2001), p. 8.

10. *Work-Life Compendium 2001*, pp. 7, 9.

11. *Work-Life Compendium 2001*, p. 7.

12. P. Kieran, "Early Retirement Trends," *Perspectives* (Winter 2001), pp. 7–13. Statistics Canada Catalogue No. 75-001-XPE.

13. C. Graham and S. Roy, "Early Retirement on the Bargaining Table," *Canadian HR Reporter* (January 27, 2003), p. 12.

14. H.G. Heneman, Jr., and G. Seitzer, "Manpower Planning and Forecasting in the Firm: An Exploratory Probe," in E. Burack and J. Walker, *Manpower Planning and Programming* (Boston: Allyn & Bacon, 1972), pp. 102–20; S. Zedeck and M. Blood, "Selection and Placement," from *Foundations of Behavioral Science Research in Organizations* (Monterey, CA: Brooks/Cole, 1974), in J. R. Hackman, E. Lawler III and L. Porter, *Perspectives on Behavior in Organizations* (New York: McGraw-Hill, 1977), pp. 103–19.

15. R. Hawk, *The Recruitment Function* (New York: American Management Association, 1967). See also P. Pakchar, "Effective Manpower Planning," *Personnel Journal* (October 1983), pp. 826–30.

16. R.B. Frantzreb, "Human Resource Planning: Forecasting Manpower Needs," *Personnel Journal* (November 1981), pp. 850–57. See also J. Gridley, "Who Will Be Where When? Forecast the Easy Way," *Personnel Journal* (May 1986), pp. 50–58.

17. Based on an idea in E.H. Burack and R.D. Smith, *Personnel Management: A Human Resource Systems Approach* (St. Paul, MN: West, 1977), pp. 134–35. Reprinted by permission. Copyright 1977 by West Publishing Co. All rights reserved.

18. G. Bassett, "Elements of Manpower Forecasting and Scheduling," *Human Resource Management* (Fall 1973), pp. 35–43, reprinted in R. Peterson, L. Tracy and A. Cabelly, *Systematic Management of Human Resources* (Reading, MA: Addison-Wesley, 1979), pp. 135–36.

19. For an example of a computerized system in use at Citibank, see P. Sheiber, "A Simple Selection System Called 'Job Match,'" *Personnel Journal* (January 1979), pp. 26–54.

20. G. Milkovich, A.J. Annoni, and T.A. Mahoney, "The Use of Delphi Procedures in Manpower Forecasting," *Management Science* (1972), pp. 381–88.

21. A.L. Delbecq, A.H. Van DelVen, and D.H. Gustafson, *Group Techniques for Program Planning: A Guide to Nominal and Delphi Processes* (Glenview, Illinois: Scott Foresman, 1975).

22. D. Brown, "Sure It's Cool, But Do You Need it?" *Canadian HR Reporter* (August 12, 2002), p. 9.

23. S. Forman, "Corporate Contenders," *Human Resources Professional* (September 1993), pp. 17, 19.

24. This is a modification of a definition found in P. Wallum, "A Broader View of Succession Planning," *Personnel Management* (September 1993), pp. 43–44.

25. Agarwal, "Human Resources Planning," p. 20 039.

26. "Early Retirement on the Bargaining Table," pp. 12–13.

27. G. Lowe, "Retiring Baby Boomers Open to Options, But Get Them Before They Leave," *Canadian HR Reporter* (March 10, 2003), p. 6.

28. O. Parker and D. Gore, "The Changing Workforce: Are We Ready?" *Canadian HR Reporter* (August 13, 2001), pp. 13.

29. P. Kieran, "Early Retirement Trends."

30. O. Parker and D. Gore, "The Changing Workforce."

31. U. Vu, "Wave of Retirement Coming, Few Organizations Getting Ready," *Canadian HR Reporter* (May 5, 2003), p. 2.

32. B. Cheadle, "High-Skill Immigrants Drive Labour Force Growth but Job Prospects Still Grim," *Canadian Press Newswire* (February 11, 2003).

33. M. Bloom and M. Grant, *Brain Gain* (Ottawa, ON: Conference Board of Canada, 2001). Cited in A. Tomlinson, "Skills and Education of Immigrants Wasted: Report," *Canadian HR Reporter* (October 22, 2001), pp. 2, 6.

34. U. Vu, "Labour Force Growth Depends on Immigrants," *Canadian HR Reporter* (March 10, 2003), pp. 1, 3.

35. U. Vu, "Massive Spike in Enrolment Creates Post-Secondary Staffing Crunch," *Canadian HR Reporter* (March 10, 2003), p. 14.

36. "Oilpatch Labour Shortage," *Canadian HR Reporter* (July 15, 2001), p. 2.

37. For more information, visit the HRDC Web Site at: www.hrdc-drhc.gc.ca.

38. Walker, *Human Resource Planning.*

39. D.A. Bratton, "Moving Away From Nine to Five," *Canadian Business Review* (Spring 1986), pp. 15–17.

40. F. Reid, "Combating Unemployment Through Work Time Reductions," *Canadian Public Policy* 12 (2), 1986, pp. 275–85.

41. M. MacKillop, "Ballpark Justice," *Human Resources Professional* (September 1994), pp. 10–11.

42. T.H. Wagar, "The Death of Downsizing—Not Yet!" Research Forum, *HR Professional* (February/March 1999), pp. 41–43.

43. S.P. Robbins, "Layoff Survivor Sickness: A Missing Topic in Organizational Behavior," *Journal of Management Education* (February 1999), pp. 31–43.

44. G. Lowe, "Retiring Baby Boomers Open to Options, but Get Them Before They Leave," *Canadian HR Reporter* (March 10, 2003), p. 6.

45. Walker, *Human Resource Planning*, pp. 355–56.

Chapter 5

1. J. Yardley, director of the Brock University Wellness Institute, cited in "Putting Theories to the Test," *Canadian HR Reporter* (November 1, 1999), p. 2.

2. R.D. Gatewood and H.S. Field, *Human Resource Selection* 5th edition (Orlando, FL: Harcourt Inc., 2001), p. 10.

3. L. Karakowsky and I. Kotlyar, "If Recruitment Means Building Trust, Where Does Technology Fit In?" *Canadian HR Reporter* (October 17, 2002), p. 21.

4. See, for example, D. Brown, "Ford, Delta Equip Staff with Home Computers," *Canadian HR Reporter* (February 28, 2000), pp. 1, 23; I. Huss and C. Kapel, "Integrated HR Strategy Needed to Recruit and Retain e-Commerce Talent," *Canadian HR Reporter* (February 14, 2000), pp. 27–29; and J. Goodings, "No Holds Barred in Fight for Talent," *Canadian HR Reporter* (May 3, 1999), pp. 1, 9.

5. R. S. Echlin, "Into the Briar Patch," *Human Resources Professional* (March 1993), p. 19.

6. D. Dahl and P. Pinto, "Job Posting, an Industry Survey," *Personnel Journal* (January 1977), pp. 40–41.

7. J. Daum, "Internal Promotion—Psychological Asset or Debit? A Study of the Effects of Leader Origin," *Organizational Behavior and Human Performance* 13 (1975), pp. 404–13.

8. "How Outsourced Recruiting Saves Time and Money—and Gets Quality Hires," *HR Focus* (September 2002), pp. 5–6.

9. See, for example, A. Harris, "Hiring Middle Management: External Recruitment or Internal Promotion?" *Canadian HR Reporter* (April 10, 2000), pp. 8–10.

10. "What the CEO Expects for 2003," *Canadian HR Reporter* (February 10, 2003), p. 2.

11. Axmith, *Survey 2000: Canadian Hiring, Retention and Dismissal Practices*, pp. 11–13.

12. *Compensation Outlook 2002* (Ottawa, ON: Conference Board of Canada). See also A. Davis, "What is the Cost of Hiring?" *Canadian HR Reporter* (June 2, 2003), pp. 12–13.

13. *Canadian Inter@ctive Reid Report* (Vancouver, BC: Ipsos Reid, 2003); and *Online Job Hunting: What the Future Holds* (Vancouver, BC: Ipsos Reid, 2002).

14. A. Tomlinson, "The Many Benefits of Online Job Boards," *Canadian HR Reporter* (July 15, 2002), pp. 17, 19.

15. "Web Spins Out New Recruiting Job Titles," *Canadian HR Reporter* (September 25, 2000), p. G3.

16. P. Lima, "Talent Shortage? That Was Yesterday. Online Recruiters Can Deliver More Candidates for Your Job Opening and Help You Find Keepers," *Profit: The Magazine for Canadian Entrepreneurs* (February/March 2002), pp. 65–66.

17. V. Hayes, "Internet Recruiting: The Revolution Goes Mainstream," *Canadian HR Reporter* (September 25, 2000), pp. G1–G2. See also D. Brown, "RBC Financial Group Brings Recruitment Back Into the Fold, "*Canadian HR Reporter* (April 24, 2003), p. 7.

18. G. Stanton, "Recruiting Portals Take Centre Stage in Play for Talent," *Canadian HR Reporter* (September 25, 2000), pp. G1–G2.

19. "Spies Like Us," *Canadian HR Reporter* (May 19, 2003), p. G2.

20. P. Lima, "Talent Shortage?"

21. U. Vu, "Security Failures Expose Resumes," *Canadian HR Reporter* (May 24, 2003).

22. P. Lima, "Talent Shortage?"

23. J. Hampton, "www.work-for-us.com," *Canadian HR Reporter* (October 23, 2000), pp. 1, 23.

24. U. Vu, "Security Failures Expose Resumes."

25. "…But Canadians are Savvy Surfers," *Canadian HR Reporter* (May 19, 2003), p. G2.

26. G. Stanton, "Recruiting Portals Take Centre Stage in Play for Talent."

27. D. Lu-Hovasse, "Headhunters: Doomed by the Mouse?" *Financial Post* (February 19, 2001), p. E4.

28. D. Lu-Hovasse, "Headhunters: Doomed by the Mouse?"

29. D. Brown, "Canadian Government Job Boards Lag on Best Practices," *Canadian HR Reporter* (January 13, 2003), p. 2.

30. V. Hayes, "Internet Recruiting: The Revolution Goes Mainstream."

31. S. Jones, "Going Global: How International Firms are Using the Internet to Recruit," *Canadian HR Reporter* (December 3, 2001), p. 21.

32. A. Tomlinson, "Energy Firm Sharpens Recruiting, Saves Money With In-House Job Board, " *Canadian HR Reporter* (March 18, 2002), pp. 7–8.

33. "Corporate Spending Millions on Ineffective Web Recruiting Strategies," *Canadian HR Reporter* (September 25, 2000), p. G5.

34. D. Brown, "Who's Looking Online? Most Firms Don't Know," *Canadian HR Reporter* (August 13, 2001), pp. 2, 12.

35. A. Snell, "Best Practices for Web Site Recruiting," *Canadian HR Reporter* (February 26, 2001), pp. G7, G10.

36. "Corporate Spending Millions on Ineffective Web Recruiting Strategies."

37. D. Brown, "Who's Looking Online?"

38. D. Brown, "Who's Looking Online?"

39. "Corporate Spending Millions on Ineffective Web Recruiting Strategies."

40. "Corporate Spending Millions on Ineffective Web Recruiting Strategies."

41. A. Snell, "Best Practices for Web Site Recruiting."

42. Pell, *Recruiting and Selecting Personnel*, pp. 16–34.

43. S. Jones, "You've Come a Long Way Baby: What the Staffing Industry Offers Today," *Canadian HR Reporter* (November 5, 2001), p. 15.

44. M. Moralis, "Shop With Care for Retail Execs," *Canadian HR Reporter* (February 11, 2002), p. G5.

45. P. Tindall, "7 Traits to Look for in Top Headhunters," *Canadian HR Reporter* (November 18, 2002), p. 10.

46. J.A. Parr, "7 Reasons Why Executive Searches Fail," *Canadian HR Reporter* (March 12, 2001), pp. 20, 23.

47. S. Jones, "You've Come a Long Way Baby."

48. A. Doran, "Technology Brings HR to Those Who Need It," *Canadian HR Reporter* (October 6, 1997), p. 8.

49. K. Barker, "Recruiting Drivers: Two Men, Two Eras, Two Completely Different Situations. The Low-Down on High-Tech Hiring at IBM in 1957 and at an Internet Service Provider Right Now," *National Post Business* (January 1, 2001), pp. 66–67.

50. G. Reamey, "HR Strategies to Attract and Keep Top Talent the Edward Jones Way," *Canadian HR Reporter* (September 25, 2000), p. G3.

51. A. Tomlinson, "Finding Talented Grads Isn't Hard if You Play the Cards Right," *Canadian HR Reporter* (November 19, 2001), pp. 9, 11.

52. N. Laurie and M. Laurie, "No Holds Barred in Fight for Students to Fill Internship Programs," *Canadian HR Reporter* (January 17, 2000), pp. 15–16.

53. L. Cassiani, "Skilled Workers Apply Within," *Canadian HR Reporter* (June 4, 2001), pp. 1, 22, 23.

54. www.hrpao.org (June 25, 2003).

55. D. Hurl, "Letting the Armed Forces Train Your Managers," *Canadian HR Reporter* (December 3, 2001), pp. 8–9.

56. L. MacGillivray, "Cashing in on the Canadian Forces, " *Workplace Today* (October 2001), pp. 40–41.

57. Canadian Forces Liaison Council (CFLC), *Why We Ask Employers to Support the Reserve Force* (Ottawa: CFLC, National Defence Headquarters, 2000); and Canadian Forces Liaison Council (CFLC), *Employers and Reservists Working Together* (Ottawa: CFLC, National Defence Headquarters, 2000).

58. Captain R. E. Grower, "Creating a Military Leave Policy," *Canadian HR Reporter* (September 25, 2000), p. G12.

59. T. Lende, "Workplaces Looking to Hire Part-Timers," *Canadian HR Reporter* (April 22, 2002), pp. 9, 11.

60. K. LeMessurier, "Temp Staffing Leaves a Permanent Mark," *Canadian HR Reporter* (February 10, 2003), pp. 3, 8.

61. J. Pearce, "Toward an Organizational Behavior of Contract Laborers: Their Psychological Involvement and Effects on Employee Co-Workers," *Academy of Management Journal* 36 (1993), pp. 1082–96. See also A. Ryckman, "The 5 Keys to Getting Top Value from Contractors," *Canadian HR Reporter* (December 2, 2002), p.25; and S. Purba, "Contracting Works for Job Hunters," *The Globe & Mail* (April 24, 2002).

62. "Flexible Staffing in the Aerospace Industry," *Airfinance Journal I Aircraft Economic Yearbook 2001*, pp. 14-17.

63. L. Corwin, "Now You See Them, Now You Don't: Using Contract Staff," *Canadian HR Reporter* (March 12, 2001), p.14; and M. Moralis, "The Unknown Executive," *Canadian HR Reporter* (February 11, 2002), pp. G1, G4.

64. M. Moralis, "The Unknown Executive."

65. M. Moralis, "The Unknown Executive."

66. "Outsourcing HR," *Industry Week* (May 15, 2000), p. 10.

67. "Outsourcing HR."

68. E. Miller, "Capitalizing on Older Workers," *Canadian HR Reporter* (June 16, 1997), p. 14. See also L. Cassiani, "Looming Retirement Surge Takes on New Urgency," *Canadian HR Reporter* (May 21, 2001), pp. 1, 10.

69. U. Vu, "The Drug Sector's Staffing Remedies," *Canadian HR Reporter* (February 10, 2003), pp. 1, 10.

70. S. B. Hood, "Generational Diversity in the Workplace, " *HR Professional* (June/July 2000), p. 20.

71. www.aboriginalbiz.com and http://aboriginal.monster.ca (June 18, 2003).

72. www.aboriginalbiz.com and http://aboriginal.monster.ca (June 18, 2003).

73. www.workink.com (June 18, 2003).

74. www.harbour.sfu.ca/scwist/jobs.html (June 18, 2003).

75. S. LeBrun, "Booklets to Connect Disabled With Work," *Canadian HR Reporter* (October 20, 1997), p. 8.

76. H.N. Chait, S.M. Carraher, M.R. Buckley, "Measuring Service Orientation with Biodata," *Journal of Management Issues* (Spring 2000), pp. 109–120; V.M. Catano, S.F. Cronshaw, R.D. Hackett, L.L. Methot and W.H. Weisner, *Recruitment and Selection in Canada*, 2nd edition (Scarborough, ON: Nelson Thomson Learning, 2001), p. 307; J.E. Harvey-Cook, R.J. Taffler, "Biodata in Professional Entry-Level Selection: Statistical Scoring of Common-Format Applications," *Journal of Occupational and Organizational Psychology* (March 1, 2000), pp. 103–118; and Y.Y. Chung, "The Validity of

Biographical Inventories for the Selection of Salespeople," *International Journal of Management* (September 2001).

Chapter 6

1. R.D. Gatewood and H.S. Field. *Human Resources Selection* (Chicago: The Dryden Press, 1990), p. 3.

2. *Angus Reid Survey for William M. Mercer Ltd.,* cited in E. Atkins, "Talent Rules," *Workplace News* (May 1999), pp. 1, 2.

3. Cited in K. Rowlands, "Marketplace: Checking References," *HR Professional* 17, no. 4 (August/September 2000), p. 12.

4. British Columbia Criminal Records Review Act; www.pssg.gov.bc.ca/criminal-records-review/index.htm (June 27, 2003).

5. J. Zeidenberg, "HR and the Innovative Company," *Human Resources Professional* 13, no. 4 (June 1996), pp. 12–5.

6. C. Kapel, "Giant Steps," *Human Resources Professional* (April 1993), pp. 13–6.

7. J.L Ashbaugh, "The Hard Case for Soft Skills and Retention," *Healthcare Executive* (March/April 2003), pp. 59–60; and D. Brown, "New Strategies Needed to Staff Oil Patch," *Canadian HR Reporter* (January 27, 2003), pp. 1, 6.

8. These guidelines are based on two sources: S.M. Sack, "Fifteen Steps to Protecting Against the Risk of Negligent Hiring Claims," *Employment Relations Today* (August 1993), pp. 313–20 and S.L. McShane, "Wrongful Dismissal Risks," pp. 20–25.

9. Gatewood and Field, *Human Resources Selection*, p. 89.

10. A. Anastasi, *Psychological Patterns* (New York: Macmillan, 1968), reprinted in W. Clay Hamner and Frank Schmidt, *Contemporary Problems in Personnel* (Chicago: St. Claire Press, 1974), pp. 102–9. Discussion of reliability based on Marvin Dunnette, *Personnel Selection and Placement* (Belmont, CA: Wadsworth Publishing Company, Inc., 1966), pp. 29–30.

11. L. Tyler, *Tests and Measurements* (Englewood Cliffs, NJ: Prentice-Hall, 1971), p. 25. More technically, "validity refers to the degree of confidence one can have in inferences drawn from scores, considering the whole process by which the scores are obtained. Stated differently, validity refers to the confidence one has in the meaning attached to scores." (See R. M. Guion, "Changing Views for Personnel Selection Research," *Personnel Psychology,* 40, Summer 1987, p. 208.)

12. Bureau of National Affairs, *Primer of Equal Employment Opportunity* (Washington, DC: BNA, 1978), p. 18. In practice, proving in court the criterion-related validity of paper-and-pencil tests has been difficult.

13. J. Ledvinka, *Federal Regulation of Personnel and Human Resource Management* (Boston: Kent, 1982), p. 111.

14. H. C. Jain, "Staffing: Recruitment and Selection" in *Human Resources Management in Canada* (Scarborough, Ontario: Prentice-Hall, 1983), p. 25 031.

15. M. Axmith, *Survey 2000: Canadian Hiring, Retention and Dismissal Practices*, p. 13.

16. S.A. Way and J.W. Thacker, "Selection Practices: Where are Canadian Organizations?" *HR Professional* (October/November 1999), p. 33.

17. S. Greengard, "Smarter Screening Takes Technology and HR Savvy," *Workforce* (June 2002), pp. 56–60.

18. T. Samson, "Tools of the Recruitment Trade," *Infoworld* (July 31, 2000), pp. 63–64.

19. I. Kotlyar and K. Ades, "E-selection: Advancements in Assessment Technology," *Canadian HR Reporter* (April 8, 2002), pp. 15, 19.

20. Way and Thacker, "Selection Practices," p. 34.

21. *Guidelines for Educational and Psychological Testing* (Old Chelsea, Quebec: Canadian Psychological Association, 1987).

22. J. Norborg, "A Warning Regarding the Simplified Approach to the Evaluation of Test Fairness and Employee Selection Procedures," *Personnel Psychology,* 37 (Autumn 1984), pp. 483–86; C. Johnson, L. Messe, and W. Crano, "Predicting Job Performance of Low Income Workers: The Work Opinion Questionnaire," *Personnel Psychology,* 37 (Summer 1984), pp. 291–99; F. Schmidt, B. Ocasio, J. Hillery, and J. Hunter, "Further Within-

Setting Empirical Tests of the Situational Specificity Hypothesis in Personnel Selection," *Personnel Psychology,* 38 (Autumn 1985), pp. 509–24.

23. *Guidelines for Educational and Psychological Testing.*

24. "Emotional Intelligence Testing," *HR Focus* (October 2001), pp. 8–9.

25. H. Kirby, "Powered by Aptitude Tests," *Works Management* (May 2001), p. 29.

26. Results of meta-analyses in one recent study indicated that isometric strength tests were valid predictors of both supervisory ratings of physical performance and performance on work simulations. See B.R. Blakley, M. Quinones, M.S. Crawford, and I. A. Jago, "The Validity of Isometric Strength Tests," *Personnel Psychology,* 47 (1994), pp. 247–74. See also B. Daniel, "Strength and Endurance Testing," *Personnel Journal* (June 1987), pp. 112–22.

27. C. Colacci, "Testing Helps You Decrease Disability Costs," *Guide to Employee Benefits, Supplement to Canadian HR Reporter* (June 14, 1999), p. G4.

28. K. Gillin, "Reduce Employee Exposure to Injury with Pre-Employment Screening Tests," *Canadian HR Reporter* (February 28, 2000), p. 10.

29. L. Young, "Employers Need to Scrutinize All Job Testing for Human Rights Violations, Supreme Court Rules," *Canadian HR Reporter* (October 4, 1999), p. 3.

30. This approach calls for construct validation, which, as was pointed out, is extremely difficult to demonstrate.

31. B. Reid, "Employee Testing Tackles Soft Skills, ROI," *Canadian HR Reporter* (September 23, 2002), p. 21.

32. J. Merritt, "Improv at the Interview: New Techniques Show Bosses How Applicants React to Stress," *Business Week* (February 3, 2003), p. 63.

33. See, for example, D. Cellar et al., "Comparison of Factor Structures and Criterion Related Validity Coefficients for Two Measures of Personality Based on the Five Factor Model," *Journal of Applied Psychology,* 81, no. 6 (1996), pp. 694–704; and J. Salgado, "The Five Factor Model of Personality and Job Performance in the European Community," *Journal of Applied Psychology,* 82, no. 1 (1997), pp. 30–43.

34. M.R. Barrick and M.K. Mount, "The Big Five Personality Dimensions and Job Performance: A Meta-Analysis," *Personnel Psychology,* 44, (Spring 1991), pp. 1–26.

35. T. Judge, J. Martocchio, and C. Thorensen, "Five-Factor Model of Personality and Employee Absence, " *Journal of Applied Psychology,* 82 (1997), pp. 745–55.

36. R. Tett, D. Jackson and M. Rothstein, "Personality Measures as Predictors of Job Performance: A Meta-Analytic Review," *Personnel Psychology,* 44 (1991), p. 732. For a related study see P. Raymark, M. Schmit, and R. Guion, "Identifying Potentially Useful Personality Constructs for Employee Selection," *Personnel Psychology,* 50, Fall 1997, pp. 723–36; and C. Fischer and G. Boyle, "Personality and Employee Selection: Credibility Regained," *Asia Pacific Journal of HRM,* 35, no. 2 (1997), pp. 26–40.

37. Tett, Jackson and Rothstein, "Personality Measures," p. 732.

38. E. Silver and C. Bennett, "Modification of the Minnesota Clerical Test to Predict Performance on Video Display Terminals," *Journal of Applied Psychology,* 72, no. 1 (February 1987), pp. 153–55.

39. Marvin D. Dunnette and W.D. Borman, "Personnel Selection and Classification Systems," *Annual Review of Psychology,* 30 (1979), pp. 477–525, quoted in Siegel and Lane, *Personnel and Organizational Psychology,* pp. 182–83.

40. I. Kotlyar and K. Ades, "E-selection."

41. F. Schmidt et al, "Job Sample vs. Paper and Pencil Trades and Technical Test: Adverse Impact and Examinee Attitudes," *Personnel Psychology,* 30 (Summer 1977), pp. 187–98.

42. Siegel and Lane, *Personnel and Organizational Psychology,* pp. 182–83.

43. J. Weekley and C. Jones, "Video-Based Situational Testing," *Personnel Psychology,* 50, 1997, p. 25.

44. Weekley and Jones, "Video-Based Situational Testing," pp. 26–30.

45. Kotlyar and Ades, "E-selection."

46. Kotlyar and Ades, "E-selection."

47. J.A. Weekley and C. Jones, "Further Studies of Situational Tests," *Personnel Psychology*, 52 (1999), pp. 679–700.

48. J. Jones and W. Terris, "Post-Polygraph Selection Techniques," *Recruitment Today* (May–June 1989), pp. 25–31.

49. J. Towler, "Dealing With Employees Who Steal," *Canadian HR Reporter* (September 23, 2002), p. 4.

50. S.L. Thomas and S. Vaught, "The Write Stuff: What the Evidence Says About Using Handwriting Analysis in Hiring," *S.A.M. Advanced Management Journal* (Autumn 2001), pp. 31–35.

51. Thomas and Vaught, "The Write Stuff."

52. B. Leonard, "Reading Employees," *HR Magazine*, April 1999, p. 4; and A. Perry and B.H. Kleiner, "How to Hire Employees Effectively," *Management Research News*, 25 (2002), pp. 3–11.

53. M.B. Currie and N. Eber, "Appealing Reasons," *OH&S Canada*, December 2002, pp. 18–21.

54. A. Tomlinson, "No Clear Cut Answer to Drug Test," *Canadian HR Reporter* (May 6, 2002), pp. 4, 11. See also *Canadian Human Rights Commission Policy on Alcohol and Drug Testing*. Canadian Human Rights Commission, June 2002.

55. C. Hoglund, "Mandatory Drug Testing," *Human Resources Professional* (January 1992), pp. 21–22.

56. "Drug Testing Can't Be Justified," *Canadian HR Reporter* (August 12, 2002), p. 3.

57. Way and Thacker, "Selection Practices," p. 34.

58. M. McDaniel et al., "The Validity of Employment Interviews: A Comprehensive Review and Meta-analysis," *Journal of Applied Psychology*, 79, no. 4 (1994), p. 599.

59. J. G. Goodale, *The Fine Art of Interviewing* (Englewood Cliffs. NJ: Prentice Hall Inc., 1982) p. 22. See also R. L. Decker, "The Employment Interview," *Personnel Administrator* 26 (November 1981) pp. 71–3.

60. Goodale, *The Fine Art of Interviewing*, p. 22.

61. Way and Thacker, "Selection Practices," p. 34.

62. McDaniel et al., "The Validity of Employment Interviews," p. 602.

63. D. S. Chapman and P.M. Rowe, "The Impact of Video Conferencing Technology, Interview Structure, and Interviewer Gender on Interviewer Evaluations in the Employment Interview: A Field Experiment," *Journal of Occupational and Organizational Psychology*, 74 (September 2001), pp. 279–298.

64. McDaniel et al., "The Validity of Employment Interviews," p. 601.

65. McDaniel et al., "The Validity of Employment Interviews," p. 601.

66. See A. M. Ryan & P. R. Sackett, "Exploratory Study of Individual Assessment Practices: Inter-Rater Reliability and Judgments of Assessor Effectiveness," *Journal of Applied Psychology*, 74 (1989), pp. 568–79, cited in McDaniel, "The Validity of Employment Interviews," p. 601.

67. A.I. Huffcut, J.A. Weekely, W.H. Wiesner, T. G. DeGroot, and C. Jones, "Comparison of Situational and Behavior Description Interview Questions for Higher-Level Positions," *Personnel Psychology*, 54 (Autumn 2001), pp. 619–644.

68. A. Pell, *Recruiting and Selecting Personnel* (New York: Regents, 1969), p. 119.

69. Axmith, *Survey 2000: Canadian Hiring, Retention and Dismissal Practices*, p. 13.

70. D.S. Chapman and P.M. Rowe, "The Impact of Videoconferencing Technology."

71. A. Huffcutt et al., "A Meta-Analytic Investigation of Cognitive Ability in Employment Interview Evaluations: Moderating Characteristics and Implications for Incremental Validity," *Journal of Applied Psychology*, 81, no. 5 (1996), p. 459.

72. Goodale, *The Fine Art of Interviewing*, p. 26.

73. Goodale, *The Fine Art of Interviewing*, p. 26.

74. McDaniel et al., "The Validity of Employment Interviews," p. 608.

75. D. Tucker and P. Rowe, "Relationship Between Expectancy, Casual Attribution, and Final Hiring Decisions in the Employment Interview," *Journal of Applied Psychology*, 64, no. 1 (February 1979), pp. 27–34. See also R. Dipboye, G. Fontenelle and K. Garner, "Effect of Previewing the Application on Interview Process and Outcomes," *Journal of Applied Psychology*, 69, no. 1 (February 1984), pp. 118–28.

76. R.E. Carlson, "Selection Interview Decisions: The Effects of Interviewer Experience, Relative Quota Situation, and Applicant Sample on Interview Decisions," *Personnel Psychology* 20 (1967), pp. 259–80.

77. See Arvey and Campion, "The Employment Interview," p. 305.

78. See, for example, M. Heilmann, and L. Saruwatari, "When Beauty Is Beastly: The Effects of Appearance and Sex on Evaluation of Job Applicants for Managerial and Nonmanagerial Jobs," *Organizational Behavior and Human Performance* 23 (June 1979), pp. 360–722; and C. Marlowe, S. Schneider, and C. Nelson, "Gender and Attractiveness Biases in Hiring Decisions: Are More Experienced Managers Less Biased?" *Journal of Applied Psychology*, 81, no. 1 (1996), pp. 11–21.

79. V. Galt, "Beauty Found not Beastly in the Job Interview," *The Globe & Mail* (April 15, 2002).

80. A. Pell, "Nine Interviewing Pitfalls," *Managers* (January 1994), p. 29.

81. T. Dougherty, D. Turban and J. Callender, "Confirming First Impressions in the Employment Interview: A Field Study of Interviewer Behavior," *Journal of Applied Psychology*, 79, no. 5 (1994), p. 663.

82. See Pell, "Nine Interviewing Pitfalls," p. 29; P. Sarathi, "Making Selection Interviews Effective," *Management and Labor Studies*, 18, no. 1 (1993), pp. 5–7.

83. J. Shetcliffe, "Who, and How, to Employ," *Insurance Brokers' Monthly* (December 2002), pp. 14–16.

84. Pell, "Nine Interviewing Pitfalls," p. 30.

85. G.J Sears and P.M. Rowe, "A Personality-based Similar-to-me Effect in the Employment Interview: Conscientious, Affect-versus Competence Mediated Interpretations, and the Role of Job Relevance," *Canadian Journal of Behavioural Sciences*, 35 (January 2003), p. 13.

86. This section is based on Pursell, Campion and Gaylord, "Structured Interviewing," and Latham et al., "The Situational Interview." See also M. A. Campion, E. Pursell, and B. Brown, "Structured Interviewing," pp. 25–42, and Weekley and Gier, "Reliability and Validity of the Situational Interview," pp. 484–87, except as noted.

87. P. Lowry, "The Structured Interview: An Alternative to the Assessment Center?" *Public Personnel Management*, 23, no. 2 (Summer 1994), pp. 201–15.

88. Steps two and three are based on the Kepner-Tregoe Decision-Making Model.

89. Pell, *Recruiting and Selecting Personnel*, pp. 103–15.

90. W.H. Wiesner and R.J. Oppenheimer. "Note-Taking in the Selection Interview: Its Effect Upon Predictive Validity and Information Recall." *Proceedings of the Annual Conference Meeting*. Administrative Sciences Association of Canada (Personnel and Human Resources Division) 12 Part 8 (1991) pp. 97–106.

91. Axmith, *Survey 2000: Canadian Hiring, Retention and Dismissal Practices*, p. 13.

92. L. Cassiani, "Upfront Checking Means Fewer Fraud Investigations After the Fact," *Canadian HR Reporter* (November 20, 2000), pp. 3, 7.

93. Axmith, *Survey 2000: Canadian Hiring, Retention and Dismissal Practices*, p. 13.

94. L. Young, "Reference Checking Skills Sorely Lacking," *Canadian HR Reporter* (January 25, 1999), p. 1–2.

95. *Axiom Survey*, cited in Young, "Reference Checking Skills Sorely Lacking," p. 1. See also C. Forbes, "Video Résumé: Seeing is Believing," *Canadian HR Reporter* (June 2, 2003), pp. 12–13.

96. "Men Lie More," *Canadian HR Reporter* (June 19, 2000), p. 7.

97. L. Cassiani, "Upfront Checking Means Fewer Fraud Investigations After the Fact," *Canadian HR Reporter* (November 20, 2000), pp. 3, 7.

98. See, for example, Axmith, *Survey 2000: Canadian Hiring, Retention and Dismissal Practices*, p. 13; and Way and Thacker, "Selection Practices," p. 33.

99. M. Stamler, "Employment Gaps, References Should be Scrutinized," *Canadian HR Reporter,* April 8, 1996, pp. 11, 15. See also P. Israel, "Providing References to Employees: Should You or Shouldn't You?" *Canadian HR Reporter* (March 24, 2003), pp. 5–6, and T. Humber, "Name, Rank and Serial Number, " *Canadian HR Reporter* (May 19, 2003), pp. G1, G7.

100. J.A. Breaugh, "Realistic Job Previews: A Critical Appraisal and Future Research Directions," *Academy of Management Review*, 8, no. 4 (1983), pp. 612–19.

101. P. Buhler, "Managing in the '90s: Hiring the Right Person for the Job," *Supervision* (July 1992), pp. 21–23; and S. Jackson, "Realistic Job Previews Help Screen Applicants and Reduce Turnover," *Canadian HR Reporter* (August 9, 1999), p. 10.

102. S. Jackson, "Realistic Job Previews," p. 10.

103. B. Kleinmutz, "Why We Still Use Our Heads Instead of Formulas: Toward an Integrative Approach," *Psychological Bulletin* 107 (1990), pp. 296–310.

104. D. Brown, "The Simple Math of Change Management," *Canadian HR Reporter* (April 24, 2000), pp. 18–19.

Chapter 7

1. B.W. Pascal, "The Orientation Wars," *Workplace Today* (October 2001), p. 4.

2. For a recent discussion of socialization see, for example, G. Chao et al., "Organizational Socialization: Its Content and Consequences," *Journal of Applied Psychology* 79, no. 5 (1994), pp. 730–43.

3. S. Jackson, "After All That Work in Hiring, Don't Let New Employees Dangle," *Canadian HR Reporter* (May 19, 1997), p. 13.

4. B. Pomfret, "Sound Employee Orientation Program Boosts Productivity and Safety," *Canadian HR Reporter* (January 25, 1999), pp. 17–19.

5. A. Macaulay, "The Long and Winding Road," *Canadian HR Reporter* (November 16, 1998), pp. G1–G10.

6. R. Biswas, "Employee Orientation: Your Best Weapon in the Fight for Skilled Talent," *Human Resources Professional* (August/September 1998), pp. 41–42.

7. J. Famularo, *Handbook of Modern Personnel Administration* (New York: McGraw-Hill, 1972), pp. 23.7–23.8. See also R. Smith, "Employee Orientation: Ten Steps to Success," *Personnel Journal* 63, no. 12 (December 1984), pp. 46–49.

8. Macaulay, "The Long and Winding Road," p. G1.

9. D. Barnes, "Learning is Key to Post-Merger Success," *Canadian HR Reporter* (July 12, 1999), pp. 16–17.

10. C. Gibson, "Online Orientation: Extending a Welcoming Hand to New Employees," *Canadian HR Reporter* (November 30, 1998), pp. 22–23.

11. D. Brown, "Execs Need Help Learning the Ropes Too," *Canadian HR Reporter* (April 22, 2002), p. 2.

12. D. Brown, "Execs Need Help Learning the Ropes Too."

13. D. Brown, "Execs Need Help Learning the Ropes Too."

14. "The Critical Importance of Executive Integration," *Drake Business Review* (December 2002), pp. 6–8.

15. V. Galt, "Training Falls Short: Study," *The Globe & Mail* (July 9, 2001), p. M1.

16. S. Mingail, "Employers Need a Lesson in Training," *Canadian HR Reporter* (February 11, 2002), pp. 22–23.

17. D Brown, "Is T&D Too Important for HR?" *Canadian HR Reporter* (February 10, 2003), pp. 22–23.

18. M. Shostak, "The Promise of New Media Learning," *Canadian HR Reporter* (April 7, 1997), pp. 15, 19.

19. A. Tomlinson, "More Training Critical in Manufacturing," *Canadian HR Reporter* (November 4, 2002), p. 2.

20. S. Harris-Lalonde, *Training and Development Outlook* (Ottawa ON: The Conference Board of Canada, 2001), p. 9.

21. D. Brown, "Lack of Skills to Blame for Project Failures," *Canadian HR Reporter* (October 8, 2001), pp. 1, 12.

22. D. Brown, "PM Calls for Business to Spend More on Training," *Canadian HR Reporter* (December 16, 2002), pp. 1, 11.

23. D. Brown, "Budget Should Include More for Training: Critics," *Canadian HR Reporter* (March 10, 2003), pp. 1–2.

24. D. Brown, "Legislated Training, Questionable Results," *Canadian HR Reporter* (May 6, 2002), pp. 1, 12.

25. N.L.Trainor, "Employee Development the Key to Talent Attraction and Retention," *Canadian HR Reporter* (November 1, 1999), p. 8.

26. D. LaMarche-Bisson, "There's More Than One Way to Learn," *Canadian HR Reporter* (November 18, 2003), p. 7.

27. Carnevale, based on K. Wexley and G. Yukl, *Organizational Behavior and Personnel Psychology* (Homewood, IL: Richard D. Irwin, 1977), pp. 289–95; E. J. McCormick and J. Tiffin, *Industrial Psychology* (Englewood Cliffs, NJ: Prentice Hall, 1974), pp. 232–340.

28. Wexley and Yukl, *Organizational Behavior and Personnel Psychology*, pp. 289–95.

29. M. Belcourt, P.C. Wright, and A.M. Saks, *Managing Performance Through Training and Development,* 2nd edition (Toronto ON: Nelson Thomson Learning, 2000). See also A.M. Saks and R.R. Haccoun, "Easing the Transfer of Training," *Human Resources Professional* (July–August 1996), pp. 8–11.

30. R.E. Silverman, *Learning Theory Applied to Training* (Reading, MA: Addison-Wesley, 1970), Chapter 8; McCormick and Tiffin, *Industrial Psychology*, pp. 239–40.

31. J. A. Colquitt, J.A. LePine and R.A. Noe, "Toward an Integrative Theory of Training Motivation: A Meta-Analytic Path Analysis of 20 Years of Research," *Journal of Applied Psychology*, 85 (2000), pp. 678–707.

32. K. A. Smith-Jentsch, et al., "Can Pre-Training Experiences Explain Individual Differences in Learning?" *Journal of Applied Psychology* 81, no. 1 (1986), pp. 100–16.

33. J.A. Cannon-Bowers, et al., "A Framework for Understanding Pre-Practice Conditions and Their Impact on Learning," *Personnel Psychology* 51 (1988), pp. 291–320.

34. This is based on K. Wexley and G. Latham, *Developing and Training Human Resources in Organizations* (Glenview, IL: Scott, Foresman, 1981), pp. 22–27.

35. K. Sovereign, *Personnel Law* (Englewood Cliffs, NJ: Prentice Hall, Inc., 1994), pp. 165–16.

36. These are based on Sovereign, *Personnel Law*, pp. 165–66.

37. K. Nowack, "A True Training Needs Analysis," *Training and Development Journal* (April 1991), pp. 69–73.

38. B.M. Bass and J.A. Vaughan, "Assessing Training Needs," in C. Schneier and R. Beatty, *Personnel Administration Today* (Reading, MA: Addison-Wesley, 1978), p. 311. See also R. Ash and E. Leving, "Job Applicant Training and Work Experience Evaluation: An Empirical Comparison of Four Methods," *Journal of Applied Psychology* 70, no. 3 (1985), pp. 572–76; J. Lawrie, "Break the Training Ritual," *Personnel Journal* 67, no. 4 (April 1988), pp. 95–77; and T. Lewis and D. Bjorkquist, "Needs Assessment—A Critical Reappraisal," *Performance Improvement Quarterly* 5, no. 4 (1992), pp. 33–54.

39. See, for example, G. Freeman, "Human Resources Planning—Training Needs Analysis," *Human Resources Planning* 39, no. 3 (Fall 1993), pp. 32–34.

40. McCormick and Tiffin, *Industrial Psychology*, p. 245. See also J. C. Georges, "The Hard Realities of Soft Skills Training," *Personnel Journal* 68, no. 4 (April 1989), pp. 40–45; R.H. Buckham, "Applying Role Analysis in the Workplace," *Personnel* 64, no. 2 (February 1987), pp. 63–55; and J.K. Ford and R. Noe, "Self-Assessed Training Needs: The Effects of Attitudes Towards Training, Management Level, and Function," *Personnel Psychology* 40, no. 1 (Spring 1987), pp. 39–54.

41. I.L. Goldstein, *Training: Program Development and Evaluation* (Monterey, CA: Wadsworth, 1974). See also S. B. Wehrenberg, "Learning Contracts," *Personnel Journal* 67, no. 9 (September 1988), pp. 100–03; M. B. Heibert and N. Smallwood, "Now for a Completely Different Look at Needs Analysis," *Training and Development Journal* 41, no. 5 (May 1987), pp. 75–79; E. G. Sorohan, "We Do; Therefore, We Learn," *Training & Development* (October 1993), pp. 47–55; M. LeBlanc, "Learning Objectives Key to Quality Safety," *Occupational Hazards* (January 1994), pp. 127–28.

42. M. Belcourt, P.C. Wright and A.M. Saks, *Managing Performance Through Training and Development*, 2nd edition (Toronto ON: Nelson Thomson Learning, 2002), p. 188.

43. Belcourt, Wright and Saks, *Managing Performance Through Training and Development,* pp. 188–202.

44. Wexley and Latham, *Developing and Training Human Resources in Organizations*, p. 107.

45. Frazis et al., "Employer-Provided Training," pp. 107–12. Four steps in on-the-job training based on W. Berliner and W. McLarney, *Management Practice and Training* (Homewood, IL: Irwin, 1974), pp. 442–43. See also R. Sullivan and D. Miklas, "On-the-Job Training That Works," *Training and Development Journal* 39, no. 5 (May 1985), pp. 118–20, and S.B. Wehrenberg, "Supervisors as Trainers: The Long-Term Gains of OJT," *Personnel Journal* 66, no. 4 (April 1987), pp. 48–51.

46. L. Burton, "Apprenticeship: The Learn While You Earn Option," *Human Resources Professional* (February/March 1998), p. 25; Frazis et al., "Employer-Provided Training," p. 4.

47. D. Brown, "New Federal Funding Promotes Skilled Trades," *Canadian HR Reporter* (February 10, 2003), pp. 1, 11.

48. U. Vu, "B.C. Proposed Changes to Trades Training," *Canadian HR Reporter* (January 27, 2003), pp. 1–2.

49. "German Training Model Imported," *BNA Bulletin to Management* (December 19, 1996), p. 408.

50. N. Day, "Informal Learning Gets Results," *Workforce* (June 1998), p. 31.

51. Day, "Informal Learning Gets Results," p. 31.

52. Harris-Lalonde, *Training and Development Outlook*, p. 16.

53. D. Manera, "Barriers to Training: Your Room Says It All," *Workplace Today* (October 2000), pp. 42–43.

54. Wexley and Latham, *Developing and Training*, pp. 131–33.

55. M. Emery and M. Schubert, "A Trainer's Guide to Videoconferencing," *Training* (June 1993), p. 60.

56. These are based on or quoted from Emery and Schubert, "A Trainer's Guide," p. 61.

57. G.N. Nash, J.P. Muczyk and F.L. Vettori, "The Role and Practical Effectiveness of Programmed Instruction," *Personnel Psychology* 24 (1971), pp. 397–418.

58. Wexley and Latham, *Developing and Training*, p. 141. See also R. Wlozkowski, "Simulation," *Training and Development Journal* 39, no. 6 (June 1985), pp. 38–43.

59. S. Lebrun, "T&D Becoming More Strategic," *Canadian HR Reporter* (February 10, 1997), pp. 1–2.

60. "Pros and Cons of E-learning," *Canadian HR Reporter* (July 16, 2001), pp. 11, 15.

61. D. Murray, *E-learning for the Workplace* (Ottawa ON: Conference Board of Canada, 2001). See also M. Rueda, "How to Make E-Learning Work for Your Company," *Workspan* (December 2002), pp. 50–53; U. Vu, "Technology-Based Learning Comes of Age," *Canadian HR Reporter* (April 21, 2003), pp. 3, 17.

62. S. Candron, "Training in the Post-Terrorism Era." *Training & Development* (February 2002), pp. 25–30.

63. D. Murray, *Keen for the Screen* (Ottawa ON: Conference Board of Canada, 2000).

64. S. Bolan, "Knowledge Is Out There," *Computing Canada* (February 23, 2001), p. 25.

65. See, for example, T. Falconer, "No More Pencils, No More Books!" *Canadian Banker* (March/April 1994), pp. 21–25.

66. W. Powell, "Like Life?" *Training & Development* (February 2002), pp. 32–38. See also A. Macaulay, "Reality-based Computer Simulations Allow Staff to Grow Through Failure," *Canadian HR Reporter* (October 23, 2000), pp. 11–12.

67. M. Shostak, "The Promise of New Media Learning," *Canadian HR Reporter* (April 7, 1997), pp. 15, 19.

68. S. Cohen, "A Guide to Multimedia in the Next Millennium," *Training & Development* (August 1997), pp. 33–44.

69. A. Czarnecki, "Interactive Learning Makes Big Dent in Time, Money Requirements for T&D," *Canadian HR Reporter* (November 18, 1996), pp. L30–L31.

70. L. Young "Self-directed Computer-Based Training That Works," *Canadian HR Reporter* (April 24, 2000), pp. 7–8.

71. These are summarized in R. Miller, "New Training Looms," *Hotel and Motel Management* (April 4, 1994), pp. 26, 30.

72. Shostak, "The Promise of New Media Learning."

73. M. Richmond, "Launching an Online Training Program," *Canadian HR Reporter* (August 9, 1999), pp. 16–17.

74. F. Manning, "The Misuse of Technology in Workplace Learning," *Canadian HR Reporter* (April 24, 2000), pp. 7, 10.

75. T. Purcell, "Training Anytime, Anywhere," *Canadian HR Reporter* (July 16, 2001), pp. 11, 15.

76. L. Cassini, "Student Participation Thrives in Online Learning Environments," *Canadian HR Reporter* (May 2, 2001), p. 2.

77. P. Weaver, "Preventing E-learning Failure," *Training & Development* (August 2002), pp. 45–50.

78. K. Oakes, "E-learning," *Training & Development* (March 2002), pp. 73–75. See also P. Harris, "E-learning: A Consolidation Update," *Training & Development* (April 2002), pp. 27–33.

79. C.R. Taylor, "The Second Wave," *Training & Development* (October 2002), pp. 24–31. See also P. Weaver, "Preventing E-learning Failure" and K. Oakes, "E-learning."

80. P. Weaver, "Preventing E-learning Failure."

81. E. Wareham, "The Educated Buyer," *Computing Canada,* February 18, 2000, p. 33. See also A. Tomlinson, "E-learning Won't Solve All Problems," *Canadian HR Reporter* (April 8, 2002), pp. 1, 6. and C. R. Taylor, The Second Wave."

82. J. Webster & P. Hackley, "Teaching Effectiveness in Technology—Mediated Distance Learning," *Academy of Management Journal* 40, no. 6 (1997), pp. 1282–1309.

83. C.D. Wetzel, P.H. Radtke & H.W. Stern, *Instructional Effectiveness of Video Media* (Hillsdale, NJ: Erlbaum, 1994).

84. J. Storck and L. Sproull, "Through a Glass Darkly: What do People Learn in Video Conferences?" *Human Communication Research* 22 (1995), pp. 197–219.

85. P. Weaver, "Preventing E-learning Failure."

86. A. Tomlinson, "Math, Reading Skills Holding Employees Back," *Canadian HR Reporter* (October 21, 2002), pp. 1, 12.

87. C. Knight, "Awards for Literacy Announced," *Canadian HR Reporter* (December 29, 1997), p. 10.

88. E. Sherman, "Back to Basics to Improve Skills," *Personnel* (July 1989), pp. 22–26.

89. N. L. Bernardon, "Let's Erase Illiteracy from the Workplace," *Personnel* (January 1989), pp. 29–32.

90. Bernardon, "Let's Erase Illiteracy from the Workplace." The PALS course was developed by educator Dr. John Henry Martin.

91. Bernardon, "Let's Erase Illiteracy from the Workplace," p. 32. SKILLPAC was created by the Center for Applied Linguistics and Dr. Arnold Packer, senior research fellow at the Hudson Institute in Indianapolis, Indiana.

92. B. Siu, "Cross-Cultural Training and Customer Relations: What Every Manager Should Know," *Canadian HR Reporter* (November 15, 1999), pp. G3, G15.

93. D. Roberts and B. Tsang, "Diversity Management Training Helps Firms Hone Competitive Edge," *Canadian HR Reporter* (June 19, 1995), pp. 17–18.

94. S. Rynes and B. Rosen, "What Makes Diversity Programs Work?" *HR Magazine* (October 1994), p. 64. See also T. Diamante and L. Giglio, "Managing a Diverse Workforce: Training as a Cultural Intervention Strategy," *Leadership & Organization Development Journal* 15, no. 2 (1994), pp. 13–17.

95. R. Koonce, "Redefining Diversity," *Training & Development* (December 2001), pp. 22–33.

96. W. Hopkins, K. Sterkel-Powell and S. Hopkins, "Training Priorities for a Diverse Workforce," *Public Personnel Management* 23, no. 3 (Fall 1994), p. 433.

97. C. Knight, "Training of, for and by the Disabled," *Canadian HR Reporter* (June 19, 1995), p. 11.

98. L. Young, "Retail Sector Seeks to Upgrade Education, Training to Solve Human Resource Woes," *Canadian HR Reporter* (February 8, 1999), p. 11. See also B. Nagle, "Superior Retail Training Blends Customer Service, Product Knowledge," *Canadian HR Reporter* (July 15, 2002), pp. 7–8.

99. D. Brown, "Is Retail Ready to Buy Training?" *Canadian HR Reporter* (July 15, 2002), pp. 7–8.

100. J. Konecny, "Certifying Good Customer Service," *Canadian HR Reporter* (December 16, 2002), pp. 1, 3.

101. P. Kulig, "LCBO Has Taste for Training," *Canadian HR Reporter* (August 10, 1998), pp. 1, 10.

102. J. Konecny, "Certifying Good Customer Service."

103. This is based on J. Laabs, "Team Training Goes Outdoors," *Personnel Journal* (June 1991), pp. 56–63.

104. Laabs, "Team Training," p. 56. See also S. Caudron, "Teamwork Takes Work," *Personnel Journal* 73, no. 2 (February 1994), pp. 41–49.

105. L. C. McDermott, "Developing the New Young Managers," *Training & Development* (October 2001), pp. 42–48.

106. A. Tomlinson, "A Dose of Training for Ailing First-Time Managers," *Canadian HR Reporter* (December 3, 2001), pp. 7, 10.

107. L. C. McDermott, "Developing the New Young Managers"; and A. Tomlinson, "A Dose of Training for Ailing First-Time Managers."

108. S. Odenwald, "A Guide for Global Training," *Training & Development* (July 1993), pp. 22–31.

109. R. Rosen and P. Digh, "Developing Globally Literate Leaders," *Training & Development* (May 2001), pp. 70–81.

110. L. Bassi, "Upgrading the U.S. Workplace: Do Reorganization & Education Help?" *Monthly Labor Review* (May 1995), pp. 37–47.

111. A. Bartel, "Productivity Gains from the Implementation of Employee Training Programs," *Industrial Relations* 33, no. 4 (October 1994), pp. 411–25.

112. Belcourt, Wright, and Saks, *Managing Performance Through Training and Development*, p. 9.

113. R.E. Catalano and D.L. Kirkpatrick, "Evaluating Training Programs—The State of the Art," *Training and Development Journal* 22, no. 5 (May 1968), pp. 2–9. See also A. Montebello and M. Haga, "To Justify Training, Test, Test Again," *Personnel Journal* 73, no. 1 (January 1994), pp. 83–87.

114. D. Kirkpatrick, "Effective Supervisory Training and Development," Part 3. Among the reasons training might not pay off on the job are a mismatching of courses and trainees' needs, supervisory slip-ups (with supervisors signing up trainees and then forgetting to have them attend the sessions when the training session is actually given), and no help in applying skills on the job. See also George B., "Measuring the Gains from Training," *Personnel Management* (November 1993), pp. 48–51; J. Spoor, "You Can Quantify Training Dollars and Program Value," *HR Focus* (May 1993), p. 3; J. Trynor, "Is Training a Good Investment?" *Financial Analyst Journal*

(September–October 1994), pp. 6–8; and S. Dolliver, "The Missing Link: Evaluating Training Programs," *Supervision* (November 1994), pp. 10–12.

115. N.L. Trainor, "Evaluating Training's Four Levels," *Canadian HR Reporter* (January 13, 1997), p. 10.

116. A. Tomlinson, "Save Training From the Axe," *Canadian HR Reporter* (April 22, 2002), pp. 1, 16.

117. B. Nagle, "ROI Gives Way to ROE," *Canadian HR Reporter* (July 15, 2002), p. 7.

Chapter 8

1. M.B. Arthur and D.M. Rousseau, *The Boundaryless Career: A New Employment Principle for a New Organizational Era* (New York: Oxford University Press, 1996), pp. 1–7. See also B. Moses, "Career Planning Mirrors Social Change," *Canadian HR Reporter* (May 17, 1999), p. G10.

2. *Employability Skills 2000* (Ottawa, ON: Conference Board of Canada, 2000).

3. J. Laabs, "The New Loyalty: Grasp It. Earn It. Keep It." *Workforce* (November 1998), pp. 34–39.

4. B. Moses, "Employee Career Planning Programs: What's in it for Organizations?" *HR Professional* (September 1985), p. 1.

5. "Workers Frustrated With Employers," *Canadian HR Reporter* (March 8, 1999), pp. 9, 12.

6. *The School-to-Work Transition: What Motivates Graduates to Change Jobs?* Statistics Canada, 2001. See also A. Tomlinson, "Unhappy Grads on the Move," *Canadian HR Reporter* (November 19, 2001), p. 10.

7. "Tech Workers Leaving the Field," *Canadian HR Reporter* (December 2, 2002), p. 16.

8. B. Moses, "Keeping Your Best People," *Canadian HR Reporter* (January 12, 1998), pp. 11, 14.

9. J. Goodings, "Most Federal Knowledge Workers Think About Quitting," *Canadian HR Reporter* (February 22, 1999), p. 3, 6.

10. These are quoted from F. Otte and P. Hutcheson, *Helping Employees Manage Careers* (Englewood Cliffs, NJ: Prentice Hall, 1992), pp. 5–6.

11. W. Enelow, *100 Ways to Recession-proof Your Career* (Toronto, ON: McGraw-Hill, 2002), p.1. See also K. Gay, "Planning Future Path is Key to a Successful Career," *Financial Post* (July 8, 1995), p. 13.

12. M. Watters and L. O'Connor, *It's Your Move: A Personal and Practical Guide to Career Transition and Job Search for Canadian Managers, Professionals and Executives* (Toronto, ON: Harper Collins, 2001).

13. For example, one survey of "baby boomers" concluded that "allowed to excel" was the most frequently mentioned factor in overall job satisfaction in an extensive attitude survey of Canadian supervisors and middle managers between 30 and 45 years old. J. Rogers, "Baby Boomers and Their Career Expectations," *Canadian Business Review* (Spring 1993), pp. 13–18.

14. E. Schein, *Career Dynamics: Matching Individual and Organizational Needs* (Reading, MA: Addison-Wesley, 1978).

15. J. Holland, *Making Vocational Choices: A Theory of Careers* (Englewood Cliffs, NJ: Prentice-Hall, 1973).

16. R. Bolles, *The Quick Job-Hunting Map* (Berkeley, CA: Ten Speed Press, 1979), pp. 5–6.

17. Schein, Career Dynamics, pp. 128–29. For a recent description of how to apply career anchor theory in practice, see T. Barth, "Career Anchor Theory," *Review of Public Personnel Administration* 13, no. 4 (1993), pp. 27–42.

18. R. Bolles, *What Color Is Your Parachute?* (Berkeley, CA: Ten Speed Press, 1976), p. 86.

19. R. Payne, *How to Get a Better Job Quicker* (New York: New American Library, 1987).

20. J. Ross, *Managing Productivity* (Reston, VA: Reston, 1979).

21. H.G. Kaufman, *Obsolescence and Professional Career Development* (New York: AMACOM, 1974).

22. D. Hall and F. Hall, "What's New in Career Management?" *Organizational Dynamics* 4 (Summer 1976), p. 350.

23. See, for example, T. Scandurg, "Mentorship and Career Mobility: An Empirical Investigation," *Journal of Organizational Behavior* 13, no. 2 (March 1992), pp. 169–74.

24. Schein, *Career Dynamics*, p. 19. See also R. Jacobs and R. Bolton, "Career Analysis: The Missing Link in Managerial Assessment and Development," *Human Resource Management Journal* 3, no. 2 (1994), pp. 55–62.

25. Otte and Hutcheson, *Helping Employees*, pp. 15–16.

26. Otte and Hutcheson, *Helping Employees*, p. 143.

27. B. Moses, "Implementing an Employee Career Development Program—Part Two: Tools to Support Career Development," *HR Professional* (December 1985), pp. 6–10.

28. T. Newby and A. Heide, "The Value of Mentoring," *Performance Improvement Quarterly* 5, no. 4 (1992), pp. 2–15.

29. Newby and Heide, "The Value of Mentoring," p. 2.

30. A.M. Young and P.L. Perrewé, "What Did You Expect? An Examination of Career-Related Support and Social Support Among Mentors and Protégés". *Journal of Management*, 20 (2000), pp. 611-632.

31. "Mentoring Makes Better Employees," *Workplace Today* (June 2001), p. 12; and S. Butyn, "Mentoring Your Way to Improved Retention," *Canadian HR Reporter* (January 27, 2003), pp. 13, 15.

32. L. Allan, "Mentoring: The Need to Move to Newer Models," *Canadian HR Reporter* (March 22, 1999), pp. 12–13.

33. L. Young, "Potential of Mentoring Programs Untapped," *Canadian HR Reporter* (April 10, 2000), pp. 1–2.

34. S. Butyn, "Mentoring Your Way to Better Retention."

35. D. Lewis, "That's Right, Double Click There, Sir," *The Globe & Mail* (May 31, 2001), p. B14.

36. D.A. Garvin, "Building a Learning Organization," *Harvard Business Review* (July–August 1993), p. 80.

37. Garvin (1994), p. 22.

38. M. Crossan, "Improvising at the Office," *The Globe & Mail* (October 3, 1997), p. C1.

39. R.C. Camp, *Benchmarking: The Search for Industry Best Practices that Lead to Superior Performance* (Milwaukee: ASQC Quality Press, 1989), p. 12.

40. Garvin (1994), p. 21.

41. D. Quinn Mills, *Labor–Management Relations* (New York: McGraw-Hill, 1986), pp. 387–96.

42. G. Dessler, *Winning Commitment* (New York: McGraw-Hill, 1993), pp. 144–49.

43. See J. Famularo, *Handbook of Modern Personnel Administration* (New York: McGraw-Hill, 1972), p. 17.

44. For a discussion, see S. Schmidt, "The New Focus for Career Development Programs in Business and Industry," *Journal of Employment Counseling* 31 (March 1994), pp. 22–28.

45. R. Tucker, M. Moravee and K. Ideus, "Designing a Dual Career-Track System," *Training and Development*, Vol. 6 (1992), pp. 55–58; Schmidt, "The New Focus for Career Development," p. 26.

46. See, for example, R. Chanick, "Career Growth for Baby Boomers," *Personnel Journal* 71, no. 1 (January 1992), pp. 40–6.

47. R. Sheppard, "Spousal Programs and Communication Curb Relocation Rejections," *Canadian HR Reporter* (November 1, 1999), p. 17.

48. L. Young, "Skills Shortage Sweeps Management Ranks," *Canadian HR Reporter* (May 22, 2000), pp. 1, 6. See also C. Reynolds, "Too Many Promotions, Not Enough Training for Middle Managers," *Canadian HR Reporter* (July 17, 2000), pp. 7, 9.

49. J. Swain, "Dispelling Myths About Leadership Development," *Canadian HR Reporter* (June 3, 2002), p. 27.

50. "Leadership Crisis Looms," *Canadian HR Reporter* (October 4, 1999), p. 18.

51. D. Brown, "Succession in An Era of Turnover," *Canadian HR Reporter* (May 21, 2001), p. 7.

52. J. Hobel, "Succession Planning on a Need-to-Know Basis," *Canadian HR Reporter* (June 5, 2000), p. 4.

53. "CEOs Talk," *Canadian HR Reporter* (June 4, 2001), pp. 17–19.

54. For discussions of the steps in succession planning see, for example, K. Nowack, "The Secrets of Succession," *Training and Development* (November 1994), pp. 49–55, and D. Brookes, "In Management Succession, Who Moves Up?" *Human Resources* (January/February 1995), pp. 11–13.

55. K. Spence, "The Employee's Role in Succession Planning," *Canadian HR Reporter* (February 14, 2000), p. 13.

56. *The Towers Perrin Talent Report: New Realities in Today's Workforce* (Toronto, ON: Towers Perrin, 2003).

57. "Managers Must Focus on Soft Skills in Tough Times," *Canadian HR Reporter* (February 11, 2002), p. 9. Centre for Creative Leadership, www.ccl.org.

58. D. Brown, "Most Firms Think Management is An Art Form – It's Not," *Canadian HR Reporter* (February 11, 2002), pp. 9, 13.

59. D. Brown, "Most Firms Think Management is An Art Form."

60. D. Yoder et al., *Handbook of Personnel Management and Labor Relations* (New York: McGraw-Hill, 1958), pp. 10–27.

61. Yoder et al., *Handbook of Personnel Management and Labor Relations*. See also Jack Phillips, "Training Supervisors Outside the Classroom," *Training and Development Journal* 40, no. 2 (February 1986), pp. 46–49.

62. K. Wexley and G. Latham, *Developing and Training Human Resources in Organizations* (Glenview, IL: Scott, Foresman, 1981), p. 118.

63. D. Kosub, "Putting Theory Into Practice," *Canadian HR Reporter* (January 13, 2003), pp. 9, 10.

64. D. Kosub, "Putting Theory Into Practice."

65. A. Tomlinson, "Find the Best Grads, Grow Them, Then Reap the Rewards," *Canadian HR Reporter* (April 8, 2002), pp. 7, 10.

66. Wexley and Latham, *Developing and Training Human Resources*, p. 207.

67. This is based on N. Fox, "Action Learning Comes to Industry," *Harvard Business Review* 56 (September–October, 1977), pp. 158–68.

68. Wexley and Latham, *Developing and Training Human Resources*, p. 193.

69. D. Rogers, *Business Policy and Planning* (Englewood Cliffs, NJ: Prentice Hall, 1977), p. 533. See also J. Kay, "At Harvard on the Case," *National Post Business* (March 2003), pp. 68–78.

70. For a discussion of management games and other non-computerized training and development simulations, see C. M. Solomon, "Simulation Training Builds Teams Through Experience," *Personnel Journal* (June 1993), pp. 100–5; K. Slack, "Training for the Real Thing," *Training and Development* (May 1993), pp. 79–89; B. Lierman, "How to Develop a Training Simulation," *Training and Development* (February 1994), pp. 50–52.

71. A. Macauley, "Strategic Plan Off Base, Do Not Pass Go," *Canadian HR Reporter* (October 23, 2000), p. 12.

72. www.workplace.ca (March 31, 2003).

73. D. McKay-Stokes, "Sleeping in the Snow Together Does Wonders for Morale," *Financial Post* (April 25, 1995), p. 20. See also L. Cassiani, "Taking Team Building to New Heights," *Canadian HR Reporter* (February 26, 2001), pp. 8, 17.

74. "MBA and Executive Development Programs," *Canadian HR Reporter* (June 3, 2002), pp. 29–31.

75. J. Famularo, *Handbook of Modern Personnel Administration* (New York: McGraw-Hill, 1972), pp. 21.7–21.8.

76. J. Hinrichs, "Personnel Testing," in M. Dunnette, ed., *Handbook of Industrial and Organizational Psychology* (Chicago: Rand McNally, 1976), p. 855.

77. D. Swink, "Role-Play Your Way to Learning," *Training and Development* (May 1993), pp. 91–7; A. Test, "Why I Do Not Like to Role Play," *The American Salesman* (August 1994), pp. 7–20.

78. This section based on A. Kraut, "Developing Managerial Skill via Modeling Techniques: Some Positive Research Findings—A Symposium," *Personnel Psychology* 29, no. 3 (Autumn 1976), pp. 325–61.

79. T. Cummings and C. Worley, *Organizational Development and Change*, (Minneapolis: West Publishing Company, 1993), p. 3.

80. Based on J.T. Campbell and M.D. Dunnette, "Effectiveness of T-Group Experiences in Managerial Training and Development," *Psychological Bulletin*, 7, (1968), pp. 73–104; reprinted in W.E. Scott and L.L. Cummings, *Readings in Organizational Behavior and Human Performance* (Burr Ridge, IL: McGraw-Hill, 1973), p. 571.

81. B. Schneider, S. Ashworth, A. C. Higgs, and L. Carr, "Design Validity, and Use of Strategically Focused Employee Attitude Surveys," *Personnel Psychology* 49 (1996), pp. 695–705.

82. "Design Validity, and Use of Strategically Focused Employee Attitude Surveys," p. 704.

83. B. Hamilton, "Developing New Leaders to Meet the Talent Shortage," *Canadian HR Reporter* (February 8, 1999), pp. 18–19.

84. *Leadership for Tomorrow: A Challenge for Business Today* (The Conference Board of Canada: Ottawa, 1999).

85. D. Brown, "Leadership Development That Pays for Itself," *Canadian HR Reporter* (April 9, 2001), pp. 7, 8.

86. D. MacNamara, "Learning Contracts, Competency Profiles the New Wave in Executive Development," *Canadian HR Reporter* (November 16, 1998), pp. G8, G12.

Chapter 9

1. R. Russell and B. Taylor III, *Operations Management* (Upper Saddle River, NJ: Prentice Hall, 1998), pp. 324–336.

2. Edward Lawler III and Susan Mohrman, "Beyond the Vision: What Makes HR Effective?" *Human Resource Planning* 23, no. 4 (December 2000), p. 10.

3. K. Jansen, "The Emerging Dynamics of Change: Resistance, Readiness, and Momentum," *Human Resource Planning* 23, no. 2 (June 2000), p. 53.

4. E. Schein, *Organizational Culture and Leadership* (San Francisco: Jossey-Bass, 1985), pp. 224–237; P. Wright, M. Kroll and J. Parnell, *Strategic Management Concepts* (Upper Saddle River, NJ: Prentice Hall, 1996), pp. 233–236. See also T. Begley and D. Boyd, "Articulating Corporate Values Through Human Resource Policies," *Business Horizons* 43, no. 4 (July 2000), pp. 8–12.

5. A. Mikkelsen and P. Oystein, "Learning from Parallel Organizational Development Efforts in Two Public Sector Settings: Findings from Research in Norway," *Public Personnel Administration* 18, no. 1 (Spring 1998), pp. 5–22.

6. The 10 steps are based on M. Beer, R. Eisenstat and B. Spector, "Why Change Programs Don't Produce Change," *Harvard Business Review* (November–December 1990), pp. 158–166; T. Cummings and C. Worley, *Organization Development and Change* (Minneapolis: West Publishing Company, 1993); J.P. Kotter, "Leading Change: Why Transformation Efforts Fail," *Harvard Business Review* (March–April 1995), pp. 59–66; and J.P. Kotter, *Leading Change* (Boston: Harvard Business School Press, 1996).

7. Kotter, "Leading Change," p. 85.

8. Kotter, "Leading Change," pp. 90–91.

9. This is based on Kotter, "Leading Change," pp. 60–61.

10. Kotter, "Leading Change," p. 65.

11. Beer, Eisenstat, and Spector, "Why Change Programs Don't Produce Change," p. 164.

12. J. Evans et al., *Applied Production and Operations Management* (St. Paul, MN: West Publishing Co., 1984), p. 39.

13. J. Intini, "Keeping Them Satisfied," *Maclean's* (October 21, 2002).

14. Based in part on J.E. Ross, *Total Quality Management: Text, Cases and Readings* (Delray Beach, FL: St. Lucie Press, 1993), p. 1.

15. B. Render and J. Heizer, *Principles of Operations Management* (Upper Saddle River, NJ: Prentice Hall, 1997), p. 96.

16. J.A. Magana-Campos and E. Aspinwall, "Comparative Study of Western and Japanese Improvement Systems," *Total Quality Management & Business Excellence*, 14 (June 2003), pp. 423–36.

17. T. Berry, *Managing the Total Quality Transformation* (New York: McGraw-Hill, 1991).

18. "Total Quality Management: The Real Challenge May be Open and Effective Communication Strategy," *Towers Perrin Focus* (Winter 1994), p. 10–11.

19. C. French, "Breaking the Information Barrier," *The Globe & Mail* (October 26, 1993), p. 25.

20. J. Thacker and M. Fields, "Union Involvement in Quality-of-Work Life Efforts: A Longitudinal Investigation," *Personnel Psychology* 40, no. 1 (Spring 1987), pp. 97–112. They conclude that unions' fears of QCs may be misplaced and that after quality-of-work-life involvement, "A majority of the rank and file members who perceived QWL—quality of work life—as successful gave equal credit for the success to both union and management. The rank and file members who perceived QWL as unsuccessful tended to blame management for the lack of success."

21. This is based on E. Adam, Jr., "Quality Circle Performance," *Journal of Management* 17, no. 1 (1991), pp. 25–39.

22. This is based on S. Caudron, "How Xerox Won the Baldrige," *Personnel Journal* (April 1991), p. 100.

23. National Quality Institute, *Canadian Framework for Business Excellence: Strategic Quality Approach* (March 2000).

24. National Quality Institute, *The Canadian Quality Criteria* (1997).

25. "Mullen Trucking Receives Canada Award for Excellence," Mullen Trucking Press Release (September 16, 2002).

26. *Dana Facility Wins NQI Canada Award.* http://bulktransporter.com/maga-zinearti...33+siteID=26+releaseid=10934. (April 2, 2003).

27. "Building a Quality Improvement Program at Florida Power & Light," *Target* (Fall 1988), p. 8.

28. *Management Systems Standards: The Story So Far* (Ottawa, ON: Standards Council of Canada, 1999).

29. B. Weller, "The New ISO 9000:2000 Standard and Organizational Excellence: Paving the Way Toward Greater Organizational Performance," *Excellence* (Summer 2001), p. 14.

30. www.iso.cg/iso9000-14000/tour (April 4, 2003); www.scc.ca/cgi-bin/pfv.cgi?/faq/30/31_e.html (April 4, 2003).

31. C. Knight, "HR's Role in ISO 9000," *Canadian HR Reporter* (February 27, 1995), p. 6.

32. R. Murakami, "How to Implement ISO 9000," *CMA Magazine* (March, 1994), p. 18.

33. L. Ramsay, "No Business Too Small for ISO 9000 Certification," *Financial Post* (August 23, 1995), p. 18.

34. See, for example, B. Dumaine, "Who Needs a Boss?" *Fortune* (May 7, 1990), p. 52; D. Hames, "Productivity-Enhancing Work Innovations: Remedies for What Ails Hospitals?" *Hospital & Health Services Administration* 36, no. 4 (Winter 1991), pp. 551–2; see also S.I. Caudron, "Are Self-Directed Teams Right for Your Company?" *Personnel Journal* (December 1993), pp. 76–84.

35. J. Harrison, "Romantic Notions of Teamwork Must Go, Says Scholar," *Canadian HR Reporter* (March 9, 1998), pp. 1–2.

36. J. Zeidenberg, "HR and the Innovative Company," *HR Professional* (June 1996), pp. 12–15.

37. J. MacMillan, "Best Practices from Honeywell: Creating an Empowering Workplace," *Excellence* (Spring 2001), pp. 5–8.

38. See R. Wellins and J. George, "The Key to Self-Directed Teams," *Training and Development Journal* (April 1991), pp. 26–31.

39. R. Majuka and T. Baldwin, "Team-Based Employee Involvement Programs: Effects of Design and Administration," *Personnel Psychology* 44 (1991), p. 806.

40. S. Johnson, "Work Teams: What's Ahead in Work Design and Rewards Management," *Compensation & Benefits Review* (March–April 1993), pp. 35–41.

41. G. Dessler, *Management: Leading People and Organizations in the 21st Century* (Upper Saddle River, NJ: Prentice Hall, 1998), pp. 476–78.

42. M. Hammer and J. Champy, *Reengineering the Corporation.* (New York: Harper Business, 1994), p. 32.

43. W.L. Tullar, "Compensation Consequences of Reengineering," *Journal of Applied Psychology*, 83, pp. 975–980. See also L. Plunkett, "How to Reengineer Process," *Workplace Today* (January 2001), p. 45.

44. H. Willmott, "Business Process Reengineering and Human Resource Management," *Personnel Review* 3, no. 3 (May 1994), p. 34.

45. M. Hammer and J. Champy, *Reengineering the Corporation*, p. 68.

46. Hammer and Champy, *Reengineering the Corporation*, p. 70.

47. Hammer and Champy, *Reengineering the Corporation*.

48. Hammer and Champy, *Reengineering the Corporation*.

49. Hammer and Champy, *Reengineering the Corporation*. See also Tullar, "Compensation Consequences of Reengineering."

50. L. Cassiani, "Women Consider Leaving for Better Work-Life Balance," *Canadian HR Reporter* (August 13, 2001), pp. 1, 14.

51. S. Singh, "When the Going Gets Tough, the Tough Hold on to Top Employees," *Canadian HR Reporter* (January 13, 2003), p. 17.

52. C. Higgins and L. Duxbury, *2001 National Work-Life Conflict Study* (Ottawa, ON: Health Canada); see also A. Tomlinson, "Employers Dependent on Unpaid Overtime: Report," *Canadian HR Reporter* (September 9, 2002), pp. 1, 3.

53. L. Duxbury, C. Higgins, and K. Johnson, *An Examination of the Implications and Costs of Work-Life Conflict in Canada* (Ottawa: Department of Health, 1999).

54. M.R. Frone, "Work-Family Conflict and Employee Psychiatric Disorders: The National Co-morbidity Survey," *Journal of Applied Psychology*, 85 (2000), pp. 888–95.

55. N. Spinks and C. Moore, "Bringing Work-Life Balance to the Table," *Canadian HR Reporter* (April 22, 2002), pp. 14–15. See also V. Galt, "Part-time Hours Help Work-Life Juggling," *The Globe & Mail* (March 30, 2001), p. B11.

56. L. Young, "Employees Losing Work–Life Battle," *Canadian HR Reporter* (August 9, 1999), p. 6.

57. J. MacBride-King, *Managers, Employee Satisfaction, and Work–Life Balance*, The Conference Board of Canada, 1999; quoted in "Managers Must Help Employees Balance Work/Home Lives," *Workplace Today* (October 1999), p. 9.

58. G.N. Powell and L.A. Mainiero, "Managerial Decision Making Regarding Alternative Work Arrangements," *Journal of Occupational and Organizational Psychology*, 72 (1999), pp. 41–56. See also D. Brown, "Work-Life Balance Programs Creating Their Own Stress," *Canadian HR Reporter* (August 14, 2000), pp. 1, 6; and K. Bachman, *Work-Life Balance: Are Employers Listening?* (Ottawa: Conference Board of Canada, 2000).

59. J. MacBride-King, *Managers, Employee Satisfaction, and Work–Life Balance*.

60. P. Kulig, "Flextime Increasing in Popularity With Employers," *Canadian HR Reporter* (September 7, 1998), pp. 1, 3.

61. K. Robertson, "Business Benefits Often Forgotten in 'Special Case' Attitude to Alternative Work Arrangements," *Canadian HR Reporter* (July 14, 1997), p. 19.

62. K.R. Yukich, *Managing a Flexible Workforce* (Toronto: Thomson Canada Ltd., 1997), p. 153.

63. Madigan, Norton, and Testa, "The Quest for Work–Life Balance," *Benefits Canada* (November 1999), p. 113.

64. K. Daly, *Family-Friendly Practices and Flexibility in Small Companies in Canada* (Guelph, ON: Centre for Families, Work & Well-Being, University of Guelph, 2000). See also D. Brown, "Flex-work Benefits Thriving in Small Businesses," *Canadian HR Reporter* (September 25, 2000), pp. 11–12, and *Small Employers Family Friendly*, www.workplace.ca (August 13, 2000).

65. S. Nollen, "Does Flextime Improve Productivity?" *Harvard Business Review* 56 (September–October 1977), pp. 12–22.

66. S. Nollen, "Does Flextime Improve Productivity?"; see also K. Kush and L. Stroh, "Flextime: Myth or Reality?" *Business Horizons* (September–October 1994), pp. 51–55.

67. B.B. Baltes, T.E. Briggs, J.W. Huff, J.A. Wright, and G.A. Neuman, "Flex and Compressed Workweek Schedules: A Meta-Analysis of Their Effects on Work-Related Criteria," *Journal of Applied Psychology*, 84 (1999), pp. 496–513.

68. J. Harrison, "Alternative Work Arrangements not so Alternative Anymore," *Canadian HR Reporter* (March 9, 1998), p. 2.

69. D. Brown, "Telework Not Meeting Expectations—But Expectations Were 'Nonsense'," *Canadian HR Reporter* (February 24, 2003), pp. 3, 11.

70. T. McCallum, "Telecommuting: Managing Work-at-Home Personnel," *Human Resources Professional* (April/May 1997), pp. 45–49.

71. N. Larin, "More Employees are Doing Homework," *Canadian HR Reporter* (December 14, 1998) p. 14.

72. N. Southworth, "Informality Governs Most Telecommuters," *The Globe & Mail* (April 4, 2001), p. B11.

73. L. Young, "Teleworking Programs Demand Extra Attention," *Canadian HR Reporter* (April 5, 1999), p. 6.

74. "The Benefits of Telework," *Canadian HR Reporter* (December 14, 1998), p. 14.

75. L. Cassiani, "Teleworkers Happy But No More Productive: Study," *Canadian HR Reporter* (November 6, 2000), p. 2. See also "The Benefits of Telecommuting?" *Canadian HR Reporter* (March 12, 2001), p. 2.

76. H. Northrup, "The Twelve-Hour Shift in the North American Mini-steel Industry," *Journal of Labor Research* 12, no. 3 (Summer 1991), pp. 261–78; C. M. Solomon, "24-hour Employees," *Personnel Journal* 70, no. 8 (August 1991), pp. 56–63.

77. "After Flexible Hours, Now It's Flexiyear," *International Management* (March 1982), pp. 31–32.

Chapter 10

1. J.T. Rich, "The Solutions for Employee Performance Management," *Workspan* (February 2002), pp. 32–37.

2. D. Brown, "Performance Management Separates Wheat from Chaff," *Canadian HR Reporter* (March 10, 2003), pp. 1, 15.

3. D. Brown, "HR Improving at Performance Management," *Canadian HR Reporter* (December 2, 2002), pp. 1, 14.

4. D. Brown, "Re-evaluating Evaluation," *Canadian HR Reporter* (April 8, 2002), p. 2.

5. M. Gibb-Clark, "Employee Appraisals Find Few Friends," *The Globe & Mail* (May 28, 1993), p. B4.

6. A.S. DeNisi and A.N. Kluger "Feedback Effectiveness: Can 360-Degree Appraisals be Improved?" *Academy of Management Executive*, pp. 14, 129–139.

7. J. Cleveland et al., "Multiple Uses of Performance Appraisal: Prevalence and Correlates," *Journal of Applied Psychology* 74, no. 1 (February 1989), pp. 130–35; I. Carlton and M. Sloman, "Performance Appraisal in Practice," *Human Resource Management Journal* 2, no. 3 (Spring 1992), pp. 80–94.

8. S. Nador, "A Properly Crafted Performance-Management Program Aids Professional Development," *Canadian HR Reporter* (May 17, 1999), p. 10.

9. For a good explanation of why reliance solely on appraisal by supervisors may not be a good idea, see K. Bhote, "Boss Performance Appraisal: A Metric Whose Time Has Gone," *Employment Relations Today* 21, no. 1 (Spring 1994), pp. 1–9.

10. J.E. Oliver, "Performance Appraisals That Fit," *Personnel Journal* 64 (June 1985), p. 69.

11. D. Brown, "HR Improving at Performance Management."

12. For a recent discussion see G. English, "Tuning Up for Performance Management," *Training and Development Journal* (April 1991), pp. 56–60.

13. C.L. Hughes, "The Bell-Shaped Curve That Inspires Guerrilla Warfare," *Personnel Administrator* (May 1987), pp. 40–41.

14. Commerce Clearing House Editorial Staff, "*Performance Appraisal: What Three Companies Are Doing*" (Chicago, 1985). See also R. Girard, "Are Performance Appraisals Passé?" *Personnel Journal* 67, no. 8 (August 1988), pp. 89–90.

15. J. Ivancevich, "A Longitudinal Study of Behavioral Expectation Scales: Attitudes and Performance," *Journal of Applied Psychology* (April 1980), pp. 139–46.

16. U. Wiersma and G. Latham, "The Practicality of Behavioral Observation Scales, Behavioral Expectations Scales, and Trait Scales," *Personnel Psychology* 30, no. 3 (Autumn 1986), pp. 619–28.

17. J. Goodale and R. Burke, "Behaviorally Based Rating Scales Need Not Be Job Specific," *Journal of Applied Psychology* 60 (June 1975).

18. K.R. Murphy J. Constans, "Behavioral Anchors as a Source of Bias in Rating," *Journal of Applied Psychology* 72, no. 4 (November 1987), pp. 573–77.

19. See M. Levy, "Almost-Perfect Performance Appraisals," *Personnel Journal* 68, no. 4 (April 1989), pp. 76–83.

20. www.halogensoftware.com/products (April 19, 2003).

21. C. Howard, "Appraise This!" *Canadian Business* (May 23, 1998), p. 96.

22. R.C. Mayer and J.H. Davis, "The Effect of the Performance Appraisal System on Trust for Management: A Field Quasi-Experiment," *Journal of Applied Psychology* 84 (1999), pp. 123–136.

23. D. Brown, "HR Improving at Performance Management."

24. Teel, "Performance Appraisal," pp. 297–28.

25. M. Waung and S. Highhouse, "Fear of Conflict and Empathic Buffering: Two Explanations for the Inflation of Performance Feedback," *Organizational Behavior and Human Decision Processes,* 71 (1997), pp. 37–54.

26. Y. Ganzach, "Negativity (and Positivity) in Performance Evaluation: Three Field Studies," *Journal of Applied Psychology,* 80 (1995), pp. 491–99.

27. T.J. Maurer and M.A. Taylor, "Is Sex by Itself Enough? An Exploration of Gender Bias Issues in Performance Appraisal," *Organizational Behavior and Human Decision Processes,* 60 (1994), pp. 231–51. See also C.E. Lance, "Test for Latent Structure of Performance Ratings Derived from Wherry's (1952) Theory of Ratings," *Journal of Management,* 20 (1994), pp. 757–71.

28. S.E. Scullen, M.K. Mount, and M. Goff, "Understanding the Latent Structure of Job Performance Ratings," *Journal of Applied Psychology,* 85 (2001), pp. 956–70.

29. A.M. Saks and D.A. Waldman, "The Relationship Between Age and Job Performance Evaluations for Entry-Level Professionals," *Journal of Organizational Behavior,* 19 (1998), pp. 409–19.

30. W.C. Borman, L.A. White, and D.W. Dorsey, "Effects of Ratee Task Performance and Interpersonal Factors in Supervisor and Peer Performance Ratings," *Journal of Applied Psychology* 80 (1995), pp. 168–77.

31. K. Murphy, W. Balzer, M. Lockhart, and E. Eisenman, "Effects of Previous Performance on Evaluations of Present Performance," *Journal of Applied Psychology* 70, no. 1 (1985), pp. 72–84. See also K. Williams, A. DeNisi, B. Meglino, and T. Cafferty, "Initial Decisions and Subsequent Performance Ratings," *Journal of Applied Psychology* 71, no. 2 (May 1986), pp. 189–95.

32. B. Davis and M. Mount, "Effectiveness of Performance Appraisal Training Using Computer Assistance Instruction and Behavior Modeling," *Personnel Psychology* 37 (Fall 1984), pp. 439–52.

33. J. Hedge and M. Cavanagh, "Improving the Accuracy of Performance Evaluations: Comparison of Three Methods of Performance Appraiser Training," *Journal of Applied Psychology* 73, no. 1 (February 1988), pp. 68–73.

34. Davis and Mount, "The Effectiveness of Performance Appraisal Training," pp. 439–52.

35. T. Athey and R. McIntyre, "Effect of Rater Training on Rater Accuracy: Levels of Processing Theory and Social Facilitation Theory Perspectives," *Journal of Applied Psychology* 72, no. 4 (November 1987), pp. 567–72.

36. M.M. Greller, "Participation in the Performance Appraisal Review: Inflexible Manager Behavior and Variable Worker Needs," *Human Relations* 51 (1998), pp. 1061–83.

37. L. Axline, "Ethical Considerations of Performance Appraisals," *Management Review* (March 1994), p. 62.

38. M. McDougall and L. Cassiani, "HR Cited in Unfair Performance Review," *Canadian HR Reporter* (September 10, 2001), pp. 1, 6.

39. "Health Worker's Performance Review Unfair," *Workplace Today* (June 2001), p. 23.

40. G. Barrett and M. Kernan, "Performance Appraisal and Terminations: A Review of Court Decisions Since *Brito v. Zia* with Implications for Personnel Practices," *Personnel Psychology* 40, no. 3 (Autumn 1987), pp. 489–504.

41. Barrett and Kernan, "Performance Appraisal and Terminations," p. 501.

42. M.M. Harris and J. Schaubroeck, "A Meta-Analysis of Self-Supervisor, Self-Peer, and Peer-Supervisor Ratings," *Personnel Psychology,* 41 (1988), pp. 43–62.

43. G.P. Latham and K.N. Wexley, *Increasing Productivity Through Performance Appraisal,* 2nd edition (Reading, MA: Addison-Wesley, 1994).

44. J. Barclay and L. Harland, "Peer Performance Appraisals: The Impact of Rater Competence, Rater Location, and Rating Correctability on Fairness Perceptions," *Group and Organization Management* 20, no. 1 (March 1995), pp. 39–60.

45. M. Mount, "Psychometric Properties of Subordinate Ratings of Managerial Performance," *Personnel Psychology* 37, no. 4 (Winter 1984), pp. 687–702.

46. V.V. Druskat and S.B. Wolff, "Effects and Timing of Developmental Peer Appraisals in Self-Managing Work Groups," *Journal of Applied Psychology* 84 (1999), pp. 58–74.

47. J. Schilder, "Office Pool Confidential," *Human Resources Professional* (November 1992), pp. 20–23.

48. M.M. Harris and J. Schaubroeck, "A Meta-Analysis," pp. 43–62.

49. W.C. Borman, "The Rating of Individuals in Organizations: An Alternate Approach," *Organizational Behavior and Human Performance* 12 (1974), pp. 105–24.

50. B.D. Cawley, L.M. Keeping, and P.E Levy, "Participation in the Performance Appraisal Process and Employee Reactions: A Meta-Analytic Review of Field Investigations," *Journal of Applied Psychology* 83 (1998), pp. 615–33.

51. J. W. Lawrie "Your Performance: Appraise It Yourself!" *Personnel* 66, no. 1 January 1989), pp. 21–33; includes a good explanation of how self-appraisals can be used at work. See also A. Furnham and P. Stringfield, "Congruence in Job-Performance Ratings: A Study of 360° Feedback Examining Self, Manager, Peers, and Consultant Ratings," *Human Relations,* 51 (1998), 517–30.

52. P.A. Mabe III and S.G. West "Validity of Self-Evaluation of Ability: A Review and Meta-Analysis," *Journal of Applied Psychology,* 67, no. 3 (1982), pp. 280–96.

53. J. Russell and D. Goode, "An Analysis of Managers' Reactions to Their Own Performance Appraisal Feedback," *Journal of Applied Psychology* 73, no. 1 (February 1988), pp. 63–67; and Harris and Shaubroeck, "A Meta-Analysis," pp. 43–62.

54. G.P. Latham, D. Skarlicki, D. Irvine, and J.P. Seigel, "The Increasing Importance of Performance Appraisals to Employee Effectiveness in Organizational Settings in North America." In C.L. Cooper and I.T. Robertson (eds.) *International Review of Industrial and Organizational Psychology,* 8 (1993), p. 103.

55. H.J. Bernardin and R.W. Beatty "Can Subordinate Appraisals Enhance Managerial Productivity?" *Sloan Management Review* (Summer 1987), pp. 63–73.

56. M. London and A. Wohlers, "Agreement Between Subordinate and Self-Ratings in Upward Feedback," *Personnel Psychology* 44 (1991), pp. 375–90.

57. London and Wohlers, "Agreement Between Subordinate and Self-Ratings," p. 376.

58. D. Antonioni, "The Effects of Feedback Accountability on Upward Appraisal Ratings," *Personnel Psychology* 47 (1994), pp. 349–55.

59. T.J. Maurer, N.S. Raju, and W.C. Collins, "Peer and Subordinate Performance Appraisal Measurement Equivalence," *Journal of Applied Psychology* 83 (1998), pp. 693–702.

60. R. Reilly, J. Smither, and N. Vasilopoulos, "A Longitudinal Study of Upward Feedback," *Personnel Psychology*, 49 (1996), pp. 599–612.

61. R. Reilly, J. Smither, and N. Vasilopoulos, "A Longitudinal Study of Upward Feedback," p. 602.

62. R. Reilly, J. Smither, and N. Vasilopoulos, "A Longitudinal Study of Upward Feedback," p. 599.

63. R. Brillinger, "The Many Faces of 360-Degree Feedback," *Canadian HR Reporter* (December 16, 1996), pp. 20–21.

64. K. Nowack, "360-Degree Feedback: The Whole Story," *Training and Development* (January 1993), p. 69. For a description of some of the problems involved in implementing 360-degree feedback, see M. Budman, "The Rating Game," *Across the Board* 31, no. 2 (February 1994), pp. 35–38.

65. C. Romano, "Fear of Feedback," *Management Review* (December 1993), p. 39. See also M.R. Edwards and A.J. Ewen, "How to Manage Performance and Pay With 360-Degree Feedback," *Compensation and Benefits Review*, 28, no. 3 (May/June 1996), pp. 41–46.

66. R. Brillinger, "The Many Faces," p. 21.

67. R. Brillinger, "The Many Faces," p. 20.

68. J.F. Milliman, R.A. Zawacki, C. Norman, L. Powell, and J. Kirksey, "Companies Evaluate Employees from All Perspectives," *Personnel Journal*, 73, no. 11 (November 1994), pp. 99–103.

69. R. Brillinger, "The Many Faces," p. 20.

70. See, for instance, G. Rich, "Group Reviews—Are You Up To It?" *CMA Magazine* (March 1993), p. 5.

71. R. Brillinger, "The Many Faces," p. 20.

72. D.A. Waldman, L.A. Atwater, and D. Antonioni, "Has 360-Degree Feedback Gone Amok?" *Academy of Management Executive*, 12 (1998), pp. 86–94.

73. P.E. Levy, B.D. Cawley, and R.J. Foti, "Reactions to Appraisal Discrepancies: Performance Ratings and Attributions," *Journal of Business and Psychology*, 12 (1998), pp. 437–55.

74. M. Derayeh and S. Brutus, "Learning from Others' 360-Degree Experiences," *Canadian HR Reporter* (February 10, 2003), pp. 18, 23.

75. A.S. DeNisi and A.N. Kluger, "Feedback Effectiveness: Can 360-Degree Appraisal Be Improved?" *Academy of Management Executive* 14, (2000), pp. 129–39.

76. T. Bentley, "Internet Addresses 360-Degree Feedback Concerns," *Canadian HR Reporter* (May 8, 2000), pp. G3, G15.

77. D. Brown, "Getting Tough With Poor Performers," *Canadian HR Reporter* (November 19, 2001), pp. 1, 14.

78. D. Brown, "Re-evaluating Evaluation."

79. See also J. Greenberg, "Using Explanations to Manage Impressions of Performance Appraisal Fairness," *Employee Responsibilities and Rights Journal*, 4, no. 1 (March 1991), pp. 51–60.

80. Johnson, *The Appraisal Interview Guide*, Chapter 9.

81. J. Block, *Performance Appraisal on the Job: Making It Work* (New York: Executive Enterprises Publications, 1981), pp. 58–62. See also T. Lowe, "Eight Ways to Ruin a Performance Review," *Personnel Journal*, 65, no. 1 (January 1986).

82. Block, *Performance Appraisal on the Job*.

83. J. Pearce and L. Porter, "Employee Response to Formal Performance Appraisal Feedback," *Journal of Applied Psychology*, 71, no. 2 (May 1986), pp. 211–18.

84. E.E. Lawler, III, "Performance Management: The Next Generation," *Compensation and Benefits Review* (May–June, 1994), p. 16.

85. Lawler, "Performance Management," p. 16.

86. M. M. Markowich, "Response: We Can Make Performance Appraisals Work," *Compensation and Benefits Review* (May–June 1995), p. 25.

87. See, for example, G. Boudreaux, "Response: What TQM Says About Performance Appraisal," *Compensation and Benefits Review* (May–June 1994), pp. 20–24.

88. Boudreaux, "What TQM Says About Performance Appraisal," p. 21.

89. See, for example, Lawler, "Performance Management: The Next Generation," p. 17.

90. D. Brown, "HR Improving at Performance Management."

91. Boudreaux, "Response: What TQM Says About Performance Appraisal," p. 23.

92. Based in part on J. E. Ross, *Total Quality Management: Text, Cases and Readings* (Delray Beach, FL: Saint Lucie Press, 1993), p. 1.

93. Ross, *Total Quality Management: Text, Cases, and Readings*, pp. 2–3, 35–36.

94. G. Boudreaux, "Response: What TWM Says About Performance Appraisal," *Compensation and Benefits Review* (May–June 1994), pp. 20–24. See also J.M. Jawahar and G. Salegna, "Adapting Performance Appraisal Systems for a Quality-Driven Environment," *Compensation and Benefits Review* (January–February 2003), pp. 64–70.

95. Lawler, "Performance Management," p. 17.

96. Markowich, "Response: We Can Make Performance Appraisals Work," p. 26.

97. Antonioni, "Improve the Performance Management Process," p. 30.

98. Antonioni, "Improve the Performance Management Process."

99. Antonioni, "Improve the Performance Management Process."

Chapter 11

1. "Aligning Work and Rewards: A Round Table Discussion," *Compensation and Benefits Review* 26, no. 4 (July–August 1994), pp. 47–63; M. Morganstern, "Compensation and the New Employment Relationship," *Compensation and Benefits Review* 27 (March 1995), pp. 37–44.

2. H. Risher, "Exclusive CBR Survey: Pay Program Effectiveness," *Compensation and Benefits Review* 31 (November/December 1999), pp. 20–26.

3. E.E. Lawler III, "Pay Strategy: New Thinking for the New Millennium," *Compensation and Benefits Review* 32 (January/February 2000), pp. 7–12.

4. S. Chadwick, "Using Rewards to Drive Commitment and Loyalty," *Canadian HR Reporter* (December 13, 1999), pp. 8–9.

5. G.S. Lowe and G. Schellenberg, *What's a Good Job? The Importance of Employment Relationships* (Canadian Policy Network Study No. W05, March 2001); *Redefining Rewards* (Toronto ON: Winter Consulting Group, 2001).

6. *The Towers Perrin Talent Report: New Realities in Today's Workforce* (Toronto ON: Towers Perrin, 2003).

7. "GM, Daimler-Chrysler Workers Ratify Agreements," *Workplace Today* (December 1999), p. 11.

8. E. Hay, "The Attitude of the American Federation of Labour on Job Evaluation," *Personnel Journal* 26 (November 1947), pp. 163–69; H. James, "Issues in Job Evaluation: The Union's View," *Personnel Journal* 51 (September 1972), pp. 675–79; Harold Jones, "Union Views on Job Evaluations: 1971 vs. 1978," *Personnel Journal* 58 (February 1979), pp. 80–85.

9. B. Ellig, "Strategic Pay Planning," *Compensation and Benefits Review* 19, no. 4 (July–August 1987), pp. 28–43; T. Robertson, "Fundamental Strategies for Wage and Salary Administration," *Personnel Journal* 65, no. 11 (November 1986), pp. 120–32. One expert cautions against conducting salary surveys based on job title alone. He recommends using job-content salary surveys that examine the content of jobs according to the size of each job so that, for instance, the work of the president of IBM and that of a small clone manufacturer would not be inadvertently compared. See R. Sahl, "Job Content Salary Surveys: Survey Design and Selection Features," *Compensation and Benefits Review* (May–June 1991), pp. 14–21.

10. See D.I. Levine, "What Do Wages Buy?" *Administrative Science Quarterly* 38 (1993), pp. 462–83.

11. Levine, "What Do Wages Buy?" pp. 462–65.

12. Levine, "What Do Wages Buy?" p. 462.

13. V. Kaman and J. Barr, "Employee Attitude Surveys for Strategic Compensation Management," *Compensation and Benefits Review* (January–February 1991), pp. 52–65.

14. M.A. Thompson, "Rewards, Performance Two Biggest Words in HR Future," *WorldatWork Canadian News* 10 (2002), pp. 1, 2, 11.

15. Job analysis can be a useful source of information on compensable factors, as well as on job descriptions and job specifications. For example, a quantitative job analysis technique like the position analysis questionnaire generates quantitative information on the degree to which the following five basic factors are present in each job: having decision making/communication/social responsibilities, performing skilled activities, being physically active, operating vehicles or equipment, and processing information. As a result, a job analysis technique like the PAQ is actually as appropriate as a job evaluation technique (or, some say, more), in that jobs can be quantitatively compared to one another on those five dimensions and their relative worth thus ascertained.

16. M.E. Lo Bosco, "Job Analysis, Job Evaluation, and Job Classification," *Personnel* 62, no. 5 (May 1985), pp. 70–5. See also H. Risher, "Job Evaluation: Validity and Reliability," *Compensation and Benefits Review* 21 (January–February 1989), pp. 22–36; and D. Hahn and R. Dipboye, "Effects of Training and Information on the Accuracy and Reliability of Job Evaluations," *Journal of Applied Psychology* 73, no. 2 (May 1988), pp. 146–53.

17. See, for example, D. Petri, "Talking Pay Policy Pays Off," *Supervisory Management* (May 1979), pp. 2–13.

18. As explained later, the practice of red circling is used to delay downward adjustments in pay rates that are presently too high given the newly evaluated jobs. See also E.J. Brennan, "Everything You Need to Know About Salary Ranges," *Personnel Journal* 63, no. 3 (March 1984), pp. 10–17.

19. R. Plachy, "The Case for Effective Point-Factor Job Evaluation, Viewpoint I," *Compensation and Benefits Review* 19 (March–April 1987), pp. 45–48; R. Plachy, "The Point-Factor Job Evaluation System: A Step-by-Step Guide, Part II," *Compensation and Benefits Review* 19 (September–October 1987), pp. 9–24; and A. Candrilli and R. Armagast, "The Case for Effective Point-Factor Job Evaluation, Viewpoint II," *Compensation and Benefits Review* 19 (March–April 1987), pp. 49–54. See also R. J. Sahl, "How to Install a Point-Factor Job Evaluation System," *Personnel* 66, no. 3 (March 1989), pp. 38–42.

20. J. B. Cunningham and S. Graham "Assessing the Reliability of Four Job Evaluation Plans," *Canadian Journal of Administrative Sciences* 10 (1993), pp. 31–47.

21. S. Werner, R. Konopaske, and C. Touhey, "Ten Questions to Ask Yourself About Compensation Surveys," *Compensation and Benefits Review* 31 (May/June 1999), pp. 54–59.

22. P. Cappelli, *The New Deal at Work: Managing the Market-Driven Workforce.* Boston MA: Harvard Business School Press, 1999.

23. "Compensation Surveys on the Internet," *Canadian HR Reporter* (February 10, 1997), p. 6.

24. This is based on F.W. Cook, "Compensation Surveys Are Biased," *Compensation and Benefits Review* (September–October 1994), pp. 19–22.

25. Cook, "Compensation Surveys Are Biased," p. 19.

26. Cook, "Compensation Surveys Are Biased."

27. S. Werner, R. Konopaske and C. Touhey, "Ten Questions to Ask Yourself About Compensation Surveys." See also U. Vu, "Know-how Pays in Comp Surveys," *Canadian HR Reporter* (April 7), 2003, p. 13.

28. S. Werner, R. Konopaske, and C. Touhey, "Ten Questions to Ask Yourself About Compensation Surveys."

29. N. Winter, "Broadbanding: Who's Using It And Why?" *Canadian HR Reporter* (December 18, 1995) p. 8.

30. Hofrichter, "Broadbanding: A 'Second Generation' Approach," *Compensation and Benefits Review* (September–October 1993), pp. 53–58.

31. D. Hofrichter, "Broadbanding: A 'Second Generation' Approach." See also G. Bergel, "Choosing the Right Pay Delivery System to Fit Banding," *Compensation and Benefits Review* 26, (July–August 1994), pp. 34–38.

32. For example, see S. Emerson, "Job Evaluation: A Barrier to Excellence?" *Compensation and Benefits Review* (January–February 1991), pp. 39–51; Nan Weiner, "Job Evaluation Systems: A Critique," *Human Resource Management Review* 1, (Summer 1991), pp. 119.

33. N. Winter, "Broadbanding: Who's Using It and Why?" p. 8.

34. B. Orr, "Competencies Key in a Changing World," *Canadian HR Reporter* (November 30, 1998), pp. 10–11.

35. G. Ledford Jr., "Three Case Studies on Skill-Based Pay: An Overview," *Compensation and Benefits Review* (March–April 1991), pp. 11–23.

36. B. Orr, "Competencies Key in a Changing World."

37. Ledford, "Three Case Studies on Skill-Based Pay: An Overview," p. 12. See also K. Cofsky, "Critical Keys to Competency-Based Pay," *Compensation and Benefits Review* (November–December 1993), pp. 46–52.

38. S. St.-Onge, "Competency-Based Pay Plans Revisited," *Human Resources Professional* (August/September 1998), pp. 29–34.

39. J. Kochanski and P. Leblanc, "Should Firms Pay for Competencies: Competencies Have to Help the Bottom Line," *Canadian HR Reporter* (February 22, 1999), p. 10.

40. C. Lee, K. Shaw and P. Bobko, "The Importance of Justice Perceptions in Pay Effectiveness: A Two-Year Study of a Skill-Based Pay Plan," *Journal of Management*, 25, 1999, pp. 851–73.

41. This is based on L. Dufetel, "Job Evaluation: Still at the Frontier," *Compensation and Benefits Review* (July–August 1991), pp. 53–67.

42. N. Winter, "Job Evaluation in a New Business Environment," *Canadian HR Reporter* (March 27, 2000), p. 17.

43. V.L. Williams and J.E. Sunderland, "New Pay Programs Boost Retention," p. 27.

44. J.R. Schuster and P.K. Zingheim, *The New Pay: Linking Employee and Organizational Performance* (San Francisco, CA: Jossey-Bass).

45. D. Yoder, *Personnel Management and Industrial Relations* (Englewood Cliffs, NJ: Prentice Hall, 1970), pp. 643–45.

46. E. Lewis, "New Approaches to Executive Pay," *Directors and Boards* 18 (Spring 1994), pp. 57–58. See also B.R. Ellig, "Executive Pay: A Primer," *Compensation & Benefits Review* (January–February 2003), pp. 44–50.

47. D. Brown, "Pay for Performance Better for Executives, Companies," *Canadian HR Reporter* (March 25, 2003), p. 2.

48. "50 Best-Paid Executives," *Report on Business Magazine* (July 2002).

49. H.L. Tosi, S. Werner, J.P. Katz, and L.R. Gomez-Mejia, "How Much Does Performance Matter? A Meta-Analysis of CEO Pay Studies," *Journal of Management* 26 (2000), pp. 301–39.

50. J. McFarland, "CEO Pay: The Globe Survey of Compensation," *The Globe & Mail* (April 23, 2002).

51. D. Olive, "Many CEOs Richly Rewarded for Failure," *Toronto Star* (August 25, 2002), pp. A1, A10–A11.

52. McFarland, "CEO Pay."

53. S. Weeks, "Batter Up. Negotiating Executive Compensation in the Big Leagues," *Canadian HR Reporter* (October 7, 2002), pp. 7–8.

54. This is based on W. White, "Managing the Board Review of Executive Pay," *Compensation and Benefits Review* (November–December 1992), pp. 35–41.

55. K. Howlett. "Pay Rules Signal Changes at OSC," *The Globe & Mail* (October 18, 1993), p. B1.

56. A. Duffy, L. Priest, and D. Israealson, "The $100,000-Plus Club," *Toronto Star* (March 30, 1996), p. A2.

57. J. McFarland, "Boards Rapped Over CEO Compensation," *The Globe & Mail* (April 24, 2002).

58. W. White and R. Fife, "New Challenges for Executive Compensation in the 1990s," *Compensation and Benefits Review* (January–February 1993), pp. 27–35.

59. P. Moran, "Equitable Salary Administration in High-Tech Companies," *Compensation and Benefits Review* 18 (September–October 1986), pp. 31–40.

60. R. Sibson, *Compensation* (New York: AMA-COM, 1981), p. 194.

61. Sibson, *Compensation.*

62. See also B. Bridges, "The Role of Rewards in Motivating Scientific and Technical Personnel: Experience at Egland AFB," *National Productivity Review* (Summer 1993), pp. 337–48.

63. M. Commanducci, "Women Make Gains in Wage Equity as Young Fall Behind," *Canadian HR Reporter* (April 20, 1998), p. 16. See also M. Drolet, "The Male–Female Wage Gap," *Perspectives* (Statistics Canada, Spring 2002), pp. 29–37; and E. Carey, "Gender Gap in Earnings Staying Stubbornly High," *Toronto Star* (March 12, 2003), p. A9.

64. www.peo.on.ca (April 29, 2002).

65. D. Brown, "StatsCan Unable to Explain Gender Wage Gap," *Canadian HR Reporter* (January 31, 2000), p. 3.

66. L. Young and D. Brown, " Last Chapter in Pay Equity Dispute Closes as Feds Buckle Under Court Decision," *Canadian HR Reporter* (November 15, 1999), p. 3. See also "Federal Government Settles Pay Equity Dispute," *Workplace Today* (December 1999), p. 9.

67. "The Never-Ending Pay Equity Case," *Canadian HR Reporter* (January 28, 2002), p. 2.

68. *Canadian Master Labour Guide 2002*, 16th ed. (Toronto: CCH Canadian Limited, 2002), pp. 549–90.

69. D. Brown, "StatsCan Unable to Explain Gender Wage Gap."

70. D. Brown, "Pay Equity Under Review," *Canadian HR Reporter* (July 16, 2001), pp. 2, 10.

71. M. Gray, "Pay Equity Through Job Evaluation: A Case Study," *Compensation and Benefits Review* (July–August 1992), p. 46

72. Gray, "Pay Equity Through Job Evaluation," pp. 46–51.

73. A. Tomlinson, "Ottawa's Pay Equity Scheme Out the Window," *Canadian HR Reporter* (June 17, 2002), pp. 1, 11.

74. M. Yao, "Inflation Outruns Pay of Middle Managers, Increasing Frustration," *The Wall Street Journal* (June 9, 1981), p. 1. See also, "The Impact of Inflation on Wage and Salary Administration," *Personnel* 58 (November–December 1981), p. 55.

75. This section based on or quoted from "The Impact of Inflation on Wage and Salary Administration," p. 55.

76. W.C. Lawther, "Ways to Monitor (and Solve) the Pay Compression Problem," *Personnel* (March 1989), pp. 84–87.

77. Lawther, "Ways to Monitor," p. 87.

78. J. Lindroth, "Inflation, Taxes, and Perks: How Compensation Is Changing," *Personnel Journal* 60 (December 1981), pp. 934–40.

79. C. Deitch and D. Dilts, "The COLA Clause: An Employer Bargaining Weapon?" *Personnel Journal* 61 (March 1982), pp. 220–23.

80. *Economic Research Institute Geographic Assessor,*® www.erieri.com (May 2, 2003).

Chapter 12

1. J. Hale and G. Bailey, "Seven Dimensions of Successful Reward Plans," *Compensation and Benefits Review* 30 (July/August 1998), pp. 71–77. See also I. Huss and C. Kapel, "Giving Employees What They Want and Linking it to Strategy," *Canadian HR Reporter* (May 8, 2000), pp. 7, 10.

2. L. Young, "Linking Pay to Performance a Global Trend," *Canadian HR Reporter* (April 19, 1999), pp. 1, 17.

3. P.K. Zingheim and J.R. Schuster, *Pay People Right!: Breakthrough Reward Strategies to Create Great Companies* (San Francisco: Jossey-Bass, 2000).

4. D. Brown, "Top Performers Must Get Top Pay," *Canadian HR Reporter* (May 8, 2000), pp. 7, 10.

5. V. Dell'Agnese, "Performance-based Rewards, Line-of-Sight Foster Ownership Behaviour in Staff," *Canadian HR Reporter* (October 8, 2001), p. 10.

6. "Giant Payout to Dofasco Employees," *Canadian HR Reporter* (March 13, 2000), p. 10.

7. *Annual Salary Increase Survey 2002.* Hewitt Associates.

8. Except as noted, this section is based on "*Non-Traditional Incentive Pay Programs,*" Personnel Policies Forum Survey, no. 148 (May 1991), The Bureau of National Affairs, Inc., Washington, D.C.

9. "*Non-Traditional Incentive Pay Programs,*" p. 3.

10. "*Non-Traditional Incentive Pay Programs,*" p. 9; and A. Czarnecki, "'Spot Awards' Incentives Easily Administered, Flexible, Affordable," *Canadian HR Reporter* (March 13, 1995), p. 15.

11. R. Murrill, "Variations on Compensation," *Compensation and Benefits Update* 4, (February 2000), p. 5.

12. "*Non-Traditional Incentive Pay Programs,*" p. 13.

13. "*Non-Traditional Incentive Pay Programs,*" p. 19.

14. "*Non-Traditional Incentive Pay Programs,*" p. 24.

15. R. Henderson, *Compensation Management* (Reston, VA: Reston, 1979), p. 363. For a discussion of the increasing use of incentives for blue-collar employees, see, for example, R. Henderson, "Contract Concessions: Is the Past Prologue?" *Compensation and Benefits Review* 18, no. 5 (September–October 1986), pp. 17–30. See also A. J. Vogl, "Carrots, Sticks and Self-Deception," *Across-the-Board* 3, no. 1 (January 1994), pp. 39–44.

16. D. Belcher, *Compensation Administration* (Englewood Cliffs, NJ: Prentice Hall, 1973), p. 314.

17. For a discussion of these, see T. Wilson, "Is It Time to Eliminate the Piece Rate Incentive System?" *Compensation and Benefits Review* (March–April 1992), pp. 43–49.

18. Measured day work is a third type of individual incentive plan for production workers. See, for example, M. Fein, "Let's Return to MDW for Incentives," *Industrial Engineering* (January 1979), pp. 34–37.

19. Henderson, *Compensation Management*, pp. 367–8. See also D. Swinehart, "A Guide for More Productive Team Incentive Programs," *Personnel Journal* 65, no. 7 (July 1986); A. Saunier and E. Hawk, "Realizing the Potential of Teams through Team-based Rewards," *Compensation and Benefits Review* (July–August 1994), pp. 24–33; and S. Caudron, "Tie Individual Pay to Team Success," *Personnel Journal* 73, no. 10 (October 1994), pp. 40–46.

20. Another suggestion is as follows: equal payments to all members on the team; differential payments to team members based on their contributions to the team's performance; and differential payments determined by a ratio of each group member's base pay to the total base pay of the group. See K. Bartol and L. Hagmann, "Team-based Pay Plans: A Key to Effective Teamwork," *Compensation and Benefits Review* (November–December 1992), pp. 24–29.

21. J. Nickel and S. O'Neal, "Small Group Incentives: Gainsharing in the Microcosm," *Compensation and Benefits Review* (March–April 1990), p. 24. See also J. Pickard, "How Incentives Can Drive Teamworking," *Personnel Management* (September 1993), pp. 26–32, and S. Caudron, "Tie Individual Pay to Team Success," *Personnel Journal* (October 1994), pp. 40–46.

22. J.P. Alston, "Awarding Bonuses the Japanese Way," *Business Horizons* 25 (September–October 1982), pp. 6–8.

23. See, for example, P. Daly, "Selecting and Assigning a Group Incentive Plan," *Management Review* (December 1975), pp. 33–45. For an explanation of how to develop a successful group incentive program, see K. Dow Scott and Timothy Cotter, "The Team That Works Together Earns Together," *Personnel Journal* 63 (March 1984), pp. 59–67.

24. L.N. McClurg, "Team Rewards: How Far Have We Come?" *Human Resource Management* 40 (Spring 2001), pp. 73–86. See also A Gostick, "Team Recognition," *Canadian HR Reporter* (May 21, 2001), p. 15.

25. W.E. Reum and S. Reum, "Employee Stock Ownership Plans: Pluses and Minuses," *Harvard Business Review* 55 (July–August 1976), pp. 133–43; R. Bavier, "Managerial Bonuses," *Industrial Management* (March– April 1978), pp. 1–5. See also J. Thompson, L. Murphy Smith, and A. Murray, "Management Performance Incentives: Three Critical Issues," *Compensation and Benefits Review* 18, no. 5 (September–October 1986), pp. 41–47.

26. D. Sidebottom, *Compensation Planning Outlook 2000*, p. 2.

27. D. Sidebottom, *Compensation Planning Outlook 2000*, p. 8.

28. B.R. Ellig, "Incentive Plans: Short-Term Design Issues," *Compensation Review* 16, no. 3 (Third Quarter 1984), pp. 26–36.

29. B. Ellig, *Executive Compensation—A Total Pay Perspective* (New York: McGraw-Hill, 1982), p. 187.

30. Ellig, *Executive Compensation*, p. 188.

31. See, for example, Bavier, "Managerial Bonuses," pp. 1–5. See also C. Tharp, "Linking Annual Incentive Awards to Individual Performance," *Compensation and Benefits Review* 17 (November–December 1985), pp. 38–43.

32. Ellig, *Executive Compensation*, p. 189.

33. F.D. Hildebrand, Jr., "Individual Performance Incentives," *Compensation Review* 10 (Third Quarter 1978), p. 32.

34. Hildebrand, "Individual Performance Incentives," pp. 28–33.

35. P. Brieger, "Shareholders Target CEO Compensation," *Financial Post* (April 7, 2003), p. FP5. See also S.M. Van Putten and E.D. Graskamp, "End of an Era? The Future of Stock Options," *Compensation and Benefits Review* (September–October 2002), pp. 29–35; N. Winter, "The Current Crisis in Executive Compensation," *WorldatWork Canadian News* (Fourth Quarter 2002), pp. 1–3.

36. R.M. Kanungo and M. Mendonca, *Compensation: Effective Reward Management* (1997), p. 237.

37. E. Redling, "The 1981 Tax Act: Boom to Managerial Compensation," *Personnel* 57 (March–April 1982), pp. 26–35.

38. D. Sidebottom, *Compensation Planning Outlook 2000*, p. 10.

39. R. Murrill, "Executive Share Ownership," *Watson Wyatt Memorandum* 11, no. 1 (March 1997), p. 11.

40. R.J. Long, "Ensuring Your Executive Compensation Plan is an Asset Rather Than a Liability," *Canadian HR Reporter* (October 19, 1998), pp. 15–16. See also D. Brown, "Bringing Stock Options Back to the Surface," *Canadian HR Reporter* (May 7, 2001), p. 2; and A. Tomlinson, "Stock Options: Last Year's Darling, This Year's Headache," *Canadian HR Reporter* (October 8, 2001), p. 2.

41. J.M. Bodley, "Incentive Plan Management in Volatile Markets," *Canadian HR Reporter* (May 17, 1999), p. 8.

42. S.J. Chadwick, "Extending Stock Option Plans to All Employees a Growing Trend," *Canadian HR Reporter* (October 5, 1998), pp. 10, 12. See also B. Cline, "Stock Option Plans...A New Trend?" *HR Professional* (June/July 1999), pp. 24–26; I. Huss and M. Maclure, "Broad-Based Stock Option Plans Take Hold," *Canadian HR Reporter* (July 17, 2000), p. 18; D. Brown, "Stock Options Grow," *Canadian HR Reporter* (March 26, 2001), pp. 1, 10; and D. Brown, "Bringing Stock Options Back to the Surface."

43. J. Staiman and C. Thompson, "Designing and Implementing a Broad-Based Stock Option Plan," *Compensation and Benefits Review* (July–August 1998), p. 23.

44. D. Jarcho, "How to Use Technology to Effectively Deliver Broad-Based Stock Option Plans," *Compensation and Benefits Review* (July–August 1998), pp. 87–90.

45. D. Brown, "CPP Investment Board Says Drop Stock Options," *Canadian HR Reporter* (March 24, 2003), pp. 1, 3.

46. "No Options at Microsoft," *Canadian HR Reporter* (August 11, 2003), p. 3. See also S.M. Van Putten and E.D. Graskamp, "End of an Era?"; E. Elliott and C. Kapel, "Market Downturn Puts Stock Options Under the Microscope," *Canadian HR Reporter* (June 17, 2002), pp. 17, 19; A. Tomlinson, "Stock Options Still Popular, Firms Picky About Recipients" *Canadian HR Reporter* (June 3, 2002); D. Brown, "Pressure Mounts to Reform Stock Option Accounting," *Canadian HR Reporter* (June 17, 2002), pp. 1, 12; D. Brown, "Stock Options: End of a Trend?" *Canadian HR Reporter* (September 9, 2002), pp. 1, 12; and "Accounting Body Calls for Options Expensing," *Canadian HR Reporter* (November 4, 2002), p. 2.

47. Basically, book value per share equals the firm's assets minus its prior (basically debt) liabilities, divided by the number of shares.

48. R. Stata and M. Maidique, "Bonus System for Balanced Strategy," *Harvard Business Review* 59 (November–December 1980), pp. 156–63; Alfred Rappaport, "Executive Incentives Versus Corporate Growth," *Harvard Business Review* 57 (July–August 1978), pp. 81–88. See also C. Graef, "Rendering Long-Term Incentives Less Risky for Executives," *Personnel* 65, no. 9 (September 1988), pp. 80–84.

49. For a discussion see I. Kay, "Beyond Stock Options: Emerging Practices in Executive Compensation Programs," *Compensation and Benefits Review* (November–December 1991), pp. 18–29.

50. J. Kanter and M. Ward, "Long-Term Incentives for Management, Part 4: Performance Plans," *Compensation and Benefits Review* (January–February 1990), p. 36.

51. R. Murrill, "Executive Share Ownership," p. 6.

52. P. Singh and N.C. Agarwal, "Executive Compensation: Examining an Old Issue from New Perspectives," *Compensation and Benefits Review* (March/April 2003), pp. 48–54.

53. This section is based on M. Meltzer and H. Goldsmith, "Executive Compensation for Growth Companies," *Compensation and Benefits Review* (November–December 1997), pp. 41–50.

54. J. Tallitsch and J. Moynahan, "Fine-Tuning Sales Compensation Programs," *Compensation and Benefits Review* 26, no. 2 (March–April 1994), pp. 34–37.

55. Straight salary by itself is not, of course, an incentive compensation plan as we use the term in this chapter.

56. J. Steinbrink, "How to Pay Your Sales Force," *Harvard Business Review* 57 (July–August 1978), pp. 111–22.

57. T.H. Patten, "Trends in Pay Practices for Salesmen," *Personnel* 43 (January–February 1968), pp. 54–63. See also C. Romano, "Death of a Salesman," *Management Review* 83, no. 9 (September 1994), pp. 10–16.

58. D. Harrison, M. Virick, and S. William, "Working Without a Net: Time, Performance, and Turnover Under Maximally Contingent Rewards," *Journal of Applied Psychology* 81 (1996), pp. 331–45.

59. G. Stewart, "Reward Structure as Moderator of the Relationship Between Extroversion and Sales Performance," *Journal of Applied Psychology* 81 (1996), pp. 619–27.

60. G. Stewart, "Reward Structure as Moderator of the Relationship Between Extroversion and Sales Performance," p. 519.

61. C. Fellman and D. Johnston, "Pay Systems that Salespeople Will Buy," *Canadian HR Reporter* (April 20, 1998), pp. 16, 18.

62. In the salary plus bonus plan, salespeople are paid a basic salary and are then paid a bonus for carrying out specified activities. For a discussion of how to develop a customer-focused sales compensation plan, see, for example, M. Blessington, "Designing a Sales Strategy with the Customer in Mind," *Compensation and Benefits Review* (March–April 1992), pp. 30–41.

63. S.S. Sands, "Ineffective Quotas: The Hidden Threat to Sales Compensation Plans," *Compensation and Benefits Review* (March/April 2000), pp. 35–42.

64. E. Maggio, "Compensation Strategies Pulling You in Different Directions?" *Canadian HR Reporter* (October 4, 1999), pp. 11, 19. See also B. Serino, "Non-cash Awards Boost Sales Compensation Plans, " *Workspan* (August 2002), pp. 24–27.

65. B. Weeks, "Setting Sales Force Compensation in the Internet Age," *Compensation and Benefits Review* (March/April 2000), pp. 25–34.

66. See, for example, W. Kearney, "Pay for Performance? Not Always," *MSU Business Topics* (Spring 1979), pp. 5–16. See also H. Doyel and J. Johnson, "Pay Increase Guidelines with Merit," *Personnel Journal* 64 (June 1985), pp. 46–50.

67. N. Winstanley, "Are Merit Increases Really Effective?" *Personnel Administrator* 27 (April 1982), pp. 37–41. See also W. Seithel and J. Emans, "Calculating Merit Increases: A Structured Approach," *Personnel* 60, no. 5 (June 1985), pp. 56–68.

68. D. Gilbert and G. Bassett, "Merit Pay Increases are a Mistake," *Compensation and Benefits Review* 26, no. 2 (March–April 1994), pp. 20–25.

69. *Merit Pay: Fitting the Pieces Together* (Chicago: Commerce Clearing House, 1982).

70. S. Minken, "Does Lump Sum Pay Merit Attention?" *Personnel Journal* (June 1988), pp. 77–83. Two experts suggest using neither straight merit pay nor lump-sum merit pay but rather tying the merit payment to the duration of the impact of the employee's work so that, for instance, the merit raise might last for two or three years. See J. Newman and D. Fisher, "Strategic Impact Merit Pay," *Compensation and Benefits Review* (July–August 1992), pp. 38–45.

71. This section based primarily on R. Sibson, *Compensation* (New York: AMA-COM, 1981), pp. 189–207.

72. D. Sidebottom, *Compensation Planning Outlook 2000*, p. 8.

73. B. Duke, "Are Profit Sharing Plans Making the Grade?" *Canadian HR Reporter* (January 11, 1999), pp. 8–9.

74. D.E. Tyson, *Profit-Sharing in Canada: The Complete Guide to Designing and Implementing Plans That Really Work* (Toronto: Wiley, 1996), pp. 200–07.

75. D. Sidebottom, *Compensation Planning Outlook 2000*, p. 11.

76. R. Murrill, "Executive Share Ownership," p. 10.

77. P. Robertson, "Increasing Productivity Through an Employee Share Purchase Plan," *Canadian HR Reporter* (September 20, 1999), pp. 7, 9.

78. S. Lebrun, "ESOP Saves the Day," *Canadian HR Reporter* (November 17, 1997), pp. 1–2. See also W. Smith, H. Lazarus, and H. M. Kalkstein, "Employee Stock Ownership Plans: Motivation and Morale Issues," *Compensation and Benefits Review* (September–October 1990), pp. 37–46.

79. B. Moore and T. Ross, *The Scanlon Way to Improved Productivity: A Practical Guide* (New York: Wiley, 1978), p. 2.

80. These are based in part on S. Markham, K. Dow Scott, and W. Cox, Jr., "The Evolutionary Development of a Scanlon Plan," *Compensation and Benefits Review* (March–April 1992), pp. 50–56.

81. J.K. White, "The Scanlon Plan: Causes and Correlates of Success," *Academy of Management Journal* 22 (June 1979), pp. 292–312.

82. Moore and Ross, *The Scanlon Way to Improve Productivity*, pp. 1–2.

83. White, "The Scanlon Plan," pp. 292–312. For a discussion of the Improshare plan, see R. Kaufman, "The Effects of Improshare on Productivity," *Industrial and Labor Relations Review* 45, no. 2 (1991), pp. 311–22.

84. B.W. Thomas and M.H. Olson, "Gainsharing: The Design Guarantees Success," *Personnel Journal* (May 1988), pp. 73–79. See also "Aligning Compensation with Quality," *Bulletin to Management*, BNA Policy and Practice Series (April 1, 1993), p. 97.

85. See T. A. Welbourne and L. Gomez Mejia, "Gainsharing Revisited," *Compensation and Benefits Review* (July–August 1988), pp. 19–28.

86. N. Winter Consulting Inc., *Alternative Compensation Practices* (1996), p. 5.

87. This is paraphrased from W. Imberman, "Boosting Plant Performance with Gainsharing," *Business Horizons* (November–December 1992), p. 77.

88. For other examples, see T. Ross and L. Hatcher, "Gainsharing Drives Quality Improvement," *Personnel Journal* (November 1992), pp. 81–89. See also J. McAdams, "Employee Involvement and Performance Reward Plans: Design, Implementation, and Results," *Compensation and Benefits Review* 27, no. 2 (March 1995), pp. 45–55.

89. J. Belcher, Jr., "Gainsharing and Variable Pay: The State of the Art," *Compensation and Benefits Review* (May–June 1994), pp. 50–60.

90. R. Masternak, "Gainsharing Boosts Quality and Productivity at a B.F. Goodrich Plant," *National Productivity Review* (Spring 1993), pp. 225–38. See also S. Hanlon, D. Meyer, and R. Taylor, "Consequences of Gainsharing: A Field Experiment Revisited," *Group & Organization Management* 19, no. 1 (March 1994), pp. 87–111.

91. L. Dunne, "Incentive Plans That Even a Union Can Love," *Canadian HR Reporter* (June 1, 1998), pp. 12, 14.

92. P.K. Zingheim and J.R. Schuster, "Value is the Goal," *Workforce* (February 2000), pp. 56–61.

93. Belcher, *Compensation Administration*, pp. 309–10.

94. D. Brown, "Variable Pay Programs Still the Way of the Future," *Canadian HR Reporter* (November 29, 1999), pp. 7, 13.

95. C. Kapel and T. Kinsman-Berry, "Seven Key Factors for Effective Incentive Plans," *Canadian HR Reporter* (October 4, 1999), pp. 12–13.

96. J. Hale and G. Bailey, "Seven Dimensions of Successful Reward Plans," *Compensation and Benefits Review* 30 (July/August 1998), pp. 71–77.

97. D. Brown, "Thanks for a Job Well Done. Can We Clean Your House for You?" *Canadian HR Reporter* (January 13, 2003), pp. 18–19.

98. The following five points are based on A. Kohn, "Why Incentive Plans Cannot Work," *Harvard Business Review* (September–October 1993), pp. 54–63.

99. P.K. Zinghein and J.R. Schuster, *Pay People Right!: Breakthrough Reward Strategies to Create Great Companies*.

100. S. Gross and J. Bacher, "The New Variable Pay Programs: How Some Succeed, Why Some Don't," *Compensation and Benefits Review* (January–February 1993), pp. 55–56; see also G. Milkovich and C. Milkovich, "Strengthening the Pay-Performance Relationship: The Research," *Compensation and Benefits Review* (November–December 1992), pp. 53–62; and J. Schuster and P. Zingheim, "The New Variable Pay: Key Design Issues," *Compensation and Benefits Review* (March–April 1993), pp. 27–34.

101. J. Cameron and W.D. Pierce, *Rewards and Intrinsic Motivation: Resolving the Controversy* (Westport, CT: Bergin & Garvey, 2002). See also G. Bouchard, "When Rewards Don't Work," *The Globe & Mail* (September 25, 2002), p. C3.

102. J. Mills, "A Matter of Pride: Rewarding Team Success," *Canadian HR Reporter* (March 8, 1999), p. 16. See also D. Hutson, "New Incentives on the Rise," *Compensation and Benefits Review* (September/October 2000), pp. 40–46; and D. Hutson, "Getting the Feel for Employee Rewards," *Canadian HR Reporter* (January 14, 2002), pp. 22–23.

103. B. Parus, "Recognition: A Strategic Tool for Retaining Talent," *Workspan* (November 2002), pp. 14–18.

104. J. Mills, "A Matter of Pride: Rewarding Team Success."

105. D. Hutson, "New Incentives on the Rise" and D. Hutson, "Getting the Feel for Employee Rewards." See also L. McKibbin-Brown, "Beyond the Gold Watch: Employee Recognition Today," *Workspan* (April 2003), pp. 44–46.

106. A. Gostick, "Flying High in a Turbulent Economy," *Canadian HR Reporter* (January 14, 2002), p. 23.

107. A. Welsh, "The Give and Take of Recognition Programs."

108. Kouzas and Posner, *Encouraging the Heart: A Leader's Guide to Rewarding and Recognizing Others*.

109. D. Brown, "Canada Wants Nurses Again, but Will Anyone Answer the Call?" *Canadian HR Reporter* (January 15, 2001), pp. 1, 14, 15.

110. Kouzas and Pozner, *Encouraging the Heart: A Leader's Guide to Rewarding and Recognizing Others*. See also B. Nelson, "Why Managers Don't Recognize Employees," *Canadian HR Reporter* (March 11, 2002), p. 9; and L. Cassiani, "Lasting Impressions Through Recognition," *Canadian HR Reporter* (March 12, 2001), p. 7.

111. J. Mills, "A Matter of Pride: Rewarding Team Success."

112. L. Young, "How Can I Ever Thank You?" *Canadian HR Reporter* (January 31, 2000), pp. 7, 9.

113. E. Wright and K. Ryan, "Thanks a Million (More or Less)," *Canadian HR Reporter* (March 9, 1998), pp. 19, 21, 23. See also "How to Sell Recognition to Top Management," *Canadian HR Reporter* (June 1, 1998), p. 21; and B. Nelson, "Cheap and Meaningful Better Than Expensive and Forgettable," *Canadian HR Reporter* (August 13, 2001), p. 22.

114. L. Davidson, "The Power of Personal Recognition," *Workforce* (July 1999), pp. 44–49. See also A. Gostick and C. Elton, "Show Me the Rewards," *Canadian HR Reporter* (March 12, 2001), pp. 7, 10.

115. V. Scott and B. Phillips, "Recognition Program Links Achievement to Corporate Goals," *Canadian HR Reporter* (December 14, 1998), pp. 22–23. See also R. Clarke, "Building a Recognition Program: Alternatives and Considerations," *Canadian HR Reporter* (November 2, 1998), pp. 17, 19; and E. Wright and K. Ryan, "Thanks a Million (More or Less)."

116. L. Davidson, "The Power of Personal Recognition."

117. D. Brown, "Recognition an Integral Part of Total Rewards," *Canadian HR Reporter* (August 12, 2002), pp. 25, 27.

118. J. Jackson, "The Art of Recognition," *Canadian HR Reporter* (January 15, 2001), p.22. See also B.P. Keegan, "Incentive Programs Boost Employee Morale," *Workspan* (March 2002), pp. 30–33.

119. S. Nador, "Beyond Trinkets and Trash," *Canadian HR Reporter* (May 20, 2002), pp. 15, 19.

120. H. Hilliard, "How to Reward Top Performers When Money is No Object," *Canadian HR Reporter* (August 13, 2001), pp. 21, 23.

121. A. Welsh, "The Give and Take of Recognition Programs"; E. Wright and K. Ryan, "Thanks a Million (More or Less)."

Chapter 13

1. Based on F. Hills, T. Bergmann, and V. Scarpello, *Compensation Decision Making* (Fort Worth, TX: The Dryden Press, 1994), p. 424. See also L.K. Beatty, "Pay and Benefits Break Away from Tradition," *HR Magazine* 39 (November 1994), pp. 63–68.

2. R.K. Platt, "A Strategic Approach to Benefits," *Workspan* (July 2002), pp. 23–24.

3. S. Beech and J. Tompkins, "Do Benefits Plans Attract and Retain Talent?" *Benefits Canada* (October 2002), pp. 49–53.

4. F. Holmes, "Talking About an Evolution," *Benefits Canada* (September 2001), pp. 30–32.

5. J. Thomas and M. Chilco, "Coming of Age," *Benefits Canada* (March 2001), pp. 36–38.

6. KPMG, *Employee Benefits Costs in Canada* (1998).

7. K. Marshall, "Benefits of the Job," *Perspectives on Labour and Income* (May 2003), p.12. Statistics Canada Catalogue No. 75-001-X1E.

8. "EI Top-Ups Common—Survey," *Canadian HR Reporter* (February 23, 1998), p. 15.

9. "EI Top-Ups Common—Survey."

10. M. Hamilton, "Much Ado About Something," *Benefits Canada,* 21 (1997), p. 67.

11. See, for example, Bialk, "Cutting Workers' Compensation Costs," *Personnel Journal* 66 (July 1987), pp. 95–97. See also H. Amolins, "Workers Must Cooperate in Return to Work," *Canadian HR Reporter* (November 3, 1997), p. 8; and C. Knight, "Ontario Businesses Ready for New WCB," *Canadian HR Reporter* (November 17, 1997), p. 9.

12. J. Goodings, "Pressure Mounts to Increase Vacation Time," *Canadian HR Reporter* (March 22, 1999), p. 3.

13. M. Rothman, "Can Alternatives to Sick Pay Plans Reduce Absenteeism?" *Personnel Journal* 60 (October 1981), pp. 788–91; Richard Bunning, "A Prescription for Sick Leave," *Personnel Journal* 67 (August 1988), pp. 44–49.

14. A. Vincola, "Working Sabbaticals Offer Employees More Than Rejuvenation," *Canadian HR Reporter* (November 15, 1999), pp. 11, 13. See also S. Salzburg Ezrin, "The Last, Best Perk?" *Canadian Business* (October 30, 1998), pp. 88–92; and K. Dorrell, "Time Out," *Benefits Canada* (April 2001), p. 21.

15. D. Gunch, "The Family Leave Act: A Financial Burden?" *Personnel Journal* (September 1993), p. 49.

16. R.E. Sibson, *Wages and Salaries: A Handbook for Line Managers* (New York: American Management Association, 1967), p. 235.

17. S. Pellegrini, "Considering Critical," *Benefits Canada* (April 2002), pp. 71–73.

18. "Employee Benefits in Small Firms," *BNA Bulletin to Management* (June 27, 1991), pp. 196–97.

19. R. Jain, "Employer-Sponsored Dental Insurance Eases the Pain," *Monthly Labor Review* (October 1988), p. 18; "Employee Benefits," *Commerce Clearing House Ideas and Trends in Personnel* (January 23, 1991), pp. 9–11.

20. S. Lebrun, "Keeping the Lid on Drug Benefit Costs," *Canadian HR Reporter* (December 16, 1996), p. 12.

21. J. Taggart, "HR's Drug Cost Nightmares," *Canadian HR Reporter* (October 21, 2002), pp. 17, 20.

22. J Curtis and L. Scott, "Making the Connection," *Benefits Canada* (April 2003), pp. 75–79.

23. M. Kirby, *The Health of Canadians—The Federal Role* (October 2002); R. Romanow, *Building on Values: The Future of Health Care in Canada* (November 2002). See also K. DeBortoli, "Kirby, Romanow Proposals Revealed," *WorldatWork Canadian News* (First Quarter 2003), pp. 1, 24–27; and D. Brown, "Romanow: Cap Payer Drug Costs," *Canadian HR Reporter* (January 13, 2003), pp. 1, 3.

24. C. Kapel, "Unitel Asks Employees to Share Costs," *Canadian HR Reporter* (June 17, 1996), p. 17. See also J. Sloane and J. Taggart, "Runaway Drug Costs," *Canadian HR Reporter* (September 10, 2001), pp. 17–18; and "Deductibles Could Be Making a Comeback," *Canadian HR Reporter* (February 26, 2001), pp. 2, 16.

25. K. Press, "Canadian Healthcare Checkup," *Benefits Canada* (June 2000), pp. 75–78. See also L. Young, "Employees Willing to Pay Higher Health Premiums," *Canadian HR Reporter* (June 19, 2000), pp. 1, 19.

26. C. Knight, "Making the Smokers Pay," *Canadian HR Reporter* (June 17, 1996), p. 17.

27. J. Norton, "The New Drug Invasion," *Benefits Canada* (June 1999), pp. 29–32. See also S. Felix, "The New Drug Dilemma," *Benefits Canada* (March 1998), pp. 35–38.

28. S. Felix, "Healthy Alternative," *Benefits Canada* (February 1997), p. 47.

29. A. Dimon, "Money Well Spent," *Benefits Canada* (April 1997), p. 15.

30. T. Boyle, "Lack of Exercise Costing Canada $2 Billion a Year, Rock Says," *Toronto Star* (August 19, 2000), p. A9.

31. T. McCallum, "Getting a Grip: Business Battles the Health Care Bulge," *Human Resources Professional* (October 1996), p. 13.

32. A. Dimon, "Money Well Spent," p. 15.

33. C. Knight, "Managing Health Care Costs," *Canadian HR Reporter* (April 22, 1996), p. 1.

34. *Flex-ability: Employer Attitudes Toward Flexible Benefits* (Toronto ON: Hewitt Associates, 2002).

35. J. Taggart, "Health Spending Accounts: A Prescription for Cost Control," *Canadian HR Reporter* (October 22, 2001), pp. 16, 18. See also "How Spending Accounts Work," *Canadian HR Reporter* (February 24, 2003), p. 16.

36. K. Gay, "Post-Retirement Benefits Costing Firms a Fortune," *Financial Post* (June 2, 1995), p. 18.

37. S. Lebrun, "Turning a Blind Eye to Benefits," *Canadian HR Reporter* (February 24, 1997), p. 2.

38. S. Pellegrini, "Keep Benefits Costs Low by Assessing Retiree Health," *Canadian HR Reporter* (June 14, 1999), pp. 9–10.

39. M. Warren, "Uncovering the Costs," *Benefits Canada* (November 1996), p. 41.

40. G. Dufresne, "Financing Benefits for Tomorrow's Retirees," *Canadian HR Reporter* (April 6, 1998), p. 11.

41. M. Warren, "Retiree Benefits Come of Age," *Benefits Canada* (May 2000), pp. 73–77.

42. A. Khemani, "Post-Retirement Benefits Liability Grows," *Canadian HR Reporter* (November 4, 1996), p. 17. See also M. Warren, "Retiree Benefits Come of Age."

43. C. Milne, "Boom, Bust and Now What?" *Benefits Canada* (July 1999), pp. 22–24.

44. S. Pellegrini, "Senior's Needs: Beyond the Public Purse," *Canadian HR Reporter* (September 6, 1999), pp. 10, 18.

45. A.N. Nash and S.J. Carroll, Jr., "Supplemental Compensation," in *Perspectives on Personnel: Human Resource Management,* H. Heneman III and D. Schwab, eds. (Homewood, IL: Irwin, 1978), p. 223.

46. K. Read, "Integration Key to Managing Lost Time," *Canadian HR Reporter* (May 18, 1998), pp. 10–11.

47. M. Cusipag, "A Healthy Approach to Managing Disability Costs," *Human Resources Professional* (June/July 1997), p 13.

48. A. Blake, "A New Approach to Disability Management," *Benefits Canada* (March 2000), pp. 58–64.

49. P. Kulig, "Returning the Whole Employee to Work," *Canadian HR Reporter* (March 9, 1998), p. 20. See also A. Gibbs, "Gearing Disability Management to the Realities of Working Life," *Canadian HR Reporter* (December 2, 2002), p. G7.

50. Curtis and Scott, "Making the Connection."

51. N. Rankin, "A Guide to Disability Management," *Canadian HR Reporter* (March 22, 1999), pp. 14–15.

52. C. Colacci, "Testing Helps You Decrease Disability Costs," *Canadian HR Reporter* (June 14, 1999), p. G4.

53. "Back-to-Work With Back Injuries," *Canadian HR Reporter* (February 9, 1998), p. 11.

54. S.B. Hood, "Repetitive Strain Injury: Preventable Plague of the '90s," *Human Resources Professional* (June/July 1997), p. 29. See also A. Cantor, "Understanding the Costs of Job Accommodation," *Back to Work* (September 1997), p. 5.

55. S. Lebrun, "Employers Take Notice of Disability Costs," *Canadian HR Reporter* (December 29, 1997), pp. 1, 24.

56. C. McMahon, "Disability Management Triumphs," *Benefits Canada* (April 1999), p. 67–73.

57. D. Dyck, "Stating Your Case," *Benefits Canada* (February 1998), pp. 55–59.

58. K. Dorrell, "Disability Champions," *Benefits Canada* (February 2001), pp. 57–59.

59. Curtis and Scott, "Making the Connection."

60. This is based on S. Felix, "The Gloom Boom," *Benefits Canada* (January 1997), p. 32.

61. "Depression Under Wraps," *Canadian HR Reporter* (November 18, 2002), p. 2.

62. M. Acharya, "Depressed Workers Cost Firms Billions, Business Panel Says," *Toronto Star* (July 21, 2000), p. C3.

63. E. Vernarec, "The High Costs of Hidden Conditions," *Business and Health* 16 (1998), pp. 19–23. See also J. Kline Jr. and L. Sussman, "An Executive Guide to Workplace Depression," *Academy of Management Executive* 14 (August 2000), pp. 103–14.

64. M. Acharya, "Depressed Workers Cost Firms Billions, Business Panel Says."

65. M. Acharya, "Depressed Workers Cost Firms Billions, Business Panel Says."

66. D. Brown, "Call to Action in War Against Mental Illness," *Canadian HR Reporter* (November 4, 2002), pp. 1, 11.

67. M. Cusipag, "A Healthy Approach to Managing Disability Costs." See also M. Burych, "Baby Blues," *Benefits Canada* (October 2000), pp 33–35.

68. B. Hayhoe, "The Case for Employee Retirement Planning," *Canadian HR Reporter* (May 20, 2002), p. 18.

69. R. Henderson, *Compensation Management* (Reston VA: Reston, 1979), pp. 289–90.

70. C. Ripsman, "Putting Together a Defined Contribution Retirement Program," *Canadian HR Reporter* (November 5, 2001), pp. 7, 8.

71. R. Headrick, "Who is Looking After the Group RRSP?" *Canadian HR Reporter* (February 11, 2002), p. 21.

72. G. M. Hall, "Pensions: Death by Regulation?" *Canadian HR Reporter* (October 4, 1999), p. 6. See also S. Smolkin, "Changing Canadian Pension Standards," *Canadian HR Reporter* (November 29, 1999), pp. 24–26; S. Smolkin, "Proposals Add to Hodgepodge of Legislative Inconsistencies," *Canadian HR Reporter* (January 17, 2000), p. 8.

73. T. Singeris and M. Mignault, "Tackling Pension Legislation Compliance," *Canadian HR Reporter* (January 31, 2000), p. 16. See also G.M. Hall, "Pensions: Death by Regulation?" See also J. Nunes, "Defined Benefit or Defined Contribution, It's Always Costly," *Canadian HR Reporter* (November 5, 2001), pp. 7, 9.

74. Sibson, *Wages and Salaries*, p. 234. For an explanation of how to minimize employee benefits litigation related to pension and health benefits claims, see T. Piskorski, "Minimizing Employee Benefits Litigation Through Effective Claims Administration Procedures," *Employee Relations Law Journal* 20, no. 3 (Winter 1994/95), pp. 421–31.

75. *The Economist* (August 5, 1978), p. 57.

76. For a classic discussion of the pros and cons of early retirement, see, for example, J. Sonnenfelt, "Dealing with the Aging Workforce," *Harvard Business Review* 57 (November–December 1978), pp. 81–92.

77. M. Banks and M. Lowry, "Changing Workforce Requires Rethinking of Pension Plan," *Canadian HR Reporter* (March 10, 1997), p. 17.

78. J. Pearce, "Switching from Defined Benefits to a Money Purchase Plan? Think Twice." *Canadian HR Reporter* (October 6, 1997), pp. 20, 23.

79. A. Shad, "When the Angry Mob Comes Knocking," *Canadian HR Reporter* (December 2, 2002), p. G6; C. Ripsman and O. Sharma, "More Than Ever, Good Governance, Smart Management Crucial," *Canadian HR Reporter* (November 4, 2002), pp. 7, 9; and L. Satov, "Time for Sponsors to Rethink Pension Plans," *Canadian HR Reporter* (October 7, 2002), pp. 22, 23.

80. B. Hayhoe, "The Case for Retirement Planning."

81. B. Hayhoe and A. Shad, "Changes to Pension Regulations in the Works," *Canadian HR Reporter* (March 24, 2003), pp. 12, 14.

82. K. Press, "Top 50 Defined Contribution Pension Funds," *Benefits Canada* (August 1999), pp. 33–42.

83. J. Thompson and P.C. Statler, "Sound Options Make for Sound Choices," *Canadian HR Reporter* (February 9, 1998), p. 10.

84. K. Press, "Top 10 Defined Contribution Pension Funds."

85. W. Babcock and C. Pitcher, " Building the Perfect Plan," *Benefits Canada* (May 2000), pp. 33–35.

86. A. Pun, "The Tide Turns on Same-Sex Spousal Benefits," *Canadian HR Reporter* (August 9, 1999), p. G4. See also "Same-Sex Legislation Rolls Out," *Canadian HR Reporter* (November 15, 1999), pp. 3, 6.

87. D. Connor, "Curtains for Early Retirement Windows?" *Canadian HR Reporter* (June 15, 1998), p. 7. See also C. Boates, "Phased Retirement," *Canadian HR Reporter* (August 10, 1998), p. G11.

88. R. Stuart and C. Graham, "Early Retirement on the Bargaining Table," *Canadian HR Reporter* (January 27, 2003), pp. 12, 15.

89. J. Chevreau, "Older Workers Plan to Stay," *National Post* (February 15, 2002).

90. D. Kadlec, "Everyone, Back in the Labour Pool," *TIME* (July 29, 2002), pp. 19–27.

91. "Phased Retirement Gaining Converts," *Canadian HR Reporter* (June 1, 1998), p. 6. See also L. Ramsay, "Pliant Pension Rules Key to Phased-In Retirement," *Financial Post* (February 9, 1995), p. 19; and " Phased-Retirement Program for N.B. Nurses," *Canadian HR Reporter* (June 16, 2003), p. 2.

92. S. Smolkin, "Bowing Out Gracefully," *Benefits Canada* (October 1996), p. 40.

93. "New Quebec Legislation for Phased-In Retirement," *Canadian HR Reporter* (August 10, 1998), p. G11.

94. D, Brown, "Growing Need for SERPs to Top Up Retirement Income," *Canadian HR Reporter* (January 15, 2001), pp. 1–2; D. Ethier, S. Hajee and I. Markham, "The SERP Solution," *Benefits Canada* (February 2001), pp. 47–49; G. Stromberg, "Supplemental Plans," *Benefits Canada* (February 2003), p. 17; and G. Schnurr, "Ottawa Increased Pension Limits but Top-ups for Top Earners Still Needed," *Canadian HR Reporter* (August 11, 2003), pp. 18–19.

95. See Henderson, *Compensation Management*, pp. 336–39. See also L. Burger, "Group Legal Service Plans: A Benefit Whose Time Has Come," *Compensation and Benefits Review* 18 (July–August 1986), pp. 28–34.

96. A. Davis, "Helping Hands," *Benefits Canada* (November 2000), pp. 117–121; and P. Davies, "Problem Gamblers in the Workplace," *Canadian HR Reporter* (November 4, 2002), p. 17.

97. F. Engel, "Lost Profits, Increased Costs: The Aftermath of Workplace Trauma," *Canadian HR Reporter* (September 7, 1998), pp. 21–22.

98. G. Kurzawa, "Cooking Up an EAP," *Canadian HR Reporter* (September 7, 1998), p. 19. See also A. Sharratt, "When a Tragedy Strikes," *Benefits Canada* (November 2002), pp. 101–105; D. Rosolen, "Situation Critical," *Benefits Canada* (November 2001), pp. 29–35; and J. Hobel, "EAPs Flounder Without Manager Support," *Canadian HR Reporter* (June 2, 2003), p.7).

99. J. Hampton, "Rougher Ride at Work: Sharp Upturn in EAP Use," *Canadian HR Reporter* (December 2, 1996), p. 25. See also A. Leckie, "Rapid EAP Growth Raises Quality Concerns," *Canadian HR Reporter* (May 8, 1995), p. 17.

100. A. Davis, "Helping Hands."

101. "Employee Benefit Costs," *BNA Bulletin to Management* (January 16, 1992), pp. 12–14.

102. "100 Best Companies to Work For," *Fortune* (January 2000).

103. C. Davenport, "Child Care Solutions for a Harried Work World," *Canadian HR Reporter* (April 21, 1997), p. 16. See also C. Eichman and B. Reisman, "How Small Employers Are Benefiting from Offering Child Care Assistance," *Employment Relations Today* (Spring 1992), pp. 51–62.

104. D. Brown, "Bringing the Family to Work," *Canadian HR Reporter* (November 6, 2000), pp. 19–20.

105. D. Brown, "Bringing the Family to Work," *Canadian HR Reporter* (November 6, 2000), pp. 19–20.

106. L. Johnson, "Effectiveness of an Employee-Sponsored Child Care Center," *Applied H.R.M. Research* 2 (Summer 1991), pp. 38–67.

107. Commerce Clearing House, "As the Population Ages, There Is Growing Interest in Adding Elder Care to the Benefits Package," *Ideas and Trends* (August 21, 1987), pp. 129–31. See also "Elder Care to Eclipse Child Care, Report Says," *Canadian HR Reporter* (August 14, 1995), p. 11. See also D. Brown, "Senate Proposes Leave Benefits for Palliative Care," *Canadian HR Reporter* (July 17, 2000), pp. 1, 6.

108. N. Spinks, "'We are Taking Gran to the Hospital': Eldercare Unpredictable, Exhausting," *Canadian HR Reporter* (December 16, 2002), pp. 7, 10.

109. P. Kulig, "Eldercare Issues Loom for Canadian Organizations," *Canadian HR Reporter* (May 4, 1998), pp. 1, 2. See also A. Vincola, "Eldercare—What Firms Can Do to Help," *Canadian HR Reporter* (June 5, 2000), p. G3; and D. Brown, "Senate Proposes Leave Benefits for Palliative Care."

110. A. Tomlinson, "Trickle Down Effects of Retiring Boomers," *Canadian HR Reporter* (June 3, 2002), pp. 1, 12.

111. K. Earhart, R.D. Middlemist, and W. Hopkins, "Elder Care: An Emerging Employee Assistance Issue," *Employee Assistance Quarterly* 8 (1993), pp. 1–10.

112. A. Vincola, "Eldercare—What Firms Can Do to Help."

113. M. Zippo, "Subsidized Employee Transportation: A Three Way Benefit," *Personnel* 57 (May–June 1980), pp. 40–41.

114. Hewitt Associates, *Survey of Educational Reimbursement Programs* (1984).

115. D. Brown, "Ford, Delta Equip Staff With Home Computers," *Canadian HR Reporter* (February 28, 2000), pp. 1, 23.

116. D. Dyck, "Make Your Workplace Family-Friendly," *Canadian HR Reporter* (December 13, 1999), pp. G5, G10.

117. "Work/Life Perks Often Avoided by Workers, Poll Finds," *BNA Bulletin to Management* (March 19, 1998), p. 81.

118. W. Burgoyne and P. Leblanc, "Pregnancy-Friendly Firms Create Loyalty, Improve Morale and Ease the Return To Work," *Canadian HR Reporter* (December 13, 1999), pp. 21–22.

119. N. Larin, "Progressive Companies Recognize Value of Family-Friendly Policies," *Canadian HR Reporter* (November 2, 1998), p. 4.

120. D. Brown, "Federal Government Jumps on Family-Friendly Bandwagon," *Canadian HR Reporter* (November 15, 1999), p. 2.

121. L. Fraught, "At Eddie Bauer You Can Have Work and Have a Life," *Workforce* (April 1997), p. 84.

122. L. Fraught, "At Eddie Bauer You Can Have Work and Have a Life," p. 84.

123. E.E. Kossek and C. Ozeki, "Work-Family Conflict, Policies, and the Job-Life Satisfaction Relationship: A Review and Direction for Organizational Behavior-Human Resources Research," *Journal of Applied Psychology* 83 (1998), pp. 139–149.

124. E.E. Kossek and C. Ozeki, "Work-Family Conflict, Policies, and the Job-Life Satisfaction Relationship."

125. B. Ellig, *Executive Compensation—A Total Pay Perspective* (New York: McGraw-Hill, 1982), p. 141.

126. P. Clark, "Relocation Perks are Tops With Executives," *Canadian HR Reporter* (June 1, 1998), p. G4.

127. "Wellness Perks Highly Valued," *Canadian HR Reporter* (November 15, 1999), p. 10.

128. J. Krauss, "Online Concierge," *Canadian HR Reporter* (August 14, 2000), p. 17.

129. M. Budman, "The Persistence of Perks," *Across the Board* (February 1994), pp. 44–46.

130. J.B. Chapman and R. Ottermann, *Employee Preference for Various Compensation and Fringe Benefit Options* (Berea, OH: ASPA Foundation, 1975). See also W. White and J. Becker, "Increasing the Motivational Impact of Employee Benefits," *Personnel* (January–February 1980), pp. 32–37; and B. Olmsted and S. Smith, "Flex for Success!" *Personnel* 66, no. 6 (June 1989), pp. 50–55.

131. M. Levy, "The ABCs of Cafeteria Plans," *Workspan* (June 2002), pp. 43–46.

132. L. Byron and R. Dawson, "Choosing Well," *Benefits Canada* (April 2003), pp. 82–85. See also A. Khemani, "Why Isn't Everybody Flexing Their Benefits?" *Canadian HR Reporter* (June 18, 2001), p. G5; D. Brown, "Everybody Loves Flex," *Canadian HR Reporter* (November 18, 2002), pp. 1, 11; and D. Woolf, "The Diversity Matrix: Responding to the Benefits Preferences of a Diverse Workforce," *Canadian HR Reporter* (July 16, 2001), p. 20.

133. J. Taggart, "Putting Flex Benefits Through Their Paces," *Canadian HR Reporter* (December 2, 2002), p. G3; L. Byron and R. Dawson, "Choosing Well"; and *Flex-ability: Employer Attitudes Toward Flexible Benefits.*

134. D. Brown, "Everybody Loves Flex."

135. *Flex-ability: Employer Attitudes Toward Flexible Benefits.*

136. For information about this program, contact Towers, Perrin, Forster, and Crosby, 245 Park Avenue, New York, NY 10167. Hewitt Associates similarly has a program called FlexSystem (Hewitt Associates, New York, NY).

137. D. Woolf, "Total Flex Appeal," *Benefits Canada* (June 1998), pp. 40–42.

138. J. Tompkins, "Moving Out: A Look at Comprehensive Benefits Outsourcing," *Canadian HR Reporter* (May 5, 1997), p. 9.

139. A. Czarnecki, "Employees Show Increasing Interest in Pension Communication Systems," *Canadian HR Reporter* (July 15, 1996), p. 18. See also J. Kopach "Today's Flexible Benefits Programs Call for Greater Employee Education," *Canadian HR Reporter* (August 9, 1999), p. G3.

140. N. Chaplick, "Enter at Your Own Risk," *Benefits Canada* (May 2000), pp. 37–39. See also M. Reid, "Legal Aid," *Benefits Canada* (June 2000), pp. 46–48; S. Deller, "Five Hot Survival Tips for Communicating Benefits," *Canadian HR Reporter* (July 13, 1998), pp. 9, 19.

141. F.G. Kuzmits, "Communicating Benefits: A Double-Click Away," *Compensation and Benefits Review* (September/October 1998), pp. 60–64. See also D. McElroy, "Six Golden Rules of Intranet Benefit Communication," *Canadian HR Reporter* (October 18, 1999), pp. 6, 9; S. Felix, "Techno-Benefits," *Benefits Canada* (January 2000), pp. 27–34.

142. C. Davenport, "Employers Twig to Value of Ongoing Pension Communication," *Canadian HR Reporter* (December 16, 1996), p. 33.

Chapter 14

1. D. Brown, "Wellness Programs Bring Healthy Bottom Line," *Canadian HR Reporter* (December 17, 2001), pp. 1, 14.

2. www.awcbc.org (June 1, 2003).

3. D. Brown, "Labour Says Some Accidents a Crime," *Canadian HR Reporter* (May 20, 2002), p. 3.

4. Statistics Canada, *Health Status of Canadians*, Chapter 6 (1994).

5. This section is based on T.A. Opie and L. Bates, *1997 Canadian Master Labour Guide* (CCH Canada Inc.), pp. 1015–34.

6. M. Pilger, "Conducting a Hygiene Assessment," *Canadian HR Reporter* (April 10, 2000), pp. G3, G4.

7. J. Montgomery, *Occupational Health and Safety* (Toronto: Nelson Canada, 1996), p. 97.

8. D. Brown, "Joint H&S Committees: An Opportunity, Not a Nuisance," *Canadian HR Reporter* (October 20, 2002), pp. 7, 10.

9. J.E. Canto-Thaler, "Employers Should Be Ready for Inspectors' Visits," *Canadian HR Reporter* (April 10, 1995), p. 8.

10. N. Keith, "Decreasing Your H&S Liability," *Canadian HR Reporter* (April 10, 2000), p. G4.

11. V. Lu, "GM Guilty in Safety Violation That Led to Worker's Death," *Toronto Star* (July 13, 2000), p. A4.

12. "Employer Jailed for H&S Violation," *Canadian HR Reporter* (April 8, 2002), p. 2. See also T. Humber, "Putting the Boss Behind Bars?" *Canadian HR Reporter* (April 7, 2003), pp. 19, 25.

13. M. Draaisma, "Pressure on for Law Making Companies Liable for On-the-Job Deaths," *Workplace News* (September 2000), pp. 1, 7. See also D. Brown, "Labour Says Some Accidents a Crime"; and "Ignoring Safety Garners 'Corporate Killing' Charge," *Canadian HR Reporter* (July 17, 2000), pp. 1, 3.

14. J. Montgomery, *Occupational Health and Safety*, p. 34.

15. P. Strahlendorf, "Tug of War," *OH&S Canada* (March 1997), pp. 36–54.

16. K. Prisciak, "Health, Safety & Harassment?" *OH&S Canada* (April/May 1997), pp. 20–21.

17. P. Strahlendorf, "What Supervisors Need to Know," *OH&S Canada* (January/February 1996), pp. 38–40.

18. A. Macaulay, "Basic Health and Safety Training Key to a Safer Workplace," *Canadian HR Reporter* (October 9, 2000), pp. 7, 9.

19. N. Tompkins, "Getting the Best Help from Your Safety Committee," *HR Magazine* 40, no. 4 (April 1995), p. 76.

20. D.S. Thelan, D. Ledgerwood, and C.F. Walters, "Health and Safety in the Workplace: A New Challenge for Business Schools," *Personnel Administrator* 30, no. 10 (October 1985), p. 44.

21. A.W. Hammer, *Occupational Safety Management and Engineering*, 3rd ed. (Upper Saddle River, NJ: Prentice Hall, 1985).

22. L. Jack, "Tunnel Vision," *OH&S Canada* (January/February 1997), pp. 31–37.

23. *A Safety Committee Man's Guide*, Aetna Life and Casualty Insurance Company, Catalog 872684.

24. J. Roughton, "Job Hazard Analysis," *OH&S Canada* (January/February 1996), pp. 41–44.

25. A. Fowler, "How to Make the Workplace Safer," *People Management* 1, no. 2 (January, 1995), pp. 38–39.

26. List of unsafe acts from *A Safety Committee Man's Guide*, Aetna Life and Casualty Insurance Company.

27. E. McCormick and J. Tiffin, *Industrial Psychology* (Englewood Cliffs, NJ: Prentice Hall, 1974).

28. E. McCormick and J. Tiffin, *Industrial Psychology* (Englewood Cliffs, NJ: Prentice Hall, 1974), pp. 522–23; Norman Maier, *Psychology and Industrial Organization* (Boston: Houghton-Mifflin, 1965), pp. 458–62; Milton Blum and James Nayler, *Industrial Psychology* (New York: Harper & Row, 1968), pp. 519–31. For example, David DeJoy, "Attributional Processes and Hazard Control Management in Industry," *Journal of Safety Research* 16 (Summer 1985), pp. 61–71.

29. McCormick and Tiffin, *Industrial Psychology*, p. 523.

30. P. Finn and B. Bragg, "Perceptions of the Risk of an Accident by Young and Older Drivers," *Accident Analysis and Prevention* 18, no. 4 (August 1986). See also O. Mitchell, "The Relation of Age to Workplace Injuries," *Monthly Labor Review* 111, no. 7 (July 1988), pp. 8–13.

31. M. Philp, "Young Workers Face High Risks," *The Globe & Mail* (July 10, 2000), p. A2. See also D. Brown, "Good Intentions—Heartbreaking Results," *Canadian HR Reporter* (November 20, 2000), pp. 1, 7.

32. "Remembering Young Workers Turned Victims," *Canadian HR Reporter* (May 5, 2003), p. 6; and D. Brown, "Many Young Workers Die Before 1st Payday," *Canadian HR Reporter* (May 5, 2003), p. 6.

33. Blum and Nayler, *Industrial Psychology*, p. 522.

34. M. Frone, "Predictors of Work Injuries Among Employed Adolescents," *Journal of Applied Psychology* 83, no. 4 (1998), pp. 565–76.

35. P. Kulig, "Behavior-Based Programs Aim to Limit Mishaps," *Canadian HR Reporter* (May 18, 1998), p. 2.

36. Miner and Brewer, "Management of Ineffective Performance," in Dunnette, ed., *Handbook of Industrial and Organizational Psychology*, pp. 1004–05.

37. G. Borofsky, M. Bielema, and J. Hoffman, "Accidents, Turnover, and Use of a Pre-employment Screening Interview," *Psychological Reports* (1993), pp. 1067–76.

38. L. Ebbs, "The Safety Culture," *Human Resources Professional* (October/November 1998), pp. 22–26.

39. L. Scott, "Measuring Employee Abilities," *Benefits Canada* (September 2002), pp. 41–49.

40. *Workers' Compensation Manual for Managers and Supervisors* (Chicago: Commerce Clearing House, 1992), pp. 22–23.

41. K. Gillin, "Reduce Employee Exposure to Injury With Pre-Employment Screening Tests," *Canadian HR Reporter* (February 28, 2000), p. 10.

42. H.A. Amolins, "Safety Perception: What Do Your Employees Really Think?" *Canadian HR Reporter* (September 21, 1998), p. 8.

43. B. Broadbent, "The Training Alternative," *OH&S Canada* (July–August 1996), pp. 36–41.

44. A group of international experts met in Belgium in 1986 and concluded that a successful safety poster must be simple and specific and reinforce safe behaviour rather than negative behaviour. See "What Makes an Effective Safety Poster," *National Safety and Health News* 134, no. 6 (December 1986), pp. 32–34.

45. "Immigrants at Higher Risk for Injury, Calgary Study Finds," *Canadian HR Reporter* (February 23, 1998), pp. 1, 8.

46. F. Wahl, Jr., "Soup's on for Safety," *National Safety and Health News* 134, no. 6 (December 1986), pp. 49–53. For a discussion of how employee involvement can impact job re-design and employee safety, see D. May and C. Schwoerer, "Employee Health by Design: Using Employee Involvement Teams in Ergonomics Job Redesign," *Personnel Psychology* 47, no. 4 (Winter, 1994), pp. 861–76.

47. M. Shaw, "Rewarding Health and Safety," *Canadian HR Reporter* (December 2, 2002), pp. 19–20.

48. J. Lutness, "Self-managed Safety Program Gets Workers Involved," *Safety and Health* 135, no. 4 (April 1987), pp. 42–45. See also F. Streff, M. Kalsher, and E. S. Geller, "Developing Efficient Workplace Safety Programs: Observations of Response Co-Variations," *Journal of Organizational Behavior Management* 13, no. 2 (1993), pp. 3–14.

49. L. Young, "Communicating Heath and Safety Where it Matters," *Canadian HR Reporter* (May 17, 1999), p. 12.

50. W. Kincaid, "10 Habits of Effective Safety Managers," *Occupational Hazards*, Vol. 58, no. 11 (November 1996), pp. 41–43.

51. "With Pay on the Line, Managers Improve Safety," *BNA Bulletin to Management*, March 20, 1997, p. 89. See also C.A. Edwards, "Discipline for Safety Infractions...Or Suffer the Consequences," *OH&S Canada* (January/February 2000), pp. 32–37.

52. D. Hofmann and A. Stetzer, "A Cross-Level Investigation of Factors Influencing Unsafe Behaviors and Accidents," *Personnel Psychology* 49 (1996), p. 329.

53. L. Scott, "Measuring Employee Abilities."

54. *Workers' Compensation Manual for Managers and Supervisors*, pp. 36–39.

55. *Workers' Compensation Manual for Managers and Supervisors*, p. 51.

56. C. Colacci, "Meet Your Return to Work Obligations With a Functional Abilities Evaluation," *Canadian HR Reporter* (April 10, 2000), p. G5.

57. A. Bierbier, "Controlling Sky-High Absenteeism," *OH&S Canada* (January–February 1996), pp. 54–63.

58. Sobeco, Ernst, and Young, *OH&S Canada* (January–February 1996), p. 10.

59. S. Ritcey, "Psychological Job Matching," *OH&S Canada* (September–October 1996), pp. 50–56.

60. M. Morales, "Canada All Talk, No Action in Wellness," *Canadian HR Reporter* (April 22, 2002), pp. 23, 29.

61. D. Dyck, "Wrapping Up the Wellness Package," *Benefits Canada* (January 1999), pp. 16–20. See also T. Wallace, "An Ounce of Prevention," *Canadian HR Reporter* (April 23, 2001), pp. 15, 19.

62. S. Pellegrini, "The Next 25 Years: Wellness," *Benefits Canada* (June 2002), pp. 83–85.

63. L. Young, "Wellness: The Future of Traditional Health and Safety," *Canadian HR Reporter* (February 28, 2000), pp. 7, 11.

64. L. Young, "Managers at B.C. Telus Held Accountable for Wellness," *Canadian HR Reporter* (February 28, 2000), p. 9.

65. S. Felix, "Wellness Workout," *Benefits Canada* (January 1998), pp. 25–30.

66. A. Tomlinson, "Healthy Living a Remedy for Burgeoning Employee Absentee Rates," *Canadian HR Reporter* (March 25, 2002), pp. 3, 12.

67. G. Lowe, "The Dollars and Sense of Health Promotion," *Canadian HR Reporter* (September 23, 2002), pp. 7–8.

68. L. Owen, "Working on Healthy Outcomes," *Benefits Canada* (February 2003), pp. 39–42.

69. D. Brown, "Canada Trails U.S. in Wellness," *Canadian HR Reporter* (June 5, 2000), pp. 1, 6. See also "Canadian Companies Lag on Wellness," *Canadian HR Reporter* (October 23, 2000), p. 17; E. Buffett, "The Wellness Myth," *Benefits Canada* (February 2002), pp. 26–27; and G. Lowe, "The Dollars and Sense of Health Promotion."

70. B. Bouw, "Employers Embrace Wellness at Work," *The Globe & Mail* (April 10, 2002). See also M. Morales, "Canada All Talk, No Action on Wellness."

71. K. Dorrell, "Making A Case," *Benefits Canada* (June 2000), p. 23.

72. This section based largely on Miner and Brewer, "Management of Ineffective Performance," pp. 1005–23.

73. "Addiction Problems in Manufacturing," *Canadian HR Reporter* (March 24, 2003), p. 3.

74. A. Chiu, "The Elements of Workplace Drug, Alcohol Policies," *Canadian HR Reporter* (March 13, 2000), p. 17.

75. S. Kennedy, "Substance Abuse Equals Absenteeism: Broad-based Workplace Initiatives Required," *Canadian HR Reporter* (April 9, 2001), p. G3.

76. A. Chiu, "The Elements of Workplace Drug, Alcohol Policies."

77. M. Johne, "Clean and Sober: Dealing With Drugs and Alcohol in the Workplace," *HR Professional* (October/November 1999), pp. 18–22.

78. Pati and Adkins, "Employer's Role in Alcoholism Assistance." See also Commerce Clearing House, "How Should Employers Respond to Indications an Employee May Have an Alcohol or Drug Problem?" *Ideas and Trends* (April 6, 1989), pp. 53–57.

79. S. Kennedy, "Substance Abuse Equals Absenteeism."

80. Based on Miner and Brewer, "Management of Ineffective Performance." The survey was conducted jointly by the American Society for Personnel Administration and the Bureau of National Affairs.

81. J. Butler, "Business, Community Create Addictions Service," *Canadian HR Reporter* (September 20, 1999), pp. 13, 15.

82. Addiction Research Foundation, "Workplace Alcohol and Drug Testing Still Risky Business," *Canadian HR Reporter* (September 8, 1997), p. 22.

83. B. Butler, "Drug Tests May Not Constitute Impairment Tests," *Canadian HR Reporter* (October 7, 1996), p. 8.

84. D.P. Church and S.D. Matthews, "Providing Alcohol at Work," *OH&S Canada* (July/August 1996), pp. 46–48.

85. Butler, "Drug Tests."

86. J.E. Canto-Thaler, "Drug Testing Remains a Murky Legal Issue," *Canadian HR Reporter* (September 9, 1996), p. 8.

87. A. Chiu, "The Elements of Workplace Drug, Alcohol Policies," p. 17.

88. D. Rosolen, "Stress Test," *Benefits Canada* (February 2002), pp. 22–25. See also A. Sharratt, "Silver Linings," *Benefits Canada* (March 2003), pp. 51–53.

89. "Nearly Half of Workers Stressed Out," *Canadian HR Reporter* (June 5, 2000), p. 6.

90. "Work Pressure Top Cause of Stress," *Workplace Today* (January 2001), p. 6.

91. P. Kulig, "Mental Health a Growing Business Concern," *Canadian HR Reporter* (October 19, 1998), pp. 1, 3.

92. "Push for Productivity Taking Its Toll," *Canadian HR Reporter* (November 6, 2001), p.15; and D. Brown, "Doing More with Less Hurts Employees and Productivity," *Canadian HR Reporter* (October 7, 2002), pp. 3, 13.

93. A. Sharratt, "Silver Linings."

94. *1999 Employment Insurance Monitoring and Assessment Report.* Human Resources Development Canada. See also D. Brown, "EI Claims From Stress and Illness Increasing," *Canadian HR Reporter* (April 24, 2000), p. 6. See also J. Santa-Barbara, "Preventing the Stress Epidemic."

95. S. Motowizlo, J. Packard, and M. Manning, "Occupational Stress: Its Causes and Consequences for Job Performance," *Journal of Applied Psychology* 71, no. 4 (November 1986), pp. 618–29.

96. J. Santa-Barbara, "Preventing the Stress Epidemic," *Canadian HR Reporter* (March 8, 1999), p. 19. See also A. Chiu, "Beyond Physical Wellness: Mental Health Issues in the Workplace," *Canadian HR Reporter* (February 26, 2001), p.4; and L. Hyatt, "Job Stress: Have We Reached the Breaking Point?" *Workplace Today* (January 2002), pp. 14, 15, 37.

97. D. Brown, "Call to Action in War Against Mental Illness," *Canadian HR Reporter* (November 4, 2002), pp. 1, 11.

98. M. Commanducci, "Brief Workplace Stress Linked to Heart Attacks," *Canadian HR Reporter* (April 20, 1998), p. 12. See also J. Gooding, "Depression a 'Clear and Present Danger' to Business," *Canadian HR Reporter* (February 8, 1999), p. 1.

99. "Longer Hours, Poorer Health," *Canadian HR Reporter* (December 3, 1999), p. 6.

100. S. Felix, "Taking the Sting Out of Stress," *Benefits Canada* (November 1998), pp. 21–24.

101. P. Crawford-Smith, "Stressed Out," *Benefits Canada* (November 1999), pp. 115–17.

102. J. Newman and T. Beehr, "Personal and Organizational Strategies for Handling Job Stress: A Review of Research and Opinion," *Personnel Psychology* (Spring 1979), pp. 1–43. See also Bureau of National Affairs, "Work Place Stress: How to Curb Claims," *Bulletin to Management* (April 14, 1988), p. 120.

103. J.K. Yardley, "Do Your Managers Roll Their Eyes When Employees Say They Are Overworked?" *Canadian HR Reporter* (April 23, 2001), pp. 18–19.

104. C. Marmer Solomon, "Stressed to the Limit," *Workforce* (September 1999), pp. 48–54.

105. T. Humber, "Stress Attack," *Canadian HR Reporter* (February 10, 2002), pp. G1, G10.

106. M. Shain, "Stress and Satisfaction," *OH&S Canada* (April/May 1999), pp. 38–47.

107. J. Hampton, "HR Execs Key to Combating Workplace Depression," *Canadian HR Reporter* (August 14, 2000), pp. 1, 3.

108. D. Brown, "Call to Action in War Against Mental Illness." See also A. Tomlinson, "Returning to Work After Attempted Suicide," *Canadian HR Reporter* (January 14, 2002), pp. 7, 9; and A. Tomlinson, "Mental Health Costs are High, But Awareness is Low," *Canadian HR Reporter* (January 14, 2002), pp. 7, 10.

109. T. Humber, "Stress Attack."

110. M. Leiter, D. Clark, and J. Durup, "Distinct Models of Burnout and Commitment Among Men and Women in the Military," *Journal of Applied Behavioral Science* 30, no. 1 (March 1994), pp. 63–64.

111. P. Carayon, "Stressful Jobs and Non-Stressful Jobs: A Cluster Analysis of Office Jobs," *Ergonomics* 37, no. 2 (1994), pp. 311–23.

112. Carayon, "Stressful Jobs."

113. Carayon, "Stressful Jobs," pp. 319–20.

114. A. Pihulyk, "When the Job Overwhelms," *Canadian HR Reporter* (January 14, 2002), p. 11.

115. M. Gibb-Clark, "The Case for Compensating Stress Claims," *The Globe & Mail* (June 14, 1999), p. M1.

116. L. Young, "Stressed Workers are Suing Employers," *Canadian HR Reporter* (May 3, 1999), pp. 1, 6.

117. D. Brown, "Liability Could Extend to Mental Damage," *Canadian HR Reporter* (October 9, 2000), pp. 1, 8.

118. A. Tomlinson, "WSIB Considers Redefining Stress," *Canadian HR Reporter* (November 19, 2001), pp. 1, 16.

119. I. Parvanova, "Repetitive Strain Injuries: Can You Afford Them?" *Workplace Today* (June 1999), pp. 36, 37, 43. See also "Ergonomics Not a Priority," www.workplace.ca/ article3/wednesday.html (September 20, 2000); and H. Tick, "Repetitive Stress Injuries a Continuing Concern," *Canadian HR Reporter* (April 22, 2002), p. 26.

120. J. Tyson, "Pointing to the Problem," *OH&S Canada* (April/May 1998), pp. 54–57.

121. J. Hampton, "RSIs: The Biggest Strain is on the Bottom Line," *Canadian HR Reporter* (February 10, 1997), pp. 15, 19. See also G. Harrington, "Pushing Ergonomics Into Place," *Canadian HR Reporter* (April 24, 1995), pp. 11–12.

122. D. Cole, "The World of Work has Changed Dramatically Since 1913… (Institute for Work and Health, 2000). See also L. Cassiani, "Control Over Work Can Reduce Work-Related Injuries, RSIs," *Canadian HR Reporter* (January 5, 2001), p. 9.

123. S.B. Hood, "Repetitive Strain Injury," *Human Resources Professional* (June/July 1997), pp. 29–34.

124. C. Knight, "Computer Tells Employees to Take a Break," *Canadian HR Reporter* (April 7, 1997), p. 9.

125. M. Morales, "Ergowatch Gives Canadian Software a Lift," *Canadian HR Reporter* (April 22, 2002), p. 27.

126. J. Purdie, "Better Offices Mean Greater Productivity," *Financial Post* (November 26, 1990), p. 35.

127. G. Harrington, "Older Workers Need Ergonomic Aid," *Canadian HR Reporter* (November 17, 1997), p. 20.

128. B. Weir, "Technology Transforms Workplace Behaviour," *Workplace Today* (October 2000), pp. 36–37.

129. N.J. Gowan, "The Case for Integration," *OH&S Canada Buyer's Guide 1997*, pp. 68–77.

130. J.A. Savage, "Are Computer Terminals Zapping Workers' Health?" *Business and Society Review* (1994).

131. D. Brown, "Killer Toxins in the Workplace," *Canadian HR Reporter* (April 23, 2001), pp. 1, 12.

132. A. Tomlinson, "Manitoba Recognizes Firefighting Cancer Risk," *Canadian HR Reporter* (June 17, 2002), pp. 2, 6. See also W. H. Glenn, "Finding the Right Balance," *OH&S Canada* (June 2002) pp. 38–43; and W.H. Glenn, "What's Killing Canadian Workers?" *OH&S Canada* (August 2002), p. 20.

133. D. Warner, "'We Do Not Hire Smokers': May Employers Discriminate Against Smokers?" *Employee Responsibilities and Rights Journal* 7, no. 2 (1994), p. 129.

134. L. Bachman and E. Buffett, "Corporate Fitness in Motion," *Canadian HR Reporter* (January 29, 2001), pp. 14, 17.

135. "EI Granted in Second-Hand Smoke Case," *Canadian HR Reporter* (May 19, 2003), p. 3. See also M.M. Finklestein, "Risky Business," *OH&S Canada* (September/October 1996), pp. 32–34.

136. R.G. Wyckham, "Regulating the Marketing of Tobacco Products in Controlling Smoking in Canada," *Canadian Journal of Administrative Sciences* 14, no. 2 (June 1997), pp. 141–65. See also "Cigarettes a B.C. Workplace Hazard," *Canadian HR Reporter* (November 7, 1997), p. 11.

137. W.H. Glenn, "Workplace Violence: An Employees' Survival Guide," *OH&S Canada* (April/May 2002), pp. 26–31.

138. G. Smith, "Violence at Work," *Benefits Canada* (June 1999), pp. 22–25. See also W.H. Glenn, "Workplace Violence"; D. Hynes, *Preventing Workplace Violence: Towards an Aggression-Free Workplace* (Conference Board of Canada, August 2001); and "Violence at Work," *Canadian HR Reporter* (June 2, 2003), p. 2.

139. "Looking Out for Trouble," *OH&S Canada* (March/April 1995), pp. 34–37. See also "Physician Abuse of Nurses," *Canadian HR Reporter* (October 22, 2001), p. 2.

140. J. Montgomery, *Occupational Health and Safety*, p. 297.

141. S.A. Baron, *Violence in the Workplace* (Ventura CA: Pathfinder Publishing, 1993), p. 98.

142. E. Newton, "Clear Policy, Active Ear Can Reduce Violence," *Canadian HR Reporter* (February 26, 1996), pp. 16–17.

143. G. Smith, *Work Rage* (Toronto: HarperCollins, 2000).

144. D. Brown, "Canadian Workplace Violence on the Rise," *Canadian HR Reporter* (May 22, 2000), pp. 1, 3. See also L. Young, "On-the-Job Harassment Precipitates Co-Worker Violence: Inquest," *Canadian HR Reporter* (March 27, 2000), pp. 1, 3.

145. D. Tona, "Coming to Terms With Tragedy at Work," *Canadian HR Reporter* (September 25, 2000), pp. 22–23.

146. "Violence Caused by Workplace Failures," *OH&S Canada* (September/October 1996), p. 15.

147. G. Smith, *Work Rage*.

148. A. Feliu, "Workplace Violence and the Duty of Care: The Scope of an Employer's Obligation to Protect Against the Violent Employee," *Employee Relations Law Journal* 20, no. 3 (Winter 1994/95), pp. 381–406.

149. K. Blair, "Employers on the Hook for Sexual Assault," *Canadian HR Reporter* (June 16, 1997), p. 5.

150. F. Engel, *Taming the Beast: Getting Violence Out of the Workplace* (Montreal: Ashwell, 1998).

151. G. French and P. Morgan, "The Risks of Workplace Violence," *Canadian HR Reporter* (December 18, 2000), pp. 27–28.

152. L.M. Bernardi, "The Legal Case Against Bullying in the Workplace," *Canadian HR Reporter* (November 5, 2001), pp. 10–12.

153. L. Martin, "Taking Action Against Workplace Violence," *Canadian HR Reporter* (April 10, 2000), p. G6.

154. "Workplace Violence: Sources and Solutions," *BNA Bulletin to Management* (November 4), 1993, p. 345.

155. *Workplace Violence: Sources and Solutions*. See also A. Tomlinson, "Re-evaluating Your Workplace: Is It Safe and Secure?" *Canadian HR Reporter* (February 25, 2002), pp. 3, 12.

156. L. Martin, "Taking Action Against Workplace Violence."

157. L. Martin and D. Tona, "Before It's Too Late," *OH&S Canada* (April/May 2000), pp. 52–53.

158. Feliu, "Workplace Violence and the Duty of Care," p. 395.

159. D. Anfuso, "Workplace Violence," *Personnel Journal* (October 1994), pp. 66–77.

160. Feliu, "Workplace Violence and the Duty of Care," p. 395.

161. Quoted from Feliu, "Workplace Violence and the Duty of Care," p. 395.

162. Anfuso, "Workplace Violence," p. 71. See also L. Martin and D. Tona, "Before It's Too Late," *OH&S Canada* (April/May 2000), pp. 52–53; H. Bloom, "Workplace Violence: The Myth that We're Helpless," *Workplace Today* (January 2002), pp. 36–37; and W.H. Glenn, "Workplace Violence."

163. D. Brown, "Canadian Workplace Violence on the Rise."

164. "Preventing Workplace Violence," *BNA Bulletin to Management* (June 10, 1993), p. 177. See also J. McCune, "Companies Grapple with Workplace Violence," *Management Review* 83, no. 3 (March 1994), pp. 52–57.

165. Quoted or paraphrased from "Preventing Workplace Violence," p. 177.

166. D. Rosato, "New Industry Helps Managers Fight Violence," *USA Today* (August 8, 1995), p. 1.

Chapter 15

1. Y. Cohen-Charash and P.E. Spector, "The Role of Justice in Organizations: A Meta-Analysis," *Organizational Behavior and Human Decision Processes* 86 (November 2001), pp. 278–321.

2. K. Blair, "How Not to Foil A Union Drive," *Canadian HR Reporter* (March 10, 1997), p. 1.

3. M. Rowbotham, "Mitigate Corporate Liability Through Employee Communication," *Canadian HR Reporter* (December 3, 2001), p. G7.

4. *Think Magazine* 55, no. 6 (1989).

5. "Big Payoff For Employee Suggestions," *Canadian HR Reporter* (September 25, 1995), p. 7.

6. P. Kulig, "The Importance of Being a Good Listener," *Canadian HR Reporter* (April 20, 1998), pp. 15, 19. See also D. Jones, "What if You Held a Survey and No-one Came?" *Canadian HR Reporter* (July 16, 2001), pp. 19, 22.

7. D. Brown, "Getting the Hard Facts in Employee Attitude and Satisfaction," *Canadian HR Reporter* (November 1, 1999), p. 2.

8. This section is based on D. McElroy, "High Tech With High Touch: A New Communication Contract," *Canadian HR Reporter* (April 7, 1997), p. G6.

9. B. Orr, "Privacy in the Workplace A Growing Challenge for Employers," *Canadian HR Reporter* (January 25, 1999), pp. 8, 10.

10. P. Israel, "Employee Misconduct ... Employer Responsibility?" *Canadian HR Reporter* (May 20, 2002), p. 5. See also "Developing Internet Policies for Employees," *Canadian HR Reporter* (November 16, 1998), p. 23.

11. A. Tomlinson, "Heavy-handed Net Policies Push Privacy Boundaries," *Canadian HR Reporter* (December 2, 2002), pp. 1, 26.

12. "We Know Where You've Been," *Canadian HR Reporter* (August 13, 2001), p. 7.

13. J. Conforti, *Privacy in the Workplace: Access to Employee Records and Monitoring of Employees in the Internet Age.* Paper presented at the Human Resources Professionals Association of Ontario Employment Law Conference, October 1999, Toronto.

14. E.A. Douthitt and J.R. Aiello, "The Role of Participation and Control in the Effects of Computer Monitoring on Fairness Perceptions, Task Satisfaction, and Performance," *Journal of Applied Psychology*, 86 (2001), pp. 867–74.

15. P. Israel, "Spying on Employees ... and It's Perfectly Legal," *Canadian HR Reporter* (April 21, 2003), p. 5. See also P. Bonifero, "Workplace Privacy and Surveillance Issues," *HR Professional* (February/March 1999), pp. 49–51.

16. "Inexcusable E-mails," *Canadian HR Reporter* (July 15, 2002), p. 2.

17. D. Brown, "10 Months to Get Ready," *Canadian HR Reporter* (February 24, 2003), pp. 1, 11.

18. R. Hiscock, "A Perspective on Canada's New Privacy Legislation," *Canadian HR Reporter* (June 18, 2001), pp. G8–G9. See also E. Kuzz, "More Rules for Employee Information Protection," *Canadian HR Reporter* (September 9, 2002), p. 16; and D. Brown, "10 Months to Get Ready."

19. N. Akerman, "Total Rewards on Guard," *Workspan* (December 2002), pp. 46–49; P.S. Eyres, "Impatience: High, Subject: Employee E-mail Policies," *Workspan* (December 2002), pp. 54–56; N. MacDonald, "You've Got E-mail Problems," *Canadian HR Reporter* (March 10, 2003), pp. G5, G10; and A. Tomlinson, "Heavy-handed Net Policies Push Privacy Boundaries." See also J. Conforti, "Privacy in the Workplace: Access to Employee Records and Monitoring of Employees in the Internet Age."

20. S. Ray and D. Holmes, "How to Discipline Without Exposure to Lawsuits," *Canadian HR Reporter* (September 6, 1999), p. 31. See also J. Miller, "Procedural Fairness Toward Disciplined Workers an Issue Before the Courts," *Canadian HR Reporter* (November 2, 1998), p. 5. See also P. Israel, "How to Tackle Poor Job Performance—and Bring Down Legal Costs," *Canadian HR Reporter* (February 10, 2003), pp. 5, 12.

21. G.A. Ball, *Outcomes of Punishment Incidents: The Role of Subordinate Perceptions, Individual Differences, and Leader Behavior.* Unpublished doctoral dissertation. The Pennsylvania State University. See also N. Cole, "Yes, Employees Can React Positively to Discipline," *Canadian HR Reporter* (November 4, 1996), p. 11; and N.D. Cole and G.P. Latham, "Effects of Training in Procedural Justice on Perceptions of Disciplinary Fairness by Unionized Employees and Disciplinary Subject Matter Experts," *Journal of Applied Psychology* 82 (October 1997), pp. 699–705.

22. D. Grote, *Discipline Without Punishment* (New York: American Management Association, 1995).

23. J. Famularo, *Handbook of Modern Personnel Administration* (New York: McGraw-Hill, 1972), pp. 65.3–65.5.

24. Famularo, *Handbook of Modern Personnel Administration.*

25. J. Towler, "Dealing With Employees Who Steal," *Canadian HR Reporter* (September 23, 2002), p. 4.

26. "Air Canada Searches Employee Rooms," *Canadian HR Reporter* (February 10, 2003), p. 2.

27. Famularo, *Handbook of Modern Personnel Administration*, pp. 65.4–65.5.

28. K. Blair, "When is a Firing Justified?" *Canadian HR Reporter* (April 21, 1997), p. 5. See also K. Blair, "Just How Just Does Just Cause Have to Be?" *Canadian HR Reporter* (November 3, 1997), p. 5.

29. E.E. Mole, *Wrongful Dismissal Practice Manual*, Chapter 7 (Toronto: Butterworths Canada Ltd., 1993).

30. Mole, *Wrongful Dismissal*, Chapter 4. See also L. Cassiani, "Dishonesty Not Always Enough to Terminate," *Canadian HR Reporter* (August 13, 2001), pp. 3, 6; and P. Israel, "Firing an Employee for Dishonesty? Put Things in Context First," *Canadian HR Reporter* (August 12, 2002), p. 5.

31. "Proving Cause for Termination Getting Harder," *Workplace Today* (January 2001), p.17; and L. Harris, "High Standards Allow Employer to Fire Threatening Employee," *Canadian HR Reporter* (October 22, 2001), pp. 8, 10.

32. T. Wagar, "Wrongful Dismissal: Perception vs. Reality," *Human Resources Professional* (June 1996), p. 10.

33. K. Blair, "Sports Editor Scores 28-Month Severance," *Canadian HR Reporter* (April 7, 1997), p. 5.

34. M.J. MacKillop, *The Perils of Dismissal: The Impact of the Wallace Decision on Reasonable Notice.* Paper presented at the Human Resources Professionals Association of Ontario Employment Law Conference, October 1999, Toronto. See also M.J. MacKillop, "Bad Faith Discharge Dismissed by S.C.C.," *HR Professional* (April/May 1998), pp. 11–12; K. Blair, "The High Cost of Bad Faith Termination," *Canadian HR Reporter* (December 1, 1997), p. 5. See also J. McAlpine, "Don't Add Bad Faith to Wrongful Dismissal," *Canadian HR Reporter* (May 6, 2002), p. 7; and P. Israel, "Cut Down on Lawsuits Just by Being Nice," *Canadian HR Reporter* (November 18, 2002), p. 5.

35. J. Miller, "Lower Courts Raise Employers' Costs With Higher Extended-Notice Damages," *Canadian HR Reporter* (May 31, 1999), p. 5.

36. M.J. MacKillop, *The Perils of Dismissal: The Impact of the Wallace Decision on Reasonable Notice*, p. 18.

37. K. Blair, "Pay in Lieu Just the Beginning," *Canadian HR Reporter* (July 14, 1997), p. 5. See also K. Blair, "Dismissal Damages, Thy Name is Mitigation," *Canadian HR Reporter* (February 9, 1998), p. 5.

38. J. McApline, "10 Steps for Reducing Exposure to Wrongful Dismissal," *Canadian HR Reporter* (May 6, 2002), p. 8.

39. E. Caruk, "What to do if a Wrongful Dismissal Action Hits," *Canadian HR Reporter* (May 6, 2002), p. 10.

40. Mole, *Wrongful Dismissal*, Chapter 3.

41. "Former TD Executive Awarded $2 Million," *Canadian HR Reporter* (February 14, 2000), p. 20.

42. This section was based on M. Rothman, "Employee Termination, I: A Four-Step Procedure," *Personnel* (February 1989), pp. 31–35; and S. Jesseph, "Employee Termination, II: Some Do's and Don'ts," *Personnel* (February 1989), pp. 36–38. For a good checklist see author Silbergeld, "Avoiding Wrongful Termination Claims: A Checklist for Employers," *Employment Relations Today* 20, no. 4 (Winter, 1993), pp. 447–54.

43. See J. Coil, III and C. Rice, "Three Steps to Creating Effective Employee Releases," *Employment Relations Today* (Spring 1994), pp. 91–94. Wrongful termination is a problem for managerial employees as well. See, for example, C. Longenecker and F. Post, "The Management Termination Trap," *Business Horizons* 37, no. 3 (May–June, 1994), pp. 71–79.

44. E.A. Lind, J. Greenberg, K.S. Scott, and T.D. Welchans, "The Winding Road From Employee to Complainant: Situational and Psychological Determinants of Wrongful Dismissal Claims," *Administrative Science Quarterly*, 45 (2000), pp. 557–90.

45. Based on Coil and Rice, "Three Steps to Creating Effective Employee Releases," p. 92.

46. W.J. Morin and L. York, *Outplacement Techniques* (New York: AMACOM, 1982), pp. 101–31; and F.L. Branham, "How to Evaluate Executive Outplacement Services," *Personnel Journal* 62 (April 1983), pp. 323–26; S. Milne, "The Termination Interview," *Canadian Manager* (Spring 1994), pp. 15–16.

47. Morin and York, *Outplacement Techniques*, p. 117. See also Sonny Weide, "When You Terminate An Employee," *Employment Relations Today* (August 1994), pp. 287–93; and Commerce Clearing House, *Ideas and Trends in Personnel* (July 9, 1982), pp. 132–46.

48. J. Zarandona and M. Camuso, "A Study of Exit Interviews: Does the Last Word Count?" *Personnel* 62, no. 3 (March 1985), pp. 47–48.

49. Quoted from Commerce Clearing House, *Ideas and Trends in Personnel* (August 9, 1988), p. 133.

50. Commerce Clearing House, *Personnel Practices/Communications* (Chicago: CCH, 1992), p. 1402.

51. D. Brown, "Shifting Attention from Recruitment to Layoffs," *Canadian HR Reporter*, September 10, 2001, pp. 1, 6.

52. *Personnel Practices/Communications*, p. 1410.

53. P. Kulig, "Temporary Employment Changing the Character of Canada's Labour Force," *Canadian HR Reporter* (November 16, 1998), pp. 1, 15.

54. "Cutting Labour Costs Without Layoffs," *Canadian HR Reporter* (December 3, 2001), p. 3. See also "Toronto Gets Work Sharing Agreements for Hotel Industry," *WorldatWork Canadian News* (Third Quarter, 2003), p. 19.

55. This is based on *Mossop Cornelissen Report* (August 1996).

56. S. Stephens, "When Two Worlds Collide," *HR Professional* (April/May 2000), pp. 27–35.

57. J. Emshoff, "How to Increase Employee Loyalty While You Downsize," *Business Horizons* (March–April 1994), pp. 49–57. See also R. Ford and P. Perrewé, "After the Layoff: Closing the Barn Door Before All the Horses Are Gone," *Business Horizons* (July–August 1993), pp. 34–40.

58. S. Stephens, "When Two Worlds Collide."

59. J. R. Nininger, *Leaving Work: Managing One of Life's Pivotal Transitions* (Conference Board of Canada, 2002).

60. *1995 Canadian Dismissal Practices Survey* (Toronto: Murray Axmith & Associates).

61. G. Golightly, "Preparing Employees for Retirement Transitions," *HR Professional* (December 1999/January 2000), pp. 27–33.

62. G. Golightly, "Preparing Employees for Retirement Transitions."

Chapter 16

1. D.G. Gallagher and G. Strauss, "Union Membership: Attitudes and Participation," in *The State of the Unions*, G. Strauss, D. Gallagher and J. Fiorito, eds. (Madison, WI: Industrial Relations Research Association, 1991), pp. v–xi.

2. Cited in Lesley Young, "Union Drives: Initiated Within, Prevented Within," *Canadian HR Reporter* (November 29, 1999), p. 14.

3. T.T. Delaney, "Unions and Human Resource Policies," in K. Rowland and G. Ferris, eds., *Research in Personnel and Human Resources Management* (Greenwich, CT: JAI Press, 1991).

4. T. Kochan and H. Katz, *Collective Bargaining and Industrial Relations* (Homewood, IL: Irwin, 1988).

5. "Wal-Mart Gets Slap on Wrist," *Canadian HR Reporter* (June 2, 2003), p. 2.

6. Based on J. Pierce, *Canadian Industrial Relations,* (Scarborough: Prentice Hall Canada Inc., 2000), p. 276.

7. P. Kumar, "Union Growth in Canada: Retrospect and Prospect" in W.C. Riddell, ed., *Canadian Labour Relations* (Toronto: University of Toronto Press, 1986), p. 103.

8. N. Spinks and C. Moore, "Bringing Work–Life Balance to the Table: Unions Adding Work–Life Balance to the Collective Bargaining Process," *Canadian HR Reporter* (April 22, 2002), pp. 14, 15.

9. J.W. Miller Jr., "Power, Politics and the Prospects for Collective Bargaining: An Employer's Viewpoint," in Stanley M. Jacks, ed., *Issues in Labor Policy* (Cambridge: MIT Press, 1971), pp. 3–10.

10. Based on "CAW Ready to Leave CLC," *Canadian HR Reporter* (June 5, 2000), p. 3; and "Union Acrimony," *Canadian HR Reporter* (August 14, 2000), p. 7.

11. T. Koeller, "Union Activity and the Decline in American Trade Union Membership," *Journal of Labor Research* (Winter 1994), pp. 19–32.

12. "You Thought Canada Was Too Unionized," *Canadian HR Reporter* (April 7, 2003).

13. L. Troy, "Can Canada's Labour Policies Be a Model for the United States?" *Proceedings of the 28th Conference of the Canadian Industrial Relations Association* (Kingston, ON: Queen's University, 1991), pp. 59–64.

14. "News Brief: Clerks Now Steelworkers," *Workplace News* (February 1999), p. 6. See also The International Association of Machinists and Aerospace Workers (IAM), "We are the IAM: Many Faces, Diverse Skills, One Union," IAM Web site: www.iamaw.org/canada/iamcanda/mainnew.html (extracted August 28, 2000).

15. E.B. Akyeampong, "Unionization—An Update," *Perspectives on Labour and Income*, Statistics Canada Catalogue No. 75-001 (Autumn 1999), pp. 45–65.

16. "Unions Show Slight Growth in 2002," *Canadian HR Reporter* (September 23, 2002), p. 2.

17. Statistics Canada, *The Rise of Unionization Among Women,* cited in Joey Goodings, "More Women Filling the Ranks of Unions," *Canadian HR Reporter* (January 11, 1999), p. 1.

18. M. Partridge, "Technology, International Competitiveness, and Union Behavior," *Journal of Labor Research* (Spring 1993), pp. 131–45.

19. L. Surtees, "Unions Unite Forces Against Northern Telecom," *The Globe & Mail* (October 18, 1991).

20. Based on D. Moberg, "Like Business, Unions Must Go Global," *The New York Times* (December 13, 1993), p. 13.

21. D. Chamot, "Unions Need to Confront the Results of New Technology," *Monthly Labor Review* (August 1987), p. 45.

22. S. Levitan and F. Gallo, "Collective Bargaining and Private Sector Employment," *Monthly Labor Review* (September 1989), pp. 24–33; B. Ettorre, "Will Unions Survive?" *Management Review* (August 1993) pp. 9–15; "Union Blasts Privatization," *The Peterborough Examiner* (Tuesday, February 8, 2000).

23. Statistics Canada, *Labour Force Survey 2000: Perspectives on Labour and Income.*

24. L. Cassiani, "Still Rare but More Managers Consider Unionization," *Canadian HR Reporter* (November 20, 2000), pp. 1, 8.

25. J. Godard, *Industrial Relations: The Economy and Society* (Toronto: McGraw-Hill Ryerson, 1994), p. 132.

26. G. Betcherman, K. McMullen, N. Leckie, and C. Caron, *The Canadian Workplace in Transition* (Kingston, ON: IRC Press, Queen's University, 1994).

27. T. Rankin, *New Forms of Work Organization: The Challenge for North American Unions* (Toronto: University of Toronto Press, 1990), pp. 150–51.

28. W.C. Hamner and F. Schmidt, "Work Attitude as Predictor of Unionization Activity," *Journal of Applied Psychology* 63, no. 4 (1978), pp. 415–521; A. Okafor, "White Collar Unionization: Why and What to Do," *Personnel* 62, no. 8 (August 1985), pp. 17–20; and M.E. Gordon and A. DiNisi, "A Re-Examination of the Relationship Between Union Membership and Job

Satisfaction," *Industrial and Labor Relations Review* 48, no. 2 (January 1995), pp. 222–236.

29. J. Brett, "Why Employees Want Unions," *Organizational Dynamics*, (Spring 1980); J. Fossum, *Labor Relations* (Dallas: Business Publications, 1982), p. 4.

30. "Union, Non-Union Wage Gap Closing," *Canadian HR Reporter* (October 21, 2002), p. 2.

31. Statistics Canada Internet site, "Unionization—An Update," extracted August 30, 2000.

32. C. Fullager and J. Barling, "A Longitudinal Test of a Model of the Antecedents and Consequences of Union Loyalty," *Journal of Applied Psychology* 74, no. 2 (April 1989), pp. 213–27; A. Eaton, M. Gordon, and J. Keefe, "The Impact of Quality of Work Life Programs and Grievance Systems Effectiveness on Union Commitment," *Industrial and Labor Relations Review* 45, no. 3 (April 1992), pp. 592–604.

33. L. Young, "Union Drives: Initiated Within, Prevented Within," pp. 2, 14.

34. "Union Targets Nova Scotia," *Canadian HR Reporter* (November 4, 2002), p. 2. See also "Where Do We Picket?" *Canadian HR Reporter* (November 5, 2001), p. 5.

35. There is an excellent discussion of the strategies used by union organizers in T.F. Reed, "Profiles of Union Organizers from Manufacturing and Service Unions," *Journal of Labor Research* 11, no. 1 (Winter 1990), pp. 73–80.

36. P. Kumar and G. Murray, *Innovations and Changes in Labour Organizations in Canada: Results of the National 2000-2001 HRDC Survey* (Human Resources Development Canada, Workplace Information Directorate, December 2002).

37. www.local40organize.com (July 15, 2003).

38. Based in part on L. Field, "Early Signs," *Canadian HR Reporter* (November 29, 1999), p. 14.

39. Young, "Union Drives: Initiated Within, Prevented Within," p. 2; and "Tactics Determined Case By Case," *Canadian HR Reporter* (November 29, 1999), p. 2.

40. M.D. Failes, "Is Silence Really Golden?" *Human Resources Professional* (August/September 1997), pp. 33, 35.

41. *Canadian Master Labour Guide,* 16th ed. (Toronto, ON: CCH Canadian Ltd, 2002).

42. A.W.J. Craig and N.A. Solomon, *The System of Industrial Relations in Canada*, 5th ed. (Scarborough: Prentice Hall Canada Inc., 1996), p. 217.

43. Craig and Solomon, *The System of Industrial Relations in Canada*, p. 218.

44. Craig and Solomon, *The System of Industrial Relations in Canada*, p. 216.

45. U. Vu, "Decertification Still a Delicate Matter," *Canadian HR Reporter* (June 16, 2003), pp. 7, 9; A. Tomlinson, "Union Decertifications on the Rise in Ontario," *Canadian HR Reporter* (July 15, 2002), p. 2; L.M. Field, "Hoping to Get Rid of Unions?" *Canadian HR Reporter* (June 16, 2003), pp. 7, 10; S. Smith, "Ontario Wants Employees to Know They Can Drop Their Union," *Canadian HR Reporter* (June 16, 2003), p. 9; G. Catherwood, "More Freedom to Communicate for B.C. Bosses," *Canadian HR Reporter* (June 16, 2003), pp. 8, 10; "Decertification Requirements," *Human Resources Advisor Newsletter*, Ontario Edition (February 1, 2002), p. 3.

Chapter 17

1. D. Yoder, *Personnel Management* (Englewood Cliffs, NJ: Prentice Hall, 1972), p. 486. See also M. Ballot, *Labour–Management Relations in a Changing Environment* (New York: John Wiley and Sons, 1992), pp. 169–425.

2. Based on R. Richardson, *Collective Bargaining by Objectives*, (Englewood Cliffs, NJ: Prentice Hall, 1977), p. 150; adapted from C. Morris, ed., *The Developing Labor Law*, (Washington, DC: Bureau of National Affairs, 1971), pp. 271–310.

3. D. Brown, "Table Talk—War Stories from the Negotiating Front," *Canadian HR Reporter* (September 9, 2002), p. 7.

4. J. Peirce, *Canadian Industrial Relations* (Scarborough: Prentice Hall Canada Inc., 2000), p. 431.

5. Adapted from R.L. Miller, "Preparations for Negotiations," *Personnel Journal* (1978), pp. 36–39, 44.

6. D. Brown, "CAW—Big Three Negotiations Set the Mark," *Canadian HR Reporter* (June 17, 2002), pp. 3, 12.

7. G. Sova, "What Unions Want," *Canadian HR Reporter* (September 9, 2002), pp. 7, 9.

8. P.G. Day, *Industrial Relations Simulation* (Scarborough: Prentice Hall Canada Inc., 1999), p. 21.

9. R. Stagner and H. Rosen, *Psychology of Union–Management Relations* (Belmont, CA: Wadsworth, 1965), pp. 95–97.

10. The section on distributive bargaining is based on R.E. Walton and R. B. McKersie, *A Behavioral Theory of Labor Negotiations* (New York: McGraw-Hill, 1965), pp. 4–6.

11. The section on integrative bargaining is based on Walton and McKersie, *A Behavioral Theory*, pp. 4–6.

12. L. Young, "Canada's Organized Labour Ready to Ally With Business," *Canadian HR Reporter* (March 13, 2000), pp. 1, 18. See also D. Brown, "Dispute Unites Union, Employers," *Canadian HR Reporter* (November 18, 2002), pp. 1, 12.

13. "Noranda Smelter Workers Agree to Freeze on Wages," *Toronto Star* (April 1, 2003), p. C4.

14. Based on C. Kapel, "The Feeling's Mutual," *Human Resources Professional* (April 1995), pp. 9–13. See also S.D. Smith, "Taking the Confrontation Out of Collective Bargaining," *Canadian HR Reporter* (September 10, 2001), pp. 11, 13.

15. "Interest-based Bargaining: Evidence from Quebec," *Worklife Report* (January 1, 2003), p. 2.

16. Based on D. Cameron, "The Interest-Based Approach to Union–Management Negotiation," *HR Professional* (February/March 1999), pp. 37–39.

17. U. Vu, "Strikes Likely in Public Sector," *Canadian HR Reporter* (February 24, 2003), pp. 1, 10; "Ontario Nurses Association and Ontario Hospital Association Begin Bargaining," *Community Action* (March 19, 2001), p. 8.

18. R.E. Fells, "Developing Trust in Negotiation," *Employee Relations,* 14, no. 1 (1993), p. 35.

19. *Viewpoints 2002: The Perspective of Business, Labour and Public Sector Leaders, Spring 2002—Labour-Management Relations in Canada* (Ottawa, ON: Canadian Labour and Business Centre). See also T.H. Wagar, "Employers More Positive Than Unions About State of Industrial Relations," *Canadian HR Reporter* (January 13, 2003), p. 5.

20. Peirce, *Canadian Industrial Relations*, p. 431.

21. Peirce, *Canadian Industrial Relations*, p. 431.

22. Cited in B. Tieleman, "Still Good Reason to Join a Union: Studies Show Union Workers Reap Better Wages and Benefits," *Financial Post* (July 5, 1999), p. C6.

23. E. B. Akyeampong, "Fact Sheet on Work Absences," *Perspectives* (Winter 2001).

24. J. I. Ondrich and J. F. Schnell, "Strike Duration and the Degree of Disagreement," *Industrial Relations* (Fall 1993), pp. 421–31.

25. D. Hasselback, "Inco Strike to Cost Firm US$20M a Month," *Financial Post* (June 5, 2003), p. FP4.

26. Gunderson et al., *Union–Management Relations in Canada*, p. 195.

27. A. Tomlinson, "Court Okays Picketing of Employers' Clients," *Canadian HR Reporter* (February 25, 2002), pp. 1, 6.

28. D. Herald, "Back to Work Doesn't Mean Back to Normal," *Canadian HR Reporter* (September 9, 2002), pp. 8, 11.

29. "Parents Look for Day Care After 3,700 Catholic Teachers Locked Out," *Canadian Press Newswire* (May 16, 2003); "Ontario Catholic School Board Refuses Arbitration with Locked-Out Teachers," *Canadian Press Newswire* (May 29, 2003); "Lockout for 70,000 Toronto Elementary Students Heads Into Third Week," *Canadian Press Newswire* (May 29, 2003); "Locked-Out Ontario Teachers File $14-Million Suit Against School Board," *Canadian Press Newswire* (May 30, 2003); "Teacher Lockout Should Have Ended

Without Government Legislation," Ontario English Catholic School Teachers' Association, www.oects.on.ca/news/nr2003/nr030603.htm (July 14, 2003).

30. "Workers End One-Day Wildcat Strike at Trenton, N.S., Rail-Car Plant," *Canadian Press Newswire* (September 24, 2002).

31. Based on Gunderson et al., *Union–Management Relations in Canada*, p. 429; and Peirce, *Canadian Industrial Relations*, p. 431.

32. Day, *Industrial Relations Simulation*, p. 11.

33. This section is based on Gunderson et al., *Union–Management Relations in Canada*, pp. 282–83.

34. S. Payette, "Yesterday and Today - Union Dues," *Workplace Gazette* (Summer 2001), p. 76.

35. Gunderson et al., *Union–Management Relations in Canada*, pp. 190–91 and 285.

36. Gunderson et al., *Union–Management Relations in Canada*, p. 191.

37. *Canadian Master Labour Guide,* 16th ed. (Toronto, ON: CCH Canadian Ltd., 2002).

38. S. Payette, "Yesterday and Today—Contract Duration," *Workplace Gazette* (Winter 2001), p. 97.

39. Day, *Industrial Relations Simulation*, p. 12.

40. "CAW-Big Three Negotiations Set the Mark," *Canadian HR Reporter* (June 17, 2002), pp. 3, 12.

41. Based on W. Baer, *Grievance Handling: 101 Guides for Supervisors* (New York: American Management Association, 1970).

42. Brown and Beatty, *Canadian Labour Arbitration*, pp. 2-1 to 2-6.

43. See J.E. Grenig, "Stare Decisis, Re Judicata and Collecteral Estoppel and Labour Arbitration," *Labour Law Journal* 38 (April 1987), pp. 195–205.

44. G. Saunders, "Union–Management Relations: An Overview," in *Human Resources Management in Canada* (Scarborough: Prentice Hall Canada Inc. 1983), p. 55 047.

45. A. Grant and J. Clarkson, "Developing Cooperative Union-Management Relationships: A Partnership Approach to Conflict," *Canadian HR Reporter* (May 7, 2001), pp. 10, 12.

46. D. Hynes, *Industrial Relations Outlook* (Ottawa, ON: Conference Board of Canada, 2002).

47. L. Cassiani, "Strength in Numbers: Unions, Management Join Forces on Training," *Canadian HR Reporter* (March 26, 2001), pp. 3, 11.

Chapter 18

1. D. Brown, "HR Issues Top of Mind for Execs Worldwide: Study," *Canadian HR Reporter* (May 5, 2003), pp. 1,9. See also A.K. Paul and R.N. Anantharaman, "Impact of People Management Practices on Organizational Performance: Analysis of a Causal Model," *International Journal of Human Resource Management* 14, no. 7 (2003), pp. 1246–1266.

2. "International Assignments," *BNA Bulletin to Management* (February 8, 1996), pp. 44–45; "International Assignment Policies and Practices," *BNA Bulletin to Management* (May 1, 1997), pp. 140–41.

3. "Short-term Global Assignments Rising," *Canadian HR Reporter* (May 7, 2001), p. 2.

4. K. Roberts, E. Kossek, and C. Ozeki, "Managing the Global Workforce: Challenges and Strategies," *Academy of Management Executive* 12, no.4. (1998), pp. 93–106.

5. K. Roberts, E. Kossek, and C. Ozeki, "Managing the Global Workforce: Challenges and Strategies," p. 94.

6. This is based on J. Fadel and M. Petti, "International HR Policy Basics," *Global Workforce* (April 1997), pp. 93–106.

7. D. Bergles, "Let Them Choose," *Canadian HR Reporter* (May 6, 2002), pp. 15, 19.

8. Paraphrased or quoted from J. Fadel and M. Petti, "International HR Policy Basics," pp. 29–30.

9. D. Bergles and L. Da Rocha, "Putting Work–life Balance into Relocation Planning," *Canadian HR Reporter* (September 23, 2002), pp. 9–10.

10. M. Tayeb, "Transfer of HRM Practices Across Cultures. An American Company in Scotland," *The International Journal of Human Resource Management* 9, no. 2 (April 1998), pp. 332–58.

11. M. Tayeb, "Transfer of HRM Practices Across Cultures. An American Company in Scotland," p. 342.

12. M. Tayeb, "Transfer of HRM Practices Across Cultures. An American Company in Scotland," p. 344.

13. M. Tayeb, "Transfer of HRM Practices Across Cultures. An American Company in Scotland," p. 345.

14. "Fifteen Top Emerging Markets," *Global Workforce* (January 1998), pp. 18–21.

15. L. Grobovsky, "Protecting Your Workers Abroad With a Global Diversity Strategy," *Canadian HR Reporter* (November 1, 1999), pp. 15–16.

16. B. Belisle and W. Cuthbertson, "Post-9/11 Challenges for Relocation, " *Canadian HR Reporter* (March 10, 2003), p. 12.

17. "Expect Corruption Overseas," *Canadian HR Reporter* (September 23, 2002), p. 9.

18. These are based on E. Gaugler, "HR Management: An International Comparison," *Personnel* (August 1988), pp. 24–30. See also Y. Kuwahara, "New Developments in Human Resource Management in Japan," *Asia Pacific Journal of Human Resources* 31, no. 2 (1993), pp. 3–11; and C. M. Solomon, "How Does Your Global Talent Measure Up," *Personnel Journal* (October 1994), pp. 96–108.

19. For a discussion of this, see Gaugler, "HR Management," p. 26; see also George Palmer, "Transferred to Tokyo–A Guide to Etiquette in the Land of the Rising Sun," *Multinational Business* no. 4 (1990/1991), pp. 36–44.

20. D. Ralston, P. Elsass, D. Gustafson, F. Cheung, and R. Terpstra, "Eastern Values: A Comparison of Managers in the United States, Hong Kong, and the People's Republic of China," *Journal of Applied Psychology* 71 (1992), pp. 664–71.

21. G. Hofstede, "Cultural Dimensions in People Management," in Vladimir Pucik, Noel Tishy, and Carole Barnett, eds., *Globalizing Management* (New York: John Wiley & Sons, Inc., 1992), p. 143.

22. Hofstede, "Cultural Dimensions."

23. Gaugler, "HR Management," p. 27. See also Simcha Ronen and Oded Shenkar, "Using Employee Attitudes to Establish MNC Regional Divisions," *Personnel* (August 1988), pp. 32–39.

24. "Comparing Employment Practices," *BNA Bulletin to Management* (April 22, 1993), p. 1.

25. This is discussed in Gaugler, "HR Management," p. 28.

26. This is based on R. Sedel, "Europe 1992: HR Implications of the European Unification," *Personnel* (October 1989), pp. 19–24. See also C. Brewster and A. Hegewish, "A Continent of Diversity," *Personnel Management* (January 1993), pp. 36–39.

27. G. Lowe, "The Quality of Work Features Prominently in Europe's Plan for Competitiveness," *Canadian HR Reporter* (May 19, 2003), pp. 6, 8.

28. G. Lowe, "The Quality of Work Features Prominently in Europe's Plan for Competitiveness."

29. Daniels and Radebaugh, *International Business*, p. 764.

30. Based on B.J. Punnett, "International Human Resources Management," in A.M. Rugman, ed., *International Business in Canada: Strategies for Management* (Scarborough, ON: Prentice Hall Canada, 1989), pp. 330–46.

31. R.L. Tung, "Selection and Training Procedures of U.S., European, and Japanese Multinationals," *California Management Review* 25 (1982), pp. 51–71.

32. Runzheimer International, *Survey and Analysis of Employee Relocation Policies and Costs* (2002).

33. Discussed in Charles Hill, *International Business*, pp. 511–15.

34. L. Hyatt, "It Takes Two: Relocating Dual Career Couples," *Workplace Today* (January 2002, p. 13).

35. M. Schell, quoted in C. M. Solomon, "Success Abroad Depends on More than Job Skills," *Personnel Journal* (April 1994), p. 52. See also J. Keogh, "A Win-win, From Start to Finish," *Workspan* (February 2003), pp. 36–39.

36. Punnett, *International Human Resources Management*, pp. 334–35.

37. L. Young, "Let's Make a Deal—When to Offer Relocation Alternatives," *Canadian HR Reporter* (June 14, 1999), pp. 18, 19. See also L. Young, "Family Relocations on the Decline," *Canadian HR Reporter* (June 14, 1999), pp. 1, 19.

38. A.M. Yeargan and R. Herod, "Managing Short-term International Assignments," *WorldatWork Canadian News* 10 (2002), pp. 1, 3, 8, 17.

39. Z. Fedder, "Short-Sighted Thinking Shortchanges Short-Term International Assignments," *Canadian HR Reporter* (September 25, 2000), p. 20.

40. Daniels and Radebaugh, *International Business*, p. 767.

41. Arvind Phatak, *International Dimensions of Management* (Boston: PWS-Kent, 1989), pp. 106–07.

42. Phatak, *International Dimensions of Management*, p. 106.

43. Daniels and Radebaugh, *International Business*, p. 767.

44. Daniels and Radebaugh, *International Business*, p. 768; Phatak, *International Dimensions of Management*, p. 106.

45. Phatak, *International Dimensions of Management*, p. 108.

46. Daniels and Radebaugh, *International Business*, p. 769.

47. Daniels and Radebaugh, *International Business*, p. 769; Phatak, *International Dimensions of Management*, p. 106.

48. Howard Perlmutter, "The Torturous Evolution of the Multinational Corporation," *Columbia Journal of World Business* 3, no. 1 (January–February 1969), pp. 11–14, discussed in Phatak, *International Dimensions of Management*, p. 129.

49. Phatak, *International Dimensions of Management*, p. 129.

50. Phatak, *International Dimensions of Management*.

51. Hill, *International Business*, p. 507.

52. Hill, *International Business*, pp. 507–10.

53. Hill, *International Business*, p. 509.

54. Hill, *International Business*.

55. Phatak, *International Dimensions of Management*, p. 113; and Charlene Marmer Solomon, "Staff Selection Impacts Global Success," *Personnel Journal* (January 1994), pp. 88–101. For another view, see Anne Harzing, "The Persistent Myth of High Expatriate Failure Rates," *International Journal of Human Resource Management* 6, no. 2 (May 1995), pp. 457–74.

56. M.A. Shaffer, D.A. Harrison, K.M. Gilley, and D.M. Luk, "Struggling for Balance Amid Turbulence on International Assignments: Work-family Conflict, Support and Commitment," *Journal of Management* 27 (2001), pp. 99–121; R. Garonzik, J. Brockner, and P.A. Siegel, "Identifying International Assignees at Risk for Premature Departure: The Interactive Effects of Outcome Favorability and Procedural Fairness," *Journal of Applied Psychology* 85 (2000), pp. 13–20; and M.A. Shaffer and D.A. Harrison, "Forgotten Partners of International Assignments: Development and Test of a Model of Spouse Adjustment," *Journal of Applied Psychology*, 86 (2001), pp. 238–54.

57. W. Arthur, Jr. and W. Bennett, Jr., "The International Assignee: The Relative Importance of Factors Perceived to Contribute to Success," *Personnel Psychology* 48 (1995), pp. 99–114; table on pp. 106–07. See also Davison and Betty Punnett, "International Assignments: Is There a Role for Gender and Race in Decisions?" *International Journal of Human Resource Management* 6, no. 2 (May 1995), pp. 411–41.

58. Arthur and Bennett, "International Assignments," pp. 105–08.

59. Arthur and Bennett, "International Assignments," p. 110.

60. G. Spreitzer, M. McCall Jr., and J. Mahoney, "Early Identification of International Executive Potential," *Journal of Applied Psychology* 82 (1997), pp. 6–29.

61. Phatak, *International Dimensions of Management*, p. 119.

62. See, for example, Blocklyn, "Developing the International Executive," p. 45.

63. L. Laroche, "Removing the Unexpected With Pre-Assignment Visits," *Canadian HR Reporter* (May 8, 2000), pp. 17, 20. See also P.M. Caligiuri and J.M. Phillips, "An Application of Self-Assessment Realistic Job Previews to Expatriate Assignments," *International Journal of Human Resource Management* 14, no. 7 (2003), pp. 1102–1116.

64. Blocklyn, "Developing the International Executive," p. 45.

65. Discussed in M. Callahan, "Preparing the New Global Manager," *Training and Development Journal* (March 1989), p. 30. The publisher of the inventory is the New York consulting firm Moran, Stahl, and Boyer; see also Jennifer Laabs, "The Global Talent Search," *Personnel Journal* (August 1991), pp. 38–44 for a discussion of how firms such as Coca-Cola recruit and develop international managers, and T.S. Chan, "Developing International Managers: A Partnership Approach," *Journal of Management Development* 13, no. 3 (1994), pp. 38–46.

66. Callahan, "Preparing the New Global Manager," pp. 29–30. See also C. M. Solomon, "Global Operations Demand that HR Rethink Diversity," *Personnel Journal* (July 1994), pp. 40–50.

67. A. Bross, A. Churchill, and J. Zifkin, "Cross-Cultural Training: Issues to Consider During Implementation," *Canadian HR Reporter* (June 5, 2000), pp. 10, 12.

68. This is based on Callahan, "Preparing the New Global Manager," p. 30. See also D. Feldman, "Repatriate Moves as Career Transitions," *Human Resource Management Review* 1, no. 3 (Fall 1991), pp. 163–78; and J. Yanouzas and S. Boukis, "Transporting Management Training into Poland: Some Surprises and Disappointments," *Journal of Management Development* 12, no. 1 (1993), pp. 64–71. See also J. Laabs, "How Gillette Grooms Global Talent," *Personnel Journal* (August 1993), pp. 64–76, and C.M. Solomon, "Transplanting Corporate Cultures Globally," *Personnel Journal* (October 1993), pp. 78–88.

69. J.S. Biteen, "Worldly Relocation Advice," *Canadian HR Reporter* (February 23, 1998), pp. 21, 22.

70. A. Bross, A. Churchill, and J. Zifkin, "Cross-Cultural Training: Issues to Consider During Implementation."

71. C. Shick, "It Wasn't What You Said, It Was How You Said It," *Canadian HR Reporter* (February 28, 2000), p. 18.

72. G. Reinhart, "Going Global," *Canadian HR Reporter* (September 25, 2000), pp. 19, 23.

73. C. Reynolds, "Global Compensation and Benefits in Transition," *Compensation and Benefits Review* (January/February 2000), pp. 28–28.

74. J. E. Richard, "Global Executive Compensation: A Look at the Future," *Compensation and Benefits Review* (May/June 2000), pp. 35–38.

75. L. Laroche, "Negotiating Expatriate Packages," *Canadian HR Reporter* (November 20, 2000), pp. 15, 19.

76. J. Stoner and R. E. Freeman, *Management*, 4th ed. (Englewood Cliffs, NJ: Prentice Hall, 1989), p. 783. See also J. Cartland, "Reward Policies in a Global Corporation," *Business Quarterly*, (Autumn 1993), pp. 93–96; and L. Mazur, "Europay," *Across-the-Board* (January 1995), pp. 40–43.

77. Hewitt Associates, "*On Compensation*," (May 1989), p. 1 (Hewitt Associates, 86–87 East Via De Ventura, Scottsdale, Arizona 85258).

78. C. Reynolds, "Global Compensation and Benefits in Transition," p. 37.

79. K. Bensky, "Developing a Workable Global Rewards System," *Workspan* (October 2002), pp. 44–48.

80. Hill, *International Business*, pp. 519–520.

81. Phatak, *International Dimensions of Management*, p. 134. See also L. Laroche, "Negotiating Expatriate Packages."

82. J. E. Richard, "Global Executive Compensation: A Look at the Future."

83. Brooks, "Long-Term Incentives," p. 41.

84. V. Frazee, "Keeping Your Expats Healthy," *Global Workforce* (November 1998), pp. 18–23. See also B. Barker and D. Schulde, "Special EAP Helps Expatriates Face International 'Culture Shock,'" *Canadian HR Reporter* (November 29, 1999), p. 20.

85. L. O'Grady, "Using Technology to De-stress on International Assignment," *Canadian HR Reporter* (September 24, 2001), pp. 8, 12.

86. A. Bross and G. Wise, "Sustaining the Relocated Employee With an International EAP," *Canadian HR Reporter* (November 29, 1999), pp. 18, 19, 21.

87. Except as noted, this is based on G. Addou and M. Mendenhall, "Expatriate Performance Appraisal: Problems and Solutions," in M. Mendenhall and G.

Addou, *International Human Resource Management* (Boston: PWS-Kent Publishing Co., 1991), pp. 364–74. See also J. Milliman, S. Taylor, and A.J. Czaplewski, "Cross-Cultural Performance Feedback in Multinational Enterprises: Opportunity for Organizational Learning," *Human Resource Planning* 25 (2002), pp. 29–43.

88. Addou and Mendenhall, "Expatriate Performance Appraisal," p. 366. See also Maddy Janssens, "Evaluating International Managers' Performance: Parent Company Standards as Control Mechanism," *The International Journal of Human Resource Management* 5, no. 4, (December 1994), pp. 853–73.

89. R. Sauer and K. Voelker, *Labor Relations: Structure and Process* (New York: Macmillan, 1993), pp. 510–25.

90. Sauer and Voelker, *Labour Relations*, p. 516. See also Marino Regini, "Human Resource Management and Industrial Relations in European Companies," *The International Journal of Human Resource Management* 4, no. 3, (September 1993), pp. 555–68.

91. Quoted from Sauer and Voelker, *Labour Relations*, p. 519.

92. S. Greengard, "Mission Possible: Protecting Employees Abroad," *Workforce* (August 1997), pp. 30–32.

93. S. Greengard, "Mission Possible: Protecting Employees Abroad."

94. S. Merkling and E. Davis, "Kidnap and Ransom Insurance: A Rapidly Growing Benefit," *Compensation and Benefits Review* (November/December 2001), pp. 40–45.

95. These are based on or quoted from S. Greengard, "Mission Possible: Protecting Employees Abroad," p. 32. See also B. Belisle and W. Cuthbertson, "Anticipate Expat Crises Instead of Responding."

96. S. Greengard, "Mission Possible: Protecting Employees Abroad," p. 32.

97. E. Bernstein, "A Floor Under Foreign Factories?" *Business Week* (November 2, 1998), pp. 126–128.

98. Definition based on Dennis Briscoe, *International Human Resource Management*, p. 65. See also Linda Stroh, "Predicting Turnover Among Repatriates: Can Organizations Affect Retention Rates?" *International Journal of Human Resource Management* 6, no. 2, (May 1995), pp. 443–56.

99. J. Keogh, "A Win–win, from Start to Finish."

100. Phatak, *International Dimensions of Management*, p. 124. See also Reyer Swaak, "Today's Expatriate Families: Dual Careers and Other Obstacles," *Compensation and Benefits Review* 27, no. 3 (May 1995), pp. 21–26.

101. D. Brown, "Companies Undervaluing Skills Learned During Relocation," *Canadian HR Reporter* (February 28, 2000), pp. 15, 21.

102. G. Reinhart, "Going Global." See also J. Hobel, "The Expatriate Employee Homecoming," *Canadian HR Reporter* (June 1, 1998), pp. G5, G11. See also J. Keogh, "A Win–win, from Start to Finish."

103. These are based on Briscoe, *International Human Resource Management*, p. 66; Phatak, *International Dimensions of Management*, p. 124; and Daniels and Radebaugh, *International Business*, p. 772. See also P. Stanoch and G. Reynolds, "Relocating Career Development," *Canadian HR Reporter* (May 5, 2003), pp. 13, 15.

104. Briscoe, *International Human Resource Management*, p. 66.

105. Phatak, *International Dimensions of Management*, p. 126.

106. H. Gregersen and L. Stroh, "Coming Home to the Arctic Cold: Antecedents to Finnish Expatriate and Spouse Repatriation Adjustment," *Personnel Psychology* 50 (1997), p. 651.

Name Index

Subject Index